SPAIN & PORTUGAL
1994

1994 Fielding Titles

Fielding's Australia 1994

Fielding's Belgium 1994

Fielding's Bermuda/Bahamas 1994

Fielding's Brazil 1994

Fielding's Britain 1994

Fielding's Budget Europe 1994

Fielding's Caribbean 1994

Fielding's Europe 1994

Fielding's Far East 1994

Fielding's France 1994

Fielding's The Great Sights of Europe 1994

Fielding's Hawaii 1994

Fielding's Holland 1994

Fielding's Italy 1994

Fielding's Mexico 1994

Fielding's New Zealand 1994

Fielding's Scandinavia 1994

Fielding's Spain & Portugal 1994

Fielding's Switzerland & the Alpine Region 1994

Fielding's Worldwide Cruises 1994

Fielding's Shopping Guide to Europe 1994

SPAIN & PORTUGAL 1994

The Most In-depth Guide to the Spectacle and Romance of Spain & Portugal

A. Hoyt Hobbs & Joy Adzigian

Fielding Worldwide, Inc.
308 South Catalina Avenue
Redondo Beach, California 90277 U.S.A.

Fielding's Spain & Portugal 1994

Published by Fielding Worldwide, Inc.

Text Copyright ©1994 A. Hoyt Hobbs and Joy Adxigian

Icons & Illustrations Copyright ©1993 FWI

FIELDING WORLDWIDE INC.

PUBLISHER AND CEO	Robert Young Pelton
DIRECTOR OF PUBLISHING	Paul T. Snapp
CO-DIR. OF ELECTRONIC PUBLISHING	Tony E. Hulette
CO-DIR. OF ELECTRONIC PUBLISHING	Larry E. Hart
PRODUCTION SUPERVISOR	Michael Rowley
PRODUCTION MANAGEMENT	Beverly Riess
EDITORIAL MANAGER	Wink Dulles
OFFICE MANAGER	Christy Donaldson

EDITORS

Linda Charlton	Kathy Knoles
Tina Gentile	Evelyn Lager
Loretta Rooney Hess	Jane M. Martin
Dixie Hulette	Peggy Plendl
Ann Imberman	Jeanne-Marie Swann
Forrest Kerr	Gladis R. Zaimah

PRODUCTION

Norm Imberman	Harold Pierson
Bryan Kring	Kip Riggins
Lyne Lawrence	Munir Shaikh
Chris Mederios	Chris Snyder
Lillian Tse	

COVER DESIGNED BY	Pelton & Associates, Inc.
COVER PHOTOGRAPHERS — Front Cover	Robert Young Pelton/Westlight
Background Photo, Front Cover	Mark Stephenson/Westlight
Back Cover	Robert Young Pelton/Westlight
INSIDE PHOTOS	Robert Young Pelton/Westlight, National Tourist Offices of Spain, and Portuguese National Tourist Office

Inquiries should be addressed to: Fielding Worldwide, Inc., 308 South Catalina Ave., Redondo Beach, California 90277 U.S.A., Telephone (310) 372-4474, Facsimile (310) 376-8064, 8:30 a.m. - 5:30 p.m. Pacific Standard Time.

ISBN 1-56952-021-6

Printed in the United States of America

Dedication

We gratefully dedicate this book to two spirits on high—Eunice Riedel, our mentor and guide, and Susan Schneider, our muse for Portugal and life.

Letter from the Publisher

In 1946, Temple Fielding began the first of what would be a remarkable new series of well-written, highly personalized guide books for independent travelers. Temple's opinionated, witty, and oft-imitated books have now guided travelers for almost a half-century. More important to some was Fielding's humorous and direct method of steering travelers away from the dull and the insipid. Today, Fielding Travel Guides are still written by experienced travelers for experienced travelers. Our authors carry on Fielding's reputation for creating travel experiences that deliver insight with a sense of discovery and style.

Unforgettable. That's what you'll say after a vacation in Spain and Portugal the Fielding way. Hoyt Hobbs and Joy Adzigian have been traveling through Europe for the past 20 years, searching for the dramatic, the little-known, the romantic attractions, and the pristine beaches that make Spain and Portugal two of the most entertaining countries in Europe. In Fielding's *Spain & Portugal*, Hoyt and Joy have created the perfect balance of entertainment and education, all in a historical context. You won't forget Spain and Portugal. Not with Fielding.

In 1994, the concept of independent travel has never been bigger. Our policy of *brutal honesty* and a highly personal point of view has never changed; it just seems the travel world has caught up with us.

Enjoy your Spain and Portugal adventure with Hoyt Hobbs and Joy Adzigian, and Fielding.

> Robert Young Pelton
> Publisher and C.E.O.
> Fielding Worldwide, Inc.

ABOUT THE AUTHORS

Hoyt Hobbs and Joy Adzigian

Hoyt Hobbs and Joy Adzigian have traveled extensively throughout Europe and North Africa since 1973. They first visited Spain and Portugal in 1975, while living in the south of France, and felt an immediate affection for the peoples and cultures of the Iberian peninsula. Their passion for art and architecture, as well as for food and wine, had met its match, and Spain and Portugal drew them back again and again.

The two wrote their first guidebook in 1979—to Egypt—when, after numerous trips, they had been unable to find a guidebook to their liking. The popular guides provided too little background and explanation, while more scholarly books hid what was interesting within reams of detail. Reviewers applauded their balanced approach. *The Library Journal* said: "...with only this book [one can] enjoy a more comprehensive, efficient, and informative tour...than is possible with any of the classical travel guides." According to *Traveler's Book Society* "...the level here is almost exactly right for the intelligent traveler....This is a book to travel with as well as to use in planning a tour...." *Business Week* simply stated that, "If a visit to Egypt is in your future, prepare for it by picking up a...copy." *The Arizona Daily Star* discribed it as a book "...for the modern-day Indiana Jones who seeks adventure in the land of the Pharaohs." "This book is a model of specific, useful, honest travel advice and concise, vivid historical exposition," noted the *Chattanooga Times*, adding that "you ought to buy this book at once." In 1981 their Egypt guide was selected for publication as the first of the Fielding's country guides. Now they have applied their successful and informative approach to Spain and Portugal.

Besides being experienced travelers, they bring an impressive array of talents to the task. Dr. Hobbs, an Associate Professor of Philosophy at Long Island University, is widely read in history, architecture and culture; Joy Adzigian, a stylist and producer, brings a background strong in literature, art and design. Both are highly knowledgable about food and wine, accepting nothing less than the best. To that end they have explored the length and breadth of Iberia, and report their findings in this lively, comprehensive guide. The authors live in New York City.

ACKNOWLEDGMENTS

A project such as this could never have been completed without substantial assistance from a large number of people and organizations. It is a great pleasure to have an opportunity to publicly thank some of them.

We owe a great debt to Pilar Vico from the Spanish National Tourist Office in New York who performed miracles without complaint. Ana Maria Osório and Maria JoãoRamires, from the Portuguese National Tourist Office, were exceedingly helpful with all our requests. Thanks to our good friends Pamela Dailey and Arthur Krystal for timely and astute editorial assistance and to Lynn and Larry Foster for helpful advice and encouragement. Donna Wayne transcribed hours of tape into readable notes, with unfailing good spirit. Dr. and Mrs. Albert H. Hobbs laid all the groundwork for this book with a lifetime of lessons. Lastly, we thank all our friends and family for their patience and we want them to know that, for better or worse, we are available again.

OCEAN

ntander

Basque Coast

aredo

Fuenterrabia

boa

N-634

Donostia

N-121

F R A N C E

PAIS BASQUE

A-68

NAVARRA

Vitoria

N-111

Estella

Pamplona

Haro

A-15

ANDORRA

N

N-122

Rio Ebro

A-68

C A T A L U N Y A

Vic

Costa Brava

A-7

Zaragoza

A-2

●**Lleida**

NII

A R A G O N

Poblet■

Rio Ebro

Tarragona

●**Barcelona**

güenza

Sitges

Costa Dorado

Rio Tajo

A-7

I   N

Costa del Azahar

SPAIN AND PORTUGAL

N

MINORCA

MAJORCA

NIII

U E V A

A-7

Valencia

Palma

diana

N-301

IBIZA

●**Ibiza**

N-322

BALEARIC ISLANDS

Alicante

Benidorm

LEVANTE

A-7

Costa Blanca

Murcia

N-301

M E D I T E R R A N E A N

N-340

Cartagena

S E A

●**Almería**

A L G E R I A

| 0 | miles | 75 |
| 0 | kilometers | 120 |

Fielding Rating Icons

The Fielding Rating Icons are highly personal and awarded to help the besieged traveler choose from among the dizzying array of activities, attractions, hotels, restaurants and sights. The awarding of an icon denotes unusual or exceptional qualities in the relevant category. We encourage you to create your own icons in the margin to help you find those special places that make each trip unforgettable.

Fielding Selection	Author Selection	Money Saver	Expensive	Quality	Warning
Homey	Luxurious	Rustic	Simple	Scenic	Business
Great Scenery	Picturesque	Beaches & Resorts	Spectacular Cuisine	Romantic	Relaxing
Museum/ Art Gallery	Artistically Important	Architecturally Interesting	History	Book Reference	Musically Interesting
Shopping	Festivals	Nightlife	Wine Tasting	Crafts	etc.
Cycling	Hiking	Golf	Tennis	Strolling	Horseback Riding
Cross-country Skiing	Downhill Skiing	Deep-sea Fishing	Fresh-water Fishing	Snorkeling & Diving	Sailing
Arrival & Departure	By Bus/Local Transportation	By Air	By Road	By Water	By Rail

TABLE OF CONTENTS

CONTENTS

INTRODUCTION

Spain welcomes tourists and is in turn embraced by more visitors than any other country in Europe. The reasons for its popularity are abundantly clear. Spain pampers travelers in paradors, warms them on sandy beaches, dazzles them with scenery and art, delights them with flavorful cuisine, and—most of all—surprises. Spain is not a European Mexico with mariachi music and Indian civilizations, but a different culture entirely—venerable, yet lively and cosmopolitan, graced by striking art and awesome architecture.

Because Spain isolated itself from world politics through the 1960s, North Americans are less familiar with it than they are with most other European countries. While the names of the Costa del Sol, Madrid, Barcelona, Seville and Grenada are generally recognized, those of Salamanca, Segovia, Santiago de Compostela, Oviedo, Burgos, or even Córdoba—any one of which would captivate most visitors—are less well known. Spain's northern and western beaches—more scenic than the overpopulated Costa del Sol and long appreciated by Europeans—are virtually barren of Americans. One of our aims is to entice you to those areas we know you'll enjoy; another is to warn you about locales overblown by their descriptions in articles or travel brochures.

In addition to guiding you to enjoyable places, we want to enhance your appreciation of them. Because Spain's long seclusion has obscured its formative historical events and figures, visitors frequently miss the significance of what they are seeing. For this reason we provide more historical and cultural background than most travel guides take time for and include specific commentaries on individual buildings and works of art.

Portugal, subordinate in size and influence to its Iberian neighbor, possesses natural beauty and historical treasures so little known that visitors need guiding to the charms of medieval Évora, Elvas, Obidos and Marvão; or to Batalha, an exquisite Gothic and Renaissance monastery; romantic Coimbra, with an ancient university; Tomar, with a mysterious 12th-century church; and Nazaré, a picture-postcard fishing village. If tourists to Spain were aware of Portugal's distinct delights and easy accessibility they surely would be drawn across the border. The finest beaches in Europe, those of Portugal's Algarve region, lie just a 2-hour drive from Seville; Lisbon, one of Europe's great capitals, can be reached in a half-day's trip from Madrid; and a day's excursion from Spain's Extremadura region to the medieval architecture of Portuguese Marvão can easily conclude with dinner back in Spain.

We bind Portugal and Spain between one set of covers to demonstrate how easily the option to visit both may be exercised. Either visited by itself, or combined with Spain, Portugal works its magic on travelers.

1994

This year Spain offers visitors two special dividends. Because the American dollar has risen on international markets, travelers will find their budgets stretching one-third further than they would have two years ago. They will also find a country prepared for them as few places in the world have ever been. Spain accomplished wonders in producing both the 1992 Summer Olympics and the 1992 World's Fair, the first time one country ever staged two such mammoth events in a single year. To enhance those productions the Spanish government granted loans to remodel hotels throughout the country, with terms so attractive that most seized the opportunity. This was only one phase of an unprecedented effort to spruce up the country for the events of 1992. Every museum and historic monument that needed renovation received it. Major roads were repaired, and routes to important sights were repaved, straightened and widened. The hundred miles of winding road from Cáceres to Guadalupe that had formerly taken three hours to travel, for example, can now be negotiated in half that time. A high speed train line was constructed to whisk riders between Madrid and Seville in three, rather than the five hours it used to take. All these improvements mean that a tourist to Spain in 1994 will be greeted by a country in better, cleaner, and fresher condition than any other in the world.

Portugal in 1994 remains what it has always been, only better. Over the past two years the cost of visiting the least expensive country in Europe, already less than half the price of France or Italy, has declined by another quarter for North American travellers. Nonetheless, Portugal provides attractive, spotless accommodations, hearty food, and surprisingly sophisticated wines for those prices— all without the crowds or formality of most European countries.

THE ARRANGEMENT OF THIS GUIDE

Following introductory chapters about trip preparation and background, we divide the sights of Spain into seven geographic areas approximating seven of Spain's traditional kingdoms. For smaller Portugal we divide its sights into three areas: central and northern Portugal—the bulk of this small country; Lisbon and its rich environs; and the Algarve with its splendid beaches.

RATINGS

Since most tourists' time and funds are limited, it's important that we not simply list what hotels, restaurants and sights are available, but provide the information to help each traveler make the best choices for himself. To ease those decisions, we use the following star ratings:

★★★★★ Outstanding anywhere in the world

★★★★ Exceptional, among the best in the country

★★★ Superior for a particular area of the country

★★ Good, a clear step above the average

★ Above average

For hotels and restaurants we provide two additional types of information. We indicate the price category of each establishment (explained under "Prices" below) and, in the case of hotels, we also specify which services they offer. Since value is an important consideration in evaluating hotels and restaurants, it affects our assignment of stars. If a hotel provides the services and style of its competitors at a savings, it earns an extra star—or even two, if its value is sufficiently outstanding. Conversely, hotels that charge higher prices than their accommodations merit are demoted by one star or more. The same point applies to the quality of food a restaurant serves. Descriptions of individual hotels and restaurants will supply the essential details, including how the rating was earned. From time to time we describe establishments without starring them, because there are regions where nothing special in a particular price range may be available.

The stars we use are based on different criteria from those assigned by national tourist bureaus and displayed outside hotel entrances in Spain and Portugal. Official stars rank a hotel by the number and kinds of services it provides, such as whether its bedrooms contain telephones, televisions, and mini-bars, or whether saunas, restaurants, or conference rooms are available. Although many of these services are incidental to a tourist, the greater their number, the greater the number of official stars a hotel receives. Official stars take minimal account of comfort, attractiveness or the quality of service.

In this guide we indicate the number of services available by assigning a class category. A 1st-class hotel will offer all the facilities one expects of any exemplary hotel. To make its services cost-effective, such a hotel will usually be large, and the price of its rooms high. 2nd-class hotels will provide televisions in every bedroom and a restaurant on the premises, but probably not saunas, conference rooms or other infrequently used extras. 3rd-class accommodations may be as comfortable as those of higher-classed hotels, but the range of services offered will begin and end with a comfortable bedroom.

As if to make their official star system more confusing, both Spain and Portugal also assign from one to four stars to establishments that are not officially categorized as hotels. However in their case, the number of stars assigned signifies a smaller number of services than those provided by similarly rated official hotels. These establishments are variously called *residencias, residentials, pensións, pensões, fondas, hostals, albergarias,* or *estalgems.* Whatever their name, they aren't officially classified as hotels because they lack some feature required by a government definition. It may be that there is no elevator, or no employee to cover the front door late at night, or simply no restaurant sharing the premises. For a traveller looking for a comfortable place to spend the night, the absence of such features seldom constitutes a deficiency, and since some of these establishments provide exceptional accommodations in every other way, they should be included in a traveler's options. We incorporate such lodgings in our hotel listings, but distinguish them from hotels by prefacing their class with the letters "R," "Hs," or "P" for *residencia, hostal, pensión,* etc.

Practical considerations dictate that not every hotel or restaurant in a city will be mentioned, and absence of a listing should not be taken to imply substandard quality. There are, for example, more than 200 hotels in Madrid alone. Attempting to discuss every hotel and restaurant in the country—in addition to being unmanageable—would defeat our desire to ease your selection. We concentrate on listing hotels convenient for the sightseer, and on including choices in all price ranges. Such selecting means that we generally do not list bad hotels, for there are enough good hotels in most of Spain and Portugal that no others merit discussion. But when a hotel that we consider deficient is conveniently located and might be booked by accident, we will describe the establishment to warn you of what to expect.

PRICES

International currency fluctuations make citing the exact costs of foreign hotels and restaurants impossible. To avoid inaccuracies, we indicate hotel and restaurant prices by less variable general categories: **Very Expensive**, **Expensive**, **Moderate**, and **Inexpensive**. Since expensive is not a relative matter to us, we use the same standards both for Spain and for less expensive Portugal. The intent is simply to be clear.

Price Category	Hotel (per night, double occupancy)	Restaurant (full meal, house wine)
Very Expensive	$200+	$100+
Expensive	$100-$200	$50+
Moderate	$50-$99	$20-$50
Inexpensive	Less than $50	Less than $20

CHANGES

The prospect of introducing Spain to visitors carries the excitement of giving a present the receiver is sure to love. At the same time it's a humbling prospect, for Spain is a huge country with beauty and history around every corner, and tiny Portugal packs its enticements densely. Our information is based on inspecting hundreds of hotels and restaurants over many visits, but we are aware that others may have improved, declined or closed too recently to be included in our reviews. If you find some treasure that we have overlooked, we want to hear about it so we can visit it for possible inclusion in future editions. Similarly, we'd appreciate hearing about instances of inadequate service in any of the establishments we list. While no hotel or restaurant treats everyone the same, egregious service or behavior is never acceptable. Your comments and suggestions are both welcome and helpful. Write us c/o Fielding Worldwide, 308 Catalina Avenue, Redondo Beach, CA 90277.

And, most important, have a wonderful trip!

PRACTICAL MATTERS

CLIMATE AND SEASONS

In latitude Portugal and Spain sit opposite that part of the United States stretching from Boston to Baltimore, but because of their proximity to the Gulf Stream and the Mediterranean Sea their climates are substantially warmer.

Portugal enjoys a Mediterranean climate, although it doesn't touch that sea. Ninety degrees is a normal summer high, with some days simmering above 100, although breezes temper this heat on the coast while northern mountains remain pleasantly cool. Summer rainfall is uncommon. In winter, frost is rare and snow unknown, except in the highest mountains where few tourists have reason to go. Winters compare to early spring in the U.S. northeast, with 50- or even 60-degree temperatures during the day, and nightly temperatures dropping to chilly 40s. Spring and autumn bring pleasant temperatures in the mid-70s, but days of steady rain.

Spain's vast geography covers several different climates. The center of Spain, sealed from the sea by mountains north, south and west, experiences weather similar to most western European countries: hot summers, cold winters (but rarely with snow), low rainfall and humidity. January temperatures average in the 40s in Madrid—11 is the record low—and rise to an average of 90 on August days. The slight rainfall averages a misleading inch per month, because most of it falls in spring and autumn. Significant precipitation falls on the

Cordillera Mountains surrounding this center, however, where six feet of moistness produces deep winter snow and good skiing.

The north of Spain, especially the northwest—Galacia, Asturias and Cantabria—makes up for the aridity of the center. Santiago de Compostela averages five feet of rain annually, with most of it falling in winter. With nearly every other day bringing some precipitation, the buildings actually grow moss. On the other hand, the northwest is warmer in winter and cooler in summer than the central plateau. August days seldom reach 90; January brings 50s on most days.

Year-round, the most pleasant temperatures in Spain are those of the eastern coast, from Catalonia to the Levant. Geographically a continuation of the French Riviera, it shares that climate, except for generally milder winters. Valencia averages 50 degrees in winter, Catalonia a few degrees less. August days reach 90, and swimming is comfortable in tepid 70-degree water through October. Almost all the rain falls in spring and autumn. Temperatures rise 4-5 degrees higher to the south in Murcia, but its most noteworthy climactic feature is an oppressive summer heat haze, called the *calina*, that turns sun and moon red and greys the sky on most days.

The southern coastline of Spain enjoys the warmest winters in mainland Europe, with temperatures averaging 55 degrees in January. Almost no rain falls on the eastern half of this coast in the summer, and not much during the rest of the year. Málaga boasts of almost 200 days of utterly cloudless skies. Coastal temperatures in August rise to mid- or even high 90s. Inland, winter temperatures average 10 degrees lower and summer temperatures a few degrees higher. Winter nights can be decidedly cool.

Snow is never a problem for the places most visitors go, but it can make the highest mountains impassable. The two major passes through the Pyrenees—Irún and La Jonquera—are never closed by snow, although smaller passes sometimes are. However, in winter, night fogs can slow mountain traffic to a crawl.

What this means for the traveler is that, no matter what the season, ideal weather exists somewhere in Spain. Spring and fall are perfect in the center of Spain, although summers can be uncomfortably hot and winters require bundling up. The northeast of Spain is best visited in summer, though spring and fall are also good, but winters bring frequent rain. Catalonia and the Levant are pleasant all year, even swimmable in early winter, at least for those used to Maine bathing. Because of heat haze, Murcia is best in seasons other than summer. Barcelona, too, is not at its most enjoyable on steamy summer days. Andalusia remains pleasant year-long, though cool on winter evenings. However, in no part of Spain is the weather ever inhospitable enough to prevent a trip.

Crowds are a consideration, too, in deciding when to visit Spain. Spain doubles its population each summer, filling beaches, hotels and restaurants. In particular, August is the time when the Spanish themselves vacation, adding their numbers to beach resorts, and closing restaurants distant from resort areas. Overall, spring would be the ideal season to cover Spain's terrain, and early summer months are preferable to crowded August.

HOLIDAYS AND SPECIAL EVENTS

The dates of holidays are important because businesses, certainly, and sights, possibly, will be closed; but holidays also offer the best opportunities to view and take part in the local color of the country.

SPAIN

National Holidays All offices closed. When occurring near a weekend, the holiday becomes a four-day weekend.

January 1, Año Nuevo (*New Year*) Everyone is in the streets on New Year's Eve, and crowds gather in Madrid's Puerto del Sol, munching grapes while waiting for the clock to reach midnight.

January 6, Epifania del Señor (*Epiphany*) Presents are given to children.

March 19, San José (*Saint Joseph's Day*) Celebrated in even numbered years only.

March 31, Jueves Santo (*Maundy Thursday*).

April 1, Viernes Santo (*Good Friday*).

April 3, Diá de Pascua (*Easter Sunday*) Processions of floats in many towns bear holy statues.

May 1, Fiesta del Trabajo (*Labor Day*).

June 25, Corpus Christi.

July 25, Santiago Apóstol (*Feast of Santiago*) Celebrated in odd numbered years only.

August 15, Asunción do la Virgen (*Assumption Day*).

October 12, Diá Nacional de España (*National Day*).

November 1, Todos los Santos (*All Saints' Day*).

December 6, Constitución Española (*Constitution Day*).

December 8, Inmaculada Concepción (*Immaculate Conception*).

December 25, Natividad del Señor (*Christmas*).

Regional Celebrations Check with the National Tourist Office of Spain for exact dates.

January 2, Granada Commemoration of the end of the Reconquest.

January 17, most towns San António (*the blessing of animals*).

PORTUGAL

National Holidays All offices closed.

January 1, Ano Novo (*New Year's Day*).

February 7, Carnaval

April 1, Sexta-feira Santa (*Good Friday*).

April 3, Easter

April 25, Dia da Liberdade (*Liberation Day*).

May 1, Dia do Trabalito (*Labor Day*).

May 25, Corpo de Cristo (*Corpus Christi*).

June 10, Dia da Portugal e da Camões (*Portugal and Camões Day*).

June 25, Corpo de Cristo (*Corpus Christi*).

August 15, Dia da Assunciõ (*Assumption Day*).

October 5, Dia da Republica (*Republic Day*).

November 1, Todos os Santos (*All Saints' Day*).

December 1, Restauraciõ da Independencia (*Independence Day*).

December 8, Imaculada da Conceicão (*Immaculate Conception*).

December 25, Dia de Natal (*Christmas*).

PASSPORTS

The single requirement for the average tourist entering Spain or Portugal is a valid passport. No shots are needed. No visa is necessary except for stays longer than 6 months, in the case of Spain, or 60 days, in the case of Portugal (though this is seldom enforced), or for employment in the country. Visa applications and information are available at the nearest Spanish or Portuguese consulate.

U. S. State Department passport agencies are located in Boston, Chicago, Honolulu, Houston, Los Angeles, Miami, New Orleans, New York, Philadelphia, San Francisco, Seattle, Stamford (CT) and Washington D.C. Federal or state courthouses also issue passports, as do many post offices.

Unexpired passports can be renewed by mail, providing that no more than 12 years have elapsed since the date of issue, and the applicant was at least 16 years old at that time. Enclose the expired passport and two full-faced photographs, two inches square, taken against a light background in either color or black-and-white, that have been signed on the back center. Include a completed application form, obtainable at one of the offices listed above, and a check or money order for $55, payable to the U.S. Passport Agency. Processing can take up to a month, after which you will receive your old passport, cancelled, and a new one valid for ten years.

First passports and replacements for those already expired must be applied for in person at one of the offices listed above. Usually the process involves two trips, one to submit the forms and a second to pick up the passport. One proof of citizenship must be presented, which can be a previous passport, a copy of a birth certificate, or a Certificate of Naturalization or Citizenship. A proof of identity is also required and may be satisfied by a driver's license or a previous passport. Credit cards are not sufficient proof of identity, but a friend of two-years' standing is. You will also need two full-faced photographs, two inches square, taken against a light background. The fee is $60 for adults eighteen and over, or $40 for minors. A charge is added for a first passport, a rush order, or a passport issued by a post office or courthouse. It can take up to six weeks for a first-time passport to arrive.

Though not publicized or guaranteed, renewals in person usually can be managed on an emergency basis in 24 hours at State Department offices. A standard passport contains 24 pages, but frequent travelers may request 48 pages at no extra cost.

CUSTOMS

Both Spain and Portugal allow visitors to carry, duty-free, any items intended for personal use. This includes one carton of cigarettes and one liter of alcohol per adult. Expensive equipment—cameras, computers, etc—should be registered with U.S. Customs before leaving the U.S. to ensure that they are not charged a duty on return. A proof of U.S. purchase will also serve.

On the return trip, U.S. customs does not charge duty on a resident's first $400 of foreign purchases intended for personal use or on gifts that accompany a traveler, assuming his last allotment was claimed one month or more before. A family is permitted to pool its individual allotments. One carton of cigarettes is also duty-free for each adult, as are 100 cigars (not Cuban, of course), one liter of alcohol, and one bottle of perfume (if sold in the U.S.). The next $1000 of personal merchandise or gifts is taxed at 10%. Above that amount, rates vary; save receipts in case of questions. Antiques with proof from the seller that they are over 100 years old are duty-free, as are one-of-a-kind paintings.

Packages mailed home, unless clearly marked "American Goods Returned" or "Gift under $50" will be assessed a duty when delivered.

CLOTHES AND PACKING

Read up on the climate and seasons, detailed above, to know what weather to expect. But note that few people in the world set thermostats as high as we do, so expect cooler interiors than at home. Air-conditioning exists in Spain and Portugal, and can be expected in expensive hotels and restaurants, but not in neighborhood restaurants or lower-priced accommodations.

Most travelers bring more clothes than they need or use, and since living out of a suitcase means having to carry it, the best advice about packing is that less is better. The Spanish are more formal in their dress than the average American or Canadian at home; the Portuguese dress somewhere between these two groups. Ties are more common on males in Spain than in the U.S. today.

Apparel that withstands wrinkling, thus needing no ironing, saves both time and money. Raincoats with linings are ideal—single garments that fend off the cool, cold and rain. Comfortable shoes are supremely important when traveling because we tend to walk much more during vacations than ordinarily. And those charming medieval lanes in Spain and Portugal are often paved with cobblestones that can bruise feet through thin-soled shoes. Although sneakers would otherwise be ideal, they are not the fashion in Spain and Portugal.

Do not be overly concerned about forgetting something. Spain and Portugal are civilized countries where almost anything forgotten or lost can be replaced. Still, it is a convenience to have things ready at hand rather than having to search for them in a store. A small sewing kit and a first aid kit fit this description. Sunglasses are needed for most seasons of the year, especially in Spain's center, its eastern and southern coasts, and in Portugal's Algarve.

MONEY

Spanish money is called *pesetas*. There are coins of 1, 2, 5, 10, 25, 50, 100, 200 and 500 pesetas and bills of 200 (uncommon), 500, 1,000, 5,000 and 10,000 pesetas. While the bills are unequivocal, coins arrive in a bewildering variety of sizes, shapes and colors. What makes things difficult is that the size of a coin does not indicate its value, nor does its color. When it is not convenient to read the denomination, thickness is the best indicator of value.

One hundred and twenty-five pesetas are presently worth about $1. Of course, with our dollar gyrating wildly, it is impossible to say what the value of the peseta will be when you read this book. Check the financial section of a good newspaper or ask your bank for the latest rate. Because of the erratic exchange rate, we quote prices in pesetas, rather than in dollars, throughout this book.

Currency fluctuations are also to be expected in the case of Portuguese money, the *escudo*. Each escudo is divided into 100 centavos, written 0$00, with the escudos to the left and centavos to the right of the dollar sign. Coins exist in denominations of 50 centavos, and of 1, 2-1/2, 5, 10 and 25 escudos, with banknotes of 20, 50, 100, 500, 1,000 and 5,000 escudos. Currently, one U.S. dollar buys 175$00 escudos, which is to say that 100 escudos is worth 57 cents, but this is certain to fluctuate.

Safety argues for carrying traveler's checks, rather than cash. Of course, traveler's checks usually cost 1% to buy, but not always. Currently American Express Traveler's Cheques are free at American Automobile Association offices for their members, and Thomas Cook Traveler's Cheques are free when travel arrangements are made through that agency. Inquire about the latest offers. And, in Iberia, exchange money only at banks—hotels, restaurants and stores give less favorable rates. Fees are charged for each transaction, which argues against numerous small exchanges, but do not convert more money than you will use, since converting back to dollars involves another exchange premium.

For some reason exchange rates are terrible here, so do not buy much foreign money before your trip. Do, however, purchase a small amount for the first day, but, if possible, not the overpriced "trip pack" offered by most banks. However, unless you land at some abnormal hour, you should be able to exchange dollars for pesetas or escudos at the airport when you arrive.

Popular credit cards are widely accepted in both Spain and Portugal. Cash machines throughout Spain and Portugal that are part of the Cirrus network will accept American bank cards that belong to that network.

COSTS

Alas, the days of truly cheap travel in Spain are gone, at least for the near future. Twenty years ago a moderate hotel charged $10 for a double and the same amount bought a pleasant dinner for two with a house wine. If a tourist worked at it, daily expenses could be kept as low as $10. Of course $10 bought more at home then too, but the loosening of government price controls on Spanish hotels and restaurants and the fall of the dollar have changed that situation even more drastically than inflation has. This is not to say that Spain costs as much as France, England or Italy. It never has, and probably never will. Spain remains one of the least expensive European countries for travelers, but today none can be considered cheap.

Comfortable double rooms in moderately priced hotels in tourist areas and resorts cost about $75 ($100 in Madrid or Barcelona). The same room in a town less frequented by tourists will be a third less. Count on $30 per person for an adequate dinner with wine. Thus, the current budget for a couple to travel modestly in Spain averages a daily minimum of $175. This does not include transportation—either getting to or around the country. It is, however, about half the figure needed for France or Italy.

Portugal remains a genuine travel bargain, always in first place among the countries of Europe. Costs will be as much as a quarter lower than Spain's. Thus, you can decrease the average daily budget for a couple to about $135 dollars, with the same caveat about adding transportation costs.

TIPPING

Scan the menu in restaurants for the words *servicio incluso*, which means your bill already includes tips. If so, a small additional gratuity is sufficient, say, 2%, or the equivalent of a dollar, whichever is greater. Otherwise, 15% is a normal tip in both Spanish and Portuguese restaurants. In elegant restaurants where a captain orchestrates the meal and a sommelier presents the wine, the captain should receive 5%, the sommelier the equivalent of $2 and the waiter 15%.

Hotels almost always include service in the bill. Still, it's gracious to leave the equivalent of a dollar per night for the maid. The concierge, doorman and porter should be tipped for specific services, say the equivalent of 50 pesetas per bag carried (or 50 escudos in Portugal), or a like amount for hailing a cab. Should service not be included in the bill, give 10% to the cashier for disbursement to the staff.

Cab drivers expect a 15% tip unless the fare was negotiated beforehand, in which case the price includes the gratuity. Ushers are not tipped, but washroom attendants should be given a small coin. Whoever opens a church or building or lights it for you should be given 100 pesetas or 100 escudos, depending on the country. A guide expects 100 pesetas or escudos per person. Hairdressers expect a 10% tip.

SHOPPING

Ceramics, leather, woven rugs, fashion, pearls, antiques and flea markets all call to the tourist's wallet in Spain.

Spain has been famous for ceramics since the time of the Moors, and its leather work so noted that "cordovan" became an English proper noun. Spain still produces colorful ceramics sold in a hundred shops and continues its tradition of fine leather, especially in Andalusia and in the famed Loewe's stores, with shoes best in Madrid, Barcelona and Seville. Madrid and Barcelona are also budding centers for haute couture. No longer is Balenciaga Spain's only internationally recognized designer; today one might add Adolfo Dominques, Alfredo Caral and Sybilla from Madrid, or, for men, José Tómas and Groc from Barcelona. Famed Majorca pearls can cost as much as 30% less in Spain. Spanish antiques have not yet escalated as precipitously as French, Italian or English articles; bargains, even in quality pieces, still exist. Costume jewelry is excellent and inexpensive. But the most entertaining shopping is to be found in local flea markets, both in Madrid and elsewhere. Discussions of each city include appropriate specific information.

In Portugal the best buys are ceramics, hand embroidery, baskets and rugs. All are finely crafted and less expensive than in the U.S. Antiques, although never cheap, remain fine buys in Portugal. And no one should miss the Feira de Ladra (Thieves' Market) in Lisbon.

One unfamiliar complication to shopping in Europe is the Value Added Tax, added to purchase prices to equalize disparities among the countries of the European Economic Community. In Spain the Value Added Tax, or IVA, is 12% on most purchases, but 33% on luxury items, while in Portugal the standard tax is a whopping 17%, with 33% for luxuries. Needless to say, such a supplement can turn a bargain into a bad buy. The good news for travelers, however, is that any foreigner who carries the merchandise home with him is entitled to a refund of the tax, provided the article cost over 47,000 pesetas or 50,000 escudos. Refund forms will be supplied by most stores or obtained at airport refund offices. Receipts and forms must be stamped by a customs official, who will ask to view the article. Refunds take a month or more to be mailed, or to be reflected on your charge card. El Corte Inglés and Galerias Preciados, the two major Spanish department stores, offer a simpler way to deal with the IVA. Any tourist who requests it receives a card entitling him to an immediate 10% deduction on every purchase, even sale items, in lieu of the IVA refund.

HOTELS AND OTHER ACCOMMODATIONS

Hotels in both Spain and Portugal are numerous and high in quality. Nowhere in the world will you find more truly grand hotels, or more delightful inns at modest rates. Service is excellent and cleanliness exemplary, with very rare exceptions. In almost every case you will get more for your hotel dollar than at home.

Unless money is not a consideration, we suggest using hotels in three very different ways. Some hotels provide such special service, views or decor, that they should be visited despite their expense—a stay can be one of the highlights of a trip. Other hotels are attractive and comfortable places to sleep at affordable prices. Last are those hotels that offer the simplest of rooms at very modest charges. Spending a few nights in one of these inexpensive places is rarely a sacrifice, especially if the savings are used to arrange a memorable stay at one of the extraordinary hotels.

Virtually every public accommodation in Spain is listed in the annual *Guía de Hoteles*, published by the Secretaria General de Turismo, and available in the U.S. at the National Tourist Office of Spain as well as at many travel agencies. The Secretaria General de Turismo rates establishments with a system of stars based on measurable features such as the percentage of rooms with private baths, air-conditioning, etc., though not for such unmeasureable qualities as comfort, efficiency and friendliness of service. These ratings provide a rough guide to price and quality, but should be read in conjunction with our descriptions and alternative star-system (see, *Introduction*, "Ratings.") A white and blue metal plaque outside the establishment will indicate its official rating and type—"H" a hotel, "HR" a *residencia*, and "Hs" a *hostale*.

First-class hotels provide a concierge, that is, a kind of ombudsman who can help with almost any problem. He (or, rarely, she) can locate tickets for almost any event, confirm travel arrangements or make them, recommend restaurants and shops, and deal with emergencies. Their knowledge and expertise are always impressive and make otherwise difficult chores effortless. The concierge should be tipped according to the number of requests, usually 100 ptas. each (or 100$00 in Portugal).

Paradors are an extraordinary Spanish institution—hotels that can enrich any trip. The first parador was built in 1926 as a hunting lodge for the wealthy, but they soon began serving tourists to Spain who demanded better than the hotels of the era provided. Faced with an oversupply of historical buildings whose owners could not afford their upkeep, the government began buying and remodeling grand edifices into hotels. The program proved immensely successful; it preserved irreplaceable structures while offering tourists a chance to eat and sleep at reasonable rates in the palaces, castles and convents in which ordinarily they could only sightsee. Eighty-six paradors now dot the country, about half of which are historical monuments, with many of the rest showcasing modern architects. Though never inexpensive, paradors tend to be less costly than other hotels of similar ratings because they are government-owned, yet with highly professional service. A night's pampered stay in a 15th century castle for about $100 strikes most people as a bargain indeed. Some paradors are truly magnificent, memorable places, such as Los Reyes Católicos in Santiago de Compostela, Olite near Pamplona, Cardona near Barcelona, San Marcos in León, Sigüenza an hour east of Segovia, and De la Reconquista in Oviedo, to mention just a few. Others offer more ordinary, but comfortable, accommodations in areas lacking sufficient hotels. A list and brochure is available from the National Tourist Office of Spain or from the booking agent for the U.S. and Canada, Marketing Ahead, Inc. at 433 Fifth Avenue, New York, NY 10016 (☎ (212) 686-9213, FAX (212) 686-0271). Note that popular paradors fill up quickly. Since many are small, one should reserve as early as possible, at least five months in advance for high seasons. Note also that parador meals are seldom adventurous or remarkable, but served in dining rooms whose style almost makes up for the unexceptional cuisine. Recently, paradors have begun serving regional cuisine, providing visitors with a convenient way to sample local specialties.

In 1940, not to be outdone, Portugal instituted a system of state-run hotels called **pousadas**. While not as many are installed in historic buildings as in Spain's case, all are well managed and eminently comfortable. Those in Óbidos, Palmela, Estremoz and Évora are outstanding, each a former castle or medieval monastery. Twenty-seven now dot the country. Reservations are advisable at pousadas, for they are popular and generally provide only a small number of rooms. Reservations can be made directly through: Empresa Nacional de Turismo, Avenida Santa Joana a Prineses, 10A, Lisbon 1700 (☎ 01 848 12 21; telex: 13609), or through any travel agent.

Portugal's unique contribution to tourist accommodations is a program of arranged stays in private manor houses throughout the country. Some are palaces, some historic buildings, others more rustic, but all provide a change from a normal hotel and its often impersonal service. Prices vary with the level of elegance, thus suiting a variety of budgets. The Portuguese National Tourist Office (☎ 212-354-4403) can supply prices; reservations may be made through Alta Tours in San Francisco (☎ 800-338-4191; Fax 415-434-2684); the main agency in Portugal is Associação das Casas do Turismo de Habitação (☎ 011-351-58-942-335).

Not all the wonderful hotels in Spain and Portugal are paradors, pousadas or manor houses. The Alhambra Palace in Granada provides as memorable an experience as the parador nearby, though the parador is the most heavily booked hotel in Spain. No hotel in the world can surpass the privately-owned Ritz in Barcelona. And both the Hostal del Cardenal in Toledo and the Rector in Salamanca far surpass the quality of their local paradors. Even if the idea of a parador or pousada seems wonderful, it's a good idea to check the ratings and descriptions of an area's other hotels before automatically booking into the parador.

If you're looking for a hotel room in person, remember that Europeans frequently ask to see a room before they register, so hotels expect it. Simple English will generally be understood. If not, a single room is *una habitación sencilla*, a double is *una habitación doble*. *Con baño* means with bath. Few double rooms contain a large bed for two (*cama de matrimonio*), though one can ask. A single room should be no more than 80% of the price of a double. The quoted price for a room in Spain includes taxes and usually, though not always, a surcharge for service. The service surcharge is always included in Portugal. In case of a dispute, asking for the *libro de reclamaciónes* (complaint book) often wins the day.

The way to sleep most cheaply in Iberia is to pay nothing for accommodations. That is sometimes possible through a system of international house exchanges. Although the location of your lodging is fixed, it can be used as a base for side trips, and sometimes cars are included in the exchange. Of course, your own home should be located in or near an area of potential interest to foreign visitors, and the odds of an agreeable arrangement improve the longer in advance that inquiries are initiated. Several companies specialize in helping with such arrangements for a fee of $35-$60:

International Home Exchange, Box 3975, San Francisco, CA 94119 (☎ 415-435-3497).

Vacation Exchange Club, 12006 111th Ave., Suite 12, Youngstown, AZ 85363 (☎ 602-972-2186).

World Wide Exchange, 1344 Pacific Ave., Suite 103, Santa Cruz, CA 95060 (☎ 408-425-0531).

RESTAURANTS

Restaurants in Spain serve filling meals at about the price of restaurants at home, and if the cost is slightly greater, the portions will be too. Spain boasts some utterly splendid restaurants that rank with the very best in the world. Zalacaín in Madrid and Arzak in Donostia (San Sebastian) both have Basque chefs, impeccable service and sublime food, at a price (about $110 dollars a person for Zalacaín, and $75 for Arzak). Because the quality of available ingredients is outstanding throughout Spain, even a modest restaurant can provide delicious tastes. Vegetables are grown for flavor, not for their capacity to survive early picking and travel, as in the U.S. Humble chicken retains the taste we have all but forgotten, and bread always tastes homemade. The Spanish love to dine out, which generates an astonishing number of restaurants. In both cities and towns, crowds wander the streets every evening, pause to study menus, and stop where their fancy dictates. Fortunately, few "tourist traps," where bad food is served at high prices, exist.

Dining costs can be reduced by ordering from the *Menú Turístico*, which all Spanish restaurants offer. This provides a 3- or 4-course meal, usually including wine, and makes up for its limited choices with savings of about half of à la carte orderings. Many places offer *platos combinados* (combination plates), a filling meal and salad all on one plate, usually including wine on the side, for five to ten dollars. Or try a sandwich (*bocadillo*) in any bar, or *tapas*, appetizers, enough for a meal in omnipresent tapas bars. Cafeterias and *auto-servicios* can be half the price of restaurants. And, when all else fails to appeal, major cities offer McDonald's and Kentucky Fried Chicken, just like at home—and at similar prices.

The bill (*la cuenta*) will already include taxes and may say *servicio incluso*, especially if you ordered a *platos combinados*, which means the tip is included. If so, a small additional gratuity is sufficient, say,

5% or the equivalent of a dollar, whichever is greater. Otherwise, 15% is the normal tip in Spanish restaurants.

The tip should be the same in Portuguese restaurants, but details of dining are otherwise quite different. First and foremost, the dinner hour ranges from 7 to 10 p.m., as compared to Spain whose restaurants begin opening for dinner each evening as Portuguese restaurants close. Portuguese food, with rare exceptions, is of a homey sort—hearty and tasty, generally either stews or plainly-done meat or fish. The flavor will be savory, for the ingredients are first-rate, but the seasoning will not be subtle. Portions will be large, and prices low. Best are fresh sardines that melt your heart as they melt in your mouth, breads to bring out the peasant in anyone, and wines of surprisingly high quality for impressively low prices. At many inexpensive restaurants the price of a meal will hover in the $20 range for a couple. With prices already so low, the tourist menus that Spain provides to cut dining costs are seldom available in Portugal. *La conta, por favor* will bring the check.

TRAVEL TO SPAIN AND PORTUGAL

BY PLANE

Direct flights to Spain presently depart from New York, Dallas/ Fort Worth (American), Miami (Iberia), Washington, DC (United), Atlanta (Delta), Toronto and Montreal (Air Canada and Iberia). Scheduled carriers include TWA, Continental, American, United, Delta, and Iberia. Iberia and TWA schedule daily flights from the New York City area to Madrid. Iberia and Delta also fly daily from New York to Barcelona through Madrid. British Airways arranges connecting flights through London to various Spanish cities; Air France provides the same service through Paris; and KLM stops over at Amsterdam. TAP flies daily to Lisbon from the New York area and three times a week from Boston, and allows a free stop over half-way at the Azores. TWA also offers daily direct flights to Lisbon throughout the year, and some flights from San Francisco. Delta flies direct from New York to Lisbon five times a week. In addition, charter flights abound.

Since airfares were deregulated, competition has led to complex, changing rates along with exotic give-aways and deals. Like specials at the supermarket, prices change continually, so that only a travel agent will know what is available at a given time. However, some principles are constant.

Prices change with the seasons and are most expensive from June through August, least expensive both from November to the middle of December and from the second of January through March.

Whatever the season, first-class fares will be the most expensive way to fly by a factor of three or four times the least expensive. For that fare, a traveler is provided free stopovers, extra leg room, and quiet. Meals are more elaborate, and drinks and headsets are free—though the high fare covers such generosity many times over. Most carriers also offer a class of fares between first class and economy, called "Business Class," "Preference Class," or some such designation, with about the same benefits as first class, except for a tad less room, and at about half the price.

Most of us cram into tourist, economy, or coach class. The names vary but not the fact that this is the low end, both of comfort and cost. Here rates grow complex.

In addition to regular economy (tourist, coach, or whatever-the-name) fares, there are also discount economy fares which reduce the number of free stopovers allowed, or else charge for them. If a flier does not plan any stopovers, he travels exactly as do those paying the full economy fares, but for less. "Excursion" fares are even lower in cost—economy-class travel with required minimum and maximum stays that happily correspond to the duration of most vacations. APEX (Advanced Purchase EXcursion) fares are special excursion fares that require full payment for tickets two weeks or so before departure. All excursion fares carry an expensive penalty for changing a reservation, and APEX fares involve a penalty for cancelling the trip. But savings, which can be half what a regular economy ticket would cost, mean that most tourists opt for such arrangements.

Stand-by fares, once the bargain-hunters treasure, have been discontinued by most airlines (Virgin Atlantic to London is an exception), because of inconvenienced and sometimes irate travelers. A true bargain hunter might, however, call airlines to check the current status.

Charter flights were once great bargains. They were also risky: if the charter company failed, the price of the paid-in-advance ticket could be lost. Since scheduled airlines have lowered their fares, the savings on charter flights today are less than they used to be, although still real. Generally there is little or no flexibility in dates of travel, and advance payment is always required. If you cancel your trip, you forfeit the entire price of the ticket, but the charter company may cancel its flight up to ten days before scheduled departure, as long as it refunds your money. So if your charter leaves as scheduled, you can be sure it will be full—the company would have cancelled otherwise. Still, we have seen one-way flights from New York to Madrid for a very tempting $200.

Ticket consolidators can provide tickets as cheaply as most charters with less risk. These firms sell the tickets that airlines were unable to at discounts. Thus, space will not be available for every flight, and never for popular times. But discounts range from 20% and more off standard fares. A sampling of consolidators is: **Access International,** 101 West 31st Street, New York, NY 10016 (☎ 212-465 0707; 800-825-3633), **Travel Avenue,** 180 North Des Plaines, Chicago, IL 60661 (☎ 800-333-3335), and **Maharaja Travel,** 393 Fifth Av., New York, NY 10016 (☎ 212-213-2020).

More offbeat for the venturesome or desperate, is generic air travel. Airhitch is the best known (2901 Broadway, Suite 100, New York, NY 11025, ☎ 212-864-2000). You register by paying a small fee and specify a range of departure dates and a preferred destination, along with alternatives. About a week before your first desired departure you are offered at least two flights meeting those specifications. If you do not accept any, your fee is forfeited; otherwise you pay the balance minus the fee. Savings can be great, as low as the lowest charters, with less money risked up front. Write or call for details and other variations on this theme.

After paying, the question remains of what to take with you. Each economy passenger is allowed two pieces of luggage, neither of which can exceed 70 pounds, and whose combined dimension (length, width, plus height) measures no more than 62 inches for one piece and 55 for the other; one carry-on with dimensions totaling no more than 45 inches; and one shoulder bag. Higher classes of fares are allowed more. These limits apply to adults and to those children paying at least half of the adult fare; children paying less than half-price fares are permitted less. If you must take more than what the airline allows, come early to the check-in and expect to pay for overweight.

Seats in the rear of a plane rock and shake more than those further forward. Tall travelers should request seats behind the door or the emergency exit, as these provide the most leg room. All told, the last row of seats is the worst, not even reclining fully. Note that foreign flights are not subject to the same non-smoking regulations as our domestic ones, so request whichever section is appropriate. One food tip is to ask for a special dietary meal both at reservation time and again when you confirm. The special diet can be kosher, low sodium, low cholesterol, or any other, but such meals generally will be prepared with more care than your seatmate's.

BY CAR

Numerous border crossings link France with Spain. The most travelled are La Jonquera from Perpignan, on the extreme east coast, and Irún from Bayonne, on the extreme west coast. Both routes avoid mountain travel through the Pyrenees and remain open 24 hours a day, even through the winter. The most interesting Pyrenees route is through the tiny country of Andorra, enticing for its duty-free shopping. Portugal connects with Spain in 14 places, but the common crossings are from Élvas to Badajoz, in the center, and from Valencia to Tui, in the north.

A car ferry links Spain with Morocco. Boats leave Ceuta, a Spanish enclave in Morocco, and Tangier, for Algeciras in Spain. The trip takes 1-1/2 hours from Ceuta, an hour longer from Tangier. Especially if bringing a car, reservations should be made in advance through a travel agent, or directly through Compania Trasmediterranea (2 Calle Pedro Muñoz Seca, Madrid, España 28011, ☎ 91-431-0700).

BY TRAIN

Express trains leave Paris every evening, arriving at Madrid 13 hours later (or at Barcelona 11-1/2 hours later). The most modern train is the Talgo which currently departs from Paris' Austerlitz station at 8 p.m., and arrives at 8:30 a.m. in Chamartin station, Madrid. The Puerta del Sol is older, and leaves at 5:45 p.m. for a 9:55 a.m. arrival in Madrid. The Talgo also leaves for Barcelona from Paris at 9 p.m. for an 8:30 a.m. arrival. Sleeping accommodations must be reserved well in advance. Trains can also be picked up south of Paris, through Biarritz for Donostia (San Sebastian) and Madrid, and through Perpignan for Figueres and Barcelona on Spain's east coast. Only the Sud Express goes direct to Portugal from France, departing from Gare d'Austerlitz in Paris.

From Lisbon, the Lusitania Express leaves at 9:45 p.m. for arrival at Madrid's Chamartin Station at 8:55 a.m. The Luiz de Camões, in the daytime, is faster by a couple of hours. In the other direction, trains leave Madrid at 1:50 and 11 p.m. for Lisbon. Part of the reason the trip takes so long is that trains have to be changed at Entroncamento because of wider-gauged Spanish rails.

PACKAGE TOURS

A package tour combines travel and hotel costs in a single price. Since the packager deals in volume, he books flights and rooms more cheaply than individuals can. Even after the packager's profit, the combination should cost less than the same arrangements made individually. On the minus side, the hotels provided are seldom the best choices in the price range and the itinerary may be rigid. Figure the costs of the tour you would arrange for yourself and see if the savings of a package tour makes it worthwhile. On your own, you can find accommodations more interesting than what the package offers, but you will have to work to select and reserve. Note that the prices cited for packages generally are *per person* in a double occupancy room.

Travel sections of newspapers often advertise package tours. Travel agents will know many more. In choosing a package tour it is important to find out whether you will be charged for any price increases that occur after you've booked. Some companies guarantee the price at booking time will not be raised. You should also ask whether you'll receive a full refund if any part of the package promised at the time of booking is not available. We list a number of packaging companies below which will be pleased to send information about their offerings:

Abreu Tours, Inc., 317 East 34th Street, New York, NY 10016 (☎ 212-661-0555 or 800-223-1580).

American Express Vacations, local American Express offices, or Box 5014, Atlanta, GA 30302 (☎ 800-241-1700).

Cavalcade Tours, 450 Harman Meadow Boulevard, Secaucus, NJ 07096, (☎ 201-617-8922 or 800-356-2405).

Cosmos Tours, 95-25 Queens Boulevard, Rego Park, NY 11374 (☎ 800-221-0090).

Cultural Heritage Alliance, 107-115 South Second Street, Philadelphia, PA 19160 (☎ 215-923-7288). Portugal only.

Getaway Vacations, Inc., 10 East Stow Road, Marlton, NJ 08053 (☎ 800-GETAWAY).

Globus-Gateway Tours, same address as Cosmo Tours, above.

Hispanidad Holidays, Inc., 99 Tulip Avenue, Suite 208, Floral Park, NY 11001 (☎ 800-488-4700; Fax 516-352-4943).

Maupintour, Box 807, Lawrence, KS 66044 (☎ 800-255-4266).

M.I. Travel, Inc., 450 Seventh Avenue, Suite 1805, New York, NY 10123 (☎ 212-967-6565 or 800-327-1515).

Odyssey Adventures, (☎ 516-569-2813 or 800-344-0013; Fax 516-569-2998).

Petrabax USA, 97-45 Queens Boulevard, New York, NY 11374 (☎ 718-897-7272 or 800-367-6611.

Plus Ultra Travel, 221 Seventh Avenue, New York, NY 10011-1806 (☎ 800-244-4741).

Portuguese Tours, 321 Rahway Avenue, Elizabeth, NJ 07202 (☎ 201-352-6112).

Skyline Travel Club Inc., 666 Old Country Road, Suite 205, Garden City, N.Y. 11530 (☎ 516-222-9090 or 800-645-6198, Fax 516-222-9322).

Spanish Heritage Tours, 116-47 Queens Boulevard, Forest Hills, NY 11375 (☎ 718-544-2752).

Sun Holidays, 26 Sixth Street, Suite 603, Stamford, CT 06905 (☎ 800-243-2057, Fax 203-323-3843).

Tour Directions International, Inc., 70 West 36th Street, Suite 1004, New York, NY 10018 (☎ 212-564-3236 or 800-423-4460; Fax 212-629-5934).

Trafalgar Tours, 21 East 26th Street, New York, NY 10010 (☎ 212-689-8977 or 800-854-0103).

Escorted package tours are a different sort of travel experience. The traveler joins a group with a leader, does everything ensemble, and leaves all the problems to someone else. Such tours are the most carefree way to travel, but do throw you in with a group of strangers and restrict your freedom to do what you want when you wish. Sometimes, however, they are led by experts on history or art and provide an education impossible to gain on one's own. Since the expenses includes a fee for the leader, this sort of tour will cost more than other package tours, probably bringing the price to about what individual arrangements would cost.

TRAVEL IN SPAIN AND PORTUGAL

Getting from one city to another in Spain or Portugal is no more difficult than getting around anywhere else. You have the same choices—car, plane, train or bus.

BY CAR

Spanish roads generally are good enough, but not what you left at home. The majority of Spanish highways are two-lane roads that would be considered good country roads in the U.S. The quality of a road and whether it is multi-laned is indicated by its letter designation. "A" followed by a number, as in A-1, means an *autopista*, a well-paved four-lane highway charging tolls (*peajes*) over most of its route. These roads will also have an "E" designation; the major arteries in Europe are being systematically numbered throughout the European Economic Community. Toll roads are privately owned in Spain and charge truly exorbitant rates, but they do not pass through low-speed-limit villages, so save both time and gas. "N" means a highway, a national road (*carratera Nacional*), and is followed by either a Roman or Arabic numeral. These are usually one lane in each direction and pass through towns and villages where speeds must be cut in half or more. "D" and "C" prefix lesser roads, acceptably paved but even slower going, generally with more curves. All roads are well marked with self-explanatory international highway symbols. Except for *autopistas*, Spanish roads present astonishing hairpin curves, especially over the mountains, but sometimes on perfectly flat terrain. These curves are usually well marked, and preceded by signs indicating an appropriate speed, but stay alert.

All of the foregoing applies to Portugal, even to its use of the same highway designations, except that Portuguese roads drop a rung below those in Spain. As if to suit their driving to the conditions, Portuguese drivers also stand a step below their Iberian neighbors, although the traffic there is lighter.

Speed limits are 120 kilometers per hour (75 mph) on *autopistas*, 100 (62 mph) on national highways, 90 (55 mph) on other roads, unless otherwise marked, and 60 (38 mph) to 40 in towns. Note that distances and speed limits in Spain will be measured in kilometers, approximately five-eighths of a mile. When passing, leave the left blinker on throughout your time in the passing lane, then signal right to return. Truckers will let you know when it is safe to pass them by signaling with their right blinker. Except for being occasionally more daring in passing, Spanish drivers are reasonably considerate and able, the Portuguese less so.

A good map of the area you plan to cover is a necessity when driving. Michelin map #990, covering all of Spain and Portugal, is recommended. Old, haphazardly developed cities can be mazes. If aiming for the center, follow signs saying "*Centro.*" Both Portuguese and Spanish authorities are serious about punishing drunken drivers, so don't take chances. And seatbelts must be worn outside of towns.

An International Driving Permit is required for foreigners driving in Iberia. Branches of the American Automobile Club can supply one. Bring along two passport-sized photos, a valid driver's license and a $5 fee. Incidentally, AAA has reciprocal arrangements with automobile clubs in Spain and Portugal that provide similar services for AAA members from the U.S. In Spain the emergency assistance number for RACE, the AAA affiliate, is ☎ (91) 593 33 33.

A car may be rented either on the spot or by making arrangements before departure. Because comparison shopping is easier from home, it's certainly the way to find the best prices. All major U.S. rental companies have Spanish and Portuguese subsidiaries. Your travel agent can make arrangements, or you can call directly for prices or reservations. Lesser known companies specialize in European rentals, but are not always as inexpensive as might be expected given the frequent "specials" offered by major rental companies. Note that Portuguese rentals will bill at 17% more than the quoted price, because of the IVA tax, and Spanish rentals will add 12%.

Although the legal driving age in Iberia is 18, some rental companies refuse to rent to people under 21, or even older. Most Portuguese rental agencies require a minimum age of 23. Check in advance. Estimate about $350 per week for a compact car with automatic transmission.

Avis: ☎ 800-331-2112.

Auto Europe: ☎ 800-223-5555, or ☎ 800-458-9503 in Canada.

Budget: ☎ 800-527-0700.

Dollar (**EuroDollar** in Europe): ☎ 800-800-6000.

Europe by Car: ☎ 800-223-1516 or ☎ 212-581-3040.

Foremost Euro-Car: ☎ 800-423-3111, in California ☎ 800-272-3299.

Hertz: ☎ 800-654-3001.

Kemwel: ☎ 800-678-0678.

National: ☎ 800-227-3876.

Sometimes the least expensive rental will be through a Spanish or Portuguese company. Additional names can be provided by the National Tourist Office of Spain or the Portuguese National Tourist Office. Some have U.S. representatives.

ATESA, Spain's largest, is represented by Reshotel Marketing, 70 West 36th Street, New York, NY 10018 (☎ 212-564-2300 or 800-423-4460).

M.I. brokers all major U.S. and Spanish companies, so can locate the best deal. M.I. Travel, Inc. 450 Seventh Avenue, Suite 1805, New York, NY 10123 (☎ 212-967-6565 or 800-327-1515).

In addition, most rental companies and major airlines offer fly/drive packages that bundle airfare and car rental prices, frequently with very attractive savings.

Renting a car for foreign use raises the issue of insurance. Rentals generally include collision insurance in the price—though this should be checked when comparing costs—but often leave a deductible of $1000 or more for damage to the rented car. In such a case, a collision damage waiver should be considered even though it can add $10 per day or more to the rental fee. Note that insurance policies covering damage waivers on rental cars at home generally do not apply to overseas rentals, although rentals by credit card often do.

A major credit card is sufficient for renting any car, but the lack of such plastic makes difficulties, here or there. Some companies will not rent at all to cardless clients; others require substantial deposits.

Gas is a major expense in Europe, costing three times what it does in the U.S. Posted gas prices are initially deceptive for Americans because they are priced by the liter (slightly more than a quart), as opposed to per gallon. "Fill her up" is *Pleno, por favor*, in Spain, or *Encha o dispósito, por favor*, in Portugal. Stations are plentiful throughout both countries.

BY PLANE

The cheapest way to fly from one city to another in Spain is to use free stopovers, if they are included in your transAtlantic fare. Sufficient free stopovers may permit you to fly without additional charge within Spain or Portugal. Check with your travel agent.

Spain's domestic airline is Avianca, affiliated with its international Iberia Airlines. Avianca offers service to all the large cities in Spain, and various bargain fares. One current special for foreign visitors is a $199 pass for unlimited flights to any locations in Spain during a 60-day period, if purchased in conjunction with a ticket to Spain on Iberia Airlines. Check for current availability, price and other specials. Barcelona is served by a shuttle plane (Puente Aereo) that leaves Madrid every hour, or half hour, and requires no reservation.

Portugal is so small that flying from one part of the country to another is rarely called for.

BY TRAIN

Trains beat planes when the distance is 200 miles or less, because train stations are located downtown while airports are not. Trains go almost everywhere in Spain, though not always directly. RENFE (Red Nacional de los Ferrocarriles Español) radiates from its hub in

Madrid to the corners of the country. Travel is convenient along any continuous radius, but requires retracing tracks to reach cities on different lines. RENFE ticket offices are centrally located in large cities.

The best trains for speed and service are international trains (EC, IC, TER, Electrotren, Pendular and Talga). Intra-country "expreso" and "rapido" come next. Seville is served by the new, high-speed AVE that takes less than 3 hours. Most cities, however, are connected by Motorail, which corresponds to our commuter train systems. Fares depend on the caliber of train and whether you choose to travel in first or second class. So many types of discounts are offered that any tourist paying full fare has simply not asked about them—round-trips, senior citizens, families, youths, and certain days of the week are all assigned one discount or another. Reservations are always advised.

If planning a substantial amount of train travel, the best buy is a pass allowing unlimited rides during a fixed period. Eurail and Interail passes are valid on Spanish trains, as well as for the rest of Europe, but for such passes to prove worthwhile you must consume a great deal of mileage. Eurail Flexipasses, issued for fewer train days at lower prices, generally prove more suitable. Even less expensive, but purely for travel within the country, are Spanish Rail Passes, called *Tarjeta Turística*. They are issued to tourists only for 3, 5 or 10 days of unlimited travel within a one-month period for fares as low as $340 for a second-class 10-day pass. Information and current prices are available from travel agents. All such unlimited tickets must be purchased before leaving the U.S. The U.S. representative of RENFE—French Rail, Inc.—is located at 610 Fifth Avenue, New York, NY 10020 (☎ 212-582-2110). A similar ticket is available for Portugal, only for use within its borders, but rarely proves economical because of the short distances involved.

For train buffs, RENFE also offers special train tours. The most famous is the Al Andalus Express, a train of beautifully reconditioned cars from the 1920s and 1930s, which includes shower rooms, a game room and a piano bar. The route varies, as does the number of days—between one and four—and service is offered only during May, June and September. Tickets are expensive—from $1000 per person for the four days, to $140 for one day, meals included—but it is an unmatchable experience. Information on this and other unique train tours is available through Marsans International (205 East 42nd Street, New York, NY 10017; ☎ 212-661-6565 or 800-223-6114).

Portuguese trains show their age and should be more efficient in such a small country. An express train runs conveniently in 5 hours to the Algarve from Lisbon, daily in the summer and four times a week during the rest of the year. Five daily trains connect Lisbon with Oporto for a 4-1/2 hour trip at less than $10. Otherwise, trains generally consume more time than do more direct buses.

BY BUS

A bus is the cheapest form of travel, beating the cost of trains by about a third. Each city, village and hamlet contains a bus station, Madrid and Barcelona three, Lisbon one. We list addresses in the "Directory" section for each city. The ticketing procedure is the same as at home. Pay as you board for a short trip or purchase a ticket in the station for a longer trip. Estimate about $6 per 100 k of ride. Although there is no provision for reservations, arriving early accomplishes the same thing.

Because there is no national bus company in Spain, numerous small firms divide up the country, so timetables and routes would fill a book, and do. The monthly *Horario Guía* lists times and routes, not only for all bus service, but also for trains and planes, and is available at any newsstand. Portugal's national bus company, the *Rodoviaria Nacional*, distributes its schedules to most hotels.

STUDENT TRAVEL

Any student or person of student age or inclination seeking information on student travel should contact the Council on International Educational Exchange (CIEE). In addition to its headquarters at 205 East 42nd Street, New York, NY 10017 (☎ 212-661-1414), branches are located near many large universities. The organization stores reams of information on work, study, education and travel programs for students. In addition it issues Federation of International Youth Travel Organization cards which discount transportation costs and museum fees, provide entrance to Youth Hostels, and offer many other benefits. To apply for a card, send two passport-type pictures, a proof of birth date, and a ten dollar fee. You need to be under 26, but not necessarily a matriculating student.

If you think you might enjoy living with a Spanish family for a week to a month, contact Experiment in International Living, Kipling Road, Box E 10, Brattleboro, VT 05301 (☎ 802-257-7751). If you'd like to investigate study abroad, the subject is covered extensively in two books—*Academic Year Abroad* and *Vacation Study Abroad*, both published by The Institute of International Education

(809 UN Plaza, New York, NY 10017; ☎ 212-883-8200). In addition, several language schools offer Spanish courses, including:

EF International Language Schools, 1 Memorial Drive, Cambridge, MA 02142 (☎ 617-252-6100) offers a nine month course in Barcelona for beginner to advanced that includes transportation and accommodations.

Escuela de Idiomas "Nerjo," Almirante Ferandiz, ☎ 73-29780. Nerja Málaga, España (☎ 52-16-87 or Fax 52-21-19) offers reasonably priced intensive courses for five days to four weeks that include living with a Spanish family.

The Hispalis Center of the Instituto de Lenguas y Cultura Española at Amor de Dios 31-2, E-41002 Seville, España (☎ 34-5-490 09 72) covers courses from beginner to advanced lasting from two to eight weeks.

Centro de Lenguas e Intercambio Cultural in Seville offers from two weeks to sixteen weeks of intensive Spanish for beginner to advanced with various accommodations. Contact Language Study Abroad at 1301 North Maryland Avenue, Glendale, CA 91207 (☎ 818-242-5263).

Centro de Idiomas at Sagasta 27, 3° Izq. 28004 Madrid, España (☎ 446-69-79 or Fax 447-22-23) offers a large variety of courses from two weeks to twenty-four and accommodations with Spanish families if desired.

Young people, 26 or under, are eligible for an especially inexpensive version of the Eurail Pass called Eurail Youthpass. It must be purchased before landing in Europe. Contact French Rail, Inc. (610 Fifth Avenue, New York, NY 10020; ☎ 212-582-2110) for details. Or, in Spain, a Youth Pass for anyone under 26 may be purchased at RENFE stations for half-price travel on designated "Blue," off-peak days.

Any young person arriving in Spain should go to Red Española de Albergues Juveniles (Calle José Ortega y Gasset 17, 28006 Madrid; ☎ 91-401-1300) for an International Youth Hostel Federation guest card (which costs about $20), and lists of available student hostels.

Young people will find living in Spain and Portugal cheaper than any other European country and much cheaper than being on their own at home. The only pleasure they might miss is the convenience of hitchhiking. Europeans generally show little consideration for those attempting the joys of the road.

FEMALE TRAVELERS

The situation for women in Spain, both native and visitor, has changed dramatically since the repressive Franco days when bare arms and short skirts were deemed illegal. Today Spanish women dress as stylishly as their counterparts anywhere in the world, and topless sunbathers on Spanish beaches are a non-event. Nonetheless, Spanish men, even if more enlightened than before, retain elements of their Latin "machismo." That means that women traveling alone can be subject to sexual harassment. But, except for large cities or resorts in Andalusia where foreign women are sometimes regarded as prey, a female tourist should encounter no more serious problems than she would at home.

Naturally, harassment is worse for women alone. The situation is complicated when ignorance of Spanish means not knowing how to respond; still, the cold shoulder is understood internationally. Rape is infinitely rarer in Spain than in the U.S., but harassment can be unpleasant and is avoided only by taking the same precautions, including avoidance of isolating situations. None of this is meant to suggest that all Spanish men are cads, only that Spain has its share and that their activity should be more censured by their society than it is at present.

The situation in Portugal is similar, though less in degree.

CRIME

When Spain was a dictatorship under Franco, and Portugal a dictatorship under Salazar, their crime rates approached zero. Today true democracy brings its worldwide accompaniments—drugs and thievery. Now Iberia calls for the same precautions as at home.

Unfortunately, more often than not, criminals prey upon tourists. As travelers we carry expensive cameras and probably more money than a local citizen on the way to work, making ourselves good marks for pickpockets and snatchers. Just as we can spot a foreign visitor by his attire and attitude, so do we become easily identifiable in a foreign land. The question is not how to stop robberies, for we cannot solve that one at home, but how to decrease the odds that we will be chosen.

Thieves congregate where tourists are, which means that the Algarve, Andalusia and Barcelona sustain Iberia's highest crime rates. Think of Seville and Barcelona as the New Yorks of Spain (though their statistics are not nearly as bad as this model suggests), and the rest of the country as comfortably safe, given normal precautions. Be a more difficult mark by carrying as little as possible, thus leaving your hands free, and by holding pocketbooks or cameras close to the body. Most important, stay alert, especially at night, and avoid deserted areas. Such precautions should be sufficient. The usual street robbery consists either of youths cornering a victim on a street, or of a quick pocketbook or camera snatch, or of one accomplice creating a disturbance, perhaps by bumping into his victim, apologizing and distracting, while a confederate grabs what he can.

Cars pose another problem. Windshield stickers indicate a rented car that may contain valuable luggage or cameras. Whenever practical, it is best to empty your car before parking; next best is to be scrupulous in hiding visible signs that luggage waits inside, or even that the vehicle has been used for a long trip. So remove scraps, cups and maps from sight. Your goal is to discourage a thief's interest in your car.

Thefts in hotels are extremely rare, and violent crimes are a tiny percentage of U.S. figures. Outside of their few high crime areas, statistics show that traveling in Spain and Portugal is far safer than traveling in the U.S. Be alert, take reasonable precautions, and no untoward event should interrupt your trip.

TIME ZONE AND OFFICIAL HOURS

Clocks in Spain are 6 hours ahead of Eastern Standard Time in the U.S.; Portugal is five hours ahead. Daylight saving time is observed both in Spain and Portugal from the last week in March to the end of September, so that during October the difference from E.S.T. declines to 5 hours, in Spain's case, and 4, in Portugal's.

The afternoon closings of shops, businesses, museums and monuments can be a tourist's bane, leaving him with nothing to do except eat and rest throughout the afternoon. Banks are generally open from 8:30 a.m. until 2 p.m. on weekdays, until 1 p.m. on Saturdays, but may close an hour earlier in summer or for the day on Saturdays. Shops in Spain and Portugal generally open at 9 or 10 Monday through Saturday, but close from 1 or 2, to 3 or 4 in the afternoon before opening again until 8 in the evening. Businesses generally have similar hours, except for being closed on Saturdays. Department stores remain open throughout the day. Museums generally close for the afternoon hiatus, and open again until 7 in the evening. Almost all museums close on Mondays and open only until 1 or 2 on Sundays. In winter most museums and monuments close at 6 in the evening, rather than 7. In Portugal bank hours run from 9:30 until 2 on weekdays and until 1 on Saturday. Restaurants open from 1 until 4 for lunch, then from 9 or so until 11:30 or midnight for dinner in Spain, and from 7 until 10 in Portugal. Of course, there are always exceptions.

August, the vacation month for most Spaniards and Portuguese, can complicate a tourist's itinerary. Especially in large cities such as Madrid or Lisbon, some museums and many restaurants close altogether or curtail their hours. The only rule is to check before setting out.

MAIL, TELEPHONES, ELECTRICITY AND MEASUREMENT

Post offices, usually located in the center of a town, open from 8 to noon and again from 5 to 7:30 p.m. on weekdays, but do not reopen in the evenings on Saturdays. However, main offices in large cities remain open all day. The mail is generally reliable, taking about a week for delivery to the U.S. Airmail postage to the U.S. cost 83 ptas. and letters within Spain, 35 ptas. Letters addressed to you can be sent to any Spanish city along with the words *Lista de Correos*. Such mail will be held until you pick it up, though it may be filed under your first name, in the Spanish style, rather than your last. In both Spain and Portugal, American Express will also hold mail free for a month for card-holders or for those who carry Amex Traveler's Cheques.

The telephone system in Spain is perfectly adequate, Portugal's less so. A local call costs 10 pesetas, or 25 escudos. To call Spain from the U.S. or Canada, dial 011 for international calls, 34 for Spain, and the Spanish telephone number, but drop the "9" in the Spanish area code. For example, the area code for Madrid is 91. To call from the U.S., dial 011-34-1-plus the local number. To call Portugal dial 011, then 351 and the local number. To call the U.S. or Canada from either Spain or Portugal, dial 009, for overseas, and 1 for the U.S. or Canada, plus the local area code and number. Calls from Spain or Portugal to the U.S. cost about twice what they do in the other direction. If you use any of the international calling cards offered by all U.S. long-distance telephone companies, however, the cost will be about the same as calling from home. As they do in this country, hotels often bill exorbitant amounts for calls made from your room, adding three or four times the actual price of the call, but the alternative of using public pay phones means dealing with Spanish-speaking operators. At telephone offices, however, an agent will place the call for you. We list local telephone office addresses with each town or city entry.

Electricity in both Spain and Portugal runs at 220 or 240 volts, compared with 110 in the U.S. Unless an appliance has a 220 volt switch, it is likely to burn out in an Iberian socket when run at twice its power. Inexpensive converters are readily available in the U.S. Make sure you also buy an adapter for European sockets, which accept thin tubes, rather than our wider prongs.

Spanish and Portuguese measures are metric, as in most of the world. Distance is measured in kilometers, volume in liters, and weight in grams.

Metric	U.S. Standard
1 kilometer	5/8 mile
1 liter	1.02 quarts
100 grams	3.5 ounces
100 kilometers	62 miles
4 liters	1.1 gallons
1 kilogram	2.2 pounds

SPORTS

SKIING

The season in Spain runs from December through May. Snow generally is abundant and good, the weather mild, and skies clear. Costs will be a good third below those in the Alps.

Val d'Aran, in the Pyranees of Catalonia, is international and sophisticated, a beautiful glacier-ringed valley. Tuca-Betrèn is the older and smaller of the two valley resorts, offering 18 slopes and trails. Modern Baqueiria-Beret is huge, with 41 slopes and trails, 19 lifts and helicopter skiing available. A total of 5000 rooms exist in the valley. For information: Oficina d'Informacio Turista de Baqueira-Beret (Apartado 60, Viella, Val d'Aran, 25530 Lérida, España: ☎ 973-64 59 59); Oficina d'Informacion Turistica (Arc del Pont, 25000 Lérida, España: ☎ 973-24 81 20).

El Formigal, almost a mile high in the Pyranees of Aragon, is new, growing and lively. Twenty-three runs and trails with 17 lifts and tows exist presently, and the open country offers miles of off-trail possibilities. For information: Oficina de Tourismo, Estacion de Formigal (Sallent de Gallego, El Formigal, 22000 Huesca, España; ☎ 974-48 81 25).

Cerler, also in Aragon, is larger and closer to the French border than El Formigal and more popular. Twenty-two trails exist at present. For information: Oficina de Turismo de Huesca (23 Calle Coso Alto, 22000 Huesca, España: ☎ 974-22 57 78).

Solynieve in the Sierra Nevada near Grenada lies at an altitude of almost 10,000 feet, yet only 60 miles from the tepid Mediterranean. The slopes here are not as demanding as some others, but snow is dependable late in the season. There is a parador. For information: Federacion Andaluza de Esquí (78 Paseo de Ronda, Veleta, 18000 Granada, España; ☎ 958-25 07 06).

Alto Campo, Pajares (with a parador) and **San Isidro** all are scenically located in the Catabrian Mountains near Santander. Snow is reliable and lasts through May. For information: Oficina de Turismo (1 Plaza Porticada, 39000 Santander, España; ☎ 942-31 07 08).

GOLF

Spaniards golfed before Sevi Ballesteros; after all he had to practice somewhere. Spain offers some very good courses, mainly in the sunny south, although not so numerous as in some countries so Spain's links grow crowded as golf's popularity increases. Recently, Portugal has carved out some handsome and challenging courses. Figure about $25 for green fees, unless the links are connected with your hotel and included in the charges, and about $10 to rent clubs. Choice courses would be:

In *Spain*:

Real Sociedat Hípica Española Club de Campo in Madrid hosted one World's Cup and three Spanish Opens. For information: Real Sociedat Hípica Española Club de Campo (Calle Fernanflor 6, 28014 Madrid, España; ☎ 91-429-8889).

La Manga Campo de Golf at Los Belones, 20 k from Cartagena in Murcia, provides gorgeous views and is superbly maintained. For information: La Manga Campo de Golf (Los Belones, Cartagena, 30385 Murcia, España; ☎ 968-56 45 11).

Golf Torrequebrada in Benalmádena Costa near Málaga offers a 5-star hotel with tennis and a casino in addition to the beautiful golf course. The small town contains very comfortable hotels at cheaper rates than the Torrequebrada, although staying there is the real experience. For information: Golf Torrequebrada (Apartado 67, Benalmádena Costa, 29630 Málaga, España; ☎ 952-42 27 42, Fax 952-44 57 02).

Hotel Byblos Andalus near Mijas outside Fuengirola possesses two difficult Robert Trent Jones courses beautifully set. This new hotel offers every facility for sport and comfort, while doubling as a spa. It does cost 30,000 plus pesetas a day to exercise as kings do and then relax. For information: Hotel Byblos Andalus (Apartado 138, Fuengirola 29650 Malaga, España; ☎ 952-47 30 50, fax 952-47 67 83).

Club de Golf Costa Brava in Santa Cristina de Arco near Barcelona is long established and a tough 18 holes. For information: Club de Golf

Costa Brava (Santa Cristina de Arco, 17246 Gerona, España; ☎ 972-83 71 50).

Real Golf de Pedreña in Santander, on a peninsula in an Atlantic bay, is Ballesteros' local course. This one requires that guests be accompanied by a member, but the Spanish are very friendly. For information: Real Golf de Pedreña (Apartado 233, 39000 Santander, España;☎ 942-50 00 01).

Real Sociedad de Golf de Neguri in Getxo (Agorta) near Bilbao is Spain's oldest course and reminiscent of Scotland. For information: Real Sociedad de Golf de Neguri (Apartado de Correos 9, Getxo, 48990 Vizcaya, España;☎ 944-69 02 00).

In *Portugal*:

Estoril Golf Club, 1 k inland from Estoril, is Portugal's oldest. The par is 69, placing a premium on accuracy, but the greens are less challenging. Mimosa and eucalyptus scent the air in these foothills of the Sintra mountains. The course is associated with the Estoril Palácio Hotel, which provides tennis too. For information: Estoril Golf Club (Av. da República, Estoril, Portugal 2765; ☎ 01 268 01 76).

Campo de Palmares near Lagos in the Algarve is a championship course that hosted qualifying rounds for the 1985 World Cup. The course ranges over sand dunes and wooded hills. So magnificent is the view from the 17th tee that it is difficult to concentrate on one's game. For information: Campo de Palmares (Lagos, Portugal 8600; ☎ 082 629 53).

Quinta do Lago in the Algarve at Almansil offers four 9-hole challenges ranked with the best in Europe, to combine in any number of 18-hole courses. Although not the most scenic in Portugal, the area offers many other activities in addition to golf. For information: Campo de Golf da Quinta do Lago (Almansil, Portugal 8100; ☎ 089 943 29).

Vilamoura Golf Club near Amansil is so stunning with its ocean views and pines that it can distract from the golf. The par 73 course is one of the most challenging in the country. The club forms part of a huge resort development offering every imaginable sport. For information: Club Golf de Vilamoura (Vilamoura, Portugal 8100; ☎ 089 355 62).

Clube de Golf do Vale do Lobo, also near Amancil, presents not one, but three different 18 hole courses. All are challenging in different ways and located in a self-contained resort that adds fine tennis. For information: Clube de Golf do Vale do Lobo (Vale do Lobo, Portugal 8100; ☎ 089 941 45).

TENNIS

Tennis has become Spain's fastest growing sport since the Sanchez brothers and sister became international stars and the Catalan Bruguerra won the 1993 French Open. The Portuguese are less enamored of the sport, although several camps exist for serious amateurs. Spain provides some cement courts but more red clay courts, like those in France. On the latter, be prepared to stay out for a while. Portugal's courts are mainly hard-surfaced. Courts rent for about $10 per hour. Some choices in the sunny south of *Spain* are:

Don Carlos Hotel outside Marbella on the road to Málaga splits hard and clay courts on which Martina and Chris once played. At a couple of hundred dollars a night you can sail, ride horses and play tennis for "free." For information: Don Carlos Hotel (29600 Málaga, Marbella, España; ☎ 952-83 11 40, Fax 952-83 34 29).

Marbella is a center for elegant sport hotels including: Los Monteros Hotel (☎ 952-77 17 00, Fax 952-82 58 46), Puente Romano (☎ 952-77 01 00, Fax 952-77 57 66), and Marbella Club Hotel (☎ 952-77 13 00, Fax 952-82 98 84).

Campo de Tenis de Lew Hoad at Mijas near Málaga is a very serious tennis camp, founded by Lew Hoad, though he no longer teaches. The courts are cement. For information: Campo de Tenis de Lew Hoad (Apartado 111, Fuengirola, 29640 Málaga, España; ☎ 952-47 48 58).

In *Portugal*'s Algarve, tennis is available at:

Roger Taylor Tennis Clinic, in Vale do Lobo, provides tennis camps as well as individual play. The 12 hard courts include 6 lit at night. Located in the Vale do Lobo resort complex, golf, swimming and squash are also available. Arrangements may be made through Roger Taylor Tennis Holidays, Ltd. (85 High Street, Wimbledon, London SW 19, 5EG, England; ☎ 089 947 97 27).

Vilamouratênis in Vilamoura opened in 1991 in a big way with 13 hard courts, some clay courts and several stadium courts. This resort offers everything for the tennis lover. For information: Vilamouratênis (Vilamoura, Portugal 8125; ☎ 089 321 25).

FISHING

Salt water fishing is so-so, but trout fishing in Spain can be fun indeed, although not for trophy fish. A license costing about $12 is required and can be purchased at the Instituto Nacional para la Conservación do la Naturaleza at Puerta de Toledo in Madrid (☎ 91-347 60 00), or in regional offices. The season runs from spring through summer in Andalusia where good trout streams surround Granada and Jaen. Ávila in New Castile and Burgos in Old Castile are centers for trout, though the season is restricted and complex. Near Gerona and Lérida, around Barcelona, clear streams and lakes run with trout and bass.

HIKING

Spain offers abundant mountain wilderness for wandering feet, plus two special national parks. **Doñana National Park**, splitting the Costa del Luz, is the vast estuary of the Guadalquivir River that crowds in winter with migrating birds, in summer with deer and bulls. It may be visited only by tours arranged in advance through Cooperativa Marismas del Rocío in El Rocío near Huelva (☎ 955-43 04 32); admission 1000 ptas. The tours leave from Matalascañas, 15 k south of Playa de Castila, on the Costa del Luz in Andalusia. No tours are offered in July or August, however. **Ordesa National Park**, in northern Aragon, provides the spectacular scenery of massive canyons cut by burbling streams. Open only from May through September, it may be visited by anyone, and is described in the chapter on Aragón and Navarre.

BOOKS

Nothing enhances a trip more than understanding what you are seeing, so read all you can before you go and while in Iberia. A very selected list follows of informative books that present the variety of Iberia:

James Michener's *Iberia* conveys a love of Spain as does no other book. Published in 1968 and widely available in paperback, it is dated now, but remains interesting.

Jan Morris turns her keen and quirky eye in *Spain* on a country she did not fall in love with. The book shows something of the darker side of Spain.

Voices of the Old Sea, by Norman Lewis is an account of the clash of the modern world with an older Spanish culture told through the events in one isolated village. The book is utterly captivating, and describes attitudes that remain present in modern Spain, even if submerged.

The classic travel book on Spain is George Borrow's *The Bible in Spain* written in 1843. If a copy is available at your library, get it. This is an opinionated, engaging old travelogue by an English Bible salesman.

For food and drink, the premier book is Penelope Casas' *The Foods and Wines of Spain*.

For Moorish art and architecture, Titus Burckhardt's *Moorish Culture in Spain* is the classic.

Washington Irving's *Tales of the Alhambra* remains evocative of these exotic buildings and times.

The Poem of El Cid is still fresh enough to enjoy, and conveys the flavor of Reconquista times.

William H. Prescott's *History of the Reign of Ferdinand and Isabella* has been the most readable book on this fascinating pair since 1838. Though long out of print, most libraries own a copy.

The best book on Columbus is Samuel Eliot Morison's *Christopher Columbus, Mariner*, accurate, though instilling great admiration for the man.

Peter Pierson chronicles the seminal king *Phillip II of Spain*, while Roger B. Merriman covers a wider canvas in *The Rise of the Spanish Empire in the Old World and the New.*

Jonathan Brown's *Velazquez, Painter and Courtier* is not just the best book on this painter, it is one of the best on any artist.

Jose Guidol is best on *Goya*.

The Spanish civil war has been extensively covered, usually from partisan points of view. A relatively balanced and moving presentation is Antony Beevor's *The Spanish Civil War.*

Gaudí is well served by two who knew him well in James Joseph Sweeney and Josep Luis Sert, *Antoni Gaudi.*

The acknowledged standard of books on Picasso is John Richardson's *A Life of Picasso*. However, it will test your interest.

Henry Myhill's *The Spanish Pyrenees* stands out among nature books.

For recent Spain, James Hooper's *The Spaniards: A Portrait of the New Spain* is good.

The following are recommended background reading for Portugal.

Written by a true writer of Portuguese extraction, John Dos Passos, *The Portugal Story: Three Centuries of Exploration and Discovery*, is a readable history.

Another good history that covers a wider scope than Dos Passos is H.A. Livermore, *A New History of Portugal.*

The best art survey is George Kubler and Martin Soria's, *Art and Architecture in Spain and Portugal and Their American Dominions: 1500 to 1800.*

Hans Christian Andersen's *A Visit to Portugal, 1866* remains interesting and enjoyable.

THE SPANISH LANGUAGE

Pronunciation is easier with Spanish than for most languages because it is highly consistent. The only problem is that not all Spaniards regularly speak Spanish. Basques talk in a separate language, as do Catalans, and some inhabitants of Galicia, so not all conversations or signs will be in that language. However, everyone can speak and understand Spanish when they choose to, and with tourists they will.

For Spanish vowels, *a* sounds like that in b*a*ck, *e* is short as in s*e*t, *i* long like pol*i*ce, *o* long like n*o*te, and *u* long like r*u*le. Spanish *ei* is pronounced as if *ey*, as in th*ey*, and *ai* is pronounced as if a long *y*, as in b*y*.

Spanish consonants generally are pronounced as in English, though there are some exceptions. *H* is always silent, *B* between vowels is pronounced like English *v*; on the other hand, *V* sounds like an English *b*. *C* usually is hard as if it were a *k*, but is lisped before an *i* or an *e*. Similarly, *G* usually is hard and slightly guttural as if it were the *ch* in loch, but sounds soft like English *h* before *e* or *i*. *J* always sounds like *h*. Doubled *LL* is pronounced like an English *y*, so *tortilla* is pronounced *torteeya*, though there should be just the hint of an l-sound. *N* is normally like the English version but when surmounted by a tilde (~) becomes *ny* as in ca*ny*on. *R* is rolled and *rr* rolled even more. Spanish *Z* is pronounced like an English *th*, so Zaragoza sounds like *Tharahotha*, with the *ho* slightly guttural. Lastly, *qu* sounds like an English *k*.

Normally the last syllable of a Spanish word receives the stress. When some other syllable should be stressed an accent is placed at that point.

WORDS AND PHRASES	
ENGLISH	**SPANISH**
Good morning (afternoon/evening)	Buenas días (tardes/noches)
Goodbye	Adios
How are you?	¿Cómo está usted?
Very well, thank you.	Muy bien, gracias.
Please/thank you	Por favor/gracias
You are welcome	De nada
Yes/no	Si/no
Pardon me	Perdón
I do not speak Spanish	No hablo Español
Do you speak English?	¿Habla usted inglés?
I do not understand	No comprendo
Miss	Señorita
Madam	Señora (married), Doña (unmarried)
Mister	Señor
Open/closed	Abierto/cerrado
Entrance/exit	Entrada/salida
Push/pull	Empujar/tirar
Today/yesterday/tomorrow	Hoy/ayer/mañana
Where is...	Dónde está...?
the toilet	el baño/sanitario
the train station	la estación de ferrocarriles
the post office	el correo
How much is it?	¿Cuánto es?
Help!	¡Socorro!

NUMBERS

ENG.	SPAN.	ENG.	SPAN.	ENG.	SPAN.
1	uno	11	once	21	veintiuno
2	dos	12	doce	30	treinta
3	tres	13	trece	31	treintiuno
4	cuatro	14	catorce	40	cuarenta
5	cinco	15	quince	50	cincuenta
6	seis	16	diez y séis	60	sesenta
7	siete	17	diez y siete	70	setenta
8	ocho	18	diez y ocho	80	ochenta
9	nueve	19	diez y nueve	90	noventa
10	diez	20	veinte		
100	cien(to)	101	ciento uno		
200	dosciento				
300	tresciento				
1000	mil	2000	dos mil		
0	cero				

DAYS

ENGLISH	SPANISH	ENGLISH	SPANISH
Monday	Lunes	Friday	Viernes
Tuesday	Martes	Saturday	Sábado
Wednesday	Miércoles	Sunday	Domingo
Thursday	Jueves		

MONTHS

January	Enero	July	Julio
February	Febrero	August	Agosto
March	Marzo	September	Septiembre
April	Abril	October	Octubre
May	Mayo	November	Noviembre
June	Junio	December	Diciembre

AT THE HOTEL

ENGLISH	SPANISH
I have a reservation	He hecho una reserva
I would like...	Quisiera...
a single room	una habitación sencilla

AT THE HOTEL	
ENGLISH	**SPANISH**
a double room	una habitación doble
a quiet room	una habitación tranquila
with bath	con baño
with a shower	con ducha
with air conditioning	con aire acondicionado
for one night only	sólo una noche
for two nights	por dos noches

ON THE ROAD	
ENGLISH	**SPANISH**
north(south/east/west)	norte(sur/este/oeste)
right(left)	derecho(izquierdo)
straight ahead	todo derecho
far(near)	lejos(cerca)
gas station	gasolinera
tires	los neumaticos
oil	el aceite
danger(caution)	peligro
detour	desvio
Do not Enter	Paso Prohibido
No parking	Estacionamento Prohibido
No passing	Prohibido Adelantar
One Way	Dirección Unica
Reduce Speed	Despacio
Stop	Alto
Toll booth	Paeje

THE PORTUGUESE LANGUAGE

In written Portuguese many words will be recognized because all Romance languages contain similarities. Knowledge of Spanish will serve you well. It is spoken Portuguese that is the problem; it sounds like some unfamiliar Eastern European language to our ears. As far as attempts to speak are concerned, have no hesitation, for the Portuguese will be pleased by the effort and strain hard to grasp your point. Understanding the natives is another matter. The language is nasal and filled with hisses and "shs" that make even words spelled the same as the Spanish equivalent sound entirely different.

A tilde over a vowel, as in ã, indicates a nasal sound with a hint of an *n* at the end. Informação, for example is pronounced almost as we say "information," though nasal and with the final *n* more hinted-at than vocalized.

As that same example shows, a cedilla beneath a *c* makes it sound like *sh*. Otherwise a *c* is hard, as if it were a *k*, unless it precedes an *e* or an *i* which makes it soft and sibilant. The sound of the letter *j* is surprising, for it is pronounced as if it were *sh*. The letter *g* is pronounced with the same *sh* sound when it precedes an *e* or an *i*, but otherwise is hard as if it were our *g*. You begin to see why the language is so full of sibilant sounds. Further, an *s* before a constant or at the end of a word is pronounced like *sh*, as is an *x* anywhere.

The combination *nh* produces the same sound as the Spanish *ñ*—that of the *ny* in English ca*ny*on—so Portuguese *senhor* sounds like the Spanish *señor*. The combination *lh* makes for a sound similar to the way we pronounce the *ll* in bil*lh*ion, so we would think *Batalha* were spelled *Batalla*. The stress within a word follows much the same principles as Spanish.

Somehow every tourist manages to communicate with and understand the Portuguese. English will be spoken at the major hotels and understood in fancier restaurants. Incidentally, any French you know is likely to serve well, because, it is the second language of Portugal.

WORDS AND PHRASES	
ENGLISH	**PORTUGUESE**
Good morning (afternoon/evening)	Bom dia (boa-tardes/boa-noite)
Goodbye	Adeus
Hello	Ola
How are you?	Como vai?
Please/thank you	Por favor/obrigado
Yes/no	Sim/não
Pardon me	Perdão
I do not speak Portuguese	Não falo Português
Do you speak English?	Fala inglês?
I do not understand	Não compreendo
Miss	Menina
Madam	Senhora (married)
Mister	Senhor
Open/closed	Aberto/fechado
Entrance/exit	Entrada/saida
Push/pull	Empurrar/puxar

WORDS AND PHRASES

ENGLISH	PORTUGUESE
Today/yesterday/tomorrow	Hoje/ontem/amanha
Where is...	Onde éstão ...?
the toilet	os casa de banho
the train station	a estação de trem
the drug store	farmácia
How much is it?	Quanto custa?

NUMBERS

ENG.	PORT.	ENG.	PORT.	ENG.	PORT.
1	um(a)	11	onze	21	vinte e um
2	dois	12	doze	30	trinta
3	três	13	treze	31	trinta e um
4	quatro	14	catorze	40	quarenta
5	cinco	15	quinze	50	cinquênta
6	seis	16	dezaseis	60	sessenta
7	sete	17	dezasete	70	setenta
8	oito	18	dezóito	80	oitenta
9	nove	19	dezanove	90	noventa
10	dez	20	vinte		
100	cem	101	cento e um		
200	duzentos				
300	trezento				
1000	mil	2000	dois mil		
0	cero				

DAYS

ENG.	PORT.	ENGL.	PORT.
Monday	Segunda-feira	Friday	Sexta-feira
Tuesday	Terça-feira	Saturday	Sábado
Wednesday	Quarta-feira	Sunday	Domingo
Thursday	Quinta-feira		

MONTHS

ENGLISH	PORT.	ENGLISH	PORT.
January	Janeiro	July	Julho
February	Fevereiro	August	Agosto
March	Março	September	Setembro
April	Abril	October	Outubro

MONTHS

ENGLISH	PORT.	ENGLISH	PORT.
May	Maio	November	Novembro
June	Junho	December	Dizembro

AT THE HOTEL

ENGLISH	PORTUGUESE
I have a reservation	Mandei reservar
I would like...	Queria...
a single room	um quarto simples
a double room	um quarto duplo
a quiet room	um quarto tranquilo
with bath	com banho
with a shower	con duche
with air-conditioning	com ar acondicionado
for one night only	so uma noite
for two nights	por dios noites

ON THE ROAD

ENGLISH	PORTUGUESE
north (south/east/west)	norte (sul/este/oeste)
right (left)	direita (esquerda)
straight ahead	em frente
far(near)	longa (perto)
gas station	estação de serviço
tires	pneus
oil	o oleo
danger(caution)	perigo
detour	desvio
Do not Enter	Entrada Proibida
No parking	Estacionamento Proibido
No passing	Proibido Ultrapassar
One Way	Sentido Único
Reduce Speed	Devagar
Stop	Alto
Toll booth	Pedagio

SPAIN

Isabeline entrance to the Museo de San Gregorio in Valladolid.

THE LAND AND THE PEOPLE

Olive grove near Toledo.

The first and second surprises about Spain's geography are its size and its altitude. Spain covers a quarter of a million square miles, making it the third largest country in Europe after Russia and France; only Switzerland can boast of a higher average altitude—in fact, one Spanish peak tops 11,000 feet. Spain's third surprise is her people. This is not a country where the sun beams idly on guitar players while tourists loll on the sand. Although there is abundant sand along Spain's 2400 miles of coast, and guitars and sun in evidence throughout, most of Spain is populated by city folk in business clothes and farmers in berets.

In shape Spain forms a shield, wider at the top and pointed at the bottom (the part that juts into the sea to reach for Gibraltar), 550 miles wide by 400 miles long. An accident of geography alone prevents Spain from belonging to Africa. A mere seven miles of sea separates Spain from Morocco, while Spain is tied to Europe in the north by a 300-mile tab of isthmus consisting of the towering Pyrenees. This mountain wall is the reason that throughout its history, Spain dealt as much with the Moors to its south as with the French to its north.

Spain separates into three horizontal climactic regions. The Pyrenees continue inland across to the northwest corner of Spain, there renamed the Cordillera Mountains, completing a mountain barrier that seals the north of Spain, holding in most rain clouds to make the north green and wet. As opposed to "wet Spain," the central part is "dry Spain." It is an immense, dusty plateau half a mile in altitude. This *Meseta* comprises La Mancha, where locals describe the climate as nine months of winter followed by three of hell. South of La Mancha a line of Sierra mountains seals the cold from Andalusia, preserving a warm Mediterranean climate.

Old provincial differences remain strong in Spain, although technically the country was unified 500 years ago, and a recent political subdivision cut up the traditional provinces into even smaller "departments." Running across the north of Spain, west to east, are the ancient provinces of Galicia, Asturias, Cantabria, the Basque provinces, Navarre, Aragòn and Catalonia.

Galicia, tucked into the northwestern corner, is hilly, misty and green, with precipitous deep inlets from the sea, like Norwegian fjords. Fishing is a major business. Inland, verdant topsoil barely covers a granite bed, making farming difficult. Farms therefore are small, raising corn, apples, lumber, and some cattle for beef. The name "Galicia" comes from the Celtic word that also gave us "Gaul" and "Wales," for originally this was the land of Celts, and the countryside does bring Wales to mind. Here, in the 8th century, shepherds followed a bright light to a crypt of ancient bones, claimed to be those of Saint James. Christian Europe rejoiced. To house these relics, one of the greatest of medieval monuments was raised on the site—the Romanesque Cathedral of Santiago de Compostela.

Asturias, **Cantabria**, and the **Basque Provinces**, running east of Galicia, present the same green and moist appearance and temperatures as Galicia, but their terrain is sedimentary rock instead of granite. Farms are consequently larger and more fertile, though growing crops similar to Galicia's. Coal mines feed Spain's heavy industry. The coast offers magnificent scenery and Donastia (San Sebastian), an elegant resort. All three provinces are home to Basques (*Vascos* in Spanish, *Euskaldi*, in Basque) in omnipresent berets, a people of enigmatic origin, language, and robust national identity. All of Spain recognizes their culinary expertise. Hard cider is the local drink (*sidra* in Spanish, *sagardua* in Basque). *Pelota, jai alai*, is the national sport, with a court in every village, though *bolos*, "boules," are not despised.

Navarre is mountainous in the northeast, hilly in the northwest, and descends into cereal plains in the south. Rough stone houses sit on the mountains, and houses dug underground nestle into the plains. Vineyards cover the southeast near Ribera, next to the famous Riojas wine area. Navarre is dotted with medieval monasteries that once provided shelter for pilgrim hordes marching to holy Santiago de Compostela in Galicia. Pamplona, famous for the running of the bulls, is Navarre's capital.

The Pyrenees run through the north of **Aragon**, descending to the basin of the Ebro River. Southern Aragon grows olives and grapes. Shut off from the tempering influence of the sea, Aragon can boil in summer and freeze in winter. This was the homeland of Ferdinand the Catholic who married Queen Isabella. Aragon too lay on the pilgrims' way to Santiago de Compostela, and abounds in ancient monasteries, the original hotels. Its major city—rebuilt in the 19th century—is Zaragoza, a friendlier town than its substantial size would suggest.

Catalonia, on the east coast, is Barcelona, and medieval and modern art. The scenic and rocky north coast, called the *Costa Brava*, turns to golden sand in the south, and becomes the *Costa Durado*. The interior is dry but fertile. Catalans are fiercely independent, speaking a language of their own related to the Provençal dialect spoken in the proximate area of France. Catalans are known for business acumen, while Catalan art is idiosyncratic, both in continuing to employ the Romanesque style later than other parts of Spain and in its avant-garde modern artists and architects: Gaudí, Sert, Miró, and Dalí.

Below this belt of northern provinces, and to the west, sits the combined traditional kingdom of Old Castile and León, the largest ancient province. Beneath it, New Castile lies east, with Exremadura to its west. Valencia hugs the coast, east of New Castile, above Murcia.

The *Meseta* begins in **Old Castile and León**. Horizons stretch wide despite low hills. To its east is La Rioja, the great wine region of Spain. Elsewhere, wheat grows, sheep and cattle graze, and people, concentrated in cities, are seldom seen. This is the land of medieval castles and of the first capitals of Spain during the Reconquest—León, Burgos, then Valladolid.

New Castile's Madrid is located almost exactly at the geographic center of the country, not far from medieval Toledo, El Escorial, Renaissance Salamanca, and Segovia with its Roman aqueduct and Disneyland castle. New Castile's southern half is called La Mancha, possibly derived from an Arabic word meaning "parched." This is the Meseta proper, an almost featureless half-mile-high plateau empty of humans except in widely separated cities. Infinite wheat fields can be seen today, but in the past the land was virtually ruined by millions of migratory merino sheep who ate every growing thing. Don Quixote can almost be seen on the distant horizon, passing the castles of Spain.

Extremadura, meaning "beyond the River Duero," is strewn with boulders which suggest Celtic dolmens at every turn. It is home more to sheep than to humans, but even the sheep head for the hills during fiery summers. The land of Extremadura nurtured most of the conquistadores who, in turn, seized any opportunity to leave its inhospitable bosom. It boasts houses of the explorers, Guadalupe's holy monastery, Mérida's Roman ruins, and Cáceres, a preserved Renaissance town.

Valencia and **Mercia** on the east coast are Extremadura's opposites. Here balmy fertile plains border a Mediterranean framed by grey mountains. Thanks to the legacy of the Moors, Valencia grows lush citrus trees, rice and olives. Perpetual sun shines on the white sands of the Costa Azahar ("Coast of Orange Blossoms") in the north, and the Costa Blanca in the south. Temperatures seldom reach 90 or descend to 40 in busy Valencia, the major city. Aridity in Murcia makes it a virtual desert, complete with stands of palms as if oases. The *calina*, a summer heat haze, can make activity difficult.

Andalusia, the southernmost part of the country, is everyone's ideal of Spain, the home of flamenco guitar and dancing. The Sierra Nevada ("Snow Mountain"), capped all year in white, holds weather along the Costa del Sol to moderate Mediterranean temperatures. West, the Guadalquivar River breaks the mountains to form a wide basin that steams in summer. Further west, behind the Costa de la Luz ("Coast of Light"), rice, sugar, and cotton extend on flat plains where fighting bulls are also raised. This is the fabled land of the Moors. A clear Andalusian sky reflects perpetually on Seville, Córdoba, Grenada and the sherry production of Jerez de la Frontera.

According to Spain's 1981 census, its population approached 40 million. Now it certainly numbers more. About 40 percent of its people live in the ten largest cities, following a world-wide demographic trend of individuals abandoning rural areas for urban dreams. Whether the migrants' dreams are realized is dubious, but they spawn boring suburbs around urban centers. A happy effect of this migration, however, is that older towns and cities have not been forced to absorb the increased population, thus preserving much of their original character. Even the centers of most Spainish cities retain their medieval or Renaissance atmosphere of narrow, crooked old streets and ancient buildings. In the context of the rest of Europe, Spain remains poor, despite enormous economic strides in the 1980s, although poverty is not evident in either the look of the cities or the stylish dress of the people. Cities and towns are sparkling, with little sign of dilapidation. Throughout the vast countryside, verdant farms cover the landscape despite the fact that only one Spaniard in six is a farmer.

The physical appearance of the Spanish range from small, dark-complected Basques in the north to slender Andalusians in the south, where one can also find the startling combination of raven hair crowning fair skin and blue eyes. The modern Spaniard is a mix of more races than he sometimes wishes to acknowledge. Originally there was a stock of Caucasian North Africans—the Iberians—plus Celts from northern Europe, along with Basques of unknown origin; then Romans intermingled, followed by German Vandals and Visigoths, and finally Moors and Jews.

The Spanish work hard. In the hot parts of the country, however, they fight a debilitating climate. Avoiding the outdoors during the heat of the day is a sensible adaptation to such temperatures, so the Spanish break to eat and rest from noon to two, or from one to three. But they come to work early and leave late to make up for the period away. You will seldom see an idle Spaniard.

Most characteristically, you will see the Spanish on their evening strolls, the *paseos*, when families come together for a walk at dusk along an avenue in each town appointed for the purpose. There is something touching about the familial closeness the ritual involves, and the affectionate attention the adults devote to their children. You will wonder how such gentle people can enjoy the blood of bullfights, or how they could have fought so violently against each other in the Spanish Civil War. You will find no easy answer: the Spanish are not a simple people.

WHERE TO GO

Beach at Santa Fe on the Costa del Sol.

Spain offers too many worthwhile sights to take in during a week or even a month: where to go requires choices. To help make these decisions, we'll describe the best things to see and what makes them worthwhile, then we'll discuss beaches, castles, cathedrals, and villages. Finally we'll propose a number of itineraries of varied length and mixed activities.

THE TOP SIGHTS

Topping any list of Spanish sights would be Andalusia's three great cities, located close enough to each other to be covered in one trip.

Granada ★★★★★ must be seen for its Alhambra Palace of the Moors. This palace, arguably the finest Muslim structure in the world, not excepting the Taj Mahal, is unlike any collection of buildings anywhere—perfect, exquisite and provoking. Together with its associated castle, fortified walls and the Generalife (the summer palace nearby), it can be seen in half a day. Add the Capilla Real (Royal Chapel) and tomb of Isabella and Ferdinand, and other sights in the city, and Granada can be explored in a day or two. An hour away lies **Córdoba ★★★★** with its Mesquita, a perfectly preserved mosque. Inside, its forest of variegated columns incongruously houses a cathedral. The Mesquita, the lovely patios of the ancient Jewish Quarter, and the other sights of Córdoba consume one day. Two hours further on waits **Seville ★★★★★**, a beautiful city that produced Expo '92, and contains the second best art museum in Spain, along with two resplendent examples of medieval Moorish-Christian architecture—the Alcázar (Fortress) and the Casa de Pilatos. At the minimum, Seville requires a three-day stay.

Next in priority is Madrid and the cities around it—Toledo, El Escorial, Segovia and Salamanca. **Toledo ★★★★★** is a virtual museum city overflowing with El Grecos, and possessing an awesome cathedral, an exquisite ancient synagogue, a fine art museum, and more. Most people try to see it all in a day, which is frenzied, but possible. Since Toledo lies within an hour of Madrid, visitors staying in the capital frequently make it a day-trip. **Madrid ★★★** is new, in Spanish terms, but cosmopolitan and fun, combining pleasing sights with great museums. Two days hardly begin to do such a large and diverse city justice. A half-hour away, for a half-day excursion, stands **El Escorial ★★★★**, an imposing complex of palace, church, and monastery from the 16th century. Another hour further along is **Segovia ★★★★★**, with a genuine castle looking strikingly like the fantasy one at Disneyland, an imposing cathedral, and a dozen Romanesque churches all set on an imposing site—a visit requiring one hurried day. **Salamanca ★★★★**, at least another full day, is surely the finest city in Spain that tourists ignore. It is a treasure-house of intricate Renaissance *plateresque* architecture, most of it preserved, along with a 16th-century classroom, on the grounds of its university. Salamanca also boasts one of the great churches in all of Spain—the Romanesque Catedral Vieja (Old Cathedral).

Barcelona ★★★★★ is a beautiful, cosmopolitan city offering much to do, pleasant walks while doing it, and fine food to enjoy afterwards. Beyond such simple pleasures, Barcelona bursts with so much architecture and art that it bids to be the one city to see in

Spain if you can see only one. There is a fine cathedral standing in a preserved medieval quarter (the Barri Gòtic); the best Medieval and Renaissance museum in Spain (the Museu de Arte de Catalunya); some of the finest examples of modern art in the Miró and Picasso museums; and the astounding Sagrada Familia cathedral by Gaudí, to mention just highlights. An absolute minimum stay in Barcelona alone demands three days; excursions to the surrounding areas, which abound in beaches, Greek and Roman ruins and medieval monasteries, can easily fill whatever additional time you have available.

Santiago de Compostela ★★★★★ presents a great Romanesque cathedral set in the most beautiful of squares. Because one travels to Santiago to see only the cathedral and squares, it would be possible to spend a half day there before continuing on one's way. But no one wants to. Everyone sits, charmed and contemplative, regretting the time of departure.

Just as grand, in a less insistent way, is the huge and flamboyantly Gothic cathedral of **Burgos ★★★★**. Burgos is a lively, lovely town that should receive at least a full day of one's time. Outside the city are a medieval convent and a Renaissance monastery, each a gem.

The "royal" cities, the successive early capitals of Christian Spain established during its centuries of reconquest, come next on the list. Traveling north from Madrid, the first of these cities (but the last chronological capital) is Valladolid. **Valladolid ★★★** is less attractive than many other Spanish cities, but houses an excellent collection of polychromed wood sculpture in a splendidly ornate Renaissance building (San Gregorio). The city also preserves the house in which Columbus died. An hour away and a little further north is the second capital of Spain, **León ★★★**. Tourists come to admire its Gothic cathedral, patterned on the French model, with acres of brilliant stained glass. While there, tourists also discover the city's atmospheric old quarter, its impressive San Marcos monastery, and its Romanesque treasure—St. Isadore's church and pantheon. **Oviedo ★★★**, the first capital of Spain, waits three hours further north. Nothing in its city limits is important enough that it must be seen, but its elegance captivates all who visit. Among other sights, Oviedo has a lovely cathedral containing 9th century relics and carvings. On the outskirts of town, however, stands a treasure. Santa María del Naranco is Spain's oldest existing civil building, the remains of an 8th century Visigothic palace. Valladolid, Léon, and Oviedo each merit a day's visit.

The state of Extremadura encompasses a variety of sights spread throughout pleasant scenery. **Mérida** ★★ preserves Roman buildings, **Cáceres** ★ is a town of Renaissance houses, **Trujillo** ★★ invites with moody castle ruins and homes of the conquistadores, while **Guadalupe** ★★★ monastery glitters mysteriously high in the mountains. Extremadura is small—a tour of the state requires only three days— and lies close to Madrid.

Pamplona ★, the university town with its famous bullring, is the capital of Navarre. It is also the center for a collection of medieval monasteries that make pleasant excursions, especially to those of La Oliva and Leyre. Both are simple Cistercian structures—the former simpler than when it was built because occupying French stripped it of decoration, the latter with a massive gloomy crypt well worth seeing.

BEACHES

So far we've said nothing about beaches, as if relaxing were not a legitimate vacation enterprise. Spain is almost surrounded by beach, close to 2400 miles of it, some on the Atlantic, but most on the Mediterranean. Europeans are well aware of both their quality and quantity, arriving in sufficient droves every summer to double the population of Spain.

The northern beaches—those on the Atlantic—look like Scandinavian fjords and are dotted with elegant resorts. A tour of these beaches can pleasantly fill a vacation. Start at Santiago and head east to the coastal **Rias** ★★, headlands cut by river estuaries to form dramatic fjords. Or follow the coast north, then east, pausing for days at Santillana del Mar, Santander, and Donastia (also called San Sebastian) to explore the **Costa Verde** ★★★, perhaps pausing too at Oviedo, a half-mile inland. Or trace the route the other way around.

On the east, the rugged **Costa Brava** ★★★ runs north from Barcelona for almost 100 miles, as cliffs and headlands are broken by tranquil coves. Though much development has taken place since the 1960s, pockets of scenic beach remain. South of Barcelona, along the 100 miles to Valencia, lies the **Costa del Azahar** ★★★, the Coast of Orange Blossoms. The land flattens, beaches widen and stretch, and the scent of orange blossoms indeed hangs in the spring air. Housing developments reach into that same air, but not to the degree that they do further south on the Costa del Sol and Costa Blanca. A few scattered towns manage to retain their charm; and beaches are ample, with Peñiscola the best. Thus, sunning opportunities run for over 100 miles both north and south of Barcelona.

Transportation is ample too. Using either trains or buses it is perfectly feasible to visit both Barcelona and its adjacent beaches without a car.

The most popular beaches in Spain, and quite possibly in all of Europe, form the southern coast of Spain. East to west spread the Costa Blanca, Costa del Sol and Costa de la Luz. The **Costa Blanca ★★★** is named for its fine white beaches, sometimes stretching for miles. Benidorm boasts of the best beaches in Spain, but the town itself is no longer attractive, and space on the sand is hard to come by at the height of the season. Nonetheless, there are pockets on this coast where crowds do not collect and bathing is scenic and tranquil. The weather is wonderful—seldom are there clouds, let alone rain. The **Costa del Sol ★★**, running from Gibraltar east to Almeria, is a different cup of tea. Beaches are gritty, pebbles in the shallows make wading difficult, and highrise developments stretch as far as the eye can see. Why then do all the people come? Because all the people come. These are Spain's most popular beaches by far and the most cosmopolitan and exciting, with crowded clubs, restaurants and bars. It is fun, and the sun shines almost every day, but such amusements are not cheap. West of Gibraltar begins the Atlantic Ocean and the **Costa de la Luz ★★**. Beaches consist of sand, rather than grit, the Atlantic sends true waves, fresh seafood is delicious, and the crowds and prices are less than on the Costa del Sol.

CASTLES

Do you want to see fortresses, the fabled castles of Spain? Here is a list of the best, all close to Madrid. **Coca ★★**, near Segovia, is the epitome of a castle; the Alcàzar in **Segovia ★★★★** looks like a fairy-tale version; and **Ávila ★★★★**, not far from Segovia, is the most complete medieval fortified town in Europe (tied with Carcassone in France). Not enough? Northeast of Coca, thirty-five miles from Valladolid, is the still-imposing castle of **Peñafiel ★★**, with parts as old as the 10th century, the rest from the 15th. South of Madrid, on the way to Andalusia, is a massive 15th-century castle in **Belmonte ★★**, complete with perimeter wall. Further afield, the Alcázar of the Alhambra in **Granada ★★★★★**, along with its perimeter walls calls to the castle lover, as do the walls of **Trujillo ★** in Extremadura. Would you like to pass the night in a castle? Near Madrid there is a large castle turned *parador* at **Sigüenza ★★★★**, or, for more intimate fortress surroundings, the parador castle at

Alarcón ★★★. Near Pamplona at **Olite** ★★★, a truly typical castle has been turned into a *parador*.

CATHEDRALS

Those looking for glorious cathedrals will find a profusion in Spain. The cathedrals in **Toledo** ★★★, **Burgos** ★★★★★ and **Seville** ★★★★ represent the best and most impressive examples the sumptuous Spanish Gothic has to offer. **León** ★★★★ presents the airier French model, and **Santiago de Compostela** ★★★★★, the acme of Romanesque. **Salamanca**'s Catedral Vieja ★★★★ is a quiet, but moving, structure. Outside **Oviedo** are two tiny 8th-century progenitors of the larger churches to come. The church at **El Escorial** ★★ and the cathedral at **Valladolid** ★★, both by the architect Herrera, are imposing neo-classical structures. Virtually every city and most towns will possess a church of interest. And monasteries range from **Poblet** ★★★, near Barcelona (entirely restored, but imposing nonetheless), to **Miraflores** ★★★ and **Las Huelgas Convent** ★★★★ (older and more charming, both are in the suburbs of **Burgos**), to **El Escorial** ★★★★ (for its classical lines), and Guadalupe ★★★ (full of religious mystery). Then there are the holy sites—**Guadalupe** ★★★, for the Black Virgin, **Santiago de Compostela** ★★★★★, for its relics of Saint James, **Ávila** ★★★, for Saint Theresa; and **San Ignacio de Loyola Monastery** ★, half an hour from Donastia, and **Javier Castle** ★, near Pamplona, for Saint Francis Xavier's and Saint Loyola's respective birthplaces.

CHARMING VILLAGES

Santiago de Compostela and **Segovia**, being large, stretch the village characterization, but both have the feel of a village and atmosphere to spare. **Trujillo** ★★ is sleepy and picturesque. **Ronda** ★★, in Andalusia, provides breathtaking vistas across the landscape. **Arcos de la Frontera** ★★, also in Andalusia, offers views almost as stunning as Ronda's from either the parador or the tiny El Convento Hotel. **Peñiscola** ★, on the Costa del Azhar, offers vistas, ★white beach for miles and a lively town. **Donostia** ★★★ on the Costa Verda is also much too large for the category, but its elegance immediately makes visitors forget that discrepancy.

ITINERARIES

Since too much of even of a good thing can tire, we recommend that days of sights be broken either by beach lolling or an extra day with nothing on the agenda in a town you enjoy. That same wisdom argues against overloading a trip with any single type of sight, whether castles, cathedrals or museums. Variety, as someone should have said, is the spice of vacations. Suggested itineraries follow, though we leave it up to you how to implement our advice to serve your interests.

The ten itineraries cover most of Spain in trips that vary in length from one week to 15 days. Any two itineraries may be combined to form trips of longer duration, and too-long itineraries may be shortened by omissions. As to the time estimates, we are aware that many travelers want to experience as much as possible and fill every minute with activity. These people will find our estimates generous. We assume a few hours every day for whims, cafe sitting, and napping. On the other hand, our itineraries are predicated on visits to only the most outstanding sights so they omit interesting and enjoyable activities for those with more time or energy. Impatient travellers can cut a day or two off our itineraries, while the thorough can add as much. Each itinerary assumes a first day consumed by travel, settling in a hotel, and gaining bearings, and a last day taken up by departure arrangements, which in some cases might involve flying into Madrid for international connections. So, a week's itinerary comprises five sightseeing days. Add to our itineraries whatever beach or rest days you wish.

IMPORTANT NOTE: Most museums in Spain are closed on Monday. If we list a museum for a day that falls on a Monday during your trip, you may wish to interchange it with another day.

MADRID, 7 days

This trip will give you the flavor of Madrid and the Prado, one of the great museums of the world, as well as El Escorial, an imposing complex.

Day 1: Travel to Madrid and settle into a hotel.

Day 2: The Museo Nacional del Prado; Jardin del Retiro, Casón de Buen Retiro.

Day 3: La Ciudad Antiqua; Plaza Mayor; Convento Descalzes Reales; Convento de la Encarnación.

Day 4: Excursion to El Escorial.

Day 5: Museo Arqueológico Nacional; shopping; Museo Lázare Galdiano.

Day 6: Palacio Real.

Day 7: Departure.

MADRID AND TOLEDO, 7 days

This trip adds remarkable Toledo to the best of Madrid.

Day 1: Travel to Madrid and settle into a hotel.

Day 2: The Museo Nacional del Prado; Convento Descalzes Reales.

Day 3: La Ciudad Antiqua; Plaza Mayor; Palacio Real.

Day 4: Museo Arqueológico Nacional; shopping; Museo Lázaro Galdiano.

Day 5: Travel to Toledo; settle into a hotel; Cathedral; Santo Tomé.

Day 6: Alcázar; El Tránsito Synagogue; Iglesia María Blanca; Santa Cruz Museum.

Day 7: Return to Madrid and departure.

Note: If an extra day is available, the fairytale castle of Segovia lies an hour north of Madrid, with El Escorial on the way.

BARCELONA, 7 days

This trip introduces the cosmopolitan city of Barcelona, its extraordinary collections of medieval and modern Spanish art, and the charm of Gaudí's architecture.

Day 1: Travel to Barcelona and settle into a hotel.

Day 2: Barri Gótic; Cathedral; Palau de la Generalitat.

Day 3: Museo de Arte de Catalunya; Fondacion Joan Miró; Museu Arqueològico, if time.

Day 4: Museu Marítim; Museu Picasso; and the Textile and Costume Museum.

Day 5: Gaudí's works, including Sagrada Familia; shopping.

Day 6: Ramblas and Palacio de la Virreina; Santa Maria del Mar.

Day 7: Departure.

Note: This itinerary assumes flying directly to Barcelona. If landing in Madrid, you may need an extra day for travel to Barcelona, depending on connections. To include Madrid, add days 2 and 3 from the Madrid itinerary, but substitute the Museo Arqueológico Nacional for the Jardin del Retiro on the second day.

MADRID AND EXTREMADURA, 8 days

This driving trip combines Madrid with a taste of the land which bred the Conquistadores. As a bonus it offers Roman ruins, a preserved renaissance town, and the holy monastery of Guadalupe.

Day 1: Travel to Madrid and settle into a hotel.

Day 2: The Museo Nacional del Prado; Museo Arqueológico Nacional, Casón del Buen Retico.

Day 3: La Ciudad Antiqua; Plaza Mayor; Palacio Real.

Day 4: Travel to Cáceres and settle into a hotel.

Day 5: Ciudad Vieja and excursion to the Roman remains at Mérida.

Day 6: Excursion to Trujillo.

Day 7:   Return to Madrid, visiting Guadalupe Monastery on the way.

Day 8:   Departure.

THE LEVANTE AND MURCIA, 8 days (or more)

This area is visited mainly for beaches—the Costa del Azahar and Costa Blanca. Valencia adds interest. Days should be added for relaxing in the sun.

Day 1:   Travel to Madrid and settle into a hotel.

Day 2:   Travel to Valencia and settle into a hotel.

Day 3:   Ciudad Vieja; Palacio de la Generalidad (only open Saturday mornings); Lonja; Museo Porvincial de Bellas Artes.

Day 4:   Museo Nacional de Ceramica; Iglesia de los Santos Janes; Colegio del Patriaca; Torres Serranos.

Day 5:   Excursion to scenic Peñiscola along the Costa Azahar, visiting Roman ruins at Sagunto on the way.

Day 6:   Travel down the Coasta Blanca to Murcia and settle into a hotel, passing through once lovely Benidorm and pausing at Gandia to see the palace of the Borgias (Borjas in Spanish).

Day 7:   Cathedral. Travel to Madrid.

Day 8:   Departure.

Note: A boat ride through underground grottoes of San José is available outside Sagunto on the way from Valencia to Peñiscola. To include Madrid, add days 2 and 3 from the Madrid itinerary, but substitute the Museo Arqueológico Nacional for the Jardin del Retiro.

SEVILLE, GRANADA, CÓRDOBA, 10 days

This trip by car or train will give you the flavor of Andalusia, the Moors, and Spanish architecture of the 14th and 15th centuries.

Day 1:   Travel to Madrid and settle into a hotel.

Day 2:   Travel to Seville and settle into a hotel. Cathedral; Torre Giralda.

Day 3:   Alcázar and gardens; Barrio de Santa Cruz; Museo Arqueológico.

Day 4:   Museo de Bellas Artes; Casa de Pilatos.

Day 5:   Travel to Córdoba and settle into a hotel. Mesquita.

Day 6:   Juderia; Alcázar and gardens; excursion to Medina el Azehara.

Day 7:   Travel to Grenada and settle into a hotel. Cathedral and Capilla Real.

Day 8:   Alhambra; Palacio Carlos V; Generalife.

Day 9:   Albaicin; Cartuja, San Juan de Dios.

Day 10: Departure.

Note: Any number of beach days on the Costa del Sol or Costa de la Luz can easily be added to this itinerary. To include Madrid, add days 2 and 3 from the Madrid itinerary, but substitute the Museo Arqueológico Nacional for the Jardin del Retiro.

OLD CASTILE, 10 days

This whirlwind trip, for which a car is necessary, includes the best castles, fine Renaissance architecture, two spectacular cathedrals and a Roman aqueduct.

Day 1: Travel to Madrid and settle into a hotel.

Day 2: Travel to Segovia and settle into a hotel, visiting El Escorial on the way.

Day 3: Roman aqueduct; Alcázar; Ciudad Vieja and Cathedral.

Day 4: Travel to Salamanca and settle into a hotel, visiting Ávila and Coca castle on the way.

Day 5: Plaza Mayor; Patio de las Escuelas; Catedral Vieja; travel to Valladolid and settle into a hotel.

Day 6: Collegio San Gregorio and the town. Travel to León and settle into a hotel.

Day 7: Cathedral; Saint Isadore; excursion to San Miguel de Escalada.

Day 8: Travel to Burgos and settle into a hotel, visiting Fromista on the way.

Day 9: Cathedral; the monastery of Miraflores; Las Huelgas convent; return to Madrid with optional stops at Santo Domingo de Silos and Pedraza de la Sierra.

Day 10: Departure.

Note: To include Madrid, add days 2 and 3 from the Madrid itinerary, but substitute the Museo Arqueológico Nacional for the Jardin del Retiro.

NAVARRE AND ARAGÓN, 10 days

This driving trip offers medieval monasteries, scenically placed churches and Pamplona.

Day 1: Travel to Madrid and settle into a hotel.

Day 2: Travel to Pamplona and settle into a hotel.

Day 3: Cathedral; Museo Navarra and Ciudad Vieja.

Day 4: Excursion to Estella and Irache Monastery, stopping at Cirauqui and Puente la Reina on the way.

Day 5: Excursion to Olite; La Oliva Monastery; scenic Ujué and the monastery of Leyre.

Day 6: Travel to Zaragoza and settle into a hotel, stopping at Tudela on the way.

Day 7: Cathedral; Lonja; Nuestra Señora del Pilar; Aljaferia.

Day 8: Excursion to Veruela Monastery; Huesca; San Juan de la Peña Monastery.

Day 9: Return to Madrid.

Day 10: Departure.

Note: The park and waterfalls of Piedra Monastery make a nice excursion from Zaragoza, stopping at picturesque Daroca on the way. Also, from spring though fall, scenic walks are possible in Ordesa National Park. To include Madrid, add days 2 and 3 from the Madrid itinerary, but substitute the Museo Arqueológico Nacional for the Jardin del Retiro. Add Burgos from the Old Castile itinerary, if time allows.

SANTIAGO DE COMPOSTELA, GALICIA, AND THE BASQUE COUNTIES, 12 days (or more)

In addition to the spectacular pilgrimage church of Santiago de Compostela, this driving trip offers rugged seacoast scenery and elegant beach resorts. Add days at Santillana del Mar, Santander, Laredo or Donostia (San Sebastian) for the beach.

Day 1: Travel to Madrid and settle into a hotel.

Day 2: Travel to Santiago de Compostela and settle into a hotel.

Day 3: Cathedral; Ciudad Antiqua; Hostal do los Reyes Católicos.

Day 4: Excursion to Pazo de Oca, to ocean inlets at Mirador de la Curota and to Cab Finisterre, the westernmost part of Europe.

Day 5: Travel via the coast to Oviedo and settle into a hotel, pausing at Mondoñedo.

Day 6: Ciudad Antiqua; Cathedral; excursion to Santa Maria del Naranco.

Day 7: Travel along the coast to Santillana del Mar, Santander or Laredo.

Day 8: Explore the town.

Day 9: Travel along the coast to Donostia (San Sebastian), detouring for San Ignacio de Loyola Monastery.

Day 10: Ciudad Vieja; Mount Igueldo.

Day 11: Return to Madrid.

Day 12: Departure.

Note: From Santiago de Compostela an excursion can be made to Osera monastery and to Orense for its Cathedral and Old Town. The

Altamira Caves lie outside of Santillana del Mar, but require advance permission to enter. Other painted prehistoric caves in the area that do not require permission are: Cueva Santimamine near Guernica on the way to Donostia; Cueva de Buxu in the Picos de Europa mountains between Oviedo and Santillana del Mar; Cueva el Castillo outside Puente Viesgo near Santillana del Mar; Cuevas Covalanas outside Ramales de la Victoria near Laredo; and Cueva Tito Bustillo outside Ribadesella on the way from Oviedo to Santillana del Mar. The road to Madrid goes through Burgos, with a magnificent Cathedral. To include Madrid, add days 2 and 3 from the Madrid itinerary, but substitute the Museo Arqueológico Nacional for the Jardin del Retiro.

THREE STAR SPAIN, 15 days

This trip covers the greatest sights in Spain, though it is light on local flavor and rest.

Day 1: Travel to Madrid and settle into a hotel.

Day 2: The Museo Nacional del Prado; the Museo Arqueológico Nacional, Casón Buen Retiro.

Day 3: Plaza Mayor; Palacio Real; excursion to El Escorial.

Day 4: Travel to Toledo and settle into a hotel. Cathedral; Santo Tomé.

Day 5: El Transito Synagogue; Iglesia María Blanca; Iglesia San Roman; Santa Cruz Museum.

Day 6: Travel to Seville and settle into a hotel. Cathedral; Torre Giralda.

Day 7: Alcázar and gardens; Barrio de Santa Cruz; Casa de Pilatos.

Day 8: Travel to Córdoba and settle into a hotel. Mesquita; Juderia; Alcázar and gardens.

Day 9: Travel to Grenada and settle into a hotel. Cathedral and Capilla Real.

Day 10: Alhambra; Palacio Carlos V; Generalife.

Day 11: Travel to Santiago de Compostela and settle into a hotel.

Day 12: Cathedral; Hostal do los Reyes Católicos.

Day 13: Travel to Barcelona and settle into a hotel. Barri Gótic; Cathedral.

Day 14: Museo de Arte de Catalunya; Museus Miró and Picasso; Gaudí's works, including Sagrada Familia.

Day 15: Departure.

Note: This itinerary assumes a departure from Barcelona. If leaving from Madrid one extra day may be needed for returning, depending on connections.

HISTORY

The tomb of Columbus in Seville Cathedral.

Although Spain is rich in history, most visitors, while appreciating the beauty of a particular palace, garden or painting, understand little of its cultural significance. One reason for such unfamiliarity is that, for much of the century, Spain isolated itself from the world community. Yet, how much more alive and exciting these sights become when one knows something about the historical times and events to which they're linked.

In this book we provide that background in two ways. Below, an historical chronology and overview gives an idea of the scope of Spain's history and a ready point of reference. The historical profiles preceding each chapter on sights add more detailed accounts of significant events and figures.

PREHISTORY TO THE VISIGOTHS (TO A.D. 711)

c. 13,000 B.C.	Prehistoric people create cave paintings at Altamira.
c. 1,300 B.C.	Iberians inhabit Spain, perhaps migrating from North Africa.
c. 1,000 B.C.	Phoenicians colonize Cádiz and Málaga.
c. 900 B.C.	Celts reach Spain, perhaps migrating from France.
c. 650 B.C.	Greeks colonize the eastern coast of Spain.
250 B.C.	Carthaginians take over the south coast.
206 B.C.	The Roman general Scipio Africanus defeats the Carthaginians, beginning six centuries of Roman rule.
19 B.C.	Caesar Augustus completes the Roman conquest of Spain.
A.D. 74	Rome bestows citizenship on the Spanish.
A.D. 380	The emperor Theodotius declares Christianity the state religion of the Roman Empire.
c. A.D. 400	Germanic tribes invade Spain.
c. A.D. 500	Visigoths conquer Spain.
A.D. 711	Muslims from Morocco conquer the Visigoths.

Civilization existed in the Iberian Peninsula for at least 1,000, and perhaps as long as 15,000, years before the Romans imposed their way of life on its inhabitants. Not only do the megalithic Celtic dolmens preserved at Antequera offer evidence of a culture that spread from Brittany and Britain at the beginning of the last millennium B.C., but the haunting cave paintings in Altimara, dating from 15,000 years ago force us to rethink our image of "primitive" cave dwellers. The Celts found two different peoples already inhabiting the land when they arrived—Iberians, perhaps originally from North Africa, and Basques, possibly from North Africa too, though this people of enigmatic beginnings may have originated in Spain.

Phoenicians landed in Spain in 1,000 B.C., but penetrated no further than the southern coast where they mined tin for the manufacture of bronze. They established permanent trading posts at Gades (Cádiz) and Malaca (Málaga), avoiding the inland territory belonging to those they referred to as "Celtiberians," mistakenly classifying two peoples as one. Greeks followed, but kept their distance by colonizing only the east coast of Spain, where major Greek ruins still remain at Empúries, north of Barcelona. In the third century B.C., as the fortunes of Phoenicia waned, its former colony, Carthage, took over control of the coast. The Romans first set foot on Spanish soil, just before the beginning of the second century B.C., when they came to attack the supply lines of the Carthaginian general Hannibal during the Second Punic War. They stayed on in Spain and set out to do what no visitor had yet accomplished—the conquest of Spain's interior.

Unlike most of Rome's opponents who fell quickly to her armies, Spain resisted for two centuries before its final defeat in 19 B.C. by Caesar Augustus. The peninsula, now a province of the Roman empire, became over time more Roman than Rome, with senators, Latin writers, and even emperors springing from its soil. In 74 A.D. the people of the peninsula were awarded Roman citizenship to acknowledge Spain's importance to the Empire. To strengthen these ties, Rome embarked on major construction projects throughout Iberia, building splendid bridges (at Alcantára), constructing huge aqueducts (still intact at Segovia), and running hundreds of miles of roads throughout the peninsula. In Mérida an elegant theater still stands beside a coliseum for gladiatorial and naval battles. The common tongue throughout the peninsula was Latin, which later evolved into both Spanish and Portuguese.

As the years passed, Rome's power declined, allowing "barbarians" to break through the Empire's border defenses. In the fourth century A.D., Franks from Germany seized present-day France. With the eastern border of the Empire vulnerable, other German tribes were free to invade and claim whatever they could. By the fifth century the Alans (originally from Iran) and the Suevi established settlements in eastern and western Iberia, respectively. Then the Vandals came, seized the south of Spain, and gave it their name, "Andalusia" (Vandal's Land). A century later, fleeing fierce Huns to their east, the mighty German tribe of the Visigoths (Western Goths) poured into Spain. They chased the Vandals across the Gibraltar straits into Africa and conquered the other Germanic tribes and indigenous people, taking command of all of Spain. With Toledo as their capital, they established an elected kingship, a caste of nobles, and a state religion—Christianity, all of which became Spanish institutions.

MOORS AND THE RECONQUEST (711-1250)

711-716	Morocco conquers Spain in the name of Islam.
722	Pelayo achieves the first Christian military victory over the Moors, initiating the reconquest.
756	Moorish Spain, led by Abd ur Rahman, secedes from the caliphate of Baghdad.

c. 800	Santiago de Compostela, alleged burial site of St. James, achieves fame throughout Europe as a pilgrimage center.
912-961	Abd ur Rahman III reigns as Spain's greatest caliph.
1072-1109	Alfonso VI reconquers most of Spain for the Christians, aided by El Cid.
1090	The Almoravids reconquer Spain for the Moors.
1147	The Almohades from Morocco conquer the Spanish Moors.
1212	Christian forces break the Moors' hold on Spain in the decisive battle of Las Navas de Tolosa.
1236-1248	Fernando III captures two of Spain's three remaining Moorish strongholds, Córdoba and Seville, leaving only Grenada under Moorish control.

A small Moroccan army crossed the Straits of Gibraltar in 711, decisively defeated the Visigoths, then chased them into small enclaves in the Pyrenees and northern Asturias. (See "Historic Profile: Moors and the Reconquest," p. 285.) The Moors' domination of Spain would last for eight hundred years—a span longer than the time that has elapsed since their final defeat in 1492. While the Dark Ages enveloped the rest of Europe, Spanish Muslims kept knowledge alive by maintaining disciplines rejected by Christians—education, philosophy, poetry, and cleanliness. Their architecture, especially in the Alhambra of **Granada** and the Mezquita of **Córdoba**, displayed a sensitivity never since surpassed. The Moors appropriated the Visigoths' horseshoe arch as their most characteristic architectural element, and, because of religious proscriptions against depicting human and animal forms, adorned their buildings with intricate geometric and floral designs in tile, wood or stucco.

With the exception of Constantinople, the Moors' capital of Córdoba soon became the largest city in Europe. But Moorish Spain remained a mere province within the Islamic empire until a dynastic change in Baghdad, the ruling center of Islam, caused the sole survivor of the previous dynasty, Abd ur Rahman, to flee to Spain where he claimed the allegiance of the Moors and forged Spain's independence. By the 10th century, under Abd ur Rahman III, Moorish Spain had reached its apex, surpassing every other part of Europe in splendor, modernity and richness. This apex, however, was short-lived. The death of his grandson created problems of succession that split the Moors' territory into separate weaker states.

In the meantime, Christians were attempting a reconquest of Spain from their northern confines. Tradition dates the beginning of the reconquest to 722 when Pelayo, a Visigoth noble, won the first Christian engagement against the Moors. But no territory was regained in this skirmish. In fact, the Reconquest owed more to the discovery of bones attributed to Saint James the Apostle by shepherds, than to such raids. By the 8th century a church and a city—both called Santiago de Compostela—had grown around the sacred site. (Saint James in medieval Spanish was *Sant' Iago.*) Santiago became a pilgrimage center, second only to the Holy Land and Rome, and drew Europeans by the hundreds of thousands to Christian Spain. Along with the pilgrims came an idea for a crusade to spread Christianity throughout the peninsula. Spain's epic reconquest, begun in this era, was followed by five centuries of struggle, both heroic and base.

Over time the northern state of Asturias conquered neighboring León. By the eleventh century these combined states annexed the land to their south, called "Castile" after all the defensive castles built there. Castile became dominant in the coalition and a genuine power in the peninsula. A separate Christian kingdom grew in Aragón, conducting its own reconquest down the eastern side of Spain. But Castile and Aragón became bitter rivals who fought against each other as often as they battled separately against the Moors. By the end of the 11th century, however, a Castilian king, Alfonso VI, was strong enough to raid as far south as the Mediterranean coast and capture Toledo, the ancient Visigoth capital. Frightened Moors called for help from Morocco. A fanatical sect called the Almoravids heeded the call and, with the exception of Valencia which was defended by the Spanish hero El Cid, reconquered all that their brethren had lost. When the religious fervor of the Almoravids abated, another fierce fundamentalist sect, the Almohades, took over and regained Valencia. This revitalization of the Moors forced the Christian rivals, Castile and Aragón, to join forces in one campaign. In 1212, to swell their ranks further, they summoned crusaders from the corners of Europe, formed an army that engaged the Islamic forces south of Toledo at Las Navas de Tolosa, and inflicted a defeat from which the Moors never recovered. After this major victory, Castile and Aragón once again parted ways.

Twenty-four years later, aided by civil wars that had sapped the Moors' strength, Castile's Fernando III was able to take Córdoba. Four years after that he seized Seville, while Aragón recaptured Valencia. The Reconquest was almost complete. Granada alone held out, though more than two centuries would pass before it fell.

FERDINAND, ISABELLA
AND COLUMBUS (1250-1516)

1369-1379	Enrique Trastámara fathers a Castilian dynasty.
1451	Columbus is born.
1454-1474	The questionable legitimacy of Enrigue the Impotent's designated heir places Isabella in Castile's line of succession.
1469	Isabella of Castile weds Ferdinand of Aragón.
1474	Isabella ascends the throne of Castile.
1479	Ferdinand ascends the throne of Aragón.
1481	The Inquisition begins.
1492	Grenada surrenders, completing the Reconquest. Spain's Jews are expelled. Columbus sails for the Indies.
1502	Spain's Moors are expelled.
1504	Isabella dies.
1506	Columbus dies.
1512	Ferdinand conquers Navarre.
1516	Ferdinand dies.

The wedding of Isabella of Castile to Ferdinand of Aragón provided Christian Spain with the unity it needed to complete the Reconquest. But first Castile was made to suffer two centuries of internecine violence and weak rulers. Foremost in its gallery of rogues was Pedro the Cruel. After Pedro killed one of his illegitimate half brothers, the other, Enrique of Trastámara, in turn murdered Pedro in 1369, and seized the throne, beginning the dynasty from which both Isabella and Ferdinand descended. By the time Isabella's half-brother Enrique IV came to power a century later, so much authority had been transferred to the nobles of Spain by successive kings that Castile had dissolved into virtual anarchy. (See "Historical Profile: Ferdinand and Isabella," p. 197.) Enrique IV claimed that his second wife's child was his heir, despite evidence to the contrary and his nickname of "the Impotent." To clear the succession for this "daughter" Enrique tried to marry his half-sister Isabella off to one prince after another, but Isabella defied him and, in 1469, secretly wed Ferdinand of Aragón. Enrique died in 1474, still protesting gossip about his daughter's paternity, but leaving Isabella's claim to the throne of Castile paramount. Five years later, with Ferdinand's ascension to his father's throne, the kingdoms of Castile and Aragón were finally united under Ferdinand and Isabella.

One of Isabella's first royal acts was to import Aragón's Inquisition to Castile. With its announced purpose of eliminating Christian heretics, the Inquisition persisted until the 19th century. What it actually accomplished, besides great personal and social disruption, was perhaps more pervasive: the esteem modern Spaniards accord "pure" bloodlines—those untainted by Jewish or Moorish ancestors.

Despite Ferdinand's generalship and Isabella's efficient organization, it required ten years of sustained warfare to subdue Grenada. On January 2, 1492 Isabella and Ferdinand walked through the gates of Grenada to conclude eight centuries of reconquest. During that same year Isabella sent Christopher Columbus on his way to the New World (See "Historical Profile: Columbus and the Conquistadores," p. 387.), and signed an order expelling all of Spain's Jews. Although Isabella lived only 12 years longer, before she died in 1504 she was to see one of her daughters marry the son of the Holy Roman Emperor—a union that would elevate Spain to the greatest power in Europe. Ferdinand survived his wife by another 12 years, during which he added Navarre, the territory that completes the map of modern Spain, to his kingdom.

HABSBURG KINGS (1519-1700)

1519-1556	Carlos V becomes the first Habsburg king of Spain.
1519-1522	Cortéz conquers Mexico.
1532-1534	Pizarro conquers Peru.
1541-1614	The life of the painter El Greco.
1547-1616	The life of Miguel de Cervantes.
1556-1598	The reign of Felipe II.
1560	Felipe II makes Madrid the capital of Spain.
1567	Revolt begins in Holland against Spain.
1571	Spain defeats the Turkish fleet at Lepanto.
1580	Felipe II gains the throne of Portugal.
1588	The Great Armada is destroyed.
1598-1621	Felipe III succeeds his father.
1599-1660	The life of the master painter Velázquez.
1609	The Moroscos (converted Moors) are expelled from Spain.
1621-1665	The reign of Felipe IV. Velázquez appointed court painter.
1648	The treaty of Westphalia wins Holland's independence from Spain.
1640	Portugal regains its independence.
1665-1700	The reign of Carlos II ends the Spanish Habsburg dynasty.

The Habsburg dynasty in Spain began and ended with a Carlos, between which three Felipes reigned. Isabella and Ferdinand's daughter Juana, despite her insanity, remained Spain's nominal ruler until her son Carlos V reached his majority. Carlos, a Habsburg on his father's side, inherited control over Holland, Belgium, Austria and Germany along with his title of Holy Roman Emperor. Born and raised in Holland, Carlos introduced Spain to the culture and art of the rest of Europe. By the time his son Felipe II succeeded him, the Low Countries, as Holland and Belgium were known, had begun a revolt that would last a hundred years and drain Spain of all its wealth from the New World. (See "Historical Profile: The Great Armada and World Power—Felipe II," p. 111.)

Felipe II established a new capital at Madrid in the center of the country, undertook massive building projects in the capital and constructed an imposing monastery at nearby El Escorial. Although he had vowed to keep his territory intact and defend the Catholic faith, his resolve was sorely tested by Protestant revolts in the Low Countries. He did defeat the Turks in a great sea engagement at Lepanto in 1571, and when, in 1580, the king of Portugal died heirless, Felipe II, with the most direct claim, for a time united Portugal's throne with Spain's. In 1588, after discovering a secret alliance between England and the rebels in the Low Countries, Felipe assembled Spain's Great Armada, intending to invade England. Only half of his ships returned. Ten years and two armadas later, Felipe died.

In 1609 his son, Felipe III, expelled all remaining Moors from Spain. In 1605 Miguel de Cervantes published *Don Quixote*, the first novel. Felipe IV succeeded his father and lost Portugal in 1640 by violating an agreement stipulating that only Portuguese administer their country. Although a low point in Spanish political history, the reign of Felipe IV witnessed the rise of most of Spain's greatest painters—Ribalta, Ribera, Murillo, Zurbarán, and, greatest of all, the court painter Velázquez.

Upon the death of Felipe IV in 1665, his son, a veritable idiot, ascended the throne. Somehow Carlos II managed to occupy his office for 35 years, but never produced an heir, and thus ended the Habsburg dynasty in Spain.

BOURBON KINGS (1700-1931)

1700-1746	Felipe V becomes the first Bourbon king of Spain.
1702-1711	Attempting to regain the throne, Habsburgs precipitate the War of Spanish Succession.
1746-1759	Fernando VI promotes Spanish neutrality.
1759-1788	Carlos III brings prosperity to Spain.

1788-1808	Carlos IV rules. The weak king and his family are immortalized by Goya.
1789	The French Revolution produces Napoléon.
1809-1813	Britain and Portugal join Spanish guerrillas against France in the Peninsular War.
1814-1833	The absolutist Fernando VII defies the first constitution.
1833-1839	The First Carlist War brings civil war to Spain.
1843-1874	The reign and exile of Isabella II.
1874-1875	The First Republic.
1875-1885	Alfonso XII regains the throne.
1898	Spain loses Cuba, Puerto Rico and the Philippines in the Spanish-American War.
1902-1930	Alfonso XIII rules as Spain's last monarch before abdicating in favor of a republic.

In 1700, the childless last Habsburg, Carlos II, named Philip of Anjou as his successor. (See "Historical Profile: Habsburgs to Bourbons," p. 459.) When Felipe V became the first Spanish monarch from the French Bourbon line (called Borbón in Spanish), his ascension precipitated a war, appropriately called the War of Spanish Succession, with the Austrian Habsburgs. Though Felipe eventually won, the war was only the beginning of two centuries of intermittent battles that would reduce Spain from a major world power to a pawn of new European leaders.

After Felipe V, Fernando VI negotiated a series of neutrality treaties to help Spain recover from the devastations of civil war. His policies were continued by his half-brother Carlos III, whose astute economic planning moved Spain forward into the 18th Century. Unfortunately he was succeeded by his son Carlos IV, an amiable dolt controlled by his wife, who, in turn, was under the spell of a favorite courtier. After the French Revolution, the unrealistic Carlos went so far as to send Spanish troops into France to attempt to restore its monarchy. His army was crushed, enabling France to force Carlos to join her later in war against Portugal and England. As the 19th century dawned, Spain entered the arena of European politics as a reluctant ally of Napoléon.

In 1808 Napoléon forced Carlos IV to resign in favor of his own brother Joseph. Outraged, the Spanish people rose in rebellion on the second of May, and fought a guerilla campaign until, four years later, aided by the British under the Duke of Wellington, they succeeded in expelling the French. The great artist Goya immortalized the era with unforgettable etchings of the horrors of war and with royal portraits of the fat Carlos IV, his determined wife and plump children.

After the expulsion of the French, Spain found itself without a king for the first time since before the Visigoths. A constitution had been written in 1812, even before the French left, and now Carlos' son was invited to return from exile to reign as Spain's first constitutional monarch. Fernando VII had other ideas, however, and upon his return repudiated the constitution and seized control as an absolute monarch. In the meantime, most of Spain's American colonies had been lost when they seized their independence while Spain was occupied by the French. More trouble lay ahead. Fernando left only an underage daughter when he died, prompting his brother Don Carlos to wage five years of the First Carlist War to press his own royal claims. In the end, the carnage and destruction gained nothing, and the daughter, Isabella II, ascended her father's throne. She proved to be nothing like her namesake, preferring sexual dalliances to governing. A putsch of the army and navy ended both her dalliances and her reign in 1868.

Since Isabella's son was too young to rule, Spain briefly enlisted two foreign relatives as its king, then opted for a kingless republic for a year. By 1875 Isabella's son was judged old enough to become Spain's constitutional king, but his untimely death, ten years later, resulted in another regency. A rebellion in Cuba at the end of the century embroiled Spain in the Spanish-American War and cost her the last two of her American possessions—Cuba and Puerto Rico—along with the Philippines. In 1902 Alfonso XIII attained his maturity and came to the throne, but the government had been so discredited in the eyes of both her citizens and her army, that only dictatorships and army putsches lay ahead.

THE SPANISH CIVIL WAR AND AFTER (1931-PRESENT)

1931-1939	The Second Republic.
1936	The Spanish Civil War begins. Madrid resists.
1937	Destruction of the town of Guernica.
1939	Barcelona and Madrid fall. End of the Spanish Civil War.
1975	Franco dies. Juan Carlos I is crowned.
1978	A new constitution is approved.
1989	Felipe Gonzalez is reelected prime minister.

By 1931 world depression had pushed Spain, a poor country at best, into even deeper economic decline. (See "Historical Profile:

The Spanish Civil War," p. 489.) When Alfonso XIII called for elections, most of the large cities voted for socialists whose platform called for a republican government without a king. Lacking support, Alfonso abdicated. For the second time in Spain's history, counting the one-year experiment of 1874, Spain found herself a republic.

The 1930s were times of radical politics throughout Europe and America. On the left, socialists, anarchists and communists in Spain gained ground in direct proportion to the deterioration of the economy, offering their new ideas in place of more traditional theories that seemed to no longer work. On the right, the fascist Spanish Falange committed political murders that caused its leader José Antonio to be jailed and martyred. One socialist government in 1931 was replaced by a different one in the election of 1933, but proved equally unable to satisfy the conflicting desires of even its own supporters. Without political direction, violence and anarchy prevailed.

In 1936 the army revolted, attempting to seize the major cities of Spain. The revolt failed in its objectives, but evolved into a civil war of army, church, royalists and fascists fighting against the government and most of the people. Generalissimo Francisco Franco led the army toward Madrid. There the citizens staunchly resisted, surprising the world and their own elected officials, who had previously fled for safety.

With Madrid firm against them, the Nationalists (as the army called itself) then adopted a strategy of conquering the rest of the country so Madrid would fall from lack of support. First they waged a successful campaign in Spain's northern Basque country, although the destruction of the town of Guernica by Franco's German allies cost the Nationalist forces much in propaganda. The next year, 1938, the Nationalists turned west and surrounded Barcelona. The Republicans tried a hopeless, if valiant, counterattack that exhausted their remaining supplies. Ironically, although the Nationalists were abundantly provisioned by fascist Germany and Italy, the democracies of America and Europe refused to aid the Republicans. Lacking rifles for its civilian troops, Barcelona fell in 1939. Madrid tumbled three month later.

Franco ruled Spain for almost three decades thereafter. He ruthlessly imprisoned Spanish liberals, but gained a great economic advantage for Spain over the war-torn countries of Europe by maintaining the country's neutrality during World War II.

With memories of the Civil War still fresh, many feared what might follow in the wake of Franco's death, but what transpired was a peaceful transition to democracy when El Caudillo died in 1975. Juan Carlos I, the son of Alfonso XIII, returned from exile, as Franco had wished, to become the constitutional monarch. He continues to reign today with his queen, Sofia. In 1979 a constitution delineating this arrangement was approved by the electorate. But in 1981 a gang of Civil Guards, a group roughly corresponding to our state troopers, attacked a session of Parliament with automatic weapons and held its members hostage. All Spain waited to hear where Juan Carlos would stand—with the rightist forces, or with the Republic. When he announced his continued support of the constitution, the Civil Guards surrendered. The next year the Socialist Party won national elections by a narrow margin, and Felipe Gonzalez was named prime minister. By Spain's next election in 1989, Gonzalez had shown himself to be less a socialist than a pragmatist and won overwhelmingly. Today, still under the leadership of Prime Minister Gonzalez, Spain stands at the center of the European political spectrum and holds a charter membership in the European Economic Community.

ART AND ARCHITECTURE

Plateresque cloister of the College of San Gregorio in Valladolid.

The Spanish love dramatic light in their paintings, delighting in its contrasts, and dark in their cathedrals, prizing its mystery. Over the centuries, Spanish painting changed, conveying emotion less with contorted bodies and copious blood than with the most subtle depictions of face and form. At their height, Spanish artists achieved true miracles of the painter's craft. Spain's architecture came to be characterized by an emphasis on solidity over openness, longitude over height, and surface decoration over architectural form.

EARLY ART AND ARCHITECTURE

PREHISTORIC, CELTIBERIAN, ROMAN AND VISIGOTH

Spain's oldest art does not suffer at all from comparison with the best work that the country produced . The finest paleolithic paintings in the world, challenging those at Lascaux across the French border, adorn the ceilings of the cave of **Altamira**. The animals depicted seem to contort and breathe. The cave can hold only fifteen people at a time, and admission is difficult to obtain, but *El Castillo* cave outside Puenta Viesgo near **Santillana del Mar** provides examples almost as striking without the need for prior arrangements. And no advance permission, only an admission charge to the *Museo Arqueologico Nacional* in **Madrid**, is required to view the artworks of the little-known Celtiberians, a people whose unique art developed in isolation from classical influences. The Celtiberian masterpiece, the lovely sculpture *Dama de Elche* with its hauntingly foreign look, captivates all who view her.

Rome's domination of the Iberian Peninsula from the second century B.C. through the third century A.D. is evidenced by its architectural legacy throughout Spain. It bequeathed Spain the *aqueduct* at **Segovia**, which is surpassed in size only by the *Pont du Gard* in France. The Roman *bridge* at **Alcantara**, though much repaired, preserves its original lines. Remains of a Roman city sprawl near **Empurias**, north of Barcelona, and at **Mérida**, in Extremadura, stands an intact *theater* beside the substantial remains of an *arena*, along with a fine museum of Roman art nearby. The *Museo Arqueológico Nacional* in **Madrid** displays classical sculpture, mosaics and sarcophagi collected from all over Spain.

The Museum also houses jewels of the Visigoths, especially the rare and fine solid gold *Crown of Reccesvinthus Rex*, with its embedded emeralds and sapphires and dangling pearls. The Visigoths began as farmers, turned migratory, then settled in Spain. Little of their art or architecture remains in their Germanic homeland, and little survives in Spain, for the Visigoths enjoyed only two centuries of dominance during which to refine their art. Their permanent buildings were almost all destroyed either by conquering Moors, or by reconquering Christians, but, miraculously, a church of the Visigoths does survive intact outside Zamora, near **Valladolid**. *San Pedro de la Nave*, harmonious in its proportions and decorated with charming carvings, dates from the 7th century.

THE MOORS

No traveler to Spain should miss the 14th century *Alhambra* in **Granada**. Familiarity with western architecture does not prepare a visitor for the experience of being transported to such a quiet, calm way of life. Rooms follow no prescribed plan, yet each attains an individual perfection while managing to compliment the rooms it adjoins. But, above all, the Alhambra presents a unique solution to the problem of merging the constructions of men with nature. At the Alhambra, nature is brought inside with stalactite ceilings that convey the sense of a starry sky, while nature herself waits just outside in the form of gardens and pools. The intricate decoration of tile walls surmounted by fantastic carved ceilings should seem busy and gaudy, yet serve instead as restful study pieces. And everywhere the sound of running water tranquilizes, for no part of the Alhambra is more than a few feet from a patio or a garden: the Moors knew secrets of peaceful architecture.

The *Mesquita* (mosque) in **Córdoba**, completed in the 10th century, shows how the Moors used their knowledge of architecture to serve religion. A striped forest of pillars and double tiered horseshoe arches creates an atmosphere of mystery and awe: this mosque has no parallel in the world. The exalted aesthetic of the Moors is evident as well in the collection of the *Museo Arqueologico Nacional* in **Madrid**. Consider the delicate ivory jar called the *Bote de Marfil*, with its sublimely harmonious decoration.

As the Reconquest advanced, some Moors found themselves behind the lines in Christian territory. Prizing their skills, the Christians engaged them, originating a style known as *Mudéjar*—Islamic art serving Christian ends. For examples of this fortunate collaboration, see the *Casa de Pilotes* and the *Alcázar* in **Seville**, parts of which bear comparison to the Alhambra, and the *El Tránsito* synagogue in **Toledo**. Less pleasing is *Mozarabic* work, done by Christians raised in Islamic territory, but liberated by their kin. The 9th century Mozarabic church of *San Miquel de Escalada* near **León** is clean and airy, but the strong straight lines of the roof clash with the curves of horseshoe arches.

ARCHITECTURE

THE RECONQUEST: ROMANESQUE

While it is not surprising that castles built to withstand assault might endure from the time of the reconquest, it is a wonder that a civilian work, a palace, remains from the 9th century. Built by

Ramiro I in the 9th century near **Oviedo**, and later used as a church—hence its name *Santa María de Naranco*—the palace suggests both the Romanesque style it prefigures, and its Byzantine source. Its rough rocks should lend a rustic crudity, but instead convey refinement and harmony. Although the barrel vaulting of the ceiling, which would become a hallmark of the Romanesque, is supported by columns, the columns are carved in patterns which never materialized in that later style. It is a seminal and fascinating structure.

So many castles were built by both Christians and Moors to defend the border which lay between them that the region was given the name "Castile." Castles, in all sizes and styles, still abound today. Those with round towers were generally designed by Christians; those with square towers usually indicate Mudéjar architects. The walls of **Ávila**, punctuated by round towers, form one of the most extensive medieval fortresses extant. By the 15th century the rule about round and square towers no longer held, defied by the powerful structure erected at **Coca**, the most typical of all the world's castles, and by the fairy-like *Alcázar* (castle) at **Segovia**.

Throughout the time of the Reconquest, religious feeling was intense in Christian parts of Spain. When, in the 8th century, bones believed to belong to Saint James were found at **Santiago de Compostela** the area became not just another pilgrimage center, but the holiest Catholic site outside of the Holy Land and Rome. By the 11th century one of the world's great churches had been erected there. Today the cathedral's splendid 18th century Baroque front belies the majesty of its Romanesque interior—a towering barrel ceiling with massive ribs supported by colossal columns—whose sheer size inspires awe. The Romanesque style commands religious awe through the power of its architecture—no filigree for these worshippers, no brightness granted by expanses of glass, no flying buttresses to permit slender columns. Introducing the cathedral is the *Door of Glory*, a masterpiece of Romanesque sculpture by Master Mateo, as he signed himself. At a time when other scultptors were fashioning staid statues, more icons than real, this genius created living beings from stone. Equally wonderous, on a smaller scale, is the *Catedral Vieja* (Old Cathedral) in **Salamanca**. A proper complement to the power of these cathedrals is *San Vincent*, a Romanesque chuch in **Cardona**, near **Barcelona**. Built at the same time as Santiago de Compostela, the purity and simplicity of the interior of this church evokes a different kind of awe. The dozen Romanesque churches sprinkled around **Segovia** inspire similar feelings.

GOTHIC

Influenced by Abbé Suger, the French lightened their churches in the 11th century with outside, "flying," buttresses that permitted less massive interior supporting columns, walls of glass to let in light, narrow ribs supporting arched ceilings, and, in place of the rounder Romanesque, pointed arches designed to raise the eye upward. Called Gothic, the new aesthetic style spread through Europe. The Spanish built one breathtaking church, complete with glorious stained glass windows, exactly on this model—the *Cathedral* at **León**. By the 13th century the Spanish had modified the French style to create a new version—wider in plan and lightened more with ornate decoration than by the brightness of windows. The cathedrals at **Burgos** and **Toledo** are masterpieces of this Spanish Gothic style, ranking among the the world's outstanding church architecture.

RENAISSANCE: ISABELINE AND PLATERESQUE

After their modification of the Gothic, Spanish architects continued to create new styles diverging from mainstream European architecture. Fifteenth century *Isabeline* buildings add a tracery of lacy decoration to otherwise bare walls, the prime example of which is the sumptuous entrance to the *Collegio San Gregorio* in **Valladolid**. The exuberance of the style, however, is most evident in **Granada** in the *Capilla Real*, where Ferdinand and Isabella are buried. In the chapel, the architect Juan Guas let his fantasies run free. There also, carved in perfect proportion by the master sculptor Bartolome Ordoñez, is the moving mausoleum of Phillip the Handsome and Juana the Mad.

In the 16th century, the Isabeline effect evolved into the famed *Plateresque*. The word "Plateresque" means "like silverwork"—intricate, chiseled, curving and precious. Plateresque refers mainly to decoration that serves no structural function and obeys no rigid symmetry, but is an appliqué attracting the eye to an otherwise undistinguished wall, window or door. The city whose architecture most epitomizes the style is **Salamanca**, a museum city of the Plateresque—and its masterpiece is the entrance to the *University*.

Secondarily, Plateresque refers to an architectural retreat from the Gothic style. Ceiling arches replace ribs and interior wall pillars substitute for outer buttresses. The plan and decoration of the interior of the *Cathedral* at **Grenada** offers a particularly interesting example. (Its exterior belongs to the following century.) The plan is a rotunda with a circular ambulatory. If more were needed to distance these curves from their pointed Gothic counterparts, the decoration—recessed portals, where frames dominate what they enclose—proclaims the Plateresque even more defiantly.

CLASSICAL AND BAROQUE

However original and striking the Plateresque may have been, it survived for only a century, ending when it lost favor among its royal patrons. As early as 1526, while the Plateresque was still at its height, Carlos V had ordered a pupil of Michelangelo to design a classical *Palace* in **Grenada**'s Alhambra precinct. Though the formality of the structure compares badly to the ethereal quality of the adjacent Alhambra, its plan of a circular courtyard within a square exterior is simple, dignified and impressive in its way, if only it were located elsewhere.

Throughout the remainder of the 16th century, Carlos' son, Felipe II, reacted against the decorative excesses of the Plateresque by originating a new style, rather than adopting an older one as his father had done. *El Escorial*, outside Madrid, was the beginning. Designed by Juan Bautista de Toledo, another pupil of Michelangelo, the monastery of El Escorial is sometimes described as a fortress. In fact it is majestic, and appears stark only when viewed from a Plateresque or Gothic perspective. When Bautista died four years into the project, he was replaced by the genius of Spanish architecture—Juan de Herrera. Untrained in architecture, Herrera followed no known style, only his feeling of what was right. The *church* in El Escorial is all his, unique and wonderful.

Herrera's originality died with him, to be replaced by a return to the ornate. The Baroque excess of the 17th century holds its own fascination, as the Spanish version, called *Churrigueresqe* (after the Churreguera family who originated it), exuberantly demonstrates. The original business of the Churriguera's was designing altars—the altarpiece in the *Convento de San Esteban* in **Salamanca** shows their extravagant work. When they turned to the larger scale of architecture, they expanded the ornate, entwined curves of their altars into buildings in which the eye can find no focus or rest, only stimulation. One acknowledged masterpiece resulted, the *Plaza Mayor*, in **Salamanca**. Uncharacteristically for plazas of the period, the buildings around this square are agreeably combined to form one of the finest ensembles in Spain.

NEOCLASSIC TO ART NOUVEAU

In the 18th century, when Bourbon rule began in Spain, Felipe V built a "little" Versailles outside **Segovia** to remind him of home.

The palace at *La Granja* is sumptuous, the gardens grand. Succeeding sovereigns built extensively in Madrid, favoring architects of classical, Italian bent. One of the best was Juan de Villanueva who designed the *Museo del Prado*. So successful was his design that it spawned descendents around the world, including the Metropolitan Museum in New York.

Although there was little to distinguish Spanish architecture through most of the 1800s, just as the century was closing, Antonio Gaudí arrived to make up for lost time. It was the era of *Art Nouveau*—dripping, draping, decorative appendages, and buildings abhorring sharp corners. To these expressions of Art Nouveau, Spain contributed its own heritage of the Gothic and Plateresque to nourish its genius Gaudí. In **Barcelona** stand his fantasies, from blocks of houses—*Casa Batlló* and *Casa Mila*—to the amusement park *Güell*, to the unfinished masterpiece of *Sagrada Família*, like no church in this world.

SCULPTURE

Romanesque sculpture in Spain followed the path of sculpture elsewhere in Europe. Figures held rigid postures, faces were caricatures, and drapery fell woodenly. Against such a landscape, the genius of Master Mateo leapt out at the viewer. By the 13th century, the time of the Gothic, sculpted figures became elongated, paralleling the upward thrust of Gothic cathedrals. They also began to bend and move. Drapery, though still not natural, was consciously used to add rhythm to compositions, and faces began to reflect the individuality, if not the accuracy, of portraiture.

In 15th century Spain, during the time of the Isabeline style, genius erupted again in the person of Gil de Siloé who decorated the monastery of *Cartuja de Miraflores* in **Burgos**. His altarpiece overwhelmed the more intricate altars of his contemporaries. In the same monastery he carved a tomb that conveys for all time the sadness of the death of the *Infante* (Prince) Don Alfonso, and, finest of all, a set of tombs for Juan II and his queen Isabel of Portugal. In his effigies, Siloé conveys the strongest emotions with the subtlest of lines.

In the 16th and 17th centuries Siloé's lead was followed by a number of great Spanish sculptors. Berruguete, influenced by the complex movements of the Greek statue of *Laocöon*, rediscovered during his time, carved tormented figures for the cathedral in **Toledo**. Although the choirstalls of that cathedral are entirely splendid, beginning with the lower parts depicting the conquest of Grenada, it is the upper stalls on the left that are by Berruguete. No one who takes the time to look can miss his work. At first, compared to the higher relief of the other stalls, his carvings seem reserved, for they are infinitely more subtle. Then, with study, they come alive. Over the center, in high alabaster relief, flies his magnificent *Transfiguration*, subtly tense and moving.

Most characteristic of Spanish sculpture is its polychromed wood. Gregorio Fernández was a master of the genre. His haunting, living faces, better executed than his mannered bodies, are exhibited in the Museum of Polychrome Sculpture at **Valladolid**. The acknowledged giant of polychrome sculpture, however, is Juan Martinez Montañés who brought the art of painted wood to its summit during the 17th century. He was called *dios de la Madera*, the god of wood. His work is displayed in the Valladolid museum, but more can be seen in the churches of **Seville**, especially in the cathedral. See his *Christ of Clemency*, the *Virgin Primisima* and the *Christ Child Lifting his Arms*, all in the cathedral, and all conveying a stark and realistic dignity. Indeed, some find them too realistic to be considered art.

To all but lovers of romantic effect, sculpture had reached its pinnacle. The master of the 18th century was Nariciso Tomé, and his masterpiece, the *Transparente*, is displayed behind the altar of the **Toledo** Cathedral. When it was finished it was considered the eighth wonder of the world, although later generations damned it for extravagance. It is a work that people either love or hate, but nonetheless came to represent the sculptural ideal in Spain.

PAINTING

Romanesque and Gothic painting in Spain can best be appreciated in the superb collection of the Museo de Arte de Catalunya in **Barcelona**. Often captivating, generally interesting, and always deeply expressive of the artist's religious feeling, early Spanish painting is remarkable for the quantity of blood it portrayed—a thinly veiled brutality. Perhaps the wars of the Reconquest that brought real blood into peoples' lives also permeated their art; perhaps Spain's Roman Catholicism, a particularly primitive, strict version, affected its artists; or perhaps the facet of the Spanish character that has always found excitement in the elaborate and bloody ritual of the bullfight migrated to its art.

By the time of the Renaissance, Spanish painting had advanced from depicting gore to enter the mainstream of European art. In fact, the greatest Spanish painters of that era all trained in Italy.

Pedro Gonzalez Berruguete suggests Giotto in his *St. Dominic Before the Inquisition*. Fernando Yanez studied with Leonardo De Vinci, but shows his own sensitivity in *Saint Catherine*, a painting remarkable for its appreciation of negative spaces. Pedro Machuca studied with Michelangelo, was greatly influenced by Caravaggio, and developed a style, especially evident in his *Madona del Suffragio*, of stark light and shadows. These paintings are included in the extraordinary Renaissance collection of the Museo del Prado in **Madrid**, a collection equally strong in both Italian and Spanish masters. Though not quite in the first rank, Spanish Renaissance painters are moving at their best and pleasing at their worst.

With the dawning of the 16th century, the quality of Spanish art underwent a dramatic change. Finally victorious in its long struggle against the Moors, Spain was free for the first time in centuries to turn its attentions outward to the rest of Europe. Spain's first sane monarch after Ferdinand and Isabella, Carlos V, had the twin luxuries of seeking out art and artists from all the corners of Europe and of introducing his countrymen to an array of artistic styles. Carlos V became the patron of the Venetian Titian, whose genius epitomized European art up to that time, and was but the first of three generations of kings, from Felipe II to Felipe IV, who together acquired one of the finest art collections ever amassed—now housed in the Museo del Prado in **Madrid**. Dürer, Botticelli, Raphael, Caravaggio, Bosch, Titian and Rubens are only the best-known of artists whose paintings are included in the superb royal collection that raised the standards of both art and its appreciation in Spain, and stimulated her own artists to rise to unequalled heights.

At the same time the first genius of Spanish painting emerged, although he was not born Spanish. Domenico Theotocopoulos, El Greco (the Greek), after studying with Titian in Italy, came to Spain from Crete, hoping to find commissions as Titian had. In 1575, at age 35, he settled in Toledo, never to leave again. El Greco had studied Byzantine icon painting in which strong outlines make thin, elongated figures stand out from their background. He introduced the device to western art, along with a palette of luminous blues and reds acquired from his Italian teachers. El Greco was a man of devotion, searching for ways to express deep religious sentiment, and succeeded as no one had before. An ego of enormous proportions allowed him to resist pressures to make his art conform: he once told a pope that if the Sistine frescos were removed, he could paint better ones.

El Greco first tried to sell paintings to Felipe II, who bought two. *The Martyrdom of St. Maurice* and *Adoration of the Holy Name of Jesus* still hang in Felipe's **Escorial**. In the latter work the great distance up and into the picture initially seems crude and childish, but, with study, the canvas opens up into eternity. El Greco drew from plastic models, not from life, producing angled figures and constant movement, but not realism. The Impressionists—especially Cézanne who copied El Greco's paintings repeatedly—learned much from him. But Felipe II found El Greco's paintings too radical and bought no others.

Thereafter, El Greco worked for wealthy private citizens and churches in **Toledo**. In the Hospital of Tavera, outside the city walls, two great works still hang. *The Baptism of Christ* is magnificent and the portrait of *Cardinal Tavera* haunting. The Museo Santa Cruz holds more than twenty El Grecos, including the famous *Altarpiece of the Assumption*. But the work most people call his best hangs alone inside the vestibule of the tiny church of Santo Tomé. *The Burial of Count Orgaz* is a late work (1586) of El Greco's and his largest. It incorporates all the original elements that El Greco developed: elongated figures, drawn as if the painter were lying down looking up at the subjects; angry, living skies; and raw emotion expressed as much in the mannered painting of fabric as in the faces of his subjects. Felipe II is painted among the apostles in heaven, El Greco himself is said to stare at the viewer as the sixth figure in the front row, and his son, Jorge Manuel, is the child on the left pointing at the burial. If you can see only one El Greco, make it this one.

El Greco did not represent a culmination of European art; he followed his own muse. In the more realistic mainstream, Spain rose to dominance in the 17th century—the Golden Age of Spanish art. It began with Francisco Ribalto (1565-1628), a Catalan, who discovered his metier late in life. His finest works are the *Vision of Saint Francis* and *Bernard Embracing Christ* in the Museo del Prado in **Madrid**. Then Jusepe de Ribera (1591-1652) burst upon the art world. Ribera is the only painter who can be compared with Velázquez in electing to paint ordinary people instead of idealized images. Ribera painted seedy characters, and used them as models to portray saints and philosophers. His figures are real like no others. It has been argued that Ribera's paintings are stronger than Velázquez', and that he was more original in his themes. According to most, his masterpiece is *The Martyrdom of Saint Bartholemew* hanging in the Museo del Prado. But equally engaging are *Joseph with the Christ Child*, *Saint Alexis* and, most striking, *Trinity*. Study the strong diagonals created by the two inverted triangles of the design, the look on the face of God as he holds his dead Son, and the drapery. Ribera is a consummate master.

Genius seemed to inspire genius as Francisco de Zurbarán (1598-1661) followed Ribera. Zurbarán's paintings were the most spiritual of all, not with the fire of El Greco's work, but possessed, instead, of a quiet, bare, intensely reflective, almost mystical quality. Zurbarán's solitary figures in white robes against dark, featureless backgrounds display his extraordinary ability to combine spirituality with utter realism. *The Crucifixion* in the Museo de Bellas Artes in **Seville** is a superior example.

When the French invaded Spain early in the 19th century, they so admired Zurbarán's work that they pried his paintings from the walls of monasteries and churches. They took almost 100 works with them back to France, now all disbursed among the museums of the world. Spain retains some fine Zurbaráns, but, alas, not the best. Also in the Museo de Bellas Artes in **Seville** is *Blessed Henry Suso* in which the German mystic Suso, stands, uncharacteristically for Zurbarán, against a landscape setting. The figure of Henry Suso is prime Zurbarán, and sublime. The Museo del Prado in **Madrid** displays the best Zurbarán collection left in Spain. Outstanding are *Saint Luke before the Crucified*, *Saint Elizabeth of Portugal*, of the luminous clothes, the striking *Virgin of the Immaculate Conception*, and the unforgettable *Saint Peter Nolasco's Vision of the Crucified Saint Peter* with Saint Peter upside down.

Contemporary with Zurbarán, though worlds apart in his career and choice of subjects, was Diego Velázquez de Silva (1599-1660), whose work represents the culmination of Spanish painting. Recognized for his genius while still a youth, Velázquez studied in Seville, and was appointed a court painter by his twenties. Two early paintings before his appointment—*The Adoration of the Magi* and *Mother Jerónima de la Fuente*, with her piercing, determined gaze—show him already a master. These hang with all the other paintings we discuss in the premier Velázquez collection, that of the Museo del Prado in **Madrid**.

At court in Madrid, Velázquez became a royal portrait painter, entering a lifelong friendship with his patron and contemporary, the lonely Felipe IV. Velázquez' portraits of the king show his human side—a homely man with thinning hair and jutting Hapsburg jaw. The portrait of Felipe's brother *The Infante Don Carlos,* demonstrates Velázquez' mastery of the portrait genre. In 1628 Peter Paul

Rubens, the most famous painter of the day visited Madrid. He had no use for any Spanish painter but Velázquez and undertook to teach him what he knew. These lessons are contained in Velázquez' disturbing *Feast of Bacchus*, in which the effete, half-naked, fair-skinned god of wine stares at us, surrounded by leathery peasants. It is a flawed painting that foreshadows Manet's *Dejuner sur l'herbe* in its shock of contrasts.

Beginning in 1629, Velázquez spent two years studying in Italy, funded by his patron Felipe. The result was two large Italinate narrative works, *The Forge of Vulcan* and *Joseph's Bloodied Coat Presented to Jacob*. The former painting is a tour de force of surfaces, from gritty floor to burnished iron to gleaming armor. Figures of the cyclops show surprisingly lean, unidealized bodies. The latter is an initially annoying painting that does not seem to work at all until one steps twenty feet away and sees it come to life.

Back in Spain, Velázquez entered a mature phase when no project was beyond him. During this period he painted the epic *Surrender of Breda*, sometimes known as *Las Lanzes* for its most striking element. The work commemorates one of the few Spanish victories in the long war with The Netherlands, and the grace with which General Spinola accepted the Dutch surrender. *Count-Duke Olivares on Horseback* is a monumental homage to his friend at court,a fellow Sevillano, in which the huge Count-Duke surveys his only military success. His depiction of *Diego de Corral y Arellano* is more subtle, the essence of portraiture. Velázquez painted everyone in the royal family and most of the jesters and dwarfs kept as pets. Most telling is his perceptive portrait of Queen Marianna , showing her unpleasant character, lightened only by touches of vermilion ribbon.

Velázquez was ambitious, rising in position with the years. Added responsibilities for collecting art for the king, decorating rooms in the Madrid palace and El Escorial, and supervising other royal painters consumed time, constricting his own artistic output. In his last phase,Velázquez determinedly painted only works that were important to him, exercised to stretch his medium. Two acknowledged masterpieces resulted. *The Fable of Arachne*, by any measure a masterpiece of complexity, depicts a weaving contest between the mortal Arachne and the goddess Minerva. Although it would be fruitless to try to decide what painting should be called the best in the world, Velázquez' last work, *Las Meninas* (Ladies in Waiting), tempts one against reason. Even Picasso drew a score of variations on this work. Like no other painting, Las Meninas makes the viewer a participant, for he stands exactly at the focus of all the activity. The picture is complex and perfect, summarizing all the painting lessons learned through the ages. Velázquez died soon after finishing *Las Meninas*, but posthumously earned the Order of Santiago he had so assiduously sought in life. A thoughtful friend—some say it was the king himself—later painted a crimson cross, the sign of the order, on Velázquez' chest in the painting.

If Velázquez poses a problem it is that he is too accomplished. Everything seems so right and undramatic that it is possible to run quickly through a gallery of his work. His mastery requires study. Fortunately his paintings all invite contemplation, for such was his genius.

Bartolomé Esteban Murillo (1617-1682) followed Velázquez and was, in his own time, considered great. Later judgments deemed him mawkish and sentimental for choosing cute urchins as his subjects, but his star has risen again. There is no question that he had every talent needed by a painter. Anyone who looks at his works displayed in the Museo del Prado can decide where to place Murillo, but no one will rank him with his predecessor. Velázquez could not be bettered.

Francisco de Goya (1746-1828) changed the direction of European painting. He first painted designs for tapestries, called "cartoons," at the royal tapestry works, before turning to portraits. By 1799 he was celebrated enough to be named painter to the king. The king happened to be a genial incompetent, dominated by his wife Maria Luisa, and her lover, Godoy. Whether Goya's portraits of the royal family are the greatest art can be argued, but if art means showing the truth, these works make a case. Goya pushed his portraits toward caricature to reveal his subjects' inner character. Paintings such as *The Family of Carlos IV* in the Museo del Prado so ruthlessly display the emptiness of the king and the ambition of the queen, who takes center stage in the group, that one wonders why they allowed such a portrait to be displayed. Perhaps they could not see what was before their eyes, or perhaps Goya's bright but washed colors seduced his clients with their elegance. Conversely, when Goya's subject was a person of quality, as in the case of his friend and father-in-law Bayeu, the portrait exudes character. Goya could also be sensual, as in *Maja Clothed*. more erotic than the same subject and pose in *Maja Nude*.

Goya's high position in the pantheon of art depends more on his fevered imagination than on his skill at portraiture. In 1808, when the French seized Spain, Goya painted two masterworks—*The Second of May* and *The Third of May*—depicting the uprising of Spanish citizens against their invaders. The first shows a battle, fierce with violence; the second, by artificially shortening the distance from the executioners' guns to the defenseless victims, shrieks of the horrors of death. Afterwards, Goya put anguish on canvas in his *Black Paintings* (named for their dominant color)—the unforgettable *Saturn Devouring One of His Sons, Dog Half-Submerged*, and *Witches' Sabbath*, for example. Equally dramatic were his series of etchings on the *Horrors of War*, and *Caprichos*, caricatures of the great and of those who believed themsleves to be. All are displayed with justifiable pride by the Prado.

Where was art to go after such geniuses? In the 20th century it became surreal or abstract, inspired by three founding fathers from Spain. The most prolific, versatile and influential modern artist surely was Pablo Ruiz Picasso (1881-1973). To those who claim modern art is not realistic because its artists lack talent, Picasso answered while a child by painting exceptional realistic works, but fought sucessfully throughout his career to create new forms of expression. Picasso, who lived in French exile most of his life, belongs to the world as much as to Spain; still, in the Museu Picasso in **Barcelona**, Spain displays a good collection of his works, stronger in early paintings than in later works. It is interesting to see the first realistic works of the teenaged Picasso and some favorite pieces from his rose and blue periods. Picasso's most dramatic, and, many would say, his finest work, the tormented *Guernica*, has finally been returned to Spain and is now displayed in Spain's new museum of modern art, the Centro de Arte Reina Sofia, in **Madrid**.

Spain does better in collecting the works of another native son, the Catalan Joan Miró (1893-1983). The Fondacio Miró in **Barcelona** presents the breadth of his work, from painting to sculpture to prints and fabrics, in a most appropriate building designed by Joseph Sert. Salvador Dalí (1904-1989), the great surrealist, has a worthy surreal gallery in the Museo-Teatro of his home town of **Figures**, northeast of Barcelona.

FOOD AND DRINK

Food markets, like this one, are typical throughout Spain.

Above all, the Spanish are robust in their tastes, adoring both hearty food and animated conversation. These preferences mean that restaurants will seem more like convivial meeting rooms than hallowed cathedrals of cuisine, and that food portions will be ample. It also means that dining customs and hours in Spain will differ from our own.

Because the Spanish enjoy their leisurely main meal at two in the afternoon and follow it with an equally lengthy rest, restaurants do not begin to reopen for dinner until nine—or in Madrid, Barcelona and Andalusia at least ten at night—occasionally with restricted menus.

Thus, an important dining consideration for visitors to Spain is not simply what to eat but when. For the most part, Americans in Spain stick to their habit of eating their main meal in the evening, causing them to search midday restaurant menus for light luncheon meals but finding few choices among listings of full dinners. At night, biding their time until the restaurants reopen, they find themselves the first arrivals, uncomfortably alone in the dining room.

Spain is relaxed about most things, including food and its availability, so it is perfectly possible to eat in Spain as you would at home. Below we explain how to find sandwiches and other light noon meals. On the other hand, it might be interesting to try eating as the Spanish do. Take your main meal at midday, then snack on *tapas* at night. That way you'll be dining during the time many shops and sights are closed for their midday break, and you can emerge fortified for serious sightseeing. You will also sleep better for it.

The Spanish begin the day lightly with a *cafe completo*, a continental breakfast of delicious strong coffee and a roll or bread. Coffee is either *solo* (black), *con leche* (with milk) or *café américano*, a weaker version. Tea made from bags is available. Most hotels charge extra for breakfast, but any bar or cafe can provide it too. Those who wish more—some eggs, for example—are talking about *desayuno* (breakfast), which is generally available at hotels, often in the form of somewhat costly, but bountiful, buffets that include cold cuts and fruit, along with ham, eggs and croissants.

At midday in any bar one can find *bocadillos* (sandwiches), consisting of rolls filled with delicious *tapas* selections, including tasty *jamon serrano* (like prosciutto). For more familiar lunch choices, stop at a cafeteria or an *auto-servicio*. Alternatively, wait until one or two o'clock to eat a full meal in a restaurant.

By early evening (seven o'clock or so) groups begin gathering in the tapas bars. The name *tapas*, which means tops or lids, derives from a time when bartenders, to protect against flies, covered a glass of wine with a small plate on which they set free appetizers. No longer free, such appetizers today costs a dollar or more. In a good tapas bar, always distinguished by a large crowd, choices will be extraordinary—slices of omelette, *chorizo* (spicy dried sausage), marinated beef, squid, clams, oysters, mussels, octopus, and shrimp, *jamón York* (boiled ham) or *jamón serrano* (air-cured mountain ham—like prosciutto but stronger), rice and potatoes. Most of the food will be cold, but not all, and *raciones*, larger plates, may be ordered. Pointing is an acceptable way to select. When it is time to pay, the waiter will count the empty plates to figure your bill. You may sample the delicacies either standing at the bar or, for higher prices, sitting at a table. The food is washed down with wine, sherry—usually a dry *fino*—or beer.

Dinner, *la cena*, is served beginning at nine or ten at night, depending on the area of Spain. However, some hotels open their restaurants earlier to accommodate our foreign habits.

FOOD

Spanish food is seldom spicy hot—in no way to be confused with Mexican food and its generous use of chilies. What distinguishes Spanish food from northern European cooking is its use of olive oil rather than the butter for sautéing. At its best, Spanish food can be as subtle as the finest French cuisine; at its worst it can be heavy or greasy; but in general, it provides tasty and satisfying fare.

The Spanish government assigns restaurant ratings, symbolized by between one and four forks, in addition to a *Lujo* (deluxe) rating, and inscribes these symbols on metal signs posted outside restaurant entrances. The ratings evaluate a restaurant's ambiance, the variety of its offerings, and the elegance of its service, but not the quality of its food or the degree of graciousness with which its diners are treated, although there is often some degree of correspondence. Menus comprise à la carte choices, but often offer either a *menú del día* or a *menú turistico* which provide complete meals at lower, fixed prices, although with a limited range of choices.

Spanish cuisine is comprised of several regional cuisines, although a famous dish from a given region will be available in most cosmopolitan centers. Common to every region is a love of seafood, rushed fresh to cities as far from the coast as Madrid. A Spaniard, on average, eats 68 pounds of fish per year. And the Spanish love garlic. If you do not sympathize, avoid dishes with names containing the words *ajillo* or *ajo*.

Andalusia is famous for its cold soup, *gazpacho*—raw vegetables, especially onion and tomatoes, blended with olive oil, vinegar and garlic. From Málaga comes the interesting white *ajo blanco*, a cold blend of garlic, ground almonds, and floating grapes. *Sopa sevillana* is a rich fish stew flavored with mayonnaise and garnished with egg. *Fritura mixta de pescados* is a mixed fry of fresh seafood. Fresh sardines (*sardinas*) can be sublime, as can trout (*trucha*), fresh from nearby streams. A hearty casserole of lima beans and ham is called *habas con jamón*.

Valencia invented *paella*, now served all over Spain. It is named for the skillet in which short-grained saffron rice is stewed with seafood, sausage, chicken and snails, all garnished with pimento. When seafood replaces the meat, the name changes to *paella marinera*. Although a description of *paella* ingredients makes it seem to call for white wine, few whites can stand up to its rich flavors.

The center of Spain, **Old** and **New Castile**, is known for roast meat (*asados*). In crisp skin, *cochinillo* (suckling pig) falls off the bone, *cordero* (lamb) is memorable when roasted over wood fires called *hornos*, and *lechazo* (milk fed lamb) is a treat. A broth in which ham chunks, vegetables and eggs swim is called *sopa castellana*, while *costido castellana* is a rich stew based on chick peas. The center for game, when it's in season, is Toledo.

Aragón and **Navarre** feature chicken and trout. *Pollo chilindron* is chicken in a peppery sauce, *trucha a la Navarra* is fried trout stuffed with *jamón serrano*.

The rest of Spain acknowledges that the **Basque Country**, where men form cooking societies, produces the finest chefs. *Pil pil*, a sort of chili sauce, is used for prawns (*gambas*) and codfish (*bacalao*). *Bacalao a la viscaina* is stewed cod in fresh tomatoes. A specialty is *merluza a la vasca*, baked hake in a casserole of clams. Basque *nuevo cochino* (Spanish nouvelle cuisine) is today the internationally "in" cuisine.

Galicia also merits a high reputation, not surprising given the superb shellfish available. *Centollas* consist of a huge local crab stuffed with its own minced meat. *Caldeirada gallega* is a heartier form of *bouillabaisse*, while *conchas de peregrino* will satisfy the scallop lover. *Empanada gallega* is a meat pie filled with either fish or meat.

Many dishes thought of as "Provençal," such as *bouillabaisse* and *cassoulet*, actually derive from **Catalonia**, where the cooking is similar to that of nearby French Provence. Mayonnaise was invented in Catalonia and brought to France in the 16th century. Pasta and snails (not in the same dish) are staples in Catalonia, though absent from menus in the rest of Spain. Fish stews are specialties—from *zarzuela de mariscos*, tomato based, to *romesco de peix*, with almonds and bread crumbs. Catalans make a delicious spicy sausage called *butifarras*. For desert, *crema cataluña* is a delectable *creme caramel*.

DRINK

Wines in Spain are as various and as frequently drunk as those in France. They can be as good as all but the very highest level of French wines, which are very good indeed, and are available at more affordable prices. In any price category below the astronomical, a Spanish wine will beat its comparably priced French counterpart. There are so many varieties of Spanish wine, however, that most of their names are unfamiliar except to specialists—a problem for the traveler who simply wants a wine to enjoy with his meal. Because its high alcohol and tannin content makes Spanish wine mature slowly, a good rule of thumb is to choose the oldest bottle in the price range you're considering.

Certain regions produce outstanding wines which are available all over Spain. Others make wines dispensed locally by the glass or carafe as *viño de la casa* or *del pais*, though even these are generally pleasant. Wine can be red (*tinto*), white (*blanco*) or rosé (*rosado*). Bottled wines are controlled to ensure quality by a *Denominación de Origen*, like the French "Appellation Controllée." *Reservas* are wines of good vintage, *Gran Reservas* are the best a given bodega (winery) bottles.

The best known of Spain's wine regions is **Rioja** in the northwest of Old Castile. Here red wines are aged in oak casks for a minimum of two years, and for as long as ten years in the case of *gran reservas*, before bottling—as opposed to the few months in a cask employed in French wine production. Its long contact with oak gives Riojas a characteristic "vanilla" taste, and the high leeched tannin content makes for long life. Rioja white wine resembles white Burgundies, although years in oak masks some of the delicacy of the grape. Wines from the northern Rioja Alta attain more subtlety and finesse than the higher (15 percent) alcohol wines of the southern Riojo Baja. With weather more consistent than that in France, an average year's production is of such high quality that fewer vintage years are declared.

For the best of the red Riojas, try any bottle of Marqués de Riscal or Marqués de Murrieta. Good, and less expensive, are Palacio's "Glorioso," Enrique Bilbao's "Viña Zaco," Gomez Cruzado's "Viña Dorana," La Rioja Alta, and CUNE, which costs even less, as do Marqués de Caceres and Paternina's "Banda Azul". For whites, Marqués de Murrieta again rates high, along with CUNE's "Monople Blanco Secco" and Bilbainas' "Viña Pacta."

Connoisseurs single out Vega Sicilia, from the area of **Valladolid**, as Spain's finest red wine. It is richly expensive (up to five figures in pesos) and difficult to find. The same company bottles a lesser wine—the equal of all but the finest Riojas—as "Valbueña," at one-third the price. And a vineyard near Vega Sicilia, Alejandro Fernandez, bottles a superb, if little known "Pesquera Tinto" at a fifth of Sicilia's price.

La Mancha in New Castile produces wine in enormous quantity but, for the most part, of little distinction. One area's wine, that of **Valdepeñas**, near the border of Andalusia, rises above the rest, however. The supply is large and no one maker stands out, but a Valdepeñas is always a safe and satisfying choice in its modest price category.

An interesting choice in white wine that goes well with seafood is a "green" wine from **Galicia**. It is named not for its color, but for the fact that a shortened growing season in this cool region brings early harvests. The wines are light, very dry and generally *petillant*, hinting at a sparkle on the end of the tongue. The best come from Albarino.

Catalonia produces most of the sparking wine in Spain, along with enjoyable still wine. The area of **Panadés**, running from the coast south of Barcelona to the Monserat Mountains, bottles surprisingly good, moderately priced reds and whites. Villafranca de Panadés, 20 miles south of Barcelona, is the center of the wine region and has installed a fascinating museum of wine in a 14th-century palace of the kings of Aragón. Here too is the huge bodega (winery) of Torres. The heavy "Sangre de Toro" is an undistinguished blend, but "Coronas" are vintage wines of strong bouquet and body. Torres' "Viña Sol" is a nice dry white. A lighter red is "Pleno" from Bodegas Cenalsa Murchante, or Jean León's "Cabernet Sauvignon," made from the famous Bordeaux grape which is allowed in Penadés, though not in Rioja, by the *Denominación de Origen*.

Most of the world's champagne comes from Penadés, though only that grown in the Champagne region of France may legally bear the name. Codorniú and Freixenet are both huge bottlers, though Conde de Caralt, Castellblanch, Rigol and de la Serra are all noteworthy. In the true champagne process, bubbles develop in the bottle over three years of storage, recorking and decanting sediment. Wines made by this process are designated *cavas* because the bottles are stored in cool caves. Sparkling wines lacking this word on the bottle are produced more cheaply in bulk vats. Spanish sparkling wine is best compared to the French *blanc de blancs*, for it does not contain the Chardonnay or Pinot Noir grapes used in French champagne. It is softer, with less bite than French champagne, but neither does it bear as high a price. A Spanish *bruto* (dry) can be enjoyed at a cost that allows it to be an everyday pleasure.

Sherry is Spain's great contribution to the world of wines. The English consume the most, and the Spanish do their part, but Americans seldom drink it, except in its sweeter versions. Yet dry sherry is a splendid aperitif, stimulating to the palate, and even serves well as an accompaniment to a meal. Sherry is made by allowing the juice of grapes to ferment in contact with air, a process that normally would produce vinegar. But at the western tip of Spain in **Jerez de la Frontera**, where sherry is produced, the juice develops a coating of yeast, a *flor* (flower), which protects against such oxidation. A richly complex wine, high in alcohol, results. The final product develops using a system called *solera*, in which huge casks, each containing one year's vintage, are stacked by year with the oldest on the bottom. As a bottle is filled from the lowest (thus oldest) cask, wine from the cask above replenishes what was removed, the next cask above replenishes that one, and so on. In this way, younger vintages acquire character from older ones. Sherry does not age in the bottle, only in the solera, and since the oldest vintage is continually replaced, a vintage year can be stretched infinitely. Visiting the bodegas in Jerez is fascinating and modestly priced, or even free.

Sherries should not be judged by cream sherry, an uncharacteristic product that develops no flor. Cream sherry is produced by sweetening *oloroso*, a dark sherry so high in alcohol that it needs no flor to protect it. Try *fino*, which is light and dry, if slightly bitter. *Amontillado*, a more mature *fino*, is amber in color and nutty in flavor. An old amontillado will be an expensive treat. Though less famous, sherry-type wines are produced in quantity in the adjoining area of **Montilla**. The grape here is the Pedro Ximenez variety rather than the Palomino grape of Jerez, and these grapes do not have their sugar content raised by sun drying. A montilla will generally be drier and possess greater finesse than a sherry, at least in the opinion of many.

The Spanish actually drink more brandy than sherry, though Spanish versions pale beside the French, and most popular brands are raw indeed. Torres, however, puts out an acceptable medium-priced brandy called "Gran Reserva," and Gonzalez Byass' "Lepanto" is worth its extra cost. Spanish beer (*cerveza*) is good, if rather light, and is ordered by the bottle (*botellin*) or draft (*cana*). Hard, sparkling cider (*sidra*) is the drink of choice in the northwest of Spain. As to Spanish whiskey, it is best to remain silent, but liqueurs are a different matter. Many of the famous ones—such as Cointreau, Benedictine, Chartreuse and the fruit liqueurs of Marie Brizard, are produced under license in Spain at the cheapest prices anywhere.

When you are not in the mood for alcohol, bottled water (*agua con gas* or *sin gas*, water with or without carbonation) is always available, as is Coca-Cola.

A list of Spanish words for commonly available restaurant dishes follows, arranged by the categories listed on most menus. Nonetheless, unfamiliar words are certain to be encountered in restaurants, so a pocket Spanish menu guide is most useful.

COMMONLY USED WORDS AND PHRASES

SPANISH	ENGLISH
ENTREMESES	**HORS D'OEUVRES**
Butifarra	Catalan sausage
Chorizo	hard, spicy pork sausage
Fiambres	cold cuts
Jamón serrano	paper-thin slices of cured raw ham, similar to prosciutto
Salchicha	fresh pork sausage
SOPAS	**SOUPS**
Ajo blanco	cold soup of ground almonds, garlic and grapes
Caldos	broths
Gazpacho	cold soup of tomatoes, cucumber, olive oil and garlic
Sopa de ajo	garlic soup
Sopa de fideos	noodle soup
HUEVOS	**EGGS**
Huevos cocido (or duro)	hard-boiled eggs
Huevos escalfado	poached eggs
Huevos frito	fried eggs
Huevos pasado por aqua	soft-boiled eggs
Huevos revuelto	scrambled eggs
Tortilla	potato omelette
Tortilla a la flamenca	Spanish omelette
Tortilla francesa	plain omelette
PESCADOS Y MARISCOS	**FISH AND SHELLFISH**
Almejas	clams
Anquila	eel
Bacalao	cod
Besugo	sea bream
Bonito or atum	tuna

COMMONLY USED WORDS AND PHRASES

SPANISH	ENGLISH
Boquerónes	fresh anchovies
Calamares	squid
Cangrejo	crab
Gambas, camerones or cigalas	prawns
Langosta	lobster
Lenguado	sole
Mejillones	mussels
Merluza	hake
Ostras	oysters
Pez espada	swordfish
Salmonetes	red mullet
Sardinas	sardines
Trucha	trout
Vieiras	scallops
CARNE	**MEAT**
Cerdo	pork
Cochinillo	suckling pig
Cordero	lamb
Higado	liver
Lechazo	milk-fed lamb
Rinones	kidneys
Solomillo	sirloin
Ternera	veal
Vaca	beef
AVES Y CAZA	**POULTRY AND GAME**
Conejo	rabbit
Faisan	pheasant
Pavo	turkey
Pato	duck
Perdiz	partridge
Pollo	chicken
VERDURAS	**VEGETABLES**
Aceitunas	olives
Alcachofas	artichokes
Aguacate	avocado
Berejenas	eggplant

COMMONLY USED WORDS AND PHRASES

SPANISH	ENGLISH
Ensalada	salad
Espinacas	spinach
Garbanzos	chickpeas
Guisantes	peas
Judias verdes	French green beans
Pepino	cucumber
Piso	fried vegetables
Puerros	leeks
Setas	mushrooms
Zanahoria	carrots

QUESOS	CHEESES

Most are local, so a complete list would be lengthy, but the following types are generally available.

Idiazabal	smoked
Manchego	fresh or smoked
Queso de Burgos	soft
Roncal	hard
Villalon	soft

POSTRES	SWEETS
Arroz con leche	rice pudding
Flan	creme caramel
Natillas	pudding

FRUITAS	FRUIT
Cerezas	cherries
Frambuesas	raspberries
Fresons	strawberries
Higos	figs
Manzanas	apples
Melocotons	peaches
Naranjas	oranges
Peras	pears
Plátanos	bananas
Pomelo	grapefruit
Sandia	watermelon
Uvas	grapes

COMMONLY USED WORDS AND PHRASES

SPANISH	ENGLISH
MISCELLANEOUS	
una botilla	bottle
una mesa	table
camarero	waiter
La cuenta, por favor	The check, please

BULLFIGHTING

Running of the bulls in Pamplona.

Despite continual predictions of its declining popularity, bullfighting remains a Spanish passion. On most days during the season, the Las Ventas bullring in Madrid is filled to its 50,000-seat capacity, and even at Spain's score of regional rings, tickets are scarce. Still, bullfighting does not engross Spanish spectators to the exclusion of other sports the way it once did. Today, in part due to the excitement generated by nationwide betting, soccer captures the largest share of Spain's sports audience, and golf and tennis, following recent international successes, grow increasingly popular. Nonetheless, as they have for hundreds of years, the Spanish retain a special place in their hearts for the bulls.

The bullfight season extends from April through October in Madrid, with fights every day during the May **Fiesta de San Isidro**, and during special weeks in other cities. In the first week in July, Pamplona holds its **Fiesta de San Fermin**, more interesting for the running of the bulls than for the calibre of the fights. In conjunction with its April Fair, Seville opens the splendid *Maestranza* bullring for two weeks at the end of the month, and presents lesser events throughout the summer. One of two different categories of fight will be offered on a given day, corresponding to professional and semi-pro. *Novilladas*, which involve young bulls and apprentice matadors, appeal primarily to those interested in spotting future talent.

But do not attend a bullfight unless you are prepared to see blood, often great quantities of it. In Spanish culture, a bull is viewed as a symbol. Although this viewpoint may be difficult to keep in mind while a team of horses drags away the bloody carcass that moments before was a proud animal, still a *corrida* is a vibrantly visual and auditory pageant, worth trying at least once.

The events of a *corrida* (bullfight) are easily described, but not so easily understood. What a corrida is *not* is a contest between a man and a bull: the bull always loses and is expected to. Of course there is the possibility that a bull may gore the matador, but such danger does not draw crowds any more than the chance of serious injury to a player brings fans to a football game. The crowd cheers the matador's mastery of the bull as much as the riskiness of his cape passes. A bullfight is a drama whose every act has been rigidly choreographed since the 18th century, a kind of ballet whose steps are as well known to the audience as they would to anyone seeing *Swan Lake* for the hundredth time. As in dance, grace and form count for everything. A bullfight is a ritual play recounting man's mastery of nature as embodied by the most powerful animal of medieval Europe.

The drama is directed by the governor of the corrida, who presides in the first row of seats opposite the bull enclosure. When he flutters his white handkerchief, trumpets blare and the procession begins. Riders in 18th-century costume and mounted on padded horses lead the parade, followed by marching bandilleros, then strutting matadors in their "suits of mirrors," waving hats at the cheering crowd. The governor tosses the key for the bull enclosure to the lead mounted *alguazil* (protector), who opens the gate to let in the first bull. The bull is huge—at least half a ton, in its prime at four to six years old and wearing ribbons on his withers to designate the ranch that bred him. Confused by the roar of the crowd and the unfamiliar terrain, the bull races about the circular arena in halts and charges. While the matadors observe him, a group of toreros play the bull with capes in order to run him through his paces, but rush for safety when his charges become too dangerous.

Next a *picador* on a padded horse stabs the bull's front withers with a lance, damaging his neck muscles so his head will droop by the time the matador engages him. A trio of *banderilleros* then run in turn at the bull, each leaping to plant a pair of ribboned darts in the neck wound until a total of six flop there. Now the matador walks magisterially alone into the ring, a long cape in hand, which he shakes to encourage charges from the colorblind bull. Deftly, and—if he is any good—with aplomb and grace, the matador makes the bull rush close enough to graze his leg, then swirls the cape away. The crowd roars "olé" in one voice in time with the charges, participating in the rhythm of the fight. As the matador conducts pass (*fäena*) after pass, "olés" can grow deafening, breaking into sustained applause for the rare virtuoso at the top of his form. The long cape is then exchanged for a shorter *muleta*, stiffened by an enclosed sword. By now the matador knows the moves of his bull, and the bull has grown confused by continually missing his quarry. The matador makes the animal rush in shorter and shorter charges until the bull stands with heaving sides. Disdainfully the matador walks away, showing his back to the beast.

The governor signals again, and trumpets announce that the matador has a fixed time to end the drama. He unsheathes his sword and moves slowly toward the victim, then quickens his pace, jumps and stabs the blade deep between the bull's shoulders into his heart. This finale is supposed to be clean and swiftly done: a single thrust that brings the bull immediately to his knees. If it is not, the crowd may demonstrate its disapproval vocally. As the bull is dying, the matador doffs his hat and bows to both the governor and the audience. An exceptional performance, as decided by the governor, can earn the matador a cheering parade around the ring and an ear cut from the bull or, more exceptionally, two ears and a tail.

While the sand is swept in preparation for the next bull, a team of horses drags out the carcass, already forgotten by the crowd engrossed in discussions of the performance. Usually a corrida consists of six fights, each lasting twenty minutes or so, the whole taking two and a half hours. It does not take that long to discern the difference between exceptional matadors and ordinary ones. The event is undeniably a splendid spectacle, often exciting and beautiful, but there is the blood and the death of a magnificent animal for our sensitivities to deal with.

THE SIGHTS

Spain's sights swell into the hundreds and include ancient ruins, historic and modern buildings, paintings, sculpture, scenery, and relaxing beaches. Describing so many attractive things to see and do raises fundamental issues of organization, although no arrangement can anticipate everyone's interests, a geographical organization seems the best solution. After tiring of the beach or a succession of museums, a reader can look through the chapter describing the sights of the surrounding area to discover fresh alternatives nearby.

We divide our descriptions into seven geographical regions. First comes Madrid and the area around it, New Castile. Next is Old Castile and León, a convenient day's drive from Madrid. Then we describe the sights of Andalusia, a longer day's drive from Madrid, followed by those of Extremadura, which lies west of Madrid and can be included on the way to or from Andalusia. The area comprising Galacia, Asturias and Cantabria is a long day's drive north of Madrid, though more convenient to Old Castile and León. The Aragón and Navarre region with its famous city of Pamplona is described next because it lies on the way to Catalonia, which, with its jewel Barcelona, consitutes the final section.

MADRID AND
NEW CASTILE

Plaza Neptuno

HISTORICAL PROFILE:
WORLD POWER AND THE GREAT ARMADA—FELIPE II

Felipe II (1556-1598) sent off the Great Armada and waged Spain's longest, most complicated war; he controlled armies, diplomats, and the first international espionage organization. Although he was the most powerful European monarch of his time, ruling Spain at the very apex of its influence, Felipe was a lonely man, so shy that his voice fell to a whisper in public. Because it was he who established Madrid as the capital of Spain and built its most awesome monument, an account of Felipe's life forms a fitting backdrop to the sights of Madrid and New Castile.

Understanding Felipe must begin with his veneration of his powerful father, the Emperor Carlos V. The child of mad Queen Juana—a daughter of Ferdinand and Isabella—and the philandering Hapsburg heir, Philip the Handsome, Carlos had been raised in the Netherlands, never setting foot in Spain until, at the age of 17, he arrived to be crowned its king. (See "Historical Profile: Ferdinand and Isabella," p. 197.) He had been cursed with a gawky frame, a sallow complexion, and a huge, jutting jaw, an inheritance unfortunately passed on to his descendants.

Carlos thirsted for empire. Soon after he ascended the Spanish throne, his Hapsburg grandfather, the Holy Roman Emperor Maximilian, died. As one of his first acts of state, Carlos spent huge sums from the Spanish treasury to insure his election as his grandfather's successor. Already reigning as Duke of Burgundy and the Low Countries, King of Castile and León, King of Arágon, and King of Naples, by age 19 he had maneuvered his way to the additional title of Carlos V, Emperor of the Holy Roman Empire. Although, counting Mexico and Central and South America, Carlos thereby assumed rule over the largest kingdom since that of the Mongols, his acquisitions changed Spain from an autonomous state into one piece of an encompassing empire.

It was not long before the Spanish demonstrated their disapproval. When Carlos left for Germany in 1520 to receive his emperor's crown, protests broke out across Spain, and unrest percolated for two years before erupting into a full-scale revolution after one of Carlos's governors retaliated by burning the commercial city of Medina del Campo. The rebels, led by the aptly named Juan Bravo from Segovia, called themselves *comuneros*, and fought resolutely for a ruler who would take Spanish interests more closely to heart. With no possibility of quelling a general uprising, Carlos acceded to the rebel's demands, agreeing to learn Spanish and take on Spanish advisors, marry a Portuguese princess, and raise any resulting children in Spain. Carlos began learning Spanish when peace was restored, but not until he had executed the ringleaders of the revolt.

After replacing his Flemish advisors with Spanish ministers, Carlos journeyed to Seville in 1526 to wed his cousin, Princess Isabella of Portugal. The two spent the summer—a far longer term than formality required—honeymooning in rooms Carlos reconstructed in the Alhambra Palace in Granada. There Felipe was conceived, to be born in the capital of Valladolid on May 21, 1527. Tenderly, Carlos sat beside Isabella through an agonizing 13-hour labor, during which she asked only that her face be veiled to hide her pain.

Felipe's need for his father's approval stemmed in part from the sense of abandonment he felt as a child during Carlos' long absences. Of the thirty-nine years that Carlos V ruled, he spent less than sixteen in Spain. Because he was a prince of many countries rather than a ruler of a unified empire, he was forced to spend his life traveling from one realm to another. Deprived of Carlos' presence, Felipe came to know his father primarily through frequent letters filled with stern advice and moral lectures.

Felipe's upbringing fell mainly to his mother until her death when he was 12; then, through his teenage years, he became the responsibility of a succession of governors assigned by his father. His child-household consisted of 51 pages, 8 chaplains, a kitchen staff, assorted cleaners and totaled 191 people, none of whom were connected to Felipe by blood or friendship. Not surprisingly, as an adult he prized solitude and felt acutely uncomfortable in company other than his family. The young prince channeled his energies into physical activity, especially dancing, fishing, hunting with his crossbow, jousting, and the new game of quoits, yet he was equally passionate about music and needlework. He read encyclopedically in Latin, Greek, Spanish and Italian, and owned books by Erasmus, Dürer, and Copernicus, as well as many cabalistic works. Although his greatest love was history, of the 41 books beside his bed when he died, 40 were religious.

Felipe resembled his father physically, with the same blond hair, pale complexion and short stature. He had thick lips, piercing grey eyes reddened from the strain of constant reading, and a protruding chin that he hid behind a beard as soon as he could grow one. Yet, he was considered handsome, and when St. Ignatius Loyola, founder of the Jesuit Order, met him, he caught a "breath of goodness and sanctity" from the young prince. [Quoted by Geoffrey Parker, *Philip II*, p. 54.]

Carlos allowed his son no more time for childhood than he had enjoyed himself. After Felipe's 16th birthday, Carlos appointed him Regent of Spain, arranged a marriage to his cousin, the Portuguese princess María Manuela, and left him in charge of Spain for the next 14 years while Carlos wrestled with problems abroad. The companionship of Felipe's new wife proved temporary, for María died two years later, after the birth of Prince Don Carlos. On Felipe's 19th birthday, Carlos decided that his son should become acquainted with his future domains and sent him on a two-year sojourn through Italy, Germany, and The Netherlands, although Felipe's aloof manner, attributable more to shyness than arrogance, made an unfavorable impression on his future subjects.

Nor were his father's political affairs going well. In 1551 France invaded Italy; Germany rose in rebellion, inflicting a severe defeat on Carlos; and Turkey invaded Spanish North Africa. Although Carlos mobilized 150,000 troops for these assorted wars, he realized that he needed an ally against France who could also help with problems smoldering in The Netherlands. He choose England and, to cement the alliance, betrothed the young widower Felipe to Mary Tudor, England's queen.

Felipe sailed to England in July of 1554 to meet his bride. Mary adored him, but, at 26, he was not equally taken with the 37-year-old queen. Soon after, Carlos, exhausted from his wars, abdicated in favor of his son and retired to a monastery at Yuste in Extremadura, to die two years later. Felipe left Mary after fifteen months of marriage, and crossed the channel to The Netherlands never to see her again. At age 28, Felipe was again alone, this time at the apex of a political empire. In his first year as monarch, Felipe won a major victory over the French at Saint Quentin on the border of The Netherlands, and won back Italy. His reign had begun auspiciously.

Felipe labored in The Netherlands for three years to untangle the problems abandoned by Carlos, before he could return to Spain. But, in marked contrast to the peripatetic style of his father, Felipe never left the peninsula again. By expanding an existing system of councils to deal with ongoing problems, and *juntas* to deal with temporary ones, he created a complex centralized government with which to control his disparate empire. He trusted no one: only he knew about everything; his ministers were informed about their areas of responsibility, nothing more. He was a slow thinker and deliberate speaker who came to prefer reading and writing to speaking and listening. Alone, without the pressure of others waiting for his words, he could reach decisions. Since most people of the time could neither read nor write, Felipe's methods seemed incomprehensible: he read every official document himself, at least in precis, and wrote every official document, at least in outline. A victim of his own mistrusting and solitary nature, Felipe assumed the burden of administering every detail of the empire, agonizing as long over the pension-claim of a single soldier as over an issue of state. The pace of government naturally slowed, and the mass of his work came, in time, to consume Felipe's every waking hour.

There were family matters to deal with as well. When Mary Tudor died in 1558, Felipe married Elizabeth of Valois, the daughter of the king of France. She was 13, exactly half Felipe's age. The marriage took place with a proxy standing in for Felipe, but Elizabeth came to Spain two years later, although two more years passed before she was judged old enough for the marriage to be consummated. Following one miscarriage, she conceived in 1566. Her concerned husband visited five times a day throughout the pregnancy and remained at her side during the labor and birth of their first daughter, Isabel. The following year Catalina was born. The next year, pregnant again, Elizabeth succumbed to fainting fits, and bloodletting so weakened her that she miscarried and died. Felipe sat with her as she expired. Now a widower three times over, Felipe sought refuge in a religious retreat.

That year, 1568, was a tragic time, for Felipe's only son and heir, by his first wife Maria Manuela, died as well. Don Carlos, the son of cousins and grandson of cousins, was the product of a constricted gene pool. He had an abnormally large head, a stammer, and a vicious personality that delighted in abusing animals and women. While at the University of Salamanca he had fallen down a flight of stairs chasing a porter's daughter, incurring serious head injuries and blindness. Trepanning by the great Flemish physician Vesalius saved his life and restored his sight, but did not improve his mental condition: once, when a shoemaker delivered boots that fit too tightly, Don Carlos forced him to eat his wares. As he grew older, he began to scheme for power, collecting money from courtiers to travel to The Netherlands, perhaps to seize control for himself. No matter how reduced his mental faculties, the royalty of Don Carlos' blood made him a danger, forcing Felipe to imprison his son. In prison Don Carlos tried a variety of suicidal means to gain his release, refusing food, eating gluttonously, undressing in cold seasons. Eventually he succeeded—in his own death, not his freedom.

Felipe married for the last time in 1570. Although he was 20 years older than the bride, his niece Ana of Austria, she nonetheless bore him four sons. Three died in childhood, but the last, a male named after his father, survived to become Felipe's heir. In 1580 both Felipe and his wife caught the flu; Ana died.

Felipe worked at pleasure, just as he took pleasure in his work. He loved art, amassing the nucleus of the present Prado collection. His tastes were greatly influenced by his father's Dutch origins, but his favorites ran to extremes. He collected the fantastic paintings of Bosch, 33 in all, as well as Titian's courtly art. Although he commissioned several works by El Greco, the *Adoration of the Name of Jesus* being the most important, Felipe eventually came to dislike the artist's work.

Felipe also enjoyed building. In 1561 he settled on Madrid as his capital, moving from Valladolid, and set about refurbishing the Alcázar for his palace. Two years later he began his most ambitious project, a palace that would also serve as a mausoleum for his father, himself, and his family, and contain a monastery to provide perpetual prayers for all their souls. So that he could personally oversee the work, the complex was constructed at San Lorenzo de Escorial, close to his new capital. Whether the plan of the building represents the cross on which Saint Lawrence died, as some say, or the Temple of Solomon, as others claim, the most intriguing part of the palace is Felipe's bedroom, for this room where he lived and worked reveals the most about his character. The chamber is tiny and austere, but contains one door that leads directly into the adjoining church so that Felipe could watch and listen to every service, even when not in formal attendance. The edifice of el Escorial covers an area the size of four football fields and was completed in just 21 years. Felipe wept from disappointment when it was finished.

Above all he enjoyed his family, the only company with whom he could truly relax. Felipe loved his wives, except for Mary Tudor, and his children, particularly his daughters, and especially Isabel. She often sat with him while he pursued his solitary tasks, silently handing him the next document that required his attention. He loved her so much that he kept her with him until shortly before his death, not arranging a marriage until she had reached the exceptionally old age of 33.

The majority of Felipe's life was spent on the affairs of his manifold territories. His statecraft is revealed in four major events: war against Turkey, the acquisition of Portugal, war in The Netherlands, and the failed attempt to conquer England.

Along with the crown of the Holy Roman Emperor came the responsibility of leading Europe's ongoing struggle with the infidel, in the form of the Ottoman Empire. After his father's death, Europe looked to Felipe to lead. Felipe began his campaign with two defeats, losing almost all his Mediterranean galleys each time, and placing the countries around the Mediterranean in imminent danger. In 1570 the Turks demanded that Venice surrender Cyprus. Venice, by the narrowest of votes, decided to fight and called on the Pope to summon Christian aid. When Felipe agreed to supply half of the money and ships in exchange for authority to appoint a commander, other countries fell in line. Felipe named Don Juan of Austria as his admiral. Don Juan was the illegitimate son of Felipe's father and a young Flemish girl, a young man Felipe had taken into his court hoping to find some enterprise worthy of his half-royal blood. In 1571, 100 Christian galleys under Don Juan bottled up a fleet of 230 Turkish ships at Lepanto in the straits of Greece. Don Juan won a resounding victory, capturing 100 enemy ships and sinking as many more. Among the Spanish sailors wounded was Miguel de Cervantes, later to write *Don Quixote*. Although the Turks were able in time to replenish their fleet, the battle of Lepanto signaled the end of their dominance of the Mediterranean. Eight years later Felipe negotiated a treaty of peace with Turkey.

Seven years after the great victory at Lepanto, the king of Portugal died. His family suffered from an astonishing mortality rate, and he left only one grandson, Don Sebastiõ, to rule after him. Don Sebastiõ had no interest in women, caring only for hunting, war, and devotions. After his coronation he set off with pomp to conquer Morocco. It was a debacle; surrounded, the entire Portuguese army surrendered when Don Sebastiõ was killed, leaving the flower of the Portuguese nobility captive. The remaining direct heir to the throne was a 66-year-old cardinal, who died four years later and left no descendants.

Now the strongest claim to the Portuguese throne was Felipe's through his mother Isabella, the daughter of Portugal's king three reigns earlier. Felipe campaigned methodically to acquire the crown. He paid the ransom for the Portuguese nobles held captive in Morocco, then lobbied extensively in the Portuguese Cortes to show the nobility and merchants how they could benefit from a union with Spain and her American empire. But Felipe's claim was challenged by the Portuguese Don Antonio, an illegitimate grandson of a former king, who found support in the common people and the clergy. Just as the Portuguese Cortes was about to decide the succession, Don Antonio seized Lisbon, forcing the assembled delegates to flee. Felipe then played his trump card. Prior to his death, the last Portuguese king had stipulated that a committee settle the succession, and, of the five members designated, three had eluded Antonio and fled from to Spain. All three voted for Felipe, who, armed with this legitimacy, invaded Portugal and conquered it in five weeks. For the first time since Roman days, the peninsula was unified. Felipe aptly remarked of his new realm, "I inherited it; I bought it; I conquered it." [Quoted in John Lynch, *Spain under the Hapsburgs,* Vol. I, p. 327.]

By this time Felipe had been at war in The Netherlands for over a decade, a conflict that would break both his health and the Spanish economy. Although The Low Countries were predominantly Catholic, significant pockets of Lutherans, Calvinists, and Anabaptists dotted the territory. Mixing politics with religion, Felipe's father had instituted an inquisition against Protestants in The Netherlands because he believed that "heretics should not only be persecuted for their beliefs, but also as creators of sedition, upheaval, riots and commotions in the state....Guilty of rebellion, they can expect no mercy." [Peter Pierson, *Philip II of Spain,* p. 44.]

Spain's economy depended on The Netherlands. Not only did the Merino wool sent there account for one quarter of Spain's exports, but, in addition, one third of Spain's imports came through The Netherlands, including ship timber brokered from the Baltic by the Dutch. Although the economy of The Netherlands depended equally on Spain, strife between Felipe and his Dutch subjects was inevitable, for the Dutch were as forceful in defending religious freedom as the Spanish were in opposing it. Three years of consecutive bad harvests through 1566 frayed nerves on both sides. Then, Felipe's decision to increase the number of Low Country bishops from four to eighteen angered the Dutch, who viewed the policy both as an expansion of the Inquisition and a strengthening of the Spanish hold on their country, while a Calvinist rampage that desecrated Catholic churches enraged Felipe.

The next year Felipe sent one of the grandees of Spain, the Duke of Alba, with 10,000 crack Spanish infantry to impose order on The Netherlands. Alba quickly ended the Calvanist rampage by arresting suspects by the hundreds. Felipe believed that The Netherlanders should pay the expenses of the campaign, and Alba imposed a new tax to that end, but the tolerance of most Netherlanders did not extend to taxes earmarked for their own persecution. War broke out again, and this time Spain could not end it.

When Alba's army attempted to win back a captured town in the southern Netherlands, they left the north undefended. Dutch privateers, known derisively as "Beggars," rushed from their haven in England to seize the undefended north, causing Alba to wheel back in an about-face. So it went for nine years. Alba could win any engagement against an army in the field, but he could not conquer the north while holding the south, or vice versa. The Dutch were everywhere that he was not.

These years of war in The Netherlands exhausted the Spanish treasury, including the millions that came from silver mines and sugar and tobacco plantations in the New World. In 1575 Felipe declared his country bankrupt. His soldiers, part Spanish, part mercenary, were not paid for as long as a year at a time, leading to 46 mutinies over the course of the war.

Anxious for improvement, Felipe replaced Alba with his own half-brother Don Juan. But there was little Don Juan could do except sign a treaty acknowledging the status quo: the south, modern Belgium, remained Spanish; and the north, modern Holland, was granted independence. Felipe refused to acknowledge the treaty, however, for he could not accept the loss of even a part of his domain. His father's advice had become Felipe's credo: "If you are forced to take a stand as champion or defender of our sacred religion, even should you lose all your kingdoms, God will receive you in glory, which is truly one goal worth striving for." [Quoted by Geoffrey Parker, *Philip II,* p. 44.] So Felipe replaced Don Juan with the capable Alexander Farnese, Duke of Parma. Over the course of seven years, from 1578 to 1585, Parma employed an astute policy of dividing-and-conquering to gain back the south including Brussels, Antwerp and Flanders. Holland still held out, but prospects looked brighter for Spain than they had for decades. Then, in 1585, the Dutch rebels signed a treaty in Nonesuch Castle with Elizabeth of England, who promised money and troops for their cause.

Relations with England became intolerably strained thereafter. Previously, Felipe had wooed England as a balance against his main rival France, despite the fact that elsewhere he gloried in the defence of Catholicism. In fact, he had supported the Protestant Queen Elizabeth even against the Pope, who twice had threatened to excommunicate her. True, Felipe had also encouraged at least three plots against Elizabeth, but such intrigues counted as statecraft in those days. Elizabeth had played a different game. She allowed Francis Drake to privateer Spanish fleets and towns in the Americas, and shifted alliances so cunningly that no one could fathom her intentions. The English Treaty of Nonesuch with the Dutch rebels could not be endured, however, with its threat of halting Spain's dearly won momentum in The Netherlands. Felipe felt he had no choice but to invade England.

He drew up plans calling for a huge Spanish fleet carrying 60,000 troops to link with Parma's army and ferry it across the Dover Straits. Once the combined Spanish forces landed on English soil he believed that English Catholics, still a majority at the time, would add their support to deliver an easy conquest. In truth, the English army was small, but the planned 60,000 Spanish troops soon fell to a more realistic 30,000, then to 20,000, and the huge fleet proved difficult to assemble.

Only England and Venice had national navies at the time; other countries hired ships as needed from private citizens. While trying to maintain secrecy, Spain scoured the Mediterranean for tonnage from Genoa, Venice and her own citizen-sailors. Spain already possessed a powerful Atlantic fleet to guard treasure ships from the New World, and had access to the ships of Felipe's new Portuguese kingdom. Altogether, Spain collected 130 ships of all sorts and sizes, of which 20 were capital ships of the line, the battleships of the day. This motley collection was the Great Armada. The Spanish referred to it during preparations as "Invincible."

Many school-day impressions of the Spanish Armada are more romantic than accurate, including the idea that a huge Spanish flotilla was defeated by a rag-tag collection of English ships. In fact, under John Hawkins, the English designed and built the best ships of the day, narrower and longer—to add speed and allow more broadside guns—and bare of raised "castles" for boarding an enemy—to lend greater maneuverability and reduce rolling. These were the ships of the future. The English could easily match the Spanish in numbers of ships, and surpass them in newness and seaworthiness. England also owned an edge in firepower with more modern, longer cannons of smaller bores that could fire 18- or 9-pound shot 1,000 yards.

Chaos attended preparations for the Armada, for collecting the thousands of men, the 100-odd ships, and the tons of stores for a campaign in enemy waters was a bureaucratic nightmare. The weight of preparation fell on Admiral Santa Cruz, the hero of a sea war in the Azores. Already in his 60s, these pressures caused him to suffer a stroke as arrangements neared completion. Desperate for a new commander, Felipe called on the Duke of Medina Sidonia, the highest grandee of Spain. Medina Sidonia had gained some fame by rescuing the port of Cádiz the previous year when a fleet led by Francis Drake had invested the town. This raid caused little damage to the city but left major problems for the Armada, since Drake seized transport ships bringing wood for the casks to hold the fleet's water and food. Hastily improvised containers would prove inadequate, later leading to virtual starvation for the sailors of the Armada.

Medina Sidonia's main qualification was his nobility. The admiral had to be someone proud officers would consider their equal or better. At first Medina Sidonia refused the command, on the reasonable basis that not only was he prone to terrible seasickness but also that he had never commanded forces either on land or sea. Medina Sidonia recommended someone else for the job but sucumbed to Felipe's persistence.

On May 9, 1588, one year later than scheduled, the Invincible Armada sailed from Lisbon proudly flying a banner that said "Arise, O Lord, and vindicate Thy cause." [cited in Garrett Mattingly, *The Armada*, p.215.] For three weeks freak storms held the ships just off the coast. After two weeks more, they had only reached Finisterre, the northernmost tip of Spain, where they put into port to repair the storm damage. Medina Sidonia wrote Felipe that the fleet was in terrible condition; he had better make peace with England. But Felipe would not be swayed. He had written about the invasion: "I am so attached to it in my heart, and I am so convinced that God our Savior must embrace it as his own cause, that I cannot be dissuaded from putting it into operation." [Quoted by Geoffrey Parker, *Philip II*, p. 57.] On July 21 the Armada steered for England.

The Armada first met the English off the coast of Plymouth, under Lord Admiral Charles Howard and Vice-Admiral Francis Drake. The Spanish immediately formed a crescent with the largest ships on the wings to embrace the enemy, awing the English sailors by the facility with which they performed their maneuver. The English stood away and pounded the Spanish beyond the reach of Spanish guns, while the Spanish tried to lure the English close enough to grapple and board where their advantage in manpower could be decisive. But never in history had such large naval forces engaged, and neither side knew quite what to do. The English strategy proved ineffectual because their guns and gunners lacked sufficient accuracy, and the gunpowder at their disposal was not powerful enough. When the rare shot hit a Spanish ship, it was usually so spent that it bounced harmlessly off the wooden hull. Nor could the Spanish board an enemy who refused to come near.

The Spanish fleet soon disengaged, unhurt, for its mission was to meet with Parma in The Netherlands and ferry troops to England, not to fight naval engagements. It anchored off Calais, as close to shore as the ships' 20 feet of draft would allow, to await Parma. The mystery of the campaign is why Parma was not at Calais, and why he had not collected the boats to ferry his troops to the Armada offshore. Perhaps he had little faith in the enterprise and did not want to waste his troops, or perhaps he feared for what would happen in The Netherlands if his army were removed. In any case, the Armada waited at anchor, and Parma didn't come.

On the night of August 7, the English floated eight blazing ships, with primed cannons waiting for the heat to set them off, toward the anchored Spanish. These fire ships caused havoc. The Spanish upped anchor and scattered, crashing into one another in the darkness. Then came a devastating squall. When the Spanish regrouped and took inventory, they found that the 50 rounds of ammunition provisioned for each cannon had been spent, seven ships of the line had been lost, one fifth of the men were disabled or dead, and their food had spoiled. There was nothing to do but go home.

Rather than return through the Channel, blocked by the English fleet, Medina Sidonia steered around the British Isles, through the North Sea, by Scotland and Ireland. Plans for the invasion had carefully considered the weather and chosen the summer for its dependable calm. Yet never in recorded history had so many severe storms occurred as in the summer of 1588. The last and most vicious gale awaited the Armada off the Irish coast. The fleet scattered with the winds, tens of ships sank, and tens more put into Ireland, too damaged to sail. Thousands of Spanish drowned or were summarily killed by the English commander in Ireland, who feared an uprising of the natives if Spanish Catholics remained in his territory.

Only half of the Invincible Armada returned to Spain, routed more by freak weather and a general's refusal to follow orders than by the enemy, but Felipe searched his soul for some act of his that had caused God to desert him. Refusing to admit defeat, in 1596 he sent off another armada, and in 1597 one more. Each time storms dispersed his fleets.

There was nothing more that Felipe could do. He began to relax his hold on the government in 1595, transferring responsibilities to his son and heir, Felipe III. He ceded The Netherlands to his daughter Isabel, finally removing that problem while saving some face. On September 13, 1598, racked with fevers and arthritis, toothless, his bedridden body a mass of gaping sores, Felipe smiled and died. He left his heir a debt of 85 million ducats, six times the yearly income of the Spanish government. Prices had quadrupled over the course of his reign. The Low Countries were gone, the Americas decimated by avarice and disease—80% of the indigenous population of Mexico had died. The crown of the Holy Roman Empire would never again grace a Spanish head.

According to contemporaries Felipe's aim had been "not to wage war so that he could add to his kingdoms, but to wage peace so he could keep the lands he had." [Quoted by Peter Pierson, *Philip II of Spain*, p. 131.] Perhaps no one could have kept such a diverse empire intact; at least it can be said of Felipe that he tried as hard as anyone could. He himself had written "I know very well that I should be in some other station in life, one not as exalted as the one God has given me, which for me alone is terrible." [Quoted by Geoffrey Parker, *Philip II*, p. 94.] Affairs in Spain worsened after Felipe died. Felipe III undermined Spain's control of Portugal; his successor caused a revolution in Spain; then came a mental incompetent who ended the line. In 1605, seven years after the death of Felipe II, Cervantes published his great *Don Quixote*, the tale of a romantic who tilted at windmills. It could well have been a parable for Felipe and his Spain.

Felipe's most visible legacies in New Castile are the imposing monastery at **El Escorial**, a building that still reflects his character, lovely gardens at **Aranjuez**, and, of course, Spain's capital city itself—Real **Madrid**, which he founded.

NEW CASTILE

The geographic, political and spiritual heart of Spain is a windswept plateau, called La Mancha, that comprises New Castile. Divided by mountains both from Old Castile in the north and Andalusia in the south, the terrain between is covered with low crops reaching to distant rolling hills. This is the fabled land over which Cervantes, in his parable about the end of chivalry, sent Don Quixote to tilt at windmills. Here Toledo, the original capital of Spain during the time of the Visigoths, endured through conquest by the Moors, and reconquest by the early Spanish. In turn, Toledo preserves precious memorials of Christian, Moor and Jew.

New Castile received its name during the Reconquest from the abundance of castles guarding this battleground between Christians and Moors. Belmonte and Calatrava castles still survive from those days, and, later, through the 15th century, more castles were built to protect Castile from Aragón's challenge from the east. But it was not until the 16th century that New Castile regained the primacy it had enjoyed during the time of the Visigoths when Toledo served as the country's capital. As Spain reached the apex of its international power, King Felipe II chose an undistinguished provincial town named Madrid as his permanent capital. He built palaces and government offices, trebling the population into that of a city. Madrid has remained Spain's capital ever since.

Madrid sits almost exactly in the center of Spain. A marker at the Puerta del Sol in Madrid reads "0 kilometers," and from it are calculated distances to every village and hamlet in the country. As Castile continued to lead Spain's effort to regain the country from the Moors, Castilian Spanish—the victor's language—spread from this center to become the tongue of modern Spain. Savants in the capital still rule magisterially on every attempt to change its vocabulary.

Today **Madrid** ★★★★★ overwhelms all other cities in New Castile in size, and its attractions can easily hold a tourist's interest for two days or a week. **Toledo** ★★★★★ outdoes this giant in both the quality and the quantity of its monuments, although its natural compactness allows exploration in just a day or two. The other fine sights of New Castile can either be arranged as day trips from Madrid, or visited during overnight stays. **El Escorial** ★★★★ is an imposing Renaissance monastery-palace only 44 k north of Madrid. Franco's huge monument to the Spanish Civil War, the **Valle de los Caídos** ★★ (Valley of the Fallen), stands nearby. The Bourbon palace of **El Pardo** ★★ lies even closer, only 13 k

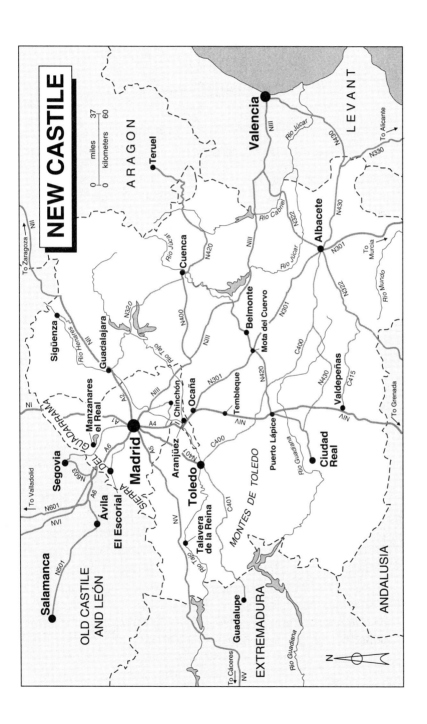

from Madrid, while the gardens of the palace at **Aranjuez** ★★ display their beauties 46 k to the south. Somewhat further afield are **Belmonte** ★★, a 15th-century castle, looking exactly as one imagines a castle should; and **Sigüenza** ★★★, displaying a wonderful 15th-century cathedral on an imposing site.

ARANJUEZ ★★

Population 35,936
Area code: 91; zip code: 28300

46 k south of Madrid on N-IV.

Entering Aranjuez is like coming into an oasis. Verdant with shrubs and leafy avenues, it is a favorite day excursion for Madrileños, especially in midsummer, when its celebrated strawberries with cream are sold by roadsides throughout town.

Before Felipe II settled on Madrid as the permanent royal capital, sovereigns would move with the seasons among several cities and palaces. Aranjuez was one such royal town, a favorite stop of Ferdinand and Isabella. Despite his preference for Madrid, Felipe II built a large palace here and surrounded it with the extensive gardens that alone have survived. Twice devastated by fire, the palace was rebuilt in the 18th century to the French tastes of the ruling Bourbon kings, who added pleasant walks and a gridded town plan.

Aranjuez' most historic moment came after Carlos IV foolishly invaded France and, when defeated, signed a treaty that allowed French troops to quarter in Spain. In March of 1808, when the French intention to seize Spain became apparent, Carlos IV fled to the Aranjuez palace on his way to escape in the Americas. He was accompanied by his Prime Minister, Godoy, a man hated by the Spanish for conceiving this foolish French policy. On the 17th of March, the citizens of Aranjuez stormed the palace and forced Carlos to discharge his minister and abdicate. Two months later the citizens of Madrid revolted on the famous night of the *Dos de Mayo*.

In the middle of the 19th century, Isabella II began the tradition of traveling by train to the greenness and strawberries of Aranjuez. Ever since, the *Trena de la Fresa* (Strawberry Train) has been a favorite Madrid summer outing. Yet the foliage and gardens are best in the spring, and it is the gardens that are Aranjuez' main attraction. Half a day will permit ample enjoyment of all the sights and gardens.

Palácio Real

Open Tues.-Sun. 10 a.m. to 1 p.m. and 3-5:30 p.m. (until 6:30 p.m. in summer). Closed Mon. and holidays. Admission: 400 ptas., to both the pal-

ace and museum, by tour only. The palace's classical brick-and-stone structure dates from the early 18th century, with many later additions. The interior today looks much as it did a century ago, despite Franco's occasional residence. Tapestries cover the walls and "Persian" carpets—Spanish copies made in Madrid—cover the floors. Opulent china, porcelain and mirrors decorate the rooms. It was in the crimson velvet throne room that Carlos IV signed his abdication.

The most interesting room is the **Porcelain Salon**, covered in colored relief tiles illustrating Chinese scenes. The royal pottery factory in Madrid's Buen Retiro Park manufactured these tiles with more pleasing effect than later ones, from the same factory, installed in Madrid's Palácio Real. The king's **Arabian Salon**, a generous reproduction of the Sala Dos Hermanos in the Alhambra, shows that even a king's smoking was restricted to a special chamber. Only about 30 of the 300 rooms in the palace are open to view, but they are sufficient to convey the idea.

Museum of Royal Robes

Same hours and ticket as for the palace. The museum shows modern copies of regal dress before the reign of Ferdinand VII, and clothing actually worn by monarchs from 1812 on. Examples of the uniforms of various Spanish military orders are also displayed. Curious furniture is on view, along with a most interesting collection of fans, some dating from the 17th century.

Gardens

The gardens are open from 10 a.m. until sunset, except Tues. Closed holidays. A ticket to all the gardens and houses costs 300 ptas.

Parterre

A "small" formal garden in the French style stretches away from the end of the palace opposite its wings.

Jardin de la Isla

Across the canal along the palace's north side on an artificial island in the Tagus River is this large informal garden—still serene—built in the 16th century for Felipe II.

Jardin del Principe

These gardens are huge and should be toured by car. Within the park—for it is more than a garden—Carlos IV, like his relative Louis XVIII in France, built a model farm so he could play at the rustic life. Signs direct you for one kilometer to the **Casa del Labrador** (Laborer's House), a classic case of royal understatement *(admission: 200 ptas.).* Laborer, indeed! These accommodations are as luxurious as any sybarite could wish. The statues are classical antiques; the mosaics mostly excavated at Merida in Extremadura; Queen Maria Luisa's dressing-room is a jewel. Signs also direct you to the **Casa de Marinos** (Sailor's House) which contains the barges of six monarchs *(admission: 100 ptas.).* Note the ceiling painted to resemble tapestry.

BELMONTE ★ ★

Population 2,811
Area code: 967; zip code: 16640

Take N-IV south from **Madrid** *for 57 k., exiting at Ocuña (11 k south of Aranjuez). 76 k on N-301 (toward Albacete) brings you to Mota del Cuervo, then 16 K on N-420 (toward La Almarcha) brings Belmonte, for a trip of 149 k. You can return to N-IV, if continuing south to* **Granada**, *by taking N-420 through Mota for a connection at Puerto Lapice in 76 k. From* **Toledo** *take C-400 south to connect with N-IV at Madridejos in 87 k. Take N-IV south for 17 k to Puerto Lapice, where N-420 goes east to Belmonte in 76 k.*

Windmills can be seen from the highway surrounding **Mota del Cuervo**, a town also containing a ruined castle(formerly run by the Order of Santiago) that is worth wandering through. But the object of the trip is Belmonte, one of the typical castles of Spain.

The **castle of Belmonte** was a fort, constructed in 1456 by Juan Pacheco, Marques of Villena, to defend his territory. It was a time of little central authority, for successive monarchs, in vain attempts to curry favor, had dissipated their power to the realm's nobles, eventually causing each grandee to assume responsibility for his own defense. Christian lords built castles as much to defend themselves against other nobles, eager to aggrandize power, as for protection from the Moors.

Some of the perimeter walls connecting the castle to the town remain, but it is the perfectly situated castle that most impresses. Hexagonally shaped, with circular towers to provide defenders good angles from which to shoot attackers, the exterior of the 15th-century castle looks today almost exactly as it did five hundred years ago.

Castle of Belmonte

Open 10 a.m.-2 p.m. and 4-8 p.m. (until 6:30 p.m. in winter). Closed the last week in August. Admission: 200 ptas. The castle was abandoned in the 17th century and not restored until the 19th. Of course during the 200 years of its abandonment all the original furnishings disappeared. The red brickwork of the central courtyard was added for 19th-century tastes, but the empty rooms inside still exude a 15th century atmosphere. Some retain lovely wood ceilings in Moorish style— *Mudejar,* carved by Moors for Christian patrons. The audience chamber ceiling is especially fine. The town **church** in Belmonte is also worth seeing for its polychrome altars and its choirstalls.

CAIDOS, VALLE DE LOS (VALLEY OF THE FALLEN) ★★

Open daily from 10 a.m. until 7 p.m. (until 6 p.m. in winter). Closed all holidays. Admission: 300 ptas., per car.

*See the directions to El Escorial. From **El Escorial** take N-601 north for 8 k to turn at the sign for Valle de los Caídos.*

This is Franco's memorial to the dead of the Spanish Civil War, though sceptics view it as a monument to himself. Regardless of the reason for the structure, its mountain setting is ruggedly beautiful amid granite outcrops and weathered pines. Inside a hill surmounted by a towering cross—four hundred feet high (with an elevator inside)—a huge underground basilica was excavated in 1959. Claims that this expensive basilica would exculpate the carnage and horrors of the civil war, clearing the consciences of both sides, are belied by the fact that Franco used Republican prisoners as forced labor to build the monument.

Franco wanted to awe—and succeeded: The nave of the underground basilica is larger than St. Peter's in Rome by a third. The cupola is huge and resplendent with bright mosaics of Spain's heros and martyrs approaching Christ and Mary. Tapestries along the nave are 16th-century Belgian depictions of the Apocalypse, appropriately, while side chapels contain copies of famous statues of the Virgin. In a crypt behind the altar repose coffins of 40,000 unknown soldiers who died in the war, but the places of honor belongs to Franco and José Antonio.

José Antonio Primo de Rivera, the son of a deposed dictatorial prime minister, led the small, quasi-fascist, Falange party during the political unrest leading up to the Spanish Civil War. (See "Historical Profile: The Spanish Civil War," p. 489.) Convicted of political murder, Antonio was incarcerated as the war broke out and died in prison at age 33, to be promoted to martyr status by Franco and his Nationalist sympathizers. Antonio's remains are buried at the foot of the altar. Nearby, under a white slab, the Generalissimo himself sleeps forever.

EL ESCORIAL ★★★★

Population 6,192
Area code: 91; zip code: 28280

From **Madrid** *take N-VI north for 16 k, then C-505 at the Las Rozas exit for 28 k. Well marked by signs, the total distance is 44 k.*

Felipe II was a complex and private monarch, deeply religious and greatly admiring of his father, Carlos V. He wanted to build a monument to God and to his father, and chose an insignificant village called San Lorenzo de El Escorial for the site. The village was chosen because it was near enough to Madrid that Felipe could travel to watch the work progress, as he often did, and for the name of the town. In his limited personal military career, Felipe had enjoyed one major success—over the French at St. Quentin in Flanders—in a battle won on August 10, the name-day of Saint Lawrence (San Lorenzo). The fact that the area contained abundant granite for building material clinched the choice.

At the time he constructed El Escorial, Felipe was the most powerful monarch in the world and put the resources of his empire to work on this, his favored project. It occupied 1,000 workmen for 21 years, and when finished contained over 1,000 doors and almost 3000 windows. Felipe wept when it was completed.

Felipe's structure was a mausoleum for his father and a pantheon for himself and his descendants. A monastery was included so monks could pray perpetually for all their souls. It also contained a palace so that Felipe could work near his father's remains, and a church, of course, for services. He commissioned Juan de Toledo, who had assisted Michelangelo and Bramante on St. Peter's in Rome, to design the building, and Felipe took an active interest in its design.

The structure stands as a reaction against the ornate Gothic, Isabeline and Plateresque styles of previous monarchs. It is monumentally simple and elegant in proportion, a brilliant solution to the problem of combining monastic austerity with the grandeur that a royal residence should express. Four years into the project the architect Juan de Toledo died, succeeded by his assistant Juan de Herrera, who carried out most of the design. To Herrera's genius is due the elegance of the details and, most significantly, the design of the awesome church inside.

The exterior of the building is worth inspection from the courtyard. The facade stretches for two football fields, and runs one and a half more in depth, yet the expanse is neither boring nor busy with detail. Corner towers reward the left and right views, broken by roofcombs half way along. Windows are arranged in asymmetrical rows to avoid monotony, and the center entrance, with its carving and columns, gives a sense of more detail than it actually presents. The effect is somber, but stimulating and quietly elegant. Plan on spending at least half a day to see everything that waits inside.

Monastery of El Escorial

Open Tues. through Sun. from 10 a.m. to 1 p.m., and from 3:30 p.m. tp 7 p.m. (until 6 p.m. in winter). Closed Mon. and all holidays. Admission: 500 ptas. Entrance is through the King's courtyard, named for the six grotesque statues of kings of Judea placed high above the church facade. Ahead is the church, to the left a former college and to the right the monastery. Back, along the right side of the church, stands a cloister and chapterhouse, and, on the church's left, the royal apartments, where we begin.

Stairs lead up to the **Battle Gallery**, a long hall of charming frescos, the former guard-room. The ceiling is elegant with Roman-style decorative tracery, a common Renaissance theme. Wall murals display various battles painted to resemble tapestry—see the top and the surrounds of the "doorways." The long wall opposite the windows shows a battle against Moors that took place in Granada in the middle of the 15th century. It is curious to find this battle depicted because the Spanish, contrary to the message of the fresco, lost. The costumes are copied from an earlier work painted during the era of the actual battle, hence providing interesting documents. Both end walls show sea battles, with accurate depictions of Spanish galleons. The window wall presents the battle of Saint Quentin, Felipe's sole personal victory.

Descending to the palace proper, the first rooms are those of Felipe's favorite daughter Isabel, and rather bare except for a portable organ. In Felipe's audience hall hang two fine Brussels tapestries and drawings of various royal residences. The next room is fronted by splendid German marquetry doors, followed by a room with a large sundial on the floor. Next comes Felipe's bedchamber where he often worked and finally died. The poor man ended his days bedridden by pain and the sores of horrendous gout. Note the door opposite which leads into the church so Felipe could attend services without moving. The throne room—with a mere stool for a throne—seems plain, especially compared to that of Felipe's successors in the Palácio Real in Madrid. Indeed, despite beautiful objects, decorations and paintings, Felipe's palace conveys the sense of a simple life. The walls, for example, are whitewashed, rather than covered in velvet as in later palaces. In an alcove rests the litter that carried the invalid king during his final years.

Stairs lead to the new **museums** where some fine paintings are displayed. There is a Bosch *Ecce Homo*, and numerous Titians and Veroneses. A recess holds charming Dürer parchment paintings of birds, animals and flowers. Five Riberas, especially *Aesop*, are symphonies of light and dark. Other rooms display *Zurbaráns*, interesting for incorporating true background scenes, instead of the monotonic fields of most of his work. The two El Grecos that Felipe purchased are also here. One in particular, the *Martyrdom of St. Maurice and the Theban Legion*, was too innovative and acerbic in color for Felipe, who never ordered another from the artist, although the painting is acknowledged today as a masterpiece. Do not miss Rogier van der Weyden's monotonic *Calvary*.

Passing behind the church, a narrow stair-tunnel, sumptuously marbled, descends to the **Panteon de los Reyes**. This pantheon was built by Felipe's successor but not finished until the reign of the following king. It has none of the feel of the rest of El Escorial, although it is moving in a different way. At the bottom of the stairs comes the double shock of the intimacy of a small round marble room combined with a seemingly infinite ceiling. All around in stacked niches are simple yet monumental porphory sarcophagi, each identical, of the great Hapsburg and Bourbon kings of Spain—Carlos V, Felipe II, and Felipe IV, Velázquez' friend and patron. Kings lie on the left, and include Isabella II who ruled, while consorts lie opposite, including Isabella's husband, Francisco Asis. Back up the stairs stretch gallery after gallery of deceased princes and princesses, including memorials to those stillborn—a reminder of the high rate of infant mortality then. At the end of the galleries is the *Pudridero* (Rotting Place), where corpses dried for ten years before internment in sarcophagi.

Next is the **church**, the masterpiece of Juan de Herrera. It exactly suits El Escorial without duplicating the style of the rest. Monumental, simple and perfect in proportion, this church by itself constitutes an architectural movement. Looking down the nave, the pillars at first seem intrusively massive before the effect of their fluting slenderizes them. Instead of the barrel vaulting characteristic of earlier churches, these pillars support a flat vault of daring span. The effect is awe-inspiring, as intended.

Subsidiary altars line both sides of the nave. In the altar to the right is a marble *Crucifixion* carved by Benvenuto Cellini. From one huge pillar hangs a painting of St. Maurice by an Italian named Cincinnato. This was the painting of St. Maurice that Felipe preferred to the masterpiece he commissioned from El Greco. The retablo behind the altar consists of 100 feet of marble and bronze designed by Herrera. On both sides kneel bronze statues—on the left, of Carlos V and his wife, daughter and sisters; on the right, of Felipe and his fourth wife Ana, along with his third wife Isabel and his first wife María, presenting

Don Carlos, the son who died. Felipe's second wife, Mary Tudor of England, is conspicuous by her absence.

If time permits, the **chapterhouse** to the right of the church is worth touring for its paintings, frescoed grand stairway and lovely cloister. Also interesting is the **library**, located to the right of the main entrance at the front of El Escorial, for its rich woodwork and rare books (including St. Teresa's diary and missals belonging to Ferdinand and Isabella, Carlos V and Felipe II).

In the same area as El Escorial is the **Casita de Abajo** ★, designed by Villanueva, the architect of Madrid's Prado Museum, for the prince who would become Carlos IV. It is situated in the new town, El Escorial de Abajo, southeast of the monastery on the road to the train station. This "Little House" is a model country cottage, resembling the Trianon at Versailles with its sumptuous interior and rich furnishings. One room is Pompeian; another is completely covered in tile.

Plaza de Colon and the Biblioteca Nacional

MADRID ★★★★★

Population 3,188,297
Area code: 91; zip code: 28000

Most travellers to Spain visit Madrid, if for no other reason than that their plane lands there. A better reason is to spend time in the **Museo del Prado**. The Prado cannot be called the best museum in the world, for it lacks broad coverage of the spectrum of world art as exhibited by the Louvre and others. What it *is*, however, is the most exhilarating of museums. The paintings it displays achieve a consistently higher average than those in most other museums, and what it omits is not a detraction. The Prado chose to delight instead of edify, to take one's breath away rather than teach a course in art history. By itself the Prado repays a trip to Spain. And Madrid, the capital of the country for the last 400 years and the seat of the kings of Spain, houses national museums in buildings that only a king could produce, along with grand fountains and vistas.

Originally called *Majerit* by the Moors, a name that twisted off Spanish tongues as "Madrid," the city was founded as a Moorish fort to guard the northern approach to Toledo. The Spanish captured the fort in 1083, discovering a statue of the Virgin Mary in a granary (*al mudin* in Arabic) during the process. Since that time the patron saint of the city has been the Virgin of Almudina. Although by no means a major town, Madrid's Virgin gave kings reason to visit from time to time. In the 14th century, Pedro the Cruel constructed Madrid's first castle on the site of the original Moorish fort. In the 15th century, Ferdinand and Isabella built a monastery, San Jerónimo el Real, and the following century Carlos V, their grandson, reconstructed Pedro's castle palatially.

In 1561, Carlos' son, Felipe II, decreed Madrid the permanent capital of Spain—*Real Madrid* (Royal Madrid). The reason is a subject of controversy, with most accounts attributing his decision to Madrid's central location. But Madrid is not exactly centered, and the centrality of a capital in Spain could not have been essential to a monarch whose territories extended far beyond the borders of this one domain. More likely the reason had to do with Madrid's proximity to the former capital, Valladolid. As the number of hearths in Valladolid increased, the supply of nearby trees became exhausted, making firewood scarce. But Madrid still had stands of timber, pure water, and few hearths. It was time to move, and Madrid was conveniently close.

With the arrival of a king and his government came tens of thousands of functionaries requiring massive public buildings to house them. Most of those original government structures, however, including the palace, burned in cataclysmic fires during the 17th century. The present palace sits on the ashes of the original and dates from the middle of the 18th century.

After its intitial influx, Madrid did not continue to grow at a steady rate. Its population exploded from 20,000 to 175,000 in its first 100 years as Spain's capital, raising it to the fifth largest city in Europe. But Madrileños exhibited a talent for choosing the losing side in almost every national controversy, which periodically caused monarchs and their courts to avoid the city and growth to stagnate. Madrileños, for example, sided with Pedro the Cruel against his half-brother Enrique of Trastámara, the founder of the dynasty from which Isabella descended; they sided with "La Beltraneja," considered illegitimate, against her aunt, later Queen, Isabella; and they sided with the Republicans against Franco. Most of Madrid's grand structures, including the Prado, were erected in a late 18th-century building spurt during the peaceful reign of King Carlos III, a monarch who earned the title "King-Mayor" for his single-handed effort to bring Madrid up to the standards of other European capitals. Historically and architecturally, Madrid is Europe's newest capital.

Napoléon's French troops seized Madrid in 1808. One month later, on the second of May, Madrileños revolted against their foreign domination. Goya immortalized the uprising in his famous *El Dos de Mayo*, and condemned the French atrocities that followed in his haunting *El Tres de Mayo*. Both hang in the Prado. During the Spanish Civil War, Madrid was a symbol to both Republicans, who strove to hold it, and to Franco's Nationalists, who attacked it in force when the war began. After a campaign of bloody battles around University City in the northwest, the determination of Madrid's citizens won the day.

Today 4 million people spread over miles of concrete suburbs. Happily, the original core of the city—the focus of virtually all the tourist's interest—remains relatively untouched by this growth. Most sights are an easy walk from this center, but since Madrid's original civil engineers never envisioned a city of such numbers, traffic can make traveling longer distances a problem. Streets are clogged, cars proceed slowly, and parking in the center is a challenge best avoided. An efficient subway system and inexpensive taxis, however, mean that driving is never necessary.

The Puerta del Sol is the midpoint of a line at whose eastern end stands the **Museo del Prado** and its **El Retiro Park** and at whose western end stands the **Palácio Real**. A mile and a quarter separates these monuments from each other, and between them lie most of the city's important sights. Along this line is the Plaza Mayor, Madrid's Ciudad Antique, and the convents of Descalzas Real and Encarnación. Even the Sunday-morning flea market, **El Rastro**, is located only a few blocks south. Less than a mile due north of the Prado, the **Museo Arqueológico Nacional** displays the treasures of Spain's early history amid the Barrio Salamanca's elegant shops. Including the Archaeological Museum with its surrounding shops, the

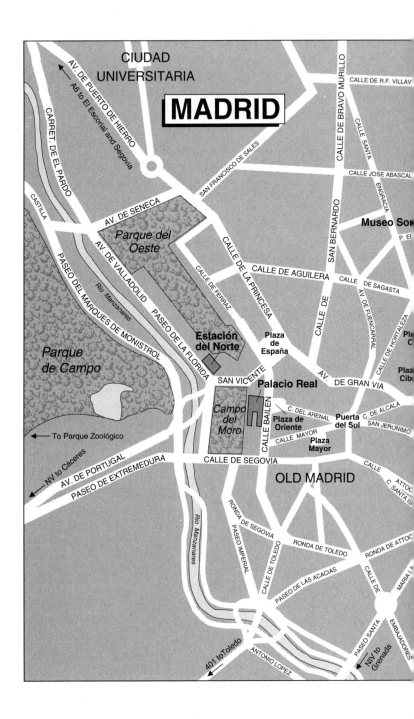

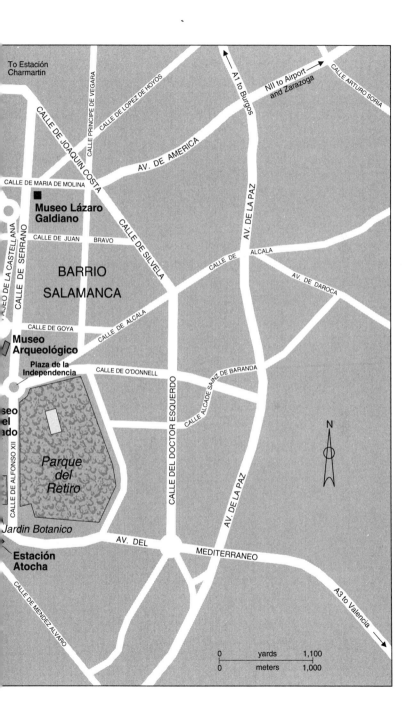

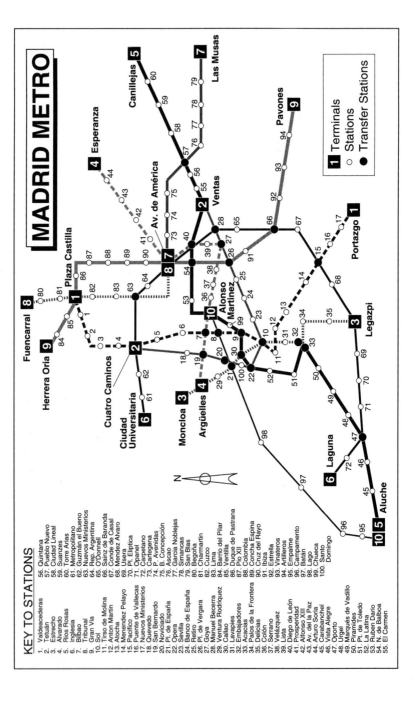

sights between those two landmarks can abundantly fill most visitors' schedules.

Madrid has always been the most lively of capitals, exuding a sense of energy and animation. One wonders when Madrileños sleep, for, drawn by 3,000 restaurants and tapas bars, they fill the sidewalks until the small hours of the night. Madrid is the culinary capital of Spain, with more restaurants offering more varieties of food than anywhere else in the country. Whatever the regional specialty—Basque, Galacian, Valencian or Andalusian—Madrid serves its cuisine as well or better than its home territory. A visitor can perform a complete culinary tour of Spain without ever leaving Madrid.

WHAT TO SEE AND DO

The **Museo del Prado** ★★★★★ is a high point, not simply of Madrid, but of Spain. The **Museo Arqueológico Nacional** ★★★ should not be missed. To experience the atmosphere of the city, take one or more **walking tours** ★ described below, preferably #1 and #2. The **Palácio Real** ★★★ is impressive for its excesses, if not its tastefulness, and almost everyone should find the associated armory and carriage museums interesting. **El Retiro** ★ park, behind the Prado, offers an array of activities throughout the summer. Museums abound. The brand-new **Villahermosa Museum** ★★★ now fills the gaps in the Prado collection. The convents of the **Encarnación** ★ and **Descalzas Real** ★★ house impressive paintings. **Museo Lázaro Galdiano** ★★ displays exquisite ivories and enamelwares, and a few exceptional paintings. The **Museo Sorolla** ★ offers a different experience—turn-of-the-century paintings of light and life. The **Centro de Arte Reina Sofia** ★★ is rapidly becoming a premier museum of modern art. And then there is shopping—elegant in the **Barrio Salamanca** ★★, and, on Sunday mornings, fun in **El Rastro** ★, Madrid's flea market.

MUSEUMS

Museo del Prado ★★★★★

Open Tues.-Sat. 9 a.m. to 6:30 p.m., (until 7 p.m. from May 15 to Oct. 15). Open Wed. night until 9 p.m. Open Sun. from 9 a.m. to 2 p.m. Admission: 400 ptas., which includes Casón del Buen Retiro. ☎ 420 26 36. Paseo del Prado. Subway: Banco de España or Antocha. Buses: 10, 14, 27, 43, 37, 45, M-6. In 1785, as a major component of his plan to beautify the capital, Carlos III commisioned the building of the stately Prado on the site of the Prado de San Jerónimo, or Saint Jerome's Meadow, formerly the gardens of Isabella and Ferdinand's monastery. The meadow had long served as a favorite promenade for the gentry of Madrid, and the king hoped to edify his strolling subjects by housing exhibits of natural science in their path. He gave the assignment to Juan de Villanueva, of neoclassical Italian bent, who designed a columned brick-and-stone structure with protruding end pavilions that generated countless similar museums around the world. Before any exhibits could be installed, however, the French invaded Spain and lodged a troop of cavalry inside, greatly damaging the interior. When the French left, Carlos' grandson, Ferdinand VII, decided to use the abandoned building to house the previously separate royal art collections under one roof. On November 19, 1817, shortly after the opening of the Louvre in Paris, the Museo del Prado first received the public.

A special aspect of the Prado collection is that, because it consists primarily of works chosen by a few Spanish kings for their own collections, it lends insight into royal tastes. Early in the 16th century, Carlos V, raised in The Netherlands before becoming Spain's king, assembled the beginning of the collection. His domains were extensive and he travelled throughout Europe, bringing a European sensibility to a Spain focused inward by its centuries of reconquest. Carlos purchased many Flemish works and, above all, paintings by the great Italian Titian, the master he admired above all others. Carlos' son, Felipe II, the enigmatic hermit-like king, greatly expanded the royal collection, adding fantastic works of Hieronymus Bosch, among others. In the 17th century, his grandson, Felipe IV, became an avid collector and also patron to the great Velázquez, whom he sent to Italy to select works for royal purchase. Felipe IV bought Rubens by the score and twice offered that artist the position of court painter, though Rubens declined each time. After Cromwell ousted Charles I from England's throne and offered the royal art collection for sale, agents of Felipe IV were the main bidders, sending home Dürer's *Self Portrait* among many others. Thus was the mass of the Prado's collection assembled.

Throughout the time of Carlos V and the collecting Felipes who succeeded him, Spain governed all of Italy south of Rome, which accounts for the Prado's superb collection of Italian masterpieces, especially those from the 16th and 17th centuries. Thanks to Carlos V and Felipe II, Dutch and Flemish works are well represented, including a major Rembrandt purchased later. Still, the focus of the collection is on the incomparable Spanish masters, assiduously gathered in homage—unparalleled in any other country—to its native artists. Because Spain was a political rival of both England and France, the Prado is weak in English painting and spotty in French. And, despite three great works by Albrecht Dürer, the collection must also be considered weak in German painting, for its artists were generally ignored by the royal collectors.

No one should miss the three Dürers, Raphael's *Portrait of a Cardinal*, Bosch's paintings, all the Zurbaráns, all of Velázquez' works, and Goya's portraits and "black paintings." In addition, the works of Berruguette, Ribera, El Greco, Pieter Bruegel the Elder, van der Weyden, Botticelli, Fra Angelico, and Titian are outstanding, although other

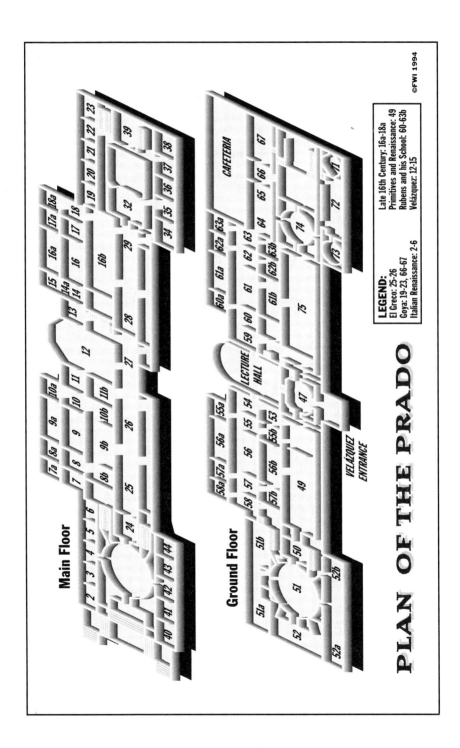

Main Floor

Ground Floor

CAFETERIA

LECTURE HALL

VELÁZQUEZ ENTRANCE

©FWI 1994

LEGEND:

El Greco: 25-26
Goya: 19-23, 66-67
Italian Renaissance: 2-6

Late 16th Century: 16a-18a
Primitives and Renaissance: 49
Rubens and his School: 60-63b
Velázquez: 12-15

PLAN OF THE PRADO

treasures will certainly call out to you as you pass. The Prado owns more than 4,000 paintings, about 1,000 of which are on loan to regional museums at any time. Since it chooses to display only a few hundred, every one will be special. Fortunately, the museum is not huge. How much time a visit requires will depend entirely on whether you wish to cover only its highlights, which can be seen in half a day, or to view its full hanging collection, which can be seen in a full day, or better still, enjoyed over a lifetime. Locations of paintings change frequently, so directions and the location of the works we describe based on our last visit may need adjusting when you arrive.

GROUND FLOOR

Left, as you enter the central "Velázquez Entrance," are paintings from the Renaissance, prefaced by medieval works. To the right hang paintings by members of the school of Rubens. Head left. You are on the way to Dürer and Bosch.

Off the long corridor of medieval paintings, three rows of rooms extend right. Work your way through the first row consisting of rooms 53, 55B, 56C, 56B and 57B.

By rooms 56B and 56C, the paintings begin to come alive. **Correa de Vivar** stands out. A sudden light comes in room 57B from *Virgin con Cabellero de Montessa*, attributed to the Italian **Pablo de San Leocadio**. Then back to room 57 in the next row. Here hang the paintings of Pedro Berruguette, the first genius of Spanish art.

Born in 1450, Pedro **Berruguette** worked in Italy before returning to Spain in 1483. He may have acquired technical mastery from his time abroad, but there is nothing Italian about his utter realism and fondness for decoration. Probably his finest work is the *Auto da Fé Presided over by St. Dominic de Guzmán*. It depicts the heretic Raymond talking to a priest who stands at the bottom of a stairway. With extended hand, the seated Saint Dominic pardons Raymond in front of a crowd that seems not to notice the event. This is the most Italian of Berruguette's works, but the colors surprise, as does the movement of the composition. Two other Berruguette paintings of Saint Dominic also deserve a look—*St. Dominic and the Albigenses* and *St. Dominic Restoring a Young Man to Life. San Pedro Martir* is a shattering work, heightened by the disquieting sight of an ax in the saint's head.

Left, in room 58, is an early innovator, the Fleming *Rogier van der Weyden* who died in 1464. His *Disposition* is a masterpiece of unforgettable faces. So too is his *Pietà*, with a striking cross soaring heavenward. This is the first religious painting to include a portrait of an artist's patron—the solemn man with clasped hands.

Pass through room 56 and into room 55 to find works of **Machuca**, a contemporary of Berruguette, which display a liveliness not seen in the previous rooms. Notice *Disposicion de la Cruz*, with its strong mood. And what a frame surrounds it—a rare preserved original frame for such an early work.

Proceed to room 54 where three extraordinary **Albrecht Dürers** wait on the far wall. *Adam and Eve*, so often reproduced, stand as tall as life—which is a surprise—on either side of the artist's *Self Portrait*. Dürer learned his trade in Italy, but his mathematical exactitude was natural, and he brought a Gothic palette of colors from his native land. This steely self-portrait must rank with the greatest of that genre, still earning admiration for the precision and profundity of its psychological self-study.

Move quickly through room 55A into 56A for a fantastic **Pieter Breugel**, the Elder," the famous *El Triunfo de la Muerte* (Triumph of Death), from 1562. Nothing signals as strongly how removed this work is from the Italian aesthetic as the subjects Breugel chose: he depicts common folk in everyday scenes. Despite the religious theme of the inevitability of death, there are no religious references. Impossible juxtapositions make the whole truly surreal, revealing Breugel's debt to countryman Bosch. Encounters with death in all its varieties cover the canvas: humans flee from armies of skeletons who attempt to force them into a box, while two lovers in the right foreground, oblivious to all around them, adore each other. Bruegel's talent and accuracy are evident; it is no wonder that he inspired the work of his two sons and that of most Flemish artists for a century to come. But his paintings pale beside those of Bosch in the next room, 57A.

No matter how often seen in reproduction, the original *Garden of Delights* still seizes the attention and amazes. **Bosch** ("El Bosco," in Spanish) was a true original. The son of a modest painter in a small Dutch village, Bosch never felt the influences of cosmopolitan life. He joined an ascetic movement called the "Brethren of the Common Life," founded on the credo that pleasure is a sure road to hell. He painted this theory with a realism that makes one wonder how he could depict pleasures so convincingly. Rather than theorizing about his sanity or contemplating how his paintings prefigure surrealism, it is best to let the eye wander, discovering details. This much is clear: the left-hand triptych shows Paradise, the center depicts earthly delight, and the right, Hell. Wonder at it.

The Adoration of the Magi calls for admiration of Bosch's artistry, his mastery of technique and detail. Yet, there is that strange city in the background looking like a modern skyscraper metropolis. *The HayCart* is easier to understand. It pictures a Dutch proverb referring to the world as a hay-cart from which each takes what he can. The poor scramble and fight to seize scraps from the central hay-cart. Christ watches from the extreme lower left, as above him nobles and high clergy approach, while monks and nuns in the foreground enjoy what they have already taken. The left panel tells the story of man's expulsion from Eden, while the right displays the tortures awaiting him in Hell.

Entirely out of order, because of the impermanence of the current hangings, Ribera's works are hung in room 51B, in the pavilion extending from the right end of the long medieval corridor. **Jusepe de Ribera** (1591-1652) is the only Spanish painter who can be compared with Velázquez in electing to paint ordinary people instead of idealized images. Ribera's subjects look so real because he used seedy characters as models for his portraits of saints and philosophers. It can be said that Ribera's pictures are stronger than Velázquez', and that he was at least as original in his choice of themes. Study his masterpiece *The Trinity*: the strong diagonals—two inverted triangles, the look on God's face as he holds his dead Son, and the drapery. See also the powerful lines of *The Martyrdom of Saint Bartholemew*, and the smiling *Archimedes*, *Joseph with the Christ Child*, and *Saint Alexis*.

Retrace your path all the way back past the center entrance, to the rooms on its right. Again three rows of rooms stretch off the long hall. The first row, rooms 61B-63B, have **Rubens** and **Van Dycks**; the second row, rooms 59-63, more Rubens; and the last, rooms 60A-63A, display various landscapes and still lives. Go further right, off room 63, past rooms 64 and 65, for a temporary installation of the great **Goya** "Black Paintings" in room 67 and 68.

These paintings, dating between 1819 and 1823, are the works of Goya's old age, and reflect a time of personal crisis. Goya had placed great faith in the enlightened ideas and secular government of the French, but his hopes for rationality among men had been dashed by France's invasion of Spain in 1808. Goya suffered a renewed attack of an illness that had earlier destroyed his hearing, and secluded himself in a house on the banks of the Manzanares river, covering its walls with paintings, called "Black" for their dominant tone. Imagine living in a house surrounded by these expressions of a bitter soul in torment. After Goya's death, the works were lifted off the walls and transferred to canvas as you see them.

See the famed *Saturn Devouring One of his Sons* and *Witches Sabbath*, but also the haunting *Dog Half Submerged*. *St. Isidore's Day* is a nightmarish self-satire of one of Goya's own exuberant, sun-filled early paintings displayed upstairs under the same name.

UPPER FLOOR

To view the rest of the collection in order requires first retracing steps through the ground floor medieval hall to the pavilion on the far right, and then climbing to the upper floor. Around the rotunda toward the back hang early Italian masterworks. You enter into room 4 in the middle to see the splendid **Fra Angelico** *Annunciation*. The contrast between the detailed, almost Flemish, reminder of the Adam and Eve story outside, with the simple architectural shapes of the building where the Annunciation takes place inside, focuses all attention on the main event. The colors take one's breathe away.

Left, in room 3, hang three parts of a four-painting series by **Sandro Botticelli**, *The Story of Nastagio Degli Onesti*. It depicts a tale from the Decameron in which Onesti, while wandering through a forest after rejection by his beloved, sees a knight murder a maiden and throwing her heart to dogs. The knight explains that he is condemned to repeat this act eternally because he killed himself after the maiden had spurned his suit. Onesti invites his own beloved and her family to a feast in the same forest so they might witness this result of rejected love. The happy aftermath is shown in the missing fourth painting. In the same room is a splendid **Mantegna**, *Death of the Virgin*.

Raphaels hang in room 2, the next room to the left. Although he might be the most talented painter who ever lived, Raphael's fame seduced him into excesses that killed him by his early thirties. To meet the demand for his work, Raphael organized a factory employing numerous assistants, which produced work of such uneven quality that questions arise about whether the master's own hand had ever touched a given painting. The Prado, however, contains several of Raphael's acknowledged masterworks. *The Holy Family with Lamb* is reminiscent of Leonardo Di Vinci but with stronger colors and more expressive faces. Felipe IV bought *Christ Falls on the Way to Calvary*, and called it the "costliest gem in the world." Again the faces, especially those of the women, are miracles of expression—from concern, to love, to anguish. Most haunting is the *Portrait of a Cardinal*. The identity of the sitter remains in question but not the depth of Raphael's psychological study or the subtle richness of his subject's red silk robes.

Turning back to view the rooms following Fra Angelico's room 4, we come to room 5 and **Andrea del Sarto**, an artist from the era of Raphael. *Lucrezia di Baccio del Fede* pictures del Sarto's wife. Stories describe her as cruel and unfaithful, but this portrait clearly shows why he kept her around. Work your way through room 6, and through three rows of rooms 7-8, A and B, for more Italian painting, including one by the genius **Caravaggio**, *David Victorious over Golaith*, of flawed composition but unearthly light.

Move into the long gallery, rooms 25 and 26, for **El Greco**. Domenicos Theotocopoulos, as he was baptized, came to Spain in 1576 after studying with Titian in Venice, and never left. El Greco had studied Byzantine icon painting in which strong outlines make thin, elongated figures stand out from their background. He introduced the device to western art, along with a palette of luminous blues and reds acquired from his Italian teachers. El Greco drew from articulated models, not from life, producing angled figures and constant movement, but not realism. The Impressionists—especially Cezanne, who copied his paintings repeatedly—learned much from him.

El Greco's best work remains in Toledo, the city he made his home. The Prado does own his finest portrait, however. *The Nobleman with his Hand on his Chest* was painted soon after El Greco landed in Spain, before the extreme elongation of figures and the fiery, yet paradoxically cool, colors of his later work. Still, there are hints of what was to come in the unknown sitter's long fingers and piercing gaze. Some of El Greco's mature work is also on view at the Prado, paintings which incorporate elongated figures, drawn as if the painter were lying down looking up at the subject; angry, living skies; and raw emotion expressed as much in the mannered painting of fabric as in the faces of his subjects. *Pentecost, The Trinity,* and especially, *The Adoration of the Shepherds* could only have been painted by this genius.

Moving down the long gallery, enter the large room 12 on the right, from which rooms 13-15 continue for the Prado's greatest painter, Velázquez.

The work of Diego **Velázquez** de Silva (1599-1660) represents the culmination of Spanish painting. Velázquez studied in Seville, and was appointed a court painter in his twenties. Two early paintings before this appointment show him already a master—*The Adoration of the Magi* and *Mother Jerónima de la Fuente*, with her piercing, determined gaze. At court in Madrid, Velázquez became a royal portrait painter, beginning a lifelong friendship with his patron and contemporary, the lonely Felipe IV. Velázquez' portraits of the king show his human side—a homely man with thinning hair and jutting Hapsburg jaw.

In 1628, Peter Paul Rubens, the most famous painter of the day, visited Madrid. He had no use for any Spanish painter but Velázquez, and undertook to teach him what he knew. These lessons are contained in Velázquez' disturbing *Feast of Bacchus*, in which the effete, half-naked, fair-skinned god of wine stares at us, surrounded by leathery peasants. It is a flawed painting that foreshadows Manet's *Déjuner sur l'herbe* in its shock of contrasts.

Starting in 1629, Velázquez spent two years studying in Italy. The result was two large Italianate narrative works, *The Forge of Vulcan* and *Joseph's Bloodied Coat Presented to Jacob*. The former painting is a tour de force of surfaces, from gritty floor to burnished iron to gleaming armor. Figures of the cyclops show surprisingly lean, unidealized bodies. The latter is an annoying painting that does not seem to work until one steps twenty feet away and sees it come to life.

Back in Spain, Velázquez entered a mature phase when no project was beyond him. During this period he painted the epic *Surrender of Breda*, sometimes known as *Las Lanzes* for its most striking element. The work commemorates one of the few Spanish victories in the long war with The Netherlands, and the grace with which General Spinola accepted the Dutch surrender. *Count-Duke Olivares on Horseback* is a monumental homage to Velázquez' friend at court, a fellow Sevillano, in which the huge Count-Duke surveys his only military success. His depiction of *Diego de Corral y Arellano* is more subtle, the essence of portraiture. Velázquez painted everyone in the royal family and most of the jesters and dwarfs kept as pets. Most charming is his perceptive portrait of *Queen Marianna* showing her determined, unpleasant character, lightened only by touches of vermillion ribbon.

Velázquez was ambitious, rising in position with the years. Added responsibilities for collecting art for the king, decorating rooms in the Madrid palace and El Escorial, and supervising the other royal painters consumed time, constricting his own artistic output. In his last phase, Velázquez determinedly painted only works that were important to him, exercises to stretch the medium. Two acknowledged masterpieces resulted. *The Fable of Arachne* depicts a weaving contest between the mortal Arachne and the goddess Minerva. In the myth, the contest results in a tie, demonstrating Arachne's ability to weave divinely, and ends with Arachne being transformed into a spider by the jealous Minerva. In Velázquez' painting, Arachne stands in the sunlit background in front of her weaving. The weaving copies a known painting, *The Rape of Europa* by Titian. Velázquez' message is that because Titian's painting is divine, painting can transcend mere craft. Velázquez was hoping at the time for a royal award never before given to a mere painter—the *Order of Santiago*; this painting was part of his campaign. Not incidentally, the painting is complex and fascinating.

Like no other painting, *Las Meninas*, Velázquez last work, makes the viewer a participant, for he stands exactly at the focus of all the activity. The princess Margaretta, her ladies-in-waiting, dog and dwarfs are all watching the subjects that the artist behind them, Velázquez himself, is painting. The models, the king and queen, are shown reflected in a mirror at the back, emphasized by the brilliant device of a courtier ascending sunlit stairs nearby. The picture is complex and perfect, summarizing all the lessons painting had discovered through the ages. Velázquez died soon after finishing *Las Meninas*, but posthumously earned the Order of Santiago he had so assiduously sought in life. A thoughtful friend—some say it was the king himself—later painted a crimson cross, the sign of the order, on Velázquez' chest in the painting.

If Velázquez poses a problem, it is that he is too accomplished. Everything seems so right and undramatic that it is possible to run quickly through a gallery of his work. His mastery requires study. Fortunately his paintings all invite contemplation, for such was his genius.

Finishing the three rows of rooms, pass through 16A-18A, all filled with Spanish works. There you can see an earlier Spanish luminary, **Ribalta**, especially the brilliantly-lit *Christ Embracing St. Bernard*, as well as **Murillo**, who followed Velázquez. Obvious comparisons with the master do not allow Murillo's works much of a chance.

Francisco de Zurbarán (1598-1661) followed Ribera, with paintings that are the most spiritual of all, not with the fire of El Greco's work, but possessed, instead, of a quiet, bare, intensely reflective, almost mystical quality. Zurbarán's solitary figures in white robes against dark, featureless backgrounds display his extraordinary ability to combine spirituality with utter realism. Outstanding are *Saint Luke before the Crucified*, *Saint Elizabeth of Portugal*, of the luminous clothes, the striking *Virgin of the Immaculate Conception*, and the unforgettable *Saint Peter Nolasco's Vision of the Crucified Saint Peter*, with Saint Peter upside down.

When the French invaded Spain in the 19th century, they so admired Zurbarán's work that they pried his paintings from the walls of monasteries and churches. They took almost 100 works back to France, now disbursed among the museums of the world. Spain retains some fine Zurbaráns, but, alas, not the best.

Returning to the front row, room 16B, we find **Titian**, so admired by Carlos V and by critics through the ages. Many of his works seem overly romantic today, but the collection is impressive and probably the best in the world. Especially memorable are *The Emperor Charles V at Muhlberg*, a portrait of his patron on horseback, and the artist's own *Self-Portrait.*

Continue through to the left pavilion, to room 19 and beyond, for someone who challenges even Velázquez, although in a radically different style. Here are the **Francisco de Goya** (1746-1828) rooms, his early and middle work prior to his last "Black Paintings."

Goya first painted designs for tapestries, called "cartoons," at the royal tapestryworks, before turning to portraits in which greys and watery colors dominate. By 1799 he was celebrated enough to be named painter to the king. The king happened to be a genial incompetent, dominated by his wife, Maria Luisa, and her lover, Godoy. Whether Goya's portraits of the royal family are the greatest art can be argued, but if art means showing the truth, these works make a case. Goya pushed his portraits toward caricature to reveal his subject's inner character. Paintings such as *The Family of Carlos IV* so ruthlessly display the emptiness of the king and ambition of the queen, who takes center stage in the group, that one wonders why they allowed such a portrait to be displayed. Perhaps these people could not see what was before their eyes, or perhaps Goya's bright but washed colors seduced his clients with their elegance. The portraits of Ferdinand VII are particularly unflattering. Goya disagreed with Ferdinand's policies so strongly that he fled Spain for voluntary exile. Ferdinand, for his part, wanted little to do with Goya. Goya's portraits of Ferdinand all incorporate the same face, because the king refused to sit for the artist.

When Goya's subject was a person of quality, however, as in the case of his friend and father-in-law *The Painter Francisco Bayeu*, the paintings exudes character and dignity. Goya could also be sensual, as in *Maja Clothed*, more erotic than the same subject and pose in *Maja Nude*. The sitter is not the Duchess of Alba, as some claim, but an unknown model. It is likely that these paintings were originally framed back to back, so the clothed version could be displayed for general viewing and the naked version turned forward for more private contemplation.

Goya's high position in the pantheon of art depends more on his fevered imagination than on his skill at portraiture. In 1808, when the French seized Spain, Goya painted two masterworks, *The Second of May* and *The Third of May*, depicting the uprising of citizens against the invaders, shown in room 39. The first depicts a battle, fierce with violence; the second, by artificially shortening the distance from the executioners' guns to the defenseless victims, shrieks of the horror of death.

Museo Arqueológico Nacional

Open Tues.-Sat. from 9:30 a.m. to 8:30 p.m. Open Sun. from 9:30 a.m. until 2:30 p.m. Closed Mon. and holidays. Admission: 200 ptas. ☎ 403 65 59. C. Serrano, 13. Entrance in the rear on Paseo de Recoletas. Subway: Colón or Serrano. Buses: 1, 5, 9, 14, 19, 51, 74, M-2. See Walking Tour #3. The National Archaeological Museum occupies the rear half of the large **Biblioteca Nacional**, with an entrance on C. Serrano. The building was opened in 1892 to celebrate the 400th anniversery of Columbus' discovery of America. Museums of archaeology abound throughout Spain, for the country is rich in artifacts of earlier civilizations, but the very best examples have been assembled for display in this national collection.

The tour begins in Room 1 with remains from Greek, Phoenician and Carthaginian settlements, then leads into a display in Room 2 of artifacts of the ancient native Iberian culture. Carthaginian influence is evident in the 4th-century B.C. *Dama de Elche*, the greatest known Iberian sculpture and the centerpiece of the room. She looks somehow foreign, of a culture outside the classical tradition, for the character of an alien aesthetic seems carved in her face. Other *damas* repose around her, almost as lovely as she. The rooms which follow contain Roman sculpture and mosaics of some interest.

The second floor begins with Visigothic jewelry. Three crowns turned into hanging votive hangings are the star attractions, and that of Reccesvinthus Rex from circa 670 B.C. is particularly outstanding. Dangling gold letters spell his name, and the crown is embedded with uncut semi-precious stones. It is the world's loss that the most splendid crown in the collection was stolen in 1921 and never recovered.

Rooms follow filled with incomparable Moorish art. The small objects, including the precious ivory box called the *Bote de Marfil*, repay study. Stucco work is also displayed, as are intricately coffered ceilings, all of which provide just a sample of the Moorish architecture that waits in Andalusia. Gothic sculpture comes next, and Renaissance objects and furniture follows. Higher floors display small collections of Egyptian and prehistoric art.

On the grounds by the entrance is an underground replica of Altamira cave. Despite every effort, it is only a hint of the real thing, but with some quiet study the animals do begin to wriggle over your head.

Palácio Real   ★ ★ ★

Open Tues.-Sat. 9 a.m. to 6:15 p.m. (until 5:15 p.m. in winter.) Open Sun. and holidays 9 a.m. until 2 p.m. Closed Mon. ☎ 248 74 04. By tour only, in Spanish or English. Admission: 325 ptas., for the palace only; 500 ptas., for the palace plus subsidiary exhibits. C. Bailén. Subway: Opera. Buses: 3, 25, 33, 39, M-4. See walking tour #2. In 1764, 26 years after the former Hapsburg palace was leveled by fire, this new palace was completed on the ashes of the old one. It was a new palace for a new dynasty. The final king of the Hapsburg line had been born mentally retarded and died childless, but, on his deathbed, willed the throne to a distant French relative, a cousin of the French Bourbon king. Thus did Felipe V initiate the present Bourbon line of Spanish monarchs. He ordered a palace, designed by the Italian architect Sachetti along classical lines, to suit his French tastes. But the building took decades to complete and Felipe died before it was finished. His son Carlos III, who did so much to make Madrid worthy of a European monarch, was the first king to inhabit the palace. Carlos took a personal interest in its decoration, even to founding a school for tile-painting in the Buen Retiro Palace, and did up his new residence in Baroque decor. While a palace is not a museum, of course, this one is filled with enough objects to serve both roles.

Entrance to the palace is through its south end where tickets are purchased, and a huge porticoed forecourt leads to the palace proper. The more expensive "Unreserved" ticket gains entry to the Library with its numismatic and music museum, the Real Farmacia (Royal Pharmacy), the Armería (Armory) and the Museo de Carruajes Reales (Royal Carriage Museum), as well as palace rooms. At least the last two museums are worth a look. Including those, it can take several hours to see the palace.

Statues of Spanish monarchs intended for the roof were placed around the grounds when it was learned they were too heavy for the safety of the building. The exterior is a solemn white. Rows of pilasters and Corinthian columns run for over a block upon an entablature, surmounted by a hint of "icing" on the roof, all producing a stately facade. But the interior is another matter.

The apartments of the palace's first occupant, Carlos III, begin at the top of a grand stairway. The ceiling of the Ambassador's Audience Chamber was painted by Mengs. Rooms lined with velvet, gilt and candalabras follow, and lead to a double throne room (one seat for the present King Juan Carlos, the other for his queen, Sofia) that tries hard to impress, but would seem more appropriate as a Hollywood movie set—though there is that Tiepolo frescoed ceiling. The dining room sits 88 comfortably. Such rooms must be seen to be believed. Two thousand rooms fill the structure, though most are off-limits to tourists. The museum of painting, porcelain and crystal displays a Bosch, four Goyas and a Velázquez amid dinner services for scores.

Outside, in the west wing of the forecourt, is the **Real Armería** (Royal Armory), containing collections of the actual armor worn by 16th- and 17th-century kings. Inside is a magnificent tent captured from the French saint-king Francis I at the battle of Pavia, and armor for men, royalty, children, horses and dogs. The long length of the jousting lances are a surprise. The finest armor are the many suits worn by Carlos V, who needed them for a reign filled with wars. All the armor is functional and at the same time artistic, a happy blend of craft and aesthetics. Of course there are amusing excesses too, such as the plating that covers half a horse and culminates in ram's horns crowning the head-piece.

South of the palace is one of the largest churches in the world, **Nuestra Señora de la Almudena**. Construction began over 100 years ago and has not yet finished. It is possible that disappointment with the results to date has quenched the builders' incentive.

Outside in the Campo del Moro, the former royal park, is a modern building which houses the **Museo de Carruajes Reales** (Royal Carriage Museum). It contains elaborately decorated carriages, primarily from the late 18th century. The one in black ebony is the only carriage to have survived the fire that destroyed the former palace in the 18th century, and dates from a century earlier. Napoleon donated the one with the crown on top. The present coronation coach still bears marks of an assassination attempt made on a former king and his bride in 1906.

Villahermosa Museum   ★★★

Open Tues.-Sun. 10 a.m. to 6:30 p.m., (until 7 p.m. from May 15 to Oct. 15). Closed Mon. Admission: 400 ptas. *420 39 44. Across from the Prado at Paseo del Prado, 8. Subway: Banco de España or Antocha. Buses: 10, 14, 27, 43, 37, 45, M-6.* This museum completes the Prado collection by filling its gaps. Both Baron Thyssen-Bornemisza and his son spent a fortune from Dutch mining and shipping profits to acquire possibly the finest, and certainly the most extensive collection of art remaining in private hands, and decided to sell the mass of it—nearly 800 paintings, sundry furniture, jewelry and statues—to Spain, thanks in no small measure to the urgings of the Baron's Spanish wife. Here these treasures will reside for our enjoyment, displayed in a tasteful palace.

The installation was not complete at our last visit and was arranged in reverse order. Modern art inhabited the first floor, fine Impressionists the second, and masterpieces from the Renaissance through the 18th-century the third. Here the familiar, powerful *Portrait of Henry VIII* by Holbein the Younger was displayed, along with the captivating *Portrait of Giovanna Tornabuoni* by Ghirlandaio.

Convento Descales Reales

Open Tues.-Thurs. 10:30 a.m. to 12:30 p.m. and 4-5:15 p.m. Open Fri., Sat. and 10:30 a.m. to 12:30 p.m., Sun. to 1:30 p.m. Closed Mon. and all holidays. By tour in Spanish only. Admission: 350 ptas.; free on Wed. Pl. de las Descalzas Reales, 3. ☎ 248 74 04. Subway: Puerto del Sol (directions in Walking Tour #2). Buses: 1, 2, 5, 20, 46, 52, 53, 74. See walking tour #2. Juana of Austria, the daughter of Carlos V, established this convent of Poor Clares in 1559. The order had been founded a century before by St. Francis of Assisi, for his disciple St. Clare. After its founding, the order petitioned the Pope for the "privilege of poverty," that is, for the right of its members to subsist on nothing but what they could beg. However, there was little begging at this particular convent. It was restricted to "Poor" Clares of the highest nobility who used it as a periodic retreat from the pressures of high society. In return for their stays they donated the sumptuous gifts now on display in the buildings around the cloister. Despite its austere exterior, the convent is a riot of decoration within. The tour passes through rooms containing fine paintings by Titian, Breugel the Elder, a splendid Zurbarán *St. Francis,* and interesting portraits of the Hapsburg royal family. Up a staircase for which "grandiose" is the only description, one enters the former dormitory hung with magnificent 17th-century tapestries. The reliquary gallery displays impressive boxes and chests. This is a special museum, small but select. Your only sense of having visited a cloistered convent is by comparison—when you step outside and around the corner to the contemporary bustle of the el Corte Inglés department store.

Convento de la Encarnación

Open Tues.-Thurs. 10:30 a.m. to 12:30 p.m. and 4-5:15 p.m. Open Fri., Sat. and 10:30 a.m. to 12:30 p.m., Sun. to 1:30 p.m. Closed Mon. and all holidays. By tour in Spanish only. Admission: 350 ptas.; free on Wed. Pl. de la Encarnación, 1. ☎ 247 05 10. Subway: Opera (directions in Walking Tour #2). Buses: 3, 25, 33, 39. See Walking Tour #2. In 1611, Margarete of Austria, wife of Felipe III, commissioned Gómez de Mora, the architect who built Madrid's Plaza Mayor for her husband, to design this convent. She and succeeding monarchs donated generously to her pet project. The art in the galleries is not up to the standards of Descalzas Reales, but there is a Ribera, a fine polychrome sculpture by Gregorio Fernandez, and pleasing 17th-century Madrid paintings.

The 18th-century church is severe in design and Baroque in decoration. A sumptuously frescoed ceiling canopies equally dazzling reliquaries—over 1000 of them—in the gallery. The contrast with the private rooms of the convent is marked, for they offer a taste of simple cloistered life in the 17th century.

Museo Lázaro Galdino

Open Tues.-Sun. 10 a.m. to 2 p.m. Closed Mon., all holidays and Aug. Admission: 350 ptas; half price on Sun. C. Serrano, 122. ☎ 261 60 84. Subway: Av. América. Buses: 9, 16, 19, 51, 89. This museum is situated in a "hole" in the subway system. The closest stop is Av. de América, six blocks due east along C. Maria de Molina. This private collection gathered by José Lázaro demonstrates what good taste and piles of money can buy. The ground floor presents a veritable history of enamelling up to the 17th century, charming ivories, fine medieval gold and silver, Renaissance jewelry and a crucifix said to be by Leonardo da Vinci. The next floor displays later statues and silver and gold work, and, with the exception of its Flemish primitives, is interesting more for its furnishings than for its paintings. Some very fine oils hang on the third floor: a moving Rembrandt portrait of his wife, Quentin Metsys, El Greco, Ribera, Zurbarán, Velázquez, Goya and Tiepolo, along with some of the best English paintings in Spain, by Gainsborough, Turner, Reynolds and Constable.

Centro de Arte Reina Sofia

Open Wed.-Mon. 10 a.m. to 9 p.m. Closed Tues. and holidays. Admission: 300 ptas. C. Santa Isabel, 52. ☎ 467 50 62. Subway: Atocha. Buses: 18, 59, 85, 86, C. Located one block northwest of the Atocha train and subway station, the building began as an 18th-century hospital. Now it houses the best of Spain's modern art, including Picasso's *Guernica*. To most experts *Guernica* is the masterpiece of 20th-century art. Painted entirely in shades of black and white, it expresses the horrors of war in its depiction of the devastation of the quiet Basque capital of Guernica. The town, in no way a military target, was carpet-bombed by wave upon wave of German planes during the Spanish Civil War. Scenes of civilians and animals contorted in agony fill the canvas. Because of Franco's involvement in the attack, Picasso would not permit this painting to be exhibited in Spain until after the dictator's regime ended. Picasso's studies for the work lend insight into its composition. If you allow it to, the painting will move you to a deep sadness.

The museum shop is worth a look for its prints and posters.

Museo Sorolla

Open Tues.-Sun. 10 a.m. to 2 p.m. Closed Mon. and all holidays. Admission: 200 ptas. Paseo del General Martinez Campos, 37. ☎ 261 60 84. Subway: Ruben Dario or Iglesia. Buses: 5, 7, 16, 40, 61, M-3. By subway walk due north for two blocks from the Ruben Dario station on Miguel Angel to Paseo del General Martinez Campos, or walk due east on Paseo del General Martinez Campos from the Iglesia station. This house was built in 1912 as the home and studio of a painter of international renown, before art history passed him by and forgot him. It is a pity. Joaquin Sorolla's paintings possess a special light, inspired by that of his native Valencia, that gives his canvases life and spirit. Displaying the works in the turn-of-the-century surroundings where the artist lived adds intimacy. Those who take the time to visit are glad they did.

Museo Panteon de Goya (Ermita de San Antonio) ★

Open Tues.-Fri. 10 a.m. to 1 p.m., and 4-7 p.m., (until 6 p.m. in winter). Open Sat. and Sun. for the morning hours only. Closed Mon. and all holidays. Admission: Free. Glorieta de San Antonio de la Florida. ☎ *542 07 22. Subway: Norte. Buses: 41, 46, 75, C.* Located three blocks north of the Estación del Norte, this chapel is a bit out of the way, but a mecca for fans of Goya. The church was built in 1798 by an Italian under orders from Carlos IV, and the king commissioned Goya, as his court painter, to decorate the cupola and vaults. The painting is early Goya and romantic, but the cupola fresco of St. Antony of Padua surrounds the viewer and draws him in. As always, Goya's crowds, especially as they lean against and upon the painted railing, seem composed of real people, rather than, as with most artists, actors hired for the drama.

Appropriately, Goya's remains—except for his head which had disappeared—were disinterred about a century after his burial in France and entombed in this church in 1908.

Real Academia de Bellas Artes de San Fernando ★

Open daily 9 a.m.-7 p.m., except Mon. and Sat., when it closes at 3 p.m. Closed all holidays. Admission: 200 ptas. C. de Alcalá, 13. ☎ *532 15 46. Subway: Sol. Buses: 3, 5, 15, 20, 51, 52. See Walking Tour #4.* The building was designed by Villanueva who also constructed the Prado. The collection inside is a hodgepodge of over 1000 works, both good and bad, but includes Goyas and four fine Zurbarán works, along with fans and furniture. Prints from original plates by masters, such as Goya, are on sale in the gift shop.

WALKING TOURS

The best way to experience any city is on foot. In Madrid, subways are convenient and taxis abundant and reasonable, so walking is seldom necessary but is certainly preferred. Each of the following walks includes a variety of sights that can be visited manageably in the time indicated.

1. OLD TOWN (LA CIUDAD ANTIGUA) ★ ★

This walk, a tour of 17th-century Madrid, will consume two hours or more, and should be taken early in the morning or late in the afternoon when the churches mentioned are open.

Plaza Mayor ★ ★. *Subway: Puerta del Sol. Buses: 3, 25, 33, 39, M-4. From the Puerta del Sol, head west on C. Mayor for two blocks, taking the third right into the Pl. Mayor.*

This huge—football-field-sized—square plaza is famed for being one of the largest and, for its arcade, the most architecturally integrated plaza in Spain. Although Felipe II had commissioned his favorite architect Juan de Herrera—responsible for such splendid neo-classical work as *el Escorial*—to design a grand square in the capital, it was not until the reign of his son that construction was begun, and then under the supervision of the architect Juan Gómez de Mora. Completed over the course of just two years, the plaza officially opened in 1620 with ceremonies to celebrate the canonization of five Spanish saints: Sta. Theresa of Ávila, St. Ignatius of Loyola, St. Francis Zavier, St. Isidro, the male patron saint of Madrid, and St. Felipe Neri. Throughout the 17th century and into the 19th, the plaza served as an arena for so many spectacles—plays, *autos-da-fě*, fireworks, royal marriage celebrations, and bullfights—that the owners of the houses forming the plaza's perimeter were required to lend their balconies to royalty during any such festivities. In the 1970s vehicles were barred from the plaza and diverted underground or around it. Thanks to the absence of traffic, today the plaza is a lively place in summer filled with crowds attending concerts and festivals, or simply milling about, and a quiet, open space in winter useful for strolls or shortcuts. Tables spring up on Sunday mornings for a stamp fair.

On the plaza's north side is the **Casa de Panaderia**, once the home of the bakers' guild, but rebuilt in 1672 after a fire. The king often sat on its second floor to observe spectacles taking place in the plaza. Today, **Felipe III ★** sculpted by the Italian Giovanni de Bologna, sits on horseback in the center of the plaza. With his beatific grin and baton of office held so insouciantly, his starched collar looks quite out of place, but is of no matter to the perching sparrows who love him dearly.

In the southwest corner of the plaza an archway leads to steps down to the **C. de Cuchilleros ★**, a strip of old *mesones* and *tabernas*, including the famous *Botín*. If you were to turn north, the street would become Cava de San Miguel, with more such dining places. (*Cava* was the name given to moats outside the original walls of medieval Madrid.) Instead turn right to the Pl. del Conde de Barajas, then left along its near edge down C. Lanzas to the **Plaza Puerta Cerrada**, an old city gate with a stone cross in the center, and surrounded by buildings with vegetable murals. Turn right again (not the acute right) on the near side up C. San Justo. Pass the convex statue-filled front of **Iglesia San Miguel**, an 18th century church of Italian Baroque style. The interior is elegant with bountiful stuccowork and a lovely oval cupola.

On the corner of the other side of the street is the **Casa de Juan de Vargas**, where Isidro, the male patron saint of Madrid, worked as a servant. Follow C. del Codo along the north side of the church. When it bends around the end of a large building, you reach the atmospheric **Plaza de la Villa ★★**. The large street bordering the plaza is C. Mayor, which leads leftward in two blocks to the Palàcio Real. The building just passed is the **Torre de Los Lujanes**, the former residence of an ancient family of Madrid grandees, in which Francis I of France was held prisoner in 1325. Of the

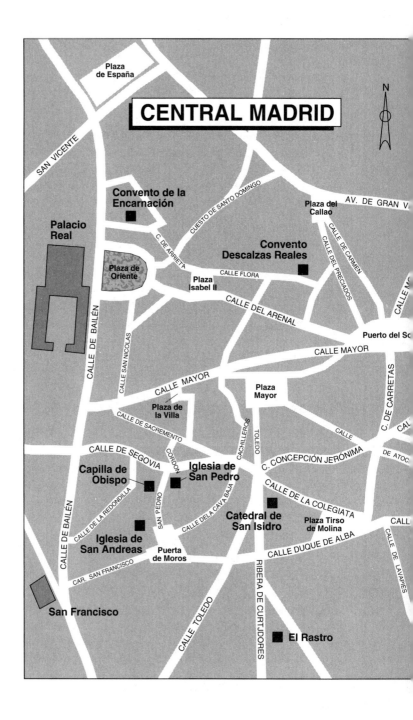

CENTRAL MADRID

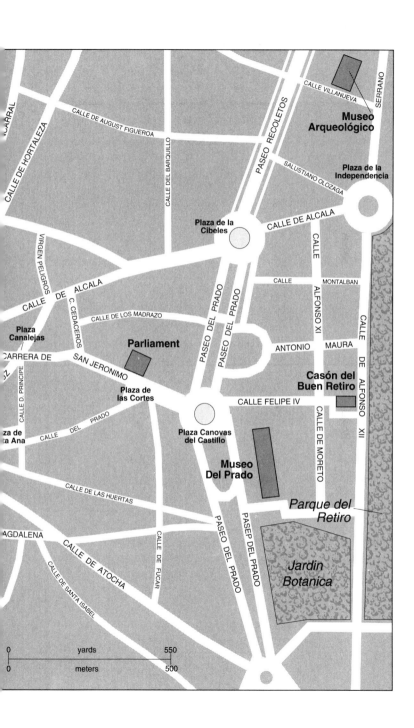

Museo
Arqueológico

CALLE VILLANUEVA

SERRANO

CALLE DE AUGUST FIGUEROA

PASEO RECOLETOS

SALUSTIANO OLOZAGA

Plaza de la
Independencia

CALLE DE HORTALEZA

CALLE DEL BARQUILLO

ARRAL

Plaza de la
Cibeles

CALLE DE ALCALA

CALLE

VIRGEN PELIGROS

CALLE DE ALCALA

CALLE

MONTALBAN

ALFONSO XI

CALLE DE LOS MADRAZO

C. CEDACEROS

Plaza
Canalejas

Parliament

PASEO DEL PRADO

PASEO DEL PRADO

ANTONIO

MAURA

CALLE DE ALFONSO

CARRERA DE

SAN JERONIMO

Plaza de
las Cortes

Casón del
Buen Retiro

CALLE D. PRINCIPE

CALLE FELIPE IV

CALLE DE MORETO

za de
a Ana

CALLE DEL PRADO

Plaza Canovas
del Castillo

CALLE XII

Museo
Del Prado

CALLE DE LAS HUERTAS

Parque del
Retiro

AGDALENA

CALLE DE ATOCHA

CALLE DE FUCAR

PASEO DEL PRADO

PASEP DEL PRADO

Jardin
Botanica

CALLE DE SANTA ISABEL

0   yards   550
0   meters   500

original Gothic building one side-door remains, the first door facing the plaza. Down into the plaza, beside Los Lujanes, is the smaller **Hemeroteca**, Periodicals Library, an annex of the City Library, with a Gothic entrance and two Renaissance tombs inside the vestibule. In the center of the plaza a 19th century statue honors **Alvaro de Bazan**, one of the heros of the naval victory over the Turks at Lepanto. The attractive large building across the way is the present **Ayuntamiento** ★ (City Hall) designed in 1640 by de Mora, the architect of the Plaza Mayor, to serve as both the meeting place for the town council and a prison—certainly an interesting combination. It is open only on Mondays from 5 to 7 p.m. for free guided tours of tapestries and furniture (☎ 542 55 12).

Walk down the plaza to the building at the end, connected by an archway to the Ayuntamiento, but pass along its side opposite the archway. This building, called the **Casa de Cisneros** ★, was built in 1537 for the nephew of Jimmenes de Cisneros, Isabella's chief minister who became the regent of Spain for a time after her death. Now much restored, it retains one fine 16th-century window at the back overlooking the lovely Pl. del Cordón. Inside is an interesting collection of furniture and tapestries, although it too is open only on Monday evenings from 5-7 p.m. Across the plaza the carved cording surrounding the door of the large **Casa de los Alfaro** signifies that it once served as a bishopric.

Continue in the same direction through the plaza and along C. Cordón. Turn down the steps on the right just after the plaza. This lets you into the **Plazuela de San Javier** ★, an atmospheric corner of old Madrid. Return to the C. Cordón and continue as it bends left to cross the C. de Segovia. On the other side stands the **Iglesia San Pedro el Vieja** ★ with a soaring 14-century Mudejar (i.e., built by Moors) tower. Inside is an exuberant retablo by José Churriguera. Off the right side of the church, as you face it, runs the C. del Principe Anglona. Follow it one block to the Pl. de la Paja, turn left down the side of the plaza to the 16th-century **Capilla del Obispo** ★ (Chapel of the Bishop) at the end. Inside, illustrating the life of Christ, is a fine polychromed wood altarpiece by a talented pupil of Berruguette. In the south wall is a superb Plateresque alabaster tomb for the Archbishop of Plasencia. Carved by the same hand, the tombs of the archbishop's parents, who paid for the chapel, flank the altar. Behind the chapel building is another religious structure. The 15th-century **Capilla de San Andrés** was reconstructed in the 18th century to house the remains of Saint Isidro, the male patron saint of Madrid. St. Isidro's remains, however, have been moved to Cathedral San Isidro discussed below.

Walk past the Capilla Obispo up the west side of the charming Pl. de la Paja by the elegant restaurants, then turn left down C. Redondilla. At its end in two blocks you come into a large street named C. de Bailén. Head slightly leftward (not a hard left onto C. Don Pedro) to the huge neo-classical 18th-century church of **San Francisco el Grand** ★★, a project of Carlos III. Inside, behind a facade by the architect Sabatini, designer of the Palácio Real, under one of the largest domes in the world (over 100 feet in diameter), are, at the east end, 15th-century choirstalls taken from El Paular monastery north of Madrid. In the first chapel on the left is a master-work painting by the young Goya, *Sermon of San Bernardino to the King of Arágon.* Request that it be lit for you. The dome and chapel ceilings were frescoed by Bayeu, Goya's father-in-law, and others.

After viewing the inside, head up the Carrera San Francisco which leads away from the front of the church. Pass through Pl. Puerta de Moros directly across to Cava Alta, observing the front of Capilla San André along the way. When Cava Alta forks, go right, then take the first left which leads into C. Toledo. Across the street you see the **Catedral San Isidro** with its massive 17th-century facade and twin towers. The inside is not special (it was gutted in 1936), except for containing the remains of St. Isidro in a silver shrine. This is only a temporary cathedral, serving until the Cathedral de la Almundena beside the Palácio Real (see Walking Tour #2) is completed. (If you turn right onto C. Estudios, instead of left onto C. Toledo, it will lead, in two blocks, to the site of **el Rastro**, the famed Sunday-and holiday-morning flea market (open from dawn until 2 p.m.) Walk north on bustling C. Toledo past San Isidro to take the second left onto C. Concepción Jerónima, then the first right onto C. Conde de Romanones. In one block you enter the Pl. de la Provincia dominated by the red **Ministerio de Asuntos Exteriores** ★ (Ministry of Foreign Affairs). Originally built in 1629 by de Moro, the architect who constructed the Pl. Mayor, it is a dignified edifice with an elegant 17th-century cloister inside. The guard may let you peek in. Here newly-arrived foreign diplomats pull up in 17th-century carriages drawn by plumed horses to present their papers. The leftward street out of the plaza returns you to the Pl. Mayor.

2. PUERTA DEL SOL, DESCALZAS CONVENT, CONVENTO DE LA ENCARNACIÓN AND PL. DE ORIENTE ★ ★

This walk should consume less than two hours, including tours of the two convents and their art. It should be taken in the morning when the convents remain open longer than they do in the afternoon. Check hours and days above. The walk leaves you in front of the Palácio Real which, if you want to include it in the tour, would add two or three hours more (and run into the mid-afternoon closings), although it could also easily be included after a pause for lunch. See the description of the Palácio above to decide.

Puerta del Sol ★. *Subway: Puerta del Sol. Buses: 3, 25, 33, 39, M-4.*

In every sense this plaza is the hub of Madrid, even of the country. Crowds bustle at every hour of the day or night. North across the oval plaza is a small bronze statue of a bear and a strawberry plant, the emblem of Madrid. East, at the entrance of C. Alcalá, is the imposing Treasury Building, the former royal Customs House. The tower with the clock, Madrid's Big Ben, was added to the former 17th-century main post office, now the reconstructed Governación (Ministry of the Interior). On the sidewalk in front a bronze plaque marks kilometer zero, from which all distances in Spain are measured. Shops of a lower caliber do their best to attract. But at the east end of the plaza, at #6, the shop called **La Pajareta** must be seen. It has been selling caramels here for over 150 years. A few doors east at #12 a store called **Casa de Diego** displays an astonishing number of umbrellas along with some fans. The window display is for tourists, but antique versions are stored away inside.

Head to the west end of the plaza and take the left of the forking streets there onto C. Arenal. Take the next left, C. Victoria, walking toward the el Corte Inglés department store, but just before you reach it, take the first right onto C. de San Martin. In a short block you enter the small Pl. de las Descalzas, for you just walked the width of the convent on your right.

See the description and hours of the Convento de las Descalzas ★ ★ *under "Museums" above.*

Return to C. Arenal and continue west (right) for two short blocks to enter the Pl. Isabela II. Across the plaza is the back of the Teatro Real, Madrid's opera house. Walking toward the plaza and right along the theater's back, you come to C. Arrieta which leads in one short block to the Convento de la Encarnación on the left.

See the description and hours of the Convento de la Encarnación ★ *under "Museums" above.*

The street that fronts the Pl. de la Encarnación leading northeast is C. de la Bola, on which a bistro called **La Bola** *at number 5 offers moderately-priced meals, if you are feeling hungry.*

Head north along the side of the convent to C. Toria. At the end of the street you face an 18th-century mansion owned by Godoy, the Prime Minister of Carlos IV and lover of his queen Maria Louisa. Today, as the **Museo del Pueblo Español** ★, it houses an interesting collection of traditional costumes from all regions of Spain. Looking right up the street you see the **Palácio del Senado** (Senate Building). Formerly an Augustinian convent, it was converted to its present use at the beginning of this century. The Palácio seems small until one recalls that the Senate is a smaller group than the Parliament, which meets in a larger building.

From here, if you have the energy for a walk of about a mile, you can head left to C. Balién, then right as it leads over a pedestrian overpass, to view the monumental vista of the **Pl. de España** *with statues commemorating Cervantes and his famous characters Don Quixote and Sancho Panza. Continue to your left into Parque del Oeste for greenery and a look at the complete Egyptian* **Temple of Debod** ★, *from Roman times. It was brought in pieces from Egypt when threatened by the rising waters of the Aswan Dam.*

From the Senate head due south through the **Pl. de Oriente** to pass the front of the **Teatro Real**, inaugurated in 1850. It is appropriately luxurious inside. This plaza owes a debt to Joseph Buonaparte, Napoleon's brother, who ordered the buildings crowding the palace to be razed. In the center of the plaza is a fine statue by the sculptor Montañés of the art collector Felipe IV, copied from a Velázquez portrait. The statue seems more heroic than what the truer eye of Velázquez permitted in his version, but the king never looked finer.

Across the street is the huge **Palácio Real** ★★★. *For a description see "Museums" above.*

3. MUSEO ARQUEOLÓGICO NACIONAL AND SHOPPING: BARRIO SALAMANCA ★★

This walk takes you to the Archaeological Museum to view superb Iberian, Visigoth and Moorish works, then through the Barrio Salamanca, Madrid's most fashionable shopping area. Expect to spend half a day—or more, if a true shopper.

The **Archaeological Museum** ★★★ *is the rear half of the large Biblioteca Nacional. The entrance is on C. Serrano. By subway, from the Colón station head east across the Pl. Colón and you will see the front of the Biblioteca to your right. From the Serrano station head south along C. Serrano for one block to reach the museum.*

See the description and hours of the Museo Arqueológico under "Museums," above.

Barrio Salamanca ★★ North of the museum C. Serrano transforms into one of the main shopping streets in Madrid. One block north (left when exiting the museum), C. Goya crosses Serrano. The two streets form one corner of an area called the Barrio Salamanca, bordered by Serrano on the west, Goya on the south, Conde de Pañalver 10 short blocks east, and José Ortega four blocks north. The Barrio Salamanca contains most of the fine department, clothing, couture, antique, art and furniture shops of Madrid, with the western half, where you are standing, the most interesting. This area, one of the first urban developments, is named for the Marqués de Salamanca who, in 1865, laid out this grid of streets which, at the time, extended beyond the existing walls of Madrid.

Here is the layout of the Barrio. C. Serrano runs north-south. A short block east and parallel to Serrano is C. Claudio Coello. Smaller streets run between. The first two after Goya, Calles Hermosille and Ayala, are the most interesting. Wander as you will. Personal favorites follow:

Beginning a few blocks south of Goya on C. Serrano and walking north on C. Serrano, you come to:

#7: Farrutx. Fine designer shoes, its own brand and others.

#26: Loewe. The very finest in leather clothing, luggage and accessories, with prices to match. Many branches throughout Spain and the U.S.

#27: Carrera Y Carrera. Fine jewelry and watches.

#28: Orlan. Leather bags, wallets, and accessories, moderately priced.

#34: Afredo Caral. Designer fashion, superbly tailored.

C. de Jorge Juan is the street that crosses Serrano south of C. Goya. A couple of shops stand out on this street.

#10: Sybilla. Off an unmarked courtyard is this impressive Spanish designer's boutique with prices that are fair for the quality.

#13: Gaitan. Handmade shoes and boots.

On C. Goya, a couple of blocks east, are two leather places worth a look.

#68: Idee. Inexpensive shoes.

#75: Sara Navarro. A high fashion designer of leather clothes, shoes and bags.

Crossing C. Goya and continuing north on Serrano:

#44: Rossy. Good costume jewelry.

#45: La Casa de las Maletas. Well crafted luggage at reasonable prices.

#47: Galarias Preciados. The Barrio Salamanca branch of this Spanish department store chain.

#48: Del Pino. Expensive costume jewelry.

#56: Talleries de Arte Granada. Fine art and furniture.

#56: Santa. Superb chocolate in a beautiful store.

#57: Cartier.

#59: Nesofsky. Fine furniture.

#63: Gonzapur Peleteria. Leather clothing at moderate prices.

#66: Gutierez. Good shoes at reasonable prices.

#66: Breton. Elegant men's clothing.

#68: Los Pequeno Suizos. Good values in shoes and leathergoods.

#76: Manuel Herrero. Stylish leather.

#78: Cacherel.

#84: Fendi.

#92: Don Carlos. Boutique for the latest young styles.

#96-8: Adolfo Dominquez. Men's clothing by the designer who gave Don Johnson his look on *Miami Vice*.

Serrano crosses C. de José Ortega Y Gasset where, by going east, you can find **Vuitton** and **Courreges**, both at number 17.

4. PUERTA DEL SOL, PL. SANTA ANA, THE CORTES, AND PL. DE CIBELES ★

This walk is light on historical buildings, but ambles through quaint streets and by shops lost in time, then lets into a charming square and, past the Senate building, to the grand open vistas of the Paseo del Prado and the Pl. Cibeles. This characteristic and attractive area is the Madrid we think of when we are away. Unless you choose to view the art in the Real Academia de Bellas Artes, the walk can be made at a time when museums are closed.

> *Start in the Puerta del Sol* ★. *For directions and a description, see Walking Tour #2.*

At the east end of the plaza two major streets fork and head further east. Take the right one, Carrera de San Jerónimo. At San Jerónimo 2, note the shop called **Gil, Successor to Antolin Quevero**. The window is a classic— cheap fans mixed with the cheapest furs and Sevillano costumes. Better material is inside, but not by much. At number 8 you pass **Lhardy**, all mahogany wood and polished brass, here for over 150 years. If you can pass the delectable window display of food without entering, you have more will power than most. Incidentally, sandwiches and tapas will not break your budget, but the dinning room in the back is expensive. At number 9 elegance continues with **Vallanueva Y Laisca**, outside all marble and brass, inside refinement. They sell small silver replicas, fine jewelry, china and war medals. The shop is on the corner of Pl. de Canalejas. Turn right around the plaza to look in an amazing shop called **La Violeta**. Yes, that is all that is sold from this exquisite stall—candied violets.

Continue across the plaza on San Jerónimo. At number 11 is **Gutierrez** for designer shoes. At number 30 a block later is **Casa Miró**, another candy store over a century and a half old, this one specializing in hard candy. At 34 is **Deogracias** for cabinets decorated to Spanish tastes, which is not everyone's.

As the street gradually widens, its name changes to Pl. de las Cortes. The **Cortes**, Spain's Parliament, is housed on the north side of the plaza in a gray building with steps leading up to Corinthian columns. The building was constructed in 1859, and its bronze lions were cast from cannons captured in Morocco in 1850. Diagonally across from the Córtez is the **Palace Hotel**, one of Madrid's finest. On the street floor of the hotel, a spacious interior courtyard is surrounded by shops and contains an airy cafe for relaxing at its center.

Continue east to the end of San Jerónimo and cross to the other side. At 48, opposite the Palace Hotel, you reach **Abelardo Linares**, a mansion filled with some of the best antiques in Spain. In a few more feet enter the Pl. Canovas del Castillo, with its fountain and views up and down the wide Paseo del Prado. Looking south is the **Museo del Prado**; to the north, the distant, lovely fountain of the Pl. Cibeles, completed at the end of the 18th century and a wonder when lit at night.

Retrace your steps back to the small park opposite the Cortes building in which is located a once-influential private club, the **Ateneo de Madrid**. Here a small street called C. del Prado forks around the park. Numerous small and interesting antique shops line this street, a slice of old Madrid, so continue to follow it west. In five blocks the narrow street opens onto the green Pl. de Santa Ana, bounded on one side by the old Hotel Victoria. At the near end and left is the **Teatro Español**, whose productions are considered the best in Madrid.

Head north past the east side of the plaza along C. Principe. In one block you return to the Pl. Canalejas, where a left turn on San Jerónimo brings you back to the Puerta del Sol. To continue the tour, cross the plaza and head north on the large street called Sevilla, which, one block later, brings you to C. Alcalá, divided by a center strip.

At number 13, back west towards the Plaza del Sol, is the **Real Academia de Bellas Artes de San Fernando ★** in a late 19th-century building designed by Villanueva, who planned the Museo del Prado. For a description of the museum and hours, see "Museums" above. Turning around to go east on C. Alcalá we pass number 15, the **Casino de Madrid**, which is not a casino at all but a private club. The late 17th-century church on the corner of C. Sevilla, **Las Calatravas**, contains an interesting retablo.

Further along, the street widens as Gran Via joins it from the northwest. Gran Via was once a fine shopping street, but now tourists visit mainly for its huge McDonald's restaurant and for the telephone office opposite that stays open day and night. Continue past the imposing Banco de España building on the south side of Alcalá, to arrive, two blocks later, at the **Ministry of Defense**, set back in its park. The ministry occupies a former palace of Godoy, prime minister under Carlos IV and great and good friend of Carlos's queen, Maria Louisa. The fountain in the **Pl. de Cibeles ★★**, which you reach next, dates from 1780.

The fountain is as lovely as the splendid vistas stretching from it down Paseo del Prado to the Museum, and up Paseo de Recoletos, its continuation. Across the plaza and south is the pretentious Main Post Office, the Palácio de Comunicaciónes, built at the beginning of this century.

5. PARQUE EL RETIRO ★

This walk is just a stroll in the park, though summertime adds mimes, clowns, jugglers and assorted other entertainment. The huge park, encompassing more than 300 acres, was originally a royal hunting preserve that contained a palace for royal vacations. Today, dotted with exposition buildings, it is part careful landscaping and part wild bushes and trees. In all, it is a restful place to amble. Note: the park closes at dusk, for it is not safe after dark.

If flora appeal, the **Jardín Botánico** waits at the south end of the Prado. In season, the roses are spectacular. (Open daily 10 a.m. to 8 p.m.; admission: 80 ptas.)

Start at the **Museo del Prado** (directions in the "Museums" section above). Walk due east from its northern end, past the Casón Del Buen Retiro, and into the park. A map at this entrance shows where sights are located, but directions hardly matter if your intent is to wander. Straight ahead in a quarter mile is the **Palácio Velázquez**, an exhibition center. To its right is the **Palácio de Cristal**, named for its glass ceiling. To its north a lake for rowing fronts a monument to Alfonso XII, in pre-World War II monumental style. The statues of monarchs you pass were those made for the Palácio Real, but considered too heavy for its roof.

EXCURSIONS FROM MADRID

EL ESCORIAL ★★★★ AND VALLE DE LOS CAÍDOS ★

El Escorial stands among the great monuments in Spain. For descriptions and hours, see the "El Escorial" and "Valle de los Caídos" headings above. Both lie about 50 k from Madrid; travel and sightseeing will consume half a day.

> *Drive along C. Grand Via heading west. As it bends north it first becomes C. Princesa, then Av. Puerta de Hierro. Signs will direct you to N-VI, going northwest. At 16 k exit left onto C-505 to El Escorial in 28 k, as the signs direct.*

> *For directions to Valle de los Caídos, see the description of "El Escorial" in this chapter.*

EL PARDO ★★

This country palace only 13 k outside of Madrid is a more tasteful version of Madrid's Palácio Real, but also not as memorable. For a description and hours see the "El Pardo" heading in this chapter. Travel and sights will take up almost half a day.

> *Take C. Grand Via heading west. As it bends north it becomes C. Princesa, then Av. Puerta de Hierro. Bear to the right on C-601 for 13 k as it parallels the Manzanares River through scrub woods into the village of El Pardo.*

TOLEDO ★★★★★

For a description and hours of the sights see "Toledo" in this chapter. Travel and sights will consume a very full day.

> *Head down Paseo del Prado to the Pl. de Emperador Carlos V, where the Atocha train station is located. Drive through the plaza, past the train station, where four roads branch ahead. Take the second one from the right, which is the one directly ahead, called Paseo de Sta. Maria de la Cabeza. Signs will lead you to N 401 for Toledo, 70 k away.*

SEGOVIA ★★★★★, ÁVILA ★★★, COCA CASTLE ★★ AND SALAMANCA ★★★★

All can be reached in two or three hours by car. See the "Old Castile and Leon" chapter.

To leave Madrid, follow the directions to El Escorial, above, but continue north instead of exiting on C-505.

WHERE TO STAY

Madrid is an expensive place to sleep, whose few inexpensive rooms go quickly. Visitors generally have to increase their budget in this city. Many factors go into choosing a hotel, but proximity to the center is an asset, permitting the enjoyable pastime of walking to most sights and restaurants. With literally hundreds of hotels to choose from, there is little reason to stay anywhere but in the old town, near it, or close by in the Barrio Salamanca, where Madrid's elegant shops gather. A very select list covering each price range is below.

VERY EXPENSIVE ($200+)

Ritz   Deluxe ★★★★★

Pl. de la Lealtad, 5. Rooms: 158. ☎ *521 28 57; FAX 532 87 76; Telex 43986.* King Alfonso XIII personally oversaw the construction of the Ritz in 1910 because he considered no existing hotel suitable for the guests to his wedding. Here you actually feel like a guest of royalty, with the stiffness that implies (ties must be worn in the bar and eating areas), but with service that is noble. No two pastel-colored rooms are the same, but all are carpeted with rugs handmade in the Royal Tapestry Factory, include embroidered linen, and most dangle their own chandeliers. Naturally the Ritz' location is special—on its own park across from the Pl. Canovas del Castillo, the Palace Hotel and the Córtez building. From it you can hit the Museo del Prado with a stone, if so inclined. Such elegance costs a king's ransom, so estimate about $600 a night for two.

Palace   1st-class ★★★★

Pl. de las Cortes, 7. Rooms: 487. ☎ *429 75 51; FAX 429 82 66; Telex 23903.* Anywhere else this would be the most elegant hotel in town, but Madrid has the Ritz too. The lobby's all-glass cupola sets the stage for its *Belle Epoque* decor and trompe l'oeil paintings. The Palace's public rooms are sumptuous, but its bedrooms are less extraordinary and so numerous that, despite superb management, the special attention for each guest the prices call for is sometimes labored. The location is as good as the Ritz and the prices are about half, though the Palace is far better than half as good.

Villa Real   1st-class ★★★

Pl. de las Cortes, 10. Rooms: 115. ☎ *420 37 67; FAX 420 25 47; Telex 44 600.* Although designed to look 19th-century, this lovely hotel was built only a few years ago. Unlike so many fancy hotels that emphasize lobbies, this one concentrates on decorating its rooms with exquisite taste. Its location is as convenient as can be.

Villa Magna   Deluxe ★★★

Paseo Castellana, 22. Rooms: 182. ☎ *578 20 00; FAX 575 31 58; Telex 229 14.* Everything a modern hotel can provide is offered by the Villa Magna, but the elegance and atmosphere of an earlier era cannot be manufactured. For this reason it takes third place to the Ritz, whose elevated prices it matches, and the Palace. What it does offer is a good location for shopping in the Barrio Salamanca. The Hotel Wellington, however, described next, offers a similar location at a third the cost.

Wellington   1st-class ★★

Velázquez, 8. Rooms: 258. ☎ *575 44 00; FAX 576 41 64; Telex 22700.* This aristocrat is well located for Barrio Salamanca shopping, yet close to the Prado and the old town. The owner is a bullfight afficionado and matadors crowd here during the season. The establishment shows signs of fading, but retains an old-world feel.

EXPENSIVE ($100-$199)

G. H. Reina Victoria   1st-class ★★★

Pl. Santa Ana, 14. Rooms: 110. ☎ *531 45 00; FAX 522 03 07; Telex 475 47.* This Madrid institution overlooks the central and lovely Plaza Ana. Recently it was taken over by the Tryp chain which improved the service and modernized it throughout. Again, as in Hemingway's day, this is the place to stay in the old town (along with the Hotel Suecia, below). Comfortable, rather than fancy, with bright rooms at prices that are fair for Madrid.

Suecia   2nd-class ★★★

Marqués de Casa Ribera, 4 (Take the street going north along the west side of the Palácio Cortes on Carrera San Jerónimo. At the back, jag west, then north again, into the little square). Rooms: 128. ☎ *531 69 00; FAX 521 71 41; Telex 22313.* The location is almost as good as that of the Victoria—in the old town, yet on a tiny quiet square. But the Suecia is new and glistening, compared to the Victoria's seasoned personality, so the options are clear, with the Victoria costing a few pestetas less. In this category the Suecia's cleanliness, maintenance and service can not be bettered in Madrid.

Tryp Ambassador   1st-class ★★★

Cuesta de Santo Domingo, 5 (near the Palácio Real, 1 block north of the Opera). Rooms: 181. ☎ *541 67 00; FAX 559 10 40; Telex 49538.* This is a most pleasant addition to Madrid's hotel inventory. As its grand stairway attests, the Ambassador is a renovated former palace from the 19th century. Bedrooms all include separate sitting areas and are pleasantly accessorized. The location is quiet and convenient to sights.

Alcalá   1st-class ★★

Alcalá, 66. Rooms: 153. ☎ *435 10 60; FAX 435 11 05; Telex 48094.*
This is a modern, softly lit, "executive-type" hotel, located near the
northeast corner of el Retiro Park. It is convenient to shopping in the
Barrio Salamanca, but a bit of a walk to the Prado and the old town.

Arosa   1st-class ★★

De la Salud, 21. Rooms: 126. ☎ *532 16 00; FAX 531 31 27; Telex
43618.* Located just south of noisy Gran Via and two blocks west of
the large C. Montera, this hotel offers a quiet atmosphere, nicely decorated rooms and an attentive staff.

MODERATE ($50-$99)

Regina   2nd-class ★★

Alcalá, 19. Rooms: 142. ☎ *521 47 25; FAX 521 47 25; Telex 27500.*
Costing only a little more than the Inglés and Paris described below,
the Regina's location is as close to the Puerta del Sol as theirs, while
its rooms stand a clear cut above them.

Inglés   2nd-class ★

Echegaray, 8. Rooms: 58. ☎ *429 65 51; FAX 420 24 23.* Although its
location is wonderful, (just off C. Prado east of Puerto del Sol, near
the Prado and the Pl. Santa Ana in the old town), and despite its offering parking (which is unusual for the area), service at the Inglés is
lackadaisical, uninterested, and even rude, and its rooms, some of
which are not air conditioned, are strangely shaped and gloomy. Even
though rooms can be large, at close to a hundred dollars a night,
they're no bargain.

París   3rd-class ★

Alcalá, 2. Rooms: 114. ☎ *521 64 96; Telex 43448.* Although superbly
located at the east edge of the Puerta del Sol, with a lobby framed in
old wood, this is a dowager of a hotel. As with the Inglés, the rooms
here are eccentric in shape and decor. The idea that a hotel room
should be bright and cheery, yet restful, seems to have faded along
with this hotel's freshness.

INEXPENSIVE (UNDER $50)

Hostale Lisboa   Hs2nd-class ★★

*C. Ventura de la Vega, 17 (just off C. del Prado, near the Victoria in Pl.
Santa Ana). Rooms: 22.* ☎ *429 98 94.* No frills, just a room to sleep in,
but the rooms are larger than the low price would indicate, and boast
new private bathrooms. The location is superb. True, the hallways and
public areas are low-wattage and the rooms sparsely and unfashionably
furnished but, for the price, one cannot do better in Madrid—and
they accept credit cards.

Mónaco   R3rd-class ★

*Barbieri, 5 (Go west on Gran Via, after its start at the intersection with C.
Alcalá, then take a right onto C. Hugo in one block. After two very short*

blocks on Hugo, jag left on C. Infantas, and take the immediate right onto Berbieri). Rooms: 32. ☎ 522 46 30; FAX 521 16 01. This one is a bit out of the way, slightly north of Gran Via. The hotel is decorated in bright red, giving it an Egyptian look (or worse). Rooms are small, but do have private baths. The neighborhood is replete with disco clubs and its strollers seem less amicable than those on the other side of Gran Via.

For a tight budget, there are numerous pensiones for $30 and under on the upper floors of the houses on **C. del Prado**, and the small streets that lead away from it. A number of short streets in the area house as many as 10 separate pensiones. For example, at C. Echegaray, 5 (across from the hotel Iglés, noted above) there are four pensiones on various floors, each of which are very inexpensive and may suit.

Your range of choices can be expanded greatly if the requirement of sleeping within walking-distance of the sights is dropped. Near the southern Legazpi subway station, the **Hostal Auto** ★ at Paseo de la Chopera, 69 (☎ 539 66 00; FAX 530 67 03) is a good moderate-inexpensive choice with parking. Near the northwestern Arguelles station, the **Hotel Tirol** ★★ on Marqués de Urquijo, 4 (☎ 548 19 00) is a fine moderately-priced pick.

In a pinch the centrally-located and moderately-priced **Moderno** on Arenal, 2 (☎ 531 09 00; FAX 531 35 50), just past the west end of the Puerta del sol, will serve. Also centrally located and moderate in price is the **Madrid**, with 72 rooms at Carretas 10, two blocks south of the Puerta del Sol (☎ 521 65 20; Telex 43142. Lower in price and ambiance is the **Fontela** at Gran Via, 11 on the third floor (☎ 521 64 00). Similar, though larger, is the **Persal** at Pl. del Angel, 12 on the second floor (☎ 230 31 08; Telex 23261), on the same square as the Hotel Victoria.

WHERE TO EAT

You can eat in Madrid for whatever you care to spend, although of course the food generally improves as the price rises. The specialties of the city are roast pig and lamb, and seafood. Below we list our favorites in various price categories, but you can also do as the Madrileños do—stroll C. del Prado (which heads west from the Pl. de las Cortes) and amble up and down its adjacent side streets until you find a place that strikes your fancy for tapas at the bar. Later, if you like what you nibbled, you can move back into the dining room for a meal.

EXPENSIVE ($50+)

Zalacaín   ★★★★★

Álvarez de Baena, 4 (north, near the Museo de Cientas Naturales). ☎ 561 48 40; FAX 561 47 32. Closed Saturday lunch, Sunday, Holy Week and August. By all standards Zalacaín is the finest restaurant in Madrid, if not all of Spain. Even the Francophilic Michelin Red Guide awards this restaurant its highest rating. The decor is dark, elegant and comfortable, like a Velázquez painting. Every attention is focused on what is arranged on each china plate, and what lays on it will taste sublime. Try the ravioli with setas, truffles and fois gras, or *bacalao tellagom*, or duck. Or for a sampling of the best, try the *Menu Degustacion*. This is a restaurant for serious connoisseurs who don't mind spending over $100 per person to enjoy an exquisite dining experience. Reservations weeks in advance are essential. *Amex, Visa and Diners Club accepted.*

El Cenador del Prado   ★★★★

C. del Prado, 4 (just off Pl. del las Cortes).☎ *429 15 61. Closed Saturday lunch, Sunday, and the first half of August.* This restaurant continually improves, and is now as elegant as any restaurant in the country. Appropriately light and airy as a garden patio, this is the home of Spanish *cocina nueva*, with a menu that changes as frequently as the chef receives inspiration. If *patatas a la importancia con almajas* (potatoes with clams) is on the menu, by all means give it strong consideration. The banana ice cream is equally outstanding. Reservations are a must.   *Amex, Visa, Diners and MasterCard accepted.*

Bidasao   ★★★

Claudio Coello, 24 (in the Barrio Salamanca) ☎ *431 20 81. Closed Saturday, Sunday, and August.* The Spanish agree that Basque cooking is the best in Spain, and Bidasao is the best Basque restaurant in Madrid. The decor of its dining rooms is modern and a little too brightly lit for our tastes, but the service is impeccable and the food first rate. Reservations advised.   *Amex, Diners, MasterCard and Visa accepted.*

Café de Oriente   ★★★

Pl. de Oriente, 2 (facing the Palácio Real).☎ *241 39 74. Closed Saturday for lunch, Sunday, and August.* The decor is glittering *Belle Époque*, the building and brick ovens date to the 18th century and the view of the palace from a terrace chair (aperitif in hand) is spectacular at night. Two dining rooms wait in the back, one for Castilian food, exceptionally prepared, the other for more elegant and expensive Basque cooking.   *All major credit cards accepted.*

Saint James   ★★

C. Juan Bravo, 12 (two blocks north of Ortega y Gasset at the north end of the Barrio Salamanca). ☎ *575 00 69. Closed Sunday.* If you crave paella, it is available at many Madrid restaurants, but this is where they do it best, along with many other Valencian rice dishes. The garden in summer is inviting, the dining room is olive drab. Prices reach the low end of expensive. Reservations are required.   *Amex accepted.*

MODERATE ($20-$50)

El Pescador   ★★★

José Ortega y Gasset, 75 (the northern limit of the Barrio Salamanca). ☎ *402 19 90. Closed Sunday, and August.* Seafood is expensive and this is perhaps the best seafood restaurant in town, so its prices must be considered fair. The decor is seafaring, with checkered tablecloths, and the food incredibly fresh. The owner is from Galicia where they know how to cook a fish. Try the *crema tres eles* (if you have never tried eels) or the *salpicon*. Lobster, though delicious, will lift you out of the moderate price category. Reservations are advised.

Visa and MasterCard accepted.

Casa Gallega

Pl. San Miguel, 8 (off C. Mayor between the Pl. Mayor and Pl. de la Villa). ☎ *547 30 55.* This is el Pescador's seafood rival. Also Galician, with a more elegant decor, its seafood seems only minutes removed from the sea. Simply-prepared things are best, and can be sublime.

Amex and Visa cards accepted.

Gure-Etxea

Pl. De La Paja, 12 (south of the Pl. de la Villa, as described in Walking Tour #2). ☎ *365 61 49. Closed Sunday, Holy Week, and August.* Here is the mecca for classic Basque cuisine, unmodified by nouvelle flair as at Restaurante Bidasao. Try a Basque staple like *baclao pil pil*, or a specialty such as *merluz Gure-Etxea*. Reservations are suggested for the airier upstairs dining room, more pleasant than downstairs.

Amex, Visa and Diners accepted.

Botín

C. Cuchilleros, 17 (out the southwest corner of the Pl. Mayor and down stairs). ☎ *266 42 17.* According to *Guinness Book of World's Records* Botín, in continuous operation since 1725, is the oldest restaurant in the world. Its specialties are roast suckling pig (*cochinillo*) and baby lamb (*cordero asado*), cooked in ancient wood ovens (*hornos*). One or the other is always on the Menu del Dia, and a price-saving when ordered that way. The decor is rough-hewn wood beams and floors. Be warned: although the roasts are first-rate, this is a tourist favorite—we could do without the crowds and the roving musicians. Reserve, or be prepared to wait in line for up to an hour.

All major credit cards accepted.

La Bola

C. de la Bola, 5 (off the Pl. de Oriente, near the Palácio Real, as explained in Walking Tour #1). ☎ *547 69 30. Closed Saturday night and Sunday in high summer.* Bola is quiet and cozy, with small dining areas and good Madrileño food, which means that *cocida Madrileño*, a stew of meat and chickpeas, is the specialty. ***No credit cards accepted.***

Hylogui

C. Ventura de la Vega, 3 (off C. de San Jerónimo, four blocks east of Puerta del Sol) ☎ *429 73 57. Closed Sunday evening, and August.* This Madrid institution contains a series of dining rooms that extend on and on, but the food is authentic Castilian and well prepared. The crowds would not come if the food were not first rate—this is the place to sample earthy Castilian cuisine. ***No credit cards accepted.***

Le Chateaubriand ★

C. Virgen de los Peligros, 1 (a large street off C. Alcalá, two blocks east of

Puerta del Sol). ☎ *532 33 41. Closed Sunday and holidays.* All dark wood and polished brass as in a typical brasserie, this restaurant bills itself as French, although it is known more for good steaks properly done.   ***Amex and Visa accepted.***

INEXPENSIVE (UNDER $20)

Luarques   ★

C. Ventura de la Vega, 16 (off C. de San Jerónimo, four blocks east of Puerta del Sol) ☎ *429 61 74. Closed Sunday night, Monday, and August.* This is the place for hearty, "peasant" fare. Beans (*fada*) are the specialties. The owners are Asturians who decorate their crowded dining room with rustic farm implements from home. Good value for the money makes this a popular place, sometimes with long waits. (But C. Ventura de la Vega bids to be the most interesting restaurant street in Madrid, and if the wait is too long at Luarques, you can move to Hylogui, described above, or to Assado or Geoymar, described below.)   ***No reservations or credit cards accepted.***

Assado   ★

C. Ventura de la Vega, 12 (off C. de San Jerónimo, four blocks east of Puerta del Sol). Even ordering the partridge will not damage your budget, and salmon or the small entrecote will leave it most healthy.
No reservations or credit cards accepted.

Geoymar

C. Ventura de la Vega, 11 (off C. de San Jerónimo, four blocks east of Puerta del Sol). Pleasantly decorated, Geoymar provides various *menus del dia* in many price ranges, starting at 1000 pesetas. All are reasonable for what they deliver.

Las Gabrieles

C. Echegaray, 17 (the next street east of Ventura de la Vega). Magnificent tiles make this bar-restaurant a feast for the eyes. The food is tastefully prepared.

McDonald's outlets are at Puerta del Sol and on Gran Via at C. Montera.

SHOPPING

The best purchases in Madrid are leather goods, including shoes, along with antiques, and men's and women's high fashion clothing. Mammoth sales are held during the second week of January and from late July through the middle of August.

LEATHER

The best quality leather clothes and accessories are undoubtedly sold by the famous Spanish firm of **Loewe**. Prices are extravagant, but the quality is superb. Note that Barcelona offers similar quality for lower prices, but that you do not save much at either location over the prices of the Loewe branch in New York. The firm maintains outlets in the best hotels but their most complete shops are at C. Serrano 26 and, for men, Serrano 34, in the

Barrio Salamanca. Less expensive and with a huge selection is **Lepanto** at Pl. de Oriente, 3 across from the Palácio Real. For high fashion shoes, **Farrutx** is a good bet on C. Serrano, 7, just south of the Museo Arqueológico. **Gutierrez** on C. Serrano, 66 has moderate prices, at a step down in quality. For good luggage try **La Casa de las Meletas** on Claudio Coello, 45 in the Barrio Salamanca.

ANTIQUES

Two of Madrid's finest antique establishments are located on either side of the Cortes building in the Pl. de la Cortes. **Gallarias San Agustin** is at San Agustin, 3 which branches off from the plaza, and **Abelardo Linares** stands at San Jerónimo 48, just west. Prices are high, but looking is free. **C. del Prado** leading off from the Pl. de las Cortes is a street filled with antique stores, some with reasonable prices. And around the el Rastro flea market numerous stores sell antiques. At 12 Ribera de Curtidores, in the heart of the market, are **Gonzalves** for brass and **José Maria del Rey** for fine antiques. At 15 is **Galería de Antiguedades**, an antique center, and at 27 is **Regalos Molina**, for ceramics (closed, for some reason on Sunday, the day that the market is held).

JEWELRY

For fine *jewelry*, try **Carrera y Carrera** at Serrano, 27, and **Del Pino** at Serrano, 48 for costume pieces. *Silver* is luscious at **Lopez**, C. del Prado, 3, and **Villanueva y Laiseca** nearby at Carrera de San Jerónimo, 9.

CRAFTS

For *crafts* the place to look is in the elegant state-owned **ArtEspaña**, which has a fine outlet at Pl. de las Cortes, 3. Prices are not low, but the finest work from all over Spain is collected under one roof. For fans and umbrellas the place is **Casa de Diego** in the Puerta del Sol at 12.

The two best shops for *ceramics* are **Antiqua Casa Talavera** (☎ 247 34 17) at Isabel la Católica, 2, just north of the Pl. Santo Domingo, a subway stop two blocks northeast of the Pl. del Oriente, and **Regalos Molina** in el Rastro at Ribera de Curtidores 27. (Ceramics prices, however, are better in Seville.)

Fine *engravings* from original plates by Goya and other great artists are sold at the **Instituto de Calcografía** in the Academia de Bellas Artes de San Fernando at Alcalá 13.

DEPARTMENT STORES

Spain has two large *department store chains*, both well represented by their Madrid branches. **El Corte Inglés** is the higher in quality of the two. Its largest store is off the Puerta del Sol on C. Preciados, another branch is in the Barrio Salamanca, at the corner of Calles Goya and Alcalá. **Galarias Preciados** can cost less and has a branch near the El Corte Inglés on C. Gran Via near the Puerta del Sol. Both chains offer English interpreters and a 10 percent discount for tourists on every purchase made, in lieu of waiting for refunds of the IVA tax.

No Madrid shopping experience would be complete without a trip to the flea market, **El Rastro**, which takes place every Sunday. The stalls set up at about 9:30 a.m., the surrounding shops open at 11 a.m. and the whole area closes at 2 p.m. It is located along the wide street Ribera de Curtidores which runs due south four blocks below the Pl. Mayor. You can take the subway to La Latina, walk a short block east, then south. The stalls in the streets mainly offer junk, but the fun is in the looking, and in the possibility of discovering a personal treasure. Stores lining both sides of the street carry generally better merchandise. Bargaining is expected, both at the stalls and in the stores, so do not assume the price quoted is the one you must pay. Watch your wallet or purse. On days of the week other than Sunday the true stores, as opposed to the street stalls, are open for more relaxed shopping.

NIGHTLIFE

Surprising for such a large and late-night city, Madrid does not offer much in the way of nightclubs and their ilk. The best flamenco in Madrid is: **El Andalus**, at Capitan Haya, 19 (☎ 556 14 39), **Café de Chinitas**, at Torija, 7 (☎ 248 51 35), and **Corral de la Pacheca** at Juan Ramon Jimenez, 26 (☎ 458 26 72). But Madrid's flamenco is not as good, and overpriced, in comparison to that in Seville. **La Scala Melia**, in the Melia Castilla Hotel, presents a Moulin-Rouge type review including topless "statues" at Rosario Piño, 7 (☎ 571 44 11). The dancing clubs in Madrid are small and tame. If you want to sample them, follow your ear through the maze of streets north of Gran Via.

The true night life of Madrid, as in most Spanish cities, consists of the evening *paseo*, and tapas bar hopping. Crowds gather at dusk to wander through the old town until after midnight, popping into whatever place a convivial-looking group has assembled. The object is not to get drunk, but to socialize and mingle. To join in, walk down C. del Prado or any adjacent side street.

SPORTS

BULLFIGHTING

Aficionados argue about which cities in Spain present the best bullfights, but most would settle on Madrid or Seville. In Madrid the season runs from April through the beginning of November, on every Sunday afternoon, but on every day during the 3-week festival of Saint Isidro in May. Tickets can be purchased at the **Las Ventas** ring at C. Alcalá, 231 (Subway: Las Ventas), or through an agency at C. Victoria, 3, off the Puerta del Sol, or through the concierge at most hotels. Tickets are always hard to find and are scalped for huge premiums during the 3-week Saint Isidro festival when the best matadors come to town.

SOCCER

The Spanish appreciate bullfighting, but they are crazy about soccer (*futbol*). Madrid fields two rival teams, but the best is usually Real Madrid whose games are played in the huge (130,000 seats) **Santiago Bernabeu Stadium** at Paseo de Castellana, 140 (Subway: Lima). Agencies in major department stores sell tickets.

DIRECTORY

AIRPORT • ☎ 411 25 45 for departures, 205 43 72 for arrivals. Barajas Airport is 12 k east of Madrid's center, not far removed for such a large city. A taxi into town costs about 2000 ptas. Alternatively, an airport bus costs 275 ptas., and leaves every 15 minutes or so, to and from the centrally located Pl. Colón, where taxis wait to carry you to your hotel. The bus stops under the plaza. Branches of Iberia dot the city, but the main office is at Pl. de Canovas, 4 (Metro: Atocha) (☎ 585 85 85).

TRAINS • RENFE's main ticket office is at C. Alcalá, 44; (☎ 429 05 18); Metro: Banco de España. Madrid has three major train stations whose service overlaps. The largest is **Chamartín** Station, located in northern Madrid (Metro: Chamartín). It serves the north and east, including France, but not Galicia (☎ 733 11 22). **Atocha** Station is located three long blocks south of the Prado (Metro: Atocha). It primarily serves the south, but also Extremadura, Portugal, and nearby northern cities, such as Ávila and Segovia ☎ 228 52 37). **Norte** Station (Metro: Norte) serves Galicia and Salamanca, but also some nearby cities to the north (☎ 248 87 16). RENFE can be called at ☎ 530 02 02 for information on all trains.

BUSES • The bus situation is complex, since eight separate stations house several times that number of independent bus companies. Try the Office of Tourism for information, or the largest of the eight stations, **Estación del Sur de Autobuses** on Av. de Canarias, 17 (☎ 468 42 00: Metro: Palos de Moguer). Generally bus fares are incredibly low by U.S. standards—for example, a round trip between Madrid and Barcelona costs in the neighborhood of $40—and only a tireless professional driver could better the 8-hour time.

DRIVING INTO MADRID • Unless your hotel is in the area between the Palácio Real and the Prado, where streets are narrow, driving should not be difficult.

From the south by **A-4 (E-5)**, the highway turns into Av. de Andalucia inside Madrid. Choose between continuing on M-30 (Av. de la Paz), which you should take if going to the east or north of the center of town, exiting on to Av. de Córdoba for the center. If aiming for the center, it is best to turn right to Pl. Arganzuela, continue straight across the plaza, and up the one-way Paseo de las Delicias which brings you into the large Pl. de Emperador Carlos V. The Atocha train station is located here. Take a true left up C. Atocha, for the area of the old town, or a less extreme left on the Paseo del Prado for beyond.

From the southwest on **A-5 (E-90)** it is straight sailing along the Av. de Portugal until signs for "Estacion del Norte." Continue after the signs to Puerta Florida, then turn right on Cuesta de San Vincente to Gran Via, then left toward the center of town.

It is straight as an arrow from the northwest on **A-6,** except that street names change as you go deeper into Madrid. A-6 is called Av. Puerta de Hierro, which changes its name to C. Princesa, then becomes Gran Via.

From the north **A-1 (E-5)** is called Av. de la Paz (also known as M-30) as it enters Madrid. Turn right on C. Alcalá just past the Plaza de Toros (bullring)—signs might say "Puente de las Ventas." Stay on Alcalá as it passes alongside el Retiro Park to end at the Pl. Puerta de Alcalá. Continue straight across on Alcalá for the center of town, or take the first left, which is C. Serrano, for the Barrio Salamanca.

From the east and the airport **N-II (E-90)** becomes **A-2,** and is called Av. de América in Madrid. Where Costa Francisco Silvela crosses, Av. de América ends. Continue on the same street, now called C. Maria de Molina. It enters a large circle, the Pl. del Dr. Manañón. Turn left here on Paseo de la Castellaña, a huge multi-laned street, for both the Barrio Salamanca and the center of town.

N-III, from the southeast, changes its name to Av. del Mediterraneo in Madrid. It changes its name again on the other side of Pl. Manero de Cavia to Paseo de la Reina Cristina, then changes its name to Paseo de la Infanta Isabel as it bends right to enter the large Pl. del Emperador Carlos V. Take the second left up Paseo del Prado, the multi-laned street, for the Barrio Salamanca, or take the street straight across, C. Atocha, for the center of town.

TRAVEL IN MADRID • Taxis are reasonable. The meter starts at 140 pesetas, then adds 65 pesetas each kilometer, although there is a surcharge of 150 pesetas at night or on holidays. Most trips from one sight to another will cost $4 or less. Taxis are white (though some are black) with a red stripe on the side. They can be flagged on the street or be found waiting at taxi stands near sights or large hotels.

Buses, though numerous and inexpensive, are slow and require exact change. The fare currently is 115 pesetas. A sign at each stop lists the numbers of those buses that pick up there.

The subway (*Metro*) is frequent, clean and quick. It does close at 1:30 a.m., however. The fare is 115 pesetas, though a 10 ride *billete del diez* cuts that in half. The various lines are designated by the end station on their route. Note that stations close at 1:30 p.m

INFORMATION • Not centrally located, the Office of Tourism is north of the Pl. de España in the Torre Madrid Building at 1, C. Princesa (see Walking Tour #3). Open weekdays 9 a.m. to 7 p.m., Saturdy from 9:30 a.m. to 1:30 p.m. (☎ 541 23 25). Another office is located in

Barajas Airport, where, if needed, attendants will provide help in finding a hotel. An office of the City of Madrid is located at Pl. Mayor, 3, but stocks little information.

CITY TOURS • The following companies provide bus tours of the sights of Madrid: **Julia Tours,** C. Captain Haya, 38 (☎ 270 43 00); **Pullmantur**, Pl. de Oriente, 8 (☎ 241 18 05); **Trapsatur**, C. San Bernardo, 23 (☎ 241 63 20). Brochures are available at most hotel desks.

EMERGENCIES

Police • in the Puerto del Sol (☎ 221 65 16; emergency: 091)

Ambulance • ☎ 734 35 00, or 230 71 45)

English speaking doctors • (☎ 431 22 29)

POST OFFICE AND TELEPHONES • Madrid's main post office is located in the Pl. Cibeles and open weekdays from 9 a.m. to 10 p.m.; Sundays from 10 a.m. to 1 p.m.; and Saturdays until 8 p.m. The Telefonica on Gran Via 28 (opposite McDonald's) is open 24 hours every day. Long-distance calls are up to 50% cheaper here than those made from hotel phones.

ADDRESSES

American Express • Pl. de las Cortes, 2 (☎ 332 50 50)

Books in English:

Turner's English Bookstore, Genova, 3 (which runs west of the Pl. Colón, near the Archaeology Museum; ☎ 319 09 26)

Washington Irving Center, Marquês de Villamagna, 8 (☎ 435 70 95), American library open Mon.-Fri. 2-6 p.m.

Car Rental Companies:

ATESA: Castellana, 243 (☎ 315 13 49)

Avis: Gran Via, 60 (☎ 247 20 48) and Paseo de la Castellana, 57 (☎ 441 05 79)

Europcar: C. Orense, 29 (☎ 445 99 30)

Hertz: Gran Via, 88 (☎ 242 10 00) and C. Doctor Fleming, 46 (☎ 457 17 72)

Embassies:

United States: Serrano, 75 (☎ 576 34 00)

Canada: Núñez de Balboa, 35 (☎ 431 43 00)

El PARDO ★★

From **Madrid** *Gran Via heads west, bends northwest and changes its name to Calle Princesa, then changes its name*

again to Avenida Puerta de Hierro. Follow signs to A-6.
Just past the University, a right fork onto C-601, leads in
13 k. to El Pardo.

This is an older, more attractive palace than those in Madrid or
Aranjuez. Half a day is plenty of time to see it and the other sights of
interest as well.

For centuries the woods around El Pardo formed a royal hunting
preserve that provided convenient outings for Spanish kings "working" in Madrid. In fact, the original building on the site was a hunting lodge built for Enrique III in 1405, before Madrid even became
the capital. After designating Madrid as his capital, Felipe II replaced
the lodge with a palace and furnished it with fine art, which rather
changed the hunt atmosphere. Fire, the scourge of so many palaces,
later burned down half of it. Since the fire occurred in 1604, however, much earlier than similar conflagrations in Madrid and Aranjuez,
its latest—present—rebuilding dates to the time of Felipe III. Thus
this is a Hapsburg structure, with Bourbon additions, as compared
to the Bourbon palaces of Madrid and Aranjuez. Still, its furnishings
are to Bourbon tastes. Today, the palace is sometimes used to enter-
tain visiting dignitaries. The residence of the present king, Juan Carlos, is nearby.

Palácio del Pardo
Open Mon.-Sat. from 10 a.m. to 1 p.m., and 4-7 p.m. (opening and closing
an hour earlier winter afternoons). Closed Sun. Admission: 350 ptas., by
guided tour only. The "Chinese" room and those with neo-classical
furniture are the most interesting. Fine Sèvres porcelain and clocks are
scattered throughout. Some of the ceiling frescos and stuccowork is
notable, and a huge collection of tapestries hangs on the walls, many,
including designs by Goya, from the Spanish Royal Tapestry Factory.

Casita del Principe
Same hours as the palace. Admission: 100 ptas. This is a twin to a similar
building in El Escorial. It too was designed by Villanueva, the architect of the Museo del Prado, for the same prince who would become
King Carlos IV. The rooms are tiny, which only intensifies the impact
of their rich decoration and furniture. The dining room is a particular
favorite. Some pleasing pastels by Tiepolo and some paintings by
Mengs adorn the walls.

Note:...The Convento de Capuchinos, on a hill to the west, contains a masterpiece of polychrome wood carving by Fernandez, and two Ribera
paintings.

SIGÜENZA ★★★

Population 6,656
Area code: 911; zip code: 19250

104 k from Madrid. Head west from Madrid toward Barajas Airport, on A2 (E90) which becomes N-II (E90), in the direction of Zaragoza. In 56 k comes Guadalajara. 48 k further, a turn left onto C-204 (there is a sign), enters Sigüenza after 26 k of winding road.

This lovely hilltop town of Renaissance houses boasts a fascinating cathedral containing a masterpiece of sculpture, and an imposing medieval fortress (now a parador) built for its bishops.

Calle de Medina leads uphill to the cathedral. Construction began on this Gothic church in 1150, although by the following century it required repairs which were not completed—in the form seen today —until the end of the 15th century. Inside, the original Cistercian shape is rather simple, while the fortress-like exterior is a mixture of all the forms that Gothic architecture passed through—but with a French feel, for the early archbishops came from there.

Cathedral ★★★

Opened by the sacristan from 11 a.m. until 2 p.m. and 4-8 p.m. (6 p.m. in winter). Apply at the Sacristy at the rear of the cathedral. Admission: 200 ptas. The sense of strength conveyed by the cathedral's exterior is continued inside by high vaulting on massive pillars. Down the left side is a lovely doorway surrounded by painted Renaissance pilasters and Mudejar designs. The adjoining chapel contains a 15th-century triptych. A jasper doorway leads to a marbled late Gothic cloister with intricate Plateresque doors, and a collection of Flemish tapestries located in a room off the north corner. Back in the church proper, after the door to the cloister, is a side altar designed by Covarrubias for Saint Librada and her eight sisters, all born on the same day, according to legend, and all martyred together. Next comes the sepulchre of Dom Fadrique of Portugal, one of the earliest examples of the Plateresque style. As the ambulatory begins, a door on the left leads into the sacristy, also designed by Covarrubias, with an astonishing painted and sculpted ceiling of thousands of staring cherubim.

Around the south side of the ambulatory, in the Doncel Chapel, waits the star of the cathedral. Don Martin de Arca was a page (*doncel*) to Isabella and died in the Granada wars. His queen commissioned this sepulcher, in the early Isabeline style, of a youth relaxed and reading. It is unlike any similar work in Spain in seeming so alive. Don Martin's parents lie in a mausoleum in the center of the chapel.

Docesan Museum ★

Open Tues.-Sun. from 11:30 a.m. to 2 p.m., and from 5-7 p.m. (During Jan. and Feb. open only Sun. and holidays). Admission: 100 ptas The museum is located in a building across from the west side of the cathedral. It contains prehistoric pieces, a collection of crucifixes, an El Greco, and a superb Zurbarán of Mary floating above Seville—alone worth the price of admission.

The Plaza Mayor ★ in front of the cathedral is surrounded by late 15th- and early 16th-century porticos and balconies. The Ayuntamiento (city hall), from 1512, is located on the south side. Calle Mayor heads steeply up to the castle from the plaza.

Looking just as a fortress should (if you ignore the windows peering through what should be solid walls), the **castle** ★, which was erected in the 12th century to protect the archbishop of Sigüenza, was renovated in the 14th. For a time it served as a prison for the wife of Pedro the Cruel because he had fallen in love with another woman while his wife-to-be was enroute to their wedding. It was too late to call off the ceremony, so Pedro went through with it, then imprisoned his new wife here. Now it is a parador, which explains its incongruous windows.

WHERE TO STAY

Parador Nacional Castillo de Sigüenza   1st-class ★ ★ ★ ★

Plaza del Castillo. Rooms: 77. ☎ *39 01 00; FAX 39 13 64; Telex 22517.* There is not a more authentically remodeled parador in Spain. Though expensive, the price is fair considering how seldom one can stay stay in a castle in which a queen was once imprisoned. The bedrooms are lovely, and some include canopied beds.

TOLEDO ★ ★ ★ ★ ★

Population 57,769
Area code: 925; zip code: 45000

*From **Madrid**, take Paseo del Prado to its southern end at the Plaza del Emperador Carlos V. Across the plaza take Paseo de Sta. Maria de la Cabeza, the middle of three branching streets. It becomes N-401 which reaches Toledo in 71 k.*

*From **Seville**, take N-IV (E5) east toward Córdoba. Continue through Córdoba, Bailén, and Valdepeñas to Madridejos (in 286 k) where you exit for C-400 to Toledo for 70 k, a total trip of 346 k.*

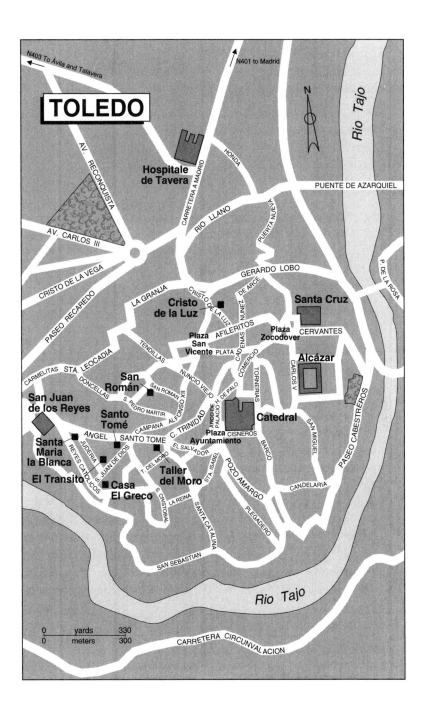

TOLEDO

N403 To Ávila and Talavera

N401 to Madrid

N

Rio Tajo

AV. RECONQUISTA

Hospitale de Tavera

HONDA

CARRETERA A MADRID

PUENTE DE AZARQUIEL

AV. CARLOS III

RIO LLANO

PUERTA NUEVA

P. DE LA ROSA

CRISTO DE LA VEGA

PASEO RECAREDO

LA GRANJA

GERARDO LOBO

DE ARCE

Cristo de la Luz

CRISTO DE LA LUZ

CADENAS NUNEZ

Santa Cruz

CERVANTES

Plaza Zocodover

TENDILLAS

Plaza San Vicente

AFILERITOS

PLATA

COMERCIO

Alcázar

CARMELITAS

STA. LEOCADIA

DONCELLAS

NUNCIO VIEJO

CARLOS V

TORNERIAS

San Román

SAN ROMAN XII

S. PEDRO MARTIR

ALFONSO XII

C. DE PALO

ARCO DE PALACIO

SAN MIGUEL

San Juan de los Reyes

Santo Tomé

CAMPANA

C. TRINIDAD

Catedral

PASEO CABESTREROS

ANGEL

SANTO TOME

Plaza Ayuntamiento

CISNEROS

Santa Maria la Blanca

REYES CATOLICOS

JUDERIA

S. JUAN DE DIOS

EL SALVADOR

BARCO

El Transito

T. DEL MORO

Taller del Moro

STA. ISABEL

POZO AMARGO

CANDELARIA

Casa El Greco

S. CRISTOBAL

LA REINA

SANTA CATALINA

PLEGADERO

SAN SEBASTIAN

Rio Tajo

| 0 | yards | 330 |
| 0 | meters | 300 |

CARRETERA CIRCUNVALACION

Toledo rises like Gibraltar from the plains of La Mancha, its peak formed by cathedral spires and the turrets of the Alcázar. The sight is unforgettable. Over millennia the river Tagus dug a ravine around three sides of Toledo, leaving the hard bluff on which the city is situated rising high above. Geography prevented the city from expanding, concentrating its treasures atop one steep hill.

The Romans were the first to appreciate the importance of Toledo's site. In 192 B.C. they fortified the hill and founded a town they called *Toletum*, from which the present name derives. In turn the Visigoths made Toledo the capital from which they ruled Spain. When the Moors invaded in 711, they aimed straight for Toledo and captured it in 712. It remained in Moorish hands for the next 300 years, though reduced in political importance by incorporation into the Emirate (later the Califate) of their capital Córdoba. Disintegration of the Califate into independent fiefdoms by 1012 left Toledo as the capital of its own Moorish state.

As a result of the Moor's toleration of other religions, Toledo contained one of the largest Jewish communities in Spain, numbering about 12,000, as well as a large Christian population. When, after centuries of harmony, the Moors attempted to extort a large sum, primarily from the Jewish community, for the defense budget, Jews cried for help to the Spanish Christian king. In 1085, Alfonso VI, aided by his general El Cid, attacked Toledo and captured the city. Under subsequent Christian kings the Jewish community thrived, making important contributions to the wealth and learning of the town. When Alfonso X the Learned established a school of translators to disseminate Arabic culture throughout Europe, it was staffed by Jews, for only they could read both Arabic and Spanish. But this happy condition ended abruptly in 1391 in a pogrom during which hundreds of Toledo Jews were murdered by Christians. Finally, in 1492, all of Spain's Jews were expelled by Ferdinand and Isabella. Ironically, the grandfather of the future Saint Theresa had moved to Ávila and converted to Christianity just before the expulsion occured.

The expulsion of the Jews marked the beginning of Toledo's decline, hastened a century later by the expulsion of those Moors who had evaded exile by converting to Christianity, stripping Toledo of many of its most accomplished citizens. What the city retained was their legacy—its buildings, and, as the seat of the Prelate of Spain, it continued to maintain the religious authority Toledo had always exercised.

No city in Spain has more to see than Toledo—one frantic day barely does it justice. Toledo is also one of the few cities in Spain were shopkeepers and their touts will urge you to enter their establishments, conveying the impression that you've fallen into a tourist trap. In truth these stores sell decent wares and, because insistence is not a natural Spanish trait, the effect is more a slight nuisance than anything serious.

> *The Alcázar is the place to begin. If driving from Madrid, go left on the Carretara de Circunvalación, crossing the Tagus where N-401 intersects, going left at the circle on the opposite side. Turn right up the winding road leading to the Alcázar. Here is the largest parking place in the city, though in summer parking can be difficult even here.*

WHAT TO SEE AND DO

The following is a list of what should not be missed.

The **Alcázar** ★ is worth a visit to see the building, some of the military museums, and the room of General Moscardo, reconstructed as it had been during the Civil War seige. The **cathedral** ★★★★ is the most sumptuous in Spain. **Santa Tomé** ★★★ houses what most consider El Greco's greatest painting. **El Greco's House and Museum** ★★ displays paintings, and is interesting as a period building. **El Tránsito Synagogue** ★★★ is a feast of Moorish decoration and so is **Santa María la Blanca Synagogue** ★★. The **Santa Cruz Museum** ★★★ is spectacular as a building and for the art it contains. **San Juan de los Reyes** ★★ was built by Isabella and Ferdinand. **San Román** ★★ is a former 13th-century Church, now a museum of Visigothic artifacts, and **Ermita del Cristo de la Luz** ★ is a small, beautifully preserved mosque from the 11th century. All are within the old town walls. The atmospheric and memorable **Hospital de Tavera** ★★ stands just outside the walls.

Note:...Toledo is an old and concentrated town comprised of a maze of alleys, rather than a grid of streets. We present the best directions we can, but when confused you should feel free to ask passersby, who are accustomed to such inquiries.

Alcázar   ★

Open Tues.-Sun. from 9:30 a.m. to 1:30 p.m., and 4-6:30 p.m. (to 5:30 p.m. in winter). Closed Mon. Calle Capuchinos; ☎ *22 30 38. Admission: 200 ptas. Entrance on the north side, furthest from the parking lot.* A fortress has occupied this location at least since Moorish times. The site so dominates both the town and the surrounding plain that military engineers loved it at first sight. Alfonso VI, who conquered Moorish Toledo, replaced the Alcázar of the Moors with his own fort, which El Cid commanded until the two separated in a quarrel. Later monarchs made the building more palace than fortress. Carlos V rebuilt it entirely in its present shape, using Covarrbuias for his architect, but it was finished under Felipe II, Carlos's son, by Felipe's favorite architect Herrera (who designed the church at El Escorial). The north facade is Herrera's. What you see today, however, is entirely a reconstruction: the historic Alcázar was completely destroyed during the Spanish Civil War.

At the outbreak of war, the Alcázar served as an army headquarters for the Nationalist side. Most of the troops were home on leave, but soon the professional soldiers and cadets who remained were joined in the Alcázar by citizens of similar sympathies. Since most of Toledo supported the opposition Republicans, its citizens surrounded the Alcázar. For two months those in the building resisted artillery, mining and siege before relief arrived at the last moment in the form of Generalisimo Franco with his army. Their stand became a symbol of determination to the Nationalists and, not surprisingly, Franco rebuilt the Alcázar after the war.

Architecturally the most interesting part of the Alcázar is its huge courtyard, which leads to entrances for various military museums. More such museums line the second floor, where the most moving display in the Alcázar is also located. There the office of General Moscardo, the defending Nationalist general, has been perfectly reconstructed as it was during the siege. You can see the dirt and bullet holes, the torn and hanging wallpaper, and the Spartan furnishings. When the Republicans surrounded the building, they telephoned the general to inform him that his son was in their hands and would be killed if he did not surrender. In a grand gesture, General Moscardo asked to speak to his son and told him to prepare for death.

After touring the Alcázar, the time of day determines what to see next. To the right is the **Hospital of Santa Cruz**, a museum that should be seen, but which is open throughout the day, and can be saved for midday when the other sights close for lunch. Toward the left (south) is the **cathedral**.

To reach the cathedral, turn left on Calle Carlos V past the Alcázar to Pascuales San Miguel which cuts across it. Turn right. The name changes to Calle Coliseo as it bends right again, then turns left as it enters the Plaza Mayor. At the end of the plaza the cathedral can be seen. A left would take you to the modern entrance, but it is worth viewing the facade first by going right instead, then left and left again into the Arco de Palácio. The cathedral facade is on the left; and on the right, angling away, is the **Episcopal Palace ★**. *Further on, beside the palace, is the* **Ayuntamiento** *(city hall), with a classical front designed by Herrera and finished by El Greco's son. Straight ahead are* **law courts ★** *from the 14th century.*

Cathedral

Open daily from 10:30 a.m. to 1 p.m., and 3:30-7 p.m. (until 6p.m. in winter, and on Sun.). Plaza Mayor; ☎ *22 22 41. Admission: 350 ptas. Entrance on the north facade.* Building began in 1227 on a typical French Gothic cathedral, but during its two centuries of construction its plan gradually changed to a squatter and broader version known as Spanish Gothic. The front, with its triangular top and asymmetrical towers, shows substantial Italian influence.

The present situation of the cathedral gives an idea of the effect of most cathedrals in the Middle Ages when they were new—all hemmed in by buildings so that no vantage permits a good view of the whole. Whether this was a calculated effect, or due to the difficulty or expense of removing neighboring buildings, is argued, but the clear result was to dramatize the openness of the interior. Before entering, a look at the outside is in order. The tall and regular tower is 15th century, showing Moorish influence, but is spoiled at the top by a later lantern and overly-intricate spire. What should have been a tower on the right became instead a dome, designed by El Greco's son in the 17th century to cover the splendid Mozarabic chapel inside. The center portal, the Pardon Door, displays the best carving of the three portals. In the center Mary offers her robe to Ildefonso, a Visigothic saint and patron saint of Toledo. The bronze door-covers are 14th century. Around the corner to the south side is the Puerta de los Leones, named for the lions on the railing columns, fronting a richly decorated portal.

Enter on the north side, through the cloisters. The interior conveys a sense of volume and strength, rather than the lightness of the soaring French Gothic. Gradually the sumptuousness of the decoration takes effect. The stained glass is of the period, multicolored and lovely; wrought iron and marble run rampant. Such richness threatens to dull the senses.

The **coro** (choir) in the center of the cathedral nave contains some of the finest wood carving in Spain. The lower row of choirstalls, carved within a decade of the event, graphically depict the Christian conquest of Granada, and constitute one of the best records of the battles. The upper tier of stalls on the left, are by the sculptor Alfonso Berruguette. They are masterpieces of bas-relief, subtly conveying a strong sense of life and movement with figures that seem to push through the wood. At the back of the choir an alabaster Transfiguration, also by Berruguette, seems to rise and hover. Wait for a tour group to come by, so that you can see the *coro* lit, or find the sacristan and offer a small gratuity.

Opposite the *coro* is the **sanctuary** and altar with its huge flamboyantly-carved polychrome retablo depicting the life of Christ. The silver statue of the Virgin in front seems lost in all the commotion. Behind the sanctuary, in the middle of the ambulatory, hangs a swirling

Baroque *Transparante* slab by Tomé that seems out of place for all its prominence. To the right (facing the Transparante) is a richly carved Gothic chapel to Santiago (usually locked). Portraits of the chapel founder and his wife hang on either side of the altar. To the left a painted Mudejar portal leads to the **Capitular** room with its intricate 16th-century ceiling of surpassing elegance. Paintings of bishops of Toledo line the room, from the first century through the 19th. Although the artistic quality of the portraits is not high, they add a pleasant decorative touch, and include one painted by Goya. See if you can pick it out.

The **sacristy** presents a gallery of art under an imposing frescoed ceiling. The first gallery contains an awesome display of El Grecos, followed by rooms with Titian's great portrait of *Pope Paul IV*, some fine Van Dykes, an uninspired Goya, and a hauntingly "pretty" *Saint John the Baptist* by Caravaggio.

You cannot miss the huge fresco of Saint Christopher, almost 50 feet high, on the west transept. Its size lends it power beyond its artistic merit, but, for visitors, the chance of a blessing from this saint of travelers cannot hurt.

The **Mozarabic Chapel** forms the front of the cathedral on the south side. The chapel was constructed in 1504 so that those who still followed the Christian service as practiced by the Visigoths would have a place to worship. Most of those who practiced the old rituals had been isolated from their brethren because they lived in Moorish territory, and were thus called Mozarabs, "almost Arabs," by the other Christians. The decor of their chapel is elegantly frescoed, but the chapel is open only for special services (usually at 9:30 a.m.). On the north side of the cathedral front is the **tesoro** (treasury), entered through a Plateresque doorway. The Mudejar ceiling is lovely. Here you can see the 16th-century silver and gilt monstrance, weighing just under 400 pounds, which is carried through the streets during the Corpus Christi festival. A sword is displayed that belonged to Alfonso VI who conquered Toledo in 1085. Nearby is the library with richly illustrated medieval song books.

Afterwards head left through the Plaza Arco de Palácio in front of the cathedral, bearing right along the Archbishopric. Take the second right which is Calle San Salvador. At the corner Santa Tomé with its wondrous El Greco lies straight ahead in one block. If time permits, first turn left, then quickly right to reach the **Taller del Moro**, *on the street of the same name.*

Taller del Moro   ★

Open Tues.-Sat. 10 a.m. to 2 p.m., and 4-7 p.m. (until 6 p.m. in winter). Open Sun. from 10 a.m. to 2 p.m. Closed Mon. Calle Taller del Moro; ☎ *22 71 15). Admission: 100 Ptas.* This is a museum displaying crafts and tools of the Moors, but it is most interesting as a building. The

14th-century structure was used by Moorish craftsmen as a workshop (*taller*), while they worked on the cathedral. It retains lovely examples of stuccowork and inlaid ceilings from the period.

From the Taller continue to the corner and turn left along Plaza del Conde. At the end turn right, then left at the crosstreet, for Santa Tomé.

Santa Tomé

Open daily 10:30 a.m. to 1:30 p.m., and 3:30-7 p.m. (until 6 p.m. in winter). Plaza Conde, 1; ☎ *21 02 09. Admission: 100 Ptas.* Gonzalo Ruiz, Count of Orgaz, a local lord of the Toledo area, donated much of the money to build this church, and was buried inside when he died in 1323. Two centuries later, in 1586, the church commissioned El Greco to portray that burial. Naturally the appearance of the Count and those who attended was by then unknown, so El Greco used the faces of Toledoans of his day. A Mudejar tower stands beside the church as its annex, and in it hangs this masterpiece, so admired that there may be a wait before admission to the small vestibule.

Recently restored to its former brightness, it now has the appearance of paint still wet. Tradition claimed that Sts. Stephen and Augustin attended the Count's burial to honor his charity, and El Greco shows them in rich capes supporting the dead Count. El Greco's son stands in front pointing to the scene. (Inconspicuously inscribed on his handkerchief is the artist's signature.) All around in various attitudes stand citizens of Toledo, including El Greco himself, the sixth figure from the left.

Return to the corner where the church begins, turning right down the hill leading to the Plaza del Conde again. But go right on San Juan de Dios, instead of entering the plaza. Two alleyways later a sign directs you left to the House of El Greco.

Casa y Museo del Greco

Open Tues.-Sat. 10 a.m. to 2 p.m., and 4-7 p.m. (until 6 p.m. in winter). Open Sun. from 10 a.m. to 2 p.m. Closed Mon. Paseo del Tránsito; ☎ *22 40 46. Admission: 200 ptas.; ticket good for Tránsito Synagogue.* Although the actual house in which El Greco lived has long since disappeared, this one was altered 100 years ago to suggest his style of living. The house is an interesting reconstruction of a 16th-century private dwelling and displays a most amazing collection of El Greco's paintings, so brightly restored that they do not seem authentic.

Return to Calle San Juan de Dios, continuing to the bottom of the street, where the Synagogue of the Tránsito stands.

Sinagoga del Tránsito

Open Tues.-Sat. 10 a.m. to 2 p.m., and 4-7 p.m. (until 6 p.m. in winter). Open Sun. from 10 a.m. to 2 p.m. Closed Mon. Calle Samuel Ha-Levi;

☎ *22 36 55. Admission: 200 ptas.; ticket good for Casa El Greco.* Of eight known Toledo synagogues, only this and Santa María la Blanca Synagogue remain. It was begun in 1364 with a grant from Samuel Ha-Levi, the Treasurer of Spain during the reign of King Pedro the Cruel. Unfortunately, but characteristically, Pedro turned on his treasurer, seized what remained of his wealth, and put him to death. After the Jews were expelled from Spain, the synagogue was transformed into a church, from which comes its present name. It fell into neglect during the 18th century, until Francisco Perez Bayer, a Hebrew scholar, undertook the work of removing later Christian overlays and restoring it to its former splendor as a 13th-century synagogue. Inside you see the loving work of centuries of restoration.

The interior is basically one large 2-story room. The balcony upstairs was for the women of the congregation. All around the upper walls, and covering the east end, run the most astonishing patterns of stucco-work, inspired by the Moors. Hebrew inscriptions praise Pedro the Cruel, Samuel Ha-Levi, and God. Above the arches in the middle of the east end is a panel of delicate roses, surrounded by lovely designs. Fifty-four lacy windows are formed of stone tracery. Above the upstairs hall hangs an intricate cedarwood ceiling, with an effect that is altogether sublime.

The large street perpendicular to C. San Juan de Dios is Reyes Católicos. Go right (north), arriving in two or three blocks at the Synagogue of Santa María la Blanca on the right.

Sinagoga Santa María la Blanca   ★★
Open daily 10 a.m. to 2 p.m., and 3:30-7 p.m. (until 6 p.m. in winter). Calle Reyes Católicos; ☎ *22 84 29. Admission: 100 ptas.* This was the principle synagogue of Toledo, rebuilt after a fire in 1250 on the site of its predecessor. Christians appropriated it in 1405, after the pogroms, and transformed it into a church of the present name. In later years it was abandoned, then used successively as a barracks, a store and a workshop. Somehow much of the interior of the original synagogue remained intact, allowing accurate restoration.

Octagonal pillars with horseshoe arches form a main aisle with two more aisles on either side. Capitals are carved with intricate designs, relieving the whitewashed columns and walls. Above the arches sophisticated stucco designs reach to the ceiling, making the whole seem more like a mosque than a synagogue, but with a sophistication that few places of worship of any religion can claim. The incongruous sanctuary and retablo were added in the middle of the 16th century.

Continue past Santa María le Blanca on C. Reyes Católicos for one block to the monastery of San Juan de los Reyes.

San Juan de los Reyes   ★★
Open daily 10 a.m. to 2 p.m., and 3:30-7 p.m. (until 6 p.m. in winter).

Calle Reyes Católicos; ☎ *22 38 02. Admission: 100 ptas.* The monastery was commissioned by Ferdinand and Isabella in gratitude for their triumph over "la Beltraneja," the pretender to Isabella's throne, and her Portuguese allies. (See *Historical Profiles: Ferdinand and Isabella.*) The monarchs' first architect, Juan Guas, finished the main structure in 1492. Ferdinand and Isabella so admired it that they planned to be buried here—before they conquered and were captivated by Granada. The whole was not completed until 1610. The facade is hung with over 100 fetters taken from Christian slaves freed during the liberation of Granada.

The restored cloister is elaborate yet graceful and its second story is especially to be appreciated. The gallery upstairs retains a fine Mudejar ceiling. The church interior is composed of one impressively open aisle. Here and there characteristic Isabeline appliqué adds decorative interest. Where the transept crosses, openwork galleries display the entwined initials of Ferdinand and Isabella, along with a yoke and an arrow (in medieval Spanish these objects start with the first letter of the two monarchs' names), and the shields of Castile and Aragón. In no uncertain terms, the Catholic monarchs left their mark on this church. Supported by an eagle, amid statues of saints, powerful friezes of royal escutcheons line the transept walls. The heads carved beneath the arches are startling.

Return through the C. Reyes Católicos to the first street on the left, Calle de Angel. Follow this for two blocks passing Santa Tomé. Take the narrow Calle Campaña across the intersection and left. Continue in the same direction across the next intersection where the street changes its name to Calle de Alfonso XII, which leads to the small Plaza Padre Mariana. Take the street leading from the left side of the plaza, Calle San Román, which quickly leads to the church of San Román around the corner.

Iglesia San Román

Open Tues.-Sat. 10 a.m. to 2 p.m., and 4-7 p.m. (until 6 p.m. in winter). Closed Sun. afternoon and all day Mon. Calle San Clemente. Admission: 100 ptas. (Good also for Museo Santa Cruz, below.) This 13th-century church demonstrates the extent to which the Moorish aesthetic dominated architecture in Toledo during its first century after passing into Christian hands. Both the outside and interior are Mudejar through and through, from the decorative brickwork to the horseshoe arches and their elaborate capitals. Today the church is a museum for Visigothic art, which is appropriate in the former capital of their domain. Note the jewelry especially. The lovely wall frescoes of the resurrection of the dead have been retained from the original church.

Return along Calle San Román, which becomes Calle Jesus y María after it crosses the intersection, then turn left at the next intersection onto Calle Trinidad. After a bend it enters the Plaza

Arco de Palácio in front of the cathedral. Continue across in the same direction, perpendicular to the cathedral, into the large Calle Hombre de Palo. It narrows into Calle Comercio lined with shops, and in two blocks leaves you in the main square of Toledo, the Plaza Zocodover, which is lively and attractive. Here a right turn will take you to the **Museo de Santa Cruz,** *or a left will lead you to* **Santa Cristo del Luz** *(descriptions below).*

Museo Santa Cruz

Open Tues.-Sat.from 10 a.m. to 7 p.m. (until 6 p.m. in winter). Mon. 10 a.m. to 2 p.m. and 4:30-6:30 p.m. Closed Sun. afternoon at 2 p.m. and all day Mon. Calle Cervantes; ☎ *22 14 02. Admission: 200 ptas. (good also for Iglesia San Román, above.)* Few museums in the world are housed in a more dramatic or beautiful building. It was built by Cardinal Mendoza as a hospital, a very sumptuous one, for the sick and orphaned of Toledo. Although the cardinal died before its completion, Isabella saw that his plans were carried through. Two fine architects of the day worked on it—Enrique Egas, on the interior, and Covarrubias, on the exterior. In truth the outside is not special, though the statue over the main portal of Cardinal Mendoza kneeling before the cross is worth a look, but the inside is magnificent. It is a huge barn in the shape of a cross of equal sides, and seems to extend limitlessly in all four directions. Overhead runs an extraordinary wood ceiling. It would be hard to believe that paintings as spectacular as the collection in Santa Cruz would have to vie for attention against an architectural background, but architecture is seldom so dramatic.

The long entry hall is lined with fine 16th century tapestries and early furniture. The Zodiac tapestries have retained their rich blues and reds, and the figures are superb. At the end of the hall hangs the magnificent pennant from Don Juan's admiral's galley, flown during his victory over the Moors in 1571 at Lepanto. Then comes a corridor devoted to El Greco, in which over 20 canvases hang. The most famous is the *Altarpiece of the Assumption*, painted a few months before he died. Here the figures are more elongated than usual and the colors more acid. The virgin holds a book containing a record of El Greco's death, added to the painting by his son. With its view of Toledo, *Saint Joseph and Child* is striking. Note the upside-down tumbling angels. On the second floor are two fine Riberas, mixed with less interesting paintings. The large *Holy Family* is reminiscent of Raphael. Tapestries depicting the history of Alexander the Great are striking, if more faded than those on the lower floor. An elegant Renaissance stair by Covarrubias leads down to a Plateresque patio, which in turn leads to small rooms housing archaeological finds.

Ermita del Cristo de la Luz

Open at any reasonable hour by applying to the gatekeeper. Cuesta del Cristo de la Luz. Admission: a tip to the gatekeeper. From the northwest side of the Plaza del Zocodover take Calle Silleria, which bends due west in one block. After the bend, take the third right onto Cuesta del Cristo de la Luz. This is a tiny, perfectly square mosque, built of brick in 922 on the site of a Visigothic church. Inside, it can be seen that pillars of the Visigothic church remain, remodeled by the Moors into superimposed arches, like those in the Córdoba Mosque. Nine individual domes cover as many bays, resulting in a surprisingly harmonious composition. The name, "Christ of the Light" comes from a story that Alfonso VI's horse stopped here, when the king conquered Toledo, and knelt. (According to some versions, it was the horse of El Cid that bowed.) Investigation uncovered a Visigothic lamp still burning inside one wall, lighting a crucifix. This indeed would have been a miracle of candle-power, for the last Visigoths had departed 300 years before.

At least one monument outside the walls of Toledo is well worth seeing, the Hospital de Tavera. The building is remarkable, as is some of the art inside.

The Hospital is due north, at the end of a large square called Paseo de Merchan. It can be walked from the Ermita del Cristo de la Luz, although it is a hike of about half a mile. To walk, head north along Cuesta del Cristo de la Luz which leads into Calle Real de Arrabal. Continuing north, pass through the Puerta Nueva de Bisagra by Covarrubias, one of the gates of Toledo. Walk along Carretaria a Madrid, by the east side of the square, to the Hospital at the garden's end. Alternatively, one can drive along the perimeter road and take a right on Carretaria a Madrid.

Hospital de Tavera ★★

Open daily 10 a.m. to 1:30 p.m. and 3:30-6 p.m.; *22 05 29. Admission: 150 ptas.* Something sad emanates from this building, perhaps because, although it was never finished, it represents the final work of three great men. This was the last building designed by Covarrubias; its stately form is a fitting memorial. He built it for Cardinal Tavera, descended from the combined great families of Medinaceli and Lerma. A double patio inside leads to a large chapel in which lay tombs of the Medinacelis—the most elegant being the tomb of Cardinal Tavera, the last work of the great sculptor Alonso Berruguette. Off the left side of the patio is a small museum of art and furniture belonging to the Dukes of Lerma. The huge dining hall displays Titian's *Portrait of Carlos V,* and a lovely Coello. In the library hangs a fine El Greco of *The Holy Family,* and a *Virgin,* unusual for actually being pretty. Ribera's *Philosophy* is nice, but the most striking Ribera—his strange painting of a bearded lady—is stashed in a small room. On the second floor is an utterly unforgettable painting by Zurbarán of the young Duke of Medinaceli, all in orange tones. On the same floor are a Tintoretto and a number of El Grecos, including his last canvas. *The Bap-*

tism of Christ by Saint John is huge and includes all the characteristics that make El Greco the most recognizable of artists.

WHERE TO STAY

While hotels in Toledo are not numerous, they span all price ranges, and their number usually proves adequate since most visitors shortchange themselves by making Toledo only a day trip. The best news is that the three finest hotels are moderately priced, with the only difficulty being to choose one over the other two.

EXPENSIVE ($100-$200)

Parador Conde de Orgaz　　　　　　　　1st-class ★★★

Cerro del Emperador (due south of the city, just off the circling road, Carratera de Circunvalación). Rooms: 76. ☎ *22 18 50; FAX. 22 51 66; Telex 47998.* This is one of Spain's modern paradors, and not our favorite by any means. True, it provides fine views of Toledo, but not spectacular enough to repay the inconvenience of being situated at such a distance from town. Nor does the staff seem overly concerned with their clients' welfare. Avoid rooms 33 and 34, in which other guests' comings and goings and the elevator's rumble are clearly audible.

MODERATE ($50-$99)

Hostal del Cardenal　　　　　　　　R2nd-class ★★★★★

Paseo Recaredo, 24 (In the northern wall of the city. The best route is to take the circular road past Paseo de Merchan, the large square that fronts the Hospital de Tavera, where a sign will point you left to parking for the hotel). Rooms: 27. ☎ *22 49 00; FAX 22 29 91.* A better hotel would be hard to imagine: small, for intimacy; in a remodeled 18th-century cardinal's mansion, for history and elegance; and with a luscious garden, for peace, quiet and beauty. For an additional charge you can have a suite with a terrace. Not that it matters, but the hotel is owned by the people who run the old taverna Botin in Madrid. There are so few rooms here, however, that reservations are a must.

María Cristina　　　　　　　　2nd-class ★★★★

Calle Margués de Mendigorria, 1 (opposite the Hospital de Tavera, north of the walls). Rooms: 65. ☎ *21 32 02; FAX 21 26 50; Telex 42827.* This hotel should be the parador—an historic building located in the precinct of an historic sight. It is beautiful, run like a Swiss watch, and clean as can be. The rooms are about as attractive as those of the Hotel Cardinal, although the location is less convenient.

Carlos V　　　　　　　　2nd-class ★★★

Calle Horno de Magdalena, 1 (between the Alcázar and the cathedral). Rooms: 69. ☎ *22 21 00; FAX 22 21 05.* The location is in the heart of the city, close to most sights; it cannot be bettered. The hotel is modern, of no great architectural distinction, but half of the rooms overlook the cathedral. The rooms are merely hotel rooms, however. And being in the heart of town puts you in the center of city noise, not so loud in Toledo as in some other places, but not the quiet of the more highly recommended choices, either.

INEXPENSIVE (UNDER $50)

Los Cigarrales   3rd-class ★ ★ ★

Carretaria de Circunvalación, 32 (half a mile west of the parador). Rooms: 36. ☎ *22 00 53; FAX 21 55 46.* Here you are presented with views as nice as those from the parador at much lower cost and with friendly service. In addition, this hotel, a remodeled country house with wood beams in the rooms and tiles on the walls, is more attractive. It is, however, outside of town.

Imperio   R3rd-class ★ ★

Calle Cadenas, 5 (one block west of the Plaza del Zocodover). Rooms: 21. ☎ *22 76 50; FAX 25 31 83.* The location is smack in the heart of medieval Toledo and the price is low enough to ease the most strained budget. The hotel is recently renovated, modern and clean, though the rooms are not memorable.

WHERE TO EAT

Toledo is no gourmet paradise, nor does it tempt you with expensive restaurants since most are moderately priced. However, it is Spain's center for game, if such is your pleasure.

EXPENSIVE ($50+)

Asador Adolfo   ★ ★ ★

Calle La Granada, 6 (head north along the facade of the cathedral to reach the restaurant in twenty paces or so). ☎ *22 73 21. Closed Sunday evening, except before holidays.* Both the attractiveness of the surroundings and the quality of the food make this the best restaurant in Toledo. Parts of the restaurant date to the 15th century. The food is typical of the area, but cooked with extra refinement and care. It may be the best restaurant for game in all of Spain. Reservations are recommended.

Amex, Diners, MasterCard and Visa accepted.

MODERATE ($20-$50)

Cardinal   ★

Paseo Recaredo, 24 (see directions above to the hotel). ☎ *22 49 00.* The garden outside is a delight, but accommodations are a bit cramped in the restaurant connected with this special hotel. You can watch the chef work in his kitchen, which is not our favorite dining view. At one time the food stood well above ordinary, though it has declined of late. *Amex, Diners, MasterCard and Visa accepted.*

La Botica   ★

Plaza de Zocodover, 13. ☎ *22 55 57. Closed Sunday nights.* Eat in style in the dinning room upstairs, or watch the passing throng from tables outside. The food is a clear cut above its competitors in the plaza, and the menu includes some original dishes, such as eggplant with cheese and shrimp. Finish with a refreshing fruit sherbet.

Hierbabuena ★

Calle Cristo de la Luz, 9 (just past the Ermita del Cristo de la Luz; see the directions to this sight above). ☎ *22 34 63. Closed Sunday night.* The Moorish ambiance and candlelight make this a pleasant dining experience. The food, however, is ordinary.

Amex, Diners, MasterCard and Visa accepted.

Casa Aurelio and Mesón Aurelio ★

Calle Sinagoga, 1 and 6 (a tiny street a few steps north of the cathedral). ☎ *22 20 97, and 22 13 92. The first restaurant is closed Wednesday and from mid August to mid September; the second is closed Monday and from mid June to mid July.* These neighbors are owned by the same family and serve comparable food. The food is well prepared and should not disappoint, especially since prices are fair. The decor is informal, though the patio of the Casa is just a bit nicer than the accommodations of the Mesón.

INEXPENSIVE (UNDER $20)

El Nido

Plaza de la Magdalena, 5 (a short block due south of the Plaza del Zocodover). The prices of its special menus are the lowest in town. The food is hearty, if undistinguished.

DIRECTORY

INFORMATION • Located in the north end of the city at the Puerta Nueva de Bisagra, by the corner of the Plaza de Merchan. ☎ 22 08 43.

TRAINS AND BUSES • The train station (☎ 22 30 99) is located west of the city on Paseo de la Rosa. Direct trains to Madrid leave 10 times per day and cost under $5. Service elsewhere involves changing trains. The local RENFE office (☎ 22 12 72) is located at Calle Silleria, 7, just west of the Plaza del Zocodover.

POST OFFICE AND TELEPHONES • The post office (☎ 22 36 11) is located at Calle de la Plata 1, which is two blocks due north of the cathedral, but hard to find, nonetheless. Telephones are available on the same street, west of the post office.

POLICE • Located in the Plaza del Zocodover at number 1 (☎ 21 34 00).

EXCURSIONS

Aranjuez ★ ★ ★ is only 43 k east of Toledo, and its gardens provide lovely walks in season. N-400 leaves east from the circular road, Carretaria Circunvalación, to take you there. A description of the town will be found under its own heading above. The monastery of **Guadalupe ★ ★ ★** lies in the mountains to the west, 178 scenic k away. See its separate description in the chapter on Extremadura. Take C-401 west from the circular road.

For the greatest variety and lowest prices in Spain on ceramics take an excursion to **Talavera de la Reina** ★, 75 k west of Toledo.

TALAVERA DE LA REINA ★

Population: 64,136
Area code: 925; zip code: 45600

From the circular road take N-403 heading northwest towad Torrijos. In 42 k this reaches N-V just before Maqueda. Heading west along N-V, signs direct to Talavera in 33 k.

Since the 15th century the name Talavera has meant ceramics. This area was famous for its designs in blue and yellow. Today it is a center for ceramics factories that produce wares in most of the traditional colors of Spain, not only in blues and yellows. Factory showrooms are located on the west side of town. On N-V coming from the west you arrive exactly where the ceramic stores line the road—stores heaped with dishes and planters, vases and tiles, and objects you had never imagined could be fabricated in that material. The prices will astonish you in the most pleasant way.

OLD CASTILE AND LEÓN

The Alcázar of Segovia.

HISTORICAL PROFILE:
FERDINAND AND ISABELLA

If Spanish monarchs were ranked by their impact on modern Spain, Ferdinand and Isabella would take first place. Before their marriage united the country's two largest kingdoms and they conquered the remainder, Spain consisted of four fiercely independent territories, ruled by separate kings. Ferdinand and Isabella initiated the exploration of the New World, completed the reconquest of Spain, and expanded the power of their office from a feudal kingship to a monarchy. Equally consequential were their more blameworthy acts: they unleashed the pro-Catholic Inquisition, and banished both Jews and Moors from Spanish soil. Ironically, given all the power they eventually commanded, Ferdinand and Isabella came to their respective thrones through miraculous circumstances. As a child, Isabella stood behind two heirs to the throne of Castile, and young Ferdinand was twice-removed from the kingship of Aragón.

Isabella's father, Juan II, the King of Castile, had married twice; Enrique IV, his son by the first wife, succeeded to the throne upon his father's death. But Juan's second wife had produced children as well: the first, on April 22, 1451, a daughter named Isabella after her mother; the second, a son. The crown would naturally pass to King Enrique's child, with the laws of succession dictating that Juan's second family become eligible—first through its male—only if Enrique were to die childless. Whether Enrique did leave a surviving child remains a mystery, but what is certain is that Isabella's ascension to the throne of Castile resulted from questions about whether Enrique's designated heir was actually his child.

Enrique began his reign in kingly fashion with raids on the Moors at Grenada. But the pleasures of monarchy—the wine, women and courtly delights—began to appeal more strongly than royal duties, and Enrique soon ceased to rule, entrusting his kingdom to ministers. When his staid wife, Blanche of Aragón (who happened to be Ferdinand's sister), paled as well in his eyes, Enrique moved to end the childless 12-year union. Claiming the impotency of both parties as his grounds, he applied to the Pope for dissolution of the marriage, thereby winning not only the annulment he desired but a nickname as well—"Enrique the Impotent".

Although Enrique next married the more lively Princess Juana of Portugal, it was not long before he tired of her and took up with mistresses, while his new wife cut a wide swathe through the ranks of the palace courtiers. One of these nobles, Beltran de la Cueva, emerged as Queen Juana's favorite. He challenged the other knights to a joust to determine whose lady was fairest, and won the test in Juana's name. For some reason this delighted the cuckolded Enrique, who celebrated the victory by endowing a new monastery. And so court life proceeded, until, 8 years after marrying Enrique, Juana gave birth to a daughter.

Although named Juana after her mother, the daughter was maliciously referred to as *la Beltraneja*, "the little Beltran girl," for few were persuaded of her royal paternity. Skeptics noted that Enrique had produced no children during 12 years of marriage to his first wife, and that their divorce had been based on his impotency. Further, the child had not been born until 8 years of marriage to a second wife, notorious for her dalliances, while Enrique himself had produced no children by any of his numerous mistresses. It appeared to many that Enrique the Impotent was appropriately titled. When Enrique assembled the nobles of Castile to recognize the child as his heir, they refused.

The Castilian nobles, their patience exhausted, demanded that Enrique acknowledge Alphonso, Isabella's brother, as heir instead. Enrique initially agreed, but repudiated the arrangement as soon as the nobles disbursed. By now, so little respect remained for the king that his effigy was defiled outside his bedroom window, and supporters of Alphonso established a separate court, saddling Castile with two kings and a civil war. Three years later, Alphonso suddenly died and the rebels offered the crown to Isabella, who refused because Enrique, the rightful king, still reigned.

In the meantime, Enrique had been trying to marry off this potential contender for the throne. An early proposal from Ferdinand to Isabella had been rejected because his prospects for inheriting Aragón's throne were slight. A match was made with Ferdinand's elder brother, however, although he died before the marriage could take place. Enrique next proposed the King of Portugal, but Isabella refused because he was too old. Finally, Enrique betrothed Isabella, without her consent, to one of Castile's main rebels, in an attempt to isolate him from the other leaders of this powerful opposition force. This lastest fiancé was not appealling. He was much older than Isabella, and had acquired a widespread reputation for vice despite presiding over a religious order. But he was eager, and applied to Rome for a release from his vow of celibacy. Fortunately for Isabella, he died while speeding towards the capital to complete their wedding arrangements. Other suitors, including Richard, soon to be Richard III of England, pursued her, as did both the brother of the king of France and a young man named Ferdinand from neighboring Aragón.

Ferdinand's course to Aragón's throne was as complex as the route Isabella had encountered in Castile. He was born on March 10, 1452, to the brother of Aragón's king. The king, however, having conquered southern Italy and finding it congenial, had taken up residence there, leaving the governance of Aragón to Ferdinand's father Juan (coincidentally of the same name as Isabella's father). Like Isabella, Ferdinand was the offspring of a second marriage, the first of which had produced an older half-brother. By rights, if Ferdinand's father were ever to become king, Carlos, the elder half-brother, would succeed him. But Juan preferred Ferdinand over his other son so strongly that he waged war to deprive Carlos of the small kingdom of Navarre, inherited from his mother. Forced to leave Spain, Carlos wandered through Italy for ten years.

Why his father so favored Ferdinand remains a puzzle. The other son, Carlos, possessed a superior intellect—he translated Aristotle's *Ethics* from the Greek—and had demonstrated a capacity for governing in Navarre. Although it is possible that Ferdinand's mother might have contrived to make her own son favored, this is doubtful given Juan's headstrong and wily character. What is clear is that Ferdinand's father—after inheriting the throne of Aragón upon the death of his childless brother—refused to recognize Carlos as his heir. The nobles of Aragón then rose in arms to force Juan to acknowledge Carlos as heir-presumptive in conformity to law. At just that moment, Carlos died suddenly of mysterious, and some would claim suspicious, causes, but even after Carlo's death, half of Aragón still refused to recognize Ferdinand and seceded. Juan, by now incapacitated by blindness, left the conduct of the resulting war to his wife and the 16-year-old Ferdinand. Victory in that campaign finally secured the throne for Ferdinand, and he began his quest for a royal mate.

When Ferdinand sent an embassy to propose marriage directly to Isabella, she promptly accepted—the alternative being another of Enrique's unsuitable candidates. Here finally was a suitor close to herself in age and station, of proven accomplishments, and comely appearance. Her acceptance of Ferdinand's proposal, however, was given without Enrique's approval. When spies informed Enrique of the match, he dispatched a company of soldiers to kidnap Isabella, and stationed troops at the border to intercept Ferdinand. A force of Isabella's partisans prevented her capture, while Ferdinand evaded border guards by disguising his attendants as traveling merchants and himself as their servant.

Isabella and Ferdinand wed on October 19, 1469, in a mansion in Dueñas, near the city of Valladolid. At 18, the bride was an acknowledged beauty, above middle height, blue-eyed and auburn-haired. Ferdinand, who stood shorter than his wife, possessed a full, square face, chestnut hair, a well proportioned body, and was younger by a year. Isabella had to borrow money from friends to pay their wedding expenses, and Ferdinand engaged in a piece of deception to ensure its completion. Because the nuptial pair were cousins, papal dispensation was necessary to set aside consanguinity restrictions. When approval did not arrive in time, Ferdinand produced a forgery. Despite Isabella's genuine desire for the marriage, she took care that her husband not exploit her position: the nuptial contract dictated that only with Isabella's authorization could Ferdinand travel beyond Castile, that he fill no positions in Castile's government without her consent, and that he could authorize no royal ordinances without Isabella's countersignature.

News of the wedding enraged Enrique, who proclaimed that Isabella had forfeited the throne of Castile by marrying without his consent. Twice more he called on the nobles to ratify "la Beltraneja" as his legitimate heir, swearing sacred oaths that she was truly his daughter. Each time they declined his request. Four years later, the king, still protesting, died.

In 1474, Isabella was crowned ruler of Castile, and Ferdinand, in Aragón at the time, was coronated by proxy. "La Beltraneja", with her new husband, the King of Portugal, mustered forces and attacked Castile. Five years of warfare ensued before Isabella's forces routed those of "La Beltraneja" in a decisive battle near Toro. That same year, 1479, Ferdinand's father died.

Against enormous historical odds, both Ferdinand and Isabella had succeeded in attaining the thrones of their separate states, forging, with their marriage, a union of mighty Castile and Aragón. At the time Castile consisted of Old Castile, land called New Castile that had been reclaimed from the Moors, and most of Andalusia. This kingdom covered the center, and encompassed more than half, of modern Spain. At the same time, Aragón, originally a small territory, had expanded by conquest to include Catalonia and the rest of the eastern seacoast—altogether about a third of Spain's present territory. Except for the small northern kingdom of Navarre, and the ten percent of Moorish land around Grenada, Isabella and Ferdinand together controlled the Spain we know today. Despite this union, however, the territory did not comprise a nation, for it lacked both common laws and common government; nor was it ruled by a unified monarchy: Isabella was Queen of Castile, while Ferdinand alone ruled Aragón. Nonetheless, their marriage created a means of future unification: one day their heir would govern all of Spain.

At the time Ferdinand and Isabella began their rule, the conquest of Grenada had been a dream of Spanish monarchs for two centuries. It was Isabella who finally achieved the goal. She mustered and supplied troops for the campaign—in effect acting as commander-in-chief—while Ferdinand served as her general in the field. In a war that lasted a decade, she managed the financing, collecting and delivering of arms, horses, mules, and food and drink for her troops —all accomplished during several pregnancies and births. In addition to this, she was inspired to establish the first field hospitals in history, and, despite the discouragement of authorities, she valued Columbus' project sufficiently to finance his explorations (see "Historical Profile: Columbus and the Conquistadores," p. 387.), bringing unheard-of fortunes to Spain in later years. But along with Isabella's accomplishments, her record includes one terrible stain.

In 1481 Spain instituted the Inquisition, although circumstances suggest that Ferdinand, more than Isabella, should be held accountable for that horrible event. (See "Historical Profile: Religion and the Inquisition," p. 413.) Later, the notorious Inquisitor General and Isabella's childhood confessor, Tomás de Torquemada, used his considerable influence to persuade her to expel Spain's Jews. Spain's Jewish population, which counted for no more than a few percent, had never been regarded as a problem for the country, and had caused no wars. But Torquemada recited old wives' tales about Jews eating Christian babies, and argued relentlessly that because Christians were being tempted to convert to Judaism, his job of prosecuting heresy had grown impossible. Ignoring the fact that the Jewish religion had never proselytized, Torquemada further demanded that all Jews— not just convicted proselytizers—be punished because "a corporation convicted of a great crime should be disenfranchised, the innocent suffering with the guilty." [W. H. Prescott, *A History of the Reign of Ferdinand and Isabella*, Vol. II, p. 139] His persistence won out. Isabella, who had demonstrated genuine compassion both for her troops and for others in need, finally signed the Edict of Expulsion in March, 1492.

Jews throughout Spain were given three months to either sell or forfeit all their property before the expulsion. Simultaneously Spanish Jews were forbidden to leave with gold or silver—that is to say money, for paper currency had yet to be invented. Perhaps 100,000 Jews departed, most to neighboring Portugal. Rather than suffer this fate, a minority chose to convert, but lying in wait for these "conversos" was the Inquisition: as Christians, they now fell within its purview. The damage Spain suffered from this expulsion is incalculable: departing Jews comprised both a sizable number of Spain's best-educated people and a large percentage of its merchants.

Despite all their accomplishments, both good and evil, Ferdinand and Isabella were less powerful than we might expect. The power of their feudal thrones depended on the consent of the nobles. Against their monarchy was poised the substantial resources of the grandees of the kingdom, two or three of whom could raise more money and larger armies than the king and queen. The Church, with its extensive land and riches, dominated by a foreign Pope in Italy, constituted another power in opposition.

Undermining the power of Spain's feudal lords required all the statecraft that Ferdinand and Isabella could summon. First they razed many of the kingdom's fortified buildings, thereby eliminating sanctuaries for potentially dissident nobles. Then they revoked awards of land and privileges that had been liberally distributed by King Enrique in a vain attempt to appease the nobles. Ferdinand and Isabella were less than consistent about this, however, for they heaped their own ample rewards upon those who had helped them conquer Grenada. Last, and most importantly, they made ability, rather than nobility, the standard by which official appointments were made, often assigning government positions to men of common birth. This innovation deprived grandees of the added power of government offices, and allowed the government to separate itself from the nobility.

While the task of curbing the nobles was not completed until later reigns, Isabella was able to realize one goal during her tenure: she wrested the Spanish Catholic church from the Pope. In 1482, Isabella and Pope Sextus IV disagreed over candidates for a vacant bishopric. For centuries Popes had controlled appointments to high Church offices, often filling them with foreigners who, not infrequently, were their relatives, as was the candidate to whom Isabella objected. After the Pope haughtily dismissed the ambassador Isabella sent to complain, she ordered all Spanish citizens to leave Rome, then announced her intention to convene a council of Christian princes to reform the Church. The vigor of her reaction so concerned the Pope that he sent a legate to mollify the Queen. When she refused him audience, the Pope capitulated, agreeing that future appointments would be made from a list proposed by the Spanish monarch. Thus, the Roman Catholic church in Spain became more nationalized than that in any other Catholic country.

Using her new ecclesiastical powers, Isabella appointed Francisco Jimenes de Cisneros as Archbishop of Toledo, the supreme prelate of Spain. Cisneros had practiced extreme asceticism as a young man, enduring the greatest privations to purify his soul. He lacked personal goals, but possessed a surfeit of ambition for his God. His purity first brought him to Isabella's attention when he served as her confessor, but refused to live amid the luxuries of her palace while fulfilling those duties.

Cisneros' first commission was to cleanse the Spanish church whose high offices were filled with nobles' sons and daughters, eager for the fortunes in revenue that accompanied these positions. Since religious belief had so little to do with their appointments, prelates commonly lived as luxuriously as any noble, enjoying mistresses and siring children. Cisneros applied an ascetic broom that swept much of the luxury and sexual activity away.

His next goal was to convert as many Moors as possible to the one true religion, as he saw it. Here his asceticism proved an impediment, for, despite the fact that the Grenada Treaty of Surrender promised religious freedom to all, he resorted to imprisonment and torture to reconvert the few Muslims who had reverted back to Islam after a time as Christians. When Islamic leaders who protested were also imprisoned, the Spanish Muslim community rose in general rebellion, which Ferdinand put down only with difficulty. But rather than chastise the instigator Cisneros, Ferdinand punished those who rebelled. In 1502, Isabella and Ferdinand expelled all Moors from Spanish lands in the same callous way that they had exiled Spain's Jews. In one stroke, Andalusia and Valencia lost almost all their farm workers, devastating Spain economically. Yet the misplaced goal of most of the country's Christians had now been accomplished— Spain was homogeneously Catholic.

Even more than their policies, the most consequential of Ferdinand's and Isabella's acts were the marriages they arranged for their children. The couple produced one son and four daughters. The eldest, a daughter named after her mother, wed the heir to the throne of Portugal, who died six months later after falling from his horse. Princess Isabella fell into a deep, seven-year depression. The youngest, Catalina, first married Arthur, Prince of Wales, and then King Henry VIII of England, to pass into history as the tragic "Catherine of Aragon."

Their only son was matched with the eldest daughter of Maximilian, the Holy Roman Emperor, with great hopes for a coalition of two mighty thrones. Tragically, the son died six months after the wedding. His wife, already pregnant, kept hopes of the union alive until she delivered a stillborn child. But Isabella and Ferdinand had another daughter, named Juana, and they arranged for her to wed Archduke Philip, Maximilian's son and heir.

They also convinced their eldest daughter, Isabella, to try another marriage after her seven-year bereavement. She was betrothed to her first husband's brother, who had since become King of Portugal. True to her mother's spirit, Princess Isabella agreed only after her fiancé promised to expel Portugal's Jews. With the death of her brother, Princess Isabella, as the eldest surviving child, added the title of heir to the throne of Spain to that of Queen of Portugal. In her person reposed the hope for a united peninsula. The poor woman, however, died in childbirth, and her sickly son survived for only two years.

Princess Isabella's death meant that inheritance of the throne of Castile evolved to Juana and her husband Philip. Philip was attractive enough to be called "the Handsome," and he brought a tidy inheritance to his marriage. From his mother's side, he had been bequeathed the Low Countries, modern-day Holland and Belgium. In February of 1500, the pair produced a son, Carlos, who was to become the next king of Spain and the Low Countries, of the Holy Roman Empire and the Americas.

Isabella did not live to see her grandson rule the largest empire since the time of the Mongols. Her health had deteriorated with the passing of each beloved child, and her final burden was an inescapable awareness that something was wrong with Juana, now heir to the throne. In 1504 Isabella was attacked by a fever, lost her taste for food and suffered from an unquenchable thirst. In this condition she wrote her last will and testament. She named Juana "queen proprietor," along with husband Philip. The laws of succession and his own children had passed Ferdinand by. But Isabella also stated that, should Juana be incapacitated, Ferdinand would act as regent. To provide for her husband, whom she genuinely loved, she offered her best jewelry and one half of the royal revenues from the New World, which, if Ferdinand had actually received it, would have been a kingly sum indeed.

Shortly before noon on November 26, 1504, in the city of Medina del Campo, Isabella died. No family attended her. Ferdinand was in Toledo on business; her few surviving children were away in foreign lands. She was 53 years old and in the 30th year of her reign. She was buried in Santa Isabella church beside the Alhambra, without any memorial, having stipulated that the money thus saved should be given to the poor. In her will she added that

Should the king, my lord, prefer a sepulchre in some other place,
then my will is that my body be there transported, and laid by his
side; that the union we have enjoyed in this world, and, through
the mercy of God, may hope again for our souls in heaven, may be
represented by our bodies in the earth.

W. H. Prescott, Ferdinand and Isabella, Vol. II, p.175.

On the evening of Isabella's death, Ferdinand resigned the throne of Castile, to which he no longer had title, then assembled the Cortes to declare Juana incompetent so he could assume the regency. The Cortes summarily affirmed Isabella's will, including Ferdinand's position as regent, but Ferdinand faced problems nonetheless. A strong minority of Castilian nobles, who regarded the unknown ways of Philip and Juana more optimistically than the known severity of Ferdinand, incited unrest in the kingdom and urged Philip to come to Spain. At the same time, both the King of France and Maximilian were menacing Spain's borders. Ferdinand responded by trying to produce an heir of his own. Within one year of Isabella's death, he wooed and married—in the same town of Dueñas in which a much younger Ferdinand had married Isabella 38 years before—an 18-year-old bride. The marriage, however, changed his situation—no longer was he the widower of the Queen of Castile, but simply Ferdinand, the King of Aragón. Voices insisted more strongly that he resign the regency of Castile.

When Philip offered to come to Spain to co-rule, Ferdinand seized the offer as his only hope of retaining a hold on Castile. But Philip landed with hardened German troops, and announced that he had changed his mind about sharing the regency, refusing even to allow Ferdinand to see his daughter. His options exhausted, Ferdinand agreed to cede Castile to Juana and Philip. The Cortes then recognized Juana as monarch, with Carlos, her son, as heir. Philip took the reins of Castile, and Ferdinand left the peninsula to sojourn in Italy.

What had caused all this maneuvering for the regency was the fact that Juana, the rightful ruler, was insane. When, for example, she heard rumors that her husband had taken a lover, Juana attacked the woman in question and shaved her bald. It seems that Philip never cared for Juana, although she was thoroughly, and insanely, smitten with him. The shaving incident was Philip's final straw; he determined to have nothing more to do with Juana. But the less he cared for her, the more intensely jealous she became. Philip filled government offices with friends from abroad and lived off the fat of Castile for two months, then caught a chill while playing ball and died. Juana sat immobile for three months in the room where he died, seldom talking, signing no official documents, and shedding no tears. Finally, she consented to bury her husband in Grenada, provided that she accompany the funeral procession.

Thus began a mad cortege. The procession moved only by night because Juana insisted that "a widow, who had lost the sun of her own soul, should never expose herself to the light of day." [W.H. Prescott, *Ferdinand and Isabella*, Vol. I, P. 268]. The daylight hours were passed observing funeral services in some monastery or church enroute. One day they stopped by chance at a convent for nuns, believing it to be a male monastery. Juana ran out screaming that everyone must leave. She spent the rest of the day guarding Philip's coffin in fields nearby, terrified lest some nun lure her dead husband away.

Almost a year to the day after he left Spain, Ferdinand returned for good. From this time until his death he ruled Castile severely in Juana's name. In 1512, preparing for one of the recurring border wars with France, Ferdinand asked permission of the King of Navarre to send troops through that small territory in the shadow of the Pyrenees. When permission was refused, Ferdinand invaded and won the final piece of land that comprises modern Spain.

As if his job were now finished, Ferdinand's health began to decline. He experienced difficulty in breathing and complained about his heart. Returning from a hunt in January of 1516, Ferdinand died in a small house in Madrigalejo, near Trujillo. He was 63 years old and had ruled Spain for 41 years. His remains were buried beside Isabella's in Grenada.

According to Machiavelli, Ferdinand had been the very model of a modern prince. His ambition was pure, undeterred by religion or other conceits. While devout Isabella toiled and bore his children, Ferdinand spawned illegitimate offspring wherever he went. He cared only for his own future: had his second marriage produced a male heir, Ferdinand would have preserved his personal power but undermined the future union of Castile and Aragón. He was acknowledged as the most astute politician in Europe of his time, possessing a cleverness that enabled him consistently to best France, though she was stronger in every way. If Isabella was loved by her subjects and fondly remembered, Ferdinand was respected and feared.

During their long, eventful reigns, Ferdinand and Isabella commissioned an astonishing number of buildings. Many survive. Of course their tomb in **Granada** is a requirement for anyone interested in the pair, but there is also a fine church, San Juan de los Reyes, and an elegant hospital, Santa Cruz, that they commissioned in **Toledo**.

Old Castile and León, however, was the stage for most of the events of their lives and is the repository for more Isabeline structures than any other area. Isabella's father, Juan II, is buried in Cartuja de Miraflores on the outskirts of **Burgos**. The nobles of Christian Spain first proclaimed Isabella as their monarch in the Alcázar of **Segovia**. She married Ferdinand in Dueñas, once a separate village, but now incorporated within the city of Valladolid. Unfortunately, the mansion in which the wedding took place no longer exists. Still surviving in **Valladolid**, however, are two of the greatest works of the architectural style that developed during their reign—Isabeline—in the portals of the San Gregorio and San Pedro churches. As young monarchs, Ferdinand and Isabella loved the monastery of San Tomás in **Ávila**, which they had built and where they had planned to be buried. Here they stayed when they could, often entertaining Torquemada, the Grand Inquisitor. After the tragic death of their only son Don Juan and his burial at San Tomás, however, it became a sad place for them thereafter. Ferdinand and Isabella also did much to encourage the University of **Salamanca** and are appropriately commemorated in the magnificent decorations in the School Square.

OLD CASTILE AND LEÓN

Madrid presents Spain's present, but Old Castile and León commemorates its past. Here, in the 10th century, Christian Spain came into being, and grew to dominate the peninsula. As the center of the Reconquest, Old Castile and León defended against counterattacks from the Moors by erecting castles and fortresses throughout its terrain, in the process earning the first half of its name—Castile. But after the Reconquest, Old Castile and León faded, letting the new capital of Madrid lead Spain into modern times. History passed by Old Castile and León, but no area of Spain preserves a greater number of monuments from the era of the Reconquest.

When the Moors swept through the peninsula at the dawn of the 8th century, they pushed the Visigoths to footholds in Asturias, just north of León. Few and powerless, these Christians struggled for two centuries to regain a mere hundred miles of land to their south. Even so, that conquest involved a victory that seems astonishing in retrospect. Abd er Rahman III, the strongest Caliph who ever ruled Andalusia, determined in 939 to finish off the remaining northern Christians. He collected an army of 100,000 men for what he called his "Omnipotent Campaign." Outnumbered by at least ten to one, Christian forces somehow managed to rout his army at Simancas, near the present city of Valladolid in Old Castile. This victory allowed Christians from Asturias to flow 100 miles south into the territory they called León, after its major city. By 910, one noble was elected king.

Now the battleground between Christians and Moors shifted further south to a 150-mile band stretching from León to just above Madrid—the territory of Old Castile. Neither the Christian King of León nor the Moorish Caliph could hold much of it for long, so local strongmen consolidated what power each could. When unification was finally effected, however, it was not by a leader from León, but by a Christian ruler from Navarre to the east. Sancho the Great of Navarre first conquered Aragón, then mastered Castile in 1029. Ironically, this unification eventuated in disharmony among the Christians that lasted for 500 years, for, when Sancho died one year after his conquest, he willed his new territory of Castile to one son, and the eastern territory of Aragón to another. Fernando I, the son who received Castile, quickly added León to his kingdom by marrying its heir, with the result that one king now ruled Castile and

León, while another governed Aragón. And so the situation would remain for centuries.

Castile and León took the lead in the struggle to reconquer the Moorish lands in the south. (See "Historical Profiles: Moors and the Reconquest," p. 283.) During this era, it functioned as a country, with all the trappings of nationhood: a capital—first at León, then Burgos, then Toledo, then Valladolid; universities—at Palencia, Salamanca and Valladolid; and numerous bishoprics, for the Christians were fervent, and their struggle with the Moors was a holy war.

Because of its leadership in the Reconquest, every Christian military success strengthened Castile and León. Before long it could count six million inhabitants which made it dominant in any Christian alliance. Leadership lasted for five centuries, until Isabella married Ferdinand from Aragón and together they defeated the last Moors in Granada. (See "Historical Profile: Ferdinand and Isabella, p. 197.") Even after, Castile and León remained the most populous region in Spain, until Felipe II moved the capital south to Madrid in 1561 to deprive Old Castile and León of its importance. Stagnation set in, people migrated elsewhere, gradually declining to the two and a half million of today, in a Spain grown four times as populous.

Old Castile and León make up one fifth of Spain. Except for mountains on its edges it is a mesa that extends the landscape of La Mancha from New Castile. Similar crops of wheat and other grains grow on similar rust-clay soil, in fields turned bright red in spring by a billion wild poppies. Today it is agriculturally rich, but it was not always so. From the 13th century until the modern era, monarchs favored the sheep production over agriculture. Flocks of northern sheep would be gathered for migrations south in the winter, then home again in the spring. These flocks numbered many millions, and royal decrees gave sheep the right to cross any land in their way. Moving multitudes stripped vegetation like locusts as they passed, leaving the soil naked to the depredations of wind and rain, and destroying what had been fertile land. Only in this century has prudent farming restored fertility, allowing farms to flourish again.

Despite the great expanse of land, dense communities developed. Most were founded during the Reconquest and required an architectural compactness that defensive walls could encircle. Population declines since the 16th century have allowed these towns to retain their character in a way that cities with expanding populations never could. These old towns make for unrivaled sightseeing.

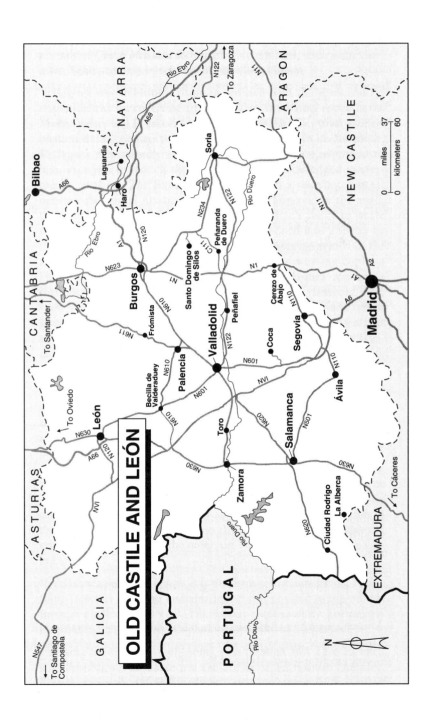

OLD CASTILE AND LEÓN

The area of Old Castile and León contains some of Spain's finest sights. **Burgos ★★★★** in the northeast boasts of a magnificent Gothic cathedral, and is itself a beautiful city that becomes irresistible when two magnificent monasteries in the suburbs are added. In the same area are an elegant Romanesque monastery at **Santo Domingo de Silos ★★★**, a Renaissance palace at **Peñaranda de Duero ★★** and the lovely town of **Soria ★★**. **Salamanca ★★★★**, in the southwest, retains its ancient university, an architectural jewel of the Plateresque, and its Old Cathedral, a preserved marvel. **Zamora ★★** and **Toro ★★**, nearby, display more Romanesque churches, while the entire town of **La Alberca ★★** seems preserved from the Middle Ages. **Segovia ★★★★★**, in the south center, is spectacularly situated to display a castle like that at Disneyland, but real. It also retains a working Roman aqueduct, an imposing cathedral, and a host of delicate Romanesque churches. In the 100 odd miles between Salamanca and Segovia lie **Ávila ★★★**, still surrounded by perfect medieval walls, and **Coca Castle ★★**, the paradigm of a medieval fortress. **León ★★★**, to the north, offers a Gothic cathedral to rival those in France, and its Old Quarter feels like the oldest in Spain. **Valladolid ★★**, in the center, is history personified. It was the capital for Ferdinand and Isabella, the city where Cervantes lived, and where Columbus died (both houses are preserved). Valladolid also offers the finest museum of wood sculpture in Spain. A splendid Romanesque church at **Fromista ★★** is in the same area (and equally close to Burgos). Lastly, the Rioja wine-growing region on the northeastern border, offers **Haro ★★** as a center for touring. The region of Old Castile and León can easily keep sightseers busy for two weeks.

ÁVILA ★★★

Population 41,735
Zip code: 05000; area code: 918

From **Madrid** *take A-6 north, exiting at Villacastin (exit 4) for N-110 west, a trip of 132 k. From* **Salamanca** *take N-501 east for 98 k. From* **Segovia** *take N-110 west for 66 k.*

The most striking feature of Ávila is its walls. No other city in Spain and few in the world can rival its imposing picture of strength and age.

A town existed on these heights long before the walls went up. But in the 11th century, when Alfonso VI drove south to take Toledo, the center of his power shifted. As he moved his fortifications southward, he ordered Ávila to be fortified. His son-in-law, Count Raymond of Burgundy, completed the project in three years, by 1091. Two thousand citizens did the work of enclosing a rectangle almost

3000 by 1500 feet with walls 10 feet thick, over 30 feet high, punctuated by 88 round towers.

A huge fort required people to defend it, so Alfonso encouraged subjects from northern Asturias to migrate, along with knights who won renown as the Knights of Ávila. The strategy evidently succeeded, for no one ever breached the walls. During the late stages of the Reconquest, the Knights of Ávila assisted in winning Zaragoza, Córdoba and Seville, and their spoils fueled the desire for a commemorating cathedral. Work in the earliest Gothic style began in 1157, in the form of a fortress stuck into the town walls. By the 15th century, Ávila attained its greatest wealth, but began to decline with the end of the Reconquest. Decline accelerated when its gentry followed the Spanish court to Madrid. The expulsion from Spain of the Moors, in 1609, sealed Ávila's fate by depriving it of most of its craftsmen.

In 1515, Teresa Sanchez de Cepeda y Ahumanda was born and, as Saint Theresa, brought fame again to Ávila. In 1522, at the age of 7, she attempted to run to the Moors, hoping to be martyred by them. She must have been an unusual little girl. Theresa's background was nobility tainted, from the Spanish point of view, by the blood of a Jewish grandfather. At puberty she began to experience mystical visions and religious dreams, all of which she wrote about exquisitely in diaries. At 19, she took the veil as a Carmelite nun. Led by visions to reform the Church, which had relaxed its views as it grew rich, she founded her own stricter version of the order, the Discalced (Barefoot) Carmelites. By the time she died in 1582, she had been interviewed by kings and earned a reputation as holy. This was confirmed by sainthood conferred only 40 years after her death.

Ávila's **walls** ★★★★ should be viewed and preferably walked. The **cathedral** ★★★ is an imposing monument; and the Romanesque basilica of San Vicente ★★ is huge and lovely. The **Monastery of Santo Tomás** ★★★ was founded by Ferdinand and Isabella and served as their palace, the mausoleum of their son, Don Juan, and the frequent residence of the Grand Inquisitor. For the Ávila of Sta. Teresa, see the **Convent of St. Teresa** ★, built on the site where she was born; the **Convent de La Encarnación** ★, where she lived as a nun for twenty years and experienced her visions; and the **Convent de San José** ★, the first for her new order. A half day is sufficient.

If arriving from **Madrid** *or* **Segovia**, *turn left off of N-501, called Av. de Madrid, after passing the Basilica of San Vincente. At the park turn left and make the first right*

*onto C. San Segundo which takes you past the town walls
and cathedral into the Pl. Sta. Teresa, for parking. If arriving from* **Salamanca** *turn left at the city walls onto Av. de
Madrid. Circle the walls until the large basilica of San
Vincente. Turn right. At the park turn left and take the
first right onto C. San Segundo which follows the town
walls, past the cathedral, and into the Pl. Sta. Teresa for
parking.*

Walls   ★★★★

These imposing barricades are almost 1000 years old, yet complete.
Of course, some reconstruction has been necessary, but overall their
character remains unchanged. For full appreciation the walls should
be viewed from a distance to gather their extent, viewed from the base
to appreciate their height, and walked along to appreciate their mas-
siveness and to feel what it would be like to defend a medieval city.

*Pass from Pl. Sta. Teresa through the gate into the old city. Once
through, turn onto the second right, following the street as it
bends left and right again until it reaches the Pl. de la Catedral.
Ahead, on the right, is the front of the cathedral, on the left is the
14th-century palace of a nobleman named Valderrabános, now a
hotel.*

Cathedral   ★★★

*Open daily from 9 a.m. to 1 p.m. and 3-7 p.m. (Opens at 10 a.m. in
winter.) Admission: 100 ptas., to the Sanctuary.* The outside of massive grey granite is a curious architectural mismash, punctuated by
rows of balls. The 14th-century left door, carved of sandstone that
weathered poorly, was moved from the west side of the church to its
present protected location. The center portal, more animatedly carved
than the others, was added in the 18th century. Most dramatic is the
back of the church, so fortresslike that it is incorporated into the town
walls.

The interior is a surprise, after the dull fortress-exterior. The nave
soars and looks up to stones surprisingly patterned in red and yellow.
Best of all, the clerestory stretches high, letting enough light inside to
see the art clearly, a pleasant change from most Spanish churches. The
altar is by Berruguette and others. At the center of the ambulatory
resides a lovely alabaster tomb of Cardinal Madrigal, a 15th-century
bishop of Ávila depicted sitting and writing. In the south (left-hand)
aisle, the sacristy still wears enough original paint to suggest what a
church of the period would look like when new—all colorful and
bright. Its rear serves as a museum, containing an El Greco portrait
and a huge monstrance (portable reliquary). A doorway further on
leads to a delicate cloister.

C. Reyes Católicos runs behind the Palacio Valderrábanos hotel (opposite the cathedral) west into the Pl. de la Victoria. The street going left across the plaza runs to the Pl. General Mola and the **Palace of Onates**, *sporting a tower complete with battlements. A gentle right along the palace leads into the Pl. la Santa where the church of the* **Convent of Sta. Teresa** *is located.*

Convento de Sta. Teresa

Open daily from 9 a.m. to 1 p.m. and from 4-7 p.m. Admission: 50 ptas. The present Baroque edifice, dating from the late 17th century, is built on land once owned by Saint Theresa's father, on which she was born and raised. Off the north transept an ornate chapel marks the place of her birth.

West of the church front is the Renaissance **Palace de Nuñez Vela** ★ *with lovely windows and an elegant patio. Back at the Cathedral, a street along its north side leads through the main gate of the walls. Outside, straight ahead, a left from the Pl. de Italia leads to the* **Casa de los Deanes**.

Casa de los Deanes

Open Tues.-Sun. 10 a.m. to 2 p.m. and 4-7 p.m. Open Sun. 11 a.m. to 1:30 p.m. Closed Mon. Admission: 200 ptas. This 16th-century palace, once the deanery of the cathedral, is now the local museum. It contains a fine triptych by Memling, along with early furniture and some attractive ceramics.

Past the Deanery, the first left runs to a park. Down the right side of the park to its end, a left along the end, brings a first right which leads to the **Basilica of San Vicente**.

San Vicente ★★

Open Tues.-Sun. 10 a.m. to 1 p.m. and 4 -7 p.m. (until 6 p.m. in winter and Sun.) Closed Mon. Admission: 25 ptas. Access is from the south side. The church commemorates the martyrdom in 303 of the child-saint Vincent and his sisters. The basilica was begun in the 12th century, but took 200 years to complete, so it mainly is Romanesque but incorporates early Gothic elements, such as ceiling ribs. The front displays unusually lively Romanesque carving around a double doorway. Inside, beneath a fine lantern tower, rests the 12th-century tomb of the Saint. The canopy is a later addition, but the carving on the tomb is of the period and depicts the martyrdom in an evocative and accomplished manner. A slab in the crypt below marks the supposed spot where the Romans killed these children. The ensemble and its display make a deeply felt memorial.

The walls lead south to the parking in the Pl. Sta. Teresa, which at its east end presents the church of **San Pedro** ★ , *a lovely Romanesque edifice, with fine lantern and rose windows. By pass-*

*ing along the north (left) side of the church, one can take the C.
Duque de Alba, which heads left, for three blocks to the* **Convento
of San José**.

Convento San José   ★

Open daily 10 a.m. to 1 p.m. and 4-7 p.m. Admission: 30 ptas. Saint
Theresa began her reform of the Church with this convent in 1562, by
offering the inhabitants a simple life of worship. Inside are tombs of
the early adherents, including that of Lorenzo de Cepeda, the Saint's
brother. A small museum displays momentos of the Saint and musical
instruments the first nuns played. It seems that Theresa played percus-
sion.

*From the Pl. Sta. Teresa parking lot, past the front of San Pedro
Church, then along its south face, the Av. de Alferez Provisional is
entered. In a few blocks it passes the* **Monesterio San Tomás**.

Monesterio San Tomás

*Open daily 10:30 a.m. to 1 p.m. and 4-7 p.m. Admission: 100 ptas.,
to the cloisters.* For a time this monastery was the favorite residence of
Ferdinand and Isabella. They commissioned it, funded it lavishly, and
spent their summers here. Isabella's former confessor, Tomas de
Torquemada, the first and most infamous Inquisitor General of the
Inquisition, often joined them. He liked the place so much that he
chose to be buried there. But tragedy struck when Ferdinand and Isabella's son, Don Juan, suddenly died. They buried him in this beloved
spot, but they could not bear to pass summers in the monastery thereafter, and turned their attentions elsewhere.

The facade displays the emblems of Ferdinand and Isabella—entwined
arrows and yokes. The Spanish names for which (*flechas* and *yugo*)
begins with their initials ("y" in the Middle Ages stood for the later
"i" as the first letter of "Isabella"). Architectural details are high-
lighted throughout by rows of balls, the peculiar Ávila style. Inside, at
the crossing of the transept, is the mausoleum of the only son of Ferdinand and Isabella, who died at 19. The delicate tomb is a Renaissance marvel by the Florentine Domenico Fancelli, who years later
carved another in Granada for the parents of the boy. The altar retablo
depicting the life of Saint Thomas in high relief is a masterpiece by
Berruguette. In the third chapel on the north side are effigies of Juan
D'Ávila and his wife, who were Prince Juan's tutors. A plain slab in the
sacristy marks the final resting place (until he goes elsewhere) of
Torquemada, the infamous Inquisitor General.

Three cloisters gird the church. The first is relatively unadorned, the
second is the "Silent Cloister," intimate and richly decorated on the
upper gallery. Stairs go up to a choral gallery furnished with finely
carved 15th-century Gothic choir stalls. Then a second flight leads to
a gallery overlooking the altar, and allows appreciation of its detail.

Beyond the Silent Cloister is the third, larger, solemn "Cloister of the Catholic Monarchs." It displays a collection of oriental objects gathered by missionary brothers. Stairs lead up to a gallery in which Isabella and Ferdinand sat in virtual thrones. Notice their coats of arms on the balustrade.

WHERE TO STAY

Ávila provides few hotels, but since few people spend the night their number usually proves sufficient. Two special hotels are included.

EXPENSIVE ($100-$200)

Palacio de Valderrábanos   1st-class ★ ★ ★ ★
Pl. de la Catedral, 9. Rooms: 73. ☎ *21 10 23; FAX 25 16 91; Telex 22481.* The building was a 14th-century palace for an early Bishop of Ávila. Were it not for the equally historic parador this would be the clear choice for spending a special night. As it is, the choices are between this hotel, located near the Cathedral, and the Parador, located by a garden near the walls. You cannot lose. The colors of the Palacio are rather loud and the interiors dark, with a feel of the thirties about the decoration. Once exceptionally grand, the hotel is showing signs of age and dust, but it remains a special place, especially when a room overlooks the cathedral.

Parador Raimundo de Borgoña   2nd-class ★ ★ ★
Marqués de Canales y Chozas, 16 (by the middle of the north wall). Rooms: 62. ☎ *21 13 40; FAX 22 61 66.* This is the former 15th-century Benavides Palace. Twelve of the rooms are in the palace, the rest in a modern addition of no special charm. Most of the furniture in the public areas is antique. The garden is lovely and leads to a stairway up to the city walls.

INEXPENSIVE (UNDER $50)

Hostale Continental   2nd-class ★ ★
Pl. de la Catedral, 6. Rooms: 54. ☎ *21 15 02.* The hotel is from a bygone era, but is clean, inexpensive, and has private baths. All in all, this is a comfortable place to lay your head.

El Rastro   ★
Pl. del Rastro, 1. (Halfway along the inside of the south wall of Ávila) Rooms: 14. ☎ *22 12 18.* Known better as a restaurant, 14 comfortable, if small, rooms are offered for the night in a Rennaisance building, and are rock-bottom in price.

WHERE TO EAT

The specialties of the area are roasts, especially lamb (*cordero*) and veal (*tenera*). The special dish of the city is a desert of candied egg yolks called *yemas*.

MODERATE ($20-$50)

El Molina de La Losa ★★★

Bajada de La Losa, ☎ *21 11 01. Closed Monday in winter.* The setting is extraordinary. Head out of Ávila, following signs to Salamanca. Just past the west end of the walls, as the road crosses a bridge spanning the gentle Adaja River, look right to see the restaurant, looking like a French country inn, on an isthmus in the river. In fact it is an ancient mill. Turn right across the bridge at the sign for the restaurant. Do not be put off by the rustic bar as you enter, the restaurant upstairs is pinewood and country furniture with gingham table cloths. There are views of the river and Ávila's walls. The lamb is delicious here, but the specialty is fish fresh from the river. ***Visa and MasterCard accepted.***

El Rastro ★

Pl. del Rastro, 1. ☎ *22 12 18.* Halfway along the inside of the south wall of Ávila is this noted restaurant, housed in a former palace, though the decor is more rustic than elegant. Roasts are the specialties. When the restaurant is crowded, as it is frequently, the service can be slow. ***Diners, MasterCard, Visa and Amex accepted.***

INEXPENSIVE (UNDER $20)

A number of inexpensive restaurants surround the large Pl. de la Victoria, located three short blocks west of the cathedral. All serve reasonably prepared food.

DIRECTORY

INFORMATION • *Located at Pl. de la Catedral, 4*, it is open weekdays from 9 a.m. to 3 p.m. and from 5-7 p.m. Open until 2 p.m. on Saturdays.

POST OFFICE AND TELEPHONES • The post office is located at *Pl. de la Catedral, 2*, with telephones next door.

TRAINS AND BUSES • The train station is located at *Av. de Portugal, 17* (☎ 22 01 88; information: ☎ 22 65 19) at the end of Av. José Antonio, northeast of the city center. Service between Madrid (2 hours, under 1000 ptas.) is frequent, as are connections to most cities in Old Castile.

The bus station is located at the intersection of *Av. Madrid and Av. Portugal*, two blocks due east of San Vicente basilica (☎ 22 01 54).

POLICE • Av. José Antonio (☎ 21 11 88).

BURGOS ★★★★

Population: 56,449
Zip code: 09003; area code: 947

From **Madrid** *A-1 (E-5) becomes N-1, reaching Burgos in 235 k. From* **Valladolid** *take N-620 (E-80) for 125 k. From* **Segovia** *take N-110 for 57 k to Cerezo de Abajo where N-1*

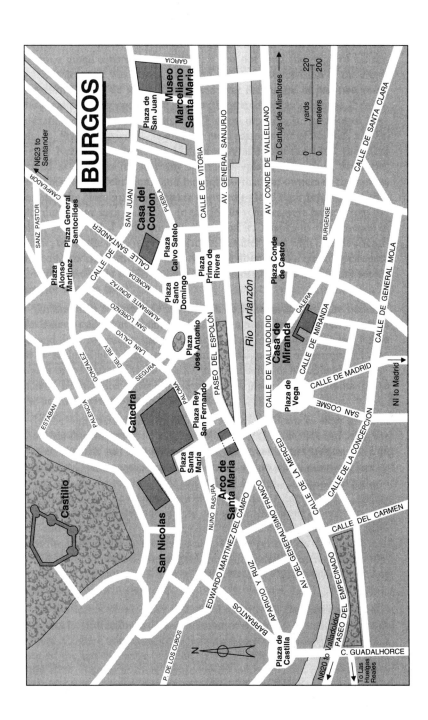

BURGOS

N623 to Santander

CAMPEADOR

SANZ PASTOR

Plaza General Santocildes

Plaza Alonso Martinez

CALLE DE SANTANDER

SAN JUAN

Casa del Cordon

Plaza Calvo Satelo

MONEDA

PUEBLA

CALLE DE VITORIA

Museo Marceliano Santa Maria

Plaza de San Juan

GARCIA

AV. GENERAL SANJURJO

Plaza Santo Domingo

ALMIRANTE BONIFAZ

SAN LORENZO

LAIN CALVO

DEL REY

GONZALEZA

PALENCIA

ESTABAN

Plaza Rey San Fernando

Plaza José Antonio

PALOMA

SEGURA

Catedral

Plaza Santa Maria

Castillo

San Nicolas

P. DE LOS CUBOS

NUÑO RASURA

Arco de Santa Maria

EDWARDO MARTINEZ DEL CAMPO

BARRANTOS

APARICIO Y RUIZ

AV. DEL GENERALISMO FRANCO

Plaza de Castilla

N620 to Valladolid

PASEO DEL ESPOLÓN

Rio Arlanzón

Plaza Primo de Rivera

CALLE DE VALLADOLID

Plaza Conde de Castro

CALERA

CALLE DE MIRANDA

Casa de Miranda

Plaza de Vega

SAN COSME

CALLE DE LA MERCED

CALLE DE LA CONCEPCIÓN

CALLE DEL CARMEN

PASEO DEL EMPECINADO

C. GUADALHORCE

To Las Huelgas Reales

CALLE DE MADRID

NI to Madrid

AV. GENERAL SANJURJO

AV. CONDE DE VALLELLANO

To Cartuja de Miraflores

BURGENSE

CALLE DE GENERAL MOLA

CALLE DE SANTA CLARA

0   yards   220
0   meters   200

N

is picked up going north for a total of 194 k. From **León**
take N-601 south towards Valladolid for 67 k to Becilla de
Valderaduey where you change to N-610 to Palencia for 61
k, and there pick up N-620 (E-80) for a total of 216 k.
From **Valladolid** *N-620 north reaches Burgos in 117 k, but*
be careful not to turn off into Palencia. From **Santander**
N-623 goes south to Burgos in 93 k. From **Bilbao** *A-68*
heads south toward Logrono. Just before Miranda in 67 k,
turn west onto either A-1 or N-1 for a continuation of 90 k.
From **Pamplona** *N-III heads west to Logrono in 92 k. There*
you take N-120 for 113 k further west.

Burgos began as a military outpost to fend off Moors, but gained
prominence when Count Fernán González briefly united the county
of Castile in 950 and made Burgos his seat of authority. The city's
importance was enhanced by Fernando I, the first king of a united
Castile and León, who named it his capital in 1037. Fifty years later,
however, Alfonso VI captured Toledo and moved the capital there.
Over the next 400 years, these two cities vied with one another for
the honor of being Christian Spain's primary city, and the capital
moved between them. Burgos undertook a cathedral in 1221, in
part to meet the "cathedral challenge" from Toledo. The rivalry became moot, however, after the conquest of Granada in 1492, when
Ferdinand and Isabella chose still another city, Valladolid, as their
capital. Burgos did not really need the status of a capital to be important, because it was situated at the crossroads of the main route to
Santiago de Compostela and to southern Spain. It was and remains a
commercial and military center.

Burgos claims El Cid as its most famous son, though, as Rodrigo
Diaz, he was actually born in Vivar, 6 miles away. When Alfonso VI
came to the throne after the suspicious death of his brother, the nobles of Castile and León appointed Diaz as their spokesperson to
force Alfonso to swear publicly that he bore no complicity in the
death. Alfonso never forgave his vassal for this, and soon found an
excuse to expel him. Homeless, Rodrigo became a mercenary soldier
and enjoyed outstanding success, campaigning both against and also
for the Moors. Soon he was known by the Arabic title of El Sidi,
"The Commander," which the Christians mispronounced El Cid. El
Cid's greatest feat was the conquest of a huge area around Valencia,
which he held for five years until he was defeated and killed by the
Moors. His wife, Doña Ximena, brought his body home, and today
it lies in the Burgos Cathedral.

The cathedral and old town lie along the Arlanzón River, which is lined on the north side with trees and flowered promenades. The old town, hemmed on its other side by a forested hill topped by a ruined castle, is relatively small. The newer city spreads east and west and across the river, but offers little of historic or scenic interest. Unlike the typical medieval hill town with a maze of cobblestoned alleys, old Burgos seems fresh and light, a place to relax as well as to enjoy the sights.

Arriving from **Valladolid** *you enter the western part of Burgos and follow the Arlanzón River on Paseo del Empecinado as far as a pedestrian bridge opposite the cathedral. Turn right here, away from the bridge, into the Pl. de Vega for parking. More parking is available at the next bridge after a right at the Pl. de Conde de Castro, where a large lot stands at the next left. From* **Madrid** *and* **Segovia** *on N-1, follow the opposite bank of the river and pass the lovely Pl. Miguel Primo de Riveira and bridge. Turn left and cross the river, then take the second left into a large parking lot. From the* **north** *you enter Burgos from the east. Cross, if necessary, to the southern side of the Arlanzón River and follow it until opposite the cathedral. Turn left into the Pl. de Vega for parking.*

WHAT TO SEE AND DO

The paramount attraction of Burgos is her **cathedral** ★★★★★, perhaps the finest Gothic cathedral in Spain, especially when considering its setting. The **Casa de Miranda** ★★ museum is also worth a look, as is the elegant facade of the **Casa del Cordón** ★, in which Ferdinand and Isabella met Columbus on his return from his second trip to the New World. Not to be missed are two exceptional early buildings in suburbs on either side of the city. **Las Huelgas Reales** ★★★★ is a magnificent convent from the 12th century, displaying clothing of the period, and **Miraflores** ★★★ is an elegant monastery from the 15th, with exceptional sculpture. The number of sights in Burgos is not great, but their quality is.

Cathedral ★★★★★

Open daily from 10 a.m. to 1 p.m. and from 4-7 p.m. Admission: 300 ptas., for the treasury and cloister. This is Spain's third largest cathedral, after Toledo and Seville, but its most imposing. It is variegated yet uniform, solidly standing as if for eternity—the finest example of the Spanish Gothic. The foundation was laid in 1221 by Fernando III, who conquered much of Andalusia and was designated a saint for his piety and compassion. The body of the cathedral was completed by the end of that century. In the 15th century a second stage of con-

struction took place. Tall spires were added to the front, the huge
Condestable Chapel was placed on the rear, a cloister built on the
side, and the other chapels decorated anew. All this was effected by
some of the great artists of the time who gathered in Burgos for this
purpose. Thus, the interior decor and some exterior work are Plateresque. Slightly later, grand ramped stairways were added around the
cathedral so that a walk to the cathedral would also include a tour of
its exterior.

Appreciation of the cathedral starts with the exterior and its front in
the **Pl. Santa María**. The intricate openwork spires soar three hundred
feet into the sky, reminiscent of the Cathedral of Cologne. In fact, the
Cathedral's first architect was from Cologne and surely imported the
design. Above the **rose window** in the center is a row of **statues** of
kings of Castile and bishops of Burgos. Over the door an incongruous
classical pediment separates a bishop leading a king on the right side
and a queen on the left, each holding real spears.

Go left up the staired ramp that climbs to the **Coronería Portal**,
located in the center of the northern side. Graceful draped statues line
both sides of the door. Under the Christ enthroned above the door is
a traditional carving of heaven and hell, with hell, as usual, the more
striking. Around the corner in a recess is the **Pellejeria Portal**, which
was once the most convenient entrance for tanners whose factories
were located on this side of the cathedral. This portal is obviously Plateresque, though more balanced than usual, and imposing. Around
the back of the cathedral is the famed **Chapel of the Condestable**,
whose octagonal order contrasts with the busy Gothic spires above.
From the rear, flying buttresses can be viewed in a lovely line. Around
the back an elegant sweep of stairs leads down and past the splendid
Sacramental Portal. Angels play while the four Evangelists write at
their desks. Note the vigorous scene of hell, and the man praying in a
boiling caldron.

Inside, the nave rises to vaulting made elegant with 15th-century ribs,
though the view down the cathedral is unfortunately obstructed by
the choir. Atop a clock high on the left is the 16th-century *Papa-
mosca*, "Flycatcher," with a bird who opens his mouth each time the
clock chimes. Proceed left. The first chapel presents a riotously overblown 18th-century retablo dedicated to Saint Tecla. It is the work of
a member of the Churriguera family who helped create the Baroque
Churigueresque style of architecture. Next is a chapel for Saint Ana,
built a century and a half earlier. It contains a lovely retablo by Gil de
Siloé. The two chapels demonstrate, respectively, ornateness as
opposed to art. At the transept, look left to a glorious diamond flight
of **Renaissance stairs**, all gilded and lovely, that leads nowhere.

Enter the nave to view the altar and choir, but look up first to see an
elegant lantern where the transept crosses the nave. Under the lantern, a slab marks the place where El Cid rests beside his wife Xemina.

The 16th-century reredos behind the high altar effectively place Biblical figures in classical niches. Though ornate, the choirstalls in the coro are well done and are unusual for having inlays. In the center of the coro is a strange 13th-century coffin of an English Archbishop named Maurice. His wood effigy is covered with embossed copper and Limoge enameling.

Continue around the left side of the apse to come to the chapel of Saint Nicolas, which contains a portable organ from the 16th century. Next is a 16th-century chapel with an **elliptical dome**, followed by two 13th-century chapels.

In the left rear is the outstanding Chapel of the Condestable. This addition to the cathedral, a medley of the Isabeline, was fashioned in 1482 for the Constable of Castile and worked on by all the great artists in Burgos. Elegant vaulting meets in a star unexpectedly filled by glass. The pillars are carved with figures of the Apostles, rendered by the Renaissance master, Gil de Siloé. Compared with the usual busy altar retablo, this one is bold and dramatic. It was carved by Gil de Siloé's son Diego. The peaceful Constable and his wife, carved by an unknown artist, face the altar. It was they who owned the Casa del Cordón (see below) where Columbus was received by Ferdinand and Isabella on his second return from the New World. Shields on the rear wall and the balastrade record the families of the Constable and his wife. To the right rear, a door leads to a sacristy in which hangs a purported da Vinci painting of Mary Magdaline.

Behind the rear of the main cathedral altar a smaller altar of three panels displays a moving depiction of Christ's walk to Calvary. The Santiago Chapel next door carries a ceiling with delicate ribs. In the south transept a magnificent Gothic paneled door on the left leads into 14th-century cloisters, with statues everywhere and more chapels at the far end. The leftmost chapel stores clerical vestments, plates and manuscripts, including the marriage contract of El Cid. The next room, the Chapterhouse, has a lovely Mudejar ceiling and displays a graceful Memling *Virgin and Child*, along with a Van Eyke. The *"Coffer of El Cid"* is bolted to the wall. This chest, purportedly El Cid's security for a loan worth far less than the gold that filled it, was found to hold sand when it was opened after his repayment of the loan. In the adjoining Sacristy is a masterpiece of sculpture by Diego de Siloé of *Christ at the Column*.

Back in the Cathedral proper, return to the front along the right side of the nave. The large chapel of the Visitation contains a carved tomb of the Bishop of Lerma, a Renaissance masterpiece of a dour faced personage. Also in that chapel hangs a delicate painting of the Madonna and Child. Notice the beautiful vaulting above. In the front chapel on the far right is a gruesome crucifixion constructed with a figure made of buffalo hide that looks for all the world like human skin.

Outside, take a look at the curious figures that make up the fountain in the plaza. Mary and her son wear real gilt crowns, while grotesques below ride fish with ears. Go up the ramped stair again, this time for a view of the **Church of San Nicolás**, *directly ahead. Look opposite the church front at the engaging Renaissance* **Palace of Castrofuerte** *with its lovely patio.*

Iglesia de San Nicolás ★

Open daily from 9 a.m. to 1:30 p.m. and from 4:30-6:30 p.m.
Although the architecture of this late Gothic church is not special, some of the art inside is. The retablo by **Francisco de Colonia** is huge and ornate, containing hundreds of stone figures depicting the life of Saint Nicholas. At the base of the altar are two fine pairs of tombs of the church's patrons, Alfonzo and Gonzalo Polanco, and their wives.

Walking directly along the face of the cathedral brings the Arch of Santa María.

Arco de Santa María ★

At this spot stood a gate through 11th-century walls that once girded the town. Today only a few stones on either side of the arch remain, inscribed here and there with Arabic writing. Past the gate looking back in the direction of the cathedral is the facade of the arch that, despite a more modern appearance, dates to 1530. Just before its construction citizens throughout Spain had risen against their new king, Carlos V, to protest his preference for foreign advisors. This was the Comuneros Revolt which forced the king to accept many of the rebel's demands. After the king agreed to the will of the people, the citizens of Burgos raised this monument to atone for their participation in the uprising.

The center figure on the top register is Count Fernán González, the first man to unite Castile. On his left is Carlos V; on his right, El Cid. Below, two legendary early judges flank Diego Porcelos, the alleged founder of the city of Burgos. He was called Porcelos (Pig) because he was one of seven siblings, which is the size of a normal pig litter. With its tiny turrets evoking a castle, the arch seems a bit of fantasy.

Stretching west is the lovely Paseo del Espolan, lined with sycamores, flowers and topiary, where the citizens of Burgos stroll. The second left leads to the **Plaza Mayor ★**, *a.k.a.* **Plaza José Antonio**. *Unusual in its oval shape, the arcaded plaza presents an attractive appearance; it houses stores and numerous cafes. On the south side stands the Ayuntamiento (City Hall), opened in 1791. Leave the east side of the Plaza, opposite the cathedral, and pass through the Pl. Santo Domingo. Take the next left onto the wide pedestrian walk, C. Santander. Turn right into the attractive Pl. de*

Calvo Sotelo for the Casa del Cordón, with the arresting carving of
a rope forming a triangle over the door.

Casa del Cordón ★

Although it is now a bank, this handsome structure was once the palace of the Constables of Castile, at which the sovereigns of the time
often stopped for extended visits. Here Ferdinand and Isabella met
Columbus to learn about his second voyage. Here, too, Philip the
Handsome, the young husband of their daughter Juana the Mad, and
father of Carlos V, died from a chill caught while playing ball with a
retainer. (See "Historical Profile: Ferdinand and Isabella," p.197.) Its
popular name "House of the Rope," obviously comes from the carved
Franciscan cord serving as a kind of tympanum to frame the coats-
of-arms of the Constables of Castile. The "dogs (?)" in the top door
corners are a whimsical touch. Altogether the facade is unique, and
the building is infused with history.

The narrow C. de Puebla exiting the northeast corner of the
plaza leads, after two long blocks, to the Pl. de San Juan and a
museum displaying the work of a noted Spanish painter from the
early part of the century. The statue in the plaza center is of Diego
Rodriquez Porcelos, legendary founder of the city. Opposite are
romantic ruins of the **Monastery of San Juan** ★ *, and, occupying*
the former cloisters, the **Casa Cultural** ★ *with a fine Plateresque*
front.

Museo Marceliano Santa María ★

Open Tues.-Sat. 10 a.m. to 2 p.m. and 4-7 p.m. (until 6 p.m. in win-
ter.) Open Sun. morning. Closed Mon. Admission: 100 ptas. The first
floor is for temporary shows, the second displays the works of a
painter from Burgos named Marceliano Santa María, who painted in a
"thirties" style. His work is clearly a cut above the ordinary, with
unusual choices of subjects, nice coloring (purples and limes), and
skillful use of light.

Across the river, three streets back and midway between the
pedestrian bridge which leads to the Arco Santa María and the
vehicular bridge upstream, stands the **Casa de Miranda** *on C.*
Miranda.

Casa de Miranda (Museo Arqueológico) ★★

Open Tues.-Fri. 10 a.m. to 2 p.m. and 4-7 p.m. Open Sat. and Sun.
11 a.m. to 1 p.m. Closed Mon. Admission: 150 ptas. The building, a
16th-century palace, is elegant with an unusual Plateresque patio containing columns that evoke the classical. Its grand staircase is imposing. The art collection is small but unusual. The tomb of Juan de
Padilla, a page of Isabella's killed during the siege of Granada, is a
masterwork by Gil de Siloé. On the first floor is a collection of Visigothic sarcophagi, and also Gothic and Renaissance tombs. On the sec-

ond floor are some extraordinary Moorish pieces, including a 10th-century ivory case for balls (perhaps for some sort of bowling), and an ivory casket from the 11th century, with Limoges plaques for Christian use affixed to the ends later. There is also an interesting altar of beaten and enamelled copper images of saints from the 12th century. The paintings vary in quality, but a weeping, Flemish style Christ is riveting.

A convent and a monastery in opposite suburbs should not be missed. **Las Helgas Reales Convent** *is 1.5 k west of the center. Take the river road on the bank opposite the cathedral (signs point to N-630) until you see signs directing you to the convent.* **Cartuja de Miraflores Monastery** *is 4 k east of the city. Follow the river road east on the side opposite the cathedral until signs direct you to the monastery.*

Convento Las Huelgas Reales   ★★★★

Open Tues.-Sat. 11 a.m. to 2 p.m. and 4-6 p.m. Open Sun. 11 a.m. to 4 p.m. Closed Mon. Admission: 275 ptas., for guided tour. Free Wed. 1.5k. west of Burgos. The convent originally was a summer residence (*huelgas* means "repose") for the first kings of Castile, but in 1187 was converted to a monastery for women of the highest rank by the queen of Alfonso VIII. She was Eleanor of Aquitaine, Richard the Lionheart's sister. The convent eventually controlled 50 manors and towns whose revenues supported the convent nicely enough that often queens would spend times of retreat here. The convent grew in size over the centuries, accruing various architectural styles. A plain 12th-century Cistercian dominates, but there are distinctive Mudejar, Gothic and Plateresque elements as well.

The convent served as a royal pantheon for the first kings and queens of Castile. Napoléon's soldiers desecrated most of the tombs during their occupation in the 19th century, but fortunately missed a few early tombs that contained clothing miraculously preserved from the 12th and 13th centuries, now on display in the convent's **Museo de Talas**. A more curious note is a strange statue with an articulated arm used to knight several early Castilian kings and nobles.

Past a Gothic arch and along the cloister, the church tower, with model castles on its top, beckons. The church is entered from a porch on which four early ornate sarcophagi still rest. The church is early 13th-century and its simple Cistercian style allows artworks clear display. Kneeling statues of the founders, Eleanor (Leonor in Spanish) of Aquitaine and Alfonso VIII, flank the altar. Royal tombs line the aisles, while the simple and moving tombs of the founders and their children are housed in the separate nun's choir. Here magnificent tapestries line the walls, and the wood floors seem too old to walk on.

The "Gothic" cloister retains enough intricate Mudejar stucco-work and wood ceiling to convey a sense of its original delicate appearance. Exquisite doors lead to the sacristy. The large chapterhouse with 9 bays displays what is said to be the standard of the Moorish commander from the battle of Las Navas de Tolosa. If only one battle turned the tide for the Christians in the Reconquest it was this victory in 1212 when Christians defeated a large army of fierce Almohad Moors. Although the "standard" is more likely a flap from a tent, it is still lovely and rich with history. This hall has seen its own history as well. It was here that Franco assembled his first government during the Spanish Civil War.

In the **Museo de Ricas Telas** (Clothing Museum), the former sewing room of the convent, clothing, jewelry and swords from the 12th and 13th century are simply displayed. Most remarkable is the equipment found with Infante Don Fernando de la Cerda, displayed in cases 8-11. But all of the clothing is striking for its intricacy and beauty. Be sure to look at the dress of María Almenar from 1196.

The Romanesque Cloister from the 12th century, the earlier of two, is simple with rounded arches. Rooms off this cloister constitute the royal apartments of the convent, with fine Mudejar decoration still intact in places. Across the garden stands the Chapel of Santiago, looking entirely Moorish, with fine wood paneling inside. A lifesize statue of Saint James sits on a throne, his articulated right arm holding a sword that can be lowered through a series of counterbalances. It was used to dub new knights, usually princes, in the early 13th century. Tradition has it that it was built so the later Fernando III would not suffer the indignity of being knighted by an inferior.

Cartuja de Miraflores

Open Mon.-Sat. 10:30 a.m. to 3 p.m. and 4-6 p.m. Open Sun. and holidays 11:20 a.m. until 12:30 and 1-3 P.M, then 4-7 p.m. Admission: free. 4 k west of Burgos. In 1442 King Juan II decided to erect a monastery on the site of one of his father's palaces to house his family's tomb. When the king died in 1454 the unfinished project was completed by his loving daughter Isabella the Catholic. She called on Juan de Colonia who worked on the second stage of the Burgos Cathedral, to help her finish the memorial to her parents. He designed a plain exterior with only a florid Gothic doorway surmounted by the founder's lion-held shields to break the monotony, making the rich interior all the more impressive.

The superb altar and marble tombs are perhaps the finest works of Gil de Siloé, and fit harmoniously. They are a rare instance of plan and execution by the same artist (with assistance on the retablo by Diego de la Cruz). Instead of the standard rectangular design, the gilt retablo presents a great circle enclosing a crucifixion. At its bottom, left and right, figures of the king and queen kneel beneath their coats of arms. But in front of the altar is the reason for the entire edifice—the paired tomb of Juan II and his wife, Doña Isabel of Portugal. Its base forms a star on which countless tiny figures, mostly characters from the New Testament, adore and watch over the recumbent king and queen above. The openwork carving is so intricate that it is difficult to believe it could be fashioned of marble. The inscription reads: "It does not have an equal in the world and constitutes the principle adornment and glory of this church."

In a niche to the left is a tomb that almost rivals this one. It was made for the Infante Don Alfonso, the son of Juan II—and Isabella's brother who would have been king instead of Isabella had he lived. But at age 14, he fell to his death from the walls of the Alcázar in Segovia, thereby allowing Isabella to ascend the throne. His tomb is masterful, if somewhat ornate, but the artistry of Gil de Siloé saves it from prettiness. The spectacled figure in the left bottom register is said to be the artist himself. In the chapel, to the left of the altar, usually hangs a splendid *Annunciation* by Pedro Berruguette, though it was not there on our last visit.

WHERE TO STAY

Burgos offers one great hotel and a number of comfortable ones of little distinction. Even the undistinguished hotels, however, charge in the expensive range. The reason is that Burgos is a prosperous city that caters to prosperous businesspeople.

EXPENSIVE ($100-$200)

Palacio Landa   1st-class ★★★★★

Carretera Madrid-Irun, at kilometer 236. Rooms: 42. ☎ *20 63 43; FAX 26 46 76; Telex 39534.* This is one of the premier hotels in Spain, with an elegance surpassed by few others, and its prices are reasonable considering what it offers. Located 3.5 k south of Burgos on N-1, it can be reached by going south on Calle Madrid, which leads away from the Santa María pedestrian bridge. The tranquil hotel is installed in part of a 14th-century castle, carted here stone by stone, and decorated inside with lovely antiques. The Palacio Landa provides whatever the heart desires, including swimming.

Condestable   1st-class ★★

C. Vitoria, 8. Rooms: 85. ☎ *26 71 25; FAX 20 46 45; Telex 395 72.* The location is good—1 block north of the river on a nice shopping street, and 4 short blocks from the cathedral. This is a modern hotel, efficiently run, with small, sleekly designed rooms and baths.

Almirante Bonifaz   1st-class ★★

C. Vitoria, 22. Rooms: 79. ☎ *20 69 43; FAX 20 29 19; Telex 39430.* This is the same type of hotel as the Condestable and equally efficient. Located on the same street, it is two short blocks further east from the cathedral.

MODERATE ($50-$99)

Del Cid   **2nd-class ★ ★ ★**

Pl. Santa María, 8. Rooms: ☎ *20 87 15; FAX 26 94 60.* This hotel stretches the moderate category, making it only in the off-season. Still it costs less at any time than the expensive hotels in town. It also has the best location possible—in the cathedral square, off to the west side. In addition, the building is a 15th-century house, rambling and full of curiosities. Recently it became affiliated with the Best Western hotel chain, and we will have to see what that does to the service. So far only the public areas have been air-conditioned. Associated with the hotel is a good restaurant, discussed below.

Fernán González   **2nd-class ★ ★ ★**

C. Calera, 17 (across the river from the old town, left from the Santa María pedestrian bridge). Rooms: 84. ☎ *20 94 41; FAX 27 47 21; Telex 39602.* This is a perfectly acceptable hotel with more atmosphere than many in town, fair prices, and views of the river, Espolón and cathedral from the front rooms. Because it is an older hotel, it offers interesting architecture and antiques. Located just across the pedestrian Santa María bridge and left onto C. Calera. The restaurant is quite elegant.

Cordón   **2nd-class ★ ★**

La Puebla, 6. Rooms: 35. ☎ *26 50 00; FAX 20 02 69.* Still another modern hotel is this one, similar to the Condestable, located one block north of it. Its small size allows greater attention to each guest, though few of the staff speak English.

INEXPENSIVE (UNDER $50)

España   **4th-class ★**

Paseo de Espolón. Rooms: 69. ☎ *20 63 40; FAX 20 13 30.* The hotel is situated beside the lovely Espolón and overlooks the river. It is modern and the staff is friendly.

Inexpensive *hostales* concentrate around the Pl. de Vega, just across the river from the Santa María pedestrian bridge. None stands out enough to earn recommendation, but most serve their purpose.

WHERE TO EAT

As in most of Old Castile, roast lamb and suckling pig are specialties, along with a local soup of lamb and shrimp.

EXPENSIVE ($50+)

Mesón del Cid   **★ ★ ★**

Pl. Santa María, 8 (to the west of the Cathedral square). ☎ *20 59 71. Closed Sunday evening.* Two ancient dining rooms on the second and third floors with hand-hewn wood framing present views of the Cathedral. Or try the pleasant terrace for fresh-air dining. The *sopa de Doña Jimena*, its version of *sopa castellana*, is recommended, as is the baby lamb with mushrooms.

Amex, Diners, MasterCard and Visa accepted.

Fernán Gonzáles

C. Calera, 19. (across the river from the old town, left from the Santa María pedestrian bridge). ☎ *20 94 42.* Located beside the hotel of the same name, this restaurant is elegant, yet more adventuresome than most in town. In addition to the usual roasts, there are *nueva cocina* specialties such as sole with shrimp sauce, and green beans with foie gras and truffles. The owner knows wines—in fact he owns several vineyards—so his selection is exemplary.

Amex, Diners Club and Visa accepted.

MODERATE ($20-$50)

Casa Ojeda

C. Vitoria, 5 (opposite the Casa Cordón). ☎ *20 90 52. Closed Sunday night.* This well-known Burgos institution, with an elegant gourmet store adjacent and a fine upstairs dining room decorated in typical Castilian style, serves classical regional cooking. The cheeses are special.   *Amex, Diners, MasterCard and Visa accepted.*

Gaona ★

Virgen de la Paloma, 41 (in the square with the stairs on the east side of the cathedral). ☎ *20 61 91. Closed Monday and from the middle to the end of November.* A patio and plants make this a pretty place. Fish and pigeon are specialties of the Basque chef.

Amex, Diners and Visa accepted.

Rincón de España

C. Nuño Rasura, 11 (at the end of Pl. del Rey San Fernando, down the stairs from the Cathedral plaza). ☎ *20 59 55. Closed Monday.* A large light room inside or a terrace with awning outside are your choices. The food is decent, if limited in variety, and can be inexpensive if ordered from a special menu.

Amex, Diners, MasterCard and Visa accepted.

INEXPENSIVE (UNDER $20)

Autoservicio Bonfin

C. Cadena (at the beginning of the Pl. del Rey San Fernando, down the stairs from the cathedral plaza). ☎ *20 61 93. Open for lunch only.* Cafeteria-style service presents a choice of sandwiches and salads, as well as fuller meals. Convenient to the cathedral for a rest, or a lunch.

DIRECTORY

TOURIST INFORMATION • Located opposite the cathedral front in the Pl. Alonzo Martínez. Open Mon.-Fri. from 10 a.m. to 2 p.m. and from 4-7 p.m., Sat. from 10 a.m. to 2 p.m. It provides a map and brochures in English.

TRAINS AND BUSES • Burgos is well served by trains because it lies on a main route between Madrid and the resort of Irun. The train station (☎ 20 35 60) lies at the end of Av. Conde Guadalhorce, a 20-minute walk northeast of the cathedral. Trains connect with León, Valladolid and Pamplona. The downtown RENFE office (☎ 20 91 31) is at C. Moneda, 21, which leads off the eastern end of Pl. José Antonio, heading northeast.

Daily bus service connects Burgos with Madrid, León, Santander, Soria and San Sebastian. The main station (☎ 20 55 75) is located at C. Miranda, 4, at the rear of the Casa Miranda, above.

POST OFFICE AND TELEPHONES • Pl. Conde de Castro, 1 (☎ 26 27 50), located across the river from the east end of the Espolón. Telephones are available at C. de San Lesmes, 18. Follow the narrow C. de Puebla exiting the northeast corner of the Pl. de Calvo Sotelo for two long blocks.

POLICE • General Vigon. ☎ 20 21 38 (091, for emergencies).

EXCURSIONS

On the route southeast to **Santo Domingo de Silos** ★ ★ ★, (which has a treasured cloister), a stop can be made at charming **Covarrubias** ★, and another at the interesting town of **Soria** ★ ★. **Peñaranda de Duero** ★ ★ due south, contains an elegant Renaissance palace in a pretty square. **Fromista** ★ ★ ★ church is a preserved Romanesque marvel, described under its own heading in this chapter.

COVARRUBIAS ★

Population: 663

Leave Burgos on Av. Madrid heading due south from the Santa María pedestrian bridge, following signs to N-1. At 9.5 k fork left onto N-234 toward Soria. In 33.5 k at Hortiguela turn right onto C110 toward Covarrubias and Lerma. In 13 k you arrive.

Still partly girded by medieval ramparts, the town is guarded by the **Doña Urraca Tower** (a.k.a. **Fernán González Tower**). It rises with an extreme batter, in the shape of a truncated pyramid. A Renaissance palace leads to a picturesque old quarter with many restored house facades. The **Colegiata** church is crammed with attractive tombs, including that of Fernán González, who first united Castile, and his wife, Doña Sancha. The associated museum (open 10 a.m. to 2 p.m. and 4-7 p.m.; closed Tues.) contains some nice works, including a Berruguette, a van Eyke and several fine primitives.

SANTO DOMINGO DE SILOS ★ ★ ★

From Covarrubias take BU-903 south for 11.5 k, turning left past Santibañez del Val to Silos in 7 k more.

All that remains of a monastery built in the 12th century is this Romanesque cloister. But what a cloister! Called the most beautiful in the world, its elegant shape and the animation of its carvings make it undeniably special. Apply at the porter's lodge; enter through the 18th-century church and descend to the lower cloister level. Take time to study the wondrous Romanesque carving on the columns, especially at the cloister corners, bases and capitals. The 14th-century painted Mudejar ceiling, though restored in large part, is still exquisite. On the north side, a sarcophagus lid in high relief, supported by three lions, stands over Saint Dominic, who reconstructed the convent early in the 12th century, and added the upper story. The small museum at the northwest corner holds an 11th-century chalice, a 10th-century manuscript, a gilt and enamel copper chest, and lovely ivories.

SORIA ★ ★

Population: 32,039

From Santo Domingo de Silos continue on BU-903 for 18 k to N-234 south to Soria in 93 k. From Burgos, take N-234 south for 145 k. Once in Soria, drive along Paseo General Yague until the postmodern Museo Numantia appears on the left.

Though its fabled charm lauded by poets has been obscured by modern buildings, Soria retains a pretty center with interesting sights.

The **Numantia Museum** ★ ★ (open 10 a.m. to 2 p.m. and 4:30-9 pm; closed Sun. afternoon and Mon.; admission: 100 ptas.) spaciously houses a good collection of Roman and Iberian pieces, especially those on the second floor from excavations at nearby Numantia. Cross C. Ferial to enter the Pl. Ramon Benito Acona. A right and quick left brings you past the Diputacion into the Pl. San Esteban with its Romanesque church of harmonious lines. **San Juan de Rabanera** ★ has Byzantine-style vaulting, and a stunning Romanesque crucifix over the altar. Outside, turn left at the back of the church to enter the Pl. San Blas y el Rosel. Directly ahead, across the plaza, is the long facade of the **Palace of the Counts of Gomara** ★. The 2-story patio inside is elegant. On the west end of the palace, the street heading north leads in one block to **Santo Domingo** ★, which has one of the finest Romanesque facades in Spain. The central portal is covered with carving that well repays study. The interior, however, was redone in the 16th century. Cross to the side of the plaza opposite Santo Domingo and go left down C. de la Aduana Vieja, passing the 18th-century **Casa de los Castejones** ★, with its Baroque doorway, after which a right onto C. Ferial returns again to the Pl. Ramon y Cajal.

PEÑARANDA DE DUERO ★ ★

Population: 821

Leave Burgos on Av. Madrid leading due south from the Santa María pedestrian bridge, and follow signs to N-1. From N-1 exit at Aranda de Duero in 79 k. to take C-111 east for 21 k. to Penaranda de Duero, a total trip of 100 k.

This walled village is dominated by a square medieval keep. But it is the **Plaza Mayor ★ ★ ★** and the palace fronting it that merits the trip. The plaza is a harmonious composition of half-timbered houses on massive stone pillars. In the center stands a stone pillory from the 15th century, unusual to see in Spain today. On the west side of the plaza stands the large **Palacio de los Condes de Miranda ★ ★** with a noble facade (open 10 a.m. to 1:30 p.m. and 4-7 p.m., until 6 p.m. in winter; closed Sun.). This is one of the great Renaissance palaces of Spain, and it combines all the architectural styles from Gothic to Mudejar to Plateresque. Inside is a lovely patio with surrounding gallery, a grand staircase and rooms with intricate wood ceilings.

COCA FORTRESS ★ ★

Population: 2,127.

*From **Segovia** take N-110 west toward Ávila, leaving west from the Pl. Azoguejo. At Villacastin in 37 k take N-VI north toward Valladolid. In about 40 k, at San Cristobal de la Vega, go right on C-603 following signs to Coca for 16 k, a total trip of 93 k. The final 7 k on D-209 is bumpy. From **Ávila** take N-110 east toward Segovia to Villacastin in 29 k. Then follow the directions from Segovia above. From **Madrid** take A-6 north, changing to N-VI at Villacastin in 83 k. Then follow the directions from Segovia above. From **Valladolid** take N-601 south toward Madrid for about 50 k, taking a left following signs for Coca in 19 k.*

This fortress is a singular example of Mudejar military architecture and one of the most famous sights in Spain. It is so often photographed because it looks just as we imagine a fortress should, if perhaps a little more massive and complex than we thought. To reach the fortress turn left just before the gate through what little remains of the town wall, or pass through the gate and turn left immediately after. In either case you end at the fortress in less than one kilometer.

Since the castle inside has been appropriated for a forestry school, only the walls can be toured, but for free. The fort dates to the 15th century and is still owned by the Duke of Alba. The surprise is that the fortress is made of fired brick. Mudejar architects made an art of laying bricks by varying the courses and colors to create patterns, and the whole feels entirely solid. The dry moat is deep and wide, the walls thick and the merloned turrets stand defiant. Despite such appearances, however, the building was never intended for defense. It was built for a funloving Archbishop as a stage for his parties.

COVARRUBIAS

See Burgos excursions.

FROMISTA ★ ★ ★

Population: 1,284

From **Burgos** *follow the directions for Valladolid, but at 5 k take N-120 west toward Osorno. In 60 k, at Osorno, take N-611 south toward Palencia for 18 k to Fromista, a trip of 78 k. From* **León** *take N-601 as if for Valladolid, but in 67 k at Becilla de Valderaduey take N-610 east to Palencia. At Palencia in 61 k take N-611 north for 32 k to Fromista, for a trip of 160 k. From* **Valladolid** *take N-620 (E-80) north to Palencia in 48 k, then follow the directions from León, for a trip of 80 k. From* **Madrid** *and* **Salamanca** *follow the directions from Valladolid. From Santander take N-611 south for 149 k.*

Today the town of Fromista seems sad and decayed, but once it was a stopping place for thousands of pilgrims on their way to the holy site of Santiago de Compostela. Still standing in the center of the village square is the pilgrim's interim destination. This church of San Martin formed part of a large abbey with accommodations for all who asked, but today just the extraordinary church remains. It was completed in 1066, before William the Conqueror landed in England. Because the village quickly declined, the abbey was abandoned by the time of the Catholic Monarchs. Thus the church has not been modified or added to, and remains the purest Romanesque.

Iglesia San Martin   ★ ★ ★

Open Wed.-Sun. 10 a.m. to 2 p.m. and 4-7pm. Open Tues. 10 a.m. to 2 p.m. Closed Mon. Admission: 200 ptas. The church was built by the widow of Sancho the Great of Navarre, the man who conquered Castile before bequeathing it to his son Fernando I, the first king of a united Castile and León. This edifice embodied the first great success of the Romanesque style in Spain after earlier essays in the form, and served thereafter as the model for Romanesque churches, though the purity of its Romanesque aesthetic is unsurpassed. Built of mammoth rough stones, every element of the church is in harmony with the rest. Inside, pure lines sweep to the cradle vaulting and carry the eye as far as a squinch-supported dome. The ribbed arches are lovely, their capitals tastefully decorated. Unfortunately, overzealous restoration in the early part of this century imparts an uncharacteristic sense of newness.

HARO and LA RIOJA ★ ★

Population: 8,581
Zip code: 26250 ; area code: 941

*From **Burgos** take either the toll road A-1 (E-5), or the toll-free parallel N-1 east toward Vitoria-Gasteiz. From the toll road, just past Miranda de Ebro in 86 k, turn south toward Logrono, exiting at exit 9 for Haro, for a trip of 112 k. From N-1, just past Miranda de Ebro in 93 k, turn south on N-232, exiting for Horo in 15 k. From **Pamplona** take A-15 northwest for 23 k, turning onto N-240 at Irurzun going east toward Vitoria-Gasteiz. The road becomes N-1 (E5) in 29 k at Alsasua. 26 k past Vitoria-Gasteiz turn onto N-232 toward Logrono, exiting at Haro in 15 k, for a trip of 146 k. From **Bilbao** take the toll road A-68 (E-804) south toward Logrono, exiting at exit 9 for Haro for a trip of 89 k. From **south of Haro**, follow the directions from Burgos.*

NOTE ... *Most bodegas close from Aug. through the first half of Sept., and most allow tours only in the morning.*

Haro is a prosperous, attractive town that serves as the capital of Rioja Alta, the finest wine region in Spain. It is a pleasant place to rest while exploring the great bodegas (wineries). Old Haro covers a hill rising from the Pl. de la Paz, circled by an arcade of glass-balconied houses surrounding an old bandstand. Dating from 1769, the stately Ayuntamiento (city hall) across the plaza is a source of information about the area. **Santo Tomás ★**, a pretty 16th-century church, sits atop the hill. The south portal is a sumptuous Plateresque carving; the interior is nicely Gothic.

But it is the wine that brings most people to Haro. Bodegas proliferate down the hill to the north, near the railway station from which they ship their wares. There the stream called Rio Oja, which gave its name to this region, enters the larger River Ebro. Bodega tours are given on an ad hoc basis, waiting for four or more tourists to assemble. The best bodegas are Lopez de Heredia, CVNE, Muga and Bilbaiñas.

Other good bodegas require a drive, but a pleasant one. Leave Haro east from the area of the bodegas, following signs to Labastida, 4 k northeast. From there follow signs to Logrono and N-232 (confusingly with the same designation as the different N-232 that passes south by Haro). On the right in 10 k pass by the picturesque hilltop village of **San Vicente de la Sonsierra** ★, surrounded by vineyards. Past Samaniego in 7 k a sign points to the road for Puerto de Herrera, which in 3 k leads into the mountains for the **Balcon de la Rioja** ★ and its panoramic views over the Rioja area. 7 k further, back on N-232, brings beautiful **Laguardia** ★ (Biasteri, in Basque). Laguardia retains its medieval village walls, gates, towers and grace. The town has ruins of a 10th-century castle, a Romanesque and a Gothic church, along with old mansions and the Bodegas Palacio, one of Spain's best. (**Marixa** ★, just outside the walls, is a nice restaurant with moderate prices, and has 10 clean rooms for equally moderate rates. ☎ 10 01 65.) From Laguardia head south toward Elciego and Cenicero. **Elciego** ★, in 4 k, is another picturesque village that hosts the bodega of Marqués de Riscal, one of Spain's premier crus—and its oldest. Across the Ebro is Cenicero, the location of Bodegas Marqués de Cáceres, producer of a modest-quality wine. From here the better highway N-232 leads northwest back to Haro.

WHERE TO STAY

In Haro or nearby are one excellent hotel and another of moderate price. Or, 16 k south in Calzada, one of those wonderful paradors beckons.

EXPENSIVE ($100-$200)

Los Augustinos   1st-class ★ ★ ★
San Agustin, 2. Rooms: 62. ☎ *31 13 08; FAX 30 31 48; Telex 37161.* This looks like a parador—it is housed in a reconstructed convent from the 14th century—though it is owned by a private chain. The hotel was completed just a few years ago and is top-grade throughout. Public spaces are nicely decorated with real and reproduction antiques, and the bedrooms are spotlessly modern.

In Calzada (16 k southwest of Haro on LO-750):

Parador Santo Domingo de la Calzada   2nd-class ★ ★ ★
Pl. del Santa, 3. Rooms: 29. ☎ *34 03 00; FAX 34 03 25.* This parador, a former palace of the kings of Navarre, was converted into a hospice for

pilgrims before its reincarnation as a hotel. The public spaces retain the old stone that breathes of history.

MODERATE ($50-$99)

Iturrimurri   **2nd-class ★★**

On N-232 1 k south of Haro. Rooms: 36. ☎ *31 12 13; FAX 31 17 21; Telex 37021. Closed the last week of December and the first week of January.* The hotel is functional and clean, with a pool of sorts, and a moderately-priced restaurant. The staff is helpful.

In Laguardia (24 k from Haro):

Marixa   **4th-class ★**

Sancho Abarca, 8 (just outside the walls). Rooms: 10. ☎ *10 01 65. Closed from the last week in December until the middle of January.* Pleasant rooms above this fine restaurant ★★ are small, but clean and attractive.

WHERE TO EAT

Local restaurants serve mainly roasts and regional dishes, but generally offer superb wine selections.

MODERATE ($20-$50)

Terete   **★★★**

Lucrecia Arana, 17 (west of the plaza). ☎ *31 00 23. Closed Sunday night, Monday and October.* This is the outstanding Haro restaurant, and is associated with a bodega. Nothing fancy—white picnic tables upstairs—but roasts are perfectly seasoned and done. The selection of wines is exemplary.   *Visa accepted.*

DIRECTORY

INFORMATION • The **Centro de Iniciativas Turisticas** in the Ayuntamiento at the end of C. Conde de Haro acts as the information office (☎ 31 27 26). Open Tues.-Sat. from 10:30 a.m. to 2 p.m. and from 5:30-8pm. Open Sun. from noon to 1 p.m.

POST OFFICE AND TELEPHONE • The post office is located on C. de la Rioja (☎ 31 08 69), along with telephones.

LEÓN ★★★

Population: 131,134
Zip code: 24001; area code: 987

From **Madrid** *take A-6 northwest, changing to N-VI at exit 1 in 57 k. Stay on N-VI for 197 k to pass Benavente where you change to N-630 for 72 k. The total trip is 326 k. From* **Ávila** *take N-110 east for 29 k past Villacastin, joining N-VI north, then follow the directions from Madrid. The total trip is 294 k. From* **Segovia** *take N-110 west to*

*Villacastin to join N-VI, then follow the directions from Madrid. The total trip is 302 k. From **Valladolid** take N-601 north for 139 k. From **Burgos** take N-620 (E-80) west for 77 k., turning on to N-610 at Magaz. N-610 enters Palencia in 11 k. Continue for 61 k past Palencia to Bacilla de Valderaduey where you go north on N-601 for 67 k to León. The total trip is 216 k. From **Salamanca** take N-630 north toward Zamora, continuing for 128 k to Caserio del Puente where you switch to N-VI going north for 6 k before rejoining N-630 for the final 72 k to León. The total trip is 206 k. From **Oviedo** take N-630 south through 115 k of slow going up and down mountains, or take the toll road A-66 after 36 k at **Campomanes** for a faster trip.*

Despite a Leonese fixation with lions, the name of their city derives from the Latin *Legio Septima*. The site was first settled by the Seventh Legion as a Roman bastion during the time of Caesar Augustus. After conquest by first Visigoths, then Moors, Christians from Asturias in the north recaptured León in 850. But the Moors took it back in 996 and burned the town. In 1002 it was retaken by the Christians—this time for good—and made the capital of a province of the same name. With such status the city became a haven for Christian refugees from Moorish territory and thus the Mozarabic center of Spain in the 11th and 12th centuries. The wonder is that there is not more fine Mozarabic architecture and art surviving, although what remains is choice. The present walls date to 1324, replacing an earlier construction that in turn replaced Roman walls. Parts of these walls still stand in the old town along with a collection of houses from the 12th and 13th centuries. Still in use, the houses' exterior plaster sometimes flakes off to reveal their original half-timbered brick.

As the Reconquest gained territory, the capital of Christian Spain moved further south and León languished. For centuries the town lay under the dust of decay. As its importance waned, the citizens of León undertook a great cathedral, perhaps in memory of other times, raising a rival to those across the Pyrenees in France. In the 20th century rich deposits of iron and coal were discovered in the mountains north of León so today the city thrives again. It is a city of modern buildings, wide avenues and fountains, yet maintains an old quarter from an entirely different age. Still, León should be a more attractive city than it is.

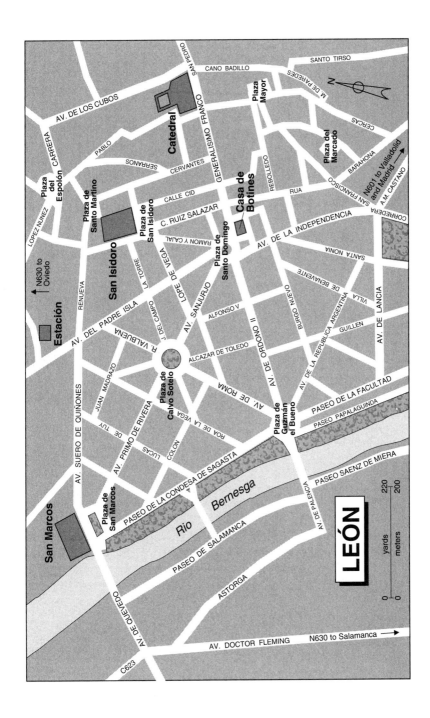

Arriving from **Salamanca** *and* **Zamora** *on* **N-630** *travel on Av. Dr. Fleming past the northern train station. After the station turn acutely right onto C. Astorga. Astorga ends forcing a left onto Av. de Palencia which crosses the Bernesga River and empties into a large traffic circle (Guzman el Bueno). Continue through the circle to Ordoño II opposite, which leads in a few blocks to another circle, Pl. de Santo Domingo, with underground parking to the right.*

From **N-601** (**Madrid**, **Valladolid** *and* **Burgos**) *drive down Alcalde Miguel Castana which soon ends at a confluence of large streets. Continue for a few blocks on the right street, Av. Independencia, until it lets into the circle of the Pl. de Santo Domingo with underground parking to the right. From the north on* **N-630** (**Oviedo**) *enter an intersection from which a right turn leads along Av. Asturia. In about two blocks, take the first left onto Av. del Padre Isla which in several blocks goes into the circle of the Pl. de Santo Domingo, with parking across the plaza.*

WHAT TO SEE AND DO

The loveliest sight in León is the elegant French Gothic **cathedral** ★★★★, with its thousand yards of stained glass windows. Noteworthy, too is the Romanesque basilica of **San Isadoro** ★★★ whose magnificent frescos from the 12th century decorate a pantheon of the earliest kings of Spain. The **old town** ★ well repays a stroll. Massive and insistently elegant, the **Monastery of San Marcos** ★★★, now one of the great hotels in the world, should be seen. It contains an archaeological museum with a few nice pieces. Near the main plaza sits a 19th-century **palace designed by Gaudí** ★. In the environs of León waits a jewel of a 9th-century Mozarabic church at **San Miguel de Escalada** ★★. A full day would allow all these sights to be seen.

León's grand wide avenues all funnel into the large Plaza de Santo Domingo, a center from which the sights radiate. Walking east on Generalissimo Franco brings you to the Pl. de Regla and, three blocks later, the **cathedral**. Walking north on C. Ramon y Caja brings **San Isidoro** in two blocks. Northwest along Av. de General Sanjurjo lies the **Monastery of San Marcos** nine blocks away.

Plaza de Santo Domingo ★

San Marcelo church ★, rebuilt in the 16th century, stands at the east end of the plaza. It contains a moving wood sculpture by Gregorio Fernandez. Facing the church's south side is the **Ayuntamiento** ★ (city hall) from 1585 with the arms of León emblazoned on its facade. Across the plaza, opposite the Ayuntamiento, is the former **Casa de los Guzmanes**, now the Diputacion, with a fine 16th-century patio and grillwork. Next to it, west, is the **Casa de Botines** ★ set back on its own lot. Now a bank, it was designed at the end of the 19th century by Antoni Gaudí as a small palace. Built to look Gothic, it shows Gaudí's mastery of that aesthetic, for it almost seems Gothic, though not exactly like any structure of that period. A walk east along Calle Generalissimo Franco past the Casa de los Guzmanes brings you to the cathedral three blocks later.

Cathedral ★★★★

Open weekdays 9 a.m. to 1:30 p.m. and 4-7 p.m. Sat. 8:30 to 1:30. Closed Sun. Admission: 250 ptas. for the museum and cloisters Begun in the middle of the 13th century and finished 150 years later, it is surprising that this church reflects so little of the Spanish interpretation of Gothic that turned most of her churches into wider, less lofty, darker structures than those north of the Pyrenees. This cathedral would suit any French town and bring glory to most.

Two equal but dissimilar towers frame the facade, with three portals beneath a great rose window. The central portal contains a vivid depiction of the fate of the damned; the left portal holds two fine depictions of prophets. A triple portal along the southern face is surmounted by a statue of Saint Froilan, the Bishop of León in the 10th century, and has lovely carvings decorating the door jambs. Continue around to the rear for a view of the buttresses flying as they support the high nave.

Inside one is struck first by soaring height, then by all the glass. Even by Gothic standards the nave is narrow, which serves to emphasize its height. Graceful piers carved to resemble bundled columns rise to an elegant ceiling traced with ribs. All around and behind in the rainbow's colors are a literal third of an acre of stained glass, the glory of the cathedral. The front rose window and that in the chapels of the apse are the oldest; those in the nave are Renaissance and later, depicting flora and minerals beneath historic personages and their crests, surmounted by the blessed. The sun transforms the interior with heavenly color.

Carved with painted alabaster reliefs, the trascoro in the center of the nave frames a central arch which gives the best view of the length of the cathedral. The altar is later, 15th century, containing a nice depiction of the Entombment on the left side. Further left is a *Pieta* by Rodger van der Weyden. Both windows in the transepts are early, with that in the south wing being especially striking. Chapels in the apse behind the altar hold tombs of early bishops. The east chapel contains the tomb of Condesa Sancha, depicting horses tearing her nephew and heir to pieces in punishment for having killed her. From the north end of the cathedral (left) a fine Plateresque doorway lets into the cloisters. Museums are installed off the left and far sides, and display a *10th-century Mozarabic Bible* and a crucifix by Juan de Juni, among other miscellanies.

Return to Pl. de Santo Domingo for the simplest route to San Isidoro. Take C. Ramon y Cajal north for two blocks to the basilica, still attached to the city walls.

San Isidoro el Real

Open Tues.-Sat. 9 a.m. to 2 p.m. and 4-8 p.m. (until 6 p.m. in winter). Open Sun. 10 a.m. to 1:30 p.m. Closed Mon. Admission: 250 ptas., for a guided tour of the Royal Pantheon. Fernando I, the first king of a united Castile and León, built a church here in the 11th century which was dedicated to St. Isidoro. This saint from Seville, not to be confused with Madrid's St. Isidro Labrador, was a 7th-century archbishop whose organization of church councils did much to define the orthodoxy of Catholicism. Fernando I transferred the saint's bones here, before dying himself the next week. Building continued under the supervision of, at first, Fernando's daughter, then his son and in turn his grandson. By then the structure had been rededicated to serve as a pantheon for the kings of Asturias, León and those of the united Castile and León.

Of Fernando's church, only the narthex survives, housing its royal pantheon. The mass of the basilica was built about a century later by his successors. The look of the front was much altered by Gothic and Plateresque additions in the 16th century, including an equestrian statue of St. Isidoro. The **portals**, however, are original and the depiction of the sacrifice of Abraham in the **tympanum** is vivid. To the east a lovely early portal depicts Christ's descent from the cross.

The uncharacteristic height of the clerestory makes the small and almost square Romanesque interior unusually light. Yet it seems claustrophobic, almost subterranean, after the light of the soaring cathedral. Huge pillars are surmounted by richly-sculpted capitals, while arches at the beginning of the nave and in the transepts show Mudejar influence. The retablo is late, early 16th-century, and overlooks a reliquary containing the bones of St. Isidoro. The north transept contains a 12th-century chapel retaining faded, but lively, **frescos**.

A doorway at the front of the basilica, left, leads to the **Pantheon of the Kings**. Carvings on the interior side of the portal and on the capitals of the columns are some of the earliest depictions of figures in all Spain. Two crypt-like rooms comprise the 11th-century structure raised by Fernando I. This is probably the first Spanish building in the Romanesque style. Here rested the remains of Alfonso V of León, Fernando I, Urrica, his daughter, and almost 20 other Infantes and Infantas, until the French desecrated the building in the 19th century. But they did not destroy the 12th-century frescos—still vibrant today thanks to the dry, airtight construction of the building. The vault ceilings depict New Testament episodes involving Christ, evangelists (with animal heads), saints and angels, and the **first Spanish nativity**

scene. A charming calendar covers one archway, showing what farming tasks should be performed each month.

The adjoining Treasury contains 10th- and 11th-century pieces, including an enamel casket, another with ivory plaques, and a Chalice of two Roman agate cups mounted together in gold.

Old Town ★

The basilica of **St. Isidoro** is in the area of the old walls, which enclose a warren of streets, ending southeast at the cathedral. Modern houses abut ancient buildings from the 13th century, which show their age by the half timbered brick exposed where plaster coatings have fallen. Another concentration of ancient houses lies in the area between the arcaded Pl. Mayor, directly south of the cathedral, and the Pl. del Mercado, to its southwest.

For a visit to the Monastery of San Marcos take the broad Av. General Sanjurjo that leads northwest out of the Pl. de Santo Domingo for 10 blocks. The walk provides lovely views of the facade as you proceed.

Antiquo Monasterio de San Marcos ★★★

The museum is open Tues.-Sat. 10 a.m. to 1 p.m. and 4-6pm. Open Sun. 10 a.m. to 1 p.m. Closed Mon. Admission: 200 ptas. In the 12th century this was the mother house of the Order of Santiago, originally established to protect pilgrims on their way to Santiago de Compostela. Three centuries later Ferdinand the Catholic, as the order's Master, drew plans to embellish the monastery to reflect the order's accomplishments during the Reconquest. The plan was finally carried out between 1513 and 1549 under the supervision of Ferdinand's successor Carlos V, in a style that was not his favorite. The present imposing facade is the result—a sumptuous Plateresque monument stretching for over a football field. The Baroque pediment added in the 18th century does not unduly disturb the original 2-story design of regular windows, friezes, engaged columns and pilasters. Santiago (St. James) on horseback strides over the elaborate main door to the left, which includes scenes from his life. The righthand door to the church is incomplete but covered with scallop shells, Santiago's symbol. All along, a row of medallions depicts assorted Biblical, Roman and Spanish personages, including Isabella the Catholic supported by Lucretia and Judith, and Carlos V supported by Trajan and Augustus.

Today most of the former monastery is given over to one of Spain's most deluxe paradors, though the church inside with its beautiful choir stalls remains open to all. Anyone can enter the hotel to look at the magnificent stone staircase leading from the lobby. The Chapterhouse, which now contains an archaeological museum under a splendid carved wood roof, and the sumptuously decorated sacristy, to the right, may be toured for a fee. Roman statuary and mosaics in the museum hold some interest, but the main treasures are the medieval works. Included are textiles and clothing, arms and religious articles, with one outstanding 11th-century Romanesque ivory, the Carrizo Crucifix, tiny, elongated, and haunting.

WHERE TO STAY

For some reason hotels are few in this substantial city, but there is the elegant parador. It is expensive, about 20,000 pesetas a night for a couple, but large enough to almost always have available rooms. However, acceptable hotels exist in every price category, so the situation should prove adequate.

EXPENSIVE ($100-$200)

Parador San Marcos   Deluxe ★★★★★
Pl. San Marcos 7. Rooms: 256. ☎ *23 73 00; FAX 23 34 58; Telex 89809.*
What hotel can improve on the entrance to the San Marcos—a sumptuous Plateresque facade stretching forever, followed by an entrance hall with a 16th-century grand staircase lined with antiques and tapestries? The whole is presided over by a chandelier that must be 10 feet tall. There is a unique feeling to walking into such a place and heading for your room, even if it is yours for only a night. Need we mention that a swimming pool is provided? Only 30 of the rooms actually stem from the old monastery, and cost more, with the rest situated in a modern wing added to the back. Even the modern rooms are large and pleasant, with ample marble bathrooms. The hotel is not faultless—service, although friendly, is not always a model of efficiency—but the entrance could not be more dramatic or the public areas more spacious.

MODERATE ($50-$99)

Quindós   3rd-class ★★★
Av. José Antonio, 24. Rooms: 96. ☎ *23 62 00; FAX 24 22 01; Telex 89693.* This modern hotel provides what a hotel should—clean comfort with willing service. It is located in a quiet neighborhood one block north of Av. Gen. Sanjurjo and a block south of the Parador San Marcos.

Riosol   2nd-class ★
Av. de Palencia, 3. Rooms: 141. ☎ *21 66 50; FAX 21 69 97; Telex 89693.* Although the modern Riosol is actually closer to the center of town than the San Marcos, it feels out of things, across the river on an unattractive street near the train station. The rooms are comfortable enough, but the service is not as professional as it should be. The hotel is located 5 blocks due west of the Pl. Santo Domingo along Av. Ordoño II, which changes it name to Av. de Palencia after it crosses the river.

INEXPENSIVE (UNDER $50)

Don Suero   3rd-class ★★
Av. Suero de Quiñones, 15. Rooms: 106. ☎ *23 06 00.* True, the rates

at this hotel barely allow it in the "inexpensive" category, but the hotel looks and acts more expensive than it is. Altogether this modern professional place is a find indeed.

WHERE TO EAT

Roast lamb and suckling pig are specialties, as with most of Old Castile. The three moderately priced restaurants below all serve good food in pleasant surroundings, though none stands much above the others.

MODERATE ($20-$50)

Nuevo Racimo de Oro

Pl. San Martin, 8. ☎ *21 47 67. Closed Sunday evening in summer and Wednesday in winter.* The restaurant looks as a mesón should. It is installed in an ancient tavern, and serves roasts from a wood fire oven, following a mandatory bowl of steaming garlic soup (served in a wooden bowl with a wooden spoon). The place is a mite touristy, but the food is delicious nonetheless, and a few dollars cheaper than the restaurants that follow. Located at the north end of the Pl. Mercado, it can be reached by walking east from Pl. de Santo Domingo to C. Rua going south, which takes you to the Pl. Mercado in three blocks.
Amex and Visa accepted.

Adonias

C. Santa Nonia, 16. ☎ *20 67 68. Closed Sunday and from the middle to the end of July.* A pleasant dining experience waits up the stairs in the green dining room with sturdy wood tables and ceramics on the walls. Regional cooking is done with care, and the service is friendly. Go south from the Pl. de Santo Domingo on C. Independencia for one block until it forks, with C. Santa Nonia going right.
Amex, Diners, MasterCard and Visa accepted.

Casa Pozo

Pl. de San Marcelo, 15. ☎ *22 30 39. Closed Sunday, the first half of July and Christmas week.* Owned by the brother of the proprietor of Adonias, there are those who consider this better and those who consider it not as good as Adonias. We find each different—this one is less formal and the food a touch more earthy—but hard to choose between. The bread is terrific. Located directly opposite the Casa Botines.
Amex, Diners, MasterCard and Visa accepted.

DIRECTORY

INFORMATION • Located at Pl. de Regla, 3, across from the front of the cathedral. Open Mon.-Fri. from 9 a.m. to 2 p.m. and from 4-6:30 p.m. Open Sat. from 10 a.m. to 1 p.m. ☎ 23 70 82.

TRAINS AND BUSES • Eight trains a day connect Madrid with León for a trip of 4-6 hours and a cost of about 2000 ptas. Connections between León and Burgos (a 2-1/2-hour ride), Valladolid (2 hours), Oviedo (2 hours), and Barcelona (1011 hours) are also convenient. One train per day goes to Salamanca. The station is located at Av. Astorga, 2.

This is about five blocks west of the Pl. Santo Domingo along Av. Ordoño II, which changes its name to Av. de Palencia after it crosses the river and runs into Av. Astorga, perpendicular to it. ☎ 22 37 04.

Most buses leave from C. Cardenal Lorenzana, 2 (☎ 22 62 00). The bus to Salamanca, however, leaves from Av. de Madrid, near the Parque de San Francisco.

EXCURSIONS

A car is required to get to **San Miguel de Escalada** ★ ★, 25 k outside of León, but it is the finest Mozarabic monument extant, and worth the short ride.

From the Pl. de Santo Dominigo head east on Generalissimo Franco, past the cathedral, to N-601. Take N-601 south toward Valladolid for 17 k. to the outskirts of Mansilla de las Mulas. A sign that should be larger points right to S. Miguel de Escalada in 12.5 k. Apply to the caretaker in the small shed in front.

Ruins of a monastery complex scattered around, though only this church survives intact. It was constructed in the 10th century by Christian refugees from Córdoba, and is the best preserved Mozarabic building in Spain. These refugees had learned their crafts and trained their eyes under the Moors and built a Christian monument with Moorish elements. The porch added in 1050 rests Moorish arches on polished columns. An elegant Moorish window cut through the covered side of the porch contrasts oddly with a sloping roof. Inside, two aisles covered with wooden vaulting line the nave, separated from the apse by three arches and a balustrade of panels carved with Visigothic birds and Moorish foliage designs. Architecturally the church is a mismash of Romanesque, Visigoth and Moorish, but in the end its charm wins out.

PEÑAFIEL CASTLE

See Valladolid excursions.

PEÑARANDA DE DUERO

See Burgos excursions.

SALAMANCA ★ ★ ★ ★

Population: 167,131
Zip code: 37001; area code: 923

*From **Madrid** take A-6 north for 37 k to exit 1 for N-VI to avoid the toll, or to exit 4 at Villacastin for a faster ride. In either case, take N-110 in 83 k at Villacastin west toward*

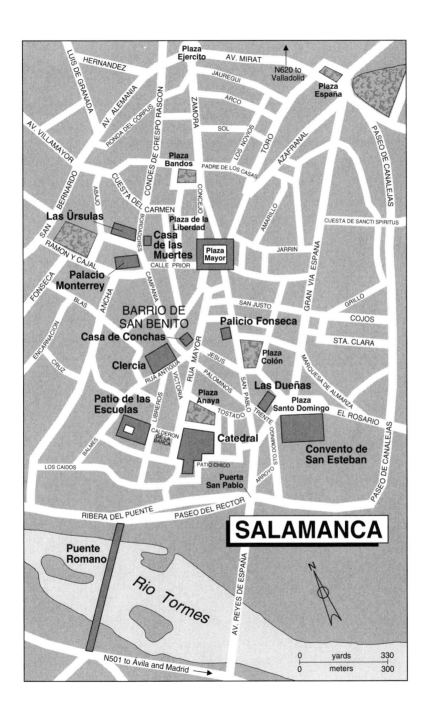

SALAMANCA

Plaza Ejercito
AV. MIRAT
N620 to Valladolid
Plaza España
LUIS DE GRANADA
HERNANDEZ
JAUREGUI
ARCO
AV. ALEMANIA
RONDA DEL CORPUS
CONDES DE CRESPO RASCON
ZAMORA
SOL
LOS NOVIOS
TORO
AZAFRANAL
PASEO DE CANALEJAS
AV. VILLAMAYOR
Plaza Bandos
PADRE DE LOS CASAS
CUESTA DEL
CARMEN
SAN BERNARDO
ABAJO
BORDADORES
CONCEJO
AMARILLO
CUESTA DE SANCTI SPIRITUS
Las Ürsulas
Plaza de la Liberdad
Casa de las Muertes
Plaza Mayor
JARRIN
SAN
RAMON Y CAJAL
CALLE PRIOR
GRAN VIA ESPANA
Palacio Monterrey
CAMPANA
FONSECA
BLAS
ANCHA
SAN JUSTO
GRILLO
BARRIO DE SAN BENITO
Palicio Fonseca
COJOS
STA. CLARA
Casa de Conchas
ENCARNACION
CRUZ
Clercia
RUA ANTIGUA
RUA MAYOR
JESUS
PALOMINOS
SAN PABLO
Plaza Colón
MARQUESA DE ALMARZA
Patio de las Escuelas
LIBREROS
VICTORIA
Plaza Anaya
TOSTADO
TRENTE
Las Dueñas
Plaza Santo Domingo
EL ROSARIO
BALMES
CALDERON DE LA BARCA
Catedral
STO. DOMINGO
Convento de San Esteban
PASEO DE CANALEJAS
LOS CAIDOS
PATIO CHICO
Puerta San Pablo
ARROYO
RIBERA DEL PUENTE
PASEO DEL RECTOR
Puente Romano
AV. REYES DE ESPAÑA
Rio Tormes
N
N501 to Ávila and Madrid

| 0 | yards | 330 |
| 0 | meters | 300 |

Ávila for 29 k, changing there for N-501 for Salamanca in 98 k. The trip covers 210 k. From **Ávila** *take N-501 northwest for 98 k. From* **Segovia** *take N-110 west for 63 k to Ávila and follow the directions from Ávila. From* **Valladolid** *take N-620 (A-80) southwest through Tordesillas and to Salamanca in 115 k. From* **north** *of Valladolid, follow directions to Valladolid and then follow those to Salamanca.*

Salamanca is truly ancient. In the early third century B.C. Hannibal attacked an important Iberian settlement here. A story goes that after the town had been successfully stormed and the men disarmed, the townswomen smuggled arms to their men in hideouts in the hills. Their bravery so impressed Hannibal that he invited the men to return. The town flourished under the Romans, but was repeatedly invaded, after Spain became Christian, by the Moors. It was recaptured by the Christians for good in 1055, although little was left after three centuries of destruction. In 1218 Alfonso IX founded the second university in Spain here, which soon swallowed up the first, in nearby Palencia, and Salamanca flourished as a university town. Salamanca became a kind of company town with the university as its prime employer and builder. It grew quickly, with most building occurring from the 15th through the 16th century, so it presents a remarkably homogeneous face. Indeed, it is a museum of Plateresque architecture, that curious Spanish appliqué of stone on plain facades, all heightened by the warm tones of the local sandstone.

By the first centennial after its founding the university had risen to be the second largest in Europe, smaller only than the University of Paris. It was large enough to contain both the Cambridge and the Oxford of its time, and possessed a better reputation than either. In this era the town was home to two great medieval painters who worked on its new cathedral. Fernando Gallego was born here, and Juan of Flanders settled here. Unlike most towns in Europe, Salamanca did not raze or renovate its former cathedral when it added a newer one, but built the new one adjoining the old, thus preserving one of Spain's great early churches.

In the 17th century, Salamanca was home to a family of altar makers named Churriguerra, who turned to the business of architecture and gave their name to an original style called Churriguerresque, a version of the Baroque. The Plaza Mayor, one of the most interesting in Spain, is their work, as is the altar in the church at St. Esteban's Monastery.

During the 18th century, Salamanca fell on hard times. The university suffered as Spain grew paranoid about the dangers of Protestantism, demanding orthodoxy above inquiry, which subverted educational standards. During the Peninsular War with Napoléon, the French destroyed many of Salamanca's buildings in fortifying the town against Wellington's approach. More recently, Salamanca served as the headquarters of the Nationalists during the early years of the Civil War. One night the university faculty was harangued by the Nationalist General Millan Astry about the virtues of blood and violence as purifiers of the soul. After this diatribe, Miguel de Unamuno, rector of the university and renowned philosopher of religion, rose uninvited to rebut Molla's views as contrary to the principles of western civilization. The audience, with Generalissimo Franco in attendance, was offended by Unamuno's disagreement with a Nationalist hero. Soon after, Unamuno was fired from his position and placed under house-arrest for life. Yet his spirit infuses the revitalized university today. The university thrives again, numbering 16,000 students, about twice its Renaissance complement.

Salamanca remains very much a university town with a youthfulness that fits oddly and nicely with its atmosphere of age. Because its medieval quarters had been destroyed it did not have to site buildings in warrens of streets as did so many Spanish towns, but instead could arrange them around plazas connected by thoroughfares. With its golden buildings amid the unhurried pace of academe, Salamanca is a most inviting city.

A circular road, variously named, leads around the old hilltop section of Salamanca. You funnel into this road from whichever direction you arrive. Salamanca is sufficiently spread out that it does not have any one place for parking hundreds of cars, and parking in the old town is difficult for anyone unfamiliar with its system of one-way streets. Follow the circular road to reach the side along the river Tormes where parking on the street is usually possible, and a short, but steep, three-block walk up the hill brings you to the cathedrals and university.

WHAT TO SEE AND DO

The **university** ★★★★ is fascinating with its sumptuous entrances, old classrooms, halls, and collection of art. The combination of the primitive **Old Cathedral** ★★★★ and the neoclassic **New Cathedral** ★★★ should not be missed. Nearby **San Esteban Monastery** ★★ combines Gothic and Plateresque details in an interesting way. The **Plaza**

Mayor ★★★ is among the most striking in Spain, and can be combined with a pleasant walk to see Plateresque mansions that dot the old city. One full day will do it all.

In the environs of Salamanca stand a number of picturesque towns that make for pleasant excursions: **La Alberca** ★★★, **Miranda del Castañar** ★, and **Ciudad Rodrigo** ★, and **Alba de Tormes** ★, where Saint Theresa is buried. Then there is a short and unusual excursion in the surrounding countryside to **Buen Amor castle**, which is not an overwhelming architectural monument, but interesting for being a castle actually lived in.

Begin in the Patio de Las Escuelas for a lesson in the Plateresque. If climbing the hill from the river, this plaza is off the left side of C. Libros, which is the second true street excluding an alley—going left.

The University   ★★★★

Open Mon.-Sat. 9:30 a.m. to 1:30 p.m. and 4-7 p.m. Open Sun. and holidays 10 a.m. to 1 p.m. Admission: 100 ptas. This patio dates from the dawn of the 16th century, a gift of Ferdinand and Isabella, by unknown architects. On first entering the plaza the larger **Escuelas Mayores** is right, and the smaller **Escuelas Menores**, a kind of preparatory school of the main university, is to the left rear. Above the double doors of the Mayores rises a great Plateresque work. The central medallion in the first register shows the benefactors, the Catholic Monarchs, with Isabella's face unidealized enough to be a genuine portrait. The middle register makes much of the double eagle crest of Carlos V, who reigned when the carving was finished, flanked by the Emperor himself and his wife. At the top are early founders and teachers at the university, flanked by Venus, Hercules and the Virtues. The carving deepens as it goes up to compensate for its greater distance from the viewer. The whole is a brilliant composition almost hidden by all the detail.

The slightly later frieze above the portal to the Menores school is simpler, and in that more elegant, though not so daring or seminal. On the bare walls next to the Menores, red-painted names can still be discerned. These are the graffiti of Renaissance graduates, said to be written in bull's blood.

Through the portal of the Mayores, where the ticket of admission to both schools is purchased, one penetrates the sixth oldest university in the Western World. The Copernican system was taught first at this university, and Isabella sent Columbus here when she wanted scholarly judgment about his proposed trip. (Incidentally, the professors concluded that Columbus' ideas were based on faulty assumptions, as indeed they were. See, "Historical Profiles: Columbus," p. 387.) Salamanca employed the first known woman professor—Beatriz de Galindo— who taught Queen Isabella Latin. Famous students included the son of Isabella and Ferdinand, and the son of Felipe II, who suffered a concussion from falling down stairs in pursuit of a maid. Hernán Cortéz attended for one year before quitting to conquer Mexico. St. Ignatius Loyola, founder of the Jesuits, and Lope de Vega, one of Spain's greatest writers, both received degrees from Salamanca, and many say that Cervantes attended. At its height in the 16th century the university consisted of 25 departments and about 7,000 students.

Enter the 15th-century cloisters covered by an original wooden ceiling of Mudejar work. Around the arcade ancient classrooms lead off. Proceeding left around the cloister, the first two rooms may readily be skipped. The next, in the corner, is called the **Hall of Fray Luis de León**, after an early famed teacher. Fray Luis had been arrested by the Inquisition for the "crime" of translating the Song of Solomon into Spanish. He returned to this classroom after five years in jail and began his lecture with the words "As we were saying yesterday..." The room remains as it was in the 16th century to show what lecture halls of the time were like. Note the pulpit with a roof which served as a sounding board for projecting the teacher's voice, and note the rough, scarred logs on which students sat, a luxury in days when it was normal for students to squat on the floor. Along the right hand wall are more comfortable seats for professors who wished to hear a lecture.

Next is the **paranifo**, or assembly hall, still used for solemn ceremonies such as the opening of the academic term and the conferring of doctorates. Arches sweep across the room with timbered ceiling between. Two 17th-century tapestries hang on the end wall framing a canopy flying a standard donated before his death by Don Juan, the student son of Isabella and Ferdinand. There is a portrait, possibly by Goya, of Carlos IV. The next hall is a 19th-century meeting room. One passes a doorway with a lovely Moorish ceiling above, then three rooms of little interest, followed by the **chapel**. Most arresting is its splendid ceiling, despite the fact that a large part of the original has been removed to a museum in the Menores School. Small though the room may be, it was the first library of the university. Today it is redone as a Baroque chapel with attractive marblework from the 18th century. Incidentally, Fray Luis is buried here, as his cenotaph on the right--hand wall indicates.

Next comes a wonderful Plateresque **staircase** with elegant "star" vaulting above. Scenes carved on the balustrade change at each flight—from pages, knights and jesters, to matrimonial scenes, to, at the top, jousts and bull baiting. The second floor gallery retains a fine ceiling and lets into an old **library** with a rich frieze high up. On the ground floor again, one room remains to inspect—the **Hall of Francisco Salinas**. He was a famed teacher of music in the 16th century and his hall is still used by music students. Fragments of a painting by Juan of Flanders remain in this memory filled room.

At the nearby **Escuelas Menores**, after passing through a Plateresque-topped portal, you enter a lovely, quiet patio, the small forerunner of every modern university's Quad. The scalloped arches, called **Sala-mancine**, that seem to reverse the expected figure and ground, are unattractive enough to be a style peculiar to only this one town in Spain. To the right is a library with the finest Mudejar ceiling left in the university complex. Across the patio a modern building serves as a sort of **museum**. It houses the remainder of the ceiling from the May-ores' chapel, along with some nice primitive paintings, some sophisti-cated works by Francisco Gallego, and, at the far end, part of a magnificent 15th-century frescoed ceiling of the *Zodiac*, a grand Renaissance work by native son Fernando Gallego.

By retracing a few step back up the C. Libreros to the first street going left, in one block is reached the Old Cathedral, right, and the New Cathedral adjoining, left. Along the way, note the walls topped with merlons, whether to keep students in or out is unclear.

New Cathedral and Old Cathedral   ★★★★
Open daily 9:30 a.m. to 1:30 p.m. and 3:30 p.m.-6:30 p.m. (the Old Cathedral closes at 6 p.m. in winter). Admission: 200 ptas., to the Old Cathedral. The entrance to the New Cathedral is on its northern face. The entrance to the Old Cathedral is from the first bay on the south inside the New Cathedral. Before rounding the **New Cathedral** to enter from the north side, it is impossible to avoid admiring the front, as extravagant a piece of late Gothic carving as ever one will see. Pierced stone carving, minute designs, friezes and balustrades which mark the cathedral's lines, culminate in an overflow of decoration around the portal. Yet the main structure is massive in appearance, with literally hundreds of small spike-like spires and countless tiny projections to lighten the look.

The foundation for the church was laid in 1513, and work finished fifty years later, though some additions were made as late as the 18th century after an earthquake weakened the cupola. Most credit for the design belongs to the late Gothic architect Gil de Hontañon and his son Rodrigo, an early exponent of the Plateresque. Together they pro-duced an interior that shocks with its harmony and lovely proportions after the riot outside. A narrow, lofty nave accompanies sweeping aisles on either side, divided by piers carved into delicate columns that rise to an elegant "star" vaulted ceiling. Atop immense arches that connect the piers runs a lovely balustrade punctuated by delicate medallions. Altogether this is an imposing church exhibiting both Gothic and Plateresque influence, without quite being the one or the other. The **coro** contains flamboyant choirstalls designed by one of the Churriguera brothers, while the **trascoro** was designed by another. But the main monument to the Churriguera family, the **cupola** and its drum with Baroque painted scenes of the life of the Virgin, is the work of both brothers together. The altar loses drama because of the distraction of two galleries that cross above it. A chapel in the apse at the right side displays a beautiful painted **Pieta** by Salvador Carmona.

A door from the first chapel on the south side leads to stairs descending to the **Old Cathedral**. This cathedral was consecrated in 1160 and is a museum of the Romanesque, with unique additions. The contrast with the New Cathedral is extreme. Undeniable elegance in the New Cathedral pales beside that of the Old, without need for the device of a narrow, high nave impossible at such an early date. Subtly pointed arches on simple columns, with higher columns dividing each, rise to equally simple groining in the ceiling. The eye is drawn along the height and length by light from a lantern at the transept. All these features were innovations for the Romanesque style. And how lovely is the execution—see the charming, unobtrusive carvings on and above the capitals.

At the altar stands a sublime early 15th-century **retablo** of 53 exquisite paintings, each in a frame. The bottom row is attributed to Francisco Gallego. Above, in a half dome, an amazing fresco of the Final Judgement leaps out of a striking black background. The statue of the Virgin on the altar is from the 12th century. Look up to the unusual lantern with its tiers of windows and flamboyant ribbing, an artwork on its own. The **St. Martin Chapel** at the west end of the nave retains delicate 14th-century frescos which cover the walls. In the south transept are a series of recesses holding delightful Gothic effigies.

From the south transept a door leads to the **cloister**, largely reconstructed, from which chapels radiate. These were used as classrooms until the University Mayores was built in the 15th century. On the east side is the **Chapel de Talavera**, for those who still followed the church rites practiced in the time of the Visigoths. The practitioners were primarily Christians in Moorish lands who had long been cut off from the remaining Christian community—hence the name Mozarabic (almost Arab) rites. The Mudejar dome is admirable as is the altarpiece by Pedro Berruguette. Next comes the **Santa Barbara Chapel** in which theology students took their final examinations, one at a time. The chair is original and much sat upon. Tradition had the students place their hands on the effigy of Bishop Lucero for inspiration and luck. What a dandy the Bishop is, with rings on every finger and fancy shoes. The Council of Castile once met in the **Santa Catalina Chapel**, which now displays lovely paintings. The original **chapterhouse** contains a Diocesan museum and some fine paintings. Note the **Santa Catalina altar** by Gallego, a lovely small gold picture of *San Pedro y San Pablo*, and the *Virgin with a Rose*. On the second floor is a fine **altar** for St. Michael by Juan de Flanders, among other works. The

Anaya Chapel on the south side of the cloister is dedicated to San Bartolome. The founders' tombs are the finest 15th-century carving and the ceiling is remarkable. Also in this chapel is an organ from the 14th century that may well be the oldest such surviving instrument, with lovely Mudejar inlay.

Exit from the churches is into the peaceful Pl. de Anaya. The street going left, C. Tostado, downhill, leads to the large C. San Pablo. Continuing straight on C. Concilio de Trento and passing the end of a large building on the left, the Las Dueñas Convent is reached.

Convento de las Dueñas　　　　　

Open daily 10 a.m. to 1 p.m. and 4-8 p.m. (until 7 p.m. in winter.) Admission: 100 ptas. The building was a palace donated to house a nunnery for women of the highest rank, hence the name Dueñas. The convent church is faced with a nice Plateresque doorway, through which one enters the cloister, the only part of the convent open to the public. But this is not an ordinary cloister. Constructed in the 16th century in the form of an irregular pentagon, the capitals of the second story gallery are carved with a profusion of grotesques to excite anyone's imagination and admiration.

The large Convento de San Esteban, across the plaza, rises above a flight of stairs. Its facade is oddly shaped and luxuriantly carved.

Convento de San Esteban　　　　　

Open daily 9 a.m. to 1 p.m. and 4:30-8 p.m. (until 6 p.m. in winter.) Admission: 100 ptas. The original church was assigned to the Dominicans when their previous home was destroyed by a flood. One of the brothers, Fra Alava, designed the present church in 1524 at the height of the Plateresque movement. Planned to present its front as dramatically as possible, it lacks towers which might distract, and leaves the sides bare. Above the round portal is a round arch framing the stoning of St. Stephan, all contained in a huge recessed curved arch, with Christ on the cross at the top. Note the delicate upper frieze of children and horses. The portico to the right of the facade is elegant Renaissance.

Entrance to the church is through a door at the end of the portico which lets onto a cloister, then the church. The interior dates to the 17th century and is unusually simple, heavy and dark. The one note of brightness and the center of attention is the high altar by the most famous of the Churriguera family, José. Massive gilt circling vines and grapes twist their way up wood columns, so massive that they almost hide figures of prophets and angels. On high is a painting by Claudio Coello of the Martyrdom of St. Stephen. It is said that 4000 pine trees died for this altar. Nothing is easier to criticize today than such a riotous excess of heavy gilt, but it must be confessed that from a distance the altar makes a dramatic statement.

Return by C. Concilio de Trento on which you came for one block to the large straight C. San Pablo. A right turn brings you in two blocks to **Fronseca Palace** ★, *now the Diputacion, on the left side. This was built for the Fronseca family in the first half of the 16th century by Rodrigo de Hontañon who helped his father design the New Cathedral. Inside, if it is possible to steal a peek, is an extremely pleasant patio with lovely carved consoles supporting the upper gallery. Continue for three blocks more along C. San Pablo to the* **Plaza Mayor**.

Plaza Mayor   ★★★

Designed in part by the Churriguera brothers, who created the Churrigueresque baroque style, and finished in 1733 (though the most imposing building, the Ayuntimiento on the north side, was added in 1755), many people consider it the most beautiful plaza in Spain. One wonders whether they have ever seen that of Santiago de Compostela. In any case, the plaza is more harmonious than most, with a unity of design that offers a reasonable solution to the problem of placing three stories of building above an arched arcade. However, this is one of those structures that the sun affects with its shadows by doubling the architectural details and making the whole too busy. On a cloudy day or early evening it is lovely. The growth holding bells on top of the Ayuntimiento was a mistake added a century later. Attractive cafes and shops ring the plaza.

Mansion Walk   ★★★

C. Prior lies outside the southwest corner of the Plaza Mayor. At the second crossing street turn right onto C. de Bordadores, in a few steps reaching the **Casa de las Muertes** ★ on your right. Here is one of the earliest examples of what came to be called Plateresque, attributed to the great architect Gil de Siloé, and more formal than later, more developed examples would become. The house belonged to the Archbishop Alonso de Fonseca whose portrait is carved over the window. When he died his nephew had tiny skulls carved just under the top window jambs, lending the present name "Death" to the house. Across the street and a few steps further along is a statue to the philosopher **Unamuno** in front of the house, now a museum, in which he died under the house arrest imposed by Gen. Franco. Directly opposite the Casa de las Muertes, set back in a square is the **Convent of Las Ursulas** ★, with an imposing octagonal turret topped by an elaborate balustrade. The convent was founded by the same Archbishop Fonseca who owned the Casa de las Muertes. He is buried inside in an elegant tomb by Gil de Siloé.

Back up the C. Prior is the **Monterrey Palace** ★. Turn right to see the elegant facade framed by two corner towers and topped by a reconstructed openwork balustrade. The palace (now owned by the Duke of Alba) was built for the Count of Monterrey, who through marriage was connected to all the best families, including the Fonsecas of the Casa de las Muertes. The Count displayed the coats of arms of all these connections on his home. Across the street is the **Iglesia de la Purisima Concepcion** ★, founded by the same Count of Monterrey. Inside is a wonderful Ribera *Immaculate Conception* over the altar, and the tomb of the Count.

Continue along C. de Bordadores which now changes its name to C. de la Compañia. The second street to the right leads into the **Barrio de San Benito** in which mansions of the old Salamanca families surround the church of San Benito. During the Renaissance these families formed bands that fought and killed each other in vendettas. Most of the tombs inside the church hold bodies that did not die of old age.

Back on C. de la Compañia one block further is the famed **Casa de las Conchas** ★ (House of the Shells). After the owner was appointed Chancellor of the Order of Santiago he was so proud that he placed four hundred scallop shells, the symbol of the order, on the walls of his house. The main door is surmounted by a Salamancine arch in which lions hold a shield with a fleur-de-lis field, the crest of the owner. The shield is repeated at the house corner. The second-story windows are as elegant as can be and the first-story windows are protected by fine Plateresque grills, each unique (with more scallop shells). On the opposite side of the street is the **Pontifical University**, also known as the Clerecia. This is a Jesuit College begun in 1617 and finished a century and a half later. It is a fine example of Baroque design.

Return around the side of the Casa de las Conchas to enter the large Rua Mayor going northeast and brings the Pl. del Corralillo in two blocks that contains the **Iglesia San Martin** ★. The building was erected in the 12th century, though many additions were added later, such as the Plateresque front. Inside is some lovely vaulting and nice Gothic tombs.

WHERE TO STAY

Salamanca provides abundant hotel choices, including one of our favorites in Spain.

EXPENSIVE ($100-$200)

Hotel Residencia Rector   R1st-class ★★★★

Paseo del Rector Esperabe, 10 (on river side of the circular road, just past the "Roman" bridge). Rooms: 13. ☎ *21 84 82; FAX 21 40 08.* The Rector is too good to be a hotel. It was a mansion until 1990, when the owners decided to make the lower floors public. As it happens, the Ferran family who own it and their architect have utterly exquisite taste. They planned rooms in which you can stay, but so beautiful and comfortable that it is difficult to consider them hotel rooms. They are huge, decorated in perfect taste, with no thought to saving costs any-where. Since the establishment is small and family-run it does not offer the services of a larger hotel, and is thus called a *residencia*. That is truly what it is. You will think you have reached heaven when you see your room (unless you happen to see the one suite, and then you will know that you are a step below). No restaurant is on the premises, but a bright nook is used for breakfasts. Of course the service is impec-cably gracious. If this sounds like your kind of hotel, reserve well ahead since it is small indeed.

Parador de Salamanca   1st-class ★★★
Teso de la Feria, 2 (from the circle road turn left at Puerta San Pablo, cross-ing the river on Av. Reyes de España; go left around the traffic circle on the other side, then take the first right). Rooms: 108. ☎ *26 87 00; FAX 21 54 38; Telex 23585.* This is not what most people expect of a parador for it is a modern building, in fact one of the first of the modern paradors, and beginning to show signs of age. It is also too far outside of town for walking. However, the reception is very professional and helpful, and the spacious rooms have enclosed balconies with lovely views of the city. It is a relaxing place to stay.

Gran Hotel   1st-class
Pl. Poeta Iglesias, 5 (opposite the southeast corner of the Pl. Mayor). Rooms: 100. ☎ *21 35 00; Telex 26809.* Grand it is not, although ren-ovations in 1991 improved it. Service is lakadaisical, yet it charges more than any hotel in town. The location, however, is good and it offers parking for a fee.

Monterrey   1st-class ★
Azafranal, 21 (three blocks northeast of the Pl. Mayor). Rooms: 89. ☎ *21 44 00; FAX 21 44 00; Telex 27836.* This is the sister to the Gran Hotel, and also charges too much in our opinion. It is in dire need of reno-vation, caters mainly to tours and the service can be icy.

MODERATE ($50-$99)

Amefa   3rd-class ★★★
Pozo Amarillo, 8 (two blocks northeast of the Pl. Mayor on the street par-allel to C. Azafranal). Rooms: 33. ☎ *21 81 89; FAX 26 02 00.* Renova-tions have just been completed with great care in this family-owned hotel. Polished wood and stone run throughout the small-scale public areas. Rooms are modest, but decent in size and outfitted comfort-ably. The full bathrooms sparkle. You cannot do better in Salamanca for anything close to this price. Service is willing and friendly, though English-speaking staff are not always available.

Condal   3rd-class
Pl. Santa Eulalia, 3 (opposite the Monterrey Hotel). Rooms: 70. ☎ *21 84 00.* The lobby is seedy, but the rooms are adequate. This is just a place to stay, and inferior to the inexpensive choices below.

INEXPENSIVE (UNDER $50)

Gran Via   3rd-class ★ ★

Rosa, 4 (near the Amefa above, one block further northeast). Rooms: 47.
☎ *21 54 01.* Nicely maintained and attractive, this would be your
best bet in the price range if the Amefa is full.

Milán   4th-class ★

Pl. del Ángel, 5 (behind the Gran Hotel). Rooms: 25. ☎ *21 75 18.* The
clean bright rooms are smaller than what one might like, and many of
the baths are only quarter tubs, so usable only for showers. If that is
not a problem for you, this hotel should suit fine. Its location is very
good.

Emperatriz   3rd-class ★

C. Compañia, 4. Rooms: 61. ☎ *21 92 00.* The building is medieval but
the rooms are new and clean. About half the rooms have showers only,
and most are a bit bare, though attractive enough.

Pensión Marina   3rd-class

C. Doctinos, 4 (on the side street going east from C. Compania). ☎ *21 65
69.* We seldom list accommodations without private bathrooms, but
this is an exception because the price is so attractive and the public
bathroom is so large and clean. Keep thinking of all the money you are
saving, when nature calls. This place is hard to miss because it is
upstairs from the Communist Party headquarters, proclaimed by a
banner above its street-level office.

WHERE TO EAT

Roast lamb and suckling pig, specialties of Old Castile, are served up
well at several restaurants, but the treat that only Salamanca offers is a special restaurant which delicately marries French with Spanish cuisine. As expected in a university town, there is a wide variety of better-than-average
restaurants as well as numerous inexpensive dining places, some serving
food only a student could love. The Pl. Mayor contains a number of stylish
bars with outdoor seating for a drink, sandwich or tapas munch.

EXPENSIVE ($50+)

Chez Victor   ★★★★

*Espoz y Mina, 26 (Pl. de la Liberdad is a small park a few steps due north
of Pl. Mayor, at whose west end is the restaurant).* ☎ *21 31 23. Closed
Sunday night, Monday, and August.* Chef Victoriano learned his craft in
France and brought the lessons home to produce some of the most
sublime cooking in Spain. The restaurant itself is just a rectangle leaving all focus on ample tables set attractively with fine linen and china.
All waits for the final decoration—food as exquisite to the eye as to
the palate. When his duties allow Victoriano circulates with the most
infectious smile, leaving orders and recommendations to his attentive
and professional, multilingual wife. The experience is close to perfect
(if only the lighting were a little less bright). The cuisine tastes closer

to French than Spanish, but is a true invention of the chef. Entrees change with the season, but if rape, skate of lovely chewy texture, or magrite of duck are available they deserve serious consideration. Appetizers are constant and both the *hojaldre de verduras y foie-gras con salsa de trufas* and *crab crepe* are outstanding. Desserts can be sublime, and include exquisite chocolate mousse, sinful chocolate tart and delicate ice creams and sherbets. Reservations are strongly recommended. ***Amex, Diners, MasterCard and Visa accepted.***

El Candil Nuevo ★★

Pl. de la Reina, 1 (one block along the second right from Calle Pozo Amarillo which leads out of the north corner of the Pl. del Mercado, on the east side of the Pl. Mayor). ☎ *21 90 27*. This "new" incarnation of a Salamanca institution unquestionably serves the best roasts and traditional Castilian food in town, and does so in the atmosphere of an old mesón. But do not overlook the fresh trout, simply prepared. If you order from the special menu, which offers a good selection, you can dine for moderate prices. Reservations are recommended. ***Amex, Diners and MasterCard accepted.***

MODERATE ($20-$50)

Le Sablon ★★

Espoz y Mina, 20 (next to Chez Victor). ☎ *26 29 52. Closed Tuesday, and July.* Its neighbor Chez Victor gets the attention, but this is a quality restaurant too, with an attractive interior of fruitwood and pink damask. The food is prepared with care and the prices are more than fair. ***Amex, Diners and Visa accepted.***

Rio de la Plata ★★

Pl. del Peso, 1 (just south of the Pl. Mayor, across from the Gran Hotel). ☎ *21 90 05. Closed Monday, and July.* Cozy with dark wood and a fireplace, and usually crowded—a good sign—the menu ranges over Castilian dishes but excels in seafood. Ordering seafood, however, can push your bill into the expensive range.

La Posada ★

C. Aire, 1 (a few steps east from the Pl. Mayor C. Pozo Amarillo runs northeast to let into a square in three blocks, from which the restaurant is a few steps to the right, opposite the tall Torre del Aire). ☎ *21 72 51. Closed the first three weeks in August.* Fortunately the cooking surpasses the decor. A neon sign announces the restaurant whose interior lives up to the expectations of such a sign. But, if game is in season, it is well worth a try, and prices are reasonable. ***Amex, Diners and Visa accepted.***

INEXPENSIVE (UNDER $20)

El Bardo

C. Compañia, 8 (by the Casa del Conchas). ☎ *21 90 89. Closed Monday and October.* The students come for the low priced menus, but the á la carte selections are generally better prepared. Prices are rock bottom.

DIRECTORY

INFORMATION • Located on C. Gran Via, 39-41. C. Gran Via is four short blocks east of the Pl. Mayor, and the tourism office is two blocks north along it. Open Mon.-Fri. from 9:30 a.m. to 2 p.m. and from 4:30-7 p.m. Open Sat. from 10 a.m. to 2 p.m. and Sun. from 11 a.m. to 2 p.m. ☎ 26 85 71. A municipal office is located in the Pl. Mayor with similar hours but less information.

TRAINS AND BUSES • Three trains per day connect Madrid with Salamanca, via Ávila, for a trip of about 3 hours. Service is more frequent to Valladolid, 2 hours away. One train goes to Barcelona (14 hrs.), and one to León (3-1/2 hrs.). Five trains daily deliver passengers to Guarda in Portugal (3 hrs.) for connections elsewhere in Portugal. The train station is located almost a half hour walk to the northeast of town on Puerto de la Estación de Ferriocarril. A RENFE office is at Pl. Liberdad, 10 (in front of the Chez Victor restaurant). ☎ 21 24 54.

Buses run frequently to Madrid, Ávila and Zamora. Two per day reach León, four reach Valladolid and five go to Cáceres in Extremadura. Two buses each day take the 11-1/2-hour trip to Barcelona, though charge more than the train. The station is located on Av. Filiberto Villalobos, 79 (☎ 23 67 17), a thirty minute walk northwest following C. Ramon y Cajal, the street that passes the Casa de las Conchas.

POST OFFICE AND TELEPHONES • C. Gran Via, 25 (two blocks north of the tourist office), ☎ 26 27 50. Telephones are available at Pl. Peña Primera, 1 (two blocks past Casa de las Muertes and right).

POLICE • In the Ayuntamiento in Pl. Mayor. ☎ 26 25 95 (091, for emergencies).

EXCURSIONS

Buen Amor Castle is close and amusing to see because it is a castle in actual use. Two picturesque towns and mountainous scenery lie half an hour to the south. Along the Portuguese border in the same area, **Ciudad Rodrigo** ★★ is a town full of history with a nice cathedral and castle. **Alba de Tormes** ★ lies just southeast of Salamanca and preserves the body of Saint Theresa in a quaint and lovely town. Atmospheric, old **La Alberca** ★★★ lies at the end of a scenic ride, with **Miranda del Castañar** ★ along the way. Not far north, **Zamora** ★★ and **Toro** ★★ both have Romanesque churches reminiscent of the Old Cathedral in Salamanca. Zamora has a castle besides. From Zamora and Toro **Valladolid** ★★★ is less than 100 k away on N-122. (See "Valladolid" below for a description.)

BUEN AMOR CASTLE

Travel around Salamanca by the circular road until reaching the north side to turn onto Paseo Dr. Torres Villarroel. Signs direct you to Zamora and N-630. At 21 k is a small sign for the castle, directing to an unpaved private road on the right. Note: on recent trips this road was a mass of potholes.

Open daily 10 a.m. to 2 p.m. and 3:30-8:30 p.m. (until 7:30 in winter.). The building began as a fort which Ferdinand and Isabella used as a headquarters during their war with Isabella's niece La Beltraneja over the right of succession. It was transformed into a palace in the 16th century by the same Archbishop Fronseca who owned the Casa Muertes in Salamanca. Today it is privately owned and a working farm. You ring the bell on the front door and the housekeeper who speaks only Spanish lets you in. Admission is free, but you are asked to buy a postcard of the castle for 100 ptas. Speaking slow Spanish, much of which will communicate, she shows you around then turns you over to her husband to complete the tour. It is not the most splendid castle in Spain, but visiting it is one of the more unusual experiences.

LA ALBERCA ★★★ AND MIRANDA DEL CASTAÑAR ★

Follow directions for the Salamanca parador, but instead of turning left at the traffic circle across the river, continue through to take the following left, opposite the pedestrian "Roman" bridge. In one block turn left again following the sign for C-512 and Veciños. Follow C-512 for 83 k to Santibañez de la Sierra. Turn right on C-515 for 10 k, turning left for **Miranda del Castanar** *2 k away. For* **La Alberca** *continue for 3 k past Miranda at which point the right forking road winds for 14 k to La Alberca.* **Ciudad Rodrigo** *can be included by returning past Miranda del Castanar to C-515 and turning left which brings you in 73 k, the first third being quite windy but scenic, to Ciudad Rodrigo.*

Miranda del Castañar ★ remains a reasonably unspoiled hilltop village consisting of houses with spreading eaves and flower-bedecked balconies. The Romanesque church and castle are worth a look.

After the winding trip to **La Alberca ★★★** it is easy to understand why this village remained isolated for so long, retaining a provincial character that most towns have lost. It was, however, discovered by tourists in the 1960s when the entire town was designated a national monument and since that time has become a bit taken with itself. Even so it remains a beautiful little town. There is little to do but wander the twisting streets to the arcaded Plaza Mayor by houses built of stone up to an adobe second story with overhanging wood balconies, bright with flowers in season. The day to come is Sunday when everyone gathers in the square in traditional dress.

CIUDAD RODRIGO ★★

Population: 14,776

From Salamanca, the most direct route is N-620 (E-80) for 89 k. To access N-620 follow directions for the Salamanca parador, but instead of turning left at the traffic circle across the river, continue to take the following left, opposite the pedestrian "Roman" bridge. For a route that includes La Alberca, see above.

Atop its hill, the city looks like the frontier outpost it was, with circling ramparts and a square towered castle. Its name "Rodrigo City" comes from Count Rodrigo Gonzalez Giron who defeated the Moors and repopulated the town. A grand **cathedral** ★ begun in the late 12th century received its last addition, the apse, in the 16th. The fine west portal contains quaint carvings of the Last Supper. Pleasant sculpture and strikingly grotesque choir stalls decorate the solid interior. The cloister off the north side consists of columns whose capitals represent fine Romanesque work, with a pure Plateresque door at the east. The **Plaza Mayor** is picturesque, with a former 15th-century mansion, now the Ayuntamiento, using towers to anchor its arcade. Near the northern rampart is the long 15th-century **Palace of Los Castros** ★, faced by Plateresque twisted columns. The severe 14th-century **Alcázar** now houses a small parador and may be entered for a look. From there the 18th-century city **ramparts** ★ can be climbed.

ALBA DE TORMES ★

Population: 4,106

Cross the river on the south side of the circular road, turning left where signs direct you to N-501, the Airport and Ávila. On the outskirts of Salamanca turn onto C-510 for Alba de Tormes in 23 k.

This town on the banks of the Tormes River was owned by the Dukes of Alba, hence its name. Today it is quiet, but with remains that shows it once was an important seat of power. The Dukes were patrons of Saint Theresa and invited her to establish one of her new convents here. It was her last work; here she died.

Immediately after the lovely **Medieval Bridge** ★, turn left to climb to the Pl. Mayor. On the left is **San Juan church** ★. The front portal and central apse of brick are 12th century Mudejar, the rest eighteenth-century. A curious 11th-century sculpture of the Apostles stands in the apse. An alley to the right leads down to the **Church of the Encarnación** ★, the last Carmelite convent founded by St. Theresa. Over the door on the facade is a too precious Plateresque scene of an angel visiting the Saint. Inside, the church is simple and stately, with the Saint's tomb at the high altar. Her heart and one arm are inside a black marble urn. To the left, funerary stones from successive tombs where she was buried before being interred here are displayed, as one person or town after another claimed her mortal remains before their final rest. At the rear of the church is a reconstruction of the cell in which she died. High on the hill is the keep from the former castle of the Alba's, all that is left of it.

ZAMORA ★★ AND TORA ★★
Population: 59,734 and 9,781, respectively

From Salamanca follow the directions for Buen Amor Castle, continuing on N-630 past its turnoff for a total of 62 k to Zamora. Toro is 33 k further east of Zamora on N-122 (E-82). For Valladolid (see description under "Valladolid" below) continue east past Tora on N-122 for 97 k.

Turn left immediately upon crossing the Duero River on Av. del Mengue. Parking is available after the road curves north by the ruins of a castle surrounded by what remains of imposing ramparts. The **castle** ★ last belonged to Urraca, daughter of Fernando I. It seems she lured one brother, who had succeeded his father to the throne, here to kill him so that another, whom she favored, could rule instead.

The gem of Zamora lies across the park—the **cathedral** ★★★. Do not be misled by the neo-classic north front; this is a 12th-century Romanesque beauty. Travel to the south end to see its original appearance. Inside the nave rises on characteristic massive piers, but uncharacteristic light streams onto the altar at the end from a lantern at the transept crossing, an idea taken from the Old Cathedral in Salamanca. Also interesting are the choir stalls, from the 15th century. Though expected Biblical scenes cover the backs, the arms and misericords contain burlesques of cloistered life and fantastic animals. Stairs from the neo-classic cloister lead up to a museum with fine tapestries.

If you like the cathedral, there is more of the same. Head northwest along C. Notarios leading away from the rear of the cathedral. In three blocks you come to **Santa Magdalena** ★ church on the left, noted particularly for its *south portal* with elaborately decorated recessed arches. Returning to the street by which we came, continue on it until it becomes C. Ramos. One block later brings a park with a lovely Renaissance palace on its right side. Today it is the city's parador, but it was a **palace for the Dukes of Alba** ★ in the 15th century. A lovely courtyard is decorated with medallions and coats of arms. One short block further lies the **Plaza Mayor**. One short block northeast is the **Casa de los Momos** with attractive windows, and the next right brings you to **Santiago del Burgos** ★, another lovely Romanesque church. Two more—**Santa Maria de la Horta** and **Santo Tomé**, lie due south.

Nearby Toro is also full of Romanesque churches, most built of brick. One in particular is noteworthy, the limestone **Iglesia del Colegiata ★★**, which boasts a glorious and almost perfectly preserved *Gothic west portal*, repainted in the 18th century to suggest its original appearance. (Open daily 10:30 a.m. to 1:30 p.m. and 5-7 p.m., until 8 p.m. in summer.) The figures of the Celestial Court and those in the Last Judgment scene are expressive as only the stiff Romanesque can be. Inside is another wondrous lantern, plus nice polychrome statuary at the nave end. The sacristy contains a painting of *The Virgin of the Fly*. Note the realistic fly on the Virgin's robe.

SANTO DOMINGO DE SILOS MONASTERY

See Burgos excursions.

SEGOVIA★★★★★

Population: 53,237
Zip code: 40001; area code: 911

From **Madrid** *take A-6 northwest to Exit #3 in 61 k, switching to N-603, past lovely landscapes, for 30 k to Segovia, for a trip of 91 k. From* **Ávila** *take N-110 northwest for 66 k. From* **Burgos** *take N-1 south, toward Madrid, for 137 k, to 3 k past Cerezo de Abajo where you switch to N-110 heading west for Segovia in 57 k more. The trip covers 194 k. From* **Valladolid** *take N-601 south toward Madrid for 109 k to Villacastin, switching to N-110 for 37 k to Segovia, a total of 146 k. From* **Salamanca**, *follow directions to Ávila, and the directions above from Ávila.*

From whatever direction Segovia is approached it is best to take a ride around the perimeter before entering the town. Such a ride shows the unusual situation of the old city, thrust precipitously above the surrounding plain in a slender ellipse. The appearance has often been likened to a ship, with the Alcázar, a fairy-tale castle, at the prow and the towers of the cathedral at the stern, while the original city walls run around most of its length. No city in Spain presents such a dramatic first look, not even Toledo.

Segovia began as Sogobriga, a major town of the Celts. The Romans captured it in 80 B.C. and it became one of their most important Spanish cities. They favored it with a great engineering feat by constructing an aqueduct two thirds of a mile long to lift water to

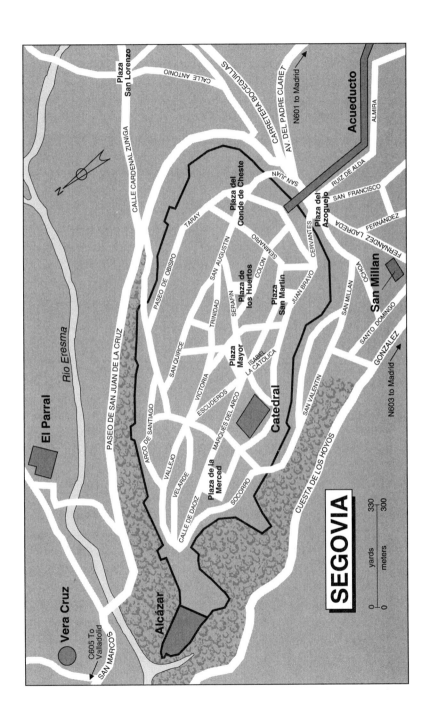

the city from the Rio Riofrio. What is remarkable is that the elevation of the city required the aqueduct to rise 92 feet (nine stories) above the ground. Also notable, the aqueduct remains in perfect condition 2000 years later and could still be used to supply the city's water.

After reconquest from the Moors, Segovia became the royal capital for a brief period. But its greatest historical claim is that it was in its Alcázar that the grandees of Spain publicly named Isabella the monarch, when her half-brother Enrique IV died, passing over his heir, La Beltraneja, as illegitimate. By this time the Alcázar was centuries old, dating to Moorish times, if not to the age of the Romans. Major reconstruction took place in the 14th century and then in the next.

Segovia boasted of a Romanesque cathedral, as did so many cities in the area at this time, but in the succeeding reign of Carlos V, the grandson of Ferdinand and Isabella, the citizens of Spain rose up against their new king for his foreign ways and burned their cathedral. This revolt, called the "Comuneros," since it was an uprising of towns, not of nobles, found one of its leaders in Juan Bravo from Segovia. In the end he was hung, though Segovia by then was cathedral-less. The city fathers hurriedly built another in the 16th century, while the Plateresque aesthetic was at its height, but for some reason designed a cathedral in an old-fashioned Gothic style. Thus Segovia today possesses the most recent Gothic cathedral in Spain, and one of the largest.

Segovia is a city that once was important but did not find continued reasons to remain so. Though by no means poor, its population today is less by twenty percent than what it was at its height in Renaissance times.

*Parking is an unsolved problem, especially in summer when hordes descend. Little space is available on the hill, and none at all in the main plaza below, Pl. Azoguejo (with the aqueduct). All we can suggest is to keep eyes peeled for any spot as you near the hill and to be prepared to walk some distance. Our tour of the old city starts in the Pl. Azoguejo, so we direct you there. From **Madrid** turn right onto Carreteria de San Rafael at the major intersection where four large avenues converge. After passing the bullring, go left onto Av. del Padre Claret, which brings you to the large Pl. Azoguejo with the aqueduct in a few blocks. From **Ávila** and **Salamanca** no changes of road are necessary. Unless you turn away, you will end up in the Pl.*

Azoguejo. From **Burgos** *or* **Valladolid** *no changes of road are necessary either; unless you intentionally deviate, you will end up in the Pl. Azoguejo.*

You cannot help looking at the **aqueduct ★★** and admiring its age and simple but functional construction. The **Alcázar ★★★**, once viewed from a distance, ranks at the top of every list of what to see. The **cathedral ★★** is well worth a visit for its imposing effect. Then there are assorted **mansions** and churches on the hill, which being less than a mile long and narrow, can be walked from end to end. Off the hill two exceptional Romanesque churches—**Vera Cruz ★★** and **San Millán ★★**, should not be missed, and the monastery of **El Parral ★** contains rich decoration. One day would be adequate to see all this, unless you add the following excursions. About ten miles south of Segovia are two 17th-century palaces: **La Granja ★★** with glorious gardens, built by a king nostalgic for Versailles, and **Riofrio ★**, an overgrown hunting lodge for royalty.

OUTSIDE THE WALLS:
VERA CRUZ, SAN MILLÁN, EL PARRAL

Go southwest from Pl. Azoguejo on Av. Fernández Ladreda, following signs to N-110 and Ávila. In three blocks the small church of **San Millán** *with a side porch, set back in its tiny square is passed. After San Millán continue on Av. Ladreda to the second street going right, Paseo Ezequiel González, which runs beside the elevated old town and provides lovely views. When it crosses the river, turn right for a moment onto C-605 heading to Segovia, and take the second left to* **La Vera Cruz** *sitting atop a hill. Return to C-605 again toward Segovia, which is named Paseo de San Juan, after it crosses the river. The first left after crossing the river takes you to* **El Parral** *Monastery.*

San Millán   ★★
Open daily 9 a.m. to 1 p.m. (only for services in winter) San Millán is the oldest (perhaps 10th century), purest Romanesque church in Segovia and one of the most charming designs in Spain. The porch outside was a place where important meetings were held; the Mudejar tower is an 11th century addition. Instead of thicker walls, external columns supporting the bays of the apse become architectural features—a local peculiarity of other Romanesque churches in Segovia. Inside, massive columns are topped with capitals carved in lovely Biblical scenes.

Vera Cruz Chapel

Open Tues.-Sun. 10:30 a.m. to 1 p.m. and 3-7 p.m. (until 6 p.m. in winter). Closed Mon. and holidays. Admission: 100 ptas. From the outside one can see that this is an unusual church—a polygon instead of the expected rectangle or cruciform shape. It was erected by the Knights Templar in the 13th century as a place for their rites, many of which were secret. In 1226 Pope Honore gave the church a piece of the True Cross, so it changed its name to La Vera Cruz. Inside, one finds a central chamber, circular in shape and two stories tall. Stairs lead up to the second story in which novice knights performed vigils while overlooking the altar. The surrounding nave is plain, except for faded 15th-century frescos. The place has a lovely feel of age. Stairs beside the altar lead up the tower for nice views of Segovia.

El Parrel Monastery

Open Tues.-Sun. 10 a.m. to 1 p.m. and 3-7 p.m. (until 6 p.m. in winter.) Closed Mon. and holidays. The facade, never completed, shows two unusual soaring columns with clustered niches at the bottom still waiting to be filled by statues. The church was built in the middle 15th century by Juan Pacheco in homage to the Virgin for her help in winning a duel. The Plateresque interior contains a sensitive reredo of Juan Pacheco praying on one side, his wife on the other. In the transept rests a Gothic effigy of his illegitimate sister beside a lovely flamboyant door to the sacristy.

Aqueduct

A tunnel at the Rio Riofrio over a mile away starts water on its way to Segovia. But the land descends into a valley as it approaches the heights of the old town, so the Romans raised the water with an aqueduct to carry it up to the hill, where it enters a tunnel again. The structure of large granite blocks secured by physics, not mortar, was completed in the first century B.C. Each block contains indentations for the grip of pincers which raised them into place. The aqueduct runs for two-thirds of a mile, reaching its greatest height of 92 feet in the Pl. del Azoguejo. It no longer functions, despite claims by the tourist authorities, but looks as if it could.

INSIDE THE WALLS

From the Pl. del Azoquejo ascend the hill by the pedestrian walk, C. Cervantes, running northwest. As it goes slightly right at the top entering C. Juan Bravo, the strange **Casa de los Picos** lies left. This 14th-century fortified mansion was studded profusely with faceted protrusions a century later to produce an armored effect. C. Juan Bravo continues past a 14th-century palace of the **Contes de Alpuente**, set back left, with nice windows and plaster decoration, then past a restored former public granary down stairs to the left, before entering the **Pl. San Martin ★**.

Facing the plaza is a Gothic house reputed to be that of **Juan Bravo** who led the uprising of the Comuneros in the 16th century, opposite his statue in the center of the plaza. Other mansions line the square, most interesting for their entrances, including the house of the **Marqués de Moya**, with intricate stucco designs around an utterly plain Romanesque door of massive stones; the Palace of the **Marqués of Lozoya**, with a Romanesque arched doorway fit for a church; and the **Palace of Quintanar**, with an arched door surmounted by a row of curious helmets. In the center stands the 12th-century Romanesque **San Martin ★**, framed by a fine porch, and with nice carving on the west front portal.

Continuing on Juan Bravo, pass the 18th-century prison, now the archive for the city. One block later pass the 16th-century church of **San Miquel** to the left, then take the right fork into the **Plaza Mayor** (a.k.a. Plaza José Antonio), lined with cafes. On its west side stands the cathedral.

Cathedral   ★ ★

Open weekdays 9:30 a.m. to 1 p.m. and 3-6 p.m. Open weekends and holidays 9:30 a.m. to 6 p.m. Open in summer daily 9 a.m. to 7 p.m. Admission: 150 ptas., for the cloister. When their old cathedral near the Alcázar was burned in the 16th century, the city fathers hired the Hontañons, father and son, who had achieved success with their neoclassical New Cathedral in Salamanca, but instructed them to design a Gothic building. This the architects did with flair, producing the last great Gothic church, but with occasional Plateresque gestures. The entrance to the cathedral is from the Plaza Mayor into the north transept. For some reason the western front of the church, with an open court that allows a fine view of the sober facade, is never used.

The cathedral impresses with soaring spaces, perfect lines, nice vaulting and light, though the trascoro is nothing but a distraction. Moreover, the flamboyantly decorated chapels are not of great merit, with the exception of a nice retablo by Juan de Juni and a triptych in the La Piedad chapel, first off the south aisle. A door in the south transept leads to the cloister, reconstructed stone by stone from the cloister of the former cathedral. As you enter, you step over the tombs of the Hotañons who designed the cathedral. The chapterhouse, off the cloister, has a late Mudejar ceiling in striking white and gold. Dramatic 17th-century Brussels tapestries are displayed, most of them designed by Rubens.

Follow **C. Marqués del Arco** *west from the cathedral entrance; a few feet later on the right pass the mansion after whose former owner the street is named. In a sixth of a mile after that come the gardens of the Alcázar with the castle itself ahead.*

Alcázar   ★★★

*Open Mon.-Sat. 10 a.m. to 7 p.m. (until 6 p.m. in winter.) Closed
Sun. and holidays. Admission: 175 ptas.* Though it looks the archetypical medieval castle, the interior today is mainly artifice. In the 14th
century a former Moorish Alcázar, probably a modification of a
Roman fort, was made into a Christian castle. Here Princess Isabella
was first proclaimed Queen of Spain. Most of Spain's medieval kings
stayed at least a while; Prince Charles of England, later King Charles
I, enjoyed a visit; and the fourth marriage of Felipe II was celebrated
inside. In 1862, after Carlos III made the palace over for an artillery
school, a fire gutted the interior. Today the inside is a fanciful reconstruction done in the 19th century. If taken with a grain of salt, it
remains fun to wander through.

Inside, furniture of the period, much armor, and some nice frescos of
medieval themes are displayed. The "King's Bedroom" is evocative
and gives a sense of how tapestries were used to insulate cold stone
walls, showing the profusion of colors in a medieval castle. The throne
room is a 19th-century fantasy of how a state room should look.

From the Alcázar gardens go straight for a few steps, then take C.
de Velarde, the left fork, which wends for three blocks before changing its name to C. Pozuelo, as it bends left to enter the Pl. de San Esteban. **San Esteban ★** is yet another lovely Segovian Romanesque
church with a beautiful side gallery. It is the latest (13th century) of
Segovia's Romanesque churches, and perhaps the most harmonious
of all, prefaced by an elegant thin front tower. The **Bishop's Palace**
opposite is covered with curious reliefs. Continue across the plaza to
pick up C. Vitoria heading east, passing the **Casa de los Hierro** in
one block on the left, with an intricate 16th-century entrance and
grotesques. The street changes its name to C. Valdelaguila as, on the
left, it passes the **Casa de Hercules**, a Dominican convent named for
the figure on its tower. A block later the street changes its name to C.
Trinidad as it passes the open and austere **San Trinidad**, yet another
Romanesque church. One block later the street passes through the
Pl. de Guevara, merging in another block with C. San Augustin.
Then it passes a 16th-century mansion housing the **Museo Provin-
cial del Bellas Artes**, before entering, two blocks later, the **Pl. del
Conde de Cheste ★**, surrounded by mansions. The **Disputacion** is
on the left, while opposite is the **Casa de las Cabezas**. Across the
plaza, left to right, are the large **Palacio del Contes de Cheste**, the
Casa de Lozoyo (with parts from the 12th century) and **Casa de
Moya**. To the right is the **Palacio Quintanar**, followed by the **Casa
de las Cadenas**, both 15th-century. Behind them is the **Iglesia San
Sebastian**, yet another of Segovia's lovely Romanesque churches,

past which is the aqueduct's end and stairs descending back to the
Pl. Azoguejo.

WHERE TO STAY

The selection is sparse, since most visitors come from Madrid and do not
stay the night. But, if they are not filled, there are choices in every category.

EXPENSIVE ($100-$200)

Parador de Segovia   1st-class ★ ★
*On Carretera N-601, 3 k north of Segovia (From the Pl. del Azoguejo take
the center of three roads fanning east, following signs to N-601 and Valladolid. Look for the parador sign.) Rooms: 113.* ☎ *44 37 37; FAX 43 73
62; Telex 47913.* This is one of the modern paradors, looking like an
overgrown Swiss chalet, that tries to impress with design. The spacious public areas are landscaped with contemporary sculpture and
crafts, and the staff is efficient, organized and helpful. All is clean, if
somehow institutional, and the ample rooms all overlook Segovia for
fine views. It possesses every facility from swimming pool to new tennis courts, but is situated half a mile from the old town.

Los Arcos   1st-class ★ ★
*Paseo de Exequiel González, 24 (one block south and another east of San
Millán). Rooms: 59.* ☎ *43 74 62; FAX 42 81 61; Telex 49823.* This
well-run modern hotel is of the business traveler sort. It incorporates
the most elegant restaurant in town. However, it is situated a good six
blocks away from the sights.

MODERATE ($50-$99)

Los Linajes   2nd-class ★ ★ ★ ★
*C. Dr. Velasco, 9 (stairs descend east of the Pl. de San Esteban). Rooms:
55.* ☎ *43 17 12; FAX 43 15 01.* The facade is 11th-century, a former
palace of nobles named Falconis. Inside it is attractively decorated and
has the cozy feel of small spaces. All rooms present glorious views over
the countryside, and the staff could not be more helpful. Without
question this is the best place to stay in Segovia. Parking is provided
for a fee at the foot of the hotel outside the city walls, but is hard to
find.

Las Sirenas   R3rd-class ★ ★ ★
*Juan Bravo, 30 (opposite Pl. San Martin, a few doors past Juan Bravo's pur-
ported house). Rooms: 39.* ☎ *43 40 11; FAX 43 06 33.* The hotel is
lovely and bright, much better than its rating or charges. Its attractiveness starts with a spacious lobby and continues to a public room
with fireplace for relaxing. The rooms are comfortable, if unmemora-
ble.

Acueducto   2nd-class ★ ★
Av. del Padre Claret, 10 (two blocks east of the Pl. del Azoguejo). Rooms:

78. ☎ *42 48 00; FAX 42 84 46; Telex 49824.* Though outside the walls, the location is close enough to walk easily, if uphill, to the sights. The hotel, however, fronts the major traffic thoroughfare of the town. This is a modern hotel with the expected services of its class, nothing more.

INEXPENSIVE (UNDER $50)

Plaza   **Hs3rd-class ★**

C. Cronista Leccea, 11 (a short block on the street leading east out of the Pl. Mayor). Rooms: 28. ☎ *43 12 28.* Small, undistinguished, but with a great location and very reasonable prices, this *hostale* is clean, the rooms tidy and the service considerate.

WHERE TO EAT

Segovia is the place for roast suckling pig and suckling lamb, served in three superior restaurants, and others besides—so many that the restaurants begin to seem pleasantly alike. This is not to disparage the food, only to note its limited variety.

EXPENSIVE ($50+)

Mesón de Cándito   **★★★**

Pl. Azoguejo, 5. ☎ *42 59 11.* Thanks to the showmanship of its former owner, this is one of the most famous restaurants in Spain. It is lodged in an 18th-century inn and consists of small timbered rooms, which display the memorabilia of years, with fireplaces. The specialty is Castilian roasts of piglet or milk-lamb whose tenderness is proved by slicing the carcass with a dinner plate. The meat is truly flavorful, but it could only be so tender if overcooked. The trout is good, as is the garlic soup, and the house wine is exceptional.

Amex, Diners, MasterCard and Visa accepted.

José María   **★★**

C. Cronista Lecea, 11 (a short block on the street leading east out of the Pl. Mayor). ☎ *43 44 84.* This time the restaurant is modern, but it still does a mean suckling pig, cut with a dinner plate as at Cándito and Duque. The difference is that the chef here does other things well too. Frogs' legs and fish are good, as are the blood sausage, or the special eggs as appetizers. The house red wine is delicious, the white more ordinary. For dessert order an orange and watch the waiter cut it artfully, before you are transported by the taste. Reservations recommended.   *Amex, Diners, MasterCard and Visa accepted.*

Mesón del Duque   **★★**

C. Cervantes, 12 (at the entrance to the old town at the top of the street running up from Pl. Azoguejo). ☎ *43 05 37.* Clearly modeled on Cándito with a similar old look, though more studied, this is the same type of place. It is hard to choose between the two. This one offers a reasonably priced special menu, however.

Amex, Diners, MasterCard and Visa accepted.

MODERATE ($20-$50)

La Oficina

C. Cronista Lecea, 10 (across the street from Restaurante José María).
☎ *43 16 43. Closed Monday in winter and all of November.* This is the
lower-priced version of the foregoing, also with an atmospheric dining
room. The choices are restricted, but cover the compulsory roast suck-
ing pig, et. al. If you order from the special menu, your meal can be
very reasonable. **Amex, Diners, MasterCard and Visa accepted.**

La Taurina

Pl. Mayor, 8. ☎ *43 05 77.* Yes, this is yet another place for roasts like
the preceding, with an attempt at the same ambience, though at even
lower prices. Ordering from the special menu can make this an inexpensive meal, and the food can be very good.
Amex, Diners, MasterCard and Visa accepted.

DIRECTORY

INFORMATION • Located at Pl. Mayor, 10. ☎ 43 03 28. Open weekdays
from 10 a.m. to 2 p.m. and from 4:30-7 p.m. Open Sat. from 10 a.m.
to 2 p.m.

TRAINS AND BUSES • The station is located at Paseo del Obispo Quesada,
a 20-minute walk due south from Pl. Azoguejo. The #3 bus from the
Pl. Mayor goes to or from the station. Twelve trains each day connect
Madrid, and three, Valladolid. ☎ 42 07 74.

The bus station is located at Paseo de Equezuile Gonzálaz, 10. Take
Av. Fernández Ladreda southwest from the Pl. Azoguejo for 5 blocks,
just past San Millán, to the Paseo and turn right. ☎ 42 77 25. Service
is excellent to and from Madrid and La Granja. Buses also go to Ávila
and to Valladolid.

POST OFFICE AND TELEPHONES • Located at Pl. del Dr. Laguna, 5 (head
east out of the Pl. Mayor on C. Cronista Lecea, taking the right fork
in one long block onto C. Serafin for 2 blocks). ☎ 43 16 11. Open
weekdays from 9 a.m. to 2 p.m. and from 4-6 p.m. Open Sat. from 9
a.m. to 2 p.m. Telephones are available at Pl. de los Huertos, 8 (next
to the post office).

POLICE • C. Perucho, 2 (☎ 42 51 61).

EXCURSIONS

Two enjoyable Segovia excursions are to two neighboring 17th-century
palaces—**La Granja** ★★ with lovely gardens and extravagant fountains,
and **Riofrio** ★, the most elegant hunting lodge anywhere. The other remarkable excursion is to **Coca Castle** ★★ one of the most characteristic
in Spain. See its description and directions under the Coca Castle listing
above.

LA GRANJA DE SAN ILDEFONSO ★ ★

From Pl. Azoguejo take the southernmost of the two streets forking east, Av. del Padre Claret, following signs to N-601 and Madrid. As the bullring comes into view, stay left. In 11 k signs lead you to San Ildefonso and La Granja.

Palace

Open daily 10 a.m. to 1 p.m. and 3-5:30 p.m. (Sun. closes at 2 p.m.) Admission: 200 ptas. Gardens: open daily from 10 a.m. to sunset. Admission: 100 ptas. Check with the Segovia Office of Tourism for the time of the fountain show. When, at the beginning of the 18th century, Felipe V, cousin to the King of France, received the Spanish throne, he built this reminder of home, his Versailles. It looks very much the French palace, especially from the back. It overlooks gardens, both formal and wild, that stretch to the horizon past a series of fountains.

Unfortunately the interior of the palace suffered from fire at the beginning of our century. The reconstructed results are still worth a look for their Versailles-like vistas through room after room and for the vast tapestry collection. In the chapel, which also suffered fire damage, are the tombs of Felipe V and his queen, Isabel Farnese. But the main attraction is the gardens and, in summer, the incredible sunset display when the fountains go on, one by one, until Fuente La Fama, the last, shoots water 130 feet in the air.

RIOFRO PALACE ★

See the directions to La Granga above.

Palace *Open the same times as La Granja. Admission: 200 ptas.* When her husband died and her son replaced her with his own queen, Felipe V's wife, Isabel Farnese, tried to outdo the La Granja palace with this one nearby. It is huge but so simple that it seems more the hunting lodge it became later, though in a pink color appropriate for its first occupant. The courtyard is grand and monumental stairways lead to sumptuous apartments. Recently much of the palace has been turned into a Museum of the Chase, with curious but sometimes interesting exhibits.

SORIA

See Burgos excursions.

TORO

See Salamanca excursions.

VALLADOLID★ ★

Population: 330,242
Zip code: 47001; area code: 983

> From **Madrid** *take A-6 north for 37 k to exit 1 for N-VI,
> to avoid the toll, or to the end at exit 6, for a faster ride. In
> either case, take N-601 north at Adanero after 122 k. You
> come to Valladolid in 82 k for a trip of 204 k. From* **Ávila**
> *take N-110 toward Villacastin for 29 k, turning north on
> N-VI for 27 k, switching at Adanero for N-601 and 82 k
> more. The trip is 140 k. From* **Salamanca** *take N-620
> (E-80) northeast for 85 k through Tordesillas, continuing
> on the same road for 30 k more. From* **Segovia** *take N-110
> west for 37 k to Villacastin, turning north on N-VI and
> continue with the Ávila directions, for a trip of 148 k. From*
> **León** *take N-601 south for 139 k. From* **Burgos** *take N-620
> (E-80) west for 125 k, skirting Palencia.*

The unusual name for the city derives from the Arabic *Belad Walid*,
"Land of the Governor," showing that the Moors considered it an
important town. Valladolid prospered due to its position in the center of miles of wheat farmland. For centuries it functioned as a second capital for the kings of Castile and León, and when Isabella
decided against the wishes of her king to marry Ferdinand from
Aragón, the two eloped to Valladolid to wed in a mansion there,
subsequently torn down. After the conquest of Granada, Isabella
and Ferdinand made Valladolid the capital of the country. But, although the future Felipe II was born in Valladolid, he moved the
capital permanently to Madrid in 1560, leaving Valladolid with only
60 years as Spain's capital.

During its brief prominence, Columbus settled to spend his last
years, and Cervantes resided for a while. Befitting its capital status, a
college was established in 1496 in the exuberant style called Isabeline, the forerunner of the Plateresque. But when the court moved
to Madrid, Valladolid declined. It regained some importance when
Napoléon made it his headquarters during the Peninsular War,
though he and his soldiers stripped the buildings of their treasures
and shipped them to France. After Napoléons' departure, Valladolid
turned to economic pursuits to recover some of its former importance, and today is a major industrial town.

Its industrial success means that Valladolid is not the loveliest of cities. What the French did not destroy, the city fathers did, by favoring

industrial development over historical preservation. Valladolid presents miles of factories, high-rise apartment and office buildings. Most merely are shelters for a large working class. Some modern Spanish cities manage to remain attractive, but Valladolid is not one of them. That is not to say the city is horrible or unbearably ugly, just that Spain spoils us to expect more.

Route **N-601** *becomes Av. Segovia which ends at the park, Campo Grande. Turn left at the park, then right at its end onto Paseo de Zorrilla, with a center divider, which lets into the large Pl. Zorrilla at the other end. Continue through the plaza to head in the same direction on C. Santiago which lets into the Pl. Mayor in 5 blocks for underground parking. From* **Salamanca** *on N-620 you reach the River Pisuerga. Turn right across the third bridge. On C. Doctrinos take the second left onto C. Santiago which leads in 4 blocks into the Pl. Mayor and underground parking. From* **León** *on N-601 you travel on Av. de Gijon to the river. Turn right on Av. de Salamanca. At the third bridge after that turn, turn left across the river and follow the Salamanca directions above. From* **Burgos** *on N-620 you reach the river on Av. de Salamanca. Cross the river and turn left three bridges later to follow the Salamanca directions above.*

WHAT TO SEE AND DO

The sight that makes a trip to Valladolid worthwhile is the former **College of San Gregorio** ★★★★, for Isabelline decoration and even more for its great museum of polychrome sculpture, in which Spain excelled. A few steps away is the lovely facade of **Colegio Santa Cruz** ★★. The **Archaeology Museum** ★ nearby is worth a visit. Valladolid's neo-classical **cathedral** ★★, which should be seen, was designed in the style of Herrera who built much of El Escorial. The **University** ★ opposite has an unusual facade. For most visitors **Columbus' House** ★★ is a must, and **Cervantes' House** ★★ is evocative. One long day covers it all.

From the Pl. Mayor, former site of bullfights and autosda-fe, head north beside the Ayuntamiento, past the Post Office, and northwest along C. Correos. Walk north one block to **San Benito church** ★, *fortresslike, but with a monumental porch. Opposite is the* **house of Alonso Berruguette**, *whose work will be admired in the Sculpture Museum. Walk one block further north to the church of* **San Miguel** ★ *which contains an elegantly simple patio. At the church turn left passing the* **Palace of the Marquesses de Val-**

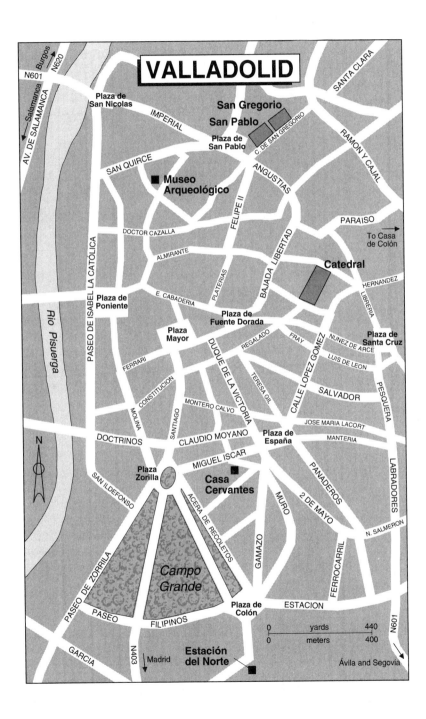

verde, *on the left, with stately decoration, and come to the Archae-*
ology Museum, on the right.

Museo Arqueológico   ★

Open Tues.-Sat. 10am to 2 p.m. and 4-7 p.m. Open Sun. 10 a.m. to
2 p.m. Closed Mon. and holidays. Admission: 200 ptas. Beside unexceptional Roman and Iberian objects, the museum contains an interesting collection of 14th-century frescoes from a church in Peñafiel.
Also interesting are oriental textiles found in the tomb of the son of
Sancho IV, and Renaissance tiles. The paintings vary in quality.

After passing a park, turn left to C. San Quirce, where a right
turn leads to the Pl. de San Pablo in 2 blocks. On one side is the
Capitana General, *a former royal palace that Napoléon appropri-*
ated for a time; on the other is the imposing facade of **San Pablo**.
Past the right side of San Pablo, in the rear, waits the extraordinary
Colegio de San Gregorio.

Iglesia San Pablo   ★★

Here is a facade of astonishing richness. It is also not quite right,
because the lower part, up to the arch over the door, is Isabeline from
1463, while the top three registers are later Plateresque. It presents a
study in the differences between these styles. Despite ornateness, the
top is orderly and static, laid out in classical squares and circles, but
the bottom half is a riot of twisting, curling forms, barely contained in
compartments that fruitlessly try for system.

The interior of the church was destroyed by the French, though
retaining lovely tombs and two handsome doorways leading off each
transept, both transitional between Isabeline and Plateresque styles.

Colegio de San Gregorio   ★★★★

Open Tues.-Sat. from 9 a.m. to 2 p.m. and from 4-6 p.m. Open Sun.
10 a.m. to 2 p.m. Closed Mon., and holidays. Admission: 200 ptas.
The entrance is sumptuous Isabeline, amusing with hairy men surmounted by bramble branches, instead of the expected carved pillars.
Above are heraldic motifs amid twisting foliage. Almost certainly Gil
de Siloé was the artist. Inside, the first court contains a window with
lovely Mudejar stucco-work, followed by a court of incredibly dense
lacy decoration on the fences and arches of the second-story gallery. A
frieze surmounted by gargoyles displays the yoke and arrow emblems
of Ferdinand and Isabella.

Right from this arcade is the entrance to the famed **Museum of Poly-**
chrome Sculpture. Of course Germans and others excelled at medieval
and Renaissance wood carving, but nowhere did the art thrive so fer-
tilely as in Spain, and there is no better collection in the country than
here. Some find the works too cloyingly realistic, but none can fault
the virtuosity. Arrows and room numbers ensure that all will be seen
in proper order.

The first exhibit is not surpassed; this is a huge retablo by Alonso Berruguette done in 1532 for San Benito church. The dismantled work requires three small rooms to display it all. It is shown at a height where it can truly be appreciated, instead of at its original elevation and distance behind an altar. Berruguette studied Michelangelo's work in Florence before returning home to produce the most evocative Spanish sculpture, culminating in this his largest and finest work. Note the large bishop with the tortured face and gnarled hands, which is Berruguette's signature. The piece goes on and on, with one masterly detail after another, leaving the viewer breathless. After room #3, a stair leads to displays above, and permits a pause to rest one's eyes.

The first rooms upstairs contain minor, early works, with some nice choir stalls, but room #15 brings Juan de Juni's **Christ's Burial**, a splendid composition, and fine Flemish retablos from the Convent of San Francisco. After completing the second floor circuit, not failing to see Pedro de Mena's **Mary Magdalene**, an early Baroque work, it is back to the ground floor and the work of the consummate master of polychromed sculpture, Gregorio Fernández, in rooms #4 and #5. The issue in Fernández' case is whether realism goes too far, becoming the sole consideration. Certainly this is true for those influenced by Fernández. His heritage is poor, but the master himself offers sensitivity amid the excessive drama. See his **Pieta, Baptism, Recumbent Christ, and Sta. Teresa**, and decide for yourself.

Through the small garden to the chapel, with its fine vaulting, are some moving funerary pieces, in addition to Berruguette's first recorded altar, badly restored.

Go east on the street fronting the Capitana General, which becomes C. de las Angustias after the intersection, to pass the brick house in which Felipe II was born. Turn left. In three blocks pass **Nuestra Senora de las Angustias** ★ *in which there is a superb altar by Juan de Juni at the end of the south transept, and pieces elsewhere by Fernández, if your appetite for sculpture still burns. Turn left at the next opportunity, reaching a square with the rear of the cathedral on the right and Santa María la Antiqua to the left.* **Sta María la Antiqua** ★ *is the oldest remaining church in Valladolid—the tower and portico being Romanesque; the rest is elegant Gothic (only open during services). Continue around to the cathedral entrance.*

Cathedral ★★

Open weekdays 10 a.m. to 2 p.m. and 4:30-7 p.m. Open weekends and holidays 10 a.m. to 2 p.m. Admission: 200 ptas. Although work commenced during the reign of Felipe II, it is questionable whether Herrera, his favorite architect, had much of a hand in the design. In the end the question is moot, because the style is obviously Herreran neo-classical, whether or not from him personally. The facade, especially the upper part, is not one of Alberto Churriguera's better efforts. But power exudes from the massive austere interior. The brilliantly colored and gilded altarpiece by Juan de Juni seems out of place amid the neo-classicism, though the figures exhibit life.

Across the park, to the east of the cathedral, is the **University** ★ . *Its flamboyantly Baroque front by Diego Tomé, exhibits the style which succeeded the Plateresque. A walk along the University's east face on C. Libreria brings another park, on the east side of which is the lovely* **Colegio Santa Cruz** ★ . *Begun in the Gothic style in 1487, by its completion the Plateresque had taken over, making this building one of the first in that style. Note the "classical" later windows and how they suit this precocious new design. The inner courtyard is sublime. C. del Cardinal Mendoza goes east, then turns north in 2 blocks to become C. Colón which leads in 2 blocks more to the Casa Colón on the left.*

Casa Colón   ★★

Open Tues.-Sat. 10 a.m. to 2 p.m. and 4-6 p.m. Open Sun. 10 a.m. to 2 p.m. Closed Mon., and holidays. Admission: free. Those who remember reading how Columbus was abandoned when his patron Isabella died or how, during the last years of his life, he sued in vain for what had been promised if he discovered new lands, will expect to find his last accommodations impoverished. Instead his last home was a mansion, all in stone. The present structure is rebuilt, but retains the original dimensions. There is something eerie about walking through these rooms to make our ideas of a legend conform to the reality of a person. In truth the museum is not much, but the experience is.

The final stop is a less pretentious house 15 minutes away that conforms more with expectations—that of Miquel de Cervantes. Retrace steps back along C. Colón and around the Pl. de Santa Cruz, following C. Fray Luis de León west for 2 blocks. Turn left (south) onto C. Lopez Gomez which leads to the Pl. España in 2 more blocks. Turn right (west) across the south end of the plaza on C. Martinez Villergas to C. Miguel Iscar. In one block turn right past a garden to arrive at Cervantes' door.

Casa de Cervantes   ★★

Open Tues.-Sat. 10 a.m. to 4 p.m. Open Sun. and holidays from 10 a.m. to 2 p.m. Closed Mon. Admission: 200 ptas. Cervantes spent only a few years here awaiting publication of his famed **Don Quixote**. When Valladolid became the capital for a short time, he bought a tract house here hastily put up by a speculator. Cervantes moved in with his family and assorted hangers-on to fill 13 rooms above a tavern, in what was then a seedy part of town. Here Cervantes was arrested after a nobleman, wounded by some assailant, was brought into the house and died. What you see today is reconstructed to a better condition than when Cervantes resided, but it is a nice presentation of a 17th-century house with furnishings.

WHERE TO STAY

There are no wonderful hotels in Valladolid, although comfortable accommodations do exist. One option, however, is to stay in the modern parador in Tordesillas, 30 k away, in a lovely park. Valladolid's greatest lack is inexpensive places to stay. Numerous *pensions* and *hostales* thrive in the area south of the university, but are mainly suited to undemanding students.

EXPENSIVE ($100-$200)

In Todesillas, 30 k west of Valladolid on N-620:

Parador de Tordesillas   2nd-class ★ ★ ★

Carretera de Salamanca, N-620. (At Tordesillas, take N-VI south for 2 k to connect with N-620 west toward Salamanca for 2 k more) Rooms: 73. ☎ *77 00 51. FAX 77 10 13.* Situated in a peaceful pine forest, this modern parador offers quiet, a pool, lovely gardens and comfortable rooms, but nothing of architectural interest. A half-hour from busy Valladolid, it serves well for relaxing.

In Valladolid:

Olid Meliá   1st-class ★ ★

Pl. San Miguel, 10 (Take C. Felipe II south from the east end of Pl. San Pablo. Turn right in two blocks onto C. de San Blas for a short block to arrive at the hotel on the right.) Rooms: 211. ☎ *35 72 00; FAX 33 68 28; Telex 26312.* This hotel is modern, large, and situated in a nice area convenient to most sights. It is probably the most comfortable hotel in town, though not in any way memorable. Parking is available for a fee.

MODERATE ($50-$99)

Roma   3rd-class ★

Héroes del Alcázar de Toledo, 8 (Walk south of the Pl. Mayor on C. Santiago for a block, then right.) Rooms: 38. ☎ *35 47 77; FAX 35 54 61.* Homey is the word for this small hotel, convenient to most sights and to the activity in the Pl. Mayor.

Imperial   3rd-class ★

Peso, 4 (From the Pl. Mayor walk a very short block along the west side of the Ayuntamiento, then turn right). Rooms: 81. ☎ *3 03 00; FAX 33 08 13; Telex 26304.* The location is just a bit better than the Roma, but in a hotel without its homey feeling. Still, the rooms are comfortable and the staff tries hard.

WHERE TO EAT

Valladolid possesses one exceptional restaurant, along with others of lesser distinction that provide satisfying food.

EXPENSIVE ($50+)

Mesón La Fragua   ★★★★

Paseo de Zorrilla, 10 (on the avenue with center divider that runs along the west side of the Campo Grande park). ☎ *3 87 85. Closed Sunday night.* Without question this is the finest restaurant in town, as patronage by Spanish royalty attests. The decor is traditional with elegant touches. Here you can order traditional Castilian roasts, superbly done, but such things are available elsewhere. This is a place to let the chef charm you with more inventive dishes. Recommended is the Rape Gran Mesón (braised skate). The wine list is choice. Reservations are necessary.   ***Amex, Diners, MasterCard and Visa accepted.***

Mesón Panero   ★★★

Marina Escobar, 1 (just west of Casa Cervantes). ☎ *30 16 73. Closed Sunday in July and August, Sunday night during the rest of the year.* La Fraqua gets more attention, and deservedly, but this place stands a good cut above the other restaurants in town. The chef is innovative and committed, even to hosting a gastronomic festival each February. Stuffed partridge is superb and the rabbit delicious. The *sopa castellana* is not prepared better anywhere.

Amex, Diners, MasterCard and Visa accepted.

DIRECTORY

INFORMATION • Located in the Pl. Zorrilla, 3 (the large plaza at the north end of the Campo Grande). It provides a much needed map. Open Mon.-Fri. from 9 a.m. to 2 p.m. and from 4-6 p.m. Open Sat. from 9 a.m. to 2 p.m. ☎ 35 18 01.

TRAINS AND BUSES • The train station is located one long block south of the southern end of the Campo Grande. ☎ 22 33 57. It offers frequent service to Madrid, and reasonable service to all the cities of Castile, except for Burgos which has only one daily train. The RENFE ticketing office is located at C. Divina Pastores, 6. ☎ 22 28 73.

Buses depart from C. Puente Colgante, 2 (in front of the bullring four blocks south of the Campo Grande off Paseo de Zorrilla which passes along its west side). ☎ 23 63 08.

POST OFFICE AND TELEPHONES • Located in the Pl. de la Arrinconada, two short blocks north of the Pl. Mayor. ☎ 33 06 60. Telephones are available at C. Gondomar, 2, one block north of Colegio de San Gregorio and west.

POLICE • Located on C. Felipe II, 10, which runs south from the Pl. San Pablo. ☎ 25 33 44.

AIRPORT • Located 14 k west of town with few direct flights, but connections throughout Spain. The local office of Iberia is on C. Gomaza, 17, which runs due south from the Pl. España. ☎ 30 26 39.

EXCURSIONS

East of Valladolid sits the massive 14th-century castle of **Pañafiel** ★ ★, lofty on its hill.

Follow the east side of the Campo Grande park. At its end turn left onto C. Estación. C. Estación soon follows the railroad tracks west. After 7 blocks turn right onto C. San Isidro, following signs to Soria and N-122. Peñafiel lies 93 k east of Valladolid.

From a distance, the imposing fortress can be seen sitting atop its steep hill, guarding the valley below, looking just as a fortress should. On the way up pass through a surprisingly large Pl. Mayor ringed with balconies for watching bullfights. The castle was constructed at the beginning of the 14th century, with a massive square keep topped by turrets added two centuries later. Two still-solid perimeter walls defended the castle then from attack. Today they help compose a perfect picture of an early medieval fortress.

ZAMORA

See Salamanca excursions.

ANDALUSIA

Street in San Roque.

HISTORICAL PROFILE:
MOORS AND THE RECONQUEST

Spain's history is unique among European countries because of its Islamic heritage. Counting from the time the Moors landed, they lived with the Christians in Spain for 781 years, which is longer than the 500 years that have elapsed since their last stronghold was captured in 1492.

But, while the arrival of Muslims in Spain early in the eighth century is well documented, the reason they came is less clear. From his base in the small Arabian city of Medina, the Prophet Mohammed conquered the nearby town of Mecca to serve as his holy capital. From there he preached conquest as a religious duty and let plunder add its own incentive. A century later, Mohammed's successors had vanquished all the lands in a broad belt from India in the east, to Morocco in the west. By the beginning of the eighth century, their quandary was whether to continue the conquest south through Africa, or north across twelve miles of water to Spain and Europe. Rumors of Spanish riches settled that issue, and the invasion began. This is one explanation.

Spanish chronicles written during the Islamic occupation, although centuries after the invasion, offer a different version. A man named Rodrigo was elected by the Visigoth nobles to become the king of Spain, thereby depriving Akhila, the heir of the former king, of his expected inheritance. Soon after, Count Julian, a vassal of King Rodrigo, sent his fair daughter Florinda to the new court for her education. One day King Rodrigo saw Florinda bathing in the Tagus and, overcome by lust, had his way with her. Count Julian vowed revenge for his daughter's dishonor. He went to Musa, the Muslim governor of Morocco, to tell him where he could land troops in secret, how the Spanish army was disposed and, in general, to convince him to invade Spain. Musa sent his lieutenant Tarik Ibn Zeyad with 7,000 men across the straits to reconnoiter. Reinforced by another 5,000 troops, Tarik engaged Rodrigo's much larger army. Incredibly, the left and right arms of Rodrigo's force were commanded by brothers of Akhila, the man who Rodrigo had deprived of the throne. When the battle began, these brothers stood aside, leaving Rodrigo's men alone to fight the Muslim army. It was a rout; Rodrigo's dusty saddle was found on the field, but his body was never recovered. Thus, the Spanish chronicles attribute the defeat to treason and treachery, to anything but an honest drubbing.

The facts are that Tarik first landed on Spanish soil in 711, on a mountain peninsula projecting off the coast. Ever since, the peninsula has borne his name—Gebal (mountain of) Tarik—Gibraltar. With only a small force, for his orders were merely to explore, he engaged and defeated the army of King Rodrigo near the coastal city of Algeciras. After Rodrigo's forces scattered, Tarik moved north to the capital of Toledo and took it easily.

Musa, concerned that his lieutenant had exceeded his orders and that spoils were falling to others, embarked the next year for Spain with 18,000 men. He met Tarik at Toledo and, after slapping him on the head with his riding crop, took personal command. In two years

Musa conquered most of Spain. The caliph of Damascus then ordered his governor, Musa, to report in person on the events of the invasion. With an immense baggage of riches and a retinue of hundreds of hostage sons of Spanish nobles, Musa paraded to Damascus where he was arrested, tried as an embezzler, and imprisoned for the rest of his life. His son carried on the conquest, seizing all that remained of Spain except a pocket here and there in the foothills of the Pyrenees, terrain not worth a fight. The whole conquest took less than seven years. Musa's son then married King Rodrigo's widow. Soon after, he was murdered in Seville's mosque, probably on orders from the caliph in Damascus who had received reports of affecting a crown and throne, and possibly of converting to Christianity. Thus ended the conquest of Spain and the family of the conqueror.

For several decades Spain was ruled by a succession of governors, known as *amirs* (commanders), appointed by the caliph in Damascus. They tested the strength of southern France with numerous raids. In 732, a major force of Muslims sacked Bordeaux and turned northeast for Paris. Near Tours, in the center of France, a large Frank army under Charles Martel blocked their advance and defeated them. This event did not end the raids, but it established the high water mark of the Muslims in Europe. Spain would be sufficient. In fact, one caliph decided that Europe was indefensible so the Muslims should abandon Spain. He died before his order could be executed.

Muslims called the territory they controlled *al Andalus*, the origin of the present name "Andalusia." Probably the word derives from "Vandal's land," although the derivation is controversial. The Muslims proceeded to create an Islamic civilization in Spain with Córdoba as their capital. Of course there remained those pockets of territory in the north that had never been subjugated and where the spirit of the Visigoths still lived, preserving memories of their kings and a time of Christian rule. The Spanish date their attempt to win back the country to 722 when Pelayo, from Asturias, defeated a Muslim force near Covadonga. It was the first victory for the indigenous people of Spain; to the Arabs it seemed nothing. In their chronicles they said

> *...a wild ass reared up against the Muslims; they defeated his army time and again, until nothing remained of it but thirty men and two women. What harm can thirty wild asses do to us.*

Quoted by Edwin Hole,
Andalus: Spain under the Muslims

It would have been more accurate to view the Spaniards as mules, for they were outstandingly stubborn. They pushed for almost eight centuries to regain what they had lost in seven years.

In the middle of the eighth century, a revolution in Damascus led by a man named Abbas replaced the ruling dynasty of Umayyads. Surviving members of the Umayyad family were systematically hunted down and killed. Only Abd er Rahman, a grandson of the former caliph, escaped. He made his way to Moroccan kinsmen of his mother and from there jumped to Spain. Civil war surrounded him because he was the sole descendent of the usurped but legitimate ruling house of Islam. By 755 he had gained control of *al Andalus.* From this time forth *al Andalus* constituted an independent kingdom, no longer ruled from Damascus. Abd er Rahman unified the quarreling Muslims, began construction of the great mosque in Córdoba, and founded the first dynasty of Muslim rulers in Spain.

While Abd er Rahman was subduing rebellious governors, the governor of Saragossa appealed to Charlemagne in France for aid. Charlemagne marched an army across the Pyrenees only to find the gates of Saragossa closed against him because the governor had changed his mind. Charlemagne set siege to the city, but a rebellion at home soon forced a return. The French retraced their steps through the Pyrenees pass of Roncesvalles. Their rear guard, commanded by Roland, the Count of Brittany, was harried by attackers all the way. His force was exterminated to the last man, an event immortalized by the medieval poem *The Song of Roland.* It was Basques who accomplished the deed, despite the poem's blame of Muslims.

At the end of the ninth century, a Spanish miracle occurred. In a field in the northwest corner of Spain, shepherds observed bright lights pointing to an ancient tomb that contained a miraculously preserved body. The bishop pronounced the bones those of St. James the Apostle. Soon a church rose over the tomb and the place was named Compostela, a possible corruption of *campus stella* (field of stars). After Rome, it became the holiest place in Europe, and the most important pilgrimage for Christians after Jerusalem. Spain grew holy, a place for Christians to defend, and a cause for crusades, while the 100,000 Europeans who came each year on pilgrimage produced an infusion of European cultures. And the rallying cry for the Reconquest was "Sant Iago," Saint James. No matter that the Bible says James died in Jerusalem.

The event was little noticed in *al Andalus,* poised for its time of greatest glory. Abd er Rahman III succeeded to the emirate in 912, and he proclaimed himself *caliph*, "successor" to the Prophet Muhammed. His Córdoba, with a quarter of a million inhabitants, was the largest city in Europe, trailing only Baghdad, Constantinople and Peking in the world. It boasted the largest library extant—some 400,000 volumes—900 public baths, and sublime architecture. Abd er Rahman III constructed a sumptuous palace in the countryside, named Medinat al Zahara after a favorite wife, that—if it still survived—would put even the Alhambra to shame.

Abd er Rahman III was blue-eyed with fair hair. He was descended from the Arab Abd er Rahman I, but his mother had been a Frank and his grandmother a Basque princess. Except for the royal blood in his veins, he was typical of those the Europeans called Moors. They were not at all the dusky blacks Shakespeare passed down to us. Fewer than 50,000 Muslims crossed to Spain during their conquest, and rather than Arab, most of them were Berbers—a race of blue-eyed, fairskinned North Africans, tending to red hair, who populate most of Morocco and Tunisia. Indeed, all those who came to *al Andalus* from Africa over the centuries probably amounted to, at most, a few hundred thousand in a population of almost six million Spanish. Intermarriage was frequent, both between conqueror and conquered, and between Christians in the north and Muslims in the south. After a few centuries of conquest, the Muslims had infinitely more Spanish than Arab in their blood.

Al Andalus, according to the Muslims, was an earthly paradise. By their legend, when God created the world, he gave five wishes to each new country. *Al Andalus* asked for a clear sky, a beautiful sea filled with fish, ripe fruit, and fair women, all granted by God. The fifth wish was for good government, which God refused because that would have made it a heaven on earth.

Al Andalus ranked as the most prosperous area in Europe. The Muslims introduced new crops—oranges, rice, cotton, and silk—that had not existed in Europe and were greatly prized. They expanded the possibilities of knowledge by teaching the art of manufacturing paper so that a man could write a book without killing a flock of sheep for vellum pages. They revived the art of glassmaking that had died with the Romans. Their architecture brought new comfort to the hot and dusty Mediterranean. Houses had blank outer walls, while rooms inside surrounded a cool courtyard filled with flowers and open to the sky. Such houses still dominate the south of Spain. The Moors also appropriated the horseshoe arch from the Visigoths and raised its use to high art in public buildings.

Their work with stucco, glazed tile, and patterned designs will never be matched.

But knowledge was the most important gift of the Muslims. The ninth through the eleventh centuries in Europe have been aptly named the Dark Ages, for the wisdom of the ancient world had long slumbered. The Muslims nurtured this wisdom and passed it on to Europe. They preserved the works of the Greek mathematicians, physicians and philosophers, especially Aristotle. They introduced the science of algebra, as well as the numbers we use today (that we call Arabic, though they were transmitted from India by the Arabs). Nor were they messengers only. Córdoba was a center of invention and learning. Here the great Jewish philosopher Maimonides was born; here too the Muslim philosopher Averröes wrote brilliant commentaries on Aristotle.

But however brightly *al Andalus* glowed, the denial of the legend's fifth wish for good government would give the Christians their chance. When the successor of Abd er Rahman III died, he left an 11-year-old heir. The reins of government fell to the vizier, a man of sufficient vigor and intelligence to seize the throne for himself. The dynasty of Abd er Rahman had ended. The usurper was dubbed *Almanzor*, "The Conqueror," for he harried the Christians as never before. He ranged through the north, sacking the cathedral of Compostela, and brought its doors and bells to hang in the Córdoba mosque. But he left no clear successor, and *al Andalus* fell apart into twenty separate states, called *taifas*, as the eleventh century dawned.

The Christians in the north now were free from the pressure of unrelenting Muslim attacks, and grew apace. By the start of the 11th century, Asturias, the last bastion of the Spanish, had added to itself the provinces of León, Castile and Galicia. All were united in the person of a man who styled himself King Fernando I. But when he died, the usual Spanish policy of dividing the kingdom among sons was followed, which had the effect of overturning the work of uniting a large territory in the first place, and was to prove the bane of the Christians. To his favorite son, Alfonso VI, he gave León, and to his eldest he bequeathed Castile, with Galicia given to the youngest. Alfonso VI and his older brother were soon at war over their shares to the detriment of the younger brother, who was forced into exile. The elder brother, however, did not sufficiently understand their sister Urraca. It seems she felt more than sisterly affection for Alfonso VI and hired an assassin to remove the sibling in his way. After his brother's death, Alfonso VI claimed Castile in addition to León, but first the nobles forced him to swear that he bore no complicity in the murder of his brother. Rodrigo Diaz de Vivar, commander of the army of León, spoke for the nobles in this affair, and matters were never cordial between Alfonso and Rodrigo Diaz thereafter. Although they cooperated in the capture of Toledo, the greatest victory up to that time by the Spanish, it was not long before Alfonso found a pretext to exil Rodrigo.

Homeless, Rodrigo Diaz became the greatest hero in Spanish history—el Cid, the mighty robber baron. He first offered his services to the *taifa* of Zaragoza, but when Alfonso came to attack Zaragoza, el Cid refused to fight against his king. Instead, he moved south to Valencia to help the Muslims defeat the Spanish count of Barcelona. When the governor of Valencia turned on him, el Cid conquered his territory, thereby gaining control of 15 percent of modern Spain. Twice, mighty Muslim armies attacked el Cid, but each time he turned them away. El Cid was later reconciled with his king and his daughters married royalty. The *Poem of My Cid*, written by an unknown author about a century after the hero's death from yet another Muslim attack, commemorated his exploits forever. The poet makes much of the dark beard of el Cid, who was "born in a good hour."

In the meantime, after the capture of Toledo, Alfonso VI swooped south. He raided throughout *al Andalus*, finally setting his foot in the sea at the southern end of Spain. Now the rulers of the petty *taifas* knew Spanish power at first hand and, fearing for their civilization, they called on Morocco for help.

There had been a revolution in Morocco shortly before this call. A puritan sect had erupted to cleanse other Muslims of the sin of luxury. Known as the people of the *rabat* ("monastery"), the Almoravids were so fundamentalist that even their men wore veils. So it was with trepidation that the pleasure-loving governors of the *taifas* of *al Andalus* sought their aid. One explained by saying that he "preferred to herd camels for the Almoravids than to guard the pigsty of Alfonso VI." [Quoted by Joseph F. O'Callaghan, *A History of Medieval Spain*.]

The Almoravids came and, together with the governors of the *taifas*, defeated Alfonso VI. Then they returned to Morocco. They came again when Alfonso VI once more threatened; this time the *taifas* did not contribute any support. A year later, in 1090, they returned to stay in sufficient force to conquer the *taifas* and assume the rule of *al Andalus*. Only Valencia held out, thanks to el Cid, but it too fell three years after his death, when his widow no longer could defend it.

For a century, the ascetic Almoravids ruled *al Andalus* until its bounty seduced them. They fell into petty factions and learned the love of luxury at the same time that their subjects rebelled against their severe rule. Across the straits in Morocco a new fundamentalist sect, called the *Almohids* ("Unitarians"), looked on these events with grave displeasure. In 1146 the Almohids came to purify the faithful of *al Andalus*.

As always, the Spanish had used civil unrest in *al Andalus* to increase their territory, but now they faced a serious unified enemy. The Almohids set out to win back what their brethren had lost, declaring a *jihad*, a holy war. Alfonso VIII (1158-1215), then king of Castile, met a huge Muslim force just south of Toledo at Alascos, and suffered the most complete defeat yet for the Spanish. His problem was that the king of Castile stood alone for Spain. Aragón and the other kingdoms each promised aid but did not deliver; instead they pressed territorial demands on the now-weakened king of Castile. Disunity in the Spanish camp would never succeed against unified Muslims.

At this darkest hour the pope saved the day. He proposed a crusade against the Infidel, a union of Christian kingdoms to oppose the holy war of the Muslims. In 1212 a large Christian army composed of one part Crusaders from other European countries, one part the army of Aragón, and one part the army of Castile marched south from Toledo. At Las Navas de Tolosa they were confronted by a Muslim force equal to their own. For two days the armies stared at each other, uncertain what to do. On July 16 the left and right side of the Christian forces commenced a pincer movement while Alfonso VIII charged the center with his own troops. The Muslim lines broke, and when the caliph fled, defeat became a rout. Alfonso VIII, who had suffered the most serious Spanish defeat, had orchestrated its greatest victory. This battle tipped the scales; never again would the Christians be seriously threatened by the Muslims. In remembrance, a tapestry from the field tent of the defeated caliph hangs today in Alfonso VIII's former palace, the monastery of Las Huelgas, near **Burgos**.

To take advantage of the collapse of Moorish power, the Christians would need unity. Indeed, the remaining story of the Reconquest is as much a tale of struggle for Christian unity as it is of battles against the Moors.

Three years after his great victory Alfonso VIII died, leaving an 11-year-old son as heir. Fortunately he also left an older daughter, Berenguela, to enforce his wishes. For the son's guardian quickly grabbed control of the government and, when the child was accidently killed while playing, the protector hid news of the death so he could maintain his power. Berenguela discovered the cover-up and sent for her own son, then living in Aragón. Although Berenguela had the best claim to the throne, she yielded the rights to her son. This new king, Fernando III, would conquer most of *al Andalus*.

Chaos reigned in *al Andalus* in the early years of the 13th century. Ibn Hud controlled most of the Islamic territory, but he faced a rebellion by Ibn al Ahmar. In this confused situation Muslims were as likely to seek Christian help as to ask for aid from their coreligionists. Muslims inside Córdoba let a band of Castilian soldiers into the suburbs of the city. Fernando III, aware of an opportunity, hurried with an army to lay siege. Although Ibn Hud raised a force to relieve Córdoba, an alliance between the rebellious Ibn Ahmar and Fernando III frightened him sufficiently to turn him back before even reaching the city. In 1236 Córdoba, the capital of *al Andalus*, capitulated to the Spanish. Fernando III carried the bells of Santiago Cathedral home again.

After Ibn Hud was assassinated by a lieutenant, the rebel Ibn Ahmar moved to Grenada and began constructing the palace we call the Alhambra. As never before, a vacuum of power existed in *al Andalus*. Fernando III took town after town, finally moving on Seville. Since the city had access to the sea through the river Guadalquivar, he collected the first Spanish navy to block seaborne supplies before settling down for a siege. Seville could look nowhere for relief and capitulated in 1248. When, independently, the king of Aragón captured Valencia, the Reconquest was almost complete. All that remained was Grenada.

The words of the poet al Rundi describe the Muslim situation at this juncture:

> *Where is Córdoba, the seat of great learning,*
> *And how many scholars of high repute remain there?*
> *And where is Seville, the home of mirthful gatherings*
> *On its great river, cooling and brimful with water?*
> *These centers were the pillars of the country:*
> *Can a building remain when the pillars are missing?*

This misfortune has surpassed all that has preceded,
And as long as time lasts, it can never be forgotten.

Quoted by Joseph F. O'Callaghan,
A History of Medieval Spain

Fernando III had done his part at warfare. Before he died, he founded a university, promoted Castilian as the official language of Spain, and revitalized the institution of the *Cortes* (Parliament).

Then for two centuries and a quarter—from 1252 to 1482—the Reconquest stopped, daunted by the remaining task of conquering Granada. Although less than 10 percent of modern Spain remained in Moorish hands, the area swelled with refugees entrenched in fortified towns. This was a time in the history of warfare when defense had the upper hand; a fortified town stood virtually impregnable. The best tactic available to the offense was a starvation-threatening siege that required vast reserves of food for the besieging army, along with financial resources sufficient to keep troops in the field for six months or more to prevent relief efforts. Nor did great incentives exist for the Christians. The Moorish king of Grenada owed an allegiance to the king of Castile that included substantial yearly tribute. For more than two centuries no Christian ruler had the vigor or the singleness of purpose to assume so difficult a task for such small advantage.

The Christians had first to set their own house in order. They were forever dividing kingdoms by inheritance and warfare at times when unified resources were demanded. Fernando III was succeeded by Alfonso X, known as *el Sabio*, "the Wise." He earned this soubriquet for the scholarship he encouraged and the works of literature and law that emanated from his palace. But his name would have been quite different if it had been based on his political ability. His father had been married to a granddaughter of Frederick Barbarossa, the Holy Roman Emperor. Alfonso emptied his treasury in an election campaign to win the title of the Holy Roman Emperor for himself. So dismayed were the nobles of Castile at this profligate waste that some rebelled while others renounced their citizenship to live among the Moors in Grenada. Eventually everyone abandoned him, including his son, who usurped the throne.

Castile seemed bent on obeying the adage that things have to get worse before they improve. The worst was Pedro IV, the Cruel. His father had a beloved mistress with whom he had fathered several children. This behavior did not please his wife, Pedro's mother. As soon as Pedro's father died, she revenged herself by killing the former mistress. This act set the tone for Pedro's reign that began in 1350 when Pedro was fifteen. One of Pedro's first royal acts was to kill one of his two illegitimate half-brothers, but the wrong one. Enrique of Trastámara, the other bastard son of Pedro's father and mistress, was the one he should have been watching. Enrique fled to Aragón before Pedro could catch him.

Pedro soon became engaged to the daughter of the duke of Burgundy, but, while waiting for his fiancée to arrive, he fell in love with María of Padilla. It was too late to stop the wedding, so Pedro went through with the ceremony and then shut his wife in the Alcázar of Toledo for eight years. Sadly, his beloved María died at 28, one of the few natural deaths in his reign. Pedro then poisoned his legal wife and declared that he had secretly married María, his mistress, ten years earlier, thus making their four children legitimate.

Pedro foraged south when he heard that his vassal, the king of Grenada, faced a Muslim revolt. He ravaged the terrain and populace along the way until those who had revolted threw themselves on Pedro's mercy. This was not a man overflowing with mercy—he killed them all. Then he began a ten-year war with Aragón. The commander of the army of Aragón was Pedro's illegitimate brother, Enrique of Trastámara, who had found refuge there from Pedro. War opened with Castilian successes, then settled into a stalemate, and ended in a papal truce. Each side then sought allies to tip the balance in its direction. The Aragonese enlisted French mercenaries who had been ravaging the south of France. Pedro allied himself with Edward of Wales, the Black Prince. The two augmented armies came together near the Castilian border where Pedro and the Black Prince won a resounding victory. But, when Pedro wanted to kill all the captured rebels, the Black Prince refused further cooperation and left.

On his own again, Pedro was no match for Enrique of Trastámara, who marched into Castile and was recognized as king by most in the large cities. Enrique moved on Toledo while Pedro set out from Andalusia to its defense. The two clashed outside the fortress of Montiel. Pedro, beaten, retreated to the safety of the fortress, and then offered a huge bribe to one of Enrique's lieutenants to help him escape. The lieutenant, who had informed Enrique of his dealings, invited Pedro to slip into his tent under cover of night. Enrique burst into the tent and struck Pedro in the face with his dagger. The two struggled and fell, with Enrique stabbing Pedro again and again until he lay still. Pedro was dead at 35.

Enrique of Trastámara, bastard son of a former king, began a dynasty in Castile from this date of 1369. One of his descendents was Isabella. Through marriages, his blood also entered the veins of the kings of Aragón and Ferdinand. Spain had to wait one more century for Isabella and Ferdinand to appear, had to endure the ravages of wars among the separate kingdoms, the scourge of the Black Death, and bloody pogroms against the Jews. But in the end, Isabella of Castile united herself and kingdom with Ferdinand of Aragón.

It was Isabella who brought the singleness of purpose to complete the Reconquest. She was filled with Christian fervor. Ferdinand contributed a calculating mind that could see beyond the intimidating costs of a major war. Their marriage united the Christian states in one formidable pair. And, ironically, the Moors precipitated their own downfall. Hassan Ali, the king of Grenada, seized the Christian border city of Zahara in 1481, which was equivalent to hurling a gauntlet. On hearing the news, prescient fakirs (holy men) in Granada moaned that "the ruins of Zahara will fall on our own heads." [W.H. Prescott, *Isabella and Ferdinand*, Vol. I. p. 318.] Don Rodrigo Ponce de León (grandfather of the discoverer of Florida), one of the mightiest nobles of Andalusia, made a surprise attack in response on Alhama, just six miles from Grenada, and won the fortress in a bloody battle. The question was whether he could hold the town against the inevitable Muslim counterattack. He called for assistance to Henrique de Guzmán, the duke of Medina Sidonia, another mighty noble and a man with whom Don Rodrigo had waged private war for a decade. Whether because of patriotism or for the promise of half of the spoils, Don Henrique heeded the call. He arrived to find Christian forces in the city girded by a Muslim force. But the Moors, fearful of being trapped between the enemy in the city and his reinforcements behind them, left the field.

So far the war had been conducted on the Christian side by nobles; it was not a national effort. Alone they could not hold a salient deep in Moorish territory. Ferdinand and a pregnant Isabella hastened to Córdoba to expand this one success into a major war. Quickly, Ferdinand mounted a frontal attack on Alhama's neighbor Loja, to diffuse the pressure concentrating on Alhama. But, after initial success, the Spanish situation deteriorated until nothing remained except ignominious retreat. From this example, Ferdinand learned the necessity of adequate preparation and the advantages of siege over frontal attack.

Just at this moment, a revolution in Grenada further weakened the Moors. Sultana Aisha, the principle wife of Hasan Ali, formed a cabal against her husband on behalf of her son. Hasan Ali fled to Málaga, which split the territory of the Moors into two opposing parts: Hasan Ali ruled the western half and his son the east, including Grenada. The Christians referred to the son, Abu Abdallah, as "Boabdil," which shows how little they understood Arabic.

Ferdinand and Isabella raised the stakes by announcing a crusade. The pope confirmed the undertaking and supplied ecclesiastical revenues in support. From the corners of Europe, crusaders poured into Spain to join against the infidel. The campaign opened with a march against Málaga in the west. To reach Málaga, the Christian army had to cross mountains down to the city, and needed local guides who knew the terrain—Moors. In these rocky defiles the flower and pretension of Spanish chivalry were cut to pieces in a surprise attack by el Zagal, "the Valiant," brother of Hasan Ali.

Heartened by his rival's victory, Boabdil chose to attack the western Christian forces himself. Ominously, his lance broke against the arch of the gate of Elvira as he left Grenada. He was defeated in a close fight at Lucena. Leaving the field, however, hemmed in by Christian forces at the rear and a river ahead, the Moors panicked. Boabdil hid but was discovered in the bushes by a common soldier and carried prisoner to Córdoba. Boabdil agreed to pay a huge tribute in gold for his release and sign a treaty providing for two year's truce.

Time was on the Christians' side. They used this respite to prepare for a final push. They built foundries for producing cannon in quantity, trained corps of engineers to mine fortified positions, and developed a new military strategy. Swiss mercenaries in the Christian camp taught the Spanish a way to fight that would make the Spanish infantry the finest in the world. The Swiss wore no armor on their backs, since they never thought of retreating, while they menaced their enemy with pikes three times the length of a man. These pikes signaled the end of knights as a military force, for these weapons could stop a charge of heavily armored cavalry.

War reopened in 1487. The Christians first captured Málaga according to a plan to close the Muslims off from the sea. Two years later they raised an army of 50,000 men to besiege the stronghold of Baeza. After seven difficult months it fell, although the Spanish lost 20,000 men, mostly to disease. With the loss of this major position, el Zagul, who had replaced his brother as king, surrendered the rest of his territory. Only Grenada under Boabdil remained in Muslim hands.

In March of 1491, 50,000 Christians came to Grenada vowing not to leave until it fell. Wooden houses were erected against the coming cold of winter, instantly creating the third largest city in Spain, named by Isabella *Santa Fé*, "Holy Faith." Then they waited, for Grenada was then the largest fortified city in the world.

After eight months of starvation, a negotiated settlement promised Grenada to the Christians sixty days hence, to allow time to pack for those who wished to leave. But insurrection in the city hastened the day of capitulation. On January 2, 1492, a small party led by the archbishop of Spain carried a cross through the gates of Grenada. When the Christians saw the cross silhouetted atop the Alhambra hill, they knew the city was theirs. Ferdinand, Isabella, and all the troops knelt on the ground to thank God. Then the nobles and the king and queen of Spain entered the city, dressed in Moorish clothes.

After completing a ten-year campaign, probably not a single Spaniard regretted its final success. But many should have mourned the passing of a large part of the variegated society of the peninsula. They would sorely miss the intellectual accomplishments of the Moors, as well as countless examples of good things that the Moors had provided. When the Spanish court first saw the Alhambra they marvelled—here was a style of living light years in advance of their own. They should have mourned themselves, too, because their treatment of the Moors was dastardly. In the treaty they promised that all Moors who wished to could remain in their land with complete religious freedom. Within ten years Christians began forcibly converting Moors, and then brutally expelled them from Spain.

Most of the architectural legacy of the Moors can be found in Andalusia, their home for almost eight centuries. **Granada's** Alhambra captures everyone's heart both for its accessible beauty and for evoking the Moors' style of life. One of the world's great mosques still stands in all its glory in **Córdoba**, and there too a 10th-century Moorish pleasure-city is under excavation at its outskirts. Although **Seville** retains little that was built for the Moors, it preserves two wonderful buildings that were sumptuously decorated by them—the Alcázar and the Casa de Pilotes. All these are monumental works in which everyone can see the stamp of the Moors, but their legacy extends as well to every whitewashed house that hides a flowered courtyard inside walls sealing it from noise and prying eyes. This design—one of the many reasons that everyone loves southern Spain—was the way the Moors chose to live in Andalusia.

ANDALUSIA

Andalusia is archetypical Spain, thus not wholly characteristic of the rest. Bullfighting, flamenco and the guitar originated here, and although each of these has become woven into the fabric of all of Spain, nowhere else are they so prominent and pervasive as in Andalusia. Here too, Gypsies, rare in the rest of the country, thrive. What makes Andalusia archetypical is that it was ruled by the Moors longest—for more than 700 years. They bequeathed to Andalusia a legacy of citrus fruits, whitewashed houses with beautiful interior patios, and, after the Christians expelled them, palaces and mosques. Thanks to the Moors, Andalusia possesses the greatest sight in Spain—the Alhambra—along with a mosque and numerous alcázars (Moorish fortresses). If there is only time to visit one area of Spain, it should be Andalusia.

Andalusia was the first part of Spain to receive foreign visitors in ancient times. Phoenicians came to mine and trade, followed by neighbors from Carthage. War between the Spanish Carthagenian Hannibal and Rome next brought Romans who came to attack the lines of supply, and stay on to rule. When Rome weakened in the fourth century A.D., "barbarian" Vandals breasted the borders of the Empire to take the south of Spain for their own. Visigoths followed a century later, pushing the Vandals across the straits into Africa, though the Visigoths continued to refer to the south as "Vandalsland." When Moors landed near Gibraltar in 710 to conquer Spain, they called their new territory *al Andalus*, approximating Vandalsland as best their language could.

When Grenada was finally recaptured, in 1492, Christians wept along with Moors, aware that a civilization superior to their own had been destroyed. *Al Andalus* possesed the greatest library in the world, and had nurtured the Jewish philosopher Maimonides and the Aristotilian philosopher Averröes. It had developed and maintained both sewage systems and public baths, none of which existed elsewhere in Europe. The Christians made a virtue of their deficiencies by arguing that cleanliness was un-Christian, but in their hearts acknowledged a culture superior to their own. Ferdinand and Isabella chose lovely Granada for their place of final rest. Their grandson and heir picked the Alhambra for his honeymoon. Christians all over Spain hired Moors or Mozarabs (Christians trained under the Moors) to design and decorate their homes and palaces.

The Moors had introduced citrus trees and rice. They cultivated the olive—first brought to Spanish shores by the Greeks—still Andalusia's most important crop. They appropriated the Roman horseshoe arch for major buildings, and adopted Roman ideas in domestic architecture to produce the typical—then as now—Andalusian house. Hidden behind a solid facade to seal out the heat, rooms surround a central open patio in which a fountain plays, and flowers perfume the air. Though the last Moors were expelled in 1609, their spirit remains alive in every Spanish whitewashed house and patio, every palace and alcázar maintained through the ages.

What lured ancient visitors—Romans, Moors, Germans, and northern Christians—was the fertile land and balmy climate of Andalusia. Hemmed by the Sierra Nevada range containing the highest peak in Spain (11,242 feet), the coast is tempered by the Mediterranean Sea for winter warmth and summer breezes. Despite insignificant rainfall, the land is well watered by the Guadalquivir (from the Arabic for "Great River Valley"), allowing two crops each year. Andalusia presents the paradox of mountains and beach, along with Moorish and Christian monuments. Spain's problem is that because Andalusia contains enough attractions to engage all of a tourist's time, the rest of the country is left comparatively touristless. Although we may mourn the situation, we agree that Andalusia draws tourists because of the wealth of its offerings.

Granada ★★★★★ tenders the Alhambra, which ranks with the greatest tourist sights in the world, in addition to the lovely Capilla Real where Ferdinand and Isabella still rest. **Córdoba** ★★★★ retains a great mosque, remains of a medieval quarter, and ruins of a pleasure city built by Abd er Rahman III. **Seville** ★★★★★, itself a beautiful city, offers a sumptuous cathedral, an alcázar and a private mansion exquisitely decorated by the Moors. In addition, the hundreds of miles of beaches constituting the **Costa del Sol** ★★ and **Costa de la Luz** ★★ are playgrounds for the European masses. Andalusia also contains the Renaissance towns **Baeza** ★★ and **Úbeda** ★★, the spectacularly situated town of **Ronda** ★★, and the home of sherry, **Jerez de las Frontera** ★.

Andalusia offers special foods and entertainments, as well. The famed Gazpacho soup was created here, probably from a Moorish recipe, as was a less well-known white soup—*ajo blanco*. Tapas originated in Seville, and Sevillian tapas still remain among the best in Spain. Deep-fried fish is a staple and, when fresh, as it generally is, can be subtle indeed. Although flamenco is a dying art, despite great efforts to keep it alive, Seville is the best place to see the real thing. If you are lucky in the performers and their mood on the night you come, you will never forget the experience.

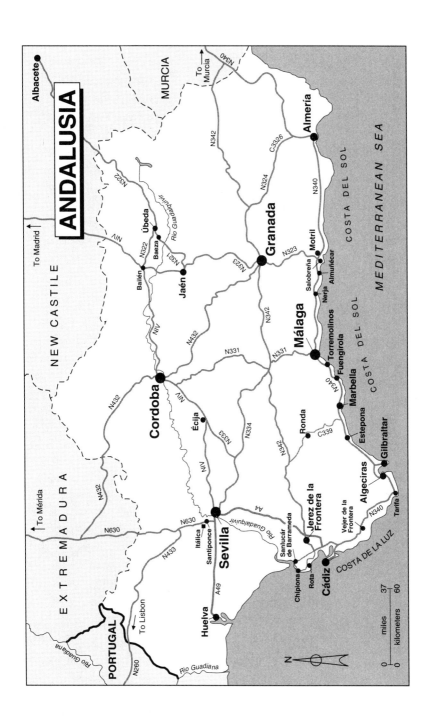

BAEZA ★ ★

Population: 14,799
Area code: 953; Zip code: 23440

From **Madrid** *take A-4 (E-5) south toward Ocaña. The highway becomes N-IV. Continue for 292 k to Bailén. (8 k before Bailén a road east leads to* **Baños de la Encina** *in 4 k, with a fine Moorish fortress.) At Bailén take N-322 east toward Úbeda for 20 k, exiting south on C-326 for 20 k to Baeza. To combine with a visit to nearby* **Úbeda**, *do not exit from N-322 after Bailén, to arrive in Úbeda in 40 k. Afterwards, take N-321 west for 9 k to Baeza. When finished with Baeza, N-321 takes you toward Jaén in 48 k, just before which N-323 heads south to Granada in 93 k. Or return to Bailén, from which N-IV heads west to Córdoba in 108 k.*

From **Granada** *take N-323 north toward Jaén for 88 k. Change to N-321 east toward Úbeda just before Jaén. Baeza is 48 k along N-321. From* **Córdoba** *take N-IV west toward Andujar and Bailén for 108 k. Follow the Madrid directions from Bailén.*

Why is tiny Baeza, off all beaten tracks, so full of Renaissance mansions and churches? Baeza was the first Andalusian city recaptured by the Christians during the Reconquest (in 1239), and before then was the capital of a Moorish *taifa*, or principality. For two centuries it served as the base from which the Christians pushed their Reconquest south, suppling shelter for the royalty and nobles of the army of Castile, and growing rich off them. After the Reconquest was complete, Baeza sat astride the main southern route, enjoying trade and prosperity. Wealthy citizens put up grand mansions in the 16th and 17th centuries, and the city added a university in 1595. But when the town of Jaén to the southwest developed into a major city, the road moved to head directly into Jaén, bypassing Baeza and turning it into the quiet town it remains today.

From **C-326** *you arrive on Acera de la Magdalena and pass a large park. Take the first right a block after the park's end onto C. José Burell. In two blocks comes another fork. Take the right hand road, C. San Pablo, which lets onto the Pl. del Generalisimo and parking. From* **Úbeda** *you travel on C. José Burell. Follow the directions above for parking.*

Baeza offers a proper **cathedral** ★, a **palace** ★ and various **Renaissance buildings** ★ with lovely facades. It has old **fountains** ★, squares and a 16th-century university. All are located near the Pl. del Generalisimo and can be seen in an hour's pleasant walk.

Walk southwest from the Pl. del Generalisimo through the large arcaded Paseo square, noting the early 18th-century **Casas Consistoriales Bajas** on the north side, built so that officials could sit comfortably during ceremonies in the square. A few steps after the southwest end of the Paseo is the attractive **Plaza de los Leones** on the left, named for the **fountain** ★ in the center. The fountain is composed of genuine antiques—the lions seem to be Roman, and the female atop the pillar is either Celtiberian or Carthaginian, bearing a likeness, according to some, of Hannibal's wife. The imposing building to the east is a 16th-century **abattoir** ★, with a lovely coat of arms for Carlos V. Moving south through the plaza we come to an arch, the **Jaén Gate**, erected in 1526 to mark the passage of Carlos V on his way to marry in Seville. Then comes the **Casa de Pópulo**, the former courthouse. The windows and medallions are Plateresque. Its six doors formerly led to six notaries' offices, but now it serves as the **Office of Tourism** and can provide a worthwhile map.

Exit from the south end of the plaza along Cuesta de San Gil, taking the first left onto C. Callejon, which enters the Pl. Santa María. The walls of the former 17th-century **seminary** on the left are covered with faint red names of graduates, painted with bull's blood. Right (south), across the plaza, is an unusual late **Gothic fountain** ★ in the form of a small arch, with the former **cathedral** beyond. Before entering the cathedral, notice the **Casas Consistoriales Altas** with an imposing pair of coats of arms—of Juana the Mad, Ferdinand and Isabella's daughter, and her husband, Philip the Handsome, the parents of Carlos V.

Cathedral

Open daily 10:30 a.m. to 1 p.m. and 4-6 p.m. Technically this is not a cathedral since, after 60 years as a bishopric, the bishop left for Jaén. The building is the same, however, as when the bishop presided. The present church, on the site of a former mosque, was raised by Fernando III, who first conquered the city. In the 16th century the interior was extensively remodeled and redecorated, but the main portal on the west front, the Puerta de la Luna with a horseshoe arch, remains from the early church. Inside are flamboyant chapels, and arches from the former mosque in the cloisters.

Head north along Cuestra San Felipe, arriving after one block at the remarkable Renaissance **Palacio del Marqueses de Jabalquinto** ★.

The golden facade is covered with Isabeline decoration—every feature seems to be growing something. Though impressive, it is more admirable in detail than overall. Inside what today is a seminary stands a more somber, elegant patio with two charming lions guarding a grand baroque stairway. Opposite the palace is the attractive Romanesque church of **Santa Cruz** ★, the only complete church dating to the time of Baeza's liberation in the early 13th century. It remains a gem, still with some frescos inside. North of the church is the imposing former **university**, dating from the late 16th century. A fine patio hides inside the plain facade, and a lovely Mudejar ceiling crowns the amphitheater.

By heading along the long west face of the university, then across its front, and turning left for a few feet, then right along C. San Pablo, in half a block you pass the 16th century **Alhondiga** (grain exchange), with an arched portico. Next turn left across the Pl. del Generalisimo to round the arcaded Paseo for a closer look at the **Casas Consistoriales Bajas** to the north. Continue along its east face on C. Gaspar Becerra for one block to the **Ayuntamiento** (city hall), a former prison, transformed in the 16th century into a sample of everything Plateresque. The arms of Felipe II are proudly displayed.

WHERE TO STAY

With a parador in Úbeda, 9 k away, and with Córdoba and Granada, an hour further, offering much more to do, few people spend the night in Baeza. Accommodations are, however, available in the quiet of this small town.

MODERATE ($50-$99)

Juanito   **2nd-class** ★

Paseo Arca del Agua (on the main road to Úbeda that begins at the Pl. de los Leones). Rooms: 21. ☎ *74 00 40; FAX 74 23 24. Closed the first half of November.* This is the best restaurant in town as well as the best hotel. The accommodations are simple, but comfortable and clean.

WHERE TO EAT

Two restaurants can be recommended, one more enterprising, the other truly inexpensive.

MODERATE ($20-$50)

Juanito   ★

Paseo Arca del Agua (on the main road to Úbeda that begins at the Pl. de los Leones). ☎ *74 00 04. Closed from November 1-15 and Sunday and Monday nights.* The chef uses the freshest ingredients in traditional specialties of the region, including *cordero con habas* and *revuelto de setas*, both recommended.

INEXPENSIVE (UNDER $20)

Sali

Passaje Cardenal Benavides, 15 (on the street going east from the Ayun-tamiento). ☎ *74 13 65. Closed Wednesday night and from the middle of September to the middle of October.* Ingredients are also first rate at this unpretentious place, and, when ordered from the special menus, meals are truly inexpensive.

DIRECTORY

INFORMATION • Located in the Casa del Pópulo in the Pl. de los Leones. ☎ 74 04 44.

TRAINS AND BUSES • The nearest train station is Linares-Baeza, 13 k out of town, which serves both Baeza and Úbeda. A bus connects with most trains.

Buses arrive from Granada and Úbeda.

POST OFFICE AND TELEPHONES • Located a short block north of the Ayuntamiento.

EXCURSIONS

Úbeda is the natural excursion from Baeza, described under its own heading below. Of course, **Granada** is only 88 k away, and **Córdoba** and **Seville** not much further. See directions under those headings.

CÁDIZ ★

Population: 157,766
Area code: 956; Zip code: 11000

*From the **Costa del Sol** on N-340, the highway divides just before reaching Cádiz. Signs adequately instruct you how to proceed. Cádiz is 123 k from Algeciras, 50 k from Conil. From **Seville** A-4 (E-5), a toll road, or N-IV which runs beside it, bring you quickly to Cádiz in 97 k or 109 k, respectively. From **Granada** take N342 (E-902) west to Antequera, then continue to Jerez de la Frontera for 155 k, where the toll road A-4 (E-5) completes the journey in 39 k more. From **Córdoba** it is best to go first to Seville, and then follow the directions above.*

Although Cádiz belongs to the Costa de la Luz, its beaches are best left undescribed. There are fine sands a ferry-ride away across the bay, however, and more inland on the isthmus. Spain's largest port retains a romantic feeling and offers sights to see, so it is not a bad place to settle for a day or two of rest.

Cádiz is old. It was founded as a port named Gades by the Phoenicians, and a port it has remained for 3000 years, for it is situated on an isthmus that carries the city out into a fine bay. In time it became the main depot for treasure ships from the mines of the New World, and it prospered, although prosperity also made for temptations and raids by Barbary corsairs, and even by Francis Drake during preparations for the Great Armada. In Napoléon's time, the French fleet was bottled up in Cádiz by Admiral Nelson. The fleet broke through the gauntlet of English ships only to sail to defeat off the Cape of Trafalgar, a few miles south.

Cádiz defies most expectations of a port. It is not grey, dirty, seedy or frightening. This is the Andalusian version of a port—whitewashed houses, with turrets, lining narrow streets that let into lovely squares. Along the sea, north and east, gardens invite promenades. While none of the sights in Cádiz are remarkable, the walking is pleasant.

POLLUTION ALERT

The beaches in the city of Cadiz are unsafe for bathing, at last report.

From whichever direction you set out for Cádiz, the narrow isthmus funnels all roads to the old town at the tip. Parking in the old town is a challenge, but when N-IV ends at the large Pl. de la Constitución, go through the city walls and turn right onto Plocia Calesas, which becomes Av. Ramon de Carranza in three blocks, and offers parking.

Walk north along Av. Carranza for half a mile to the Pl. de España. Take C. Antonio Lopez going left, just past the Disputacion, which brings you to the palms of the lovely **Plaza de Mina**, the former garden of a convent, in four short blocks. The **Office of Tourism** is located at the north corner of the plaza at C. Calderon de la Barca, 1 (open Mon.-Sat. 9 to 2 p.m.). A map is available for navigating the maze of Cádiz' streets. Head northwest along C. Calderon de la Barca for two blocks to the ramparts and gardens for lovely views. Return to the east side of the plaza for the **Museo del Bellas Artes y Arqueológico**.

Museo del Bellas Artes y Arqueológico   ★

Open Mon.-Fri. 9 a.m. to p.m. and 5:30-7:30 p.m. Open Sat. 9 a.m. to 1:30 p.m. Admission: 300 ptas., to both museums. As its name describes, this building combines two separate museums. The archaeological collection, consisting of local finds, is not outstanding, but there is a headless Roman female statue which was worshiped for a while as a Virgin, and a nice Roman sarcophagus. It is the paintings in the fine arts section, however, that make a visit worthwhile. There are canvases by Rubens, Cano, Murillo and Ribera, and an extraordinary collection of Zurbaráns. The Zurbaráns come from a group of saints he painted for the Monastery at Jerez, and form one of his few remaining intact series. In all there are 21, some sublime.

For Goya frescos, head two blocks along C. Rosario, which leaves the south end of the plaza, to **Santa Cueva**, *a late 18th-century church.*

Leaving from the west end of the Pl. de Mina, C. San José goes southwest to the Pl. San Antonio in one block and a jag right. The main shopping street, C. Ancha, heads southeast. Further southwest on C. San José is the **Church of San Felipe Neri** (open only during services). It was in this church that the First Republic was proclaimed, although King Fernando VII promptly renounced its constitution when he returned to the throne. On the east side, adjacent to the church, is the **Museo Historico ★** with an admirable ivory and mahogany model of Cádiz as it looked at the end of the 18th century. It presents much the same appearance as today, if less battered by time and weather (open Tues.-Fri. 9 a.m. to 1 p.m. and 4-7 p.m.; admission: free). To see a modern grand building in an exuberant Mudejar style, head west along C. Sacramento that runs beside the museum for two short blocks to the **Teatro Manuel de Falla**. Otherwise, take C. Sacramento southeast for 5 blocks into the Pl. Castelar. Across the plaza, at the southeast corner, C. de Santiago leads past the baroque **Iglesia Santiago** and into the Pl. de la Catedral, after two blocks more. To the west of the cathedral with its golden dome stands a medieval town gate.

Cathedral ★

Open Mon.-Sat. 10 a.m. to 1 p.m. Admission: 200 ptas., to the cathedral museum. Entrance on C. Acero. The mass of the cathedral was in place by the middle of 18th century, though it was not finished until a century later. The baroque facade is well matched by gilt and stucco inside. Manuel de Falla, whose music incorporated so much Andalusian folklore and songs, is buried in the crypt. The museum contains about as much silver and gold as one is ever likely to see, and a monstrance (portable reliquary) that may outdo all the rest in Spain, which is saying a great deal. There are some decent paintings by Ribera and Zurbáran, among others.

WHERE TO STAY

A hotel development is rising on the thin strip of isthmus leading to the old city. But if you want to stay out of town, there are nicer places elsewhere along the coast. We recommend accommodations in the old town.

EXPENSIVE ($100-$200)

Atlántico   **1st-class ★ ★**

Duque de Nájera, 9 (off the circular road around the old town, at its most western end). Rooms: 153. ☎ *22 69 05; FAX 21 45 82; Telex 76316.* This six-story, clean, white modern structure is more reminiscent of nice motels in the States than of a parador, but, like all paradors, the rooms are comfortable and, in this one, most windows offer pleasant views across the bay. Situated in the Parque Genoves, at the tip of the peninsula, one feels surrounded by country quiet in the heart of town.

MODERATE ($50-$99)

Francia y Paris   **2nd-class ★**

Pl. de San Francisco, 2 (one block due south of the Pl. de Mina along C. Rosario). Rooms: 69. ☎ *21 23 19; FAX 22 24 31.* This former town house has been thoroughly and tastefully modernized inside. However, while the rooms are certainly adequate, one gets the feeling that the public spaces got more than their share of the decorating funds. The location is convenient to all the sights and quiet, but without ocean views.

WHERE TO EAT

It is hard to better Cádiz fried sardines whether from stalls along the harbor in the southeast corner of the old town or in almost any local restaurant. We list two fancier restaurants. Naturally, both specialize in seafood, and seafood is not inexpensive.

EXPENSIVE ($50+)

El Faro   **★ ★**

C. San Félix, 15 (at the southwest tip of the old town, a block north of the sea wall). ☎ *21 25 01.* The owner adds hanging hams to an Andalusian decor to let you know his place is serious about food. Here you do not need to stick to plain seafood. The sauces and marinades are tastefully done, and the chef knows meat as well. This is a popular place, so reservations are advised.

                    Amex, Diners, MasterCard and Visa accepted.

El Anteojo   **★**

C. Alameda de Apodaca, 22 (directly north of the Museo de Bellas Artes, near the sea wall). ☎ *22 13 20. Closed Monday and from the first three weeks of February.* Views across the bay from the terrace are so lovely that the food does not have to be good. In fact the food is at least good, especially if you stick to the always fresh seafood, simply prepared.

MODERATE ($20-$50)

El Sardinero   ★

Pl. San Juan de Dios (this large plaza is two blocks east of the Pl. de la Catedral along C. Pelota). ☎ *28 25 05. Closed Monday.* A number of decent seafood restaurants line this square, so it is fun to walk around and choose, though el Sardinero's Basque chef elevates it above the rest. A simple place, but the food is good.

DIRECTORY

INFORMATION • On C. Calderon de la Barca, 1, which actually is on the Pl. de Mina, at the north end.

TRAINS AND BUSES • The station is located on Av. del Puerto, off Plocia Calesas, just north of where the old town begins.

Buses to Seville are frequent, but only leave once a day for Granada and Córdoba. The station is just east of the Pl. de España in Pl. de Hispanidad. ☎ 21 17 63. A different bus line serves the nearby coast towns: Transportes Los Amarillos is located on Av. Ramón de Carranza near the parking place. ☎ 28 58 52.

BOAT TO PUERTO SANTA MARÍA • The fine beach across the bay at Puerto Santa María is served by four boats per day in season. Boats leave the harbor near the train station and the parking, for a 150 ptsa. trip, each way. Information is available at the tourism office.

CÓRDOBA ★ ★ ★ ★

Population: 284,737
Area code: 957; Zip code: 14000

From **Madrid** *take A-4 (E-5) south toward Aranjuez, which becomes N-IV. At Bailén, after 298 k, N-IV turns west to Córdoba, 108 k further away. From* **Granada** *take N-432 to Córdoba in 163 k. From* **Seville** *take N-IV (E-5) to Córdoba for 142 k.*

As their capital, Córdoba rose with the Moors to glory, but it was already familiar with such status. The Romans had made it the seat of their southern province of Baetia, as they called Andalusia, 800 years before. Córdoba became the largest city in Roman Spain, and here the great Latin writer, Seneca the Elder, was born. Later, its archbishop Hosius presided over the Church Council of Nicea, from which came the famous creed.

Under the Moors Córdoba became the shining light of medieval Europe. By the tenth century, its population had reached half a million—double its size today—at a time when neither London nor Paris approached 100,000. The streets were paved and lighted, public baths were open to all, 50 hospitals served the sick, and a third of a million mansions, houses and stores filled the city. Nor was Córdoba merely large and modern. While the Dark Ages eclipsed science in the rest of Europe, Córdoba served as its reservoir of learning. Córdoba's library housed a quarter of a million volumes at a time when books elsewhere in Europe were rare as hen's teeth, and only one Christian in a hundred could read. Of course the Moors had an advantage—they knew how to make paper while the rest of Europe wrote on costly sheepskin—and Córdoba had 29 public schools. The

great Jewish philosopher Moses Maimonides was born and lived in Córdoba, as did the great Aristotilian scholar Ibn Rushd, known to the West as Averröes, who produced sophisticated commentaries on the master. Later his works were translated into Latin to produce the scholastic thought, which Abelard, Duns Scotus and Thomas Aquinas developed to lift Europe into the Renaissance. Algebra and so-called Arabic numbers (actually transmitted to the Arabs from India) were disseminated from Andalusia to the rest of the continent. Without the Moorish culture in Andalusia—indeed, without Córdoba—the west would have remained in its Dark Ages for centuries longer, with unpredictable results.

In 1236, the Christians captured Córdoba, ending its preeminence. Even after the reconquest, Córdoba retained fame for its tooled, embossed and colored leatherwork, so desired throughout Europe that "cordovan" became a common noun in English. But never again would the city shine as it once had.

Arriving from **Madrid** *or from the direction of* **Jaén***, travel along Paseo de la Rivera beside the Guadalquivir River. After passing the gardens of the Alcázar you arrive at a "T." Continue right onto Av. de Conde de Vallallano. Stay along the boulevard gardens on Paseo de la Victoria, though if a spot for parking presents itself, as it usually does, take it. Otherwise continue to the circle, taking Ronda de los Tejares northeast. At the third right turn onto C. Cruz Conde, whose second right onto C. de Robledo leads to parking. From both* **Seville** *and* **Granada** *you come to a large traffic circle and proceed northwest to cross the bridge over the Guadalquivir River, which funnels into Av. de Conde de Vallellano. Then follow the directions above.*

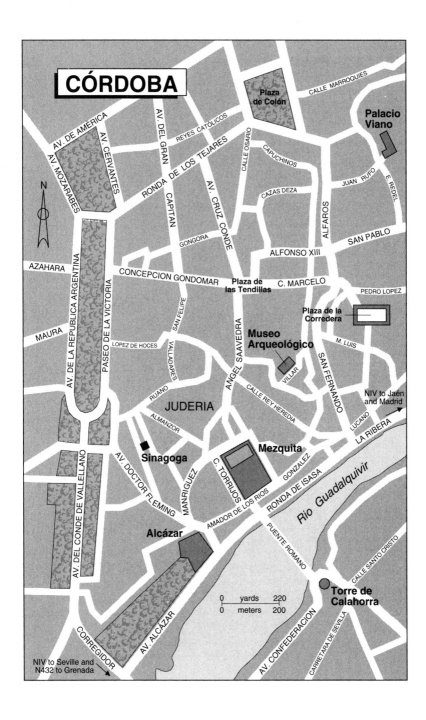

CÓRDOBA

Plaza de Colón

CALLE MARROQUIES

Palacio Viano

AV. DE AMÉRICA
AV. CERVANTES
AV. MOZARABES
AV. DEL GRAN CAPITAN
REYES CATÓLICOS
RONDA DE LOS TEJARES
AV. CRUZ CONDE
CALLE OSARIO
CAPUCHINOS
CAZAS DEZA
GONGORA
JUAN RUFO
E. REDEL
ALFAROS
SAN PABLO

N

ALFONSO XIII

AZAHARA
AV. DE LA REPUBLICA ARGENTINA
PASEO DE LA VICTORIA
CONCEPCION GONDOMAR
Plaza de las Tendillas
C. MARCELO
PEDRO LOPEZ

MAURA
LOPEZ DE HOCES
SAN FELIPE
VALLADARES
Plaza de la Corredera

Museo Arqueológico

M. LUIS

RUANO
ANGEL SAAVEDRA
VILLAR
SAN FERNANDO

JUDERIA
ALMANZOR
CALLE REY HEREDIA
NIV to Jaén and Madrid
LUCANO
LA RIBERA

Sinagoga
Mezquita
GONZALEZ
Rio Guadalquivir

AV. DEL CONDE DE VALLELLANO
AV. DOCTOR FLEMING
MANRIGUEZ
C. TORRIJOS
AMADOR DE LOS RIOS
RONDA DE ISASA

Alcázar
PUENTE ROMANO

CALLE SANTO CRISTO

Torre de Calahorra

0 yards 220
0 meters 200

CORREGIDOR
AV. ALCÁZAR
AV. CONFEDERACION
CARRETARA DE SEVILLA

NIV to Seville and N432 to Grenada

WHAT TO SEE AND DO

The sight for which Córdoba is world-famous is the **mezquita** ★★★★★, or mosque, one of the greatest raised by Islam. It is located a short block north of the Guadalquivir River. Around the mosque crowd remains of the old medieval quarter, a twisting maze of streets, called the **Juderia** ★★ that extends five blocks north of the mosque, two blocks west and one block east. A medieval **synagogue** ★ and an **archaeological museum** ★ lie within the Juderia, and lovely flowered patios can be glimpsed through doorways and grills. On its west side rise the remains of old city **walls**. An **alcázar** ★ overlooks the river one block southwest of the mosque, and a block upstream from it is the so-called **Puente Romano**, little of which is Roman.

There should be more to see in Córdoba, given its former splendors. But the mosque alone repays a trip, the other sights are concentrated in a small area, and everywhere orange trees perfume the air. In addition, evocative ruins of a pleasure city built by Caliph er Rahman wait at **Medinet Azahara** ★★★, 10 k outside the city. One full day does justice to Córdoba.

The best approach to the mosque is through the medieval quarters, the Juderia, to acquire some feel for life as it was then. Make your way to the grand boulevard of Córdoba, the gardened Paseo de la Victoria. Head a few blocks south to reach the beginning of the reconstructed town walls. Follow these walls to their gate, the **Puerta de Almodovar**, watched over by a statue of Seneca.

Juderia   ★★

Turn immediately right through the town gate, hugging the walls along C. Maimonides. Whitewashed houses, many with lovely interior patios and flowers, line the lanes. In one long block is the **synagogue** ★, on the right (open Tues.-Sat. 10 a.m. to 2 p.m. and 3:30-5:30 p.m., opening and closing an hour earlier in winter; closed Mon. as well as Sun. afternoons; admission: 75 ptas.). With the two in Toledo, this is the last surviving synagogue in Spain. It dates to the 14th century and is tiny, though with fine Mudejar stucco work along the upper walls and balcony.

Across from the synagogue is a touristy reconstructed **Zoco** (souk, "market"), interesting only for a look at the building, with craftsmen working around an open patio, and containing a museum of bullfighting. Turn east across its southern face, passing first the statue of Maimonides and then the **Capilla de San Bartolome** on the right, with vaulting and Mudejar work inside. At the end of C. Cardenal Salazar, C. Almanzor Romero leads southeast to the corner of the **mesquita** ★★★★★ (mosque). Along its northern face, beside the bell tower, is its normal entrance. See the description below.

After the mesquita, head east along its north face to take the alley going left, just before the corner of the walls, called C. Velázquez

Bosco. Almost immediately take the right that leads past the truly beautiful **flowered patios** ★ on either side and into an alley heading south, called the Calleja de las Flores. Córdoba takes great pride in its patios, holding a contest during the first two weeks of May. The alley lets into C. Encarnación which goes east for a block to C. Rey Heredia. Jag right, then left onto Cale Horno de Cristo which leads to the **archaeological museum** ★.

Mezquita   ★★★★★

Open daily 10 a.m. to 1:30 p.m. and 4-7 p.m. (until 5:30 in winter). Admission: 400 ptas. Approximately one-third of the present structure was completed by Abd er Rahman in 785, after he purchased a Christian church on the site and razed it to erect his mosque in one year. He saved pillars from the former church, which the Christians had in turn appropriated from earlier Roman and Visigoth buildings, to incorporate in the structure. This earliest stage of the mosque covered half of a football field—75 yards by 25 wide—and employed the innovation of creating aisles by superimposing two tiers of arches, for height and spaciousness. Over the next 200 years three additions were made, each incorporating the superimposed arches, to quadruple the original size to 200 yards long (counting 50 yards of courtyard) and 130 wide.

The plan is typical of mosques the world over. First comes a courtyard with a basin for ritual ablution, followed by the mosque proper—a rectangular building with a special niche in one wall, called a *mihrab*, that indicates the direction of Mecca. Toward this niche the congregation bows in prayer. What is unique about this mosque is the addition, made in the 16th century, of a cathedral inside. At that time, all aisles of the mosque but two were sealed off, depriving the mosque of its original open feeling, and the flat, carved and painted wooden ceiling was replaced by vaulting. (A portion of this original ceiling has been restored near the mihrab.) Today the building is the most incongruous of structures—an Oriental mosque encasing a Gothic cathedral. Upon seeing the intrusive cathedral, Carlos V, who initially authorized its construction, berated the city fathers by saying, "You have built here what you might have built anywhere else, but you destroyed what was unique in the world." (Ironically, this same king had destroyed sections of the Alhambra to make room for a palace there.)

The Puerta del Perdon entrance was added to the enclosing walls in the 14th century, though in a style—except for the coats of arms of Córdoba and Spain high on the outer side—thoroughly suitable to the mosque. The side facing the courtyard is wholly Moorish in flavor, and lovely. The courtyard itself, with rows of shading orange trees and a large ablution basin centrally placed near the long wall, looks much as it would have in the tenth century. (Incidentally, the oranges are as bitter as can be.) Directly across from the Pardon Gate is the entrance to the mosque proper.

Inside stands a magical forest. Pillars like trees stretch in every forward direction into the distance. Originally 850 of them, all different—of marble, jasper, porphyry, and breccia—supported arches that alternated limestone and brick to make red and white stripes. About half the pillars—the rest were displaced by the cathedral—remain, enough to produce an effect like no other building in the world. The pillars came mainly from looted older buildings in Spain, but some were shipped from Carthage in North Africa and a few from as far as Constantinople. Having been appropriated from different buildings, the pillars varied in height and required bases of individual elevation to even them out. The vast majority of the capitals are concrete replicas, with a few marble originals bearing traces of original gilt near the mihrab.

The route to the mihrab is straight ahead, against the south wall of the mosque, although it involves passing the cathedral (as quickly as possible). The **Villaviciosa Chapel** is situated just in front of the mihrab. Unfortunately it has been sealed off recently, though it is possible to peer through the grill. Probably this chamber was intended for the caliph and his immediate family, but it was remodeled in a Mudejar style in the 14th century when it received a lovely dome, reminiscent of that prefacing the mihrab. Adjoining, on the left, is the **Capilla Real**, again a 14th-century addition of harmonious Mudejar work. Directly ahead is the **mihrab**.

The mihrab was constructed in 965 using Byzantine craftsmen, probably from Greece, hence the glittering mosaics. The mihrab proper is the tiny closet through the horseshoe arch. Preceding it are three bays forming an enclosure for the caliph and his family. The wooden ceiling prefacing this enclosure is the only remainder of the tenth-century original that first covered the whole mosque. Three domes above the caliph's enclosure are original designs of intersecting arcs that form an octagonal center, all inlaid with mosaics to present arabesques on a gold field. Brilliant mosaics make the walls rich, but the most splendid are the arabesques framing the archway to the mihrab. That octagonal chamber, into which one cannot enter, consists of carved marble walls and a dome formed by an elegant plaster shell. So successful was the design of this mihrab that it became the standard throughout the Muslim world.

The **cathedral**, insistently placed in the midst of this oriental splendor, cannot be entirely ignored. It is a mishmash of every ornate style from Gothic to baroque, as if competing with the elegance of the mosque by overwhelming the viewer. On its own it is impressive, if overblown, with fine workmanship throughout. Ignoring the gilded stucco roof, the coro encloses fine baroque choir stalls, and the pulpits are baroque masterpieces—note the bull who cranes to hear the sermon. But nothing can excuse the travesty of placing this florid Christian structure inside one of the world's greatest works of architecture. Some say that the mosque is large enough and sufficiently grand that it absorbs the cathedral without loss, but most will find the cathedral so disturbing that the experience of the mosque is undermined. Carlos V's assessment is sadly accurate.

Museo Arqueológico Provincial ★

Open Tues.-Sat. 10 a.m. to 2 p.m. and 6-8 p.m. (until 7 p.m. in winter). Open Sun. 10 a.m. to 1:30 p.m. Closed Mon. and holidays. Admission: 250 ptas. The museum is housed in the 16th-century palace of Jerónimo Páez, with a rich Renaissance portal, though the patio on the other side is simple. Exhibits are arranged chronologically to instruct in art history. Rooms to the right present prehistoric material, including several endearing Iberian lions. Further on are interesting Roman mosaics. The second floor presents a Moorish collection, mainly excavated from Medinat Azahara nearby. Amid lovely capitals, the star is a bronze inlaid stag from a fountain in Medinat Azahara, donated to the caliph by the emperor of Constantinople.

*Walk due south to the river and the so-called **Roman bridge**. The bridge does rest on Roman foundations, though its present form derives from Moorish construction in the eighth century, much restored since. On the opposite bank is the **Torre de Calahorro**, from the 14th century. It was recently taken over by an artist and made into a museum of models of ancient Córdoba with inane verbal descriptions. (It closes at 7 p.m. in summer, 6 p.m. in winter, all day Sun. and Mon., and costs 250 ptas.) A model of the mosque when new almost makes a visit worthwhile. Downstream in two blocks is the Alcázar.*

Alcázar ★

Open Tues.-Sat. 9:30 a.m. to 1:30 p.m. and 5-8 p.m. (until 7 p.m. in winter). Open Sun. 9:30 a.m. to 1:30 p.m. Admission: 200 ptas. The original alcázar of the Moors stood east of the present structure, on the spot where the present bishopric faces the mosque. In the 13th century Alfonso X the Learned built a palace in the gardens of the original alcázar, which was substantially modified in the succeeding century to what exists today. Later the building served as the office of the local Inquisition and its prison until the 19th century. Although the interior is not of great interest, there are some mosaics inside and nice Moorish baths. The gardens with pools, flowers and cypresses make for peaceful strolling.

Palacio de Viana ★★

Pl. de Don Gome. Open Mon., Tues., Thurs., and Fri. 9 a.m. to 2 p.m. and 4-6 p.m. (Opens and closes an hour earlier winter afternoons). Closed Wed. and weekends. Admission: 250 ptas. The simplest course is to take a taxi, which should not cost more than $3, for the mile ride from the mosque. Normally one hardly bothers with an 18th-century palace in Spain, unless it was built by a king, but the reason for seeing this one is its dozen patios, in some ways the loveliest in this city of fine patios. In addition, there are nearly 50 rooms open to the public to show how the very rich once lived.

WHERE TO STAY

Córdoba serves nicely as a place to spend a night or two, with good choices in every price category. The problem is that the city does not have any excess of hotels, which can be a problem in busy seasons. It is best to reserve ahead.

EXPENSIVE ($100-$200)

Aldarve   1st-class ★★★★

Magistral González Francés, 15 (facing the east wall of the mosque). Rooms: 103. ☎ *48 11 02; FAX 47 46 77; Telex 76594.* All white in the style of a new Moorish villa, the elegance of the decor and the beauty of its patio make it unrivaled in Códoba. The hotel is attentively run. The most difficult problem for a guest is to choose between a room facing the elegant interior patio and one facing the mosque. Parking is available for a fee.

El Califa   R2nd-class ★★

Lope de Hoces, 14 (a block north, and short block east, of the Melia Córdoba). Rooms: 67. ☎ *29 94 00; FAX 29 57 16.* The street on which the hotel resides is lovely, filled with orange trees. The building is attractively modern with an elegant granite reception area. Rooms are tastefully decorated; the service is good; prices lie at the bottom of the expensive range, and parking is available for a fee.

On the Carretera de El Brillant, 4 k north of Córdoba:

Parador de la Arruzafa   1st-class ★★

Av. de la Arruzafa. Rooms: 94. ☎ *27 59 00; FAX 28 04 09; Telex 76695.* This is a modern parador, looking too much like a Miami Beach hotel of the second or third class. Of course it is clean and well maintained, but its best feature is lovely gardens to provide peace and quiet, albeit outside of town. A swimming pool and tennis courts are available.

Maimónides   R2nd-class ★★

Torrijos, 4 (opposite the east side of the mosque patio). Rooms: 83. ☎ *47 15 00; FAX 48 38 03; Telex 76594.* We remember happier days for the Maimónides. Actually it probably remains the same, but over the years other hotels have improved. It still enjoys a perfect location and views of the mosque from the front rooms, but is in need of a sprucing up. Parking is available for a fee.

Los Gallos Sol   2nd-class

Av. Medina Azahara, 7 (two blocks north and one east of the Melia Córdoba). Rooms: 115. ☎ *23 55 00; FAX 23 16 36; Telex 76566.* This hotel is a good ten years overdue for a facelift, still looking 70s modern. It is a pleasant enough place, but nothing outstanding, and a rather long walk to the sights.

Husa Gran Capitán   1st-class

Av. de América, 5 (the avenue runs across the north end of the Victoria Gardens.) Rooms: 99. ☎ *47 02 50; FAX 47 43 48; Telex 76662.* If you are part of a tour, you probably are staying here already; otherwise you probably wouldn't want to. Overrated is a term invented for such establishments. The rooms are large but uninviting and overlook either an ugly, noisy street or an unattractive courtyard. The staff tries. Parking is available for a fee.

Meliá Córdoba   1st-class

Jardines de la Victoria. (located at the southern end of the gardens that begin where the city walls end. See the arrival directions.) Rooms: 106. ☎ *29 80 66; FAX 29 81 47; Telex 76591.* This is supposed to be the grand hotel of Córdoba, but it does not come close. The decor reminds one of the fifties; the lobby is dreary, and the building is situated by a simple park that few of the rooms overlook.

MODERATE ($50-$99)

González   3rd-class ★ ★ ★

Manriquez, 3 (on the street running west from the northwest corner of the Mosque). Rooms: 16. ☎ *47 98 19.* A delightful hotel at most reasonable prices, this one is heartily recommended. The lobby is white with light wood, punctuated by antiques, especially the lovely chandelier. Altogether this hotel feels perfectly Andalusian, clean and fresh, and is situated on an equally lovely street.

Marisa   R3rd-class ★

Cardenal Herrero, 6 (along the north wall of the mosque). Rooms: 28. ☎ *47 31 42.* This hotel is simple and pleasantly, if not memorably, decorated. The small size lends a homey feel, and the location is just as good as more costly alternatives.

Selu   R2nd-class

Eduardo Dato, 7 (a block due north of the el Caliph hotel). Rooms: 118. ☎ *47 65 00; FAX 47 83 76; Telex 76659.* This is a functional modern hotel recently renovated. Parking is available for a fee.

INEXPENSIVE (UNDER $50)

Serrano   3rd-class ★ ★

Pérez Galdós, 6 (just off the right side of the Av. Gran Capitan which runs due north of the Juderia, a block south and two east of the hotel Gran Capitan). Rooms: 64. ☎ *47 01 42; FAX 48 65 13.* Modern without being stark, this hotel is a charmer. It is situated on a quiet street of pleasant art galleries. The 5-block walk to the Juderia is not too much to ask for such pleasing accommodations.

Andalucia   3rd-class ★ ★

José Zorrila, 3 (just north of the Juderia and a short block east of the major

Av. del Gran Capitan that runs due north of the Juderia). Rooms: 40.
☎ *47 60 00.* The hotel is modest, the location good and the prices very fair, which is not a bad combination.

Sénica   HsR4th-class ★

Conde y Luque, 7 (the street runs east-west 2 blocks north of the mosque). Rooms: 10. ☎ *47 32 34.* Clean as a whistle and with a lovely courtyard for breakfast, what more can you ask for a low price? A room with bath costs extra, but breakfast is included. Reservations are a must.

El Triunfo   Hs3rd-class

Cardinal González, 79 (at the southwest corner of the mosque, near the river). Rooms: 44. ☎ *47 55 00.* Just a tad higher-priced than the foregoing and not on as pleasant a street, this establishment is also clean as can be, and convenient to the sights. Noise sometimes becomes a problem, however. Reserve to avoid disappointment.

WHERE TO EAT

One can eat well in Córdoba, although it is difficult to dine cheaply. The regional specialty is a somewhat thicker, more garlicky version of gazpacho called *salmorejo* in which ham and eggs are included. The other specialty is *rabo de toro*—oxtail stewed in heavy tomato sauce—which no one should disparage without trying.

EXPENSIVE ($50+)

Mesón Bandolero   ★★

Torrijos, 6 (next door to the hotel Maimonides). ☎ *41 42 45.* The room is lovely, with brick arches forming intimate dining areas, and a patio filled with palms for outdoor eating. Tables are set with linen and sparkling brass serving plates. None of this elegance is surprising, given that this restaurant is affiliated with the so tasteful hotel Aldarve. Although the food is carefully prepared and covers specialties of the region, our hearts insisted on this recommendation for the beauty of the place more than the food.

Amex, Diners and Visa accepted.

El Caballo Rojo   ★★

Cardenal herrero, 28 (opposite the northwest corner of the mosque). ☎ *47 53 75.* Dining is upstairs in a huge 50s kind of place that is noisy because hordes of people are enjoying themselves. The menu claims dishes based on ancient recipes, some of which are tasty indeed, such as *ajo blanco* and *rape mozárabe*. A complimentary sherry aperitif settles you in, and ordering from a special menu can hold down prices.

Amex, Diners, MasterCard and Visa accepted.

El Blasón   ★★

José Zorrilla, 11 (near the hotel Andalucia). ☎ *48 06 25.* Whitewashed walls and tiled floor lend a perfect Andalusian feel, and a patio filled with greenery invites. Service is excellent. There is a reasonably-priced special menu, plus a more expensive *menu de degustación* to put the chef through his paces.

Amex, Diners, MasterCard and Visa accepted.

El Churrasco ★

Romero, 16 (the street heading northwest from the northwest corner of the mosque). ☎ *29 08 19. Closed Thursday and August.* Again, white walls with brick arches characterize this restaurant, this time with iron chairs and an indoor garden under a skylight. The specialty after which the restaurant is named is a kind of barbecued pork that, along with other grilled dishes, draws a crowd. The *salmorejo* soup is delicious. *Reservations are strongly recommended. Amex, Diners, MasterCard and Visa accepted.*

DIRECTORY

INFORMATION • On C. Torrijos, 10, which frames the west side of the mosque, in the Palacio de Congresos y Exposiciones. The staff is helpful with information on Andalusia in general, as well as on Córdoba. ☎ 47 12 35.

TRAINS AND BUSES • The train station is located one mile north of the mosque on Av. de América. For information: ☎ 49 02 02. The RENFE ticket office is at Ronda de los Tejares 10, which cuts across Av. Gran Capitan, about six blocks north of the Juderia. ☎ 47 58 84.

There is no central area for bus departures because the routes are divided among several companies. The tourist office provides information and schedules. For Seville and Jaén call ☎ 47 23 52; for Madrid, Valencia or Barcelona the number is ☎ 29 07 69; for Granada and Málaga call ☎ 23 64 74.

POST OFFICE AND TELEPHONES • The post office is at 15 C. Cruz Conde, which runs north from the large conflux of streets at the Pl. de las Tendillas, just north of the Juderia. Telephones are located in this same plaza at number 7.

POLICE • Campo Madre de Dios, 5, a wide street about ten blocks east along the river. ☎ 25 14 14; for emergencies 091.

AIRPORT • Córdoba's small airport is 6 k outside of town, with limited flights, none international. For information contact Iberia (☎ 47 12 27) at Ronda de los Tejares, 3, near the RENFE office above, under "Trains."

EXCURSIONS

Medina Azahara, located about 11 k from Córdoba, is an excavated pleasure city, built by the first caliph of el Andalus, Abd er Rahman III. It is atmospheric and contains some lovely buildings reconstructed from the ruins.

From the hotel Melia Córdoba, make a circuit around the north end of the Victoria garden heading south. Take the first right on

Av. Medina Azahara, which becomes C-431. In 8 k, bear right as a sign directs to reach the ruins in 3 k more.

Medinet Azahara ★★★

Open Tues.-Sat. 10 a.m. to 2 p.m. and 6-8 p.m. (opening and closing two hours earlier on winter afternoons). Open Sun. and holidays from 10 a.m. to 1:30 p.m. Closed Mon. Admission: 250 ptas. Caliph Abd er Rahman III, mightiest of the Moors, began work in 936 on a city terraced on a hill to afford beautiful views. He named it for his favorite wife, az Zahara. Records tell of construction crews numbering in the ten thousands, of a garrison to hold a 12,000-man army, and of lovely gardens with a zoo. It must have been an Arabian Nights place, perhaps rivalling the Alhambra, and certainly surpassing it in size and age. Yet it endured for less than a century, because it was razed by Berbers who felt betrayed by one of Abd er Rahman III's successors. Over the ensuing centuries, the site was looted for building materials by Christian kings and aristocracy for their own building projects.

Excavations began in 1944, and reconstruction—still underway—began a decade later. The area contains a small city, and the Spanish government is in no hurry. The grand gate to the town and **plaza** inside have been reconstructed enough to give a sense of their design, but most impressive is the **Salon Rico**. The walls have been re-erected, some of the original carved stones replaced, and the floor reconstructed. It is an imposing structure, and the carved designs in stone are interesting for their more realistic portrayal of nature, compared to the abstraction of later Alhambra stucco. The **mosque** nearby is also worth a look. The site is a place to wander through and dream of other times and other worlds.

COSTA DE LA LUZ ★★

These are the beaches left to the Spanish after Europeans appropriate the rest. So do not come here expecting excitement and international flavor—stick with the Costa del Sol for that. What you will find is fine beaches, much better than those on the Costa del Sol, and villages that retain their character. You will also find a large part of Spain on holiday here beginning from the middle of July through August. Accommodations are difficult to obtain during that time, but even then enough beach exists that quiet places can be found for communing with sea and sun. At other times accommodations should not pose any problem, and the beach remains warm well into October.

The Costa de la Luz extends west from Gibraltar to the Portuguese border, over 200 k in length. Naturally such a large area includes much variation, but to generalize, the beaches improve the further west they go, while the atmosphere turns transparent, earning the name "Coast of Light."

We describe the towns beginning in the east and going west. The first half, to Cádiz, is traversed by N-340 (E-5) west, beginning from Gibraltar (described in a separate heading below). Decent roads connect all the towns, though traffic can crawl in August. It is also possible to cover the route using local buses, but with much transferring involved.

ALGECIRAS

Population: 86,042
Area code: 956; Zip code: 11200

Located across the bay from Gibraltar, 13 k away by the road around Algeciras bay, the port of Algeciras affords the best views of the Rock and offers transportation by car ferry to both Tangier and Ceuta in Morocco. The city itself is grey overall, though with nice public gardens inside the first perimeter wall. It contains a decent cathedral and ruins of a Moorish fort, but no beaches.

TARIFA ★

Population: 15,220
Area code: 956; Zip code: 11380

N-340 goes right into town, 21 k southwest from Algeciras.

Tarifa is the southernmost part of Spain, not excepting Gibraltar, and only 15 k off the coast of Morocco—visible on clear days. It is also exposed to ocean winds that make it a windsurfer's dream and often a beach sitter's nightmare, because of blowing sand. However, the beaches extending west for 10 k from the town are lovely. The old town still retains parts of its Moorish walls and gates. On the sea, just east, are remains of a Moorish castle from the tenth century with a later fortified tower.

17 k west from Tarifa, a turn left down a small road toward the ocean leads to the fine beach of **Bolonia** *with bars and eating places, and extensive ruins of the Roman town of Baelo Claudia (closed Sun. afternoons and all Mon.).*

WHERE TO STAY

The nicest Tarifa accommodations are outside town on N-340, with a few cheaper places inside the town.

MODERATE ($50-$99)

Balcón de España   2nd-class ★★★
La Peña 2-Northeast 8 k on Carretera de Cádiz (mailing address: Apartado 57). Rooms: 40. ☎ *68 43 26; FAX 68 43 26. Open only from April 15 to the end of Oct.* This lovely little place provides a pool, tennis and patios, and must be reserved well in advance. It is near good beaches, and even its meals are special.

La Codorniz   4th-class ★★
6.5 k on Carretera de Cádiz (N-340). Rooms: 35. ☎ *68 47 44; FAX 68 34 10.* This is the best choice after the Balcón. It is equally clean and friendly, and also near good beaches. During high season it too fills up weeks in advance.

WHERE TO EAT

Try fried fish at any stall for delicious, inexpensive eating. For inexpensive sit-down-meals, try the line of restaurants just west of the city walls. At the next higher price level there is the **Balcón**, mentioned under the hotels above, and the attractive **el Rincon de Manolo**, on the same highway, about 1 k closer to town.

ZAHARA DE LOS ATUNES ★

Population: 1,891
Area code: 956; Zip code: 11393

30 k from Tarifa, turn left on the small road with a sign for the town, 11 k toward the coast.

This little fishing town, just being discovered, owns a long, lovely beach that is seldom crowded.

WHERE TO STAY

New hotels will probably change the situation, but for the time being choices are few.

EXPENSIVE ($100-$200)

Sol Atlanterra   1st-class
4 k east on the road to Atlanterra. Rooms: 284. ☎ *43 90 00; FAX 43 30 51; Telex 781 69). Open May through Oct.* Huge, and Miami-Beach looking, the hotel offers every service in a compound all its own. The question is why someone would come all the way to Spain to stay in a compound.

MODERATE ($50-$99)

Antonio   4th-class ★
1 k east on the road to Atlanterra. Rooms: 30. ☎ *43 91 41; FAX 43 91 35. Closed Nov.* This hotel is heavily booked, and with good reason. Here you are not part of a herd, the views are lovely, and good meals are available on the terrace.

WHERE TO EAT

Fried fish from stalls near the port are wonderful, but full meals can be had at the **Antonio** hotel, mentioned above, with lovely views, or from **Cortijo de la Plata**, about 4 k from town along the same east road.

VEJER DE LA FRONTERA ★★

Population: 12,100
Area code: 956; Zip code: 11150

Just off N-340, 71 k from Algeciras, or 50 k from Tarifa.

This is one of the most beautiful villages remaining in Spain— whitewashed houses atop a hill encased by ramparts, from which views of the countryside are stunning. Partially restored ruins of a **Moorish fortress** share the hill with the Gothic and Mudejar **Iglesia de San Salvador**, above an atmospheric labyrinth of a **Medieval Quarter** against the ramparts. There is no beach here, but the golden sands of Conil are only 12 kilometers away.

WHERE TO STAY

Only one is worth considering, but that one is special and reasonably priced.

MODERATE ($50-$99)

Convento de San Francisco   2nd-class ★★★
La Plazuela. Rooms: 25. ☎ *45 10 01; FAX 45 10 04.* The restoration of this 17th-century convent has been painstakingly and tastefully done by the family who owns it. Do not be put off by the entrance or lobby, nor by the fact that as a small establishment it does not offer every service. You are here for the rooms—lovely large bedrooms constructed from former monks' cells. Although not air-conditioned, night breezes usually encourage sound sleep.

CONIL DE LA FRONTERA ★★

Population: 13,289
Area code: 956; Zip code: 11140

Past Vejer on N-340 in 14 k is a left turn to the coast and Conil in 2.5 k.

This town is transforming quickly from a quiet fishing port into a resort, and the reason for the change is golden beaches that stretch to the horizons in both directions, and lining an exceptionally calm Atlantic. Hotels have begun to charge resort prices.

WHERE TO STAY

We list three small hotels, each with some character, unfortunately with prices higher than their official classification would lead one to expect.

EXPENSIVE ($100-$200)

la Gaviota   3rd-class ★

Pl. Nuestra Señora de las Virtudes. Rooms: 15. ☎ *44 08 36; FAX 44 09 80. Open Feb-Oct.* At least for the price you get a suite with cooking facilities. This is your place if you intend to dine in. The apartments are booked well before the high season.

Don Pelayo   3rd-class ★

Carreteria del Punto, 19. Rooms: 30. ☎ *44 20 30; FAX 44 50 58.* In a quiet area, and with nice sized rooms, this is probably your best choice, unless the idea of an apartment appeals.

Tres Jotas   3rd-class

C. San Sebastian. Rooms: 39. ☎ *44 04 50; FAX 44 04 50.* This is a functional place with good service and prices a tad lower than those above. But it is a tad less nice as well.

CÁDIZ ★

See the description under that heading above.

EL PUERTO DE SANTA MARÍA ★

Population: 61,032
Area code: 956; Zip code: 11500

From Cádiz head south along N-IV, splitting off to follow signs to Puerto Real, as it wraps north around the bay to el Puerto in 22 k.

The Rio Guadalete splits the town in two with **sherry bodegas** lining the south bank—offering tours and free samples in the mornings —and a fishing harbor lining the north. Also on the north bank is a lovely promenade leading to a restored **Moorish castle** with an attractive mansion beside it, and a pair of nice churches. About a tenminute walk north along the water, or a short drive, is the **Playa Puntillo**, a long stretch of fine beach.

WHERE TO STAY

Hotels are pricey.

EXPENSIVE ($100-$200)

Monasterio de San Miguel   1st-class ★★★

C. Larga, 27. Rooms: 132. ☎ *54 04 40; FAX 54 26 04.* This 18th-century convent recently was made over with luxury trappings as a hotel. It provides the extra features of an elegant cloister and church. This one is deluxe all the way.

MODERATE ($50-$99)

Los Cántaros   **2nd-class** ★
Curva, 2. Rooms: 39. ☎ *54 02 40; FAX 54 11 21.* The staff treats the clients well at this homey place. Prices are fair for what is offered.

WHERE TO EAT

Walk along the C. Ribera del Marisco for fresh fish from any outdoor bar. The city also offers a fine restaurant.

MODERATE ($20-$50)

El Patio   ★
Rufina Vergara, 1. ☎ *54 05 06.* A treat for the eyes, this restaurant, on a quiet square, is a former 18th-century inn arranged around a lovely patio. The food is good, without attaining excellence, at fair prices.
                              Amex, Diners, MasterCard and Visa accepted.

ROTA

Population: 25,291
Area code: 956; Zip code: 11520

From Puerto de Santa María head north along the coast on C-441 for 21 k, turning south at the sign for Rota, 6 k away.

There is a large U.S. naval base just outside the town which has resulted in fast food restaurants, cheap souvenir shops and resentment among the citizens that sometimes flares into protest. On the other hand, a series of truly lovely beaches runs for miles north of the town. But all this hardly matters, because accommodations are almost impossible to secure and expensive when gotten.

CHIPIONA

Population: 12,500
Area code: 956; Zip code: 11550

A lovely coast road goes north from Rota to join C-441 in 7 k, for another 8 k to Chipiona.

Chipiona is famous for curative waters which are piped into the fountain of the **Iglesia de Nuestra Señora de Regla**. In general, they attract an older Spanish crowd. Otherwise, this is a basic charming resort community with miles of lovely beaches constituting the **Playa de Regla**, running south of the lighthouse from Av. Regla. But decent hotels are scarce.

SANLÚCAR DE BARRAMEDA ★

Population: 48,390
Area code: 956; Zip code: 11540

9 k east of Chipona on C-441.

Sanlúcar has grown a grey band of boring houses around the older part of town, but retains character in the center. At the mouth of the Guadalquivir, it enjoys a nice river beach by the warmest of waters. This also is the port for shipping manzanilla sherry, so bodegas offer free tours and tastes. There are enough interesting churches and two palaces to occupy one's time.

WHERE TO STAY

Accommodations are difficult to find, since most of the hotels are small, though pleasant.

MODERATE ($50-$99)

Palacio de los Duquess de Medina Sidonia　　　　★★★★★
Conde de Niebla, 1. 3 Suites.☎ *36 01 61.* The Medina Sidonia family is one of the most illustrious in Spain—their ancestor commanded the Great Armada. The present duchess lets out a few rooms to us commoners in the renovated barn of their local mansion. Each suite has a fireplace and magnificent views. With only three rooms to rent, reservations are essential and the Palacio does not offer the services of a proper hotel. But if you are one of the lucky ones, you will talk about it for years.

Posada del Palacio　　　　　　　　　　　3rd-class ★★★
Caballeros, 11. Rooms: 13.☎ *36 48 40; FAX 36 50 60. Closed from the second week of Jan. until Feb.* A true find and newly renovated, the location and hotel have character and the clients are treated as guests.

Tartaneros　　　　　　　　　　　　　　R2nd-class ★★
Tartaneros, 8. Rooms: 22. ☎ *36 20 44; FAX 36 00 45.* This is a very comfortable hotel with a few extras in the rooms, such as a TV, to justify its price.

Los Helechos　　　　　　　　　　　　　R3rd-class ★
Pl. Madre de Dios, 9. Rooms: 16. ☎ *36 13 49; FAX 36 96 50.* This hotel feels like home, as it should because it is a house made into a hotel. Homey touches endear it. Parking is available for a fee.

WHERE TO EAT

Two good choices are on the Bajo de Guia beach. Both are well known and packed during high season, when reservations are essential.

MODERATE ($20-$50)

Bigote　　　　　　　　　　　　　　　　　　　★
Bajo de Guia. ☎ *36 26 96.* Little work went into the decor, but some-

one spends a lot of time searching for the freshest fish. Order any seafood, simply done, and you will be gratified.

Amex, Visa, and MasterCard accepted.

Mirador Doñana ★

Bajo de Guia. ☎ *36 42 05. Closed from the middle of Jan. through the middle of Feb.* The terrace offers views of the scene. Seafood is perfectly done. The large shrimp called *langostinos* are memorable, though not cheap.

The coast immediately north of Sanlucar consists of the huge **national park of de Doñana ★ ★**, with no public roads, so coastal passage northward is impossible. One has to circle the park by travelling to Seville and then west. However, the beaches further west have little to offer compared to those discussed.

From Sanlúcar C-441 east toward Lebrija reaches Las Cabezas de San Juan in 47 k, where the toll road N-IV heads speedily to **Seville***, 39 k away.*

COSTA DEL SOL ★ ★

The Costa del Sol is an international playground in which the Spanish are vastly outnumbered by visitors from Britain and Germany. What originally drew foreigners was the promise of warmth through seemingly limitless sunny days. They came in huge numbers, as did both older Americans and British to retire in the sun, forming compounds where most of the inhabitants speak no Spanish, and miles of high-rise hotels that line both the beaches and hills behind. The 120 mile stretch between Motril on the east and Gibraltar on the west that forms the heart of the Costa del Sol can no longer be described as attractive, and is more international than Spanish. Its beaches are shale, pebbles or grey grit, not the golden sand we dream of, and the waters can be more than a little polluted. (Search for areas flagged with "EC," which indicates that the water attains European Community cleanliness standards.) Why then does the Costa del Sol continue to be one of the most popular vacation spots in the world? The answer is simple: people come because it is where the people come. In high season it is an exciting, three-ring circus of crowds and activities, by night a constant round of parties and clubs. It is a people-place, not an historic or scenic area.

Of course the coast is not uniform. **Málaga ★**, the largest city in the area, roughly divides the Costa del Sol in half. It serves most people as a place to land or detrain then quickly leave, although it does possess some attractions. The towns to its east are the least crowded and remain more Spanish than international. Just west of Málaga is **Torremolinos** ★, the package vacation capital of the coast, to which young, working-class English flock in endless streams. Think of it as a Fort Lauderdale, with all the crowds and excitement that implies. Yet ten kilometers west is the family resort of **Fuengirola**, and twenty kilometers further is **Marbella** ★★ and its neighbor **San Pedro de Alcantara** ★, resorts for the beautiful people, yachts, golf and astronomically expensive luxury hotels. At the extreme west end is unique **Gibraltar** ★, still as British as it can be.

During July and August almost every beach, hotel and restaurant is crowded, and hotels raise their prices to twice those of other seasons. At other times accommodations are more reasonable, though the reason for coming—the excitement—pales. The entire coast is serviced by highway N-340 which traverses every city and town and slows traffic to a crawl. Predictably, this highway holds the record every year for the most accidents in Spain. Local buses also connect the entire coast, as does an electrified train. Flights to the coast land at Málaga, in the center, or at Gibraltar 120 k away on the western end. We describe the locales starting from the eastern end of the Costa del Sol and make our way west.

SALOBREÑA ★

Population: 8,119
Area code: 958; Zip code: 18680

*From **Granada** N-323 reaches Salobreña after a 65 k ride of lovely mountain views. From elsewhere, get to Granada and follow that same road.*

The town hangs on a steep hill 2 k inland from a nice beach (by the standards of the area), but offers charm and views to repay the need to walk uphill and down. Mountains rise behind the town and a plain stretches in front to the sea, while sugarcane plantations spread all around. Uphill is a fine restored **Moorish castle** which offers shaded **walks** and concerts in the summer.

WHERE TO STAY

Unfortunately accommodations are scarce in town, although two quiet places sit just outside.

MODERATE ($50-$99)

Salobreña   **2nd-class** ★
On N-340 4 k west toward Málaga. Rooms: 80. ☎ *61 02 61; FAX 61 01 01.* The hotel is not terribly attractive, but it offers every amenity

including a pool and tennis courts at a reasonable price for the area, and the views are attractive.

INEXPENSIVE (UNDER $50)

Salambina   4th-class ★★★

On N-340 1 k west toward Málaga. Rooms: 13. ☎ *61 00 37; FAX 61 13 28.* This little charmer presents lovely views over cane fields to the sea. Its prices are reasonable. Rooms should be booked well ahead for a stay in high season.

ALMUÑÉCAR ★

Population: 16,141
Area code: 958; Zip code: 18690

A 15 k drive west from Salobreña on N-340.

The bad news is the beach (shale) and the sea-water (less than crystal clear). The good news is that the old center of town retains charm and history and a nice promenade along the beach, unfortunately lined by high-rises. And prices have not risen as high here as elsewhere along the coast. Extensive remains of a Roman aqueduct lie a half-mile west.

WHERE TO STAY

Quite a number of moderate and inexpensive hotels are available, from which we offer a selection.

MODERATE ($50-$99)

Goya   R3rd-class ★

Av. de Europa. Rooms: 24. ☎ *63 05 50; FAX 63 11 92. Closed from the middle of Jan. to the middle of Feb.* The hotel is well maintained by staff that try to make your stay pleasant.

Playa de San Cristóbal   R3rd-class ★

Pl. San Cristobal, 5. Rooms: 22. ☎ *63 11 12. Open from the middle of March to Oct.* This is an endearing little hotel, family run, with homey touches.

INEXPENSIVE (UNDER $50)

Carmen   R4th-class ★

Av. de Europa, 8. Rooms: 24. ☎ *63 14 13.* Prices are low and the rooms are comfortable.

NERJA ★★

Population: 12,012
Area code: 952; Zip code: 29780

22 k west on N-340 along a lovely stretch of road.

By the not so remarkable expedient of keeping developments outside town, Nerja has been able to combine popularity and attendant crowds while preserving its attractiveness. Nerja is most famous for its **Balcón de Europa**, a clifftop promenade above the sea, so dubbed by King Alfonso XII when he paused to admire the view. Four kilometers east is a series of remarkable caves, the **Cuevas de Nerja**, large enough to hold summer concerts inside. (Open 9:30 a.m. to 6 p.m. in summer; from 10 a.m. to 1:30 p.m. and from 3-6 p.m. the rest of the year. Admission: 300 ptas.)

WHERE TO STAY

Good choices are unfortunately few.

EXPENSIVE ($100-$200)

Parador de Nerja   1st-class ★★★
Playa de Burriana-Tablazo. Rooms: 73. ☎ *252 00 50; FAX 252 19 97.* This is a modern-style parador of no architectural distinction but with a lovely garden that provides fabulous views, like those of the Balcón de Europa. A few of the rooms share this view, but most overlook a central patio. An elevator descends to the rocky beach, and tennis courts are available.

Balcón de Europa   2nd-class ★
Paseo Balcón de Europa, 1. Rooms: 102. ☎ *252 08 00; FAX 252 44 90; Telex 79503.* This modern businessperson-type hotel would not be noteworthy were it not for its situation atop the cliffs.

MODERATE ($50-$99)

Portofino   4th-class ★
Puerta de Mar, 4. Rooms: 12. ☎ *52 01 50.* Open March through Oct. Better known for its restaurant, this establishment offers a few nice rooms and the same view from the clifftop that the other hotels charge a bundle for.

MÁLAGA ★

See the description under its separate heading.

TORREMOLINOS ★

Population: 29,000
Area code: 952; Zip code: 29620

Some refer to this as the Costa del Sol for lower classes. If true, then these are the people who have the most fun. The city thrives on a mix of British, Americans, Germans and Scandinavians, from bank tellers, to secretaries, to outright crooks (since British extradition laws make Spain a partial asylum), most wearing very little and/or something outrageous. Shops that run from the most camp souvenir galleries to eccentric shoppes, as well as restaurants and hotels, have sprung up to service the motley crowd. Here you can drink or eat in English pubs, dine on authentic smorgasbord and sauerbratten, and dance until dawn, when it is time to squeeze into a spot on the body-to-body beach. The experience is entirely bizarre, and fun if in the proper mood.

WHERE TO STAY

Hotels deal mainly in package tours which means their standards are below what the individual traveller expects. Of course, if vacancies exist, hotels are willing to rent to individuals, at a higher price. There is little to choose between establishments, except price, so we list the relevant information by category.

EXPENSIVE ($100-$200)

Meliá Torremolinos   1st-class
   Av. Carlotta Alessandri, 109. Rooms: 281. ☎ *238 05 00; FAX 238 05 38; Telex 77060.*

Pes Espada   1st-class
   Via Imperial, 11. Rooms: 205. ☎ *238 03 00; FAX 237 28 01; Telex 77655.*

Alhoa Puerto-Sol   1st-class
   Via Imperial, 55. Rooms: 418. ☎ *238 70 66; FAX 238 57 01; Telex 77339.*

Meliá Costa del Sol   1st-class
   Paseo Maritimo. Rooms: 540. ☎ *238 66 77; FAX 238 64 17; Telex 77326.*

Cervantes   2nd-class
   Las Mercedes. Rooms: 393.☎ *238 40 33; FAX 238 48 57; Telex 77174.*

Don Pablo   1st-class
   Paseo Maritimo. Rooms: 443. ☎ *238 38 88; FAX 238 37 83; Telex 77252.*

MODERATE ($50-$99)

Sidi Lago Rojo   2nd-class
   Miami, 5. Rooms: 144. ☎ *238 76 66; FAX 238 08 91; Telex 77395.*

Don Pedro   2nd-class
   Av. del Lido. Rooms: 272. ☎ *238 68 44; FAX 238 37 83; Telex 77252.*

Isabel   2nd-class
   Paseo Maritimo, 97. Rooms: 40. ☎ *238 17 44; FAX 238 11 98. Open Mar. through Nov.*

Don Paquito   R3rd-class
   Av. del Lido. Rooms: 49. ☎ *238 78 58; FAX 238 37 83; Telex 77252.*

FUENGIROLA

Population: 30,606
Area code: 952; Zip code: 29640

16k. west along N-340.

This town is a lesser version of Torremolinos, without the compensations of liveliness and camp. Move on.

MARBELLA

Population: 67,882
Area code: 952; Zip code: 29600

27 k west of Fuengirola, and 43 k west of Torremolinos.

The contrast between the two previous towns, and this one could not be greater. Its name comes from *mar bella*, "beautiful sea," which is a slight exaggeration, but Marbella has grown into a haven for the rich and for those living richly for a week or two. The average income here ranks with the highest in Europe, and society pages the world over report on summer happenings. Hotels and villas line the beach for ten miles in each direction, and the huge yacht basin of Puerto Bañus, 7 k west, is filled all summer with almost 1000 impressive boats. Befitting the clientele, everything is expensive, although if money is not an object, one can live as well here as anywhere in the world.

WHERE TO STAY

These include the most luxurious hotels in the world, some with one or more world-class golf courses, others with every sport imaginable, some that act as spas that pamper, and others combining all of the above. But the cost of a double can breast $500 per-night. For this one area in Spain we include a category above the Very Expensive, for doubles that cost over $300 per night. Hotels do exist at more reasonable levels, however.

VERY VERY EXPENSIVE ($300+)

Los Monteros   Deluxe ★★★★

On N-340 going east toward Málaga, 5.5 k outside of town. Rooms: 171. ☎ *277 17 00; FAX 282 58 46; Telex 77059.* If you want the most expensive of a very expensive lot, this is the place. Deluxe in every way, including a superb restaurant with French flavor. The atmosphere, on the other hand, is very British, and the garden is simply awesome.

Puente Romano   Deluxe ★★★★

On N-340 going west toward Gibraltar, 3.5 k outside of town. Rooms: 184. ☎ *277 01 00; FAX 277 57 66; Telex 77399.* Another wonderful garden, this time containing a real Roman bridge. Rooms are housed in separate buildings that dot the grounds. The service and accommodations are deluxe in every way, and the tennis pro is Manolo Santana.

Marbella Club   1st-class ★ ★

On N-340 going west toward Gibraltar, 3k. outside of town. Rooms: 95. ☎ *277 13 00; FAX 282 98 84; Telex 77319.* This was the first of the grand hotels in the area, the one that turned Marbella into the haunt of the jet set. The surrounding grounds could hardly be more lovely, but the rooms are a mixed lot—from fabulous to barely adequate. Considering its prices, the place needs work.

MODERATE ($50-$99)

Naguele   R4th-class ★ ★

On N-340 going west toward Gibraltar, 3.5 k outside of town. Rooms: 17. ☎ *77 16 88. Open March through Oct. 15.* The irony is perfect: this hotel is just yards away from the two previous choices whose guests pay almost ten times as much. Of course you do not get their gorgeous gardens, private beach or luxury rooms, but you do get the same quiet location. Note the small number of rooms, however—reservations are a must.

Lima   R3rd-class ★

Av. Antonio Belon, 2. Rooms: 64. ☎ *277 05 00; FAX 286 30 91.* The architecture is not memorable, but the comfortable rooms are within two blocks of the beach.

WHERE TO EAT

Per square kilometer, Marbella offers more superb restaurants than anywhere else in Spain. Though such fine meals are not inexpensive, prices tend to be fair, and far less than what the hotel rates would lead one to expect.

EXPENSIVE ($50+)

La Hacienda   ★ ★ ★ ★

9 k east along N-340 and an additional 1.5 k north. ☎ *283 12 67. Closed Mon., Tues., and from the third week of Nov. to the last week of Dec.* The restaurant is housed in an elegant villa overlooking the sea. The food is sublime. The chef is Belgian, and his lamb matches the best we ever tasted. Reservations are required.

Amex, Diners, MasterCard and Visa accepted.

La Fonda   ★ ★ ★

Pl. Santo Cristo, 10. ☎ *277 25 12. Open for dinner only, and closed Sun.* The restaurant is situated on a lovely square, in a lovely old house filled with lovely things—all contributing to the romance. The food ranges over French, Spanish and Austrian (the nationality of the owner). Every dish is close to perfect, and the deserts defy description. Reservations are required.

Amex, Diners, MasterCard and Visa accepted.

ESTEPONA ★

Population: 24,261
Area code: 952; Zip code: 29680

28 k west of Marbella on N-340, and 84 k west of Málaga.

Although the town itself is drab and developers have arrived in force, a pleasant flowered promenade remains along the pebble beach and the plazas retain their charm. Estepona is still a fishing village, maintaining the largest fleet on the coast.

WHERE TO STAY

In and around this town are some of the best values on the coast.

MODERATE ($50-$99)

Santa Marta   **3rd-class ★★★**
11 k east along N-340 to Marbella. Rooms: 37. ☎ *278 07 16. Open April through Oct.* The hotel consists of bungalows around a beautiful garden, similar to some of Marbella's very, very expensive hotels. Although the rooms are by no means grand, and some are fading, the setting is as quiet and almost as lovely as those expensive hotels provide, at a small percentage of their price.

Buenavista   **P2nd-class ★**
Paseo Maritimo, 180. Rooms: 38. ☎ *80 01 37.* Nothing grand here, but basic accommodations at fair prices produce a good deal.

From Estepona N-340 goes west to San Roque in 35 k, the last part of which is scenic. Signs direct to La Linea, 7 k south, the border for Gibraltar, and the end of the Costa del Sol.

GIBRALTAR ★★

Population: 28,339
Area code: 956; no zip code

From **Seville** *take either N-IV or the toll road A-4, (E-5) south toward Jerez in 84 k. Continuing past Jerez toward Cádiz, pick up N-340 at San Fernando in 38 k. N-340 takes you to La Linea, the border, in 119 k. From* **Granada** *take N-342 for 92 k to exit #1 at Salinas, where you pick up N-351 to Málaga for 60 k. From Málaga follow the slow coast road N-340 for 120 k to the border. From* **Córdoba** *take N-331 for 116 k to N-334 for 1 k east before picking up N-331 again for a 57 k ride to Málaga. The slow coast road, N-340, leads to the border in 120 k.*

The "Rock," which natives refer to as "Gib," does indeed look like the Prudential logo. It is a spit of land 4 miles long by half a mile wide, ninety percent of which is taken up by precipitous mountain. This was one of the two ancient Pillars of Hercules, paired with the comparable peak of Gebel Musa directly across the straits. The Phoenicians promoted a legend that the world ended at these straits in order to frighten others away from their colonies further west. The name "Gibraltar" comes from *Gebel Tarik*, Tarik's Mountain in Arabic, named after the leader of the first Moorish incursion into Spain. It was seized by the English in 1704, during the War of Spanish Succession, ostensibly on behalf of the Hapsburgs, but more likely so the British could control a base in the Mediterranean. Ever since, this British colony has been a sore spot in Spain's side.

For decades the Spanish tried to isolate Gibraltar by barring entry from Spain. But in 1985 the border at La Linea was opened and is now crossed by thousands of tourists, many attracted by Gibraltar's freeport status for duty-free liquor and VAT-free goods. Officially the currency is the British Pound Sterling, but Spanish pesetas are accepted everywhere. Gibraltar has pleasant beaches on its east side, the town on its west side and the Rock in between with its caves and "apes". Half a day covers everything.

From the border at La Linea you cross the end of the airport field and funnel into Main Street, lined with pubs and duty free shops. At the end of the street is the **cable car ★ ★ ★** station *(closed Sun.)* for a ride to the top of the rock. Buy a one-way ticket and walk to additional sights on the way down. Halfway to the top the cable car stops at the **Apes' Den ★ ★**. The half-tame monkeys, called apes because they are tailless, are a mischievous lot, so watch cameras and anything loose they might grab. Feedings are at 8 a.m. and 4 p.m. The top of the Rock presents unrivaled views overlooking Europa Point where the Atlantic and Mediterranean Oceans meet. On clear days Morocco is visible, 11 miles away.

From the top take Saint Michael's Road south to **Saint Michael's Cave**. This was a hospital during the Second World War but now serves as an eerie auditorium where summer concerts are held. Follow Queen's Road north to its end for Upper Town Road and the **Gibraltar Laser Experience ★** *(closed Sun.)* which recreates World War II events and displays paraphernalia, all in a tunnel used for shelter during that war. Below it are the remains of a **Moorish castle** from the 14th century. Steep alleys lead to the northern end of Main Street. At Bomb House Lane on the right is the **Gibraltar Museum** *(closed Sun.)*, with exhibits depicting the history of Gibraltar, as well as some nicely preserved Moorish baths. Opposite the museum stands the **tourist office**. The **Governors' Residence** is at the next Main Street corner. Here, one of those **Changing of the Guard** ★★ ceremonies is presented on Tues., starting at about 10:20 a.m., as only the British do them.

WHERE TO STAY

Hotels tend to be expensive on Gibraltar, though a few are moderate in price. The British reduced their military garrison by half in 1990 and it remains to be seen what impact that will have on the hotel situation.

VERY EXPENSIVE ($200+)

The Rock Hotel   1st-class ★★★★

3 Europa Road. Rooms: 143. ☎ *730 00; FAX 730 13; Telex 2238.* This is the luxury hotel of Gibraltar, looking as a British colonial hotel should, with a huge terrace and ceiling fans. Refurbishing in pinks and oranges was completed recently to sustain its preeminent position on Gib. It overlooks the town from a lovely garden, with views over town and sea.

EXPENSIVE ($100-$200)

Caleta Palace   1st-class ★★

Catalan Bay Road (on the west side of the isthmus). Rooms: 153. ☎ *765 01; FAX 710 50; Telex 2345.* This is the hotel for relaxing in style near some of the best beach on the isthmus. Every room presents beautiful sea views.

MODERATE ($50-$99)

Bristol   4th-class ★★

10 Cathedral Square. Rooms: 60. ☎ *768 00; Telex 2253.* Located by the cathedral in the heart of town, with a nice garden, this hotel manages to convey the sense of a colonial hotel. Wood paneling helps, as does the comfortable furniture in ample rooms. However, the prices were pushing the "moderate" limit when last we visited, and may have passed it by the time you arrive.

Queen's Hotel   4th-class ★

1 Boyd Street. Rooms: 24. ☎ *740 00.* Easy to find, next to the cable car station, this hotel has little character, but a game room, sun deck and agreeable service. The bedrooms are clean as a whistle and nicely decorated.

WHERE TO EAT

None of the more expensive places seem worth their charges, but the pubs and fish-and-chips places remain fun for a meal or two.

DIRECTORY

INFORMATION • Located in Cathedral Square, near the governor's residence. ☎ 764 00.

POST OFFICE AND TELEPHONES • The post office is at 102 Main Street, four blocks north of the governor's residence.

POLICE • The main station is on Irish Town Street, ☎ 725 00.

GRANADA ★★★★★

Population: 262,182
Area code: 958; Zip code: 18000

*From **Madrid** A-4 (E-5) runs south to Ocaña in 63 k, where N-IV (E-5) continues south to Bailén in 235 k more. From **Bailén**, N-323 (E-902) reaches Granada in 130 k, for a total trip of 427 k. From **Córdoba** N-432 goes directly southeast to Granada in 166 k. From **Seville** N-334 east toward Antiquera changes its designation to N-342 at Salinas before completing a trip of 251 k.*

Only Granada, in all the world, presents the Thousand and One Nights in palpable reality. Although Grenada was not among the major cities of the Moors during most of their 700-year stay in Spain, it was their last capital and thus the culmination of their artistry, so impressive that Christian conquerors could not bear to destroy it. And so the last palace of the Moors, the Alhambra, remains standing today.

Granada first attained prominence when Jaén was captured by the Spanish in 1246, forcing the Moorish ruler of the principality—consisting of the southern coast of Spain from Algeciras to Almeria—to move his capital southward. He chose Granada, which thus became the final capital of the dynasty of Nasrids, for his family name was Ibn el Ahmar Nasir. He learned from this defeat to deal with the Christians rather than to fight them. His successors used diplomacy to stave off the Christians, even allying with them to capture Seville, and by doing so prospered. But the Christians seized piece after piece of the rest of the Moorish empire, until Granada remained the last bastion, swollen with refugees from lost domains. Granada grew to 200,000 souls by the 14th century, about four times the London of those times, and building began on the Alhambra Palace.

Toward the end of the 15th-century revolt weakened Granada. Caliph Muley Hassan fell in love with a Christian woman named *Zoraya* (Morning Star), who had converted to Islam. This love threatened the position of his principal wife who fled with her young son before the caliph could repudiate her. She returned with supporters angered by the caliph's severe tax policies, deposed the old caliph and placed her son Abu Abdallah, known to the Christians as Boabdil, on the throne. Granada's rule fell to a child-king, who reigned over subjects divided into those supporting the young calif and those supporting the previous one. It was a perfect time to attack; Isabella and Ferdinand declared war. Twice Boabdil sallied forth with his army, and twice was captured and forced to cede territory. After the second loss, he vowed never to leave Granada again. By 1491 the Christians had cut Granada off from the sea and all other avenues of supply, and sat down for a siege. Eight months later, on January 2, 1492, the city surrendered and Boabdil marched away with tears in his eyes. The Catholic monarchs entered the city dressed in Moorish clothes. Seven hundred and eighty-one years of Moorish domination had ended.

Within decades the Christians expelled the Moors from Spain and burned most of Granada, including all its mosques. Only the Alhambra remained untouched, for its beauty lent it sanctity. Although Ferdinand and Isabella chose this city as their final resting place, decline continued. The final blow was the expulsion in 1609 of the Moroscos, people of Moorish descent, depleting Granada of most of its population. The city numbered less than 50,000 citizens by the 18th century. But through good times and bad, the stream of visitors never abated. The most famous tourist was Washington Irving, who lived for three months in the ruins of the Alhambra Palace, and there began his evocative *Tales of the Alhambra*. Today both tourism and revitalized agriculture have again brought prosperity to Granada.

Situated in the low foothills of the Sierra Nevada, the city encompasses three peaks in a row—the Alhambra sits on the middle and highest, beside which the smaller hill of Sacromonte rises, and Monte Mauror stands to its south. Most of the city proper lies in the valley below these hills and west, although the Albaicín, the old quarter, nestles between the two hills of the Alhambra and Sacromonte. Views from the lower city show the Alhambra shining atop its hill against a backdrop of the snow-clad Sierra Nevada.

Granada also retains a significant Gypsy population, as all visitors discover. The women sell flowers, while the men hover around. They can be very insistent; and valuables should be carefully watched.

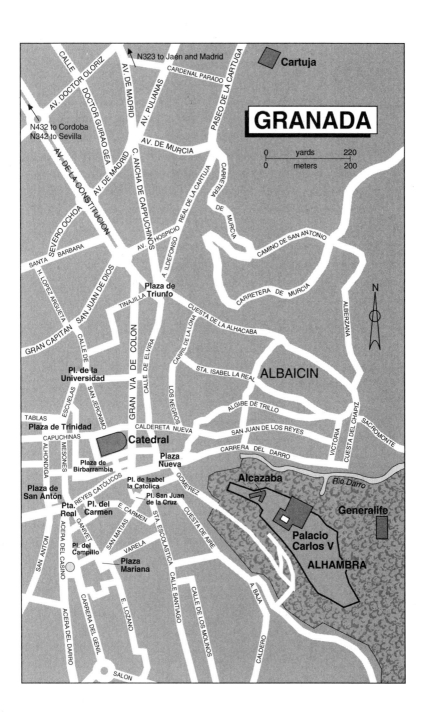

Cartuja

GRANADA

| 0 | yards | 220 |
| 0 | meters | 200 |

N323 to Jaén and Madrid

CARDENAL PARADO

CALLE

AV. DOCTOR OLORIZ

AV. DE MADRID

AV. PULIANAS

DOCTOR GUIRAO GEA

N432 to Cordoba
N342 to Sevilla

PASEO DE LA CARTUJA

AV. DE MURCIA

C. ANCHA DE CAPPUCHINOS

AV. DE MADRID

AV. DE LA CONSTITUCION

CARRETERA

DE

MURCIA

AV. HOSPICIO

A. ILDEFONSO

REAL DE LA CARTUJA

CAMINO DE SAN ANTONIO

SANTA BARBARA

H. LOPEZ ARGUETA

SEVERO OCHOA

SAN JUAN DE DIOS

Plaza de
Triunfo

TINAJILLA

CUESTA DE LA ALHACABA

CARRETERA DE MURCIA

ALBERZANA

N

GRAN CAPITAN

CALLE DE

GRAN VIA DE COLON

CALLE DE ELVIRA

CARRIL DE LA LONA

CUESTA DEL CHAPIZ

SACROMONTE

Pl. de la
Universidad

STA. ISABEL LA REAL

ALBAICIN

ESCUELAS

SAN JERONIMO

LOS NEGROS

ALGIBE DE TRILLO

VICTORIA

TABLAS

Plaza de Trinidad

CALDERETA NUEVA

SAN JUAN DE LOS REYES

CAPUCHINAS

ALHONDIGA

MESONES

Plaza de
Birbarrambia

Catedral

Plaza
Nueva

CARRERA DEL DARRO

Alcazaba

Rio Darro

Plaza de
San Antón

REYES CATOLICOS

Pl. de Isabel
la Catolica

GOMEREZ

Pta.
Real

Pl. del
Carmen

E CARMEN

Pl. San Juan
de la Cruz

STA. ESCOLASTICA

CUESTA DE AIRE

Generalife

SAN ANTON

ACERA DEL CASINO

GANIVET

SAN MATIAS

Pl. del
Campillo

VARELA

Plaza
Mariana

**Palacio
Carlos V**

ALHAMBRA

CARRERA DEL GENIL

E. LOZANO

CALLE SANTIAGO

CALLE DE LOS MOLINOS

A. BAJA

ACERA DEL DARRO

SALON

CALDERO

Parking is available on the Alhambra hill, but parking in the city below is far from the sights. The best course is to begin at the Alhambra, walk or taxi down, then taxi back up to your car.

*From **Madrid** and north, Granada is entered on Av. de Madrid, which arrives at a traffic circle just after passing the University on the left. Take Av. de la Constitutión to the left. At the next intersection, in one very long block past a park, go left on Av. del Hospicio, then right at the first opportunity onto Av. Andaluces. Round the circle at Pl. del Triunfo to continue out the opposite end on C. Elvira. Elvira ends in about ten blocks at C. Reyes Católicos. Turn left here into the Pl. Nueva, and take the first right onto the narrow Cuesta de Gomerez, which leads through the gate to the Alhambra precinct. Signs direct to the Alhambra Palace and parking.*

*From **Córdoba** and west Granada is entered on Av. de la Constitución. After passing a large park on the left, follow the directions from Madrid above. From the **Costa del Sol** and south traffic is funnelled into Acara del Casino which ends at the large Pl. Puerta Real. Take the large street right, Reyos Católicos, for about eight blocks to the Pl. Nueva. Take the right at the far end of the plaza, the narrow Cuesta de Gomerez, for 6 blocks through the gate to the Alhambra Precinct. Signs direct to the Alhambra Palace and parking.*

The **Alhambra Palace** ★★★★★ ranks at the top of any list of the most beautiful and fascinating buildings in the world. As a bonus the **Alcazaba** ★, a 13th-century fortress, stands beside it, the stunning Renaissance **palace of Carlos V** ★★ abuts it, and the lovely summer palace of the Moors, the **Generalife** ★★★, perches above. The Alhambra Precinct alone requires rushing to complete in half a day. Below the Alhambra, in the city proper, is the moving and elegant **Capilla Real** ★★★★, the burial place of Ferdinand and Isabella, beside an impressive **cathedral** ★. The old quarter of the **Albaicín** ★ is worth exploring, for it is a maze of whitewashed houses with beautiful patios that affords lovely views of the Alhambra above. Two churches merit a look—the **Carthusian Monastery** ★, north of the city center, and **San Juan de Dios** ★, not far from the cathedral. By hurrying and hitting only highpoints, Granada can be experienced in a day, but is much more enjoyable in two.

ALHAMBRA PRECINCT

A steep climb begins before passing through the entry gate to the precinct. This gate, the *Puerta Las Granadas* (Pomegranates' Gate) was erected by Carlos V in 1536 on the site of a former Moorish portal. Past this entrance waits an enchanted forest, where all becomes suddenly quiet with nothing visible but stately elms, planted by the duke of Wellington in the 19th century. Signs direct pedestrians to the **Puerta de la Justicia**, their entrance, and cars to the **Puerta de Coches** by a roundabout, but scenic route. One combined ticket serves all the sights. The proper order in which to visit the various sights is an issue. The best course is to see the palace of Carlos V first, for it pales after the Alhambra, and the same point holds for the Alcazaba. Then see the Alhambra, followed by the lovely walk to the gardens of the Generalife. However, this timing is made difficult by the fact that tickets now include set times of entry to the Alhambra and palácio. Do not miss your appointed time, for the ticket is invalid thereafter.

Open Mon.-Sat. from 9 a.m. to 8 p.m. (closes at 6 p.m. in winter). Open Sun. from 9:30 a.m. to 6 p.m. Illuminated on Wed. and Sat. nights from 8-10 p.m., for a separate charge of 300 ptas. Admission: 525 ptas. for the Alhambra Palace, Alcazaba, Generalife and palace of Carlos V; free after 3 p.m. on Sun.

The palace of Carlos V lies directly ahead, if entering from the Puerta de la Justicia, or to the left, if entering from the Puerta de Coches.

Palacio de Carlos V

Because he so loved the site Carlos V wanted a palace of his own adjoining the Alhambra, though his love was not so pure that it prevented him from destroying about a third of the Alhambra Palace—all the private royal rooms—to gain space. As his architect he used the Italian Machuca who had trained with Michelangelo, to plan a severely neoclassical structure. The design is wholly elegant, so much that it seems too austere to inhabit, although it delights as pure design. The plan is a circle inside a square. The outer face emphasizes two stories with rows of regular windows distinguished by alternating piedmonts and circles above, and separated by Ionic pilasters on the upper story. Inside comes the shock of a huge open circular patio, formed of simple Doric columns below and Ionic columns above with recesses intended for statues. On at least one occasion a bullfight was held in this patio. The original plan included a huge dome to cover the central patio, but the building was never finished and seems never to have been inhabited, in fact, by Carlos V or by anyone else.

To the left, on the ground floor, is the **Museo de Art Hispano-Musuleman** *(open Mon.-Fri. 10 a.m. to 2 p.m., with a separate admission charge).* It contains objects found in the Alhambra area, including many pieces of original decoration, a cistern with lions attacking gazelles and a huge blue pitcher almost as tall as a person. On the second floor is the **Museo de Bellas Artes** *(open Tues.-Sun. 10 a.m. to 2 p.m., with a separate admission charge).* It displays works done by Granada artists, including paintings by Cano, but also a fine Limoges enamel triptych of the Crucifixion from the early 16th century.

Alcazaba ★

To the left (west) of the palacio de Carlos V is an open area known as the Pl. de los Aljibes (cisterns). The reservoir beneath was constructed by the Catholic monarchs to collect water, for the Christians did not know how to work the existing Moorish system. The Alcazaba stands to the left (west) of this plaza.

A fortress (alcazaba) has existed on this eminently defensible site since the tenth century, though the present structure dates from the 13th. The fortress adds a 12-foot thickness of wall to that surrounding the entire Alhambra precinct. Sturdy square towers gave defenders secure places from which to fire down on attackers. The tower in the northwest corner, called the **Torre de le Vela**, was the one from which Cardinal Mendoza, sent ahead to ascertain that the town was safe, raised the flag of Christian Spain to signal that the city was theirs. Today it offers splendid views over the city and the Alhambra Palace, with the Sierra Nevada behind. A plaque nearby quotes the haunting lament of a Moorish poet: Nothing is sadder than to be blind in Granada.

Alhambra Palace ★★★★★

Ibn el Ahmar Nasir (a.k.a. Muhammad I), founder of the Nasrid dynasty, began a palace on this site in the 13th century, but little of the original remains. Of what survives, the Court of Myrtles was built for Yusuf I in the middle of the 14th century, the Court of the Lions for Muhammad V near the end of that century, and the Tower of the Infantas for Muhammad VII at the close of the 14th century.

The facade is of no architectural interest, for Islamic palaces are intended as private places, hiding all the luxury from public view. Further, tradition called for each new ruler to add rooms of his own, rather than occupy his predecessor's quarters. Thus, the palace is a compound consisting of numerous rooms, rather than a unified structure. The Alhambra did separate into three areas. One contained the living accommodations for the caliph. That part was destroyed to build Carlos V's palace. Another area consisted of public rooms for ceremonies—such as audiences with the caliph or his ministers—and for music, or other entertainments. Several of these survive—the Mexuar, Hall of the Ambassadors, Kings' Chamber, Hall of the Two Sisters and Abencerrajes Gallery. A final part sheltered the close staff of the caliph, most importantly his harem. Note that the names today applied to the rooms are generally fanciful and give little indication of the original names or uses.

No consideration was given to permanence or future generations in designing these rooms, they served only for the enjoyment of one owner. Construction was of brick, wood and, especially, stucco, molded and carved into the most intricate designs, then painted and gilded, but eminently perishable. In 1591 gunpowder exploded outside the walls near the Court of the Lions, causing great damage. In the 19th century French troops left explosives when they retreated from bivouac here, which fortunately did not go off. But in general, centuries of neglect exacted a heavy toll on such fragile materials.

Reconstruction has been under way for almost a century. If what you see looks too new to be original, that is because it is, but all has been restored with the greatest authenticity to suggest the original look. Still, the original feeling would have been different from what you see today, for the rooms would have been furnished, Persian carpets would have lined the floors, metal and glass lanterns would have provided soft light off brightly painted decorative wood and stucco. The miracle of the Alhambra is that despite reconstruction and the loss of furniture and paint it still captivates as no other buildings can. Very likely its appeal is for the way of life this architecture presents, so different from anything Western. There is no attempt to awe with size, only with beauty. No room is further than a few feet from an outdoor patio playing water for both its sight and sound, and gardens are never more than a step away.

Entrance is into the **Mexuar**, from the Arabic *Mashwar*, "audience chamber." The balcony was added by Isabella and Ferdinand and still bears original traces of 15th-century painted design. At the end of the room Isabella and Ferdinand added an oratory which involved lowering the original floor, for Christians preferred to stand to look out of windows, while Moors sat. The exit door on the left was cut through the walls for tourists.

That doorway leads to the **Patio de Cuarto Dorado**, redecorated in Mudejar style after the Reconquest, but with an elegant low fountain. Across the patio is the facade of the **Palace of Comares**, from 1370, which serves as a fine sample of the Alhambra aesthetic. Simple rectangular portals are surrounded by the most refined carved stucco designs. Windows above are fitted with intricate wooden screens, *mashrabia*, to allow the ladies of the court to see out without being seen. The left portal goes to royal apartments, the right once admitted to administrative offices, no longer existing.

Take the left portal into a small room then go left again into the glorious **Patio de Los Arrayanes** (Court of the Myrtles). A central reflecting pool is filled by small fountains at either end and lined by Myrtle bushes. By reflection the pool doubles the arcades at both ends to emphasize the harmony of simple arches and ornate decoration. The center arch is higher than the others to display a more ornate arch behind it that leads into an end room. Around the sides of the pool are four sets of chambers for wives, with alcoves for their divans, but little surviving decoration. The room at the far end (south) was destroyed to construct the palace of Carlos V. Before entering the near end, notice the exquisite carved design of its original doors. They lead into the apartment for the caliph, the **Sala de la Barca**, with alcoves on either end for divans, showing that it served as a bedroom. A lovely wood ceiling above has a half dome on either end so the caliph could see "stars" as he closed his eyes. At the rear is the magnificent **Solón de Embajadores** (Room of the Ambassadors), the audience chamber of the palace. Here the caliph would sit, framed and made dazzling by its light, in the recess of the center window to receive embassies. Decoration on the walls, of amazing complexity, would have been even more startling with original paint, and almost prevents the eyes from rising to an astonishing ceiling that ascends to a dome symbolizing heaven.

Return to the Patio de los Arrayanes and follow the left side to the next to last portal, the open one. Before going though into one of the great wonders of the Alhambra, enter the end arcade for a look at the basement of the palace of Carlos V, just to remember how cold Christian architecture became two centuries after the Alhambra. It seems altogether inhuman after a taste of the Alhambra.

Through the portal, after a small chamber for a caliph's wife, comes the **Sala de los Mozárabes**, whose ceiling was once highly praised but suffered great damage from an explosion. But it is difficult to concentrate on this room when the **Patio de los Leones** beckons. The hall opens to a pavilion of slender columns with unique capitals supporting stalactite arches and domes. Across the way, past the fountain, is its twin. The fountain rests on the backs of twelve charming lions who give the patio its name. Various state apartments ring the patio with entrances off a columned arcade. On the center of the right side is the **Sala de los Abencerrajes**, named for a clan who supported Boabdil and his mother in their rebellion against the reigning caliph. Tradition says the former caliph murdered the leaders of this family before ceding his throne, and sees remains of that blood in stains on the floor. The doors are lovely and the stalactite ceiling is a wonder. At the far end of the patio is the **Sala de los Reyes**, three rooms in a row, named for the painting of ten seated Moors over the central room. (The Christians thought Moors had kings.) Given Islamic strictures against painted figures, these 14th-century paintings on leather probably were executed by Christians. Off to the left side of the patio is the **Sala de**

las Dos Hermanas (Two Sisters), fancifully named for two marble slabs in the pavement, although the room may indeed have once formed part of the harem. It possesses the most amazing of the surviving stalactite, or honeycombed, domed ceilings said to contain five thousand individual cells. How it manages to be beautiful amid the incredible detail is one of art's mysteries. The walls too are rich in decoration. The Arabic inscription that looks so elegant, actually commemorates the circumcision of a caliph's son. Opposite the entrance, a window retains the only surviving Moorish shutter in the palace, although most windows originally had them.

A portal at the rear lets into the **Sala de los Ajimeces**, named for the windows of its porch that give a lovely view of the **Patio de Lindaraja** below, originally with a reflecting pool like the other patios. Once more the ceilings are worth admiration. A corridor at the end leads across the patio to rooms remodeled by Carlos V. It was here that Washington Irving stayed to study the beauties and myths of the Alhambra. At the far end of these apartments a modern corridor runs to the **Tocador de la Reina** (queen's dressing room) in a tower, remodeled by Elizabeth of Parma, wife of Felipe V, and hung with paintings. Stairs descend to a patio with four cypresses. A sign points to **baños** (baths). Here was the original *hamman*, or bath, of the palace, in the form of a later remodeling by Carlos V.

Cross the Patio de Lindaraja to enter the main gardens of the Alhambra. Ahead and to the left is the **Torre de las Damas**, the oldest surviving part of the palace—dating from the beginning of the 14th century—and not in the best condition. The pool is watched over by two Moorish lions rescued from a hospital in the city below. The pavilion is simple, since columns have replaced the original carved stucco piers in the rear wall, but the tower retains some fine workmanship inside. Several other towers in the Alhambra walls are worth visiting, especially the **Torre de la Captiva** (Imprisoned Woman), a miniature palace three towers further along the walls, and the **Torre del las Infantas** (Princesses), next in line and late in period but sumptuously decadent.

From the Torre de las Infantas, it is worth a minute to return in the direction of the palace to visit the **Parador de San Francisco** in the center of the gardens. Once this was a convent in whose chapel the bodies of Isabella and Ferdinand rested while waiting completion of their tombs in the Capilla Real in the lower town. Return to the Torre de las Infantas where a gate, a little further along the wall, lets out to a cypress-lined walk up to the Generalife.

Generalife ★★★

This was a summer retreat for the caliph and his court, placed higher on the Alhambra hill to capture breezes. Originally, it would have been rustic and a working farm, though today it has been reconstructed into formal gardens. The building is arranged around a central court in which omnipresent water flows. Both short sides of the building contain graceful pavilions. A gallery for views over the Alhambra Palace runs along the near long side. On the far side were apartments for the caliph and his entourage. Compared to the luxuries of the palace, the Generalife is simple and fresh.

While a taxi back to the city is not expensive, it is pleasant to walk from the Alhambra hill, if feet are not too tired. Simply head downhill. After a couple of hundred yards to the gate of Puerta las Granada, Cuesta de Gomerez leads to the Pl. Nueva in about five blocks. A left turn onto the large C. Reyes Católicos brings the busy Pl. de Isabel la Católica in five blocks more to. Head right along Gran Via de Colón to take the second left down C. de los Oficios. The **Palacio Madraza** *is passed on the left, with painted 18th-century facade. It was Granada's university under the Moors. Inside is an octagonal Mudejar room with nice decoration and dome, and the Sala de Babildos with a fine ceiling. (Open 9 a.m. to 2 p.m.; admission is free.) On the right, a little further along the alley, is the entrance to the* **Capilla Real***, and still further along is the* **Cathedral***.*

Capilla Real

Open daily from 10:30 a.m. to 1 p.m. and 4-7 p.m. (to 6 p.m. in winter). Admission: 150 ptas.; Sun. free. In her will Isabella asked to be buried with Ferdinand at whichever place he chose. Ferdinand selected Granada, the site of his greatest victory. In 1506, two years after Isabella's death, a mausoleum was begun by Enrique de Egas under Ferdinand's direction and finished in 1521, five years after Ferdinand's death. The art this chapel contains, the beauty of the tombs, and their historical importance makes this one of the most moving sights in Spain.

Behind an uninspired facade lies an interior of every element of the developed Isabeline style. Emblems of the Catholic monarchs are everywhere, including their well-known arrow and yoke motif. Entry is through the sacristy—two simple rooms made splendid by the art in them. The paintings are the original collection of Isabella and demonstrate both her religious devotion and surprisingly refined aesthetic taste. Here are some masterpieces, seldom reproduced, from the 15th century and earlier. The paintings include a wonderful *Cristo Muerto* by Roger van der Weyden, a very interesting Botticelli, a fine *San Juan Evangelista* by Berruguette, and four spectacular Memlings, among others. Also on display are the crown and scepter of Isabella, some needlework by her own hand, and the sword of Ferdinand. Banners flown by the Christian army in the conquest of Granada adorn the walls.

The chapel itself seems surprisingly small for figures that loom so large in western history. Near the entrance in the finest Italian marble are the effigies of Ferdinand and Isabella. Further back and standing slightly higher are effigies of their daughter, Juana the Mad, and her husband, Philip the Handsome—the parents of Carlos V. The effigies of Ferdinand and Isabella hold the greatest interest for the personages represented, and suggest true if idealized likenesses of that famed pair. The faces are difficult to see without a ladder—climb the pulpit for the best look. Nonetheless, the other pair of effigies—of Juana and Philip —is artistically superior, the masterpiece of Bartolome Ordoñez. The actual lead coffins lie unadorned in the crypt below, each under its corresponding effigy. The small fifth casket holds a niece of Juana's. The retablo at the altar is among the first in the Plateresque style, and its panels depict the capture of Granada and the conversion of the infidels. Kneeeling painted statues of Ferdinand and Isabella that seem to be true portraits, flank the retablo.

Cathedral   ★

Same hours and ticket as the Capilla Real; Sun. free. The entrance is west on C. Gran Via de Colón. After finishing the Capilla Real, its architect Egas was commissioned by Carlos V to design an adjoining cathedral. To Carlos the chapel was not sufficiently impressive to memorialize his illustrious grandparents. Seven years later the great architect Diego de Siloé took over the job, though the cathedral was not finished until 1714. Given its purpose and the talent that worked on it, the cathedral should be wonderful. Unfortunately, it is not a success, although interesting in its parts.

The main facade is due to Granada's great artist, Alonso Cano (buried inside). It is simple in design but heavy in feeling. Inside, soaring ceilings seem to bear down on too massive piers. What is original about the interior is the main altar, in a huge circular niche with arches cut through to a circular ambulatory. The effect, though interesting, detracts from the importance of the altar. The upper gallery in the rotunda above the altar contains some fine paintings by Cano, and the stained glass higher up is the finest 16th century work. But the loveliest part of the cathedral is the doorway in the south transept. This was the original door to the Capilla Real and is harmonious Isabelline work.

The streets south of the cathedral are known as the **Alcaicería**. *They formed the silk bazaar under the Moors, but it burned in 1843. Today is it reconstructed as a den of souvenir shops. The baroque church of* **San Juan de Dios** *is nearby, and the charming quarter of the* **Albaicín** *is not far. For the church, follow C. San Jerónimo that goes north from the middle of the north face of the cathedral. In about eight short blocks, turn right on the large C. San Juan de Dios for two blocks to the church on the left.*

San Juan de Dios ★

Open daily 10 a.m. to 1 p.m. and 2-6 p.m. Admission: 150 ptas. Juan de Robles was a Portuguese of Jewish descent who devoted his life to the sick and needy. He was cannonized for founding the Order of the Knights Hospitallers. The adjoining hospital was established in his memory in 1552, two years after his death, and the church was added in the 18th century. The facade is admirable and the inside is a glittering baroque fantasy, culminating in the Churrigueresque high altar. The patio of the still-functioning hospital that precedes the church is a painted Renaissance beauty.

For the Albaicín, return to the Pl. Nueva.

Albaicín ★

The Albaicín is the surviving part of Moorish Granada and covers the slope facing the Alhambra. Still a maze of twisting alleys and whitewashed houses—some dilapidated, some with splendid patios inside, and some veritable mansions—the Albaicín offers something worth seeing at every step.

Head east along the Pl. Nueva, passing the early 16th-century **Audiencia** in the northwest corner. The **Pl. Santa Anna** is reached in one block, containing a church by Diego de Siloé from 1548, with a graceful tower and fine portal. From the north side of the church the Carrera del Darro leads east along the banks of the Darro River. The Albaicín hugs the north side of the steeply rising hill.

After the second bridge, **Moorish baths** (*Baños Arabes*) stand at number 31 (open 10 a.m. to 2 p.m. and 3-6 p.m.; admission free). Nothing of the decoration remains except star-shaped ceiling vents that once contained colored glass. About two blocks further on the left is the **Convent of Santa Cataline de Zafra** from 1540 which incorporates a Moorish house. The **Casa de Castril** from 1539 follows at number 43, with a splendid facade of scallop shells and a phoenix. The house belonged to Bernardo Zafra, a treasurer to Queen Isabella, and today is the local archaeological museum (open Tues.-Sat. 10 a.m. to 2 p.m.; admission: 200 ptas.). The patios inside are lovely, although the collection is of minor interest. Opposite is **Santes Pedro y Pablo** with a fine Mudejar ceiling from 1576.

Walk five short blocks along the continuation, called the Paseo de Padre Manjon, pausing for awesome views of the Alhambra walls on high. At the end, Cuesta del Chapiz goes left. The **Casa de Chapiz** at number 14 is a 16th-century Morosco house with lovely garden. Going right, the Camino del Sacromonte leads up the hill of that name. Here Gypsies lived in caves furnished as homes. Some still live in these caves, others preserve them as tourist traps. The homes are interesting to see, but beware the Gypsies—carry no more cash than you can afford to lose. Otherwise, continue along Cuesta de Chapiz to the first true street going left. It winds to reach the church of **San**

Nicholas in about three blocks, from whose terrace are the finest views of the Alhambra. Then wander back through the Albaicín to admire patios fortuitously glimpsed through vestibules and gates along the way.

La Cartuja is 2 k north of the center of town and reached by driving west from the Pl. Nueva along Carrera del Darro. After the street changes its name to Passeo del Padre Manion, it turns north and changes its name again to Cuesta del Chapiz. It bends left, then turns right and changes its name again to C. Pages, before ending at a "T." Go left on Carretera de Murcia as it winds up the hill to the monastery.

La Cartuja ★

Open daily 10 a.m. to 1 p.m. and 4-7 p.m. (closes at 6 p.m. in winter). Admission: 150 ptas. This church was redecorated in 1662 at the height of the baroque period and stands as one the finest examples of that exuberant style, a constant surprise to the eye. In a way it brings one back to Europe after a visit to the Moorish Alhambra. The altar is a swirl of brown and white marble, frosted by molded stucco, beneath a painted dome. The sacristy is admirable for its marquetry doors, vestment chests and walls inlaid with silver, tortoiseshell and ivory. In the monastery proper hangs a series of paintings by a former monk—martyrdoms that luxuriate in blood.

WHERE TO STAY

Granada provides a good selection of hotels, but it is also heavily visited, so it is wise to reserve ahead in busy seasons. Your choices will be between staying on the Alhambra Hill, for its quiet and views, or sleeping in the city below. In the city proper ask for rooms in the back of hotels to minimize noise.

On the Alhambra hill:

EXPENSIVE ($100-$200)

Alhambra Palace · 1st-class ★★★★

Peña Partida, 2 (continue on the main road on the Alhambra hill to the circle where signs direct you left for the Alhambra, but turn right). Rooms: 132. ☎ 22 14 68; FAX 22 64 04; Telex 78400. The hotel was done at the turn of the century in Moorish style with arches, bright tiles, and wooden ceilings that make it a fantasy appropriate to its location. The terrace bar faces the Sierra Nevada, and the rooms overlook either the town or the same beautiful mountains. Rooms are large and comfortably designed, although the public spaces are showing signs of wear. We like this hotel a great deal, but have heard complaints about sloppy service and mis-additions on the bill.

Parador de San Francisco · 1st-class ★★★★

Alhambra (in the palace precinct, follow the signs). Rooms: 38. ☎ 22 14 40; FAX 22 22 64; Telex 78792. This was a monastery built at the end of the 15th century, but for its first two decades employed the monks in watching and praying over the bodies of Ferdinand and Isabella while they awaited completion of the Capilla Real. Today's parador faces its own lovely patio on one side and the Alhambra gardens on the other. A better location can hardly be imagined. Rooms in the original wing have character, antiques and very expensive prices; those in the new wing are more ordinary at lower charges. This is the most heavily booked parador in Spain, with a long waiting list. Reserve very early if you want to insure getting a room.

Alixare   2nd-class ★

Av. de los Alixares (continue straight when signs for the Alhambra Palace direct you left). Rooms: 162. ☎ 22 55 75; FAX 22 41 02; Telex 78523. At the furthest reaches of the Alhambra hill, this hotel offers quiet and a pool. It is otherwise undistinguished and often filled by package-tour groups.

MODERATE ($50-$99)

América   4th-class ★ ★

Real de la Alhambra, 53 (fifty feet south of the Parador). Rooms: 13. ☎ 22 74 71. Open Mar.-Nov. 9. This flower-bedecked gem beats the location of the government parador by fifty feet. It is an utterly charming place to stay, but already discovered, so its few rooms must be booked months in advance. Recently the management has required that guests take their meals here.

In the city proper:

EXPENSIVE ($100-$200)

Meliá Granada   1st-class ★ ★ ★

Angel Ganivet, 7 (due south of the cathedral on a street running southeast from the large Pl. Puerta Real). Rooms: 197. ☎ 22 74 00; FAX 22 74 03; Telex 78429. A modern, businessperson's hotel that is professionally managed, pristine, and charges fair prices.

Victoria   2nd-class ★ ★

Puerta Real, 3 (this main plaza of the city is a few blocks east of the cathedral along C. de Reyes Católicos). Rooms: 69. ☎ 25 77 00; FAX 26 31 08; Telex 78427. This Granada establishment that never was the best in town, but always pleasant, has acquired charm with the years. The location is first rate, although on a very noisy square, and the unassuming lobby hides more interesting, rather posh, public spaces and rooms recently redone.

Kenia   2nd-class ★ ★

C. Molinos, 65 (at the southeast extreme of the city). Rooms: 16. ☎ 22 75 06. Ensconced in a former small mansion located in a quiet part of town, the rooms are simple, but the garden is lovely and the prices are low. As it is some distance from the sights, it is best for those with a car.

Inglaterrra 2nd-class ★

Cetti Meriem, 4 (this street is directly behind the rear of the cathedral, off C. Gran Via de Colón). Rooms: 36. ☎ *22 15 58.* Brand new in 1992, we await reports, but the spaces looked comfortable when we saw them.

MODERATE ($50-$99)

Macía 3rd-class ★ ★

Pl. Nueva, 4 Rooms: 40. ☎ *22 75 36; FAX 22 35 75.* An absolute gem of a reasonably-priced hotel, located on the pleasant Pl. Neuva. Floors are marble, the rooms light and airy, and the prices are low.

Sacromonte 3rd-class ★

Pl. del Lino, 1 (Walk away from the facade of the cathedral on C. Marqués de Gerona for 3 blocks to C. Alhondga, then turn left for 2 blocks.). Rooms: 33. ☎ *26 64 11; FAX 26 67 07.* This very pleasant hotel is located in the heart of town on a quiet plaza. Rooms are white with pink bedspreads, and somewhat spartan for our taste.

INEXPENSIVE (UNDER $50)

Hostal-Residencia Britz P3rd-class ★

Cuesta de Gomerez, 1 (on the Pl. Neuva). Rooms: 22. ☎ *22 36 51.* The rooms are decorated with more style than one usually sees in this price range, and as clean as anyone could want.

Hostal-Residenica Lisboa P3rd-class

Pl. del Carmen, 27 (this is the plaza off C. de los Reyos Católicos just before the Pl. Real). Rooms: 28. ☎ *22 14 13.* The hotel is under the same management as the Britz, which accounts for the same spic -and-span look. But the rooms are less attractive.

WHERE TO EAT

Granada has a reputation as a gourmet wasteland. In fact there are several fine restaurants in town and outside; it is only the average that could stand improvement.

EXPENSIVE ($50+)

Ruta del Veleta ★ ★ ★

Carretera de Sierra Nevada, 50; 6 k southeast of Granada (from the Pl. Real head south along Carrera del Genil, left on Paseo del Salón, then continue on Paseo de la Bomba following signs to Pico del Veleta and Sierra Nevada). ☎ *48 61 34. Closed Sun. eve.* Granada's loveliest restaurant is this one, outside the city. The dining room spreads blue and white ceramics around and overhead to lend both elegance and hominess. The food is first rate, wines superb, and service polished. Reservations are strongly advised.

Amex, Diners, MasterCard and Visa accepted.

Cunini ★ ★

Pescaderia, 9 (two short blocks south of the cathedral front). ☎ *25*

07 77. Closed Mon. evening. The decor is simple but precise, and the seafood is perfectly prepared. Without question this is the best seafood restaurant in town.

MODERATE ($20-$50)

Sevilla

Oficios, 12 (in the alley opposite the Capilla Real). ☎ *22 12 23. Closed Sun. evening.* This is the most famous restaurant in Granada, as celebrity pictures indicate, although not particularly touristy. It is charmingly decorated with tiles lining intimate dining rooms. This is the place to try Andalusian specialties, such as *sopa sevillana* (mayonnaise soup), *cordero al la pastoril* (spicy lamb stew) and *rape a la granadina* (monkfish in a shrimp and mushroom sauce). Reservations are advised.   ***Amex, MasterCard and Visa accepted.***

Alcaicería

Placeta de la Alcaiceria (down an alley to the left off C. de los Oficios). ☎ *22 43 41.* Three lovely dining areas surround a patio, all white and green and light. The good taste extends to the food.

DIRECTORY

INFORMATION • Located at C. Liberos, 2, across from the southwest corner of the cathedral front. Open Mon.-Fri. 10 a.m. to 1 p.m. and 4-7 p.m., Sat. from 10 a.m. to 1 p.m.

TRAINS AND BUSES • The train station at the end of Av. Andaluces can be reached by following Gran Via de Colón north for a mile and a half (☎ 20 33 22). Trains connect with Madrid 3 times a day, taking from 7 hours on the fastest, which costs about 4000 ptas, to 8 and a half hours on slower trains for half the price. Seville is served twice a day for 1500 ptas., and connections are possible for other destinations. The downtown RENFE office is at C. de los Reyes Católicos, 63 (☎ 22 31 19).

Several bus companies divide the available routes, which means that the place of departure depends on the destination. Alsina Gráells handles most of the Andalusia destinations, at Camino de Ronda, 97, a half mile due west of the cathedral (☎ 25 13 58). More distant routes are the domain of Bacoma on Av. Andaluces, 10, near the train station (☎ 28 42 51). A trip to Madrid costs as much or more than the low cost train fare. Bus #11 goes to both bus stations and the train from Gran Via Colón and Puerta Real.

POST OFFICE AND TELEPHONES • The main post office is at Puerta Real, the main traffic plaza, south of the cathedral. Telephones are available at C. de los Reyes Católicos, 55. It remain open until 10 p.m.

POLICE • The main station is in Pl. del Carmen, the northeast corner of the Puerta Real (092, for emergencies).

AIRPORT • A small airport 17 k outside of town serves Madrid, as well as some other Spanish cities. The Iberia office is at Pl. de Isabel la Católica, 2, one block south of the cathedral along Gran Via de Colón (☎ 22 14 52).

EXCURSIONS

Granada is a good base from which to visit **Úbeda** and **Baeza**, both described under separate headings in this chapter. The **Costa del Sol**, described above, is also near. The natural tour is to visit **Córdoba**, less than two hours northwest, and/or **Seville**, three hours due west. The scenic town of **Ronda** is another good trip. Descriptions can be found under the respective headings in this chapter.

ITALICA

See "Excursions" under Seville city listing

JEREZ DE LA FRONTERA

See "Excursions" under Seville city listing

MÁLAGA ★

Population: 503,251
Area code: 952; Zip code: 29000

From **Madrid** *either head for Granada or Córdoba and follow directions from there. From* **Granada** *take N-323 south toward Motril, but at Salobreña in 65 k go west along N-340 for 92 k. From* **Córdoba** *take N-331 south toward Antiquera for 116 k. Go east on N-321 for 8 k to pick up N-331 south again for 35 k more. From* **Seville** *take N-334 east for 159 k to Antiquera and follow the preceding directions.*

In ancient times the quarries of Málaga were famed far and wide, even supplying most of the stone for the great cathedral of Sancta Sophia in Constantinople. Under the Moors Málaga served as the port for Granada and thus became a major target for Ferdinand during his effort to isolate Granada from reinforcements and supplies. Naturally the Moors had strongly fortified the city against such a possibility, but Ferdinand captured Málaga in 1487 after a difficult siege. To send a message to Granada, he killed all its defenders with ceremony.

At the time Málaga's cloudless skies made it a garden lauded by Arab poets. Wine, apricots, oranges, and later sugarcane, helped keep Málaga rich. But those who tended the garden were Moors, and when they were expelled in the 16th century, Málaga fell on hard times. In the 18th century demand for Málaga's sweet wine helped it recover, though Málaga suffered again when tastes in the next century turned to drier French versions. Tourism in recent days has helped. Málaga also boasts of a famous native son, Pablo Picasso, although his family moved away when he was ten.

Málaga is the major city of the Costa del Sol. Since it has no beaches to speak of, most people use it as a transit hub without bothering to look at the town. The city may not be attractive overall but it contains handsome sights, certainly worth part of a day to explore. Be alert in the evening, however, because street robberies are too prevalent. One should see the ruins of the Moorish **Alcazaba**★ and nearby **Gibralfaro**, with quiet walks and gardens, the **Cathedral** and **Museo de Bellas Artes**. All lie within an area of five blocks. Málaga is split, on a north-south axis, by the River Guadalmedina. To its west lie most places of interest. In fact the sights all cluster by the Puerto (Port), along which runs a pleasant park with underground parking at its eastern end in the Pl. de la Marina.

From the **Airport** *and from the* **western Costa del Sol** *watch for signs to Av. de Andalucia as you approach one of the rare clover leafs in Spain. Head east to the Pl. de la Marina and parking. From* **Granada and north** *one-way streets complicate matters. The city is entered on Av. de Jorge Silvela along the Guadalmedina. At the second bridge one-way streets force the crossing of the river. Take the first left to parallel the river, but at the next bridge, go right for one block on C. Marmoles, taking the next left to a large traffic circle. Go left again along Av. de Andalucia, which enters the Pl. de la Marina and parking. From the* **eastern Costa del Sol** *the city is entered on Paseo de Marítimo which reaches a large traffic circle after passing the hospital. Head left along the Paseo del Parque, at the end of which is the Pl. de la Marina and parking.*

Additional parking lies two blocks north along Cortina del Muelle which runs east.

From the Pl. de la Marina walk north to the edge of the park. There C. Molina continues north for two blocks to the

cathedral. Or take the next main street to the east, C. Mar-
qués de Larios, which also heads due north. This is the main
shopping street of Málaga, bordered by interesting stores.
The **office of tourism** *is on the right in about three blocks.*
An alley going right, just past the office of tourism, leads to
the cathedral.

Cathedral

Open daily 10 a.m. to 1 p.m. and 4-5:30 p.m. Admission: 50 ptas., to the
choir and treasury. Original designs for the cathedral were drawn by the
famed Diego de Siloé in 1528 in a neoclassical style, but the single
completed tower shows that it is not finished yet. Money ran out.
Some would say rather that funds were cut off when the church elders
saw what it looked like. It is not the most attractive of cathedrals,
although interesting enough for a look. The interior is overly dark, as
could be said for many others in Spain, but the massive Corinthian
columns make an impact with their girth. The various chapels and
altar hold little of interest, but the choir is quite another story. The
stalls consist of the finest wood carving by masters of that genre—by
Pedro de Mena (buried nearby) and Alonso Cano, among others—admirable for exquisite details.

From the front of the cathedral walk due north beside the
baroque **Bishopric***. At the end of the Pl. turn right (east) along C.*
Cister by the **Sagradio***, formerly the site of the city mosque, now*
with a nice Isabeline north face. At its west end C. San Agustin
heads northeast for two blocks to the Museo de Bellas Artes.

Museo de Bellas Artes

Open Tues.-Sat. 10 a.m. to 1:30 p.m. and 5-8 p.m. (closes an hour
earlier in winter). Open Sun. 10 a.m. to 1:30 p.m. Closed Mon.
Admission: 100 ptas. The building itself is interesting—the former
palace of Buenavista. Inside, is a varied collection, from Roman mosaics, to paintings by Zurbarán and Ribera. The paintings are on loan
from the Prado, and thus not of the first class, but childhood drawings
by Picasso are simply wonderful.

Turn right after the museum for two blocks to the **Pl. de la**
Merced*, passing the church of* **Santiago** *with a Mudejar tower on*
the way. The buildings around the plaza with peeling shutters
harken to the turn of the century, and a plaque at number 15 on
the north edge of the plaza marks the house where **Picasso** *was*
born. Go south from the plaza along C. Alcazabilla, passing
remains of a **Roman theater** *on the right. At the end of the street*
stands the large **Aduaña***, from the end of the eighteenth century.*
To the left is the **alcazaba***.*

Alcazaba   ★

*Open Mon.-Sat. 11 a.m. to 2 p.m. and 5-8 p.m. (closes an hour earlier in
winter). Open Sun. 10 a.m. to 2 p.m. Admission: 100 ptas.* Although
restored from the foundations up, the buildings and, especially the
gates and fortifications, are evocative, a kind of second-rate Alhambra
which betters some first-rate efforts in other styles. The walls were
built in the 11th century and show clever tactics to concentrate attackers in a winding entrance. Inside, a small inner palace was built over
the course of the 11th-14th century and remains admirable in reconstruction. It contains a museum of material from the Visigothic era
through the Moorish, including fine ceramics. The double fortress
wall leads steeply up to the **Gibralfaro** (mountain lighthouse), actually
ruins of a castle from the 14th century. The parador stands beside it.
The gardens are pleasant and views of the town and its setting are
striking.

WHERE TO STAY

Since few people stay overnight the choices usually prove adequate.

EXPENSIVE ($100-$200)

Parador Málaga-Gibralfaro   2nd-class ★ ★
On the Gibralfaro hill. Rooms: 12. ☎ 222 19 03; FAX 222 19 02.
Although this is a modern building, its stone covered with ivy lends an
older look, but it is the views over the town and sea, along with the
quiet, that makes this an excellent choice. However, it is not air-conditioned, nor does it have all facilities usually found in paradors. That
is not to say that the service is in any way lacking. A minibus goes up
and down from the city.

Málaga Palacio   1st-class ★
*Corina del Muelle, 1 (off the northeast corner of the Pl. de la Marina).
Rooms: 225. ☎ 221 51 85; FAX 221 51 85.* The glitter has faded from
this older hotel, but it still retains its fine location and views of the
park from the rooms that face it.

Los Naranjos   2nd-class ★
*Paseo de Sancha, 35 (about one half mile due east of the Paseo del Parque).
Rooms: 41. ☎ 222 43 19; FAX 222 59 75; Telex 77030.* The name
comes from the small orange grove in front, a nice touch that heralds
the attention given throughout this admirably run little hotel.

MODERATE ($50-$99)

Las Vegas   2nd-class
Paseo de Sancha 22 (just before Los Naranjos). Rooms: 107.☎ 221 77 12.
The building is nothing remarkable, but the garden around the pool
is nice. If you get a room at the back with ocean views, you will enjoy
your stay.

INEXPENSIVE (UNDER $50)

Victoria   **P3rd-class ★**

C. Sancho Lara, 3 (on a side street off the main shopping street C. Marqués de Larios). Rooms: 13. ☎ *221 77 12.* The location is super and the price is right. The rooms are not memorable, but they are squeaky clean.

WHERE TO EAT

Think fried fish and walk to the east end of the Paseo del Parque, then a block further for the area known as Pedragalejos. Here unassuming places serve delectable fried fish for a pittance.

EXPENSIVE ($50+)

Café de Paris   **★ ★**

C. Vélez Málaga, 8 (east of the Paseo del Parque and a soft right onto Paseo Canovas del Castillo). ☎ *222 50 43. Closed Sun.* No question that this is the best food in town, owned by a former chef at some of Spain's finest restaurants. Try the *menu de degustacion* to sample his wares. Seafood is the star, of course, and prepared with care. Reservations and jacket and tie are required.

Amex, Diners, MasterCard and Visa accepted.

Antonio Martín

Paseo Marítimo, 4 (a block south of the Cafe de Paris). ☎ *222 21 13. Closed Sun. eve.* The ocean view from the terrace makes this old institution a pleasure. Fish simply prepared is your best choice, for the kitchen can be erratic with sauces. Reservations are strongly advised.

Amex, Diners, MasterCard and Visa accepted.

INEXPENSIVE (UNDER $20)

La Cancela

C. Denís Belgrano, 3 (C. Molina Larios is the street that passes the facade of the cathedral and ends a block later at C. Granada. The restaurant lies down an alley off C. Granada.) ☎ *222 31 25. Closed Wed.* Two eclectically decorated small dining rooms immediately make you feel at home. The food is standard, but hearty, and modestly priced.

DIRECTORY

INFORMATION • Located on Pasaje de Chinitas, 4, off C. Marqués de Larios, the main shopping street that heads due north from the Pl. de la Marina. ☎ 221 34 45.

TRAINS AND BUSES • The train station is west of the port, across the river on C. Cuarteles (☎ 231 25 00). The RENFE office is at C. Strachan, 2 (just west of the southern face of the cathedral (☎ 221 31 22). Connections can be made almost anywhere in Spain.

The central bus terminal is at Paseo de los Tilos, just past the train station. This is a large hub for bus routes and offers frequent service to most destinations (☎ 235 00 61).

POST OFFICE AND TELEPHONES • A post office branch is located across the street south from the front of the cathedral, but the main office is just across the river on Av. de Andalucia (☎ 235 91 07). Telephones are available across from the cathedral at Calle Molina Larios, 11.

POLICE • The telephone number is ☎ 221 50 05.

AIRPORT • Electric trains (Ferrocarril) go the 10 k to and from the airport every half hour. The best stop is the Centro/Alameda station, located a block north and slightly west of the Pl. de la Marina. Buses also make the trip on the same schedule, leaving from the cathedral. Málaga airport handles both international and national flights (☎ 223 11 69). The Iberia office is at Molina Lario, 13 ☎ 213 61 26).

EXCURSIONS

The **Costa del Sol** is the natural excursion from Málaga. See a description under that heading.

RONDA ★ ★

Population: 31,383
Area code: 952; Zip code: 29400

From **Seville** *the fastest route, though not the most direct, is to go south either on the toll road A-4 (E-5) or on the free N-IV to Jerez for 90 k, then east on N-342 to Algodonales for 70 k, where C-339 heads south for lovely views and some hairpin curves along 43 k of road. From* **Córdoba** *head south on N-IV for 12 k, where N-331 splits off. Follow N-331 to just short of Antiquera in 116 k, then west for 3 k along N-334 and an exit onto N-342 to Algodonales in 90 k. Take the scenic C-339 south to Ronda in 43 k. From* **Granada** *take N-342 west past Antiquera, switch to N-342 for 90 k to Algodonales. Take C-339 south for 43 k to Ronda.*

Ronda is one of those special places that almost everyone loves. It could hardly be more unusual in its situation. The old city stands on a bluff with precipitous drops on three sides, and the fourth side is separated from the newer part of town (post-Reconquest) by an incredible slice of 300-feet-deep gorge. From this aerie, views over the valley and distant hills are nothing short of stupendous.

Everyone, beginning with the Celts, made a stronghold of the impregnable old city, but it was the Moors who left the most lasting remains. Only surprise and the use of metal cannonballs for the first time in Spain allowed Ferdinand to capture it in 1485. Ronda was the center of a revolt by the Moors against forced conversions to Christianity a decade after the fall of Granada. The insurrection was put down with great difficulty and loss of life. Expelling the Moors quelled such threats in Ronda, but then the remaining citizens turned to banditry, safe in their fortress fastness, causing two centuries of problems for the police.

Little Ronda had a seminal impact on the sport of bullfighting. A corporation was founded here in 1493 to supervise such events, which at the time still pitted mounted men against bulls. In the beginning of the 18th century, the local Romero family invented a new way to fight on foot using capes and a team of assistants, and killing the bull at the end with a sword thrust. The modern, stylized form of bullfighting was thus invented in Ronda. At first fights were held in the Pl. de la Ciudad, by sealing off the streets, then a special ring for the purpose was built in 1785, the second oldest in Spain (after Seville).

Being close to Gibraltar and enjoying cool summer breezes, Ronda has always been a favorite of the English. Hence, the very British hotel Reina Victoria was built here in 1906, for officers vacationing with their families. Here Rainer Maria Rilke, the great German poet, stayed for several months in 1912 recovering from an illness, and began his *Spanish Elegies*. Hemmingway visited frequently, and the substantial ashes of Orson Welles are buried on a bull farm outside of town. Today, the tourists arrive on weekends, but weekdays remain serene.

> *The town is entered on C. de Sevilla. To cross the Puente Nuevo into the old town a turn must be made at some time to the parallel street to the right, C. Jerez, which changes its name to San Carlos. Across the bridge the name again changes to C. Arminan. Parking is where you find it. If all else fails, city parking is just to the right of the Puente Nuevo in the Mercadillo, or new town, side.*

The old town, called the Ciudad, is less than half a mile long by a quarter wide, so no one can get lost by too much. On the other hand, it conforms to the Moorish layout of winding streets and alleys so everyone gets lost at least a little. That is to say, it is a place for wandering. Start at the far (southern) end of the Ciudad, at the **Alcazaba**.

Not that there is much to see of the old Moorish fort, for the French demolished it in 1809, but it is a romantic site with nice views. Follow the main street, called C. Nuñez at this point, back in the direction of the new town for two blocks. As the street bends right go left into the main square, the **Pl. de la Ciudad** ★. It was in this place that the modern form of bullfighting was first practiced. At the north end of the plaza is the church of **Santa María la Mayor** ★ (open at the caretaker's whim; 50 ptas. donation). This is a mosque done over with the trappings of a 17th-century Christian church, as the recently uncovered mihrab in the vestibule shows (now with a statue of the Virgin inside). The church tower once was the minaret. Inside is a mixture of Gothic nave and gilded baroque high altar.

Leave by a small street running from the east side of the church. Go east to a "T" where C. Ruedi de Gameros goes north for one block to the **Mondragon Palace** ★, imposing with twin graceful turrets. This is probably a Renaissance rebuilding, on the site of the former Moorish palace, in which Ferdinand and Isabella stayed after taking the town, while Isabella gave birth to a daughter. Today it houses exhibitions, so one can enter to admire its two handsome patios with glazed tiles and Mudejar stucco tracery. Do not miss the gallery in the rear with lovely artesonado ceiling and dramatic views of the valley.

Retrace steps back to the church and go east to the main street, here called C. Arminan, but take the first right into a pretty square with a striking little **minaret** standing alone to show that there once was a mosque nearby. Take C. Marqués de Salvatierra from the northeast corner of the plaza for two blocks to the **Casa del Marqués de Salvatierra** on the right. The Renaissance facade displays "savages" over the portal and may be visited (open daily 10 a.m. to 1 p.m. and 4-7 p.m.; admission: 150 ptas., for guided tour). Downhill to the right one passes two bridges, the first on Roman foundations, the second claimed to be Moorish. Further down the ravine are some of the finest **Moorish baths** ★ remaining in Spain (open Tues.- Sat. 10 a.m. to 1 p.m. and 4-7 p.m.; open Sun. 10 a.m. to 1 p.m.; admission: free). On the return up the hill, continue past the Casa del marqués de Salvatierrra toward the Puente Nuevo, and pass the **Casa del Rey Moro**. Although called the House of the Moorish king, it obviously dates from the early 18th century.

Continue over the Puente Neuvo along C. San Carlos to the **Pl. de Toros** ★, the bullring, in two blocks. It was completed in 1784, and surely is the most charming in Spain, which is why it has so often been featured in movies (open daily from 10 a.m. to 6 p.m.; admission to the ring: 75 ptas., to the museum: 100 ptas.). One block further on C. San Carlos brings the lovely gardens of the Alamenda Tajo on the left. From here a dramatic walk along the cliffs leads to the Victorian hotel with the apt name of Hotel Reina Victoria, worth looking in and walking through the gardens in the rear.

WHERE TO STAY

To fully experience Ronda one has to spend the night in the **Hotel Reina Victoria**. But if $100 in season is too much, there is a less expensive choice.

EXPENSIVE ($100-$200)

Reina Victoria   1st-class ★ ★ ★ ★ ★

Av. Dr. Fleming, 25 (on entering town take the first right to the hotel). Rooms: 89. ☎ *287 12 40; FAX 287 10 75.* Built in 1906 by an English company for British guests, there is nothing so charmingly colonial anywhere else in Spain. It truly does seem Victorian, with the grace, charm and decor of that era. Today it is run by the Husa chain, caters to tour groups and has just been completely renovated, but retains its old feeling. The gardens are lovely, with views that cannot be matched. Try very hard to get a room at the back with a balcony overlooking the valley.

INEXPENSIVE (UNDER $50)

El Tajo   R2nd-class ★

Cruz Verde, 7 (off Carrera de Espinel, four blocks east of the Plaza de Toros). Rooms: 67. ☎ *87 62 36.* For the modest price you get a comfortable room that is spotlessly clean

WHERE TO EAT

Although there are a number of inexpensive restaurants in the Mercadillo (new town), none stands out compared to two moderately priced places, also in the Mercadillo, serving better food.

MODERATE ($20-$50)

Don Miguel   ★ ★

Pl. de España, 3 (at the Puente Nuevo). ☎ *287 10 90. Closed Sun., and the last two weeks in Jan.* Two terraces offer such dramatic views of the Tajo Gorge that they may be too much for those subject to vertigo. If bothered, feast your eyes on the baby lamb on your plate and all will be well, for it is superb. Reservations are advised on weekends.
                        Amex, Diners, MasterCard and Visa accepted.

Pedro Romero   ★

Virgen de la Paz, 18 (opposite the Pl. de Toros). ☎ *287 11 10.* Named after the founder of modern bullfighting, naturally the restaurant is decorated with memorabilia of the bullring. Somehow it is attractive and homey. Of course you should try the *rabo de toro* here, and for

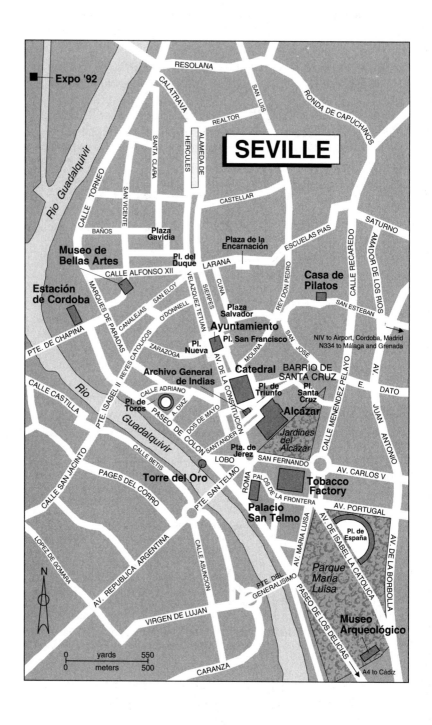

desert there is a special caramel custard *al coco* (with coconut) that should not be missed. ***Amex, Diners, MasterCard and Visa accepted.***

DIRECTORY

INFORMATION • Located in the Pl. de España at number 1, which is the Pl. just before the Puente Nuevo. Open Mon.-Fri. from 10 to 2:30 p.m. ☎ 287 12 72.

TRAINS AND BUSES • The train station is on Av. Andalucia in the northeast corner of the Mercadillo. The bus station is off the same avenue four blocks west. However, different companies with different routes and schedules use the building. ☎ 287 22 64.

POST OFFICE AND TELEPHONES • The post office is located at C. Virgin de la Paz, 20, opposite the Pl. de Toros.

POLICE • On C. Espinel, 39, east of the Pl. de Toros (☎ 287 13 70; emergency: ☎ 091).

SEVILLE ★★★★★

Population: 653,833
Area code: 95; Zip code: 41000

*From **Madrid** either aim for Córdoba or Granada and follow the directions from there. From **Granada** take N-342 west for 92 k past Antequera, then take N-334 northwest for 159 k to Seville. From **Córdoba** take N-IV (E-5) southwest for Seville in 142 k.*

Seville does not have the best art museum or cathedral or Moorish architecture, but it is second best in all these arenas and, thus, places high on total points. Since it is a beautiful city with lovely vistas and orange and palm trees lining streets punctuated by quiet parks, it is a tourist's delight.

Seville has been large and important since the time of the Iberians, thanks to its safe situation inland along the Guadalquivir River that formed an easy road to the sea. Julius Caesar himself fortified it in 45 B.C. and it grew to one of the most important Roman towns in Spain, as still impressive ruins at nearby Italica attest. In fact, it bred two Roman Emperors—Trajan and Hadrian. Seville was the first capital of the Visigoths, before Toledo took over that position. Under the Moors, Seville placed second behind Córdoba until 1023, when the kingdom split into principalities, and Seville's independence left it free to grow and to surpass the former capital. For two centuries her prosperity was unrivaled, then, in 1248, Seville was conquered by the great Christian warrior Fernando III, later sainted for his accomplishments. Saint Fernando was buried here in 1252.

Naturally many Moors fled Seville after this early conquest. Their property was divided among Fernando's followers, making many rich overnight, creating a class of Andalusian nobles whose wealth and power were immense. Thus arose, for example, the dukes of Medina Sidona, one of whom almost financed Columbus' first voyage, and another of whom admiralled the Invincible Armada. In the early 14th century, Seville was the favorite city of the notorious king Pedro the Cruel, who remodeled the palace of the Moors into the striking Alcázar we see today.

Riches from the New World brought great prosperity to Seville, for this was the port to which the treasure ships sailed to unload their silver, gold and tobacco, much of which remained in local pockets. Carlos V came to Seville to meet and marry his bride, Isabel of Portugal, remodeling rooms in the Alcázar for his honeymoon suite. In 1647 a plague attacked, ran rampant for five years and reduced the population by one third. This, combined with declining trade from the New World, began a slide that was climaxed by the silting up of the Guadalquivar River, handing preeminence thereafter to Cádiz, Spain's New World port.

Nonetheless, life continued in Seville. Spain's finest artist, Velázquez, was born here in 1599, as was Murillo in 1618. Zurbarán became an adopted son. The French writer Beaumarchais visited in 1764, and wrote a story about a Seville roué named Don Juan that inspired Mozart's *Don Giovanni*. Mozart followed with *The Marriage of Figaro*, inspiring Rossini's *Barber of Seville*. Later Prosper Merimée wrote about a Gypsy in Seville who enchanted a soldier, which became Bizet's *Carmen*. Seville's Tobacco Factory served as the model for Carmen's place of employment. In the present century, textiles and metallurgy have returned prosperity to Seville.

Seville is famed in Spain for its Easter festivities, when nightly processions of hooded and robed penitents march behind floats of bejeweled and flower-bedecked Saints and Virgins. Bands and bystanders break out into song as the processions pass. This is followed two weeks later by the April Fair, a week of celebrations. Tents are set up outside the town to which Sevillaños ride on horseback in costumes like those in *Carmen* and celebrate with food, wine and parties throughout the night. In association with these festivities are a month of bullfights with the finest matadors, as well as impromptu nightly dancing, including flamenco. It is a festive and memorable time to visit, but a period when all hotels are booked full at prices twice their usual charges.

Seville also hosted the World's Fair of 1992, Expo '92. In fact this was the city's second World's Fair. Its first, celebrated in 1929 as the Ibero-America Exposition, was rather a dud because of the world financial collapse that year. The recent fair occupied the island of La Cartuja, just north of the city-center.

Arriving from the north or east on **N-IV**, *or from the* **Airport**, *one travels along Av. Aeropuerto which becomes Av. de Kansas City (yes, that is its name) as it goes through the city. When it ends in a "T," go left along Av. Luis Morales which changes its name to Av. San Francisco Javier near the university on the right. Take the next right along C. Enramadilla, which narrows, then widens, and is called Av. Carlos V. As it passes the bus park, parking is available to the right.*

Arriving from **Málaga** *on* **N-334** *enter the city along Av. de Andalucía, passing through one huge, clover-leafed intersection and then two other major intersections. At the third intersection with the Soccer Stadium, visible to the right, turn right along Av. Luis Morales, and follow the rest of the directions above.*

Arriving from **Cádiz** *or* **Jerez** *on N-IV from the south along Av. de Jerez, the corner of the large Parque de Maria Luisa is soon reached. Turn right at the park onto C. Muñoz León, which follows the edge of the park under the new name of C. Borbolla. Continue for one block past the park's end, make a left onto Av. Carlos V, and parking to the left in two blocks.*

From **Mérida** *traffic is funnelled across the Guadalquivar River on Av. de Cristo de Expiración. Take the first right after the bridge, along a street that soon is named Paseo Cristobal Colón. Bear left at the Torre del Oro, the polygonal stone tower, onto Almirante Lobo which feeds in one long block into the busy circle called the Puerta de Jerez. Continue through the circle, take the large street opposite, C. San Fernando, by the gardens of the Alcázar. At the end of the gardens, continue through the traffic circle onto Av. Carlos V. Parking is at the second right.*

Seville offers an abundance of interesting things to see amid one of the most beautiful cities in the world. The **Alcázar ★★★★** and the **Casa de Pilatos ★★★** are both wonderful hybrid Moorish palaces, built for Christians by Moorish artisans—Mudejars. The **Cathedral ★★★** is among the finest in Spain, and the largest. Seville's **Museo de Belles Artes ★★★** houses the second best collection in Spain, including remarkable Zurbaráns and one of Velázquez' finest paintings. The **Museo Arqueológico ★** displays lovely finds from nearby Roman Italica. The **Barrio Santa Cruz ★**, the old quarter, retains lovely plazas, flowered patios and elegant houses. There are admirable buildings—the **Archivo General de Indias**, the **tobacco factory**, the **Ayuntamiento ★** and the complex called the **Pl. de España**. Last, but not least, the remains of Expo '92 on the island of La Cartuja have been turned into an amusement park. It is quite impossible to see Seville in less than two days.

> *Proceed west along Av. de Carlos V from the parking to cross the Pl. de Juan de Austria. Across the plaza the still westward street is called C. San Francisco. Pass the gardens at the rear of the Alcázar on the right and the huge university building on the left. This was the former* **tobacco factory***, famed as the model for Carmen's place of employment. At one time 10,000 workers rolled Cuban cigars here, but now it constitutes a part of the University of Seville and only the carving of the story of tobacco around the main door betrays its former function. At the end of the street stands the magnificent grand* **Hotel Alfonso XIII***. Turn right along C. San Gregoro into the* **Pl. de Contratación***, the hub of numerous sights. The* **Office of Tourism** *is down the alley to the right. The square building to the left is the* **Archivo General de Indias***, and ahead is the* **Cathedral** *with the* **Giralda Tower** *visible above its west side. To the right is the* **Alcázar***, and between the cathedral and the Alcázar is the entrance to the* **Barrio Santa Cruz***.*

THE CATHEDRAL AREA

Cathedral and Giralda Tower   ★★★

Open Mon.-Sat. 11 a.m. to 5 p.m., Sun. 2-4 p.m. Closed Jan. 1 and 6, May 30, Aug. 15, Dec. 8 and 25. Admission: 300 ptas., to the cathedral and Giralda Tower. After conquering Seville, the Christians at first used the mosque of the Moors for religious services, but in 1401 decided to build their own cathedral, and finished the project in the remarkably quick time of a century. A member of the building committee is said to have exclaimed: "Let us build a cathedral so immense that everyone who sees it will take us for madmen." What they constructed was the largest Gothic cathedral in the world, save perhaps the still unfinished Saint John the Divine in New York. To build it they razed the mosque, though left its Patio of Oranges for a cathedral cloister, and its minaret for a bell tower. The main portal of the facade is modern, surrounded by two others of the period, the left one being the best.

On the east face of the cathedral, to the rear, rises the **Torre Giralda** ★★ (Weathervane Tower). Here too is the entrance to the cathedral and the ticket counter. The tower is the minaret from the adjacent mosque of 1198. Originally it was topped by four golden balls which fell in an earthquake. When the cathedral went up, a bell tower was added to the top of the minaret surmounted by a statue which turns in the wind and symbolizes Faith. Altogether, the tower stands over 300 feet high, as handsome and harmonious a structure as can be imagined up to the place where the arcade of the belfry begins. (Use a hand to block the top and its harmony will be apparent.) The tower may be climbed by walking up interior sloping ramps, and provides the best view of the cathedral and surrounding city. Note that each bell in the clarion is named.

The vast size of the cathedral interior is not at first apparent. The light is dusky because the stained glass windows are unusually high, the piers seem less massive because they are formed into smaller columns, and the doubling of the aisles on each side of the nave is not immediately apparent. Further, as with so many Spanish cathedrals, the central coro blocks any grand view down the nave. Nonetheless the cathedral is a football field long, almost equally wide and the vaulting above the nave soars 185 feet into the air.

Entering by the south transept one confronts the impressive **tomb of Christopher Columbus**. The coffin is carried by four figures representing the original four kingdoms of Spain—Castile, Aragon, Navarre and León. The work was cast in the 19th century. Whether Columbus' body actually lies in the coffin is a subject of great controversy. It is known that he died in Valladolid and that his body was carried to Santo Domingo for burial. The Spanish say that the corpse was disintered, taken to Havana, then returned here to prevent capture during the Spanish-American War. In Santo Domingo they claim that Columbus' remains never left.

The **high altar** is fronted by an ornate Plateresque gilt screen which seems to double the gilt of the awesome Gothic retablo, the largest in Spain. Its details are difficult to study from a distance. In the apse behind the high altar is the large **Capilla Real**, a Plateresque marvel. High up, Fernando III, the conqueror of Seville, is shown receiving the keys to the city. On the chapel altar stands a silver and bronze shrine for the king's remains. These remains proved incorruptible, so

Fernando was declared a saint, and is carried in processions during Easter week. Above the shrine stands a small Virgin, said to be a gift from Louis IX of France that Fernando carried with him in battle. To the left is the effigy of King Alfonso X, the Wise, Fernando's son, and opposite is Fernando's wife, Beatrice of Swabia. The striking dome above consists of radiating heads of martyrs spiralling to the apex. Stairs in the chapel lead to a vault below (generally closed) in which coffins hold remains of Pedro the Cruel and his "wife" Maria de Padilla. Ironically, resting beside Pedro is his half-brother Fadrique Trastámara, who Pedro killed, and whose brother avenged the death by killing Pedro and then founded the dynasty that bred both Isabella and Ferdinand.

To the left, facing the Capilla Real is a chapel with a retablo by Zurbarán. To the right, in the corner, is a lovely oval room with a fine frescoed ceiling, the **Chapterhouse**. Church vestments are displayed adjoining. Further along is a neoclassical **Sacristy** with a painting by Zurbarán, and an adjacent **treasury** displaying numerous relics, including the actual keys to the city presented to St. Fernando—silver gilt by the Moors, iron gilt by the Jewish community. In the center of the nave stands an ornate **coro** with fine Gothic choirstalls. Between the coro and the front door to the cathedral lies a **tombstone for Columbus' son Hernando**.

Before finishing with the cathedral a quiet treat awaits through a door on the right side that gives access to the **Patio de los Naranjos**, the courtyard for the former mosque. Inside is the original basin for the mosque, perhaps appropriated from a Visigothic fountain. The chapel to **Our Lady of Granada** has a fine Mudejar ceiling, and up red marble stairs is stored the **Columbus Archives** of books owned by the discoverer, many annotated in his hand, donated to the cathedral by his son Hernando.

Alcázar   ★★★★

Open Tues.-Sat. 10 a.m-5 p.m. Open Sun. 10 a.m. to 1 p.m. Closed Mon. Admission: 600 ptas., exact change. Across the Pl. de Triunfo from the cathedral, past square battlement towers, and through an unassuming gateway with a tiled lion above, is the entrance to the Alcázar. These walls are all that remain of a Moorish palace from 1176. In 1366 Pedro the Cruel replaced that palace with a smaller one of his own. But he so admired the Moorish aesthetic that he borrowed artisans from the caliph of Granada to construct it. Here Pedro lived with his "wife" Maria de Padilla (see "Historical Profile: The Moors and the Reconquest" p.285) and here he murdered Fadrique of Trastámara, his half-brother. On another occasion he invited the emir from Granada to dinner and killed him for his jewels, one of which, a giant uncut ruby, found its way into the British royal crown. Later Isabella gave birth to her only son while she and Ferdinand resided here. Carlos V, their grandson, married his wife in the Hall of the Ambassadors. A hundred years later, Velázquez' patron Felipe IV, restored the Alcázar, although an earthquake and fire in the 18th century did substantial damage and subsequent restoration has been crude at times. Nonetheless, this is the oldest continually occupied palace in Europe (the present king and queen often stay), and one of the finest remaining examples of Mudejar architecture.

Through the gate one enters the **Patio de Montería**. On the left is the **Sala de Justicia** with plaster coats of arms around the walls, and a remarkable wooden ceiling above. Further left, though presently closed, is the lovely **Patio de Yeso**, one of the few remaining parts of the original Moorish palace. From the Patio de Monteria, three **stone arches** (possibly Roman) straight ahead lead to the **Patio de Leones**, with patterned pavement and the handsome **palace of Pedro the Cruel** across the way.

The main facade, with its arcaded wings on two sides, presents an almost Byzantine look, due to a deep overhanging eave above the entrance. Below the eave, blue tiles bear an Arabic inscription saying that there is no conqueror but God, a secret putdown by the Moorish craftsmen of their Christian master. The right-hand wing was built by Ferdinand and Isabella as a center to deal with matters concerning the New World. Starting in this Isabeline wing, a vestibule hung with nice tapestries leads to a room for audiences and finally a small **chapel** with ornate coffered ceiling. The picture above the altar shows Mary protecting dim figures of Native Americans under her cloak. The blond-haired figure beside her on the right is thought to be Columbus. Outside, at the far end, a grand stair leads to **royal apartments** on the second floor. Left of the landing is the intimate **Oratory of Isabella** with a remarkable tile depiction of Mary visiting her cousin St. Isabella. Rooms of varying styles and age follow, including the **banquet hall** with a lovely ceiling, built by Carlos V for his wedding feast. But the finest of the rooms is **Pedro the Cruel's bedroom** with intricate carving in perfect Mudejar style, and an alcove for his bed.

The treasure of the Alcázar is Pedro's palace. Enter through the main portal into a **vestibule** that presents an elegant vista of a row of horseshoe arches. Bright tiles (unfortunately modern) line the walls halfway up, intricate painted stucco runs along the high walls and through the arches, and a complex coffered ceiling hangs overhead. Turn left from the vestibule into the **Patio de las Doncellas** (Maids of Honor), the center of the palace. If only Carlos V had not added the classical second story to the patio it would be a jewel. Ignore that second story and enjoy the multilobed arches, brilliant tiles and the rhythm of the arches, not ignoring the ancient original doors. Of course there is a fountain in the center for the sound of water, and vistas through the patio sides of surrounding rooms.

Cross to the right side to see the so-called **Salón de los Reyes Moros**, which of course was intended for Christian, not for Moorish kings. In any case it displays nice woodwork, fine wooden doors and alcoves for beds.

Cross to the far side to enter the **Salón de Carlos V**, with a fine coffered ceiling that replaced the original Mudejar one. This is followed by a long room that ends at the triple arches of the **Peacocks**, named for the tiled birds above the arches, a fantasy of pattern on pattern. Through the peacock arches waits the most splendid room in the Alcázar, the **Salón de Ambajodores**, in which Carlos V is said to have held his wedding. The room seems more a jeweler's work than that of tilers or plasterers, for the complexity of the intricate designs stretches belief. Above is a dome that has no equal in the world. Throughout there is the shock of western motifs—seashells over the arches, castles and lions above portraits of the kings of Spain around the ceiling—that makes sense in a room designed for Christians by the Moors.

Off this room and through another for Felipe II, the small **Patio de las Muñecas** (dolls) is entered, named for two tiny faces on the capital of one of the columns. For many this is the favorite of all the areas of the Alcázar, because of its human scale, despite the intricacy of designs which seem to rise to the heavens. On one side is a room called **Isabella's bedroom**, on another, the bedroom for her new baby, **Don Juan**.

Return through the vestibule to the Patio de Leons. Turn right along a gallery to the **Patio de María de Padilla**, the site of a Gothic palace older than Pedro's, though much remodeled. Here are a suite of rooms known as the **palace of Carlos V**.

The **Emperor's Room** with non-Moorish tiles halfway up the walls and groined vaulting above seems rather a mishmash, but the **Tapestry Room** displays an amazing series of tapestries depicting a battle that Carlos fought in Tunis. Two hundred years later Felipe V ordered copies made of all the tapestries, which is our good fortune, because the originals disappeared and today you see these perfect copies.

What would a Moorish palace be without gardens? The Alcázar has its own in the rear, planted with exotic trees and dotted with ornamental waterways. Directly behind the Alcázar, first passing the aptly named **Grotesque Gallery** to the left, is the beautifully tiled **Carlos V Pavilion**. After the gardens, the Alcázar is exited through a garage in which two seventeenth-century carriages are parked. Note the use of leather straps as shock absorbers.

Archivo General de Indias

Open Mon.-Sat. 10 a.m. to 1 p.m. Closed Sun. Admission: free. On its own square between the cathedral and Alcázar, this impressive building was designed in 1572 by Herrera, the architect of the Escorial. Originally it was an exchange where merchants conducted business, but it was remodeled in the 18th century into an archive for the masses of material relating to the discovery, administration and trade of New World. Almost 40,000 files, going back to Columbus' time, are stored on the second floor, along with changing exhibits of maps and documents of general historical interest. It is worth the climb for a look.

Barrio Santa Cruz ★

This quarter is what remains of the Moorish layout of Seville, crowding houses along meandering alleys. Located next to the Alcázar and the mosque, this would have been the most densely populated part of the city during the time of the Moors. Long after the Moors and Jews who lived here had been expelled, this area again became a most desirable place to live. Today the quarter's real estate is expensive and the glistening whitewashed houses are perfectly maintained. The barrio is a place for strolling past cafes, artisans' shops and lovely patios to come suddenly into charming squares. The whole area can be explored in a half hour's leisurely walk.

The barrio begins alongside the east face of the Alcázar complex, extending in a rectangle for about 5 blocks east. Exit from the Alcázar to the right around the building, following its east face, to arrive in one block at the **Pl. Elvira**, with fountain and benches. Continue along the Alcázar side, turning right at the wall that borders the Alcázar gardens to follow Callejon del Agua past some of the nicest houses in the barrio. A short left turn at the end of the wall brings us to the attractive **Pl. Alfaro**. This is where Figaro supposedly serenaded Rosina on her balcony. To the right of the plaza a short street lets into the attractive **Pl. Santa Cruz**. From here you can wander north and west again to see more of the barrio, or retrace your steps to the Alcázar for the next sight.

WEST OF THE CATHEDRAL

Covering about 4 blocks to the west of the cathedral are a few nice things to see—the **Hospital de la Caridad***, the* **Torre del Oro***, and the* **Pl. de Toros***.*

The wide Av. de la Constitutión runs along the west side of the cathedral. Head south, turning right on C. Santander just after passing the Archivo de Indias. Turn right at the next corner on C. Temprado to view the **Hospital de la Caridad** on the right. It was founded in 1674 by Don Miguel de Manara who decided, after spending the first part of his life in pleasure and debauchery, to devote his remaining time to helping the poor. Some claim he was a model for the character Don Juan. The building is subdued baroque in style and its church contains a series of paintings by Murillo, along with two gruesome canvases by Leal. Manara is buried in front of the altar of the church. (Open Mon.-Sat. 10 a.m. to 1 p.m. and 3:30-6 p.m.; Sun. 10 a.m. to 1 p.m.; admission: 200 ptas.). On the opposite side of the street is the **Teatro de la Maestranza**, Seville's new opera house.

Back on C. Santander continue for one block to its end at Paseo de Cristobal Colón and the river. Left is the impressive **Torre del Oro**, so named for the gold hued tiles that used to decorate its sides. It was built in 1220, along with a twin across the river (no longer standing), to control river traffic. At night a chain between the two towers could be raised to close the river. The smaller tower on top and steeple are later additions. Today the structure functions as a naval museum (open Tues.-Fri. 10 a.m. to 2 p.m.; weekends to 1 p.m.; closed Mon.; admission 25 ptas.).

Two blocks north along Paseo Cristobal Colón is the **Pl. de Toros de la Maestranza ★**, Seville's bullring. Built in 1763, it is the oldest and most beautiful in Spain. Across the river C. Betis, a riverfront street with the feeling of a resort, is festive with cafes, restaurants and shops.

NORTH OF THE CATHEDRAL

Two worthwhile sights lie north of the cathedral area. Each is eminently walkable—at a distance of roughly half a mile—though the **Museo de Bellas Artes** *is west and the* **Casa de Pilatos** *is east, which makes the combined trip closer to a mile. If the walk sounds too long, take a taxi for one leg of it. We describe the entire walk from the cathedral but it can be followed in the reverse direction, of course.*

From the northern face of the cathedral, C. Hernando Colón leads due north for one block into the Pl. San Francisco. Running along the left side of the plaza is the most unusual **Ayuntamiento ★**, completed in 1564. The facade is a riot of Plateresque decoration, so much adorned that the building seems too slight to bear it. The surprise is the other side, barely embellished at all, for that side was redone in the 19th century when styles had changed. Running away from the north end of the plaza is the pedestrian shopping street of C. Sierpes, lined with attractive stores. A bust of Cervantes marks the spot of the former debtors' prison in which the writer began *Don Quixote.* One block along C. Sierpes, down an alley to the left, is the church of **San José** (1766), a gaudy little structure with the most baroque of altars. Returning to Sierpes and continuing across on C. Sagasta for a block to the west, the attractive Pl. Salvador and the church of **San Salvador** presents itself. The church was completed in 1712 on the site of the first great mosque of Seville. Its bell tower is the former minaret from 1079, and the facade incorporates original arches of the mosque. Only a foot or two of the arch columns show, demonstrating how much the ground has risen in nine hundred years. For the **Casa de Pilatos** (see the description elsewhere) continue across the plaza and due west for five blocks.

Return to C. Sierpes and continue north to the **Palacio de la Condesa de Lebrija**, on the right for two blocks. The interior is not of the first order, but it has three patios with mosaics from nearby Roman Italica, and a rather nice artesonado ceiling over the stairs. C. Sierpes ends in one block more, when it reaches the busy C. Martín Villa. Slightly right is the department store el Corte Inglés. The **Museo de Bellas Artes** (see description) is left along Martín Villa, which becomes C. Campaña for a block, then becomes C. Alfonso XII before reaching the museum 3 blocks later.

Casa Pilatos ★★★

Open daily 9 a.m. to 6 p.m. Admission: 500 ptas. to the ground floor, and 500 ptas. to the upper floor. On the right day, when the crowds are small and the mood proper, this can be one of the most memorable sights in Spain. It should not be viewed through the aesthetics of the Moors. Theirs was an ornate look of patterns heaped upon patterns but always with lightness and elegance. This palace for the Marqués of Tarifa was completed in 1540, and partially modelled on the House of Pontius Pilate, which the Marqués had visited in Jerusalem. You will not notice any Roman or near Eastern features, but you will see is a riot of Mudejar design. Here are the elements of Moorish architecture—bright patterned tiles, carved stucco filigree and textured wood ceilings, all taken to their extreme. The result is brash compared to the Moor's delicacy, but wonderful on its own terms.

Past a Plateresque portal and entrance courtyard, the drama begins with the central patio—Moorish arches on the lower level, Gothic balustrade and arches above, bright tiles on the walls and Roman statues inhabiting the corners. In the center stands a fountain, not a low, unassuming water trickling device, but a strong architectural statement. The fantasy continues in rooms leading from this patio, culminating in the southwest corner in the stairway to the upper story, with its remarkable ceiling. The second floor is more prosaic, with rooms of varying later periods and some antiques. Only part can be visited, because the present owner, the Duque de Medinaceli, still lives in one wing.

Museo de Bellas Artes ★★★

Open Tues.-Fri. 10 a.m. to 2 p.m. and 4-7 p.m.; Sun. 10 a.m.-2 p.m. Closed Mon. Admission: 200 ptas. This is the second best art museum in Spain, which still leaves it at a far remove from the Prado. The art is housed in a former convent, with three delicate patios, constructed in 1612, but thoroughly restored in the early 19th century. Its collection of works was rescued from nearby convents during the 19th century when many religious orders were suppressed in Spain. Extensive remodeling was still under way at our last visit, with no end in sight. At that time only a selection from the collection was hung in three rooms. The selection and arrangement was not the full permanent one, and will have been changed.

The collection is weighted heavily toward artists from Seville, including some of the finest work of her adopted son Zurbarán. A canvas by Pacheco, teacher and father-in-law of Velázquez, of a man and woman praying is worth a look. Pacheco is universally condemned as a journeyman artist, with good reason, but this work is inspired. Two Velázquez are owned by the museum and one, *The Portrait of Cristo-*

bal Suarez de Ribera, by itself repays the admission charge. It is among the most profound portraits ever done. Equally strong is the Zurbarán collection, which rivals that of the Prado. *Saint Hugh and the Carthusian Monks at Table* is interesting, *The Apotheosis of Saint Thomas Aquinas* is a miracle of perspective and design (with Zurbarán himself peering at the viewer, behind the kneeling Carlos V), and the *Virgin of the Caves,* in which those magical Zurbarán monks in white kneel to a Virgin with astonishing pink roses at her feet, is unforgettable.

There is a nice Goya *Portrait of José Duarzo,* and a fine statue of *Saint Bruno* by Montañes, as lifelike as wood can be. The museum owns an extensive collection of Murillo and of Valdés Leal, a Sevillano taken with Ruben's historical style, as well as some charming 19th- and early 20th-century work by local artists.

SOUTH OF THE CATHEDRAL

Southward past the baroque **Palacio de San Telmo** *an imposing arc of buildings borders a canal at the* **Pl. España,** *built for the aborted 1929 Seville World's Fair. The lovely* **Parque de Maria Luisa** *harbors the* **Museo Arqueológico, Museo de Atres y Costumbres Populares** *and the* **Pabillon Real**.

Av. de la Constitución runs south from the west side of the cathedral and ends in the grassy Puerta de Jerez. Continuing south past the Hotel Alfonso XIII Av. de Roma arrives in one block at the **Palacio de San Telmo**. The Churrigueresque portal is admirable. This was the residence of the dukes of Montpensier who donated the palace grounds—now the Parque de María Luisa—to the city. They also donated this palace, although the city has not yet decided what to do with it. Around the end of the palace, head southeast along its remaining gardens to Av. del Peru. In two blocks after passing the **Teatro Lope de Vega**, one of the buildings of the 1929 World's Fair, you arrive at Av. María Luisa, across which is the **Parque de María Luisa**. Walk south through the park, part wild, part formally arranged, to the south end past attractive villas left over from the 1929 World's Fair. Just before the end, comes the **Museo de Artes y Costumbres Populares** ★ with interesting exhibits of crafts, furniture and costumes (open Tues.-Sun. 10 a.m. to 2 p.m.; admission: 250 ptas.). In a few yards more the park ends, facing the **Museo Arqueológico** across the street.

Museo Arqueológico   ★

Open Tues.-Sun. 10 a.m. to 2 p.m. Closed Mon. Admission: 250 ptas. The finest Roman finds in Spain are displayed here. In the basement are shown artifacts from earlier cultures, including a famous hoard of gold from the sixth century B.C. found at Carambola, fine Phoenician statues and ceramics. The ground floor displays Celtiberian statuary, although none as wonderful as in Madrid, with the exception of some charming bulls and lions. Here too are fine Roman mosaics and statuary from nearby Italica.

Head east then north along the eastern edge of the park on Av. de Isabel la Católica, to pass the monumental **Pl. de España**. *This was Spain's pavilion for the 1929 World's Fair, and is a fantasy worth viewing. By continuing along Av. de Isabel la Católica, you return to the huge university building (the former tobacco factory), past which are the gardens of the Alcázar and the cathedral area again.*

Discovery Park, Isla de la Cartuja ★
This island is in the Guadalquivir, north of the cathedral square opposite the Museo de Bellas Artes. Open Tues.-Thurs. 7 p.m. to 2 a.m., Fri.-Sat. 10 a.m. to 4 a.m., and Sun. 10 a.m. to midnight. Admission: 2000 ptas., 1500 ptas. for children or senior-citizens. Here are remains of the 1st-Class World's Fair of 1992, in case you missed it. The fair commemorated the 500th anniversary of Columbus' discovery of the New World, and its theme was "The Age of Discovery." For this mammoth event, a lake was dug on the island with other water works to provide natural air conditioning. Now it is a huge theme-park that can be fun and educational for children of all ages.

The exhibition centers on the 15th-century monastery of **Santa Maria las Cuevas**, where Columbus reputedly explained his theories to the monks. From here begins the Way of Discovery, that includes a **Pavilion of the 15th Century** to show what life was like in Columbus' time in various parts of the world. The **Discovery Pavilion** presents the great inventions and discoveries that formed the modern world, including an audiovisual presentation with moving seats. The **Navigation Pavilion** traces the history of maritime exploration, and lets you "walk on water." The **Puerto de Indias** reconstructs a 15th-century port with shops, taverns and crafts of the era. There are miles of nature sights, and cable cars, catamarans, a circus, and an impressive fireworks and laser show at night.

WHERE TO STAY

During normal times, Seville has sufficient beds for all her guests, but not for Easter week or the *fiera* that follows it. You are already too late for lodgings in Seville for these events, though you can commute from Madrid, Málaga, Córdoba or Granada. At any other time beds should be readily available, although at prices almost a third higher than usual for Spain. Inexpensive rooms are hard to find.

VERY EXPENSIVE ($200+)

Alfonso XIII  Deluxe ★★★★★
San Fernando, 2 (on its own grounds opposite the rear of the Alcázar gardens). Rooms: 149. ☎ *422 28 50; FAX 421 60 33; Telex 72725.* Utterly deluxe and perhaps the most romantic hotel in Spain, the Alfonso was built so that aristocrats would have a place to stay while visiting the 1929 World's Fair. The style is Mudejar with elegant glazed tiles, mar-

ble and mahogany everywhere. The hotel surrounds a central patio that offers as lovely a spot for a drink as anyone could wish for. Of course the hotel location is perfect, and it is managed by the CIGA chain, which speaks well for the quality of service. It is, however, very expensive, passing thirty thousand pesetas for a double.

Las Casas de la Juderia   A2nd-class ★★★★

Pl. Santa Maria la Blanca (This plaza runs north-south at the eastern end of the Barrio Santa Cruz. The hotel is a block north.). Rooms: 29 suites. ☎ *441 51 50; FAX 442 21 70.* Four houses near the Barrio Santa Cruz were combined and gutted to produce a small number of beautiful apartment suites, styled with elegance. In addition to one, two or three bedrooms each has a dining-room, and a kitchen, including clothes washer and drier. The furniture is fine antique reproductions, and many rooms overlook lovely internal patios. For a party of travellers who would need more than one hotel room, a suite with two or three bedrooms could actually prove a bargain.

Tryp Colón   1st-class ★★★

Canalejas, 1 (two blocks south of the Museo Bellas Artes). Rooms: 211. ☎ *422 29 00; FAX 422 09 38; Telex 72726.* This is the other grand old hotel of Seville, also built for the 1929 World's Fair. The lobby is dramatically lit by a stained glass dome and the hotel has been recently remodeled to maintain its place near the top. However, it is not the Alfonso XIII either in luxury, location or romance. Unfortunately it tries to match its prices.

Meliá Sevilla   1st-class ★

Av. de la Borbolla, 3 (just east of the northeast end of Parque de Maria Luisa). Rooms: 366. ☎ *442 15 11; FAX 442 16 08; Telex 730 94.* This is a modern high-rise hotel, all gleaming metal and polished stone, and thoroughly impersonal. The rooms are comfortable, but it is a bit of a hike to the sights and the cost of a room is high. The buffet breakfast does include champagne, however.

EXPENSIVE ($100-$200)

Donna Maria   1st-class ★★★

Don Remondo, 16 (head to the east end of the cathedral and go northeast along C. Don Remondo for less than half a block). Rooms: 61. ☎ *422 49 90; FAX 422 97 65.* This gem of a small hotel is as conveniently located as a hotel can be—you can hit the cathedral with a rock, if inclined. The decor is luxe and homey at the same time, and prices barely push into the expensive category.

Inglaterra   1st-class ★★

Pl. Nueva, 7 (this lovely plaza fronts the west side of the Ayuntamiento, a block due north of the cathedral). Rooms: 116. ☎ *422 49 70; FAX 456 13 36; Telex 72244.* This is a staid hotel, with an atmosphere that belies its modern architecture. The service is superior and the rooms are eminently comfortable, but it seems expensive for what it provides.

Alcázar   2nd-class

Meléndez Pelayo, 10 (across the street from the northeast end of the Alcázar gardens). Rooms: 96. ☎ *441 20 11; Telex 72360.* This is a modern hotel of no distinction except that the location is convenient to the sights and the bedrooms are larger than most.

MODERATE ($50-$99)

Murillo   3rd-class ★★

Lope de Rueda, 9 (Located in the heart of the Barrio Santa Cruz where no car can go. A porter will carry your luggage from the Pl. Santa Cruz, however.) Rooms: 57; 14 apartments are also available. ☎ *421 60 95; FAX 421 96 16.* This lovely little hotel is beautifully decorated in the character of Andalusia. The public areas are warm with dark woods and the bedrooms are bright and clean.

La Rábida   3rd-class ★

Castelar, 24 (from the northwest corner of the cathedral go west along C. Garcia de Vinuesa for one block, then right for two blocks along C. Castelar). Rooms: 87. ☎ *422 09 60; FAX 422 43 75; Telex 73062.* This is a converted townhouse with atmosphere. A pleasant patio resides inside which some of the rooms overlook. The bedrooms are modern and comfortable, a good choice that would be even better if the staff cared more.

Bécquer   2nd-class ★

Reyes Católicos, 4 (This street runs away from the Puente Triana, a.k.a. Isabel II, the bridge just north of the Pl. de Toros. The hotel is at the beginning of the street.) Rooms: 120. ☎ *422 89 00; FAX 421 44 00; Telex 72884.* The hotel dates from the 60s, and is beginning to gain the charm that comes with age and good maintenance. Marble and dark woods in the lobby provide some elegance, and the service is more than adequate. If only the rooms had a little more character.

INEXPENSIVE (UNDER $50)

Goya   P2nd-class ★★

Mateos Gago, 31 (the street goes due east from the east face of the cathedral and reaches this hotel in two blocks). Rooms: 20. ☎ *421 11 70.* This would be a find, if it had not already been found, with so few rooms that it is essential to book in advance. The building with its gay awnings is charming, the rooms are clean and there is a garden on the roof. The location is better than that of the Alfonso XIII for about a sixth of its price.

WHERE TO EAT

Seville's reputation is that of serving the best food in Andalusia. Here tapas were invented, and some of the best can still be found. Eating is one of Seville's genuine treats. On a fine afternoon or evening, a pleasant outing is to cross the river over the bridge near the Torre del Oro and turn right along C. Betis. The atmosphere is that of a summer resort and restaurants, many with views of the river and the sights, serve quite good food. For recommendations look for the C. Betis address in the selections below. If feeling in a picnic mood, have a cup of gazpacho to go from **Gaspaciaria** at C. Hernando Colón, 7, just north of the cathedral.

EXPENSIVE ($50+)

Egaña Oriza

San Fernando, 41 (at the southeast tip of the Alcázar Garden). ☎ *422 72 11. Closed Saturday at lunch, Sunday, and August.* This restaurant is the most innovative and acclaimed in Seville. The bar at the entrance serves sublime tapas. The dining room is comfortably large, modern and tan, brightened by light from a two-story glass wall. The food is Basque nouvelle, unique and subtle. Here you are in the chef's hands and they are good hands indeed. Reservations are essential.

Amex, Diners, MasterCard and Visa accepted.

San Marco

C. Cuna, 6 (follow C. Sierpes, the pedestrian shopping street, to its northern end and turn right onto C. Martín Villa, right again in one block onto C. Cuña to the restaurant at the corner on the right). ☎ *421 24 40. Closed Sunday and August.* The restaurant is housed in a century-old townhouse and decorated in a vaguely Venetian style, with tables elegantly set. The menu ranges over Italian, Continental and some Andalusian dishes, all done with care. To begin, have ravioli stuffed with seabass, with pheasant and foie gras or with crabmeat, or a salmon and crab tart with caviar. Bream on a bed of fennel or goose confit Lyon style are among the succulent entrees. Leave room for desert.

Amex, Diners, MasterCard and Visa accepted.

Asador Ox's

C. Betis, 61 (opposite side of the river, opposite the cathedral). ☎ *427 95 85. Closed Sunday and August.* Although the chef is Basque, the restaurant specializes in grilled fish and meats, all perfectly done. Installed in a small townhouse, the restaurant's light decor lends a fresh feeling.

Amex, Diners, MasterCard and Visa accepted.

La Albahaca

Pl. Santa Cruz, 12 (in the Barrio Santa Cruz, one block north of the eastern end of the Alcázar Gardens). ☎ *422 07 14. Closed Sunday.* This is the intimate, romantic place people imagine in Seville, all tiles and greens in an elegant small mansion. The food and service will not disappoint. Sea bass with fennel and bonito are just two specialties, and how does tangerine mousse sound for desert?

Amex, Diners, MasterCard and Visa accepted.

Florencia

Av. Eduardo Dato, 49 (this avenue runs due east from the northern tip of the Alcázar Gardens, though it begins with the name of C. Demetrio de Rios, a walk of about four long blocks). ☎ *453 35 00. Closed August.* The dining room, done in peach and light greys, feels elegant without being intimidating. The menu tends to the nouvelle, with a menu de degustación to sample the chef's proudest wares.

Amex, Diners, MasterCard and Visa accepted.

La Isla

C. Arfe, 25 (cross Av. de la Constitutión at the southern end of the cathedral and take the first right down C. Arfe, little more than an alley). ☎ *421 26 31. Closed Monday, and from the middle of August to the middle of September.* Newly installed in a modern setting of salmon and black lacquer, this is the best pure seafood restaurant in Seville. Start with the house paella, followed by the fish of your choice, and you will hardly notice that the service lacks graciousness.

Amex, Diners, MasterCard and Visa accepted.

Rio Grande

C. Betis, 61 (opposite Ox's). ☎ *427 39 56.* The view from the terrace is the thing here, especially at night when lights sparkle on the river. Although the menu ranges over international dishes, we suggest sticking with the Andalusian ones, such as paella and gazpacho which are done well. *Amex, Visa, Diners and MasterCard accepted.*

MODERATE ($20-$50)

Los Alcázares

C. Miguel de Manara, 10 (la few steps west of the Alcázar front, across from the Archivo de Indias). ☎ *421 31 03. Closed Sunday.* The decor is typical Andalusian and the menu covers the expected, but the bill will be less. For the price and basic Spanish food, this is a good place.

Amex, Diners, MasterCard and Visa accepted.

Modesto

C. Cano y Cueto, 5 (C. Santa Maria la Blanca forms the eastern border of the Barrio Santa Cruz. The restaurant's street runs east from its southern end). ☎ *441 68 11. Closed Wednesday.* This is a popular, unassuming place that serves superior tapas. If you're in the mood for a full meal, the dining room upstairs is pleasant with white walls and blue-and-white tiles, more intimate than the tables outside. Fried fish is delectable, as are the specials.

Amex, Diners, MasterCard and Visa accepted.

Hostería del Laurel

Pl. Venerables, 5 (this plaza is exactly in the center of the Barrio Santa Cruz). ☎ *422 02 95.* The outside looks like a mesón should, and the inside continues the theme with hanging hams and garlic above heavy wooden tables. The food is standard Spanish cuisine, but agreeable.

Amex, Diners, MasterCard and Visa accepted.

INEXPENSIVE (UNDER $20)

Pizzeria San Marco

C. Betis, 66 (just south of Ox's). ☎ *428 03 10.* Yes it is a pizzeria, but all modern and shining, and heavily patronized by the locals. The most expensive pasta is under $10, and tasty.

EVENINGS OUT

Seville is the best place to see flamenco and maintains three permanent *tablas* for the art. Each is a small place, seating an audience of fifty or fewer, so reservations are always a good idea and can be arranged by most hotels.

Los Gallos

Pl. Santa Cruz, 11. ☎ *421 69 81.* Too intimate, but puts on the most authentic flamenco, and prides itself on the best performers.

El Arenal

Dos de Mayo, 26. ☎ *421 64 92.* Will serve you dinner, or not, as you wish, and the show is often good.

El Patio Sevillano

Paseo de Colón, 11. ☎ *421 41 20.* Mixes other kinds of folk dance and songs with flamenco.

Understand that pure flamenco can be very intense. In fact the aim is to throw one's soul to the audience; performers are judged by the depth of their feelings. It is part dance, part guitar music, part singing and part rhythmic clapping. The dancing should be familiar, but the singing is strangely guttural and as earthy as the human voice can become. Guitarists can be amazing virtuosos, and the clapping incredible. Given a good group of performers, the experience will be unforgettable. Current prices range from 2500-3000 ptas., which includes one free drink. Usually there are two shows, one at about 9:30 p.m., the other at midnight, but check.

DIRECTORY

INFORMATION • Located on Av. de la Constitución, 21B, just south of the cathedral. Open Mon.-Sat. from 9:30 a.m. to 7:30 p.m. and Sun. from 9:30 a.m. to 2 p.m. ☎ 422 14 04.

TRAINS AND BUSES • The station for most destinations is Santa Justa at the intersection of José Laguillo and Av. Kansas City (☎ 441 41 11). A cab is necessary. However, trains for Cádiz and west leave from Estación de San Bernardo, a half mile northeast of the Alcázar Gardens (☎ 423 22 55). The RENFE office is on C. Zaragoza, 29, about three blocks north of the Pl. de Toros (☎ 422 26 93).

As usual, several bus companies split up the routes, but most depart from the Estación de Autobuses (☎ 441 71 11) at Pl. de San Sebastian, which is a long block east of the former Tobacco Factory. See the office of tourism for schedules and the various companies.

POST OFFICE AND TELEPHONES • The main post office is at Av. de la Constitución, 32, west of the Archivo de Indias. Telephones are available at the Pl. Nueva, 3, which is on the west side of the Ayuntamiento, and open weekdays to 10 p.m., though closed for lunch. Sat., it closes at 2 p.m.

POLICE • The main station is at the Pl. de la Gavidia (☎ 422 88 40; ☎ 091 for emergencies).

AIRPORT • Seville's San Pablo Airport (☎ 451 61 11) connects with major European cities and most Spanish airports, but few international destinations. It is located 12 k east along N-IV. Take Av. Menéndez Pelayo north from the Alcázar Gardens to the end of the gardens and then right onto C. Demetrio de Rios, which becomes Av. de Eduardo Dato as it travels along the Gardens of la Buhaira. Turn left on Av. Luis Morales two blocks past the gardens which brings you to the train station, and Av. Kansas City to the right, that takes you to N-IV. Iberia is located at Almirante Lobo, 3 (☎ 422 89 01). This street runs to the river from Puerta de Jerez, the plaza at the western corner of the Alcázar gardens. Buses connect from there with flights.

SHOPPING • Among the best buys in Spain are ceramics made in Seville, partly because their prices are low, partly because the quality of work and design is high. You can get a taste of the wares by walking along the pedestrian mall of C. Sierpes. At #30 is **Cerámica Sevillaño**, with fine designs, and at #66 **Sevillarte**, equally good. **Martian** at #6 sells thicker, more folk-like pieces. If you like what you see, try **Cerámicas Sevilla** on Pemiento, #9, which runs beside the wall to the Alcázar Gardens in the Barrio Santa Cruz. Around the corner, at Gloria, #5, this outlet continues. The wares are part Moorish-inspired with gold rims and part Renaissance blues on white, and blues and greens on white. The supply is so large this shop seems to be a factory, but it is not. For the factories and their outlets, you have to cross the river over Puente Isabel II, the bridge just north of the Pl. de Toros. Directly off the bridge you come to C. San Jorge, and the heart of the ceramic outlets area. Prices are incredibly low, and most companies will ship. Try **Cerámica Santa Ana** at #31, **Cerámica Ruiz** at #27, and **Cerámica Montalvan**, especially for tiles, around the corner at Alfareria, #21.

Interesting too are the fans, including some very expensive antiques, at **Casa Rubio** on C. Sierpes, #56. Further down Sierpes, at #73 is a leather shop named **Bolsos Casal** with copies of expensive name-bags for women at modest prices. For the horsey set there is a superb leather store, **El Caballo**, on C. Antonio Diaz, #7, at the end of the street on the east side of the Pl. de Toros. A nice branch of Artespaña displays well-made furniture and accessories in the Pl. de la Gavidia, just north of the el Corte Inglés department store at the end of C. Sierpes.

EXCURSIONS

Roman remains at **Itálica** lie 9 k north, for a half day of exploring. **Jerez de la Frontera**, the home of sherry, waits an hour south for a pleasant half day of free or inexpensive samples. Of course, magical **Córdoba** and **Granada** are within a few hours east, and described under their respective headings in this chapter. For an excursion of two or three days, consider the area of **Extremadura**, due north, which has not yet become inundated with tourists and is described in a later chapter. Also, the Portuguese border and beginning of the Algarve beaches are 175 k away; Lisbon is 417 k distant.

For **Itálica** *cross the river on the Puente de Chapina, the third bridge north of the cathedral area, travelling west along C. Ordiel on the west bank. Follow signs to Santiponce and Mérida. About 3 k outside of town turn north on N-630. Follow signs 1 k past Santiponce for Itálica.*

For the **Algarve** *follow the directions for Itálica but do not turn north on N-630. Continue west instead on A-49 (E-1). After 3 k, switch to N-431, just before Huelva in 92 k, and a further journey of 63 k to Portuguese border.*

For **Lisbon** *follow the directions to Itálica and continue past it along N-630. Just before Zafra in 134 k turn west on N-432 (E-102) to Badajoz in 79 k at the border. West from Badajoz on N-4 (E-90) brings you to Cruzamento de Pagoes in 152 k. There go south on N-10 (still E-90) to Setubal in 35 k and the highway E-1 to Lisbon 50 k away.*

For **Extremadura** *follow the directions to Itálica and continue past it along N-630. You come to Mérida in 194 k.*

For **Jerez** *follow Av. de la Palmera leading south from the southern end of the Parque de Maria Luisa. You are given the choices of the toll road A-4 or the free N-IV toward Cádiz, reaching Jerez in about 70 k.*

Itálica   ★

Open Tues.-Sat. 9 a.m. to 5:30 p.m., Sun. 10 a.m. to 4 p.m. Admission: 250 ptas. This Roman town was among the earliest in Spain, founded in 206 B.C. by Scipio Africanus as a place of retirement for the veterans among his troops. By the second century A.D. it had grown to a population of 10,000 and stood among the most important towns in Spain. Two emperors were born here—Trajan and Hadrian. Prosperity ended with the arrival of the Visigoths who favored nearby Seville. Itálica then became a quarry for marble and stone materials, even for mosaics to use as decoration in later Christian mansions. The surprise is that anything remains, and quite a bit does, though only a fifth of the site has been excavated so far. There is a huge amphitheater that once seated 40,000, a theater, two baths, a forum and a network of streets. Here and there some remaining mosaics are fenced off, but the major works and all the statuary are carted off to museums in Madrid and Seville as soon as they are uncovered.

JEREZ DE LAS FRONTERA

Population: 176,238. Area code: 956; Zip code: 11400. Arrival is along Av. Alcade Alvaro Domecq, though at C. Guadalete one-way signs force a right onto C. Beato Juan Grande, which becomes Alameda Cristina in one block. Continue one block and turn slightly left. Then one-way signs again force a right fork onto C. Larga. Again comes a fork and a right on C. Lanceria to the garden of the Pl. del Arenal. Turn right then left around the garden, take the first right into the Pl. Monti. Turn left at the end of the plaza past the gardens of the Alcázar. Follow them to their end for parking beside the Alcázar.

NOTE... *Almost all bodegas close Aug., and are closed on weekends.*

Jerez is a corruption of the Arabic name *Xerex*, which in turn was a corruption of the Roman Caesaris, which eventually gave us "sherry" in English. Jerez is a rather quiet and pleasant town, a place to see a nice Alcázar, some mansions, a sherry bodega or two, and even some elegant dressage similar to the Vienese Lippizaners. As to the bodegas, most open only for the morning between 10 a.m. and 1 p.m., or so, close all of August, and most charge an admission of between 250 and 400 ptas. For this you get a tour of almost an hour and samples. Most of the tours are in English.

After a look at the restored **Alcázar**, a stop can be made at the oldest bodega in Jerez, **Gonzalez Byass**, on the street west of the Alcázar, at C. Manuel Maria Gonzalez, 12 (☎ 34 00 00). Return to C. Manuel Maria Gonzalez and follow it north. As it bends east around the gardens, take the first left to the **Colegiata church** ★ with a fine baroque stair and portal. In the sacristy hangs Zurbarán's *Sleeping Girl*, a worthwhile work seldom seen or reproduced. North of the church we arrive in the Pl. del Arroyo, a.k.a. Pl. de Domecq. At its west end C. San Ildefonso runs north to the bodega of **Pedro Domencq**, one of the largest shippers. In this instance reservations are required (☎ 33 19 00). At the east end of the Pl. Arroyo is the huge **Palacio de Marquesse de Bertemati**. Following its south side for a block brings the charming **Pl. del Asunción**. At its south end is the **Casa del Cabildo Vieja**, late 16th-century with an ornate facade. A small archaeological museum is housed inside. On the east side of the plaza is **San Dionisio**, a redone Moorish-Gothic church, still with a nice Mudejar tower and fine artesonado ceiling above the nave. Four or five blocks northeast of the plaza is the house of **Ponce de León** (1537) with a pretty patio.

For more bodegas stop by the **office of tourism** for a map and information. It is located two blocks north of the Pl. Arenal gardens at C. Alameda Cristina, 7 (☎ 31 05 37). You need a cab to get to the **Real Escuela de Andaluza de Arte Equestre** on Av. de Duque de Abrantes (☎ 31 11 11), to see Lippizaner-like dressage. Shows are Thurs. from noon to 1:30 p.m. and tickets are available at the box office for 1100-1400 ptas., depending on seats.

ÚBEDA ★ ★

Population: 28,717
Area code: 953; Zip code: 23400

From **Madrid** *take A-4 (E-5) south toward Ocaña. Along the way the highway becomes N-IV. Continue for 292 k to Bailén to take N-322 east toward Úbeda for 40 k. To combine with* **Baeza**, *close by, take N-321 west for 9 k to Baeza. After Baeza, N-321 wends to Jaén in 48 k, just before which N-323 heads south to Granada in 93 k. Or, return to Bailén, from which N-IV heads west to Córdoba in 108 k.*

From **Granada** *take N-323 north toward Jaén for 88 k, changing to N-321 east toward Úbeda just before Jaén. Úbeda is 57 k along N-321. From Córdoba take N-IV west toward Andujar and Bailén for 108 k. From Bailén take N-322 east toward Úbeda for 40 k.*

Like its sister city Baeza, Úbeda was taken early by the Christians during the Reconquest, and became wealthy as a staging post for battles further south. In the 16th century, it invested those profits on monuments and palaces, unfortunately just as a new road to thriving Jaén was about to turn Úbeda into a backwater. These lovely building are spread around, but one perfect concentration in the Pl. Vázquez de Molina constitutes one of the finest single assemblages of Renaissance architecture in Spain.

The city does its part to encourage tourists by clear signs directing traffic to the *Zona Monumental*, the major sights within the old city walls. Úbeda also offers crafts in a Gypsy quarter nearby. All can be seen in two hours.

The place to begin is the harmonious open Pl. Vázquez de Molina. Due north is the **Casa de las Cadenas**, now the city hall, named for the chains around the forecourt, and built for a secretary to Felipe II. Its front is imposing with classical columns and surprising, out of place, caryatids. Wander around the back for a look at its lovely patio and a stop at the **tourist office** next door for a fine brochure and map. In the Pl. Molina again, the mansion next to the Casa de las Cadenas is the **Palacio del Condestabel Dávalos ★**, a 17th-century renovation of a structure a century older. Its long, restrained front is made harmonious by two elegant lines of windows. This is one of the first historic buildings made into a parador, in 1930, and is still splendid inside. Opposite, to the south of the plaza, is the church of **Santa Maria de los Reales Alcázares**. Behind it are remains of the

Moorish **Alcázar** for which it is named, but the church is mainly 16th-century inside, with notable painted ironwork and unusual ceilings of arabesques painted blue.

At the east end of the plaza stands the unusual **Capilla del Salvador**. (If closed, apply to the first door on the right.) This church once formed part of a great palace designed for Carlos V, but only it and some ruins behind remain. The front is a truly original design by the architect Vandaelvira from plans by Gil de Siloé. Two round towers at the corners seem much too small and low, until the eye rises to the triangular pediment above, and grasps the triangular design. The portal is styled as a Roman arch with scenes carved around and above. The inside suffered great damage during anticlerical raids at the outbreak of the Spanish Civil War, including the destruction of most of the church treasures and art, but has been reconstructed to its original neoclassical look. The theatrical high altar behind fine ornamental ironwork contains what remains of Berruguette's original retablo, and the sacristy is a glorious Italianate masterpiece of coffered ceiling, medallions, graceful caryatids and atlantes.

Walk north from the front of the chapel up C. Horno Contador passing the **Casa de los Salvajes** on the left in one block. The reason for the name is evident in the men dressed in animal skins holding the coat of arms of a local bishop. A short block further brings the Pl. Primero de Mayo, the main square. Across, well displayed, sits the church of **San Pablo ★**. The west front portal is accomplished 13th-century work; the south portal is a lovely Isabeline design. Inside, the chapels command attention with fine iron grillwork, stucco vaults and doorways.

Continue from the rear of the church northeast along C. Rosal. The **Casa Canastero**, in a short block, was a bishop's mansion, with two carved soldiers, bearing the owner's coat of arms. More mansions line the previous street, C. Montiel. Ahead stand the city walls and a 14th-century **Mudejar gate**. Outside the walls the street is renamed Cuesta de la Merced, and changes its name again after going through a square to C. Valencia. Here is the Gypsy quarter and crafts of pottery, ironwork and esparto grass.

If time permits, the huge **Hospitale de Santiago** at the intersection of C. Obispo Cobos and the road to Jaén is worth seeing. It was built in 1575 by the architect who executed the Capilla el Salvador. A large statue of St. James as the Killer of Moors rises above the entrance, and inside is a classical colonnaded patio with a grand staircase covered by original frescos.

WHERE TO STAY

While there is no need to stay the night in Úbeda with Granada and Córdoba an hour away, there is no reason not to enjoy the lovely parador either, or some less expensive accommodation.

EXPENSIVE ($100-$200)

Parador Condestable Dávalos   1st-class ★ ★ ★

Pl. Vázquez de Molina, 1. Rooms: 31.☎ *75 03 45; FAX 75 12 59.* This parador is one of the loveliest smaller ones, and situated on a pretty square. The patio is elegant, the common spaces are homey with working fireplaces, the stairway to the rooms is grand, and the ample rooms have wood ceilings and commodious baths.

MODERATE ($50-$99)

La Paz   3rd-class ★

Andalucia, 1 (at the northeast corner of the old city walls). Rooms: 51. ☎ *75 21 46; FAX 75 08 48.* The hotel is modern and the rooms are simple, but with homey touches. A stay here also provides an opportunity to investigate the city walls.

WHERE TO EAT

Pickings are slim for a town of this size, with only one place we can recommend.

MODERATE ($20-$50)

Cusco

Parque de Vandevira, 8. ☎ *75 34 13. Closed Monday night and from the middle of July through August.* The place is simple and so is the food, but it is prepared with care. And the bill will not shock.

Visa and MasterCard accepted.

DIRECTORY

INFORMATION • Pl. del Ayuntamiento, 2, next to the rear of the Ayuntamiento. ☎ 75 08 97. Open Mon.-Fri. 10 a.m. to 1:30 p.m. and 6-8 p.m. Open weekends 10 a.m. to 1:30 p.m.

TRAINS AND BUSES • Buses leave C. San José 9 times a day for the train station at Linares-Baeza 20 k away. Buses are frequent to Baeza (under $2) and connect with less frequency to Córdoba, Seville and Madrid.

POST OFFICE AND TELEPHONES • On C. Trinidad, just north of the walls. ☎ 75 00 31.

POLICE • In the Ayuntamiento. ☎ 75 00 23.

EXCURSIONS

The natural excursion is the one to Baeza. Granada, Córdoba, and even Seville are an hour or two away. See the respective descriptions under separate headings in this chapter.

EXTREMADURA

The Roman bridge at Mérida.

HISTORICAL PROFILE:
COLUMBUS AND THE CONQUISTADORES

Christopher Columbus was born Cristoforo Colombo in Genoa, Italy in 1451, the son of a master wool weaver. Attracted more by the tales of sailors in this seaport town than by the prosaic looms to which he was apprenticed, he grew into a romantic, dreaming of fabled kingdoms. Physically, he was tall, with high cheek bones, an aquiline nose, ruddy complexion and striking red hair—that turned white by the age of 30. It is likely that the blood of an ancient barbarian who had invaded Italy flowed in his veins.

The first records of Columbus at sea occur only after the sale of his family's house and business in 1473, when he was 22. Columbus worked for his father, as youths of the time generally did, until something caused the family business to fail, in effect setting Columbus free. The next year Columbus sailed to North Africa as a deckhand, and a year after to the Aegean. In 1476, he joined a merchant convoy to Portugal, but his ship was attacked by pirates off the Lisbon coast and sunk. Columbus swam to shore and made his way into the city, which was then a center for maritime exploration. After a quick return to Genoa, he set out to Lisbon again for a new life.

He resided for eight years among a community of Genoese in Lisbon where he and his brother sold maps. Here he taught himself Portuguese, Spanish and Latin. In a public chapel near his shop, he met Felipa Perestrello e Moniz, the daughter of a deceased aristocratic sea captain, and fell in love. They married in 1479, and Diego, their first son, was born the next year. Columbus sailed with Felipa for a stay with her relatives in Madeira, and later—probably thanks to friends of her father—joined an expedition sailing to West Africa's Gold Coast. These voyages sent Columbus to farther reaches than all but a handful of his contemporaries.

Felipa's contacts gained Columbus an audience with the king of Portugal in 1484, to whom Columbus proposed his grand plan to sail west to Cathay, to Cipango (Japan) and India, and trade there for precious spices, pearls and gold. Although the Portuguese king declined to support this expedition, he left open the possibility of reconsideration. However, when word arrived that Bartholeme Dias had rounded Africa, the king no longer had reason to explore a westward course to India, for one of his own captains had opened an eastward route.

There is no mystery about how Columbus came to the idea of reaching the Indies by sailing west. Educated people of the time all knew these lands lay somewhere across the Atlantic, for even then, belief in a flat earth was confined to the ignorant. Columbus differed only in his assessment of the practicality of such a trip. He thought the East lay 2400 miles west of the Azores, the westernmost lands known to Europeans—a voyage of less than three months—while conventional wisdom estimated the distance at 10,000 miles. It was one thing in those times to cruise along a coastline for a month or more, but quite another matter to sail for long periods out of sight of land. Although the astrolabe existed, its use required data from prior voyages, so uncharted waters could only be traversed by imprecise compass dead-reckoning. The longer the voyage, the further off course errors would take a ship, and errors were unavoidable. Educated people believed that Columbus' project was possible, but, if the distance was 10,000 miles, too risky to undertake. Because Columbus placed Japan a thousand miles closer to Europe than most cartographers, he figured that the Indies were one quarter as distant as others thought, for, by decreasing the size of each degree of latitude, he lowered the scholarly estimate of the world by 25%. Of course, Columbus was wrong: 2400 miles west of the Azores lay the Virgin Islands, not Japan.

Felipa died in 1485, leaving Columbus to raise his 5-year-old son. Unable to generate interest in his plan at the Portuguese court, Columbus sailed to Spain. On landing, he placed his child in the monastery of la Rabida, near modern Huelva, a step that would prove crucial to making his eventual voyage possible. In nearby Seville, he met Enrique de Gúzman, the Duke of Medina Sidona, a hero of the Reconquest. Enrique agreed to underwrite Columbus' voyage, but then fought a private quarrel that caused the king and queen to exile him from Seville. Columbus next turned to Luis de la Cerda, the Duke of Medina Celi, who owned a merchant fleet, and gained his support. Columbus required no more money than a wealthy person of the time could afford—less than $100,000 by today's standards —and unfailingly convinced those who heard his arguments. Only scholars resisted him. But Luis thought the enterprise should have royal approval, so he asked permission of the queen.

Queen Isabella invited Columbus to explain his proposal in person, and they met in nearby Córdoba. She was interested enough to consider royal sponsorship, but first submitted the matter to a commission for study. In the meantime, she provided Columbus with housing and a stipend. Columbus waited six years, as the royal stipend dwindled away, until the commission issued its report: the enterprise was indeed possible, but it was based on factual errors that made it impractical.

A desolate Columbus returned to the monastery of la Rabida to collect his son, intending to sail for France or England to try for sponsorship. But first he told his tale to the abbot of the monastery, Juan Perez, and produced another convert. The abbot, who had once been confessor to the queen, asked Isabella to reconsider. She sent for Columbus, supplying a mule and money for his transport to meet in Santa Fé, outside Granada which she was then besieging.

Presumably this recall meant that Isabella had changed her mind and was now willing to support Columbus, yet after their meeting she dismissed him again. The suspicion is that, after gaining approval in principle, Columbus cooled the queen's ardor by asking for excessive rewards. We know he demanded that he be raised to noble rank, named Admiral of the Ocean Seas (the highest maritime office in Spain), appointed governor-general of any lands he should discover, and receive one-tenth of all the profits realized from his explorations. As Columbus rode off on his mule, the royal treasurer Santangel changed Isabella's mind again by pointing out that the necessary funds were available in a dormant account. The titles and percentages should not be a sticking point, since they would be granted only if Columbus were successful and in that event would be merited. Isabella sent for Columbus one last time and agreed to underwrite his expedition.

Columbus sped to Palos de la Frontera, beside the monastery, for that city had been fined for a communal misdeed and owed the crown the services of two caravels. These were the *Niña* and the *Pinta*. Each was about 70 feet long by 23 wide, the size of a modern coastal yacht. Columbus bought another vessel, the *Santa María*, which was 50% larger, although less sea-worthy, for his flagship. The *Niña* and *Pinta* carried crews of 24 and 26 respectively, while the *Santa María* carried 40. Crews consisted primarily of men from nearby towns, and included a sailor sentenced to death for killing a man in a brawl, and three of his friends caught engineering his jailbreak. One *converso*, (former Jew) was hired because Columbus thought his knowledge of Hebrew and Arabic would be helpful in conversing with the Great Khan of China.

Preparations were completed by August 2, 1492, but Columbus waited one day more because, on this deadline for all Jews to leave Spain, the seas were congested with ships. On August 3rd his tiny armada set sail for the Azores, where they restocked before entering uncharted waters. Throughout the voyage Columbus kept two ship's logs, a real one and another—for the eyes of the crew—that shaved 10% from the distance traveled to make the men feel less distant from home. As it happened, the fake log proved the more accurate. After two months they arrived at the place where Columbus had assured the crews that Japan lay. No land was sighted. The sailors, whose fears had been calmed by Columbus' certainties, now threatened mutiny, for if they sailed much farther, their provisions would not last the return trip. Columbus talked them into continuing for two days more. The next day signs of land were spied—a floating log and a carved stick. The second day, October 12, a sailor caught sight of one of the islands of Bermuda.

Columbus sailed around the Caribbean looking for China and Japan, and seeking gold. He landed on Cuba and at the Dominican Republic. Then he returned, hitting the Azores by superb dead-reckoning. After reprovisioning, he sailed to Portugal, but left hurriedly, fearful of poisoning by the king whose eastern monopoly to India was threatened by Columbus' discoveries. Thirty-two weeks after he had set out, he docked again at Palos, then crossed Spain with 6 captured Indians (as he called them), colored birds, masks and trinkets of gold. When Columbus arrived in Barcelona, where the court was then in residence, the king and queen wept with him in joy over his success.

Columbus captained three subsequent voyages to explore, colonize, and bring Catholicism to the New World natives. On the second voyage, he carried horses, cows and pigs, none of which existed in the New World. In return his men brought back 500 slaves and syphilis to Europe, although not without first leaving smallpox and measles behind. He sighted the mainland of South America on his third voyage, the first European to do so. But he had no inkling that he had discovered a new continent; he assumed all major land masses must already be known by the enlightened time of the 16th century.

With each succeeding voyage Columbus' star, which had shone so brightly at his first success, grew more tarnished. Colonization had not succeeded: one village was obliterated by Indians, another by disease. Under his command, but not always by his order, natives were killed, enslaved, tortured and raped. He had to contend with the wildness of the terrain, the natives, and his own men, a combination that would test any governor's ability. On his third voyage, based on stories from jealous lieutenants, Columbus was arrested in Santa Domingo and carted back to Spain in chains, only to be forgiven by his sovereigns in person. The worst ignominy was his return from his fourth voyage to no fanfare at all, in part because his benefactor, Isabella, lay dying. After her death, King Ferdinand rescinded many of the honors and much of the money Isabella had promised Columbus. The last years of Columbus' life were consumed petitioning for what he had originally been promised. On May 20, 1506, the severely arthritic Columbus died. The coat of arms he designed said simply: To Castile and León, a New World given by Columbus.

The New World still remained to be conquered. Mexico and Peru contained Indian kingdoms that would test any European power, but the Spanish conquistadores were extraordinary men who performed what can only be called "miracles." Most of them came from Extremadura, on the Portuguese border—hard men bred by a harsh environment.

In 1519, an expedition set out for Mexico under the command of Hernán Cortés. Five hundred men, 15 horses and 2 cannons were landed on the island of Cozumel, then ferried to the mainland. This force was able to hold off and defeat thousands of Indians at a time, thanks in part to the Indians' fear of horses, which they had never seen, and in part to a prophecy that their god Quezalcoatl would return as a white man flying over the sea. Cortés burned his ships, to force resolve on his men, then captured Montezuma, the emperor of Mexico, and defeated his armies. Hundreds of pounds of gold and an empire were gained in the process.

Cortés was born in **Medellin** in Extremadura, to a family of lesser nobility. A sickly child, he studied law for two years at the University of Salamanca before quitting, to his parents' grave displeasure. He was a strong-willed young man, determined to win fame as a soldier, so he signed on for a war in Italy. Before embarking, tales about the New World turned his head, however, leading him to spurn his commission and to sail westward instead. After his conquests, he retired to Medellin where he lived for 11 years more, dying at the ripe age of 63.

In 1512 an ill-fated Spanish expedition landed near modern Panama. Indians killed most of the force; the rest were left under the command of a young lieutenant named Francisco Pizarro. But reinforcements arrived, including a young stowaway named Vasco Núñez de Balboa who was fleeing creditors. After convincing the soldiers to appoint him as their leader, Balboa set off into the jungle and discovered the Pacific Ocean. In full armor he walked into the sea to take possession for Castile. Balboa also had been born in Extremadura, in the town of **Jerez de los Caballeros**. Unfortunately, his triumph was short-lived. Envy of his discovery and charges of theft caused the Governor-general of the Americas to order Pizarro to arrest and behead Balboa in 1530.

Pizarro thus became the commander of Central America, an uncharted jungle that held no excitement for him. At age 50 he turned his attention south to modern-day Peru. Using trickery, he captured the ruling Inca and, by governing the country through him, conquered an empire the size of Europe, with a population of five million—all with an army of 180 men and 27 horses. The Inca ruler offered one of the world's great bribes for his freedom—enough gold and silver to fill a room 17 feet by 12, as high as Pizarro could reach. Pizarro accepted 13,000 pounds of gold and 26,000 pounds of silver, then burned the Incan ruler at the stake. Later, Pizarro was repaid in kind—assassinated by masked Spanish soldiers. He too was an Extremaduran, from **Trujillo**. Born illegitimate to a hidalgo captain of infantry and a humble mother, he was raised with the captain's legitimate children and took one half-brother with him to Peru. The brother survived to bring riches home to Trujillo, along with an Inca princess wife.

With such conquests came unheard-of fortunes. American silver and gold mines annually produced the equivalent of the Spanish royal income from all other sources combined, although, unforgiveably, millions of natives perished from starvation and disease to mine this treasure. The great irony is that Spain was not enriched by her new wealth at all. She had become embroiled in a decades' long war in the Netherlands that consumed all her resources. The gold and silver unloaded from galleons in Seville was immediately transported north to fund Spain's army. All in vain, for Spain lost the war.

EXTREMADURA

The name of the province means "Beyond the Duero (River)." Like its name, the land conjures up extremes. The area is generally poor, though three great rivers course through it, for their tributaries do not spread far from the main beds, a millennia-old condition that the Spanish government began correcting in the 1950s with dams and canals. The hard land of Extremadura produced hard men—as exemplified by the Spanish adventurers who conquered the great Indian civilizations of the New World. These men seized any opportunity to leave rather than face the prospect of scratching a living from unproductive fields. Hernán Cortés, conqueror of the Aztecs and Mexico, came from Medellin; Francisco Pizarro, conqueror of the Incas and Peru, came from Trujillo; and many of their less famous soldiers emigrated from Extremaduran villages and towns.

Extremadura comprises the western edge of Spain. Geographically it would be natural for Extremadura to belong to Portugal. Mountains block it from the rest of Spain in the north, east and south, yet it blends unbroken with the land across its western border. The Romans ignored the border in the early centuries of the Christian era and placed their capital of Lusitania, as they called later-day Portugal, at Mérida in Extremadura. There the finest Roman ruins in Spain still remain. When Portugal became a nation by breaking away from Spain in the 11th century, it seized what land it could but was unable to take control of Extremadura, leaving it in Spanish hands.

The southern half of Extremadura presents an exotic landscape of flat land strewn with huge boulders that look like the dolmens and menhirs of the Celts. A white and chalky soil supports acres of olive groves standing immobile around these prehistoric rocks, with an effect that is serene. Hills emerge in the north, leading to mountains, as the land grows greener and scenic in more standard ways. As the difficulties of scraping a living would suggest, Extremadura is the least populous area of Spain, and thus is more given over to wildlife than elsewhere in Spain. Here you see buzzards, falcons, and hawks circling in the air and storks by the score settle on rooftop nests. The sounds of castanets heard in many towns are merely storks conversing.

Extremadura is the part of Spain least visited by tourists, which means it is less spoiled and bustling than the rest. Yet, there are sights enough here to repay a two-day pause on the way to or from Andalusia. **Mérida** ★★ preserves a Roman theater of elegant design, and an arena. A new museum dramatically presents some of the best

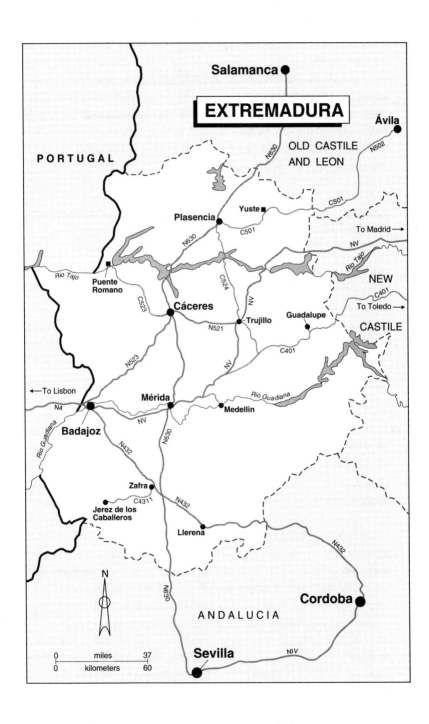

Roman art in Spain. The medieval walls of **Cáceres** ★★ enclose the most complete and homogeneous assemblage of Renaissance mansions in Spain. Charming **Trujillo** ★★, the home of Pizarro, offers its own Renaissance mansions above a lovely Plaza Mayor, along with castle ruins and history. **Guadalupe** ★★★ perches its atmospheric monastery loftily atop a mountain. Inside is the famed Black Virgin amid riches endowed by the Conquistadores. From the south, a pleasant route north toward Toledo and Madrid can be followed that includes Mérida, Cáceres, Trujillo and Guadalupe, or the route may be traversed in reverse.

CÁCERES ★★

Population: 71,852
Area code: 927; zip code: 10000

From **Madrid** *N-V southwest runs straight to Trujillo in 261 kilometers. From* **Trujillo** *head west on N-521 for 49 kilometers to Cáceres. From* **Mérida** *N-630 leads north to Cáceres in 71 kilometers. From* **Andalusia** *see the directions to Mérida. From* **Guadalupe** *C-401 leads to Zorita in 53 kilometers. Go north on C-524 for 28 kilometers to Trujillo, and follow the directions from there. From* **Toledo** *follow the directions to Guadalupe.*

The Romans called it Colonia Norbensis Caesara which the Spanish shortened to Cáceres. It was an early and persistent battleground fought over by Christians and Moors. The nucleus of the famed Order of Santiago, the most distinguished society in Spain, was formed here in 1170 to muster knights devoted to the Reconquest. By 1229, when Christians had taken control of the city for good, Cáceres was producing company after company of soldiers—first to fight against the Moors, later to conquer the Indian civilizations in the New World. Soldiering proved lucrative for some of these men who returned from campaigns to erect houses to announce their wealth and status to all. By the end of the 16th century, when no worlds remained to conquer, Cáceres ceased raising mansions, indeed ceased to grow. The happy result for today's visitor is that the old part of the town is the most homogeneous, best preserved Renaissance quarter in Spain. The mansions had been built primarily in the most privileged area—that within the old city walls—and filled those two acres so densely that few stores or modern buildings found room to locate. Thus, although not especially beautiful or imposing, an almost perfect picture of the Renaissance survives in the old quarter.

> *From* **Madrid** *or* **Trujillo** *turn left at the bullring. Be careful to obey one-way signs as they funnel arrivals into the large Pl. del General Mola in front of the old walls and parking. From* **Mérida** *follow Av. de España with its center island. At its end, the street changes its name to C. San Antón. Take the next right onto C. Donoso Cortés which lets into the Pl. del Santa Clara, against the old city walls. Turn a hard left, almost doubling back, to follow the walls into the large Pl. del General Mola and parking. From* **Portugal** *enter the Pl. de América and take a right on Av. de España with a center island. Then follow the directions from Mérida.*

> *Purple signs saying "Ciudad Monumental" point the way.*

WHAT TO SEE AND DO

The preeminent sight of Cáceres is the **Renaissance Quarter** ★★★ contained inside the old walls. Outside, the **church of Santiago** ★, where the Order of Santiago was founded, also is worth seeing for a fine retablo.

From the spaciousness of the Pl. de General Mola the old **walls** present an imposing face. Although substantially restored now, the foundations are Roman, parts are Moorish, and the remainder date to the 15th century. Towers protrude from the walls so that defenders could shoot back at an enemy storming the walls. Of the two towers on either side of the main gate, that on the left rests on Roman foundations, and that on the right in adobe derives from the Moors in the 12th century. The curving stairs and gate, called the Arco de la Estrella, were designed by a member of the baroque Churriguera family in the 17th century. The **Office of Tourism** lies to the right, where an essential map is available.

A short block through the gate brings the 16th-century **Episcopal Palace**, on the left, with medallions of the Old and New World flanking its portal, interesting for depictions of geography as it was then known. We have entered the Pl. de Santa María. To the right stands the large **Mayoralgo Palace** with elegant windows and a nice patio inside. More awaits in the plaza, but first turn left down C. Conilleros to the **Casa de los Toledo-Moctezuma**, with an unusual domed tower. Now a bank, the house once belonged to a lieutenant of Cortés who married the daughter of the Aztec emperor Montezuma, and built this edifice with her dowry. Go south along the walls to the **Torre de los Espaderos** (Armorers) on the right at the next corner. Like most of the towers in the city this one was truncated by Isabella to lessen violent feuds among the city's families, each of which had raised a tower for defense.

Exit the walls through the Scorro Gate for a look at the church of Santiago by following C. de Godoy, which heads northwest. In one block the **Palacio de Godoy** is passed, with a fine corner balcony, to enter the **Plaza de Santiago**. During the 12th century, in an earlier church on the site, the forerunner of the Order of Santiago was established. So prestigious did it become that 400 years later Velázquez would devote his time and effort to try to gain membership in the order. The present church is 16th century, built by Rodrigo Gil de Hontañon, the last great Gothic architect. Inside, a splendid retablo in high relief by Berruguette surrounds Santiago Matamore (St. James, the Slayer of Moors) with scenes from the life of Christ. Note the anguished faces and elongated bodies that are Berruguette's signature. Return through the walls again, and head directly west along C. Tiendas to return to the Pl. de Santa María.

Passing the **Torre de Carvajal**, on the left, cross to the **Catedral de Santa María**. Sixteenth-century Gothic, the church is elegant within and without. The retablo consists of refined figures, difficult to discern in the interior gloom. Head along the north side of the cathedral to exit the plaza from the west and enter the Pl. de San Jorge.

On the left is the **Palacio de los Golfines de Abajo**, one of two palaces in the quarter owned by this family. The facade becomes elegant through Mudejar designs, especially the windows and their surrounds. Its owner was permitted to display the coats of arms of Ferdinand and Isabella after they had enjoyed his hospitality. Continue west across the plaza to pass the **Residencia de Luisa de Carvajal**, on the left, and walk around the north face of the **Iglesia de San Francisco Javier**, with an imposing 18th-century facade. Pass the **Torre del Sol**, from the 15th century, with a nicely carved family crest over the arch, to reach the rear of the church of San Mateo. Along its south side stands the 15th-century **Casa de las Ciqüeñas** (House of the Storks), now occupied by the military, retaining the only intact tower that Isabella permitted. If the guard allows, peek into the patio to see its delicate arches. To the left is the former **Casa de las Veletas** (House of the Weathervanes). It houses a small museum of archaeological exhibits —the costumes and utensils for everyday use are especially interesting, as is a 12th-century cistern from the original Moorish Alcázar that serves as its basement. (Open Tues.-Sun. 9:30 a.m. to 2:30 p.m. and 5-7 p.m. Closing on Sun. at 2:30. Admission: 200 ptas.)

Return north to view the 15th-century **church of San Mateo** with its striking tower. In the austere interior rest the noble families of the city. Walk north along the church facade to the **Casa de Ulloa** and turn left (west) down the typical C. Ancha. In less than a block on the left is the **Casa do Comendador de Alcuescar**, with a Gothic tower, nice window decoration and a fine balcony. Beside it stands the former **Casa de Sanchez de Paredes**, now a parador, which may be entered for a look around.

Turn right at the walls at the end of the street, and right again at the next corner onto C. del Olmo. At the end of the block on the left is the other house of the Golfines family, the **Palacio dos Golfines de Arriba**, with an imposing tower. Both this and the **Casa Adanero** opposite have lovely patios. Go left around the Palacio dos Golfines to reach the walls and turn right to come to the **Casa de la Generala** in one more block. Another block brings a return to the Arco de la Estrella from which the tour began.

WHERE TO STAY

The hotel situation in Cáceres is tight. The area does not see enough foreign tourists to warrant substantial hotel construction, though the Spanish arrive on weekends to fill available beds. Choices are few and reservations are advised.

EXPENSIVE ($100-$200)

Parador de Cáceres   1st-class ★ ★ ★
C. Ancha, 6 (inside the walls at the middle of the west wall—entrance from the Pl. de Santa Clara). Rooms: 27. ☎ *21 17 59; FAX 21 17 29.* Here you can sleep in one of the mansions you came to see. The house was built in the 15th century, became a restaurant a century ago, and in 1989 was transformed into a parador. It is stark inside, but quiet. Patios abound, as do suits of armor.

MODERATE ($50-$99)

Extremadura   2nd-class ★ ★
Av. Virgen de Guadalupe, 5. (This street is the continuation of N-521 from the north, as it bends south. The hotel is opposite the large Parque del Príncipe.) Rooms: 68. ☎ *22 16 00; FAX 21 10 95.* This is a pleasant hotel of the modern sort, fronted by the rough stone of the old city. It has a swimming pool and has just been renovated. Service is good and the prices are more than fair.

Alcántara   2nd-class
Av. Virgen de Guadalupe, 14 (opposite the Extremadura). Rooms: 67. ☎ *22 89 00; FAX 22 87 68.* This hotel loses in the competition with its sister across the street. It has seen better days, but not for a while.

INEXPENSIVE (UNDER $50)

Goya   Hs2nd-class ★
Pl. General Mola, 33. Rooms: 15. ☎ *24 99 50.* The staff is helpful and there are fine views of the stately city walls from most rooms—not a bad combination for a low price.

Almonte   Hs3rd-class
C. Gil Cordero, 6 (a few steps west of the Pl. de America). Rooms: 90. ☎ *24 09 26.* Attractive and with enough rooms that at least one should be available, this hotel also provides parking for a fee.

WHERE TO EAT

In general Extremadura is not a place for gastronomes. However, two of the best restaurants in the province are located in Cáceres standing as exceptions to that rule. The area is known for game and pork.

EXPENSIVE ($50+)

Atrio

Av. de España, 30. (Actually the restaurant is a jag north from this main street with center island.) ☎ *24 29 28. Closed Sun. night.* In a shopping mall cul de sac, the building is all forest green. The interior is yellow and white, sleek, and surprisingly elegant for provincial Spain. The chef tries to make everything special to justify high prices, adding truffles to most dishes. Still, the service is professional and the quality of the food is first rate. **Amex, Diners, MasterCard and Visa accepted.**

MODERATE ($20-$50)

El Figón de Eustaquio ★★

Pl. San Juan, 12. (This quiet plaza is one block from the west end of the Pl. del General Mola.) ☎ *24 81 94.* Many consider this the best restaurant in the province. There is nothing nouvelle about the food, but local dishes are inventively and tastefully prepared. Prices will be expensive, if ordering à la carte, but moderate if one of the special menus is selected. The restaurant is attractive, consisting of a number of rooms on an intimate scale. At lunchtime it is extremely busy, and reservations are required. **Amex, MasterCard and Visa accepted.**

DIRECTORY

INFORMATION • Located to the right of the main city walls' gate at Pl. del General Mola, 33. Though English is not spoken, the staff is willing. Weekday hours run from 9 a.m. to 2 p.m. and 6-8 p.m., opening and closing an hour earlier on winter afternoons. Sat. 10 a.m. to 2 p.m.

TRAINS AND BUSES • The train station is located on Av. Alemania, 3 k south of town on the road to Mérida. Though the station is small, service is good to and from Madrid because Cáceres lies on the main train route to Portugal. ☎ 22 50 61.

The bus station is located across the street from the train station. Service is surprisingly good for a city of this size, with most cities on the western side of Spain accessible. ☎ 24 59 54.

POLICE • Av. Virgen de la Montaña, 3, just east of the Av. de España. ☎ 22 60 00.

EXCURSIONS

From Cáceres, **Trujillo**, **Mérida** and **Guadalupe** each are an hour or two away. See the descriptions under separate headings in this chapter. **Lisbon** is 349 k west. Medieval **Marváo** lies 117 k west on N-521, just over the Portuguese border. See the "Central and Northern Portugal" chapter for a description.

GUADALUPE ★ ★ ★

Population: 2,765
Area code: 927; zip code: 10140

*From **Madrid** take N-5 southwest to Talavera de la Reina
in 131 k. Turn south on N-502 to Guadalupe in 106 k.
From **Cáceres** take N-521 to Trujillo in 49 k. From **Trujillo**
take C-524 for 28 k to Zorita, and go east on C-401 for
51 k to Guadalupe. From **Mérida** take N-V northeast to
Miajads in 51 k and then C-401 for 75 k.*

Legend has it that at the beginning of the 13th century a shepherd
found a cow, apparently dead, in the mountains beside the Guadalupe River. As he knelt to examine the cow, Mary suddenly appeared
telling him to summon the priest, for a sacred image of herself lay
buried beneath the animal. The cow revived, and a blackened
3-feet-high image of the Virgin Mary and her Son soon was un-
earthed—the Black Virgin of Guadalupe. Alfonso XI invoked the aid
of this icon during a crucial engagement with the Moors 50 years
later. After victory, he built a grand monastery for her sanctuary,
which became a famous pilgrimage center. Here Isabella and Ferdinand signed the documents authorizing Columbus' explorations,
and Columbus brought Indians from the Americas to be baptized in
the fountain facing the church. In gratitude for their successes, the
Conquistadores heaped riches on the church of this Virgin, to make
it the most richly adorned church in Spain. Yet, by the 19th century
the monastery was abandoned by the monks who had inhabited it,
and fell into disrepair. Franciscan friars took it over at the start of this
century to restore it to its former glory. It has become a center of pilgrimages once again as the symbol of *hispanidad*, the cultural ties
linking Spain with Latin America.

Part of the allure of the Virgin and her monastery is their remote-
ness high on a peak of the Sierra de Guadalupe. Though access in
this day of motor transport is no effort, the rugged scenery is wondrous, and the final sight of the monastery clinging to its wild peak
puts the traveler in the proper frame of mind. Though there are no
monuments to see other than the monastery and its church, the village surrounding the monastery has been famed for copper work for
centuries. Products are on sale in numerous shops.

Monasterio Guadalupe

*Open daily 9:30 a.m. to 1 p.m. and 3:30-7 p.m. Admission: 200 ptas.,
for the guided tour in Spanish of approximately one hour. Although
the core of the building is late 14th-century, additions were made*

though the 18th. The complex is a jumble because geography crowded each addition within a limited perimeter.

The **fountain** in the middle of the picturesque Pl. Mayor in front of the church was used to baptize the first Americans brought to Europe. The church facade is flamboyant 15th-century Gothic. Two towers in rough stone with crenelated battlements guard either side, and fortress walls surround the whole. Bronze doors from the 15th century illustrate the events of Mary's life.

The church may be toured on one's own for free; the tour of the monastery requires a guide and fee. Entrance for the monastery tour is to the left.

The **church** proper was built in the 14th century, and is among the oldest monastery churches in the country. The interior retains its original proportions and dimensions, but with later decorative additions, such as the 18th-century balustrade at the top of the nave and 16th-century wrought iron grille facing the sanctuary. The classical retablo is 17th-century work by El Greco's son and another artist. In a splendid dress (changed daily), the Black Virgin, the reason for all this show, looks down from on high, brightened by spotlights.

The tour of the **monastery** comes first to a 15th-century Mudejar-style cloister with two stories of horseshoe arches. A tiled brick fountain in the center wears a remarkable spire. The former rectory displays a collection of extravagant church vestments, all sewn by the Hieronymite monks with exquisitely rich and ornate handwork. A fine Gothic cloister lies beyond, but is not normally included in the tour. It can be seen from the hotel Hospederia, next door.

The Chapterhouse, with fine artesonado ceiling, stores medieval choirbooks, some with delicate illustrations. Paintings are displayed as well, including small panels by Zurbarán. The tour passes through the church next, along the second floor choir (note the organ cases), to enter a splendid 17th-century sacristy. Here is the only series of Zurbarán's paintings remaining in the place for which they were designed—a truly remarkable series of eight works. The room itself is sumptuous with mirrors and gilt and shows the simplicity of these paintings in a far different way than would the plain walls of a museum. The tour then wends through a series of chapels, each more ornate than the last. In the first is another fine Zurbarán, after the next comes an octagonal room with ornate reliquaries. Rich jasper stairs lead up to a room with interesting full length paintings of Biblical figures by the 17th-century Neopolitan, Luca Giorano. Finally the tour enters the closet-sized 17th-century Camarin. A garish marble dais from 1953 spins and the Virgin herself is there.

WHERE TO STAY

Other than on feast days, the few hotels prove sufficient, as most tourists hurry on to their next stop. Although there is little to see other than the monastery, those who rush away miss two of the more interesting hotels in the country.

MODERATE ($50-$99)

Parador de Guadalupe   1st-class ★★★

C. Marqués de la Romana, 10 (opposite the monastery). Rooms: 40. *36 70 75; FAX 36 70 76.* Pilgrims have slept here since the 15th century. Isabella stayed too, signing her contract with Columbus in these rooms. The surviving Mudejar decorations are lovely, as is the patio, but bedrooms have been decorated more recently in a restful Moorish style. The hotel is quiet, provides fine views of surrounding mountains and valley below, and offers a pool.

Hospederia del Real Monasterio   3rd-class ★★★

Pl. Juan Carlos I (at the rear of the monastery, opposite the church). Rooms: 40.  *36 70 00; FAX 36 71 77.* This hotel is installed in former rooms of the monastery, and surrounds the lovely Gothic cloister, which may be entered from the bar. The shock is that the monks run it. Accommodations are eminently comfortable. Much of the furniture was made by the brothers, and the wood beams in the rooms are ancient. Prices are also very reasonable—a third less than the Parador, which itself is reasonably priced.

INEXPENSIVE (UNDER $50)

Cerezo   Hs3rd-class ★★★

Gregorio López, 12 (about a block east and uphill from the monastery). Rooms: 15. ☎ *36 73 79.* There are no better accommodations at these prices in the country. Rooms are comfortable, clean, many with scenic views, and the owners are true hosts. Even the food is good, and inexpensive.

WHERE TO EAT

Guadalupe offers two of the least expensive restaurants serving decent food in all Spain. Try the monk's cooking at the Hospederia for under $20, or walk up to the hotel Cerezo to spend even less.

DIRECTORY

INFORMATION • There is no office as such, nor the need in such a small village, but the Ayuntamiento can provide information. It is uphill along Av. Don Blas Perez, the main street of the village.

TRAINS AND BUSES • No trains, but buses leave from below the village for Madrid (at 9 a.m. and 3:30 p.m.), Trujillo and Cáceres (at 6:30 a.m. and 4:30 p.m.).

POLICE • Located in the Ayuntamiento. ☎ 36 70 06.

EXCURSIONS

Trujillo, **Cáceres** and **Mérida** are easily reached from Guadalupe. See directions and a description under the appropriate separate heading in this chapter. **Toledo** is less than 200 k away on C-401.

MÉRIDA ★ ★

Population: 41,783
Area code: 924; zip code: 06800

From **Seville** *take N-630 north for 197 k.* From **Cáceres** *take N-630 south for 71 k.* From **Trujillo** *take N-V south for 88 k.*

Mérida was founded by soldiers from Caesar Augustus' Spanish campaigns in 23 B.C. as their retirement village. They called it Emerita Augusta (Augustus' Veterans), from whose first half the present name evolved. Augustus' son-in-law donated a theater to the new town that seated 6,000, and the citizens added two aqueducts and a racecourse, plus an arena for chariot races and sea battles that could hold 14,000 spectators. Mérida prospered at the crossroads from Salamanca to Seville, and from Toledo to Lisbon. It also administered the large Roman territory of Lusitania, which encompassed later-day Portugal. Under the Visigoths and Moors it remained an important city, but lost that importance when Portugal broke away from Spain. Indeed, one of Mérida's claims to fame is that it is one of the few cities in Spain that Isabella and Ferdinand never visited.

Today Mérida seems more a large village—albeit with a certain vitality—than a city. All seems ordinary until one reaches the top of the hill and looks on the remains of ancient Rome. The Roman **theater** ★ ★ is among the most elegant anywhere and the **arena** ★ is imposing. In addition, Mérida has just completed a lovely **museum** ★ to house some of the finest Roman art in Spain. Ruins of the Moorish **alcazaba** are evocative, and from its walls one can view a still-functioning **Roman bridge**.

From the south and **Seville**, *cross the River Guadiana on the old Roman Bridge. A left turn on the far bank brings parking. From* **Cáceres** *follow Av. Via de la Plata until the small Albarregas river (more a stream) is crossed, passing a Roman aqueduct on the left to arrive at a fork. Take the right fork and continue on C. Calvario for three long blocks until it ends at C. Almendralejo. Turn right to the bank of the Guadiana, then go left at the circle onto Av. del Guadi-*

*ana and parking. From **Trujillo** comes an interchange at the outskirts of town. Take Av. Juan Carlos I, heading southwest. In about five blocks (passing faint remains of the Roman racecourse on the left) this ends. Go right on Av. de Extremadura, which changes its name to C. de Almendralejo and leads to the banks of the Guadiana River. Go left at the circle there along Av. del Guadiana for parking.*

WHAT TO SEE AND DO

Alcazaba

Open Mon.-Fri. 9 a.m. to 2 p.m. and 4-8 p.m. (closes an hour earlier in winter). Open Sat. from 9 a.m. to 2 p.m. Admission: 200 ptas.; ticket good for the Roman precinct as well. Walk downstream along the river (south) for approximately one block. The entrance is on the north side, away from the river. The Romans built a substantial fortress here, so well-constructed that successive Visigoths and Moors had only to repair and maintain it. After the Moors it fell into disrepair and suffers now from 1000 years of neglect, exacerbated by a French gutting in 1808. What you see today is the fortress walls and the cistern, the rest being mainly a dusty field. It is worth a climb down dank stairs to the Moorish cistern, added in the 10th century. It descends to the depth of the river so its water table would keep the cistern filled during a siege. Note the Roman-style vaulting in the passageway, Corinthian capitals atop Visigothic columns, and Visigoth pillars used as lintels. A walk on the walls gives nice views of the river—often with sheep and cattle gently grazing nearby—and of the long Roman bridge with 64 arches.

*Walk left from the Alcazaba entrance to the Pl. de España at the corner, the main square of the town surrounded by shops and restaurants. Here, at the west end of the plaza is the **Hotel Emperatriz**, a former 16th-century palace with a huge interior patio. Walk along the near side (south) of the plaza to C. Santa Eulalia, the major shopping street. In two and a half blocks, turn right on C. Francisco to see the Roman **Temple of Diana**, with a nice Corinthian peristyle. Continue for two more blocks up C. Santa Eulalia, turning right onto C. José Ramon Melida, where stores are passed that sell local red incised pottery and handsome reproductions of Roman blue and green glass. The attractively modern brick building in two blocks is the **Museo Nacional de Arte Romano**. At its end lies the precinct of the **Roman ruins**.*

Museo Nacional de Arte Romano   ★

Open Tues.-Sat. 10 a.m. to 2 p.m. and 5-7 p.m. Opens and closes an hour earlier winter afternoons. Open Sun. 10 a.m. to 2 p.m. Closed Mon., and holidays. Admission: 200 ptas. For Spain this is a daringly modern building in which to display ancient art, and it suits almost perfectly one of the best collection of Roman material in the country, all excavated from this area. The ground floor shows statues, including a lovely Ceres taken from the Roman theater (a copy stands there in place of this original). The next floor is for less interesting ceramics, glassware and coins. The top floor houses some nice mosaics and several fine busts. In the basement are original Roman *thermae* (steam-baths).

Monumentos Romano   ★★

Same hours as the Roman Museum above. Admission: 200 ptas. The theater is surely Spain's most beautiful remembrance of Rome. Most of it dates to 23 A.D., including the seats for 6,000, the entranceways formed of stones so carefully fitted that they required no mortar, and a pit in the front for the chorus. The elegant towering stage wall was added in the second century A.D. Beyond the stage wall reposes a garden and portico where the audience could stroll during intermission. It all seems so civilized. Today, classical plays are still performed during summer evenings. (Check at the Office of Tourism for times and prices.) North of the theater stands a large arena that could hold 14,000 spectators at chariot races, gladiatorial combats and mock sea battles (for which the floor was flooded). A low wall protected the spectators in the front row, the most expensive seats, from wild animals sometimes employed as contestants during gladiatorial contests. The cavern in the center of the arena floor presumably held the machinery for producing such shows.

C. Francisco, on which the Temple of Diana is situated, would lead to the local parador if followed north, away from the temple. The **parador** *inhabits a former baroque convent. C. de Almendralejo, at the rear of the parador, leads east in five blocks to the small* **Iglesia de Santa Eulalia**. *It dates to the 13th century and contains Visigothic pillars in its nave from an even older church.*

WHERE TO STAY

Mérida provides surprisingly few hotels for a town of its size and tourist interest.

EXPENSIVE ($100-$200)

Parador Via de la Plata   1st-class ★★

Pl. de la Constitución, 3 (signs direct you). Rooms: 82. ☎ *31 38 00; FAX 31 92 08.* The outside of this former convent is unassuming, but the interior adds baroque decorative touches to combed whitewashed walls for a nice effect. The former chapel is now a restful lounge and there is a simple patio in the center. Bedrooms are comfortable and pleasant; the service is attentive. There is private parking and a lively restaurant.

MODERATE ($50-$99)

Cervantes   **3rd-class ★**

C. Camilo José Cela, 8 (just off the north corner of the Pl. España). Rooms: 30. ☎ *31 49 01; FAX 31 13 42.* Although the accommodations are nothing special, the hotel is centrally located and professional.

Emperatriz   **2nd-class**

Pl. de España, 19. (The plaza is one block from the Roman bridge.) Rooms: 41. ☎ *31 31 11; FAX 30 03 76.* This is a strange place. It is a former huge mansion from the 17th century, inside of which stands an awesome, soaring patio, with rooms rising through three stories around it. For years, however, the hotel had been unbelievably seedy, incorporating a disco and arcade games which disturbed the guests. We could not even look at a room during our last visit because the hotel was under renovation, as it had been for two years. What you might find when you come is anyone's guess. We can only tell you that, in the past, the rooms worsened as the floors went higher.

INEXPENSIVE (UNDER $50)

Guadiana   **Hs3rd-class**

Pl. de Santa Clara (the plaza directly west of the Pl. de España). Rooms: 12. ☎ *31 32 07.* The rooms are large for this price category, although bare for our taste. They are perfectly clean and sufficiently comfortable.

WHERE TO EAT

Mérida locals enjoy a meal out, so they keep several good restaurants in business.

MODERATE ($20-$50)

Nicholás   **★★**

Félix Valverde Lillo, 13 (this street runs parallel to, and to the west of, the main shopping street, C. Santa Eulalia). ☎ *31 96 10. Closed Sun. night, and the middle three weeks in Sept.* In its own town house, this is easily the most elegant restaurant in town. The cuisine is that of the region—partridge with truffles, and good pork.

Amex, Diners and Visa accepted.

INEXPENSIVE (UNDER $20)

Briz   **★**

C. Félix Valverde Lillo, 5 (near Nicholás). ☎ *31 93 07.* This is an unassuming place that serves fine food at very reasonable prices. The stews are the thing here—either lamb or partridge.

Casa Benito

C. Santa Eulalia, 13. ☎ *31 55 02.* As with the other restaurants in town, the menu covers hearty regional dishes. This place is especially popular at lunch for its reasonable fixed-price menus, but goes à la carte at night.

DIRECTORY

SHOPPING • Mérida sells inexpensive reproductions of blue and green Roman glass goblets and vases. On the street leading to the Roman precinct, C. José Ramon, **Reproduciones Romanes** at #40 and **Copias Romanes** at #20, both provide nice selections, especially the latter. They also sell the local incised brown-red pottery. **Greylop** #24 has the best pottery selection. Across the street at number 13, **Mascara** sells endearing puppets and other quality crafts.

INFORMATION • Located by the Roman precinct on C. María Plano. ☎ 31 53 53.

TRAINS AND BUSES • The train station is located on C. Cordero, one block north of Santa Eulilia Church. ☎ 31 81 09. Service is frequent to Cáceres, Badajoz on the Portuguese border, and Madrid. Otherwise, it is spotty.

The bus station lies one kilometer across the Roman bridge on Av. de la Libertad. Buses serve more cities, more frequently, than do the trains. ☎ 25 86 61.

POST OFFICE AND TELEPHONES • Located in the Pl. de la Constitución, where the parador is. ☎ 31 24 58.

POLICE • The offices are in the ayuntamiento in the Pl. España. ☎ 31 50 11.

EXCURSIONS

Cáceres, **Trujillo** and **Guadalupe** are the main Spanish sites of interest nearby. Each is described under its own heading in this chapter. **Seville** lies three hours south. The spectacular fortifications of **Elvas** lie 81 k west on N-V (N-4 for the final 15 k), and beautiful **Evora** is 89 k further on (turning south onto N-18 after Estremoz), both across the Portuguese border. In fact, **Lisbon** is only 312 k west. See the descriptions in the "Central and Northern Portugal" and "Lisbon and Environs" chapters.

TRUJILLO ★ ★

Population: 9,445
Area code: 927; zip code: 10200

From **Madrid** *N-V going southwest runs (fairly) straight to Trujillo in 261 k. From* **Guadalupe** *take C-401 west to Zorita in 51 k, then join C-524 going north to Trujillo in 28 k. From* **Cáceres** *N-521 goes straight to Trujillo in 49 k. From* **Seville**, *follow directions to Mérida. From* **Mérida** *N-V goes east to Trujillo in 88 k.*

Trujillo is said to have conceived twenty American nations. While that is an exaggeration, this village contributed far more than its share to the conquest of the Americas, for it was the home of Francisco Pizarro. Pizarro, an illegitimate son of a noble family, left his work as a swineherd to seek a fortune in the New World. When he reached Peru, he followed the strategy that Cortés had employed in Mexico. Under the protection of a truce, he captured the Inca Atahualpa, and ruled his empire through him until he was strong enough to grab the reins himself, thereby accumulating riches that are incalculable in modern terms. Rivalry with a lieutenant led Pizarro to kill him, only to be murdered in turn by the dead man's supporters. But his half-brother Hernando and various compatriots from Trujillo survived, to return with sufficient treasures to make their hometown wealthy for a while.

Trujillo had been an unimportant village before the Conquistadores left to seek their fortunes. When they returned, each built a mansion as impressive as his booty would allow. This new wealth provided only a one-time injection into the economy of the town, which settled back into obscurity after its building boom in the 16th and 17th centuries. Today Trujillo offers mansions similar to those of Cáceres, though less densely and—thanks to their whitewashed facades—less austerely. They surround one of the most pleasant, expansive plaza mayors in Spain. Above the plaza, majestic ruins of a 12th-century Moorish fortress look down. Trujillo is an engaging village.

*From **Madrid** and **Guadalupe** the road funnels into the Pl. del General Mola. Go straight through onto C. San António, which enters the Pl. San Miquel in one block. Continue through to C. Sofrago, which changes its name to C. Silleria, then enters the Pl. Mayor, where parking should be available. From **Mérida** Trujillo is entered along Carreteria de Badajoz. Continue across the large Av. de la Encarnación, following the side of a park along C. Pardos. Continue straight through the small Pl. de Aragon along C. Romanos, which is named C. Parra when it bends right, and leads into the Pl. Mayor for parking. From **Cáceres** the town is entered along Av. Ramon y Cajal. Bear left at the park onto C. Ruiz de Mendoza. Angle left at the small Pl. de Aragon onto C. Romanos, which is named C. Parra when it bends right, and leads to Pl. Mayor for parking.*

WHAT TO SEE AND DO

Begin in the lovely **Plaza Mayor ★**. The plaza is irregular in shape, almost forming a triangle. Varying levels are linked by broad flights of stairs for variety. At the north center strides a powerful bronze **statue of Francisco Pizarro**, sculpted in 1927 by two American artists. Its twin resides in Lima, Peru, the city Pizarro founded. To the left (west), in an arcade, is the **Office of Tourism** which provides a map.

At the northeast side of the plaza stands the 16th-century Gothic church of **San Martín**, with a soaring nave and numerous Renaissance tombs. An arcade on its south side once served as a communal meeting place. Opposite is the **Palacio de San Carlos**, from the early 17th century, now a convent. The bell at the door will bring a nun (if rung at any normal Spanish museum hour) to show off an arched inner court with stored Visigothic fragments, and interesting vaults of the basement. (A donation is in order.)

South around the plaza is the mansion of the **Marquesa de Piedras Alba**. At the southwest corner of the plaza stands the **Palacio de la Conquista**. De la Conquista was the Marquis' title conferred on Francisco Pizarro's brother Hernando, who survived to return from Peru wealthy. Once home, he built this mansion with an extraordinary number of grilled windows. At the corner balcony is a series of busts of the family. On the left are Francisco with his wife, Yupanqui Huaynas, daughter of the Inca. On the right are Hernando and his bride, Francisca (Francisco's daughter). Part of the mansion is open to visitors (open daily 10:30 a.m. to 2 p.m. and 4:30-6 p.m., tip the guide). Proceeding west by the mansion, you reach the former **ayuntamiento** (town hall), from the 16th century, with an old reconstructed triple arcade. Through the central arch the **Palacio de Pizarro de Orellana**, now a school, preserves a fine patio with an elegant Plateresque upper gallery.

Passing the front (south), follow C. Almenas due west to the restored town walls and one of the original seven gates, the **Gate of San Andres**. Once through and past San Andres Church, the remains of **Moorish baths**, now a stagnant reservoir, are faced. Turn right into the quiet, almost abandoned old town, then left along C. de la Paloma going north, and prepare for a climb. In two blocks you arrive at the Gothic **Santa María**, restored in the 15th century. The bell tower remains from the original Romanesque structure. (If closed, apply at the house to the right of the steps.) Inside, the church is pristine Gothic, with lovely vaulting. The retablo at the altar is a Spanish masterpiece by the great Fernando Gallego, from Salamanca. A hundred peseta coin is necessary to illuminate it. All around are the tombs of the great families of the city. The upper choir is fronted by an elaborate balustrade with coats of arms of Ferdinand and Isabella at each end to indicate their seats, should they be in residence.

Follow the church facade to the east side, and walk north to its rear, across from which is the **Pizarro Museum**. (Open daily 10 a.m. to 2 p.m. and 4-6 p.m.; closed on holidays; admission: 100 ptas.). This is the former home of Francisco Pizarro's father. It is unlikely that the illegitimate Francisco was born here, though he did spend a good deal of his childhood playing with his legitimate brothers in this place. Some of the rooms are nice, although the so-called museum has little to show.

The steep lane continues up to the top of the hill to massive twelfth-century crenelated walls of the **Castillo** (Castle). So far only the Moorish curtain-walls with their square towers have been restored. The area is a peaceful place to wander, watch the birds, and look over the countryside.

Return down C. Santiago that runs from the southwest corner of the fortress walls. In a long block you reach the town walls and, prefaced by two stately towers, the **church of Santiago** built into the walls. Pass through the Santiago gate in the walls to return to the Pl. Mayor.

WHERE TO STAY

Trujillo is a pleasant place to spend a night, since it has enough life and activity, yet not too much. Unfortunately, the town offers few hotel rooms.

EXPENSIVE ($100-$200)

Parador de Trujillo　　　　　　　　　　　　　　**1st-class ★★**

Pl. de Santa Clara (two blocks due east of the Pl. Mayor). Rooms: 46. ☎ *32 13 50; FAX 32 13 66.* This time the parador is installed in a former 16th-century convent. Befitting its convent heritage, it is less formal than many paradors and correspondingly more inviting and relaxed. All rooms focus on a simple central cloister, now a patio, providing a pleasant atmosphere, with antiques around.

MODERATE ($50-$99)

Las Ciqüeñas　　　　　　　　　　　　　　　　**2nd-class ★**

Carretaria N-V, (about 2 k east of town). Rooms: 78. ☎ *32 12 50; FAX 32 13 00.* This is a clean, modern hotel with extra facilities, yet modest prices.

INEXPENSIVE (UNDER $50)

Mesón la Cadena　　　　　　　　　　　　　**Hs3rd-class ★★**

Pl. Mayor, 8. Rooms 8. ☎ *32 14 63.* The building is a 16th-century mansion. Rooms above the mesón are pleasant and comfortable, with views of the plaza and the town walls. This is a find, indeed.

WHERE TO EAT

You can dine reasonably well in this town for very little money.

MODERATE ($20-$50)

Hostal Pizarro　　　　　　　　　　　　　　　　**★★★**

Pl. Mayor, 13. ☎ *32 02 55.* This restaurant is an institution, not only of Trujillo, but of all Extremadura. The chef and waitress are two sisters who inherited this place long ago from their father. Together, they serve the most authentic Extremaduran home cooking. Partridge casserole is delicious, and the roast lamb is quite good. The prices will please you almost as much as the food does.

INEXPENSIVE (UNDER $20)

Mesón la Cadena   ★

Pl. Mayor, 8. ☎ *32 14 63.* Whitewashed walls are made charming by local ceramics, creating an atmosphere far more deluxe than the prices. While à la carte selections can bring the bill above the inexpensive category, numerous *platos tipicos* fit comfortably within it.

Mesón la Troya

Pl. Mayor, 10. ☎ *32 13 64.* There is not much to choose from between these neighbors. Both are attractive, reasonably priced and serve tasty food. We slightly prefer the Cadena; see if you agree.

DIRECTORY

INFORMATION • Installed in an arcade on the left of the Pl. Mayor. The hours are variable.

BUSES • The station is at Carretera a Badajoz, four or five blocks south of the Pl. Mayor. ☎ 32 12 02. It serves the towns of Extremadura and offers frequent trips to Madrid.

POLICE • In the ayuntamiento on C. Hernandez Pizarro, before the bus station. ☎ 32 01 08.

EXCURSIONS

Cáceres, **Mérida** and **Guadalupe** are all short excursions from Trujillo. See the respective descriptions in this chapter.

GALICIA, ASTURIAS, AND CANTABRIA

View across the Plaza Obradoiro in Santiago de Compostela.

HISTORICAL PROFILE: RELIGION AND THE INQUISITION

Spain's Catholic roots are old and deep. Even before the Pope bestowed the name *los Reyos Católicos* (the Catholic Monarchs) on Ferdinand and Isabella in the 15th century, Spain had taken pride in being a Catholic country. Its Visigothic rulers had converted to Catholicism as early as the sixth century. After the Moors conquered most of Spain in the eighth century, only the northern fringe of the country remained under Christians rule, yet much of the population in the rest of the country maintained its Catholicism. For the next 800 years, Catholics in Spain lived alongside Islamic neighbors. Moors were tolerant of other religions, freely allowing Jews, persecuted by the Christian world, to make homes in their territory, so as the Christians regained land from the Moors, they inherited a Jewish and Moorish minority, making Spain a melting pot of religions. The story of religion in Spain is the tale of how the country changed from the most tolerant in Europe into the least.

Until the end of the 15th century, religion neither qualified nor disqualified anyone for a vocation. Despite the proximity of three religions, unlike more homogeneous France and Germany, Spain bred no Christian heresies. Then, at the end of the 14th century, pogroms exploded throughout the south of Spain and in Barcelona to the north. Christian mobs, either jealous of Jewish economic success or frightened by stories of Jewish atrocities, killed thousands of Jews. Throughout Spain, fearful Jews converted to Christianity, becoming known as *conversos.*

Anti-semitism was far from sanctioned by the government. A Jew in the 15th century could still occupy an important position—one, in fact, was in charge of supplying Ferdinand's troops during the Grenada campaign, and another served as Isabella's court physician. Isabella had said "all the Jews in my realms are mine and under my care and protection and it belongs to me to defend and aid them and keep justice." [Henry Kamen, *Inquisition and Society in Spain*, p. 12.] Yet, by 1478 she had instituted the Spanish Inquisition, and 20 years later signed an edict expelling all of Spain's Jews.

What changed Isabella's attitude and why did she order an inquisition? While it is certain that clerics urged their monarchs to impose an inquisition, Isabella and, even more, Ferdinand did not always do what Rome's clergy directed. Circumstantial evidence suggests Ferdinand as the driving force behind the Inquisition, with Isabella following his lead.

Because an ongoing inquisition had existed in Aragón before Castile's more infamous one, Ferdinand of Aragón had firsthand acquaintance with its operation, while Isabella of Castile did not. Since Ferdinand's character was one of shrewdness, while Isabella was more other-worldly and sentimental, the fact that the Spanish Inquisition was instituted immediately before Castile began its costly war against Granada becomes significant. In fact it seems likely that the Spanish Inquisition was instituted by Ferdinand as an economic policy. Strikingly, over 90% of those tried by the Inquisition were former Jews, although they constituted only a few percent of the population. The reason for such concentrated persecution could not have been that only former Jews committed heresies, but rather that they controlled a disproportionately amount of the country's wealth. During the early years of the Inquisition, all seized assets became the property of the Crown, a policy which contributed substantially to the national revenue. In 1482 the Pope issued a bull stating:

> ...that in Aragón, Valencia, Mallorca and Catalona the Inquisition has for some time been moved not by zeal for the faith and the salvation of souls, but by lust for wealth, and that many true and faithful Christians, on the testimony of enemies, rivals, slaves and other lower and even less proper persons, have without any legitimate proof been thrust into secular prisons, tortured and condemned as relapsed heretics, deprived of their goods and property and handed over to the secular arm to be executed, to the peril of souls, setting a pernicious example, and causing disgust to many.

> **Quoted by Kamen, *op. cit.*, p. 34**

Whatever the causes, in 1478, granting a petition signed jointly by Ferdinand and Isabella, Pope Sixtus IV issued a bull establishing the Spanish Inquisition in Castile. Two years later it was announced that the first tribunal of the Inquisition was en route to Seville. Four thousand households fled before the inquisitors arrived, confirming, at least in the minds of its proponents, the need for such a tribunal.

The Spanish Inquisition was modeled after earlier inquisitions in France. It consisted of itinerant tribunals acting as courts of law, overseen by a supreme council under the direction of an Inquisitor General. The first Inquisitor General was Isabella's former confessor, Tomás de Torquemada. Because prevention of heresy was the expressed purpose of the Inquisition, only Christians could be tried. But the true "purpose of the trial and execution [was] not to save the soul of the accused but to achieve the public good and put fear into others." [Contemporary source quoted by Kamen, *op. cit.*, p. 161.] That is, the goal was not justice, but discipline—both for the accused and for the community.

A tribunal would arrive at a town and call for a high mass, which the populace was required to attend. There townspeople all swore an oath to support the Inquisition's business. After reading an edict listing heresies, an invitation was then extended to the audience to denounce themselves or their neighbors. In the early days of the Inquisition a 30-day grace-period was extended during which immediate confessions were lightly punished. Usually enough denunciations were received to give the tribunal sufficient work.

Heresy included sacrileges of the slightest sort. One man was arrested for smiling when a friend said the words "the Virgin Mary;" another for urinating against the wall of a church; yet another for shouting during a card came that "even with God as your partner you won't win this game." [Kamen, *op. cit.*, p. 162.] The slightest suspicion that a citizen practiced Judaism caused his arrest. Wearing finery on Saturday, the Jewish Sabbath, could do it, as could refusing pork when dining out, or even washing on a Jewish holiday. Sex was another area of concern to the tribunals. Five percent of all those convicted by the Inquisition were convicted of bigamy; homosexuality and bestiality are crimes; but even saying that sex was no sin served as grounds for arrest.

Once testimony against an accused person had been obtained, the evidence was sent to theologians to determine if it constituted a heresy. If it did, the accused was arrested and imprisoned. Upon his arrest an inventory was made of his assets so they could be seized until his case had been decided. Although the Inquisition resorted to torture to force confessions, it should be noted that all European criminal courts of the time did likewise, and the Inquisition was more sparing of this device than was civil justice. Torture was used only on those accused of the most serious heresies, about one third of the cases.

Three forms of torture were employed. The *garrucha*, or hoist, involved being hung by the wrists with heavy weights tied to the feet, then raised and dropped until abruptly caught by the rope. The *toca*, water torture, involved stuffing a towel in the mouth, then pouring containers of water down the open throat. The *potro*, or rack, consisted of progressively tightening cords around the accused's body. According to the rules of the Inquisition, a confession gained through torture did not count as truth unless the subject repeated his confession on the day following. All details of a torture session were meticulously recorded.

One account of a woman accused of refusing pork and of changing her bed linen on Saturdays runs as follows:

> *She was ordered to be placed on the* potro. *She said, "Señores, why will you not tell me what I have to say? Señor, put me on the ground—have I not said that I did it all?" She was told to tell it. She said "I don't remember—take me away—I did what the witnesses say." She was told to tell in detail what the witnesses said. She said, "Señor, as I have told you, I do not know for certain. I have*

said that I did all that the witnesses say. Señores, release me, for I do not remember it." She was told to tell it. She said, "Señores, it does not help me to say that I did it and I have admitted that what I have done has brought me to this suffering—Señor, *you know the truth*—Señores, *for God's sake have mercy on me.*

Kamen, *op. cit.*, **p. 176.**

Trials were conducted in secret. Anyone arrested was presumed guilty since the evidence had already been heard and judged heretical—the accused could only try as best he could to prove his innocence. Yet, as the above account indicates, he would not know the charges against him or even who had brought them. This made defense near to impossible, and only after someone confessed could he be assisted by a lawyer, appointed by the tribunal. The judicial process was, in effect, a series of audiences broken up by periods of prison confinement, rather than a continuous trial, and the normal period from incarceration to conviction or release was 3 years, though there were cases that pended for 20.

At the end waited the *auto da fé*, or "ceremony of faith." Public *autos da fé* were very popular, consisting of colorful processions through the main streets of town by the members of the tribunal, followed by guards, and all the accused. The dress was striking, looking like nothing so much as brightly colored Klu Klux Klan outfits —except for the black worn by those sentenced to die.

After stirring speeches by members of the tribunal and public confessions by the accused, sentences were read. Four different sentences were possible. First, an accused person could be acquitted. But since this amounted to an admission that the tribunal had made a mistake, its usual form was to suspend the judicial process without acknowledging the innocence of the accused. A second sentence was penance, which could encompass anything from a fine, to a prison term, to enforced wearing of a *sanbenito*, a yellow robe with crosses that marked the wearer as a former heretic. The third type of sentence was reconciliation, reserved for more serious crimes. Punishment could include banishment, service as a galley slave, seizure of one's assets, or public flogging—in any combination. Relaxation was the most serious sentence, reserved for those who did not repent of their crimes or who had relapsed into evil ways. About 2% of the accused were "relaxed." The penalty was to be tied to a stake then roasted alive, unless the criminal confessed at the last moment, in which case he was strangled before being burned.

Not every Spaniard supported the Holy Office, as the Inquisition was called. A contemporary wrote:

> *Those newly converted from the Jewish race, and many other leaders and gentry, claimed that the procedure was against the liberties of the realm, because for this offence their goods were confiscated and they were not given the names of witnesses who testified against them.*
>
> *As a result the conversos had all the kingdom on their side, including persons of the highest consideration, among them Old Christians and gentry.*

Kamen, op. cit., p. 37.

This chronicler surely is correct in saying that some people in high places, both lay and ecclesiastic, were opposed to the Inquisition, but he is surely wrong when he says that the "kingdom" was against it. A truer description of the situation was that "it is only the lords and leading persons who wage this war against the Holy Office, and not the people." [*Op. cit.*, p. 256.] Common citizens never attacked the officials of the Holy Office, never raised their common voice against it; they approved. The Inquisition began in 1480 and was not disbanded until 1834. To outlive generations of monarchs and church leaders, it must have had popular support.

On rare occasions, however, entire towns rose against the Inquisition. In 1484 the city of Teruel locked its gates against the tribunal, causing the Inquisition to excommunicate all the citizens. In response, the clergy of Teruel secured papal letters lifting the censure, but were set upon by Ferdinand with an army to force the town to submit.

Perhaps the most dramatic opposition occurred in 1485 when the inquisitor Pedro Argües was assassinated as he knelt in prayer. The deed was probably arranged by *conversos* and was not unexpected, since Fra Argües wore chain mail beneath his robes and a steel helmet under his clerical hat. However, the murder only strengthened the inquisitors' resolve and increased the numbers of their adherents.

Effects of the Inquisition ran deep through Spanish society. Although it began as an attack on former Jews, Jew and non-Jew alike were at risk, for anyone at all could be accused. The Inquisition gave rise to the concept of *limpieza de sangre*, purity of blood, that caused everyone to rush to geneologists to prove the absence of Jewish ancestors in his family tree. In almost every case this involved deception, for it was rare for a family of any standing in Rennaisance Spain to be without even a drop of Jewish blood. A royal secretary reported that all the noble lines of Castile, including Isabella and Ferdinand, had *converso* ancestors, along with half the high government officials and four Spanish bishops in Aragón. [Kamen, *op. cit.*, p. 19.] The first Inquisitor General, Tomás de Torquemada, and Saint Teresa of Ávila came from *converso* families. The effect of the Inquisition has been long. Even today it is not uncommon for a Spaniard to take pride in the "attribute" of not having Jewish blood.

GALICIA, ASTURIAS, AND CANTABRIA

These three ancient provinces top the western half of Spain in a belt 500 miles long, but, in parts, only 30 miles deep. Although each province is different, all offer a similar range of attractions to the tourist. The whole area borders an Atlantic lined with rocky inland peaks, and receives more rainfall than anywhere else in the country—thereby earning the name "Green Spain." Its population stems from ancient roots, and both its folklore and languages differ somewhat from the rest of Spain.

Galicia, tucked into the northwest corner of Spain, sits atop Portugal. Bordered by the Atlantic on two sides, it is the wettest area of Spain, though inland areas remain dry most of the summer. It is green and wooded. Because it sits on a rift in the earth that caused prehistoric folding and splitting, hills and mountains cover most of the terrain, and the coast is crinkled into inlets with hills on either side, like Norwegian fjords or Scottish firths. Overall, Galicia presents a landscape more associated with Scotland than with Spain, and the comparison is not inaccurate.

In the eighth century B.C., Celts from northern France migrated to Galicia, perhaps even before another group migrated to Britain to become the Welsh and early Scottish. They named the area Gaelia (from which Galicia derives), the root word for both "Gaul" and "Wales." They brought musical instruments, similar to bagpipes, and legends, including that of the Holy Grail. Romans made fast work of their territory, however—conquering, then leaving, with little permanent imprint. In the fifth century A.D. the Germanic tribe of Suevi settled permanently, though they were defeated by the Visigoths a century later. So isolated was Galicia that the Moors barely stopped by when they were conquering the rest of Spain, permitting the area to be the earliest to return to Christian ways. In the beginning of the ninth century shepherds found an uncorrupted body reputed to be Saint James (Sant' Iago). The site of Santiago de Compostela and this body became a great pilgrimage center in the Middle Ages, and remains so today.

Asturias, the center province of this northern belt, is considered the first kingdom of Spain. The Visigoths, chased to this extremity by the Moors, began their Reconquest from here. Thus, the Asturian city of Oviedo may be called the first capital of modern Spain. Within its confines is located the pantheon of the earliest kings; on its out-

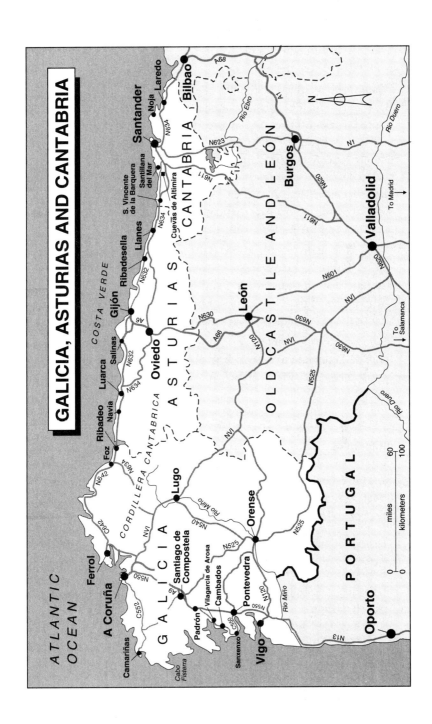

skirts stand the oldest remains of a palace, the remodeled church of Santa Maria del Naranco. But the area is infinitely older than this. The cave of Altimira and others nearby contain paleolithic paintings from fifteen thousand years ago.

Cantabria province is the Basque homeland. The origin of the Basques and their language is unknown, although it is clear that they hunted whales off the coast of Greenland as early as the ninth century. They are proud of their ancient heritage, traditions and language, and are fiercely independent. Basque industriousness contributes to the prosperity of the region, aided by rich deposits of iron ore. Their chefs are renowned. And their beautiful coast, with the elegant resorts of Santillana del Mar, Santander and Donastia (San Sebastián) is evidence of the good fortune of the Basques.

In Galicia many people speak Gallego, a language akin to Portuguese. Basque (Euskera) is spoken in Asturias and Cantabria. Though Spanish is understood and spoken by all, in some instances town names on road signs will not be written in Spanish. In this text we use the place-names a traveler is most likely to see.

The premier sight of the area is the Romanesque cathedral of **Santiago de Compostela** ★ ★ ★ ★ in Galicia. Galicia also offers lovely beaches—the **Rias Altas** and **Rias Bajas** ★ ★—which are generally uncrowded and infinitely more scenic than their Mediterranean counterparts. Asturias provides competition with the beaches of its **Costa Verde** ★, in addition to offering prehistoric paintings in **Altimara** and other caves ★, amd along with the quiet sophistication of **Oviedo** ★ ★, incorporating the oldest civilian Christian works in Spain. Cantabria provides the elegant resorts of the **Basque Coast** ★ ★ ★—**Santander** ★, **Santillana del Mar** ★ ★, and beautiful **Donostia** ★ ★ ★ (San Sebastián).

BASQUE COAST ★ ★ ★

Sweeping around the French border, the Bay of Biscay forms 250 k of Basque Coast. Indeed, "Biscay" is a corruption of *Vizcaya*, the Spanish word for Basque. Steep cliffs line the bay, broken by estuaries. Where they find shore-room, fishing villages face the sea, while green hills climb behind.

This is the country of Basques, those who speak Euskera, a language of no known relatives or origin. The people are notoriously independent—place names printed in Spanish are spraypainted overnight with Basque equivalents. The Basque separatist movement claims several political murders each year, though violence is sup-

ported by only a small proportion of the people. Fortunately, the
danger for visitors is slight, as the target is always the Spanish government or its agents, not tourists or ordinary citizens. Even though
the political situation will be evident because of omnipresent painted
slogans, it should not otherwise affect a visit. What is more likely to
be remembered is the food, for Basque cuisine is extraordinary.

The Basque coast might well contain the best beaches in Spain, in
addition to beautiful scenery, superior food, and elegant resorts—all
with smaller crowds than will be encountered elsewhere. What it
lacks is the stark light of the south, for the days are frequently misty.
Instead a mellow atmosphere shows the dark blue sea and deep
green hills to rich effect. The coast is anchored at the west end by the
expensive and sophisticated resort of Santander, and at the east end
by beautiful and elegant Donostia (San Sebastián). In between, a
score of lovely villages wait patiently for those who prefer quiet to
sophistication. We begin our description with Santander at the western end of the Basque Coast, 30 k from Santillana del Mar, where
the Costa Verde (discussed below in this chapter) ends. Hotel and
restaurant recommendations are grouped together following the discussion of towns and route.

> *From* **Santillana del Mar** *C-6316 west joins N-611 in 8 k
> for a 17 k trip to Santander. From* **Burgos** *take N-623
> north for 123 k. From* **Valladolid** *take N-620 for 58 k to
> Palencia, then N-611 for 209 k. to Santander. From*
> **Madrid** *follow the directions to Burgos, then follow the Bur-
> gos directions. From* **Pamplona** *take N-240 north to Tolosa
> in 64 k, changing there for N-I north for 22 k to Donostia
> (San Sebastián), then follow the route below backwards.*

Santander ★ caters mainly to the Spanish who seek elegance and
such sophisticate entertainment as theater and dance. It has a casino
for gambling, beautiful ocean promenades and fine beaches, but
does not offer old buildings, quaintness or charm. A tornado in
1941 threw the ocean upon the city, causing a fire that destroyed
most older buildings, so today the edifices glisten newly. An intelligent ordinance passed after this cataclysm, imposed a five-story limit
on the height of buildings and set aside land for gardens and walks,
to produce the modern, attractive city of almost 200,000 citizens.

Santander spreads in a thin line along the bay, leading out to
Magdalena Point. Almost a century ago its citizens subscribed to
build a **palace** to attract Alfonso XIII, whose summer residency did

much to popularize the resort. Now the palace is an annex of the local university, providing summer classes in Spanish. The best beaches ring this point. Fine beaches also line the northern area called El Sardinero, the home of the **Gran Casino del Sardinero**. Golf is across the bay at Pedreña; an airport lies 7 k south of the city.

From Santander take N-634 east. It cuts inland across the Ajo Cape to reach lovely **Laredo** *in 48 k. However, by avoiding the cape one misses* **Noja ★**, *10 k deeper in the cape, with a spectacular beach called Playa Ris. If interested, look for the turn-off about 38 k after Santander.*

Laredo ★ was once a sleepy fishing village that happened to have a wonderful beach to its west. Today it has grown into a true resort with an August population swollen to ten times the 10,000 souls off-season. High-rise buildings now line the beach, which remains as fine as it ever was, although less scenic. On the last Friday of August Laredo holds its "Battle of the Flowers," when flowered floats parade through the mass of winding streets that constitute the town.

28 k of beautiful drive further west along N-634 brings picturesque **Castro Urdiales**.

The quiet village of **Castro Urdiales ★★** huddles on a peninsula around castle ruins and a 14th-century church, all framed by mountains that sweep around the beach and bay. The site is lovely. The town retains a less assuming character than those nearby, except for copying Larado with its own Battle of the Flowers on June 25.

After Castro Urdiales comes a boring stretch of road leading to **Bilboa**, *a city of half a million holding little interest for a tourist. The city can be skirted by joining highway A-8 going east. Exit at Amorebieta (exit 18) to take C-6313 toward Gernika.*

When squadrons of German planes carpet-bombed Gernika (Guernica) during the Spanish Civil war it became an international symbol of atrocity. Gernika was neither a military center nor of any strategic importance. It was, and remains, merely a symbol for the Basques. Whether for this reason, or simply to practice their bombing, German planes killed hundreds of civilians and their animals during a surprise raid on April 26, 1937. Thus, there is little that is old in Gernika, but the stump of the original Oak Tree, under which the Basque parliament traditionally met to have their rights acknowledged by Spanish sovereigns, remains in the town plaza, beside a newer tree planted after the bombing.

Leaving Gernika, take C-6212 northeast toward **Gauteguiz de Arteaga**, *with a restored 15th-century castle. From Arteaga the coast road going north presents lovely views and passes by the resort of* **Playa de Laida**, *then peaceful* **Elanchove** *in a fine bay, before reaching* **Lekeitio** *(Lequeitio) in about 35 k.*

What could be more picturesque than a village tucked into a bay cut into the foot of a small mountain? Suppose we add a fleet of brightly colored boats, and two wide beaches spreading to either side of the harbor? For good measure, throw in a flamboyant 15th-century church with flying buttresses standing atop other buttresses, and you have the postcard-village of **Lekeitio ★★★**.

12 k west along C-6212 brings **Ondárroa ★**, *which is hardly less picturesque than Lekieto, on a spit of land jutting out into the sea.* **Matriku** *(Motrico), 4 k further on, is losing its attractiveness to modern developments.* **Deba** *(Deva), in another 4 k, retains a fine beach. Here pick up the larger road, N-634, for 9 k to* **Zumaya** *(Zumaia), with surf. South of the town C-6317 bears left toward Zestoa and* **Azpeitia**, *in 16 k, for an excursion to the birthplace of San Ignacio de Loyola, founder of the Jesuit Order.*

The 16th-century church in the town of Azpeitia retains the baptismal font from an earlier building, at which Inigo Lopez Recade was baptized. After a decade of killing, he joined the priesthood and adopted the name Ignacius of Loyola. Still later he founded the Society of the Jesuits. Several noteworthy mansions surround the church, but west of the town is the site of the saint's birth, now the **Sanctuary de Loyola**, a monastery. The monastery encloses the house of his family, the Santa Casa. Important rooms—such as the one in which he was born, the one where he convalesced from wounds, and the one in which he experienced his conversion, have been made into chapels.

From Zumaia N-634 leads east to **Guetaria ★** *with a street of medieval houses leading to a lovely 15th-century church.* **Zarauz ★**, *a fashionable resort, is 3 k further east. Lovely villas with gardens line the beach, and two nice Renaissance palaces stand in the village. In 3 k the express*

E-10 is joined for a 13 k trip to Donostia (San Sebastián), the jewel of the coast.

Donostia ★★★ nestles between two small mountains that face a bay of elegant proportions, looking something like a scallop shell. It is a *Belle Époch* resort, much frequented by the French. Nonetheless, it was an Englishman who, in 1896, built the Miramar Palace for Queen María Christina that first brought cachet to the city. Intelligent planning since created a city of elegant walks, parks, bridges and buildings, that never ceases to delight the eye. Add the fact that there are more superb restaurants in this city of under 200,000 than in all of Madrid, combines to equal a perfect resort—although at a cost, for elegance is expensive.

Resting atop a hill at the foot of Mount Igueldo, the **Miramar Palace** is under renovation today, but its fine gardens are open for strolling. The palace faces the mile-long curve of **La Concha beach** that must be counted among the most beautiful in the world. At the west end of the beach towers Monte Igueldo, with splendid views from the summit. At the east end stands Monte Urgull, at the tip of a peninsula. A lovely promenade lines the length of the beach for pleasant walks. Most sights, however, cluster near Monte Urgull.

Where La Concha beach ends on the east, a garden grows around the present **Ayuntamiento**. The building was formerly the city casino, built before the turn of the century, but, during the time of Franco, when games of chance were banned, the unused structure was taken over by the city. Inside it is a glittering mass of marble and glass. At the end of the gardens of this Parque Alderdi Eder, the elegant shopping street of **Av. de la Libertad** runs east-west. Two blocks north of the park, and one block east, is the main square of the town, the **Pl. de la Constitución**. It is a friendly place, busy with groups of strollers. The balconies still retain numbers from the days when bullfights were held in the plaza and balconies were rented to fans. Three blocks north of the Pl. de la Constitución is the city museum—**Museo San Telmo** ★. Formerly it was a monastery; now it houses a nice collection of Basque art through the ages, along with paintings by El Greco, Goya and others. (Open in summer Mon.-Sat. 9 a.m. to 9 p.m.; Sun. 9 a.m.-1 p.m. Other seasons, 10 a.m. to 1 p.m. and 3:30-7 p.m.; Sun. 10 a.m. to 1 p.m. Admission: 100 ptas.)

Beside the museum stands the 18th-century church of **Santa María**, with a sober interior and inebriated chapels. A steep path northwest of the church leads upwards to the fortress of **Castillo de Santa Cruz del la Mota**, which guards the summit of Monte Urgull.

The castle, from the 16th century, illustrates how buildings changed from secure places of lodging for important persons to fortresses designed to withstand heavy bombardment by cannon. A military museum inside is of little interest.

Proceeding east, then north, from the Museo San Telmo brings the **Paseo Nuevo**, an attractive promenade around the peninsula of Ugull. At its end is the **Palacio del Mar**, an oceanographic museum. (Open daily 10 a.m. to 1:30 p.m. and 3:30-7:30 p.m., to 8 p.m. in summer; closed Mon. from the middle of Sept. to the middle of May. Admission: 200 ptas.) East of the museum, in three short blocks, is the Urumea River, spanned by four ornate **deco bridges** from the turn of the century. Near the first of these, the Puente de Kursaal, a park surrounds the **Victoria Eugenia Theater** and the **María Cristina** Hotel, both Victorian palace-like structures from early in our century.

The sights do not endear Donostia to the traveler as much as its elegant, peaceful ambiance—even when the city is filled with summer crowds. There is a style here seldom encountered today.

N-1 leads east of Donostia in 20k. to **Hondarribia** ★ *(Fuenterrabía). This lovely town overlooks Hendaye across the French border. Because of its border location, it is fortified by 15th-century walls. It retains several blocks of Renaissance mansions along the C. Mayor, ending at the Palacio de Carlos V, finished in the 16th century, but now a handsome parador.*

We list hotels and restaurants beginning with the western end of the Basque coast, following our route east.

SANTANDER

WHERE TO STAY

Real 1st-class ★ ★ ★ ★
Paseo Perez Galdos, 28 (in el Sardinero, but on Los Peligros beach). Rooms: 125. ☎ *(942) 27 25 50; FAX (942) 27 45 73; Telex 39012.* Without question this turn-of-the-century hotel with splendid views of the bay is the premier hotel in the city, but its prices are astronomical—close to 40,000 pesetas per night.

Rhin R3rd-class ★ ★
Av. Reina Victoria, 153 (at the southern end of el Sardinero beach). Rooms: 95. ☎ *(942) 27 43 00; FAX 27 86 53.* You can stay five nights here for the cost of one at the Hotel Real. The accommodations are comfortable, the views lovely, and the beach is right across the street.

México   R3rd-class ★ ★

C. Calderón de la Barca, 3 (opposite the bus station). Rooms: 35. ☎ *(942) 21 24 50.* Tasteful decor makes this hotel special. That, and the moderate prices, make it a find. However, it is quite a walk to el Sardinero.

WHERE TO EAT

El Molino   ★ ★ ★

In Puente Arce, 13 k southwest. ☎ *(942) 57 50 55. Closed Sun. night, and Mon.* Though installed in a 17th-century mill with the original works in place, the renovation is elegant. The food is of the first order—expensive, but worth every peseta.

Amex, Diners, MasterCard and Visa accepted.

Bodiga del Riojano   ★

Rio de la Pila, 5 (off C. Santa Lucia, four blocks north of the port). ☎ *(942) 21 67 50.* Atmospheric with dark woods and old wine barrels, this restaurant serves wholesome food at modest prices.

LAREDO

WHERE TO STAY

Risco   2nd-class ★ ★

Alto de Laredo (1 k south on the old road to Bilbao). Rooms: 25. ☎ *(942) 60 50 30. The restaurant is closed on Wed., except in July and Aug.* The views from this small establishment on a bluff overlooking the village are spectacular. Prices are moderate, and the restaurant is the best in the area.   *Amex, Diners, MasterCard and Visa accepted.*

Ramona   4th-class ★

Alameda José Antonio, 4. Rooms: 10. ☎ *(942) 60 71 89. The restaurant is open from the middle of June through the middle of Sept.* It is the moderate prices—of both the rooms and food—that make this hotel stand out. Accommodations are most comfortable, and the food savory.

NOJA

WHERE TO STAY

Montemar   3rd-class ★ ★

On the Ris beach. Rooms: 61. ☎ *(942) 63 03 20. Open from the middle of June through the middle of Sept.* Located on the beach, this restful, comfortable hotel with its own tennis court cannot be bettered for its moderate price.

CASTRO URDIALES

WHERE TO STAY

Miramar   2nd-class ★

On the beach. Rooms: 34. ☎ *(942) 86 02 00.* The views are lovely and the accommodations comfortable at this moderately priced establishment.

LEKEITIO (LEQUEITIO)

WHERE TO STAY

Beitia   3rd-class ★

Av. Pascual Aboroa, 25. Rooms: 30. ☎ *(94) 684 01 11. Open from the third week in Apr. through the second week in Oct.* This is a clean and restful moderately priced hotel, set in the most picturesque of fishing villages.

DEBA (DEVA)

WHERE TO STAY

Miramar   2nd-class ★

C. Arenal, 24. Rooms: 60. ☎ *(943) 60 16 60.* Views of the coast are lovely, the rooms are comfortable and clean, and the prices are moderate.

ZARAUZ

WHERE TO STAY

Alameda   3rd-class

Gipuzkoa. Rooms: 39. ☎ *(943) 83 01 43; FAX 13 24 74.* This is a professionally run place that soothes with a lovely terrace for tranquil views. Moderate prices are reasonable for all it offers.

DONOSTIA (SAN SEBASTIAN)

WHERE TO STAY

María Cristina   Deluxe ★★★★★

Paseo República Argentina. Rooms: 139. ☎ *(943) 42 49 00; FAX 42 39 14; Telex 38195.* This is a hotel for the aristocracy, built with the finest materials from the turn of the century—mahogany woodwork, onyx baths, and Carrera marble columns. It is situated in an extensive park and remodeled throughout in 1989. Aristocracy comes at a price, however—about 25,000 pesetas per night.

De Londres y de Inglaterra   1st-class ★★★

Kalea Zubieta, 2 (just south of the Parque Alderdi Eder, where the ayuntamiento is located, facing La Concha beach). Rooms: 145. ☎ *(943) 42 69 89; FAX 42 00 31; Telex 36378.* Views of the sea, the gorgeous beach and two hills that anchor each end of the bay are unrivaled from this elegant hotel. Want more? There is a casino next door. The views and elegance are not inexpensive, but cost half as much as the María Cristina.

Niza   R2nd-class ★★

Kalea Zubieta, 56 (west of the Hotel de Londres, facing the beach). Rooms: 41. ☎ *(943) 42 66 63; FAX 42 66 63.* Here you enjoy the same magnificent views offered by the Hotel Londres, for a moderate price.

You do not partake of as much elegance, but do get a comfortable room.

Hostal Residencia Easo

Kalea San Bartolome, 24 (two blocks south of La Concha beach, behind the hotel Niza). Rooms: 11. ☎ *(943) 46 68 92.* Clean, comfortable, largish rooms, close to the beach, makes this hotel is a true bargain at its inexpensive rates.

WHERE TO EAT

Arzak ★★★★★

Kalea Alto de Miracruz, 21 (east of the city, on the way to Hondarribia). ☎ *(943) 27 84 65; FAX 27 27 53. Closed Sun. night, Mon., the last half of June, and Nov.* The only question about this restaurant is whether it is the first or the second best in all Spain. When you eat here, however, the issue seems settled in Arzak's favor. It was Chef Jean Arzak who created Basque *nueva cucina*, and he presents a menu of dishes every one of which is innovative and perfect in its way. Considering the succulence of the food and the elegance of service, prices are correct, though, of course, very expensive. Reservations weeks in advance are a must.   ***Amex, Diners, MasterCard and Visa accepted.***

Akelarre ★★★★

Passeo del Padre Orcolaga, 56, in the barrio de Iqueldo (east of the city on the slopes of Mount Iqueldo). ☎ *(943) 21 20 52; FAX 21 92 68. Closed Sun. night, Mon., the first week of June, and Dec.* Anywhere else this restaurant would stand above all others, but Donostia has Arzak too. Views are exceptional from the slope of Mount Igueldo and the food is sublime. Start with mushrooms and asparagus spears. Some justly rave about the *lubina* (sea bass with green peppers), but the *salmonetes* (red mullet) make a choice between two utterly wonderful options. Prices are in the expensive range, but below those at Arzak. Reservations are required.   ***Amex, Diners, MasterCard and Visa accepted.***

Panier Fleuri ★★★★

Paseo de Salamanca, 1 (at the mouth of the Urumea River). ☎ *(943) 42 42 05. Closed Sun. night, Wed., the first three weeks in June, and the last have of Dec.* Since the chef was recently named the best in the country, this restaurant would be a standout in any part of Spain, but here the competition keeps every establishment on its toes. There is a definite French accent to the Basque food here, but every dish is utterly delectable. As with the preceding, prices are in the expensive range, and reservations are required.

Amex, Diners, MasterCard and Visa accepted.

Alotza ★★

Kalea Fermin Calbeton, 7 (just south of the Pl. de la Constitución). ☎ *(943) 42 07 82. Closed Mon.* While this establishment is not in the league of the preceding, its prices are moderate and the food remains innovative. The atmosphere is less formal too, for a relaxed meal.

HONDARRIBIA (FUENTERRABIA)
WHERE TO STAY

Parador el Emperador   2nd-class ★★★★
Pl. de Armas del Castillo. Rooms: 36. ☎ *(943) 64 21 40; FAX 64 21 53.*
This castle presents a monolithic face of awesome power. It had to be strong when built in the 11th century, situated as it was on the border with France. Carlos V renovated it early in the 16th century, and the Spanish government remodeled the inside into a parador 20 years ago, to convey the atmosphere of medieval times as no other parador. Although it costs in the expensive range, it is a very special place to spend a night. Reserve far in advance.

WHERE TO EAT

Ramón Roteta   ★★★
In Irun, 3 k south of town. ☎ *(943) 64 16 93. Closed Sun. evening, Thurs., the last half of Feb., and Nov.* Lodged in an elegant mansion, this restaurant serves food elevated both in style and price. Poached eggs with truffles are sublime, and the rice with vegetables and clams is outstanding.   ***Amex, MasterCard and Visa accepted.***

COSTA DEL RIAS (GALICIAN COAST) ★★

Rias are deep cuttings made in the coast by river estuaries. Since the sea's pounding hammers the land down, views can be remarkable from surrounding hills. Here are beaches (often of fine sand, sometimes littered with shells) without the crowds of the Costa del Sol. Though swimming in the Atlantic tests all but New Englanders, the southernmost rias, called the Rias Bajas, provide more temperate bathing, and are unquestionably the most attractive, for here the coast rises high on either side, making extensive panoramas. Five separate southern rias shape the Galician coast, from the latitude of Santiango south to the Portuguese border, into the thumb and fingers of a hand. We describe these five rias, from north to south. C-550 follows their contours and makes for a scenic day's trip by car. This road was much in need of repair on our last visit; proceed carefully, if driving. Surprisingly good bus service visits all the coastal towns. After a description of the route and its sights, we offer recommendations for sleeping and eating.

From Santiago de Compostela take N-550 west for 18 k to Padrón.

Padrón stands at the head of the Ria de Arousa, where, according to legend, winds blew Saint James ashore to began a seven-year sojourn in Spain. In the Church of Santiago, beside a bridge over the

Sar, the stone where the ship is supposed to have moored sits beneath the altar.

> *From Padrón, a turn west on C-550 goes to the Ria Muros y Noia, with good beaches and few tourists, or a turn south on C-550 goes to four other rias over a route that provides more interest along the way.*

> **Ria Muros y Noia***: C-550 wends with little scenic interest to Ribera, a fishing town at the end of a cape in 42 k. The road then cuts across the cape to Porto do Son. Do not miss the romantic* **Castro de Barona** ★ *on the way. This is an ancient Celtic fortress on a small isthmus, with lovely surrounding beaches that generally are deserted. Noia, at the head of the ria, is 20 k further on.*

In **Noia**, the picturesque 14th-century **Santa María a Nova** stands amid an ancient cemetery that contains some 10th-century tombstones inscribed with runes. **San Martin**, facing the sea, wears some nice statues on its facade. There are decent beaches around Noia, but better ones lie further on.

> *The most scenic area is the north side of the ria. Fine beaches surround Muros, 36 k away, entered across a 14th-century bridge.*

Charming **Muros** ★ is a fishing village divided by alleys, with arcaded streets and the pretty Gothic church of **San Pedro**. Fine beaches line Point Louro.

> *A visit to* **Cabo Finisterre** ★, *the westernmost part of Europe and the end of the world to the ancients, is a scenic excursion. Continue north from Muros on C-550 along a lovely stretch of coast to Corcubion, 42 k. away. The village of Finisterre is 13 k west, and 2 k further is the windswept cape, with its lighthouse overlooking the sea. The beaches are gorgeous.*

> **Ria de Arousa***: From Padrón, C-550 going southwest reaches* **Villagarcia de Arousa** *in 25 k, with a green promenade along the sea, plus a magnificent restaurant.* **Cambados** ★, *in 10 k, is a lovely town with an unforgettable square, two sides of which are formed by the 16th-century palace of Fefinanes. There is a lovely parador, but no beaches. This matter is taken care of in 15 k at* **O Grova**

(El Grove) ★, *and the gorgeous pine island of* **A Toxa** *(La Toja)* ★, *off its coast. Beaches are plentiful in this favored resort area. The island of A Toxa has recently been subjected to luxury hotel developments.*

Ria de Pontevedra: *C-550 proceeds south through the resort village of* **Sanxenxo** *(Sangenjo), and the more typical fishing village of* **Combarro** *to reach* **Pontevedra** *in 35 k. Alternatively, one can drive directly from Padrón along N-550 in a fast 37 k.*

Pontevedra is a sleepy town of some size (65,137 population) that does well as a base for exploring the rias. It preserves an old section in a small area opposite the Burgo Bridge. Here is **Santa María la Mayor**, a late 15th-century Plateresque church for fishermen. (Note the reliefs at the rear of the west end.) The **Museo Provincial**, five blocks southeast on the Pl. de Lena, consists of two former mansions tied together by an arch. The pre-Roman—especially the Celtic—material is most worthwhile. This museum tries hard to interest by reconstructing parts of famous ships, and modeling antique kitchens (open daily 11 a.m. to 1:30 p.m. and 5-8 p.m.; admission: 200 ptas.). Near the northeast edge of the Jardines Vincenti are romantic ruins of the 14th-century convent of **Santo Domingo**.

Still on C-550, now going southwest, quickly pass Marin, then miles of beaches to reach **Hio** ★ *near the end of the cape in 28 k, with a fine Romanesque church with more miles of nice beach.*

Ria de Vigo: *South of Hio the scenery grows more lovely with each kilometer until reaching the outskirts of Vigo in 51 k. This industrial city can readily be skirted for the scenic 18 k ride to* **Panxón**, *a charming fishing village.* **Playa América** *is a modern resort lining the bay with its ribbon of fine sand beach.* **Baiona** *(Bayona), at the west end of the bay, houses its popular parador in the former 16th-century fortress of Monte Real, atop a hill with magnificent views. Fine beaches continue to Cape Silleiro. There is little scenery south of this place, though* **Tui** *(Tuy)* ★ *in 61 k, at the Portuguese border, is a charming town with nice mansions and a fortress-like 13th-century cathedral.*

We list especially pleasant accommodations and restaurants beginning in the north at Ria de Muros y Noia, then working south.

MUROS (RIA DE MUROS Y NOIA)

WHERE TO STAY

Murandana   **R3rd-class ★**
Av. Marina Española, 107. Rooms: 16. ☎ *(981) 82 68 85.* A pleasant-enough place at a moderate price, offers inexpensive meals besides.

VILLAGARCIA DE AROUSA (RIA DE AROUSA)

WHERE TO STAY AND EAT

Chocolate   **★★★**
Av. Cambados, 151 (actually in the town of Vilaxoan). ☎ *(986) 50 11 99. Closed from the last week in Dec. to the last week in Jan., and Sun. nights.* This is a delightful restaurant, serving some of the finest food in Galicia for prices that rise just above the moderate. It also offers 18 tastefully decorated rooms.

CAMBADOS (RIA DE AROUSA)

WHERE TO STAY

Parador del Albariño   **2nd-class ★★**
Paseo de Cervantes. Rooms: 63. ☎ *(986) 54 22 50; FAX (986) 54 20 68.* This parador is almost rustic, built in the style of the manor houses of the area, and prices are barely on the wrong side of the expensive category.

WEST OF VILAGARCIA (RIA DE AROUSA)

WHERE TO STAY

Pazo el Revel   **2nd-class ★★★**
Camino de la Iglesia, in Vilalonga. Rooms: 21. ☎ *(986) 74 30 00; FAX 74 33 90. Open June through Sept.* This hotel is installed in a 17th-century manor house, with a lovely garden behind for quiet, containing a pool and tennis courts. You cannot do better for a moderate price.

O GROVE AND A TOXA (RIA DE AROUSA)

WHERE TO STAY

Mar Atlántico   **2nd-class ★★★**
In San Vincente del Mar, 9 k south of O Grove. Rooms: 34. ☎ *(986) 73 80 61; FAX 73 82 99.* Set in a sylvan pine forest, here you feel the cares of the world fall away, not impeded by charges barely in the moderate category.

Louxo   **1st-class ★★★**
Island of A Toxa. Rooms: 96. ☎ *(986) 73 02 00; FAX 73 27 91.* The hotel sits in a magnificent park with views, and offers every sports

facility. Although it charges in the expensive range, it is half the price of the Gran Hotel nearby, and the rooms are nicer here.

WHERE TO EAT

La Posada del Mar
C. Castelao 202, in O Grove. ☎ *(986) 73 01 06. Closed Sun. eve, and from the middle to the end of Dec.* The dining room offers views across the channel to the pretty island of A Toxa. Seafood is fresh as can be, and prices are moderate.

COMBARRO (RIA DE PONTEVEDRA)

WHERE TO STAY

Stella Maris 2nd-class ★
On C-550, before Combarro. Rooms: 27. ☎ *(986) 77 03 66.* This is a pleasant little hotel with some views at an attractive moderate price.

PONTEVEDRA (RIA DE PONTEVEDRA)

WHERE TO STAY

Parador Casa del Barón 1st-class
Pl. de Maceda. Rooms: 47. ☎ *(986) 85 58 00; FAX 85 21 95.* This parador is a remodeled 18th-century mansion, which was never attractive, but prices are barely expensive.

WHERE TO EAT

Doña Antonia ★★★
Soportales de la Herreria, 9 (the second floor). ☎ *(986) 84 72 74. Closed Sun., and the first three weeks of July.* This is a gourmet's dream. The food is elegant and superb, at a cost that will only hurt for a little while. **Visa, Diners, MasterCard and Amex accepted.**

Casa Solla ★★★
Carretera de La Toya (2 k west of town). ☎ *(986) 85 60 29. Closed Sun. eve, Thurs. eve, and Christmas week.* Pity the person who must choose between this restaurant and Doña Antonia. This one is more syvan, with a lovely garden, but the food is no less spectacular. Want proof? Try the creamed oysters. **Visa accepted.**

BAIONA (RIA DE VIGO)

WHERE TO STAY

Parador Conde de Gondomar 1st-class ★★
1.5 k outside Baiona. Rooms: 124. ☎ *(986) 35 50 00; FAX 35 50 76; Telex 83424.* This luxury parador is built to look like an 18th-century mansion, and is located inside the walls of a genuine ancient castle. It offers swimming, tennis, and romantic views of the sea. For all this it costs just a touch more than the average parador.

COSTA VERDE ★

This Asturian coast is as pretty as any in Spain, and beloved by the Spanish. Bluffs line the shore, broken by clean sandy inlets for protected bathing. The coast is long, extending from Ribadeo at the border of Galicia for 300 k east to San Vincente, where the Basque Coast begins. However, we describe a route that extends past these political boundaries for 50 k or so on either side. It does not seem proper, for example, to bring you to within 30 k of beautiful Santillana del Mar, then not mention it. The coast is roughly divided in two by Gijon, from which either the less spoiled western half or the more elegant eastern half can be explored. As the coast is so long, we divide our description into western and eastern routes, followed by recommended places to stay and eat.

*From **Oviedo** the toll road A-66 leads to Gijon in 29 k. From **León** follow directions to Oviedo. From **Santiago** it is possible to come from the western end of the coast by taking the toll road A-9 north to Betanzos for 57 k, then taking N-VI east to Baamonde for 47 k, and, finally, N-634 northeast to Ribadeo in 90 k.*

WESTERN COSTA VERDE

Gijon is a city of a quarter of a million people bordering a wide bay. It consists largely of modern buildings, since the Civil War destroyed most of its older structures. Today it prospers as one of the main ports for shipping the coal from mountains to its south, and the steel manufactured in its outskirts. While it offers fine sand beaches, surprising to come upon after the commercial bustle of the rest of the city, they can become polluted during the height of summer.

*Head west from Gijon on N-632 (or avoid Gijon altogether by taking the west branch of A-8) to **Avilés** in 25 k. Once Avilés ranked with the prettiest towns in Spain, but large steelworks have put an end to that today. 3 k further the village of **Salinas** ★ emerges from the pines. It is an attractive resort town with the longest beach on this coast.*

*For an excursion to prehistoric cave paintings, at Soto del Barco west on N-632 in 13 k, take N-633 south in the direction of Cornellana. Following signs for **San Román** in 13 k. The cave is above the town, and contains a lovely painting of a wounded stag and yellow horse.*

West on N-632, after Avilés, comes **Cudillero** *in 20 k, after taking C-2 north for one k. The village is picturesque and proud of its castle, though there are no worthy beaches. Next on N-632, in about 30 k, comes* **Cadavedo***, a pretty small town with nice beaches, but few accommodations. 30 k more, as the road changes designation to N-634, brings lovely* **Luarca***.*

Luarca ★ lines the mouth of the Rio Negro, where it opens into a lovely bay in the sea. The town consists of charming whitewashed slate roofed houses, set along cobbled alleys. At the end of the estuary is a lighthouse, a church and a fascinating cemetery, while a path leads above the bay for fine views. A decent beach borders the cliffs.

Signs to La Coruña return one to N-634 going west. **Navia** *in 20 k is a new town and fishing port.* **Topia de Cassiego** ★*, in 20 k more, presents a splendid beach with good surfing to the west of this sleepy fishing village. In 10 k, after crossing the Rio Eo, we arrive at* **Ribadeo***.*

Technically **Ribadeo** ★ sits across the border in Galicia, and it is a more substantial town than its population of under 10,000 would suggest. It offers a quaint fisherman's quarter, a lighthouse, a castle, a parador and an attractive beach. On the hill 2 k outside the town is the Hermitage of Santa Cruz, and fine views of the coast. Northwest of Ribadeo range miles of fine beach and few tourists.

From Ribadeo N-634 meets N-642 going north in 19 k toward Foz. In about 3 k signs direct to **San Martin de Mondoñedo** ★★*, a church from the beginning of the 12th century. It is all that remains of a former monastery. The style is the earliest form of Romanesque, with a timber roof, and outer buttresses. The capitals inside are carved in charming scenes and the stone retablo is endearing.* **Foz** ★ *is a busy little port with two fine beaches separated by a headland. White sand beaches amid lovely scenery lie 40 k north around the town of* **Vivero***. Unfortunately, accommodations here are scarce.*

EASTERN COSTA VERDE

From Gijon (see above), head east on a pretty stretch of N-632 to **Villaviciosa** ★ *in 30 k. This village of charming streets is the cider capital of Asturia, with a nice church in* *the Pl. Mayor, and restaurants from which refreshing cider is available. 18 k more brings* **La Isla** ★ *on a huge bay ringed with numerous beaches. In 21 k comes* **Ribadesella**.

Ribadesella ★★ offers pleasant accommodations and a splendid beach. On the outskirts a marvellous cave called **Cueve Tito Bustillo**, contains paleolithic paintings of the age of Altimara, and, in some cases, of that quality. (Open 10 a.m. to 1 p.m. and 3:30-6:30 p.m.; closed Mon., and summer weekends; admission: 200 ptas. Only four hundred people allowed per day.)

5 k west of Ribadesella, just before Nueva, N-632 feeds into the better N-634. From Nueva to Santillana del Mar almost 100 k west, fine beaches line every kilometer of the route. The first town worthy of note along the way is **Llanes** ★, *a quiet resort with good beaches, dotted with interesting rock formations, a nice church and a castle. After 15 k of road bordered by shore and mountains comes the village of* **La Franca** ★, *on the outskirts of which a lovely cliff frames a beautiful beach. In another 18 k comes* **San Vincente de la Barquera**.

San Vincente ★★ is blessed with a huge beach that led to its development as a resort, but without losing its attractiveness. The town is filled with old arcaded houses, has several nice mansions, a castle and interesting remains of a 13th-century convent.

A few kilometers outside of San Vincente turn left onto the coastal road C-6316, which brings **Comillas** *in 10 k.*

Comillas ★ has long been a resort whose visitors have included King Alfonso XII. The town is attractive, with a charming Plaza Mayor and fishing port. It also contains a set of neo-Gothic buildings from the end of the 19th century, including a Moorish style **pavilion by Gaudi** (now a restaurant). To all this it adds miles of beaches to the west, 5 k outside of town.

Continue west on C-6316 for 19 k to elegant **Santillana del Mar**.

Santillana ★★★ has been called the prettiest village in Spain and well it might be—except on weekends when the tourists descend. Exception must be taken to its name however, for it is several kilometers from the sea. At the northern end of the main street stands the late 12th-century **Collegiate Church of Santa Julliana** (whose corrupted name denominates the village). The facade is elegant Romanesque on the east end, and the interior contains interesting vaulting. In the choir four lovely Romanesque statues hide inside a 17th-century Mexican silver altarfront. The cloisters are quietly moving. Throughout the length of the village stand elegant **mansions** from the 15th-17th centuries. Half a mile to the south is a **zoo** which houses several European bison, exactly like those depicted on the ceiling of **Altamira Cave**. That cave lies 2 k southwest, but can be entered only by official permission that takes months to secure.

8 k to the west C-6316 joins the better N-611 for a speedy 25 k trip to **Santander** ★ . *See the Basque Coast above for a description.*

We list restaurants and hotels for the Costa Verde in the order of our route, starting with Gijon and going west, then covering the eastern half.

GIJON
WHERE TO STAY

Parador El Molina Viejo   1st-class ★
Parque Isabel la Católica (east of the center of the city). Rooms: 40. ☎ *(985) 37 05 11; FAX 37 02 33.* This parador is installed in a cider mill from the 18th century, and for all its first-class rating, provides simple accommodations. The rooms overlooking the park are preferred. Although an expensive place, it is not prohibitively so.

WHERE TO EAT

Casa Victor   ★
C. Carmen, 11 (near the train station, by the port). ☎ *(985) 34 83 10. Closed Sun. eve, Thurs., and Nov.* The restaurant looks like many a mesón in the area but serves the best seafood in town. Victor, the owner, is a thoughtful restauranteur who modifies the traditional fare of the region with nueva touches.

Amex, Diners, MasterCard and Visa accepted.

LUARCA
WHERE TO STAY

Gayoso   2nd-class ★ ★
Paseo de Gomez, 4. Rooms: 33. ☎ *(985) 64 00 50; FAX 47 02 71. Closed Nov. through Apr.* This hotel is seasoned and atmospheric, the rooms large, and wooden balconies add just the right touch. It pushes just past the moderate price category.

Casa Consuelo   3rd-class ★
On N-634, 6 k west. Rooms: 35. ☎ *(985) 64 08 44; FAX 64 16 42.*

Closed from the middle of Sept. through the first week in Oct. Situated nicely, with fine views, this hotel is a good buy for a very moderate price.

WHERE TO EAT

Leonés ★★

Paseo Alfonso X el Sabio, 1. ☎ *(985) 64 09 95.* The decor is best described as "quaint," but the food is special. We think often of the scrambled eggs with shrimp, spinach and a hearty tang of garlic, not to mention the apple sherbet.

Amex, Visa, Diners and MasterCard accepted.

TAPIA DE CASARIEGO

WHERE TO STAY

Palacete Pañalba 1st-class ★★

C. El Cotarelo, in Figueras, 2 k from Casariego. Rooms: 12. ☎ *(985) 62 31 50.* Contained in a luxurious *modernista* mansion, the hotel is tasteful, reserved, quiet, and costs in the moderate range.

RIBADEO

WHERE TO STAY

Eo 2nd-class ★

Av. de Asturias, 5. Rooms: 24. ☎ *(982) 11 07 50; FAX 11 00 21. Open Apr.-Sept.* The modern parador in town offers no charm and falls second to this restful, well-run place. When you add the fact that this establishment charges in the low-moderate range—so you pay about half as much as at the parador—the choice is clear.

WHERE TO EAT

O Xardin ★

C. Reinante, 20. ☎ *(982) 11 02 22. Closed Mon. in winter, and from Christmas through Jan.* Aptly named "The Garden," this is a relaxed, bistro place that serves inventive, well-prepared food at a moderate price. **Diners, MasterCard and Visa accepted.**

VIVERO

WHERE TO STAY

Ego 2nd-class ★

At the Playa de Area on C-642, 2 k north. Rooms: 29. ☎ *(982) 56 09 87; FAX 56 17 62.* This is a well-maintained hotel that provides beach and ocean views for a moderate price.

LA ISLA

WHERE TO STAY

Astuy 2nd-class ★

On the beach, 3 k east. Rooms: 52. ☎ *(942) 67 95 40; FAX 67 95 88.*

Closed from mid Jan. to mid Feb. This hotel sits opposite a lovely beach and charges a moderate price for clean and comfortable accommodations.

RIBADESELLA

WHERE TO STAY

Grand Hotel del Sella   1st-class ★ ★

Paseo de la Playa. Rooms: 82. ☎ *(985) 86 01 50; FAX 85 74 49. Open Apr.-mid Oct.* Views of the town and bay from the rooms facing the water are lovely. Other rooms are contained in an 18th-century mansion, and a tennis court and pool are available. Prices are expensive.

Ribadesella Playa   2nd-class ★

Paseo de la Playa, 34. Rooms: 17. ☎ *(985) 86 07 15; FAX 86 02 20. Closed Jan.* The views are as lovely from this former mansion as from the Grand Hotel down the beach, but at a moderate price. This hotel is less grand, but very comfortable.

LLANES

WHERE TO STAY

Don Paco   2nd-class ★ ★

Posade Herrera, 1. Rooms: 42. ☎ *(985) 40 01 50; FAX 40 26 81. Open June-Sept.* The hotel is a former 17th-century palace beside the town ramparts. Rooms facing the sea provide beautiful views, but are comfortable, with prices at the high end of the moderate range.

LA FRANCA

WHERE TO STAY

Mirador de la Franca   3rd-class ★ ★

On the beach, 1 k west of town. Rooms: 52. ☎ *(985) 41 21 45; FAX 41 21 53. Open April through the end of Sept.* This is a lovely little place beside a fine beach, offering views and quiet at a moderate price.

SAN VINCENTE DE LA BARQUERA

WHERE TO STAY

Miramar   3rd-class ★ ★

1 k north of San Vincente. Rooms: 15. ☎ *(942) 71 00 75. Open Mar. through the middle of Dec.* Views of the ocean and surrounding mountains are stunning from this charming little hotel. All this, and quiet too, comes at a moderate price.

COMILLAS

WHERE TO STAY

Josein   3rd-class ★

C. Manuel Noriega, 27. Rooms: 23. ☎ *(942) 72 02 25. Open Apr.-Sept.*

The views of the beach and sea are worth more than the moderate price charged. Rooms are comfortable and clean.

Hosteria de Quijas   3rd-class ★ ★
On N-634 near Reocín. Rooms: 13. ☎ (942) 82 08 33. Closed from the last week in Dec. through the fourth of Jan. The hotel reposes in an elegant 18th-century mansion that makes one feel like a baron. There is a pool, though the beach is some distance away. This is the way to live, and at a moderate price.

WHERE TO EAT

El Capricho de Gaudí   ★
Barrio de Sobrellano. ☎ (942) 72 03 65. Closed Mon., and Feb. To be frank, the food is not extraordinary and on the expensive side, but the building is a treat. It was designed by Gaudí in 1885 as a summer pavilion, in a style composed of Moorish elements carried to their extremes. You can peek in, of course, without dining.
Amex, Diners, MasterCard and Visa accepted.

SANTILLANA DEL MAR
WHERE TO STAY

Parador Gil Blás   2nd-class ★ ★ ★
Pl. Ramón Pelayo, 11. Rooms: 56. ☎ (942) 81 80 00; FAX 81 83 91. This parador is situated amid noble Renaissance mansions, and is one itself, from the 17th century. Baronial in every way, the edifice oozes atmosphere. Prices are in the expensive range, and the rooms are heavily booked.

Altimar   2nd-class ★ ★
C. Cantón, 1. Rooms: 32. ☎ (942) 81 80 25; FAX 84 01 03. Here you also get to stay in a baronial mansion, also from the 17th century, but at a moderate price that makes up for the fact that the mansion is a little smaller and the service not as grand as at the parador.

OVIEDO ★ ★ ★

Population: 190,123
Area code: 985; zip code: 33003

From **León** *take N-630 north for 115 k. The road winds through scenic mountains, and can consume three hours, if there are trucks—and there always are. Alternatively, one can take N-120 west for 8 k to pick up the toll road A-66 north to save almost an hour. From* **Gijon** *on the Cantabrian coast take A-66 west, then south for 29 k.*

Oviedo, situated over a pass through the Cordillera Mountains and less than 20 miles from the sea, was established as a defensive outpost to keep the Moors from the little territory remaining to the

Spanish Christians. Nonetheless, by the middle of the eighth century the Moors had utterly destroyed the town. Alfonso II, one of the earliest Spanish kings, then rebuilt the city and moved his court there in 810. Thus Oviedo is one of, if not the oldest, capitals of the kings of Spain. Alfonso also built two churches. One, Santullano, survives in its original form. In the other, Alfonso built a special shrine to contain the sacred relics of the Visigoths that Christians managed to carry away from Toledo when the Moors seized that capital. Centuries later, this old church was replaced by a Gothic cathedral, but the original shrine was preserved in the newer structure, and exists today. Alfonso's successor, Ramiro I, built a summer palace on the slopes of Mount Naranco nearby. One hall of that palace survives in the somewhat altered form of a church. Thus, Oviedo was on course to become a proper capital when Christians captured León, to the south, to which the court moved, never to return. Since 1388, however, the heir to Spain's throne has been designated Prince of Asturias, in remembrance of the historical importance of this province.

Oviedo languished until the 19th century when coal deposits in the Cordillera Mountains began to be exploited, bringing prosperity to the area. Oviedo again became what it had been centuries before, a kind of capital of the Asturian region—this time more an economic than a political center. Today Oviedo exudes an attractive comfort and, despite its largish population, seems a small town. The city centers on a lovely park, the Parque de San Francisco, filled with ponds, fountains, flowers, aged trees and strolling people. Along its north side runs an avenue of attractive stores and banks; a block back from its west side stands the elegant town parador; and a block from its east corner stretches a small old quarter, containing many of the sights for tourists.

Come to relax in Oviedo. The distances to sights are eminently manageable on feet, the park calls for strolls and leisurely rests, and the food is good. What is worth seeing will take no more than half of one day, but most visitors are in no hurry to leave.

The finest sight in Oviedo is **Santa María del Naranco ★★**, the former hall of Ramiro's palace. It is 4 k northwest of town on a mountainside with lovely views. A hundred feet away is **San Miguel de Lillo ★**, an equally ancient church. The Gothic **cathedral ★★** is one of the highlights of the city proper. Inside is preserved the Cámera Santa, a ninth century shrine of hoary Christian relics. Renaissance mansions surround the cathedral. The **Archaeological Museum ★** nearby is worth a stop, as is the **Museo de Bellas Artes**

de Asturias. Several blocks northeast stands **Santullano** ★, a 9th-century church. West of the park is the former Hospital of the Principality of Asturias, now a special **parador**, with an elegant baroque facade.

Arriving from **León** *and* **south** *on N-630 the town is entered on Av. León. Continue straight as the street changes its name to Calvo Sotelo. It passes along the edge of the large Parque de San Francisco, on the left. Parking lies at the end of the park, down the first left across C. Fruela straight ahead.*

From the **north** *on A-66 continue straight onto C. Victor Chavarn, which changes its name to Alcalde G. Conde and enters a plaza in one block. Take, not the acute left, but the gentle left which brings C. Arguelles in one block. Turn right and take the first left to parking, just before the park.*

From the **northeast on N-634** *C. Jovellanos winds and changes its name to C. Arguelles. Take the first left to parking, just before the park.*

Head east from the northeast corner of the park along C. San Francisco. In one block the 17th-century **Old University** *stands on the right. A jag left, then immediately right, brings the attractive plaza of Alfonso II. Immediately left is the 17th-century* **Valdecarzana Palace**, *and at the southwest corner stands the* **Casa de la Rua**, *a 15th-century house. Proceed ahead to the cathedral.*

WHAT TO SEE AND DO

Cathedral   ★★
Open Mon.-Sat. 10:15 a.m. to 1 p.m. and 4-7 p.m. (to 6 p.m. in winter). Open Sun. from 4-7 p.m. Admission: 200 ptas. to the Cámera Santa. Pl. Alfonso II El Castro. The original cathedral was begun in 781 and finished in 802. In 1388, the city decided to replace that church with a larger Gothic structure that was not finished until the 16th century. Of the early church, only two pieces remain. South of the present facade stands San Tirso, which is just a window frame from the 9th-century church. And inside the present cathedral is the Cámera Santa (Holy Chamber).

The facade is blackened with a grime that adds to the feeling of age, if not attractiveness. The soaring south tower is a Gothic masterpiece, but the incomplete north tower and empty niches around the portals produce an air of incompleteness about the whole.

The interior seems small, but well proportioned and light. Overall, this is a most sedate flamboyant Gothic church. Chapels lining both sides of the nave are later baroque additions, as is the ambulatory which displays photographs of the reconstruction of the Cámera Santa. Poorly restored, the 16th-century retablo looks better from the length of the nave than close at hand. The north transept (left) contains a fine late Gothic chapel to house remains of some of the earliest kings of Spain in marble sarcophagi so eroded that the names and decoration can no longer be discerned.

The south transept (right) leads to the Cámera Santa. This "Holy Chamber" was built in 810 by Alfonso II to house sacred relics the Visigoths carried away with them when the Moors conquered Toledo and most of the rest of Spain. In the 12th century the Cámera was masterfully redecorated in the Romanesque style. The chapel was bombed during the Spanish Civil War, but reconstructed afterwards. In 1977 thieves stole its priceless treasures, though the culprits were apprehended on their way to France, and most of the treasures regained. Today the Cámera Santa consists of one doorway and a tiny apse displaying treasures. It is housed in the former cloister, which currently serves as a gallery of revolving art exhibits, though also displaying some medieval tombs.

Cámera Santa: The vault of the main chamber rests on Romanesque statues of apostles serving as columns. They compare with the great work of Master Mateo in Santiago, whose influence is probable. A sublime figure of Christ watches over the doorway. In the tiny apse, more a large niche, reside the priceless treasures for which the Cámera, indeed the cathedral, were erected. Precautions to prevent a recurrence of the 1977 robbery prevent any close viewing of these artworks. But there in the center is the Cruz de los Angeles, a bejeweled Maltese cross from 808, probably used for ceremonies during the reign of Alfonso II. On the side rests the Cruz de la Victoria, from 910, actually a sheath to protect the oak cross carried by Pelayo in the first Christian victory over the Moors. There is a coffer covered in silver with Arabic writing, early reliquaries, ivory diptyches and silver and gold plate.

South past **San Tirso**, *with its 9th-century window, comes the 18th-century palace of Velarde, now housing the* **Museo de Bellas Artes de Asturias**. *Although not of the first rank artistically, the paintings inside form a charming collection of unfamiliar works. Continuing south would bring the Pl. Mayor and the picturesque* **Pl. de Daoiz y Velarde**, *the town market, west of it.*

Returning to the cathedral and walking behind, leads to the **Provincial Archaeological Museum** ★, *housed in an 18th-century convent. (Open Tues.-Sat. 10 a.m. to 1:30 p.m. and 4-6 p.m. Open Sun. 11 a.m. to 1 p.m. Admission: free.) What is special* *about this museum is its display of fragments and reproductions of early Asturian art, as a preparation for the Asturian art you see in the Cámera Sancta and the churches at Naranco.*

North from the front of the Museum brings C. Azcarrega. Cross this large street and head northeast along C. Martinez Vigil for 5 blocks to Santullano at the end of a small park.

Santullano ★

Open Tues.-Sun. 10 a.m. to 1 p.m. and 4-6 p.m. Admission: free. If closed, apply at the Presbytery. This church is among the oldest in Spain, dating from the early tenth century, the times of the Asturian kings. The exterior is charming, with a wide porch in front and three square apses in the rear. The inside is small but elegant and preserves traces of frescoes on the walls, reminiscent of late Roman work.

*A block west of the west end of the Parque de San Francisco is the city's **parador** housed in the former Antiquo Hospital del Principado from the 18th century. The harmonious, almost classical front is surmounted by a baroque extravaganza of a coat of arms above the door.*

Santa María del Naranco ★★

Open daily (Mon.-Sat. in winter) 10 a.m. to 1 p.m. and 3-7 p.m. (to 5 p.m. in winter). Admission: 150 ptas. On the precipitous slopes of the hill of Naranco Alfonso II built a summer palace early in the ninth century to catch the breezes and lovely views. A hundred feet north he erected a small church, San Miguel de Lillo. Over the centuries the palace fell to ruin and disappeared, all except for one part that was made into a second church. Today, two ancient churches stand on this hill, though one, Santa María, began life as the hall in an Asturian palace.

Take C. Calvo Sotelo along the eastern edge of the park for 4 blocks past the park. At the large intersection take Av. del Padre Vinjoy going right. Follow the second right onto the major thoroughfare of Av. Hernandos Menéndez Pidal, which changes its name to Av. de Colón, after a park. Cross a bridge over train tracks, continuing straight along the smaller C. Ramiro I. In two short blocks a sign directs left up Av. de los Monumentos to Naranco in less than 4 k.

The first impression of Santa María is of a building with too many architectural elements for its tiny size. Gradually one becomes aware that this is caused by an unfamiliar aesthetic, not by detail, for the building is harmonious. Remodeling from a palace into a church occurred in the early tenth century and consisted of adding some religious carving inside and outer walls where needed, for the hall was neither the front nor back of the palace. In other words, the present structure retains its architectural elements from the time when it was the palace audience hall, thus providing a glimpse of life in the ninth century.

The structure conveys a sense of strength despite its size. Constructed of local stone, buttressing pilasters strengthen the long walls. The main room stand over a low first floor, probably to raise it above the damp. Outer porches at either end provide fresh air and peaceful views. Inside, note the cradle vaulting of the ceiling, the medallions hanging around the top of the walls, and the pillars carved in twisted columns. This building prefigures the Romanesque, but with elements such as the foregoing, that are unique contributions to architecture.

A hundred feet further up the hill is the original church of the palace, **San Miguel de Lillo**, also dating to the ninth century. Its plan is simple: a narrow nave to emphasizes the height. The window tracery is exceptional, as are carvings on the entrance door jambs and column bases.

WHERE TO STAY

Oviedo is not equipped for tourists as much as most other Spanish cities, instead its hotels cater mainly to business people at a rate they can afford. There are abundant hotel choices at the expensive level, but few at lower rates.

EXPENSIVE ($100-$200)

De La Reconquesta   1st-class ★ ★ ★ ★ ★
C. Gil de Jaz, 16 (one block west of the west end of the Parque de San Francisco). Rooms: 142. ☎ *24 11 00; FAX 24 11 66; Telex 84328.* This is one of our favorite hotels in Spain. The outside is stately yet with a touch of humor in the baroque coat of arms affixed to the harmonious front. The interior is elegant through and through with a huge central patio that expansively invites. Bedrooms are large, tastefully decorated and comfortable; the bathrooms are luxurious. All this and service that is close to perfect too—attentive, helpful but not obsequious. Unlike other paradors this one is managed by the Italian CIGA company, which owns and manages some of the grand hotels of Europe. There is always a rub, of course—the charges are very expensive, over 20,000 pesetas per couple per night.

Principado   2nd-class ★
C. San Francisco, 6 (east of the east corner of the Parque de San Francisco). Rooms: 70. ☎ *21 77 92; FAX 21 39 46; Telex 84003.* This hotel offers no history or stunning architecture, but provides a comfortable stay at half the price of La Reconquista. The rooms were renovated in 1989.

MODERATE ($50-$99)

Tropical   R3rd-class
C. 19 de Julio, 6, second floor (The Pl. de Porlier is a short block north of the northwest corner of the Parque de San Francisco. C. 19 de Julio runs from its east side.) Rooms: 44. ☎ *21 87 79.* As mentioned, accommoda-

tions below the expensive level are difficult to find in this city. This hotel is not special, but has the advantage of lower rates than most, almost low enough to be considered inexpensive.

WHERE TO EAT

Catering to businesspeople has a happy effect on Oviedo's restaurants. The town boasts two that serve exceptional food and one that is pure fun.

EXPENSIVE ($50+)

Casa Fermín   ★★★

C. San Francisco, 8 (west of the northwest corner of the Parque de San Francisco). *21 64 52. Closed Mon* Relaxing pinks and greys provide a background for greenery and bright skylights in this most elegant of Oviedo's restaurants. Because the owner is a promoter of the food of his region, the menu consists of *fabada* (beans in a tomato sauce), clams with fois gras *en papillote*, and seafood. Everything is prepared with care and style, and the prices are fair. Reservations are advised, especially on weekends. *Amex, Diners, MasterCard and Visa accepted.*

Trascorrales   ★★★

Pl. de Trascorrales, 19 (two blocks south of the cathedral in the marketplace). *22 24 41. Closed Sun, and the second half of Aug.* Although the decor is rustic with dark wood and copper pots, it is tasteful. The food is aggressively *nueva cocina*, and inventiveness abounds. Strawberries in a sauce of sugar and pepper is not something that would occur to most, but try them and be transported. Reservations are recommended. *Amex, Diners, MasterCard and Visa accepted.*

MODERATE ($20-$50)

El Raitan   ★

Pl. Trascorrales, 6 (opposite the restaurant Trascorrales). *21 42 18. Closed Sun. eve.* This looks like a rustic inn, and waitresses dress appropriately so that everyone relaxes here and has a good time. There are no choices to make. From wine and soups through dessert, everyone is served the same eight-or nine-course meal (we lost count), with family style service allowing seconds and thirds. Some of the bean dishes seem a little too similar to others, but do not worry. In an instant that dish will be taken away and something different will replace it. Be hungry. Reservations are advised. *Amex, Diners, MasterCard and Visa accepted.*

DIRECTORY

INFORMATION • The office is located at Pl. Alfonso II, one block west of the park (☎ 21 33 85). The staff is helpful and speak English.

TRAINS AND BUSES • The RENFE station is located on C. Uria (☎ 24 33 64). The station is three long blocks northwest of the park. RENFE trains go south to León and Madrid, and due west to Barcelona and points between. FEVE, a different railway company, serves the north. The FEVE station is on C. Económicós (☎ 28 01 50), a two minute walk left of the RENFE station.

There are two main bus companies. ALSA, which serves the south, is located in the lower level of a shopping mall on Primo de Rivera, 1 (☎ 28 12 00). It is three blocks due north of the park. Turytrans (☎ 28 50 69) is located opposite the FEVE train station, and serves much of the north.

POST OFFICE AND TELEPHONES • The main post office is at C. Alonso Quintanilla, which is two blocks north of the park. Telephones are available in Pl. de Porlier, behind the University, a long block east of the park.

POLICE • The main police station is on C. General Yague, 5 (☎ 21 19 20), which is a distance from the center of town.

AIRPORT • Oviedo uses the Gijon airport, 47 k away. The Iberia office is located on C. Uria, two blocks northeast of the park.

EXCURSIONS

From Oviedo the **Verde** and **Basque Coasts** both are within 75 k. See the descriptions above in this chapter. **León** lies 115 k south on N-630, with the rest of Old Castile below. See the descriptions in the "Old Castile and León" chapter.

SAN SEBASTIÁN (DONASTIA)

See the description under "Basque Coast" above.

SANTANDER

See the description under "Basque Coast" above

SANTILLANA DEL MAR

See the description under "Costa Verde" above

SANTIAGO DE COMPOSTELA ★ ★ ★ ★ ★

Population: 93,695
Area code: 981; zip code: 15700

The best route from **Madrid** *is N-VI all the way to Lugo, 453 k to the northwest. Be alert near Benavente, lest you lose the road. At Lugo head west on N-547 for 107 k to Santiago. From* **León** *take N-120 west for 38 k to Astorga,* *where N-VI is picked up going northwest to Lugo, 169 k away. There take N-547 going west for a further 107 k. From **Oviedo** take N-634 west, which follows the coast for 81 k then heads inland to Lugo, 71 k further. At Lugo take N-547 going west to Santiago in 107 k. From Portuguese **Porto** the coast road N-13 is the more scenic route. It reaches the border at Valenca do Minho in 128 k, though requires a short span on N-113 going north. From the border take N-550 to Santiago in 105 k.*

Legend tells of a sea voyage by the Apostle Saint James whose boat was driven by storms to the mouth of the Ulla river. He anchored in the present city of Padrón and began preaching Christianity to the locals. Seven years later he returned to Jerusalem where he was killed by Herod. According to the legend, however, disciples brought James' body back to Spain and buried it near the place where his ship originally had landed. Through the troubled times of invasions by Visigoths and Moors the location of the body was forgotten, until 813 when a shining light drew shepherds to the spot. A cult grew around the venerated remains. Thirty years later, during an engagement between a band of Christians and Moors, a knight mysteriously appeared whose standard bore a red cross on a white field. He routed the infidels, then disappeared as mysteriously as he had come, but several knights claimed to recognize him as Saint James—Santiago. This event fixed the epithet *Matamoro*, "Slayer of Moors," to Saint James, and made him the patron saint of the Reconquest.

By the 11th century, pilgrims by the hundreds of thousands (two million, in the record year) from all the corners of Europe walked as far as 1000 miles to visit those sacred remains. These travellers, seeking to atone for some sin or to receive help for a personal problem, wore a kind of uniform. Enclosed by long hooded cloaks, they carried a stave taller than a man, tied a gourd for water to the stave and wore a broad hat with three scallop shells attached. Such shells were the symbols of the Saint, and the pilgrims were referred to as those who "took the cockleshell." The route was hard and unfamiliar, so in 1130 a monk named Aimeri Picaud wrote history's first guide book to describe the roads, climate and sights, as well as the manners and customs of people along the way. Monasteries and hospitals grew up along the route to provide simple accommodations for weary pilgrims. Among the famous pilgrims were Charlemagne, el Cid and Saint Francis of Assisi.

Because of Spanish wars against France, Holland and England in the 16th century, the number of pilgrims declined drastically. In 1589 Francis Drake raided La Coruña, 50 miles from Santiago, frightening the Bishop of Santiago so much that he hid the sacred relics for safety. Afterwards, incredibly, no one could remember where. It was not until 1879 that they turned up again, were duly certified as authentic by the Pope, and the pilgrimages recommenced. In any year when the Feast of Saint James (July 25) falls on a Sunday, special indulgences are granted to pilgrims. At that time, they arrive in numbers that pass one million.

The entire area around the Cathedral of Santiago is a national monument. A newer town surrounds it, heavily populated by university students. On weekends, as a kind of initiation rite, male students in ancient capes roam the plazas serenading women. If the woman is pleased, she contributes a bright ribbon that the student pins to his cape; if displeased, she douses him with water. All the sights lie in a radius of a few blocks of the cathedral.

Parking is an unsolved problem in Santiago, compounded by one-way streets, unmarked dead-ends and a lack of direction signs.

*From **Lugo**, the **airport** and **east** the city is entered on C. Concheiros which is soon renamed San Pedro. At Puerto de Camino turn left onto C. Virgen de la Cerca. As it bends right the street receives the name C. Fuente de San Antonio and reaches parking in the Pl. de Gelmirez Galicia on the right in three blocks. The lot is four blocks due south of the cathedral. For additional parking closer to the Cathedral, continue straight, though the street changes its name to C. Mola. In two blocks a park is reached. Go right, then left along its border, C. Pombal. Take the first right which forks off from Pombal. When the street bends right, parking lies both left and right in one block.*

*From **Portugal** and **south** N-550 continues straight on Av. Rosalia de Castro until reaching the end of a park. Turn left and left again to follow the park, now on C. Pombal. Take the first street that forks right from Pombal. When this street bends right, parking lies to both on the left and the right in one block.*

WHAT TO SEE AND DO

Cathedral of Santiago   ★★★★★

Open Mon.-Sat. 10 a.m. to 1 p.m. and 4-7 p.m. Open Sun. 10 a.m. to 1:30 p.m. Admission: 200 ptas., to the museum. A church was erected to protect the remains of Saint James immediately after their discovery in 815. It was enlarged a hundred years later, only to be destroyed during a raid by the Moors in 997. The present edifice was begun in the 11th century and finished by the 13th, although a new facade was added in the 18th century. Plazas surround the front, back and most of both sides to show off this cathedral better than any other in Spain.

No other plaza in Spain can match the spacious **Pl. de Obradorio** (Work of Gold) ★★★★ in front of the cathedral. Opposite the cathedral is the ornate former **Palacio de Rajoy** from 1772, now the ayuntamiento. To the west is the imposing facade of the **Hospital Real** ★★, a pilgrim hostelry from 1511, now one of the greatest paradors. Its Plateresque facade was added in 1687. To the East is the **Colegio de San Jerónimo**, in the Romanesque style, but from the 17th century. And to the north is the cathedral, rising two flights above the Plaza to dominate everything else. In between, a vast field of open space keeps these magnificent buildings at a slight distance, both in space and time.

The so-called Obradoiro facade of the cathedral is perhaps the most successful example of the Churrigueresque style. Though replete with twistings, intricate knobs, spikes and vines, as the style dictates, the strong thrust of the two towers' rising, creates an effect like flames shooting up to the sky. The facade was added to the original front of the cathedral by Ferdinand Casas y Novoa in 1750. Fortunately, the original front was not torn down to make way for the new. Now it remains inside, protected from the elements as any great work of art should be.

A 12th-century Romanesque cathedral resides beyond the facade. Just inside the entrance is the original entrance to the cathedral, one of the masterpieces of Western art. It is known as the **Door of Glory** and consists of a series of statues and scenes by a sculptor named Mateo who died in 1217. The central shaft which presents the figure of Santiago above the Tree of Life, shows Mateo himself kneeling at the base. Centuries of pilgrims, thankful to have completed their pilgrimage, wore away the impress of five fingers in this central pillar. Above the main door is *Christ in His Glory*, surrounded by an orchestra of church elders. The arches are supported by Apostles, and the columns rest on monsters. (Traces of painting, visible here and there, are newer—16th century.) The left door presents the tribes of Israel, and the right, the Last Judgement. Choose your own entry, after admiring both the reserve of the presentation of these most passionate of religious themes and the elegance of their execution.

The interior is surprisingly plain and dark to those used to Gothic and later cathedrals. The Romanesque lacks the gallery of windows known as the clerestory which let light into later churches. Nor does it employ pointed arches and rising ribs in the vaulting to carry the eye upwards, or carved columns or balustrades to add variety. It takes but a moment, however, for the utter simplicity and huge scale of this cathedral to work its magic.

A portal to the right leads to the Plateresque **Reliquary Chapel**, with effigies of the earliest kings and queens of Spain. To its right is the **Treasury**. Amid countless crucifixes, the bejeweled bust of Santiago Alfeo stands out. But the reason for the church lies ahead, at the end of the nave. The high **altar** is lit by a dome added in the 15th century from which a huge censer, called the **botafumeiro**, is swung on special days through the energies of eight men. The 18th-century altar contains a 13th century seated statue of Saint James, elaborately attired. Ascending stairs on the right side allow the faithful to kiss the hem of his gown. Descending stairs on the right side lead to a plain **crypt** in which rests the body of Saint James and two of his disciples. This crypt actually is part of the foundation of the original ninth century basilica. Excavations have shown that beneath it lies an ancient Roman and Suevian necropolis, which suggests that the name Compostela, instead of being a corruption of the Roman *campus stella* (field of stars), comes directly from the Roman *compostela* (cemetery).

In the right hand transept is the entrance to the cloister. But first study the tenth-century depiction of Santiago Matamoro, to its right above a door leading to the sacristy. This is the earliest portrayal of Santiago as the Slayer of Moors. The plain **cloister** is late Gothic by Gil de Hotañton. Across it waits the entrance to the cathedral **museum**. The library displays the huge Botafumeiro, while the chapterhouse shows 17th-century and earlier Spanish tapestries, and allows fine views of the plaza and its buildings. There too is the papal letter certifying that the remains in the crypt indeed are those of Saint James. In the basement are various archaeological bits, some excavated from earlier churches on the site.

Exit from the south transept through the **Puerta de las Platerias** (Goldsmith's Door) ★. This too is an early eleventh-century Romanesque work, without the elegance of the Door of Glory, but with exuberance to take its place. Unfortunately some of the carving is obscured by additions on either side of the portal. Ahead and slightly left is the **Casa de la Canonica** (Canon's House), now a monastery. Rounding the rear of the cathedral we come to the **Puerta Santa**, a door added in the 17th century which incorporates far older sculpture by Mateo, originally intended for the cathedral choir. We now are in another lovely square, the **Pl. de la Quintana**. Stairs lead up to a baroque 17th-century mansion on the right, the **Casa de la Parra**, now a gallery rotating exhibits of modern art.

Ahead, across the Pl. de la Inmaculada, stands the **Convento de San Marin Pinario ★**. The facade facing the plaza, completed in the 18th century, sends massive classical columns to the roof. The church, further north, is more ornate. Its decaying interior remains dramatic with a wide nave covered by a daring coffered vault. The Churrigueresque retablo is by the architect of the cathedral facade, Casas y Novoa. The choirstalls are lovely 17th-century work.

Continuing the circuit of the cathedral, pass along the alley of the Pasaje Glemirez, which goes under an archway to return to the Pl. Obradoiro. To the left of the arch is the **Palacio Gelmírez ★**, the former Bishop's Palace. Parts are as old as the 12th century. Several rooms may be visited, including the kitchen, Salon de Fiestas, and the huge Salon de Synod. A visit is most worthwhile. (Open daily through the summer Mon.-Sat. 10 a.m. to 1 p.m. and 4-7 p.m.; admission: 50 ptas.)

In the plaza, the huge building forming the north side is the **Hotel de los Reyes Católicos ★★**, a former hospice for pilgrims built by Ferdinand and Isabella in gratitude to Saint James for their victory over the Moors. The design of the building is a cross within a square which affords four lovely patios, each different from the other. A nice chapel sits exactly in the center. The Plateresque facade with stunning doorway and harmonious window moldings was added in 1678. Today it is one of the most luxurious of all the paradors. (Free tours available daily 10 a.m. to 1 p.m. and 4-6 p.m.)

Calle Franco ★ heads south from the south end of the plaza, between the cloisters of the cathedral and the San Jerónimo College. Old buildings and new shops and restaurants run for 6 blocks down to the pleasant Pl. del Toral, with its fountain. A return to the Pl. Obradoiro can be made along **Rua del Villar**, which runs parallel to C. Franco, also with old houses and nice shops.

Santa María del Sar   ★

Open Mon.-Sat. 10 a.m. to 1 p.m. and 4-6 p.m. Closed Sun. Admission: 100 ptas. The church is located about 1.5 k southeast of the old town. South of the circular road, Av. Fuente de San Antonio, C. Castron d'Ouro becomes C. de Sar. As it passes beneath the bypass road, the church lies to the right. This is a church of the same 12th century era as the cathedral. Incongruous buttresses were added in the 12th century, for reasons that become evident as soon as one steps inside. Before doing so, however, look at the remaining cloister gallery with elegant carved small paired arches. There reside the tombs of priors through the 15th century.

The inside startles, because the pillars of the nave all lean inward. It transpired that this ground near a river could not support the burden born by the pillars, hence the need for outside buttresses. The effect is strange indeed.

WHERE TO STAY

There are beds in Santiago in every price category. If our selections should be full, C. Franco and Rua del Villar, mentioned above, each has numerous *hotel residencias* for low prices.

EXPENSIVE ($100-$200)

Reyes Católicos   Deluxe ★★★★★

Pl. de España (Obradoiro). Rooms: 136. ☎ *58 22 00; FAX 56 30 94; Telex 86004.* This may be the most deluxe of all paradors. If you are lucky enough to get a room in the front overlooking the plaza, you will never want to leave. But if you are among the less fortunate, your room will look onto one of four lovely patios, which requires no sympathy. The only problem with this hotel is that it is very expensive, passing 20,000 pesetas per night in high season, although worth every cent. Simply wandering the halls and patios is a pleasant excursion. It is amusing to think that the elegant dining room served as a maternity ward when the hotel was a hospital in the 18th century.

Araguaney   1st-class ★★★

Alfredo Brañas, 5 (the street runs parallel to the park, ten short blocks roughly south of the Cathedral). Rooms: 64. ☎ *59 59 00; FAX 59 02 87; Telex 86108.* This is the opposite of the Reyes Católicos—as modern as the other is aged—but deluxe, nonetheless. It is all chrome, marble and glass, with a heated swimming pool, whose glass bottom forms the ceiling of a discotheque. Bedrooms are comfortably sized. Prices equal those at the Reyes Católicos.

MODERATE ($50-$99)

Windsor   Hs1st-class ★★

República de El Salvador, 16-A (directly behind the Araguaney, a block further south). Rooms: 50. ☎ *59 29 39.* Dark woods and floral prints make this an inviting little hotel. True, it is located on a busy shopping street and caters to tour groups, but the service is considerate, and prices are low compared to others in this category.

Compostela   1st-class ★

Calvo Sotelo, 1 (at the corner of Av. Fuente de San Antonio and C. Horno, seven blocks directly south of the cathedral where the new town begins). Rooms: 99. ☎ *58 57 00; FAX 56 32 69; Telex 82387.* This is a bit of a dowager today, needing sprucing up. Certainly it does not merit its official rating. But the prices are those of a 2nd-class hotel and it is a professional establishment. Are its lights dim to save on electricity?

Gelmírez   1st-class ★

C. Horneo, 92 (this street runs due south from the end of the old town). Rooms: 138. ☎ *56 11 00; FAX 56 32 69; Telex 82387.* Although the lobby is not memorable, the bedrooms are pleasant and good sized. The furnishings are fairly new; the decor covers a lot of browns and greens. Being a largish hotel, the service can be spotty.

INEXPENSIVE (UNDER $50)

Mapoula   Hs2nd-class ★★

C. Entremurallas, 10, "third floor" (at the southern edge of the old town, just before Av. Fuente de San Antonio). Rooms: 10. ☎ *58 01 24.* Fortunately, there is an elevator to carry you four flights up to what the Spanish call the third floor (the ground floor is not counted). The rooms are bright, white and clean. There are no special views, but the location is good, the price is right, and the decor is pleasant. The only problem is that the hotel is often full, as one would expect.

Universal   R2nd-class ★

Pl. de Galicia, 2 (at the east end of the street with the Hotel Araguaney). Rooms: 54. ☎ *58 58 00.* This is a step up from the usual low-priced hotel. The bedrooms are larger, as are the bathrooms, and the furniture has some style. But the prices are higher too, meriting the inexpensive category only out of season.

Suso   Hs2nd-class ★

Rua do Villar, 65. Rooms: 9. ☎ *58 66 11.* This little second floor hotel is located close to the cathedral in an old building. The rooms are modest, but comfortable. Service is willing, but there is a bar to take care of in addition to the rooms. Prices are genuinely inexpensive.

WHERE TO EAT

Galicia is known for octopus and shellfish, a hearty vegetable soup called *caldo gallego*, and *empanadas*, a sort of turnover. By all means try a *viño verde*, a "green wine," with seafood. As an alternative to our recommendations you can wander down C. Franco, and Rua del Vilar parallel to it, both of which are lined with small attractive restaurants.

EXPENSIVE ($50+)

Toñi Vicente   ★★★

Av. Rosalia de Castro, 24 (this artery is a kind of continuation of C. Franco). ☎ *59 41 00. Closed Sun.* This is a comet just arrived on the restaurant scene in Santiago. It is as elegant as anyone could wish and the food is truly spectacular. Baked sea brill is sublime and the deserts are memorable.   ***Amex, Diners, MasterCard and Visa accepted.***

Anexo Vilas   ★★

Av. Villagarcia, 21 (C. Marinez Anido runs along the south side of the Herradura park in the new town. It changes its name to C. Rosalia de Castro before coming to a large intersection. The righthand road, Av. Romero Donallo, arrives at this restaurant at its first left). ☎ *59 86 37. Closed Mon.* The second best-prepared food in town is served here. Sr. Vilas, the owner, tirelessly promotes the cooking of Galicia. After you try the sardinas *Mama Sueiro*, sardines with peppers and garlic, you may well become a promoter too.   ***Amex, Diners and Visa accepted.***

Don Gaiferos   ★

C. Nueva, 23 (the street that goes south from the Pl. de la Quintana, behind the Cathedral cloisters). ☎ *58 38 94. Closed Sun. and the last week in Dec.* The decor was the most tasteful in town before Toñi Vicente. The cooking is more international than regional, competent, but not exceptional. ***Amex, Diners, MasterCard and Visa accepted.***

MODERATE ($20-$50)

Reyes Católicos

Pl. Obradioros, 1. ☎ *58 22 00.* This recommendation is unusual for it is not for the hotel restaurant, but for the bar and the platos combinados it serves. These are the most expensive and best we've had. A bill for two with wine will push $40. For the money you will be served a plateful of simply done food of the highest quality, and get to wander through the elegant hotel. The bar is left from the entrance, through the huge lounge. ***Amex, Diners, MasterCard and Visa accepted.***

Nova Gallihea

C. Franco, 56. ☎ *58 27 99.* This is a restaurant for locals, with no concessions to tourists. The decor is nothing much, the restaurant tiny, but the food is authentic home cooking, if your home is in Galicia. Ordering one of the special menus will keep costs moderate.

San Clemente

Pl. San Clemente, 6 (this little plaza is downstairs at the south end of the ayuntamiento from the Pl. Obradioro). ☎ *58 08 82. Closed Sun. eve.* Seafood is what makes this restaurant special, and seafood is not inexpensive, but the crowds here demonstrate that the quality is good and the prices are fair.

Alameda

Puerta Fajera, 15 (at the bottom of C. Franco, bordering the park). ☎ *58 66 57.* The restaurant is its own sylvan building, all in green and white, situated by the park, with tables outside for views. The food is good, and there are special menus to hold down the cost. ***Amex, Diners, MasterCard and Visa accepted.***

INEXPENSIVE (UNDER $20)

O'Sotano

C. Franco, 8 (in the basement). ☎ *56 50 24.* The biggest problem with this restaurant is its popularity—which can lead to both crowding and noise. There are no complaints about how good the food is for the price. In fact, prices are low enough that you can order à la carte, instead of being restricted to special menus.

DIRECTORY

INFORMATION • The main office is located on Rua del Vilar at number 43. ☎ 58 40 81. There is a smaller office at the north end of the ayuntamiento in the Pl. Obradioro.

TRAINS AND BUSES • The train station is just south of the main circular road, Av. de Lugo, a 15 minute walk south of the cathedral. ☎ 52 02 02.

Three trains per day go to Madrid, others cover most destinations in the area.

The bus station is at C. San Cayetano, a 20-minute walk northeast of the Cathedral. Service to sights in Galicia is good, but slow for longer distances. ☎ 58 77 00.

AIRPORT • Santiago Airport (☎ 59 74 00)is 11 k east of town on N-547, the road to Lugo. There are direct flights to European capitals, and good connections with all of Spain. Buses to Santiago meet the flights. The Iberia office is located on C. General Pardiñas at 24, which is west of C. Horno, the main street of the new town. Buses leave here for the airport. ☎ 59 05 51.

POST OFFICE AND TELEPHONES • Located to the right of C. Franco, two blocks from the Pl. Obradioro. ☎ 58 12 52.

POLICE • Located behind the Post Office. ☎ 58 11 10.

EXCURSIONS

A pleasant day can be spent at the beach at a nearby scenic ria—a sea inlet, like a Norwegian fjord. See descriptions under the **Costa del Rias** heading above. For garden fans, **Pazo de Oca** is a country estate 25 k south.

South on N-525 toward Orense (Ourense) for 27 k, a sign directs a right turn for Valboa and the Pazo de Oca just after crossing the Ulla River.

Pazo de Oca   ★
Open from 9 a.m. to 1 p.m. and from 4 to 8 p.m. Opens and closes an hour earlier in winter. At the end of the road stands a typical manor house of the area. Behind it, terraces descend to a lily pond and a still lake on which a stone boat seems to float. Deep greens, rust colored moss, and eerie stillness pervade.

NAVARRE AND ARAGÓN

The portal of the Holy Sepulcher in Estella.

HISTORICAL PROFILE:
FROM HAPSBURGS TO BOURBONS

When the ascetic, industrious Felipe II passed the scepter to his son, the monarchy changed completely. Felipe III was as profligate with his court and person as his father had been abstemious, and lacked all common sense.

Disdaining such realities as a bankrupt treasury, Felipe III attempted to conquer England, which his father had been unable to engineer with vast financial resources at his disposal. In 1599, he sent 50 ships toward the British Isles, only to see them dispersed by a tempest. In 1601, 33 Spanish galleons landed in Ireland, where their troops were defeated easily by the English. The reduced numbers in these flotillas show Spain's changed fortunes from the glorious days of Felipe II's 136-ship Invincible Armada. However, these follies of Felipe III ceased in 1603 when Queen Elizabeth died, for her successor, James II, as a Catholic, was no enemy.

Felipe III turned next to Portugal where, through a complete lack of sensitivity, he began undermining the union forged by his father, who had sworn that only native Portuguese would fill important Portuguese offices. Filipe III appointed Spaniards to the governing council of Portugal, as well as to vacant bishoprics. When he traveled to Portugal for his first and only visit in 1619, he charged the extravagant cost of the trip to the Portuguese. This insult, when added to Portugal's loss of a rich empire in the Far East to the Dutch and English (whom the Portuguese viewed as enemies of Spain, not themselves), bred resentment that erupted into revolution and Portuguese independence in the next reign.

Felipe III also expelled the Moriscos—Moors who had converted to Christianity. Because the half-million Moriscos were hard-working farmers who made Andalusia and Valencia bloom, their eviction cost Spain a significant percentage of its agricultural production, in addition to five percent of its population. All told, Felipe III proved ruinous for an already ailing Spain, weakening both its empire and economy. In fact, one of Felipe's seemingly inconsequential acts would prove fatal to the Hapsburg dynasty he headed. He arranged a marriage between his son and the daughter of the King of France, thereby introducing French blood into the Spanish royal line to give France a future claim on the throne.

In 1622, 16-year-old Felipe IV succeeded his father. He stood tall and thin, and looked more resolute than he was because of his thrusting Hapsburg jaw. Both he and his French bride, Isabel de Bourbon, loved spectacles. The two delighted in *autos-da-fé*, theater performances, bull fights, and parades. Often one or the other would play childish tricks, such as loosing snakes into the audience. When Felipe was a child, his tutor had been the duke of Oliveres, and their friendship grew as the youngster matured. Oliveres assumed the position of chief minister in the new government.

Oliveres' principle policy was to centralize Spanish power in the monarchy, a goal that ran counter to ancient currents of separatism throughout the country, still comprised of independent provincial *cortes* (parliaments), laws, and taxation. Oliveres brought Felipe IV to the cortes of Aragón and of Valencia to exhort concessions against their own independence. But he could make no headway against Catalonia, and when the French invaded the Catalan territory of Rousillon, the citizens of Barcelona refused even to billet Spanish troops on their way to win it back. This spark set off a civil war in 1640.

But first there was revolution in Portugal. Portugal's most powerful noble, the Duke of Bragança, owned one third of the country and was feared by Oliveres, who once tried to kidnap him. Switching tactics, Oliveres sought Bragança's loyalty by bribing him with power by giving him command of the Portuguese army. Oliveres had been correct in mistrusting Bragança who, in 1640, turned his troops against the Spanish and liberated the country in 24 hours, thus ending Spain's 60-year union with Portugal.

While Felipe's energies were focused on Portugal, Catalonia asked France to take over. The French jumped at the chance and, when the Spanish army returned from Portugal, they were defeated easily by the French at Lerida.

Oliveres' policies had cost Spain Portugal and precipitated civil war, leaving Felipe IV no choice but to fire his friend, who died insane 3 years later.

In 1646, Baltasar Carlos, Felipe's heir, died. Felipe, who had lost his first wife, then married his deceased son's betrothed, Mariana of Austria. Although the loss of Portugal bothered Felipe IV greatly, the French army occupying secessionist Catalonia was more serious. It cost a decade of civil war before Felipe's troops finally recaptured Barcelona in 1651. Another decade of preparation was required before Felipe felt ready to invade Portugal. But, by that time, the Duke of Bragança, now calling himself the King of Portugal, had formed an alliance with England that had brought him an English wife and army. In 1663, his combined forces decisively defeated the Spanish. News of the defeat hastened Felipe's own death, which went unmourned by his people. In fact, were it not for the long association between Felipe IV and his friend the painter Velásquez, few would remember this king. Instead he seems more real than any other Spanish monarch because the canvases of the great Velásquez immortalized the sad king and his family.

Felipe IV left a 4-year-old cretin as his heir. Carlos II suffered from premature senility, never learned to speak or eat normally, but survived against all expectations to reign for 35 years. With Carlos II the line of Hapsburgs had run dry, for although he married, he was incapable of siring children. All Europe now eyed Spain rapaciously, knowing that some non-Spaniard could eventually acquire the crown. On his deathbed, Carlos named Philip of Anjou, the grandson of Louis XIV of France as his heir.

Thus the 18th century began with a Bourbon king on the Spanish throne, known to the Spanish as Felipe V. But the Hapsburg family was not yet ready to concede. Archduke Charles, of the Austrian Hapsburgs, supported his competing claim with an army that landed at Barcelona in 1702. This opened the War of Spanish Succession in which Austrians, aided by opportunistic England, fought the Spanish for almost a decade. In the first battle, Felipe V was defeated at Barcelona then, while retreating, the English entered Spain from Portugal to capture Madrid. Felipe rushed back, retook the capital, then returned west to defeat the Austrians at Almansa. In his absence, Madrid was once again taken, so he wheeled and recaptured it. Thus were battles both won and lost during this war, but neither side could gain any decisive victory. Hostilities ended in 1711, simply because the combatants were exhausted. Felipe had survived the attack on his throne, losing only the peninsula of Gibraltar to the English, but the tired Spanish king retired in 1724 to La Granja, a model of Versailles he had built to remind him of home. His rest lasted only 7 months, for his heir died of smallpox, forcing the old king back to his throne for another 20 years. He died, deranged, in 1746.

Felipe V's second son and successor, Fernando VI, demonstrated that Bourbons could administer as well as defend their country. He promoted Spanish neutrality and simplified an overly complex tax structure, to allow the economy to recover from decades of war and the high taxes it cost. Unfortunately, Fernando bore a Bourbon proclivity for mental illness, dying in 1759. His half-brother, Carlos III, carried on.

Carlos III was 43, robust and ruddy, when he came to the throne. His passion was hunting, and he dressed so as to be ready in a moment to grab a gun and chase after wolves. Yet he proved an able king. One of his first concerns was the lawlessness rampant in Madrid, both robberies and crimes of passion. The very costume of the time prevented arrest and prosecution—men walked in street-length black cloaks and wide-brimmed slouch hats, which concealed both their identities and whatever weapons they might carry. Carlos outlawed the long cloaks and sent police armed with knives to reduce illegal lengths on the spot. In response, the citizens rebelled and chased the king from Madrid. But when Carlos made such cloaks and hats the uniform of the Royal Executioner, street fashions changed immediately.

Carlos followed the lead of France and other European countries in expelling the Jesuit Order. This allowed him to modernize university curricula, controlled until then by Jesuits and grown archaic under their direction. He also decreed it was no disgrace for *hidalgos* (noblemen) to work, a revolutionary step. In Spain one man in three considered himself an hidalgo and, however impoverished, maintained status by never dirtying his hands. Under Carlos, new businesses, including weaving, received government assistance, whereas before Spain had sent its abundant wool for weaving to England and Flanders, buying the finished product back at higher prices. Carlos' measures so invigorated the economy that the population of Spain increased by one sixth. Carlos III died at age 72, in 1788, of a depression that all Bourbons seemed heir to.

Carlos IV was entirely unlike his father. Dull and amiable, he was a creature of his more enterprising wife. She, in turn, was smitten by a soldier of the Royal Guard, Manuel Godoy. Godoy was dubbed a duke at 25, and soon after named prime minister of Spain.

In 1789 the world's crowned heads trembled at news of the French Revolution. The bumbling Spanish king with his shrewish wife and immature prime minister decided to play at war to restore the French monarchy. When the French executed their king, Godoy invaded France. A humiliating defeat left Godoy no option but to sue for peace. However, for failing at generalship, Godoy was awarded the title "Prince of the Peace" by his adoring queen. Then France and Spain joined in arms against England. Godoy, with the help of 15,000 French troops, invaded England's ally Portugal and conquered it in 3 weeks. He sent his queen an orange branch from her new territory to earn the name "War of the Oranges" for the campaign. But Spain paid dearly for this victory, for off the coast at Trafalgar, Lord Nelson sank the combined French and Spanish fleets.

Nor was Spain's alliance with France going well. Napoléon sent 100,000 troops to Spain, ostensibly to protect it from attack, but actually to surround the garrisons of major northern cities. When Napoléon demanded that northern Spain be ceded to him, even Carlos could see that he was about to be reduced from ally to subject. He fled with his court to Aranjuez. There his son Fernando stirred up the citizens to ransack Godoy's mansion in search of the architect of the foreign policy that threatened Spain's independence.

Although Godoy escaped by hiding in a rolled carpet in his attic, the mob moved to the Aranjuez palace where a frightened Carlos IV abdicated in favor of his son, Fernando. However, Fernando found the French in control of the capital, Madrid, so he crossed the border into France to seek Napoléon's recognition and assistance. Once the mob disbursed, Carlos reconsidered his abdication and, independently, with his queen and Godoy, set out to visit Napoléon as well. All the contestants for Spain's crown now called on the Corsican General to adjudicate between them. Napoléon's judgment was that Fernando should renounce his claim and Carlos do so as well, so that his own brother Joseph could rule instead. Then he arrested the lot.

Spain received the news that a Frenchman was now their ruler on the second of May, 1808. On this day, the *Dos de Mayos*, the citizens rose up against their invaders. With Spain's royal family away in France, juntas of private citizens organized defenses and raised militia, hounding Joseph from Madrid in ten days. It took the presence of Napoléon, backed by 300,000 French troops, to reinstate him. Still the citizens fought, not major battles which they could not win, but little wars—*guerrillas*. Eventually, England sent Wellington to Portugal with enough troops to win Portugal, although insufficient to threaten the French in Spain. But when Napoléon left for his ill-fated invasion of Russia in 1810, Wellington was able to hammer successfully at the French, finally chasing them north of the Pyrenees three years later. Wellington followed the retreating French to defeat Napoléon at Belgium's Waterloo in 1814.

Now Spain was free again, but without a king for the first time since the Visigoths. Delegates from Spain, the Philippines, and all the American colonies met in Cádiz to draw up the first constitution in her history. The delegates offered Fernando VII the office of constitutional monarch, but when he returned to Spain to accept the crown, he revoked the constitution and arrested every delegate he could find. Fernando remarried late in life, producing one child, a daughter. To ensure the continuation of his line he altered the laws of succession so that a woman could inherit the throne. Nonetheless, civil war broke out after his death in 1833 between partisans of Isabella II and those favoring Fernando's brother, Don Carlos ("the Carlists"). Five more years of strife left Isabella II in control. During her reign she followed her father's lead in suppressing all liberality and constitutional government, although her preference was for sexual adventures above governing. In 1868, a putsch of the navy and army ended her rule.

Isabella left a 12-year-old son. After an interim reign and a Second Carlist War over his succession, Alfonso XII was summoned from school at England's Sandhurst to be crowned king at age 17. He died at 27, in 1886, leaving a pregnant wife. Alfonso XIII was thus born a king. As Alfonso grew, he watched the last of Spain's overseas possessions fall away.

A mysterious explosion had sunk the United States battleship Maine in the harbor of Havana, provoking the United States to declare war on Spain. Within a year, Cuba was independent and the Philippines were a protectorate of the United States. Spain managed to avoid the horror of World War I by neutrality, but the radical political parties that unbalanced Europe in the first part of the 20th century—communist, anarchist and socialist—came to infect Spain as well. The time of monarchies had passed. In 1931, elections showed that Alfonso XIII had lost the support of his people. He abdicated and moved to France.

NAVARRE AND ARAGÓN

Navarre, tucked between the Basque counties and northern Aragón, is tiny. Not 100 miles long in any direction, Navarre could be contained five times over by Aragón. However, size is the major geographic difference between the two states. Both border the Pyrenees, are precipitously mountainous at their northern ends, descend to plains in the south, and suffer climates that are perhaps the worst in Spain. Since both are landlocked, away from the tempering influences of the sea, they see snow in winter and burn from a searing summer sun.

Despite geographic similarities and a shared history up to the 11th century, the two states later separated for 400 years before reunion by Ferdinand in 1512. Surprisingly, during the time of its greatest hero, Sancho III, smaller Navarre dominated not only Aragón but all of Christian Spain. Having conquered kingdoms from Catalonia through Aragón, along with Old Castile and León, he called himself "King of the Spains." On his deathbed in 1035, however, Sancho willed Aragón to one son, Navarre to another, Catalonia to a third and Old Castile to a fourth. After much jockeying among these four powers, Old Castile merged with León, while Aragón dominated Navarre and Catalonia. Navarre retained enough authority, however, for its king to arrange a marriage in 1191 between Berengaria, daughter of King Sancho VI, and Richard the Lionheart.

From the 13th through the end of the 14th century, Aragón played a major role in European politics. Aragón's control of Catalonia brought suzerainty over its territories in southern France between Rousillon and Nice. In 1282, Sicily, which ruled Italy south of Naples, offered its crown to the king of Aragón to prevent French usurpation. By the end of that century the armies of Aragón had completed the reconquest of the eastern coast of Spain as far south as Valencia. Thus, Aragón controlled one third of Spain, almost one quarter of France, and half of Italy. But when its King Ferdinand married Isabella, the monarch of Castile, in 1469, the identity of Aragón submerged in a larger confederation. By that time Navarre had broken away.

The king of Navarre had died childless in 1234, and the citizens of Navarre voted that his nephew, the French count of Champagne, be offered the throne. For three centuries after, Navarre's crown—the prize of marriage alliances—was passed among various French no-

ARAGON AND NAVARRA

bles, ending with Jean, Duc d'Albret, in 1512. These transfers of power were orchestrated by kings of France anxious for a friendly neighbor on their southern border, an area controlled by archrival Spain. The Navarrese, hoping to avoid digestion by Aragón and Castile, were glad for a strong protector. In 1512, Ferdinand ended Navarre's independence when his conquering army engulfed it en route to war with France.

Although the provinces of Aragón and Navarre cover more than 10% of Spain, they contain less to attract tourists than their size would suggest. Navarre's capital of **Pamplona ★** is famed for its running of the bulls during the feast of San Fermin. Although a city of no particular attractiveness, it does contain a Gothic cathedral and an interesting museum of Navarrese art. Since the French controlled Navarre during the Middle Ages, hundreds of thousands of French pilgrims passed through Navarre on their way to Santiago de Compostela, leaving behind ancient Romanesque monasteries built for their convenience. **Olite ★**, **La Oliva ★★** and **Leyre ★★** survive, as does one town so filled with medieval buildings as to still convey the atmosphere of those times—**Estella ★★**, called "La Bella." As for Aragón, its vast expanse is more likely to be driven through by tourists on their way to Barcelona than stopped at for sightseeing. Aragón does offer **Zaragoza ★★**, a major city which contains the Moorish palace of Aljaferia and a splendid cathedral. There is a truly ancient monastery situated amid spectacular scenery at **San Juan de la Peña ★★** and a perfect ancient castle at **Loarre ★**. In addition, **Ordesa National Park ★★** offers miles of rugged scenic beauty, while the palace where Ferdinand was born still stands in **Sos del Rey Católico ★**.

ESTELLA ★★

Population: 13,086
Area code: 948; zip code: 31200

From **Pamplona** *take N-111 west by following C. Bosquecillo that cuts between the Jardines de la Taconera and the gardens of the Ciudadela.* **Puente la Reina**, *in 24 k, presents a fine Romanesque church from the 12th through 14th centuries on the town outskirts of Estella is 21 k further. From* **elsewhere in Spain**, *follow the directions to Pamplona in its section below, and then follow the directions above.*

The town, which pilgrims dubbed "Estella la Bella," grew overnight. In the 11th century, the king of Navarre offered tax-free status to anyone who would settle there, for he needed bodies to reside in the southern part of his territory to oppose Moorish attacks. Ordinary people came, as did merchants, and a town of separate quarters, or parishes, sprang up in which emigrés migrating from the same area of Spain lived together. When the kings of Navarre took up residence during the 12th century, Estella became a royal town and the host to hordes of pilgrims on their way to Santiago de Compostela. Competing parishes vied with each other to raise ever more splendid churches, a contest whose results remain for our appreciation.

Cross the tiny Rio Ega, following signs to the main, though small, plaza of the town—**Plaza de San Martín**. This is the heart of the ancient *barrio franc*, or French Quarter. To the right, dating from the 12th century, is the **Palacio do los Reyes do Navarra**, one of the oldest secular structures in Spain. Although much restored, it contains one fine Romanesque capital depicting Roland in battle with the Moorish giant Farragut. It also houses the **Tourist Office**. On the opposite side of the plaza stands the 16th-century former **ayuntamiento** emblazoned with a coat of arms. Elegant **San Pedro de la Rua ★** overlooks the plaza (open daily 11:30 a.m. to 1 p.m. and 5:30-7 p.m. admission: 100 ptas.) The church is 12th-century Romanesque, fronted by a lovely portal of Mudejar design. Instead of crowds of holy figures, delicate arabesques surround an unusual scalloped arch. Inside, Gothic elements compete with the Romanesque design in three separate apses. At the church center rises a charming column of entwined serpents, and a baroque chapel on the left is devoted to a relic of Saint Andrew, preserved from 1270. The second bay on the right leads to remains of a wonderful cloister with masterfully carved columns. Sadly, half of this cloister was blown up by mistake when Felipe II destroyed an adjacent castle that he feared would serve as a stronghold of the Navarrese independence movement. **Santo Sepulcro**, at the end of the street, presents a pure Gothic portal with a moving *Last Judgment*.

On the other side of the river, beside C. Mayor, is the quarter settled by Navarrese, which still retains much medieval atmosphere. The quarter's proudest possession is the 12th-century Romanesque **Iglesia de San Miguel Arcangel ★**. The north portal is as intensely Christian as can be, serving as an antidote to the "foreign" flavor of San Pedro. Scores of Biblical figures crowd for room around the doors. Note especially the statue columns carved in high relief.

Outside of Estella, 3 k south as directed by a sign from N-111, stands the massive **Monastery of Irache** ★. Its foundation is truly ancient, dating from the tenth century. Later, Cistercian monks built one of the first pilgrim hospitals here, and in the 16th century Benedictines founded a university that functioned for almost 300 years. The church is open for guided tours (Tuesday-Sunday 9:30 a.m. to 1 p.m. and 3-7 p.m. admission: 100 ptas.). Its facade is 17th-century, as is the cupola inside that prefaces an apse from the 12th century. The Plateresque cloister seems somehow cold.

WHERE TO STAY

Irache   **R2nd-class★**

Carretera Pamplona-Logroño, N-111, k 43 (1 k west on N-111). Rooms: 74. ☎ *(948) 55 11 50.* This is the only good choice in the neighborhood. It is moderate in price, modern, clean and comfortable, and supplies tennis courts and a pool.

WHERE TO EAT

Navarra   ★

C. Gustavo de Maeztu, 16. ☎ *55 10 69. Closed Sunday evening, Monday, and the 2nd half of December.* The attractiveness of the place justifies its expensive prices. It is decorated as a medieval inn surrounded by a pretty garden. The trout Navarra is delectable.

LA OLIVA MONASTERY ★ ★

From **Pamplona** *take N-121 south toward Zaragoza by following Av. de Zaragoza as it leaves the large hub of the Pl. del Principe de Viana. In 40 k comes* **Olite** *with its fine castle. 17 k south of Olite take C-124 east for an attractive drive of 18 k through the countryside.*

French monks completed this Cistercian monastery in the 12th century, the first built outside their homeland. From its inception it counted as a major missionary center in Spain. Cistercian buildings are characterized by simplicity, foregoing the decorative embellishments of the Romanesque and Gothic styles, and the simplicity of La Oliva became intensified after its abandonment when its treasures were stripped. Today the Cistercians have returned to restore it. (Open daily 9 a.m. to 8 p.m., 6 p.m. in winter; admission: 100 ptas.)

The plain facade is enhanced by a single band of sculpture above the central portal. Austerity inside produces a solemn effect. Pointed arches are a surprise in a 12th-century structure, either a peculiarity of this Romanesque design or the first example of the Gothic in

Spain. The adjacent cloister is an interesting mishmash of 15th-century architecture grafted onto an older structure.

See "Olite" for accommodations and dining.

LEYRE ★ ★

From **Pamplona** *take N-121 south toward Zaragoza by following Av. de Zaragoza as it leaves the large hub of the Pl. del Principe de Viana. 5 k outside the city take N-240 heading east. In 35k C-127 heads south for* **Sangüesa** *and* **Sos del Rey Católico***, a detour of 24 k. (both described below). Continue on N-240 for Leyre, looking for the turn-off to Monasterio Leyre in 16 k.*

On the way to the monastery of Leyre, Sangüesa and Sos del Rey Católico are worth a stop. Tiny **Sangüesa**, 7 k along C-127, is filled with mansions. Beside the town bridge stands **Santa María la Real**, a former royal chapel from the 13th century. The present *ayuntamiento* was formerly the **Palace of the Princes of Viana**; the main street is lined with attractive classical houses, leading, two streets after the bridge, to the imposing baroque **Palace of Vallesantoro** on the right.

Seven k east is the birthplace of Francis Xavier. Born Francisco **Javier** in 1506, he cooperated with Ignatius Loyola in founding the Order of Jesuits. Later he travelled to Japan, becoming one of its first Western missionaries, and personally converted several hundred thousand Buddhists, although he died as he was about to enter China on a similar mission. In the 16th century, soon after his death, the house in which he was born was replaced by a castle that contains some nice murals. It may be toured daily 9 a.m. to 1 p.m. and 4-7 p.m. A simple *Son et Lumiere* is presented Sat., Sun. and holidays at 10:30 p.m., during June and July. Admission: 100 ptas., for the sound and light show.

Sos del Rey Católico lies a further 13 k south on C-127. A walled village, all of which has been declared a national monument, remains under restoration. There are a number of lovely mansions and the **Palacio de Sada** in which Ferdinand was born—although substantially altered a century later. There is also a modern parador charging moderate prices:

Parador Fernando de Aragón   **1st-class ★ ★**
Rooms: 65. ☎ *(948) 88 80 11; FAX: 88 81 00).*   *Expensive.*

The ancient **monastery of San Salvador de Leyre**, just off N-240, is beautifully situated beside a valley reservoir framed by rocky hills. This was the spiritual center of medieval Navarre. A great Romanesque church, consecrated in 1057, served as the royal pantheon for her kings and counted most of Navarre among its dominions as sources of revenue. In the 13th century, however, Aragón gained control of Navarre and favored San Juan de la Peña as a religious center, diverting revenues from Leyre. Nonetheless, Cistercian monks undertook the job of enlarging the church with a grand Gothic vault. By the 19th century the site was abandoned, but Benedictines have been in residence since 1954, restoring the convent.

The western portal of the church from the 12th century is justly famous. Carvings cover every inch. Many figures are archaic, but possess great charm. The most imposing part of the church, however, is the crypt below it. Entry is forbidden, but 100 ptas. will illuminate it so it can be seen through the grille. It was built in the 11th century to provide a foundation for the original church, and is composed of large rough-hewn blocks that form a cavern of arches. Massive columns buried deep into the earth for support show only a foot or so above the floor. In the church above, the most striking feature is the later (13th-century) high Gothic vault. The first several bays, however, remain from the earlier church. A modern chapel contains the pantheon of the earliest kings of Navarre, formerly interred in the crypt. The bones of ten kings and queens lie in wooden caskets inside.

LOARRE CASTLE

See San Juan de la Peña below for a description and directions.

OLITE ★

Population: 2,829
Area code: 948; zip code: 31390

*From **Pamplona** take N-121 south toward Zaragoza by following Av. de Zaragoza as it leaves the large hub of the Pl. del Principe de Viana. Olite is reached in 40 k. (See also "La Oliva Monastery" and "Leyre" above.)*

Charles III, king of Navarre, ordered a castle built here in 1406. Charles was also the count of Evreux in France, so he employed French architects. What arose was a fantasy that blended solid stone walls for strength with the elegant apartments of a palace. From that time until Ferdinand conquered Navarre in the 16th century, Olite was the main fortress of the Navarrese kings. Dominated by this castle, the entire village today retains a medieval atmosphere, not yet spoiled by crowds of tourists.

The village is entered through an arched gateway; then the turrets of the **castle** ★ come into view. Fifteen towers mark the perimeter walls. Originally the castle inside contained a roof garden, a lions' den, an aviary, and a small courtyard used for bullfights. It has been much remodeled over the centuries and today houses a parador for which some original stuccowork and painted marquetry ceilings have been restored. The Gothic **Santa María la Real**, formerly the royal chapel, stands beside the castle with a fine 14th-century facade. Nearby **San Pedro**, in many ways artistically superior to Santa María, although in the Romanesque style, has a richly carved 12th-century portal.

WHERE TO STAY

EXPENSIVE ($100-$200)

Parador Principe de Viana   2nd-class ★ ★ ★

Pl. de los Teobaldos, 2. Rooms: 43. ☎ *(948) 74 00 00; FAX: 74 02 01* This parador conveys more of the feeling of a castle than any other. There are grand halls, hidden stairways, parapets, tapestries, and suits of armor—all a great deal of fun for a price just over the expensive line.

MODERATE ($50-$99)

Casa Zanito, 3rd-class

C. Mayor, 16 (second floor). Rooms: 15. ☎ *(948) 74 00 02. Closed from the last week of December through the first week of January.* The accommodations are comfortable and unassuming, if a little small, but their price hugs the low end of the moderate category, and a decent moderately priced restaurant waits downstairs.

WHERE TO EAT

Try Casa Zanito, above, for a moderate meal, or, for a memorable dining experience at prices that barely pass into the expensive, read on:

MODERATE ($20-$50)

In Tafalla, 5 k north of Olite on N-121:

Tubal   ★ ★ ★

Pl. de Navarra, 2 (on the second floor). ☎ *(948) 70 08 52. Closed Sunday night, Monday, and from the last week of August through the first week of September.* This unassuming restaurant may be the best in Navarre. Every dish is prepared with exquisite taste. If the cod with garlic and crab does not make your mouth water, the partridge salad should. Save some room for fresh ice cream.

Amex, Diners, MasterCard and Visa accepted.

ORDESA NATIONAL PARK ★★

*From **Zaragoza** take N-350 north toward Huesca, then past it to Sabinanigo, for a total of 141 k. Take N-260 north to Biescas, for 15 k, at which point N-260 turns east for a lovely 23 k drive to Torla and the entrance to the park. From **Pamplona** take N-121 south toward Zaragoza by following Av. de Zaragoza as it leaves the large hub of the Pl. del Principe de Viana. 5 k outside the city take N-240 heading east. In 113 k Jaca is reached. Continue east on N-330 for 18 k to Sabinanigo. Go north on N-260 for 15 k to Biescas, staying on N-260 as it turns east for 23 k to Torla and the entrance to the park.*

Although Spain contains a number of parks and wildlife preserves, Ordesa is its most dramatic, recognized since 1918 as a natural treasure. The park cannot be driven through; it consists of a number of well-marked hiking trails that cover its most attractive sights. These trails range from easy walks to more demanding hikes, though most lie within the abilities of the average person. The scenery is breathtaking—waterfalls, gorges, caves, precipitous peaks, mountain meadows, and stands of fir and beech. Chamois, boar, and mountain goats share the beauties. The park includes a restaurant that serves inexpensive meals, a tourist office nearby (open July and Aug.), and a modern parador:

Parador de Monte Perdido   2nd-class ★★
Valle de Pineta, 22350 Huesca. Rooms: 24. ☎ *(974) 50 10 11.* This modern parador wins no design awards, but the point is the spectacular scenery. Its restaurant is more adventurous than most.

NOTE...*The trails are passable only from May through Sept., with the first and last of these months unpredictable. Check with the Oficina de Turismo de Huesca* ☎ *(974) 22 57 78).*

The Circo Soaso walk covers most of the dramatic scenery. Hiking is not difficult, though the complete circle covers 28 miles. It begins at the Cadiera refuge.

PAMPLONA ★

Population: 183,126
Area code: 948; zip code: 31000

The most direct route from **Madrid** *is A-2 west toward Guadalajara, which receives the designation N-II after Alcalade Henares. In 151 k, at Medinaceli, take N-111 north to Soria. Passing through Soria and around Logroño, N-111 reaches Pamplona in 281 k more. From* **Burgos** *take N-1 west toward Gasteiz (Vitoria) for 115 k and continue on the same road for 72 k past Gasteiz to Pamplona. From* **Segovia**, **Valladolid**, **León**, *and* **Salamanca**, *follow directions to Burgos in the "Old Castile" chapter, and the directions from Burgos above. From* **Donostia** *(San Sebastian) take N-240 south for 86 k. From* **Zaragoza** *take N-232 or the toll road A-68 west toward Logroño. The toll road splits just past Murchante in 86 k. Take N-15 north to Pamplona in 78 k. By N-232, connect with N-121 outside Castejon, which is followed north to Pamplona for 85 k. From* **Barcelona** *follow directions to Zaragoza, then the Zaragoza directions above.*

The city's name derives from Pompey, for he refounded the city by settling Basques here in 77 B.C. Both Goths and Francs captured it during the fifth and sixth centuries. The Moors held it for 50 years until liberation by Charlemagne in 748. Angered because he did not receive sufficient pay for this service, Charlemagne then sacked the city and tore down its walls. In retribution, the citizens attacked his rear guard at the pass of Roncesvalles as he was returning to France in 778, massacring it to the last man, and giving rise to the medieval epic *The Song of Roland*.

By the ninth century Pamplona was chosen capital of the county of Navarre, which became a kingdom under Sancho I. Though small, the kingdom and its capital prospered until 1512 when Ferdinand conquered it to incorporate Navarre into the larger political entity of Spain. A French force arrived in 1521 to besiege Pamplona. Although the siege was sucessfully resisted, one of the defenders, Iñigo Lopez de Recalde, was wounded with momentous consequences. During idle time spent recovering from his wounds, Iñigo was struck with the idea of an army for Christ. As St. Ignacio de Loyola he founded the Jesuit Order.

The best known fact about Pamplona is its running of bulls, made famous by Ernest Hemingway in *The Sun Also Rises*. This takes place during the annual festival of San Fermin from July 6-14, which commemorates the martyrdom of a local saint who died in the 3rd century. Bullfights occur very evening during the festival, and every morning at 7 a.m. a rocket announces that the bulls for the evening's fights have been loosed from their corral to run the 1,000 yards through the barricaded streets of the city to the bullring. Brave and foolhardy citizens wearing traditional red and white neckerchiefs test their courage by running ahead of the herd, ducking into building entries as bulls near. During the festival the population of Pamplona triples, as do the prices of the hotels, although the price hardly matters, since all rooms have been booked months before.

The rest of the year Pamplona is a quiet city, except for occasional boisterous students from the local university. Although it is lined by grand avenues, the city is not particularly attractive. It does retain a small old quarter, but its character has been obliterated by restaurants and shops. Considering everything, Pamplona is probably better visited than stayed in, especially with such wonderful accommodations as those at Olite, less than 40 k away.

The bullring borders an old quarter that is less than half a kilometer square. Here are the city **cathedral** ★, imposing enough for a visit, and the **Museo Navarra** ★, with a fine collection of murals. Of course the **Plaza de Toros** ★ should be seen, along with the ruins of the walls of the city fortress, **La Ciudedela**. Half a day suffices.

From **Madrid** *and from* **Burgos**, *Pamplona is entered on Av. Bosquecillo which runs through the large park of the Ciudadela. Take Av. del Ejercito right at the end of the park, which in two long blocks presents parking on both the left and the right. From* **Zaragoza** *arrive on Av. de Zaragoza, which leads into a large traffic circle called Pl. del Principe de Viana. Take Av. del Conde Oliveto that leaves the plaza going west. At the next large intersection, in two short blocks, parking can be found both to the left and to the right. From* **Donostia** *(San Sebastian) drive through the Jardines de la Taconera along Recta de Taconera, after leaving the river Arga. When this street turns slightly right and changes its name to Yarques, parking is available in one block on both its left and right sides.*

The parking lots border the citadel called **La Ciudadela**. This pentagonal fort was built in the 16th century by Felipe II. Now it is surrounded by acres of gardens. A walk west for four blocks along the attractive Paseo de Sarasate, planted in the center, leads to the heart of the city in the **Pl. del Castillo**, with the large **Disputacion** (Provincial Council Building) at its south end. To its north are a maze of twisting streets that constitute the old quarter of Pamplona. From the northern corner of the plaza, C. Chapitela leads to the Pl. Mercaderes in one block. C. Santo Domingo leads from its northwest corner to the **Museo Navarra** ★ in two blocks. Along its side are remains of the **town walls** that provide nice views of the river Arga and the city. Behind the museum is the corral where the bulls are kept before letting them run the streets to the bullring. From the west end of the plaza, Mercaderes C. Curia leads to the **cathedral** ★ in three short blocks. Two blocks south and one block west of the Pl. del Castillo is the famed **bullring** of Pamplona.

WHAT TO SEE AND DO

Museo Navarra ★

Open Tues.-Sat. 10 a.m. to 1:30 p.m. and 5-7 p.m. Open Sun. for the morning hours. Admission 200 ptas. The museum is housed in a 16th-century building, once the charity hospital of Misericordia. The museum displays Roman mosaics found in the area. Most are purely geometric, the carpets of the time, but the third gallery contains a fine mosaic depicting the Cretan fable of Theseus and the Minotaur. Gallery four displays the Romanesque period in elegant capitals from the 12th-century cathedral of Pamplona, torn down in favor of the present one. Those capitals in the center of the room are masterpieces of composition and detail.

The second floor presents early paintings. The first three galleries reconstruct the Palace of Oriz to show its unusual 16th-century monochrome wall panels. Succeeding galleries present a collection of stately murals from the 13th through 15th centuries, taken from various churches in the surrounding area. Furniture occupies the third floor, along with a few paintings, including a fine Goya of the Marqués de San Andrian. Do not miss the fine 2nd-century mosaic in the courtyard.

On the way to visit the cathedral, turn west for a few steps from the Pl. Mercaderes to see the church of **San Saturnino**. *The Last Supper carved on the north door of this Romanesque church is remarkable.*

Cathedral ★

Open daily in summer 8 a.m. to 1:30 p.m. and 4-8 p.m. Open in winter 8 to 11:30 a.m. and 6-8 p.m. Admission: 100 ptas., to the Museum and cloister, open only in the summer. This cathedral was built over the course of the 14th century, to replace an earlier Romanesque edifice. However, at the end of the 18th century, a front was added that combined baroque decoration with a classical design, producing the present disconcerting look.

Inside, however, the church is pure Gothic, of a style peculiar to Navarre. The nave does not soar as high as other Gothic churches, and the coro has been removed to allow a view down to the altar. Ceiling ribs are plain and the walls bare. The altar is faced by an intricate iron grille, before which stands an elegant marble tomb of Carlos III, the last great king of Navarre, and his wife, carved by a Frenchman. The cloisters are elegant Gothic. On its east side is the Barbazan Chapel, with lovely vaulting, named for the bishop entombed in it. On the south side is an unforgettable door, carved all around with precious Biblical scenes. The 14th-century refectory of the cathedral now is the diocesan museum, worth seeing for its medieval kitchen as well as for a collection of polychromed statuary.

Bullring ★
The structure suggests the Coliseum in Rome. Appropriately, fronting the entrance is a bust of "Papa" Hemingway, who did more than anyone to bring renown to this city.

WHERE TO STAY

Higher-priced hotels in Pamplona tend to charge more than their services merit, and during the Feast of San Fermin, all prices triple. The best values are in lower-priced establishments. As an alternative to staying in Pamplona, consider Olite (described previously). There you can spend the night in a medieval castle converted into a parador, while a wonderful restaurant waits nearby.

EXPENSIVE ($100-$200)

Iruña Palace-Tres Reyes   1st-class ★ ★
Jardines de la Taconera (at the north border of the gardens surrounding the Ciudadela). Rooms: 168. ☎ *22 66 00; FAX: 22 29 30; Telex: 37720.* Most rooms overlook a lovely garden. They are eminently comfortable, and the service is good, yet the hotel is modern with no special charm. All told, such a room would be fair at $100 a night, but not at half again that much.

Yoldi   2nd-class ★
Av. San Ignacio, 11 (three blocks south of the Pl. del Castillo). Rooms: 48. ☎ *22 48 00; FAX 21 20 45.* Recent renovations have made this one of the more attractive hotels in town. It remains a comfortable, quiet place to stay.

Ohri   3rd-class ★
C. Leyre, 7 (a block and a half south of the bullring). Rooms: 55. ☎ *22 85 00; FAX 22 83 18.* The location is good, the rooms comfortable. Its

small size allows individual attention for each guest, but it over-charges, in our opinion.

La Perla **2nd-class**
Pl. del Castillo, 1. Rooms: 68. ☎ *22 77 06.* The location is wonderful —on the main square in the heart of town. This hotel is the city's old-est and was a favorite of both Hemmingway and Henry Cabot Lodge. But time has passed and the hotel has not kept up—now it is seedy and uncomfortable. Front rooms, however, provide good views of the run-ning of the bulls.

Maisonnave **2nd-class**
C. Nueva, 20 (two blocks west of the Pl. del Castillo). Rooms: 152. ☎ *22 26 00; FAX: 22 01 66; Telex: 37994.* The location is superior, the hotel modern, and the rooms comfortable, but there are more rooms than the small staff can handle. Such deficiencies would be easier to over-look if the prices were moderate.

MODERATE ($50-$99)

Eslava **R3rd-class ★**
Pl. Virgin de la O, 7 (beside the Jardins de la Taconera). Rooms: 28. ☎ *22 22 70; FAX 22 51 57.* If you get one of the rooms overlooking the val-ley, you will be pleased indeed. Even if you are not, the room will be attractively old, with wood-beamed ceilings. The hotel is quiet and reasonably priced.

WHERE TO EAT

Food can be quite good in Pamplona, after all this is Basque country. Dishes range from stews to simply grilled fish and meat. During the Festi-val of San Fermin, the loser of the previous evening's contest (when it is the bull) is available around town in stews.

EXPENSIVE ($50+)

Josetxo **★★★**
Pl. Principe de Viana, 1 (on the major traffic circle, four blocks south of the Pl. del Castillo). ☎ *22 20 97. Closed Sundays, and August.* This formal and elegant restaurant bears a longstanding reputation as the best in Pamplona. Today Hartza, below, provides stiff competition, but Josetxo remains first-rate. Fish are the specialties, including crab and omnipresent hake, but the pigeon should not be overlooked. Reserva-tions are advised. ***Amex, Diners, MasterCard and Visa accepted.***

Hartza **★★**
C. Juan de Labrit, 19 (opposite the bullring, to the north). ☎ *22 45 68. Closed Sunday evening, Monday, August, and Christmas week.* Elegant enough in its lovely townhouse, nonetheless, this restaurant is a little less "stiff" than Josetxo. Its menu tries fewer selections, but each is exceptional—ingredients are the best and the chef's touch is delicate. Reservations are strongly advised. ***Amex, Diners, MasterCard and Visa accepted.***

MODERATE ($20-$50)

Otano

C. San Nicolas, 5 (one block along the street that leaves the west side of the Pl. del Castillo). ☎ *22 70 36. Closed Sunday evening.* The restaurant is located above the bar and decorated as everyone imagines a Spanish eatery should be. The food is hearty and features regional specialties.

INEXPENSIVE (UNDER $20)

Iruna

Pl. del Castillo, 44. ☎ *22 20 64.* The art deco decor is gorgeous, and the hearty food can be inexpensive if one is careful in ordering.

DIRECTORY

INFORMATION • Located on C. Duque de Ahumada, 3, a block east of the Pl. del Castillo. English is spoken, travel information is current, and the staff will help with hotel accommodations. ☎ 22 07 41.

TRAINS AND BUSES • The Estación de Rochapea is located on C. Rochapea, 2 k from the center of town. The number 9 bus goes there for 50 ptas. from the Paseo do Sarasate, the wide boulevard running west of the Pl. del Castillo. Train service is frequent both to Madrid and to Barcelona. ☎ 12 69 81.

Buses depart from Av. Conde Oliveto, 4, which is one block west of the main traffic circle, Pl. del Principe de Viana. ☎ 21 36 19.

POST OFFICE AND TELEPHONES • Located at Paseo Sarasante, 9, the wide boulevard running west of the Pl. del Castillo. ☎ 22 12 63. Telephones are available around the corner from the Tourist Office at C. Cortes de Navarra.

POLICE • The municipal police are located on C. Monasterio de Irache, 17, which is outside the center of the city. ☎ 11 11 11.

AIRPORT. • The local airport is 7 k south of the city, and provides service to large Spanish cities. ☎ 31 72 02.

EXCURSIONS

Pamplona is a center around which monasteries and castles from the early Middle Ages congregate. The medieval town of **Estella** ★★, filled with churches and mansions, is less than 50 k southwest. (See the separate description.) **La Oliva** ★★ is an elegant 12th-century monastery readily combined in a half-day tour with the nearby town of **Olite** ★ and its splendid castle. (Each is separately described.) **Leyre** ★★, 50 k east, is a 12th-century monastery favored by the kings of Navarre that houses their remains. Nearby are **Sangüesa**, filled with medieval mansions, **Sos del Rey Católico** ★, with the palace in which Ferdinand the Catholic was born, and **Javier**, the birthplace of Saint Francis Xavier. (All three are described above under the heading of "Leyre.") Another 50 k in the same direction is the oldest monastery of all, **San Juan de la Peña** ★★, on an astonishing site, along with the truly romantic **castle at Loarre** ★. (Both are described below under "San Juan de la Peña.") For a change of pace, a national park at **Ordesa** ★★ provides opportunities for hikes with incredible scenery (described above under its own heading.).

SAN JUAN DE LA PEÑA ★★

From **Zaragoza** *take N-350 north toward Huesca, then past it to Sabinanigo, for a total of 141 k. Follow N-330 east for 18 k to Jaca. Continue east, now on N-240, for 11 k Turn south on C-134 for 5 k to San Juan. From* **Pamplona** *take N-121 south toward Zaragoza by following Av. de Zaragoza as it leaves the large hub of the Pl. del Principe de Viana. 5 k outside the city take N-240 heading east. In 92 k Puenta de la Reina de Jaca is reached. 10 k further east take C-134 south for 5 k to San Juan.*

For the **Castillo de Loarre** ★, one of the most atmospheric in Spain, continue 9 k south to Bemues. Take N-330 south to join N-240 south for 25 k to Ayerbe. Turn east as a sign directs for 7 k to the village of Loarre.

Monastery of San Juan de la Peña   ★★★

Open Tues.-Sun. 10 a.m. to 2 p.m. and 4-7 p.m. (opening and closing an hour earlier in winter). Closed Mon. (closed Tues. in winter). Sometime during the 9th century, a hermit named Juan chose a barely accessible cliff (Peña) for his hermitage. He must have had an eye for scenery. A full-fledged monastery existed by the 10th century, along with a lower church built into the cliff wall. In the 11th century the monks adopted the Cluniac reforms and built another church in an early Romanesque style above the first. The order was considered the holiest in Aragón, conducting the burial of its kings from the 11th to the 14th centuries. In the 17th century, rich revenues and growing membership led to another church being erected higher up the mountain. The French pillaged this third church in 1809, however, although fortunately leaving the earlier churches intact.

Built in the first part of the 10th century, the crypt, partly underground, is actually the original church on this site. The Sala del Concilio served as the monks' dormitory and is massive. The church itself is unique, a design of *Mozárabs* (Christians taught by the Moors). Two aisles are demarcated only by great arches and lead to dual apses that are mere niches cut into the mountain rock. Remains of 10th-century murals can be detected on walls and the undersides of the arches.

Stairs lead to an upper story and courtyard that constitute a pantheon of early Aragónese nobility. The tombs, which line the left wall, are marked by simple plaques surrounded by a border of balls. Only coats of arms indicate the occupants who range from the 11th-century founder of the Kingdom Aragón, Inigo Arista (with a cross and four roses), through 14th-century nobles.

The upper church was built in the late 11th century in the earliest Romanesque style. Living rock forms part of the roof over a single aisle. Off the north wall a chapel decorated in the 18th century serves as a pantheon to the kings of Navarre from the 11th through the 14th centuries. Outside, a lovely Romanesque cloister is bordered by the face of the cliff on one side and a sheer drop on the other. The capitals are carved in a seminal Romanesque style and depict biblical history through the time of the Evangelists. On the left side reposes a 15th-century chapel, sorely out of place.

From Ayerbe, 4 k of rocky road and hairpin curves are rewarded at the end by a castle aerie, with serene views. **Loarre Castle** ★ was built into the cliff face at the end of the 11th century by Sancho Ramirez, the king of Aragón and Navarre. Later a religious order was installed inside. Fronted by almost a third of a mile of stout wall that follows the curves of the mountainside, this fortress meets all expectations. A massive keep leads by a covered stairway to a magnificent chapel with elegant columns. The rest of the castle is a maze of winding passageways, with battlements that are brilliantly designed defensive structures. All it needs is King Arthur.

ZARAGOZA ★ ★ ★

Population: 590,750
Area code: 976; zip code: 50000

*From **Madrid** take A-2 west toward Guadalajara, which receives the designation N-II after Alcalade Henares. In 328 k Zaragoza is reached. From **Burgos** take N-1 west toward Logroño for 89 k. After Miranda, turn south on N-232 toward Logroño, continuing past Logroño to Zaragoza in 170 k more. From **Pamplona** take either N-121 or the toll road A-15 south for 85 k to Castijon. There take either N-232 or the toll road A-68 south for 95 k more. From **Barcelona** take A-7 south toward Tarragona. After 62 k take N-2 west toward Lleida (Lerida) which brings you to Zaragoza in 234 k.*

The flat plains of southern Aragón, well watered by the Ebro river, grow miles of wheat and corn. Zaragoza is the commercial center for this vast region. Romans first founded a town on the site in 25 B.C., which they named Caesar Augusta, from whose sounds the present name derives. Fifteen years later, according to tradition, the Virgin Mary appeared to Saint James beside the river, standing on a pillar of jasper, which she left behind to mark the event for some reason. Soon a church rose around the pillar, still preserved, although now it resides inside Nuestra Señora del Pillar, an 18th-century rebuilding of the far earlier church. In the second week of October, the city celebrates its "Pillar" festival with parades, lantern-lit processions, and, of course, bullfights.

In the eighth century the Moors captured Zaragoza. By the 11th century it had became a rich and important *taifa* (principality) within the Moors' domain. Its ruling family of Benihud built a palace, like that of the Alhambra, only more substantial for these colder climes. This Aljaferia, after much remodeling through the ages, has been restored to something of its former state, and is a wonder. In the first part of the 12th century, however, Alfonso I recaptured Zaragoza for the Christians. Zaragoza remained the capital of Aragón from that time until the end of the 15th century when Ferdinand married Isabella and Aragón ceased to exist as a kingdom. During the Peninsular War against Napoléon, the French attempted to capture Zaragoza, but the citizens held firm through a 2-month siege. The city still refused to capitulate when the French, after reinforcements, stormed the walls. The fighting turned hand to hand and proceeded through the town, house by house. Only by dynamiting most of the buildings were the French able to quell the citizens. By that time the city lay in ruins with half of its 100,000 citizens dead.

Zaragoza's recovery from this ruin is remarkable. The population has grown to ten times the number the French left living, and the city has expanded to several times its 19th-century size. Although much that was historical and interesting has been lost, today Zaragoza is a thriving commercial center that preserves a few treasures for the tourist.

The sight that makes Zaragoza worth a stop is the **Aljaferia ★★★**, which preserves marvelous Moorish stuccowork and ceilings. A complex beside the river consists of a huge **Cathedral ★**, **Nuestra Señora del Pillar ★** containing the venerated pillar and a rare example of a Renaissance secular building—the **Lonja ★**. In addition, the tasteful **Museo Camon Aznar ★** is well worth a look.

*From **Madrid** the city is entered on Av. de Madrid. As the avenue emerges from a tunnel, the Aljaferia is on the left, and parking should be available on the streets around it. From there take Av. Conde de Aranda for about eight* *blocks until it ends at the large Av. Cesar Augusto. Take this avenue left for 6 blocks until it enters the Pl. del Pillar. Arriving from **Pamplona** on A-68, go left when it ends at the Pl. del Toros. If arriving from Pamplona or **Burgos** on **N-232**, keep left to travel along Av. de Navarra which ends at the Pl. del Toros. In both cases, in one block a left will bring the Aljaferia, a right will follow Av. Conde de Aranda for 8 blocks until it ends at the large Av. Cesar Augusto. A left on this avenue for 6 blocks brings the Pl. del Pillar. From **Barcelona** the city is entered on Av. Cataluña. After crossing the Rio Ebro, you'll find the Pl. del Pillar is on the right.*

Along the huge rectangle of the Pl. del Pillar are **Nuestra Señora del Pillar** and the **Lonja**. The **Cathedral** is due west, in a continuation of the plaza. Two blocks south of the plaza at C. Espoz y Mina, 23, is the interesting **Museo Camon Aznar**. The **Aljaferia** is a distance from the plaza. From the extreme west end of the plaza, head south along Av. Cesar Augusto for six blocks. Then turn left on Av. Conde de Aranda for eight blocks more, for a total of about 1 k.

WHAT TO SEE AND DO

Nuestra Señora del Pillar ★
Open daily 9:30 a.m. to 2 p.m. and 4-7 p.m. Admission: 200 ptas., to the museum. The present structure, replacing a much older church, was built in 1680 to house the sacred pillar and image of the Virgin. It was designed by the son of Felipe II's great architect, Herrera. The son did not inherit his father's genius but designed an innovative structure nonetheless. His quadrangular plan features a huge dome surrounded by smaller tiled cupolas added a century later. Inside, columns seem excessively massive, as if the architect were unsure of his calculations so made them overly safe. The most interesting feature is the ten frescoed cupolas—the one in the center of the north nave was painted by the young Goya, who was born nearby. Ornate chapels line the aisles leading to the high altar backed by a fine marble retablo by Damian Forment. Beside the altar is the Santa Capilla surrounded by marble columns. In a niche on the right is the sacred pillar supporting an extravagantly robed Virgin. Her attire is changed daily. Columbus is said to have taken a piece of the pillar with him for luck on his first voyage to The New World. The pillar is kissed by the faithful from outside the chapel rear. Three bombs that landed on the chapel during the Civil War (but did not explode) hang nearby to demonstrate the pillar's power.

To the east of N.S. del Pillar is the huge reconstructed **Ayuntamiento** *with ornate eaves. To its west is the* **Lonja**.

Lonja ★

Open during exhibitions only from 10 a.m. to 1 p.m. and 5-8 p.m. Open Sun. and holidays during exhibitions from 11 a.m. to 2 p.m. Admission: free. Most medieval commercial towns had a central building where commodities were brokered. This is one of the few surviving, to give a sense of civil architecture in the 16th century. The hall is a Gothic structure with Plateresque decorative elements. Twenty-four columns surmounted by grotesques support the ceiling, surrounded by a frieze that records the raising of the building.

West of the Lonja is the huge **Palace of the Archbishop** *and the Cathedral.*

Cathedral ★

Open daily 9 a.m. to 2 p.m. and 4-6 p.m. Admission: 200 ptas., for the Treasury, the Tapestry Museum, and the Pillar Museum. The Cathedral is most notable for its size. A baroque facade was added in the 18th century to the Gothic interior. Today all architectural styles from the Gothic to Mudejar, through Plateresque and Churrigueresque sprinkle the inside. In a most unusual touch, the marble floor below depicts the vaulting overhead. To the left of the altar and its retablo of fine Gothic work is a tomb of Archbishop Juan of Aragón, a brother of Ferdinand the Catholic. A slab in black stone nearby marks the location of the heart of Don Baltasar Carlos, the son of Felipe IV who Velásquez painted so often. The Parroquieta Chapel holds a fine 14th-century tomb carved in Burgandian style, covered by a lovely Mudejar ceiling. Paintings in the Treasury include works of Ribera, Zurbarán, and Goya, while the adjacent Tapestry Museum displays a grand collection of Gothic and later works. The *Betrothal of Anne of Brittany* is a masterpiece.

Museo Camon Aznar ★

Open Tues.-Sat. 10 a.m. to 1 p.m. and 5-9 p.m. Open Mon. 10 a.m. to 1 p.m. and Sun. 11 a.m. to 2 p.m. Admission: free. In this former Palace of Pardo is stored the art collection of a famous Spanish art historian with impeccable taste. The works include an Andrea del Sarto of *Four Saints*, an unusual El Greco still life, a fine Zurbarán crucifixion, along with works by Ribera, Ribalta, Rembrandt, and Van Dyck. There is a rare Velázquez sketch and a profound Goya self-portrait.

Aljaferia ★★★

Open Tuesday-Sat. 10 a.m. to 1:30 p.m. and 4:30-6:30 p.m. Open Sun. 10 a.m. to 2 p.m. Closed holidays. Admission: 200 ptas., for the guided tour. The Moorish prince of Zaragoza built this palace in the eleventh century. After Zaragoza was reconquered by the Christians, it became the palace of the kings of Aragón, with much remodeling of original rooms and decor. Later it served as an administration center and courts of the local arm of the Inquisition, later still, as an army barracks. The huge building recently underwent extensive restoration, resulting in a Moorish first floor and a Gothic and Renaissance second floor. All told, this building contains some of the more exquisite rooms to be seen in Spain.

Of exceptional interest is the *musallah*, private mosque, on the first floor, which rivals parts of the mosque in Cordova. The *mihrab* is a gem, as is the stucco filigree. A grand staircase from 1492 leads up to the Christian apartments. Of the former throne room only a magnificent ceiling remains, containing the entwined initials of Ferdinand and Isabella. Another fine ceiling crowns the room of Santa Isabel (Isabel of Portugal), an altogether charming room. The juxtaposition of Moor and Christian architecture just a floor apart provides much food for thought.

WHERE TO STAY

As a major city, Zaragoza includes a full complement of hotels. Since it is not a major tourist stop, however, most hotels are of the businessperson sort, and charge expense-account prices.

EXPENSIVE ($100-$200)

Gran Hotel   1st-class ★ ★ ★

C. Joaquin Costa Canalejas, 5 (twelve blocks south of N.S. del Pillar). Rooms: 138. ☎ *22 19 01; FAX: 23 67 13; Telex: 58010.* For once this name fits—this Belle-Époque hotel has been declared a national monument. It was renovated ten years ago, and will soon be due again. The service is costly but exceptional.

Goya   1st-class ★

C. Cinco de Marzo, 5 (on the first street to the west along the grand avenue Paseo de la Independencia, due south of N.S. del Pillar). Rooms: 148. ☎ *22 93 31; FAX: 23 47 05; Telex: 58680.* This hotel offers quiet and professional service but without the atmosphere of the Gran. It charges less as well, and is located more conveniently for the sights.

MODERATE ($50-$99)

Ramiro I   2nd-class ★ ★

C. Coso, 123 (C. San Vicente de Paul heads south from the west end of the cathedral. In four blocks C. San Jorge goes west one block to this hotel.) Rooms: 101. ☎ *29 82 00; FAX 39 89 52; Telex: 58689.* This hotel charges less than normal for its class. It is an older establishment with most conveniences, although it is somewhat understaffed. Still, the rooms are comfortable and a good value.

INEXPENSIVE (UNDER $50)

Conde Blanco   3rd-class ★ ★

C. Predicadores, 84 (this street goes west from the Mercado de Lanuza, the market a block south of the west end of the Pl. del Pillar). Rooms: 87.

☎ *44 14 11; FAX 28 03 39.* The locale is quiet and attractive, conveniently situated between the sights of the Pl. del Pillar and those of the Aljuferia. The hotel is modern and very professionally run. Please do not tell the management that its prices are too low.

WHERE TO EAT

Zaragoza possesses a large number of elegant restaurants but boasts of one superior establishment with very fair prices.

EXPENSIVE ($50+)

Costa Vasca   ★ ★ ★

Teniente Coronel Valenzuela, 13 (follow directions to the Hotel Goya and continue to the west end of its street to reach the attractive Pl. de Salamanca and this restaurant). ☎ *21 73 39. Closed Suday and the last 3 weeks of August.* A more pleasant dining experience is hard to find. The chef greets you as you enter a tastefully decorated intimate room. Tapas are sublime, but all the food is of the first order, seafood especially. All this and fair prices too make Costa Vasca a popular place. Reservations are strongly recommended.

Amex, Diners, MasterCard and Visa accepted.

INEXPENSIVE (-$20)

Tres Hermanos

C. San Pablo, 45 (turn west on block south of the Mercado de Lanuza, the market a block south of the west end of the Pl. del Pillar). ☎ *44 10 85. Closed Tuesday.* We cannot guarantee gastronomic heights but can assure that cost will be low. The sign outside translates as "Economical Meals," and those are what you get. The restaurant is downstairs and generally crowded.

DIRECTORY

INFORMATION • Located in the Torreón de la Zuda-Gloneta Pio XII, which is at the west end of the Pl. del Pillar. The staff is helpful and speaks English. ☎ 39 35 37.

TRAINS AND BUSES • Estación Portillo is located on Av. Clave, 4 blocks south of the Aljaferia. As the major city in the region, Zaragoza offers convenient schedules to most of Spain. The RENFE office is located at C. Clemente, 13, a street which leaves the grand boulevard Paseo de la Independencia heading east.

POST OFFICE AND TELEPHONES • Located on the grand boulevard Paseo de la Independencia, 33 (☎ 22 26 50).

POLICE • ☎ 49 91 76; emergency: ☎ 092.

AIRPORT • Zaragoza's airport is 9 k west of the city on N-232. It's a substantial terminal serving the major cities of Spain (☎ 32 62 62). Buses, for under 100 ptas., connect with the Pl. de San Francisco. The Iberia office is located at C. Canfranc, 22-24 which goes west from the Pl. de Aragón at the southern end of the Paseo del la Independencia (☎ 21 82 50).

EXCURSIONS

All the excursions from Pamplona described above are as easily visited from Zaragoza. See the description under "Pamplona excursions" to make a choice. Descriptions of the individual sights include directions from Zaragoza.

CATALONIA AND THE LEVANT

Gaudí's Casa Batlló in Barcelona.

HISTORICAL PROFILE:
THE SPANISH CIVIL WAR

The Civil War of 1936-39 ranks with the blackest events in Spain's history. It began as a military putsch that degenerated on both sides into atrocities of unprecedented proportions. Even today, no Spanish town remains unscarred by its effects.

By 1936 a century of army coups had set the stage for civil war. From the time of Napoléon's defeat in 1813 through the Spanish-

American War in 1898, 37 relatively bloodless coups had been attempted—12 successfully—as one general seized power after another. Because each new government appeased only conservative constituencies—land owners and the Spanish Catholic Church—Spain entered the 20th century as the least-developed country in Europe. Industry was negligible; land magnates controlled vast acreage and hosts of tenant farmers; the Church owned a third of the nation's wealth; with one general for every 100 troops, the army barely functioned.

In 1920 the Spanish Army lost 14,000 troops in a humiliating ambush in Morocco. Another 7,000 died the following week. Spain had been disgraced; her citizens were angry. A commission was convened to assess the responsibility for the slaughter, but before a report could be released, the Captain-General of the state of Catalonia, Miguel Primo de Rivera, staged a coup. His corrupt dictatorship lasted for ten years until the army withdrew its support in 1930, forcing his resignation. Just as world depression hit Spain, creating even greater unemployment and social unrest, King Alfonso XIII formed a new government. The next year, civil turmoil compelled the King to call for general elections. Most of the votes went to monarchist candidates, due largely to the combined urging of Catholic priests and the strong-armed tactics of large landowners coercing thousands of peasants. Nonetheless, all the large cities except Cádiz voted against the King. Realizing that a country cannot be governed without the cooperation of its cities, the army withdrew support from Alfonso XIII, who abdicated and went into exile.

Thus, amid economic depression and growing unrest, the tragic Second Republic began. Over a million farm workers lived in near slavery, possessing no land of their own, but hiring out for the pitiful wages decreed by farm owners. Most of these people were so impoverished that they had never in their lives tasted meat. Decades of outlawed unionism had fostered resentment among a million laborers who knew that workers in other countries enjoyed better conditions than theirs. At the same time, various regions of Spain, especially Catalonia and the Basque areas, resented attempts to diminish their *fueros*—ancient rights of independence and rule by consent.

Grievances varied. Some cried for agricultural reform, the division of the 10,000-acre farms into smaller plots for starving farmers. Some opposed the centrism of the national government, preferring regional autonomy. Still others objected to the stranglehold of the Spanish Catholic Church on education and morals—although at the time Spain was the least Catholic of all Catholic countries, with only one citizen in five regularly attending mass.

It was an era of political upheaval throughout the world, disturbing old certainties. Communists revolutionized Russia, while fascists replaced socialists in Germany and Italy. Everywhere politics polarized into left or right. In Spain, the largest organization on the left was the anarchists, who resented all forms of government, believing that people would cooperatively work out problems on their own. Many laborers and teachers agreed with the anarchists, but a large number followed the socialists, who argued that raising wages, providing health needs, and offering proper education were the duties of any government. The next largest group on the left were the Marxists, introduced into Spain by Paul Lafargue, Marx's own son-in-law. Marxists believed in communally-owned enterprises instead of private property. However, because Marxist theory gave little weight to the political power of peasants while encouraging a centrist state, most Spaniards felt it offered no solution to their problems. Finally, there were communists, divided into those who followed Trotsky and those who followed Stalin and took orders from Russia. In 1931, perhaps 10,000 Spanish considered themselves Stalinists.

The largest party on the right was the CEDA, the Catholic party. Next came the Carlists, who supported a return to monarchy under Prince Don Carlos. Last was a small group, called the Falange Español, "Spanish Phalanx," led by José Antonio Primo de Rivera, the son of the former dictator. His was a paramilitary organization, schizophrenically supporting anticapitalist social reforms along with fascist ideals of cleansing society through brutality.

At the beginning of the Second Republic, the temper of the government was mainly socialist. One of its first acts was to separate the church from the state. When the prelate of Toledo responded with a sermon calling for the return of the monarchy, leftists burned 20 churches in reply. The new government agreed to permit home rule for the Catalans, but not for the Basques. Little headway was made on the grave issue of agricultural reform. After an election was called in 1933, opponents of the regime won a majority of seats and immediately overturned all policies of the previous government. Basques rose in Asturias, demanding autonomy, but were violently put down by soldiers. Thirty thousand political prisoners soon crowded the jails, for anger and frustration had turned into violence.

Both the left and right formed "fronts," coalitions of individual parties from the same end of the political spectrum. In 1936, the

Popular Front—consisting of socialists, Marxists, and communists—won a general election, thanks to the support of anarchists, even though monarchists elected more delegates than any other single party. A liberal government was formed, while the right called for a coup d'état. After police shot a Civil Guard thought responsible for a bomb thrown at the President of the Republic, the Guard's funeral erupted into a running gun battle between Falangists and socialists. Falangists attempted to assassinate the Deputy Speaker of the Cortes; then they tried to kill the most prominent socialist in Catalonia. When the Falangists machine-gunned laborers in Madrid, the government closed its offices and arrested their leader, José Antonio. This arrest, and massive strikes in Madrid and in Barcelona helped anarchists and socialists increase their popular base. The Spanish Army, worried about anarchy, separatism, and a departure from Catholic ideals, grew agitated.

The Spanish Army consisted of 30,000 hardened colonial troops protecting territory that Spain controlled in north Morocco, as well as untrained home forces. Francisco Franco y Bahamonte, the son of a Galician naval paymaster, had chosen the army over his father's service because so few navy ships and opportunities survived the Spanish-American War. He had risen to the rank of general in charge of the Spanish Foreign Legion, whose motto was *Viva la Muerte* ("Long Live Death"). Franco, a small man with a pot belly and squeaky voice, was brave, but always cautious. Because of questions about his loyalty during such turbulent times, the government had posted him far from Spain in the Canary Islands.

After months of plotting, an army rebellion rose in Spanish Morocco on July 18, 1936. The next day, after an English pilot had flown Franco to Morocco to lead the army over the straits to Spain, the sailors of the fleet refused to transport the soldiers. Instead, in the first major airlift in history, the army was flown by German and Italian airplanes to Spain. On the mainland, garrisons of troops attempted to seize major cities. With the army in rebellion, the government was helpless, but private citizens defied the troops. By sheer numbers the people succeeded in resisting more often than not, so that by the end of the first week, only Seville, Cádiz, Jerez and Algeciras in the south, and Pamplona, Burgos, Vallodolid, and the territory of Galicia in the north, were held by the army. As a putsch the uprising was a failure, now it was a case of surrender or war. The army held a horizontal strip across the north, minus the Basque region, and a small area in Andalusia.

Except for police of questionable loyalty, the Republican government commanded no forces. Should it arm the citizens? All the major parties—anarchists, socialists and communists—demanded weapons, but the government feared the anarchy of a country in arms. People acquired weapons by force or purchase anyway, and formed themselves into troops.

If it was to be war, Franco's army would need supplies. He turned to Italy and Germany. Mussolini, favoring a fascist regime in Spain to oppose the British Mediterranean fleet, supplied planes and troops. A total of 50,000 Italian troops entered the fray. Hitler, too, desired a fascist regime in Spain, viewing it as a strategic threat to France's southern border, and a base for German U-boats. Also, civil war in Spain would provide an opportunity to field-test his equipment and soldiers. Hitler supplied the latest German aircraft to make up the infamous Condor Legion, along with tanks, artillery, and a host of military advisers.

The Republican government needed supplies from other countries, too, because Spain had no substantial war industry. Initially, France sold the government outmoded materials at inflated prices, but soon closed its borders to further sales. The socialist Prime Minister of France, Léon Blum, should have sympathized with the kindred government of Spain, but his shaky administration feared antagonizing French rightists. The British maintained a facade of neutrality, as the Prime Minister, Anthony Eden, argued that aiding the Republic would only lead to more German and Italian supplies for the rebels. In fact, high-ranking members of the British government maintained close social ties to the Spanish nobility and openly preferred fascism to liberal policies. In the end, Eden sent the English navy to support Franco. Although the United States Neutrality Act prevented aid to any belligerent, Ford and General Motors sent 10,000 trucks to Franco, none to the Republic, and DuPont delivered as many bombs. Because of Franco's pro-Catholic views, the rebels gained the support of Joseph Kennedy, who exerted a powerful influence in the U.S. government on their behalf. In the final analysis, leaders of the free world feared a "red menace" more than fascism, since leftists were intent on doing away with class privileges.

With nowhere else to turn, the Republic petitioned Stalin for supplies. His image required that he not refuse, but, feeling weak because he had just purged his army, he feared Hitler's displeasure. So he dribbled insufficient aid with great fanfare. Still, as the Republic's only supplier (except for Mexico), Russia strengthened the hand of the Spanish Stalinists, who gradually gained control of both the government and its armed forces. By refusing aid to the Spanish Republic, the democracies pushed it further left.

In an attempt to gain international approval, both sides waged a propaganda campaign. Franco's army began to refer to itself as Nationalist. Its adherents claimed that Republicans killed 20,000 priests and raped nuns by the hundreds over the course of the war. Later, the number was reduced to 7,937 killed, and no rapes were substantiated. But, undeniably, genuine atrocities were committed by the Republican side—army officers were executed as they left their homes, businessmen and priests were murdered. Most Republican killing took place in the early days of the war, when the passion for retribution was most intense. Conflicting propaganda makes truth elusive, but an estimate of 10,000 civilian murders by Republicans is generally accepted.

Nationalist atrocities were of a different order. Soldiers killed at least ten times as many civilians as the Republicans, doing so systematically over the course of the war less with the intention of punishment than to exterminate liberals. "Your women will give birth to Fascists," their graffiti boasted.

The war opened with a Nationalist attack on Madrid. By November 8, 1936, the city was virtually surrounded, its fall imminent. No one expected citizens with guns to match professional soldiers. The Nationalists concentrated their attack on the western suburbs, around the University, where Madrileños had been reinforced by an army of anarchists from Barcelona, the anarchist center. Also defending the city were the first of the International Brigades that would eventually number 35,000 troops. These primarily working-class people—enlisting to fight fascism—had been recruited from Europe and America by the communists, but included as many non-communists as party members in their ranks. This motley collection of untried troops traded a lack of military training for determination, and, against all expectations, held off the Nationalists.

The Republican government was as surprised as anyone at this valiant defense—anticipating the fall of Madrid, its members had fled to Valencia. The battle for Madrid settled into a stalemate, and, when Nationalists tried to bomb the city into submission, the first such attempt in history, resistance only hardened.

Yet Madrid would have fallen, had Franco not diverted his forces for a propaganda expedition. The army garrison in Toledo failed to capture that city, and had been under civilian siege in the Toledo Alcázar for two months. Eleven hundred defenders and 500 civilian sympathizers became a symbol of Nationalist determination. Franco's first priority was relieving the Toledo garrison, an action that delayed his arrival in Madrid by three weeks. By then Republican reinforcements had arrived.

Blocked at Madrid, the Nationalists next planned to conquer the rest of the country, causing Madrid to fall for lack of support. As 1937 began, the Nationalists commanded 100,000 army troops and an equal number of Carlist and Falangist militia, along with 10,000 German and 50,000 Italian regulars. Republican troops comprised 320,000 men and women, though at any given time half of these irregular troops were away on leave. The Nationalists aimed first at the northern Basque region.

The Nationalist campaign went smoothly except for a horrible incident at Guernica. The city of Guernica was a Basque symbol of no military importance, six miles behind the front. On April 26, between 4:30 and 7 p.m., wave upon wave of German planes systematically destroyed the town. First came a carpet of high explosive bombs, then strafing, and finally a torrent of incendiary shells. The carnage, illuminated by burning houses, was the most horrifying the world had seen. One third of the citizens suffered injuries; 1,654 people died. Miraculously, one of the few survivors of the raid was the sacred oak tree of the Basques, under which their treaties had traditionally been signed. The Nationalists disavowed responsibility for the massacre, pointing fingers at German pilots. In Paris, the Spanish painter Picasso immortalized the horror in his *Guernica*, considered one of the great modern paintings.

By 1938 armies on both sides had grown to 700,000. The Nationalists drove toward the sea on the east and reached it with ease. Catalonia and its capital of Barcelona was now cut off, while Madrid formed an isolated pocket in the west.

Generally in war, defense is less costly of lives and material than offense. In defending their homes, the Republicans proved to be staunch fighters, but the Republican government, anxious for the publicity of major victories, time and again used their untrained troops to launch ineffective offensive campaigns. In defense of Barcelona, the Republicans threw nearly 200,000 men at the Nationalist circle around the city. Initial success was followed by a slowing and finally a stoppage of the advance. Bogged down, the citizen-soldiers became fodder for an uncontested Nationalist air force and artillery, and by the time they retreated back to Barcelona, the Republicans had lost 70,000 troops and tons of irreplaceable equipment. A quarter of a million troops now remained to defend Barcelona, sharing only 40,000 rifles. The Pope urged Franco to wait until after the Holy Season to attack, but on December 23, Franco entered Barcelona behind 300,000 well-armed troops. Half a million refugees fled him into France. Madrid fell on March 31, 1939, and Franco announced the official end of the Civil War on April 1. Now Spain was Franco's problem.

Generalissimo Franco, *El Caudillo* ("The Leader"), immediately enacted the Law of Political Responsibilities, which stated that all persons guilty of subversive activities from October 1, 1934 to July 18, 1936, as well as those who opposed the National Movement, either actively or passively, were criminals. This law made everyone who opposed the coup, in word or deed, and those who simply lived in a community that opposed it, guilty of a serious crime. Franco bragged that he possessed a list of a million liberal criminals. Two hundred thousand people were executed over the first five years of the regime, and a like number were imprisoned and used as forced labor to reconstruct the battered country. In the new Spain, a man could be fined for walking the streets without a hat or jacket, a woman for bared arms in public. Everyone went to church, for not to do so was grounds for arrest.

Since all electoral candidates were members of Franco's FET party, Franco ruled until his death on November 20, 1975. His Spain, with its subsidized hotels, cheap food from a depressed economy, and trains that always ran on time, was a heaven for tourists. Although he supplied Hitler with Spanish ores to repay the cost of German supplies during the Civil War, Franco kept Spain officially neutral during World War II. He cut crime to minuscule proportions by jailing suspects along with the guilty. Throughout his reign he warned of the anarchy that only he kept at bay. After his death, the Third Republic commenced peaceably and in an orderly fashion. The Spanish economy blossomed, but then so did crime, as it seems to in all democracies.

CATALONIA AND THE LEVANT

However natural it may be to think of Spain as culturally homogeneous, that conception is frequently misleading and never more so than in Catalonia's case. Catalonia (called "Catalunya" locally) is the most European part of the Iberian peninsula. It has as much in common with the south of France as with the south of Spain—as well it should, for the two were joined throughout much of their history.

Catalonia was the second place in the Iberian Peninsula to receive foreign settlers. The Greeks colonized Empüries in the sixth century B.C., and there introduced the olive into Spain. Two centuries later Carthagenians followed. Their attack on the Roman colony at Segunto, in the second century B.C., brought Roman armies to Spain in retaliation, to destroy the bases of their Carthagenian enemy Hannibal, and stay to conquer the peninsula. Tarragona, south of Barcelona, functioned as the Roman headquarters in Spain. Goths emigrated in the fifth century, followed by Moors in the eighth. Unlike their sojourn in the rest of Spain, however, the Moors held Catalonia for only a short time.

To rid itself of Moors, Catalonia appealed to the great King of the Franks, Charlemagne. He sent his son Louis le Debonair, Count of Toulouse, who freed Catalonia from the Moors in 801 and united it with his territory in southern France. His father, Charlemagne, organized the combined territories into what he called the Spanish Marches, merging Catalonia with the part of France later known as Languedoc (from Language of Oc, for the non-Parisian language spoken there). But, less than a century later, Catalonia turned the tables when Wilfred the Hairy, the first Count of Barcelona, took Toulouse. In 987, as the rest of France united in recognizing the usurper Hugh Capet as King, Barcelona and its French territory refused to acknowledge his claim, thereby declaring itself separate from the rest of the kingdom of France.

These Catalan and southern French territories remained united for 700 years, preserving their independence by playing off the neighboring powers of France and Aragón against each other. Indeed, for a golden three centuries it was Catalonia that controlled Aragón, rather than the other way around. When an Aragónese king died childless, in 1137, his brother, Ramiro, was forced to abandon monastic life to rule. Ramiro betrothed his daughter Petronila to Ramón Berenguer IV, the Count of Barcelona, then returned to his cloistered existence. Berenguer IV thus became Regent of Aragón and, when Ramiro died in 1172, Berenguer's 10-year-old son was crowned Alfonso II, the King of Aragón.

At the time both Castile and Aragón were separately attempting to reconquer territory from the Moors. It would sometimes happen that both kingdoms had designs on the same city, but it would not do for a Christian king to rescue a city from the Moors then have to defend it from attack by another Christian king. In 1179 Alfonso II, negotiated a treaty with the King of Castile that drew a vertical line from Logroño in the north through Alicante in the south to demarcate separate spheres of conquest. Two reigns later, Jaume I earned the name "Conqueror" by taking Valencia, thereby giving Catalonia and Aragón control of the eastern coast of Spain. Including Jaume I's seizure of the Balearic Islands three years earlier, Catalonia had established itself as a power in Europe.

Jaume's successor Pedro III married the only child of King Manfred, ruler of Sicily which controlled all of Italy south of Rome. When the French attempted to impose claims on Sicilian territory, the Italians rose against them, and Pedro came to their aid with an army. Since he was in Italy with troops at his command, he seized the throne of Sicily for Catalonia. Now Catalonia controlled the south of France, one third of Spain and half of Italy. Catalan troops next went to the aid of Constantinople, beleaguered by the Turks. In return, the Pope granted them the territory of Turkey, though in name only, since the Turks who actually controlled the country did not agree. A small force also landed in Greece and were ceded Athens by the Pope.

Catalonia's Mediterranean dominance lasted only 50 years. Pedro IV left two sons when he died, both of whom expired childless, so the throne reverted—never to return to Catalonia—to an Aragónese in 1410. Turks regained control of Greece and the Catalans came home from Turkey.

Yet Catalonia continued to govern substantial territory in the south of France for two centuries more. The two areas shared a language, customs, and cuisine. Provençal, as it is known in France, or Catalan, as the related tongue is known in Spain, was the favored tongue of the troubadours during the Middle Ages, for it lent itself superbly to poetry. Catalonia considered itself a Mediterranean country facing east, rather than west into Spain, and fought fiercely to remain independent of the hegemony that powerful Castile created throughout the rest of the country, resisting every effort to impose Castilian

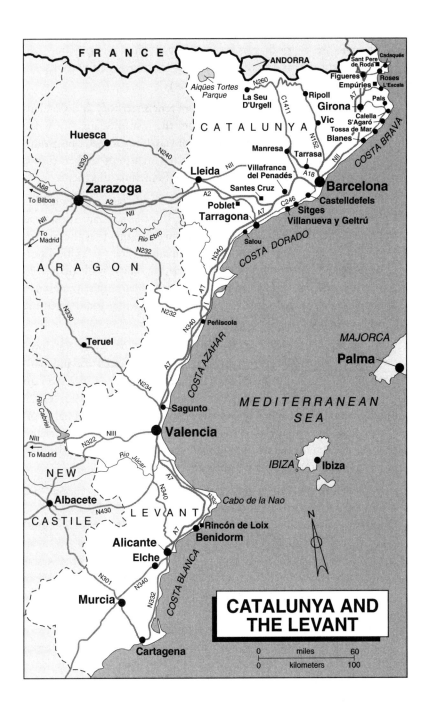

CATALUNYA AND THE LEVANT

Spanish as its language. When forced to recognize Castilian Kings, the Catalans swore an oath that was a model of non-commitment: "We, who are as good as you, swear to you, who are no better than us, to accept you as king and sovereign lord, provided you observe all our liberties and laws—but if not, not."

In 1639 France invaded Catalonia's French territory and Catalans enlisted to fight alongside troops from the rest of Spain. But when the Spanish King ordered the people of Catalonia to billet his troops in their houses, they took the command as an affront to their rights, declaring war on Spain, and inviting the French to join them.

Too strong for Felipe to expel, French troops occupied Catalonia and much of Aragón for over a decade. But the Catalans soon tired of their new overlord, and were as jealous of rights that the French usurped as they had been of those the Spanish tried to. As local support eroded, the French saw the handwriting on the wall and agreed to leave Catalonia. However, the 1669 treaty that ratified the French departure ceded them those Catalan territories that today form the south of France.

As late as the 1930s, during the Spanish Civil War, Catalonia fought against the Nationalists and Franco as much for independence from the rest of Spain as against dictatorial government. Franco made them pay dearly. He imposed Castilian as the official language on all of Spain, and made writing Catalan a prisonable offense. Today, Catalonia is a semi-autonomous territory of Spain, similar to a state in the U.S., and its official language is the old, French-sounding, Catalan.

Beautiful **Barcelona** ★ ★ ★ ★ ★ is the treasure of Catalonia, and for most people one of the highlights of all Spain. One reason it is so enjoyable is that its entertainments are so varied. It offers a well-preserved medieval quarter and a fine cathedral in the Barri Gòtic, an exceptional museum of medieval art in the Museo de Arte de Catalunya, fine museums for the modern art of both Picasso and Miró, and the eccentric, lovable architecture of the genius Gaudí. There is more to Catalonia than the capital, however. **Empúries** ★ ★ preserves rare Greek ruins, and **Tarragonab** ★ ★ displays extensive Roman remains. **Poblet** ★ ★ ★ and **Santa Cruz** ★ ★ monasteries are grand medieval edifices. Beaches of great appeal line 600 miles of coast—the scenic **Costa Brava** ★ ★, the golden Costas **Azahor** ★ ★ and **Dorada** ★ ★, and the sandy stretches of the **Costa Blanca** ★ ★. South in the Levant is the major metropolis of **Valencia** ★ ★, with enough variety to repay a day's visit, while staying on the Costa Azahor, to its north, or the Costa Blanca, to its south.

BARCELONA ★ ★ ★ ★

Population: 1,754,900
Area code: 93; zip code: 08000

*From **Perpignan** in France both the toll A-9, and the free N-9, reach the Spanish border at La Jonquera in 20 k. There they continue in Spain under the new names of A-7 and N-II and reach Barcelona after 160 k. From **Zaragoza** the toll road A-2 east joins A-7 in 137 k. for a further trip of 62 k. Alternatively, there is the free N-II which reaches Llerida (Lérida) in 142 k. and Barcelona in a further 156 k. From **Pamplona**, **Madrid**, **Valladolid**, and west, follow directions to Zaragoza, and the directions from that point above. From **Valencia** the best routes are the parallel coast roads A-7 (toll) and N-340. They reach Barcelona in 331 k. Note that N-340 can be slow going when beach towns are crowded in summer.*

Legend has the city founded by Hannibal's father, the Carthagenian general Hamilcar Barca, and derives the city's name from his. In reality the city descends from a Roman colony established in the time of Augustus, named Faventia Julia Augusta Paterna Barcino. Shortened to Barcino, the name transmographied into Barcelona. The original town comprised a low hill just inland from the sea—the present Barri Gòtic—as it would for almost 1,000 years. Franks captured Barcelona from the Romans in A.D. 263, and when the Romans recaptured it they surrounded the hill by a cyclopian wall that still exists in scattered pieces. In 874, after the French had expelled the Moors and annexed Catalonia in the process, Wilfredo el Velloso (the Hairy) was named the Count of Barcelona and granted independence by the ironically named French king, Charles the Bald. From that time forth, Barcelona maintained preeminence in Catalonia.

The city grew and prospered both because its location on the eastern coast made it a funnel through which most of the Mediterranean trade flowed into Spain, and because its people were singularly hard-working and blessed with sound business sense. Barcelona remains the busiest port in Spain, its second largest city, and a more substantial business center than the country's political capital, Madrid. In both the middle of the 18th and the middle of the 19th

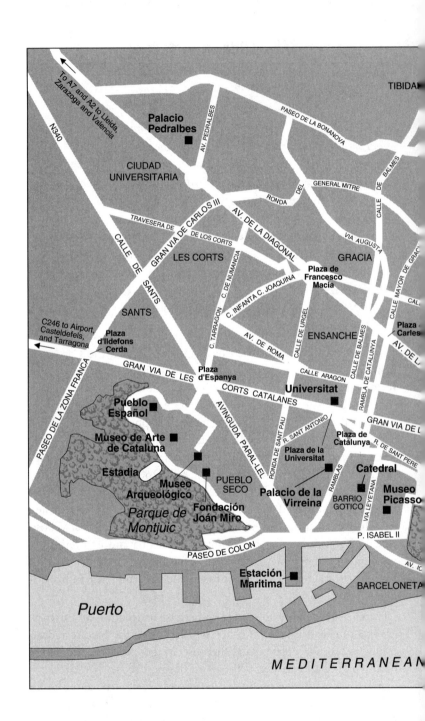

PASEO DEL VALLE HEBRON

BARCELONA

VIA FAVENCIA

VIA JULIA

a
eo
di

Parque Grüell

ESERA DE DALT

SAN ANDRES

To A7
and Girona

C. CAMELIAS VIRGEN DE MONTSERRAT

PASEO DE FABRA Y PUIG

CALLE DE FELIPE II

AV. DE LA MERIDIANA

CALLE SAN ANDRES

E GRACIA

CONGRESO

agrada
Familia

AV. GAUDI

CALLE DE SAGRERA

AV. DE LA MERIDIANA

N

za de
oros

CALLE ARAGON

ATALANES   **Plaza de les
Glories Catalanes**   SAN MARTIN

CALLE GUIPUZCOA

Besós

Rio

P. CARLOS II

CALLLE ALMOGAVARES

CALLE PEDRO IV

A19

rque de la
dadela

seo de
Moderno

SAN ANDRIA
DE BESOS

To Mataró
and Costa
Bravo

PUEBLO NUEVO

BADALONA

SEA

| 0 | yards | 1,100 |
| 0 | meters | 1,000 |

centuries Barcelona undertook imposing urban renewals. The first entailed tearing down most of the ancient walls to construct a wide thoroughfare along the western edge of the Barri Gótic, primarily for promenades. The thoroughfare followed a sometime stream and permanent sewer and was named the Ramblas, perhaps from the Arabic *raml*, meaning "stream." The second project produced a great extension of the city north of the Barri Gótic. Called the Eixample (Extension) and supervised by the architect Ildefons Cerda, it was a marvel of rational city planning with grand avenues that more than doubled the city's size. Today, Barcelona spreads both north and south of this extension, following the coastline.

The visitor will spend most of his time in the center of this sprawling metropolis. The port of Barcelona lies on the sea midway between the north and south halves of the city. Immediately south of the port rises the abrupt hill of Montjuïc. Here are several fine museums and the arenas from the 1992 Olympics. Two blocks inland from the port and running for ten blocks further west is the original heart of Barcelona, the Barri Gótic, containing the cathedral and other medieval buildings. Its south border is formed by the lovely Ramblas, which changes its name every few blocks. South of the Ramblas is a maze of streets called the Barri Xines (Chinese Quarter), the former red-light district, now much toned down, although still not the safest place after dark. West of the Barri Gótic, beginning at the landmark Plaça Catalunya, stands the 19th-century urban development Eixample, with boulevards, elegant stores, and buildings by Gaudí. Northwest of the Barri Gótic a park blooms where an 18th-century fortress once stood, called the Ciudadela, providing space for a zoo and the Museum of Modern Art. Barcelona's atmosphere is one of industry, quiet excitement and good taste.

Catalan will be the language most often heard. It sounds something like French and many words will be understood by those familiar with that tongue. Spanish is understood by all, French by most, and English by a large number of Barcelona residents, particularly those who service customers. Street names use *Avinguda* for Avenue, *Carrer* for Street and *Plaça* for Plaza.

Convenient underground parking is generally available in a large lot under the square behind the Boquería, the main food market. It is one block west of the Rambla St. Josep, and thus near the Barri Gótic.

From the **Airport** *22 k south of the city Barcelona is entered on Av. de Gran Via. Continue past the hill of*

Montjuïc on the right. Turn right one block after the University on the left onto Rambla de Catalunya. Continue east along the Rambla dels Etudis with a center island. After a church and the market on the right in four blocks, take the first right onto C. Hospital, and then right again into the parking lot.

From **France** *and north, Barcelona is entered either on Av. Meridiana which funnels into Av. de les Corts Catalanes, or on Av. Catalanes in the first place. However, at Pl. de les Glories Calalanes it becomes one-way, forcing a detour north (right) to follow the parallel C. Diputacio for 14 blocks to Pl. Gracia. One block later turn left (east) onto the Rambla de Catalunya. Continue east along the Rambla dels Etudis with the center island. After a church and a market on the right in four blocks, take the first right onto C. Hospital, and the first right again into the parking lot.*

From **Madrid**, **Zaragoza** *and west Barcelona is entered on an avenue that changes its name from Reial, to Miró, to Colblanc, to Creu Coberta, then enters the large traffic circle of Pl. d'Espanya. Take Av. Gran Via leaving the circle toward the northeast. Turn right one block past the University on the left onto Rambla de Catalunya. Continue east along the Rambla dels Etudis with its center island. After a church and the market on the right in four blocks, take the first right onto C. Hospital, and the first right again into the parking lot.*

WHAT TO SEE AND DO

The pleasures extended by Barcelona encompass a wider spectrum than any other city in Spain. High on any list would be the sights of the **Barri Gòtic**—the cathedral ★★, the **Frederic Marés Museum** ★, the **Museum of the City of Barcelona**, the **Palau de la Géneralitat** ★, and the buildings of the **Plaça del Rei** ★. The **Ramblas** ★★ call for leisurely strolls. Nearby is the 14th-century church of **Santa Maria del Mar** ★★, off **Carrer Montcada** ★, a street of Renaissance mansions. On the summit of **Montjuïc** stands the **Museu d'Arte de Catalunya** ★★★, of wondrous medieval art, the ultramodern **Fundació Joan Miró** ★, and the **Olympic** stadia. In the newer part of the city, the Eixample, tower fantastic buildings by **Gaudí** ★★, including the incredible **Sagrada Família** ★★★ church. In the Parque de la Ciudadela, northeast of the Barri Gòtic, is a **zoo**, while the extensive **Picasso Museum** ★ is passed on the way. In such a large city, the most convenient plan is to visit sights by area, and we organize them that way.

The **Bus Turistic** provides convenient transport to most of the sights, leaving from the Pl. Catalunya at the west end of the Ramblas every half hour starting at 9 a.m., until the end of September. The bus stops at fifteen sights around the city, at any one of which passengers may get off to board again half an hour later for the next circuit. Multilingual members of the Tourist Board ride along to answer questions. The cost for a full days ride is about $10, or $7 for half a day, payable on boarding.

POLLUTION ALERT

Bathing in and around Barcelona is not recommended. Pollution levels can be dangerous.

BARRI GÓTIC

This quarter is named for the dense concentration of Gothic buildings that create a medieval atmosphere in the area, more than survives in any other city in the world. It encompasses the original city of Barcelona before its expansion, and includes traces from Roman times, pedestrian walks and a charming square.

At the corner of C. Hospital at the end of Rambla Sant Josep stands the small Pl. de la Boquería on the north side of the street. C. Boquería, more a shopping arcade than a street, heads north for a bit more than three blocks before changing its name to C. Coll and entering the charming Plaça Sant Jaume.

Plaça Sant Jaume ★

Two Gothic buildings form the east and west borders of the plaza. On the east is the much restored **Ajuntament** (City Hall), generally with banners hanging from the second-story windows of its 19th-century facade. Its northern face along C. de la Ciutat is from the 15th-century. A dramatic black and gold mural by the 20th-century artist and architect Josep Sert resides inside, along with an impressive Gothic hall where the Consell de Cent, the ruling body of Barcelona, once met. Unfortunately, permission is required to see anything more than the building's rather ordinary courtyard. On the west side of the plaza stands the **Palau de la Géneralitat ★**, formerly a grand 15th-century palace and, until recently, Catalonia's seat of government. Plans are in progress to open the palace to visitors, and may be in effect by your arrival, although no hours had been set at our last visit. Walk west from the plaza along the north face of the palace to the entrance on C. Bisbe Irurita. Inside is an elegant Renaissance patio, an imposing 16th-century hall, and a lovely chapel dedicated to Saint George, the dragon-slayer—a patron saint of Barcelona as well as of England. A weathered 15th-century medallion of that saint on C. Bisbe Irurita marks the outside entrance to the patio.

The narrow C. Bisbe Irurita is bordered on the right side by the **Casa de los Canonigos** *(Canons), connected to the Palau de la Géneralitat by a covered passageway overhead that looks eminently medieval, although constructed in 1926. At the end of Bisbe the plaza of the cathedral opens,* **Plaça Nova***. Turning back to face the cathedral, the* **Palacio de Bisbe** *on the right contains two soaring plain towers of a more weathered stone than the rest, grizzled because they remain from the fourth-century Roman walls of the town. The open plaza before the cathedral is the place to see the local folkdance, the Sardana, danced to the accompaniment of fife and drum by parishioners leaving mass on Sunday.*

Cathedral ★ ★

Open daily 7:30 a.m. to 1:30 p.m. and 4-7:30 p.m. Admission: 200 ptas. Cloister Museum open daily 11 a.m. to 1 p.m. Admission: 50 ptas. Although the cathedral was constructed in the 14th century, its facade is more recent—late 19th-century—designed to suit the Gothic interior. Inside, the church is harmonious in proportion, though wider in feeling than even the normally wide Spanish Gothic churches. The whole is unfortunately dulled by blackened stone and a less spacious clerestory than eyes would wish. In the center a trascoro in marble carved after designs by the great Bartolomé Ordoñez illustrates the martyrdom of Saint Eulalia by Romans in the 4th century. She was a native of Barcelona and is the patron saint of the cathedral. The coro it contains is admirable. Two tiers of high stalls are surmounted by individual spires. The upper tiers are emblazoned with the coats of arms of France, England, Portugal, Hungary, Poland, Sweden and The Netherlands, for here Carlos V convened kings to join his exclusive club—the Knights of the Golden Fleece.

Stairs at the foot of the altar descend to a crypt preserving remains of Saint Eulalia in a fine 14th-century marble sarcophagus attributed to Giovanni Pisano, but more likely by an unknown north Italian. The Gothic door to the sacristy and museum leads to wooden coffins of the cathedral founders, Ramón Berenguer I and his wife. Off the south transept stand unusual cloisters. Magnolias and palm trees surround a pond in which geese play in memory of their Capitoline ancestors. A small museum in the chapter house on the west side exhibits a collection of paintings. Most admirable is the composition and faces of *Pieta* by Bartolomé Bermijo, with a most human-looking bespectacled priest.

Pass around to the north side of the cathedral to follow the narrow C. dels Contes de Barcelona along its flank. At number 10 on the left is the Frederic Marès Museum.

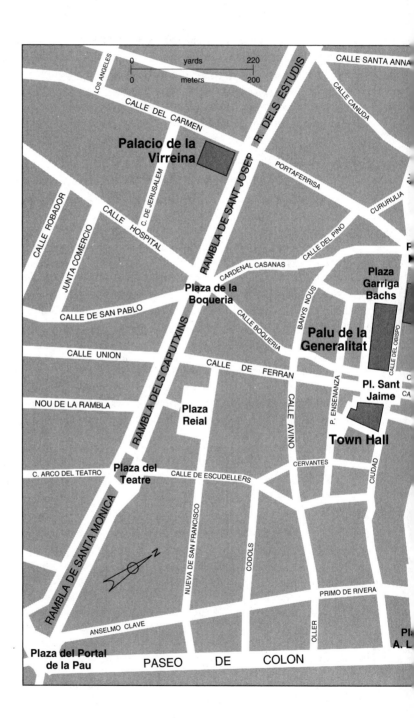

CENTRAL BARCELONA

Museu Frederic Marès ★

Open Tues.-Sat. 10 a.m. to 2 p.m. and 4-7 p.m. Open Sun. 10 a.m. to 2 p.m. Closed Mon. Admission: 250 ptas. The heart of the collection was gathered by a Catalan artist named Marès, who reconstructed the Gothic tombs of the Aragón kings at Poblet Monastery (described under that heading). The top floor of the museum is a melange of everyday objects and advertisements that capture the spirit of design in the early part of this century. Displayed in the basement are early stone sculptures, including Roman, Moorish, Romanesque and Gothic pieces, gathered by this inveterate collector. On floors in between, is mounted a fine collection of polychromed wood sculpture—mostly from Catalonia, but also from elsewhere in Spain.

Continue along C. dels Contes de Barcelona to take the first left into the Pl. del Rei.

Plaça del Rei ★

The plaza is named for the 14th-century royal palace of the Kings of Aragón that occupies the far left of the square, down a flight of stairs. One enters an immense arched Gothic audience hall, the Saló del Tinell, with a reconstructed wood–ceiling. Among other rooms that may be visited is one with splendid murals of the Catholic Monarchs attending Columbus, for somewhere in this palace, perhaps in the Saló del Tinell, the Catholic Monarchs received Columbus after his first trip to the New World to hear the first news of his amazing discoveries. *Open Tues.-Sat. 10 a.m. to 2 p.m. and 4-7 p.m. Open Sun. 10 a.m. to 2 p.m. Closed Mon. Admission: free.*

Next to the palace stands its **Capilla de Santa A'gata**, spare and moving with a fine altar. The chapel is entered from the building on the right side of the plaza, the 15th-century Casa Padillàs, now the **Museu d'História de la Ciutat**. The purpose of the museum is to show models of early buildings and various stages of Barcelona's growth, but, in the course of moving the building from its original site in the Eixample and digging a new foundation, Roman and Visigoth structures were discovered. So the most interesting sights reside in the basement where these ancient remains are displayed. (Hours for the Museu are the same as for the palace, and admission is free.) The building on the near left side of the plaza is the 16th-century **Palau del Lloctinant**, now housing an astonishing collection of medieval records. For the average tourist a look in the courtyard at the grand stairway with its lovely ceiling will suffice.

Continue along C. dels Contes de Barcelona to the second left onto C. Libreteria. Take the second left again to enter the grassy Pl. Berenguer el Gran. Here one has the best look at the remaining **Roman walls**, *for the Chapel of Saint Agatha was built into them, and would have lost an outer wall if this part of the Roman fortification had been torn down along with the rest. The walls were 27*

*feet thick in parts and 60 feet high, though not quite so elevated
here. Return to the Pl. del Rei and go away from it along the apse
of the cathedral. At the end of the apse, tiny C. Paradis turns left.
As it bends right, the CEC Mountaineering Club stands at number
10. Walk inside to see the four pillars remaining from the Roman*
Temple of Augustus.

MONTJUÏC

*Commanding both city and sea, this steep hill seems to call for a
fortress. In more peaceful times its abundant land provides space
for museums and athletic stadia, though for centuries it served as
the cemetary for the city. The name presumably derives from Mons
Iovis, Mount Jupiter in Latin. The best entrance, if driving, is from
the Pl. Espanya. Head down the Ramblas to the sea. Turn right at
the statue to Columbus and right again in one short block onto Av.
del Paral-lel, which ends in about fifteen blocks in the Pl. Espanya.
A grand vista to the left leads up an equally grand stairway to the
Palau Nacional. The fountains are lighted at night and play to
music on Sat. and Sun. at 10 p.m. in summer, 9 p.m. in winter. To
the right of the start of the palace stairs is a reconstruction of the
German Pavilion designed by Mies van der Rohe in 1929. Its Bau-
haus elegance seems most ordinary today, although it caused an
uproar when new because of its extreme contrast with the palace's
grandeur.*

*If car-less, Montjuïc is best reached by the funicular (cable car)
that runs from 11 a.m. to 9:30 p.m., in summer, only on weekends
in winter, and costs 100 ptas. Walk toward the sea from C. de
l'Hospital along Rambla Caputxins for 2 blocks. Turn right on C.
Nou de la Rambla for 7 short blocks to Av. del Paral-lel and the
funicular station. You exit on the hill near the Fondacio Miró. Follow the directions below in reverse.*

Palau Nacional, Museo de Arte de Catalunya   ★ ★ ★
Open Tues.-Sun. 9 a.m. to 2 p.m. Closed Mon. Admission: 500 ptas.
The grand boulevard leading from the Pl. Espanya, the fountains, the
van der Rohe German Pavilion, and the palace itself all were built for
a world's fair hosted by Barcelona in 1929. Today the palace houses
the Museu d'Arte de Catalunya, one of the world's great assemblages
of medieval art. Its collection of Romanesque painting is unsurpassed.

The reason for the excellence of the collection is that its works were
appropriated by the government during the early 1900s from
Romanesque and Gothic churches throughout Catalonia to protect
the art both from thieves and the elements. Although one way to

amass a great collection, these seizures denuded parish churches throughout Catalunya.

Romanesque paintings alone fill 34 rooms. Special notice should be paid to the charming 12th- and 13th-century works, such as frescos from Pedret, Bohi, and Santa María, and especially to the *Pantocrator* fresco from Sant Clemint de Taull, with a precocious use of foreshortening and haunting gaze. Note the Byzantine feeling combined with attempts at portraiture. The Gothic period blossoms with the *Nativity* of Lluis Borrassa, and the precision of Bernat Martorell, then ascends to genius in Lluis Dalmau's *Verge dels Consellers*, and culminates in the retablos of Jaume Huguet. Although weakest in artworks from periods after the Gothic, the museum possesses paintings by Ribalta, Velázquez and Zurbarán, a fine Ribera, and lesser works by el Greco and Tintoretto.

Poble Espanyol

Open daily 9 a.m. to 8 p.m. Admission: 500 ptas., 250 ptas. for children Follow the road west from the palace, Av. dels Montanyans, and turn right at the first opportunity. This "Spanish Village" is another survivor from the 1929 World's Fair. It is a collection of replicas of houses in different styles, presenting the variety found through Spain, amid a melange of souvenir and crafts shops, restaurants, and even amusement rides. Viewing these replicas makes sense only for those who cannot see the real thing. The admission charge is steep, but the experience is pallid. For unfathomable reasons, the Spanish love it.

Museu Arquaeològic ★

Open Tues.-Sat. 9 a.m. to 1 p.m. and 4-7 p.m. Open Sun. 9:30 a.m. to 1 p.m. Closed Mon. Admission: 200 ptas., free on Sun. Go east from the palace, taking the left fork along Passeig de Santa Madrona. This museum displays notable and rare Carthagenian jewelry discovered in the Balearic Islands, along with a fine selection of Celtiberian pieces. The collection is strong in Roman and Greek artifacts, mainly from excavations at nearby Empüries—note the bronze panther head and the *Venus of Empüries*. Interesting too are reconstructions of a Roman kitchen and atrium. The fittings of an actual Roman catapult are also on view.

Fundació Miró ★

Open Tues.-Sat. 11 a.m. to 7 p.m. Open Sun. 10:30 a.m. to 2:30 p.m. Open Thurs. evening to 9:30 p.m. Closed Mon. Admission: 400 ptas. Return along Santa Madrona back to the fork to curve around left. Turn left at Av. de Miramar for a few yards. The all-white building designed by Josep Sert provides part of the pleasure, for it is perfectly suited to the bright colors of the art on its walls. Sert also designed the notable Fondaçion Maeght in Provence. The artist, Joan Miró, was born in Barcelona, but lived in France in self-imposed exile during Franco's years. It was he who donated most of the artworks in the museum, and the money to house them. The collection spans the breadth of his work, from sculptures, to tapestries, to mobiles, to precisely designed colorful paintings. The building is bright and airy, and the art makes one smile.

Return along Av. de Miramar for the 70,000 seat Olympic Stadium, swimming pool, and other stadia. Note the covered stadium of impressive Japanese design. Ahead on Av. de Miramar is the teleferique (cable car) that, for 150 ptas., rides up to the **Parc d'Atracciones***, a rather tame amusement park, then continues up to the* **castle** *at the summit of Monjuïc for 100 ptas. more. (The cable car runs weekdays from noon to 3 p.m. and from 4-8:30 p.m.; weekends from 11:30 a.m. to 8:30 p.m. In the winter it opens only on weekends.)*

Castell de Montjuïc

Open Tues.-Sat. 10 a.m. to 2 p.m. and 4-7 p.m. Open Sun. 10 a.m. to 8 p.m., or to 2 p.m. in winter. Closed Mon. Admission: 50 ptas. The fortress was built in 1640 by the citizens of Barcelona during one of their rebellions against the rest of Spain. Although the English captured it, followed later by the French and by Franco, it presents an imposing front. Unrivaled views over the city and sea are presented from the roof, but housed inside is the usual collection of military museums.

THE RAMBLAS ★ ★

The Ramblas consist of a wide pedestrian island bordered by two narrow streets. Citizens love to passeo *past kiosks selling newspapers, magazines, books and erotic comics, flower stalls, bird sellers, and impromptu entertainers. Every block or two the Ramblas change their name. None of the sights along the way are spectacular, but the walk continually presents precious surprises, and for many this will be the Barcelona remembered longest. Note that the Ramblas turn more seedy at night and function as the city drug center. We start from the beginning of the Rambla Sant Josep, one long block west of the C. de l'Hospital.*

On the southwest corner at number 99 stands the 18th-century **Palau de la Virreina**, built by a viceroy to Peru who skimmed a fortune from Peruvian silver, though named for his widow. It presents revolving exhibitions and contains a permanent stamp collection on the top floor. (Open Tues.-Sat. 10 a.m. to 2 p.m. and 4:30-8:30 p.m.; open Sun. 10 a.m. to 2 p.m., Mon. 4:30-9 p.m. Admission is variable, but free to the stamp collection.)

Continue down Rambla Sant Josep toward the sea. On the right, half way along the block, is the entrance to a huge covered food market, called the **Boquería ★**, roofed in 1870's girdered ironwork. Walk through the market and out the rear entrance to see the 18th-century **Antic Hospital de la Santa Creu** across the parking lot. No longer a hospital, its patios are tranquil. Returning to the Rambla, a sidewalk mosaic by Miró is located near the corner. Crossing C. de l'Hospital and the next street, C. de Sant Pau, brings the opera house of Barcelona at the next corner—the **Gran Teatre del Liceu**, one of the few buildings for true opera in Spain. While it is not impressive outside, inside all is sumptuous gold gilt and red velvet. (Open for tours on summer weekdays at 11:30 a.m. and 12:15 p.m. Admission: 200 ptas.) On opening night in 1892, an anarchist threw two bombs into the audience, though performances have been more ordinary since.

At Rambla del Caputxins, cross C. la Unio. On the left side of the street C. Colom leads into the **Plaça Reial** ★. This is one of the few true plazas in Barcelona, surrounded by an arcade of homogeneous buildings. Palm trees wave and a fountain of the three graces decorates the center. Its streetlamps were designed by Gaudí. Today the square is slightly seedy with bars all around, but on Sundays it comes to life with a philatelic and numismatic market. Continuing a few feet down the Ramblas, turn right onto C. Nou de la Rambla. At number 3 is the **Palau Güell** ★ ★, an early building by Gaudí. Since it now functions as a museum (for theater memorabilia), it is the rare civil building by this eccentric architect open to the public. Don't miss it! (Open weekdays 11 a.m. to 2 p.m. and 5 p.m. to 8 p.m., weekend 4-8 p.m. Admission: 200 ptas.)

The Rambla grows less attractive from this point on. At its end stands a solemn statue of Columbus pointing over the wrong sea. To his left, the first street north, C. Banca, holds the **Museu de Cera de Barcelona**, one of those wax museums that every large European city seems to have. (Open Mon.-Sat. 11 a.m. to 2 p.m. and 5-8 p.m. Admission: 400 ptas.) To Columbus' right, in a barn of an old building, is the **Museu Maritim** ★. The building, called the Drassens Reials, is worth the visit. Dating from the 14th century, it is the only surviving medieval shipyard in Europe. The collection inside features an exact model of the galley *La Real*, flagship of Prince Don Juan during the great battle of Lepanto in 1571. (Open Tues.-Sat. 10 a.m. to 2 p.m. and 4-7 p.m. Open Sun. 10 a.m. to 2 p.m. Admission: 200 ptas.) Floating in the harbor opposite the far side of the Maritime Museum is a replica of Columbus' flagship, the **caravel Santa Maria** ★. Its tiny size is a shock that evokes appreciation for the courage of those who sailed so insubstantially past the end of the known world. The ship may be toured, using the ticket from the Maritime Museum. (Open daily 9 a.m. to 2 p.m. and 3 p.m. to sunset.)

Along the water, north of the port, stands Barcelona's latest example of urban development. It was constructed to serve as the 1992 Olympic village, and then to be sold for expensive condominiums. Beside the ocean stretches a wide ocean promenade and beach.

Note:...Despite its relatively clean appearance, the port area of Barcelona can be dangerous. It is best avoided from the onset of dusk.

THE EIXAMPLE

The area known as the Eixample was constructed above the western end of the Barri Gòtic in the middle of the 19th century to proclaim a modern age for Barcelona. Streets run straight as arrows, intersecting at right angles to form the clean lines of a grid. Its design represented both the rationality and egalitarianism of the time through orderly homogeneity. By the original plan, each block would be a square of the same size, every 200 hundred squares would contain a hospital, every 25 a school. However, the plan was only haphazardly carried through. The buildings raised along these streets were commissioned by individuals and companies, but all aimed to incorporate the latest ideas in architecture—to express the spirit of the modern. Hence, the young Gaudí found several commissions here, along other noted Catalan architects of his era. Most of these designs no longer remain, as changing ideas of what was contemporary led to replacement by later buildings. But enough survive to give this area the most extensive collection of art nouveau architecture in the world.

Guided tours of *Modernista* architecture are given Tuesday, Wednesday and Thursday at 3 p.m. by the Guide Bureau at 54 Via Laietana (☎ 310 77 78), just east of the Picasso Museum. The tours take about two hours and cost $7. The Bureau will arrange individual tours at other times.

Passeig de Gracia was and remains the most elegant street of the Eixample. Today it is lined with buildings for stylish shops, banks, and fancy apartments. But one side of a single block of Passeig de Gracia retains enough early 20th-century buildings to earn the playful name "Manzana de la Discordia" ★—the Block of Discord.

The principle of this early modern movement was the opposite of that which governed later 20th-century design. Clean lines, smooth and shiny materials, the simplest and straightest shapes all characterize design in our time, but the Barcelona *modernista* movement from the late 19th-century found inspiration in the curves and irregularities of nature, not in mathematical precision. To our eyes such buildings seem playful, full of unexpected turns and details, to serve as an antidote for the uniform simplicity whose familiarity has bred, if not contempt, at least a kind of boredom. The proof that we hardly look at contemporary buildings lies in how arresting these earlier fantasies seem.

> *P. de Gracia begins at the Pl. de Catalunya with its fountains. The plaza lies four blocks west of the Pl. Nova, fronting the cathedral. It is also the western terminus of the Ramblas, about three blocks west of the Rambla Sant José. P. de Gracia leaves the northwest corner of the plaza and heads north along the el Corte Inglés department store.*

Three blocks north along Passeig de Gracia, bordered by street lamps designed by Gaudí, brings C. del Consell de Cent. Here begins the "Block of Discord." Stay on the east side of P. de Gracia for the full view of the buildings opposite, then cross to inspect their details. First, at number 35, is the **Casa Lleó Morera**, designed by a famed Gaudí contemporary named Domènech i Montaner. Only the upper two floors remain from his design, but grow enough flowers and beasts to give a sense of how exotic and Gothic in feel it must have been. The interior is more elegant than what the exterior leads one to expect and incorporates the finest craftsmanship. Although the building is commercial, among its clients is the Patronat de Turisme on the third floor in a stunning apartment. Perhaps some question about the promotion of tourism will occur to you; if so, call ☎ 302 06 08.

At number 41 stands the pyramid topped medieval-looking **Casa Amatller**, designed by another Gaudí contemporary—Puig i Cadafalch. The interior is again elegant, though not open to the public. The art institute on the second floor, however, often responds to sincere inquiries to show visitors around their office. The **Casa Batlló** next door at number 43, is Gaudí's exercise in blue-green tiles. This was Gaudí's interpretation of the cave of St. George's dragon, with balconies suggesting skulls. The front doors seem to undulate as if made of soft material—understandably Salvador Dali admired them. Admission requires advance permission, but a quick peek from outside is allowed.

Two blocks west, occupying the corner of the west side of the street at number 92, is Gaudí's most imposing building, an apartment complex named **Casa Milà**, though known familiarly as "La Pedrera" (The Stone Quarry). The exterior looks like a massive fortress melting. Ironwork balconies are intricate assemblages of matted vegetable-like matter, each unique. Chimneys on the roof are reminiscent of the shapes that children make by dripping wet sand. In this case a free tour, at least of the roof, is available to the public. (Tours on Tues.-Sat. at 10 a.m., 11 a.m., noon, 1 p.m. and 4 p.m.)

North in 11 blocks along C. de Provence waits the incomparable Gaudí church of Sagrada Família, but a slight detour presents two more *modernista* buildings. Continue along P. de Gracia to turn right at the next corner to reach the **Pilau Quadras** at Av. Diagonal 373. This is another building by Puig i Cadafalch, whose interior with its sculpture and mosaics is stunning, and entrance is free, for it is now a museum of musical instruments. (Open Tues.-Sun. 9 a.m. to 2 p.m.) One block east along the Diagonal on the opposite side of the street at 416 stands the huge **Casa de les Punxes**, like a Gothic castle.

> *Continue one block further on Diagonal to take C. Provenca that forks off to the left. It leads in six blocks to Sagrada Família.*

Sagrada Família   ★ ★

Open daily 8 a.m. to 9 p.m. (closes at 6 p.m. in winter). Admission: 400 ptas. Work began on a rather ordinary neo-Gothic church in 1882. Two years later the architect resigned and Gaudí won the commission to complete it, remaining his favorite project until he died in 1926. Work proceeded slowly, since funds were inadequate, and private commissions would take Gaudí away from work on the church for years at a time. For the last ten years of his life Gaudí lived in a small room on the church grounds, for the project consumed him, although he spoke of it as requiring two centuries to complete. In 1926, absent-mindedly crossing a street, he was struck by a trolley and killed. Since then the issue has been whether or not to finish the church. Gaudí left an awesome, but roofless structure, too incomplete to function as a church, of a design so personal that no one could complete it as he would have. Anarchists burned all of Gaudí's plans during the Civil War. Nonetheless, work, financed in large part by admission fees, has been under way since 1979 to finish the church. The intent is to be as faithful to Gaudí's conception as possible, but Gaudí himself worked from the inspiration of the moment as much as from blueprints.

Only the west facade of three envisioned by Gaudí was completed by the time of his death, but what an awesome facade it is, of a spirit recognizably Gothic, translated into modern idioms. The facade represents Christ's birth, and tells that story in carved scenes that seem to grow from the stone around the portals. Study the fine details and wonder at the overall conception. Fear of the power of an unrestrained imagination causes some people to feel a strong aversion to the building, but most agree that the building is spiritual, awesome and playful, a wholly unforgettable experience.

NORTH OF THE BARRI GÓTIC

Via Laietana forms the north border of the Barri Gótic. It can be reached either by going north one block from the Pl. Nova in front of the cathedral, or by continuing through the Pl. Sant Jaume along C. Jaume I for 4 very short blocks. At Pl. de l'Angel where Via Laietana intersects with C. Jaume I, C. de la Princesa heads north.

Turn down the third right along C. de Montcada, onto **C. Montcada ★** *, a street declared a national monument for all the mansions that line it. At number 15, on the right is the* **Palau Berenguer d'Aguilar***, a 15th-century mansion that houses the* **Picasso Museum***. Opposite is the 14th-century* **Palau dels Marques de Llio***, at number 12, displaying an extensive collection of Spanish clothing and other apparel. More 15th-century mansions stand at numbers 14, 23 and 25, ending with the Baroque* **Palau Dalmases** *at number 20.*

Museo Picasso ★

Open Tues.-Sun. 10 a.m. to 7:30 p.m. Open Sun. 10 a.m. to 3 p.m. Admission: 500 ptas. Two things make this an interesting museum. Of course the first is the artworks displayed. Although it is far from the finest assemblage of Picassos, and does not contain many of the artist's more familiar works, the collection is the largest such assemblage in the world, strong in childhood drawings, paintings of the seminal

"Blue Period," and includes Picasso's wonderful cubist variations on Velázquez' great *Las Meninas.* The second note of interest is that the building is composed of two 14th-century mansions remodeled and joined. Against all expectations they provide a fine setting for the modern art on their walls.

On the right, at the end of C. Montcada, stands the rear of the church of **Santa Maria del Mar***.*

Santa María del Mar

Open Mon-Fri. 9 a.m. to 1 p.m. and 5-8 p.m. Admission: free. Finished in the 14th century, this church epitomizes the Gothic style as interpreted in Catalonia. It is Barcelona's most dramatic church. Although the west octagonal tower was not added until the 19th century, the remainder of the outside is early, and celebrated for its west portal. Note the solid buttresses surrounding the church, so different from the "flying" French versions. The interior was gutted of later Baroque decoration during the Spanish Civil War, which restored its original Gothic lines. The nave is high, the vaulting unusually wide, and the adjoining aisles narrow to emphasize spaciousness. Pillars are set more widely than in any other Gothic church in order to carry the eye to the apse behind. The high altar is formed of soaring columns connected by narrow arches, instead of a solid wall. Chapels along the aisles seem somewhat denuded, although fine stained glass windows provide their own decoration.

Return to C. Montcada and continue across on Passeig del Born to reach the beginning of the **Parc de la Ciutadella** *in four blocks.*

Parc de la Ciutadella

At the beginning of the 18th-century, after Barcelona had taken sides against the national government once again, an angry Felipe V razed blocks of houses to build a fortress to cow the citizens. A century and a half later the citizens got back at him by razing his fortress to turn it into a lovely city park, and placed museums and a zoo within its ample confines.

The layout is as follows. Ahead on the left is the **Geology Museum**, of interest to those who know about such things. A short distance to its left stands the **Castell del Tre Dragons**, originally a modernism cafe erected by Domènech for the 1888 Exhibition held in the park, but now a museum displaying almost every kind of stuffed animal. The building is most interesting architecturally as a harbinger of the *modernista* movement. (Open Tues.-Sun. 9 a.m. to 2 p.m. Closed Sun. Admission: 250 ptas.) To the right of the Geology Museum is the **Umbraculo**, a lovely conservatory of tropical plants. Straight ahead in about two blocks' distance are the gardens and lakes of the park, including the **Font de Aurora**, a work on which Gaudí assisted. Directly to the right of the lakes and fountains stands the **Palau de la Ciudadela**, what remains of the fortress of Felipe V after the rest was torn down. Today the palace houses the Catalan Parliament and the **Museum of Modern Art**. Pre-modern would be a more accurate name for the museum, for despite an occasional Picasso or Miró, most of the works are by earlier Catalans. (Open Tues.-Sat. 9 a.m. to 7 p.m. Open Sun. 9 a.m. to 3 p.m., and Mon. 3-7 p.m. Admission: 500 ptas.) Continuing south, is the **Parc Zoológic**. While there may be larger collections of animals elsewhere, only this zoo offers an albino gorilla. His name is *Copito de Nieve* (Snowflake), and the dolphin and orca show enchants everyone. (Open daily 9:30 a.m. to 7:30 p.m.; closes at 5 p.m. in winter; admission: 700 ptas.)

PARQUE GÜELL ★

In 1900, funded by his patron Güell, Gaudí began work in the western outskirts of Barcelona on a planned community of houses—a housing development—to express his ideas of urban design. He planned a grand entrance area, spaces for 60 houses, shaded walks and a shopping plaza. Gaudí personally designed every element including furniture for the houses that were completed—nothing was bought ready-made. Such painstaking design took time, so, by the 14th year of the project, only the entrance to the park, the agora-like market, a grotto, pagoda, some walks and one house had been finished, in which Gaudí lived. Güell decided he could pour no more money into the project, so it remains in precisely that state today.

> *By car drive west along P. de Gracia for two miles to the large green Pl. Fernando Lesseps. Turn right around the plaza along Travesera de Dalt. Take the second left onto Av. de la Muntanya. The sixth right along C. Olot crosses the entrance to the park. By public transportation, take the green line, number 3, toward Montbau, getting off at the Lesseps stop. There, on Pl. de Gracia, #24 bus goes to the park entrance.*

No one would think from the entrance that it introduced a housing development. The ironwork gates are intricate, the staircase grand, although bordered by homier mosaic walls, while at the top stands a classical structure of ionic columns. Walking up, one discovers that the columns are formed of mosaics guarded by a sumptuous blue dragon. The pavilion at the end, formed of a forest of columns, was intended as a community shopping area, quite unlike any mall in most of our experiences. Look at the undulating ceiling, a fantasy of mosaics. Walks behind this pavilion lead to a square lined by Gaudí benches peacefully overlooking all of Barcelona. Wander over bridges, elevated paths, and through the grotto to the **Casa-Museu Gaudí**, at the rear of the park. Inside are many of the designs, including furniture, that Gaudí constructed for his planned community. The park is open in summer daily 10 a.m. to 9 p.m., or to 6 p.m. in winter. The Casa-Museu Gaudí is open daily 10 a.m. to 1:30 p.m. and 4:30- 7 p.m. Admission to the park is free. The museum costs 150 ptas.

WHERE TO STAY

In order to host the 1992 Olympics, Barcelona built 12 major new hotels to increase rooms in the city by a third, and ease some of the hotel pressure in Barcelona. Unfortunately, prices have not declined with this increased supply. Room costs in Barcelona stand right behind Marbella as the second highest in Spain, and burden visitors' budgets. Prices, in fact, average one whole category above what they would elsewhere. That is to say, a modest hotel in Barcelona will charge expensive prices. On the other hand, Barcelona does tender some wonderful hotels.

The premier location would be on or near the Ramblas, convenient to sights and shopping. But given that Barcelona provides a subway system, it is possible to stay outside of this center, if near a subway stop, and commute. Such a location is second best, however, to the Ramblas area with its opportunity for serendipitous walks.

VERY EXPENSIVE ($200+)

Ritz  Deluxe ★★★★★

Gran Via de les Corts Catalanes, 668 (Corts Catalanes cuts across the top of the Barri Gótic one block west of Pl. Catalunya. The hotel is one block west and three north of Pl. Catalunya.) Rooms: 161. ☎ *318 52 00; FAX 318 01 48; Telex 52739.* By any measure the Ritz ranks with the finest hotels in the world. It was built in the belle époque style of 1919, and a recent face-lift has made its elegance dazzle again. The entrance—all chandeliers, gilded mirrors and flowers—is as grand as can be. In this case, the hotel is not merely a lobby—its rooms are among the most spacious and beautiful in Spain. Many contain marble fireplaces (though never lit), and huge baths in bathrooms the size of rooms in other hotels. Even if its rooms were merely ordinary, the Ritz would still be worth a stay for the service. You will find no more attentive staff and knowledgeable concierges anywhere. Of course it costs in the 40,000 peseta range, but that is only money.

Condes de Barcelona 1st-class ★★★★

Passeig de Gracia, 75 (6 blocks west of the Pl. de Catalunya). Rooms: 109. ☎ *215 06 16; FAX 216 08 35; Telex 51531.* The building is the former mansion of the Batllós for whom Gaudí also designed a building further down the passeig. The renovation is exquisite, from elegant marble lobby to modern stylish rooms. Its location is conveniently for boutique shopping, though a 6-block walk to the center of town. This hotel is very popular despite rooms in the 20,000-ptas. range, and should be booked well in advance.

Rivoli Rambla 1st-class ★★★

Rambla dels Estudis, 128. Rooms: 87. ☎ *302 66 43; FAX 317 50 53; Telex 99222.* The Art Deco style is perfect for Barcelona, the hotel is small enough for intimacy and the location is superior. All that prevents us from praising this establishment even more is the small size of the rooms for such high prices.

Claris 1st-class ★ ★ ★

Pau Claris, 150 (1 block north and 2 west of the Pl. de Catalunya) Rooms: 124. ☎ 487 62 62; FAX 215 79 11. The building is splendid 19th-century neoclassic. Antiques abound inside, from English to Hindu, to French; and a Japanese garden adds just the touch for this eclectic mix. The owner loves Egyptian antiquities—thus the framed pages from the *Description d'Egypt* on the walls and a small museum of his collection. Don't worry, the bedrooms are tastefully new.

Avenida Palace 1st-class ★ ★

Gran Via de les Corts Catalanes, 605 (one block north of Pl. Catalunya). Rooms: 211. ☎ 301 96 00; FAX 318 12 34; Telex 54734. This fine hotel was built in 1952 in the grand Rococo style of an earlier era. Inside, all is marble, brass and lovely stuccowork, with a pair of elegant stairways leading off from the lobby. The rooms are very comfortable, if somewhat overdone. The location beats that of the Ritz at half the price.

Majestic 1st-class ★ ★

Passeig de Gracia, 70 (five blocks west of the Pl. de Catalunya). Rooms: 336. ☎ 488 17 17; FAX 488 18 80; Telex 52211. Think of this as two hotels, each with a fine location for shopping, but the front rooms, in a former townhouse, are spacious and attractive, while the back rooms, in a huge extension, are drab and overlook nothing.

Princesa Sofía 1st-class ★ ★

Plaça Pius XII (opposite the university, two miles southwest of the center along Av. Diagonal). Rooms: 511. ☎ 330 71 11; FAX 330 76 21; Telex 51032. Of the modern hotels in Spain this one ranks with the best managed—service is surprisingly good considering the large number of rooms. Recently redecorated, the rooms themselves are both spacious and comfortable. However, the hotel is located too far from the center for walking (though the Maria Cristina subway stop is a block away), and its prices approach the elevated ones at the Ritz.

EXPENSIVE ($100-$200)

Gran Derby 1st-class ★ ★ ★ ★

C. Loreto, 28 (Follow Av. Diagonal northwest to Pl. Francisc Macia, a circle with fountain. Take the left onto Av. J. Tarradellas, then the first right onto Av. de Sarria for a short block to C. Loreto.) Rooms: 43. ☎ 322 20 62; FAX 410 08 62; Telex 97429. The hotel is expensive and, although situated in a quiet neighborhood, is both three miles from the center of town and a fair distance from the nearest subway stop. It is recommended because the rooms are superbly tasteful and huge. All include a separate sitting room, and 2-bedroom suites are available. For two couples traveling together, or for a family, such an arrangement could almost prove cost-effective.

Regente 1st-class ★ ★ ★

Rambla de Catalunya, 76 (five blocks west of Pl. de Catalunya). Rooms: 78.

☎ *215 25 70; FAX 487 32 27 Telex 51939*. Although its townhouse-intimacy, tastefully decorated rooms and lovely roof terrace all deserve raves, its prices do not.

Montecarlo 2nd-class ★ ★ ★

Rambla dels Estudis, 124. Rooms: 73. ☎ *317 58 00; FAX 317 57 50; Telex 93345.* The look of the marble entrance and wooded reception area is the way we think of Barcelona. Accommodations are sufficiently comfortable, and the prices, for a change, are fair.

Colón 1st-class ★ ★

Av. de Catedral, 7 (across the plaza fronting the cathedral). Rooms 147. ☎ *301 14 04; FAX 317 29 15; Telex 52654.* After a recent renovation, the Colón again offers comfort and style. In some ways we preferred the eccentric, if threadbare, former look, for we see enough Laura Ashley at home. Its location is most convenient, although the bells of the cathedral chime outside the windows. Sixth-floor rooms with balconies over the plaza are preferred.

Gran Via 2nd-class ★ ★

Gran Via de les Corts Catalanes, 642 (one block west of the Pl. de Catalunya). Rooms: 53. ☎ *318 19 00; FAX 318 99 97.* The hotel is a turn-of-the-century mansion retaining some of the original decor, including a grand neoclassic staircase. The breakfast area is a hall of mirrors. Guest rooms are not quite up to the elegance of the rest of the building, but are sufficiently comfortable. Front rooms have views, but also noise.

Rialto 2nd-class ★ ★

C. Ferrán, 42 (one block south of the Pl. de Sant Jaume in the Barri Gòtic). Rooms: 128. ☎ *318 52 12; FAX 315 38 19; Telex 97206.* This hotel, along with the Suizo and Gótico that follow, is owned by the Gargallo Company and similar in tasteful decors, intimacy and the best locations possible. All three would be ideal, if they charged a little less.

Gótico 2nd-class ★ ★

C. Jaume I, 14 (three short blocks north of the Pl. de Sant Jaume in the Barri Gòtic). Rooms: 83. ☎ *315 22 11; FAX 315 38 19; Telex 97206.* White walls and floors set off dark wood furniture in this elegant little hotel, otherwise similar to the Rialto and Suizo. Similar also is a price scale set higher than it should be. A better location would be hard to imagine.

Suizo 2nd-class ★ ★

Pl. del Angel, 12 (across the street from the Gótico above). Rooms: 48. ☎ *315 41 11; FAX 315 38 19; Telex 97206.* Perhaps because it is smaller than its two sisters above, we slightly prefer the Suizo. Like the others, the decor is perfect, the service respectful, and the prices are a tad high.

Gaudí   2nd-class ★

C. Nou de la Rambla, 12 (a few steps south of the Rambla Caputxins, opposide the Palau Güell). Rooms: 73. ☎ *412 26 36.* This hotel is recommended for its superb location and for a unique view from the rooms on upper floors. The rooftop of the Palau Güell opposite is a fantasy of shapes that can only be seen from these hotel windows. Otherwise, this hotel is ordinary, although at the bottom of the expensive range.

Regencia Colón   2nd-class ★

C. Sagristans, 13 (a half block west of the Hotel Colón). Rooms: 55. ☎ *318 98 58; FAX 317 28 22; Telex 98175.* This is the annex for the Hotel Colón discussed above. It lacks the charm and views of its sister, but provides a fine location and comfort at half the price.

MODERATE ($50-$99)

Nouvel   4th-class ★

C. Santa Ana 18-20 (the street goes north from the western end of Rambla Estudis). Rooms: 76. ☎ *301 82 74.* This hotel is attractively decorated in a *modernista* style. Rooms are basic but ample for the price, and the service is conscientious.

Mesón Castilla   3rd-class ★

C. Valldoncella, 5 (at the western end of Rambla Estudis C. Tallers angles left leading to the hotel in four blocks). Rooms: 56. ☎ *318 21 82; FAX 412 40 20.* The neighborhood is quiet and lovely, more of an asset than the rooms. Although the location requires a 4- to 6-block walk to the sights, the stroll is pleasant enough to repay the exercise. Rooms are comfortable enough, though of no great distinction.

San Augustín   3rd-class ★

Pl. Sant Agusti, 3 (this plaza is one block south of the Rambla Sant Josep along C. de l'Hospital). Rooms: 77. ☎ *318 17 08; FAX 317 29 28; Telex 98121.* Proximity to the Ramblas and sights make this hotel worth considering, although its prices are moderate only out of season. It is also across the street from the market. Rooms are ordinary.

Cortés   3rd-class

C. Santa Ana 25 (across the street from the Nouvel described above). Rooms: 46. ☎ *317 91 12; FAX 301 31 35; Telex 98215.* Basic accommodations are provided in a neighborhood convenient to both sights and shopping. The hotel is not as attractive as the Novel, but is comfortable and slightly less expensive.

INEXPENSIVE (UNDER $50)

Lausanne   P2nd-class ★ ★

Av. Portal de l'Angel, 24 (just east of the southern end of the Pl. Catalunya). Rooms: 17. ☎ *302 11 39.* For the low price, the rooms have size and style, and the management is most professional. The location is good, if a few blocks from the sights. This much for the price is a true find in Barcelona.

Rey Don Jaime I   4th-class ★
C. Jaume I, 11 (just south of Pl. Jaume in the Barri Gótic). Rooms: 30. ☎ *315 41 61.* Its location in the Barri Gótic is the most notable feature of this hostale. The staff is willing, but the rooms are undistinguished.

Australia   Hs2nd-class ★
Ronda Universitat, 11 (the street goes north across the western end of Pl. de Catalunya). Rooms: 23. ☎ *317 41 77.* Named for the country in which the owner lived for 20 years, this hostale exhibits exceptional concern for guests. The location is not far from the sights, adjacent to an extension of the University of Barcelona.

Palacios   P2nd-class ★
Gran Via de les Corts Catalanes, 629bis (opposite the Office of Tourism, one block west and two north of the Pl. Catalunya). Rooms: 25. ☎ *301 37 92.* The rooms have more style than usual in this price range. Not all the bathrooms have showers, but such a room can be requested.

Oliva   P2nd-class ★
Passeig de Gracia, 32, 4th floor (on the "Block of Discord" near Gaudí's Calla Batllo). Rooms: 16. ☎ *317 50 87.* The rooms are somewhat more spacious than this price range usually provides, and it is fun to stay on this street of elegant shops and unusual architecture.

WHERE TO EAT

By mingling French ideas with Spanish, Barcelona serves some of the best food in Spain. *Bullabesa* (*suquet de peix,* in Catalan), the French fish stew bouillabaisse, is available, but the specialty stew is *zarzuela de mariscos,* a "comic opera" of seafood. Since the south of France influences Catalan cuisine, Italian dishes make their way onto Barcelona menus. *Pan con tomate,* bread soaked with olive oil and spread with tomato, is the usual appetizer; pastas, such as macaroni, will also be seen. Catalans dine very late. The normal dinner hour is 10 p.m., and restaurants do not open in the evening much before that hour. Although Barcelona boasts a large number of the finest restaurants in all Spain, exalted prices make it possible for a diner to pay 20,000 pesetas at the most expensive. Of course, no one is forced to splurge, for Barcelona also contains modest restaurants where good meals are available for 3000 pesetas. And there is a MacDonald's, among other inexpensive eateries.

Before dinner consider a champagne bar, called a *xampanyeria,* to sample glasses of various Spanish brands while munching *tapas.* A rather elegant one is **La Cava del Palau** at C. Verdaguer i Callis, 10 (go north from the front of the cathedral to Via Laietana in one block, west for a block along Laietana, right along C. Sant Pere, to the first left). Munch on cheeses, pâtés, smoked fish or caviar. (Closed Sun.) A more earthy example is **El Xampanyet** at C. Moncada, 22 (head north from Pl. Jaume in the Barrio

Gótico to reach C. Prinesa which leads to the Picasso Museum in three blocks and C. Moncada). (Closed Monday.)

EXPENSIVE ($50+)

Neichel ★★★★★

Av. de Pedralbes, 16bis (Av. Pedralbes heads northwest from Pl. Pius XII, which is at the southern end of Diagonal. The restaurant is in the third alley on the right.) ☎ *203 84 08; FAX 205 63 69. Closed Sunday, Christmas week, Holy Week and August.* To cite one restaurant as the best in Barcelona is certain to provoke argument. With some trepidation we offer this one. True, it is not so beautiful as some others, since it is installed in a modern housing complex. Also, the cooking is as French as Spanish, since its owner hails from Alsace. But the food is sublime. The *menú de degustación* is very expensive, but presents the best the restaurant offers, and that is exceptional indeed. Save room for extraordinary deserts. Reservations are required.

Amex, Diners, MasterCard and Visa accepted.

El Dorada Petit ★★★★

C. Dolors Monserda, 51 (Located about 4 k northwest of Pl. Catalunya in the area known as Sarria—it is best to take a taxi.) ☎ *204 51 53. Closed Sunday and the middle two weeks of August.* Undeniably this restaurant stands among the best in Barcelona, and most people place it at the top. The food is insistently *nueva cocina*, inventive and the most beautiful we have ever seen. Housed in a turn-of-the-century summer house with a lovely garden for summer dining, the decor is as elegant as the food. It is the prices that concern us, for they seem designed more to make the restaurant exclusive than to earn a fair profit. Reservations are required. *Amex, MasterCard and Visa accepted.*

Botafumeiro ★★★★

C. Mayor de Gracia, 81 (Mayor de Gracia is the continuation of Pas. de Gracia, after it crosses Diagonal. The restaurant is located 4 blocks further along the street.) ☎ *218 42 30. Closed Sunday night, Monday, Holy Week, and August.* The restaurant is named after the giant censor swung in the cathedral of Santiago de Compostela, for the owner is from Galacia. He has fish flown to Barcelona daily. Need we mention that this is the best pure seafood restaurant in the city, and some say the country? The decor is functional white and light wood, for this is a no-nonsense restaurant. Order *mariscos Botafumeiro*, a cascade of shellfish of every variety, and we think you will agree. Reservations are advised. *Amex, Diners, MasterCard and Visa accepted.*

Azulete ★★★

Via Augusta, 281 (Via Augusta is a large avenue 1 k west of Diagonal. The restaurant is in the same Sarria neighborhood as El Dorada Petit.) ☎ *203 59 43. Closed Saturday lunch, Sunday, holidays, Holy Week, the first two weeks of August and Christmas week.* A former conservatory serves as the dining room, decorated with trees and flowers around a fountain to create the most romantic dining place in Barcelona. The chef is a woman with a delicate touch and so inventive that the menu changes seasonally. This is not just a pretty place—the cooking can match the best in the city. And the prices, though high, are slightly lower than the competition. Reservations are strongly advised.

Amex, Diners, MasterCard and Visa accepted.

Via Venito   ★★★

C. Ganduxer, 10 (heading southwest along Diagonal, turn right at the second street past the traffic circle Pl. Francesc March). ☎ *200 72 44. Closed Saturday lunch, Sunday and the first three weeks in August.* Always ranking among the most beautiful Barcelona restaurants—with its Belle Époque decor—and standing with the best for the caliber of its food, Via Venito lately has begun charging prices that strike us as too high. Despite its name, the cuisine is Catalan of the *nueva cocina* sort. The dishes are elegant to the eye and sublime on the palate. Reservations are required.   *Amex, Diners, MasterCard and Visa accepted.*

La Dama   ★★★

Avinguda Diagonal, 423 (three blocks south of the intersection of Diagonal with P. de Gracia). Convenient to the boutiques of Passeig de Gracia, this is a most elegant restaurant, housed in an architectural statement —an art nouveau building that contributes to the experience. The food is first rate, getting better all the time, and *nueva* to the core. However, prices reach into the stratosphere.

Amex, Diners, MasterCard and Visa accepted.

La Odisea   ★★★

C. Copons, 7 (one block east of el Corte Inglés department store on Pl. Catalunya). ☎ *302 36 92. Closed Saturday lunch, Sunday, Holy Week and August.* Although less celebrated than a number of other Barcelona restaurants, we think this food merits inclusion with the best. Dark red walls make the decor more masculine than some of the prettier establishments, and the space is small. The chef is known more for taste and style than for inventiveness. Scrambled eggs with caviar, ravioli in cheese sauce, and liver salad with mushrooms and vinegar are exquisite. Unlike most of the other fine restaurants, this one can be walked to from the center of town. Reservations are required.

Amex, Diners and Visa accepted.

Agut d'Avignon   ★★

C. Trinitat, 3 (From the Rambla de Caputxins go north along C. Ferrán, bordering the Pl. Reial. One block after the plaza turn right onto C. d'Avinyo to find this restaurant a few steps later in a cul-de-sac on the right.) ☎ *302 60 34. Closed Holy Week, and Christmas week.* Dark wood, rush-caned chairs and white walls create a first impression of a mesón. A closer look at the venerable antiques shows the restaurant to be more elegant than that. Seating is on five small levels. The cuisine is more traditional Catalan than the *nueva cocina* so in vogue elsewhere. Mussels in garlic cream sauce are delectable; meat and game generally are combined with some fruit sauce. The food is good, although not at the outstanding level of some others, but a convenient Barri Gòtic location and comfortable surroundings make it worth consideration. Reservations are advised.

Amex, Diners, MasterCard and Visa accepted.

MODERATE ($20-$50)

Set Portes

Passeig Isabel II, 14 (in the port, two blocks left of the end of Via Laietana). ☎ *319 30 33.* Seven doors do indeed front the street, opening onto a large mirrored, marble-floored dining area. The specialty is seafood which is amazingly reasonable for the quality and quantity. Fish paella and the house version of zarzuela are excellent and bountiful enough to share. Note that this area is not safe at night, so commuting by taxi is recommended. Reservations are advised.

Amex, Diners, MasterCard and Visa accepted.

Senyor Parellada

C. Argenteria, 37 (the street leads northeast from Via Laietana, just north of the Pl. Jaume). ☎ *315 40 10. Closed Sunday, holidays and August.* The restaurant is dignified without being stuffy and serves well-prepared Catalan dishes at very fair prices—an excellent value all the way around. *Amex, Diners, MasterCard and Visa accepted.*

Brasserie Flo

C. Jonqueres, 10 (C. Jonqueres heads southwest off Via Laietana west of the cathedral. The restaurant is located a block south of the back of the el Corte Inglés department store beside Pl. Catalunya.) ☎ *319 31 02.* Opened by a group of expatriate French who missed home-cooking, this is a most authentic brasserie. It is installed in an old warehouse that somehow feels French. Pâtés and the choucroute are the real thing. Reservations are advised.

Amex, Diners, MasterCard and Visa accepted.

La Caracoles

P. Escudellers, 14 (the street runs east from the Pl. Reial at the end of Rambla Caputxins) ☎ *302 31 85.* This venerable Barcelona institution is much favored by tourists, so musicians come with the meal. Despite its popularity, the rustic surroundings are relaxed and it serves hearty Catalan food prepared well. Of course, try the snails (caracoles), but fried fish, mussels and paella are tasty too. No reservations are taken, and there may be long waits.

Amex, Diners, MasterCard and Visa accepted.

Font del Gat

P. Santa Madrona (on Montjuïc between the Fundacio Miró and the Museu Arqueológic). ☎ *424 02 24. Closed Monday, except for holidays.* This is the place for lunch while visiting Montjuïc. The restaurant is nicely styled inside, but dining on the terrace is the most pleasant. Even if the food is ordinary, the views are special.

INEXPENSIVE (UNDER $20)

Egipte   ★
C. Jerusalem, 12 (directly behind the Boquería market off Rambla Sant Josep). ☎ 317 74 80. Closed Sunday. No frills here, just good food of the homey variety. The reason for the Egyptian motif is anyone's guess. There are crowds at lunch, but also numerous low-priced special menus. Prices are very fair, and no reservations are taken.

No credit cards.

Agut   ★
C. Gignas, 16 (follow C. Ciutat from the north side of the Ajundament in Pl. Jaume in the Barri Gótic to C. Ample, just before reaching the port. Jag left then right.) ☎ 315 17 09. Closed Sunday evening, Monday, and the month of July. This one is almost too good to be true. It offers fantastic value for food that is genuinely well prepared—and has done so for 75 years. It looks as it should, incorporating a kind of fifties decor in a place that is older. Of course nothing is perfect. The neighborhood should be walked with caution at night.

No reservations or credit cards.

Pitarra
C. d'Avinyò, 56 (d'Avinyó runs east from C. Ferrán halfway between the Rambla Caputxins and the Pl. Jaume in the Barri Gótic). ☎ 301 16 47. Closed Sunday. While the food is at least acceptable, what makes this place special is the variety of inexpensive special menus.

Raim D'or Can Maxim
C. Bonsucces, 8 (Bonsucces goes south from the west end of Rambla Etudis). ☎ 302 02 34. Closed Sunday. This place is always crowded because the food is good and the prices low. The gazpacho is tasty, although only served at lunchtime.

Cafe de l'Academie
C. Lledo, 1 (east of the north side of the Ajuntamient off the Pl. Jaume in the Barri Gótic). ☎ 315 00 26. Open for breakfast and lunch only. Come here for delicious sandwiches (of the French style with small amounts of meat), with a background of recorded classical music.

McDonald's
C. Ferrán, 1-3 (on the Rambla de Caputxins). The real thing.

SHOPPING

Barcelona is the best shopping city in Spain—for selection, trendiness and lovely avenues made for walking. That is not to say everyone will buy, for it is not—with some exceptions—a city of bargains. What it is is a city well designed for the activity. Store hours generally run from Mon.-Fri. from 9am to 1:30 p.m. and from 4 or 5-8 p.m. Many stores open Saturday for the morning hours, but do not reopen in the afternoon. Stores are closed on Sun.

Fine **boutiques** for clothing, leather, jewelry, and shoes, many on the cutting edge, are concentrated in an area bordered by P. de Gracia on the east, Rambla de Catalunya a block south, Pl. Catalunya to the north and Diagonal 9 blocks west. It is perfectly possible to cover the whole area in a leisurely late afternoon and early evening.

The area begins with a branch of **El Corte Inglés** department store, for moderate-priced clothing, at the Pl. Catalunya. **Loewe's** extravagant leather is at P. de Gracia, 35. At 53-55 a mall, called **Boulevard Rosa**, in the street floor of the building contains over 100 fine boutiques. Also at 55 is **Centre Permanent D'Artesana**, displaying works by fine artisans from around Catalunya. **Rodier** is at 66, **Fiorucci** at 76. **Adolfo Domíngues**, the designer who gave Don Johnson his look on *Miami Vice*, has a shop at 89, with clothes for women as well. Turn west on C. Mallorca for some special stores. At the corner of Rambla de Catalunya, at 100, is **Groc**, an outstanding designer for men. Across the street at C. Mallorca 242 stands **José Tomas**, another fine men's designer. Further along C. Mallorca is an extraordinary showplace of furniture design. **B.D. Ediciones de Diseno**, at 291, is run by architects who sell museum quality designs by the greats, living and deceased, such as chairs and furniture fittings by Gaudí. The building that houses the store is a monument too, designed by the *modernista* architect **Domènech i Montaner**. At number 258 on C. Corsega, which is the last street along Passeig de Gracia going south before Diagonal, is a shop named **Urbana** which stocks fixtures reclaimed and restored from *modernista* buildings. It displays everything from light fixtures to mantels, armoirs and door knobs, each an artwork.

For **trimmings and costume jewelry** at great prices, walk from the Rambla Sant Josep to the Pl. Jaume along C. Boquería, which changes its name to C. Call. This is the wholesale trimmings and accessories area with store after store, though only a few will sell to the retail buyer.

There are two areas for **antiques**. One is in the Barri Gótic in the area just south of the cathedral along the tiny streets of C. Banys Nous and C. del la Palla. Art Nouveau jewelry can be surprisingly affordable in some of these tiny shops. For fine **lace**, try **L'Arca de l'Avia** at Banys Nous, 20. Behind the cathedral on C. Franeria is **Grafiques el Tinell**, for **prints** from old woodblocks and etchings, some handcolored. On Baixada de la Libreteria, 2, the next street to the east, is **Papirum** which sells antique and handcolored **paper** and end-papers.

The second antique area is just west of the Barri Gótic on C. Montcada. From the Pl. Jaume in the heart of the Barri Gótic go north through the Pl. Angel to follow C. Princesa. The fourth right is C. Montcada, with the **Picasso Museum** selling a large selection of **prints**, **shirts**, etc., on the corner. For four short blocks antiques shops line both sides of the street going south. Also on this street is a fine shop for **handcrafts** called **1741** at number 2, and an outlet of **Fondacion Maeght**, the great French **art gallery**, at 25. Lastly, an **antiques market** is held in the square in front of the cathedral on Thurs. from about 10 a.m. until 2 p.m., or so.

Espadrilles, the traditional rope-soled canvas shoes of Catalonia, can be purchased at **La Manual Lapargalera** on C. d'Aviryo, just after it turns east from C. Ferrán on the way to the Pl. Jaume in the Barri Gótic.

Yes, there is a large **flea market** in Barcelona. It consists of more junk than jewels, but you never know. It is called **Els Encants**, and takes place in the Pl. de les Glories Catalanes which is on Gran Via Corts Catalanes about 15 blocks north and one block west of the Pl. Catalunya. The red line 1 metro from Pl. Catalunya toward Santa Coloma stops at the Glories station right at the market. Markets take place Mon., Wed., Fri. and Sat. beginning at dawn.

DIRECTORY

INFORMATION • There are several convenient branches of the Office of Tourism. All provide a map and a complete list of Barcelona hotels. One office is located at the airport, another on Gran Via del Corts Catalanes, 658 (one block west and two north of Pl. Catalunya), another at Pl. Porta de la Pau (where the Ramblas ends at the port) The telephone numbers are: ☎ 325 58 29, 301 74 43, 310 37 16, respectively. All are open Mon.-Fri. 9 a.m. to 7 p.m. and on Sat. from 9 a.m. to 2 p.m. The Barcelona Tourism Board at 35 P. de Gracia (☎ 215 44 77) is especially helpful with information about sights.

CITY TOURS • Both Julià Tours at Ronda Universitat, 5 (☎ 317 64 54) and Pullmantur at Gran Via, 635 (☎ 318 02 41) offer half-day tours of Barcelona for about 4000 ptas.

U.S. CONSULATE • Via Laietana, 33 (☎ 319 95 50).

CANADIAN CONSULATE • Via Augusta, 125 (☎ 209 06 34).

AMERICAN EXPRESS • Av. Roselló, 257 (☎ 217 00 70).

TRAINS AND BUSES • Estació Central De Sants is located at Pl. Països Catalanes, in the southwest (☎ 490 02 02). Lines red 1 and green 3 of the metro both stop at Sants-Estacio. The downtown RENFE office is at P. de Gracia, 13 (☎ 322 41 42).

Barcelona is served by five different bus companies, with as many terminals. There is no system to the separation of routes. Check with the Office of Tourism, or ☎ 245 25 28.

POST OFFICE AND TELEPHONES • The main post office is at the end of Via Laietana near the port at Pl. d'Antoni Lopez (☎ 318 38 31). Telephones are available at C. de Fontanella, 4, at the east end of el Corte Inglés by the Pl. Catalunya.

POLICE • The Centro de Atencion Juridico Polcial (☎ 317 70 20) where English is spoken is at C. de la Ramblas, 43, which runs west from Rambla Caputxins.

AIRPORT • International and domestic flights all arrive at El Prat de Llobregat Airport, 14 k south of the city (☎ 401 31 31). TWA and Iberia both fly directly to the U.S. A taxi will cost about 2000 ptas. and take half an hour. Trains leave to and from the airport every 30 minutes for a 15-minute trip that costs 220 ptas. The Barcelona terminus is Esatació Central De Sants, well-connected by metro. An Iberia shuttle bus also leaves from there every hour or so.

EXCURSIONS

The closest good beach is at **Sitges**. See the description under **Costa Dorada ★** in this chapter. Charming beaches also lie north about 100 k along the **Costa Brava ★★**, also described in this chapter. Extensive Roman ruins are found at **Tarragona ★** and **Empüries ★**, while **Santes Creus ★** and **Poblet ★★** are two extraordinary medieval monasteries. Each is described under its own heading below.

For **Sitges** *and the* **Costa Dorada** *head southwest along Grand Via de Corts Catalanes to the freeway toward the airport. Past the airport the road becomes the coastal C-246 which reaches Sitges in 43 k. The fastest route to* **Tarragona**, **Santes Creus** *and* **Poblet** *is to go to the port, head south on Pas. de Colom, which becomes Pas. de Josep Carner and lets onto A-7 toward Tarragona after 84 k. For Poblet and Santes Creus, after 49 k change to A-2 toward Llerida. At exit 11, Vila-Rodona, leave the highway for Santes Creus. For Poblet leave the highway at exit 9, Monblanco, and take N-240 toward Llerida for 6 k. For the* **Costa Brava** *and* **Empüries** *take Gran Via de Corts Catalanes northeast to Pl. de les Glories Catalanes where Av. Meridiana heads north toward the Autopista, but take N-II north toward Girona instead. For the Costa Brava take exit 9 at Videres and aim for the coast and Sant Feliu de Guixols along C-253 and C-250. For Empüries continue past Girona to exit 5 at Viladamat, then 16 k toward the coast to L'Escala with Empüries on its outskirts.*

Trains to **Sitges** *leave frequently from Estació De Sants. The trip takes less than an hour and costs about 350 ptas., round trip.* **Tarragona** *is served very frequently by train for an hour and a half trip costing 450 ptas.* **Poblet** *is reached by train to Llerida for a trip of 3-plus hours and a cost of 850 ptas, then by bus for an hour.* **Santa Creus** *is further along that same bus route. Two buses per day travel the two-and-a-half-hour trip to* **Empüries** *for about 1000 ptas. They are operated by Sarfa (☎ 318 94 34), located at Pl. Duc de Medinacelli, 4, in the port area.*

COSTA DEL AZAHAR ★★

Perfumed by acres of orange groves, the resorts of the Costa del Azahar begin where the Costa Dorada ends, and stretch south past Valencia to the Cabo de la Nao, a distance of 260 k. The resorts are a mixed lot—some charming, some overdeveloped—but the sand beaches are the finest in Spain. We describe the coast beginning at Benicarlo, below where the Costa Dorada ends, and work our way south past Valencia. N-340 follows the coast.

BENICARLÓ

Population: 16,587
Area code: 964; zip code: 12580

Benicarló is on N-340, 28 k south of San Carles de la Rápita.

Once attractive, the town is today overbuilt, although it does offer a parador, a small port and decent beaches.

WHERE TO STAY

Parador Costa del Azahar　　　　　　　　　　　1st-class ★★
Av. del Papa Luna, 5. Rooms: 108. ☎ *47 01 00; FAX 47 09 34.* Hotel gardens run down to the sea to produce a feeling of peaceful quiet. The hotel itself is modern and of no special distinction. Tennis and a pool are provided, for a price that just passes the expensive.

PEÑISCOLA ★★★

Population: 3,077
Area code: 964; zip code: 12598

South of Benicarlo 7 k along the scenic unnumbered coastal road.

On a small peninsula (which gives the town its name) Peñiscola snuggles tiny whitewashed houses against a solemn castle on a hill. Cars are not allowed in the narrow twisting streets. The village is charming, and the **castle**, which was the home of the antipope Luna during his exile in the 15th century, is worth a look. What is less charming is the stretch of high-rises that line the beach on either side of the peninsula. However, finer, whiter sand beaches do not exist elsewhere in Europe and they run for miles.

WHERE TO STAY

EXPENSIVE ($100-$200)

Hostería del Mar　　　　　　　　　　　　　　1st-class ★★★
Carretera de Benicarlo (on the road to Benicarlo, 1 k north of the peninsula). Rooms: 85. ☎ *48 06 00; FAX 48 13 63; Telex 65750.* This hotel is affiliated with the national paradors and outdoes most of the modern ones in style. White wall and dark wood lend a Castilian look, but most dramatic are the views over the sea and peninsula. Tennis is available.

INEXPENSIVE (UNDER $50)

Marina   **4th-class ★**

Av. José Antonio, 42. Rooms: 19. ☎ 48 08 90. Open from April-October. No views, but restful, comfortable rooms should satisfy most people, and the prices should please.

ALCOCÉBER ★★

Population: 2,703
Area code: 964; zip code: 12579

From Peñiscola CS-500 leads away from the coast to N-340. After 16 k on N-340 a small road leads to the beach.

Don't tell anyone about this place, for it has yet to be fully discovered. The town remains fairly quiet and two fine crescent beaches still have empty spots.

WHERE TO STAY

MODERATE ($50-$99)

Aparthotel Jeremías-Romana   **3rd-class ★★**

1.5 k south on the beach. Rooms: 39. ☎ 41 44 11; FAX 41 24 11. The moderate price buys not a bedroom, but a suite, which is all this hotel consists of. The aura is calm, ocean views are provided, and the beach is super. Tennis is available.

INEXPENSIVE (UNDER $50)

Jeremías   **4th-class ★**

1 k south on the beach. Rooms: 38. ☎ 41 44 37; FAX 41 24 44. Open from March to the end of October. Just as quiet, and in as lovely a spot by the beach as the Jeremías-Romana, this hotel offers comfortable rooms at very affordable prices. Tennis is available.

BENICASIM ★

Population: 4,705
Area code: 964; zip code: 12560

From Alcocéber return to N-340 going south for 32 k.

Developers came in force decades ago, attracted by the spectacular setting of wide beaches with mountains seeming to rising just above them. The mountains and beaches remain, enlivened today by crowds. Because development of this area began in the seventies, hotels in Benicasim are somewhat dated-looking but charge seventies prices to make accommodations a bargain today.

WHERE TO STAY

MODERATE ($50-$99)

Orange   2nd-class ★ ★

Gran Avenida. Rooms: 415. ☎ *39 44 00; FAX 30 15 41. Telex 65626. Open April through October.* Looking like an overblown chalet, this huge hotel, surrounded by a lovely garden, is only 100 yards from the sea. It lacks tasteful decor but makes up for it with low prices for the rooms. Ask for one with a sea view. Tennis is available, along with most other facilities.

Voramar   2nd-class ★ ★

Passeo Pilar Coloma, 1. Rooms: 55. ☎ *30 01 50; FAX 30 05 26. Open April through September.* Though lacking the garden, this hotel otherwise is more attractive than the Hotel Orange. Bedrooms overlooking the sea have ample balconies. The hotel is on the beach and offers tennis courts.

SAGUNTO ★

Population: 52,759
Area code: 96; zip code: 46500

Sagunto is 65 k from Benicasim by N-340.

Known as *Seguntum* in Roman times, the Carthagenian siege of this town in 218 B.C. precipitated the Second Punic War. After the Romans won, they rebuilt the town. Although Sagunto has no beach, it has ruins enough to repay a visit of an hour or two.

Climb the hill to the Moorish **alcazaba** with excavations of Roman remains inside. On the way is an **amphitheater** sufficiently restored to be used for festivals. The ruins are a mix of Roman, Visigothic and Moorish, and fun to sort through. (Open Tues.-Sat. 10 a.m. to 2 p.m. and 4-6pm; open Sun. 10 a.m. to 2pm; closed Mon.; admission: 200 ptas.)

VALENCIA

See the description below under a separate heading.

From Sagunto the speedy toll A-7 whisks to Valencia in 25 k.

EL SALER ★

Area code: 96; zip code: 46012.

From Valencia take the autopista V-15 for 12 k south, then the coast road for 2k .

Despite proximity to Valencia and a dramatic location on a sandbank with sea on one side and a huge fresh-water lagoon on the other, el Saler has so far escaped overdevelopement. Two expensive hotels are here, one for the golf enthusiast.

WHERE TO STAY

EXPENSIVE ($100-$200)

Sidi Saler   1st-class ★ ★
> *On the beach 3 k southeast of town. Rooms: 272.* ☎ *161 04 11; FAX 161 08 38; Telex 64208.* This is a modern super-luxury resort that charges expensive, but fair prices, considering all the style and services—including an indoor pool as well as an outdoor one, and tennis too.

Parador de el Saler   1st-class ★ ★ ★
> *Near the beach 7k. south of town. Rooms: 58.* ☎ *161 11 86; FAX 162 70 16; Telex 610 69.* The raison d'etre for this modern parador is the golf course it sits amid. A pine forest runs beside it and beach is near, so activities are not restricted to golfing.

GANDÍA

Population: 52,646
Area code: 96; zip code: 46700

From el Saler the scenic coastal road joins N-332 in 24 k at **Cullera***, with a beach development. 26 k further is Gandía.*

Gandía's claim to fame is that it was the duchy of the Borja family. One Borja became a pope (Alexander VI), another was his notorious son, known to us through the Italians as Caesare Borgia, still another was the Pope's equally notorious daughter, Lucretia. All were born, not in Gandía but in Jativa, 20 k inland, except for the great-grandson of Pope Alexander VI, Francisco Borja. He reversed the family reputation by becoming the vicar-general of the Jesuit order, and leading a saintly life for which he was canonized. He was born in the **Palacio del Santo Duque** in Gandía, which can be toured. (Open daily for guided tours at 10am, 11 a.m., noon, 5 p.m., 6 p.m. and 7 p.m.; in winter at 11 a.m., noon, 4:30 p.m. and 5:30 p.m.; admission: 100 ptas.) Six k east of Gandía is its port with a beach development running north.

WHERE TO STAY

EXPENSIVE ($100-$200)

Bayren I   1st-class ★ ★
> *Passeig Maritim Neptu, 62 (at the beginning of the beach). Rooms: 164.* ☎ *284 03 00; FAX 284 06 53; Telex 61549.* The outstanding feature of this hotel is its grand terrace with splendid sea views. Accommodations are deluxe, but of no great style.

Gandía is 36 k from Cape Nao, the start of the Costa Blanca, described below.

COSTA BLANCA ★

The Costa Blanca is endowed with fine beaches and a perfect climate that is virtually rainless, indeed cloudless. Beginning in the 1960s, these attractions drew developers the way a dying animal lures vultures. Natural beauty that once thrilled now is covered in concrete, but the fine beaches remain, along with the weather, and here and there a pocket of serenity so far has escaped ruin. Water and air along this coast remain warm enough through October for sunning and bathing. We describe the better resorts starting in the north at Denia on Cape Nao and running southwest to Capo de Palos, a coastline of 250 k. The most charming resorts lie at the start of this route, on Cape Nao, a craggy promontory that dives into the sea, broken here and there by coves and beaches. Cape Nao stands only 135 k west of the island of Ibiza, and ferries run to and from Denia. The most extensive beaches, on the other hand, are at the southern end of the coast.

*From **Valencia** the fast toll A-7 speeds south to Alicante. At exit 62 backtrack on N-332 for 3 kilometers to Onda, from which a road heads east to the coast for 9 kilometers. From the eastern end of the **Costa del Sol** at **Almeria** N-340 winds 139 kilometers to Vera where 11 kilometers toward Garrucha on the coast brings a scenic coastal road that reaches Agulas in the north in 38 kilometers. Follow the description of the Costa Blanca in reverse. From **Madrid** the fastest route is to go to Valencia and follow the directions above.*

DENIA

Population: 22,162
Area code: 96; zip code: 03700

Denia has seen history from the Iberians on. In fact its name derives from Roman Dianium, for the goddess Diana. Nothing of this past remains on view, though there are ruins of a 13th-century medieval castle on the hill above town. This is very much a family resort, and its long pleasant beaches are highly developed. Ferries to Ibiza (☎ 578 42 00) and Formentera (☎ 578 53 62) leave the port. Afternoon hydrofoils reach Ibiza in an hour and a half (about $50), while evening ferries take five hours (about $40).

WHERE TO STAY

MODERATE ($50-$99)

Rosa   **3rd-class ★**

On the road to Las Marinas, 2 k northeast of town. Rooms: 30. ☎ *578 15 73; FAX 578 15 73. Closed Dec. and Jan.* This peaceful little place is not far from a beach, and has a terrace, swimming pool and tennis court, all for a modest price.

JÁVEA ★

Population: 10,964
Area code: 96; zip code: 03730

The steep and winding, but scenic, coast road reaches Jávea in 10 k.

The old town huddles around a 16th-century fortified church inside ramparts and Moorish gates, but the beach is a modern development. Wonderous grottos line the coast around Jávea and a safari park is located at Vergel a few k inland (open 10 a.m.-7:30 p.m. in summer, until 6 p.m. in winter). Six k east stands Cape San Antonio with fine views to Ibiza on a clear day. A scenic coast road runs for 12 k southeast to Cape Nao, again with spectacular views of sea and promontory.

WHERE TO STAY

EXPENSIVE ($100-$200)

Parador Costa Blanca   **1st-class ★★**

On the beach 4 k southeast of town). Rooms: 65. ☎ *579 02 00; FAX 579 03 08.* Paradors do find the best locations. This one is surrounded by a garden amidst a palm grove with beach to the north and south. The hotel itself is modern and unexceptional.

MORAIRA ★★

Area code: 96; zip code: 03724

No good road goes directly to Moraira from Jávea. Return to N-332 and go south for 6 k, then follow signs east for Moraira in 9 k.

Moraira is so secluded the developers haven't found it. Hurry. A promontory to the south forms a sheltered cove, and the village gathers around an old watchtower above a little harbor.

WHERE TO STAY
MODERATE ($50-$99)

Moradix   **3rd-class ★**

1.5 k west of town. Rooms: 30. ☎ *574 40 56 FAX 574 45 25. Open from Mar.-Oct.* This is a secluded, pleasant place providing comfortable rooms, views of the sea and appealingly low prices.

WHERE TO EAT

El Girasol   **★★★**

1.5 k on the road to Calpe. ☎ *574 43 73. Closed Mon. off season, and from Jan. through Feb.* In this elegantly restored villa are served the best meals along the Costa Blanca. Fish are the stars, served with a slightly French touch—expensive, but memorable.

Amex, Visa, Diners and MasterCard accepted.

CALPE ★★

Population: 8,000
Area code: 96; zip code: 03710

Return from Moraira to N-332 for the 12 k drive south to Calpe.

The Peñón de Ifach, a miniature version of Gibraltar, rises from the sea, connected to the coast by a spit of land lined by sand beaches on both sides. So far so good. But the beaches are divided by a solid concrete row of highrises of no appeal. Still, Calpe has that scenic rock, and is not as crowded as most other resorts.

WHERE TO STAY
MODERATE ($50-$99)

Venta La Chata   **3rd-class ★**

On the road toward N-332, 4.5 k north of town. Rooms: 17. ☎ *583 03 08. Closed from the middle of Nov.-the middle of Dec.* This is a charming little place that charges unusually low rates—the perfect antidote to the modern highrises. Accommodations are rustic, but atmospheric, and terraced gardens looking to the sea are a lovely touch. Further, the hotel restaurant provides tasty meals at inexpensive prices.

ALTEA ★

Population: 11,108
Area code: 96; zip code: 03590

A gorgeous 11 k stretch of N-332 connects Calpe to Altea.

This is a romantic little fishing village of whitewashed houses surrounding a church with a blue-tiled dome. On every side except the sea, mountains shelter its tiny cove. But the developers have arrived.

WHERE TO STAY

MODERATE ($50-$99)

Altaya 3rd-class

Calle Generalisimo, 115 (in the port). Rooms: 24. ☎ *584 08 00. Closed Jan. and Feb.* The hotel is situated in the town proper, which provides a sense of being in Spain, not offered by the expensive highrises. Rooms are fairly comfortable and their price barely passes the moderate.

WHERE TO EAT

Monte Molar ★★

Take N-332 northeast for 2.5 K and a left for 1 k. ☎ *584 15 81. Closed Wed. in winter, and from the middle of Jan. through the middle of Mar.* The restaurant is absolutely gorgeous and elegant, with a pretty terrace overlooking the sea. The food is expensive and memorable. For seafood, try the timbale of fish with asparagus; for meat, the magret of duck with mushrooms; and for fun, the snails with rice. Every dish is perfect. Reservations are strongly advised.

Amex, Diners, MasterCard and Visa accepted.

BENIDORM

Population: 25,544
Area code: 96; zip code: 03500

A pretty stretch of N-332 leads to Benidorm in 10 k, though it lies 2 k off the highway.

Picture a rocky promontory with a village of whitewashed houses along twisting alleys, add two crescent white sand beaches on either side. Now picture characterless highrise hotels all around so that the village is hidden, and add enough beds—all full during the summer—for a third of a million package-tour vacationers. This is Benidorm. One must stay on the beach, near the old town, to see what was once attractive about Benidorm, and this guides our recommendations.

The **Casino Costa Blanca** (☎ 89 07 00) with gambling is on N-332, 1.5 k south of town.

WHERE TO STAY

EXPENSIVE ($100-$200)

Cimbel 1st-class

Av. de Europa, 1 (on the Playa de Levant). Rooms: 144. ☎ *585 21 00; FAX 586 06 61; Telex 68275.* This large modern hotel is similar to others, except it is on the beach and close to the old town. A front room is essential.

MODERATE ($50-$99)

Bilbaíno 3rd-class ★ ★

Av. Virgen del Sufragio, 1 (on the Playa de Levant, where it begins at the Promentorio del Castillo). Rooms: 38. ☎ *585 08 04 FAX 585 08 05. Open Mar.-Nov.* For our money this is the best location in town. Facing the sea, one sees only beach and the character of the village on the promontory. Inexpensive meals are also served.

PLAYA DE SAN JUAN ★

Population: 10,522
Area code: 96; zip code: 0354

N-332 going west from Benidorm arrives at Alicante in 45 k, where a 7 k backtrack along the coast reaches Playa de San Juan.

The fine sand and its extent makes this beach so popular. Development is still expanding, but it is hard to fill such a long beach. Swelled by arrivals from Madrid, however, the Spanish manage to cover most of it themselves during August. There is nothing of scenic interest except the sea, but an extensive nightlife exists. The sun and water make this an attractive alternative to staying in Alicante, for those who wish to see the sights of that city.

WHERE TO STAY

EXPENSIVE ($100-$200)

Sidi San Juan 1st-class ★ ★ ★

It is its own compound without a street address. Rooms: 176. ☎ *516 13 00; FAX 516 33 46; Telex 66263.* This deluxe modern compound on a private beach is surrounded by wonderful gardens. The hotel is deluxe in every way and, all things considered, well worth its high price for the beauty, seclusion and comfort.

MODERATE ($50-$99)

Almirante Pocardy 2nd-class ★

Av. de Niza, 38. Rooms: 64. ☎ *565 01 12; FAX 565 71 69.* This is the best value on the beach. This hotel is peaceful, offers sea views, a pool and tennis, along with comfortable rooms.

ALICANTE ★

Population: 251,387
Area code: 96; zip code: 03000

From the direction of Benidorm Mount Benacantil is soon passed, with parking just below it on the Passeo de Gomiz along the beach before the port. If full, continue along the Esplanada de España for additional parking.

Alicante is the major city of the Costa Blanca. Coincidentally, given its location on the "White Coast," the city name is apt, for it derives (with a prefaced Arabic "Al") from its Roman name—Lucentum, "Place of Light." People visit Alicante for the activity of a city and for castle ruins high on a hill, not for its beaches. A couple of fine churches add to the appeal.

The interesting sights lie at the bottom of, and on, Mount Benacantil, east of the port. Walk the lovely palm-lined Esplanade do España in the direction of the steep hill, turning left at its end, where the sea wall begins on the right. Two short blocks lead to the **Ayuntamiento** in golden stone with twin towers. The style is Churrigueresque, from the middle of the 18th century. Entry is permitted to see a rococo chapel and ornate hall. (Open daily 9 a.m. to 3pm; admission: free.) A short block north is **San Nicolás de Bari**, a serene neo-classical cathedral with a lovely cupola. Go west for one long block on Calle Mayor, the street of the Ayuntamiento, to the church of **Santa María**. The facade is a wedding cake of swirling baroque decoration. Continue along the sea side of the church, down steps, to an elevator that climbs Mount Benacantil to **Castillo de Santa Bárbara ★**. The castle is an accretion from the 13th-16th centuries, built on much older foundations. It has drawbridges, a moat and dungeon—as any respectable castle should—and splendid views. (Open Sun.-Fri. 9 a.m.-9 p.m.; in winter open Sun.-Fri. 10 a.m. to 1 p.m. and 5-8pm; open Sat. 10 a.m. to 1pm; closed Mon., in winter. Admission: 50 ptas.)

WHERE TO STAY

Staying at the beach in Playa de San Juan (discussed above), 7 k east, is an option to rooming in the city, though Alicante can be a fine host too.

EXPENSIVE ($100-$200)

Residencia Palas   2nd-class ★

Pl. Ayuntamiento, 6. Rooms: 53. ☎ *520 66 90.* The choice between this hotel and its sister (below) is between larger bedrooms and more attractive public spaces. The public areas in the Residencia are nothing to speak of, but the bedrooms are large and comfortable. Location on the plaza is congenial, and prices of both Palas hotels barely enter expensive territory, so both are values.

Palas   2nd-class ★

C. Cervantes, 5 (one short block east of the Pl. Ayuntamiento and a short block toward the sea). Rooms: 49. ☎ *520 93 10.* Chandeliers and antiques lend an old-world aura to the public spaces. Rooms are attractive, in a regency style, though not as large and relaxing as at its sister hotel.

WHERE TO EAT

For inexpensive dining wander the old town at the foot of Mount Benacantil. For superb food, try the first recommendation below.

EXPENSIVE ($50+)

Delfin ★★

Expanada de España, 12. ☎ *521 49 11.* A lovely terrace looks over
the port and palms of the esplanade. The upstairs dining room is
bright and elegant. Cuisine is *nueva* with a distinctly French touch,
and comprises both seafood and meat. Every dish is delicate, sophisticated and special. Reservations are strongly advised.

Amex, Diners, MasterCard and Visa accepted.

MODERATE ($20-$50)

Rincón Castellano ★

*Calle Manero Molla, 12 (two blocks inland from the center of the
Explanada España).* ☎ *521 90 02. Closed Thurs.* Nothing pretentious, just traditional red-checkered tablecloths that promote a
friendly atmosphere. Given the name, naturally the cooking is Castilian, including copious, tasty roast lamb. Prices are reasonable, and can
be kept at an inexpensive level by careful selection. No reservations are
accepted. **Amex, Diners, MasterCard and Visa accepted.**

SANTA POLA ★

Population: 12,022
Area code: 96; zip code: 03130

*From Alicante follow the water south and signs for the
airport. A few k outside of the city, take N-332 along the
coast. Exit 20 k from the city, as signs direct, for a 1 k trip to
Santa Pola on the coast.*

Fine sand beaches lined by pine trees, call out for bodies. People
answer the call both for the beaches and the fish restaurants along
the harbor. The offshore island of Tabarca is regularly served by ferries for it offers marvelous sand.

WHERE TO STAY

MODERATE ($50-$99)

Polamar 2nd-class ★

Playa de Levant, 6. Rooms: 76. ☎ *541 32 00; FAX 541 31 83.* Comfortable and fairly priced, this hotel offers views and a terrace.

GUARDAMAR DEL SEGURA ★

Population: 5,708
Area code: 96; zip code: 03140

N-332 reaches Guardamar in 30 k.

Guardamar seems to have infinite sand beaches, stretching both north and south of the town. That is all there is, but if beach is the priority, here it is in spades.

WHERE TO STAY

MODERATE ($50-$99)

Guardamar   **3rd-class** ★

Av. Puerto Rico, 11. Rooms: 52. ☎ *572 96 50; FAX 572 95 30.* Our choice for the views and the comfortable rooms, but the pool seems a gilding of the lily in this beach-town.

LA MANGA DEL MAR MENOR ★

Area code: 968; zip code: 30370.

From Guardamar take N-332 south for 59 k to El Algar, then the coast road toward Cabo de Palos for 17 k.

A 20-k-long sandbar forms a huge lagoon called the Mar Menor (Small Sea) that is calm for water skiing. A resort lines the sandbar, though some of its modern buildings have style.

WHERE TO STAY

EXPENSIVE ($100-$200)

Sol Galua   **2nd-class** ★

Hacienda Dos Mares and Grand Via. Rooms: 177. ☎ *56 32 00; FAX 56 32 54; Telex 67119.* This comfortable modern hotel sits on a promontory with spectacular views over both lagoon and sea. Prices are very fair for its class.

COSTA BRAVA ★ ★

Potentially, the "Wild Coast" is Spain's most scenic. Overbuilding since its discovery in the 1960s, however, has spoiled much of it and summer crowds pose problems, yet parts still retain a stunning beauty. Officially the Costa Brava begins at Lloret de Mar, about 60 k north of Barcelona, and continues north for 130 k of cliffs, secreted coves and resorts all the way to the French border. What makes this coast special is that geography produced small inlets that make its resorts intimate rather than sprawling miles of beach. Finding accommodations in August without reservations is practically impossible, although September should prove relatively easy—and the water remains warm. May and even June see some vacant rooms. Winter, although beautiful, is chilly and few hotels open. We trace a route that begins in the south at Lloret and ends at the French border.

From Barcelona take N-7 north toward Girona. Leave the highway at Videres (exit 9) and aim for the coast and Sant Feliu de Guixols along C-253 and C-250. Lloret de Mar is south from Sant Feliu along 49 k of scenic, but winding, coast road.

LLORET DE MAR

Population : 10,480
Area code: 972; zip code: 17310

There is nothing quaint about Lloret. It is serious enough about being a resort to bloat by ten times in August. People come for the beach, which is pleasant and clean, and for the crowds. Lloret is not characteristic of the rest of the coast.

WHERE TO STAY

If rooms are available, Lloret offers some good values.

MODERATE ($50-$99)

Excelsior   **2nd-class ★**
P. Mossen J. Verdaguer, 16 (directly behind the beach promenade, by the gardens). Rooms: 45. ☎ *36 41 37; FAX 37 16 54; Telex 97061. Open Apr.-Oct.* This well-run hotel provides views over gardens to the sea from front room. The price is reasonable.

Marsol   **2nd-class ★**
P. Mossens J. Verdaguer, 7 (directly behind the beach promenade, by the gardens). Rooms: 87. ☎ *36 57 50; Telex 57173. Open Mar.-Oct.* A fine location, a pool, air-conditioning, and reasonable rates, all make this hotel worth considering.

At Platja de Fanals, 2k. south of town:

Surf Mar   **2nd-class ★**
Rooms: 216. ☎ *36 53 62; FAX 37 15 45. Open Apr. to the last week in Oct.* A magnificent expanse of lawn surrounds the hotel complex, which is otherwise distinguished mainly by its low prices. Here the beach is less crowded than in town.

TOSSA DE MAR ★★

Population: 2,969
Area code: 972; zip code: 17320

The corniche road north from Lloret to Tossa and beyond to Sant Feliu de Guixols offers an amazing variety of scenery, from cliff-top views over the ocean to forests and coves. Tossa is 12 k north of Lloret.

Tossa is fortunate in its site and manages to retain character amidst numerous vacationers. The town surrounds a horseshoe bay in which a nice beach nestles, with a cape and lighthouse at one end, along with remains of 12th-century town walls. Vila Vella, the old town, was designated a national monument for its charming alleys that run beside golden Renaissance walls, towers and fishermen's houses, huddled on the cape.

WHERE TO STAY

Tossa provides abundant accommodations in the inexpensive to moderate range. A few stand out.

MODERATE ($50-$99)

Mar Menuda   **2nd-class ★ ★**

Platja de Mar Menuda (at the beginning of the northern beach). Rooms: 40. ☎ *34 10 00; FAX 34 00 87. Closed Jan. through Feb.* This is a quiet, restful hotel with a lovely shade terrace over the sea. The prices push the limit of the moderate category, but are worth it. There is even a pool and a tennis court.

Áncora   **R2nd-class ★ ★**

Av. de la Palma, 4 (at the north end of the Platja Gran). Rooms: 58. ☎ *34 02 99.* A peaceful patio and quiet location make this hotel stand out. Low prices and a tennis court add to the attraction.

INEXPENSIVE (UNDER $50)

Sant March   **R3rd-class ★**

C. Nou, 9 (two blocks back from the Platja Gran). Rooms: 30. ☎ *34 00 78. Open May-Sept.* Situated on a quiet street, this hotel offers affordable comfort.

SANT FELIÚ DE GUÍXOLS ★

Population: 15,485
Area code: 972; zip code: 17220

The corniche road provides 23 k of magnificent scenery and hairpin curves on the way from Tossa to Sant Feliu.

Sant Feliú is attractively circled by hills sheltering its bay. It enjoys great popularity as a resort, popularity that comes more from its conviviality than its beach, which is nothing to speak of. Instead, everyone buses to the magnificent beach of S'Agaró 3 k to the north. The town **church** was remodelled inside in the 14th century, but its wonderful facade with a charming arcade remains intact.

WHERE TO STAY

Given its popularity, Sant Feliú is woefully short of hotels, which makes reservations imperative.

VERY EXPENSIVE ($200+)

In S'Agaró, 3 k north:

De la Gavina   **Deluxe ★ ★ ★**
Pl. de la Rosaleda. Rooms: 74. ☎ *32 11 00; FAX 32 15 73; Telex 57132.* This modern beach complex, surrounded by pines on a magnificent beach, was built to satisfy every desire for pampered quiet. All is deluxe, as befits the Relais and Châteaux chain, and the furniture is worth a fortune, which is about the magnitude of the bill.

EXPENSIVE ($100-$200)

Murla Park   **2nd-class ★ ★**
P. dels Guíxols, 22 (at the northern end of the platja). Rooms: 89. ☎ *32 04 50; FAX 32 00 78; Telex 57364. Closed from the middle of Oct. through the first week in Dec.* This hotel provides quiet and some nice views over the bay. It is efficiently run.

INEXPENSIVE (UNDER $50)

Rex I   **3rd-class ★**
Rambla del Portalet, 16 (two streets back from the platja). Rooms: 25. ☎ *82 18 09. Open June-Sept.* The Rex is well managed and provides more pleasant rooms than comparable establishments at this price.

WHERE TO EAT

Befitting its popularity, Sant Feliú supports two superior, though expensive, restaurants.

EXPENSIVE ($50+)

Eldorado Petit   **★★★**
Rambla Vidal, 23 (about halfway to the beach along the Rambla). ☎ *32 18 18. Closed Wed. from Oct.-Apr., and Nov.* This is the original establishment that went bigtime in Barcelona. The food is almost as beautiful and inventive here, but in more relaxed surroundings, and although the prices are expensive, they are not in the stratosphere of the Barcelona flagship.   *Amex, MasterCard and Visa accepted.*

Can Toni   **★★★**
C. Sant Martiria, 29 (well back from the beach, near the bus station). ☎ *32 10 26. Closed Mon. from Oct.-May.* Though lacking the grand style of Eldorado Petit, the chef here is truly talented and creative. For its informality and fine food, this is one of our favorite places.
     Amex, Diners, MasterCard and Visa accepted.

PALAFRUGEL ★

Population: 15,030
Area code: 972; zip code: 17200

From Sant Feliú C-255 winds north past S'Agaró and Palamos to Palafrugel in 23 k.

Although not on the beach, Palafrugel serves as the hub for several beach communities within a 5-k radius. One of these, **Calella**, offers a string of adorable beaches, another, **Llafranc**, has magnificent coastal views, but, **Tamariu**, surrounded by umbrella pines, is less crowded and the most lovely. Still another beach, **Aigua Blava**, lies in a secluded cove surrounded by azure sea, and has a parador. Lastly, **Begur** offers a medieval castle. A 50 minute walk from Calella brings the Castell i Jardins de Cap Roig, a fine botanical garden formed of a maze of flowers and tropical plants. (Open daily Mar.-Dec. 9 a.m. to 9pm; admission: 200 ptas.) Good ceramics are produced in **La Bisbal**, 12 k along C-255 on the way back toward Girona.

WHERE TO STAY

Each of the surrounding beach villages offers some fine accommodations, when they are not filled.

EXPENSIVE ($100-$200)

In Aigua Blava:

Aigua Blava   1st-class ★★★
Platja de Fornells. Rooms: 85. ☎ 62 20 58; FAX 62 21 12; Telex 56000. Closed from the middle of Feb. through Nov. This hotel wins easily over the parador nearby. The Aigua Blava is less expensive, superbly managed and situated in a formal garden overlooking the cove. It offers a pool and tennis, all for prices that are eminently fair.

Parador de Aiguablava   1st-class ★★
Rooms: 87. ☎ 62 21 62; FAX 62 21 66. Views over the cove and coast are nothing short of magnificent. This is a modern-style parador with the expected fine accommodations and good service.

In Tamariu:

Hostalillo   2nd-class ★
C. Bellavista, 22. Rooms: 70. ☎ 61 02 50; FAX 61 02 17. Open May through Sept. Of the options in Tamariu, we prefer this one for its lovely terrace looking over the cove. Considering that it is the best hotel in town, its prices are fair.

MODERATE ($50-$99)

In Calella:

Garbí   2nd-class ★
Av. Costa Daurada, 20. Rooms: 30. ☎ 61 40 40; FAX 61 58 03. Open from the middle of Apr. through Oct. Situated in a lovely pine forest, this hotel provides quiet along with generous accommodations.

Santroc   3rd-class ★
Pl. Atlantic, 2, in Barri Sant Roc. Rooms: 48. ☎ 61 42 50; FAX 61 40 68. Open from Apr. through the middle of Oct. This is another

peaceful little hotel, this time above the beach, with spectacular views from the terrace over coast and sea, although its cost pushes the moderate priced category.

In Llafranc:

Casamar　　　　　　　　　　　　　　　　　　　**3rd-class ★★**

C. Nero, 3. Rooms: 20. ☎ *30 01 04; FAX 61 06 51. Open from the middle of Apr. to the middle of Oct.* This little gem provides splendid views over the cove at prices that are lower than the preceding.

L'ESCALA ★

Population: 4,048
Area code: 972; zip code: 17300

Follow signs to **Pals** ★, *a 14th-century farming community, lovingly restored. Continue north along C-260 through Torroella with a 13th-century castle, then through flat fields to L'Escala after 27 k.*

Although L'Escala offers decent beaches, its main attraction is the extensive classical ruins nearby at Empúries. The ruins are a walkable 2 k from town, and are described under a separate heading in this chapter.

WHERE TO STAY

MODERATE ($50-$99)

Nieves-Mar　　　　　　　　　　　　　　　　　**2nd-class ★**

P. Martim, 8. Rooms: 80. ☎ *77 03 00; FAX 10 36 05; Telex 98532). Open Feb. through Nov.* With a pool, tennis courts and nice views of the sea, this is the best choice in town and reasonable for what it offers. Simple fresh fish are done well in its modestly-priced restaurant, and fish soups are delicious.

CADAQUÉS ★

Population: 1,547
Area code: 972; zip code: 17488

Head north to Castello d'Empúries, with an exceptional provincial Gothic church from the 13th century. Continue toward Roses on C-260, but in 7 k follow signs left to Cadaqués, 10 k further on.

This is the archtypical fishing village, as pretty as the nicest postcard of quaint whitewashed houses surrounding a little harbor. The town is lively, but suffers from a beach that, though attractive, is composed of uncomfortable stones. The village gained fame when Salvador Dali built a summer house here, attracting a collection of artists, including Picasso, Utrillo and Duchamp. His house, ornamented with egg-shaped decorations, is opposite the Port Lligat hotel. Fans of Dali, or anyone interested in the exotic, should take a trip to **Figueres**, 25 k inland, the town where Dali lived for his final years. There the pink Dali Museum is decorated with huge boiled eggs and bubble gum, preceded by a pile of tractor tires. The inside is better seen than described. (Open Oct.-Mar. daily 11:30 to 6pm, and July-Sept. 9 a.m. to 9pm; admission: 500 ptas.)

WHERE TO STAY

EXPENSIVE ($100-$200)

Playa Sol   **2nd-class ★**

Platja Pianch, 3. Rooms: 49. ☎ 25 81 00; FAX 25 80 54). Closed Jan. through the middle of Feb. This modern hotel presents pretty views of the village. The garden is attractive and the hotel offers tennis and a pool.

MODERATE ($50-$99)

S'Aguarda   **2nd-class ★**

Carreteria de Port-Llegat, 28 (on the way to Port-Llegat, 1 k north of town). Rooms: 28. ☎ 25 80 82; FAX 25 87 56). Closed Nov. Pleasant views and surroundings add to the comfortable, fairly-priced rooms.

WHERE TO EAT

EXPENSIVE ($50+)

La Galiota   **★★**

C. Narciso Monturiol, 9. ☎ 25 81 87. Open July through Sept., and weekends during the rest of the year. In addition to being the best place to eat in town, this is the trendiest. Pictures by Dali line the walls. However, the restaurant is not pretentious either in decor or cuisine—the simplest things, such as leg of lamb, can be sublime. Reservations are strongly advised.   ***Amex, Diners and Visa accepted.***

The remaining 38 k of coast are breathtakingly scenic, but do not offer beach towns as pleasant as those described. **Port de la Selva**, *9 k along, is a fine natural harbor in a huge bay. Another 6 k brings* **Port de Llanca**, *with a long beach subject to winds. Nine k south of Llanca are the marvellous ruins of the 11th-century* **Monestir de Sant Pere de Roda ★**. *Views up and down the coast are stupendous. (Open daily 10 a.m. to 2 p.m. and 4 p.m. to dusk; admission: 150 ptas.) From Llarca, 21 k along N-260 brings the French border at the town of* **Port Bou**.

COSTA DORADA ★ ★

The Costa Dorada consists of mile after mile of golden sand, after which the coast is named. Beginning at Castelldefeis, 25 k south of Barcelona, it ends at Sant Carles de la Rápita, where the river Ebro forms a delta at the sea, 150 k south. C-246 follows the northern part, changing to N-340 from Calafell south. We describe the sights starting from the northern end.

From **Barcelona** *take the freeway toward the airport. Past the airport the road becomes the coastal C-246 which reaches Castelldefels in 23 k. From* **Valencia** *take either the toll A-7 or the free N-340 (which crawls through coastal towns in the summer) 183 k to Tortosa and follow the description below in reverse.*

CASTELLDEFELS

Population: 24,559
Area code: 93; zip code: 08860

This and Sitges, which follows, are the two most popular resorts for Barcelonans. Both are crowded, yet retain enough attractiveness to draw visitors, and pine hills behind its enormous beach make sunning in Castelldefels particularly sylvan. The town contains a Romanesque church and the keep from a medieval castle. Since this beach is a day outing for Barcelonans and many own houses in the town, however, the hotel situation is terrible.

SITGES ★★

Population: 11,850
Area code: 93; zip code: 08870

This is one of the most appealing towns in Spain. It contains an attractive harbor, a lovely sea promenade, whitewashed houses and a long golden beach. In addition, it has a couple of nice museums including the **Casa Llopis**—for dolls and furniture.

WHERE TO STAY

Proximity to Barcelona seems to have infected hotels here with its high price disease.

EXPENSIVE ($100-$200)

Terramar   1st-class ★ ★
P. Maritim, 80 (at the southern end of the beach). Rooms: 209. ☎ *894 00 50; FAX 894 56 04; Telex 53186. Open May-Oct. On its own little square overlooking the beach, this is a most comfortable hotel. The views are nice and tennis is available as well.*

Subur Maritim   **2nd-class** ★

P. Martim, 72 (on the beach at the bottom of Pas. Dr. Benapres).
Rooms: 45. ☎ *894 15 50; FAX 894 04 27; Telex 52962.* This intimate place is watched over by an attentive staff. Views of the beach
and ocean are pleasant and the garden around the pool is peaceful.

MODERATE ($50-$99)

Romantic y la Renaixenca   **4th-class** ★ ★ ★

C. Sant Isidre, 33 (three blocks back from the northern end of the
beach). Rooms: 55. ☎ *894 83 75; FAX 894 81 67). Open Apr.*
through Oct. These two buildings are managed as one hotel and provide the opportunity to stay in a *modernista* house. The garden is lush
and, yes, romantic. Accommodations are comfortable, if a little
cramped, but the prices are fair indeed.

VILAFRANCA DEL PENEDÈS AND SANT SADUMI D'ANOIA ★

Take C-420 inland for 22 k to Penedès. Sant Sadumi lies
11 k north of Penedès on C-243.

This is an excursion for those interested in wine. Penedès is the
still-wine capital of Catalonia with a wonderful museum of the grape
in the **Museu dei Vi** on the Pl. Jaume. The museum occupies the
ground floor of a 14th-century palace of the kings of Aragón. (Open
daily 10 a.m. to 2 p.m. and 4-6pm; admission: 200 ptas.) Sant Sadumi seems to have nothing but champagne on its mind as sign after
sign points to some *cava* producer. In addition, since the town first
attained prosperity at the turn of the century, it is a virtual museum-
town of the *modernista* style. Codorniu's cellars and the house of the
family are superior examples.

VILLANOVA I LA GELTRÚ ★

Population: 43,560
Area code: 93; zip code: 08800

From Sitges the attractive coast road leads to Villanueva
in 7 k.

Golden sand is framed by boulders around a bay, while olive and
palm trees lend shade. An enchanting museum, the **Casa Papiol**, sits
in the northern end of the town. The museum reconstructs living
conditions for the well-to-do at the turn of the 19th century, and is
fascinating for the details.

WHERE TO STAY

A town of this size should provide more hotels, but, at least, the prices
begin to decline as the distance widens from Barcelona.

MODERATE ($50-$99)

Sovli 70   3rd-class ★

P. Ribes Roges, 1. Rooms: 30. ☎ *815 12 45; 815 70 02. Closed from the second week of Oct.-the first week of Nov.* Here, prices are reasonable and there are views over the lovely beach.

C-246 is joined a few k south of La Geltru and leads to el Vendre, at which point the road is designated N-340 and reaches Tarragona in 27 k.

TARRAGONA

See the description under its own heading below.

SALOU

Population: 16,450
Area code: 977; zip code: 43840

From Tarragona follow signs to A-7, but take the freeway south toward Salou, before entering the toll road. Salou is 10 k on the freeway.

Salou is much enjoyed by the Tarragonians, who cover its long expanse of sand in the high summer. Pleasant flowered promenades, lined by palms, follow the beach. A glut of building, however, has virtually swallowed up what was once a fishing port.

WHERE TO STAY

Because Salou is accustomed mainly to day-trippers from Tarragona, its hotels are few, but reasonable.

MODERATE ($50-$99)

Carabela Roc   2nd-class ★

C. Pau Casals, 108 (on the platja de la Pineda, 7 k east). Rooms: 96. ☎ *37 01 66; FAX 37 07 62; Telex 56709. Open from the second week in Apr.-Oct.* This charmer is nestled amid pines near a fine long beach.

Planas   3rd-class

Pl. Bonet, 3 Rooms: 100. ☎ *38 01 08. Open from the middle of Apr. through Oct.* A pleasant terrace and low prices are the best features of this modest hotel.

CAMBRILS DE MAR ★

Population: 11,211
Area code: 977; zip code: 43850

A coast road covers the 8 k to Cambrils.

By the few added kilometers it lies further from Tarragona, Cambrils manages to retain more character. It includes a pretty marina, and is less developed overall. Cambrils also beckons gourmets, thanks to a family named Gatell whose various members run three separate excellent restaurants.

WHERE TO STAY

Prices are more than fair.

MODERATE ($50-$99)

Mónica   2nd-class ★★

C. Galcerán Marquet, 3. Rooms: 56. ☎ 36 01 16 FAX 79 36 78. Open Mar. through Nov. Its palm grove garden makes this choice stand out. Reasonable prices and comfortable rooms do not hurt either.

WHERE TO EAT

EXPENSIVE ($50+)

Casa Gatell   ★★

P. Miramar, 26. ☎ 36 00 57. Closed Sun. night, Mon. and the middle of Dec.-Jan.

Can Gatell   ★★

P. Miramar, 27. ☎ 36 03 31. Closed Mon. night, Tues., and from the middle of Oct. through the middle of Nov. These relatives, side by side, manage to produce fine dishes night after night, so it is hard to choose between them. Both are good choices to sample authentic paellas, or the Spanish version of bouillabaisse. Any good fish restaurant is going to be somewhat expensive, but these are sure to please. (The family runs yet another restaurant, **Eugenia**, on Consolat de Mar, 80, that is prettier, a bit less expensive, and not so tasty in food as these two. ☎ 36 01 68.)

SANT CARLES DE LA RÁPITA ★

Population: 9,960
Area code: 977; zip code: 43540

The next point of interest after Cambrils is 65 k south. Either join the toll road A-7 or the free N-340 heading south toward Tortosa. If travelling by A-7, exit at Amposta (exit 41), the next town after Tortosa, and take N-340 from there. In 13 k further comes Sant Carles.

Sant Carles perches on the edge of the Ebro delta, which is one thing that makes it special. This low land grows tons of rice, and each fall millions of migrating birds harvest the last pickings on their way to wintering in Africa. Virtually all the coastline of the delta is beach by any definition. The second thing that makes Sant Carles special is that it is a planned community—planned in the middle of the 19th century, by Carlos III who created so much of Madrid. This was to be the model port of Spain, since it was situated in a huge protected bay. Construction of a rational gridded town commenced, but for some reason the expected trade never arrived. Perhaps Spain had enough harbors already. So today it sits, all prettied, waiting for ships that will never come, instead receiving sun- and nature-lovers.

WHERE TO STAY

Prices are fair.

MODERATE ($50-$99)

Juanito   **4th-class ★ ★**

On Platja Miami, 1 k south. Rooms: 35. ☎ 74 04 62. Open Apr.-Sept. Quiet (because it is out of town), on the beach for lovely views, and with a terrace for lounging, this is our favorite choice in Sant Carles.

If full, take your pick between the following serviceable, modestly priced hotels:

Miami Park   **2nd-class**

Av. Constitución, 33. Rooms: 80. ☎ 74 03 51. Open Apr. through Mar.

Llansola   **3rd-class**

C. San isidro, 98. Rooms: 18. ☎ 74 04 03. Closed Nov.

Plaça Vella   **3rd-class**

C. Arsenal, 31. Rooms: 21. ☎ 77 24 53; FAX 74 43 97.

EMPURIES ★ ★

One route to Empüries is described in the Costa Brava itinerary above, along with accommodations. From **Barcelona** *the quickest route is along the toll A-7 past Girona to exit 5, then turning toward the coast to Viladamat and L'Escala. A sign points along a paved road to Empüries 1 k before L'Escala. The trip covers 145 k.*

Open Tues.-Sun. 10 a.m. to 2 p.m. and 3-7 p.m. From the middle of Sept.-May open from Tues.-Sun. 10 a.m. to 1 p.m. and 3-5 p.m. Closed Mon. Admission: 150 ptas. A helpful guidebook in English costs 500 ptas.

Empüries is the one place in Spain where significant Greek remains can be explored. While the ruins are not extensive, neither are they abundant in Greece itself. The experience is heightened by the fact that the site, having drastically declined by the third century A.D. and been abandoned in the eighth century, is not surrounded by modern buildings—thus freeing the imagination to humanize the stones. There are also extensive remains of a Roman city located on a gentle hill overlooking the sea and pleasant beaches, and guides in togas to show you around.

Phoenicians settled here first in the sixth century B.C. on what was an offshore island, now joined to the mainland. Greeks arrived in the fourth century B.C. and built their *Neapolis* ("New Town") about an eighth of a mile south of that first settlement. It became the major Greek colony on the peninsula, from which both the grape and olive were introduced to Spain and western Europe. In 49 B.C. Julius Caesar built a retirement town for his Roman veterans higher up the hill. As Roman power declined, beginning in the third century, invasions so depleted both cities that they fell readily to the Moors in the eighth century, and were abandoned thereafter.

The Greek city, lowest on the hill, is entered through a cyclopean gate south of the Museum. Immediately to the left stands its sacred precinct with remains of the Temple of Aesculapius, the god of medicine. Just north a tall watchtower rises, from which lookouts could scan the sea. At its feet lie remains of the town cisterns, including a reconstructed water filter. Directly to the right of the gate run the colonnades of the Temple of Zeus Serapis, a combined Greek and Egyptian god of the sun and fertility. The town meeting place—agora—stood 100 yards north of this gate. Behind it is a reconstruction of the stoa, or roofed market. Ruins of a very early Christian basilica lie just to the north.

The extensive Roman town spreads up the hill and across a road. Much remains to be excavated, though two houses with mosaics have been cleared and are interesting studies as early versions of the typical patioed Spanish houses of today. The forum, lined by porticos, lies south of these houses. Temples and shops would have surrounded this plaza. An amphitheater can be discerned 100 yards further south.

POBLET MONASTERY ★ ★ ★

Poblet and **Santes Creus** *monasteries, being 30 k apart, are readily combined in one trip. From* **Barcelona** *take the toll A-7 west for 62 k, where it divides. Take A-2 toward Lleida to exit 11, Vila-Rodona. Santa Creus is 3 k north of Vila-Radona. For Poblet continue to exit 9, Montblanc. Go west for 6 k on N-240 to L'Esplung de Francoli and Poblet. From* **Zaragoza** *and west both monasteries lie on the route to Barcelona, and the directions above may be followed.*

Open daily 10 a.m. to 12:30 p.m. and 3-6 p.m. (or to 5
p.m. in winter). Admission: 500 ptas., for guided tours.

Poblet is an architectural masterpiece and the most complete example of a Gothic monastery in Spain. It has won international awards for the quality of its restoration.

The monastery was founded by Ramón Berenguer IV in the middle of the 12th century to thank God for success against the Moors. For this, he brought Cistercian monks from his territories in southern France to create a cloistered community. Poblet was favored through the 15th century by the kings of Aragón, who established a residence for retreats and made the monastery their royal pantheon. But, during the Napoleonic Wars and the anticlerical times that followed in the 19th century, Poblet was abandoned and desecrated. Cistercians returned in 1940, restoring the monastery ever since.

After passing through the gates in two perimeter walls, the Romanesque Chapel of Santa Catalina, from the time of the founder, lies on the left. Directly ahead is the baroque 18th-century church front, with two tall towers. The huge, solemn adjoining cloister contains a large hexagonal fountain and pavilion. The church interior, in the simple Cistercian style, is mainly 13th-century. Its pride is the tombs of the House of Aragón that repose on either side of the transept crossing.

Architecturally unique, the royal tombs are placed on low archeways from which the sarcophagi and effigies angle down toward the viewer. They date from the middle of the 14th century. On the left are effigies of Jaume I, who reclaimed Valencia from the Moors; Pere IV, with two wives; Fernando I; and Martin I. On the right are effigies of Alfonso II, Juan I, and Juan II, with their respective wives. Because the sculpture is lovely and moving, it is a shock to learn that the originals were utterly destroyed and that what we now see are carvings by the Catalan artist Frederic Marès, dating from this century. They are, however, faithful to the original aesthetic.

The tour continues through the monastery kitchen, refectory, and an elegant chapterhouse, to the huge dormitory and adjoining royal palace from 1400. A smaller dormitory nearby has been converted into a museum that shows the state of the monastery before reconstruction.

SANTES CREUS MONASTERY ★ ★

See the encompassing directions to nearby Poblet Monastery above.

Open daily 10 a.m. to 1 p.m. and 3-7 p.m. (to 6 p.m. in winter). Admission: 300 ptas., for guided tours.

Santes Creus was founded as an annex to Poblet monastery (described above) by the same king, at about the same mid-12th-century date, and—like Poblet—for Cistercian monks from France. Similarly, it was favored by the kings of Aragón and served as a royal pantheon for several. It too was abandoned and suffered damage in the middle of the 19th century, but restoration began in this century and continues. The lovely Gothic architecture and completeness of Santes Creus are rivaled in Spain only by Poblet.

A baroque gateway through perimeter walls lets into the principle courtyard, surrounded by outbuildings now privately owned. The former bishopric with a patio serves today both as the ayuntamiento and the local school. At the far end stands the 13th-century church, with battlements added a century later. Entrance through the south side lets into a grand cloister. Though restored, the original liveliness of the carvings on the capitals prefigured the later, more flamboyant Gothic, and makes the cruder fountain pavilion and basin seem out of place. Tombs of the nobility of Aragón fill wall niches.

The church interior is severely simple in the Cistercian style. A high nave is raised on massive square pillars. Light is admitted through a 13th-century lantern at the transept crossing and through original rose windows at either end of the church—the one in the apse being particularly lovely. Left and right of the altar are the royal tombs. On the left, beneath a canopy, reposes Pere III. His son Jaume II and wife are to the altar's right. These effigies represent the very finest carving of the 14th century. Later, Plateresque decoration was added below.

The adjoining chapterhouse is properly solemn, and the dormitory above forms an elegantly simple gallery surmounted by a timber roof. Outside, to the right, is a lovely, simple cloister from the 12th century. A passage leads to the kitchens and refectory, then to the royal palace with an elegant patio and fine stairway.

TARRAGONA ★ ★

Population: 111,869
Area code: 977; zip code: 43000.

One route to Tarragona is described under the **Costa Dorada** *heading above. From* **Barcelona** *the most speedy route is to take the toll road A-7 west for 97 k. From* **Zaragoza** *and west the toll A-2 leads in 214 k to exit 11 at Valls where a connection in 8 k to N-240 brings Tarragona in 16 k more. Slower, but toll-less, is to take N-II for 142 k to Lleida, where N-240 leads to Tarragona in 90 k more. From Valencia the toll A-7 leads to Tarragona in 257 k, while the free N-340 consumes twice the time because of its route through coastal resorts.*

Today Tarragona is Catalonia's third city, but once it was the principle city in all of Spain. Caesar Augustus made it the Roman capital of that part of the Iberian peninsula controlled by the Romans and called Terraconensis, in which some find the source of the present name. But non-Roman remains of massive stone walls show that a town long preceded that Roman one. The original settlement was an Iberian town which the Carthaginians took, resettled, and called Tarchon, a more likely source for the present name. In any case, under the Romans, Tarragona prospered greatly, enjoying a population probably twice that of today. Saint Paul is said to have visited to begin the process of Christianizing Western Europe. Tarragona became the original and primary bishopric of Spain—a primacy that lasted until passing to Toledo in the eleventh century. In 711 the Moors razed the city so completely that it remained deserted for 300 years. It rose again to become the major eastern city of Spain, but because it served as a center for rebellions, it was repeatedly sacked —in 1643, 1705, and 1811. These assaults stunted growth, allowing Barcelona, and even Valencia and Terrasa, to eventually surpass it.

Tarragona possesses a fine collection of Roman artifacts displayed in the **Museu Arqueològic ★** ; the **Praetorium ★** where Caesar Augustus stayed and Pontius Pilate was born; a lovely walk, called the **Passeig Arqueològic ★**, along city walls that are Roman with earlier remains and later additions; ruins of a huge **circus maximus**; and an imposing Gothic **cathedral ★**. There is also a cemetery with sarcophagi of the earliest Christians, called the **Necropolis Paleocristia ★**; a cute port below terraced houses, and a splendid Roman mausoleum, **Centcelles ★**, 5 k west of town. Tarragona is a pretty city, as yet undiscovered by tourists, that well repays a half day's visit.

POLLUTION ALERT

Tarragona's beaches are not considered safe for bathing.

From the **Costa Dorada** *the city is entered on Via Augusta, which funnels into Rambla Vella after a slight right. In 5 blocks comes a hospital on the right, followed by the old city walls. Take the next right for parking. From* **Barcelona**, **Zaragoza** *and west, the city is entered along N-240 which funnels into the major traffic circle of Pl. Imperial Tarraco. Take Rambla Nova with a center strip, opposite the side of the circle that was entered. In 2 blocks comes a major intersection where a gentle left should be made onto Av. Pau Casals. The third right, C. López Peláez leads to parking one block later on the left. From* **Valencia** *on A-7, cross the Francoli River along Av. Ramón i Cajal. When this street crosses the large intersection with Rambla Nova (with the center strip), continue straight across. The name of the street is now Av. Pau Casals, and the third right, C. López Peláez, leads to parking in one block on the left.*

Rambla Vella, a few steps south of the parking place, divides the new part of Tarragona from the older section on the north side of the Rambla. Walk a half block to the beginning of the walls and follow them northwest for two blocks to the Portal de Roser. Here begins the Passeig Arqueológic between the walls, but first pass through the gate into the Pl. Pallol to see a few remains of a **Roman forum**.

Passeig Arqueologic ★

Open Tues.-Sat. 9 a.m. to 1:30 p.m. and 3-8 p.m. (to 6 p.m. in winter). Open Sun. 10 a.m. to 1 p.m. Admission: 100 ptas. This walk along the city walls presents an opportunity to see the different stages of their construction. The walk also passes pretty gardens and provides views over the countryside. Of course the lowest part of the walls, composed of massive stones, is the oldest—pre-third-century B.C., and probably built by Carthage. It supports a Roman wall of regular construction built by Scipio Africanus in the third century B.C. Above are Visigothic and medieval additions. The outer wall is an 18th-century English structure.

The walk ends at the portal de Sant Antoni, which lets into the old quarter. Following the walls south leads to the Museu Arqueologic in three blocks.

Museo Arqueologic ★

Open Tues.-Sat. 10 a.m. to 1 p.m. and 4:30-8 p.m. (to 7 p.m. in winter). Open Sun. 10 a.m. to 2 p.m. Closed Mon. Admission: 100 ptas. The exhibits all were found at Tarragona and in the surrounding area, and most are Roman. The statuary is not outstanding, but the mosaics, especially an appropriately haunting Medusa, are striking. Some smaller articles on the second floor hold interest.

The tall Gothic building adjoining is the praetorium.

Praetorium ★

Open Tues.-Sat. 10 a.m. to 1 p.m. and 4:30-8 p.m. (to 7 p.m. in winter). Open Sun. 10 a.m. to 2 p.m. Closed Mon. Admission: 100 ptas. Though looking Gothic because of restoration in the Middle Ages, this building is a first century B.C. palace that sheltered historical figures of a magnitude that seem mythical. Caesar Augustus is known to have slept here, and Pontius Pilate, later praetor of Judea, was probably born within these walls during his father's term as governor of Tarragona. A thousand years later kings of Aragón also resided here. Today the building serves as a museum of the city's history, with exhibits that are of small interest. But the basement remains Roman, and includes mysterious tunnels and vaults. On the first floor is a sarcophagus of Hippolytus, salvaged from the sea and claimed to be third-century B.C. Greek.

The cathedral is 2 blocks northeast along C. Santa Anna, which crosses the front of the museum, and a left along the picturesquely arcaded C. Merceria.

Cathedral ★

Open daily 10 a.m. to 12:30 p.m. and 4-7 p.m. (to 6 p.m. in winter). Admission: 150 ptas., including guide This 14th-century cathedral was raised during the transitional period between Romanesque and Gothic styles. The facade presents a lovely Gothic central portal flanked by smaller round Romanesque doors.

Entry is through the large cloister on the north side. Although the interior vaulting is Gothic, this earliest part of the church is primarily Romanesque. Moorish influence is apparent in the geometric pierced-work in arches and in the polylobed arches closest to the cathedral. In fact a tenth century mihrab penetrates the west gallery, amid Roman architectural fragments. The cathedral was built on the site of a former mosque (which replaced an even earlier Roman Temple of Jupiter), from which this "prayer niche" survives. Although most of the capitals of the arcade are merely foliated, a few are charmingly carved. Everyone's favorite, in the second bay on the east, depicts a cat's funeral conducted by rats. The museum off the east gallery displays a fine collection of tapestries, including the beautiful Gothic *La Bona Vida* (The Good Life).

Dusky light inside the cathedral slowly reveals the immense size of the church—a football field in length (one of the biggest in Catalonia), seeming even higher than it is because the side aisles reach only halfway up the nave. Though severe in feeling, all the decorative work is first-rate and to be savored. Most outstanding is the intricate and delicate high altar retablo by Pere Joan and Guillermo de la Mota. It depicts the life of Saint Tecla who was converted by Saint Paul then suffered persecution from everyone, including her mother. Several times she was saved from death by Divine intervention.

After visiting the cathedral, go around the back to see the **Chapel of Sant Pau**, *on what is reputed to be the site where Saint Paul first preached. Rebuilt in the middle of the 13th century, the chapel shows signs of much greater age.*

From directly in front of the cathedral descend C. Mayor past antique stores to reach the Pl. de la Font, named for the fountain. This is the site of the Roman **Circus Maximus**, *still under excavation (entrance is free). When new in the first century A.D., the circus was a narrow oval, 350 feet long, seating 25,000 spectators.*

Walk to the western end of the Rambla Vella to turn right along P. de les Palmeres to the balcony overlooking the sea at the first corner. Called the **Balcó de Mediterràni**, *its view of city and sea are lovely. Toward the beach below can be seen the Roman* **amphitheater**. *Stairs to the left descend to the structure, in which one is free to wander. Ruins of a 12th-century Romanesque church stand in the center.*

For the **Necropolis Paleocristia** ★ *walk 7 blocks northwest up the gardened Rambla Nova to its end. West along Av. Ramón i Cajal for a half mile, almost to the river, brings the necropolis on the left. This large cemetery from the earliest Christian times contains a large number of tombs, sarcophagi, and urns, some reused from the pagan Romans. More are displayed in the museum. (Same hours as the Museu Arqueològic; admission: 100 ptas.)*

The **Centcelles Mausoleum** ★ *requires a car or taxi for the 5 k trip. Take Av. Ramón i Cajal across the river, following signs to A-7 and Valencia. Turn off onto the road marked for Reus. In Constanti turn right onto C. de Centcelles, unpaved, for half a mile, turning left just before the village of Centcelles. Two large buildings, monumental, but incongruously tiled in pink, stand in a modern vineyard. Inside, a large cupola is covered with wonderful* *mosaics depicting early Christian themes. The mausoleum belonged to a wealthy Roman of the fourth century.*

WHERE TO STAY

Prices remain reasonable in Tarragona, although the selection is sparse and lacks character.

EXPENSIVE ($100-$200)

Imperial Tarraco   1st-class ★★

P. Palmeres (at the end of Rambla Vella). Rooms: 170. ☎ *23 30 40; FAX 21 65 66; Telex 56441.* This crescent of a modern hotel stands just above the Balcó de Mediterràni for postcard views over the town and sea. A room with a sea view is the whole point of the hotel, so insist on one. The rooms are comfortable, if a little bare, and include a private balcony. This is the best hotel in town and reasonably priced for its category.

MODERATE ($50-$99)

Lauria   2nd-class ★

Rambla Nova, 20 (a block from the end of the Rambla, near the Balcó de Mediterràni). Rooms: 72. ☎ *23 67 12; FAX 23 67 00.* This businessperson's hotel is sleek, well located and some rooms provide distant sea views.

España   4th-class ★

Rambla Nova, 49 (a block north of the Hotel Lauria). Rooms: 40. ☎ *23 27 07.* This modern townhouse with an excellent location charges attractive prices. Rooms are comfortable, and the outer ones have balconies.

WHERE TO EAT

For the best, freshest, seafood, head for the port and innumerable restaurants. Our favorite, La Puda, is described below. The port stands at the southwest end of the beach—by heading due south from the Rambla Nova the walk is less than half a mile.

MODERATE ($20-$50)

La Puda   ★★

Muelle Pescadores, 25 (across from the pavilion where the fishermen dock). ☎ *21 15 11.* Completely unpretentious with sea-blue walls and white tablecloths, this restaurant serves the best fish in town for the fairest prices. Start with an appetizer platter of the day's catch, followed by the house fish soup, or whatever claims your fancy. No reservations are taken. *Amex, Diners, MasterCard, and Visa accepted.*

La Galería   ★

Rambla Nova, 16 (near the Hotel Lauria). ☎ *23 61 43. Closed Wed. night, Sun., and Sat. and Sun. lunch in summer.* The cuisine is inventive and remarkably inexpensive. The decor is attractively Belle

Époque with artwork by the chef, who will also decorate your plate with a lovely entree. The sauces are good. Reservations are required on weekends. ***Amex, Diners, MasterCard and Visa accepted.***

DIRECTORY

INFORMATION • A municipal Tourist Office is located at C. Major, 39, opposite the cathedral steps (☎ 23 89 22).

TRAINS AND BUSES • The station is in the port at Pl. de la Pedrera ☎ 23 36 43). Trains run almost continually to Barcelona, but only three per day cover the four-hour run to Valencia, and four do the eight-hour trip to Madrid. RENFE had a convenient office at Rambla Nova, 40 (☎ 24 02 02).

The bus station is located on Pl. Imperial Tarraco, at the top end of the Rambla Nova (☎ 22 20 72). Service is more frequent and faster to Valencia than by train.

POLICE • ☎ 23 33 11.

EXCURSIONS

Tarragona stands in the middle of the **Costa Dorada**, described above. **Barcelona**, to the north, and **Valencia**, to the south are natural trips, described in this chapter.

VALENCIA ★ ★

Population: 751,734
Area code: 96; zip code: 46000

From **Barcelona** *the toll A-7 is much faster than the free N-340, which crawls through beach resorts for the 257 k trip. From the* **Costa Dorada** *the same route is preferred, covering about 200 k. From* **Madrid** *N-III leads directly in 351 k. From Almeria at the end of the* **Costa del Sol** *N-340 reaches Alicante in 299 k, outside of which the toll A-7 completes the remaining 179 k.*

Valencia has been a garden since the time of the Greeks, with the usual succession of masters—Cathagenians, Romans, Visigoths, then Moors. In the 11th century Valencia declared herself an independent Moorish state, but, in 1094, El Cid gathered an army of Christians and dissatisfied Moors to seize the heavily fortified city for himself. Over the next five years he personally controlled this fief, one of the richest areas in Spain, and died defending it during one of the Moor's repeated efforts to take it back. (Legend has it that, even after his death, el Cid's troops set his dead body astride a horse to frighten attackers away.) Three years later, the Moors regained their hold, and el Cid's wife, who had assumed command of his forces, left Valencia. Moors retained the city for only century, until Jaume I of Aragón recaptured it for the Christian side.

Through war and peace Valencia prospered, for it is Spain's most fertile region—on a huge well-irrigated plain favored by continual warm weather. Only in the 17th century did it decline, when expulsion of the Moors' descendents drained it of farmers. But decline was only temporary, for it was not long before immigrants from poorer parts of Spain replaced the lost workforce. Today Valencia is the third-largest city in Spain, spreading across a wide level landscape. It is comfortably pleasant in winter, but can steam uncomfortably in midsummer.

Valencia presents an unattractive face to arriving visitors. Sprawling modern suburbs and factories seem to extend forever, surrounding and hiding Valencia's attractions, almost all of which nestle in a bend in the river Turia at the core of the city. There is an interesting **Cathedral ★**, containing the Holy Grail (it is claimed); rare civil Gothic architecture in the **Lonja de la Seda ★** and the **Palacio de la Generalidad ★**; the **Colegio del Patriarca** with a choice collection of paintings (though requiring special permission); two fine *modernista* buildings in the **Estación**, and the bustling **Mercado Central** (Central Market). Not far away, beside a pleasant garden, is the **Museo Provincial de Bellas Artes**, one of Spain's better museums of painting. Spain's finest ceramic collection is housed in the **Palacio Marqués Dos Aguas ★**, a building so ugly that it is not to be missed. Valencia can provide a day's enjoyment by any reckoning.

POLLUTION ALERT

At last report Valencia's beaches are not safe for swimming.

Parking is available in Pl. Zaragoza, the square in front of the Cathedral. From the **airport** *and* **Madrid** *a dry watercourse is crossed to travel along Av. del Cid. It changes its name to San José Calasanz, after crossing the perimeter road (Av. de Pérez Galdos) before entering the large Pl. España. Take C. San Vicente Martir across the plaza, going northeast to the Pl. de Zaragoza and parking in 12 blocks. From* **Barcelona** *and the* **Costa Dorada** *follow signs for "Centro" and cross the riverbed to travel along the wide Av. de Peris y Valera. Turn right on C. Sueca to reach the huge, four-lane Gran Via Germanias and turn left (a momen-*

tary right is necessary first). The street bends under the train tracks to enter the large intersection of the Pl. España. Take San Vicente Martir heading northeast to the Pl. de Zaragoza and parking in 12 blocks. From the **Costa del Sol** *the city is entered along Av. de Auslas March. Turn left at the intersection to follow the large Av. de Peris y Valero which bends along an elevation over the train track. At the end of the elevation take San Vicente Martir on the right to the Pl. de Zaragoza and parking in 12 blocks.*

WHAT TO SEE AND DO

Cathedral ★

Open daily 10 a.m. to 1 p.m. and 4-6 p.m. (in winter for the morning hours only). Admission: 100 ptas. to the museum. Most of the Cathedral was built in the 14th and 15th centuries, the Gothic era. Plateresque and Baroque decorations that were applied later to the interior as in so many Spanish churches, have in this case been removed to leave the simpler Gothic original. The main facade is a strange bird —remodeled in the early 18th century in a Gothic style to blend with the interior. More striking is the adjoining octagonal Gothic tower, called the Miguelete, with a pierced upper story lined with tracery. It is unique.

Inside, the revealed Gothic superstructure, stripped of decoration, seems plain. The first chapel on the right with elegant vaulting is the original chapterhouse. On the altar stands a small purple agate cup, surrounded by alabaster reliefs. According to legend, this is the true Holy Grail used by Christ at the Last Supper. Indeed it is an old cup, certainly dating to Roman times, that had been venerated for centuries in northern Catalonia before its donation to the Cathedral. The chains nearby were captured by an Aragonese fleet in the 15th century from the port of Marseilles, though why they should be displayed in a church is a puzzle. The museum off this chapel contains a number of early Valencian polychromed sculptures, a dark Zurbarán, a lovely Carravagio *Virgin*, and two special large Goyas of St. Francisco Borja, the saintly member of that otherwise venal Borja family.

Returning to the church proper, the 16th-century high altar betrays a large debt to Leonardo da Vinci. The camborio at the crossing uses alabaster for panes instead of glass. Chapels in the left aisle are interesting, with some good paintings here and there. The treasury contains much goldwork, including a piece by the master, Benvenuto Cellini.

Proceed around the Cathedral to view the outside. The earliest part, the south facade, is Romanesque, while the north facade is badly weathered Gothic. A huge **Archbishop's Palace** *is connected* *to the south face. Off the north side stretches the lovely* **Pl. de la Virgin** *with a neoclassic fountain of a reclining colossus in the center. To the right, connected to the Cathedral by an arcade, is the* **Basilica de Nuestra Señora de los Desamparados** *(Our lady of the Forsaken), with a venerated gilt statue of the Virgin inside. This building, completed in 1667, was the first Spanish lunatic asylum, and possibly the first in the world.*

To the right of the plaza, fronted by orange trees, is the Gothic **Palau de la Generalitat ★**. In this 15th-century building the Cortes of Valencia sat to impose the "general" tax, for which the building was named. The facade is elegant, though the second tower is 20th century. Inside is a fine patio, a splendid hall with lovely tiles, 16th-century murals and an artesonado ceiling, and two tower rooms with wondrous gilt and painted ceilings. (Open weekdays 9 a.m. to 2 p.m. Admission: free, but by advance permission only. ☎ 332 02 06.)

Continue along the street fronting the palace, **C. Caballeros**. The door-knockers of many mansions lining this street are high so a horseman could reach them without dismounting. Some Gothic patios (such as numbers 22 and 23) are visible through doorways. After number 41, turn left down the tiny C. Abadadia San Nicholas to **Iglesia San Nicolás**. Although this was one of the oldest churches in the city, during the 16th century it was redecorated inside and out in the most flamboyant Churrigueresque style. The interior is a Baroque extravaganza.

Return to C. Caballeros, to take C. Bolseria, the third left. It leads downhill in three blocks to the Pl. del Mercado. The **Mercado Central**, after which the plaza is named, is on the right—a modernista production of tiles and glass from 1928. Inside is a collection of over a thousand stalls, divided into two sections, one for meat and produce and another for fish.

Across from the Mercado is the Gothic Lonja de la Seda.

Lonja de la Seda   ★

Open Tues.-Fri. 10 a.m. to 2 p.m. and 4-8 p.m. Open weekends 10 a.m. to 1 p.m. Closed Mon. Admission: free. Valencia became the center for silk that Moors introduced into Spain. Late in the 15th century, to proclaim their prosperous status, silk merchants erected this building as a bourse to manage and trade their goods. The richly decorated result is one of the finest surviving examples of Gothic civil architecture. A center tower divides the facade into halves, one side with the arms of Aragón and elaborate tracery, the other with an ornate upper gallery. The large Salon de Contratación inside, where

contracts were bought and sold, supports a lofty ceiling on unusual
Gothic twisted columns. A stairway from the Orange Tree Courtyard
leads up to the Salon de Consular del Mar (Maritime Court), covered
with a wonderful carved gargoyle ceiling of the period, brought here
from the former town hall.

*Continue along the plaza, which lets into Av. Maria Cristina at
the end, and leads in four blocks to the bustling garden Pl. del Pais
Valenciano (a.k.a. Pl. de Ayuntamiento), with the* **Ayuntamiento**
*on the right. Although its facade is early 20th-century, the interior
is 18th. An elegant Salo de Festes is left of the entrance. There is a
small museum containing miscellany along with some fine ceramics. (Open Sun.-Fri. 9 a.m. to 1:30pm; Admission: free.) The*
Office of Tourism *with a worthwhile map is located in this building.*

Two blocks ahead the imposing **Estación del Norte** *can be seen,
a modernista marvel worth the walk.*

*From the north end of the Pl. Valenciano take C. Barcas going
right. Turn left at the old theater building onto C. Poeta Querol.
The second left at a church on C. Salva brings the 19th-century
university complex. To its north stands* **Colegio del Patriarca**, *a
former 16th-century seminary. Inside, around an elegantly simple
patio, are rooms with fine tiles. The second floor consists of a
choice museum with charming Valencian primitives, a superb Van
der Weyden triptych, a Caravaggio, Ribaltas and an El Greco.
(Open daily 11 a.m. to 1:30 pm, but only on weekends in winter;
admission: 100 ptas.)*

*Return to C. Querol, continuing north to the next corner after
the church. Here, on the left around the corner, is an unforgettable
building—the Palacio Marqués de Dos Aguas.*

Palacio Marqués de Dos Aguas
*Open Tues.-Sat. 10 a.m. to 2 p.m. and 4-6 p.m. Open Sun. 10 a.m. to
2 p.m. Closed Mon. Admission: 200 ptas.* Erected in the 18th century, this is the most Baroque civil building in Spain. The main portal
is surrounded by an incredible assemblage, including two alabaster
atlantes pouring water in an obvious pun on the Marqués' name.
Originally, the facade was covered in murals as well. Inside is an
exceptional ceramics museum, with over 5000 pieces on display, perhaps the best collection in a country famous for that art. It must be
admitted, however, that it is difficult to concentrate on ceramics amid
the extravagance of gilt, marble, and murals in the palace rooms. Such
bad taste has seldom been surpassed, and the opportunity to see it is
special.

Continue to the end of the street, and right around the Gothic church of **San Martín**, *coated in Baroque decoration although sporting a 15th-century bronze equestrian statue of the saint over the door. Head toward the Cathedral and along its right (south) side, this time rounding the right side of the Archbishop's Palace to view the* **Almudín** *at its rear. This was the public granary from the 16th century and now houses a museum of paleontology.*

Walk north to the Puente Trinadad, crossing the riverbed. On the other side, to the right on C. San Pio V is the Fine Arts Museum.

Museo Provincial de Bellas Artes ★

Open Tues.-Sat. 10 a.m. to 2 p.m. and 4-6 p.m. Open Sun. 10 a.m. to 2 p.m. Closed Mon. Admission: 200 ptas. For the scope and quality of its paintings this museum ranks at least as the third best in Spain. For the art of Valencia it is first-rate. The ground floor, however, is dedicated to sculpture and mosaics of a secondary sort. It is the second floor that shines, beginning with a series of rooms emphasizing medieval primitive paintings from the area surrounding Valencia. The paintings are unrestrained in their graphic depictions of blood and gore, yet refreshingly innocent, somehow. The contrast with the rampant imagination displayed by Bosch's *Los Improperios* (The Mockers) in gallery 30, drawn by a more tutored hand, is instructive. (The centerpiece of this triptych hangs in El Escorial.) Juan Macip and Juan de Juanes represent the Renaissance well. Extraordinary canvases by Ribalta in gallery 37 lead the way to Ribera in gallery 40. One gallery is devoted to Goya, and another to a single painting—a haunting Velázquez self-portrait.

WHERE TO STAY

Though not numerous, hotels in Valencia usually prove adequate because the number of tourists is also small. Rooms are fairly priced. In such a sprawling city, however, a location close to the sights is important and guides our selection.

EXPENSIVE ($100-$200)

Reina Victoria   1st-class ★★

C. Barcas, 4 (the street heading east from the Pl. Valenciano). Rooms: 97. ☎ *352 04 87; FAX 352 04 87; Telex 64755.* With its light and airy look the hotel suggests a French hostelry of the 1930s. Recently refurbished, the comfortable bedrooms all wear deep pile rugs and chintz bedspreads. Service is exemplary.

Excelsior   2nd-class ★

C. Barcelonina, 5 (behind the Palacio Marqués de Dos Aguas). Rooms: 67. ☎ *351 46 12.* Wood panelling in the lobby lends a homier atmosphere than most hotels evoke. The rooms are comfortable with brass headboards, and the prices, almost a third less than the Victoria, make this an appealing choice.

Inglés   2nd-class ★

C. Marqués de Dos Aguas, 5 (across the street from the palace). Rooms: 62. ☎ 351 64 26; FAX 394 02 51. The building is a former palace, but the bedrooms, though comfortable, are by no means deluxe. The location is first-rate, however.

MODERATE ($50-$99)

Bristol   R2nd-class ★

C. Abadia San Martin, 3 (at the end of the street of the Palacio Marqués de Dos Aguas). Rooms: 40. ☎ 352 11 76. This is a comfortable, intimate hotel, without frills. It is well maintained, the bedrooms are comfortable, and the location is super.

Continental   R2nd-class

C. Correos, 8 (one block along the street that leaves the center of the Pl. Valencianos, heading east). Rooms: 43. ☎ 351 09 26; FAX 351 09 26. This hotel occupies the upper two floors of a townhouse, and provides comfortable bedrooms, although not much more.

INEXPENSIVE (UNDER $50)

Moratín   Hs3rd-class

C. Moratin, 15 (off C. Barcas which runs east from the north end of the Pl. Valencianos). Rooms: 12. ☎ 352 12 20. This is about the best of a short supply of inexpensive accommodations. It is clean and the service is friendly.

WHERE TO EAT

Valencia is the birthplace of paella, and restaurants here compete with one another for the most tasty version. Other specialties are rice dishes in countless varieties, for this is where the rice is grown, and produce is invariably fresh and delicious. Valencians also love their shellfish, hence the many restaurants with *marisqueria* in their name. These will necessarily be expensive, but the quality will be high. While *nueva cocina* is available, it is generally better elsewhere.

EXPENSIVE ($50+)

El Plat   ★★

C. Conde de Altea, 41 (1 block south and 1 west of the eastern end of Gran Via Marqués, which is the large center divided road 2 blocks south of the Estación del Norte). ☎ 35 15 11. Closed Mon. and holiday and Sun eves. This restaurant specializes in paella, serving the best in the city. It is an unpretentious place, but serious about food, and there are other local specialties as well.   Reservations are not taken.   ***Amex, MasterCard and Visa accepted.***

Rio Sil   ★

C. Mosén Femades, 10 (take the second left from the southeast corner

of the Pl. Valencianos and walk to near the end of the tiny street).
☎ *52 97 64. Close the first half of July.* Closer to the sights than El
Plat, this restaurant also does paella extremely well. The decor is
vaguely nautical and there are tables outside.

MODERATE ($20-$50)

El Timonel ★

C. Felix Pizcueta, 13 (three blocks east of the Estación del Norte).
☎ *352 63 00. Closed Mon., Holy Week, and Aug.* The interior is
reminiscent of a yacht, a little hokey, but this is probably the best
shellfish restaurant in town and worth the walk. Reservations are
advised for diner.   *Amex, Diners, MasterCard and Visa accepted.*

INEXPENSIVE (UNDER $20)

La Romeral ★

*Gran Via Marquês del Turia, 62 (Gran Via Marqués is the large center
divided road 2 blocks south of the Estación del Norte. This restaurant
is situated 2 blocks from its eastern end.)* ☎ *395 15 17. Closed Mon.
and Aug.* This local place serves well-prepared dishes for amazingly
low prices.

DIRECTORY

SHOPPING • Valencia is the home of the Lladró pottery works that produces those cute, pricey, glossy white figurines with a touch of blue or
pink. Naturally stores all over town sell them, but for the aficionado
Valencia is unique in having a Lladro factory outlet that handles Naos,
the cheaper line as well. Prices are almost half of retail. Although the
pieces are seconds, usually their imperfections are so minor that only
an expert can tell. The unmarked store is in a suburb of the city called
Tavernes Blanques, so a taxi is the only means of getting to C. 1 de
Mayo, 32.

Antique and **books** stores surround the Lonja. A **flea market** is held
Sun. in the streets behind the Cathedral.

INFORMATION • Located in the Ayuntamiento in the Pl. Valencianos
(☎ 351 04 17).

TRAINS AND BUSES • The Estación del Norte is on C. de Játiva, two blocks
south of the Pl. Valancianos (☎ 352 02 02). Service is good to most
destinations in Spain.

The bus station (☎ 349 72 22) is located at Av. de Menéndez Pidal,
13 (across the river, north of the sights). Bus # 8 from the Pl. Valencianos goes there.

POLICE • Gran Via de Ramón y Cajal, 40 (south of the Estación del
Norte). ☎ 351 08 62.

AIRPORT • Valencia's airport serves European capitals as well as all of
Spain. It is 10 k southwest of town. Bus #15 leaves hourly from the

bus station. Iberia (☎ 352 97 37) is on C. de la Paz, 14 (just east of the Pl. Zaragoza in front of the cathedral).

EXCURSIONS

Valencia divides the **Costa del Azahar** from the **Costa Blanca**, its natural excursions. Both are described above. The nearest good beach is outside **El Saler**, described in the Costa del Azahar section.

PORTUGAL

*A view along Lisbon's Rua Augusta to the Triumphal Arch of the Praça do
Commércio*

THE LAND AND
THE PEOPLE

Children

Portugal occupies the western fifth of the Iberian Peninsula, and comprises a rectangle 137 miles wide (at its widest) by 350 miles long. Its geography is mountainous north and east—along the Spanish border—sloping down to plains on the west, before rising again in low mountains at the southern Algarve. Flowers, trees, and scenic rolling hills contrast with the generally more ascetic landscape of Spain.

The river Minho separates Portugal's northern border from the province of Galicia in Spain. Between the Minho and the parallel

Douro river 200 k south of it, the land is mountainous granite, although covered in dense vegetation. Small villages nestle in warmer valleys, where lyre-horned oxen can still be seen pulling wooden wheeled carts. The Douro River cuts through this plateau. Along its banks grow the grapes for port wine, before shipping west down the river to the natural port of Oporto, and the sea.

South of the Douro dense mountains continue in the east, although the land lies low along the coast. Castles and fortified walls on the east still defend mountain villages from the Spanish as they have for eight centuries, while sheep graze and farmers raise grapes for the fine wines of the Dão region. Rice paddies on the low western coast stretch for uninterrupted miles, protected from sea salt by sand dunes anchored by pines. The river Tejo (Tagus) cuts Portugal roughly in half. Its alluvial banks raise olives, grapes, vegetables and wheat. Rice grows on spreading plains where horses and black fighting bulls roam. Lisbon begins at the Tejo estuary, just before the river enters the Atlantic. On the coast, both north and south of Lisbon, cliffs surround sand beaches and quaint fishing villages.

South of the Tajo is the department of Alentejo, comprising almost a third of Portugal. Flat and poorly watered by nature, artificial irrigation has turned this area into the granary of Portugal. Clustered forests of cork oaks break the flatness, one-third of all those in the world, from which Portugal sells more cork products than any other country. Away from the forests, rolling hills cradle houses dazzlingly whitewashed, topped by orange tile roofs that grow ornate, eccentric chimneys. Occasional windmills turn in the breeze.

The southernmost part of Portugal is called the Algarve, named from the Arabic word for west, for this was the western extremity of the Moors' territory. Minor mountains separate the Algarve from the Alentejo, but they are tall enough to constitute a barrier that allows the Atlantic Ocean to temper weather and produce a semitropical climate. Vegetation is lush with camillias and citrus groves. Rolling sand beaches on the eastern coast turn to spectacular cliffs on the west framing smaller beaches, and ending in the sheer windswept bluffs of Capo de São Vicente, the southwestern extremity of Europe. Not surprisingly tourists have discovered the mild climate, beautiful beaches, and crystal ocean—and arrive in droves each summer.

Portugal owes its mild climate to the warmth of the Atlantic's Gulf Stream. This can produce summer temperatures of over 100 on the coast, though subdued by continual sea breezes. Mountains remain pleasantly cool, but the inland plains of the Alentejo grow stifling and airless in mid-summer when temperatures of 120 are not unknown. Winters are clear and mild, generally in the 50s, with only occasional frost and rare mountain snow. Winter nights, however, reach freezing in the higher mountains. Spring and autumn bring pleasant temperatures, in the 60s and 70s, but also rains, more in the north than further south.

The last census in 1981 gave Portugal a population of just under ten million, when including the islands of Madeira and the Azores. This number incorporates almost a million expatriates from the African colonies of Angola, Guinea and Mozambique who returned in 1975 to raise the country's population by 10% in six months. Portugal boasts only one metropolis—Lisbon, in which one Portuguese in ten lives, and one additional true city—Oporto, with a population of a third of a million. In Portugal a family of visiting tourists can raise the population of towns by percentage points.

Despite major efforts to industrialize, Portugal remains a country of farmers. One in five still earns his living from the land. Sixty percent of Portugal's industry is located in Lisbon and Oporto, leaving the majority of the country either empty or in farms. Fishing remains a major industry, with sailors routinely harvesting catches off the Newfoundland Banks in North America as they have since time immemorial, as well as from local seas. Portugal is one of the largest producers of tungsten and mines significant quantities of uranium, but must import all its oil, and has built the usual ugly refineries in Lisbon, Oporto and Sines.

As a people the Portuguese seem surprisingly quiet, in contrast to southern Spanish exuberance. Nonetheless, they go out of their way to help anyone who asks. They know that their language seems Greek to everyone else and strive hard to understand a visitor's English. Portuguese all understand Spanish, though they are offended when a Spaniard speaks to them in his language while a guest in their land, for centuries of conflict are not readily forgotten. Of course they do not take the same offense when a tourist tries Spanish if English fails.

Portuguese work so hard that it is difficult to find one at rest, outside of the men in local bars in the evening. They show the depths of their feelings when they cry during *fado* songs. But most outstanding is their simple sincerity, plain on their faces and in their eyes. The Portuguese are hard to dislike.

WHERE TO GO

The walls of Óbidos.

The major sights of tiny Portugal can be managed in two weeks by car, with slower trains or buses adding one week more. Such a schedule would be hurried and permit only waving at beaches while passing, without a single day for indolent basking. Thus, three weeks (or even four) would approach an ideal—sightseeing combined with days of relaxing. Because fine beaches can be reached in a day from anywhere in Portugal, travellers are permitted great flexibility in their plans.

THE TOP SIGHTS

As the most visited city in Portugal, **Lisbon** ★★★★ must be mentioned first. Although it is not memorably beautiful, it contains atmosphere, two excellent museums, and—in its Belém suburb—a wonderful monastery that exemplifies Portugal's outstanding contribution to world architecture—the Manueline style.

Portugal's most elegant sight is the monastery at **Batalha** ★★★★★. From its inception at the dawn of the 15th century through completion a century later, doting kings provided Portugal's finest architects and sculptors, sparing no expense to create a marvel. The ensemble comprises an unusually harmonious whole, graceful in all details. Batalha's lovely buildings—an easy day-trip from Lisbon—should not be missed. A visit can also include the nearby village of **Alcobaça** ★★★ with a fine monastery of its own, that contains the romantic tombs of Inês de Castro and her lover, Pedro the Cruel.

Évora ★★★★ comes next, not because it offers any single essential sight, but because of such a number of attractions contained in the lovely package of the town itself. Because Évora is located at Lisbon's latitude two-thirds of the way across the country, a tourist could leave Lisbon early one morning, see Évora's sights before dark, stay the night in Estremoz at one of Portugal's most elegant pousadas, and spend the next day touring the fortified towns of **Estremoz** ★, **Evoramonte** ★, and lovely **Elvas** ★★. **Marváo** ★★, discussed below, can easily be added on for one more day.

Tomar ★★★ ranks high on any list. The monastery consists of a mysterious 12th-century church of the Knights Templar, embellished by sublime cloisters. What makes a visit even more appealing is proximity to **Almourol** ★★—Portugal's most romantic castle—sitting, as in a fairy-tale, in the waters of the Tajo river. Less than half an hour away, too, is the pilgrimage site of **Fátima** ★. And Tomar is near enough to Lisbon to be visited as a day-trip from the capital.

Next comes **Sintra** ★★★, both for its enchanted mountain site, and for offering not just one, but three, castles—one from the 10th-, one from the 16th-, and one fantasy from the 19th-century. It lies a mere 30 k from Lisbon. If one wished to spend the night, the baroque royal palace of **Queluz** ★ could also be visited on the way to Sintra or on the return to Lisbon.

Although **Marváo** ★★ is just a fortified hilltop village, of which Portugal possesses scores similar in age and condition, it differs by being the most charming and certainly the one to see, if only one is possible. All there is to do here is to walk through the village soaking up atmosphere. Marváo is a breeze of a day-trip from Évora, or can be reached directly from Lisbon in 5 hours by car.

Because of its one perfect square, **Viseu** ★★ comes next. A stately cathedral stands on one side, a fine museum on another, and a perfect Portuguese baroque church graces the opposite end. Nearby, the site of Portugal's first university—parts of which are Renaissance—overlooks the attractive town of **Coimbra** ★★★. A trip to Viseu can also be combined with a visit to **Guarda** ★, a village situated in the center of a score of other medieval fortified hilltop villages, each one filled with atmosphere.

Braga ★★, in the far north, is a city of baroque churches, lovely parks and—at Bom Jesus—a flight of stairs that needs to be seen to be believed. Nearby **Guimaráes** ★★ contains the country's oldest surviving castle, where the first King of Portugal was born. A stop at **Oporto** ★★ on the way would be natural, to enjoy both its 19th-century character and free samples of port.

From Oporto or Braga, **Bragança** ★★ is an easy trip. It offers not just old buildings that might be seen elsewhere, but—isolated behind mountains in an almost forgotten area of the country—a glimpse of an older way of life.

BEACHES

Portugal's southern extremity, the **Algarve** ★★★, consists of 200 k of the finest beaches in Europe. The water is an unpolluted vibrant blue-green; the beaches are the finest white sand; and the cliffs behind form exquisite rock formations and picture-postcard coves. Such perfection naturally attracts hordes of sunseekers, yet the Algarve's prices are surprisingly low—generally lower than the less entrancing resorts along Spain's coast. Best of all, there remain areas at the western end of the Algarve that the crowds have not yet discovered. The Algarve is an easy day's travel from either Lisbon or Évora.

Fine beaches are also available within an hour's drive south of Lisbon outside of **Setubal**, and there are elegant resorts an hour west at **Estoril** ★, with a casino, and at neighboring **Cascais** ★, although ocean pollution can sometimes cause problems at both. Near Batalha is the famous beach of **Nazaré** ★, attractive but crowded during the summer. About 20 miles west of Coimbra stretch long lovely beaches at **Figueira da Foz** ★. Last, but far from least, half-way between Coimbra and Oporto, less than 100 k west of Viseu, is the beach town of **Aveiro** ★★, situated on a huge lagoon and cut by canals.

ITINERARIES

The five itineraries that follow offer different tastes of Portugal in trips of five to eleven days. They comprise sightseeing and travel through the countryside, but do not include any leisure at the beach. In particular, none incorporate a stay at any of the truly beautiful beaches of the Algarve. Obviously, relaxed time by the sea adds to the pleasure of a vacation. Given that beaches line the west and south of Portugal and that Portugal is narrow west to east, at almost any time during an itinerary one can break away to the ocean. The best beaches, those of the Algarve, are readily combined either with Lisbon or Évora. For example, in the "Lisbon, Évora, Marvão and Tomar" or "The Best of Portugal" itinerary, instead of travelling to Évora on day 4, a turn can be made south to the Algarve instead. After sufficient sun and sand, one can continue to Évora to rejoin the itinerary.

LISBON, 5 days

This tour covers all the highlights of Lisbon and leaves time for shopping and strolling.

Day 1: Travel to Lisbon and settle into a hotel.

Day 2: Castello de São Jorge, the Alfama, the Cathedral and the Rossio.

Day 3: São Roque, Igreja do Carmo, shopping in the Chaiado, and a visit to the Calouste Gulbenkian museum. If time allows, add the Estufa Fria in the Parque Eduardo VI.

Day 4: The Belém Tower, Hieronymite monastery, Carriage Museum, and Museum of Popular Art (all located in the suburb of Belém, 3 k from the center), stopping en route at the Museu Nacional de Arte Antiga.

Day 5: Departure.

LISBON AND ITS ENVIRONMENTS, 7 days

This trip adds the elegance of Batalha and enchantment of Sintra to the best of Lisbon.

DAY 1: Travel to Lisbon and settle into a hotel.

DAY 2: Castello de São Jorge, the Alfama, the Cathedral and the Rossio.

DAY 3: The Belém Tower, Hieronymite monastery, Carriage Museum, and Museum of Popular Art, stopping en route at the Museu Nacional de Arte Antiga.

DAY 4: São Roque, Igreja do Carmo, shopping in the Chaiado, and a visit to the Calouste Gulbenkian museum. If time allows, add the Estufa Fria in the Parque Eduardo VI.

DAY 5: Travel to Batalha for the monastery, visiting Alcobaça on the way.

DAY 6: Travel to Sintra for its palaces, visiting Queluz on the way.

DAY 7: Departure.

LISBON, ÉVORA, MARVÃO AND TOMAR, 7 days

DAY 1: Travel to Lisbon and settle into a hotel.

DAY 2: Castello de São Jorge, the Alfama, the Cathedral and the Rossio.

DAY 3: The Belém Tower, Hieronymite monastery, Carriage Museum, and Museum of Popular Art, stopping en route at the Museu Nacional de Arte Antiga.

DAY 4: Travel to Évora and settle into a hotel; Roman temple; Cathedral and mansions.

DAY 5: Travel to Tomar, visiting Elvas and Marvão on the way; settle into a hotel.

DAY 6: Convent of Christ; return to Lisbon, visiting the castle of Almourol on the way.

DAY 7: Departure.

Note: If additional time is available, instead of returning to Lisbon on day 6, continue to Batalha, visiting Alcobaça on the way. On the return to Lisbon visit Sintra and Queluz, if time allows.

LISBON AND NORTH, 10 days

DAY 1: Travel to Lisbon and settle into a hotel.

DAY 2: Castello de São Jorge, the Alfama, the Cathedral and the Rossio.

DAY 3: The Belém Tower, Hieronymite monastery, Carriage Museum, and Museum of Popular Art, stopping en route at the Museu Nacional de Arte Antiga.

DAY 4: Travel to Batalha, visiting Sintra and Alcobaça on the way; settle into a hotel.

Note: If the Batalha pousada is full, accommodations generally are available in Leiria 10 k north.

DAY 5: Tour the monastery; travel to Tomar, visiting the castle of Almourol on the way; tour the monastery; settle into a hotel.

DAY 6: Travel to Viseu, visiting Coimbra on the way; settle into a hotel.

DAY 7: Cathedral; Museu Grão Vasco; tour of the village; travel to Braga; Cathedral; settle into a hotel.

DAY 8: Museu Biscainhos; tour of the town; Bom Jesus; travel to Oporto, visiting Guimarães on the way; settle into a hotel.

DAY 9: Cathedral; São Francisco; Palacio Bolsa; tour of the port lodges; travel to Lisbon, arriving late; settle into a hotel.

DAY 10: Departure.

Note: If an extra day is available, on day 8 travel to Bragança instead of Oporto; settle into a hotel. On day 9 walk the town, the castle, the Domus Municipalis, and travel to Oporto, settling into a hotel. Days 9 and 10 above become days 10 and 11.

THE BEST OF PORTUGAL, 11 days

DAY 1: Travel to Lisbon and settle into a hotel.

DAY 2: Castello de São Jorge, the Alfama, the Cathedral and the Rossio.

DAY 3: The Belém Tower, Hieronymite monastery, Carriage Museum, and Museum of Popular Art, stopping en route at the Museu Nacional de Arte Antiga.

DAY 4: Travel to Évora and settle into a hotel; Roman temple; Cathedral and mansions.

DAY 5: Travel to Tomar, visiting Elvas and Marvão on the way; settle into a hotel.

DAY 6: Convent of Christ; travel to Batalha, visiting the castle of Almourol on the way; settle into a hotel.

Note: If the Batalha pousada is full, accommodations are generally available in Leiria 10 k north.

DAY 7: Tour of Batalha monastery; travel to Viseu; settle into a hotel; Cathedral; Museu Grão Vasco; tour of the village.

DAY 8: Travel to Braga; settle into a hotel; Cathedral; Museu Biscainhos; tour of the town; Bom Jesus.

DAY 9: Travel to Sintra, visiting Guimarães along the way; settle into a hotel.

DAY 10: Visit the three castles of Sintra; travel to Lisbon; settle into a hotel; São Roque, Igreha do Carmo, shopping in the Chaido, and the Calouste Gulbenkian museum, if time and energy allow.

DAY 11: Departure.

HISTORY

The tomb of Inês de Castro in Alcobaça's Santa Maria Monastery.

An understanding of Portuguese history enhances any visit. Here we present an outline, to which details will be added in the historical profiles that preface each chapter on sights.

PREHISTORY THROUGH THE BIRTH OF PORTUGAL (9000 B.C.-A.D. 1139)

c. 9000 B.C.	Neolithic occupation.
c. 1300 B.C.	Iberians migrate from North Africa.
c. 900 B.C.	Celts migrate from northern France.
138 B.C.	Rome defeats Virianthus.
19 B.C.	Augustus completes the conquest of the peninsula.

c. A.D. 400	German Suevi migrate to Portugal.
c. A.D. 500	Suevi fend off the Visigoths.
A.D. 711	Muslims invade from Morocco.
A.D. 1095	Henri of Burgundy becomes the Count of Portucale.
A.D. 1107-1185	The span of Afonso Anriques.
A.D. 1139	Afonso Anriques titles himself the king of Portugal.

Until Portugal became independent in the 12th century, the course of her history was little different from Spain's. While Portugal does not possess Spain's remarkable cave art, evidence exists of indigenous paleolithic people from about the same 10,000 B.C. era. Iberians who migrated from North Africa at the beginning of the first millennium B.C. settled the whole peninsula, Portugal included, as did the Celts four centuries later. A Celtic village, in fact, has been reconstructed in Citânia de Briteiros, near Braga. But little was known about these people before the Romans arrived in the second century to write descriptions of who and what they found. They described various tribes around the peninsula, including a particularly warlike group known as Lusitanians, after whom the Romans named a province in the center of latter-day Portugal. Romans knew the fighting spirit of these people well, for the Lusitanians had fought as mercenaries with Hannibal in Italy, so when the Romans set out to conquer the peninsula, they were not surprised that this tribe gave them more trouble than all the rest. The Lusitanian chief Virianthus defeated every Roman army sent against him, and was subdued only by treachery.

Rome finally prevailed in 19 B.C., then set out to civilize the country with roads, buildings, and its Latin language, that evolved into Portuguese. They left a gem of a temple at Évora. But by the fifth century A.D., Rome's decline allowed German tribes to divide up their Empire. The Suevi grabbed latter-day Portugal and were the only tribe to resist Visigothic hordes a century later.

Moors from across the Straits of Gibraltar conquered the peninsula in the eighth century, leaving only small enclaves of Visigoths in the extreme north. From these confines began five centuries of reconquest, moving at a snail's pace until a powerful king, Alfonso VI, came to the throne of Castile. Alfonso captured the Visigoth capital of Toledo, as well as Lisbon, and raided as far as the southern extremity of Spain. His successes frightened the Moors to calling on Morocco for assistance in the form of a fierce, fundamentalist sect, called the Almoravids, who rolled back Alfonso. Alfonso asked France for help. Among those who answered his call was Henri of

Burgundy, a relative of the French King. Henri helped stem the tide and was rewarded with northern Portugal, the territory known as *Portucale*, from which the modern name of the country derives.

This was the age of feudalism, which meant that Henri ruled his county on behalf of the King of Castile. When Henri died, however, his wife refused homage until compelled, and even then her son, still in his minority, claimed that her fealty did not include his. In time that son, Afonso Henriques, came of age, assumed his father's title, and refused homage until defeated in battle by the King of Castile. Then another invasion by Moroccans pressed Castile hard, although Afonso Henriques stemmed their advance in his territory. With that success and the continued distraction of his overlord, in 1139 the Count began to title himself Afonso I, the King of Portugal. From that moment on, with only a 60-year hiatus, Portugal has been independent of Spain.

THE BURGUNDIAN DYNASTY (1140-1385)

1185-1211	Sancho I completes the reconquest of Portugal.
1211-1223	Afonso II, the Fat, attacks the power of the Roman Catholic Church.
1277-1325	Dinis I revitalizes agriculture and founds the University of Coimbra.
1357-1367	Pedro I, the Cruel, breeds an illegitimate son from whom the succeeding House of Avís descends.
1367-1383	Fernando I rules with the scheming Leonor Telles.
1385	João, Master of the House of Avís, seizes the throne.

Initially Afonso's kingdom consisted of the northern third of modern Portugal only, but the rest was soon added through his conquests and those of his son, Sancho II. Afonso himself took Lisbon, already a major city because of its harbor. He also captured much of the south from the Moors, although they managed to win some of it back. When he died in 1185, he had founded a dynasty that would last for two centuries, and he left illegitimate children from whom Portugal's remaining two dynasties would descend. Thus, Afonso Henriques is aptly named the father of his country.

By the death of his son Sancho II in 1211, the reconquest had been completed. Thus Portugal was intact almost 300 years before Spain accomplished that goal. Sancho's son, Afonso II, tried to increase the monarch's power by curbing the power of the Church tied to Rome, but was excommunicated for his efforts, and died early. When his young heir came under the influence of Castile, he was overthrown by Afonso's brother, who convened the first parliament to include representatives from towns—the nascent middle class.

His son, Dinis I, gave land to the common farmer, who previously had subsisted as a mere serf, thus earning the sobriquet *Dom Dinis Labrador* (Dinis the Farmer). In addition, he founded Portugal's first university at Lisbon, which later moved to Coimbra. With all this he had time to write respectable poetry, and proved to be the best monarch of the Burgundian line. Two reigns later came Pedro I, the Cruel. Between murders Pedro found time to sire a number of illegitimate children, one of whom he installed as the abbot of the religio-military order of Avís, something like the Knights Templar. That abbot would one day be King.

Fernando I succeeded Pedro. His early death left his heiress daughter Beatrice under the control of his widow, Leonor Telles. Leonor openly took up with a courtier and married off Beatrice to the King of Castile. Many were upset, both at Leonor's morals and her politics. One day the Master of the House of Avís came to the palace to kill Leonor's paramour, then he incited a crowd to proclaim him Regent and, finally, King. Thus did João I, formerly the abbot Master of the Order of Avís, become King of Portugal in 1385, and the founder of a dynasty.

THE HOUSE OF AVÍS (1385-1588)

1385-1433	The reign of João I.
1394-1460	The life of Prince Henry the Navigator.
1419	Discovery of the Madeira Islands.
1431	Discovery of the Azores.
1487	Bartolemeu Dias rounds the Cape of Good Hope.
1495-1512	The reign of Manuel I, the Fortunate.
1497-1498	Vasco de Gama reaches India.
1519-1521	Magellan circles the globe.
1580	The last king of the Avís line dies.

João I was fortunate to marry a special woman, the English Philippa of Lancaster, who raised four exceptional boys. When old enough they joined in an invasion of Ceuta on the Moroccan coast. Most of the credit for their successful conquest was paid to one son—Dom Henrique, who devoted the remainder of his life to encouraging maritime exploration, for which he became known to the English-speaking world as Prince Henry the Navigator. He financed expeditions that discovered the Madeira and Azore Islands, still territories of Portugal today, and other voyages that made their way down most of the African coast. His older brother succeeded their father as King in 1433, but died five years later mourning a third brother who had been captured in Morocco. The fourth, and last, brother travelled to the corners of Europe, something seldom done in those times.

Two reigns later the King, João II, received Columbus to hear his plan to sail west to India, but declined to back him, in part because Bartolemeu Dias had rounded the Cape of Good Hope, giving the Portuguese one route to India. João II died without heirs, bringing the throne to the son of an adopted child of Dom Henriques. Manuel I, called the Fortunate, presided over many of the great Portuguese discoveries. Vasco de Gama reached India, establishing Portuguese colonies, and Pedro Cabral discovered Brazil. Portugal grew rich, allowing Manuel to build extensively in a flamboyant style named after him. Splendid examples survive in the Belém Tower, the Hieronymite Monastery, the Convent at Tomar and parts of the great Cathedral at Batalha. Intricate designs displayed the exotic flora and fauna discovered by the Portuguese explorations.

Manuel's son married the daughter of the Spanish monarchs Ferdinand and Isabella, while in turn Manuel's sister went to Spain to marry the heir to that throne. The exchange cost Portugal a great deal. The Spanish required that Portugal institute an inquisition like their own, and Manuel's new daughter-in-law gave Spain a future claim on the Portuguese throne. The next Portuguese monarch died pursuing chivalric romance in Morocco, leaving no heirs. The only remaining Portuguese in line for the throne was his uncle, a cardinal, who died in 1580 without children.

SPAIN AND THE HOUSE OF BRAGANÇA (1580-1910)

1580-1640	Spain rules Portugal.
1640-1656	The Duke of Bragança recaptures the throne.
1706-1750	Architecture flowers under João V.
1750-1777	The indolent José I cedes governing to Pombal.
1755	Lisbon is razed by the Great Earthquake.
1808-1821	The court goes into exile in Brazil.
1808-1812	The Peninsular War.
1825-1836	Civil war erupts over the succession.
1908	King Carlos I and his heir are assassinated.
1910	Manuel II abdicates, ending the monarchy.

When the last Avís died childless, Felipe II of Spain gained the throne of Portugal, but to ensure popular acceptance, he agreed that the Portuguese government would be staffed only by Portuguese. While this arrangement lasted, Spain ruled Portugal, but 60 years later Felipe's descendent of the same name appointed Spaniards to government positions, inciting the Portuguese. The most powerful Portuguese noble of the time was the Duke of Bragança, who the Spanish tried to seduce with power by giving him control of the Portuguese army. He turned his troops against the Spanish in 1640, conquering all of Portugal in a matter of weeks, thereby founding the Bragança dynasty, Portugal's last, as João IV.

Half a century later, after independence had been consolidated, João V came to the throne. Supported by gold and diamonds from Brazil, he built ostentatiously throughout Portugal. Especially splendid are the palaces at Mafra and Queluz, near Lisbon, and the library at Coimbra, an ideal of its type. His son, José I, lacking all ambition, trifled while a favorite minister named Pombal ruled the country. In 1755, after Lisbon was leveled by an earthquake, Pombal resurrected the city, which still bears his orderly stamp.

Since 1386 Portugal had been tied by treaty in a "strong, perpetual and true league of friendship" with England. When Napoléon declared war on England, this treaty embroiled Portugal in the conflict. Napoléon invaded in 1808 to deprive the English of Portuguese bases, and England sent the future Duke of Wellington to drive him out, though the royal court of Portugal sailed to its colony of Brazil as soon as the French came near. Wellington chased the French from Portugal by 1811, and from Spain two years later. But the royal court had found the weather and society of Rio de Janero more congenial than Lisbon, and remained abroad for another decade.

By the time a king returned to Portugal in 1821 he found that a constitution rejecting absolute rule had been drafted in his absence. In the end, the monarchy fell victim to increased political awareness of the people. In 1908 the King and his heir were assassinated. The King who followed would be the last. An uprising by the navy sent him into exile in 1910, making Portugal a republic.

THE REPUBLIC (1910-)

1910-1926	Liberal governments replace one another.
1926	A military coup installs General Carmona.
1928	Salazar enters the government.
1932	Salazar becomes Prime Minister.
1968	Incapacitated, Salazar is replaced.
1968-1974	Marcelo Caetano takes over.
1974	The flower revolution brings socialism.

1975   The African colonies are given independence.

1976   A new constitution is enacted.

With no tradition or principles of democratic rule, Portugal had a stormy time with republican government, switching ministers and parties several times a year. At the same time the economic situation deteriorated, deepened by the cost of Portugal's joining the Allies in World War I. The situation had grown desperate by the 1920s. In 1925 three separate military coups were attempted; in 1926 one succeeded.

The military government drafted a civilian, Antonio de Salazar, to solve crushing economic problems. At first he succeeded brilliantly, so much so that he became Prime Minister by 1932, and promulgated a new constitution in which only his party could field candidates, to become dictator, in fact, if not in title. Salazar kept Portugal out of World War II, from which it profited greatly, but by the 1960s, economic trouble had brewed again. At the same time, voices for independence in her African colonies of Angola, Mozambique and Guinea could no longer be stilled. During this crisis, Salazar suffered an incapacitating stroke from which he never recovered, and eventually died in 1970. His replacement was a party faithful—Marcelo Caetano. Caetano tried to hold the African colonies with 50,000 troops, a huge drain for small Portugal, but too few to quiet the voices of independence. Almost everyone except the government could see that the expensive military enterprise was not working.

The army revolted in 1974, filling the streets of Lisbon with flower-draped tanks in the so-called "Flower Revolution." A realistic general who recognized the futility of armed intervention in Africa became president and freed the colonies as his first official act. Much strife remained before Portugal settled into orderly political processes—a communist government that had to be ousted by a popular uprising, and governments that changed themselves capriciously. During the 1970s Portugal seemed the most politicized of countries, but now appears set on a moderate socialist course.

ART AND ARCHITECTURE

The nave of the church at Batalha Monastery.

Expect atmosphere and charm from Portuguese art rather than genius. Évora, Lisbon, and, especially, Batalha surround the visitor
with late medieval architecture of a distinctive style—part Gothic,
part intricate Manueline, interposed with lively sculpture. Hardly a
city or town fails to provide at least one plaster building of pleasing
proportions, whose details are picked out by darker stone—the Portuguese national style. Gilded wood dances intricately inside churches, while *azulejos*—painted glazed tiles, brighten the walls. No one

comes to Portugal primed to study familiar art, but everyone leaves with happy eyes.

ROMAN TO ROMANESQUE

Rome left a souvenir of her occupation in the form of a lovely second-century temple to Diana in the center of **Évora**. Archaeologists uncovered a Roman city at **Conimbriga**, with the largest private houses known from Roman times, and fine mosaics.

Following conquest by the Moors in the eighth century, came five centuries of reconquest by the Christians, gaining back land piece by piece. Often, when Christians conquered Moors, they put them to work designing buildings. A splendid example of such *mudejar* architecture survives from the tenth century—**São Pedro de Lourosão** outside **Olivera do Hospital** near Coimbra. Predating the time of towering cathedrals, its low ceiling rests on horseshoe arches atop ancient Roman columns. Elegant paired windows separated by delicate columns are of a typical Moorish style called *ajimeses*.

The 12th century ushered in the Romanesque architectural style. Named for the use of Roman architectural elements, churches in this style rest barrel vaults on round Roman arches. Portugal possesses three exceptional examples. *Sé Velha* (Old Cathedral) in **Coimbra** was designed in the middle of the 12th century as a fortress church, for it was a time of war and Coimbra defended the front. An imposing facade with just one window is topped by triangular merlons to protect defenders as they shot at attackers. Massive piers inside support the ceiling while Byzantine columns define the galleries, but the altarpiece and cloisters are later by a century or more. This church "in armour" epitomizes medieval times. In **Tomar** the magnificent *Convento do Cristo* is surrounded by sturdy 12th-century walls. All of the convent is wonderful, but the centerpiece is the oldest part, the 12th-century *Charola*, a 16-sided church of the Knights Templar, modeled on the Mosque of the Rock in Jerusalem. An octagon inside rises two stories to a dome separated by an ambulatory from the polygon of the building walls. This solid stone church echos of crusading knights. In **Bragança**, miraculously, a civil building survives from the 12th century—the *Domus Municipalis*, City Hall. Its five sides are pierced by multiple Romanesque round arches, playing against medallions that ring the roof. Since the interior of the structure is composed of a single imposing room, one wonders how city government could have functioned.

Castles survive in abundance from these early times. The most romantic is **Almourol**, perfectly situated on an island in the Tagus

River, near Tomar. Approachable only by boat, it looks as a fairy castle should, with stout walls and soaring towers. High on a hill in **Leiria**, Afonso Henriques, the first King of Portugal, constructed another castle in the early 12th century. Purists point out that the castle was modified later, but it looks magical nonetheless.

GOTHIC AND MANUELINE

By the end of the 12th century the Gothic style swept through Europe. Round arches gained points reaching up to ever-higher ribbed vaults resting on thinner supports to add lightness and a heavenly upward thrust to buildings. In **Alcobaça** the church of *Santa Maria Monastery* dates from this era and has been lovingly freed of later additions. It is particularly interesting because few churches remain in its Cistercian mold. Supports are massive in this case, although they lift typically ribbed vaulting above, and, uncharacteristically, beams connect the arches. The church stretches inordinately long and thin, a tunnel of devotion. In the southern transept lies the greatest Portuguese Gothic sculpture, the tombs of Pedro I and Inês de Castro, discussed later.

More typically Gothic is the 14th-century church in **Santa Maria de Vitoria** monastery at **Batalha**. The monastery was commissioned by João I, founder of the house of Avís, in gratitude for God's help in defeating the Spanish. Complete with rose window, buttresses, pinnacles and mammoth door outside (unfortunately with only copies of the original statues, except for the central *Christ in Majesty*), the plain interior sweeps upward to a forest of ribs in the vaulting. This is flamboyant Gothic at its most harmonious.

The other buildings of the monastery are magnificent Gothic structures too, but decorated in the 15th and 16th centuries in a new style. Portugal grew rich from her overseas colonies during the reign of Manuel I, "the Fortuate," and built on a grand scale. An original style developed that celebrated the sea and the foreign flora and fauna Portugal had just discovered. The term *Manueline* refers not to building plans or structures, but to the decoration, its profusion and representation of ropes, knots, ship's masts, palm trees, acorns, leaves and flowers, or even playful designs. Decoration became a wonder of its own, a feature on which light could play.

The first Manueline building is the *Church of Jesus* at **Setúbal**. Inside, huge pillars unexpectedly twist in spirals to support a flamboyantly ribbed ceiling. The *Royal Palace* at **Sintra** contrasts Manueline wings with a rich mudjar center, famed for its wood ceiling. But the *Hieronymite Monastery* at **Belém**, outside Lisbon, represents the culmination of the style. The church interior is a grotto of tapering columns rising to webs of crossed vaulting above. The cloister outside is Manueline at its most sophisticated. For a harmonious mix of Gothic structure and Manueline decor see *Santa Maria de Vitoria* monastery at **Batalha**, noted before, whose *Claustro Real* (Royal Cloister) and the *Capelas Imperfeitas* (Unfinished Chapels) use rich decorations to play superbly against Gothic structures. Beneath intricate stone canopies in the *Capela do Fundador* (Founders Chapel) repose the bodies of João I, his wife Philippa, and Prince Henry the Navigator, their son. Yet the most famous example of the Manueline is the often-pictured window surround of the nave in the *Convent of Christ* at **Tomar**. Amid the masts, knots, seaweed and chains, a window barely can be discerned. This was the apex of Manueline exuberance.

NEOCLASSIC AND BAROQUE

The Manueline style lasted only 100 years, replaced by a neoclassical reaction against extravagant decor in the late 16th century. In **Lisbon** *São Vencente de Fora* is simple, classically perfect and original in its coffered ceiling. Lovely *ajulejos* (painted tiles) cover the walls, some depicting the capture of Lisbon from the Moors. At **Coimbra** *Santa Clara a Nova* suggests the Parthenon of Rome. It is visually harmonious, though moving toward profuse decoration again.

In the beginning of the 18th century, King João V promised to build a monastery if God would grant an heir. He repaid his debt with the sumptuous palace/monastery at **Mafra**. Portugal's wealth then was due to the gold and emeralds discovered in her colony of Brazil, allowing João to lavish millions on this palace. A German architect, known to the Portuguese as João Frederico Ludovice, designed a baroque masterpiece whose walls run two miles in circumference. Marble, elegant in color and tone, covers all.

In 1755 an earthquake leveled much of **Lisbon**. Reconstruction was managed by Prime Minister Pombal, giving a name—*Pombaline*—to classical open squares and boulevards, especially Lisbon's grand *Terreiro do Paço* (Terrace of the Palace), elegantly lined with buildings and centered on a statue of the King, José I.

By the end of the century, a busier baroque style dominated, exemplified by the *Royal Palace* at **Queluz**, outside Lisbon. Although inspired by Versailles, its feel is quite different, thanks to its rose stucco facade. The mirrored throne room, however, and the queen's boudoir do suggest the original. This is one of the few palaces designed for a queen—Maria I—and looks it.

SCULPTURE

Sculpture in Portugal is omnipresent and frequently of high quality. Of the early sculpture, everyone's favorite is the tombs of Pedro I and his beloved Inês de Castro in the monastery in **Alcobaça**. While still a prince, Pedro fell in love with the Spaniard Inês, but his father had her murdered, probably because he mistrusted her Spanish connections. When Pedro came to the throne, he viciously killed her assassins, then moved Inês' body to Alcobaça, where he constructed his own tomb facing hers so she would be his first sight on the Day of Resurrection. These tombs lie in opposite transepts of the church. Inés' effigy, borne by six angels, looks beautiful enough to explain Pedro's passion. The carving of the Last Judgment at Inês' feet is sublime. Pedro's tomb is emblazoned with an intricately designed wheel of fortune at his head and scenes of his last moments at his feet. The tombs are not to be missed.

The place to study medieval sculpture is in the *Museu Machado de Castro* in **Coimbra**. The wing to the right on the ground floor traces the progression to the Renaissance. One favorite is an early limestone knight in heavy armour astride his equally sturdy steed, that belies its small size. Among other interesting Renaissance pieces, the left wing displays the genius of Nicholas Chanterene, a Walloon by birth, but the great sculptor of the Manueline period. His *Virgin Reading* and *Entombment of Eight Personages* provide a foretaste of the exceptional sensitivity he exhibited in masterpieces elsewhere. In **Coimbra**, in the church of the *Monastery of Santa Cruz*, tombs by Chanterene of Afonso Henriques and Sancho I, the first two kings of Portugal, flank the altar. Originally painted, they still exude strength in restful sleep. Chanterene is largely responsible for the west door of the church at the *Hieronymite Monastery* at **Belém** in the outskirts of Lisbon, which includes a statue of Prince Henry the Navigator and effigies of Manuel I and his queen. The overall harmony of conception is remarkable for a time when the placement of statues was dictated by architecture.

Names of sculptors are seldom known in Portugal and attributions to individuals become dubious because most pieces were produced in workshops, but, here and there, an exceptional artist can be picked out. In the late 16th century two Portuguese brothers named Gaspar and Domingos Coelho produced a masterpiece in **Portalegre**. The high altar of the *Cathedral* places panels in an arched frame, a pleasing classical aberration during a time of gilded excess.

By the 18th century, rococo gilded wood ran riot through churches. *São Francisco* in **Oporto** is the outstanding example. It looks as if the carvers covered every space with gilded wood and were not satisfied, so they covered their gilded wood with more. In **Aveiro**, near Oporto, the chancel of the church of *Convento de Jesus das Barrocas*, now a museum, includes a remarkable marble mosaic.

One final sculpture deserves mention, because every visitor to **Lisbon** sees it—the statue of José I in *Terreiro do Paço* square. Construction of the palace at Mafra required so much carving that a school was established to train sculptors. Joaquim Machado de Castro emerged as its most gifted pupil. To make certain that his rebuilding of Lisbon would receive royal commendation, Pombal wanted a statue of the King displayed centrally and called on de Castro to create this "pretty" king atop a small horse. The bronze work is of the highest order, amazingly intricate in detail, but the conception does not seem like one that would please the sitter. Nonetheless it did. José was apparently happy to see himself as a chubby, effete boy on a pony.

PAINTING

Painting in Portugal holds interest because the works, so little known or reproduced, come as fresh surprises. In fact Portugal bred scores of competent artists whose work is admirable, but gave birth to only one genius—Nuno Gonçalves.

The place to begin any study of Portuguese painting is in the *Museu Nacional de Arte Antiga* in **Lisbon**. The second floor displays great works by foreign artists, including a fine *Temptation of Saint Antony* by Bosch, the splendid *Saint Jerome* by Dürer, and the magnificent *Twelve Apostles* by Zurbarán. Portuguese paintings take up the third floor. No one can fail to be arrested by the huge six-panel polyptych called *The Adoration of Saint Vincent* by Nuno Gonçalves, from the middle of the 15th century. Saint Vincent, the patron saint of Lisbon is portrayed full-figure in the middle of both center panels as he receives homage from the court, bishops and representatives of all strata of society. In the left center panel Alonso V kneels with his son beside him, the future João II, and Prince Henry the Navigator stands behind. Queen Isabel kneels opposite, the king's mother behind her, and standing in the rear left is probably the artist himself. The crowded composition presents wondrous faces of almost startling realism. Alas, this is the only known work of Gonçalves' genius.

Gonçalves' talent soars above that of his 15th-century peers displayed on the same floor. The great Flemish artist Jan van Eyck's visit to Portugal in 1428 gave rise to a host of Portuguese imitators. Thus, except for Gonçalves, early Renaissance painting in Portugal consists either of charming primitives or of van Eyck imitations. By the next century, however, Portugal found its stride. The greatest Manueline painter was Jorge Afonso, whose altar painting of *Christ Appearing to the Virgin* in the church *Madre de Deus* in **Lisbon** is a balanced portrayal of wondrous, peaceful faces. In the ambulatory of the *Templars' church* in **Tomar**, hangs his *Resurrection*, with Christ floating above the city of Lisbon. Gregorio Lopes is famed for his backgrounds which make intricate frames for unexceptional figures. The *Museu Nacional de Arte Antiga* in **Lisbon** displays his *Virgin and Child with Angels*, a striking work. On the other hand, Cristovão Figueiredo painted faces as well as anyone, as his *Entombment* in the same museum shows. But the most haunting painting in the museum is by an unknown artist—*Portrait of a Lady with a Rosary*, worthy of Zurbarán.

"The Grand Vasco," Vasco Fernandes, mastered light. His *Pentacost* in the sacristy of the church of **Mosteiro de Santa Cruz** in **Coimbra** is dramatic and monumental. Fernandes worked mostly in **Viseu**, the best place to see and appreciate his art. *Museu Grão Vasco*, named for him, holds his masterpieces—five altars from the cathedral. *Saint Peter on his Throne* is masterful for spatial illusion, while *Calvary* crowds peasants and German soldiers in an assemblage for the eye to wander over and the mind to contemplate.

Domingos António de Sequieira (1768-1837) was Portugal's Goya, an exile—like Goya—because of his liberal political views. He won a gold medal in Paris by besting Delacroix and Gericault, among other luminaries. Much of his finest work is displayed in the *Museu Nacional de Arte Antiga* in **Lisbon**. *Saint Bruno at Prayer*, simple and intense, employs bold foreshortening. *Count do Farrobo* is perceptive and forceful. The *Portrait of the Viscount of Santarem and Family* is complex, subtle in tone, and arresting. His charcoals are luminous. Sequieira indeed was a master, and a fitting culmination for Portuguese art.

In 1955 Portugal received one of the greatest gifts of art that has ever been donated. Calouste Gulbenkian, an Armenian from Turkey, brokered oil for Iraq to become one of the wealthiest men in the world. He was an avid collector of art who could afford the best, and lived his last fifteen years in Portugal, dying in 1955, but leaving a museum in **Lisbon** to house his collections. The *Calouste Gulbenkian Museum* ranks with the major museums of the world, and contains the finest collection ever amassed by a single person. Its collection of oriental carpets and oriental ceramics unfailingly interest. The museum houses European paintings from medieval times to the 20th century, with its greatest strength from the 17th century through Impressionism. The collection of art nouveau Lalique glass is unsurpassed. Visiting this museum to see its choice selection of great European paintings provides a fine context for the Portuguese art seen elsewhere around the country—the Portuguese artists compare surprisingly well.

FOOD AND DRINK

Homemade bread.

Tourists don't need to revise their dining habits in Portugal as they do in Spain—meals here are served at the same times as at home. They will find the food heavy, but enjoy the flavors, and, especially, the freshness of the fish. Portuguese restaurants generally cost less than those in Spain, which adds to the pleasure, and are similarly rated with forks on a plaque outside of the restaurant to indicate a price level and range of offerings, with four and five forks signifying the high end. Like the Spanish, the Portuguese sauté in olive oil and use garlic generously. (Say *sem alho* to request no garlic.) A gross comparison of the two cuisines would find many similar dishes, but give the nod to Spain for subtlety and to Portugal for spices. After all, the Portuguese first brought Eastern spices in quantity to Europe, and favor cumin, coriander and paprika today.

Breakfast (*pequeno almoço*) is a light meal, consisting of bread or a roll (*bolo*) and tea (*chá*) or coffee—*café solo* (black), or *café com leite* (with milk). Full lunch (*almoço*) may be eaten in a restaurant, or sandwiches and simple platters munched in a *cervejaria* (beer hall). *Pastelarias* (pastry shops) serve more than just sweets. There are tapas-type bars, called *tascas*, serving delectables after work. Restaurants open for dinner (*jantar*) at seven and close at ten, later in Lisbon. A *menu do dia* will offer a multicourse meal at a set price lower than the regular menu, which is a la carte. *Parato do dia* is the daily special.

FOOD

Bread lovers will think they've reached heaven in Portuguese restaurants. Corn bread (*pão de milho*) is not sweet or coarse, but fragrant with just a hint of corn. If you have never had barley bread (*pão do centeio*), here is your chance. *Pão de broa* is a rye bread against which all others will be compared. There are scores of others, some regional, some available nationally, but every one delectable.

The menu (*lista* or *ementa*) will start with appetizers, either individual choices, such as *presunto* (proscuitto-type cured ham), or a combination (*acapipes* or *entrada*) that should include wonderful bread.

Soups (*sopas*) come in great variety and can be hearty enough for a light meal. The most famous is *caldo verde*, a potato soup including sausage and lightly cooked kale. *Sopa a alentejana* is the most garlicky of garlic soups, usually with an egg poached in the broth. *Sopa de mariscos* is a seafood bisque, *caldeirada* a seafood chowder. Hearty bean soup is *sopa de feijões*. In addition, the Portuguese make their own version of *gazpacho*, and if it is *a alentejana*, it will have ham or sausage added. For something lighter try *canja de galenha*, chicken and rice soup.

Fish (*peixe*) often is the best menu choice, whether broiled or fried. Freshness makes its taste a revelation for many of us. In addition to plain fish, there are interesting combinations to try. The Portuguese live on codfish (*bacalhau*), often serving it with just potatoes, which is bland, but they also offer *bacalhau dourado*, in a tomato, onion and garlic sauce, or *lisbonense*, in a cream sauce, or any of 100 other versions. *Cataplana* is clams stuffed with sausage and bacon, and delicious. *Sardinhas assadas* are the world's best sardines.

Meat (*carne*) and poultry (*ave*) can be interesting. In fact a simple grilled chicken (*frango*) will have a flavor that was lost when we began mass-producing our fowl. Try one with *piri-piri* sauce, a hot sauce with a kick. One flavorful specialty, and an original combination, is *porco a alentejana*—pork marinated in wine and spices to which clams are added. Suckling pig (*leitao*) roasted (*assado*) is invariably good. Lamb (*cordiero*) or kid (*cabrito*) cooked over wood can be superb. Avoid beef.

Portuguese cheese (*queijo*) is delicious, especially *serra*, mild *Castelo Branco*, and *alentejo* made from sheep's milk. *Cabreiro* is a goat cheese—*beja* salty, or *serpa* somewhat sharp. *Flamengo* is similar to Gouda.

Deserts (*sobremesas*) go beyond the universal flan (*flã*), though they tend to cloying sweetness. If such is your fancy, try *pudim Molotov*, a meringue with sweet topping, *touçinho do ceu* or *sonhos*. *Arroz doce*, rice pudding is always available. Fruit (*fruta*), especially oranges, will generally prove an excellent choice.

DRINK

As wine prices rise, people are forced to search out lesser known, more affordable varieties. Now Portugal is being discovered as a producer of superior wine. Do not judge Portuguese wine by Mateus—those omnipresent flagons of semisparkling, slightly sweet rosé wine—or by Lancers in the pottery bottle. Portugal can do much better.

In the center of the country, around the city of Viseu, is the large production area of **Dão**, bottling reds and whites in quantity. Here wine is aged for 5-7 years in oak to create smooth vintages of great body, similar to burgundy. These are good, modestly priced wines. The reds are best drunk after at least five years, the whites no older. The largest bottler is SOGRAPE whose "Grão Vasco" is reliable, but J.M. Da Fonseca's "Terras Altas" ranks a level higher. Pinhel, nearby, produces wines of similar character but with more finesse. A good Pinhel can stand up to a second growth French wine at a third or even a quarter of its price.

The best wine areas surround Lisbon. **Colares**, near Sintra, grows grapes in sand dunes. At the turn of the century this sand warded off the great attack of *phylloxera* that destroyed all vines through France and Europe, forcing a grafting of traditional vines to American roots resistant to the plague. Only the wines of Colares still grow from the native European root stock. The reds of Colares count among Portugal's best, dry and rich in tannin. Unfortunately, vines are rapidly giving way to seaside bungalows, causing supplies to dwindle and prices to rise. The best whites come from Buçelas and Carcavelos, whose territory is unfortunately small. The wines are light, dry, and fruity. Near Lisbon, but south, vines grow around the city of Setubal. J.M. da Fonseca produces two reds, "Periquita" and "Palmela." There are wine connoisseurs who dismiss "Periquita" as ordinary, but we have found it satisfactorily smooth, if light, and an exceptional buy. "Palmela" is lighter, more like a bordeaux despite the burgundy bottle shape, and is considered a value by almost everyone.

For a different experience, try one of Portugal's **green wines** (*vinhos verdes*). These are grown in the extreme north where cool temperatures shorten the growing season. Grapes are picked young—"green"—hence the name. A chilled white will be light and dry, even astringent; the reds, also chilled, are an acquired taste. Monção holds first place among the regions producing such wine.

Portugal's most famous wine is **port**, named for Oporto, the place from which it has been shipped since the 18th century. Port is intensely rich, so much so that it is sipped from a glass holding only a small amount. It is a fortified wine—brandy is added to arrest grape fermentation and raise the alcohol content to 20 percent. Vintage ports come only one year in five on average and are not ready for drinking until they are a minimum of ten years old. People either love their mix of rich flavors or find them cloying. Crusted port is a blend of years, lighter than vintage port, and ready for drinking in five years or so. The most accessible of the ports is called tawny, matured in casks rather than bottles until pale maroon in color and delicate. Darker-colored ruby port is a younger, cheaper version. White ports are gaining in popularity; dry and chilled they make a nice aperitif. Taylor, Cockburn, and Sandeman each bottles acceptable dry versions. The other famous Portuguese fortified wine is **Madeira**, from the island of that name, so rich it suggests a syrup.

Most of the wine in Portugal is sold as *vinho da casa*, house wine, or *vinhos da região*, regional wine, and will be better than it costs. It can be red (*tinto*), white (*branco*), or rose. Beer (*cerveja*) can be excellent; try Sagres brand. Water is *água*.

A list of Portuguese words for commonly available foods follows, arranged by the categories on most menus. A pocket guide to Portuguese food will still prove helpful since the available variety is large.

COMMONLY USED WORDS AND PHRASES

PORTUGUESE	ENGLISH
SOPAS	**SOUPS**
Caldeirada	fish chowder
Caldo verde	potato and kale soup
Canja de galenha	chicken and rice soup
Sopa a alentejana	garlic soup with egg
Sopa de feijão	bean soup
Sopa de marisco (or de peixes)	seafood bisque
OVAS	**EGGS**
Ovos cozido	hard boiled
Ovos mal pasados (or quentes)	soft boiled
Ovos estrelados	fried eggs
Ovos escalfados	poached eggs
Ovos mexidos	scrambled eggs
PEIXE E MARISCOS	**FISH AND SHELLFISH**
Ameijoas	clams
Anchovas	anchovies
Arenques	herring
Atum	tuna
Bacalhau	codfish
Camarões	shrimp
Caranguejo	crab

COMMONLY USED WORDS AND PHRASES

PORTUGUESE	ENGLISH
Carabineiros (or gambas)	prawns
Cataplana	clams stuffed with sausage and bacon
Eiros	eel
Espadarte	swordfish
Linguado	sole
Mexilhões	mussels
Ostras	oysters
Pescada	hake
Robalo	sea bass
Salmão	salmon
Salmonete	red mullet
Sardinhas	sardines
Truta	trout

CARNE	MEAT
Assado	roasted
Chouriço:	spicy smoked sausage
Cordeiro	lamb
Costeleta	chop
Cozido	boiled
Figado	liver
Grelhado	grilled
Panado	fried in breadcrumbs

COMMONLY USED WORDS AND PHRASES

PORTUGUESE	ENGLISH
Porco	pork
Presunto	cured ham similar to proscuitto
Rins	kidneys
Salsicha	fresh sausage
Salteado	sautéed
Vitela	veal

AVES E CACA	POULTRY AND GAME
Faisão	pheasant
Frango	chicken
Ganso	goose
Pato	duck
Veado	venison

LEGUMES	VEGETABLES
Alcachofra	artichoke
Alface	lettuce
Alho	garlic
Arroz	rice
Batata	potato
Beringela	eggplant
Broculos	broccoli
Cenoura	carrot
Cogumelos	mushrooms

COMMONLY USED WORDS AND PHRASES

PORTUGUESE	ENGLISH
Couve	cabbage
Ervilhas	peas
Espinafres	spinach
Feijae	beans
Salada	salad
SOBREMESA	**DESSERT**
Arroz doce	rice pudding
Bolos	pastries
Flã	creme caramel
Gelado	ice cream
Pudim	pudding
FRUTA	**FRUIT**
Ananás	pineapple
Cerejas	cherries
Figos	figs
Framboesas	raspberries
Laranja	orange
Limão	lemon
Maçã	apple
Melão	melon
Morangos	strawberries
Pêssgo	peach
Pêra	pear

THE SIGHTS

We divide the sights of Portugal into three sections. There is enough to see in Lisbon and a 100-k radius around it to comprise one section. These sights include medieval monasteries, baroque palaces, and charming towns and beaches, in addition to cosmopolitan Lisbon. The Algarve is assigned a section of its own because it consists not of monuments, but of an uninterrupted string of beaches that can be enjoyed either for their own sake or as a respite during a tour of other parts of the country. The remainder of Portugal—the largest part of the country—comprises the third section.

Anyone landing in Lisbon will want to look first at the chapter *Lisbon and its Environs*. Travelers arriving from Spain may be interested first in the chapter *North and Central Portugal*. Rather arbitrarily, we have placed northern and central Portugal before the chapter on Lisbon and its environs. The Algarve has been placed at the end so it can be consulted at any time during a journey through Portugal.

Prefacing each of these three chapters is a short historical profile describing one of the major historical periods in Portugal. It is hoped that such information will add life to the sights.

CENTRAL AND
NORTHERN
PORTUGAL

The stairs to Bom Jesus near Braga.

HISTORICAL PROFILE:
THE BIRTH OF PORTUGAL

A country such as Italy is naturally defined by water on three sides and mountains on the fourth. Geographically, the Iberian Peninsula looks as though it too should comprise a single country—it makes no cartographical sense that Portugal, one slice of the Iberian peninsula, be separate from Spain. Portugal's northern border meanders between the two countries through minor mountains that do not demarcate, to leave a chunk of Spain atop Portugal. Although the Atlantic marks a natural end west and south, the long eastern border wanders haphazardly, following one river for a while, then drifting to the next, following no logic or order.

What are the reasons for the existence of such an erratic border, or any border at all? A difference in language does not provide the explanation, for the division of Iberia caused the separation of languages, rather than the other way around. The Portuguese people attribute their independence to a national hero, Afonso Henriques, who dared to proclaim himself king. But Portugal's boundaries remained stable for centuries after his death, despite continual wars with Spain. The answer seems to be that, rather than any crucial event or person, Portugal owes its nationhood to a series of battles going the right way at the right times over a span of centuries.

This is not to say that every difference between Spain and Portugal is the effect rather than the cause of their being separate countries. The historic stock from which the Portuguese descend differs slightly from Spain's. During the 16th and 17th centuries Portugal's commercial concerns lay in Africa and the Far East while Spain focused on America to the west. And Portugal's long alliance with England was one factor in keeping the nations apart. But history's accidents were also essential, for in the beginning Spain and Portugal were joined.

When the Romans came to the peninsula in the second century B.C., they found a mixture of people there—those known as Celtiberians—and endeavored to colonize them. Rome's most formidable opponents were a group called Lusitanians, who inhabited the area that would later become Portugal. They were led by a hero named Virianthus who, despite inferior numbers, regularly out-generalled the Roman troops sent to subdue him. Only after the Romans had bribed three of Virianthus' lieutenants to assassinate him, were the leaderless Lusitanians subdued, along with the other tribes occupying the peninsula. For administrative reasons the Romans then organized all of Iberia into smaller provinces, many of which developed the separate identities they would possess thereafter. One province, Lusitania, corresponded to the northern half of Portugal. Its major city, Olissipo, would later become Lisbon.

By the third century A.D., Rome's decline opened her empire to "barbarians." German tribes crossed the far borders and migrated down to the peninsula—Vandals took the south, Alans the east coast, and Suevi seized the area of Lusitania, which they found congenial in soil and climate to their native Germany. When fiercer Visigoths followed two centuries later, they conquered all of the peninsula except the territory of the Suevi, thus leaving a different population stock for Portugal than for Spain.

In 711, Islamic Moors conquered the peninsula, naming Portugal *al Garbi*, "the West," from which comes the modern name Algarve for their last outpost, Portugal's southern coast. Reconquest by Christians slowly won the peninsula back, mostly under the leadership of Castilian kings. Alfonso VI, at the time of El Cid, freed Lisbon in 1070, and reestablished a bishopric at Braga to the north. His success so frightened the Moors, however, that they called for help from their brethren in Morocco, the Almoravids, who chased Alfonso VI back to his former territory. Alfonso called on France for assistance.

In 1095, the son-in-law of the King of France came with reinforcements, including his cousin, Henri of Burgundy. After some military success, Alfonso VI gave Henri his illegitimate daughter Teresa as payment for his services, and her dowry included the title of Count of Portucale, the northern part of later-day Portugal. The territory was named after the Roman town of Portucale, *Portus Cale*, the port of Cale. Later the town's name would be shortened and made more Portuguese-sounding as "Porto," but "Portucale" remained the term for the original Christian lands and for all that they would win from the Moors, which is to say, the whole of Portugal.

Henri established his court at Guimarães, in the extreme north, near the bishopric of Braga. To encourage the economy he set aside a street for foreign merchants, and rebuilt the cathedrals of Braga and Oporto nearby. With wife Teresa's help, he also produced a son, Afonso Henriques.

Henri died in 1112, when his son Afonso Henriques was only five. His mother acted as regent for the young count. But when the king of Castile, Alfonso VII, called on his nobles to pay feudal homage for their territories, Teresa refused. Alfonso VII compelled her homage by force, although Afonso Henriques claimed that his mother did not speak for him. She had taken a lover and given birth to another child by that time, estranging herself from her son. Soon after, Afonso Henriques began grabbing the reins of government, leading, by his early twenties, to war with his mother. When Afonso defeated her army, she fled north into Galacia followed by Afonso with his army.

This incursion into his territory was too much for the king of Castile, who attacked Afonso Henriques, defeated him, and forced the homage this vassal had so long withheld.

Then another Muslim sect from Morocco, the Almohades, conquered their brothers in the peninsula and pressed hard against the king of Castile. Afonso Henriques met one detachment of Almohades at Oric in 1139 and defeated them. Feeling powerful, he assumed the title of king of Portugal. Of course, the king of Castile did not agree, but he was too occupied with powerful Moors to do anything about the matter. In 1179, Afonso Henriques gained the pope's recognition of his title, in return for a small annual tribute. Except for one interlude four hundred years later, the country remained independent of Spain from that time forth.

Afonso Henriques is described as fair complexioned, bearded and a giant of a man—as founders are wont to be imagined. He married Mafalda, the daughter of the count of Savoy. His territories originally comprised a little less than the northern half of modern Portugal, but he set out to expand them south by conquering the land still held by the Moors. In 1140, with the aid of Crusaders on their way to the Holy Land, he besieged Lisbon but retired upon payment of a tribute. In 1177, he enlisted English, Normans, Flemings and Germans on their way to the Second Crusade to attack Lisbon again, promising booty and land to those who would help. Witnesses claimed that Lisbon contained 150,000 men, women and children behind strongly fortified defenses. The city stood firm against the attackers' catapults, which delivered up to 5000 missiles during one ten-hour period, and the walls resisted their rams and fortified ladders. For 17 weeks of siege, the city held out before surrendering on October 23, 1147. Many of the crusaders accepted King Afonso's offer of land, settling north of Lisbon.

After this success, Afonso Henriques continued the conquest south, at one point controlling all but the southernmost quarter of the country. But the Moors fought back, first retaking, then losing land, as fortunes on both sides changed. Afonso Henriques also tried to carry conquest north into the Spanish territory of Galicia, where he was defeated, suffered a broken leg when a town portcullis fell on him, and endured the ignominy of capture by the king of Castile. He gained his freedom by payment of ransom, but his injury ended his wars. He died in 1185, at nearly 80, after 57 years on the throne, and left his son Sancho I a kingdom.

Sancho continued the effort to conquer southern Portugal, gaining the major city of Silves in 1189 with help from yet another itinerant army of crusaders. But the Moors retook the city two years later. Sancho came to the throne at 31 and died in 1211 at 57. His son Afonso II, the Fat, concerned about the power of the church, began investigating ecclesiastical abuses. The Pope responded by excommunicating him. After a reign of only 12 years, Afonso died of leprosy, leaving an heir who was 12.

The boy, Sancho II, remained under the thumb of advisors who encouraged him to marry the widow of an Andalusian captain. This frightened many Portuguese who feared Spanish influence at the court. With the backing of the nobles, his uncle petitioned the Pope to declare the marriage illegal. The Pope ordered Sancho to abandon his wife and accused him of a catalogue of crimes it would seem impossible for one so young to have accomplished. When Sancho refused to leave his wife, the Pope designated uncle Afonso as king in his stead. Afonso III captured his nephew's wife, to make certain that no heir could be bred, then chased Sancho to Castile. With the church's backing, Afonso III was able to complete the conquest of the south, once and for all. He convened the first Cortes which included representatives of towns, the nascent middle class, in addition to nobles and clergy.

His son Dinis I succeeded to the throne when Afonso III died in 1277. The new king was known as *Rei Lavrador*, "the Farmer King," for his interest in agriculture. To increase production, he decreed that anyone who raised crops for ten years on the same land be given title to the land, which made many who had lived as serfs free, land-owning citizens. He also founded the first Portuguese university, originally in Lisbon, then moved to Coimbra when the rowdiness of the students caused complaints from Lisbon's citizens. He had time to compose poetry and to marry Isabella, the daughter of the king of Aragon. In her time she was considered saintly, partly for her sanguine acceptance of Dinis' philandering, and was later canonized. In 1325 Dinis died after a golden reign of 46 years.

Dinis I was the star of the house founded by Afonso Henrique. With his successor, Afonso IV, the end would begin.

CENTRAL AND NORTHERN PORTUGAL

The two chapters that follow are devoted respectively to the Algarve—for lovely beaches—and to Lisbon and its rich environs, leaving most of Portugal's area to be covered in the present chapter. However, that task is not as daunting as it might seem. The distance from Évora in the south to Bravães in the extreme north is 250 miles, about the distance from New York City to Washington, and Portugal seldom stretches wider than 100 miles. Thus the area is not excessively large, and we concentrate on sights of interest to average travellers, relegating more specialized locales to excursion sections.

Starting south at the latitude of Lisbon, **Évora ★★★★** stands halfway across the width of the country, about two hours from the capital. It is probably the most beautiful town in Portugal, with a day's pleasant sights to be savored. Nearby are **Elvas ★★** and **Marvão ★★★**, both fine examples of fortified hilltowns from Medieval times. **Tomar ★★★**, 150 k northeast of Lisbon, preserves the mysteries of a 12th-century church of the Knights Templar embellished by splendid Manueline and Renaissance additions. In the same area, in the middle of the Tagus River, waits the most romantic castle in Portugal, **Almourol ★★**. **Coimbra ★★★** with a grand site and Medieval university lies just over two hours north of Lisbon. There are beaches nearby at **Figueira da Foz ★** and at **Aveiro ★★**, and the best Roman ruins in the country at nearby **Conimbriga ★**. **Viseu ★★★**, 125 k northeast of Coimbra, is the perfect Portuguese town, containing the features that most do, but more attractively than the rest. It also boasts of a fine art museum displaying two little-known but superior Portuguese painters from the Renaissance. Little **Guarda ★★**, by the Spanish border 66 k east of Viseu, is a center for a large concentration of atmospheric hilltop villages fortified in the Middle Ages. **Oporto ★★** is a mere 120 k north of Coimbra, even less from Viseu. It retains the character of its 19th-century port wine exporting industry. About 50 k north stands **Braga ★★**, a town of baroque splendors, within a hundred k of the northern border of Portugal. Nearby, in **Guimarães ★★**, is the castle in which the first king of Portugal was born, thus earning its title of the birthplace of the country. Near the eastern border with Spain,

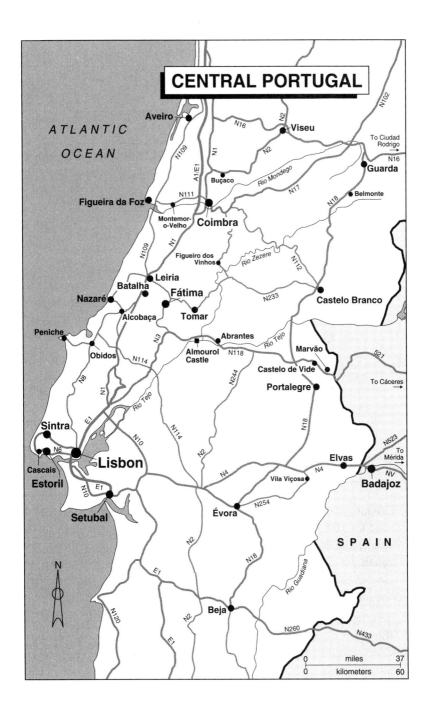

CENTRAL PORTUGAL

ATLANTIC OCEAN

Aveiro

N16

N2

Viseu

To Ciudad Rodrigo

N16

Guarda

Buçaco

Rio Mondego

N17

N18

Belmonte

Figueira da Foz

N111

Montemor-o-Velho

Coimbra

N109

N1

Figueiro dos Vinhos

Rio Zezere

N112

Leiria

Batalha

Fátima

N233

Castelo Branco

Nazaré

Alcobaça

Tomar

Peniche

Abrantes

Rio Tejo

Marvão

521

Obidos

N114

Almourol Castle

N118

Castelo de Vide

To Cáceres

N8

N1

N244

Portalegre

Rio Tejo

N18

Sintra

N10

N114

N523

To Mérida

N6

Elvas

NV

Lisbon

Cascais

E1

N2

N4

Vila Viçosa

N4

Badajoz

Estoril

N10

E1

Setubal

Évora

N254

N2

SPAIN

N18

Rio Guadiana

N

Beja

N260

N433

N120

N2

E1

miles 0 — 37

kilometers 0 — 60

250 k due east of Oporto, the town of **Bragança** ★★, which bred Portugal's last ruling dynasty, reposes in blissful isolation.

ALMOUROL CASTLE

See "Tomar excursions."

ARRAIOLOS

See "Évora excursions."

AVEIRO ★★

Population: 29,646
Area code: 034; zip code: 3800

From **Lisbon** *A-1 runs north for 82 k to a leg of 12 k on N-366 before joining N-1 toward Coimbra and Oporto. After 119 k, just past Condeixa-a-Nova the autoestrada A-1 may be taken for 74 k to an exit for Aveiro 14 k west. From* **Coimbra** *A-1 can be joined for a 74 k run to the Aveiro exit, then a jag west for 14 k. From* **Oporto** *A-1 runs south for 46 k to the Aveiro exit and a turn west for 14 k. From* **Guarda** *N-16 heads north then west for 68 k to* **Viseu**, *then continues west for 70 k to cross the autoestrada for a final leg of 14 k. Thus, Aveiro can serve as a stopover on the way to Oporto and north. Parking is available along the Canal Central and its extension, the Canal do Cojo, in the city center.*

Aveiro stands beside a huge lagoon extending north for 45 k and west for 10 k to the ocean. It is an unusual city crisscrossed by canals, near good, empty beaches, a city with the flavor of a dutch burgh. Its canals are plied by high bow, flat bottomed, punted boats, not dissimilar to gondolas—except for brightly painted bow emblems and the fact that they serve not as water-taxis, but as seaweed collectors.

Aveiro had its ups and downs. Until the end of the 16th century it thrived as a cod fishing port. In the 17th century, however, a storm closed Aveiro's lagoon from the sea and it quickly silted up, leading to two centuries of economic depression for the city. Because of the loss of its port and the malarial marshes that formed after the silting, Aveiro's population declined by two thirds, then, in 1808, the sandbar was breached by engineers, making Aveiro a port once again.

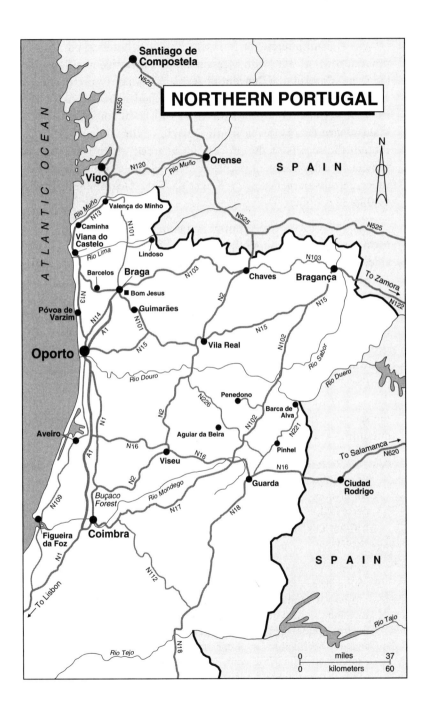

NORTHERN PORTUGAL

Today the city lives off fish, plentiful salt from the huge lagoon for the salted cod of Portugal, and seaweed for fertilizer.

Aveiro's main interest for tourists will be her beaches, but it is an unusual town as well, with pleasant sights. Attractive mansions line the **Canal Central**; the **Convent of Jesus** ★ contains a pretty church and museum with worthwhile paintings; and a boat tour of the **ria** ★★ (estuary) is a pleasant outing with local color to see. The **Vista Alegre** factory is 7 k south, outside of Ilhavo on N-109. Although the secrets of the process are guarded, there is a museum showing the development of this ware from clumsy beginnings. (Advance permission is necessary: Lugar da Vista Alegre, 3830 Ilhavo; ☎ 034 32 23 65.)

The sights of Aveiro are central and compact. The main square of town is the Praça da República. Here is the tourist office which provides information about boat trips through the lagoon. The 16th-century church of **Misericordia** flanks the east side of the square, with a nice doorway, tiled facade, and *azulejos* inside. Opposite is an elegant 17th-century **Town Hall**, beside the Pr. Humberto Delgado, which is actually a wide bridge over the Canal Central. Eastward stretches the shaded main avenue of town, Dr. Lourenço Paixinho; westward the Canal Central runs toward the lagoon. Boats quietly ply the water (which can, however, emit a foul smell on summer days). Following Rua da Grande Guerra south by the church front, the second left leads to the Convent of Jesus housing the regional museum.

Convento de Jesus and Museu de Aveiro   ★

Open Tues.-Sun. 10 a.m. to 12:30 p.m. and 2-5 p.m. Closed Mon. Admission: 350$00. The church was built in the 15th century but decorated in the early 18th. The interior contains some of the finest baroque gilded work in Portugal, finding its apex in the vaulted front chancel.

At the end of the 15th century the city received Donha Joana, the young sister of King João II. She was a celebrated beauty who had captivated Louis XI of France and almost married Richard III of England, but had decided to give up this world to enter a convent in Aveiro. She devoted the last 18 years of her life to sewing hair shirts, and was beatified for it. Scenes from the life of Saint Joana line the church walls. The choir contains the memorable tomb of this saint, a tomb that required 12 years to manufacture, as the intricacy of the polychrome marble mosaic demonstrates. But with all its intricacy, it manages to be moving. The adjoining museum is a mixed lot of sculpture, polychrome wood, crucifixes, and Vista Alegre porcelain. Best are the primitive paintings, including a 15th-century portrait of Saint Joana, which some attribute to the great Nuno Gonçalves.

The closest beach is **Praia de Barra**, on the sandbank due west. Proximity to Aveiro makes it crowded, though other beaches remain serenely secluded. 26 k south along N-109 and then a 5 k run west on N-334 brings **Praia de Mira**, a most attractive beach livened by stilted houses. Here fishing boats are still hauled by teams of oxen, as they once were in more famous Nazarré. Northern beaches require circling the lagoon on N-109 to Estarteja in 20 k, then turning west on N-109-5 to Torreira on the sandspit. Although opposite Aveiro, São Jacinto can only be reached by road through this circle through Torreira. Alternatively, there is a ferry. **Torreira** retains its fishing village atmosphere as ox-teams haul in the nets. **São Jacinto** is also small, but with more life and good swimming water.

WHERE TO STAY

For those moving quickly onward, a hotel in town is probably best, and Aviero offers a number of good values, but value also characterizes the beach hotels. Unless otherwise indicated, the establishments below are in the city of Aveiro.

EXPENSIVE ($100-$200)

In Águeda 24 k southeast:

Palácio de Águeda   1st-class ★ ★ ★ ★
Scenic N230 heads east from Aveiro before angling southerly along the Vouga river to Águeda in 22 k. Take N1 south for 2 k to Quinta da Borralha. Rooms: 48. ☎ *60 19 77; FAX 60 19 76; Telex 37823.* This hotel looks as all Portuguese hotels should. It is a former manor house of Count Borralha, renovated by a Frenchman with perfect taste. Formal gardens stretch behind, rooms are ample, all facilities are available, and the setting is restful. Live like a noble for a night.

On the sandspit between Torreira and São Jacinto:

Pousada da Ria   2nd-class ★ ★ ★
Bico do Muranzel. Rooms: 19. ☎ *483 32; FAX 483 33; Telex 37061.* Water on three sides adds drama to this modern building, whose plentiful windows make the most of the setting. Views of the ocean and fishing-boats in the lagoon provide restful days. Tennis is available too, at this heavily booked pousada.

MODERATE ($50-$99)

In Torreira:

Estalagem Riabela   2nd-class ★ ★
Rooms: 35. ☎ *481 37; FAX 481 47; Telex 37243.* Views of the lagoon, plus tennis and restful scenery at a truly modest price make this a special hotel.

Imperial   1st-class ★

*Rua Dr. Nascimento Leita (on the square beside the Convento de Jesus).
Rooms: 107.* ☎ *221 41; FAX 241 48; Telex 3794.* This is an unexceptional-looking modern hotel, but the bedrooms are comfortable without offensive decor, and views of the lagoon and convent gardens lie outside the window.

Paloma Blanca   R1st-class ★★

*Rua Luís Gomes de Carvalho, 23 (near the east end of Av. Dr. Lourenço
Peixinho and the train station). Rooms: 50.* ☎ *38 19 92; FAX 38 18 44;
Telex 37353.* The house is a former Moorish-style mansion with modernized, tastefully decorated rooms. The focus of the rooms is on a lovely garden. Don't tell the owner his prices are too low.

INEXPENSIVE (UNDER $50)

Arcada   3rd-class ★

*Rua Viana do Castelo, 4 (on the north edge of Pr. Humberto Delgado over
the canal, just north of the Pr. da República). Rooms: 49.* ☎ *230 01; FAX
218 86; Telex 37460.* The location is central and the hotel has been modernized recently. It occupies the 2nd-4th floors of an attractive building, but the bedrooms are a dreary tan and noise can be a problem. Still, the bedrooms are comfortable and include TVs.

WHERE TO EAT

Restaurant choices in Aveiro are not numerous, but those that exist are authentic.

MODERATE ($20-$50)

Centenario   ★★

*Largo do Mercado, 9 (opposite the covered market, halfway along Av. Dr.
Lourenço Peixinho).* ☎ *227 98. Closed Tuesday, and the first two weeks
of May.* Although its prices hover at the bottom of the moderate level, this restaurant, with its modern paneled dining room, looks like much more. A must to begin is *Sopa do Mar*. Fish and meat are equally good, so order any of the specials with security.

MasterCard and Visa accepted.

DIRECTORY

INFORMATION • Located in the main square of Pr. da República above the bank of Fonsecas & Burany (☎ 236 80).

TRAINS AND BUSES • Both trains and buses are served by the station at the east end of Av. Dr. Lourenço Peixinho (☎ 244 85). Service is frequent to Lisbon, Coimbra and Oporto.

BOM JESUS

See Braga excursions.

BRAGA ★ ★

Population: 64,113
Area code: 053; zip code: 4700

Braga is north of **Oporto** *by A-1 or N-14 for 54 k. From Vigo in* **Spanish Galicia** *take A-9 south for 32 k to Tui on the border, then N-13 in Portugal south for 68 k to Viana do Castelo. From there N-113 merges with N-103 for a 47 k run to Braga.*

Verdant hills and a fertile valley brought Braga prosperity before the Romans came. When they arrived, they established Braga as the capital both of northern Portugal and of present-day Galicia in Spain. Through most of its history, however, Braga was better known for religion than for political power. When Suevi barbarians conquered Portugal they were converted to Christianity through synods at Braga and made the city both a bishopric and their capital. After Reconquest from the Moors, the Pope resolved a power struggle between the bishop of Braga and his counterpart in Santiago de Compostela in Braga's favor, designating Braga as the seat for all of Spain and Portugal—"Primate of the Spains." Primacy did not last, however, going early to Toledo in Spain and to Lisbon in Portugal by the 18th century. Yet Braga remained the most devout and conservative city in Portugal. In the 18th century, perhaps to make up for the loss of ecclesiastic power, two successive bishops undertook a reconstruction of the city and its numerous churches—all in the baroque style. Wide avenues were cut, gardens planted, and fountains were placed all around. The reconstruction of the churches is to be deplored—most lost their aesthetic interest—but the city does present a handsome face as a result of its renewal. There is enough to see in the city to merit half a day, and sights in the environs will more than fill the remainder.

From **Oporto** *the traffic interchange of Pr. do Condestavel is soon reached. Bear right along Av. da imaculada Conceicão for five blocks until reaching the wide Av. de la Liberdade for a left turn. The avenue ends at Pr. da República, with a park to its right. A parking lot lies beside Av. Central, the appropriately named road through the park's center.*

At Rua do Souto, which forms the south border of the park, turn east for a block to the chapel of **N. S. de Penha de França** on the south side of the street, which retains nice *azulejos*. Proceeding east along Rua do Souto, after crossing the wide Av. de la Liberdade the **Torre de Menagem** stands on the right side. This tower formed part of a 14th-century fortress that once guarded the medieval city walls. The first street angling left, Rua San Marco, leads past the **Casa da Gelosia** on the left, for an opportunity to admire rare remaining examples of *mashrabiya*, latticed Moorish windows to let women look out without being seen. Across the next intersection stands a very Baroque **Igreja Santa Cruz**. Turn left through the Largo Carlos Amarante for two short blocks to look at the *azulejos* facing the **Casa do Raio** at the corner on the right. Return to Santa Cruz church, bearing left to take the first right past **Capela dos Coimbras** with a Manueline tower. Rua do Souto is regained by a short walk north. Across the street is the imposing former **Episcopal Palace** with components from the 14th, 17th and 18th centuries. Now it's a superb library which includes a document confirming Afonso I as Portugal's first king. The courtyard is worth entering for a look at an ornate yet graceful fountain of castles, cherubs and spouting waters. West of the Archbishop's palace stands the fine 18th-century **Camara Municipal** (City Hall), with the **Museu Casa dos Biscainhos** behind it, and south is the large complex of the **cathedral**.

WHAT TO SEE AND DO

Cathedral   ★ ★

Open daily 8:30 a.m. to 6:30 (in winter closes an hour earlier and for lunch from 12:30 to 1:30 p.m.). The treasury is closed Mon. Admission: 200$00, for a guided tour in Portuguese to the pendant chapels and treasury. Entrance to the cathedral is through a courtyard on the north side, a right turn through the cloister and a final left turn. Although this is Portugal's oldest cathedral, built in the 11th-12th centuries, later additions and decoration hide most of the original structure. In the dark interior, a simple nave fights the distraction of 18th-century gilt in the chapels. At the front of the cathedral the chancel vaulting and altar are intricate and focus on a 14th-century Virgin. A chapel to the right incorporates a polychrome altar carved to represent a painting by Rubens. The chapel to the left of the chancel is lined with fine 18th-century *azulejos*. At the rear of the cathedral a Manueline baptismal font stands and, opposite, a chapel contains the bronze 15th-century tomb of a prince named Dom Afonso.

Exiting the cathedral into the cloisters again, the entrance to the treasury opens immediately left. Although the works inside are poorly displayed and ill-conserved, genuine treasures lurk. The plain iron cross, called the Cruzeiro do Brazil, was carried with Pedro Alvares Cabral when he discovered Brazil. There are curiosities, such as brain cases— one containing the sixth-century grey matter of the first bishop—and

platform shoes for a very short bishop, but also an astonishing number
of beautiful early crosses and coffers, from the 10th through the 12th
century. The *coro alto* is entered from the treasury and features inlaid
choir seats and two incredibly ornate 18th-century organs.

Saint Catherine's chapel at the north end of the cloisters holds votive
offerings of body parts. The King's Chapel, with elegant Gothic vaulting, is entered from the east side of the cloister. The tombs of Henri
of Burgundy and his wife Teresa of Castile, the parents of Afonso I,
the first king of Portugal, are 16th-century. The legs of Henri's effigy
have been partly amputated, apparently to allow it to fit into a smaller
space somewhere else. Also on view is the gruesome mummy of
Bishop Lourenço Vicente. After blessing the troops before the battle
of Aljubarrota in 1385, he entered the fray himself and received a slash
on his cheek in the melee. The scar is faithfully reproduced on his
effigy. At the east end of the courtyard are two more Gothic chapels.
The first depicts the life of Saint Gerald, the first archbishop of Braga,
in lovely 18th-century *azulejos*. On the left side is the entrance to the
Chapel of Glory, a marvelous 14th-century structure covered in
Mudejar decoration, including fine frescos. The charming tomb of
Bishop Pereira, who built the chapel, lies in the center.

Museu Biscainhos

*Open Tues.-Sun. 10 a.m. to 12:30 and 2-5:30 p.m. Closed Mon. and
holidays. Admission: 200$00.* The house in which this museum is
lodged dates from the middle of the 17th century and was the grand
mansion of the Biscainhos family for two centuries. The rooms and
furniture inside reflect the refinements of noble life. Groundfloor
exhibits display finds from Roman excavations three blocks south of
the casa (one may observe the ongoing excavation there for free). A
passage leads past stables to lovely gardens in the rear. Here is buried
a horse, shot by the mansion's last owner, which had belonged to a
commoner the owner's daughter had married against his wishes. After
shooting the steed in anger, the owner walked away from his house
forever.

IN THE OUTSKIRTS

Bom Jesus

*Buses marked "02 Bom Jesus" leave frequently from Largo Carlos
Amarante, at which the aforementioned church of Santa Cruz stands
on the corner, for the 6 k trip to Bom Jesus. By car turn left at the end
of the wide Av. da Liberdade onto Av. João XXI. Watch for a sign
about 1 k outside of town for a right turn to Bom Jesus, a further 5 k.*
It is not often one travels just to see flights of stairs, but these are
among the most extraordinary stairs ever constructed. The lower
flights were built beginning in the first quarter of the 18th century,
the final flights were added fifty years later, all during the height of the
baroque style. The view up shows how surpassingly elegant architecture can be, for the otherwise busy double flights of the second tier

form repetitive patterns of complex harmony. Although the first three flights seem ordinary at first, details gradually emerge that make them special. One notices that the banister's end at the bottom whips around pillars. A fountain stands at the beginning of the remarkable second tier, heralding others along the way. From this point a double stair crisscrosses at every landing, ornamented with statues of Old Testament figures and small obelisks. The final stage is flanked by chapels to the three virtues. While the church on top is not sufficient reason for the climb, the countryside views and formal gardens certainly are.

Citânia de Briteiros ★

Frequent city buses marked "Ruães" stop at Briteiros. They leave from near the church of São Vicente on the street of that name, which is a continuation of Av. de Liberdade. Occasional buses depart from Bom Jesus, above. By car, from Bom Jesus go east along N-103-5 for 9 k to Sobreposta, at which N-309 goes south for the final 4.5 k. Briteiros is a rare excavated site of pre-Roman Celtiberians, a people about whom little is known. The town existed from the third century B.C. through the first century of the Christian era and represents the Celtiberian's last bastion against the Romans. It is a large site, serenely situated on a hill, surrounded by remains of an extensive town wall. Over 100 dwellings are known and represented by a few courses of their walls, but several conical houses with thatched roofs have been reconstructed to show what the rest would have looked like. The dry stonework is superb. A visit is a must for those interested in archaeology, and pleasant for those who enjoy sylvan excursions.

WHERE TO STAY

Those visiting Braga have the option of sleeping at one of two memorable pousadas located 22 k to the southwest in Guimarães. Braga itself offers nothing as splendid, but does provide values in low-cost accommodations. In addition, there are two special hotels nearby in Bom Jesus, with splendid views—although providing nothing whatsoever to do at night except eat.

MODERATE ($50-$99)

In Bom Jesus:

Do Elevador 1st-class ★ ★ ★

Rooms: 25. ☎ *67 66 11; FAX 67 66 79; Telex 33401.* The public rooms contain elegant antiques and the bedrooms are tastefully modern. The hotel's incredible views alone would make a stay a great pleasure, but to add a final incentive, very good, moderately priced meals are also provided.

Do Parque 1st-class ★ ★

Rooms: 49. ☎ *67 66 79; FAX 67 66 79; Telex 33401.* The building is a 19th-century mansion recently converted to a hotel by the same people who own Do Elevator. The decor here is similarly elegant and perhaps even more lovely. While this hotel doesn't offer the countryside views of its sister, it substitutes a lovely garden in their place.

In Braga:

Turismo Dom Pedro 1st-class ★★
Praceta João XXI (at the south end of Av. da Liberdade). Rooms: 132. ☎ *61 22 00; FAX 61 22 11; Telex 32136.* This is the best hotel in town, modern and spotless, with balconies overlooking a park. It's an exceptional value, with rates that barely climb into the moderate category.

Carandá 2nd-class ★
Av. da Liberdade, 96. Rooms: 100. ☎ *61 45 00; FAX 61 45 50.* This brand-new and tasteful hotel charges unexpectedly low prices. Bathrooms are modern, the bedrooms are air-conditioned, and there are fine views of the city.

WHERE TO EAT

As with its hotels, Braga restaurants are not fancy, but represent excellent values.

MODERATE ($20-$50)

O Inácio
Campo das Hortas, 4 (this small park is a few steps south of the Museu Casa Biscainhos, discussed above). ☎ *61 32 25. Closed Tuesday and from the middle of April through the middle of September.* Rough stone walls and hand-hewn beams lend O Inácio the rustic look of an old tavern, although the food is prepared with greater care than the image suggests. Daily specials are recommended; and the wine selection is choice, which generally proves a proprietor's concern for his clients' dining experience. ***Amex, Diners, MasterCard and Visa accepted.***

INEXPENSIVE (UNDER $20)

Abade de Priscos
Pr. Mousinho de Albuquerque, 7 (a garden square one block due north of the parking lot). ☎ *766 50.* This small, intimate, family-run restaurant serves exceptional food that is remarkably low-priced for its quality.

DIRECTORY

INFORMATION • Located at the corner of Av. da Liberdade and Rua do Souto, by the park (☎ 225 50).

TRAINS AND BUSES • Located at Largo da Estacão (☎ 221 66), four blocks due west of the cathedral. Take Rua Dom Diogo Sousa west, continuing as it is renamed Rua Andrade Corvo. Connections are frequent to most cities, but require a change of trains at Nine. The bus station is located at Central de Camionagem (☎ 234 33), which is reached by going north from Av. da Liberdade for about four blocks. Service to Oporto and Guimarães is frequent, but less so for greater distances.

POLICE • Campo de São Tiago (☎ 719 50), which is at the end of Rua do Anjo that runs southwest from the church of Santa Cruz.

EXCURSIONS

Barcelos ★ for crafts, **Bravães** ★★ for an extraordinary Romanesque church, **Guimarães** ★★ for an atmospheric medieval walled town and **Viana do Castelo** ★ for beaches—all summon the tourist to travel a few miles from Braga. Guimarães is described under its own heading in this chapter.

BARCELOS ★

Population: 4,031
Area code: 053; zip code: 4750

Barcelos lies 22 k west of Braga on N-103.

Barcelos is an attractive village famous for two things: a huge market-day that takes place every Thursday, and naive, brightly painted pottery in the shape of fantastic figures.

The market is held in the huge main square, the Campo da República. On Thursday mornings the acreage fills with thousands of people, as many selling as buying. Then, as noon passes, the crowd melts away. The range of offerings is vast—from pottery, sewn-work, pillows, painted ox yokes, and old and new clothing to rugs, furniture and even animals.

The symbol of Barcelos pottery has its origin in the Middle Ages. A passing pilgrim accused of theft was brought before a judge in the midst of his meal. To corroborate his innocence, the pilgrim called upon the judge's lunch—an uneaten roast rooster—to crow. It purportedly did, giving rise to the over-cute rooster trademark of Barcelos potters, displayed throughout Portugal. (Incidentally, this same tradition exists in Spain.) More interesting work is done, however, by a few fine artisans in the village who craft amusing figures, often with animal heads. The **Tourist Office** in one of the towers of the village wall on Rua Duques de Bragança doubles as a crafts center with a large selection, but smaller shops dot the village as well.

BRAVÃES ★★

Population: 653

Scenic N-101 goes north to Ponte da Barca in 33 k. From there N-203 goes west to Bravães in 5 k.

The little church of São Salvador makes a trip to this tiny community worthwhile. The church is unadulterated Romanesque from the 12th, or possibly even the 11th century. While Romanesque churches seldom incorporate carvings on their portals—at most some simple lamb-of-God scene—for some reason this one is a riot of charming semi-primitive art, including figures of bulls and monkeys. Even the south portal is carved—with griffins and the Holy Lamb. In the dark interior reside more naive carvings on capitals that frame windows, along with rare original murals. This church should be a national treasure included on most tourists' itineraries. Instead, being located in a village of no particular note, it remains lonely and desolate. *(If it's closed, apply at the café across the plaza.)*

VIANA DO CASTELO ★★

Population: 15,336
Area code: 058; zip code: 4900

N-103 west reaches Viana in 47 k.

This elegant resort town is situated on the north bank of the River Lima estuary at the foot of green hills. Viana owes its appearance to the prosperity it achieved at the height of King Manuel's reign, when prosperous citizens built their mansions in the Manueline style. Then prosperity dissolved, so the 16th-century mansions were never replaced by more up-to-date styles. The central **Praça da República**, with surrounding mansions and center fountain, is one of the loveliest squares in Portugal. Three blocks west, along Rua Manuel Espregueira, stands a fine 18th-century palace, which, since it's now the municipal museum, may be toured. (Open Tues.-Sun. 9:30 a.m. to noon and 2-5 p.m.; closed Mon.; admission: 100$00.)

The beach along the river is gravelly, but a ferry from the port goes to an island off-shore and the attractive Praia do Cabedelo. In addition, there are pristine beaches a short car-ride north.

WHERE TO STAY

As with most resorts, the hotel-escudo does not go as far as elsewhere.

MODERATE ($50-$99)

Viana Sol   **1st-class ★**
Largo Vasco da Gama (near the river, three blocks southwest of the Pr. da República). Rooms: 65. ☎ *82 89 95; FAX 82 89 97; Telex 32790.* The hotel's attraction is that it provides a full range of facilities at moderate prices. Bedrooms are spare but pleasant.

INEXPENSIVE (UNDER $50)

Viana-Mar   **R2nd-class ★**
Av. dos Combatentes da Grande Guerra, 215 (one block west of the Pr. da República). Rooms: 36. ☎ *82 89 62; FAX 82 98 62.* This comfortable little hotel offers good value for the money.

WHERE TO EAT

Viana is not a gourmet's mecca, but the recommendation below stands out.

MODERATE ($20-$50)

Os 3 Potes   ★ ★

Beco dos Fornos, 7 (just off the east side of the Pr. da República).
☎ *82 99 28. Closed Monday.* Installed in the 16th-century public bakery of the town, the remodeled restaurant retains a rustic feel, along with some delicate touches. The food is extraordinary for the modest price, and simple *caldo verde* is delicious. However, on summer weekends folk dancing can be a trifle touristy.

MasterCard and Visa accepted.

BRAGANÇA ★ ★ ★

Population: 14,662
Area code: 073; zip code: 5300

From **Braga** *N-103 goes east presenting lovely lake views to Chaves in 127 k. From here a slower-going, ill-repaired, N-103 continues for the final 96 k of mountain scenery. From* **Oporto** *N-15 east runs through villa Real and directly to Bragança in 250 k. From* **Viseu** *N-2 goes north to villa Real in 108 k. From there N-15 east reaches Bragança in 140 k. From* **Coimbra** *and south one has the option of going to Oporto and following the directions above from there, or of going to Viseu and following its directions. The latter route is slower, but more scenic. From* **Guarda** *take N-16 north to Celorico da Beira in 22 k, then N-102 north to Macedo de Cavaleiros in 172 k. Just north of that town N-15 goes northwest to Bragança in a final 41 k. From Spanish* **Zamora** *(which is 62 k north of Salamanca) N-122 goes west to the border where it changes its designation to N-218 for a trip of 114 k.*

By **train** *from Oporto the trip takes eight hours, for the train does not average as much as 20 mph, but the views are awesome and the carriages are turn-of-the-century wooden ones (with primitive restrooms) that fascinate railway buffs.* **Buses** *are faster by a factor of two.*

Bragança is tucked into the northeast corner of Portugal, a good 200 k from any area of interest to tourists. It lies in the heart of the province called Trás-os-montes, "behind the mountains" and indeed it is behind in many senses. The area is poor—because rolling hills keep farms small and unprofitable—and isolated politically and socially from the rest of Portugal by its mountain barrier. The inhabitants live in a different time from ours, and the reason for visiting is to view this older way of life. Farmhouses throughout the countryside are hand-built of stone, with slate, tile or thatched roofs, and nestle into bucolic hillsides covered in grass and scrub. Wood-wheeled carts—pulled by lyre-horned oxen and driven by bearded men—will often be seen.

The town of Bragança is known for the imposing walls of its citadel, its ancient **keep** ★, its early medieval **town hall** ★, and its importance for Portuguese history. During the 17th century when the Spanish controlled Portugal, the duke of Bragança was the most powerful man in the country. He led the opposition against this foreign domination, and, after defeating the Spanish, became King João II. His was to be the last dynasty in Portugal, enduring until the revolution of 1910.

Bragança stands at an elevation of half a mile, but is still surrounded by an amphitheater of hills. All roads converge on the cathedral square, with parking below the citadel high upon its hill (parking is also available beside the citadel entrance). Given the insistent draw of the medieval citadel above, the 16th-century cathedral need detain no one. Head up toward the ramparts along Rua do Conselheiro Abilio Beca to reach the **Museu do Abade de Baçal**.

Museu do Abade de Baçal

Open Tuesday-Sunday 10 a.m. to 12:30 p.m. and 2-5 p.m. Closed Monday and holidays. Admission: 200$00. This house is a former 16th-century bishop's palace remodeled two centuries later. Two bishop's litters and archaeological pieces are displayed on the ground floor, including, in the garden, two strange, crudely carved rocks called *berrões.* Generally just over a yard long, and usually depicting either boars or bulls, several hundred of these carvings have been discovered in the countryside of Trás-os-montes province. Their function —and the culture and dates of the carvers—is unknown. Certainly they are pre-Christian, in purpose if not date.

Several second-floor ceilings of the palace are notable, including one unusual ceiling carved with fruit. Rooms display ecclesiastical paraphernalia—some elegant, some curious—as well as paintings—some nice work by Abel Salazar, from this century—and ethnographic pieces—including a scold's bridle with a tongue depressor to silence the offender.

Continuing up toward the citadel, the first church passed on the right is **São Vicente** ★, in which Dom Pedro claimed to have married his mistress Inés de Castro. (See "Historical Profile: The Birth of Portugal.") The present 17th-century facade covers a much older structure. Inside is a fantastic three-dimensional Christ flying across the ceiling, done in the 19th century. (*It should be noted that churches in Bragança are not easy to get into. Luck will find them open, otherwise all that can be done is to ask anyone who passes.*) Just before the citadel, to the left, is **São Bento ★** with a nice Renaissance portal. The nave is a wooden barrel-vault covered in Renaissance tromp l'oeil. The chancel is sheltered by a fine Mudejar ceiling.

The crenellated walls around the citadel arc of indeterminate age, but appear to be 15th-century renovations of earlier fortifications. If so, they are in remarkable repair. The **castle ★** consists mainly of a tall square keep with turrets and towers around it. It was built by Dom Sancho I in 1187 and reinforced in the 15th century. There is a drawbridge, a dungeon and tiny doorways leading to unexpected rooms and corridors. The so-called Torre de Princesa actually held a queen captive—Dona Leonor, the wife of Dom Jaime—who was suspected of infidelity. The keep now serves as a military museum.

To the left of the castle is **Santa Maria** with another painted nave ceiling. Beside it is a unique pentagonal structure, the **Domus Municipalis ★**. It is the oldest surviving town hall in Portugal, if not in the world, dating to the 12th century. The present orange tile roof is incongruous, and the building has often been restored, but it retains its original plan of a single large chamber. Clearly its function was not to house various officials, but to serve as a meeting hall for general discussion of municipal affairs. Below the hall is a large cistern for supplying water to the citadel during times of siege.

WHERE TO STAY

There are few hotels in Bragança. Although there are also few tourists, those who come generally stay the night, making room availability uncertain. It is best to reserve before arrival.

MODERATE ($50-$99)

Pousada de São Bartolomeu   1st-class ★ ★
Estrada de Turismo (0.5 k southwest, above the citadel). Rooms: 16. ☎ *224 93; FAX 234 53; Telex 22613.* This pousada was built in the late 1950s and retains the charm of that era, but its best feature is a perfect view of the citadel. Craft pieces from the region are used for decoration. The bedrooms are wood with cork ceilings for soundproofing. It is a peaceful place, with balconies for meditative views.

Bragança   2nd-class ★
Av. Dr. Francisco de Sá Carneiro. Rooms: 42. ☎ *225 79.* This modern hotel primarily serves businesspeople, but its location is central and

the bedrooms are comfortable, with some providing views of the citadel. It's a reasonable choice if the pousada is full.

INEXPENSIVE (UNDER $50)

São Roque   **R2nd-class ★**
Rua da Estacada, 26-7 7th-8th floors. Rooms: 36. ☎ *234 81; FAX 269 37.* Most of the rooms look out to the citadel and are decorated pleasantly. They are clean and comfortable, for a price that approaches a steal.

Albergaria Santa isabel   **R1st-class**
Rua Alexandre Herculano, 67. Rooms: 14. ☎ *224 27; FAX 269 37.* Despite a jolly blue-and-white-tiled facade, the hotel seems sad inside. Perhaps because it has seen better days. The São Roque above, under the same management, is a much better buy.

WHERE TO EAT

No one travels to Bragança to dine.

MODERATE ($20-$50)

Lá em Casa
Rua Marquês de Pombal. ☎ *221 11. Closed Moday.* Rustic bare stone walls and crockery decoration lend a homey feel. The cooking is more adventurous than at the competition.

Plantório
Estrada Cantarias. ☎ *224 26.* This large modern place offers fine views of the citadel and is popular with local businesspeople. The food is tasty, if unexciting, but the wine list contains bargains.

BRAVÃES

See Braga excursions.

BUÇACO FOREST

See Coimbra excursions.

CASTELO BRANCO

See Marvão excursions.

CASTELO DE VIDEO

See Marvão excursions.

COIMBRA ★ ★ ★

Population: 79,799
Area code: 039; zip code: 3000

*From **Lisbon** the autoestrada A-1 can be taken north for
79 k to Aveirasade Cima, where a north turn on N-366
connects with N-1 in 12 k. Follow N-1 for a final 133 k.
From **Batalha** take N-1 north for 81 k. From **Oporto** the
autoestrada A-1 runs south to exit #9 in 92 k. Here a short
extension east leads to N-1 south for the final 9 k.*

*Frequent **trains** from Lisbon reach Coimbra-B station in
2 hours, from which another train goes to the downtown
Coimbra-A station. From Oporto the trip consumes less
than 2 hours. **Buses** take almost a third longer.*

Coimbra, Portugal's third largest city, tumbles along a steep river-
bank by the gently flowing Mondego river. The city is situated midway between Lisbon and Oporto, making it a convenient stop along
the way. To encourage visits the city offers a fine museum—the
Museu Machado de Castro ★ ★, an intriguing **university
quarter ★**, plus mansions, monasteries and churches, including the
most imposing **Romanesque church ★ ★** in the country. Portugal's
most extensive Roman remains stand nearby at **Conimbriga ★**,
while the enchanted forest of **Buçaco ★** and a vast beach at **Figueira
da Foz ★ ★** both lie less than an hour away. All this makes Coimbra
popular with tourists, but it is large enough to absorb them graceful-
ly.

Although Coimbra has been occupied since Roman times, in its
earliest days it was an insignificant appendage of nearby Conimbriga,
the administrative seat of a Roman province. Repeated sackings—
first by barbarian Suevi, then by Moors—caused Conimbriga to be
abandoned in the ninth century. Many of its remaining citizens fled
to this site, making it a kind of descendant of the abandoned Roman
town. Even Coimbra's name is probably a corruption of "Conimbriga." When he assumed his crown in 1139, Afonso I, Portugal's
first king, chose Coimbra—then the largest city in Christian hands—
as his capital. It remained the capital for two centuries breeding the
first six kings after Afonso, until the court moved permanently to
Lisbon in 1255. Portugal's original university was established in
Coimbra in 1308. Later it, too, moved to Lisbon, but complaints
about boisterous students returned it to Coimbra, where it remains,

dominating the town both literally, high on the hill, and figuratively, as the major institution in the city.

The city divides into three parts. Above the east bank stands the university quarter—the Bairro Alta, site of the medieval city; at its feet lies the Baixa, or lower town; and, lastly, on the west bank of the river sprawls the newer town, which retains some old monasteries and churches that originally stood outside the medieval city. We divide our discussion of the sights into those on the Bairro Alta hill, which comprise most of what is noteworthy, and those located elsewhere. We suggest starting with the university, as walking downhill is always easier.

> *Parking is a problem in Coimbra. Two options exist. From* **Lisbon** *Coimbra is entered on the east bank of the river. The road runs to the Ponte Santa Clara which crosses to the west bank. Turn left along Av. Emidio Navarro, with a divided center in which parking may be possible. If full, continue to the plaza in front of the train station, where the avenue ends. Turn right there through the Largo das Ameias, then take the first left along Av. Fernão de Magalhães. Parking is often available in two blocks in a large square on the right. From* **Oporto**, *by continuing straight, one travels along Av. Fernão de Magalhães. After passing through the large plaza of Largo do Arnado, bear right to continue on Av. Magalhães, and parking should be available in the large park on the left in three blocks. If full, continue along Av. Magalhães for two more blocks where it ends at the Largo das Ameias. Turn right, then take the next left along Av. Emidio Navarro, where parking often is available in the center divider.*

WHAT TO SEE AND DO

BAIRRO ALTA AND THE UNIVERSITY

> *It is best to taxi up this hill, then walk down. Begin at the Porta Ferrea of the Velha Universidade (Old University). Ask the taxi to stop in the Pr. Dom Dinis, then turn west between two colleges.*

Velha Universidade ★

> *Opening times of various buildings are different, and some require small admission charges, but the hours from 10 a.m. to noon and 2-5 p.m. will find everything open.* During its first two centuries, the university passed between Coimbra and Lisbon, but finally settled here in 1537 under orders from King João III. Before then, the university

only offered degrees for priests and was mediocre by any standard. Dom João, determined to raise its quality, first donated his Coimbra palace to house the university magnificently, then hired Andre de Resende from the University of Paris to whip the faculty into shape. In his inaugural address the new rector accused the faculty of gross ignorance and sloth. Pursuant to his quest for excellence, the king offered impressive stipends to attract scholars of international repute, including Erasmus. Although Erasmus declined, other fine academicians accepted, lifting the University's caliber of instruction. A school of Liberal Arts was established, expanding the student population beyond just prospective clergy, and soon after a college of law was opened, followed by a college of pharmacy. By the end of the century, about 1500 students, mostly non-cleric, were in residence and the reputation of the university ranked with the very best in Europe. Although the university was to suffer ups and downs over the following centuries—at times even selling degrees for a fee—today, with an enrollment of almost 15,000 students, it stands again as the premier Portuguese institute of higher learning. Famous residents have included Luis Vas de Camões, Portugal's greatest poet, Saint Anthony of Padua, and Dr. António Salazar, who served as a professor of economics before becoming Portugal's dictator. Today some students still wear the traditional uniform of black capes with ribbons on the sleeve to indicate their college. Light blue indicates science; darker blue, Liberal Arts; violet, pharmacy; yellow, medicine; and red, law. Students in their final year sport wider ribbons than underclassmen.

Through the 17th century Porta Ferrea (Iron Door) the grey Patio das Escolas presents the most interesting buildings of the university. As it's used as a parking lot, the effect of the plaza's size and perspective is diminished today. In the center stands a statue of João III, who donated his palace, which lies ahead, to house the old university. Naturally, the palace was much altered for the purpose. To the left is São Pedro College, a 16th-century addition to the university. To the right an imposing gallery, the Via Latina, is enriched by a later ornate central portal with stairs to ascend to the gallery. Off the gallery are lecture rooms and the Sala dos Capelos—a former royal audience chamber in which academic ceremonies are held—beneath the gaze of portraits of Portugal's kings.

Returning to the courtyard and continuing counterclockwise leads to the clumsy clock tower in the corner. It summoned students to their classes and earned the name "Goat Tower." Continuing, the former palace is passed, at whose approximate center is a fine Manueline portal, leading into the University Chapel. The chapel ceiling is painted and *azulejos* line its walls, but the most impressive feature is the 18th-century organ, a fantasy of gilded wood. A few steps further is the entrance to the library. (If the door is closed, ring the doorbell.) It was a gift from King João V in 1724, whose coat-of-arms is blazoned over the door. There is no library in the world that can compare with its always ornate, sometimes elegant, finely crafted baroque decoration that covers every surface. It simply must be seen. At the library's end is a portrait of its royal donor encased in the most ornate frame imaginable. All three rooms are awesome, making one wonder how readers surrounded by such visual stimulation could concentrate.

Proceed back through the Porta Ferrea, through its plaza, then left (north) along Rua de Miranda which passes between several colleges of the university to open up into the large Largo da Feira, down a flight of stairs. Nestled between university buildings on the north side of the square is the **Se Nova** *(New Cathedral). To the left of the square is the former* **bishop's palace** *and the church of* **São João de Almedina**, *both built in the 12th century, although the bishop's palace was modified in the 16th. Today the palace houses the excellent* **Museu Machado de Castro**. *Note the* **Moorish tower** *by the entrance.*

Museu Machado de Castro   ★★
Open Tues.-Sun. 10 a.m. to 12:30 p.m. and 2-5 p.m. Closed Mon. Admission: 200$00. Largo Dr. José Rodrigues. This museum displays the best collection of native sculpture in the country, and some fine painting and objets d'art in a building that adds its own interest.

The collection begins to the right side of the entry courtyard with early sculpture. A Visigoth angel hovers charmingly. A mounted knight resting a mace on his shoulder is outstanding both as a composition and as a rare secular work from the Gothic era. More 15th-century work follows, of which an assemblage of three knights in mail at the Sepulcher, and a pregnant Virgin by Master Pero stand out. In the 16th century Coimbra became the artistic center of Portugal by enticing Nicolas Chanterene, Jean de Rouen (Ruão) and Philippe Houdart (Hodart) from France, where they were joined by the Portuguese Castilho brothers—João and Diogo. Their sophisticated work betrays a strong Italian influence, and is of the highest quality. Among other things, what attracted them to Coimbra was easily worked fine white limestone from nearby Ança. This group initiated Renaissance sculpture in Portugal and are responsible for most of the fine Manueline carving throughout the country. The museum displays an admirable assemblage of their work. See Chanterene's *Virgin Reading*, Rouen's *Entombment*, and Houdart's *Paschal Feast*. By the 17th century, wood replaced stone as the medium of choice and, with a few exceptions, the quality of sculpture declined.

The ceilings on the second floor deserve as much attention as the exhibits. A representative display of Coimbra pottery shows its development from the 17th century on. The best paintings are in two rooms devoted to Renaissance religious paintings by Portuguese and Flemish artists. Quentin Matsys is always interesting, and, on the Portuguese side, there are compelling works by the Master of Sardobal (or his school), the Master of Santa Clara, and three sensitive paintings by Josefa de Obidos.

The basement is formed of the remains of an eerie Roman cryptoporticus, a two-story platform (the lower story of which is closed) which originally elevated the Roman forum that existed on this site. Today Roman and Visigothic artifacts are displayed in the nooks and crannies of this structure.

Walk around the river end of the museum along Rua de Borges Carneiro which winds in a block to the Old Cathedral.

Se Velha   ★★

Open daily 9:30 a.m. to 12:30 p.m. and 2-7 p.m. Admission: 50$00 to the cloister. Largo de Sé Velha. This church was erected when Coimbra first became the capital of Portugal in the 12th century. That the town did not yet feel safe from attack by the Moors is evidenced by the fortress facade of the church, complete with merlons on top. Overall it's the most imposing Romanesque church in the country. The main facade (west) is pure Romanesque, the later north portal is one of the first constructed in the Renaissance style, and the apse includes a rare and lovely Romanesque gallery.

The interior is awesome in size. Here the second and third kings of Portugal were anointed. The fine Gothic retablo of the Assumption of the Virgin rising above the four Evangelists was carved by two Flemings. Its surrounding foliage contains charming figures, including a pig playing the bagpipe. The chapel in the south transept (to the right) holds a semicircular retablo by a member of the Coimbra school, and the chapel of São Pedro to the left, lined by nice *azulejos*, contains a crumbling retablo of the life of Saint Peter by Jean de Rouen.

Cloisters lie through the first door in the south aisle, and up. These are very early, 13th-century Gothic, although the bays are filled with tracery, as would become the style two centuries later. In the first chapel on the left is a fine font carved by Jean de Rouen. The chapterhouse contains the tomb of Dom Sisnando, the first Christian governor of Coimbra after its reconquest. There are indications that he was of Moorish blood.

Descend the stairs of Escades de Quebra-Costas opposite the cathedral front, and take an immediate right along the narrow Rua de Sobre-Ripas to reach two mansions standing across from each other. On the left side of the lane is the 16th-century **Casa Sub-Ripas**, *privately owned, with a Manueline doorway; on the right side is the* **Casa do Arco**. *In a few steps further, the lane passes beneath an arch to reach the* **Torre do Anto**, *remaining from the old city walls. Today it houses the Coimbra Regional Handcraft Center, an extensive display of local crafts. As it is an artists' cooperative, the*

*pieces are for sale as well as for looking. Return to the beginning of
the lane again to head down across the little square for a right turn
through the* **Almedina gate**, *surmounted by a tower. This gate is
12th century, part of the medieval city walls, and still bearing the
Moorish name of "The City." After angling left, a cross street is
reached. Turn right onto the main shopping street of Coimbra,
Rua Visconde da Luz, to reach the Pr. 8 de Maio and the* **Mosteiro
de Santa Cruz** *in approximately four blocks. This is the lower town
(Baixa).*

ADDITIONAL SIGHTS

Mosteiro de Santa Cruz

Open daily from 9 a.m. to noon and from 2 p.m. to 6:30 p.m. Admission: 100$00 to the sacristy and cloister; Pr. 8 de Maio. The original
monastery, built in 1131 before Portugal had a king, preceded even
the Old Cathedral. Portugal's first two kings—Dom Afonso I and his
son Dom Sancho I—were buried here. However, the church needed
major renovations by the beginning of the 16th century, and the
result of that rebuilding is what one sees today. As the burial place for
the first kings, this church held a special place in royal hearts, and,
although small, it is richly endowed with art. The plaza itself is pleasantly girded by houses of the 17th and 18th centuries.

The church facade was designed by Diogo de Castilho and decorated
with statuary by Jean de Rouen and Nicholas Chanterene. These three
were the shining lights of a special assembly of artists who gathered in
Coimbra in the early 16th century, and were responsible for much that
is wonderful in Manueline art. Sadly, the stone has weathered badly,
and what remains is spoiled by an 18th-century doorway, so it is difficult to appreciate what should have been a seminal piece of architecture.

Fortunately, there is no problem with deterioration inside. A Manueline ceiling covers a nave lined with *azulejos*. The octagonal pulpit is
an extraordinary piece of carving, probably by Nicholas Chanterene.
On either side of the altar lie the tombs of Kings Afonso I and Sancho
I, left and right, respectively. They had been buried in the courtyard
in front of the church, but were disinterred and installed in new tombs
early in the 16th century. It is thought that Diogo de Castilho
designed the anachronistic Gothic tombs and that Chanterene did the
carving. Left of the altar is the entrance to the sacristy. Some of the
paintings are worth attention, but the period furniture is perhaps
more interesting. The cloister is unusually simple Manueline, with bas
relief for the most part instead of the usual high relief. Stairs lead up
to the *coro alto* which contains choir stalls carved and gilded along the
top. The work is superior.

ACROSS THE RIVER

The ruins of **Santa Clara-a-Velha** ★ stand less than half a mile across the river. Cross on the Ponte Santa Clara and continue past the left turn to Lisbon for the next left turn onto a lane. Here are atmospheric ruins of a lovely 14th-century Gothic church, destroyed by the floods of the river Mondego and time. Half buried in silt, the skeleton manages to convey greater age than the church of the Santa Cruz monastery, which is actually two centuries older. Just west of the ruins is the **Portugal dos Pequenitos** park. It presents child-sized models of all of Portugal's famous monuments, plus exotic buildings from former colonies. Adults feel like Gulliver; children enjoy it almost as much. (Open daily 9 a.m. to 7 p.m., or 5 p.m. in winter; admission: 200$00 for adults, 50$00 for children.)

WHERE TO STAY

Hotels in this city are not the best. Perhaps its sizable student population has something to do with the situation, but the fact is that the best hotels attain only the second-class category, and they aren't numerous. An option is to stay at perhaps the most extraordinary hotel in Portugal in the nearby Buçaco forest or at hotels at the resort of Figueira da Foz.

MODERATE ($50-$99)

Astória   2nd-class ★

Av. Emidio Navarro, 21 (on the avenue that parallels the river, just north of the bridge). Rooms: 64. ☎ *220 55; FAX 220 57; Telex 42859.* This is a 1920s hotel with the froufrou of the era to lend individuality and interest. It is in fine repair and the bedrooms are comfortable.

Dom Luís   2nd-class ★

Quinta da Verzea (on N-1 to Lisbon, 2.5 k south of town). Rooms: 104. ☎ *44 15 10; FAX 81 31 96; Telex 52426.* This is the newest hotel and most stylish in the area. It's outside the city, however, but offers views.

Oslo   2nd-class

Av. Fernáo de Magalháes, 25 (near the Coimbra-A train station). Rooms: 30. ☎ *290 71; FAX 206 14.* This is a pleasant enough place, but with the cold feeling of Scandinavian decor, and too much noise. Rooms at the back are preferred for this reason.

Bragança   2nd-class

Largo das Ameias, 10 (the square in front of the Coimbra-A train station). Rooms: 83. ☎ *221 71; FAX 361 35; Telex 52609.* The Brangança is a modern box of no charm, but could serve for a night.

INEXPENSIVE (UNDER $50)

Domus   R3rd-class ★

Rua Adelino Veiga, 62 (1 block north and 1 east of the beginning of Av. Fernáo de Magalháes). Rooms: 20. ☎ *285 84.* The 2nd-floor hotel provides large, clean, erraticly decorated bedrooms that are true bargains.

Almedina **R2nd-class**

Av. Fernáo de Magalháes, 203 (four blocks north of the Coimbra-A train station). Rooms: 43. ☎ 291 61. Functional, clean and very inexpensive—all of which makes us wish there were more character about the place.

WHERE TO EAT

Chanfana, goat stewed in red wine, and leitao, suckling pig, are specialties of the area. Restaurants provide good value for the money, but not memorable food.

INEXPENSIVE (UNDER $20)

Trovador ★

Largo da Sé Velha, 17 (by the north face of the Old Cathedral). ☎ 254 75. Closed Monday. The atmosphere is inviting rather than elegant, although the waiters sport bow ties. The food is quite good, especially the chanfana. Fado is performed late on weekends.

Pedro dos Leitões ★

On N-1 in the village of Mealhada, 21 k north of Coimbra. ☎ 220 62. This little village is the roast suckling pig center for the country. Restaurants line the road, all announcing leitao assado. This large establishment is generally mobbed for lunch. It roasts the little critters over glowing coals, pricing the pig by weight, so you can satisfy either a large or a small appetite.

O Alfredo ★

Av. João das Regras, 32 (just across the Ponte Santa Clara). ☎ 44 15 22. Tasty seafood is served in a simple setting, along with well-prepared meat dishes.

Dom Pedro

Av. Emidio Navarro, 58. (Along the river, south of the bridge). ☎ 291 08. Closed Monday and holidays. With a splashing fountain in the center, the restaurant tries hard for style. The food is pleasant enough, but betrays the same lack of taste that the decor exhibits.

Diners, MasterCard and Visa accepted.

DIRECTORY

SHOPPING • Coimbra is known for pottery, producing a faience brightly decorated with animals and birds. The best place to view the selection, and perhaps to buy, is at the **Artensanato da Região de Coimbra** in the Torre de Anto at Rua de Sub-Ripas, 45 (discussed above). A good shop for modern copies of elegant 16th-to 18th-century patterns is **Jorge Mendes** at Pr. do Comercio, 9 (at the foot of the Almedina gate).

INFORMATION • Located in Largo da Portagem, which is beside the Ponte Santa Clara, the office can provide a helpful map (☎ 238 86).

TRAINS AND BUSES • A shuttle connects the downtown Coimbra-A station at Largo das Amenias, upriver from the bridge (☎ 349 98), with the Coimbra-B station outside of town. Trains beyond the surrounding area all leave from Coimbra-B. Lisbon, Oporto and Figueira da Foz are well-served, and five trains go to Viseu daily. A high-speed train, the Alpha, reaches Lisbon in 2-1/2 hours, but requires advance reservations.

Buses leave from Av. Fernão de Magalhães, about ten blocks north of Coimbra-A train station (☎ 270 81). Service is not as frequent to large cities as the train, but much better for smaller ones.

POLICE • Located on Rua Olimpio Nicolau Rui Fernades (☎ 220 22).

EXCURSIONS

Extensive Roman ruins lie at **Conimbriga** ★, only 15 k southwest. The lovely **forest of Buçaco** ★, with sylvan walks, holds the most wonderful hotel in the country, a former royal retreat. **Figueira da Foz** ★ is a resort with vast beaches and a casino, 45 k west. Further afield, but within a 100 k radius are **Tomar** ★★★, **Aveiro** ★★ and **Viseu** ★★★, each described under separate headings in this chapter, along with **Batalha** ★★★★★, described in the "Lisbon and its Environs" chapter.

Conimbriga   ★

Open daily 10 a.m. to 1 p.m. and 2-8 p.m.; until 6 p.m. in winter. The museum opens at 10 a.m. and closes at 6 p.m.; closed Mon. in winter. Admission: 300$00 (200$00 in winter).

Leave Coimbra by crossing over the Ponte Santa Clara bridge to the west bank of the Mondego and taking the first left to N-1 and signs for Lisbon. After 15 k turn left onto N-347 toward Condeixa-a-Nova, for a sign in about 2 k.

An Avic Mondego bus leaves opposite the hotel Astoria on weekdays at 9:05 a.m., on weekends at 9:35 a.m. The return from Conimbriga leaves at 12:55 p.m. on weekdays, but not until 6 p.m. on weekends. More frequent service leaves from the Coimbra bus station to and from Condeixaa-Nova, which is a walkable 2 k from the ruins.

Originally, Conimbriga lay on the main road between the two large Roman centers of Braccaria (modern Braga) and Olissipo (now Lisbon), and prospered from trade and the good farmland surrounding it. The city was founded in the first century, or a little before, but artifacts dug from the site show that Celts preceded the Romans by as much as 900 years. The city's heyday came in the third century A.D. when huge villas were constructed. By the end of that century, fear of barbarians caused a defensive wall to be built that consumed parts of these splendid villas for building material. By the fifth century the town had fallen to the Suevi and was gradually abandoned thereafter. This exodus accounts for the preservation of the remains, for there has been no construction since on the site. Excavation began almost 100 years ago, although so far only about one-third of the site has been dug and the most important city monuments have just recently been made available to tourists.

It is best to start in the museum, whose maps, maquettes and artifacts give orientation and a sense of what will be seen. The entrance to the ruins passes the **House of the Fountains** ★ on the right, named for the unusually large pond in the center with provisions for water jets, instead of the small pools found in most Roman dwellings. Fine mosaics cover the floors, including hunting scenes and a chariot drawn by four horses. Through the city gates and to the right is the **House of Cantaber**, one of the largest houses known from the Roman world. There are several pools and, at the rear, private baths, a great luxury in this era of public bathing. The path continues to the city forum, donated by the emperor Flavian. Other remains are difficult to decipher.

Buçaco Forest ★

Follow Coimbra's river road, Av. Emidio Navarro, to take a right through the plaza, Largo das Ameias, in front of the train station. Turn left at its end onto Av. Fernão de Magalhães which connects with N-1 going north to Oporto. At Mealhada, the suckling pig capital, in 21 k turn east onto N-234 which reaches Luso in 7 k. Signs *direct to the forest entrance. Five buses daily stop at Buçaco on their way to Viseu. The last bus from Buçaco leaves at 6:45 p.m.* Buçaco National Forest crowns a peak of the Serra do Buçaco. Something is enchanted about its lovely waterways interspersed with palms, its ancient trees and vales of ferns. Monks thought so, and chose the forest for their solitary contemplations as early as the sixth century. Popes thought so, and from far away in Italy forbade women to enter the forest, while decreeing excommunication to anyone damaging a tree. Kings thought so, and supported royal hunting lodges on its grounds for centuries, before erecting a final royal retreat in 1910. There is nothing to do except walk—cars aren't allowed—and little to observe except nature, which, if the season is right, will overpower with mimosas, camellias, magnolias, hydrangeas, and lilies-of-the-valley. True, there is the odd little chapel to come upon unexpectedly, and also, smack in the center, a gingerbread confection of a former royal palace, designed by an Italian who had worked on theater sets. It seems the king wanted a Manueline building three centuries after the style had become passé, so he was given a stage set. This fantasy of Renaissance times is a wonder to wander through and to spend a day in, which one can. It now serves as a hotel for 60 fortunate guests who reserved months in advance.

Palace Hotel do Buçaco   1st-class ★ ★ ★ ★ ★

Foresta do Buçaco. Rooms: 62. ☎ *(031) 93 01 01; FAX 936 09; Telex 93450.* Expensive at the 20.000$00 level, and worth every centavo, for there is no more sylvan setting in the country, and no greater fantasy to inhabit. Hours can be pleasurably spent wandering inside to discover murals, suits of armor and splendid *azulejos*. The bedrooms are luxurious, yet induce the deep sleep of the countryside. Fixed price meals are moderate in cost, served in a dining room that must be seen and, appropriately, are more refined than the usual hotel fare.

FIGUEIRA DA FOZ ★

Population: 13,397
Area code: 033; zip code: 3080

Follow Coimbra's river road, Av. Emidio Navarro, to take a right through the plaza in front of the train station, Largo das Ameias. Turn left at its end onto Av. Fernão de Magalhães which connects with N-1 going north to Oporto. In just a kilometer or two look for the turn onto N-111 west which reaches Figeira in 45 k. About halfway, the romantic ruins of the castle of Montemor-o-Velho *are passed.*

Figueira da Foz is one of the most popular resorts in Portugal, but mainly with the Portuguese and Spanish, rather than non-Iberians who have yet to make its discovery. Its appeal is a huge 2-mile-long beach. There is little to do but walk, swim and bask, although the village is prosperous and attractive, and a casino opens in the afternoon. At the northern end of the beach, two miles away, is the almost unspoiled fishing village of **Buarcos ★**.

WHERE TO STAY

Catering mainly to Portuguese, prices at these hotels have not yet risen to international levels.

EXPENSIVE ($100-$200)

Grande Hotel da Figueira   1st-class ★
Av. 25 de Abril (on the promenade by the beach). Rooms: 91. ☎ *221 46; FAX 224 20; Telex 53086.* This is the fanciest hotel in town, all modern glass and marble, but a bit antiseptic in feel. Still, the bedrooms are comfortable, some have lovely sea views, and prices are barely expensive.

MODERATE ($50-$99)

Aparthotel Atlântico   2nd-class ★
Av. 25 de Abril (near the Grande Hotel). Apartments: 70. ☎ *240 45; FAX 224 20.* Although the architecture is undistinguished, this highrise presents lovely views over the ocean. Each apartment includes a sitting room and kitchenette—all at a very fair price.

INEXPENSIVE (UNDER $50)

Nicola **R1st-class**
Rua Bernardo Lopes, 36 (the street leading from the river past the casino).
Rooms: 24. ☎ 223 59. Although showing signs of wear, the hotel is
clean and its bedrooms comfortable.

WHERE TO EAT

Grilled seafood is the thing to eat, and there are several moderately
priced places to enjoy it.

MODERATE ($20-$50)

Tubarão ★
Av. 25 de Abril (on the promenade, at the southern end). ☎ 234 45.
Plain, almost without decoration, the restaurant impresses as being all
business, and the business is grilling fish.

Tamargueira ★
Estrada do Cabo Mondeo (outside of Buarcos, 3 k north). ☎ 225 14.
Fishing implements announce what this rustic restaurant serves. The
terrace with ocean views is most pleasant, and the grilled fish is fresh,
but soups are good as well.

CONIMBRIGA

See "Coimbra" under "Excursions."

ELVAS ★ ★

Population: 13,507
Area code: 068; zip code: 7350

Situated beside the Spanish border, Elvas is just 22 k west
of **Badajoz** along the Spanish N-V and the Portuguese N-4.
Mérida lies just 66 k further east along N-V. From **Évora**
take N-68 northeast to Estremoz in 46 k, then turn east on
N-4 for an additional 43 k. From **Lisbon** head south past
Setubal on the autoestrada for 50 k. Join N-10 going east
for 21 k to meet N-10 north toward Cruzamento de Pegões
for 14 k. Turn east on N-4 for 37 k to Montemoro-Novo,
and continue on N-4 for the remaining 111 k. From **north
of Lisbon** follow Lisbon directions until reaching A-1. Exit
A-1 at villa Franca, 35 k north of Lisbon, for N-10 going
to Cruzamento de Pegões in 49 k. There N-4 goes east to
Elvas in 148 k. From **south of Lisbon** follow directions to
Évora, then the directions above from there.

> *By* **train** *Elvas is just over five hours from Lisbon. Connections can be made from Marvão, but the trip takes more than three hours. There is an express bus from Lisbon that beats the train. A bus from Évora takes under two hours.*

Standing by the Spanish border, Elvas' traditional business has been to defend Portugal against invasion. Its fortifications are not, as so often seen in Portugal, quaint relics of romantic struggles against Moors, but serious 17th-century ramparts that found good use during a siege as recently as the 19th century. Given the continual threat of attack, naturally the town of Elvas huddled within its fortified walls, which meant that houses had to be small and streets narrow and jumbled in quaint ways. Because Elvas was regained from the Moors a century later than Lisbon, Moorish remains are more in evidence. The occasional gateway or tower whose elegance catches the eye is surely a Moorish structure.

For its imposing fortifications Elvas is well worth a visit. Cobbled streets and tiny houses add atmosphere, but Elvas is not so full of monuments as to detain a visitor for long. After an hour or two wandering, most people are happy to have come, but have seen enough to leave satisfied.

Approaching the old town, there are fine views of Elvas' beautiful **aqueduct** ★ to the west. It took almost a century to build, not completed until the early 17th century, and runs for five miles, 100 feet high in places, forming an elegant, if somewhat clunky, line of arches and tiers that still carry water to the city. The old town is entered through a gate in the south rampart wall. Inside, Rua de Olivença leads up to the main square, the **Praça da República**, paved in geometric shapes. The former town hall stands on the near side, housing the **tourist office**, and the **cathedral** stands opposite (north). Manueline lateral portals are decent work, but badly weathered. To the right of the cathedral a small street leads behind it into the pretty **Largo Santa Clara**. In the center of the triangular-shaped square a **pillory** dangling iron hooks stands as a reminder of times when punishment was public. On the near (south) side of the square stands the octagonal-shaped church of **Nossa Senhora da Consolação**. It was built in the 16th century during the Manueline era to duplicate the shape of an earlier Templar church that stood on the same site or nearby. Inside, it is a glory of colored *azulejos*, which line the walls and even the cupola, that is supported by gilded marble columns. At the north end of the square a **Moorish gate** beneath a logia is flanked by twin towers. Passing through this gate, ascend to the Largo da

Alcaçova, then bear left, then right at the "T," to walk the lovely little Rua das Beatas to the **castle**. Original construction was Moorish, but it was reworked from the 14th through the 16th centuries. The old governor's residence displays a reconstructed kitchen and bedroom. (Open Fri.-Wed. 9:30 a.m. to 12:30 and 2:30-7 p.m.; until 5:30 p.m. in winter. Closed Thurs.)

For a different route back to the Olivença gate, go left from the castle, following the walls. A drive around the fortifications shows them to their best effect, including another fortress just southeast, the **Forte de Santa Luzia**—star-shaped to force attackers into crossfire from the walls.

WHERE TO STAY

Elvas is short on hotels, but there are elegant accommodations in Évora and a regal pousada in Extremoz, all described in the Évora section in this chapter.

MODERATE ($50-$99)

Pousada do Santa Luzia   1st-class ★ ★
Av. de Badajoz (at the end of N-4, as it enters the town). Rooms: 16. ☎ *62 21 94; FAX 62 21 27; Telex 12469.* This white, villa-like hotel became a pousada recently, after failing as a private enterprise. The first floor is all spacious public rooms looking out on a fountained courtyard. Upstairs and annex bedrooms are all decorated colorfully and pleasingly. Not the most elegant, it entices with a relaxed atmosphere.

Dom Luis   1st-class ★
Av. de Badajoz (at the end of N-4, as it enters the town). Rooms: 90. ☎ *62 27 56; FAX 62 07 33; Telex 42473.* This is a modern hotel that is showing signs of wear, but it still offers comfortable bedrooms and more amenities than its prices would suggest.

INEXPENSIVE (UNDER $50)

Estalgem Don Sancho II   R2nd-class ★
Pr. da República, 20 (the main square within the walls). Rooms: 26. ☎ *62 26 86; FAX 62 47 17.* This friendly hotel, located in the heart of town, offers bedrooms that, although small, are cozy and attractively furnished with near-antiques. Meals served in the appealing downstairs restaurant are the best bargains in town.

WHERE TO EAT

For bargain dining, try the Estalgem Don Sancho II, mentioned above. For more expensive, but still moderately priced meals, see the selections below.

MODERATE ($20-$50)

Pousada de Santa Luzia   ★

Av. de Badajoz (at the end of N-4, as it enters the town). ☎ *62 21 94.* The pousada bills itself as offering the best cooking in Europe. While this is a laughable exaggeration, the cuisine is much better than at the average pousada. *Ensopado de borregoi* garlicky mutton, green pepper and bread stew, and shellfish stew are good specialties. Would that the dining room were more attractive.   ***Major credit cards.***

Don Quixote   ★

On N-4 3 k east of town. ☎ *62 20 14.* This restaurant specializes in fish, served in a bright, convivial dining-room.   ***Major credit cards.***

ÉVORA ★ ★ ★ ★

Population: 35,117
Area code: 066; zip code: 7000

From **Lisbon** *head south past Setubal on the autoestrada for 50 k. Join N-10 going east for 21 k to meet N-10 north toward Cruzamento de Pegões for 14 k. Turn east on N-4 for 37 k to Montemor-o-Novo. A few k outside that town N-114 bears southeast to Évora in 30 k. From the* **Algarve** *take N-264 north from Albufeira for 70 k to Ourique, outside of which N-391 heads east, then north, to circle Beja in 60 k. Take N-18 north for the final 78 k. From* **Guarda** *take N-18 south past Castelo Branco, Portalegre and Estremoz for 289 k. From* **north of Lisbon** *follow Lisbon directions until reaching A-1. Exit A-1 at villa Franca, 35 k north of Lisbon, for N-10 going to Cruzamento de Pegões in 49 k. There N-4 goes east to Montamor-o-Novo in 37 k, from which N-114 reaches Évora in 30 k.*

Direct **trains** *from Lisbon depart four times daily and take about three hours. Trains from Faro consume just under six hours (costing less than 1000$00). All told the bus is better, with expresses from Lisbon taking only two-and-a-half hours. From Elvas there are two daily departures and the trip takes almost two hours.*

To put the matter simply, Évora is the most wonderful city in Portugal. It is a kind of Portuguese Florence—with bright houses topped by red-orange roofs—as well as a Portuguese Seville—gloriously flowered. UNESCO declared the town a world treasure.

Évora thrived during Roman times and was designated a *municipium*, giving it the right to coin money. Later, the Moors conquered and held it for 450 years. It was liberated in 1166 by an outlaw knight named Geraldo Sem-Pavor (Gerald, the Fearless), whose reputation in Portugal is similar to El Cid's in Spain. To storm the town he impaled lances in the walls for his troops to climb like stairs. Once in Portuguese hands, the royalty found Évora more congenial than Lisbon, and spent as much time in residence as their duties permitted. During this period—from the 14th through the 16th centuries—Évora flourished as Portugal's Athens, a city filled with palaces, churches and arts. But when the Avis dynasty died out in 1579 and the Spanish took over Portugal, Évora became a forgotten city consigned to preserving relics from its time of glory.

All the sights lie within the walls of the old city, and most are concentrated at the very center. They comprise monuments marking every era of greatness—from a Roman temple to 16th-century mansions. At least a day is required to savor them properly. Anyone arriving during the last week in June will find Évora at its most festive. This is the fair of São João which includes folk dancing, stalls selling food and others offering local crafts.

Parking is generally possible in the Pr. do Giraldo; if full, there are two more lots in two blocks along Rua Nova, which runs east from the northern end of the plaza.

Arrivals from **Lisbon** *reach the city walls, but are prevented by one-way streets from proceeding further east. Turn left along the Estrada da Circunvalacão for a quarter of a mile to turn right through the next entrance into the walls. Inside, the street first is called Rua Candido dos Reis, then Rua João de Deus, then it enters the Pr. do Giraldo for parking. From the* **Algarve and south** *turn left onto Rua A. J. D. Almeida at a large intersection one block before reaching the city walls. It leads to a traffic circle in two blocks; take the left hand road, Estrada do Circunvalacão past gardens to turn right through the walls along Rua da República, which arrives in five blocks at the Pr. do Giraldo for parking. From* **Guarda**, **Estremoz** *and* **northern** *areas turn right at the city walls along Estrada da Circunvalacão, through the aqueduct and then left at the next entrance through the walls. Inside the walls the street is first called Rua Candido dos Reis, then Rua João de Deus, before entering the Pr. do Giraldo for parking.*

Start at the **Pr. do Giraldo**, the main square, almost exactly in the center of the walled town, where a fine 16th-century fountain plays in the center. The **Office of Tourism** is located near the middle of the west side of the plaza. On the east side, a low arcade covers the sidewalk. About half way along, Rua 5 de Outubro leads uphill past crafts shops to open wide in the Largo Marquês de Marialva, fronting the **cathedral**. Adjoining the cathedral on its left side is the **Museu de Évora**.

WHAT TO SEE AND DO

Cathedral ★★★

Open Tues.-Sun. 9 a.m. to noon and 2-5 p.m. Closed Mon. and holidays. Admission: 150$00. The cathedral was begun late in the 12th century and finished by the middle of the 13th in the earliest Gothic style. With a few exceptions, it retains its original design. The monolithic facade flanked by square towers presents a fortress face, broken by the deeply recessed porch of the entrance. Each side of the entrance is lined by a 14th-century series of the Apostles, all of whom seem to have the same face. The interior is disconcerting because its stone blocks are picked out with bright mortar, producing a checkerboard effect that fights with the solidity that should be conveyed. Still, the lantern above the transept crossing is elegant and the fine rose windows lighting the transepts are original. Not so the retablo. The original is now displayed in the Museu de Évora; what presently overlooks the altar is an 18th-century work in marble, quite out of keeping with the style of the cathedral. At the end of the north transept a carved portal with a marble head is attributed to Chanterene. The glory of the treasury, whose entrance is off the south transept, is a 13th-century French ivory statue of the Virgin that opens to show events from her life, although an odd wooden replacement-head sits on her shoulders. In addition to the usual sacerdotal vestments and ecclesiastical plate there is an impressive cross in gilded, enameled silver studded with over 1000 precious and semi-precious stones. The door to a fine cloister stands near the main entrance. The heaviness of the cloister reflects a Romanesque aesthetic, although lightened by circles of Moorish open tracery. Statues of Evangelists stand in each corner. At the southeast corner a chapel contains the moving sepulcher of the founding bishop of the cathedral, his head held gently by angels. All the carving in this chapel merits appreciation.

Museu de Évora ★★

Open Tues.-Sun. 10 a.m. to 12:30 p.m. and 2-5 p.m. Closed Sun. and holidays. Admission: 200$00. The museum is housed in the former bishop's palace from the 17th century. Sculpture is displayed chronologically on the ground floor. A fragment of Roman bas-relief of a vestal virgin's lower half is notable for the subtle depiction of a diaphanous dress. There are some fine medieval tombs and outstanding Renaissance carving by Nicolau Chanterene, especially the effigy of Bishop Afonso. Displayed on the second floor is a good collection of Portuguese primitive painting. The main attraction is in room 2—a colorful 13-picture series of the life of the Virgin from the late 15th century, which originally had served as the retablo of the cathedral. It is Flemish work, by the look, although Italian buildings serve as backgrounds.

A part of the 16th-century building at the northwest corner of the largo belonged to Vasco da Gama before his appointment as Viceroy of India. Later the building housed the first Office of the Inquisition in Portugal. Proceeding northward past the museum, enter another large plaza, the Largo Conde de villa-Flor. In its center, framed by the open plaza, is a **Roman Temple**. *West of it is the* **Convento dos Lóios** *beside the* **Igreja de São João Evangelista**, *and beyond it, north, is the* **Palace of the Dukes of Cadaval** *beside a garden affording views of the countryside over remains of the Roman town walls.*

Templo de Diana

This lovely second-century temple in the ornate Corinthian style, is called Diana's temple, although there is no evidence proving who was worshiped in it. The marble capitals and bases sandwich granite columns. The temple owes its fine state of preservation to its continued use through the centuries, so its stones were not carted away for building material. During one period it served as a fortress; at another, as the municipal slaughterhouse.

Paço dos Duques de Cadaval

Open Tues.-Sun. 10 a.m. to noon and 2-6 p.m. Closed Mon. Admission: 150$00, for a ticket good for São João Evangelista as well. The palace was built in the 14th century, incorporating a turret from the medieval city walls as its northern tower. The facade was substantially remodeling in the 17th century. Two kings—João III and João V—lived inside, but the palace has evolved today to the Cadaval family, who also own the Church of Saint John the Evangelist across the square. A museum inside displays a gallery of the dukes, along with two fine Flemish bronze plaques.

Igreja de São João Evangelista ★★

Same hours as the Paço dos Duques de Cadaval above. This church contains some of the finest **azulejos** in Portugal. The facade was remodeled after the 1755 earthquake, but the church was erected 200 years before by Rodrigo de Melo, the Count of Olivença. The flamboyant Gothic entry is original. Inside, the nave is lined with chapels forming a pantheon of the Melo family. But it is the amazing *azulejos* that captivate. They are by the greatest artist in the medium, Antonio Oliveira Bernardes, at the height of his powers in 1711. Note the *tromp l'oeil azulejo* window! The sacristy holds some unexceptional paintings, but also one of a Pope whose eyes not only follow the viewer, but whose feet seem to as well.

The convent of São João now is a most elegant pousada. The former chapterhouse door ranks with the great portals in Portugal.

Next to the cloisters of São João stands a large library from 1805 connected by an arch to the bishop's palace. Pass under the arch and turn left to be faced by a **Manueline mansion** *with a mashrabiya balcony (for looking out without being seen). Continue past a tower next to the* **Palaco do Condes de Bastos***, originally a Moorish palace, although the facade is 15th century. Parts of first-century Roman town walls are visible. Returning to the rear of the cathedral and passing around the apse, continue south along the charming Rua do Cenáculo. In one block take the right arm of the "T," Rua da Freina de Baixo, which leads to the* **mansion of Garcia de Resende** *on the left side in a short block. The Manueline decoration of the second-floor windows is admirable. Turn right to pass between two towers of the Medieval town wall into the picturesque* **Largo das Portas de Moura***. A fine Renaissance fountain plays in the center of the square and a number of elegant houses border it. Especially grand is the 16th-century* **Corovil mansion** *at the southern end, with twin arcades and horseshoe arches.*

Return toward the two towers, turning left just before reaching them to travel two blocks along Rua Misericordia, past the rococo **Igreja da Misericordia***, into the small Largo de Alvaro Velho. At its southwest end, steps lead down the picturesquely arched* **Travessa da Caraça** *to enter the Largo de Graca with a* **Renaissance church** *of the same name whose facade is done in Italian classical style, topped by four rising atlantes. Leaving the largo by its west end opposite the church, turn left for a few feet along Rua da República to take the first right into the Pr. 28 de Maio, dominated by* **Igreja de São Francisco***.*

Igeja de São Francisco ★

Open Mon.-Sat. 9am to 1 p.m. and 2:30-6 p.m. Open Sun. 10 a.m. to 11:30 a.m. and 2:30-6 p.m. Admission: 25$00. The grandiose entry portico is formed of rounded, pointed and horseshoe arches, which about covers the genre. Inside, the aisleless nave is dizzyingly high. Here again, the stones are picked out by white mortar, the peculiarity of this town. Except for the altar—with two galleries to either side— the church is relatively free of decoration which lets the architecture speak loudly and well. But what everyone remembers about this church is not elegance but its gruesome chapterhouse, entered from the left of the altar. Here the bones of perhaps 5000 dead have been collected as a reminder of what awaits us all. The sign at the entrance translates: "We bones who are here await your bones."

Opposite the church is the **Museu de Artesanato**, *a collection of handcrafts that is actually a store. At the lower end of the square is a public garden bordered on the south by part of the imposing 17th-century town walls. A bandstand in the park presents summer concerts beside ruins of one royal palace and a copy of part of another. The Pr. do Giraldo, from which we began, is two blocks due north of the church of São Francisco, along Rua da República which passes behind it.*

WHERE TO STAY

Évora has long been in the tourist business and can usually accommodate as many visitors as wish to spend the night. The establishments are all rather small; no 100-room hotels exist. There is an exceptional pousada in town, however, and the most wonderful pousada in the country is 46 k away in Estremoz, described under "Excursions."

EXPENSIVE ($100-$200)

Pousada dos Lóios   1st-class ★ ★ ★

Largo Conde de villa Flor (beside the Cathedral). Rooms: 32. ☎ *240 51; Telex 43288.* Installed in a 16th-century convent, the elegance of its surroundings make this one of the finest pousadas. Rooms surround a lovely two-story cloister, used for dining in the summer. One of the great doorways in the world, a Gothic-Moorish fantasy, leads to the former chapterhouse. Bedrooms include rugs from nearby Arraiolos, although the furniture is more comfortable than elegant. To say that its location is convenient to the sights is an understatement. It is one.

MODERATE ($50-$99)

Riviera   R1st-class ★

Rua 5 de Outubro, 49 (the street that leads east from Pr. do Giraldo). Rooms: 22. ☎ *233 04; FAX 204 67.* This hotel, a former townhouse, enjoys an ideal location near the sights on a street lined with nice shops. It could be more tastefully decorated but is otherwise a fine choice.

Planicie   2nd-class ★

Largo Álvaro Velho, 40 (1 block south from Pr. do Giraldo along Rua da República, and 2 short blocks east along Rua M. Bombarda). Rooms: 33. ☎ *240 26; FAX 298 80; Telex 13500.* The exterior is attractively Renaissance-looking, and the location is good—in a lovely square, near the sights. The interior is not up to the promise of the exterior, however. Public rooms are coldly marbled and the bedrooms are spare and carpetless. Some rooms have views. The hotel is affiliated with the Best-Western chain.

Albergaria Vitória   R1st-class ★

Rua Diana de Lis (1 block south the Estrada Circunvalaca, at the southwest corner of the old town). Rooms: 48. ☎ *271 74; FAX 298 80; Telex 44875.* This is a modern hotel of no architectural character, but it offers comfortable rooms and balconies for views of the lovely town. Although located outside the old town, this problem is solved with a car or taxi ride.

INEXPENSIVE (UNDER $50)

O Eborense   R2nd-class ★ ★

Largo da Misericordia, 1 (1 block south from Pr. do Giraldo along Rua da República and 2 short blocks east along Rua M. Bombarda). Rooms: 29. ☎ *220 31.* This delightful little hotel is installed in a 16th-century townhouse on a pleasant square near the sights. The decor is eccentric but fun. Bedrooms are reasonably comfortable, but without luxuries.

Santa Clara   2nd-class

Travessa da Milheira, 19 (2 blocks west from the Pr. do Giraldo along Rua Serpa Pinto, and 1 short block north). Rooms: 51. ☎ *241 41; Telex 43768.* This is a simple hotel that offers the necessities at reasonable prices.

Policarpo   R3rd-class

Rua da Freiria de Baixo, 16 (beside the Miseracordia church, 1 block south of the Cathedral, near the two towers of the Largo das Portas de Moura). Rooms: 16. ☎ *224 24.* This is a former nobleman's house that functions today as a bare-bones hotel. It is atmospheric, dark, and far from spic-and-span, but those with a sense of adventure who enjoy out-of-the-ordinary places will love it. So, too, will those trying to save money. Bedrooms are large, but the decor varies from pleasant to atrocious.

WHERE TO EAT

Nothing in Évora draws the gourmet. But tasty meals are available for modest prices, although there is little variety—all the restaurants try for old tavern looks and serve similar dishes.

MODERATE ($20-$50)

Fialho   ★

Travessa das Mascarenhas, 14 (north of the Pr. do Giraldo for about 5 blocks to the Pr. J. A. de Aguiar, from which this little lane goes north). ☎ *230 79. Closed Monday, the first three weeks of September, and from the last week of December until after New Years.* The restaurant has the look of an old tavern, with crockery hung on the walls. The food is traditional Portuguese, and, while not exceptional, it is tasty and authentic. Reservations are recommended.

Amex, Diners, MasterCard and Visa accepted.

Cozinha de Santo Humberto

Rua da Moeda, 39 (this street leaves the west side of Pr. do Giraldo).

☎ *242 51. Closed Thursday, and November.* The building dates from several centuries ago, and anything old the owner could find is hung on the walls. Flowered tables and comfortable seating are pluses, although the food could be better.

Amex, Diners, MasterCard and Visa accepted.

Guião

Rua da República, 81 (1 block south of the Pr. do Giraldo). ☎ *224 27. Closed Monday and from the middle of November to the middle of December.* As with most restaurants in Évora, this one is decorated as an old tavern, although somewhat more tastefully than others. The food is traditional Alentejo, which means that pork with clams is one specialty, and the meals are filling.

Amex, Diners, MasterCard and Visa accepted.

DIRECTORY

INFORMATION • Located in the Pr. do Giraldo (☎ 226 71). This is a most pleasant office with a staff that speaks English.

TRAINS AND BUSES • The train station (☎ 221 25) is located half a mile to the southeast of town along a continuation of Rua da República.

The bus station (☎ 221 21) is near the church of São Francisco on Rua da República.

POLICE • Located just east of the north end of Pr. do Giraldo (☎ 220 22).

EXCURSIONS

Marvão ★★, pretty as a medieval postcard, lies northeast along N-18 for 105 k to Portalegre, then 16 k further north on N-359. Its sights are described under its own heading in this chapter. **Elvas ★**, only 89 k northeast, is similar in its medieval-Moorish character to Évora and also described under its own heading in this chapter. Direction in reverse preface the "Évora" description.

Attractions at a nearer hand include the embroidered carpet-making village of **Arraiolos**, the medieval town of **Estremoz ★** with craft pottery and the most elegant pousada in the country, the fortified town and Gothic castle of **Evoramonte ★**, and the similar, but more evocative fortified village of **Monsaraz ★**. Note that this area has the highest concentrations of mystical Celtic dolmens—tombs built of massive boulders—and menhirs —circular places of worship formed by a rock ring—in the country. They may be seen in their splendid isolation in the countryside. The Tourist Office provides a map of locations.

ARRAIOLOS

Population: 3,567

Follow the Estrada de Circunvalacão northward to turn left on N-114-4 for 12 k to take a right turn north on N-370 for the final 10 k.

For practical purposes Arraiolos consists of one main street lined with shops selling *tapete*. They sell the rugs which Arraiolos has been sewing for four centuries. In the 16th century, when the Portuguese acquired a taste for carpets they found in the East, embroidery production was begun in this area of Portugal to sate that appetite. In the beginning, designs were oriental or Persian, but turned to Aubusson styles in the 18th century. Originally the products were used for throws or wall hangings, rather than as carpets. Then, as now, the rugs were sewn with pure wool colored by natural dyes on linen canvas. Thus, they are durable, hold their color well, and do not burn readily. Because production even today is all by hand, a square yard will take a month for one woman to sew, resulting in the not-so-surprising prices of almost 20.000$00 per square-yard. Pillow covers are available for a more affordable 4.000$00. Examples of Arraiolos' rugs are displayed in a small museum on the second floor of the town hall, located beside the office of tourism in the main square.

EVORAMONTE ★

Population: 935

> *Follow Évora's Estrada de Circunvalacão northward to turn left on N-18, toward Estremoz. Evoramonte lies north about 33 k along N-18. Signs for "Castelo d'Evoramonte" in the modern village point to a steep road up to the castle.*

Tiny Evoramonte's moment in history came in 1834 when, a few miles away, Prince Pedro and his younger brother Miguel duked it out for the Portuguese crown. After winning, Pedro signed a treaty with his brother in a house in Evoramonte that still proudly commemorates the event with a plaque. The village castle and walls were built long before, in the 14th century on Moorish and Roman foundations. As with many such castles, renovation occurred in the 16th century, but, unlike most, the renovation did not significantly change the style from the massive Gothic original. What is startling about this castle is the vanilla color of a preservative painted over its walls. Otherwise, this is a fine castle with four cylindrical towers that offer breathtaking views.

ESTREMOZ ★

Population: 7,869
Area code: 068; zip code: 7100

> *Follow Évora's Estrada de Circunvalacão northward to turn left on N-18, passing Evoramonte (discussed above) to reach Estremoz in 46 k.*

Estremoz, surrounded by 17th-century ramparts, is famous for two things. It produces unglazed jars of eccentric shapes, and it boasts a fine medieval palace, now Portugal's most regal pousada.

Three kings worked on the castle keep, finished by King Dinis in 1258. An octagonal room on the third floor has fine windows, and the platform on the tower roof provides extensive views. King Dinis later constructed a palace beside the keep for his lovely wife Isabel of Spain, who became a saint. She died in what is called the audience chamber. An explosion at the end of the 17th century wrecked most of the palace, but it was subsequently restored, and finally transformed into a pousada.

Although the town's eccentric water jars are curiosities, more charming examples of ceramic work in the form of naive little figures and animals are also produced—on sale around town.

WHERE TO STAY

Pousada da Reinha Santa Isabel   **1st-class ★ ★ ★ ★ ★**

Largo Dom Dinis. Rooms: 23. ☎ *226 18; FAX 239 82; Telex 43885.* Save up for this one and reserve months in advance. It's your chance to walk where kings walked and slept, if not in the same room, at least in the same building, where they dreamed. A saint also spent time here, and the king granted Vasco da Gama an audience but did not invite him to stay the night. Antiques abound amid velvets and marble; the entrance hall impresses; and the corridors transport. Most of the rooms include canopied beds and the views that royalty came to see. Of course it's expensive, but the experience and the unobtrusive pampering make it worth every escudo.

MONSARAZ ★

Population: 1,290

Follow the Estrada de Circunvalacão southward around Évora to turn right on N-18 going south toward Beha. In about 15 k N-256 bears east for 40 k, where a sign just before the Guadiana river directs a 4 k turn left to Monsaraz.

Beginning in the 13th century almost all towns near the Spanish border were fortified for defense. Monsaraz was no different. But when fortification ceased to be important, Monsaraz had nothing else to offer, so it has stayed the way it always was—today for our enjoyment. The village consists of just four cobblestone streets, lined with houses that are small and individual as only very old houses of the same general style can be. Many bear arms of the owners and most retain their outside stair—a style dating from the 16th-17th centuries. Its ruined castle was rebuilt in the 13th century and given an outer massive perimeter wall in the 17th. Few places in the world so preserve the atmosphere of a Renaissance village.

EVORAMONTE

See "Évora" under "Excursions."

FIGUEIRA DA FAZ

See "Coimbra" under "Excursions."

FLOR DE ROSA

See "Marvão" under "Excursions."

GUARDA ★

Population: 14,803
Area code: 071; zip code: 6300

From **Lisbon** *take the autoestrada A-1 north for 79 k to Aveirasade Cima where it connects with N-336 that leads to N-1 in 12 k. Continue on N-1 to Coimbra in 133 k. There take N-117, which heads southeast for a bit before turning northeast. The road is scenic, but slow going, for 138 k to Celorico da Beira. On the outskirts of that town, N-16 east completes the final 22 k. From* **Viseu** *take N-16 east for 68 k. From* **Coimbra** *pick up the Lisbon directions above. From* **Oporto** *take either the autoestrada or N-1 south to Albergens-a-Velha in 46 k. There take N-16 east to Guarda in a further 133 k. From* **Évora** *N-18 leads northeast to Estemoz in 46 k and continues through Portalegre and Castelo Branco to reach Guarda in a total of 289 k. From* **Tomar** *go south on N-110 to the outskirts of Entroncamento to pick up N-118 going east. In 76 k it reaches Alpalhão where N-18 leads to Guarda in 160 k more. From the* **Algarve** *either the directions from Lisbon or from Évora may be followed, with the former being quicker and the latter more scenic. In either case it is a distance of about 450 k. Guarda is a straight drive from Spanish* **Salamanca** *along*

N-620 which changes its designation at the Portuguese border to N-16. The distance is 157 k.

Trains *leave from Lisbon four times a day for a trip of 6-1/2-8 hours, depending on the train. The trip is 3 hours from Coimbra.*

At two-thirds of a mile above sea level Guarda is the highest town in Portugal, so it's cool in summer but bitter in winter. The reason for its name (Guard) is evident from this summit. Since fortification in the 12th century, Guarda's job has been to guard against Spanish incursions, for it is only 60 k from a border that once moved to and fro. Guarda forms one component of an incredible string of 20 similarly fortified crests within a 100-k radius that, in Medieval times, formed a sort of Maginot Line. Granite-grey Guarda is not the most attractive of these towns, but it offers the best accommodations in the area so it serves as a base for the fortress tours described under "Excursions."

Guarda's principle square, **Largo Luis de Camões**, is surrounded by 16th- through 18th-century houses and contains the town **Cathedral**. Construction began at the end of the 14th century, under the direction of the architect of Batalha cathedral, which explains its flying buttresses, clerestory and spires. Work dragged on for a century and a half, by which time Boytec, the Manueline architect, arrived to add his gargoyles and twisting columns. After an exterior constricted by two octagonal towers, the inside seems vast, although it has little lightness about it. The limestone retablo in high relief is attributed to Jean de Rouen. Whether or not the attribution is correct, the work lacks the life that characterizes most his work.

Remains of the **castle** look down upon the plaza. Little of the original stands except for the massive tower keep. Downhill and to the north (right), beside the town walls, stands the **church of Misericordia** with a most elegant 17th-century baroque facade. It faces across to one of the original town gates, the **Torre dos Ferreiros**.

WHERE TO STAY

Although only two hotels are worth consideration, between them they contain 150 bedrooms which should easily satisfy the demand.

MODERATE ($50-$99)

De Turismo   **1st-class ★★**

Av. Coronel Orlindo de Carvalho (at the end of the town gardens). Rooms: 105. ☎ *21 22 05; FAX 21 22 04; Telex 53760. The look of a traditional* inn invites you into tasteful, comfortable bedrooms. The hotel is efficient in a quiet way that breeds confidence.

Filipe   **R1st-class** ★

Rua Vasco da Gama, 9 (in the square with Miseracordia Church). Rooms: 45. ☎ *21 26 58; FAX 21 64 02; Telex 53746.* At prices one third less than de Tourismo, bedrooms here are certainly adequate and reasonably comfortable.

WHERE TO EAT

Both of the hotels above serve quite good food. The dining room of the Felipe is the more attractive of the two, and its cooking is more interesting.

EXCURSIONS

Attractive **Viseu** ★★ lies 68 k west along N-16. **Coimbra** ★★★ with its ancient university is conveniently close. Take N-18 west for 22 k to Celorico da Beira, where N-17 leads slowly and scenically to Coimbra in 138 k. **Évora** ★★★★ and **Oporto** ★★ can be reached in a half-day and a day, respectively. All are described under their own headings in this chapter. But the reason for the trip to Guarda is the score of castles in the countryside around it. Note that there is no requirement that all twenty must be seen. A sameness begins to grow about them because all repose in tiny towns perched on hilltops, and all date from the same medieval era. Nonetheless, some have features that distinguishes them from the rest, so the whole group would constitute an instructive two-day excursion. A car is the only means of transportation that can reach every one. We divide our description into a larger group of fortresses located, for the most part, south of Guarda and a smaller group located to the north. Of the two tours, the southern one covers the more interesting sights.

THE SOUTHERN FORTS

*South on N-18 brings **Belmonte** in 22 k, just off that main road.*

Belmonte   ★

The granite **fortress** was constructed by King Dinis in the 13th century and looks so right that it seems a movie set. (Open daily 9 a.m. to noon and 1-5 p.m.) The church of **São Tiago** stands beside the keep. Its interior contains tombs of the ancestors of Pedro Alvares Cabral, who was born in Belmonte and discovered Brazil. Two k north of Belmonte along N-18, a road to the right toward Comeal da Torre shortly brings **Torre Centum Cellas**, a curious Roman tower. The three-story square tower is constructed of granite without mortar and dates at least to Roman times. Its function is debated, but its abundant windows argue against a fortress or watchtower.

Continue south for 12 k on N-18 toward Talxoso, but turn left (east) on N-18-3 toward Caria just before it. A few k further west brings Sortelha on its hill.

Sortelha ★

All in granite and surrounded by boulders of the same material, the town huddles inside 13th-century fortified walls. Most of the houses are empty, as is the imposing castle, artfully fitted into the living stone. The scene is memorable.

An excursion further south to the even more boulder bestrewn village of Monsanto is possible. If interested, continue east on N-18-3 to Santo Estavão, where N-233 south leads through Nenamacor to Monsanto in 38 k.

Monsanto ★★

Mammoth boulders seem to perch precariously on the steep side of the hill to which Monsanto clings. Boulders fill the town too, and its houses—constructed of the same granite material—seem almost to be boulders themselves. A castle was built here in the 12th century, but its top was blown off by an explosion in the 19th. Today it is a romantic ruin of granite walls and stairs, covered in lichen. The view seems to extend forever.

Otherwise, continue east from Sortelha on N-18-3 to Santo Estavão, where the road changes its designation to N-233 and goes east, then bends north to Sabugal in 13 k.

Sabugal ★

This time the castle is a bit later—14th century. It is also quite complete since it has been restored. The five sides of the keep are unusual, and the ensemble of fortifications forms a pretty picture. (If it is closed, apply at the town hall.)

Continuing north on N-233, the highway N-16 is met in 56 k crossing to Spain. Turn right here to pass **Castelo Mendo** *with some castle ruins in a few k on the left just before crossing the Rio Coa, and* **Castelo Bom**, *with one tower of its castle remaining, just before joining N-332 north to Almeida.*

Almeida ★

This peaceful village displays formidable 18th-century fortifications in the form of a six-pointed star. This style is named Vauban, after its originator, who is said to have worked on Almeida. Monolithic in design, the walls force attackers to concentrate on areas where they were targets for fire from walls on two sides. Almeida's fortifications are double: should one wall be breached, another could still be defended. In spite of the cleverness of the construction, the fort was stormed—once by the Spanish and later by the French. Some attractive mansions dot the town within the fortifications

THE NORTHERN FORTS

From Guarda take N-221 northeast for 48 k to Castelo Rodrigo.
Or, from Almeida continue north on N-332 which meets N-221 in
about 17 k at Castelo Rodrigo.

Castelo Rodrigo

Do not be misled by the quiet and intimacy of this little village within
fortified walls—its early citizens had passion. In the 16th century,
when the lord of their castle helped Felipe II of Spain acquire the Portuguese crown, the populace set fire to his castle. So today it is a ruin,
with a bit of romance about it.

Take N-222 north for about 26 k to Castelo Melhor.

Castelo Melhor

The little village clings to the side of a rocky peak below a fine medieval wall steadied by strong round towers. Alas, the castle inside is
gone, replaced by grass.

Continue on N-222 as it descends and bends to meet the high-
way N-102. Take the highway south (left) for about 21 k to the vil-
lage of Marialva.

Marialva   ★

The old walls above the modern village gird the ghost town of an earlier village. The castle and walls date to the beginning of the 13th century, and the old village seems to have been abandoned for at least two
centuries since. An absolute time-warp is contained within the walls
—there are remains of the castle keep, a tower wall, a church with a
Manueline doorway, a 15th-century pillory and various aged houses,
all empty.

Continue south along N-102 to Tancoso, just right of the high-
way.

Trancoso

In the 13th century King Dinis strengthened the original ninth-cen-
tury walls and built a castle inside. Here he married his 12-year-old
bride, Isabel of Castile, who later became a saint. As a wedding
present Dom Dinis gave the village to his bride. Although it still
retains some 16th-century houses, the walls at the northern end with
their castle and squat keep are more interesting. (If it's closed, apply
at the town hall.)

Continue south along N-102 to Celorico da Beira in 13 k. Here
N-16 can be taken east back to Guarda in 22 k. For the insatiable,
there is castle keep standing in busy Celorico.

GUIMARÃES ★ ★

Population: 22,092
Area code: 053; zip code: 4800

See the directions to Braga. Guimarães is 22 k southeast of Braga along N-101.

Guimarães is Portugal's birthplace. Henri, duke of Burgundy, came to Spain to help Alfonso VI of Castile battle the Moors and received the king's illegitimate daughter as a reward. Henri and Teresa married in 1095 and were given the County of Portucale, as northern Portugal was then known, for a wedding present. At the time Guimarães was not even a village—only the site of a monastery—but the newlyweds took one of the monastery towers, fit it out as a palace, and settled in residence. In that tower of Mumadona monastery, their son Afonso was born in about 1110. After his father's death, he declared his territory independent from Spain and assumed the first title of King of Portugal.

Today Guimarães thrives on weaving, cutlery manufacturing and tanning. Handwork still is practiced in the form of ox yokes, embroidery, and linen damask. Industrial Guimarães surrounds the older sights, leaving the center attractive with gardens and monuments. Parking is where one finds it, but should be available at the Paço dos Duques on the green hillside below the castle.

*From **Braga** Rua de São Gonçalo funnels into Rua de Gil Vicente, which bends left after passing the post office and receives the name Av. Henrique Delgado. Either the first or second right thereafter will lead to the castle.*

WHAT TO SEE AND DO

Castelo ★ ★

Open daily 10 a.m. to 12:30 p.m. and 2-5 p.m. Admission: free. Old walls of indeterminate great age surround a castle consisting of a massive keep amid seven towers of various heights, topped by triangular merlons that make the whole look fierce. The original tower was remodeled in the 11th century to serve as a palace in which Afonso I, the first king of Portugal, was born. Additions over the centuries greatly expanded that original; then the whole became a prison early in the 19th century. Soon after, the complex was abandoned and used as a quarry for public buildings throughout Guimarães. Prime Minister Salazar decided that this was one of the most historic buildings in the nation and, in 1940—recapturing as many of its stones as could be found—set about restoring it.

With so much alteration, it is no longer clear which tower was the original—the one in which the first king was born—or even if that tower still exists. Regardless, the monolithic complex is suitably awesome for a national monument.

Just outside the walls is the Romanesque chapel of **São Miguel** from the 12th century. Inside, a font from an earlier church is said to be that used to christen Afonso. Below the grassy hill is the Palace of the Dukes of Braganza.

Paço dos Duques de Braganza   ★★

Open daily 10 a.m. to 5:30 p.m. Admission: 300$00 for a guided tour, 200$00 in winter. The building is an early 15th-century palace built for the first duke of the powerful Bragança family that would later rule Portugal. The duke decided to build a new palace because the castle on the hill was not modern enough for his needs. Four buildings, each with a corner tower, form a cloister in the center. Since he employed a French architect, the style is that of the late Gothic in Burgundy. The large number of brick chimneys (39) was unusual and remains a striking feature. In the 17th century the palace was abandoned and suffered horribly until Prime Minister Salazar ordered its repair in 1940, at the same time the castle was receiving similar treatment. In the case of the palace, because Salazar intended to live in it, renovation—rather than restoration—was performed. The present structure, therefore, provides an interesting study of the difference between fixing the old without depriving it of its look of age, and making the old perfect again. Today the building functions as a museum displaying the noble lifestyle of some indeterminate century, for there are pieces inside from the 14th through the 19th centuries, in a building without the nicks and wear of its age.

It is the superb furnishing that are of primary interest—from Aubusson and Gobelins tapestries, to antique Persian carpets, Chinese porcelain, and 17th-century Portuguese furniture. In addition, the ceilings in the dining Hall and banquet hall are wonders. Three still lifes by Josepha de Obidos should be sought out.

Proceed downhill by taking the first left, **Rua Santa Maria,** *which passes the front of the Convent do Carmo. Many of its houses are 14th and 15th century. A square is soon passed with the former* **convento de Santa Clara**, *now the town hall. Continuing, the Largo de São Tiago is reached, at the end of which stands the 16th-century* **Paços do Concelho**, *a former town hall. Past it the Largo de Oliveira is entered, at whose east side is the church and convent of* **Our Lady of the Olive Tree**.

Nossa Senhora da Oliveira   ★

Museum open Tues.-Sun. 10 a.m. to 12:30 p.m. and 2-5 p.m. Closed Mon. Admission: 200$00, free on Sun. This convent is the descendant of the original 10th-century monastery that Henri of Burgundy and his wife found occupying this site. As its name indicates, the founding had something to do with an olive tree. Legend has it that in the 7th-century Visigothic nobles approached the shepherd Wamba in his fields to beg him to be their king. By way of refusal, he thrust his staff into the ground and vowed that he would not become king unless his olive staff flowered. It did and he did, and in the tenth century a monastery commemorating the miracle was constructed on this spot.

An unusual 14th-century Gothic porch prefaces the church. The church facade is of the same era, although the tower is 16th-century Manueline. The church interior was redecorated in this century and is of little interest. What is of interest are the Romanesque cloisters whose second floor serves as a fine museum. Called the Museu Alberto Sampaio, it can be entered just south of the church.

An astonishing collection of rich ecclesiastical plate is displayed. Also on view is a tunic that João I, the first king of the House of Avis, wore in the battle of Aljubarrota where he defeated Portuguese nobles and their Spanish allies to secure his throne. The most amazing work on display is a 14th-century gilt triptych altarpiece donated by João after that battle. While one story claims that he captured it from the Spanish, another contends that he commissioned it afterwards. Whatever its origins, it is a masterpiece displaying the Nativity in the center panel, the Annunciation and presentation at the temple on the left panel, and the Magi and shepherds on the right. In addition, chalices, monstrances and elegant crosses all fight for attention.

A grand vista at the end of the square leads down to the church of **Santos Passos,** *majestic from a distance, although of little interest inside. Walk toward it to take the second right along the Alameda da Liberdade gardens for one block to the church of São Francisco to the left.*

São Francisco ★
Open Tues.-Sun. 10 a.m. to 12:30 p.m. and 2-5 p.m. Closed Mon. Admission: free. Of the original 15th-century church only the main portal and apse remain, the rest being 17th century. One cannot fail to notice the tile-covered mansion next door that seems to alert that the reason to enter the church is for sublime blue-and-white Delft *azulejos* lining the chancel walls.

For those interested in archaeology a walk to the **Marins Sarmento Museum** *is in order. Continue to the west end of the Alameda gardens, where the* **Office of Tourism** *is found. Turn right to walk through the plaza, continuing north along Rua Paio Galvão, which passes more garden to reach the Gothic* **São Domingos** *in one block on the left, with the museum installed in its cloisters.*

Museu Martins Sarmento

Open Tuesday-Sunday 10 a.m. to noon and 2-5 p.m. Closed Mon. Admission: 200$00. Named for the archaeologist who began the excavation at Citânia de Briteiros (see "Braga" under "Excursions"), this museum displays the smaller objects found there and elsewhere in the area. Included are two headless statues of Celtiberian warriors holding round shields, and—most dramatic of all—the Colossus of Pedralva, all ten feet of him. Some of the smaller bronze pieces are surprising, such as dolphins and a hermaphrodite figure.

WHERE TO STAY

For moderate and inexpensive accommodations, Braga is a better bet than Guimarães. But for memorable rooms at very fair prices—considering the quality—stay in one of Guimarães' two pousadas.

EXPENSIVE ($100-$200)

Pousada de Santa Marinha da Costa · · · · · · · · · · · · · · · 1st-class ★ ★ ★

Estrada de Penha (2.5 k east, directed by abundant signs). Rooms: 50. ☎ *51 44 53; FAX 51 44 59; Telex 32686.* Do not judge this one by its whitewashed exterior suggesting a factory. Actually, it is a former convent, founded in the 12th century but completely restored in the 18th. Inside it is grand, but even more impressive is the elegant taste. In fact it would be difficult to decide whether this or Rainha Santa Isabel in Estremoz is the most elegant of the pousadas. The fortunate will stay at both. Hallways are grand enough to ride horses through, as happened in olden days, and many bedrooms include canopied beds. As this is the flagship of the entire pousada chain, the service is always on its efficient toes. The only surprise will come when you look at the bill—the price of a room barely crosses the expensive line.

Pousada de Santa Maria da Oliveira · · · · · · · · · · · · · · · 1st-class ★ ★

Rua Santa Maria. Rooms: 16. ☎ *51 41 57; FAX 51 42 04; Telex 32875.* If two pousadas served the same town one would hope for a difference in what each offered. This one is for city mice. It is constructed from a block of old townhouses, now joined by interior corridors, so it has the feel of an old town inn. Although there is nothing grand about the accommodations, there is much warmth and atmosphere.

MODERATE ($50-$99)

Fundador Dom Pedro · 1st-class

Av. Don Afonso Henriques, 740 (due south of the Tourist Office, at the end of the Alameda gardens). Rooms: 63. ☎ *51 37 81; FAX 51 37 86; Telex 32866.* If both pousadas are full, this is a perfectly comfortable option, although modern—in fact the only highrise in town—and lacking atmosphere.

WHERE TO EAT

Of the two pousadas, the food is more exciting at Pousada da Oliveira, where meals are moderate in cost.

EXCURSIONS

A pleasant two-stop outing is possible for those interested in lace and a stroll through a pretty town. Take Rua Dona Constanca de Noranha, the road that follows the southern edge of the park containing the castle, which leads to N-101 toward Amarante. In 7.5 k comes **Trofa** where, on a nice day, all the women will be tatting on their doorsteps or in the plaza. Feel free to inspect their wares. A command of Portuguese is unnecessary; the will to communicate finds a way.

In 25k more, the town of **Amarante** ★ is entered. It lies pretty-as-a-picture along the clear Tamega River. Its newest houses are 18th century. Wooden balconies overhang the river which is spanned by a fine massive bridge. There is a 16th-century church, if some sighseeing objective is necessary, but the most pleasant course is to walk and stop frequently just to look around.

LEIRIA

See "Batalha" under "Excursions" in the "Lisbon" chapter.

MARVÃO ★ ★ ★

Population: 309
Area code: 045; zip code: 7330

*From **Lisbon** go north along the autoestrada for 35 k to Garregado, where N-3 is picked up going north. N-3 ends in 91 k at Torres Novas, becoming N-118. Go east for 86 k to Alpalhão. Continue east, though the highway designation is now N-246, reaching Castelo de Vide in about 18 k. Watch for a sign for Marvão going left in about 7 k. From **Évora** take N-18 north for 105 k to Portalegre. Outside that city N-359 leads to Marvão in 16 k. From **Coimbra** and **Oporto** get to **Leiria**, 70 k south of Coimbra along N-1. From Leiria take N-113 east which winds for 25 k to join N-243 to Torres Novas in 30 k more. From there the Lisbon directions apply.*

*   **Train** *service is infrequent, although connections can be made from Lisbon, Elvas and Portalegre to Beira, then a 10 k bus ride.*

Portugal possesses a surplus of fairy tale hilltop villages surrounded by medieval walls commanded by ancient castles. The description of Guarda in this chapter covers ten such sites, and an equal number more could have been added. However, everyone agrees that

Marvão is the most charming of the lot—the one to see, if seeing just one. Marvão exudes a calming atmosphere and shows prettiness at every hand, but there is not much to see in the tiny village. Sufficient variety in nearby excursions, however, justifies a stay overnight.

Since one is accustomed to villages nestling in valleys, the initial sight of Marvão is surprising—perched atop a steep hill with the houses seeming to strain to reach even higher. The reason, of course, was for defense. The village castle was raised at the close of the 13th century and surrounded by curtain walls. A second wall was added around the whole in the 17th century. From the access road—that circles all arrivals around the peak—the village seems utterly impregnable. And so it has proven to be. Dazzlingly whitewashed houses, sporting orange tile roofs, cling to the walls. Hardly any are newer than the 17th century. A walk through the cobbled street to the castle is no different today than it would have been three centuries ago, save for the odd TV aerial and telephone wire.

Rua do Espirito Sant leads to the castle past handsome wrought-iron balconies. Four successive fortified gates must be passed to reach the fortress, which essentially consists of one massive keep. On a clear day the view from the walls is as fine as any in the country—looking east one sees Spain, a mere 5 miles away. Next to the castle stands a white chapel that contains both the **Office of Tourism** and the **Museu Municipal**, whose most interesting exhibit is mannequins in local costumes. (Open daily 9 a.m. to 12:30 p.m. and 2-5:30 p.m. Admission: 200$00.) The Office of Tourism maintains a list of inexpensive bed-and-breakfast rooms let by local citizens.

WHERE TO STAY

Other than bed-and-breakfast rooms, there are only two hotels. Both are fine choices, but heavily booked.

MODERATE ($50-$99)

Pousada de Santa Maria   3rd-class ★★★
Rua 24 de Janeiro, 7. Rooms: 29. ☎ *932 01; FAX 934 40; Telex 42360.* Three old town houses were joined to create this pousada. Its comfortable decor and spectacular views make this one of the nicer places to stay in all of Portugal. There is no attempt at elegance or grandeur, just cozy relaxation.

INEXPENSIVE (UNDER $50)

Estalagem Dom Dinis   R2nd-class ★
Rua Dr. Matos Magalhaes. Rooms: 8. ☎ *932 36.* This is a quiet, inviting place, with comfortably solid furnishings. A cheerful reception sets just the right tone.

WHERE TO EAT

While the food is somewhat better at Dom Dinis, the views from the relaxing Pousada dining room so enhance the dining experience that it must be the first choice. Prices are moderate.

EXCURSIONS

Past **Portalegrbe**, famed for tapestry, is the intriguing Knights' Templar monastery of **Flor de Rosa** ★, an outing of 36 k each way. **Castelo de Vide** ★, with a spa and ancient Jewish quarter, is only 12 k to the west, and a further 83 k would bring **Castelo Branco** and its incredible embroidered bedspreads.

PORTALEGRE

Population: 15,876
Area code: 045; zip code: 7300

Take N-359 southwest for 16 k. The road leads into Largo A. J. Lourinho. The tapestry workshop is one short block south and another east.

The city first acquired renown in the 16th century for sewing exquisitely detailed tapestries. A century later silk brought real prosperity and led to a clutch of fine 18th-century houses. But the tapestry work—still using woolen thread—continued and is produced today in a workshop in an old monastery. A tour takes the visitor through all the steps, from making a slide of the work to be copied, to projecting it on graph paper (indicating thereon the color of each stitch), to viewing actual pieces in the making. None can be purchased, since all work is by commission, but nothing except the cost stands in the way of commissioning a piece for oneself. (Open for tours except Sun. 9:30-11:30 a.m. and 2:30-5:30 p.m.)

FLOR DE ROSA ★

Population 394

After 2 k from Portalegre on N-18 toward Alpalhão, take N-119 west to Crato. There take N-245 north for 2 k.

The present town is so small as to be dwarfed by the massive ancient fortified monastery in its midst. The monastery is surrounded by a crenellated wall, and its buildings resemble small forts. Knights Templar of Malta constructed the monastery in the middle of the 14th century. On the right stands an elegantly simple church with a most impressive nave. The small cloister is lovely. This is a favorite spot for those who take the small trouble to come here; one generally has the complex all to oneself.

CASTELO DE VIDE ★

Population: 2,558
Area code: 045; zip code: 7320

From Marvão regain the highway N-246, south of the village. Go west for 11 k.

Standing even higher than Marvão, Castelo de Vide presents a similar picture of whitewashed houses. The main square, **Praça Dom Pedro V**, is ringed with 17th-century buildings and an 18th-century mansion. Beside the church of Santa Maria in the square, a sign shows the way up to the castle. To the right is the **Judiaria**, the ancient Jewish quarter. The Judiaria is a jumble of small houses, many with two entrances, one for business and one for family. Houses are small and crowded together because an ordinance decreed that Jews had to live separately from Christians, locked inside their quarter each night.

Uncharacteristically, the **castle** lies inside its own walls outside those of the village. Its keep suffered damage from an explosion, but the 12th-century tower that leads to it is of interest. On the site is a 17th-century **church** with nice *azulejos*. Downhill from the Judiaria is a picturesque square, the **Fonte da Vila**, whose fountain waters are reputed to possess curative value and certainly taste sweet.

CASTELO BRANCO ★

Population: 24,287
Area code: 072; zip code: 6000

From Marvão continue past Castelo da Vide on N-246 for 25 k to Alpalhão. There take N-18 north for 58 k. Head straight through the city along Av. 1 de Maio which feeds into Rua de Se. Rua de Se bends left, then changes its name to Campo da Patria, as it climbs to the gardens of the former Bishop's palace.

The gardens of the former Episcopal Palace are a formal fantasy of clipped ornamental hedges, pools and unexpected statues. To the left is the Episcopal Palace itself, with the **Museu Tavares Proença** installed inside. Its most interesting exhibits are a series of *colchas*, embroidered bedspreads, for which this town has been famous since the 16th century. The spreads are linen, embroidered with brightly colored figures in large-stitched silk thread. Originally, young women made them for their trousseaux. There is a workshop, connected with the museum, where pieces may be commissioned.

MONSANTO

See "Guarda" under "Excursions."

MONSARAZ

See"Évora" under "Excursions."

OPORTO ★ ★

Population: 335,916
Area code: 02; zip code: 4000

From **Lisbon** *the autoestrada north joins N-1 at Care-gado in 40 k for a drive north of 152 k, to just south of Coimbra, where the autoestrada A-1 speeds to Oporto in a final 120 k. From* **Coimbra** *a drive north on N-1 of 9 k allows a connection to the autoestrada A-1 for the final 131 k. From* **Évora** *take N-114 northwest to Montemor-o-Novo in 30 k, where N-4 goes west to Cruzamento de Pegões in 37 k. There N-10 goes northwest to Vial Franca de Xiro, where N-1 is picked up and the Lisbon directions may be followed. From the* **Algarve** *follow directions to Lisbon, but to skirt the city, at Maratecs take N-10 north, instead of N-10 west to Setubal. Continue past Cruzamento de Pegões in 14 k toward Villa Franca de Xira in a further 49 k, where N-1 is picked up and the remaining Lisbon directions may be followed. From* **Braga** *take N-14 south which reaches the autoestrada A-4 in about 10 k. The remaining trip is 54 k. From* **Viseu** *take N-16 due west for 65 k to the autoestrada A-1, which goes north to Oporto in a further 46 k. From* **Tomar** *get to Coimbra and follow directions from there.*

Train *service is frequent from most parts of the country, although most trains end in the de Campanha station, which is a distance from the center of the city. Change there for a five-minute ride to the Estacão São Bento in the heart of the city. A Lisbon express train takes about three hours, about twice the time from Coimbra. Buses almost double those times, although they are as convenient as trains from*

*nearer departures, such as Braga and Viseu. At four-and-
a-half hours, the bus beats the train from Guarda.*

*Of course, a plane is fastest. Pedras Rubras airport is 14 k
south of the city. A taxi costs less than 3000$00. The #56 bus
takes about 45 minutes to reach Pr. de Lisbōa, one block west
of Av. dos Aliados, and costs less than $1.*

A Roman settlement originally occupied the south bank of the
wide mouth of the Douro River. The north bank of the river was its
port, although, gradually, another town grew around the port. The
towns were respectively called Cale and Portus (The Port). By the
tenth century, after the Moors had been chased south of the Douro,
the northern territory now in Christian hands combined the two
Roman names to call itself Portucale. Thus, too, the fiefdom inherited by Afonso I and over which he styled himself king, was called
Portucale. Since Christian reconquest of the rest of the country involved adding more and more territory to this original area, the
name came to designate the entire country, and was later transmuted
into "Portugal."

The present city of Oporto—in Portuguese, simply *Porto*—occupies the site of the Roman town of Portus, sprawling down the long,
steep north bank of the Douro, 6 k from the sea. With almost a million people in the extended agglomeration, it is easily the second
largest city in Portugal and the one most devoted to commerce.
Oporto has a long history of independence. In the 13th century its
citizens disputed the right of the king to impose tariffs on their shipping. In response, the king established a royal city on the opposite
bank, now called Villa Nova de Gaia, and wrangled an agreement
that a third of the shipping—upon which he was allowed to impose
taxes—would depart from his city. Much later, when Lisbon fell
meekly to Napoleon in 1808, Oporto held out, setting up a junta to
rule in the king's place when the court fled to exile in Brazil. A year
later, Napoleon's General Soult captured Oporto, but the English
under Wellesley, later the duke of Wellington, regained it four
months later. In 1820, Oporto's citizens rebelled against the occupying English to adopt the first liberal constitution in Portugal.
Eight years later, when Miguel I returned from two decades of pleasant exile in Brazil to reign as an absolute monarch, the city revolted
again—siding with Miguel's brother in his successful fight for the
crown. Finally, in 1890 Oporto began the antimonarchist republican
rebellion that bore final fruit in Lisbon in 1910, when the last monarch was expelled.

Portugal in general, but Oporto in particular, has a long history of close ties with England. In the 17th century, France closed its borders to imports of English clothing, and in response Charles II forbade the importation of French wines, leaving English thirsts unslaked. The English began sending their cloth to Portugal, returning with wine from Oporto. This arrangement was formalized in the Methuen Treaty of 1703, which stipulated that the two countries would remain perpetual friends. Soon Englishmen came to Oporto, bought up inland vineyards along the Douro, and formed shipping companies for the wine that floated to Oporto. Whether to prevent spoilage or to satisfy the English palate for sweet wine, a method was developed for adding grape brandy to the wine to stop its fermentation while half of the grape sugar remained. It produced a sweet, fortified wine of as much as 30% alcohol that is called after its place of embarkation, *port*. To earn the name, wine originally had to age in Villa Nova de Gaia, across the river from Oporto. Famous port houses, such as Sandeman, still maintain "lodges" (warehouses) there today, although aging now is permitted anywhere along the Douro littoral.

Oporto today presents the face of a 19th-century commercial port—full of granite-trimmed buildings, few more than three storeys high. The heart of the city is the wide, gardened, Av. dos Aliados, which runs five blocks inland from, and perpendicular to, the river. All of the sights lie south of this landmark. The **Cathedral** ★, with a fine altar, stands two blocks directly south; the church of **San Francisco** ★, the non-plus-ultra of the Baroque, borders the river to the southeast and soars beside the **Palácio da Bolsa** ★, containing one overwhelming hall in the style of the Moors. Lining the river in front of San Francisco is the **Cais (quay) de Ribeira**, the oldest and most picturesque quarter. Across the river in Villa Nova de Gaia stretches a row of **port lodges** ★ for free tours and tastings. Upriver from the lodges stands the architecturally interesting **Convento de Nossa Senhora da Serra do Pilar**. All told, there is less to see in Oporto than its size might suggest, but the ambiance of the city is different from any other in Portugal and the sights are pleasant enough for a day's stay.

One-way streets complicate entry into the city. Centralized parking is available at the north end of the Av. dos Aliados, north of the imposing town hall, on either side of the grand church of Trinidade.

From **Lisbon** *and south on the autoestrada A-1 the Ponte da Arrabida is crossed leading to a cloverleaf on the north bank. Exit here, following signs for "Centro" by heading east along Rua do Campo Alegre. The street ends at a "T;" take Rua de Julio Dinis right. R. Dinis ends at the garden of the Crystal Palace; turn left along Rua do Dom Manuel II. After passing the 18th-century Carranças Palace, the road ends at a "T." From here the going is trickier to describe than to follow, for one-way streets offer few choices. Go right on Rua Alberto Aires de Gouvela for one block, turn left on Rua da Restauracão, which soon follows the edge of the garden of João Chagas past the rear of a university complex. At the east side of the university buildings is the Pr. de Lisbõa whose southern edge is followed on Rua dos Clericos, which in two blocks lets into the Pr. de Liberdade with a fountain in the center. Turn left along Rua dos Almada—with the garden in the center—for 5 blocks, passing the city hall to reaching the large church of Trinidade. Parking is available both to the right and to the left of the church.*

From **N-1** *the course is simpler. Ponte de Dom Luis I is crossed to reach Av. Vimara Peres, which changes its name after passing the Cathedral on the left to Av. de Dom Afonso Henrigues. Then it passes the São Bento train station and ends at the Pr. de Liberdade. Go north along Rua do Almada—with the garden in the center—for 5 blocks, past the city hall to the front of the large church of Trinidade. Parking is available both to the right and to the left of that church.*

From **Braga** *and the* **airport** *the simplest course is to turn left on N-12, the Estrada Circunvalacão, at a large traffic circle. Take the first exit to the right onto Rua do Amial which changes its name successively to Rua do Vale Formoso, Rua de Antero de Quental and Rua de Lapa, before entering the large Pr. da República. Turn left at its end, then right at its corner to pass a church before taking soft left. This ends in a "T." Go right on Rua de Camões to find parking to the right side, opposite the Trinidade church.*

*If parked beside the Trinidade church, walk downhill past the neo-Renaissance city hall (to the right of which is the **Office of Tourism**) for three blocks along the gardens in the center of Rua do Almada. At the end of the gardens is the Pr. da Liberdade, an animated plaza with a statue of Pedro IV in the center. Turn right at the southeast corner to enter the Pr. de Almeida Garrett, where the **train station of São Bento** is left. Extensive blue azulejos inside show scenes from Portuguese history. Continue south along Av. de Dom Afonso Henriques to turn right in one long block at the intersection with Rua Saraiva de Carvalho. Here, atop its knoll, is the cathedral.*

WHAT TO SEE AND DO

Cathedral ★

Open daily 9 a.m. to 12:30 p.m. and 2-5:30 p.m. Admission: 50$00 to the cloisters. Of the 12th-century Romanesque fortress church in which João I married Philippa of Lancaster in 1387, little can be seen, since so many decorative additions have been added. The central window of the facade is lovely Romanesque, but the portal is Baroque. Baroque is the dominant theme of the interior, and the space is lovely. A treasure graces the Chapel of the Holy Sacrament in the north (left) transept. A retablo and altar front of chased silver from the 17th century is a marvel of mannered figures that seem to move in the dim light. A door at the end of the south transept leads to a solemn 14th-century cloister whose upper tier was wrapped in lovely *azulejos* in the 17th century.

*Toward the river in the cathedral plaza is a fine 18th-century **Old Bishop's Palace**, now an office building. A lane behind the apse of the cathedral leads downhill to cross the access road to the Ponte de Dom Luis I for the church of **Santa Clara**, covered inside in 18th-century carved gilt. The ceiling is elegant. Remains of the old **city walls** stand behind the church. If the above sights do not appeal, descend the western flank of the cathedral hill to the Pr. Infante Dom Henrique which lays at the rear of the church of **São Francisco**. Adjacent to the north side of the church is the **Palácio da Bolsa**.*

Igreja São Francisco ★

Open Mon.-Sat. from 10 a.m. to 1 p.m. and from 2 p.m. to 5 p.m. (in winter closed from 12:30-2 p.m., but open to 7 p.m.) Closed Sun. Admission: 100$00. Rua da Bolsa, 44. Be prepared for a shock behind the Gothic exterior. The inside, decorated from the 17th through the 18th centuries, is the most dazzling and fantastic of all the baroque edifices in Portugal. Gilt is everywhere in dizzying profusion. When your eyes begin to smart, it's time to leave.

Palácio da Bolsa   ★

Open Mon.-Fri. 9 a.m.-6 p.m. Open Sat. and Sun. 10 a.m. to noon and 2-5 p.m. (in winter open Mon.-Fri., closes noon to 2, open until 5:30 p.m.). Admission: 200$00, for guided tour. This is the Stock Exchange, built in 1834 on the ruins of the convent of neighboring São Francisco. What makes a visit worthwhile is a hall, called the Salon de Arabe. The huge oval room took 18 years just to decorate in a style loosely derived from the Alhambra in Spain. The ornateness is luxuriant, and the inlaid parquet, besides being fine work, still exudes a pleasant smell.

Past the west end of the Bolsa a right and an immediate left brings the Largo São João Novo, named after the church there. Opposite the church is the **Museu de Etnografia i Historia**. *Exhibits are a mismash of 19th-century and early 20th-century curiosities and folk pieces that are unfailingly interesting. (Open Tues.-Sat. 10am to noon and 2-5 p.m. Closed Sun., Mon., and holidays. Admission: free.)*

Returning to the Pr. Infante Dom Henrique at the rear of the church of São Francisco, descend Rua da Alfandega that leaves its southeast corner. On the right the house where Henry the Navigator was purportedly born, now hosting art exhibits, is passed. Further downhill and right at Rua da Reboleira is the **Center of Traditional Arts and Crafts**, *for a look or a purchase. Down to the river and upstream (east) is the area called* **Ribeira**, *a seedy but atmospheric district.*

Vila Nova de Gaia   ★

This is the name for the area across the river where port wine is warehoused in what the trade calls "lodges." They line the bank opposite the center of Oporto, all clearly marked by neon company signs. One can walk or taxi—taxis are entitled to a surcharge for crossing the river—across the lower level of the Ponte de Dom Luis I. Do not fail to notice the lovely **Maria Pia railway bridge** upstream (east), designed by Gustave Eiffel of tower fame, and the newer **Arrabida road bridge** downstream, crossing in a single span measuring 1000 feet.

All the lodges offer free guided tours and samples. Buses #57 and #91 go to them. All are open on weekdays from either 9am or 10 p.m. to noon and from 2-5 p.m. A few, such as Sandeman and Real Vinicola, are open on Sat. as well. Note that three such tours bring most people to the edge of intoxication. A few of the better ones are:

Sandeman *Largo Miguel Bombarda, 2.* ☎ *30 40 81.*

Ferreira *Av. Diogo Leite, 70.* ☎ *30 08 66.*

Real Vinicola *Rua Azevedo Magalhães, 314.* ☎ *30 54 62.*

Calem *Av. Diogo Leite, 2.* ☎ *39 40 41.*

WHERE TO STAY

Oporto recently added a spate of luxury hotels to remedy a lack at that level, although all charge very high prices. With the exception of the truly elegant infante de Sagres they are gleaming modern hotels that, in our opinion, are not worth their lofty rates. Better values exist in Oporto's moderately priced lodgings.

VERY EXPENSIVE ($200+)

Infante de Sagres   1st-class ★ ★ ★ ★
Pr. Dona Filipa de Lencastre, 62 (one block west of Av. do Almada, about half way along). Rooms: 74. ☎ *201 90 31; FAX 31 49 37; Telex 26880.* The Infante is one of the great hotels of Europe and, unquestionably, the most luxurious in Oporto. Although built in the 1950s, no cost was spared to make it as grand and lovely as it could be, with rich and elegant paneling and wrought iron throughout. Its list of guests include the royal, great and famous. The bedrooms are large, with marble bathrooms, although their decor is not up to the exalted standards of the public spaces. What is truly outstanding is the service, for there are as many people providing service as spending the night.

Le Méridien Porto   1st-class ★ ★ ★
Av. da Boavista, 1466 (about 2 k west of the center). Rooms: 232. ☎ *600 19 13; FAX 600 20 31; Telex 27301.* Every service is efficiently provided by this modern hotel that lives up to the fine reputation of the Méridien chain. However, its size precludes the impeccable service of the Infante above, it charges more, and it's a 10-minute taxi ride from the sights.

EXPENSIVE ($100-$200)

Dom Henrique   1st-class ★ ★
Rua Guedes de Azevedo, 179 (1 block east of the Trinidade train station, which is just north of the Trinidade church at the top of the Rua do Almada). Rooms: 112. ☎ *200 57 55; FAX 201 94 51; Telex 22554.* This, too, is a modern hotel with all services, as opulent as the preceding. But it's close enough to the sights to walk and charges at the bottom, rather than at the top, of the expensive range. Some rooms have fine views over the city.

Porto Sheraton   1st-class ★ ★
Av. da Boavista, 1269 (across the street from the Méridien). Rooms: 253. ☎ *606 88 22; FAX 609 14 67; Telex 22723.* Newer even than its neighbor the Méridien, the Sheraton provides an expected modern look and services. For those pining for home it might be a good choice, and it charges about half of the price of the Infante.

MODERATE ($50-$99)

Albergaria Miradouro   R1st-class ★★

Rua da Alegria, 598 (3 blocks east and 2 north of the Trinidade train station, which is just north of the Trinidade church at the top of the Rua do Almada). Rooms: 30. ☎ *57 07 17; FAX 57 02 06.* This 13-story modern building in a quiet neighborhood offers dramatic views of the city and the river traffic for a modest price. The decor is tasteful and the walk to sights is downhill. Its Portucale restaurant is one of the best in the city.

Albergeria São João   2nd-class ★★

Rua do Bonjardim, 120 (although one-way in the wrong direction, Rua de Fernandes goes east from the Trinidade church to reach the hotel in 4 blocks). Rooms: 43. ☎ *208 02 61; FAX 32 04 46.* This hotel occupies the top floor of a modern building, yet it is cozy with antiques and a fireplace. The bedrooms are large and intelligently laid out so that each includes a sitting area. The location is convenient to the sights.

Castor   2nd-class ★

Rua das Doze Casas, 17 (a half block north and a short turn west from the Miradoro above). Rooms: 63. ☎ *57 00 14; FAX 56 60 76; Telex 22793.* This is a tasteful, contemporary and quiet hotel, with comfortable bedrooms that could, however, be larger. Walking to the sights is feasible.

Grand Hotel do Oporto   2nd-class ★

Rua de Santa Catarina, 197 (Rua de Dr. Magalhães Lemos runs east from the middle of Rua do Almada. A left turn onto Santa Catarina in 2 blocks brings the hotel.) Rooms: 100. ☎ *200 81 76; FAX 31 10 61; Telex 22553.* "Grand" is stretching it, but the hotel tries with a marble lobby and crystal chandeliers. The bedrooms are surprisingly bright and comfortable, and the location is good.

INEXPENSIVE (UNDER $50)

Rex   R1st-class ★★★

Pr. da República, 117 (this major plaza is 1 block west of the Trinidade train station). Rooms: 21. ☎ *200 45 48; FAX 38 38 82; Telex 20899.* This converted townhouse overlooks a gardened, serene square. The house is a neoclassic charmer with marble staircase, paneled wood and intricate stucco ceilings. Really, it *is* inexpensive, despite its more luxurious look. The bedrooms are lovely, with painted stucco ceilings, and larger than most.

Albergaria Girassol   R2nd-class

Rua do da Bandeira, 133 (1 block east of the southern end of Rua do Almada). Rooms: 18. ☎ *200 18 91.* The hotel occupies the top floor of a building and provides adequate bedrooms for modest prices. The location is most convenient.

Peninsular **3rd-class**

Rua do da Bandeira, 21 (a few steps north of the São Bento train station). Rooms: 50 (a few lack private baths). ☎ *200 30 12; FAX 38 49 84.* The neon sign out front does not bode well, but the bedrooms are more pleasant than that introduction. The location is prime.

WHERE TO EAT

What can one say about the food in a city most famous for tripe? If one likes tripe stewed with spicy sausage and white beans (*tripas a moda do Oporto*) obviously one can say a good deal. On the whole, the food is hearty, rather than gourmet—as in *bacalhau a Gomcs*, casserole of cod, onions and potatoes, or *caldeirada*, fish stew in tomatoes and onion. Almost any restaurant along the Ribeira will do a good job on such dishes—and at a moderate cost. Wash it all down with a *vinho verde.*

EXPENSIVE ($50+)

Portucale

Rua da Alegria, 598 (3 blocks east and 2 north of the Trinidade train station, which is just north of the Trinidade church at the top of the Rua do Almada). ☎ *57 07 17.* The dramatic view alone would make this place special, but it also serves the best food in the city. The dining room is pleasantly decorated with modern hangings, and the tables are attractively dressed with good linens, silver and china, and flowers. Despite the stunning views, there is an intimate feeling. The *cabrito a serrana,* kid stewed in red wine, is cooked nowhere better.

Amex, Diners, MasterCard and Visa accepted.

MODERATE ($20-$50)

Mesa Antiga

Rua de Santo Ildefonso, 208 (Leave the southeast corner of Pr. da Liberdade at the southern end of Av. do Almada on Rua de do da Bandeira. In 1 block, round the church to enter Rua de Santo Ildefonso for 1 block). ☎ *200 64 32. Closed Saturday and the last two weeks of September.* Old wood and blue-and-white *azulejos* create the proper cozy atmosphere for food that is prepared with care. This is a family-run place, where the main work is done in an improbably small kitchen. Try the tripe, or sole in delectable green sauce, or any daily special.

MasterCard and Visa accepted.

Aquário Marisqueiro

Rua Rodrigues Sampaio, 179 (a step or two east of the Pr. do General H. Delgado, which fronts the city hall). ☎ *200 22 31. Closed Sunday and holidays.* This is fish heaven. Clams are good, as is shellfish *açorda*—a bread thickened stew—and sole done any which way.

O Escondidinho

Rua de Passos Manuel, 144 (2 blocks east of the middle of Av. do Almada). ☎ *200 10 79. Closed Sunday.* The place exudes an old club atmosphere with its blackened beams, fireplace and antique ceramics on the walls.

The waiters are informal, although they know their business and will recite the day's specials, which, unfortunately, range from very good to bland. A steak is always a good choice, as are charcoaled sardines.

Amex, Diners, MasterCard and Visa accepted.

INEXPENSIVE (UNDER $20)

Taverna de Bebobos ★★

Cais da Ribeira, 25. ☎ *31 35 65. Closed Sunday and March.* This restaurant is well over 100 years old and tiny, which contributes to the coziness and makes reservations imperative. The cuisine is typical Portuguese, done better than at all but a few much more costly restaurants.

Chez Lapin ★

Cais da Ribeira, 42. ☎ *264 18.* Like its neighbor Bebobos, this, too, is tiny and eclectically decorated. Naturally, the specialty is rabbit, in a white sauce, but fish are fresh and good as well.

Standard Bar ★

Rua Infante Dom Henrique, 43 (the street on the south edge of São Franicisco). ☎ *239 04. Closed Sunday.* This is a small, crowded place that serves only a few dishes, but at very low prices. The cod *açorda*, bread stew, is wonderful.

DIRECTORY

INFORMATION • Located at Rua Clube dos Fenianos, 25 (☎ 31 27 40) on the west side of the city hall. Lots of advice is available about port tastings, boat trips up the Douro and vineyard tours.

AIRPORT • Pedras Rubras international airport is 16 k north of the city (☎ 948 21 44). A taxi will cost under 2.000$00. Buses #44 and #56 connect with the central Pr. do Lisbõa. The main TAP office is at Pr. Mouzinho de Albuquerque, 105 in the Boavista rotunda (☎ 69 98 41), which is a mile east of the Pr. da República at the top of the Av. do Almada.

TRAINS AND BUSES • Three separate train stations are located in Oporto. Local trains, such as those to Guimarães, embark from the Trinidade station north of the city hall. Most other trains depart from the inconvenient Estacão Campanhã (☎ 56 41 41), at the east edge of the city. There is, for example, a 3-1/2-hour express to Lisbon. The station can easily be reached by a 5-minute connection from the central Bento station a few steps southeast of Pr. da Liberdade at the southern end of Av. do Almeda. Service is very good to almost anywhere in Portugal.

There also are three separate bus depots. The main one is Garagem Atlantico (☎ 200 69 54) on Rua Alexandre Herculano at Rua Alexandre Herculano, 366 which is west of the Estacão de São Bento. It serves most of the country and handles the national RN lines. Another depot, Estacão de Camionagem, is used for shorter trips. It is located at Pr. do Dona Felipa de Lencastre (☎ 200 61 21), which is one block east of the Av. do Almada, by the Infantes hotel. The third depot is little used.

POST OFFICE AND TELEPHONES • The main post office (☎ 38 02 51) is on the east side of Pr. do General H. Delgado by the city hall. Telephones are available until 11 p.m.

POLICE • The main station (☎ 268 21) is located on Rua Alexandre Herculano, which runs southeast of the Estacão de São Bento.

EXCURSIONS

The most peaceful Oporto excursion is a *cruise* up the Douro river—and the most ideal cruise is to Pinhão with an overnight in Regua. Including all meals for two days and sleeping accommodations, the trip costs about 20.000$00 per person. This and shorter trips are conducted by Endouro at Muro dos Baalhoeiros, 104 (☎ 32 42 36). Or, for those with less money or time, there are cruises of the river bridges offered by Cruzeiro das Tres Pontes. Boats depart hourly from a dock in Villa Nova de Gaia, behind the Ferreira port lodge. Service runs from May through Oct.; between 10 a.m. and 6 p.m. except Sun.

Oporto is 50 k from the fine beach and canals of **Aveiro**, and 65 more from elegant **Viseu** with a fine museum. **Braga** and its Baroque churches is 70 k north, and **Guimarães**, Portugal's birthplace, is 24 k southwest of it. All are described under separate headings in this chapter. There is also the pottery town of **Barcelos** and the lovely site of **Amarante**, both described under Braga "Excursions."

TOMAR ★ ★ ★

Population: 14,821
Area code: 049; zip code: 2300

From **Lisbon** *take the autoestrada A-1 north to Carragado for 45 k where N-3 can be picked up going northeast. In 91 k, at Entroncamento, N-110 goes north to Tomar in 19 k. From* **Coimbra** *take N-1 south for 70 k to Leiria, where N-115 goes southeast through Fátima to Tomar in 45 k. From* **Batalha** *take N-1 north for 11 k to Leiria and follow the preceding directions. From* **Marvão** *get back to N-246 and go west to Alpalhão for 25 k where N-118 continues west for 67 k to Rossio, where N-3 goes west to villa Nova da Barquinha in 29 k. Two k west N-110 goes north to Tomar in 19 k.*

Trains *run often enough from Lisbon and take two hours, including a change at Santarém. It takes almost as long* *from closer Coimbra. The bus is slower by almost an hour from Lisbon.*

Tomar, a quaint town of cobblestone streets, straddles the river Nabão. Its quaintness, however, is not what draws tourists. In woods above the town, a church established for secret rites was embellished over the centuries by some of the greatest architecture in Portugal. And, nearby, on an island in the center of the Tagus river, reposes the 12th-century castle of Almourol peering above its wooded slope, the most romantic castle in Portugal.

When Jerusalem was captured during the Second Crusade in 1119, a group of French knights created the Order of Knights Templar for the purposes of defending the Holy Sepulcher to the death, and of protecting pilgrims in Palestine. Despite such vows, Jerusalem was soon lost, but the order continued, now as a military arm of the Catholic Church. Within a century 20,000 members could be counted, 9,000 castles throughout Europe were under its control, and most of Europe's banking lay in its grasp. Kings begged the help of the order for their wars and tread carefully in its presence, lest they antagonize such immense power. The order answered to no authority below the pope. Individual members, subject only to the Master of their order, strode the streets of Europe in white tunics blazoned with a red Maltese cross, afraid of no one, up to and including the rank of king. The rites of their order were shrouded in deep mystery, known to no outsider.

In 1128 the Knights Templar were given land to erect a castle in Portugal by Dona Teresa, the mother of the first king of Portugal. Their contribution to her son Alfonso's military success against the Moors was substantial. In 1147 the order traded their original land for acreage at Tomar and there built a castle on a hill, completed in 1160. A church followed two years later; then all was surrounded by fortress walls. By the 14th century, however, the power of the order had become too threatening to people in high places. Phillip V of France arrested the master of the Knights Templar in 1307 and executed him. Pope Clement V decreed the disbanding of the order five years later. But a sympathetic King Dinis resurrected it in Portugal in 1320, by creating a similar organization with a new name—the Order of Christ. Later, Prince Henry the Navigator, as a second son, was given charge of this order in lieu of a throne. Its Maltese cross glowed fiery red on the sails that Henry sent searching for undiscovered worlds. Prince Henry added to the Templar church at Tomar, Manuel I supplied a building done in the Manueline style—including the most ornate, most photographed window in the country—and João III changed the order into a monastic brotherhood for which he contributed cells for the monks and a solemn neoclassical cloister. Additions were made over the course of five centuries, but none disturbed the lines of the 12th-century octagonal Templar church. This church and its later embellishments are what brings the visitors to Tomar.

The Convent of Christ reposes atop a wooded park on the west bank of the Nabão. Rua Serpa Pinto crosses the Ponte Velha and leads to the main square, Pr. da República. Here the 15th-century church of **São João Babtista** *has an imposing later Manueline tower and a most elegant door. Parallel to R. Pinto, and three blocks south (left), Av. Dr. Candido Madureira climbs to the Sete Montes park, after passing the* **Office of Tourism***. The road through the forest zigzags up to the 12th-century walls of the precinct to pass through a gate beside which stands the keep of the original castle. To the right are ruins of a palace built by Prince Henry. Parking is available.*

Convento de Cristo

Open daily 9:30 a.m. to 12:30 p.m. and 2-6 p.m. (closes at 5 p.m. in winter). Admission: 300$00. The complete monastery is a confusion of buildings, because it is formed of additions over the span of five centuries, and all the additions were constrained by the desire to be close to, but not impinge on, the original Templar church. This goal is illustrated by the strange angle of the cloister walls protruding to the right of the stairs to the entrance, and in the constricted entrance to the church. The present entrance was added in the 16th century, designed by a Spaniard in his splendidly native Plateresque style. Nearby, a plaque marks the original entrance.

The entrance leads into the nave, with the original octagonal Templar church, known as the *Charola*, to the right. Although many authorities claim the Charola was modeled on the Holy Sepulcher in Jerusalem, its polygonal shape and cupola match the Islamic Dome of the Rock more than any Christian prototype. Eight faintly painted piers support a two-story octagon with an altar in the center. Coats of arms may be discerned painted on the cupola above. Except for a few paintings, some choir stalls and a number of 16th-century polychrome statues of saints leaning against the piers, little decoration survived the damage wrought by the occupying French in the 19th century. Enough remains to give a sense of the original look, but not of its original functions. Some say the knights attended services on horseback, while others claim that this was a place for vigils by novice knights. There are stories telling how the orientation of the building and details of its design provide secret messages about the location of buried treasures. But, for most people the pleasure of seeing an unusual architectural design from the hoary early Middle Ages suffices without detailed rationales.

The nave was added early in the 16th century to form a more typical church, although its construction required breaking through the west wall of the Charola. Exuberant Manueline decoration makes the hall airy, in contrast with the more imposing charola. A doorway to the north leads to the Cloistro do Cemitario, named for two 16th-century tombs laying within—one being that of Baltasar de Faria, the first Inquisitor-General of Portugal. The cloister was built by Prince Henry the Navigator and later covered by *azulejos*. On its right another of the seven cloisters of the monastery, the Cloistro da Lavagem, contains tanks for water. On its left is the sacristy with a small museum.

A portal from the south side of the nave lets out to the splendid two-story Cloistro Principal, added by João III in the middle of the 16th century. Its Renaissance neoclassicism derives from the Italian Palladio, as its unadorned sweeping arch and columns suggest. A spiral stair from the ground floor leads up to the terrace of the adjoining Santa Barbara cloister for a view of the window that epitomizes the extreme of Manueline ornateness. The window is actually the central window at the end of the church nave seen from the outside. It was carved in 1510, although the identity of the artist is unknown. At the bottom a bust of a sea captain sprouts the roots of a cork tree that rises through seaweed, coral and pieces of chain up masts framing the window sides. Above are symbols of Manuel I—a shield and a cross between two spheres. "Cables" run from the window to two turrets, one wrapped in chain, the other in ribbon. If the latter is seen as a garter, then the turrets might represent the orders of the Golden Fleece and of the Garter, respectively.

The remainder of the convent is used as a hospital by the military and is presently off limits to tourists.

WHERE TO STAY

Tomar provides perfectly acceptable hotels, but another option is the Pousada de São Pedro or the Estalagem Vale da Ursa, both in forests on lakes.

MODERATE ($50-$99)

In Castelo do Bode:

Pousada de São Pedro   **2nd-class ★**

Castelo de Bode (take N-110 south for 7 k, then N-358 east for a final 7 k). Rooms: 15. ☎ *38 11 75; Telex 42392.* The building was erected in the 1950s to house engineers constructing the Castelo de Bode dam. Today it is a pousada that offers quiet and lovely lake views. The bedrooms betray their spartan origins, but the public spaces are restful and the restaurant produces quite good food.

Near Cernache do Bonjardim:

Estalagem Vale da Ursa   **R1st-class ★★**

On N-238, 10 k southwest of Cernache do Bonjardim (Take N-238 northwest of Tomar for 30 k to the Zezere river.) Rooms: 12. ☎ *995 11; FAX 995 94.* This spanking new hotel offers quiet, tennis and fishing. The bedrooms are pleasant and all feature terraces overlooking the reservoir. Fresh fish in the restaurant can be sublime.

In Tomar:

Dos Templários   **1st-class ★**

Largo Candido dos Reis, 1 (beside the public garden). Rooms: 84. ☎ *32 17 30; FAX 32 21 91; Telex 14434.* The best feature of this hotel is its views of the convent on the hill. Otherwise, it provides the services expected of its category and ordinary bedrooms, but, considering its moderate prices, there is no reason to complain.

Residencial Trovador   **R1st-class**

Rua Dr. Joaquim Ribeiro (near the bus station). Rooms: 30. ☎ *32 25 67; FAX 32 21 94.* This hotel is pleasant enough and the service is friendly, but it lies outside the center of the old town and lacks the views of the Templários, which makes it the second choice.

INEXPENSIVE (UNDER $50)

Residencial União   **R2nd-class ★**

Rua Serpa Pinto, 91 (near the Pr. da República). Rooms: 21. ☎ *31 28 31.* This hotel's airy, tastefully decorated rooms all incorporate sparkling bathrooms. In the most expensive high season, the rooms are a bargain; out of season—at 20% less—they can only be called a steal.

Pensão Luanda   **R2nd-class ★**

Av. Marquês de Tomar, 13-15 (across the public gardens). Rooms: 14. ☎ *31 29 29.* The location offers attractive views and the hotel itself is modern, clean and hospitable. Prices are incredibly modest.

WHERE TO EAT

With two exceptions, restaurants in Tomar specialize in blandness. The best choice is located 2 k outside of town.

MODERATE ($20-$50)

Chico Elias   **★★**

Algarvias (take N-349-3 west toward Torres Novas for about 2 k. The restaurant is announced by no sign, so one must look for a grey farmhouse with a green door on the right side of the road.) ☎ *310 67. Closed Tuesday.* The decor is utterly rustic, but the cooking is inventive and tasteful. Among the delectable entreés are cod with pork, rabbit stewed in a gourd, and a stew of snails, sausage and ham. Reservations are essential.

Chez Nous   ★

Rua Dr. Joaquim Jacinto, 31 (between the two river bridges). ☎ *31 47 43.*
Closed Tuesdsay. Unlike the other restaurants in town that strive for
blandness, the French taste of the owner irrepressibly infuses his food.
There are interesting beef dishes, and cod combinations that even the
Portuguese never thought of.

EXCURSIONS

Fátima ★ of the miracles lies on the way to **Batalha ★ ★ ★ ★ ★** and
its incredible monastery, a trip of 50 k. Both are described in the Lisbon
chapter under "Batalha." The charming fortified hilltop town of
Marvão ★ ★ ★, described under its own heading in this chapter, is 130 k
east. Directions are included in the beginning of the Tomar section.

The most romantic Tomar excursion is to the castle of **Almourol ★**,
which sits atop a wooded isle in the middle of the Tejo river. It seems the
stuff of fairy tales.

> *Drive south from Tomar on N-110 for 8 k to turn east on the*
> *scenic N-358-1 to Constancia in 15 k. Turn right (west) at the*
> *bridge onto N-3 for 3.5 k, where a sign directs a left turn to the*
> *castle, reached after 1 k.*

Castelo Almourol   ★

The tiny island in the Tajus is improbably densely wooded, and the
castle flies above the trees. It is a perfect fortress, straight from all our
imaginations—ten golden-hued stone towers that anchor walls surrounding a massive square keep. Because the island is a hill, castle
parts stand at different elevations to lend the false perspective of a
larger structure, and, early in the morning when mist envelopes the
river, the castle floats in a dream.

A Roman fortress first crowned the site before the Knights Templar—as part of a strategy of recapturing land from the Moors and
then raising defensive castles so they could not take it back—built the
present castle in 1171. In little more than a century the Moors had
been driven so far south that the castle lost its purpose and was abandoned. Abandoned it remains, although an appropriately old boatman
is pleased to row visitors either out to the castle or around it for a
nominal fee.

VIANA DO CASTELO

See "Braga" under "Excursions."

VISEU ★ ★ ★

Population: 21,454
Area code: 032; zip code: 3500

*From **Lisbon** A-1 runs north for 82 k and leads to a leg of 12 k on N-366 before joining N-1 toward Coimbra and Oporto. After 119 k, just past Condeixa-a-Nova, the autoestrada A-1 may be taken for 74 k to an exit for Aveiro and N-16. N-16 leads to Viseu in 65 k, with a final 2 k on N-2 as signs direct. From **Oporto** take the autoestrada A-1 south for 46 k to the exit for Aveiro and N-16, which goes east to Viseu in 65 k, with a final 2 k on N-2 as signs direct. From **Coimbra** take N-1 north for 9 k to a connection east for the autoestrada A-1. Take A-1 north toward Oporto, but change in 50 k at the exit for Aveiro and N-16 going east for a final 65 k, the last 2 k on N-2 as signs direct. From **Guarda** take N-16 which begins north then turns west for 68 k.*

*   **Trains** from Lisbon and Coimbra require changes and take 5 hours and 1-1/2 hours respectively. From Oporto the trip consumes just under four hours. Buses travel in about the same amount of time.*

Viseu is a peaceful, attractive town that serves as the capital of the Dão wine region. In many ways it is a typical Portuguese town, but somehow the typical features seem more enchanting in Viseu. There are the usual stands of 16th-century houses, a large cathedral and cathedral square. But the 16th-century houses, untypically, are arranged on wide streets to show them to fine effect; the cathedral is grand; and its square is expansive and surrounded by especially imposing buildings. And, while every town in Portugal seems to display a pretty whitewashed baroque church with details picked out by contrasting stone, Viseu's Miseracordia church is the most lovely of them all. Unique to Viseu were the two Renaissance artists who lived and worked here, combining forces to decorate the cathedral. Today their production is enshrined in a fine museum.

Gaspar Vaz joined Vasco Fernandes in Viseu in the early part of the 16th century. Probably they came together to decorate the cathedral altar. Led by these masters, a school of painting known as the Viseu School arose that produced the finest Portuguese paintings of the era. In particular, the later works of Vasco Fernandes excel in sensitive portraiture and vibrant color. To the Portuguese he is known simply as "O Grão Vasco," the Great Vasco.

From **Lisbon**, **north** *and* **west** *N-2 becomes Av. Emidio Navarro as the Pavia river is crossed. Turn right at the first plaza along Av. Cap. Silva Pereira, which reaches the major intersection of Largo de Santa Cristina in three blocks. A left turn would lead to parking in two blocks, but parking is often available in the more interesting main plaza, Pr. da República (a.k.a. Pr. Rossio), by continuing straight for two blocks. From* **Guarda** *N-16 becomes Rua 5 de Outubro in the town and goes straight to the major intersection of Largo de Santa Cristina. Here a sharp left would lead to parking in two blocks, but parking is often available in the more interesting main plaza, Pr. da República (a.k.a. Pr. Rossio), by continuing straight for two blocks.*

The splendid cathedral square, Adro da Sé, stands on the highest part of the town, anchoring the convoluted streets of the old town rising to meet it. Two blocks below, the tree-lined, small park of the Pr. da República faces town hall. From the northwest corner of this plaza, Rua Nunes de Carvalho climbs to meet the cathedral, passing through a remaining gate in the original town wall just before disgorging in the cathedral square. This square is an open plateau overlooking the town. On its east side stands the grey cathedral; beside it, on the north, is the former Bishop's palace, now the **Grão Vasco Museum**, and on the west is the lovely **Miseracordia church**.

WHAT TO SEE AND DO

Cathedral

Open daily 9 a.m. to noon and 2-7 p.m. The treasury closes at 5 p.m. Admission: 100$00, to the treasury. Little that is visible remains from the 12th-century original, remodeled, as was the case with so many churches in Portugal, in the 16th and 17th centuries and then redecorated in the 18th. Twin towers outside remain from that original church, but topped by 18th-century crowns. The 17th-century facade seems an afterthought, as bored looking Evangelists march around the portal. Yet, a surprisingly elegant space waits inside. Although the aisles were removed in the 16th century, the original Gothic columns remain, and overhead, the ceiling was redone with graceful ribs in the form of ropes, knotted at intervals. Keystones present the coats of arms of the first bishop, Alfonso V, and of King João II. The barrel ceiling above the altar was painted in the 17th century, and a century later the original altar retablo by Vasco and others was removed to the Grão Vasco museum in favor of a sumptuous baroque confection.

Azulejos line the north transept (left) leading to a sacristy, roofed by charmingly painted wood, and to stairs up to the high choir, whose stalls are lovingly carved into fanciful animals. From here the upper level of a fine Renaissance cloister may be entered. Before descending to the ground floor, a visit to the chapterhouse and the cathedral treasury is worthwhile. Among miscellany the treasury contains two lovely 13th-century Limoge coffers and a 12th-century Bible. The experience will be heightened if the guide is the sacristan, who delights in performing slights of hand. The ground floor of the cloisters blends neoclassical arches on Ionic columns with 18th-century *azulejos* on the walls. The chapel of Our Lady of Mercy has a fine retablo in low relief of the Descent from the Cross. Note the elegant Gothic doorway that leads back to the cathedral.

Museu Grão Vasco   ★★★

Open Tuesday-Sunday 9:30 a.m. to 12:30 p.m. and 2-5 p.m. Closed Mon. Admission: 200$00, free on Sunday. The ground floor displays fine carvings, a collection of Virgins of lesser interest, ceramics, Arraiolos carpets, and a small group of fine early paintings. The second floor is devoted to furniture and ecclesiastic plate, with a few nice watercolors by the 19th-century painter Alberto de Sousa. But it is the third floor for which the museum is proudly named. Here are the paintings of Vasco Fernandes, the Grand Vasco, who spent his last 30 years in Viseu creating his finest work. In room 1 is part of the former retablo of the cathedral. The work is by several hands as the lower figures reveal. *Saint Peter* on his throne and the *Martyrdom of Saint Sebastian* with a background reminiscent of Holland show a fine aptitude for the painters art, although whether these were painted by Vasco Fernandes or by Gaspar Vaz remains in dispute. Room 2 is entirely devoted to the Grand Vasco, and the *Crucifixion* in luminous reds and yellows is memorable. Room 3 contains two masterworks by Gaspar Vaz, a triptych of the Last Supper and *Christ in the House of Martha.* Room 4 presents a fine series of 14 panels from the cathedral retablo depicting the life of Christ. Note Balthasar in the *Adoration of the Magi* panel depicted as an Indian from newly discovered Brazil.

Igreja de Misericordia   ★

Although the interior is of slight interest, the exterior, completed in 1775, presents—silhouetted against the open sky—the Portuguese baroque church par excellence. Elegant stone window-surrounds echo the curves of the central roofcomb. The towers are stately and the balcony above the door is a fine touch. This example makes it evident that an earlier gap between ecclesiastic and secular architecture has narrowed. For without its small cross and towers, this facade could well front a lovely mansion.

Stairs by the south end of the cathedral apse lead down to **Rua Direita**, *lined with fine 18th-century houses. In two short blocks the street intersects with another. Turn back left along* **Rua dos**

Andrades *to traverse three short blocks of 16th-century houses interspersed with crafts' shops. Rua Direita continues right from this meeting and soon arrives at Rua Formosa, a right turn on which leads back to the Pr. da República.*

WHERE TO STAY

Except for festival times, hotels in Viseu are adequate to the demand. None are grand, but all offer good value for low prices. The following are close enough to inexpensive that none lesser need be considered.

MODERATE ($50-$99)

Grão Vasco   1st-class ★

Rua Gaspar Barreiros (on a park half a block south of the Pr. da República). Rooms: 100. ☎ *42 35 11; FAX 270 47; Telex 53608.* This low, modern building frames a swimming pool and a pleasant park. Bedrooms are somewhat larger than most and tastefully decorated with reproductions.

Moinho de Vento   2nd-class ★

Rua Paulo Emilio, 13 (2 blocks then a short right along Rua de M. Bombarda, which leaves the southwest corner of Pr. da República). Rooms: 30. ☎ *42 41 16; FAX 42 96 62; Telex 52698.* Although lacking a pool and garden, the Moinho is otherwise as good a choice as the preceding. Bedrooms are more modern but not quite as large, although perfectly comfortable and available at a most engaging price.

INEXPENSIVE (-$50)

Avenida   3rd-class

Av. Alberto Sampaio, 1 (a few steps west of the south end of the Pr. da República). Rooms: 40. ☎ *42 34 32; FAX 267 43; Telex 52522.* The highly individual and very eclectic decor at this hotel sometimes works and sometimes doesn't. A similar description applies to the rooms, some of which are splendid (for the low charges) while others are off--putting, but each is different.

WHERE TO EAT

Cooking in Viseu is more adventurous than in many similar towns. Moderately priced treats lie in store for anyone dining at the following choices. Of course, one should have a bottle or a carafe of Dão to wash down the meal.

MODERATE ($20-$50)

O Cortiço

Rua Augusto Hilário, 43 (a few steps southeast from the statue of Dom Duarte below the Cathedral square). ☎ *42 38 53.* Rustic with granite walls, this restaurant serves the most imaginative cuisine in town. The service could be more gracious, but the wine-fed rabbit and the veal with rice are delicious.   ***Amex, MasterCard and Visa accepted.***

Trave Negra

> *Rua dos Loureiros, 40 (three blocks down the hill northeast from the Cathedral on the corner of Av. Emidio Navarro where N-2 leads into town).* ☎ *261 38.* This is a candle- and lantern-lit place serving well-considered food with elegant touches.

> ***Amex, Diners, MasterCard and Visa accepted.***

INEXPENSIVE (UNDER $20)

Cacimbo

> *Rua Alexandre Herculano, 95 (One block east of the Pr. da República, R. Herculano runs south).* ☎ *228 94.* Come here for the roast suckling pig in the window.

EXCURSIONS

Viseu is centrally situated for a large number of other sights of interest. There's the fortified hill town of **Guarda** 68 k to the east, **Aveiro** for beaches an equal distance to the west, the medieval university of **Coimbra** 65 k west and 74 k south, **Oporto** 65 k west and 46 k north, with baroque **Braga** 54 k beyond that. All these are described under their own headings in this chapter.

..LISBON AND ITS ENVIRONS

A Lisbon street car.

HISTORICAL PROFILE:
THE RISE AND FALL OF THE HOUSE OF AVÍS

The Portuguese royal House of Avís came into existence because an abbot seized the throne from his cousin, the rightful heir. The dynasty ended two centuries later when its penultimate ruler fell victim to chivalrous fantasies, leaving the throne to a childless cardinal. Over the 200 years it flourished, however, the House of Avís bred two outstanding figures—Dom Henriques, known in English as

Prince Henry the Navigator, and Manuel I, patron of Portugal's contribution to world architecture, the Manueline style.

Half a century of political and romantic intrigues coalesced to produce João, the first Avís king, and provide him with an opportunity to usurp Portugal's crown from his 13-year-old cousin, Beatrice. The chain of events began when Afonso IV, who succeeded to the throne in 1325 (see "Historical Profile: The Birth of Portugal," p. 611.), tried to meddle in Castilian politics. Factions in Castile were jockeying for power during the minority of a child king, when Afonso decided to throw Portugal's support behind one faction by marrying his son Pedro to the daughter of its leader. The bride-to-be came to Portugal to wed her fiancé, accompanied by an entourage of ladies-in-waiting, including Inês Pires de Castro, the daughter of the Chamberlain of Castile. Pedro duly married his espoused, but had eyes for no one but the fair Inês. It was not long before attraction blossomed into a love affair that came to the King's attention, who banished Inês. Five years later, after Pedro's wife died of complications following the birth of a son, Pedro brought Inês back and sired several children with her, infuriating his father. Historians disagree over whether the King himself hired three assassins or merely closed his eyes to someone else's intrigue, but the result in either case was the murder of Inês.

Inconsolable, Pedro took up arms against his father but lost; they remained estranged until a death-bed reconciliation. As soon as he became king, Pedro disinterred Inês' body, dressed her in regal robes, and forced the nobles of the realm to kiss her hand in homage as their queen. Then he buried her in a lovely tomb in the monastery of Alcobaça and commanded that his tomb be constructed facing hers, so she would be his first sight on resurrection. He next sought her murderers, and, finding two of them hiding in Spain, tore the heart from the chest of one, and from the back of the other—which helped earn him the epithet "the Cruel."

However deep his affection for Inês may have been—for he never remarried—it did not prevent Pedro from enjoying other women. He took up with Teresa Lourenço and fathered a fateful illegitimate son, João, who took vows on his majority, as master of the religio-military Order of Avís. It was this João who would later seize the Portuguese throne to establish the Avís dynasty.

King Pedro's son Fernando, by his Castilian wife, inherited the throne when Pedro died. Fernando was 24, handsome, impetuous, and more interested in wars than governing, which he left to a favorite courtier. The courtier arranged for the king to marry his niece, despite the fact that she was already married. The lady's husband was no fool, for he fled across the border into Spain, permitting King Fernando and Leonor Telles de Meneses to wed. In the meantime, Juan Fernández Andeiro, a clever Spanish diplomat who had been concluding alliances with England on Portugal's behalf, returned to the Portuguese court and fell in with Leonor. When Leonor became pregnant, rumors called Andeiro the father. Leonor believed that João, master of Avís, was the source of those rumors. Although the 20-year-old abbot was highly regarded at court and by the people, on the queen's orders he was chained in the castle of Évora until the English duke of Lancaster interceded.

When King Fernando died of a disease that caused his premature aging, his heir Beatrice was left in Leonor's care. Possibly influenced by the Spaniard Andeiro, Leonor quickly married Beatrice to the king of Castile, who thereupon claimed the title of king of Portugal, rather than that of consort of Portugal's Queen. The prospect of Spanish control roused the Portuguese middle classes, although most of the nobles did not object to a change in the nationality of their ruler. In this charged atmosphere, João, released from imprisonment, came to Leonor's chambers to speak privately with Andeiro. Upon meeting Leonor's lover, João murdered him and, in order to rally the populace, sent a retainer through the streets of Lisbon crying "They are killing the master." The big lie worked. A mob gathered, clamoring that João should be king, pressuring the Council of Portugal to name him regent.

As soon as he received the office of regent, João arrested Leonor and exiled her. At the same time, he enlisted English forces to counter the Castilian king's mobilization for war. More than 50 of the towns and most of the Portuguese nobles supported Leonor and Beatrice, the legitimate heir, so the king of Castile encountered little resistance when he marched to Lisbon to lay siege. At this dark hour, João's forces were saved by an outbreak of plague racing through the crowded, unsanitary camp of the besiegers, to decimate their ranks. The Spanish returned home to regroup. João used this respite to win over Portugal's populous northern area and gain the backing of the Cortes for his ascension to the throne. In 1385, the House of Avís crowned its first king.

When the Castilian army returned the next year, 15,000 Spaniards met less than half as many Portuguese, plus a hundred or so English knights, in battle near Batalha, north of Lisbon. The Portuguese had lined a forward ditch with stakes and counted on streams on either side to protect their flanks. The Spanish, confident in their numerical superiority, charged, but were turned back in disarray and defeated within an hour. João vowed to build an abbey near the site of the battle in gratitude. This abbey of Batalha (battle) was the first flamboyant Gothic building on the peninsula, an architectural masterpiece raised by Houget, an English architect. Therein João would be buried.

João allied himself with John of Gaunt, duke of Lancaster and father to the future Lancasterian line of English kings, to press a claim of John's to the throne of Castile. Together they invaded, but, rather than fighting, John sold his rights to the reigning monarch of Castile for cash. All João received for his services was John's daughter Philippa. João was angry at this betrayal; nonetheless, to his great benefit and Portugal's, he married Philippa.

Philippa had been raised in the most intellectual court of the era, one that included Geoffry Chaucer among its luminaries, to stand with the rare educated women of her time. Unlike most men, she could both read and write, and proceeded to raise her children in an intellectual atmosphere. She gave birth to five sons, though the first died in infancy. The second son, Dom Duarte, was designated the Infante and would succeed his father. The fourth son was Dom Henrique, known to the English-speaking world as Prince Henry the Navigator.

João had seized a throne bankrupt from civil wars; the coinage of his kingdom had been debased to one two-thousandth of its former value. But João I had the advantage of four virile sons eager to help. By 1415 the boys were old enough to plan an attack on the Moroccan city of Ceuta. Tragically, on the eve of their departure, their mother caught the plague, but even dying she urged them on. Ceuta was captured, giving Portugal its first push towards international power.

Most of the credit for the massive invasion went to Dom Henrique who was rewarded with the dukedom of Viseu for his efforts. He was already master of the religio-military Order of Christ and a rich man from his various estates, yet he set up residence at Sagres, near the furthest extremity of Europe, where he could best dream about lands beyond those known to Europeans. Dom Henriques was devout, celibate and ascetic—he drank no alcohol and owned few personal possessions. He established a kind of school for navigation, stockpiling information gathered from all the foreign ships that put in at Sagres on their way to destinations farther north in Portugal.

He personally underwrote numerous voyages of exploration along the African coast, and colonized the fertile island of Madeira. His expeditions returned with gold to fill the royal treasury and sugar to trade in Europe.

João I died in 1433 on his 77th birthday, exactly 48 years after the battle near Batalha that had secured his throne. His son Duarte I reluctantly accepted the crown, but was too sensitive for the task and died five years later mourning an abortive expedition that left one of his brothers a hostage of the Moors. His heir, Afonso V, although only six at the time, would reign for 43 years. In the beginning a pawn of the nobles, at the end Afonso became embroiled in the morass of Castilian politics involving Henrique the Impotent, Henrique's purported daughter Juana, and Isabella the Catholic. (See "Historical Profile: Ferdinand and Isabella, p. 197.") Afonso died in 1481, just as he had decided to retire. During the next reign, Prince Henry the Navigator, feeling death's approach, adopted Afonso's brother— from whom a king would later ensue—as his heir. In 1460 Henry died. A courtier sent to examine his body three weeks after death found it uncorrupted, except for the tip of his nose—a sufficient defect to prevent the possibility of sainthood. Henry was buried near his father in Batalha.

Upon ascending the throne, Afonso's son João II was faced by nobles grown powerful during his father's distracted reign. The Duke of Bragança, descendant of an illegitimate son of the founder of the House of Avís, controlled 50 towns and could raise an army of 13,000 men from among his retainers. João accused the duke of negotiating a secret treaty with Castile, tried and beheaded him. Then he went after Portugal's next most powerful noble, the Duke of Viseu, whose father had acquired the title by being adopted by Prince Henry the Navigator. João II either killed the duke himself or ordered the deed. In either case, the duke's death left just one son remaining of five Henry's adopted son had sired, for three others had died in childhood. History would call the survivor "The Fortunate," for Manuel was to become Portugal's most notable king.

In 1493, King João II admitted 60,000 Jews into Portugal after their expulsion from Spain. He charged each a tax for admittance and, for the price, permitted one year's residency. Sometime about 1483 he also gave an audience to a Genoese named Christopher Columbus who proposed sailing west to China and India, but João declined to support the project. João's only son died of a fall from his horse, followed, soon after, by João's own death in 1495 after an attack of dropsy.

With no surviving heir, the throne passed to the remaining child of Prince Henry's adopted son, the king's cousin, Manuel. At 26, Manuel I was thin, green eyed and fair, with arms that dangled ape-like to his knees. He was fond of display. After restoring their former lands to the country's important nobles, he called them all to the palace so that they could form a splendid court—and be easily watched. He commissioned a spate of buildings in a new style that combined flamboyant Gothic elements with the Spanish plateresque and was called, after him, "Manueline." Craftsmen who knew the Arabic arts incorporated the flora and fauna of newly-discovered lands in these decorations. He revised Portuguese law, but had little use for parliamentary sessions.

Manuel married the widowed daughter of Ferdinand and Isabella and, after she died in childbirth, married another of their daughters, with whom he had ten children. As one condition of the marriages, Spain required that Portugal expel its Jews. Manuel appreciated the importance of Jews for the economy of Portugal, so he tried to convert as many as possible in order not to lose them. His measures included taking Jewish children away from their parents to indoctrinate them in the Christian faith.

In 1495, excited and jealous about Columbus' discoveries, Manuel ordered a fleet commanded by Vasco de Gama to find India by sailing west, which Columbus had not accomplished. Bartolemeu Dias, the first explorer to round the tip of Africa, designed four ships for de Gama, two of which returned 2-1/2 years later laden with rich spices—the first ships to circumnavigate the globe. Soon the Portuguese would found colonies in Goa, India, the Congo, and Sumatra and Malaya—the Spice Islands. Five years later they "discovered" Brazil. For a time Portugal would be rich, well able to fund Manuel's passion for building, and the country would rise among the powers of Europe.

When Manuel's heir, João III, was 14, Manuel arranged with Carlos V of Spain that the boy marry Carlo's sister. Manuel, recently widowed for the second time, so liked the girl when he met her that he instead married her himself. Manuel died in 1521. João III then married a second of Carlos' sisters and sent his own sister back to marry Carlos. Through this merging of families, the Spanish would one day gain access to the throne of Portugal.

In 1557, soon after starting an inquisition in Portugal modeled on Spain's, João III died, preceded by his own son, who had left only a five-year-old named Sebastião to be the next king. Next in line for the throne in this depleted family was João III's brother Henrique, a Cardinal who raised Sebastião. The young king's pleasures ran to swimming, riding, fighting with swords, and other military exercises. A childhood illness caused symptoms of developing impotence and outbreaks of peculiar behavior—including the opening of his ancestors' tombs to meditate upon their bones. Sebastião also grew fixated on the idea of a holy war against infidels. When he finally organized a ludicrously unrealistic chivalrous expedition against Morocco, it seemed almost fitting that he lose his life in the invasion.

Sebastião's death left 60-year-old Cardinal Henriques as the sole living member of the House of Avís. The death of this childless Cardinal in 1758, after a reign of only a few months, brought the 200-year-old royal House of Avís to an abrupt and anticlimactic end.

LISBON AND ITS
ENVIRONS

Lisbon owed its early growth and importance to geography. As the River Tejos (Tagus in English) nears the Atlantic Ocean it spreads into an estuary lake, then narrows to channel its way for a final nine miles to the sea. Lisbon, on the inland side of this channel, is protected by land barriers against both the elements and seaward attack.

In the twelfth century B.C. Phoenicians built a town upon São Jorge, the steepest hill in what was to become Lisbon. They called their settlement *Alis Ubbo* (the Serene Harbor), from which the present name of Lisbon derives (Lisboa, in Portuguese). By 205 B.C., after the Second Punic War, Romans replaced the Carthaginian descendents of those Phoenicians and were followed in turn by various Germanic tribes, eventually dominated by the Visigoths in A.D. 457. In 714, on their way to subjugate the peninsula, the Moors conquered Lisbon and held it for the next four hundred years.

To recapture Lisbon from the Moors, Afonso Henrique, the first king of Portugal (see *Historical Profile: The Birth of Portugal*), enlisted knights passing on their way to the Second Holy Land Crusade by promising them spoils and land. In 1147 an army of Portuguese, English, Normans, Dutch and Germans besieged strongly fortified Lisbon, which, with a reputed population of 60,000 families, would have been the second-largest city in western Europe. After four months, the starving Moors called for a truce, which the besiegers accepted, but used as a ploy to attack the city. After Lisbon had been taken, most of Afonso's foreign entourage were satisfied with their spoils and continued on to Palestine, but some accepted his offer of land and remained. An Englishman, Gilbert of Hastings, for example, was consecrated as the first bishop of Lisbon. A century later, in recognition of its importance, Afonso III moved the capital of Portugal from Coimbra to Lisbon, where it has remained ever since.

Vasco de Gama sailed to India from Belém outside of Lisbon in 1497, and his successful trip ushered in a golden age for all of Portugal, but especially for its capital. For two centuries, comparatively tiny Lisbon was the richest city in Europe. The population had been about 50,000 before rich spice cargos began to flow into its harbors, but doubled in the first 25 years of the Portuguese monopoly of this trade, then tripled after a century. Although the countryside was depopulated by this exodus to the capital, and farming suffered, profits from trade allowed the king to import enough foodstuffs and wool for his country. The immensity of these profits also allowed Manuel I to build as no king had been able to before or since. His architects created a new style, the Manueline, which proclaimed the prosperity in ornately carved decorative motifs, incorporating the flora and fauna of India and the Spice Islands. The preeminent example of this style—the Heronymite Monastery—resides in Lisbon's Belém suburb.

In 1531 and again in 1597 severe tremors shook Lisbon, harbingers of a catastrophe that finally occurred in 1755 while all Lisbon was at mass on All Saints' Day. As the earth shook, houses quivered then fell to heaps of rock and dust. Fires erupted throughout the city. When citizens ran toward the open area of the harbor to avoid the flames, they were swallowed by a tidal wave four stories high. The epicenter of the earthquake lay under Lisbon, but its tremors were felt as far away as Scotland and Jamaica. Although impossible to estimate with accuracy, it seems that over the course of a few hours Lisbon lost between a quarter and a third of its population. The city had been levelled.

The king, José I, was fortunate to have been vacationing in Belém because his Lisbon palace collapsed. Most of his ministers cowered immobilized in the face of this unprecedented cataclysm. One alone displayed vigor, for which he would later receive the title of the Marquis of Pombal. He collected the dead and sailed their bodies on barges out to sea, to prevent plague. He stationed soldiers to stop looting. He tore down the remains of damaged buildings along with whole structures to make space for the first rational urban renewal in Europe, preceding Haussman's remodeling of Paris by a century. On the site of the king's former palace Pombal built a grand plaza, the Praça do Comércio, with a statue of King José prominently displayed in its center. Running inland from the plaza, a series of parallel avenues replaced the earlier medieval maze, each comprising stores and factories relating to a single trade, after which the streets are still named. Buildings of a harmonious design, many by the architect Eugenio dos Santos, were erected around the plaza and along the new avenues. To pay the huge expense of this project, a general tax of 4% was imposed on the citizens of the city. But, seduced by the immense resources he controlled, Pombal grew into a dictator, dismissed by the succeeding monarch and charged with embezzlement.

In 1908 the fate of the monarchy was sealed when both the king and his heir were murdered by an assassin's bullets on the site of Pombal's Praça do Comércio. Two years later the kingship fell for good after a naval bombardment of the palace. And two-thirds of a century later, in 1974, tanks with flowers in their guns rolled down Pombal's grand avenues to depose the successor to the dictator António Salazar during Portugal's "Flower Revolution."

With a population of just over one million, **Lisbon** ★★★★ today is the smallest capital in western Europe. Were it not for its so-called seven hills—which seem more like hundreds to tired feet and pumping heart—it would also be the most manageable. Though virtually no monuments in central Lisbon survived the earthquake of 1755, the city retains grand 18th-century avenues and plazas, along with some quaint quarters, such as the Alfama. It houses the best museums in the country and, in neighboring Belém, the paradigm structures of the fabulous Manueline architecture, fortunate survivors of the quake.

Day trips by car, bus or train from Lisbon can take in all the variety that Portugal offers. Seventy miles north of Lisbon is the most harmonious collection of buildings in the county, the memorable Gothic monastery at **Batalha** ★★★★★, by itself worth a trip to Portugal. Just south of it is the well-known fishing village of **Nazaré** ★, that is always described as a picture-postcard, although it is difficult to spot the village today amid the crowds of tourists. A few kilometers away in **Alcobaça** ★★★ is the sublime medieval church and monastery of Santa Maria. A lovely medieval walled town lies twenty miles farther south of Alcobaça at **Óbidos** ★★. Twenty miles north of Lisbon stands a sumptuous baroque monastery at **Mafra** ★, while royal palaces at lovely **Sintra** ★★★ and **Queluz** ★ are even closer. Fine beaches wait at **Cascais** ★ and **Estoril** ★, ten miles west. **Setúbal** ★ lies on the sea 30 miles south of Lisbon and contains the first Manueline church, while beaches stretch nearby. Using three days for Lisbon, eight days would cover the sights of the area.

ALCOBAÇA ★★★

Population: 5,383
Area code: 062; zip code: 2460

Directions from **Lisbon** *are included in the "Excursion" section of that city. From* **Coimbra** *take N-1 south for 85 k to Cruz da Legua (with pottery for sale along the streets) where N-8 goes west for 16 k.* **Batalha** *is 4 k on N-1 north of Cruz da Legua.* **Nazaré** *is 14 k northwest along N-8-4.*

The reason for the existence of the town and for the tourists to throng here is the Abbey of Santa Maria, containing the finest church in Portugal. Even the fruit trees for which the area is famed were first planted by its monks. The monastery was founded by the first king of Portugal, Afonso I, to repay a vow to God for helping capture the major city of Santarém from the Moors. Work began in 1178 and finished in the first quarter of the 13th century for a cloistered order of Cistercians sent from France by Saint Bernard himself. Thus, the style of the buildings is the earliest, most monumental, and simplest Gothic.

Inside is a relic of one of Portugal's great romances. At the beginning of the 14th century, Dom Pedro, heir to the Portuguese throne, was betrothed to a Castilian princess. A lady-in-waiting named Inês de Castro travelled with Pedro's bride to Portugal, and the young groom fell instantly in love—not with his wife-to-be, but with the noblewoman who accompanied her. Aware of his son's infatuation, Pedro's father banished Inês from the kingdom. When Dom Pedro's wife died five years later, Pedro brought Inês back to live with him, fathering two children with her. The King was upset at this flouting of his command, at the begetting of royal children without the sanction of the church, and at the fact that the children's mother was Spanish. The King sent, or at least allowed, assassins to kill Inês. As soon as the throne came to Pedro he had two of the assassins viciously murdered, then disinterred Inês' remains, dressed her in regal robes, and ordered the nobles of the realm to kiss her skeletal hand as the reigning queen of Portugal. He buried her in high state in the Monastery of Santa Maria at Alcobaça and constructed his own tomb there, too, with his feet facing hers so that his first sight on the Day of Resurrection would be his beloved.

Mostairo de Santa Maria   ★★★

Open daily 9 a.m. to 7 p.m. (to 5 p.m. in winter). Admission: 350$00 to the abbey (250$00 in winter). The church facade was greatly changed by Baroque additions in the 17th and 18th centuries, but the central portal is original, although not its statues. To the left extends a wall hiding ranks of cells that once housed 100 monks. The interior of the church was altered over the centuries, but desecration by the French during the Peninsular War led to a restoration that removed later additions to reveal the pure, awesome Cistercian original—one of Portugal's most moving sights.

An unusually narrow nave serves to accentuate the football field of length that makes this the largest church in the country. Columns are close-set and massive. Engaged pillars along the aisles are curiously truncated ten feet above the floor to gain space for the congregation, but at the same time providing a lovely perspective. Lighted only by the rose window of the nave and two others in the transepts, and barren of surface decoration and even side chapels, the effect is a purity that seems more modern than its venerable age. To the left of the entrance is the Sala dos Reis containing statues—of no great artistic merit—depicting the kings of Portugal, in addition to *azulejos* portraying Afonso's victory at Santarém and the history of the monastery.

In the south transept (left) lies the 14th-century tomb of Inês de Castro resting on a pride of lions with human faces, including, it is reputed, that of one of her assassins. Opposite, in the north transept, is the man who loved her, Dom Pedro. As Pedro commanded, they lie feet to feet. Carved of soft limestone in a florid Gothic style, both effigies were damaged by the French, as is apparent in the plaster reconstruction of Inês' nose. She does look beautiful, nonetheless, protected by six gentle angels surrounding her. A frieze at the top of the sarcophagus interweaves the coat of arms of Portugal with that of the de Castro family. Tomb sides depict scenes from the life of Christ. Carved on the end of the tomb's head is a crucifixion scene. Appropriately, the finest carving faces Pedro: at the foot end is a most realistic scene of the Last Judgement.

The effigy of Pedro looks severe, lending credence to his nickname "the Cruel." The sides of his tomb present scenes from the life of Saint Bartholomew, his patron saint, while the head-end shows Pedro's last moments. The carving at the foot is an exceptional composition of the wheel of fortune, whose details repay study. On both tombs is written *Atéão fim do mundo*—"until the end of the world."

A chapel off the south transept contains the tombs of Afonso II and III, from the 13th century, along with a strange—and mutilated—terracotta group surrounding St. Bernard, carved by a monk in the 17th century. Behind the high altar a charming Manueline door seems to grow vegetation as it leads to a sacristy with reliquaries emptied of their contents by some pillager or other. A door in the north aisle leads to a lovely 14th-century cloister of silence, whose upper story was added two centuries later. Arches between twisted columns are capped by roses. The chapterhouse, which may be entered from the north side of the cloister, is a room of round-arch doorways and windows, and graceful vaulting, though lined by distracting terra-cotta statues produced by monks in the 18th century. Stairs lead to a cavernous Gothic dormitory. From the west side of the cloister the monastery kitchen may be entered. A stream running through it was intended for washing dishes rather than, as some say, to provide the monks with fish. The huge fireplace and chimney were tiled in the 18th century. Next to the kitchen is the solemn space of the refectory whose stairs, built into the end wall, lead to a lector's pulpit.

WHERE TO STAY

There is a comfortable, moderately priced hotel just up the hill in front of the Monastery, and a serviceable, inexpensive pension nearby.

MODERATE ($50-$99)

Santa Maria   **2nd-class ★**
R. Dr. Zagalo. Rooms: 31. ☎ *59 73 95; FAX 59 67 15; Telex 40143.* The hotel is modern and reasonably attractive. Bedrooms are spotless, and some have balconies overlooking the monastery.

INEXPENSIVE (UNDER $50)

Coracoães Unidos   **P2nd-class**
R. Frei António Brandão, 39 (the street leads out of the square in front of the monastery). Rooms: 16, but only 8 with baths. ☎ *421 42.* The bedrooms are basic, but clean, and the management is cheerful.

DIRECTORY

TRAINS AND BUSES • The station is 5 k away in Valado dos Frades, though frequent buses transport to Alcobaça. Buses from the train station also run frequently to Nazaré.

The bus station (☎ 422 21) is on Av. Manuel da Silva Carolino, a 5-minute walk to the monastery—left, then downhill and another left. Service is frequent to Batalha and Nazaré.

EXCURSIONS

The **Museu Nacional do Vinho** (☎ 422 22) stands 1 k outside of town on N-8, the road to Batalha. Guides show exhibits of the history of wine production. There is no tasting, but wine may be purchased at the end of the tour. However, the tours are generally given in Portuguese. *(Open Mon.-Fri. 9 a.m. to 12:30 p.m. and 2-5:30 p.m.; admission: free).*

BATALHA ★★★★

Population: 7,683
Area code: 044; zip code: 2440

Directions from **Lisbon** *are included in the "Excursion" section of that city. From* **Coimbra** *take N-1 south for 81 k. From* **Nazaré** *N-8-4 leads east through Alcobaça to Cruz da Legua (with pottery for sale along the streets) in 30 k, where N-1 north reaches Batalha in 4 k. From* **Tomar** *take N-358-2 south to N-118 west toward Torres Novas in 19 k, shortly after which N-243 bears west for 34 k to join N-1 north for the final 4 k.*

The town is aptly named by the Portuguese word for battle, for its founding was due to a fight that changed the course of Portuguese history. A mighty army from Castile had invaded to contest the claims of King João I—who had usurped the throne of Portugal one year previously. (See "Historical Profile: The Rise and Fall of the House of Avís," p. 693.) On August 14, 1385, the Castilian army lined the plain of Aljubarrota, 12 k south of Batalha, swelled by a large body of Portuguese nobles rebelling in support of the prior royal house. The army brandished sixteen of the new weapons of the day—cannons. The 20-year-old João I, with no artillery and backed by a much smaller complement of knights—although aided by citizen-soldiers and 500 Englishmen—faced this host almost twice his numbers with trepidation. He vowed that if success came his way he would endow a monastery, for it seemed that only a miracle could win the day. João won a resounding victory, and construction of a monastery began three years later in this valley near the site.

The first stage of construction comprised the church, founder's chapel, royal cloister and chapterhouse, finished by 1436. The first architect, Afonso Domingues, was Portuguese, but the second, Houguet, was Norman who lent a feeling of the English Gothic, reminiscent—in those areas where perpendiculars are emphasized by pillars and spires—of Westminster Cathedral. King João's son Dom Duarte finished the founder's chapel and added an octagonal chapel

behind the apse, that was never completed. In turn, his successor added a second cloister named—after himself—the Afonso V Cloister. Manuel I decorated various parts of the whole in the exuberant style named for him, before turning his attention to his own Heronymite monastery outside Lisbon. His successor, João III, added dormitories and yet a third cloister (subsequently destroyed), before stopping work for good in 1550 to concentrate on his own building at Tomar. A century and a half of building by the mightiest monarchs of Portugal created a monastery of surpassing majesty.

Mostairo de Santa Maria da Vitoria　　　★ ★ ★ ★ ★

Open daily 9 a.m. to 6 p.m., (to 5 p.m. in winter). Admission: 400$00 to the abbey (250$00 in winter). The exterior limestone, weathered to a warm ocher, culminates in a flamboyant facade of scores of small spires, but no tower or belfry. To the right is the dome of the founder's chapel; cloister walls spread left. A lovely flamboyant window surmounts the richly carved main portal filled with copies of the original statues. Buttresses and lacy balustrades run in all directions. There is no focus for the eye, a characteristic of this structure built by various sovereigns with different ideas.

The church interior startles with plainness after the exuberance outside. Yet that same simplicity allows the grand sweep of the vaulting to soar. Dappled colors from the stained glass (modern, except for Manueline glass at the end in the chancel) swathe the floor, and great piers seems to anchor the ceiling from possible flight.

To the immediate right is the moving **Capela do Fundador** (Founders Chapel), a square room lit by an octagonal lantern. Under delicate stone canopies beneath the lantern lies the joint tomb of the founder, João I, and his wife, Philippa of Lancaster (see "Historical Profiles: The Rise and Fall of the House of Avís," p. 693). The king wears the insignia of the Order of the Garter, founded by Philippa's father, Edward III of England. In a charming touch, he is depicted holding his wife's hand. The rear wall contains the tombs of the exceptional sons of these parents. On the left, a tomb holds the few remains of Dom Fernando, who had been left a hostage after an abortive attack on Tangier. Humiliation and imprisonment led to his death, probably of dysentery. His heart, cut out of his body by compatriots as it hung from the walls of Fez, was embalmed and brought here. The third tomb from the left, bearing a Gothic canopy, is that of Dom Henrique, duke of Viseu, known as Prince Henry the Navigator. His features here look quite different from those painted by Nuno Gonçalves, in his masterpiece of *Saint Vincent* in Lisbon.

The artistic highlight of the monastery is the **Claustro Real** (Royal Cloister), entered through the north wall of the church by the transept. Erected by Afonso Domingues, the first architect of Batalha, in pure, elegant Gothic style, Manuel I found it cold in feeling and ordered his architect Mateus Fernades to add riotous Manueline embellishments to the columns and insert tracery to half-fill the arches. Manuel had a good eye—the combination is superb. The **chapterhouse** is entered from the east side of the cloister. The boldness of its 60-foot expanse of unsupported vaulting amazed contemporaries. According to one story, the architect used convicts to build it, since the dangers of its unproven construction were considered too great to risk the lives of honest men. Another story says the architect had to sleep beneath the vaulting for one night to convince doubters of its safety. Safe it is, for it survived the shaking of Lisbon's 1755 earthquake. Today the room contains Portugal's Tomb of the Unknown Soldier, perpetually guarded. The east window is lovely 16th-century glass.

From the northwest corner of the Royal Cloister the adjacent **cloister of Dom Afonso V** may be entered, after a pause to inspect the Manueline **lavabo** on which carved foliage seems to grow its own foliage. This slightly smaller cloister makes a nice contrast to its larger neighbor, for it is pure Gothic, and most elegant. Exit from its southeast corner to the outside, then round the chapterhouse to enter the **Capelas Imperfeitas**.

The chapel is entered through one of the great doorways in Portugal. Manuel's architect Mateus Fernandes covered every inch of this soaring Gothic portal with decoration. On the door columns, carved iron chains become knotted ropes, and then plants. "Inside" (a strange term for a roofless room) the simple original design of Dom Duarte is apparent—an octagonal rotunda radiating seven chapels. He died before it was complete. Under Manuel I, Mateus Fernandes planned an octagonal roof supported by pillars, but was taken off the job before its completion, leaving stumps of the pillars, profusely carved, and a structure still unroofed. In 1533, in reaction to his father's exuberant decoration, Manuel's son added a somber balcony, but nothing more. And so it remains, somehow more moving in its incompleteness than the finished rooms. Although intended as a pantheon for the kings who succeeded João I, the chapel contains only the tomb of Dom Duarte and his wife, Leonor of Aragón, opposite the entrance, along with those of a noble and an infante (prince).

WHERE TO STAY

Surprising for a town so popular with tourists, hotel choices are few. Only one can be recommended, so reservations are strongly advised.

EXPENSIVE ($100-$200)

Pousada do Mestre Afonso Domingues   ★
Across the square from the monastery. Rooms: 21. ☎ *962 60; FAX 962 60; Telex 42339.* This is a low-slung modern pousada. Bedrooms are comfortable, though lacking style, but prices are barely expensive. Fortunately, the soundproofing effectively muffles noise from the highway.

WHERE TO EAT

All the town restaurants are ordinary and touristy. The best choice is the Pousada, which serves moderately priced food with some style.

EXCURSIONS

Nazaré ★ and **Alcobaça** ★★★ are close by. See the directions from Alcobaça. The pilgrimage site of **Fátima** ★ is near—18 k east on N-336.

FÁTIMA ★

Population: 7,298
Area code: 049; zip code: 2495

Fátima and Santiago de Compostella in Spain constitute the great pilgrimage sites of the peninsula, with Fátima receiving greater numbers. On May 13, 1917, the sky lightened and three young children saw the Virgin Mary standing in an oak tree. Their report was met with disbelief by most, but the children said that Mary promised to return on the same day of each ensuing month, pledging a miracle for her final appearance. Increasingly large crowds gathered on the 13th of each month to hear Mary call for peace, a particularly appropriate message for the time of World War I. On October 13, the sixth and final month, 70,000 people had collected in a driving rainstorm. At noon the sun came out, spun in orbit and plummeted toward the earth. Then everything returned to normal, with no evidence of the rain.

The **Basilica of Fátima** stands at the end of an immense esplanade. This neo-classical church can hold 300,000 inside, but only those who are suitably attired—no shorts, no bare arms, no slacks on women—are permitted entrance. Inside, two of the three children who first saw the vision are buried. The square in front is larger than Rome's Saint Peter's Cathedral. The **Capelinha das Apariçoães** on the esplanade is a modern structure surrounding the site of the original visitation. Alas, the oak tree is no more. The **Museu-Vivo Apariçoães**, which provides a sound-and-light show of the miraculous events, stands on the park grounds. Near the park, on R. Jacinto Marto, is the **Museu de Cera de Fátima**, a wax museum that attempts, sometimes in eerie ways, to make the events real.

Note that the 12th and 13th of each month are pilgrimage times. The town fills to overflowing on those dates in May, and almost so every October.

CASCAIS ★

Population: 29,882
Area code: 01; zip code: 2750

ESTORIL ★

Population: 25,230
Area code: 01; zip code: 2765

> *Directions from* **Lisbon** *are included in the "Excursion" section of that city.*

These two towns provide the closest beaches to Lisbon. Formerly separate, a continuous community along the bay now links Cascais with its sister Estoril. Both were fishing villages that became resorts for the wealthy in the 19th century. Elegance remains, mixed with fishermen who always lived here, and a commuter population from Lisbon.

Cascais offers three fine sand beaches—crowded, but less polluted than those at Estoril. The bay water is not the cleanest. A less-crowded beach lies west of town. Cascais is somewhat less expensive, and more genuine than Estoril. On the edge of its promontory stands a former Fort and Royal Palace, which cannot be visited because the president of Portugal holds receptions there. Cascais has a reputation for good shopping. The main shopping street is R. Frederico Arouça, one block south of the train station.

Estoril is the more sophisticated of the two towns. Houses are fancier and the town hosts horse races and sailing regattas. A large tropical garden of a park in the center is overlooked by the **Estoril Casino**, one of the largest and most luxurious of its kind in the world. Beaches are fine sand, difficult to spot among the crowded bodies.

For much better beaches, head west around the cape for Praia Guincho, 9 k west of Cascais (buses leave from the train station). This beach is immense, pollution-free and relatively uncrowded. Winds are continual and sometimes strong, which makes for dramatic oceans and a strong undertow that the locals take in stride. Cabo da Roca, the westernmost point of Europe, can be seen 8 k farther west. The Office of Tourism there will provide a paper, if one asks, certifying one's visit. The moderately priced **Refugio da Roca** serves excellent soup.

WHERE TO STAY

Hotels come in all price ranges in these resorts, but the best values are in Cascais.

VERY EXPENSIVE ($200+)

In Cascais:

Albatroz   1st-class ★ ★ ★
R. Frederico Arouca, 100 (one block south of the train station). Rooms: 40. ☎ 248 28 21; FAX 284 48 27; Telex 16052. The hotel grew around a 19th-century ducal palace on the water, and dukes and their ilk still guest at this special place. Cary Grant stayed, as did Grace Kelly and Prince Rainier. The bedrooms are not grand, although recently redone with superb taste. Views are splendid and the staff pays attention to every detail.

In Estoril:

Palácio   1st-class ★ ★
R. do Parque Estoril (just east of the park). Rooms: 162. ☎ 468 04 00; FAX 468 48 67; Telex 12757. As its name and reputation says, this hotel is grand and elegant, even set in its own gardens, although only some of the rooms are air-conditioned. The service is attentive and the staff is omnipresent, but though the cost is 20% less than the Hotel Albatroz, the Albatroz is a better choice.

EXPENSIVE ($100-$200)

In Praia do Guincho:

Do Guincho   1st-class ★ ★ ★

Rooms: 31. ☎ *487 04 91; FAX 487 04 31; Telex 43138.* This luxury hotel is incorporated into the towers of a 17th-century fortress. Bedrooms with their vaulted ceilings are small but replete with charm. Staying here produces a wonderful sense of isolation.

In Cascais:

Cidadela   1st-class ★ ★

Av. 25 de Abril (the coast road). Rooms: 130. ☎ *483 29 21; FAX 486 72 26; Telex 16320.* The hotel faces its own garden overlooking the sea. Public rooms and bedrooms are huge and tastefully done. Duplex suites contain kitchenettes, dining rooms, living rooms and two or three bedrooms, each with a private bath. Suites are bargains for families or couples travelling together.

Estalagem Senhora da Guia   1st-class ★ ★ ★

Estrado do Guincho, the coast road, 3.5 k west of Cascais. Rooms: 28. ☎ *486 92 39; FAX 486 92 27; Telex 42111.* The heirs of the Sagres beer brewery built this imposing villa in 1970. When the heirs left, a family took it over for use as a hotel and decorated it in fine taste. Each bedroom is different, but all are pleasing. Views of the coast are grand.

MODERATE ($50-$99)

In Cascais:

Casa da Pérgola   2nd-class ★ ★ ★

Av. Valbom, 13 (a half block southwest of the train station). Rooms: 10, only 8 with private bath. ☎ *484 00 40. Open April-October.* Many will agree that these are the most wonderful accommodations in the area. The century-old private villa has a garden patio and a marble entrance. Elegant antiques furnish the public spaces. Because this house was not built as a hotel, bedrooms are all different, but each is decorated with taste.

INEXPENSIVE (UNDER $50)

In Estoril:

Smart   R3rd-class ★

R. José Viana, 3. Rooms: 16, some without baths. ☎ *468 21 64.* The hotel is a large house, recently remodeled, with a patio garden on a street of villas. Bedrooms are clean and functional, and most have televisions, unusual for this price category.

WHERE TO EAT

Both Cascais and Estoril are filled with restaurants, although most are expensive and few offer good value. However, there is a fine restaurant at the Guincho beach.

EXPENSIVE ($50+)

In Praia do Guincho:

Porto de Santa Maria ★★★

Estrada do Guincho. ☎ *487 02 40. Closed Monday.* This restaurant is by no means elegant, though fresh flowers at the door help. It is a functional place dedicated to serving the freshest seafood. A huge aquarium displays the shellfish selection, which is priced by weight. There are several cascades of fish and shellfish, and shellfish with rice is a specialty.

LISBON ★★★★

Population: 826,140
Area code: 01; zip code: 1100

The autoestrada A-1 from **Oporto** *and* **Coimbra** *also rings the* **airport**, *7 k north of the city. It bends west along the southern edge of the airport where it is called Av. Craveiro Lopes. Just before the racetrack, turn right at the large interchange to travel along Av. Campo Grande, with a center island. At the second traffic circle (the Pr. Duque de Saldanha) bear rightward along the wide Pereira de Melo for 3 blocks until it enters the circle of the Pr. Marqués de Pombal, with a park to the right. Turn south (left) along Av. de Liberdad, lined with flowers, to skirt the Pr. dos Restauradores and enter the Pr. Rossio. Take the rightmost of the parallel streets heading south toward the river, R. do Aurea, which ends in 6 blocks in the huge plaza of Praça do Comércio with parking. From* **Setúbal** *and* **south**, *the soaring span of the Ponte 25 da Abril is crossed to become Av. de Ponte in the city. Exit at the first opportunity. Follow the port east along Av. 24 de Julho, which leads in 3 miles to the huge Praça do Comércio with parking. From* **Cascais** *and* **Estoril** *by the coastal N-6 Belém is entered along Av. Marginal, which changes its name to Av. de India and finally to Av. 24 de Julho as it follows the river and port. It deposits traffic in a few miles in the huge Praça do Comércio with parking. By the inland road and from* **Sintra** *along N-7, the autoestrada becomes Av. Duarte Pacheco, then changes* *its name to Av. Joaquim de Agular before reaching the large traffic circle of Pr. Marquês de Pombal. From there follow the Oporto directions.*

In 1975, Lisbon received three-quarters of a million *retornados*, people of Portuguese descent fleeing the former African colonies of Angola, Mozambique, Guinea and Cape Verde, that had just gained independence. Such numbers were a huge bite for tiny Portugal to swallow, as the population of the country swelled by 10% in a matter of months. About half of these immigrants stayed in Lisbon, increasing its population by a quarter, and the digestion of this influx is not complete.

Shantytowns now exist in Lisbon's outskirts and have spread across to the south bank of the Tejos; the city suffers from beggars, street people, and an aura of poverty. Nonetheless, nothing but another earthquake will change the character and appearance of an 18th-century city and major European capital.

Despite the fact that so little remains from before 1755, Lisbon seems the oldest of all the European capitals. The heart of the city is Pombal's 18th-century urban renewal, unchanged in feeling since his day. Elsewhere in the city's center, steep hills make avenues and tall buildings impractical, thus preserving old alleys lined by the only buildings that suit them—originals from the 18th-century that all but touch each other across the lanes. Palaces and mansions may be preserved in other cities, but only Lisbon managed to save whole blocks of ordinary houses—now blackened by age—from the 18th century. Economic stagnation helped, for Portugal was not a participant in the Industrial Revolution that generated factories and abundant housing for an exploding middle class, changing the landscape of cities throughout the rest of Europe in the 19th century. Lisbon still exhibits both faces of an 18th-century city—imposing expanses designed for royalty, and crowded warrens left to the lower class.

All Lisbon funnels into the lowland valley called the Baixa, where Pombal's Praça do Comércio (known familiarly as the *Terreiro do Paço*, Terrace of the Palace) leads north from the river over a grid of avenues to the Praça Rossio. On either side hills rise. To the right, facing inland, is the steep bluff of São Jorge with the castle of the same name on its summit. As the bluff descends toward the river, the most characteristic quarter of the city, the famed Alfama, covers its sides. To the left, a gentler hill rises to the Bairro Alto (the High Quarter), a place of shops and restaurants, with the better stores on

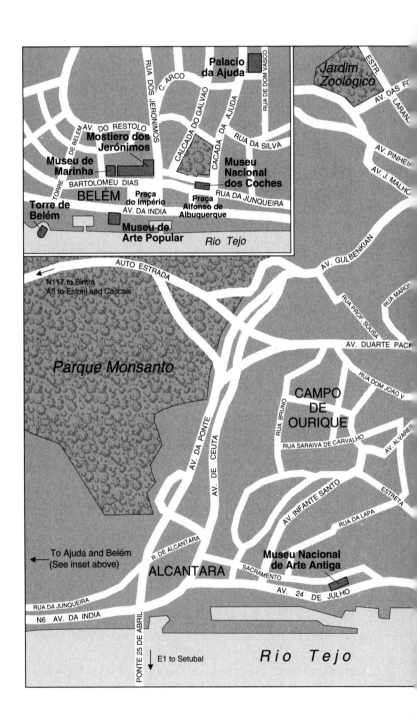

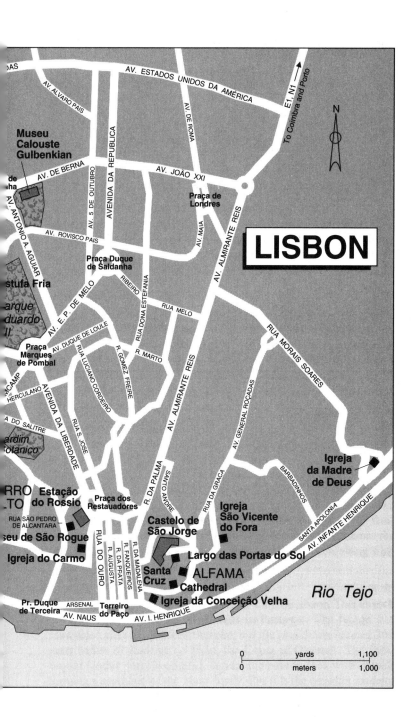

slopes near the Baixa, in a quarter named Chiado. Farther north the grand avenue of Liberdade parades to the plaza of the Marquês de Pombal, followed by the large park of Eduardo VII, around which modern Lisbon sprawls. The former suburb of Belém, now incorporated into the city, lies four miles to the west along the river. Scenic Lisbon does not spread far.

As with any city, Lisbon's charms are best savored on foot. Its steep hills, however, exact a stiff price on lungs and legs. To help, Lisbon runs charming old yellow streetcars and double-decker buses imported from England, whose stops are marked by large signs with clearly posted routes. Even more convenient are the taxis—the least-expensive in western Europe. Meters in these black cars with green-blue roofs start at 130$00, and for local trips are unlikely to run beyond 500$00 (about $3.50). A 15% tip is the norm. When their roof lights are lit, taxis can be hailed on streets, but are more readily found in stands beside hotels or monuments. Buses charge by the number of zones traversed, starting at 125$00. Streetcars do the same but start at 105$00. *Módulos*, ten-trip tickets, cut these costs in half. Even cheaper are special tourist passes for 4 days at 1000$00, that may be purchased at the Santa Justa funicular just south of Pr. Rossio. Judicious use of wheeled transportation will confine walking to downhill or at least to level ground. Even so, many sidewalks in Lisbon are composed of cut tiles in enchanting designs that can batter feet through thin soles.

Lisbon's pleasures extend beyond traditional sights. They include walking the lanes of the **Alfama ★** to taste the city life of the non-rich as it was two centuries ago, and strolling the Baixa along wide avenues. The most pleasant of the traditional sights is the **Castelo de São Jorge ★★**, both for the ramble along its walls and for the views of the city, river and sea below. The architectural highlights of the city are the **Mosteiro dos Jerónimos ★★★★** and the **Torre de Belém ★★**, both Manueline masterpieces in the suburb of Belém. Lisbon holds the two best art museums in Portugal—the **Museu Nacional de Arte Antiga ★★★★** for Portuguese painting, Bosch, Durer and Zurbarán, along with collections of silver and gold; and the **Museu Calouste-Gulbenkian ★★★** for special Islamic art, superb 18th-century French painting, and an enormous collection of Lalique glass. The **Museu de Marinha ★★** (Maritime Museum) has some interesting displays, while the **Museu Nacional dos Cochas ★★★** (Coach Museum) is probably the best of its kind anywhere. Lisbon has no magnificent churches, but some pretty ones. The **Cathedral ★** conveys a Romanesque feel, **São**

Roque ★★ has one amazing chapel, **Igraja do Carmo ★** (whose ceiling fell in the earthquake) conveys an eerie sense of olden times, but, best of all is **Igreja da Madre de Deus ★★★** for its beautiful *azulejo* tiles. The **Museu do Arte Popular ★★** in Belém should not be missed for its survey of craftwork from all the provinces of Portugal. An unexpected treat is the **Estufa Fria ★**, the so-called "cold greenhouse" in Parque Eduardo VII at the end of Av. de Liberdade that houses a lush collection of tropical plants amid waterfalls and grottos. A busy three days is necessary for seeing the sights of Lisbon.

Sensible groupings of sights by proximity are possible. Combine a visit to the Castelo de São Jorge, at the top of the hill, with a walk through the Alfama spilling down its side, and a tour of the Cathedral and the Igraja da Conceicão at the bottom. A second grouping includes Pombal's complex of the Praça do Comércio, leading down the avenues to the Praça Rossio, an excursion up to the Bairro Alto, then down again along Av. de Liberdade to the Parque Eduardo VII and the botanical Estufa Fria. Both of the preceding could be combined in one exhausting day. A trip to the suburb of Belém covers the Mosteiro dos Jerónimos, Torre de Belém, Museu de Marinha, and Museu Nacional dos Cochas. The Museu Nacional de Arte Antiga is on the way to Belém, and can readily be included for one long day. The Museu Calouste Gulbenkian and the wonderful *azulejo* tiles of the church of Madre de Dios both require separate outings, for, although not greatly distant, neither is close to other sights.

Castilo de São Jorge　　　★★

Open daily 8 a.m. to sunset. Admission: free. Taking a taxi up to the castle, then walking down through the Alfama is best, although bus #37 also goes to the castle. It was on this hilltop that the Phoenicians first settled, though no one records who lived here before. The Romans also established a city on this hill, whose remains are still under excavatation. Visigoths raised the massive perimeter walls of the castle and probably built the ten towers, although the Moors restored and strengthened both. The ruined palace inside the walls was built by Dom Dinis in the 13th century and it served as the principal royal palace of the Portuguese kings until the 16th century when Manuel I built a new one—since destroyed by the earthquake—in the lower city. The São Jorge palace then became a prison, abandoned in the present century.

Contained within its walls is a pleasant garden populated by rare white peacocks, black-necked swans, ducks, ravens and the occasional flamingo. Walk the ramparts for the best orientation to the city. Southeast, spilling down the hill, is the Alfama quarter. To the east, lying in a valley, are the orderly avenues and plazas of Pombal's Baixa, with the Praça do Comércio beside the river, and the Av. de Liberdade stretching north to the large park of Eduardo VII. The Bairro Alto rises directly east. Even farther east and south, the graceful bridge of the Ponte 25 da Abril—with the longest single span in Europe—can be seen stretching cross the Tejos.

ALFAMA ★

From São Jorge Castle head to the church of Santa Cruz on the grounds. Walk east behind its apse to take R. de Santa Luzia going right downhill. It bends and narrows to stairs that enter the open plaza of Largo das Portas do Sol. Or take a taxi from town directly to Largo das Portas do Sol. Trolleys #28 and #12, as well as bus #37 also stop there. The route described can be followed in reverse from the Cathedral, though it is uphill in that direction.

The Alfama is archetypical Lisbon, which means that not everyone will enjoy it. It is dirty, noisy, unattractive, slightly dangerous (beware of pickpockets), beflowered and quaint. It presents a slice of life from the 18th century—the low life of fishermen and the underclasses. Buildings squeeze against one another, wash hangs from windows, braziers in doorways waft the scent of food, and children run in mobs. The point of a visit is mainly to taste the activity, not to view monuments, so the best times are mornings and late afternoons when the neighborhood is busy.

The original name of the quarter probably was the Arabic *al Hammam*—the baths. Until the great earthquake it was peopled by the well-to-do, but the lower classes grabbed the buildings that survived destruction and made it their bairro. Before that cataclysm, most of Lisbon would have looked the way the Alfama does today.

The best introduction to the quarter is the plaza of **Largo Das Portas do Sol**. It is named for the gate into the Moorish city that faced the rising sun. On the right, at the southern end of the plaza, is the **Fundacão Ricardo do Espirito Santo Silva**. This museum of decorative arts, housed in a 17th-century palace of the Counts of Azurara, contains a fine collection of 17th- and 18th-century furniture in rooms around a courtyard. The foundation supports a school in the annex, where students today relearn old crafts. *(Open Tuesday-Saturday 10 a.m. to 1 p.m. and 2:30-5 p.m.; Admission: free, though a tip is expected.)* **Santa Luzia**, opposite, has some nice tiles inside which depict the Praça do Comércio before the earthquake.

From the museum, walk west (across the plaza) to descend the steps of Beco de Santa Helena on the right. Halfway down take the first left along Beco do Garces then left again to ascend R. do Picão, which enters **Largo do Salvador**. At number 22 is a rare remaining 16th-century mansion, formerly belonging to the Counts of Arcos. Its balcony is later baroque. Return to the southern end of the largo to take the small **R. da Regueira**, which forks left of the R. do Picão on which we entered. It is a street of small shops and restaurants. At **Beco das Cruzes**, the first alley on the right, is an 18th-century house with carved ravens supporting an overhanging second story. A few feet down Beco das Cruzes a nice *azulejo* panel surmounts a door on the left, and an old arch crosses the street farther along. A few steps more down R. da Regueira sees it open to a fountain on whose left are the steps of the **Beco do Carneiro**—so narrow that houses almost touch across the alley—with a nice view from the top. Return to the fountain to follow **R. de San Miguel** opposite Carneiro, as tiny antique shops line the way. **Beco da Cardosa**, the second left, is worth ascending for a short way to see 16th- to 18th-century houses branching off its blind alleys. A few steps more along R. de San Miguel brings the church of **San Miguel**. Inside is some fine baroque woodwork. A few steps south of the Largo de San Miguel, which fronts the church, is the most animated street of the quarter, the **R. de San Pedro**, crossing. Head along it to the right into **Largo de San Rafael**, with one tower remaining from the 14th-century walls of the city. West of the largo, R. de João da Praça leads in two blocks to the **Cathedral** of Lisbon.

Cathedral ★

Open daily 9 a.m. to noon and 2:30-6 p.m. Open Mon., Wed. and Fri. to 7:30 p.m. Admission: 100$00 to the museum and cloisters. From the northern end of the Praça do Comércio go east two blocks to R. da Madalena which runs north-south. Three blocks north at the church of Madalena turn right on R. de Santo Antonio da Sé for three short blocks. (Another route is described in the Alfama section above.) Bus #37 and streetcars #28 and #11 stop at the Cathedral.

After capturing Lisbon from the Moors in 1147, Afonso Henrique ordered a cathedral to be built for his English bishop. By the end of that century a Romanesque cathedral was completed, including defensive capabilities for a city that did not yet feel safe from attack. Over the centuries Gothic additions were appended, and later, baroque decoration. After the cathedral suffered great damage in the 1755 earthquake it was reconstructed to its earlier style, producing the bare but imposing church on view today.

The facade is particularly harmonic, with massive crenellated towers and small rounded Romanesque apertures for the rose window, bells and entry portals. It is all quite stately. Inside, the nave is a pure Romanesque barrel on plain pillars that leads to a simple lantern at the crossing. The aisles paralleling the nave, however, are surmounted by an elegant Gothic triforium. To the left, upon entering, is a baptismal font dating from 1195 at which Saint Anthony of Padua is said to have been christened. The church altar is 18th-century; behind it is a fine 14th-century Gothic ambulatory. The third chapel on the right (south) contains endearing 14th-century tombs of Lopo Fernandes Pacheco and his wife. The carving is simple and charming, with pains for small things, such as the hair, but caricatures for the clothing and the dogs at their feet. Just to the right is the entrance to a lovely, though damaged, 13th-century cloister. Farther right in the south transept is the entrance to the sacristy, which serves as the treasury. It contains relics of Portugal's patron Saint Vincent in a lovely mother-of-pearl casket.

Santo António da Sé, *on the site of the birthplace of Saint Anthony of Padua, is west of the Cathedral facade.*

BAIXA

This is the Lisbon built by Pombal after the great earthquake. Its straight lines and ordered vistas reflect the rationalism of the 18th century—one of Pombal's rules was that buildings could have no overhangs or curves. The intent was to construct a commercial district anchored at either end by large plazas for public gatherings. It remains more or less the same today, despite the office buildings and banks that have replaced the old shops, and the herd of cars that fills the formerly dramatic expanse of the Praça do Comércio. Nonetheless, the area invites promenades in the same way that the Champs Elysée does in Paris.

Praça do Comércio   ★

The Baixa begins by the river with the Praça do Comercio. However, most Lisboetas call it Tereiro do Paço (Terrace of the Palace), commemorating the site of the royal residence before the 1755 earthquake. The huge plaza is lined by pink arcades housing government offices on three sides and by the sea on the fourth. In the center, toward the south, stands an equestrian **statue of José I**, king during Pombal's era. Machado de Castro cast this large work in the finest 18th-century style, reminiscent of similar statues of the French Sun King. As it happened, King José was ill during the statue's creation so he did not sit for the artist, which perhaps explains the ornate helmet with a visor that all but obscures his face. A bronze medallion in the front depicts Pombal. When Pombal was removed in disgrace from office the craftsman who made the medallion was ordered to destroy it. Unable to melt down his own work, he hid it instead, and later it was found and replaced. In the northeast corner of the plaza King Carlos I and his heir were assassinated in 1908.

Rossio

A handsome **triumphal arch** in the northern arcade of the Praça do Comércio leads out to a series of parallel avenues each built for one trade. They lead north in seven blocks to the main square of the city known to all as the **Rossio**, although its official name is Praça Dom Pedro IV. The statue in the center of this square is actually of Maximilian. A ship transporting the statue from France to Mexico had sailed into Lisbon when word arrived of Maximilan's death. The Portuguese were able to buy the now useless statue for a pittance, and changed only a few details. Before the 1755 earthquake, this plaza was the city center where bullfights and autos-da-fe were witnessed by crowds. The palace of the Inquisition stood at the north end of the plaza, replaced in the middle of the 19th century by the present **Teatro**

Nacional. Two central baroque fountains imported from France are surrounded by flower stalls and cafes.

To the left of the Teatro Nacional is one of the train stations of Lisbon, the **Estação de Rossio**. Its quaint facade from the 19th century mimics either the Manueline or the Moorish, amid such exuberance that it is difficult to tell which. North of the station is the **Pr. dos Restauradores**, commemorating, by a central obelisk, those who rose against the Spanish in the 17th century to regain independence from Spain. In the northwest corner of the plaza is the huge **Palácio Foz** which now serves as the Direccão-General do Turismo. At its north end the Calcada da Gloria funicular lifts up to the Bairo Alto.

Bairro Alto

In this quarter Pombal tried to construct his usual grid of avenues, but the curves of the hill defeated his efforts. Today it is a place for cafes and, especially on its southern slopes, called the Chiado, the site of Lisbon's best stores. In 1988 terrible fires destroyed a score of shops including Lisbon's two largest department stores, and the area has not completely recovered, although plenty of establishments remain. A funicular (for 25$00) entered beside the Palácio Foz rises to the terrace of São Pedro de Alcantara, from which fine city views spread. Running west from the north end of the terrace is **R. Dom Pedro V**, where Lisbon's best antique shops crowd together for two blocks.

R. San Pedro de Alcantara, beside the terrace, leads south in one block to the 16th-century **Igreja São Roque** ★ ★. Its unremarkable exterior encases as elegant a baroque interior as one is likely to see, and includes what may be the most sumptuous and costly chapel in the world. The nave's flat wooden ceiling is a tromp l'oeil vault, painted with scenes of the Apocalypse. Four ornate chapels line each side. Proceeding down the right side, note lovely *azulejo* and a fine painting in the third chapel. The chapel of São João Baptista is left of the high altar, and unique in the world. In 1742 King João V commissioned a chapel of semi-precious stones to be built in Rome. Upon its completion, it was blessed by the Pope, dismantled, transported on three ships and reconstructed again in Lisbon in 1750. Lapis lazuli dominates, but there are elements of porphyry, amethyst and several sorts of marble. What appears to be a painting above the altar is also of stone, a finely detailed and polished mosaic, as are the others in the chapel. Note the chandeliers and their "chains." After a look at the sacristy *azulejos*, exit the church for an inspection of its treasures in the **Museu de São Roque**, to the right of the church entrance. One bowl consists of more than thirty pounds of gold, a miter is covered in Brazilian diamonds, and a pair of gilded silver candlesticks together approach one ton. *(Open daily 10 a.m. to 5 p.m. The museum is closed on Monday Admission: 25$00, free on Sunday.)*

Continue along the street, which now is named R. da Misericordia, for three blocks to the corner with a pair of churches framing R. Garrett that goes left between them. Over its three blocks **R. Garrett** collects the finest stores in the city, with others on surrounding streets. Take the third left up Calcada do Sacramento for one block to Largo do Carmo, at whose corner rise the atmospheric ruins of the **Igreja do Carmo ★**.

Construction on this Carmelite church began at the end of the 14th century, though problems with its foundation delayed construction for fifty years. The second-largest church in Lisbon after the Cathedral, it was built in the finest Gothic style, but the great earthquake toppled its ceiling. For some reason the church was never rebuilt, so it serves today as dramatic evidence of that cataclysm. One part functions as a kind of museum. A pleasant garden inside is open to the sky, silhouetting the skeleton of the church. *(Open Monday-Saturday 10am to 1 p.m. and 2-5 p.m. Closed Sunday and holidays. Admission: 150$00.)*

At the east end of R. do Carmo, past scars of the 1988 fire, is an elevator, called **anta Justa**, that descends from the Chiado to the Rossio area again. The elevator is reminiscent of Eiffel's famous Paris tower, for it is the same type of girdered construction from 1898. **Avenida da Liberdade** runs straight for almost exactly one mile from the Plaça de Restauradores to the Parque Eduardo VII. It was laid out in the 19th century for promenades by the well-to-do, and, originally, was walled and gated for their protection. The gates and walls are gone today but the promenade presents lovely vistas, bordered by palms and water gardens, with playful mosaics on the sidewalks. However, the hotels and office buildings that line it are not of great interest, so a taxi might be in order to reach the park at its end.

The park, **Parque Eduardo VII**, is named for Queen Victoria's son who visited Lisbon several times, partly to shore up the shaky monarchy of Carlos I, who was assassinated despite these efforts. At the northwest corner of the park grows the tropical lushness of the **Estufa Fria ★**. Called the "Cold Greenhouse" because wooden shutters instead of glass maintain the temperature, it is an acre of plants, ferns and flowers connected by paths, tiny bridges, fountains, ponds and streams. The Estufa Quente (Hothouse) nearby maintains desert flora and well earns its name in the summer. *(Open daily 9 a.m. to 6 p.m.; to 5 p.m. in winter; admission: 57$00.)*

BELÉM

Belém is a 20-minute taxi ride 8 k along the river west of the center of Lisbon. It is served by buses #12, #14, #27, #28, #29, #43 and #49, and trolleys #15, #16 and #17. Faster public transportation is the 10-minute train that departs every 15 minutes from the Cais do Sodré station, along the river five blocks due west of the Praça do Comércio.

Belém is Portuguese for Bethlehem. It was the original port of Lisbon from which the maritime explorers sailed into the unknown and to which the fruits of their discoveries arrived, enriching Lisbon beyond the dreams of most countries in the world. Some of this bounty stayed in Belém. Manuel I constructed the **Mosteiro dos Jerónimos** ★★★★ in thanks for Vasco da Gama's opening of the spice trade, and deducted a tax of 5% from all that trade to pay for the construction. It was the first complete Manueline structure. Then he built a fortress in the river to protect the shipping—the **Torre de Belém** ★★. Within three blocks of these two sights are the **Museu do Arte Popular** ★★, for an exposure to Portuguese crafts, the **Museu de Marinha** ★★ (Maritime Museum), and the **Museu Nacional dos Cochas** ★★★ (Coach Museum). Each of these sights is described below. Buses #27 and #43 from the Pr. Pombal stop at the Mosteiro dos Jerónimos.

Torre de Belém

Open Mon.-Sat. 10 a.m. to 6:30 p.m. (in winter to 5 p.m.) Open Sun. 10 a.m. to 2 p.m. Closed Mon. and holidays. Admission: 400$00 (250$00 in winter) Sun. free. In the river off the riverine Av. Marginal at Av. Torre de Belém. When it was constructed in 1521, the tower stood farther out in the river whose bank, after centuries of silting, has since come out to meet it. It was planned both for a river lookout and as an armed fortress to defend Portuguese shipping. It looks suitably robust, but elegant at the same time, with its lovely porch, delicate third-story terraced windows and precious Moorish-influenced details. The inside is plainer and more Gothic in feel, with stone spiral staircases and bare walls.

Museu de Arte Popular

Open Tues.-Sun. 10 a.m. to 12:30 p.m. and 2-5 p.m. Closed Mon. and holidays. Admission: 200$00.) Along the river two blocks east of the Torre de Belém. In a building left over from the 1940 Lisbon World's Fair are displayed the arts and crafts of Portugal, arranged by region. Here is the place to acquaint oneself with the range and talent of Portugal's folk artists and perhaps to prepare a shopping list and itinerary.

Mosteiro dos Jerónimos

Open Tues.-Sat. 10 a.m. to 6:30 p.m. (in winter to 5 p.m.) Open Sun. 10 a.m. to 2 p.m. Closed Mon. and holidays. Admission to the cloisters: 400$00 (250$00 in winter). From the Museu Popular head north across the gardens of the Pr. Imperio, on the other side of which the monastery stands. Henry the Navigator built a small monastery on this site in the 15th century, replaced by Manuel I early in the 16th century with a richly endowed Hieronymite Monastery. The original plans were drawn by the architect Diogo Boytac, who was taken from a commission at Setúbal for the job. Seventeen years into the building he was succeeded by João de Castilho and the French sculptor, Nicolas Chanterene, to whom most of the decoration is due. By good fortune the earthquake of 1755 caused only slight damage, so this masterpiece remains in essentially its original state.

The white limestone monastery consists of a compound whose south side, facing the Pr. Imperio, is the south wall of the church of Saint Mary, while a grand cloister extending north completes the sides of a square. An elegant porch on the southern side is decorated with a canopy containing innumerable statues of knights who sailed with Vasco de Gama. Below, on the central pillar, is a carving of Prince Henry the Navigator. The west portal, the entrance to the church, includes a statue of Manuel I across from his wife Maria, the second of the daughters of Ferdinand and Isabella he married, accompanied by their respective patron saints, with Biblical scenes above.

The church interior is vast, with aisles as high as the nave. Exquisite vaulting is raised on paired columns whose diameters decrease for perspective as they march to the front of the church. The tomb of Vasco de Gama on the back of a lion rests by the doorway, while another tomb opposite honors Camoães, Portugal's great poet, though his body actually lies in an unmarked pauper's grave. The star vaulting at the transept crossing is audacious. In the end chancel are royal tombs borne on elephants. Here is Manuel I, the Fortunate, to whom all of this is due.

Exit through the west entrance to enter the cloisters through the gift shop. The cloisters enclose a large space in a two-story arcade of wide arches punctuated by spires. The vaulting is fine and the sculpture incredibly rich. It is the galaxy of animals, vegetables and ropes carved on columns and walls here that earn this monastery its fame. The second story is elegant, if less exuberant. A doorway leads to the upper choir of the church, with 16th-century stalls handsomely carved from Brazil wood.

Museu da Marinha

Open Tues.-Sun. 10 a.m. to 5 p.m. Closed Mon. and holidays. Admission: 200$00; free on Wed. Entrance is at the west end of the Hieronymite Monastery. This museum consists mainly of ship models, fascinating for those willing to devote the time and attention to study them. In the entrance are three anchors from Columbus' Niña. Note the models of ships from the era of the great discoveries. These are caravels, a Portuguese invention, and the type of ship that Columbus chose as well. Their lateen rigs allowed sailing much closer to the wind than the square sails used previously. Without this improvement Africa could not have be rounded by sail. Some of the uniforms on display are splendid in a Gilbert and Sullivan way.

Museu Nacional dos Coches

Open Tues.-Sun. 10 a.m. to 1 p.m. and 2:30-5:30 p.m. Closed Mon. and holidays. Admission: 400$00. R. de Belém parallels the south face of the Hieronymite Monastery and leads eastward in two blocks to the *museum.* Housed in the former royal riding school on the grounds of the Palace of Belém (which is now the home of the president of Portugal) is this museum filled with nothing but amazing coaches. These gilded fantasies stand parked in long rows. It should be remembered that their function was to impress, and one must admit that the least of them would turn heads if it rolled by today. Favorites are the coach of José I, the king at the time of the great earthquake, the huge carriages of João V, a 17th-century French litter, and the miniature coach of Carlos I, used when he was a child, adding pathos to the thought of his later assassination. Amid all the gilt below, do not fail to look up at the lovely ceiling frescos.

Museu Nacional de Arte Antiga ★★★★

Open Tues.-Sun. 10 a.m. to 1 p.m. and 2:30-5 p.m. Closed Mon. and holidays. Admission: 200$00; free Sun. morning. The museum is located along the river by the Jardim 9 de Abril at 95 R. das Janelas Verdes, which is halfway between Belém and the Praça do Comércio in the heart of Lisbon. A walk along the river from the Praça do Comércio would cover less than a mile and a half, although a taxi is certainly quicker. Trolley #19 or buses #27, #40, #49 or #54 pass by. This certainly is the finest museum extant of Portuguese painting, and includes much more. It is housed half in the 17th-century palace of the Count of Alvor, where Pombal lived for a while, and half in a modern addition whose west end provides the entrance. Inside and downstairs is the chapel of Santo Alberto, preserved from a former convent on this site. Its wooden sculpture is admirable, as are its *azulejos.* Rooms follow displaying Portuguese furniture, tapestries and carpets. Before entering the old building, opposite the entrance, ascend to the mezzanine to view a fine collection of porcelain, both from, and inspired by, the Far East. Two early 17th-century screens from Japan show the arrival of the Portuguese, the first people of European physiognomy that the insular Japanese had seen. The name for these screens comes from the Japanese word for "southern barbarian," and oversized noses show what most impressed the Japanese about these foreigners. Also on the mezzanine are collections of gold pieces and polychrome sculpture.

The second floor is devoted to Portuguese painting, including the one acknowledged masterpiece of the nation. It is a polyptych of six wood panels painted in the middle of the 15th century for the Lisbon church of Saint Vincent, which no longer exists. The artist is Nuno Gonçalves, and this is his only certain work. The painting is a collection both of portraits of famous Portuguese and of representations of segments of lower society, listening to Saint Vincent, pictured in the center of both middle panels. Important figures have been identified in the central panel in which Saint Vincent holds a Bible. King Afonso V kneels at the saint's feet, his heir stands behind, and next back, beside the saint, is the mustachioed Prince Henry the Navigator. Kneeling on the other side is Afonso's wife in front of the sister of Ferdinand of Spain, Afonso's mother, and behind her, farthest left, is the presumed portrait of the artist. All the faces are lusciously alive and one wonders where this artist gained a skill to rank with the European geniuses of the period.

The great Flemish painter Jan van Eyck visited Portugal in the early 15th century to influence a century of Portuguese artists. Most notable among his artistic descendents is Frei Carlos, from the following century, and his *Annunciation*, which bears comparison with the master. Of a different vein are the charming Portuguese primitives, especially an anonymous 15th-century *Ecce Homo* with a shrouded upper visage, and *Vision of Hell* in which hell is a kitchen presided over by an Indian Satan. Further on are rooms dedicated to Domingos de Sequeira, from the 19th century, a sort of Portuguese Goya. Like Goya he lived in exile and produced wondrous drawings and etchings, in addition to oils. His paintings appeared in Paris exhibitions where he bested Delacroix and Gérricault, among others. Outstanding are his portraits of the viscount of Santarém and his family, the young count of Farrobo, and the artist's own children.

Past the bookstore on the ground floor of the new building, the old building begins with a superb collection of silver tableware, mainly French, from the firm of Germain. French furniture follows. Across a landing is the entrance to the museum's European masterpieces. The stars are a Dürer painting of Saint Jerome, which once hung in the Hieronymite Monastery, and an astonishing Bosch of *The Temptations of Saint Anthony*. Saint Anthony is painted four times throughout the picture, never once looking at all sorts of sinners who surround him, each demonstrating sins by excess. There is a lovely *Virgin and Child with Saints* by Holbein the Elder, an interesting Bruegel depiction of beggars, and a fine self-portrait by Andrea del Sarto. Of the Spanish paintings, the best is probably Ribera's *Martyrdom of Saint Bartholomew*, although there is also a Velázquez portrait of Maria of Austria and a Zurbarán canvas of the twelve apostles.

Museu Calouste Gulbenkian   ★★★★

Open Tues.-Sun. 10 a.m. to 5 p.m. Open 2-7:30 p.m. on Wed. and Sat. in summer. Closed Mon. and holidays. Admission: 200$00; free Sun. The museum is located in Lisbon's north, about a half-mile north of the end of the Parque Eduardo VII. Av. de Alcantara, which is renamed Av. António Augusto Aguiar, follows the east edge of the park and leads to the Pr. da Espanha and the Parque de Palhava, where the museum is located. Trolleys #24 and #27, and buses #16, #26, #31 and #56 all stop nearby. Before World War I the Armenian Calouste Gulbenkian negotiated an agreement to broker all the oil Iran sold to the West for a 5% commission. This made him one of the richest private citizens in the world. During World War II, however, Britain made him unwelcome when he resisted requests to sever his ties with the Iranian embassy in Vichy France. Portugal welcomed him on the rebound. In return he became a citizen and established a billion-dollar foundation, the largest in Europe, to aid Portuguese arts. He also donated his private art collection to the country. Gulbenkian had been a passionate collector, desiring only the best; his tastes were wide and his pockets incredibly deep. His great coup was to purchase several works, including two Rembrandts, from the Hermitage during the late 1920s, when Russia needed hard currency. In breadth and quality his collection was the finest remaining in private hands until he died in 1955 and bequeathed it to Portugal. Using Gulbenkian's money, the present building was erected in 1969, designed expressly for the works it displays.

What makes this museum special is that it is at once modest in size and astonishingly high in quality, to allow and encourage study. Gulbenkian was not a collector who strove to complete a series, but a lover of art who purchased individual works simply because they captivated him. Consequently, it is a museum of stars, rather than one providing examples of the breadth of any single art genre.

Of the Egyptian, Greco-Roman and Mesopotamian art, the very first exhibit, an Old Kingdom alabaster bowl of elegant proportions, stands out. Those with an interest will find the Greek coins superb. One highlight of the museum is its collections of Middle-Eastern carpets, Korans and ceramics. The European art collection begins with several jewel-like medieval ivories and illustrated medieval manuscripts, including a fine *Book of Hours*, but moves quickly to paintings. Outstanding early works are van de Weyden's *Saint Catherine*, Dirk Bouts' *Annunciation*, and a haunting *Portrait of a Young Girl* by Domenico Ghirlandaio. After a fine Hals, a good Van Dyke portrait, and a Ruysdael landscape, are the two fine Rembrandt's—*Alexander* (sometimes called *Pallas Athene*), and the disturbing face in the *Portrait of an Old Man*. The 18th- and 19th-century French paintings and sculpture are choice, including a Fragonard, the fine De La Tour pastel of *Duval de l'Epinoy*, a nice Houdin sculpture of Diana, and several Corots. French furniture ranges from elegant to ornate. An impressive display of costly silver tableware leads to rooms of English painting and later French canvases—by Manet, Fantin-Latour, Renoir and Dégas, among others. The exhibit ends with an overwhelming exhibit of Lalique art nouveau glass.

Igreja da Madre de Deus, and Museu Nacional do Azulejo ★★★

The museum is open Tues.-Sat. 10 a.m. to 5 p.m. Open Sun. 10 a.m. to 2 p.m. Closed Mon. and holidays. Admission: 200$00; free on Sun. Located one block inland from the river, about 4 k west of the Praça do Comércio, at R. Madre de Deus, 4. Trolleys #3, #16, #24, #27, and buses #13, #18 and #42 stop there. This monastery was founded at the beginning of the 16th century by Donha Leonor, the widow of King João II. Here *azulejo* tiles can be seen in situ inside the exquisitely decorated little church, and their development explained by displays in the *azulejo* museum in its cloisters.

Although the church (to the right of the entrance) was substantially rebuilt after the great earthquake, much of the earlier art survived inside, along with the outside Manueline west entrance. Twisted columns lining the portal support an arch in which fishnets and pelicans entwine. The fishnet was Leonor's symbol, the pelican was her husband's. Inside all seems stunningly rich. Lower walls are lined with 18th-century Dutch *azulejos*, deeper blue than the Portuguese examples. The walls above are crowded with paintings of Saint Francis, on the right, and Saint Clare, on the left. Overhead, the barrel-coffered ceiling also contains paintings, this time primitives of the life of the Virgin. The altar is gilded baroque and holds a fine pulpit.

There is more. Steps lead down to the surviving part of the original church whose walls are lined by 16th-century *azulejos* from Seville. The main, renaissance cloister extends off this chancel, and beyond it is a lovely, earlier Manueline cloister. The *azulejo* museum is entered from the main cloister, but first climb to the upper gallery for more of the church. Here the chapel of Saint Anthony is tiled with 18th-century *azulejos* depicting the saint's life, above which are more early primitive paintings. Next comes the *coro alto*, the nun's choir, all in gilt, with still more paintings, and finally the sacristy, lined by Portuguese *azulejos* from the 18th century and still more 16th century primitives.

The *azulejo* museum uses actual tiles along with pictures to provide excellent instruction in the development of that art. The reason for the pictures is that the finest examples of these tiles are still affixed to buildings throughout Portugal. The Portuguese had picked up the idea of decorative tiles from the Moors, either from those still living in Spain or those met in Morocco when the Portuguese came to conquer Cueta in the early 15th century. By the end of the 16th century the Portuguese were manufacturing their own. The first were predominantly blue—*azul*—hence the name. By the 17th century, the Portuguese had mastered the art and scenes, generally of outdoor life, became immensely popular. Demand remained strong until architecture changed to a simpler neo-classical style at the close of the 18th century, although subsequently it picked up again.

WHERE TO STAY

Lisbon provides a reasonable number of hotels so that accommodations generally pose no problem. However, during Christmas, Easter week and June and July, reservations should be made well in advance. Hotels in Lisbon are among the most expensive in the country, although not exorbitant by European or American standards. Fine hotels at more modest prices are also available.

VERY EXPENSIVE ($200+)

Ritz   1st-class ★ ★ ★ ★

*R. Rodrigo da Fonseca, 88 (one block east of the Parque Eduardo VII).
Rooms: 310.* ☎ *69 20 20; FAX 69 17 83; Telex 12589.* The Ritz has
been the best in town since a famous hotel named the Aviz closed a
decade ago. Modern outside, its elegance is all within, consisting of
exquisite furniture and appointments. It may have the finest bathrooms in Europe. Although its reputation derives from the fine
appointments and all of the suites are utterly elegant, many of the simple bedrooms are more ordinary. A suite with a park view is well worth
the additional escudos. However, the simple bedrooms cost almost
$300 for a double.

Le Meridien Lisboa   1st-class ★ ★ ★

*R. Castiho, 149 (on the east edge of the Parque Eduardo VII). Rooms:
331.* ☎ *69 09 00; FAX 69 32 31; Telex 64315.* This member of the
well-regarded French chain is elegantly modern in its dress of marble
and chrome, and the favorite of many business people. All rooms have
lovely views of the park, but should be larger for the price, which
matches the Ritz.

Lisboa Sheraton   1st-class ★ ★

*R. Latino Coelho, 1 (3 blocks along Av. Pereira de Melo that runs west
from the southern end of the Parque Eduardo VII). Rooms: 385.* ☎ *57
57 57; FAX 54 71 64; Telex 12774.* The Sheraton is the tallest building
in Lisbon, so views are spectacular from the top floors. Otherwise, it
provides what familiarity with the chain would lead one to expect.
However, it has the audacity to outcharge the Ritz, as if to seek
panache by being the highest-priced hotel in the city.

EXPENSIVE ($100-$200)

York House   R1st-class ★ ★ ★ ★

*R. das Janelas Verdes, 32 (opposite the Museu Nacional de Arte Antiga).
Rooms: 45.* ☎ *396 25 44; FAX 397 27 93; Telex 16791.* The York is the
most charming and comfortable hotel in Lisbon. The only reason not
to stay here is if it is full. This *residencia* is remodeled from a 16th-cen-
tury convent whose renovation was done in the best of taste. All furnishings are perfect. Its location is far enough from the heart of the
city for relative quiet and close enough to taxi to in minutes. The best
rooms are those overlooking the beautiful courtyard. Classed as a residencia, mainly because it lacks an elevator, in every noticeable regard
its service is first class. An annex in a townhouse down the street adds
17 more rooms decorated in a Victorian style. Bedrooms there are
larger than those in the main hotel and 15% less, but the ones fronting
the street can be noisy. The main hotel is preferred.

Veneza   2nd-class ★ ★ ★

Av. da Liberdade, 189. Rooms: 38. ☎ *352 26 18; FAX 352 66 78.* This
19th-century mansion has just opened as one of Lisbon's most stylish

hotels. Although there is an odd contrast between elegant marble stairs in the lobby and bedrooms done in a homey green with white wicker, the former impresses and the later welcomes. This hotel combines elegance, hominess and a fine location in one intimate package.

Avenida Palace   1st-class ★ ★ ★

R. 1 de Dezembro, 123 (halfway between the Pr. Rossio and the Pr. dos Restauradores). Rooms: 100. ☎ *346 01 54; FAX 342 22 84.* This century-old hotel, conveniently located for visiting the sights, presents crystal chandeliers, brocaded walls, curtains and handwoven carpets to suit its grand age. The staff wears tails. Bedrooms have recently been redone and are attractive, if somewhat nondescript. The only drawback is a bustling, noisy location.

Dom Manuel I   2nd-class ★ ★ ★

Av. Duque d'Avila, 189 (just north of the Parque Eduardo VII). Rooms: 64. ☎ *57 61 60; FAX 57 69 85; Telex 43558.* Behind a modern facade waits a superbly styled interior that make this our choice if the York is full. It becomes even more attractive when the low price for its category is factored in. The bedrooms are tasteful, if slightly on the small side. The location is near the Gulbenkian Museum, but a distance from the heart of the city.

Principe Real   2nd-class ★ ★ ★

R. da Alegria, 53 (a few steep blocks west from the Av. da Liberdade, beside the Jardim Botanico. Rooms: 24. ☎ *346 01 16; FAX 342 21 04; Telex 44571.* Each bedroom is different and tasteful, with fresh flowers in every room—this is the hotel to which the Ritz sends its overflow. The location is pastoral near a lovely park, and prices are reasonable for its style.

Lisboa Plaza   1st-class ★ ★

Travessa do Salitre, 7 (halfway along the Av. da Liberdade, and a step west). Rooms: 112. ☎ *346 39 22; FAX 347 16 30; Telex 16402.* The art nouveau decor lends a special quality, and the bar comes from a more relaxed and gracious era. Bathrooms are grand and bedrooms were recently renovated for comfort. The location is convenient for walks.

Mundial   1st-class ★ ★

R. Dom Duarte, 4 (1 block east of the Praça do Comércio). Rooms: 147. ☎ *886 31 01; FAX 87 91 29; Telex 12308.* A superior location and views of the Castelo de São Jorge from the back rooms (which are also quieter) make this a choice to consider. Bedrooms are comfortable and ample, with a quietly tasteful decor. The management is efficient. Rooms are often available here when other choices are full, not because it is a lesser option, but because few Americans and Europeans know about the hotel.

Tivoli Jardim   1st-class ★

R. Julio Cesar Machado, 7 (behind its sister the Tavoli Lisboa at Av. Liberdade 185) Rooms: 119. ☎ *53 99 71; FAX: 355 65 66; Telex 12172.*

Although bedrooms are small and basic, the lovely garden around its sister hotel with both tennis court and pool make this a pleasant place to stay. Its sister, the Tavoli Lisboa, charges too much to be recommended, but the Jardim is quieter as well.

Altis   1st-class
R. Castilho, 11 (5 blocks along Av. da Liberdade from the Praça do Comércio and two blocks west). Rooms: 307. ☎ *52 24 96; FAX 54 86 96; Telex 13314.* This is a comfortable-enough, sleek, modern hotel with a convenient location. Since its prices push slightly past the expensive limits, this one should be considered only if better choices are full.

MODERATE ($50-$99)

Dom Carlos   2nd-class ★ ★ ★
Av. Duque de Loule, 121 (fronting its own park two blocks east of the Pr. de Pombal). Rooms: 73, plus 17 suites. ☎ *53 90 71; FAX 352 07 28; Telex 16468.* The recently remodeled Dom Carlos uses yards of glass to take full advantage of a garden outside. The bedrooms are Scandinavian and wood panelled, with Portuguese touches. This is a comfortable and efficient hotel that charges a quarter of the fee of many of its neighbors.

Albergaria da Senhora do Monte   1st-class ★ ★
Calçada do Monte, 39 (on a hilltop just north of the São Jorge hill). Rooms: 28. ☎ *886 60 02; FAX 87 77 83.* Views of the castle, city and river are perhaps the best available, and the hotel is pleasantly decorated. Bedrooms are comfortable and all incorporate terraces for views. The rooms at the back, however, provide the views worth coming for. While the bedrooms are not air-conditioned, they seldom need it. Admittedly, the location is not the most central, but the modest price saves enough for plenty of taxi rides.

Da Torre   2nd-class ★
R. dos Jerónimos, 8 (located beside the Mosteiro Jerónimos in Belém). Rooms: 50. ☎ *363 62 62; FAX 364 59 95.* This modern hotel is furnished with style and taste. It is endearing and would be recommended more strongly except for the cool service. Its location is perfect for touring the Belém area, and the center of town 6 k away can be reached in 15 minutes by taxi (or half an hour by public transport). The bedrooms are not air-conditioned.

Capitol   2nd-class ★
R. Eça de Queiroz, 24 (off the southeast corner of the Parque Eduardo VII). Rooms: 58. ☎ *53 68 11; FAX 352 61 65; Telex 13701.* This hotel offers the quiet of a peaceful street by a small park. Emphasis is on the bedrooms, which have a spacious feeling, in part because they are sparsely furnished. Some have pleasant balconies and all are air-conditioned.

Roma   2nd-class ★

Av. de Roma, 33 (near the Roma metro stop, 2 k north and 1 k east of the Parque Eduardo VII) Rooms: 265. ☎ *796 77 61; FAX 793 29 81; Telex 16586.* Debits arc that this hotel stands at a distance from the center of town on a noisy street, and lacks intimacy. Assets are the low prices for its class, and the fact that rooms should be available. The hotel is light and spacious and the bedrooms are comfortable, some even large. Downtown is 15 minutes away by subway or taxi. All bedrooms are air-conditioned.

Principe   2nd-class

Av. Duque d'Avila, 301 (1 long block north of the Parque Eduardo VII). Rooms: 68. ☎ *53 61 51; FAX 53 42 14; Telex 43565.* The bedrooms are roomy and the rate for children under nine is only half the listed charge. Half of the bedrooms are air-conditioned and many have balconies. The hotel is European in flavor, but otherwise nondescript.

INEXPENSIVE (UNDER $50)

Imperador   R3rd-class ★

Av. 5 de Outubro, 55 (a quarter of a mile north of the northeast corner of Parque Eduardo VII, one block west and north of the Saldanha metro stop). Rooms: 43. ☎ *352 48 84; FAX 352 65 37.* The rooms are spotless and comfortably decorated in muted colors. Front rooms overlook a small garden.

Nazareth   R2nd-class

Av. António Agusto de Aguiar, 25 (at the northeast corner of the Parque Eduardo VII). Rooms: 32. ☎ *54 20 16; FAX 356 08 36.* This one is for those who appreciate camp. The fourth-floor hotel has a lobby decorated as a fortress with fake vaulting on the ceiling and wrought ironwork. Not surprisingly, the bedrooms are slightly eccentric too, many with steps up or down to the adjoining bathroom.

Horizonte   R2nd-class

Av. António Agusto de Aguiar, 42 (at the northeast corner of the Parque Eduardo VII). Rooms: 52. ☎ *53 95 26; FAX 56 25 29.* This *residencia* is a former apartment house fronted by an impressive stairway. Bedrooms are arranged around a central stairway and are clean and comfortable, despite the worn look of the lobby.

WHERE TO EAT

As expected of a capital, Lisbon contains the most elegant restaurants in the country. But visitors are not forced to pay the cost of elegance because of the number and variety of modestly priced alternatives available.

EXPENSIVE ($50+)

Tágide   ★★★★

Largo da Academia Nacional de Belas Artes, 18 (two blocks south of the R. Garrett in Chiado). ☎ *347 18 80. Closed Saturday night and Sunday.* This is our choice for the finest restaurant in Lisbon. Spacious windows of this former townhouse look over the port and reflect crystal chandeliers from an elegant off-white dining room. (Request a window table.) Service is elegant and the dishes, if anything, surpass expectations. Start with salmon pâté or cold stuffed crab. Graduate to grilled baby goat with herbs, pork with clams and coriander, or supreme of halibut. Either the souffle with hot chocolate sauce or dessert crepes will cap a superb meal. A couple will spend about 15.000$00 with wine, which is a bargain for such exquisitely prepared food. Reservations are necessary.

Amex, Diners, MasterCard and Visa accepted.

Casa da Comida

Travessa das Amoreiras, 1 (4 blocks west and 3 south of the Parque Eduardo VII). ☎ *388 53 76. Closed Saturday lunch, Sunday and August.* There is a lovely planted patio for summer and a roaring fire in winter to make one feel at home. The decor is elegant with homey touches. Portuguese gourmets come here when they are not dining at Tágide, to argue over which is the better restaurant. The food is slightly nouveau, with delicate servings, and specialties include a succulent cascade of shellfish and a turbot with green pepper, preferable to the roast baby kid with herbs that is better at Tágide. Prices are about the same as Tágide and reservations are necessary.

Amex, Diners, MasterCard and Visa accepted.

Conventual

Pr. das Flores, 45 (in the western side of the Bairro Alto, best to take a cab). ☎ *60 91 96. Closed Saturday lunch, Sunday and August.* Although the food may be a touch more refined at the preceding, Conventual attains very high standards for more typical Portuguese specialties, and prices are about 30% less. Greatly adding to the experience is the place itself—a former convent—and the exquisite taste of the owner who spreads her collection of antiques all around. Prices hover at the bottom of the expensive range. Reservations are strongly advised.

Amex, Diners, MasterCard and Visa accepted.

Gambrinus

R. das Portas de Santo Antão, 25 (on a tiny square behind the Teatro Nacional just north of Pr. Rossio). ☎ *32 14 66.* There is no question that this is the best seafood restaurant in Lisbon, nor that it is the most expensive restaurant in Portugal. A dinner can cost 50% more than at Tágide. The fish and shellfish are invariably fresh and done to a turn, as they should be at these prices. Reservations are advised.

Amex and Visa accepted.

Aviz

R. Serpa Pinto, 12-B (around the corner from R. Garret in the Chiado). ☎ *32 83 91. Closed Saturday lunch, Sunday and August.* This is the most deluxe restaurant in the country. It serves very good food, but has declined recently and the service seems distracted. The restaurant, saved by its chef, is all that remains of Lisbon's former most elegant hotel. Mahogany panelling, black leather, marble columns and chandeliers lend a men's club atmosphere to the lounge. Three dining rooms are more intimate and turn-of-the-century grand. In general the dishes betray a French taste, despite being specialties of the restaurant. For example, vichyssoise Rothschild adds shrimp to the classic recipe.   *Amex, Diners, MasterCard and Visa accepted.*

MODERATE ($20-$50)

Sua Excelencia

R. do Conde, 42 (1 block due north of the National Museum of Ancient Art). ☎ *60 36 14. Closed Saturday lunches, Wednesday in September, and Sunday lunches in August.* This restaurant is entirely the child of its owner, Francisco Queiroz. No sign announces it. When the doorbell is rung, the owner greets you, escorts you to a table in a colorful room with tile floor, then recites the menu of the day. Selections depend on what is fresh in the market. Sr. Queiroz speaks enough English to convey what is necessary, and one can be certain that whatever is selected will be carefully prepared. Reservations are necessary.

Amex, Diners, MasterCard and Visa accepted.

Pap'Açorda

R. da Atalaya, 57 (from the church of São Roque in the Bairro Alto head west along Trav. da Queimada to take the fifth left). ☎ *346 48 11. Closed Sunday.* This restaurant specializes in the hearty food of the Alentejo. Naturally the specialty is *açorda*, a delicious stew of fish, bread, and eggs seasoned with coriander. Reservations are necessary on weekends.   *MasterCard and Visa accepted.*

Comida de Santo

Calçada do Eng. Miquel Pais, 39 (just off the Jardim Botanico in the Bairro Alto. R. Dom Pedro V heads that way). ☎ *396 33 39.* With such close ties to Brazil, Portugal would naturally have restaurants offering that cuisine, and de Santo is clearly the best. Sample any of the variety of dishes cooked in palm oil and coconut milk—some are very spicy, but others are mild. This different and delectable dining experience all takes place in a tropical atmosphere. Reservations are advised.

Amex, Diners, MasterCard and Visa accepted.

Sancho

Travessa da Gloria, 14 (just off Av. de Liberdade, 1 long block north of the Pr. Restauradores). ☎ *346 97 80. Closed Sunday and holidays.* Cozy with stucco walls, fireplace, leather furniture and wood-beamed ceiling, this restaurant provides relaxed enjoyable meals. Shellfish are specialties, and expensive, but there are moderately priced meat courses as well.   *Amex, MasterCard and Visa accepted.*

Restaurante 33

R. Alexandre Herculano, 33A (1 long block south and 2 west of Pr. Rossio at the Parque Eduardo VII). ☎ *54 60 79. Closed for Saturday lunch, and Sunday.* This establishment looks English with its sedate panelling, but presents well-prepared Portuguese food, accompanied by a singer on weekends. Reservations are advised. ***MasterCard and Visa accepted.***

INEXPENSIVE (UNDER $20)

Bota Alta

Travessa da Queimada, 35 (the street heads west from the church of São Roque in the Bairro Alto) ☎ *32 79 59. Closed Sunday.* The only problem with this place is that it is well known for its tasty food and good value, so waiting in line can be expected. It is a small, bistro place with a smoke-stained ceiling. The *caldo verde* is delicious. Of course there is cod in many varieties, but also daily specials.

No reservations are taken.

Cervejaria da Trindade

R. Nova de Trindade, 20-B (off R. Garrett in the Chiado) ☎ *342 35 06.* The room once formed part of a convent and then a brewery, although now it is a beer hall owned by the Sagres beer company. Even if prawns are ordered, the meal should be inexpensive, and filling and tasty. A tourist menu is offered for $10. Wash it down with a *mista*, a mixture of light and dark beer.

Pastelaria Bénard

R. Garrett, 104. ☎ *347 31 33. Closed Sunday.* This is the most fashionable of the dozen tea houses in Lisbon. Tea and cakes are the specialties, but there is a small selection of heartier foods. Best for lunch.

Xêlê Bananas ★

Pr. des Flores, 29 (from R. da Escola Politecnica, which is a continuation of R. Dom Pedro V in the Bairro Alto, take a left on R. San Marcal at the Botanical Gardens, then the third right). ☎ *395 25 15. Closed Saturday lunch and Sunday.* The pretty square opposite adds to the pleasure of the dining experience. The restaurant looks more expensive than it is, and Lisboetas know that well.

Bonjardim

Traversa de Santo Antão, 11 (a narrow street beside the post office building in Pr. dos Restauradores). ☎ *342 74 24.* Noted for roast chicken, this establishment is sufficiently successful to support two additional outlets on the same street. Fish soup and the pork *alentejana* aren't bad either.

Great American Disaster

Pr. Marquês de Pombal, 1 (on the ground floor of the Varig building in front of the Parque Eduarto VII). ☎ *51 61 45.* Here are served the best hamburgers in Lisbon. ***Amex, Visa and MasterCard accepted.***

SHOPPING

Lisbon entices shoppers with handcrafts, not high fashion. Ceramics are lovely and reasonable, and Portuguese carpets are famous, though never cheap, as is needlework from the Azores and Madeira. Stores generally open at 9 a.m., close at noon, reopen at 2 p.m. and close at 7 p.m. Many are closed on Saturday.

Gold, by law of at least 19 karats, is reasonable by U.S. standards, as is **silver**. The Portuguese specialty is filigree work. **Sarmento**, at R. Aurea, 251, in the Baixa has a distinguished century-old reputation. For sterling tableware the top quality is **Joalharia Ferreira Marquês**, occupying numbers 7-9 in the Rossio.

The best concentration of **antique** stores is along R. Dom Pedro V in the Bairro Alto (see direction under "Sights"). Much of the material is religious. An outstanding selection of antique *azulejos* is contained at **Solar**, at #70, along with other old things. A fascinating store for browsing is the **Centro Antiquaro do Alecrim** for drawings from old books, many handcolored. It is located at R. do Alecrim, 48-50 (near Sant'Anna, described below). What could be more typical of Portugal than a souvenir of **cork**? **Casa das Corticas**, at R. Escola Politecnica #4, the continuation of R. Dom Pedro V, sells nothing else and has invented surprising, if not always serious, uses for the material.

For **ceramics** and **azulejos**, besides the fine antique ones at Solar mentioned above, see **Sant'Anna** occupying #95-7 on R. do Alecrim, the southern continuation of R. de San Pedro de Alcantara that leads from R. Dom Pedro V to R. Garrett. In addition to a large selection of tiles, the store also carries its own line of ceramic pieces—boxes, planters, candelabra, etc. Its only true competitor is **Fabrica Ceramica Viuva Lamego**, a fair distance away at #25 Largo do Intendente (by the Intendente metro stop in the north of the city). Designs here are more colorful, but less sophisticated, than at Sant'Anna.

For fine bone **china**, there are several outlets of the well-known **Vista Alegre** factory. The best is at Largo do Chiado, 18, one block north of R. Garrett. In addition to prices that are about half those in the U.S. for the china, exquisite French Baccarat **crystal** is also sold at a great discount. Unfortunately, the outlets do not ship. For the well-known Portuguese crystal, Atlantis, the place to go is **Cristalissimo** at R. Castilho, 149, in the Meridien hotel.

The finest **embroidery** is sold in Lisbon, brought from the islands of Madeira and the Azores, which remain bastions of the craft. The best-known shop is **Madeira House** at R. Augusta 131-5 in the Baixa. The selection is large, but not quite up to the quality carried at **Madeira Superbia** on Av. Duque Loulé, 75-A (the street that leads east from Pr. Pombal in front of the Parque Eduardo VII). The highest quality of all is carried by the prestigious **Principe Real** at 12-14 R. da Escola Politécnica (the continuation of R. Dom Pedro V).

Needlepoint carpets from the village of Arraiolos are famous enough to lend their name to the style. Several stores in Lisbon sell arraiolos, but one is superior in selection, quality and honesty. Most people do better buying from **Casa Quintão** on R. Ivens, 30-4 (off R. Garrett in the Chiado), than in the village where the rugs are made. If $2000 sounds like a lot for an eight-by-ten-feet carpet, price comparable ones in the U.S.

For **handcrafts** of great variety at inexpensive prices from all the regions of Portugal go to **Filartesanato**, which is in the Feira Internacional de Lisboa toward Belém on the waterfront west of the Tejos bridge, Ponte 25 de Abril.

Then there is the famed Lisbon **flea market**, the *Feira da Ladra* (Thieves' Market). It is held Tuesdays and Saturdays, from early morning until sunset. All the stalls are open-air and fill the Campo de Santa Clara, three blocks east of São Jorge. Trolley #28 and bus #12 stop there. As with any such market, 99% of the goods are uninteresting, but there is that remaining percent, and the hope of a treasure. Diligance can uncover interesting craftswork. Bargaining is expected.

ENTERTAINMENT

The two characteristic Portuguese entertainments are bullfights and *fado*, both presented best in Lisbon.

Bullfights in Portugal are a different proposition from their Spanish counterparts. The purpose is not to kill the bull, and fighting is done with lances from horseback. The audience comes to admire the graceful movements and skills of the horse and rider. Since tradition dictates 18th-century dress for the participants, these events constitute memorable spectacles. Teams arrive in carriages and emerge in embroidered vests with flourishes of tricornered plumed hats. The second half of the show consists of a group of men who try to throw the bull. Matches are held from Easter through October. In Lisbon they take place in Campo Pequeno near a metro stop. But the best events are held in the suburb of Vila Franca de Xira, which can be reached from the Santa Apolónia Station, on the river west of the Alfama. Although one pays a 10% premium, the most convenient way to secure a ticket is from the ABEP kiosk in Pr. dos Restauradores or at Av. da Liberdade 140.

Fado, literally "Fate," means a deep song, a Portuguese passion comparable to flamenco in Spain—though consisting only of earthy singing, for there is no dancing involved. Readers of a certain age may remember the song "Lisboa Antiqua," which was a popularization of one *fado* tune. Performances generally take place in a cafe and consist of a singer, almost always a woman, playing plaintive songs on a guitar accompanied in a husky voice. Melodies betray old Middle-Eastern tonalities. The husky sounds tend to disconcert those unfamiliar with the genre at first, though most listeners take to it increasingly as an evening progresses. *Fado* houses generally serve dinner until about 10 p.m., after which the show begins. Dinners are often expensive, but it is not necessary to eat in order to watch the show. One can arrive at 10 p.m. to listen, paying only a drink minimum. After-dinner reservations should be attempted, but are quickly exhausted. A short description of the more authentic *fado* houses—most are in the Bairro Alto—follows.

Senhor do Vinho

R. do Meio-a-Lapa, 18 (west of the Bairro Alto; best visited by taxi).
☎ 397 74 56. Closed Sunday and the last week in December.
Although both the food and drinks are more expensive here than at
most houses, the food is probably the best of all the fado houses and
the singing tends to be authentic.

Amex, Diners, MasterCard and Visa accepted.

Lisboa a Noite

R. des Gaveas, 69 (this street is the first left off Trav. da Queimada
which heads west from the church of São Roque). ☎ 346 85 57.
Closed Sunday. The expensive food is better than most, and this time
it is the owner, Fernanda da Maria, a famous fadista, who sings and
sings very well.   **Amex, Diners, and MasterCard accepted.**

Mascote de Atalaia

R. da Atalaia (from the church of São Roque in the Bairro Alto head
west along Trav. da Queimada to take the fifth left.) This is the real
thing—no food, no professional entertainers, no tourists, just wine
with the locals to listen to whichever fadistas drops in. The quality is
unpredictable, but the expense is low.

DIRECTORY

INFORMATION • The main office is in the Palácio da Foz on the north side
of Pr. dos Restauradores (☎ 346 63 07). Be sure to take one of the
maps they offer. There is another office at the airport (open 24 hours),
and one at Santa Apolónia station.

CITY TOURS • Star, affiliated with American Express, offers half-day tours
for about 4000.00, departing at 9:30 a.m. and 2:30 p.m. It is located
at Av. Sidónio Pais, 4 (☎ 53 98 71), near the Pr. Pombal, and at Pr.
Restauradore 14 (☎ 346 25 01).

TRAINS AND BUSES • There are four separate train stations in Lisbon.
International trains and trains from the north use Santa Apolónia station (☎ 86 41 43; information: 87 60 25). The station is a
15-minute walk along the river east of Praça do Comércio. Rossio station handles passengers from Sintra and Estremadura, the near north.
It is located west of Pr. Rossio (☎ 87 60 25). Electric trains serving
the near beaches Estoril and Cascais leave from Cais do Sodré (☎ 37

01 81) by the river just west of the Praça do Comércio. The cost is less
than $1. Trains for the Algarve and south leave from Sul e Sueste in
Barreiro (☎ 87 71 79) on the south bank of the river. Tickets include
the price of a ferry that leaves the bank at the Praça do Comércio.

The main bus depot is Rodoviária Nacional at Av. Casal Ribeiro, 18
(☎ 53 77 15) near the Pr. Duque de Saldanha (an 8-block walk from
the Pr. Pombal along P. de Melo). Three buses go daily to Faro in the
Algarve, two expressos go to Oporto, and 14 leave for Coimbra.

POST OFFICE AND TELEPHONES • A main post office is in the Pr. dos Restauradores, 58 (☎ 34 70 05). Telephones are available as well.

POLICE • ☎ 346 61 41. Emergencies: ☎ 115.

ADDRESSES

U.S. Embassy • Av. das Forcas Armadas (☎ 726 66 00)

Canadian Embassy • Av. da Liberdade, 144 (☎ 347 48 92)

American Express • Handled by Star, Av. Sidonio Pais, 4A (☎ 53 98 71)

AIRPORT • Portela airport is 8 k northeast of the center of the city and handles both international and domestic flights. By taxi (about 700$00) the trip should take half an hour in traffic. Linha Verde (Green Line) buses depart from the Santa Apolona train station and make stops along Av. de Liberdade for under $2. Most airlines have offices in Pr. Marquês de Pombal, including TAP at #3-A (☎ 57 50 20).

EXCURSIONS

Lisbon serves as a hub for some special excursions. The longest is to **Batalha** ★★★★★, 120 k north. Batalha monastery is the premier Gothic and Manueline structure in the country, outshining even Lisbon's Mostiero dos Jerónimos. With a two-hour train ride each way the visit will consume a day, but by car other sights—such as the picturesque village of **Nazaré** ★ and the monastery of **Alcobaça** ★★★, with special sculpture—could be combined in one excursion. By train lovely **Óbidos** ★★, a walled medieval town, requires a change at Caçem and a trip of almost three hours each way. At less than 100 k away, travel time by car should be an hour and a half. The huge baroque palace complex at **Mafra** ★ is a half-day excursion including a train ride of an hour and a half each way. By car it can be combined with Portugal's version of Versailles at **Queluzb** ★, otherwise a separate train trip. The beauty of **Sintra** ★★★ was immortalized by Byron and can be reached by frequent trains in 45 minutes. For beaches, there are elegant ones at **Cascais** ★ and **Estoril** ★, near to each other as well as to Lisbon, half an hour away. Long, uncrowded beaches surround **Setúbal** ★, 55 miles south of Lisbon, a 45-minute train ride with frequent service. All the foregoing sights are described under their own separate headings in this chapter.

At greater distances, requiring a hotel transfer from Lisbon, there is **Coimbra** ★★★ and the green north; **Tomar** ★★★, **Marvão** ★★, **Elvas** ★ and **Évora** ★★★★ to the east; and the **Algarve** beaches to the south. These sights are described in the "Central and Northern Portugal" chapter, with the exception of the Algarve which has a chapter of its own.

By car, for **Cascais** *and* **Estoril** *follow the river west to scenic N-6 for 25 k, another 2 k for Cascais. For* **Sintra** *take R. Joaquim de Aguiar west from Pr. de Pombal. The street becomes Av. Eng. Duarte Pacheco from which, near the end of the huge Parque Flor-*

estal, N-117 goes north to meet an extension of N-6 for Sintra in 23 k, the final few k. on N-249. For **Mafra** *stay on N-117 for 40 k until it joins N-9 for a final 8 k. For* **Queluz** *stay on N-117 for 8 k.*

For northern points go east at Pr. Pombal on Periera de Melo, which reaches the circle of Pr. Saldanha in three blocks. Take Av. da República north as it becomes Campo Grande with a planted center strip. After the race course on the right, turn left on Mel. Craveiro Lopez, which bends around the airport and changes its name to Est. de Sacavém. Continue along the autoestrada A-1. Exit at Carregado in 37 k. For **Tomar and east** *take N-3 northeast. Exit in 91 k at Entroncamento to take N-110 19 k to Tomar. Take N-1 north for northern destinations. For* **Óbidos** *exit at Rio Maior in 49 k. Take N-114 northwest to Caldas da Rainha in 22 k, turning south on N-8 for the final 7 k. For* **Alcobaça** *exit from N-1 at Cruz da Legua in 84 k to take N-8 west for 16 k. For* **Batalha** *stay on N-1 for 99 k.*

For destinations **east and south** *of Lisbon take the Ponte 25 Abril by following the river west to Av. de Ceuta then north for two blocks to the circle of Largo de Alcantara and turning west to reach the ramp. Autoestrada A-2 reaches* **Setúbal** *in 50 k. From there N-10 east for 35 k to Cruzamento de Pegões joins N-4 to* **Évora** *in another 67 k. For the* **Algarve** *take N-10 from Setúbal for 21 k to Marateca to join N-5 south for 31 k to Alcácer do Sal, where the designation becomes N-120. Bear right in 18 k to continue on N-120 along the coast to the western Algarve in about 180 k. Alternatively, continue to Brandola to take N-259 southeast, turning south on N-262 in about 20 k toward Azinheira dos Barros, and stay on the road as it becomes N-264 for a leg of 204 k.*

MAFRA ★

Population: 10,153
Area code: 061; zip code: 2640

40 k north of **Lisbon**, *directions for Mafra are included in the "Excursion" section of Lisbon. If coming from* **Óbidos and north** *along N-8 turn west at Malveira for 8 k.*

The monument here is a palace-monastery, again a king's offering in return for a favor from God. It was commissioned by João V in thanks—after three heirless years of marriage—for the birth of his daughter. Construction began in 1717 on this baroque palace-church-monastery complex covering ten acres. Eighteen years and two German architects later the monastery was completed—built, it is said, of Brazilian gold and diamonds.

The king wanted to overwhelm, and drained a rich treasury to do so. Fifty thousand workers were employed at the height of the construction. There are over 800 rooms in the complex, faced by 4500 windows. The length of the facade exceeds 200 yards. In the center is the classic pediment and high belltowers of the basilica, from either side of which the wings of the palace stretch to terminate in bulbous domed extensions. Most of the stone is marble. The left (south) wing housed the Queen and her staff, the right was for the King, and night visits entailed an appreciable walk.

Mosteiro de Mafra   ★★
Open Wed.-Mon. 10 a.m. to noon and 2-5 p.m. Closed Tues. Admission: 300$00, for guided tours of the palace (200$00 in winter. Entrance to the complex is through the Queen's door, the third left from the basilica. The **basilica** is elegant in proportion and consists of a fine barrel-vault ceiling on fluted columns, culminating in a large rose-and-white cupola. All the decoration is rich marbles. In particular the ornate sacristy is virtually a museum of marble's variety.

The **palace** may be visited only by a guided tour. When inspecting the ornate furniture keep in mind that when João VI fled to Brazil in 1807 to avoid capture by the French, he took the best furniture from this palace with him. What we see today is his rejects. Special rooms include a trophy room in which everything is made of antlers or skins; the mirrored queen's dressing room; the audience chamber with a trompe l'oeil ceiling; and an ornate throne room.

The **monastery** which, at its height, held 300 monks, surrounds a courtyard behind the basilica. Its gilded rococo library is astounding.

WHERE TO STAY

Albergaria Castelão   3rd-class ★
Av. 25 de Abril (opposite the palace). Rooms: 35. *81 20 50; FAX 516 98; Telex 43488.* This is a hotel of no pretensions, with very comfortable bedrooms. Its price is comfortably moderate, and it serves the best meals in town, at reasonable prices.

NAZARÉ ★

Population: 10,265
Area code: 062; zip code: 2450

Directions from **Lisbon** *are included in the "Excursion" section of that city. From* **Coimbra** *and north, see the directions under* **Alcobaça**.

For decades Nazaré has been described as a picture-postcard village. Naturally, people flocked to see it, until their numbers almost completely obscure the picture. Once fishermen pulled their boats out of the surf by ox-teams. Crowned by long black-stocking caps on their heads, the men wore trousers so often mended with patches that they seemed a kind of tattersall. Women wore seven petticoats of different colors under flared skirts and covered their heads with colorful scarfs above large gold earrings. But today a new harbor obviates the hauling of boats from the water, and finding a local person in traditional apparel, amid the swarms of summer tourists, is difficult.

Still, a fine beach remains, and locals are discernable in winter. A special boat is peculiar to this one town in Europe. Descended from Phoenician caiques, the brightly striped boats have a high prow with a pair of magical signs—most often large eyes—painted on opposite sides to ward off evil. Models are sold throughout the village, as are heavy fisherman's sweaters.

The modern town runs along the beach. Parallel alleys of whitewashed cottages at the north end house the fishermen and display clothing on omnipresent washlines. North of the beach, upon a cliff served by a funicular (in season only), stands the tiny original town, called the **Sitio**. Here is the attractive church of **Nossa Senhor da Nazaré**, with a vast interior whose transepts are covered in a profusion of 18th-century *azulejos*. By repute, the statue of the Virgin inside was brought here in the fourth century from Palestinian Nazare, hence the name of this village. South of the church, at the cliff edge, is the **Ermida da Memoria**, a tiny chapel covered floor to ceiling with *azulejos*. It commemorates the spot where a noble in hot pursuit of a stag, watched the deer fall over the cliff and realized that he could not prevent his own horse and self from following. However, his prayer to the Virgin of Nazaré was heard and answered. His horse miraculously stopped at the edge. The view over the new town and sea is lovely.

WHERE TO STAY

None of the hotels in Nazaré will break a reasonable budget, but rooms are almost impossible to secure in the summer. Reservations are a must during that season.

MODERATE ($50-$99)

Riba-Mar   **P3rd-class ★**

R. Gomes Freire, 9 (on the northern end of the beach). Rooms: 23. ☎ *51 11 58; Telex 43383). Closed the last week of December.* This hotel's decor reflects local character and offers pleasant views of the beach from room balconies. Bedrooms are comfortable and feel like those at an inn. Tasty, but inexpensive, meals are served in the restaurant.

Maré   **2nd-class**

R. Mouzinho de Albuquerque, 8 (a block behind the Riba-Mar). Rooms: 36. ☎ *56 12 26; FAX 56 17 50; Telex 15245.* The modern lobby is a cozy introduction to bedrooms that are serviceable, but nothing more.

Praia   **2nd-class**

Av. Vieira Guimarães, 39 (opposite the market, beside the bus station). Rooms: 40. ☎ *56 14 23; FAX 56 14 36Telex 16329. Closed December.* This hotel is an unattractive six-story '60s-modern building that provides reasonably comfortable accommodations, although pushing the moderate category.

WHERE TO EAT

The beach is lined with moderately priced restaurants. Two of the better ones are described below.

INEXPENSIVE TO MODERATE (UNDER $50)

Beira-Mar

Av. da República, 40 (near the Mar Bravo). ☎ *56 13 58. Open March-November.* Although meat dishes are available, most clients come for the fish. A wait for tables may be necessary at this very popular place.

Mar Bravo

Pr. Sousa Oliveira, 75 (next to Riba-Mar). ☎ *55 11 80. Open in season.* Special menus keep the prices in this popular restaurant low.

ÓBIDOS ★ ★

Population: 825
Area code: 062; zip code: 2510

Directions from **Lisbon** *are included in the "Excursion" section of that city. From* **Coimbra**, *and north, take N-1 south for 120 k to Rio Maior, then turn northwest along N-114 for 17 k to Caldas da Rainha, and finally south on N-8 for 8 k.*

Óbidos is so quaint that it hardly seems real. This tiny walled town surrounding a proper castle has changed hardly at all since the middle ages. Originally a sea bay lapping the hill of the town necessitated a fortress to guard against seaborne attacks. When the Moors seized the fortress they surrounded the small village that had grown around the fortress with perimeter walls. After Christians reconquered the village in 1148, they fitted the fortress out as a castle and several times restored the village walls—the last time being in the 16th century. By then the bay beside the town had entirely silted up, leaving the fortifications without any purpose, and reducing the importance of the village, which preserved it from change. In 1228 King Dinis paused at Óbidos on his way elsewhere. His wife so admired its charm that he gave it to her as a present. By tradition Óbidos remained a fief of each Queen of Portugal until 1833.

The village is so small that it takes only an hour to savor, but the maze of curling streets should not be attempted by car. Park beside the main gate, the Porta da Vila, and tour the four streets on foot.

Azulejos mark a shrine just inside the Porta da Vila. The main street of the village is the narrow R. Direita, on the left with a center gully. It twists past little whitewashed houses—roofed in orange tiles, with flowers on windowsills and by doorways—to lead into the main square of the village around a pillory and fountain in the center. The tree-shaded **Church of Santa Maria** ★ dates to the late 17th century, but the Romanesque portal shows earlier antecedents. In 1444, 10-year-old Dom Afonso V married his 8-year-old cousin here. The walls are covered with floral *azulejos*, the ceiling is painted with arabesques, fanciful Brazilian natives, and cherubs. On the left wall is an unexpected finely-detailed renaissance tomb. To the right of the main altar are captivating 17th-century paintings by a woman from Seville, named Josefa de Óbidos who was cloistered nearby. *(Open daily 9:30 a.m. to 12:30 p.m. and 2:30-7 p.m.; in winter to 5 p.m.)*

The **municipal museum** ★ is also located in the square. In truth the museum is not very interesting except for one room devoted to the paintings of Josefa de Óbidos. There is an admirable quality of passion about the paintings, conveyed by their diffused light and subtlety. *(Open Tuesday-Sunday 9:30 a.m. to 12:30 p.m. and 2-5 p.m.; admission: 200$00.)*

R. Direita ends at a church, beside which an arch leads into the castle courtyard, now used for parking. To the left, stairs ascend the crenelated **ramparts** for a walk with nice views of the countryside. A fortunate hole in the walls looks out on one of the charming windmills of the area. The **castle** ★ itself is suitably imposing. Square towers anchor its corners, the right-hand one being the castle keep, while round towers incongruously line the rear. In the 16th century the castle was outfitted as a palace when the Manueline door and front windows were added. Today it serves as one of Portugal's most atmospheric pousadas. Anyone can walk inside for a look.

WHERE TO STAY

Although few visitors spend the night in Óbidos, the village contains not one, but three special hotels.

EXPENSIVE ($100-$200)

Pousada do Castelo   1st-class ★ ★ ★

Paço Real. Rooms: 6, plus 3 suites. ☎ *95 91 05; FAX 95 91 48; Telex 15540.* Not only does this hotel feel like a castle, it's the genuine article. Up a stone stair to the baronial hall, with a suit of armor along the way, stone corridors lead to rooms with wood ceilings and windows deeply set in the thick castle walls. Here one can be a knight for a night. But only a few have the chance, since just nine parties can be accommodated at a time. Booking must be done months ahead for this justifiably popular pousada. Expensive meals are served in the dining room, also baronial with its beamed ceiling. Meals are not the best value, but if one is staying elsewhere, a lunch or dinner here does provide a leisurely look at the inside of the castle.

MODERATE ($50-$99)

Estalagem do Convento   2nd-class ★ ★

R. Dom João de Ornelas (just outside the town walls). Rooms: 31. ☎ *95 92 17; FAX 95 91 59; Telex 44906.* Installed in a modest former convent, country furniture makes this hotel special. Large wooden pieces line the corridors and inhabit some of the rooms. The bedrooms are very comfortable. Good food is served in the restaurant for a very moderate price.

Albergaria Rainha Santa Isabel   3rd-class ★ ★

R. Direita. Rooms: 20. ☎ *95 91 15; FAX 95 91 15; Telex 14069.* Installed in one of the old houses in the heart of the village, this hotel provides a sense of the aged village atmosphere. Bedrooms are cozily furnished and there is an elevator for the upper floors.

WHERE TO EAT

The pousada is at hand for expensive dining in a medieval atmosphere, and the Hotel do Convento offers tasty food, but the best value in the village is described below.

Alcaide   ★

R. Direita. ☎ *95 92 20. Closed Monday and November.* The dining room is festooned with ivy and the tables are dressed with checkered cloths; a balcony outside overlooks an orchard. The owner is from the Azores so menu choices include unusual dishes. Everything is tasty, and the prices hug the low end of the moderate scale.

Amex, Diners, MasterCard and Visa accepted.

QUELUZ ★

Population: 47,864
Area code: 01; zip code: 2745

Only 12 k north of **Lisbon**, *directions for Queluz are included in the "Excursion" section of Lisbon.* **Sintra** *is 15 k west along N-6.*

By a tradition going back to the mid-17th century, the second son of Portugal's king was given the use of a hunting lodge at Queluz. In 1747 the second son was Dom Pedro, who extensively rebuilt the lodge to transform it into a summer palace. His wife, Maria, had been betrothed to Louis XV and greatly admired Versailles, where she had lived for a while. Much of the present palace was constructed by an imported French architect as a sort of Portuguese Versailles, complete with formal gardens. By a tortuous course Maria eventually came to the throne, and this palace was her favorite residence—and the place to which she was confined when she went insane. Although the palace is surrounded by apartment buildings today, the interior transports the visitor into the baroque age.

Palácio Real de Queluz

Open Wed.-Mon. 10 a.m. to 1 p.m. and 2-5 p.m. Admission: 400$00 for guided tour of the palace, 200$00 in winter. The Ambassadors' Hall is covered with a fine painting of a concert. Lovely *azulejos* of oranges line the corridor. A very French boudoir of the queen prefaces the columned boudoir of the later regent, Dona Carlota, painted with scenes from *Don Quixote*. The breakfast room, next, is charming. After a mirrored dining room with a fine Arraiolos carpet, come three rooms for princesses and a music room with almost-perfect acoustics. Glass and crystal in profusion characterize the throne room. The chapel contains paintings by the queen and her sisters. The formal gardens outside are serene.

SETÚBAL ★

Population: 97,762
Area code: 065; zip code: 2900

55 k north of **Lisbon**; *directions are included in the "Excursion" section of Lisbon. Since the autoestrada A-2 runs from just east of Setúbal straight to Lisbon, it is on the preferred route to the capital from either the east or south. See directions from specific individual locations in appropriate chapters.*

The industrial center and port of Setúbal makes it the third-largest city in Portugal. Although the city is not particularly attractive, neither is it as ugly as its economic functions might suggest. What makes it worth a stop is the intriguing small church of Jesus, the first Manueline building, and the fine beaches in its environs.

*From **Lisbon**, **south** and **east**, Setúbal is entered along Estrada da Graça which feeds into the continuation of Av. Luisa Todi, with a planted center strip. In a few blocks the large park of Das Escolas appears on the right. Here parking is available.*

From the parking lot head east for one long block along Av. Luisa Todi to turn left on Av. 22 de Dezembro, which reaches the church of Jesus in about the same distance. From the bus station on Av. 5 de Outubro or the train station just east, head west along Av. 22 de Dezembro for about four blocks.

Igreja de Jesus   ★ ★

Open Tuesday-Sunday 9 a.m. to noon and 2-5 p.m. Closed Monday and holidays. Admission: free. This hall-church was begun in the last decade of the 15th century by Boytac, the architect who originated the Manueline architectural style. He finished the church, but not the adjoining convent, because his master called him for the grander commission of the Hieronymite monastery in Belém. Given the shock of the interior even today, one can imagine how inventive the device of twisted columns would have seemed at the time. True, the columns are merely two pillars twisted into one mass, but they appear to grow down from the ceiling rather than support it from the ground, as columns had always done in the past. The effect is arresting, and led to the twisting, living shapes of the developed Manueline style.

A wainscotting of lovely *azulejos* from the 17th century follows both walls, and a particularly harmonious design of tiles lines the altar.

Outside is a cloister with a monastery surrounding it, now serving as the **Museu da Cidad**. On the ground floor are some nice *azulejos*. The upper floors are devoted to wonderful primitive paintings attributed to an anonymous "Master of Setúbal." Clearly influenced by the stiff figures of van Eyke, the artist managed to convey a compassion in the faces that is his (or her) own.

WHERE TO STAY

Unless one sleeps in the castle described below, there is no reason to spend the night in Setúbal when pleasant beach accommodations are so close (as described in "Excursions" below). If castles appeal, there is a lovely one, also described below, 8 k north of Setúbal in Palmela.

EXPENSIVE ($100-$200)

Pousada de São Filipe   1st-class ★ ★

R. São Filipe (From Av. Luisa Todi take the second right after the Parque das Escolas. Almost immediately turn left on Estrada do Castelo de São Filipe which winds up to the pousada.) Rooms: 14. ☎ *52 38 44; Telex 44655.* The Spanish built this castle at the end of the 16th century to defend the kingdom of Portugal which they had appropriated and to cow the citizens in the city below with its guns. They chose a spot with a wonderful view that visitors to the pousada now enjoy. Guests stay in the former guards' quarters in bedrooms that are charmingly rustic. Getting to them requires wandering the castle corridors, which is no chore at all. Reservations are usually necessary.

In Palmela:

Pousada do Castelo de Palmela   1st-class ★ ★ ★

From Setúbal, take Av. Cinco de Outubro east from the church of Jesus. Turn left in 4 blocks onto Av. Portela, which becomes N-252. Just before the auto-estrada, take N-379 going west.) Rooms: 28. ☎ *235 12 26; FAX 233 04 40; Telex 42290.* This is a hotel whose grounds merit half a day's sightseeing. It is situated in the confines of Palmela castle whose fortress dates from Afonso I in the 12th century. West of the castle is the 15th-century monastery in which the pousada is lodged. A former mosque, made over into a church, in turn destroyed in the 1755 earthquake, stands in ruins in front of the castle. Around the whole are crude perimeter walls built by the Moors, surrounded by a complex 17th-century outer wall. The pousada is an example of the most tasteful sort of renovation, preserving the feel of the renaissance monastery while providing every modern comfort. On the other hand, the bedrooms, lodged in monks' cells, are spartan, although their views are anything but.

EXCURSIONS

There are beaches south on the peninsula of Troia, and beaches west along the Serra da Arrabida mountain range.

TRÓIA

The 8-k strip of sand and pine trees that separates the river Sado from the ocean is a highly developed beach resort, including an 18-hole Robert Trent Jones golf course. Despite the development of this peninsula, unspoiled beach remains on the ocean side and south, and moderate accommodations are available.

A car ferry leaves the commercial port of Setúbal (the Doca Comércio) every half hour in season (every hour out-of-season) for a 20-minute trip.

Aparthotel Tróia, **Rosamar** and **Magnoliamar** are three hotels forming the Torralta complex, which includes every amenity from a baby-sitting service to golf. All are apartment hotels, sleekly modern and charmless, but their prices are moderate. ☎ *442 22, for the former,* ☎ *441 51 for the latter two.*

SERRA DA ARRÁBIDA

The Arrábida mountain range lines the 40-k southern coast of the Setúbal peninsula, forming high limestone cliffs over the ocean, broken by sandy coves. The scenery is dramatic.

Follow Av. Luisa Todi west to N-379-1. After about 20 k signs for **Portinho do Arrábida** *point to a steep and narrow 1 k descent. For safety it is best to leave one's car at the top, though the walk back is tiring. The bay forms a perfect curve of fine white sand embracing clear waters. Unfortunately, there are no hotels, although some private houses accept guests.*

After Portinho N-379-1 climbs north for 6 k to meet N-379 going west. 5 k of rough road leads to Santana, just past which a left turn toward the south brings Sesimbra in 2 k.

SESIMBRA

Sesimbra remains a thriving seaport, although the developers have arrived. Its lovely beaches are less spoiled, however, than comparable ones elsewhere, and the fishermen are real. A ruined castle stands high upon the hill.

EXPENSIVE ($100-$200)

Do Mar   1st-class ★ ★

R. Combatentes do Ultamar, 10 (west of town). Rooms: 168. ☎ *223 33 26; FAX 223 38 88; Telex 13883.* This is a luxury resort complex terraced down a hill. The architecture is interesting, including an aviary in the lobby. Rooms are starkly modern and comfortable, but the bathrooms could be larger. However, ocean views atone for any imperfection.

MODERATE ($50-$99)

Espadarte   3rd-class

Av. 25 de Abril. Rooms: 80. ☎ *223 31 89; Telex 14699.* Some of the rooms are noisy, all are small, some are dingy and old, while others brand-new. But the low price and a balcony overlooking the sea makes a stay worthwhile.

N-379 continues west for 12 k to Cabo Espichel, an awesomely wild and windy cape.

SINTRA ★ ★ ★

Population: 20,574
Area code: 01; zip code: 2710

Sintra is located 28 k northwest of **Lisbon***; directions are included in the "Excursion" section of Lisbon. From* **Mafra** *take N-9 south for 23 k.*

The magical mountains surrounding Sintra are lush with camellias, gardenias, bougainvilla and eucalyptus in season. Byron lauded this "Eden" in *Childe Harolde* and wrote his mother that it is "perhaps the most delightful (village) in Europe." There is also a Black Forest quality about the mountains, which appropriately shelter a castle worthy of King Ludwig of Bavaria. All in all, Sintra is one of the highlights of Portugal. In the most dramatic setting imaginable, Sintra offers a palace, a fantasy castle and a ruined fortress of the Moors. A day would cover the sights comfortably. While tourists arrive by the bus-full, they are absorbed into the vastness of surrounding nature.

Actually three Sintras wrap around the mountain. The Vila Velha clusters near the Palácio Real of Portugal's kings. Separated to the north is the new town, called Estefania, with the bus and train station along the way, and to the south is the formerly separate town of São Pedro, which hosts a famous crafts market.

From **Lisbon** *N-249 becomes the winding Estrada de Chão de Meninos, then Av. D. F. de Almeida, to end at Largo de Albuquerque. Turn left here along R. Dr. Alfredo Costa which bends right to change its name to Av. Volta do Duche, leading into the parking of the Pr. de República beside the Palácio Real. From* **Mafra** *Av. Henrique Salgado leads into the Largo de Albuquerque, from which point the Lisbon directions can be followed.*

Palácio Real

Open daily 10 a.m. to 1 p.m. and 2-5 p.m. Admission: 400$00 for guided tour. Kings and queens favored the mountain air of Sintra for their summers since the end of the 14th century. Even before, the Moors had built a summer palace on the spot, which Dom João I tore down to build the central, and oldest part of the present palace. Additions were made over the years—including the left 16th-century wing added by Manuel I—producing a jumble of styles, all dominated by two clumsy conical chimneys. Individual windows are lovely.

Magnificent rooms inside are sprinkled with some of the finest *azulejos* in the world. Past the kitchen in the Sala dos Arabes is the first example of these—blue, green and white Mudejar tiles, among the oldest in the country, imported from Spain in the first decade of the 16th century. The adjacent chapel has an *azulejo* floor and a fine ceiling. After the Sala de Afonso VI, whose *azulejo* floor is said to have been worn away by that king's pacing during 9 years of imprisonment, comes a Chinese room with an ivory pagoda donated by the Emperor of China in 1809. The Sala dos Brasoães is roofed by a remarkable artesonado ceiling of the coats of arms of Portugal's first families. The one blank octagon held the blazon of the Coelho family, erased for their part in a conspiracy against João II. Farther along is the Sala das Sireias with lovely *azulejos* of mermaids playing instruments. Next is the Sala de Pegas (Magpies), named for the birds on the ceiling which hold a rose and the legend *Por bem* ("for the good"). Tradition had João I ordering the multiple images after being caught by his wife in the act of presenting a rose to a lady of the court and uttering "It's all for the best," a story that hardly makes sense. More likely, the magpies represent the King, and the rose represents his Queen who was indeed from the House of Lancaster. Across the central patio the Sala dos Cisnes can be admired. Named for the swans embellishing the magnificent ceiling, the woodwork is also masterly.

There are various options for the 3 k, almost-vertical climb to the Castelo dos Mouros and the Palácio da Pena atop the highest peaks in the Sintra mountains. The most pleasant journey is to walk, encouraged by the thought that the return is downhill. A map is available from the tourist office. Alternatively, a taxi will cost about 2000$00 for the round trip. In summer buses travel daily at 10:45 a.m., 3 p.m. and 4 p.m. for 150$00. For romantics there are horse-drawn carriages that will cost about 4000$00. By car head west (uphill) from the palace, past the post office on R. Pedroso. At the Estalagem dos Cavaleiros, now boarded up, where Byron stayed, turn sharply left and just as sharply right at the next opportunity. The road twists and winds back on itself until reaching a parking place. From here a 10-minute walk remains up to the Moors' Castle. For the Palace of Pena continue to a "T," then turn right as signs direct.

Castelo dos Mouros ★

Open Tues.-Sun. 8 a.m. to sunset. Closed Mon. Admission: free.
Although called a castle, this was actually a fortress. It was built in the eighth or early ninth century, then captured by Christians in the 12th. Since then it has fallen into romantic ruins, although the perimeter wall remains with corner towers. Some restoration was attempted in the 19th century, but given up. On a clear day there are heavenly

views from atop a tower inside the walls. Also on the grounds is a Romanesque chapel dating to the twelfth century Reconquest.

Palácio Nacional da Pena   ★★

Open Tues.-Sun. 10 a.m. to 1 p.m. and 2-4:45 p.m. Closed Mon. Admission: 400$00. Queen Maria II came to the throne in 1836 and married Friedrich of Saxe Coburg-Gotha, an old titled German family of three cousins, each of whom married queens. Cousin Leopold became King of the Belgians, cousin Albert was the consort of Queen Victoria in England and Fernando II, as the Portuguese know him, became the king of Portugal. A tinge of homesickness led him to import a German architect to build a palace at Sintra. What resulted is a fantasy that outdoes Ludwig of Bavaria's fairytale castles from a quarter of a century later. It is part Moorish, part Gothic, part baroque, tinged with Manueline—a confection of crenellations, minarets, turrets and drawbridges—a castle for the child in us all. Over the drawbridge and through a tunnel are remains from a Manueline monastery with fine *azulejos* and a lovely alabaster altar. The rooms of the palace remain almost exactly as they were in 1910 when the royal family fled to exile. Their taste, however one evaluates it, is therefore evident to all.

WHERE TO STAY

We sympathize with anyone who does not want to leave Sintra after a short day. Mountain nights are wonderful, the Moors' Castle is lighted, and there are a number of exceptional accommodations in the area.

EXPENSIVE ($100-$200)

Palácio de Seteais   1st-class ★★★★

Av. Bocage, 8, Seteais (1.5 k outside Sintra on N-375, which is reached by going west from the palace on R. Pedroso). Rooms: 30. ☎ *923 32 00; FAX 923 42 77; Telex 1441.* No hotel in Portugal feels as much like a French chateaux. This one was built in the 18th century by a Dutch businessman, but taken over by the Marquis of Marialva before transformation into a hotel. The appropriately long driveway leads up to the palace atop a hill. Most rooms overlook palatial formal gardens, with views to the sea on clear days. All the rooms are perfect, including the bedrooms fitted with antiques or look-alikes. Three bedrooms incorporate hand-painted murals. There is a pool and two tennis courts. Everything is perfect—except the coolness of the management, and the fact that reservations almost certainly will be needed. Go for an overpriced lunch or just a cocktail to see the place, if you cannot spend the night.

Quinta de São Thiago   2nd-class ★★★

Estrada de Monserrate (about 1 k further along the road past the Palácio de Seteais above, then a marked turn along a steep bumpy road). Rooms: 14. ☎ *923 29 23.* This is a lovely 16th-century villa owned by a British and Portuguese couple who extend themselves for their guests. Much of the furniture is antique and there is the feel of staying in an elegant house rather than a hotel. A swimming pool and a tennis court are provided, but not air conditioning. Reservations should be made in advance.

Quinta da Capela   **2nd-class ★ ★**
Estrada da Monserrate (about 2 k further along the road past the Palácio de Seteais above, past Monserrate, then look carefully for a marked turn). Rooms: 10. ☎ 929 34 05; FAX 929 34 25. On the other hand, this 16th-century building looks more like a farm than a villa. But, inside it is delightful. Two outlying cottages contain kitchenettes, although the bedrooms in the main house are more elegant. There is a tiny old chapel in the garden, a pool and lovely views.

Tivoli Sintra   **1st-class ★**
Pr. da República. Rooms: 75. ☎ 923 35 05; FAX 923 15 72; Telex 42314. This hotel of modern design is an affront to its surroundings, but the traditional decor inside is more successful. Bedrooms are unusually large, comfortable, and the balcony views are sylvan.

MODERATE ($50-$99)

Central   **3rd-class ★**
Pr. da República, 35. Rooms: 14. ☎ 923 09 63. Its charm is its old-fashionedness. Each bedroom is individually decorated with homey pieces of furniture.

Estalagem da Raposa   **4th-class ★**
R. Dr. Alfredo Costa, 3 (along the street that leads to Estefania, the new town, near the train station). Rooms: 8. ☎ 923 04 65. The inviting look is that of a private house, set back from the street by a garden. Bedrooms are comfortable and clean.

INEXPENSIVE (UNDER $50)

Casa Adelaide   **3rd-class**
Av. Guilherme Gomes Fernandes, 11 (just before R. Dr. Alfredo Costa bends left, turn right into Largo Virgilio Horta, then left again past the police station). Rooms: 10. ☎ 923 08 73. The rooms are homey and some provide views.

WHERE TO EAT

The moderately priced food in the restaurant of the **Tivoli Sintra** is probably the best in town, but there is little ambiance to the dining room. The dining room at the **Palácio de Seteais** has ambiance to spare, but over-priced, unimaginative food. Galeria Real below combines the two.

MODERATE ($20-$50)

Galeria Real
R. Tude de Sousa (on the main street in São Pedro). ☎ 923 16 61. Closed Monday evening. This is a pretty, second-floor restaurant located in a warren of antique shops. The ceiling is hand-painted beams, the floors

tiled, and flowers decorate each table. Codfish souffle is the delicious specialty. Otherwise the menu is not adventuresome.

INEXPENSIVE (UNDER $20)

Alcobaça ★

R. da Padarias, 7 (the street runs uphill from the tourist office, just west of the Palácio Real). ☎ *923 16 51. Closed Wednesday and December.* This is an eminently local place that serves standard Portuguese dishes at very fair prices. If the cooking wasn't good, it wouldn't be so crowded.

SHOPPING

A large crafts fair is held in the township of São Pedro on the second and fourth Sunday of the month, providing examples of all the local arts. For those who miss the fair, samplings of local crafts are on sale at **Central Bazaar** next to the Hotel Central in the Pr. da República in front of the palace.

DIRECTORY

INFORMATION • Located at the south end of the Pr. da República (☎ 923 11 57).

TRAINS AND BUSES • The train station is located on Av. Dr. Miguel Bombarda (☎ 923 26 05), halfway between the Vila Velha and the new town of Estefania. Trains serve Lisbon every 15 minutes, stopping at Queluz. Trains connect with Óbidos, but connections elsewhere are difficult.

The bus station is across the street from the train station and is best for surrounding towns.

POST OFFICE AND TELEPHONES • Located across from the Office of Tourism (☎ 923 11 57).

POLICE • Located in Largo Dr. Virgilio Horta, which is to the left of R. Dr. Alfredo Costa that connects the Vila Velha with Estefania (☎ 923 34 00). For emergencies: ☎ 115.

EXCURSIONS

Sintra is readily combined with **Mafra**, 20 k north or with **Queluz**, 20 k east. Descriptions are contained in this chapter, under those respective headings. For Mafra, follow the directions at the beginning of the Sintra entry in reverse. For Queluz see the directions in the "Excursion" section of the Lisbon description.

A pleasant excursion for those interested in wine is to the remarkable vineyards of **Colares**, 6 k west of Sintra. What makes its wines special is that vine roots are buried deep in sand which protected them from the phylloxera blight that struck Europe in 1865. All other vines in Europe succumbed and had to be grafted to American roots that were immune to the blight. Today only a Colares red is made from true European grapes. The

Adega Regional de Colares promotes these wines and may be visited. Purchases are possible.

THE ALGARVE

The beach at Praia da Rocha.

HISTORICAL PROFILE:
THE END OF THE MONARCHY AND ITS AFTERMATH

When the last survivor of the house of Avís died in 1580, the only
direct claim to the crown belonged to Felipe II of Spain, who bribed
and lobbied his way to the throne, bringing 60 years of Spanish rule
to Portugal. Although Spanish rulers initially respected Portuguese
institutions and left the governing of the country to native Portuguese, they increased their control as time passed, fostering growing

resentment. What followed seems more a soap opera than academic history.

The most powerful Portuguese noble of the time was the Duke of Bragança, the overlord of a third of a million people. Fearing that he might serve as a rallying point for rebellions, the Spanish tried to seduce him with power, giving him license to raise troops to preserve civil order. The Duke used the distraction of a civil war in Spain to turn these troops against the Spanish and conquer Portugal in a matter of days. He crowned himself João IV in 1640, beginning Portugal's long last dynasty.

A number of Portuguese nobles still believed, however, that their fortunes lay with Spain and resettled across the border. The commander of the Portuguese colony of Ceuta in Morocco handed its control to Spain, which has kept it ever since. By 1656, after inconclusive battles and vain attempts at diplomacy, João died, still seeking international recognition for himself and his monarchy. At age 13 his son Afonso VI was crowned king. Some childhood disease had partially paralyzed Afonso's left arm and leg and slowed his speech and understanding. When he married the daughter of the Duke of Savoy, he celebrated alone in bed by eating while his bride entertained the guests. His wife soon departed for a convent to petition the Pope for an annulment, circumstances that permitted no heir to ensue. Afonso's obvious incompetence forced him to resign in favor of his normal brother Pedro who, after the annulment of Afonso's marriage, married his brother's wife and took control of the state.

In time Pedro's son João V came to the throne, a well-educated, shy young man. He married Maria Ana, a daughter of the Archduke of Austria. When three years had passed with no heir, João promised God that he would build a magnificent monastery if his wife were delivered of a child. After his wish was fulfilled, João constructed the sumptuous monastery-palace of Mafra. To produce the skilled craftsmen that project required, he established a school for artisans, one of whom was Joaquim de Castro, who later sculpted Lisbon's most famous statue, that of José I in the center of the Terreiro do Paço square. João built hospitals and fountains, founded libraries, and created Portugal's Royal Academy of History. He died in 1750.

João was succeeded by José I, as indolent a man as any king who ever reigned. He spent his days playing cards, listening to opera, or making outings to the estuary at Belém. At 8 p.m. he would return to his Lisbon palace but not present himself for affairs of state until 11 p.m. Official business consisted of signing papers; he left governing to a virtual dictator—Sebastião José de Carvalloe Melo, Count of Oeiras and Marquis of Pombal, nicknamed "the Pasha."

Despite his titles, Pombal descended from a mere cavalry officer, but he had used an uncle in the government and a marriage above his station to achieve the post of prime minister by the time he was 31. He claimed expertise in economics, a sorely needed science in a country bankrupt from the long effort to free itself from Spain. Pombal found inspiration in England's dynamic middle class and capitalist system, and tried to impose a similar economy on Portugal. Portugal, however, lacked both England's traditions and its significant middle class, so he was able to establish only the semblance, not the substance, of an English economy. A company created to control the Brazilian trade, for example, modeled on Britain's East India Company, went quickly bankrupt.

Pombal's power, so strong that he ruled as a virtual dictator for a quarter of a century, stemmed from his fortitude after the great earthquake in Lisbon in 1755. The ground shook for ten minutes, followed by two series of aftershocks, then fire, and finally a tidal wave that reached as far as the shores of England. The heart of the city was leveled. For nine months the king and court lived in tents, immobilized by an awareness of the magnitude of the destruction and daunted by the problem of how it could be repaired. Pombal stepped forward to rebuild the capital. He constructed broad avenues leading from the Terreiro do Paço, where the former palace had stood, and lined them with classic buildings in place of former rococo structures. In the center of the main square he placed a cherubic statue of his king.

The king appreciated Pombal's achievement. In turn, Pombal, empowered, set out to further increase his control at the expense of the powerful nobles. An attempted assassination of the King gave Pombal his opportunity to harass them, although there were voices that murmured that the ambush had about it more of the feel of Pombal than of the nobles. Pombal suspended the normal rules of justice for this case he called "regicide" while his investigators and police interrogated one lord after another. When the inquiry was over, the mighty had been cowed and a score had lost their heads. Now almost all offices of power, in both the government and the church, were held by a relative or a henchman of Pombal. Pombal reorganized the educational system to teach Portuguese instead of Latin grammar for the first time. He established a Royal Board of Censorship which proscribed the writings of Hobbes, Locke, Voltaire, and any others who intimated that a king's power might be less than absolute.

When King José I died in 1777, his daughter, as regent, called Pombal to visit and summarily fired him. Five years later, under indictment for, but as yet unconvicted of embezzlement, Pombal died. If Portugal verged on bankruptcy before Pombal, it reached destitution after him. Pay for civil servants fell months in arrears; the royal bulls, horses, and mules were sold to raise cash, and worse was to come.

Revolution in France had elevated Napoléon to Emperor. He soon pressured Portugal to renounce her ancient alliance with England, with whom he was at war. When Portugal agreed only to neutrality, Napoléon invaded, frightening the royal family and court to board 15 ships for Brazil, where they set up a monarchy in exile. England did not forsake her old ally, sending 16,000 troops under Sir Arthur Wellesly for Portugal's defense. They defeated the French, who withdrew to Spain, which Napoléon had taken in the meantime. Again the French invaded Portugal, but this time Wellesly followed them back to Spain where he defeated them at Talavera. Wellesly was rewarded for his victory with the title of Duke of Wellington. When, in 1810, the French attempted one more time to take Portugal, Wellington's troops met them in the stately forest of Buçaço and sent them home for good.

Even after this Peninsular War had ended, Portugal's monarch remained abroad enjoying the congenial climate of Brazil. A regency tried to rule with English assistance, but the liberalism sweeping Europe erupted into a revolution in Portugal, producing a new kind of Parliament based on proportional representation rather than inherited titles. The members invited the king to return, providing that he accept the status of constitutional monarch. King João VI returned in 1821 after a 13-year sojourn abroad, leaving his eldest son, Dom Pedro, as his regent in Brazil. João formally accepted a new constitution, but his wife and his second son, Don Miguel, remained unrepentent absolutists. When the King left Lisbon to quash a revolution they had fomented in Sintra, the frightened Parliament, without its monarch in attendance, dissolved itself. João VI died in 1826 after granting Brazil independence.

The son who had remained behind in Brazil thus became Pedro II, Emperor of Brazil, and simultaneously Pedro IV, King of Portugal. Pedro preferred his life in Rio de Janeiro to prospects in his homeland, so he agreed to give his Portuguese crown to his brother Don

Miguel, the absolutist, if he would marry Pedro's daughter, Maria. Miguel took over the government in 1828 but neglected to marry his niece. To protect Maria's inheritance, Pedro abdicated his Brazilian crown to come to reclaim Portugal. Miguel besieged him in Oporto, but Pedro broke through and rushed to Lisbon. By 1834, with help from the English and Spanish, Pedro IV was again the King of Portugal. In the three months left of his life, he restored the constitution and, following the lead of other European countries, confiscated the lands belonging to the monasteries.

Maria II was 15 when her father died, no age to control the powerful forces of liberalism, anarchy, and radicalism rampaging through Portugal and the rest of Europe. She endured strife and continual threats of revolt until her death in 1853, which preceded the death of her son and heir Pedro V by only 8 years. Pedro's brother Luis I, however, managed a reign of 28 years until 1889. He was blessed with an able prime minister, Fontes, who worked a miracle by building roads and railroads, laying a telephone cable to Brazil, and, at the same time, significantly reducing the national debt.

The reign of Luis' son Carlos I was abruptly curtailed, along with the life of his heir, by an assassin in 1908. Antimonarchical republicanism was in the air. Carlo's second son, Manuel II, would be the last king. Though republicans had little success in taking over the Parliament through elections, they managed to infiltrate the ranks of the navy. In 1910 warships bombarded the palace. Manuel escaped to England and a republic was proclaimed.

The republican rebels of 1910 were idealists opposed to all that the monarchy represented. They regarded religion as a superstition, yet maintained an unfailing faith in the worth of individuals—whether or not their value had been demonstrated. Republicans cancelled saints' days as official holidays and opened new universities for education at a nominal fee. They allowed just one political party, their own, in elections they invariably won.

When problems began to surface, as they must for any form of government, republican ideals got lost in simpler, more violent solutions. After a minor incursion by advocates of the deposed King, the government arrested hundreds while severely limiting freedoms of the press and speech. Bayonettes became the normal tools for ending workers' strikes. Whenever the Parliament became intransigent, governments were created during vacation adjournments. Governments came and went with the seasons—four in 1919, seven in 1920, and five in 1921—while the *escudo* fell to one-twentieth of its prerevolutionary value. For idealistic reasons, Portugal entered World War I on the side of the Allies. Afterwards, she had to stand in line with those on the losing side to beg the League of Nations for financial assistance.

To say the least, democracy was not working and everyone knew it. In 1925 three attempted army coups failed; then, in 1926, one succeeded. Gomes da Costa, a general in the Great War, formed a new government, assigning Dr. António de Oliveira Salazar, a professor of economics at Coimbra University, to the all-important post of Finance Minister. Salazar had resisted earlier offers of government posts and demanded extraordinary powers to buy his acceptance of this one, including veto power over any proposed government expense. In office, Salazar turned annual deficits into surpluses and reduced the long-term debt, earning great respect for his expertise. By 1932 he was named President of the Council, or Prime Minister.

Ironically, the last king of Portugal died on the day that Salazar accepted his post in the government that he would rule as a dictator. Salazar was a strange man, so private that little is known of his personal life. Perhaps asexual, he never married but adopted a son and daughter. Salazar's first act as Prime Minister was to produce a new constitution. According to his model government, the Parliament consisted of two houses—an assembly elected by direct suffrage plus a "corporate chamber" in which representation was based on economic power. Consistent with the tenets of fascism, businesses were organized into federations, workers into unions, and professionals into orders, each represented by parliament delegates. But only one party was recognized, Salazar's National Union (UN). To keep order, Salazar created the PIDE, secret police, which soon enlisted 20,000 informers.

Salazar's sympathies lay with Franco during the Spanish Civil War, and he provided the Nationalists with supplies, although he committed no Portuguese troops. In World War II, he maintained neutrality against pressure from both sides for more partisan commitments. He sold essential ores to Hitler but allowed Allied ships to put into Portuguese ports. After the war, he constructed three dams to electrify Portugal and a quarter of Spain as well, and used some of the water for irrigation. However, by the 1960s his economic miracle no longer was effective. Portugal had fallen badly into debt again, while her colonies in Africa posed equally severe problems.

Portugal still controlled Guinea, Mozambique, and Angola. Angola alone covered half a million square miles with a population almost as large as Portugal's. But countries all over Africa had begun crying for independence and, one by one, receiving it. Only Portugal decided to fight to retain her colonies, committing fifty thousand troops to Africa, where, as a foretaste of the United States' experience in Viet Nam, they fought guerrillas they could not catch. The undertaking was expensive, the conscription it necessitated was extremely unpopular, and nothing stemmed the inevitability of the independence movement.

In 1968 António Salazar suffered a stroke, causing brain damage from which he never recovered. He was replaced by Dr. Marcelo Caetano, a founding member of Salazar's party. Salazar himself did not die until 1970, still believing he controlled the government because no one had the courage to tell him otherwise. Caetano called for elections the next year, the first in which women voted, but the slates still comprised only candidates acceptable to the ruling party. As combat in Africa continued, unrest in the universities and among junior officers in the army increased.

On April 24, 1974 the citizens of Lisbon woke to find their streets filled with flower-bedecked tanks. This bloodless "flower revolution" exiled the government to Brazil and elevated General Spinola, a hero of the campaign in Guinea, to the presidency of a leftist government. Spinola, as a military man, appreciated that force could not hold Portugal's colonies. He granted independence to them all in 1975.

Spinola appointed Avelino Gonçalves, a Marxist, as his Minister of Labor. Gonçalves used his position to manipulate appointments in the government-controlled media until communists ran this powerful resource. Using this propaganda base, Gonçalves was able to raise himself to the position of president of the Council (prime minister), forcing Spinola to resign. Gonçalves purged the military and universities—telling students that they could fire professors they disliked, which the students happily did. It was again a time of economic crisis as 700,000 refugees from former African colonies flooded into Portugal, 300,000 to Lisbon alone. By the time of its 1975 elections, Portugal had become intensely politicized, as if making up instantly for centuries of deprivation. Posters on every available wall covered other posters to a measurable depth. On the evening of the election, one could walk any street in the country and stay informed—every radio and television was tuned to the results. The communists were soundly defeated by the socialists, but Gonçalves refused to step down. Risings began in the north, and farmers in the south marched on Lisbon, threatening a food blockade. In 1976 the military removed Gonçalves.

One of the army officers who had led this putsch became president, and he chose as his prime minister a longtime socialist—Mario Soares. Numerous changes in governments have taken place since 1976 by normal democratic process, without army uprisings or civil disturbances. It may be that Portugal at last has found democracy. Over the years, Soares has been voted out of office and then voted back in. Presently he again serves as prime minister.

THE ALGARVE

With clear skies all summer, breezes that make a 90-degree sun pleasant, and 200 k of transparent water lining white-sand beaches, the popularity of the Algarve seems inevitable. And popular it is—especially among the English and the Germans—but its celebrity is recent. In 1960, the area contained accommodations for about 60,000 visitors; today hotel capacity passes a quarter of a million beds, while private accommodations double that number. Yet enough beaches exist to cradle half a million people comfortably. The peculiar herding instincts of our species dictates that some towns will crowd with humans, while others, equally or more appealing, will remain relatively deserted. In sum, the crowd situation in the Algarve is not intolerable, especially considering that by whatever standard beaches are assessed, these are the best offered in Europe. Development has added some of the world's premier golf courses, luxury accommodations, and fine restaurants. The Algarve can be expensive at such places, but bargains exist too that make the Algarve beaches potentially the lowest priced in Europe as well as the best.

The name Algarve comes from the Arabic *al Garb*, which means "the west." This is where the Moors made their last stand in Portugal, retaining possession until the middle of the 13th century. The orange, lemon, and almond trees covering the landscape; the water-wheels for irrigation; and the whitewashed houses with their cool interior patios beneath peculiar pierced-work chimneys are all the Moors' legacy. Sadly, the 1755 Lisbon earthquake did great damage to the Algarve, destroying all but a few of the Moors' actual buildings.

Much later, Prince Henry the Navigator set up his "school" of navigation in Sagres, near Cabo São Vicente, the western end of the Algarve, because that windswept cape is the southwesternmost piece of Europe and, according to the ancients, the edge of the world. Henry's collection of maps and reports compiled from visiting sailors enabled him to send his caravels on explorations to expand the world.

The Algarve coast separates into three geographic areas. From Faro east to the Spanish border, the land is low, and dunes and lagoons line the sea. A ribbon of sandbars just off the mainland calms the water and serves as splendid beaches. The center, from Faro west to Lagos, is lined by sandstone cliffs that open to modest bays and harbors. From Lagos to the western end of the Algarve at Cabo de São Vicente, high granite cliffs break into grottoes and wild rock formations, cut by small coves that are exceptionally scenic. Only the center—from Faro to Lagos—sees excessive crowds. Secluded beaches exist both east of Faro and west of Lagos, with Olhão and Tavira on the east and Sagres on the west excelling. Whether crowded or not, the sand is white and fine all along the coast. Temperatures are the highest in Portugal, partly because the Algarve is southern and partly because high hills behind the coastline contain the heat. They contain the moisture too, which makes the Algarve lush, and temper winter cold so that the area seldom experiences temperatures below sixty on winter days. Nor is the ocean polluted, although during the summer, when fresh water levels are lowest, bottled water is generally safer to drink than tap water. July and August are the peak months for tourists, and hotel reservations are necessary during that time, but as more days intervene from the peak, advance arrangements become less crucial.

The resorts and villages of the Algarve are each unique. Beginning with Faro, the main arrival city of the coast, we describe them below. Taking Faro as a central point, we cover the resorts going east from Faro followed by those going west. The major coastal road N-125 runs inland west of Faro but connects with the resorts by feeder roads. Although trains parallel the coast, for the most part they run inland, stopping only at a handful of coastal towns. Local buses serve every village, but often with frequent, time-consuming stops.

From **Lisbon** *auto-estrada A-2 reaches* **Setubal** *in 50 k. From there N-10 east for 21 k reaches Marateca to join N-5 south for 31 k to Alcáçer do Sal, where the highway designation becomes N-120. For the more scenic route, bear right in 18 k to continue on N-120 along the coast to the western Algarve in about 180 k, although it is faster to continue to Brandola and take N-259 southeast, turning south on N-262 in about 20 k toward Azinheira dos Barros. Stay on the road as it becomes N-264 for a leg of 204 k. The trip of 272 k takes less than 5 hours except in busy summer, and ends near Albufeira, roughly the center of the Algarve. The recommended route, however, is to Évora to see some of Portugal's finest sights, spend the night, and travel on. Directions to Évora are included in the "Excursion" section of "Lisbon"; the leg from Évora to the Algarve is described below. From* **north of Lisbon***, skirt Lisbon by turning east onto N-10 just before Vila Franca de Xira (a crafts center for brass, rugs, and objects made of horn), 35 k before the*

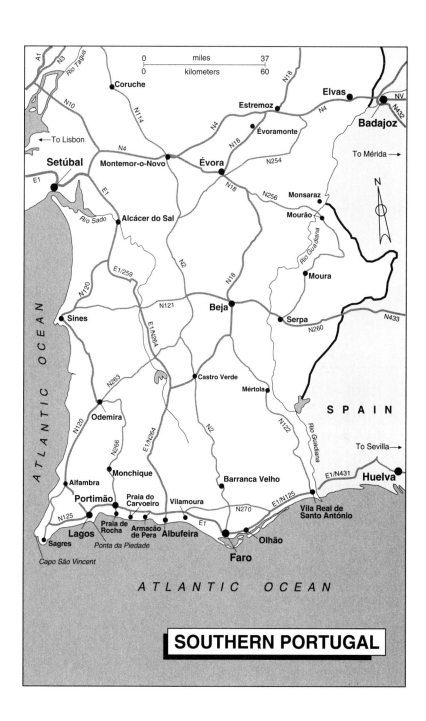

SOUTHERN PORTUGAL

capital. In 49 k N-10 reaches Cruzamento de Pegões where attention is required in order to remain on N-10 for a southern swing of 14 k. to Marateca, from which the Lisbon directions apply. From **Évora** *N-18 heads southeast toward Beja, 78 k away. Continue south along N-391 for 60 k to Ourique, where a final leg on N-264 ends near Albufeira after 79 k. From* **Spain** *the shortest drive is from Ayamonte, which is a direct 159 k from Seville. A car-ferry (with long waits in high season) crosses the Guadiana River to Vila Real de Santo Antonio at the eastern extreme of the Algarve. From north of Andalusia follow directions to Évora, then the directions above.*

Daily **flights** *of 40 minutes connect Lisbon with Faro. The train from Lisbon to Faro takes about 7 hours, with the bus taking as long and being only slightly cheaper. Express buses cut the time to 4-1/2 hours, although they cost more than the train.*

FARO

Population 28,622
Area Code 089; zip code 8000

Because Faro is the capital of the Algarve and serves as the airport for the area, it is crowded with tourists. Despite its pretty harbor area and interesting old town to its south, a shantytown rings its outskirts. Although more attractive villages exist elsewhere in the Algarve, accommodations in Faro are generally scarce because many who land here venture no further. As a result, its island beach, although attractive, is covered with sunbathers. Bus #16 serves this beach from the Office of Tourism in the harbor. The better shops congregate on the pedestrian Rua Santo António.

WHERE TO STAY

Reservations anywhere along the Algarve are strongly advised in high season, but nowhere is this admonition more important than for Faro, even for a stay of one night.

VERY EXPENSIVE ($200+)

La Réserve   1st-class ★ ★ ★

Estrada de Esteval (11 k west along N-125). Rooms: 20 apartments. ☎ *904 74; FAX 904 02; Telex 56790. Closed from the second week of November through the first week in December.* For those familiar with the Relais et Chateaux association, it is sufficient to say that this hotel is a member, one of two in Portugal. The association is comprised only of elegant, luxury estates. This hotel is uncharacteristically modern, rather than one of the historic properties usually affiliated with the group, but it is luxurious anyway. Every apartment provides cooking facilities and a sea view. Two swimming pools and a tennis court in a lush garden complete the complex. Prices are high, but the comfort and elegance provided are higher. Conveniently alongside stands the finest restaurant (described below) in the Algarve.

EXPENSIVE ($100-200)

Eva   **1st-class ★ ★**

Av. da República (occupying the north end of the harbor). Rooms: 150.
☎ *80 33 54; FAX 80 23 04; Telex 56524.* Clearly the first choice for anyone staying inside the city of Faro, this eight-story modern hotel overlooks the yacht harbor and beyond. Bedrooms are pleasant, the management efficient, and there is a roof-top pool. The hotel is also a bargain because its prices just touch the expensive category.

MODERATE ($50-99)

Faro   **2nd-class**

Pr. Don Francisco Gomes, 2 (at the center of the harbor). Rooms: 52.
☎ *80 32 76; FAX 80 35 46; Telex 56108.* This is a grey, factorylike, modern building whose bedrooms are comfortable if unimaginative. Rooms with balconies overlooking the harbor are best.

INEXPENSIVE (UNDER $50)

Casa de Lumena   **2nd-class ★ ★**

Pr. Alexendre Herculano, 27 (two blocks east of the port). Rooms: 12.
☎ *80 19 90; FAX 80 40 19.* The hotel is lodged in the house of Portugal's former sardine king, who was the richest man in town. The establishment is humbler, however, than what its history might suggest. Although by no means grand, it is run by an English couple who keep it spotless. Some of the original furnishings remain, here and there, and the decor is eccentric, to say the least. All told, the hotel is a great bargain.

Albacor   **2nd-class ★**

Rua Brites de Almeida, 23-5 (two blocks east of the port, a stone's throw from the previous hotel Lumena). Rooms: 38. ☎ *80 35 93; Telex 56778.* The bedrooms are perfectly clean, the location is central, and balconies are available, which is quite a list of assets for a hotel in this price range.

WHERE TO EAT

Restauranteurs in Faro act as though the tourists will come whether they try hard or not, so most do not. The following are the only restaurants that can be recommended.

EXPENSIVE ($50+)

La Réserve ★★★

Estrada do Esteval (see the hotel of the same name above). ☎ *902 34; FAX 904 02; Telex 56790. Closed Tuesday, and from the second week of November through the first week in December.* This restaurant ranks with the finest in the country, both for the quality of its French-inspired dishes and the elegance of their presentation. Salmon marinated in mustard and duck Vendome are memorable, as is the smoked scabbard fish. Furthermore, two can dine and be pampered for half of the cost of a fine Lisbon restaurant.

Naturally reservations are required.

Cidade Velha ★★

Rua Domingos Guieiro, 19 (beside the city hall and cathedral, 1 block east of the port). ☎ *271 45. Closed for Saturday lunch, and Sunday.* This is the leading restaurant in Faro proper. It is a romantic place installed in a former bishop's mansion, decorated with pink tablecloths, fresh flowers, and soft lighting. The food is inventive and very good indeed. All that prevents us from recommending it more strongly is the fact that a few dollars more would buy a meal at La Réserve above.

MasterCard and Visa accepted.

FROM FARO WEST TO THE SPANISH BORDER

OLHÃO ★

Population: 34,573
Area code: 089; zip code: 8700

8 k east of Faro.

This town is the largest fishing port in the Algarve, and consists of white cubical houses with external stairs and roof terraces, causing the town to be referred to as a cubist city. Olhão contains poor sections, and the town is too large to be called charming, but so far tourists are few and three superb beach islands wait nearby—Ilha da Armona, Ilha do Farol and Ilha da Cualatra, with the first two being the best. Ferries leave the harbor frequently during the season. The problem with Olhão is that, with so few tourists, not many hotels have been built, and those that exist are not particularly appealing. Nothing is perfect.

WHERE TO STAY

MODERATE ($50-99)

Ria-Sol   **3rd-class**
Rua General Humberto Delgado, 37. Rooms: 52. ☎ *70 52 67; Telex 56923.* This hotel is a step up from the pensãos, but not distinguished.

INEXPENSIVE (UNDER $50)

Bicuar   **3rd-class**
Rua Vasco da Gama, 5 (about 2 blocks from the Office of Tourism). Rooms: 12. ☎ *71 48 16.* Rooms at this tiny establishment are small but tasteful, and most provide small terraces.

Helena   **3rd-class**
Rua Dr. Miguel Bombarda, 42 (down the street and left from the Office of Tourism). Rooms: 20. ☎ *70 26 34.* Bedrooms are large for the price, but the place shows signs of wear.

TAVIRA ★★

Population: 7,282
Area code: 081; zip code: 8800

22 k east from Olhão along N-125; 31 k east of Faro.

There is no prettier town on the coast. Glistening white houses sprawl along the estuary of the Asseca river, then rise up a gentle hill, while twenty charming churches punctuate the scene. A Roman bridge spans the river below; the ruins of a Moorish alcázar, with gardens inside, crown the hill; an offshore sand spit provides 10 k of beach opportunities to stay far from the madding crowd. The bus marked "Quatro Aguas" leaves from the movie house in the Pr. de República, for a 10-minute ride to the ferry. Santa Luzia, 1 k south, is an even nicer, less crowded beach.

WHERE TO STAY

There are few hotels, which is part of the charm of Tavira.

MODERATE ($50-99)

Quinta do Caracol   **3rd-class ★**
Bairro do São. Rooms: 7 apartments. ☎ *224 75; FAX 231 75.* Seven white bungalows surround a garden and pool for the most pleasant accommodations in Tavira.

Eurotel Tavira   **2nd-class**
Quinta das Oliveiras (3 k east on N-125). Rooms: 80. ☎ *32 43 24; FAX 32 55 71; Telex 562 18.* This is a self-contained beach development with pool and tennis courts in a modern setting. The prices are low for the type and facilities, though package tours often book all the rooms.

INEXPENSIVE (UNDER $50)

Princesa do Gilão   **R3rd-class** ★
Rua Borda de Agua de Aguiar, 10 (just across the river). Rooms: 14.
☎ *226 65.* Clean rooms with tiled floors and nice views of the village
make this a pleasant place.

Lagoas   **P3rd-class** ★
Rua Candido dos Reis, 24 (just across the river). Rooms: 17. ☎ *222 82.*
This pension has spotless rooms, an accommodating management,
and views of the village.

VILA REAL DE SANTO ANTÓNIO

Population: 13,379
Area code: 081; zip code: 8900

> *Bypassing overdeveloped Monte Gordo, Vila Real lies 23 k*
> *east on N-125.*

The only reason for visiting Vila Real is that the Andalusian route
to the Algarve passes through this first Portuguese town across the
Spanish border. There are no beaches. This dreary town lives on
tuna fishing and daytrippers from Spain. Trains and buses connect to
the rest of the Algarve, however.

WEST FROM FARO TO CABO SÃO VICENTE

LOULÉ ★

Population: 8,595
Area code: 089; zip code: 8100

> *From Faro head west along N-125 where a sign for Loulé*
> *in about 7 k points inland along N-125-4 for another 7 k.*

This town is included as a pause for those interested in crafts. It is
not a beach town. Loulé is a center for baskets, mats, and hats of
palm and esparto, as well as for copperware, fine wrought iron, some
pottery, and beautiful colored harnesses (although the latter are hard
to find these days). It is no chore to search through the shops that
huddle under the ancient fortress in the center of the town. While
there, notice the lacy chimneys that seem almost artworks, certainly
with that order of individuality. Saturday is market day, but individual craftspeople in the town sell every day but Sunday.

VILAMOURA ★

If coming from Loulé, return to N-125 and continue west for about 9 k. 11 k west of Faro.

Vilamoura is the most ambitious resort venture in Portugal and perhaps Europe. It consists of not one championship golf course but three, and boasts manicured lawns, gardens, a casino, and spanking luxury hotels vying to outdo one another. Every comfort is available at a price. The scenic beauty is Portugal's as is the land, but a guest has to remind himself that he is neither in the U.S. nor in several similar complexes around the world. Costs are high—all the hotels charge 20,000$00-30,000$00 for a double, more or less, except the two finds we list below. Breakfast and golf privileges are included, as they should be. Although views over the ocean are dramatic, the nearest beach is 4 k away at Quarteira. That beach is fine but its scenery consists of highrise apartments and hotels.

WHERE TO STAY
VERY EXPENSIVE ($200+)

Vilamoura Marinotel   1st-class ★ ★ ★
Beside the marina. Rooms: 387. ☎ *38 99 88; FAX 38 98 69; Telex 58827.* This huge complex is insistently ultramodern, with every gadget a hotel can have. The grounds and views are lovely.

Dom Pedro Golf   1st-class ★ ★
Rooms: 261. ☎ *38 96 50; FAX 31 54 82; Telex 56870.*

Dom Pedro Marina   1st-class ★ ★
Rooms: 155. ☎ *38 98 02; FAX 31 32 70; Telex 56307.*

Atlantis Vilamoura   1st-class ★ ★
Rooms: 313. ☎ *38 99 37; FAX 38 98 69; Telex 56838.*

Although the preceding are separate hotels, they are similar enough that comments about one apply to the others. All are first class in every modern way, have lovely lawns (except for the Marina), and fine views.

MODERATE ($50-99)

Motel Vilamoura Golf   1st-class ★ ★ ★
On the Pennick golf course grounds). Rooms: 52. ☎ *30 29 77; FAX 38 00 23 Telex 15872.* Despite the name, this is not a motel. It is a modern, low-slung hotel surrounding a large patio with two pools and decorated in tiles and mosaics. It is impossible to get any closer to the golf course, and tennis is nearby. In such a luxurious area, this "motel" is a bargain indeed.

Estalagem da Cegonha   2nd-class ★ ★
Centro Hipico de Vilamoura (on N-125, 7 k toward Faro). Rooms: 10.

☎ *30 25 77.* This old inn of indeterminate age is situated beside Vilamoua's stables. The rooms are charming and comfortable, and the greatest bargain in Vilamoura.

QUARTEIRA

Population: 8,905
Area code: 089; zip code: 8125

13 k from Faro along N-125, a 6 k feeder road leads toward the coast and this resort.

Quarteira's blessing and curse is that it contains one of the longest pure beaches on the coast. The original fishing village now is lost among blocks of high rise apartment buildings, and the beach is barely discernible between the crowd of sunning bodies. With so many lovely areas along the coast, it is something of a mystery why people choose this place. It is difficult for an overnight visitor to find accommodations because the high rises consist of apartments leased by the week or month, leaving few true hotels. About the only reason for selecting Quarteira is to play golf at the spectacular courses in Vilamoura, 4 k away, without paying the prices of the luxury hotels there.

WHERE TO STAY

As noted above, the choices are few.

MODERATE ($50-99)

Dom José   **2nd-class ★ ★**
Av. Infante de Sagres. Rooms: 134. ☎ *30 27 50; FAX 30 27 55.* This modern nine-story hotel is a walled complex, with more conveniences than its rating would suggest. Its good value makes it popular and thus difficult to book.

Atis   **2nd-class**
Av. Infante de Sagres. Rooms: 72. ☎ *38 97 71; FAX 38 97 74; Telex 56802.* This hotel is tucked into the rows of high rises, but with a beach-view balcony, accommodations should prove acceptable.

ALBUFEIRA ★

Population: 17,218
Area code: 089; zip code: 8200

After regaining N-125 from Quarteira, look for the feeder road to Albufeira in 19 k.

Take the crowds away and this would be the perfect Algarve town. Fishermen's houses cling together along cobblestone alleys on a cliff overlooking a working beach lined with brightly colored skiffs. The beach is connected by a tunnel carved from rock to another beach backed by contorted cliffs and facing a transparent sea. Albufeira is the most popular Algarve resort, especially with the younger set, so one cannot eliminate either the people or their noise.

WHERE TO STAY

Packagers consume most of the hotel space, making accommodations difficult to find.

EXPENSIVE ($100-200)

Montechoro   1st-class
3.5 k northeast of the village. Rooms: 410. ☎ *526 51; Telex 56288.* This is an attractive Mediterranean-looking, self-contained resort complex, of pools, tennis and squash courts, saunas, gym, and restaurant. The idea is that you never need leave. Nor did you have to fly to Portugal for this.

Clube Mediterrâneo da Balaia
Praia Maria Luisa (7k. east). Rooms: 300. ☎ *58 66 81; FAX 53 78 47. (Reservations should be made through Clube Mediterrâneo do Viagens, Av. António de Aguiar 24 in Lisbon;* ☎ *53 83 09.)* This is a Club Med facility, with every activity imaginable and communal dining. The price includes all meals and there is a minimum stay of a week.

Sol e Mar   2nd-class ★
Rua João Bernardino de Sousa (at the top of the town). Rooms: 74. ☎ *58 67 21; FAX 58 70 36.* This hotel provides the best accommodations in the village proper. All bedrooms include balconies with unobstructed ocean views.

MODERATE ($50-99)

Estalagem do Cerro   E2nd-class ★ ★
Rua Samor Barros. Rooms: 83. ☎ *58 61 91; FAX 58 61 74; Telex 56211.* Half of this hotel is modern, half more rustic, but altogether the accommodations offer much more than expected in the price range, including sauna, Jacuzzi, Turkish bath, and gym. Of course there is a pool too. It perches atop a hill for views, which means a steep 10-minute walk to the beach.

Rocamar   2nd-class ★
Largo Jacinto d'Ayet (along Rua Samora Barros). Rooms: 83. ☎ *58 69 90; FAX 58 69 98; Telex 56211.* Out of town far enough for quiet but near the best beach, this modern angular hotel offers standard rooms but exceptional views.

Baltum   3rd-class ★
Av. 25 de Abril (near the main beach). Rooms: 50. ☎ *58 91 02; FAX 58 61 46.* This hotel offers modern conveniences and a quieter location than most for reasonable rates. There is a too-noisy annex in the village as well.

WHERE TO EAT

Restaurants are everywhere in this village; the cheapest ring the harbor.

MODERATE ($20-50)

O Montinho ★★

In Montechoro, 3.5 k northeast. ☎ *51 39 59. Closed Sun., and from the second week of January through the first week of February, and from the middle of November to the middle of December.* The French-influenced cuisine here is the best food near Albufeira. It is served in a converted old farmhouse, tastefully restored with rustic accents. A reasonably priced *menu de degustation* is the best way to sample the chef's specialties. Reservations are strongly advised.

Amex, MasterCard and Visa accepted.

A Ruína ★

Cais Herculano (near the fish market). ☎ *51 20 94.* Despite the rustic atmosphere of its bare stone walls, wood tables, and dripping candles, to call this restaurant a "ruin" is true hyperbole. The customers come for the seafood, which is incredibly fresh and fairly priced.

PRAIA DA ROCHA ★

Area code: 082; zip code: 8500

N-125, if coming from Albufeira, leads to Portimão in 30 k. Praia da Rocha lies at the end of a 2 k feeder road to the coast.

This is the beach for the city of Portimão, a grey, sardine-canning town with nothing but fresh sardines to attract the visitor. Its beach is quite another matter. It is flat, golden, long, spotted with the eccentric boulders that suggested its name, and backed by varicolored cliffs that rise 200 feet behind. This beach will not, however, be a personal discovery, as the high rises forming a solid line in front of the cliffs prove. It is only the first of a series of beaches that stretch to Lagos 18 k away. West along Av. Tomas Cabreira comes Praia do Vau in 3 k, then Praia dos Tres Irmãos in 4.5 k and Praia de Alvor in 5 k, followed, after a deviation inland, by Meia Praia in 14 k. All are long and lovely and attract an upscale crowd to their expensive hotels.

WHERE TO STAY

This popular resort offers accommodations in all ranges.

VERY EXPENSIVE ($200+)

Algarve 1st-class ★★★

Av. Tomás Cabreira (on the cliff at about the middle of the beach below). Rooms: 220. ☎ *41 50 01; FAX 41 59 99; Telex 57347.* The Algarve is a luxury hotel perched so close to the edge of a cliff that its terrace is cantilevered over it. Decoration is all aglitter; every service is available. By a quick count, the number of people on staff equals the number of guests. Prices are more reasonable out of season.

EXPENSIVE ($100-200)

Bela Vista   1st-class ★ ★

Av. Tomás Cabreira (just west and toward the sea from the Jupiter below). Rooms: 14. ☎ *240 55; FAX 41 53 69; Telex 57386.* This hotel is a century-old former summer home of a wealthy family and has been a hotel for half a century. Although it is not maintained as it once was, enough grandeur remains to make an adventure of investigating the rooms and halls. However, the price is high, thus the unattractive furniture in the public areas is unconscionable. Bedrooms all are different in style and price. If the only availabilities are in the annex, go elsewhere.

Júpiter   1st-class

Av. Tomás Cabreira (on the corner of the road from Portimão where it meets this cliffside street). Rooms: 180. ☎ *41 50 41; FAX 41 53 19; Telex 57346.* At half the cost of the Algarve hotel nearby, this hotel is about half as good. Bedrooms are nothing special, and the service is about what is expected for the category.

MODERATE ($50-99)

Avenida Praia   2nd-class ★

Av. Tomás Cabreira (toward its west end). Rooms: 61. ☎ *41 77 40; FAX 41 77 42; Telex 56448.* The views are about the same from this comfortable hotel as from others charging several times as much.

LAGOS ★

Population: 10,054
Area code: 082; zip code: 8600

N-125 runs inland from Portimão to Lagos in 18 k.

Lagos is the gateway to the western Algarve and one of the larger resorts, although small by most measures. It is able somehow to absorb tourists while remaining itself throughout the summer invasion. Having one of the widest bays on the coast helps. Sheltered by promontories both east and west, the town lines the estuary of the river Bensafrim to command the bay and attract tourists with a gorgeous beach so often photographed that for most people it represents the Algarve.

It was from Lagos that King Sebastião set out in 1578 to conquer Morocco. (See "Historical Profile: The Rise and Fall of the House of Avís," p. 693.) This romantic who dreamed of God and chivalry died in battle, as he surely would have wished, but neglected to leave any heirs. His death created a vacuum that let the Spanish take over Portugal, and the Portuguese have longed for their chivalrous king ever since. A modern statue of Dom Sebastião in the main square enhances his myth by presenting the young king like a spaceman.

Although razed along with so many other Portuguese towns in the 1755 earthquake, Lagos preserves a quantity of 18th-century houses built immediately afterwards. The old part of town, just inland from the ancient fort and the gardens at the river mouth, contains many. The Pr. da República opens up at the north end of the riverine gardens. Under the arches of the **customs house** bordering the square, slave auctions were held, one of the sorriest aspects of the Portuguese explorations. No sign marks these events. One block west from the church in the Pr. da República is the chapel of **Santo António**, with a wood facade and an interior that is a rococo gem and whose charming polychrome altar survived the quake. Adjoining stands the **Museu Municipal**, displaying an eccentric collection that ranges from Roman mosaics to mutant animals preserved in jars. There is, as they say, something for everyone. (Open Tues.-Sun. from 9 a.m. to 12:30 and 2-5 p.m.; closed Holidays; admission: 200$00.)

As to beaches, **Praia de Dona Ana** is a fantasy of rocks carved into wild shapes by the sea and mysterious grottoes washed by green waters. It lies 2 k due south. Here the **Ponta da Piedade** (Point of Piety) presents stunning views. To walk, follow the river road, Av. dos Descobrimentos, west to a sign for Praia de Pinhão. At this point beach paths lead to Praia Dona Ana. Alternatively, motorboats from the port take sightseers to explore the grottoes. The **Office of Tourism** on the river at Largo Marquês de Pombal has details. For a wide stretch of sand there is Meia Praia—all 4 k of it—to the east of Lagos.

WHERE TO STAY

The option to stay in town rather than on the beach is a viable one—for the town is pleasant—but so is the beach. Hotels average a cut above most along the Algarve coast because Lagos hosts tourists a cut above those at other resorts.

EXPENSIVE ($100-200)

De Lagos   1st-class ★ ★ ★

Rua Nova da Aldeia (on a hill near the bus station, opposite the port).
Rooms: 317. ☎ *76 99 67; FAX 76 99 20; Telex 57477.* This luxury complex sprawls over a hilltop. The architecture is varied enough for interest and the feeling is more homey than in comparable complexes. Bedrooms are very comfortable and all have views either of the town,

the pool, or the lush courtyard. Guests are automatically enrolled in
the Duna Beach Club on Meia Praia beach that the hotel owns. A jit-
ney regularly makes the 5-minute trip from the hotel. Golf is available.

MODERATE ($50-99)

Casa de S. Gonçalo de Lagos   **R1st-class ★**
Rua Cândido dos Reis, 73 (in the heart of the old town). Rooms: 13.
☎ *76 21 71; Telex 57411.* The layout is somewhat unconventional, as
is the decor, but all is decorated with style, and the roof terrace is sylvan. If it were not for the noise of revellers from the bars nearby, this
hotel could be strongly recommended. Avoid street-level rooms for
that reason.

Meia Praia   **2nd-class ★ ★**
On the beach of Meia Praia, 4 k east. Rooms: 66. ☎ *76 20 01; Telex
57489. Closed from November through the middle of April.* This is a
pleasant hotel on a quiet part of the beach. Lovely gardens for relaxing
and a feeling of isolation contribute to its atmosphere. Two tennis
courts are provided in addition to a pool. The bedrooms could be
more attractive, but those with sea views are decorated by the planet's
best decorator.

São Cristovão   **2nd-class**
*Rossio de São João (on the main intersection at the edge of town). Rooms:
80.* ☎ *76 30 51; Telex 56417.* This modern hotel is well run and offers
comfortable bedrooms at a very fair rate. The problem is its location,
both because of the traffic and the distance from the beach.

Marazul   **R3rd-class ★ ★**
*Rua 25 de Abril 20, 13 (one block south of the Pr. Marquês de Pombal).
Rooms: 18.* ☎ *76 91 43; FAX 76 99 60; Telex 58760. Closed from the
last week in November to the end of December.* Attractive, centrally
located, and immaculate, this is a pleasant place to stay. Prices are
moderate, although street rooms can be noisy.

Lagosmar   **R2nd-class**
*Rua Dr. Faria e Silva, 13 (just north of the Pr. Marquês de Pombal).
Rooms: 45.* ☎ *76 37 22; FAX 76 73 24.* In the same area as the Mara-
zul and with more rooms, this is a perfectly adequate second choice.

WHERE TO EAT

Inexpensive restaurants congregate along Ruas Lopes and Sociro da
Costa, stretching north of the museum.

EXPENSIVE ($50+)

Alpendre
*Rua António Barbosa Viana, 17 (1 block west of the Pr. Marquês de Pom-
bal).* ☎ *76 27 05. Open in season only.* This is the most celebrated restaurant in town, once praised by *Gourmet* magazine. We do not know
why. Although the restaurant is a fine one, such praise is excessive—

restaurants that flambé everything prize effect above subtle flavors. The dining room is attractive, but a sort of Musak that intrudes on the mood is played. Reservations are necessary.

Amex, Diners, and MasterCard accepted.

MODERATE ($20-50)

Dom Sebastião ★

Rua 25 de Abril 20, 20-2 (1-1/2 blocks south of the Pr. Marqués de Pombal). Closed Sunday off season and from the middle to the end of December. This restaurant enjoys great popularity because it serves good Portuguese food. Specialties include shellfish, which can run up the bill. The wine list is superb. The dining room has the feel of an old, comfortable inn and offers fine value for the price.

SAGRES ★

Population: 2,032
Area code: 082; zip code: 8650

From Lagos, west N-125 deteriorates, as fewer tourists and towns result in less upkeep. In 23 k, Vila do Bispo is reached; N-125 ends and N-268 is picked up going south for a final 10 k to Sagres.

There is a beautiful empty beach at **Pria do Castejo***, reached by a signposted right turn (west) after Vila do Bispo. Here breezes tend to make the temperature comfortable on the hottest days. A beach restaurant grills the freshest of fish.*

Sagres is the only true town on the Sagres Peninsula, a land—as the sparse vegetation indicates—of constant wind. Here lived Prince Henry the Navigator, whose energies and finances fueled the Portuguese exploration of the world. Living at the southwesternmost tip of Europe, Prince Henry came as close as his duties allowed to participating in those discoveries. The present village of Sagres on the sheltering east side of a small promontory is newer, consisting of but three streets paralleling the water, and is popular with fishermen, backpackers and nature lovers. Scenic coves around the town provide beach shelter from the wind. Prince Henry lived about 5 k west of the village at the naked extremity of Cabo Vicente. Today as then, the cape is desolate, and awesome for it. Sir Francis Drake destroyed Henry's monastery in a raid just before the time of the Spanish Armada and burned his great maritime library so that nothing but nature and a lonely chapel are today as Henry knew them. A 16th-century monastery has been partly reconstructed, inside of which stands a 14th-century sailors' chapel and a compass marked on the grounds, dating from after Henry's day. A tourist office and a spartan youth hostel also reside. Close to the cliff edge, a lighthouse presents awesome views of waves whipped into froth by wind and rocks.

WHERE TO STAY

Accommodations are easier to come by here than elsewhere along the coast.

EXPENSIVE ($100-$200)

Pousada do Infante   1st-class ★ ★

Ponta da Atalaia (halfway between the harbor and Mareta beach). Rooms: 23. ☎ *642 22; FAX 642 25; Telex 57491.* This pousada is styled as a villa and gleams white atop a cliff. There is a beach below and the terrace presents the ocean stretching infinitely. Bedrooms are comfortable but worn and badly arranged because the balconies look over one another rather than the sea. A tennis court and a pool are provided. All told, there are better values in the moderate category below.

Baleeira   2nd-class

On the cliff above the village. Rooms: 118. ☎ *642 12; FAX 644 25; Telex 75467.* The views are lovely, but the bedrooms are not. Some are small and most have linoleum floors. There is a dramatic pool and a tennis court, however, and prices barely crest the expensive.

MODERATE ($50-$99)

Dom Henrique   R1st-class ★ ★

Sítio da Mareta (on the cliff above Mareta beach). Rooms: 15. ☎ *641 33.* The views here surpass those of the pousada at a third of its price. This hotel is just a large house with guest rooms to rent. They are very comfortable and the more expensive ones have ocean and beach views. The management is very accommodating.

Motel Os Gambozinos   3rd-class ★

At the Praia do Martinhal, 3.5 k northeast, off N-125 at the sign for "Martinhal". Rooms: 17. ☎ *643 18.* If the idea of a cozy deserted beach appeals, here it is. The tastefully decorated hotel is run by a Dutch couple with the cleanliness one would expect of such proprietors.

Estalagem Infante do Mar   E1st-class ★

Praia da Salema (17k. east, above the village of Salema). Rooms: 16. ☎ *651 37; FAX 574 51.* Salema is a weathered fishing village in a sheltered bay whose cliffs nestle a fine beach. This hotel is rustic and bright. The bedrooms are spotless and comfortable, and many have fine sea views from their balconies.

WHERE TO EAT

Sagres village is full of tiny inexpensive restaurants. For food that is a cut above, one has to travel 5 k to Cabo São Vicente.

MODERATE ($20-$50)

Fortaleza do Beliche   ★

5 k along the road to Cabo Vicente. ☎ *641 34.* This establishment is run by the national pousada system and offers four rooms for sleeping, but is primarily a restaurant. It is installed in a tiny fort, hence the name. The decoration is rather phoney Henry-the-Navigator in theme, but the service is courteous, the food is good, and the view sublime.

HOTEL QUICK REFERENCE LIST

(BY REGION)

Because dollar prices vary as the peseta floats internationally and as local ordinances change, instead of specific dollar amounts we use the following price-categories:

Very Very Expensive (VVExp) $300+ per double per night

Very Expensive (VExp)   **$200-299** per double per night

Expensive (Exp)   **$100-199** per double per night

Moderate (Mod)   **$51-99** per double per night

Inexpensive (Inexp)   **$50 or less** per double per night

SPAIN

MADRID AND NEW CASTILE

	Phone # FAX #	Class	Price	Rooms	Stars
Madrid	**91+**				
Alcalá Alcalá, 66 Madrid 28009	435 10 60 435 11 05	1st	Exp	153	**
Arosa De la Salud, 21 Madrid 28013	532 16 00 531 31 27	1st	Exp	126	**
G. H. Reina Victoria Pl. Santa Ana, 14 Madrid 28012	531 45 00 522 03 07	1st	Exp	110	***
Hostal Auto Paseo de la Chopera, 69 Madrid 28045	539 66 00 530 67 03	3rd	Mod	24	
Hostale Lisboa Ventura de la Vega, 17 Madrid 28014	429 98 94	Hs2nd	Inexp	22	**
Inglés Echegaray, 8 Madrid 28014	429 65 51 420 24 23	2nd	Mod	58	*
Mónaco Barbieri, 5 Madrid 28004	522 46 30 521 16 01	R3rd	Inexp	32	*

MADRID AND NEW CASTILE

	Phone # FAX #	Class	Price	Rooms	Stars
Palace Pl. de las Cortes, 7 Madrid 28014	429 75 51 429 82 66	1st	VExp	478	****
París Alcalá, 2 Madrid 28014	521 64 96	3rd	Mod	114	*
Regina Alcalá, 19 Madrid 28014	521 47 25 521 47 25	2nd	Mod	142	**
Ritz Pl. de la Lealtad, 5 Madrid 28014	521 28 57 532 87 76	Deluxe	VVExp	158	*****
Suecia Marqués de Casa Ribera, 4 Madrid 28014	531 69 00 521 71 41	2nd	Exp	128	***
Tirol Marqués de Urquijo, 4 Madrid 28008	548 19 00	3rd	Mod	35	
Tryp Ambassador Cuesta de Santo Domingo, 5 Madrid 28013	541 67 00 559 10 40	1st	Exp	181	***
Villa Magna Paseo Castellana, 22 Madrid 28046	578 20 00 575 31 58	Deluxe	VVExp	182	***
Villa Real Pl. de las Cortes, 10 Madrid 28014	420 37 67 420 25 47	1st	VExp	115	***
Wellington Velázquez, 8 Madrid 28001	575 44 00 576 41 64	1st	VExp	258	**
Sigüenza	**91+**				
Parador Castillo de Sigüenza Plaza del Castillo Sigüenza 19250	39 01 00 39 13 64	1st	Exp	77	****

MADRID AND NEW CASTILE

	Phone # FAX #	Class	Price	Rooms	Stars
Toledo	**925+**				
Carlos V Calle Horno de Magdalena, 1 Toledo 45001	22 21 00 22 21 05	2nd	Mod	69	***
Hostal del Cardenal P. Recaredo, 24 Toledo 45003	22 49 00 22 29 91	R2nd	Mod	27	*****
Imperio Calle Cadenas, 5 Toledo 45001	22 76 50 25 31 83	R3rd	Inexp	21	**
Los Cigarrales Carretaria de Circunva- lación, 32 Toledo 45000	22 00 53 21 55 46	3rd	Inexp	36	***
María Cristina Calle Margués de Mendigorria, 1 Toledo 45003	21 32 02 21 26 50	2nd	Mod	65	****
Parador Conde de Orgaz Cerro del Emperador Toledo 45002	22 18 50 22 51 66	1st	Exp	76	***

OLD CASTILE AND LEÓN

	Phone # FAX #	Class	Price	Rooms	Stars
Ávila	**918+**				
Hostale Continental Pl. de la Catedral, 6 Ávila 05001	21 15 02	Hs2nd	Inexp	54	**
Palacio de Valderrábanos Pl. Catedral, 9 Ávila 05001	21 10 23 25 16 91	1st	Exp	73	****
Parador Raimundo de Bor- goña Marqués de Canales y Cho- zas, 16 Ávila 05001	21 13 40 22 61 66	1st	Exp	62	***

OLD CASTILE AND LEÓN

	Phone # FAX #	Class	Price	Rooms	Stars
Rastro, El Pl. del Rastro, 1 Ávila 05001	22 12 18	Hs2nd	Inexp	14	*
Burgos	**947+**				
Almirante Bonifaz C. Vitoria, 22 Burgos 09004	20 69 43 20 29 19	1st	Exp	79	**
Condestable C. Vitoria, 8 Burgos 09004	26 71 25 20 46 45	1st	Exp	85	**
Cordón La Puebla, 6 Burgos 09004	26 50 00 20 02 69	2nd	Mod	35	**
Del Cid Pl. Santa María, 8 Burgos 09003	20 87 15 26 94 60	2nd	Mod	30	***
España Paseo de Espolón Burgos 09003	20 63 40 20 13 30	4th	Inexp	69	*
Fernán González C. Calera, 17 Burgos 09002	20 94 41 27 47 21	2nd	Mod	84	***
Palacio Landa Carretera Madrid-Irun, kilometer 236 Burgos 09000	20 63 43 26 46 76	1st	Exp	42	*****
La Rioja Region	**941+**				
Iturrimurri N-232 1 k south of Haro Haro 26200	31 12 13 31 17 21	2nd	Mod	36	**
Los Augustinos San Agustin, 2 Haro 26200	31 13 08 30 31 48	1st	Exp	62	****
Marixa Sancho Abarca, 8 Laguardia 01300	10 01 65	4th	Inexp	10	*

OLD CASTILE AND LEÓN

	Phone # FAX #	Class	Price	Rooms	Stars
Parador Santo Domingo de la Calzada Pl. del Santo Calzada 26250	34 03 00 34 03 25	2nd	Exp	61	****

León 987+

Don Suero Av. Suero de Quiñones, 15 León 24002	23 06 00	Hs2nd	Inexp	15	**
Parador San Marcos Pl. San Marcos 7 León 24001	23 73 00 23 34 58	Deluxe	Exp	256	*****
Quindós Av. José Antonio, 24 León 24002	23 62 00 24 22 01	R3rd	Mod	96	***
Riosol Av. de Palencia, 3 León 24009	21 66 50 21 69 97	R2nd	Mod	141	*

Salamanca 923+

Amefa Pozo Amarillo, 8 Salamanca 37002	21 81 89 26 02 00	R3rd	Mod	33	***
Condal Pl. Santa Eulalia, 3 Salamanca 37002	21 84 00	R3rd	Mod	70	
Emperatriz C. Compañia, 4 Salamanca 37001	21 92 00	3rd	Inexp	61	*
Gran Hotel Pl. Poeta Iglesias, 5 Salamanca 37001	21 35 00	R1st	Exp	100	
Gran Vía Rosa, 4 Salamanca 37001	21 54 01	R3rd	Inexp	47	**
Milán Pl. del Ángel, 5 Salamanca 37001	21 75 18	R4th	Inexp	25	*
Monterrey Azafranal, 21 Salamanca 37001	21 44 00 21 44 00	R1st	Exp	89	*

OLD CASTILE AND LEÓN

	Phone # FAX #	Class	Price	Rooms	Stars
Parador de Salamanca Teso de la Feria, 2 Salamanca 37008	26 87 00 21 54 38	1st	Exp	108	***
Pensión Marina Calle Doctinos, 4 Salamanca 37001	21 65 69	P3rd	Inexp	11	
Residencia Rector Paseo del Rector Esper- abe, 10 Salamanca 37008	21 84 82 21 40 08	R1st	Exp	13	*****
Segovia	**911+**				
Acueducto Av. del Padre Claret, 10 Segovia 40001	42 48 00 42 84 46	2nd	Mod	78	**
Las Sirenas Juan Bravo, 30 Segovia 40001	43 40 11 43 06 33	R3rd	Mod	39	***
Los Arcos Paseo de Exequiel González, 24 Segovia 40002	43 74 62 42 81 61	1st	Exp	59	**
Los Linajes C. Dr. Velasco, 9 Segovia 40003	43 17 12 43 15 01	R2nd	Mod	55	****
Parador de Segovia Carretera N-601, 3 k north Segovia 40003	44 37 37 43 73 62	1st	Exp	113	***
Plaza C. Cronista Leccea, 11 Segovia 40001	43 12 28	Hs3rd	Inexp	28	*
Valladolid	**983+**				
Imperial Peso, 4 Valladolid 47001	33 03 00 33 08 13	3rd	Mod	81	*
Olid Meliá Pl. San Miguel, 10 Valladolid 47003	35 72 00 33 68 28	1st	Exp	211	**

OLD CASTILE AND LEÓN

	Phone # FAX #	Class	Price	Rooms	Stars
Parador de Tordesillas Carretera de Salamanca, N-620 Tordesillas 47100	77 00 51 77 10 13	2nd	Exp	73	***
Roma Héroes del Alcázar de Toledo, 8 Valladolid 47001	35 47 77 35 54 61	3rd	Mod	38	*

ANDALUSIA

	Phone # FAX #	Class	Price	Rooms	Stars
Baeza	**953+**				
Juanito Paseo Arca del Agua Baeza 23440	74 00 40 74 23 24	2nd	Mod	21	*
Cádiz	**956+**				
Francia y París Pl. de San Francisco, 2 Cádiz 11004	21 23 19 22 24 31	2nd	Mod	69	*
Parador Atlántico Duque de Nájera, 9 Cádiz 11002	22 69 05 21 45 82	1st	Exp	153	**
Córdoba	**957+**				
Aldarve Magistral González Francés, 15 Córdoba 14003	48 11 02 47 46 77	1st	Exp	103	****
Andalucia José Zorrila, 3 Córdoba 14008	47 60 00	3rd	Inexp	40	**
El Califa Lope de Hoces, 14 Córdoba 14004	29 94 00 29 57 16	R2nd	Exp	67	**
González Manriquez, 3 Córdoba 14003	47 98 19	3rd	Mod	16	***

ANDALUSIA

	Phone # FAX #	Class	Price	Rooms	Stars
Husa Gran Capitán Av. de América, 5 Córdoba 14008	47 02 50 47 43 48	1st	Exp	99	
Los Gallos Sol Av. Medina Azahara, 7 Córdoba 14005	23 55 00 23 16 36	2nd	Exp	115	
Maimónides Torrijos, 4 Córdoba 14003	47 15 00 48 38 03	R2nd	Exp	83	**
Marisa Cardenal Herrero, 6 Córdoba 14003	47 31 42	R3rd	Mod	28	*
Meliá Córdoba Jardines de la Victoria Córdoba 14004	29 80 66 29 81 47	1st	Exp	106	
Parador de la Arruzafa Av. de la Arruzafa Córdoba 14012	27 59 00 28 04 09	1st	Exp	94	**
Selu Eduardo Dato, 7 Córdoba 14003	47 65 00 47 83 76	R2nd	Mod	118	
Sénica Conde y Luque, 7 Córdoba 14003	47 32 34	Hs4th	Inexp	10	*
Serrano Pérez Galdós, 6 Córdoba 14001	47 01 42 48 65 13	3rd	Inexp	64	**
Triunfo, El Cardinal González, 79 Córdoba 14003	47 55 00	Hs3rd	Inexp	44	

Costa de la Luz

Conil de la Frontera	956+				
Don Pelayo Carretera del Punto, 19 Conil de la Frontera 11140	44 20 30 44 50 58	3rd	Exp	30	*
Gaviota, La Pl. Nuestra Señora de las Virtudes Conil de la Frontera 11140	44 08 36 44 09 80	3rd	Exp	15	*

ANDALUSIA					
	Phone # FAX #	Class	Price	Rooms	Stars
Tres Jotas C. San Sebastian Conil del la Frontera 11140	44 04 50 44 04 50	3rd	Exp	39	

El Puerto de Santa María 956+

Cántaros, Los Curva, 2 El Puerto de Santa María 11500	54 02 40 54 11 21	2nd	Exp	39	*
Monasterio de San Miguel C. Larga, 27 El Puerto de Santa María 11500	54 04 40 54 26 04	1st	Exp	132	***

Sanlúcar de Barrameda 956+

Los Helechos Pl. Madre de Dios, 9 Sanlúcar de Barrameda 11540	36 13 49 36 96 50	R3rd	Mod	16	*
Palacio de los Duquess de Medina Sidonia Conde de Niebla, 1 Sanlúcar de Barrameda 11540	36 01 61	NR	Mod	3	*****
Posada del Palacio Caballeros, 11 Sanlúcar de Barrameda 11540	36 48 40 36 50 60	3rd	Mod	11	***
Tartaneros Tartaneros, 8 Sanlúcar de Barrameda 11540	36 20 44 36 00 45	R2nd	Mod	22	**

Tarifa 956+

Balcón de España Carretera de Cádiz: Apar- tado 57 Tarifa 11380	68 43 26 68 43 26	2nd	Mod	40	***
Codorniz, La Carretera de Cádiz Tarifa 11540	68 47 44 68 34 10	4th	Mod	35	**

ANDALUSIA

	Phone # FAX #	Class	Price	Rooms	Stars
Vejer de la Frontera	**956+**				
Convento de San Franciso La Plazuela Vejer de la Frontera 11150	45 10 01 45 10 04	2nd	Mod	25	***
Zahara de los Atunes	**956+**				
Antonio Carretera de Atlanterra Zahara del los Atunes 11393	43 91 41 43 91 35	4th	Mod	30	*
Sol Atlanterra Carretera de Atlanterra Zahara de los Atunes 11393	43 90 00 43 30 51	1st	Exp	284	

Costa del Sol

Almuñécar	**958+**				
Carmen Av. de Europa, 8 Almuñécar 18690	63 14 13	R4th	Inexp	24	*
Goya Av. de Europa Almuñécar 18690	63 05 50 63 11 92	R3rd	Mod	24	*
Playa de San Cristóbal Pl. San Cristóbal, 5 Almuñécar 18690	63 11 12	R3rd	Mod	22	*
Estepona	**952+**				
Buenavista Paseo Marítimo, 180 Estepona 29680	80 01 37	P2nd	Mod	38	*
Santa Marta 11 k east along N-340 to Marbella Estepona 29680	278 07 16	3rd	Mod	37	***
Marbella	**952+**				
Lima Av. Antonio Belón, 2 Marbella 29600	277 05 00 286 30 91	R3rd	Mod	64	*
Marbella Club Carretera de Cádiz Marbella 29600	277 13 00 282 98 84	1st	VVExp	95	**

ANDALUSIA	Phone # FAX #	Class	Price	Rooms	Stars
Monteros, Los Carretera de Cádiz Marbella 29600	277 17 00 282 58 46	Deluxe	VVExp	171	****
Nagueles Carretera de Cádiz Marbella 29600	77 16 88	R4th	Mod	17	**
Puente Romano Carretera de Cádiz Marbella 29600	277 01 00 277 57 66	Deluxe	VVExp	184	****
Nerja	**952+**				
Balcón de Europa Passea Balcón de Europa, 1 Nerja 29780	252 08 00 252 44 90	2nd	Exp	102	*
Parador de Nerja Playa de Burriana-Tablazo Nerja 29780	252 00 50 252 19 97	1st	Exp	73	***
Portofino Puerta de Mar, 4 Nerja 29780	52 01 50	4th	Mod	12	*
Salobreña	**958+**				
Salobreña Carretera de Málaga Salobreña 18680	61 02 61 61 01 01	2nd	Mod	80	*
Salambina Carretera de Málaga Salobreña 18680	61 00 37 61 13 28	4th	Inexp	13	***
Torremolinos	**952+**				
Alhoa Puerto-Sol Via Imperial, 55 Torremolinos 29620	238 70 66 238 57 01	1st	Exp	410	
Cervantes Las Mercedes Torremolinos 29620	238 40 33 238 48 57	2nd	Exp	238	
Don Pablo Paseo Marítimo Torremolinos 29620	238 38 88 238 37 83	1st	Exp	443	

ANDALUSIA				
Phone # **FAX #**	**Class**	**Price**	**Rooms**	**Stars**
Don Paquito Av. del Lido Torremolinos 29620 238 78 58 238 37 83	R3rd	Mod	49	
Don Pedro Av. del Lido Torremolinos 29620 238 68 44 238 37 83	2nd	Mod	272	
Isabel Paseo Marítimo, 97 Torremolinos 29620 238 17 44 238 11 98	2nd	Mod	40	
Meliá Costa del Sol Pasero Marítimo Torremolinos 29620 238 66 77 238 64 17	1st	Exp	540	
Meliá Torremolinos Av. Carlotta Alessandri, 109 Torremolinos 29620 238 05 00 238 05 38	1st	Exp	109	
Pes Espada Vía Imperial, 11 Torremolinos 29620 238 03 00 237 28 01	1st	Exp	205	
Sidi Lago Rojo Miami, 5 Torremolinos 29620 238 76 66 238 08 91	2nd	Mod	144	
Gibraltar 956+				
The Rock 3 Europa Road Gibraltar 730 00 730 13	1st	VExp	143	****
Caleta Palace Catalán Bay Road Gibraltar 765 01 710 50	1st	Exp	153	**
Bristol 10 Cathedral Square Gibraltar 768 00	4th	Mod	60	**
Queen's Hotel 1 Boyd Street Gibraltar 740 00	4th	Mod	24	*
Granada 958+				
Alhambra Palace Peña Partida, 2 Granada 18009 22 14 68 22 64 04	1st	Exp	132	****

ANDALUSIA					
	Phone # FAX #	Class	Price	Rooms	Stars
Alixare Av. de los Alixares Granada 18009	22 55 75 22 41 02	2nd	Exp	162	*
América Real de la Alhambra, 53 Granada 18009	22 74 71	4th	Mod	13	**
H-Residencia Britz Cuesta de Gomerez, 1 Granada 180010	22 36 51	P3rd	Inexp	22	*
H-Residencia Lisboa Pl. del Carmen, 27 Granada 18014	22 14 13	P3rd	Inexp	28	
Inglaterra Cetti Meriem, 4 Granada 18010	22 15 58	2nd	Exp	36	*
Kenia C. Molinos, 65 Granada 18008	22 75 06	2nd	Exp	16	**
Macía Pl. Nueva, 4 Granada 18010	22 75 36 22 35 75	3rd	Mod	40	**
Meliá Granada Ángel Ganivet, 7 Granada 18009	22 74 00 22 74 03	1st	Exp	197	***
Parador de San Francisco Alhambra Granada 18009	22 14 40 22 22 64	1st	Exp	38	****
Sacromonte Pl. del Lino, 1 Granada 18002	26 64 11 26 67 07	3rd	Mod	33	*
Victoria Puerta Real, 3 Granada 18005	25 77 00 26 31 08	2nd	Exp	69	**
Málaga	952+				
Málaga Palacio Corina del Muelle, 1 Málaga 29015	221 51 85 221 51 85	1st	Exp	225	*
Naranjos, Los Paseo de Sancha, 35 Málaga 29016	222 43 19 222 59 75	2nd	Exp	41	*

ANDALUSIA

	Phone # FAX #	Class	Price	Rooms	Stars
Parador Málaga-Gibralfaro Monte Gibralfaro Málaga 29016	222 19 03 222 19 02	2nd	Exp	12	**
Vegas, Las Paseo de Sancha 22 Málaga 29015	221 77 12	2nd	Mod	107	
Victoria C. Sancho Lara, 3 Málaga 29015	222 42 23	P3rd	Inexp	13	*
Ronda	**952+**				
Reina Victoria Av. Dr. Fleming, 25 Ronda 29400	287 12 40 287 10 75	1st	Exp	89	*****
Tajo, El Cruz Verde, 7 Ronda 29400	87 62 36	R2nd	Inexp	67	*
Seville	**95+**				
Alcázar Meléndez Pelayo, 10 Sevilla 41004	441 20 11	2nd	Exp	96	
Alfonso XIII San Fernando, 2 Sevilla 41004	422 28 50 421 60 33	Deluxe	VExp	149	*****
Bécquer Reyes Católicos, 4 Sevilla 41001	422 89 00 421 44 00	2nd	Mod	120	*
Casas de la Judería, Las Pl. Santa María la Blanca Sevilla 41004	441 51 50 442 21 70	A2nd	VExp	29	****
Donna María Don Remondo, 16 Sevilla 41004	422 49 90 422 97 65	1st	Exp	61	***
Goya Mateos Gago, 31 Sevilla 41004	421 11 70	P2nd	Inexp	20	**
Inglaterra Pl. Nueva, 7 Sevilla 41001	422 49 70 456 13 36	1st	Exp	116	**

ANDALUSIA					
	Phone # FAX #	Class	Price	Rooms	Stars
Meliá Sevilla Av. de la Borbolla, 3 Sevilla 41004	442 15 11 442 16 08	1st	VExp	366	
Murillo Lope de Rueda, 9 Sevilla 41004	421 60 95 421 96 16	3rd	Mod	57	**
Rábida, La Castelar, 24 Sevilla 41001	422 09 60 422 43 75	3rd	Mod	87	*
Tryp Colón Canalejas, 1 Sevilla 41001	422 29 00 422 09 38	1st	VExp	211	***
Úbeda	*953+*				
Parador Condestable Dávalos Pl. Vázquez de Molina, 1 Úbeda 23400	75 03 45 75 12 59	1st	Exp	31	***
Paz, La Andalucía, 1 Úbeda 23400	75 21 46 75 08 48	3rd	Mod	51	*

EXTREMADURA					
	Phone # FAX #	Class	Price	Rooms	Stars
Cáceres	*927+*				
Alcántara Av. Virgen de Guadalupe, 14 Cáceres 10001	22 89 00 22 87 68	2nd	Mod	67	
Almonte C. Gil Cordero, 6 Cáceres 10001	24 09 26	Hs3rd	Inexp	90	
Extremadura Av. Virgen de Guadalupe, 5 Cáceres 10001	22 16 00 21 10 95	2nd	Mod	68	**
Goya Pl. General Mola, 33 Cáceres 10001	24 99 50	Hs2nd	Inexp	15	*

EXTREMADURA

	Phone # FAX #	Class	Price	Rooms	Stars
Parador de Cáceres C. Ancha, 6 Cáceres 10003	21 17 59 21 17 29	1st	Exp	27	***

Guadalupe   927+

	Phone # FAX #	Class	Price	Rooms	Stars
Cerezo Gregorio López, 12 Guadalupe 10140	36 73 79	Hs3rd	Inexp	15	***
Hospederia del Real Mon- asterio Pl. Juan Carlos I Guadalupe 10140	36 70 00 36 71 77	3rd	Mod	40	***
Parador de Guadalupe C. Marqués de la Romana, 10 Guadalupe 10140	36 70 75 36 70 76	1st	Mod	40	***

Mérida   924+

	Phone # FAX #	Class	Price	Rooms	Stars
Cervantes Camilo José Cela, 8 Mérida 06800	31 49 01 31 13 42	3rd	Mod	30	*
Emperatriz Pl. de España, 19 Mérida 06800	31 31 11 30 03 76	2nd	Mod	41	
Guadiana Pl. de Santa Clara Mérida 06800	31 32 07	Hs3rd	Inexp	12	
Parador Vía de la Plata Pl. de la Constitución, 3 Mérida 06800	31 38 00 31 92 08	1st	Exp	82	**

Trujillo   927+

	Phone # FAX #	Class	Price	Rooms	Stars
Mesón la Cadena Pl. Mayor, 8 Trujillo 10200	32 14 63	Hs3rd	Inexp	8	**
Las Ciqüeñas Carretera N-V Trujillo 10200	32 12 50 32 13 00	2nd	Mod	78	*
Parador de Trujillo Pl. de Santa Clara Trujillo 10200	32 13 50 32 13 66	1st	Exp	46	**

GALICIA, ASTURIAS, AND CANTABRIA

	Phone # FAX #	Class	Price	Rooms	Stars
Basque Coast					
Castro Urdiales	942+				
Miramar Playa Castro Urdiales Castro Urdiales 39700	86 02 00	2nd	Mod	34	*
Deba	942+				
Miramar C. Arenal, 24 Deba 20820	60 16 60	2nd	Mod	60	*
Donastia	943+				
De Londres y de Inglaterra Kalea Zubieta, 2 Donastia 20007	42 69 89 42 00 31	1st	Exp	145	****
H. Residencia Easo Kalea San Bartólome, 2 Donastia 20007	46 68 92	Hs3rd	Inexp	11	*
María Cristina Paseo República Argentina Donastia 20004	42 49 00 42 39 14	Deluxe	VExp	139	*****
Niza Kalea Zubieta, 56 Donastia 20007	42 66 63 42 66 63	2nd	Mod	41	**
Hondarribia	943+				
Parador el Emperador Pl. de Armas del Castillo Hondarribia 20280	64 21 40 64 21 53	2nd	Exp	36	****
Laredo	942+				
Ramona Alameda José Antonio, 4 Laredo 39770	60 71 89	4th	Mod	10	*
Risco Alto de Laredo Laredo 39770	60 50 30	2nd	Mod	25	**
Lekeitio	942+				
Beitia Av. Pascual Aboroa, 25 Lekeitio 48280	684 01 11	3rd	Mod	30	*

GALICIA, ASTURIAS, AND CANTABRIA

	Phone # FAX #	Class	Price	Rooms	Stars
Noja	**942+**				
Montemar Playa Noja Noja 39180	63 03 20	3rd	Mod	61	**
Santander	**942+**				
México Calderón de la Barca, 3 Santander 39002	21 24 50	R3rd	Mod	35	**
Real Paseo Pérez Galdós, 28 Santander 39005	27 25 50 27 45 73	1st	VExp	125	****
Rhin Av. Reina Victoria, 153 Santander 39005	27 43 00 27 86 53	R3rd	Mod	95	**
Zarauz	**943+**				
Alameda Gipuzkoa Zarauz 20800	83 01 43 13 24 74	3rd	Mod	39	

Costa del Rias

		Class	Price	Rooms	Stars
Baiona	**986+**				
Parador Conde de Gondomar Baiona 36300	35 50 00 35 50 76	1st	Exp	124	***
Cambados	**986+**				
Parador del Albariño Paseo de Cervantes Cambados 36630	54 22 50	2nd	Exp	63	**
Combarro	**986+**				
Stella Maris Carretera C-550 Combarro 36993	77 03 66	2nd	Mod	27	*
Muros	**981+**				
Murandana Av. Marina Española, 107 Muros 15250	82 68 85	R3rd	Mod	16	*

GALICIA, ASTURIAS, AND CANTABRIA

	Phone # FAX #	Class	Price	Rooms	Stars
O Grove	**986+**				
Louxo Isla A Toxa O Grove 36980	73 02 00 73 27 91	1st	Exp	96	***
Mar Atlántico San Vincente del Mar O Grove 36980	73 80 61 73 82 99	2nd	Mod	34	***
Pontevedra	**986+**				
Parador Casa del Barón Pl. de Maceda Pontevedra 36002	85 58 00	1st	Exp	47	*
Vilagarcia de Arousa	**986+**				
Chocolate Av. Cambados, 151 Vilaxoan Vilagarcia de Arousa 36600	50 11 99	4th	Inexp	18	**
Pazo el Revel Camino de la Iglesia Vilalonga 36990	74 30 00 74 33 90	2nd	Mod	21	***
Costa Verde					
Comillas	**942+**				
Hostería de Quijas Carretera N-634 Comillas 39520	82 08 33	3rd	Mod	13	**
Josein C. Manuel Noriega, 27 Comillas 39520	72 02 25	3rd	Mod	23	*
Gijon	**985+**				
Parador El Molina Viejo Parque Isabel la Católica Gijon 33203	37 05 11 37 02 33	1st	Exp	40	*
La Franca	**985+**				
Mirador de la Franca Playa La Franca La Franca 33590	41 21 45	3rd	Mod	52	**

GALICIA, ASTURIAS, AND CANTABRIA

	Phone # FAX #	Class	Price	Rooms	Stars
La Isla	**942+**				
Astuy Playa La Isla La Isla 39195	67 95 40	2nd	Mod	52	*
Llanes	**985+**				
Don Paco Posade Herrera, 1 Llanes 33500	40 01 50 40 26 81	2nd	Mod	42	**
Luarca	**985+**				
Casa Consuelo Carretera N-634 Luarca 33792	64 08 44 64 16 42	3rd	Mod	35	*
Gayoso Paseo de Gomez, 4 Luarca 33700	64 00 50 47 02 71	2nd	Exp	33	**
Ribadeo	**982+**				
Eo Av. de Asturias, 5 Ribadeo 27700	11 07 50 11 00 21	2nd	Mod	24	*
Ribadesella	**985+**				
Grand Hotel del Sella Paseo de la Playa Ribadesella 33560	86 01 50 85 74 49	1st	Exp	82	**
Ribadesella Playa Paseo de la Playa, 34 Ribadesella 33560	86 07 15 86 02 20	2nd	Mod	17	*
Santillana del Mar	**942+**				
Altimar C. Cantón, 1 Santillana del Mar 39330	81 80 25 84 01 03	2nd	Mod	32	**
Parador Gil Blás Pl. Ramón Pelayo, 11 Santillana del Mar 39330	81 80 00 81 83 91	2nd	Exp	56	***
San Vincente de la Barquera	**942+**				
Miramar San Vincente de la Barquera 39540	71 00 75	3rd	Mod	15	**

GALICIA, ASTURIAS, AND CANTABRIA

	Phone # FAX #	Class	Price	Rooms	Stars
Tapia de Casariego	**985+**				
Palacete Pañalba C. El Cotarelo, Figueras 33794	62 31 50	1st	Mod	12	**
Vivero	**982+**				
Ego Playa de Area C-642 Vivero 27850	56 09 87 56 17 62	2nd	Mod	29	*
Oviedo	**985+**				
Principado C. San Francisco, 6 Oviedo 33003	21 77 92 21 39 46	2nd	Exp	70	*
Reconquesta, De La C. Gil de Jaz, 16 Oviedo 33004	24 11 00 24 11 66	1st	Exp	142	*****
Tropical C. 19 de Julio, 6 Oviedo 33002	21 87 79	R3rd	Mod	44	
Santiago de Compostela	**981+**				
Araguaney Alfredo Brañas, 5 Santiago de Compostela 15701	59 59 00 59 02 87	1st	Exp	64	***
Compostela Calvo Sotelo, 1 Santiago de Compostela 15702	58 57 00 56 32 69	1st	Mod	99	*
Gelmírez C. Horneo, 92 Santiago de Compostela 15702	56 11 00 56 32 69	1st	Mod	138	*
Mapoula C. Entremurallas, 10 Santiago de Compostela 15702	58 01 24	Hs2nd	Inexp	10	**
Parador Reyes Católicos Pl. de España Santiago de Compostela 15705	58 22 00 56 30 94	Deluxe	VExp	136	*****

GALICIA, ASTURIAS, AND CANTABRIA

	Phone # FAX #	Class	Price	Rooms	Stars
Suso Rua do Villar, 65 Santiago de Compostela 15702	58 66 11	Hs2nd	Inexp	9	*
Universal Pl. de Galicia, 2 Santiago de Compostela 15706	58 58 00	R2nd	Inexp	54	*
Windsor República de El Salvador, 16-A Santiago de Compostela 15701	59 29 39	Hs1st	Mod	50	**

ARAGÓN AND NAVARRE

	Phone # FAX #	Class	Price	Rooms	Stars
Estella	*948+*				
Irache Carretera Pamplona-Lo- groño, N-111, k 43 Ayegui 31200	55 11 50	R2nd	Mod	74	*
Ordesa National Park	*974+*				
Parador de Monte Perdido Valle de Pineta, Huesca 22350	50 10 11	2nd	Exp	24	**
Olite	*948+*				
Casa Zanito C. Mayor, 16 Olite 31390	74 00 02	3rd	Mod	15	
Parador Principe de Viana Pl. de los Teobaldos, 2 Olite 31390	74 00 00 74 02 01	2nd	Exp	43	***
Pamplona	*948+*				
Eslava Pl. Virgin de la 0, 7 Pamplona 31001	22 22 70 22 51 57	R3rd	Mod	28	*

ARAGÓN AND NAVARRE

	Phone # FAX #	Class	Price	Rooms	Stars
Iruña Palace-Tres Reyes Jardines de la Taconera Pamplona 31001	22 66 00 22 29 30	1st	Exp	168	**
Maisonnave C. Nueva, 20 Pamplona 31001	22 26 00 22 01 66	2nd	Exp	152	
Ohri C. Leyre, 7 Pamplona 31001	22 85 00 22 83 18	3rd	Exp	55	*
Perla, La Pl. del Castillo, 1 Pamplona 31001	22 77 06	2nd	Exp	68	
Yoldi Av. San Ignacio, 11 Pamplona 31002	22 48 00 21 20 45	2nd	Exp	48	*
Sos del Rey Católico	**948+**				
Parador Fernando de Aragón Sos del Rey Católico 50680	88 80 11 88 81 00	1st	Exp	65	**
Zaragoza	**976+**				
Conde Blanco C. Predicadores, 84 Zaragoza 50003	44 14 11 28 03 39	3rd	Inexp	87	**
Goya C. Cinco de Marzo, 5 Zaragoza 50004	22 93 31 23 47 05	1st	Exp	148	*
Gran Hotel C. Joaquín Costa Canalejas, 5 Zaragoza 50001	22 19 01 23 67 13	1st	Exp	138	***
Ramiro I C. Coso, 123 Zaragoza 50001	29 82 00 39 89 52	2nd	Mod	101	**

CATALONIA AND THE LEVANT

	Phone # FAX #	Class	Price	Rooms	Stars
Barcelona	**93+**				
Australia Ronda Universitat, 11 Barcelona 08002	317 41 77	Hs2nd	Inexp	23	*
Avenida Palace Gran Vía de les Corts Ca- talanes, 605 Barcelona 08007	301 96 00 318 12 34	1st	VExp	211	**
Claris Pau Claris, 150 Barcelona 08009	487 62 62 215 79 11	1st	VExp	124	***
Colón Av. de Catedral, 7 Barcelona 08002	301 14 04 317 29 15	1st	Exp	147	**
Condes de Barcelona Passeig de Gràcia, 75 Barcelona 08008	215 06 16 216 08 35	1st	VExp	109	****
Cortes C. Santa Ana 25 Barcelona 08002	317 91 12 301 31 35	3rd	Mod	46	
Gaudí C. Nou de la Rambla, 12 Barcelona 08001	412 26 36	2nd	Exp	73	*
Gótico C. Jaume I, 14 Barcelona 08002	315 22 11 315 38 19	2nd	Exp	83	**
Gran Derby C. Loreto, 28 Barcelona 08029	322 20 62 410 08 62	1st	Exp	43	****
Gran Vía Gran Vía de les Corts Ca- talanes, 642 Barcelona 08007	318 19 00 318 99 97	2nd	Exp	53	**
Lausanne Av. Portal de l'Angel, 24 Barcelona 08002	302 11 39	P2nd	Inexp	17	
Majestic Passeig de Gràcia, 70 Barcelona 08008	488 17 17 488 18 80	1st	VExp	336	**

CATALONIA AND THE LEVANT

	Phone # FAX #	Class	Price	Rooms	Stars
Mesón Castilla C. Valldoncella, 5 Barcelona 08001	318 21 82 412 40 20	3rd	Mod	56	*
Montecarlo Rambla dels Estudis, 124 Barcelona 08002	317 58 00 317 57 50	2nd	Exp	73	***
Nouvel C. Santa Ana 18-20 Barcelona 08002	301 82 74	4th	Mod	76	*
Oliva Passeig de Gràcia, 32 Barcelona 08008	317 50 87	P2nd	Inexp	16	*
Palacios Gran Vía de les Corts Catalanes, 629bis Barcelona 08007	301 37 92	P2nd	Inexp	25	*
Princesa Sofía Plaça Pius XII Barcelona 08028	330 71 11 330 76 21	1st	VExp	511	**
Regencia Colón C. Sagristans, 13 Barcelona 08002	318 98 58 317 28 22	2nd	Exp	55	*
Regente Rambla de Catalunya, 76 Barcelona 08008	215 25 70 487 32 27	1st	Exp	78	***
Rey Don Jaime I C. Jaume I, 11 Barcelona 08002	315 41 61	4th	Inexp	30	
Rialto C. Ferrán, 42 Barcelona 08002	318 52 12 315 38 19	2nd	Exp	128	**
Ritz Gran Vía de les Corts Ca- talanes, 668 Barcelona 08010	318 52 00 318 01 48	Deluxe	VExp	161	*****
Rivoli Rambla Rambla dels Estudis, 128 Barcelona 08002	302 66 43 317 50 53	1st	VExp	87	***

CATALONIA AND THE LEVANT

	Phone # FAX #	Class	Price	Rooms	Stars
San Augustín Pl. Sant Agusti, 3 Barcelona 08001	318 17 08 317 29 28	3rd	Mod	77	*
Suizo Pl. del Angel, 12 Barcelona 08002	315 41 11 315 38 19	2nd	Exp	48	**

Costa del Azahar

Alcocéber	964+				
Aparthotel Jeremías-Ro- mana Playa de Alcocéber 12579	41 44 11 41 24 11	3rd	Mod	39	**
Jeremías Playa de Alcocéber 12579	41 44 37 41 24 44	4th	Inexp	38	*

Benicarló	964+				
Parador Costa del Azahar Av. del Papa Luna, 5 Benicarló 12580	47 01 00 47 09 34	1st	Exp	108	**

Benicasim	964+				
Orange Gran Avenida Benicasim 12560	39 44 00 30 15 41	2nd	Mod	415	**
Voramar Passeo Pilar Coloma, 1 Benicasim 12560	30 01 50 30 05 26	2nd	Mod	55	**

El Saler	96+				
Parador de el Saler El Saler 46012	161 11 86 162 70 16	1st	Exp	58	**
Sidi Saler Playa Saler 46012	161 04 11	1st	Exp	272	***

Gandía	96+				
Bayren I Passeig Maritim Neptu, 62 Gandía 46730	284 03 00 284 06 53	1st	Exp	164	**

Peñiscola	964+				
Hostería del Mar Carretera de Benicarló Peñiscola 12598	48 06 00 48 13 63	1st	Exp	85	***

CATALONIA AND THE LEVANT

	Phone # FAX #	Class	Price	Rooms	Stars
Marina Av. José Antonio, 42 Peñiscola 12598	48 08 90	4th	Inexp	19	*

Costa Blanca

Alicante	96+				
Palas C. Cervantes, 5 Alicante 03002	520 93 10	2nd	Exp	49	*
Residencia Palas Pl. Ayuntamiento, 6 Alicante 03002	520 66 90	2nd	Exp	53	*

Altea	96+				
Altaya Calle Generalísimo, 115 Altea 03590	584 08 00	3rd	Mod	24	

Benidorm	96+				
Bilbaíno Av. Virgen del Sufragio, 1 Benidorm 03500	585 08 04 585 08 05	3rd	Mod	38	**
Cimbel Av. de Europa, 1 Benidorm 03500	585 21 00 586 06 61	1st	Exp	144	

Calpe	96+				
Venta La Chata Carretera Valencia, km 150 Calpe 03710	583 03 08	3rd	Mod	17	*

Denia	96+				
Rosa Pda. Marines, 98 Denia 03700	578 15 73 578 15 73	3rd	Mod	30	*

Guardamar del Segura	96+				
Guardamar Av. Puerto Rico, 11 Guardamar del Segura 03140	572 96 50 572 95 30	3rd	Mod	52	*

CATALONIA AND THE LEVANT

	Phone # FAX #	Class	Price	Rooms	Stars
Jávea	**96+**				
Parador Costa Blanca Playa del Arenal, 2 Jávea 03730	579 02 00 579 03 08	1st	Exp	65	**
La Manga del Mar Menor	**968+**				
Sol Galua Hacienda Dos Mares and Grand Vía La Manga del Mar Menor 30370	56 32 00 56 32 54	2nd	Exp	177	*
Moraira	**96+**				
Moradix Moncayo, 1 Moraira 03724	574 40 56 574 45 25	3rd	Mod	30	*
Playa de San Juan	**96+**				
Almirante Pocardy Av. de Niza, 38 Playa de San Juan 03540	565 01 12 565 71 69	2nd	Mod	64	*
Sidi San Juan Playa San Juan Playa de San Juan 03540	516 13 00 516 33 46	1st	Exp	176	***
Santa Pola 96+					
Polamar Playa de Levant, 6 Santa Pola 03130	541 32 00 541 31 83	2nd	Mod	76	*

Costa Brava

Cadaqués	**972+**				
Playa Sol Platja Pianch, 3 Cadaqués 17488	25 81 00 25 80 54	2nd	Exp	49	*
S'Aguarda Carretera de Port-Llegat, 28 Cadaqués 17488	25 80 82 25 87 56	2nd	Mod	28	*

CATALONIA AND THE LEVANT

	Phone # FAX #	Class	Price	Rooms	Stars
L'Escala	**972+**				
Nieves-Mar P. Martim, 8 L'Escala 17130	77 03 00 10 36 05	2nd	Mod	80	*
Lloret de Mar	**972+**				
Excelsior P. Mossen J. Verdaguer, 16 Lloret de Mar 17310	36 41 37 37 16 54	2nd	Mod	45	*
Marsol P. Mossens J. Verdaguer, 7 Lloret de Mar 17310	36 57 50	2nd	Mod	87	*
Surf Mar Platja de Fanals Lloret de Mar 17310	36 53 62	2nd	Mod	216	*
Palafrugel	**972+**				
Aigua Blava Platja de Fornells Palafruget 17255	62 20 58 62 21 12	1st	Exp	85	***
Casamar C. Nero, 3 Llafranc Palafruget 17211	30 01 04 61 06 51	3rd	Mod	20	**
Garbí Costa Daurada, 20 Calella Palafrugel 17210	61 40 40 61 58 03	2nd	Mod	30	*
Hostalillo C. Bellavista, 22 Tamariu Palafrugel 17211	61 02 50 61 02 17	2nd	Exp	70	*
Parador de Aiguablava Aiguablava Palafrugel 17255	62 21 62 62 21 66	1st	Exp	87	**
Santroc Pl. Atlantic, 2 Barri Sant Roc Palafrugel 17210	61 42 50 61 40 68	3rd	Mod	48	*

CATALONIA AND THE LEVANT

	Phone # FAX #	Class	Price	Rooms	Stars
Sant Feliú de Guíxols	**972+**				
De la Gavina Pl. de la Rosaleda S'Agaró Sant Feliú de Guíxols 17220	32 11 00 32 15 73	Deluxe	VExp	74	***
Murla Park P. dels Guíxols, 22 Sant Feliú de Guíxols 17220	32 04 50 32 00 78	2nd	Exp	89	**
Rex I Rambla del Portalet, 16 Sant Feliú de Guíxols 17220	82 18 09	R3rd	Inexp	25	*
Tossa de Mar	**972+**				
Áncora Av. de la Palma, 4 Tossa de Mar 17320	34 02 99	R2nd	Mod	58	*
Mar Menuda Platja de Mar Menuda Tossa de Mar 17320	34 10 00 34 00 87	2nd	Mod	40	**
Sant March C. Nou, 9 Tossa de Mar 17320	34 00 78	R3rd	Inexp	30	*
Costa Dorada					
Cambrils de Mar	**977+**				
Mónica C. Galcerán Marquet, 3 Cambrils de Mar 43850	36 01 16 79 36 78	2nd	Mod	56	**
Salou	**977+**				
Carabela Roc C. Pau Casals, 108 Salou 43840	37 01 66 37 07 62	2nd	Mod	96	*
Planas Pl. Bonet, 3 Salou 43840	38 01 08	3rd	Mod	100	

CATALONIA AND THE LEVANT

	Phone # FAX #	Class	Price	Rooms	Stars
Sant Carles de la Rápita 977+					
Juanito Platja Miami Sant Carles de la Rápita 43540	74 04 62	4th	Mod	35	**
Llansola C. San Isidro, 98 Sant Carles de la Rápita 43540	74 04 03	3rd	Mod	18	
Miami Park Av. Constitución, 33 Sant Carles de la Rápita 43540	74 03 51	2nd	Mod	80	
Plaça Vella C. Arsenal, 31 Sant Carles de la Rápita 43540	77 24 53 74 43 97	3rd	Mod	21	
Sitges 93+					
Romantic y la Renaixenca C. Sant Isidre, 33 Sitges 08870	894 83 75 894 81 67	4th	Mod	55	***
Subur Maritim P. Martim, 72 Sitges 08870	894 15 50 894 04 27	2nd	Exp	45	*
Terramar P. Maritim, 80 Sitges 08870	894 00 50 894 56 04	1st	Exp	209	**
Vilanova i La Geltrú 93+					
Sovli 70 P. Ribes Roges, 1 Vilanova i La Geltrú 08800	815 12 45 815 70 02	3rd	Mod	30	*
Tarragona 977+					
España Rambla Nova, 49 Tarragona 43003	23 27 07	4th	Mod	40	*
Imperial Tarraco P. Palmeres Tarragona 43003	23 30 40 21 65 66	1st	Exp	170	**

CATALONIA AND THE LEVANT

	Phone # FAX #	Class	Price	Rooms	Stars
Lauria Rambla Nova, 20 Tarragona 43004	23 67 12 23 67 00	2nd	Mod	72	*

Valencia   96+

	Phone # FAX #	Class	Price	Rooms	Stars
Bristol C. Abadia San Martín, 3 Valencia 46002	352 11 76	R2nd	Mod	40	*
Continental C. Correos, 8 Valencia 46002	351 09 26 351 09 26	R2nd	Mod	43	
Excelsior C. Barcelonina, 5 Valencia 46002	351 46 12	2nd	Exp	67	*
Inglés C. Marqués de Dos Aguas, 5 Valencia 46002	351 64 26 394 02 51	2nd	Exp	62	*
Moratín C. Moratín, 15 Valencia 46002	352 12 20	Hs3rd		12	
Reina Victoria C. Barcas, 4 Valencia 46002	352 04 87 352 04 87	1st	Exp	97	**

PORTUGAL

NORTHERN AND CENTRAL PORTUGAL

	Phone # FAX #	Class	Price	Rooms	Stars

Aveiro   034+

	Phone # FAX #	Class	Price	Rooms	Stars
Arcada Rua Viana do Castelo, 4 Aveiro 3800	230 01 218 86	3rd	Inexp	49	*
Imperial Rua Dr. Nascimento Leitão Aveiro 3800	221 41 241 48	1st	Mod	107	*
Palácio el Águeda Quinta da Borralha Borralha 3750	60 19 77 60 19 76	1st	Exp	48	****

NORTHERN AND CENTRAL PORTUGAL

	Phone # FAX #	Class	Price	Rooms	Stars
Estalagem Riabela Torreira Murtosa 3870	481 37 481 47	2nd	Mod	35	**
Paloma Blanca Rua Luís Gomes de Car- valho, 23 Murotsa 3870	38 19 92 38 18 44	R1st	Mod	50	**
Pousada da Ria Bico do Muranzel Murtosa 3870	483 32 483 33	2nd	Exp	19	***
Braga	**053+**				
Carandá Av. da Liberdade, 96 Braga 4700	61 45 00 61 45 50	2nd	Mod	100	*
Do Elevador Bom Jesus Braga 4700	67 66 11	1st	Mod	67	***
Do Parque Bom Jesus Braga 4700	67 66 79 67 66 79	1st	Mod	49	**
Turismo Dom Pedro Praceta João XXI Braga 4700	61 22 00 61 22 11	1st	Mod	132	**
Bragança	**073+**				
Albergaria Santa Isabel Rua Alexandre Herculano, 67 Bragança 5300	224 27 269 37	R1st	Inexp	67	
Bragança Av. Dr. Francisco de Sá Car- neiro Braganca 5300	225 79	2nd	Mod	42	*
Pousada de São Bartolomeu Estrada de Truismo Bragança 5300	224 93 234 53	1st	Mod	16	**
São Roque Rua da Estacada, 26-7 Bragança 5300	234 81 269 37	R2nd	Inexp	36	*

NORTHERN AND CENTRAL PORTUGAL

	Phone # FAX #	Class	Price	Rooms	Stars
Buçaco	**031+**				
Palace Hotel do Buçaco Foresta do Buçaco Buçaco 3800	93 01 01 936 09	1st	Exp	62	*****
Coimbra	**039+**				
Almedina Av. Fernão de Magalhães, 203 Coimbra 3000	291 61	R2nd	Inexp	43	
Astória Av. Emidio Navarro, 21 Coimbra 3000	220 55 220 57	2nd	Mod	64	*
Bragança Largo das Ameias, 10 Coimbra 3000	221 71 361 35	2nd	Mod	83	
Dom Luís Quinta da Verzea Coimbra 3000	41 15 10 81 31 96	2nd	Mod	104	*
Domus Rua Adelino Veiga, 62 Coimbra 3000	285 84	R3rd	Inexp	20	*
Oslo Av. Fernão de Magalhães, 25 Coimbra 3000	290 71 206 14	2nd	Mod	30	
Elvas	**068+**				
Dom Luís Av. de Badajoz Elvas 7350	62 27 56 62 07 33	1st	Mod	90	*
Estalgem Don Sancho II Pr. da República, 20 Elvas 7350	62 26 86 62 47 17	R2nd	Inexp	26	*
Pousada do Santa Luzia Av. de Badajoz Elvas 7350	62 21 94 62 21 27	1st	Mod	16	**
Estremoz	**068+**				
Pousada da Reinha Santa Isabel Largo Dom Dinis Estremoz 7100	226 18 239 82	1st	Exp	23	*****

NORTHERN AND CENTRAL PORTUGAL

	Phone # FAX #	Class	Price	Rooms	Stars
Évora	**066+**				
Albergaria Vitória Rua Diana de Lis Évora 7000	271 74 298 80	R1st	Mod	48	*
Eborense, O Largo da Misericordia, 1 Évora 7000	220 31	R2nd	Inexp	29	**
Planicie Largo Álvaro Velho, 40 Évora 7000	240 26 298 80	2nd	Mod	33	*
Policarpo Rua da Freiria de Baixo, 16 Évora 7000	224 24	R3rd	Inexp	16	
Pousada dos Lóios Largo Conde de Villa Flor Évora 7000	240 51	1st	Exp	32	****
Riviera Rua 5 de Outubro, 49 Évora 7000	233 04 204 67	R1st	Mod	22	*
Santa Clara Travessa da Milheira, 19 Évora 7000	241 41	2nd	Inexp	51	
Figeira da Foz	**033+**				
Aparthotel Atlântico Av. 25 de Abril Figeira da Foz 3080	240 45 224 20	2nd	Mod	70	*
Grande Hotel da Figueira Av. 25 de Abril Figeira da Foz 3080	221 46 224 20	1st	Exp	91	*
Nicola Rua Bernardo Lopes, 36 Figeira da Foz 3080	223 59	R1st	Mod	24	
Guarda	**071+**				
Filipe Rua Vasco da Gama, 9 Guarda 6300	21 26 58 21 64 02	R1st	Mod	45	*

NORTHERN AND CENTRAL PORTUGAL

	Phone # FAX #	Class	Price	Rooms	Stars
Turismo, De Av. Coronel Orlindo de Car- valho Guarda 6300	21 22 05 21 22 04	1st	Mod	105	**
Guimarães	**053+**				
Fundador Dom Pedro Av. Don Afonso Henriques, 740 Guimarães 4800	51 37 81 51 37 86	1st	Mod	63	
Pousada de Santa Maria da Oliveira Rua Santa Maria Guimarães 4800	51 41 57 51 42 04	1st	Exp	16	***
Pousada de Santa Marinha da Costa Estrada de Penha Guimarães 4800	51 44 53 51 44 59	1st	Exp	50	****
Marvão	**045+**				
Estalagem Dom Dinis Rua Dr. Matos Magalhães Marvão 7330	932 36	R2nd	Inexp	8	*
Pousada de Santa Maria Rua 24 de Janeiro, 7 Marvão 7330	932 01 934 40	3rd	Mod	29	***
Oporto	**02+**				
Albergaria Girassol Rua do da Bandeira, 133 Porto 4000	200 18 91	R2nd	Inexp	18	
Albergaria Miradouro Rua da Alegría, 598 Porto 4000	57 07 17 57 02 06	R1st	Mod	30	**
Albergeria São José Rua da Alegria 172 Porto 4000	208 02 61 32 04 46	2nd	Mod	43	**
Castor Rua das Doze Casas, 17 Porto 4000	57 00 14 56 60 76	2nd	Mod	63	*
Dom Henrique Rua Guedes de Azevedo, 179 Porto 4000	200 57 55 201 94 51	1st	Exp	112	**

NORTHERN AND CENTRAL PORTUGAL

	Phone # FAX #	Class	Price	Rooms	Stars
Grand Hotel do Oporto Rua de Santa Catarina, 197 Porto 4000	200 81 76 31 10 61	2nd	Mod	100	*
Infante de Sagres Pr. Dona Filipa de Lencastre, 62 Porto 4000	201 90 31 31 49 37	1st	VExp	74	****
Méridien Porto, Le Av. da Boavista, 1466 Porto 4100	600 19 13 600 20 31	1st	VExp	232	***
Peninsular Rua do da Bandeira, 21 Porto 4000	200 30 12 38 49 84	3rd	Inexp	50	
Porto Sheraton Av. da Boavista, 1269 Porto 4100	606 88 22 609 14 67	1st	Exp	253	**
Rex Pr. da República, 117 Porto 4000	200 45 48 38 38 82	R1st	Inexp	21	***
Tomar	**_049+_**				
Dos Templários Largo Candido dos Reis, 1 Tomar 2300	32 17 30 32 21 91	1st	Mod	84	*
Estalagem Vale da Ursa Cernache do Bonjardim Sertá 6100	995 11 995 94	R1st	Mod	12	**
Pousada de São Pedro Barragem do Castelo de Bode 2300	38 11 75	2nd	Mod	15	*
Pensão Luanda Av. Marquês de Tomar, 13-15 Tomar 2300	31 29 29	R2nd	Inexp	14	*
Residencial Trovador Rua Dr. Joaquim Ribeiro Tomar 2300	32 25 67 32 21 94	R1st	Mod	30	
Residencial União Rua Serpa Pinto, 91 Tomar 2300	31 28 31	R2nd	Inexp	21	*

NORTHERN AND CENTRAL PORTUGAL

	Phone # FAX #	Class	Price	Rooms	Stars
Viseu	**032+**				
Avenida Av. Alberto Sampaio, 1 Viseu 3500	42 34 32 267 43	3rd	Inexp	40	
Grão Vasco Rua Gaspar Barreiros Viseu 3500	42 35 11 270 47	1st	Mod	100	*
Moinho de Vento Rua Paulo Emilio, 13 Viseu 3500	42 41 16 42 96 62	2nd	Mod	30	*
Viana do Castelo	**058+**				
Viana-Mar Av. dos Combatentes da Grande Guerra, 215 Viana do Castelo 4900	82 89 62 82 98 62	R2nd	Inexp	36	*
Viana Sol Largo Vasco da Gama Viana do Castelo 4900	82 89 95 82 89 97	1st	Mod	65	*

LISBON AND ITS ENVIRONS

	Phone # FAX #	Class	Price	Rooms	Stars
Alcobça	**062+**				
Coracões Unidos R. Frei António Brandão, 39 Alcobça 2460	421 42	P2nd	Inexp	16	
Santa Maria R. Dr. Zagalo Alcobça 2460	59 73 95 59 67 15	2nd	Mod	31	*
Batalha	**044+**				
Pousada do Mestre Afonso Domingues Batalha 2440	962 60 962 60	1st	Exp	21	*
Cascais	**01+**	(See also Praia do Guincho)			
Albatroz R. Frederico Arouca, 100 Cascais 2750	248 28 21 284 48 27	1st	VExp	40	***

LISBON AND ITS ENVIRONS

	Phone # FAX #	Class	Price	Rooms	Stars
Casa da Pérgola Av. Valbom, 13 Cascais 2750	484 00 40	2nd	Mod	10	***
Cidadela Av. 25 de Abril Cascais 2750	483 29 21 486 72 26	1st	Exp	130	**
Estalagem Senhora da Guia Estrado do Guincho Cascais 2750	486 92 39 486 92 27	1st	Exp	28	***
Estoril	*01+*			(See also Praia do Guincho)	
Palácio R. do Parque Estoril Estoril 2765	468 04 00 468 48 67	1st	VExp	162	**
Smart R. José Viana, 3 Estoril 2765	468 21 64	R3rd	Inexp	16	*
Praia do Guin- cho	*01+*				
Do Guincho Praia do Guincho Cascais 2750	487 04 91 487 04 31	1st	Exp	31	***
Lisbon	*01+*				
Albergaria da Senhora do Monte Calçada do Monte, 39 Lisboa 1100	886 60 02 87 77 83	1st	Mod	28	**
Altis R. Castilho, 11 Lisboa 1200	52 24 96 54 86 96	1st	Exp	307	
Avenida Palace R. 1 de Dezembro, 123 Lisboa 1100	346 01 54 342 22 84	1st	Exp	100	***
Capitol R. Eça de Queiroz, 24 Lisboa 1000	53 68 11 352 61 65	2nd	Mod	58	*
Dom Carlos Av. Duque de Loule, 121 Lisboa 1000	53 90 71 352 07 28	2nd	Mod	73	***

LISBON AND ITS ENVIRONS

	Phone # FAX #	Class	Price	Rooms	Stars
Dom Manuel I Av. Duque d'Ávila, 189 Lisboa 1000	57 61 60 57 69 85	2dn	Exp	64	***
Horizonte Av. António Agusto de Aguiar, 42 Lisboa 1100	53 95 26 56 25 29	R2nd	Inexp	52	
Imperador Av. 5 de Outubro, 55 Lisboa 1000	352 48 84 352 65 37	R3rd	Inexp	43	*
Lisboa Plaza Travessa do Salitre, 7 Lisboa 1200	346 39 22 347 16 30	1st	Exp	112	**
Lisboa Sheraton R. Latino Coelho, 1 Lisboa 1097	57 57 57 54 71 64	1st	VExp	385	**
Meridien Lisboa, Le R. Castiho, 149 Lisboa 1000	69 09 00 69 32 31	1st	VExp	331	***
Mundial R. Dom Duarte, 4 Lisboa 1100	886 31 01 87 91 29	1st	Exp	147	**
Nazareth Av. António Agusto de Aguiar, 25 Lisboa 1000	54 20 16 356 08 36	R2nd	Inexp	32	
Príncipe Av. Duque d'Ávila, 301 Lisboa 1000	53 61 51 53 42 14	2nd	Mod	68	*
Príncipe Real R. da Alegría, 53 Lisboa 1200	346 01 16 342 21 04	2nd	Exp	24	***
Ritz R. Rodrigo da Fonseca, 88 Lisboa 1093	69 20 20 69 17 83	1st	VExp	310	****
Roma Av. de Roma, 33 Lisboa 1700	796 77 61 793 29 81	2nd	Mod	265	*

LISBON AND ITS ENVIRONS	Phone # FAX #	Class	Price	Rooms	Stars
Tivoli Jardim R. Julio Cesar Machado, 7 Lisboa 1200	53 99 71 355 65 66	1st	Exp	119	*
Torre, Da R. dos Jerónimos, 8 Lisboa 1400	363 62 62 364 59 95	2nd	Mod	50	*
Veneza Av. da Liberdade, 189 Lisboa 1200	352 26 18 352 66 78				
York House R. das Janelas Verdes, 32 Lisboa 1200	396 25 44 397 27 93	R1st	Exp	45	****
Mafra	**061+**				
Albergaria Castelão Av. 25 de Abril Mafra 2640	81 20 50 516 98	3rd	Mod	35	*
Nazaré	**062+**				
Maré R. Mouzinho de Albuquer- que, 8 Nazaré 2450	56 12 26 56 17 50	2nd	Mod		
Priaia Av. Vieira Guimarães, 39 Nazaré 2450	56 14 23 56 14 36	2nd	Mod	40	
Riba-Mar R. Gomes Freire, 9 Nazaré 2450	51 11 58	P3rd	Mod	23	*
Óbidos	**062+**				
Albergaria Rainha Santa Isa- bel R. Direita Óbidos 2510	95 91 15 95 91 15	3rd	Mod	20	**
Estalagem do Convento R. Dom João de Ornelas Óbidos 2510	95 92 17 95 91 59	2nd	Mod	31	**
Pousada do Castelo Paço Real Óbidos 2510	95 91 05 95 91 48	1st	Exp	9	****

LISBON AND ITS ENVIRONS

	Phone # FAX #	Class	Price	Rooms	Stars
Palmela	**065+**				
Pousada do Castelo de Palmela Palmela 2950	235 12 26 233 04 40	1st	Esp	28	***
Sesimbra	**065+**				
Espadarte Av. 25 de Abril Sesimbra 2970	223 31 89	3rd	Mod	80	
Do Mar R. Combatentes do Ultamar, 10 Sesimbra 2970	223 33 26 223 38 88	1st	Exp	168	**
Setúbal	**065+**				
Pousada de São Filipe R. São Filipe Sctúbal 2900	52 38 44	1st	Exp	14	**
Sintra	**01+**				
Casa Adelaide Av. Guilherme Gomes Fer- nandes, 11 Sintra 2710	923 08 73	R3rd	Inexp	10	
Central Pr. da República, 35 Sintra 2710	923 09 63	3rd	Mod	14	*
Estalagem da Raposa R. Dr. Alfredo Costa, 3 Sintra 2710	923 04 65	4th	Mod	8	*
Palácio de Seteais Av. Bocage, 8 Seteais 2710	923 32 00 923 42 77	1st	Exp	30	****
Quinta da Capela Estrada de Monserrate Seteais 2710	929 34 05 929 34 25	2nd	Exp	10	**
Quinta de São Thiago Estrada de Monserrate Seteais 2710	923 29 23	2nd	Exp	14	***
Tivoli Sintra Pr. da República Sintra 2710	923 35 05 923 15 72	1st	Exp	75	*

LISBON AND ITS ENVIRONS

	Phone # FAX #	Class	Price	Rooms	Stars
Tróia	*065+*				
Aparthotel Tróia Tróia Setúbal 2900	442 22	2nd	Mod		
Magnoliamar Tróia Setúbal 2900	441 51	2nd	Mod		
Rosamar Tróia Setúbal 2900	441 51	2nd	Mod		

ALGARVE

	Phone # FAX #	Class	Price	Rooms	Stars
Albufeira	*089+*				
Baltum Av. 25 de Abril Albufeira 8200	58 91 02 58 61 46	3rd	Mod	50	*
Clube Mediterrâneo da Bal- aia Praia Maria Luisa Albufeira 8200	58 66 81 53 78 47	NR	Exp	300	
Estalagem do Cerro Rua Samor Barros Albufeira 8200	58 61 91 58 61 74	E2nd	Mod	83	**
Montechoro Montechoro Albufeira 8200	526 51	1st	Exp	410	
Rocamar Largo Jacinto d'Ayet Albufeira 8200	58 69 90 58 69 98	2nd	Mod	83	*
Sol e Mar Rua João Bernardino de Sousa Albufeira 8200	58 67 21 58 70 36	2nd	Exp	74	*

ALGARVE

	Phone # FAX #	Class	Price	Rooms	Stars
Faro	**089+**				
Albacor Rua Brites de Almeida, 23-5 Faro 8000	80 35 93	2nd	Inexp	38	*
Casa de Lumena Pr. Alexendre Herculano, 27 Faro 8000	80 19 90 80 40 19	2nd	Inexp	12	**
Eva Av. da República Faro 8000	80 33 54 80 23 04	1st	Exp	150	**
Faro Pr. Don Francisco Gomes, 2 Faro 8000	80 32 76 80 35 46	2nd	Mod	52	
Réserve, La Estrada de Esteval Faro 8000	904 74 904 02	1st	VExp	20	****
Lagos	**082+**				
Casa de S. Gonçalo de Lagos Rua Cândido dos Reis, 73 Lagos 8600	76 21 71	R1st	Mod	13	*
Lagos, De Rua Nova da Aldeia Lagos 8600	76 99 67 76 99 20	1st	Exp	317	***
Lagosmar Rua Dr. Faria e Silva, 13 Lagos 8600	76 37 22 76 73 24	R2nd	Mod	45	
Marazul Rua 25 de Abril 20, 13 Lagos 8600	76 91 43 76 99 60	R3rd	Mod	18	**
Meia Praia Meia Praia Lagos 8600	76 20 01	2nd	Mod	66	**
São Cristovão Rossio de São João Lagos 8600	76 30 51	2nd	Mod	80	
Olhão	**089+**				
Bicuar Rua Vasco da Gama, 5 Olhão 8700	71 48 16	R3rd	Inexp	12	

ALGARVE				
Phone # FAX #	Class	Price	Rooms	Stars
Helena Rua Dr. Miguel Bombarda, 42 Olhão 8700	70 26 34	R3rd	Inexp	20	
Ria-Sol Rua General Humberto Delgado, 37 Olhão 8700	70 52 67	3rd	Mod	52	
Praia da Rocha	**082+**				
Algarve Av. Tomás Cabreira Portimão 8500	41 50 01 41 59 99	1st	VExp	220	***
Avenida Praia Av. Tomás Cabreira Portimão 8500	41 77 40 41 77 42	2nd	Mod	61	*
Bela Vista Av. Tomás Cabreira Portimão 8500	240 55 41 53 69	1st	Exp	14	**
Júpiter Av. Tomás Cabreira Portimão 8500	41 50 41 41 53 19	1st	Exp	180	
Quartiera	**098+**				
Atis Av. Infante de Sagres Quartiera 8125	38 97 71 38 97 74	2nd	Mod	72	
Dom José Av. Infante de Sagres Quartiera 8125	30 27 50 30 27 55	2nd	Mod	134	**
Sagres	**082+**				
Baleeria Sagres 8650	642 12	2nd	Exp	118	
Dom Henrique Sítio da Mareta Sagres 8650	641 33	R1st	Mod	15	**
Estalagem Infante do Mar Praia da Salema Sagres 8650	651 37 574 51	E1st	Mod	16	*

ALGARVE	Phone # FAX #	Class	Price	Rooms	Stars
Motel Os Gambozinos Praia do Martinhal Sagres 8650	643 18	3rd	Mod	17	*
Pousada do Infante Ponta da Atalaia Sagres 8650	642 22 642 25	1st	Exp	23	**
Tavira	*081+*				
Eurotel Tavira Quinta da Oliveiras Tavira 8800	32 43 24 32 55 71	2nd	Mod	80	
Lagoas Rua Candido dos Reis, 24 Tavira 8800	222 82	R3rd	Inexp	17	*
Princesa do Gilão Rua Borda de Agua de Aguiar, 10 Tavira 8800	226 65	R3rd	Inexp	14	*
Quinta do Carcol Bairro do São Tavira 8800	224 75 231 75	3rd	Mod	7	*
Vilamoura	*089+*				
Atlantis Vilamoura Vilamoura 8125	38 99 37 38 98 69	1st	VExp	313	**
Dom Pedro Golf Vilamoura 8125	38 96 50 31 54 82	1st	VExp	261	**
Dom Pedro Marina Vilamoura 8125	38 98 02 31 32 70	1st	VExp	155	**
Estalagem da Cegonha Centro Hipico de Vilamoura Vilamoura 8125	30 25 77	2nd	Mod	10	**
Motel Vilamoura Golf Vilamoura 8125	30 29 77 38 00 23	1st	Mod	52	***
Vilamoura Marinotel Vilamoura 8125	38 99 88 38 98 69	1st	VExp	387	***

SPECIAL RESTAURANTS
(By Region)

NOTE: Because restaurant prices are not fixed, we use the following price categories:

Very Expensive (VExp) $100+ for dinner for two with house wine

Expensive (Exp)   **$50-100** for dinner for two with house wine

Moderate (Mod)   **$20-50** for dinner for two with house wine

Inexpensive (Inexp)   **$20 or less** for dinner for two with house wine

Closing days are indicated by the obvious day abreviations of M, T, etc., with Su for Sunday and Th for Thursday. In some cases an establishment closes only for lunch or only for dinner, which we indicated with M/1 (*closed Monday for lunch*), or T/d (*closed Tuesday for dinner*).

Note, most resort restaurants close for one month or for the season in winter, while other restaurants generally close for one month in summer. Check the listing in the text for specifics.

SPAIN

MADRID AND NEW CASTILE				
	Phone #	Price	Stars	Closed
Madrid	**91+**	(Many restaurants close in August)		
Bidasao Claudio Coello, 24	431 20 81	Exp	***	S, Su
Bola, La C. de la Bola, 5	547 69 30	Mod	**	Su, S/l
Botín C. Cuchilleros, 17	266 42 17	Mod	**	
Cafe de Oriente Pl. de Oriente, 2	241 39 74	Exp	***	Su, S/l
Casa Gallega Pl. San Miguel, 8	547 30 55	Mod	***	
Cenador del Prado, El C. del Prado, 4	429 15 61	Exp	****	Su, S/l
Chateaubriand, Le C. Virgen de los Peligros, 1	532 33 41	Mod	*	Su
Gure-Etxea Pl. De La Paja, 12	365 61 49	Mod	***	Su

MADRID AND NEW CASTILE

	Phone #	Price	Stars	Closed
Hylogui C. Ventura de la Vega, 3	429 73 57	Mod	*	Su/l
Laurques C. Ventura de la Vega, 16	429 61 74	Inexp	*	M, Su/l
Pescador, El José Ortega y Gasset, 75	402 19 90	Mod	***	Su
Saint James C. Juan Bravo, 12	575 00 69	Exp	**	Su
Zalacaín Álvarez de Baena, 4	561 48 40	VExp	*****	Su, S/l

Toledo   *925+*

	Phone #	Price	Stars	Closed
Asador Adolfo Calle La Granada, 6	22 73 21	Exp	***	
Botica, La Plaza de Zocodover, 13	22 55 57	Mod	*	Su/l
Cardinal Paseo Recaredo, 24	22 49 00	Mod	*	
Casa Aurelio Calle Sinagoga, 1	22 20 97	Mod	*	W
Hierbabuena C. Cristo de la Luz, 9	22 34 63	Mod	*	Su/l
Mesón Aurelio Calle Sinagoga, 6	22 13 92	Mod	*	M

OLD CASTILE AND LEON

	Phone #	Price	Stars	Closed
Ávila *918+*				
Molina de La Losa, El Bajada de La Losa, 12	21 11 01	Mod	***	M
Rastro, El Pl. del Rastro, 1	22 12 18	Mod	*	
Burgos *947+*				
Autoservicio Bonfin C. Cadena	20 61 93	Inexp		All eves.

OLD CASTILE AND LEON				
	Phone #	Price	Stars	Closed
Casa Ojeda C. Vitoria, 5	20 90 52	Mod	**	Su/d
Fernán Gonzáles C. Calera, 19	20 94 42	Exp	***	
Gaona Virgen de la Paloma, 41	20 61 91	Mod	*	M
Mesón del Cid Pl. Santa María, 8	20 59 71	Exp	***	Su/d
Rincón de España C. Nuño Rasura, 11	20 59 55	Mod	*	M
La Rioja Region 941+				
Terete Lucrecia Arana, 17 Haro	31 00 23	Mod	***	M, Su/d
León 987+				
Nuevo Racimo de Oro Pl. San Martin, 8	21 47 67	Mod	**	W. or Su/d
Adonias C. Santa Nonia, 16	20 67 68	Mod	**	Su
Casa Pozo Pl. de San Marcelo, 15	22 30 39	Mod	**	Su
Salamanca 923+				
Bardo, El C. Compañia, 8	21 90 89	Inexp		M
Candil Nuevo, El Pl. de la Reina, 1	21 90 27	Exp	**	
Chez Victor Espoz y Mina, 26	21 31 23	Exp	****	M, Su/d
Posada, La C. Aire, 1	21 72 51	Mod	*	
Rio de la Plata Pl. del Peso, 1	21 90 05	Mod	**	M
Sablon, Le Espoz y Mina, 20	26 29 52	Mod	**	T

OLD CASTILE AND LEON

	Phone #	Price	Stars	Closed
Segovia	**911+**			
Mesón de Cándito Pl. Azoguejo, 5	42 59 11	Exp	***	
José María C. Cronista Lecea, 11	43 44 84	Exp	**	
Mesón del Duque C. Cervantes, 12	43 05 37	Exp	**	
La Oficina C. Cronista Lecea, 10	43 16 43	Mod	*	M
La Taurina Pl. Mayor, 8	43 05 77	Mod	*	
Valladolid	**983+**			
Mesón La Fragua Paseo de Zorrilla, 10	33 87 85	Exp	****	Su/d
Mesón Panero Marina Escobar, 1	30 16 73	Exp	***	Su/d

ANDALUSIA

	Phone #	Price	Stars	Closed
Baeza	**953+**			
Juanito Paseo Arca del Agua	74 00 40	Mod	*	Su, M/d
Sali Passaje Cardenal Benavides, 15	74 13 65	Inexp		W/d
Cádiz	**956+**			
El Anteojo C. Alameda de Apodaca, 22	22 13 20	Exp	*	M
Faro, El C. San Félix, 15	21 25 01	Exp	*	M
Sardinero, El Pl. San Juan de Dios	28 25 05	Mod	*	M
Córdoba	**957+**			
Blasón, El José Zorrilla, 11	48 06 25	Exp	**	

ANDALUSIA

	Phone #	Price	Stars	Closed
Caballo Rojo, El
Cardenal Herrero, 28	47 53 75	Exp	**	
Churrasco, El
Romero, 16	29 08 19	Exp	*	Th
Mesón Bandolero
Torrijos, 6	41 42 45	Exp	**	

Costa De La Luz
El Puerto de Santa María	956+			
El Patio
Rufina Vergara, 1	54 05 06	Mod	*	
Sanlúcar de Barrameda	956+			
Bigote
Bajo de Guia	36 26 96	Mod	*	
Mirador Doñana
Bajo de Guia	36 42 05	Mod	*	

Costa Del Sol
Marbella	952+			
La Hacienda
9 k east along N-340	283 12 67	Exp	****	M, T
La Fonda
Pl. Santo Cristo, 10	277 25 12	Exp	***	Su, +
lunch

Granada 958+
Alcaicería
Placeta de la Alcaicería	22 43 41	Mod	*	
Cunin
Pecsaderia, 9	25 07 77	Exp	**	M/d
Ruta del Veleta
Carretera de Sierra Nevada, 50	48 61 34	Exp	***	Su/d
Sevilla
Oficios, 12	22 12 23	Mod	**	Su/d

Málaga 952+
Antonio Martín
Paseo Marítimo, 4	222 21 13	Exp		Su/d
Café de Paris
C. Vélez Málaga, 8	222 50 43	Exp	**	Su

ANDALUSIA	Phone #	Price	Stars	Closed
La Cancela C. Denís Belgrano, 3	222 31 25	Inexp		W
Ronda	**952+**			
Don Miguel Pl. de España, 3	287 10 90	Mod	**	Su
Pedro Romero Virgen de la Paz, 18	287 11 10	Mod	*	
Seville	**95+**			
Albahaca, La Pl. Santa Cruz, 12	422 07 14	Exp	**	Su
Alcázares, Los C. Miguel de Manara, 10	421 31 03	Mod	*	Su
Asador Ox's C. Betis, 61	427 95 85	Exp	**	Su
Egaña Oriza San Fernando, 41	422 72 11	Exp	****	Su, S/l
Florencia Av. Eduardo Dato, 49	453 35 00	Exp	*	
Hostería del Laurel Pl. Venerables, 5	422 02 95	Mod		
Isla, La C. Arfe, 25	421 26 31	Exp	**	M
Modesto C. Cano y Cueto, 5	441 68 11	Mod	*	W
Pizzeria San Marco C. Betis, 66	428 03 10	Inexp	*	
Rio Grande C. Betis, 61	427 39 56	Exp		
San Marco C. Cuna, 6	421 24 40	Exp	***	Su
Úbeda	**953+**			
Cusco Parque de Vandevira, 8	75 34 13	Mod		M

ESTREMADURA				
	Phone #	Price	Stars	Closed
Cáceres	**927+**			
Atrio Av. de España, 30	24 29 28	Exp	*	Su/d
Figón de Eustaquio, El Pl. San Juan, 12	24 81 94	Mod	**	
Guadalupe	**927+**			
Hospederia del Real Monas- terio Pl. Juan Carlos I	36 70 00	Mod	**	
Cerezo Gregorio López, 12	36 73 79	Inexp	**	
Mérida	**924+**			
Briz C. Féliz Valverde Lillo, 5	31 93 07	Inexp	*	
Casa Benito C. Santa Eulalia, 13	31 55 02	Inexp		
Nicholás Félix Valverde Lillo, 13	31 96 10	Mod	**	Su/d
Trujillo	**927+**			
Hostal Pizarro Pl. Mayor, 13	32 02 55	Mod	***	
Mesón la Cadena Pl. Mayor, 8	32 14 63	Inexp	*	
Mesón la Troya Pl. Mayor, 10	32 13 64	Inexp		

GALICIA, ASTURIAS, AND CANTABRIA				
	Phone #	Price	Stars	Closed
Basque Coast				
Donastia	**943+**			
Akelarre Passeo del Padre Orcolaga, 56	21 20 52	Exp	****	M, Su/d
Alotza Kalea Fermin Calbeton, 7	42 07 82	Mod	**	M

GALICIA, ASTURIAS, AND CANTABRIA

	Phone #	Price	Stars	Closed
Arzak Kalea Alto de Miracruz, 21	27 84 65	VExp	*****	M, Su/d
Panier Fleuri Paseo de Salamanca, 1	42 42 05	Exp	****	W, Su/d
Hondarribia	**943+**			
Ramón Roteta Irun	64 16 93	Exp	***	Th, Su/d
Laredo	**942+**			
Ramona Alameda José Antonio,4	60 71 89	Mod	*	
Risco Alto de Laredo	60 50 30	Mod	**	W
Santander	**942+**			
Bodiga del Riojano Rio de la Pila, 5	21 67 50	Mod	*	
Molino, El Puente Arce	57 50 55	Exp	***	M, Su/d

Costa del Rias

O Grove	**986+**			
Posada del Mar, La C. Castelao 202	73 01 06	Mod	*	Su/d
Pontevedra	**986+**			
Casa Solla Carretera de La Toya	85 60 29	Exp	***	Su
Doña Antonia Soportales de la Herreria, 9	84 72 74	Exp	***	Su/d, Th/d
Vilagarcia de Arousa	**986+**			
Chocolate Av. Cambados, 151	50 11 99	Exp	***	Su/d

Costa Verde

Comillas	**942+**			
Capricho de Gaudí, El Barrio de Sobrellano	72 03 65	Exp	*	
Gijon	**985+**			
Casa Victor C. Carmen, 11	34 83 10	Mod	*	Th, Su/d

GALICIA, ASTURIAS, AND CANTABRIA

	Phone #	Price	Stars	Closed
Luarca	985+			
Leonés Paseo Alfonso X el Sabio, 1	64 09 95	Exp	**	
Ribadeo	982+			
O Xardin C. Reinante, 20	11 02 22	Mod	*	M
Oviedo	**985+**			
Casa Fermín C. San Francisco, 8	21 64 52	Exp	***	M
Raitan, El Pl. Trascorrales, 6	21 42 18	Mod	*	Su/d
Trascorrales Pl. de Trascorrales, 19	22 24 41	Exp	***	M
Santiago de Compostela	**981+**			
Alameda Puerta Fajera, 15	58 66 57	Mod	*	
Anexo Vilas Av. Villagarcia, 21	59 86 37	Exp	**	M
Don Gaiferos C. Nueva, 23	58 38 94	Exp	*	Su
Nova Gallihea C. Franco, 56	58 27 99	Mod	*	
O'Sotano C. Franco, 8	56 50 24	Inexp	*	
Reyes Católicos Pl. Obradioros, 1	58 22 00	Mod	**	
San Clemente Pl. San Clemente, 6	58 08 82	Mod	*	Su/d

ARAGÓN AND NAVARRE

	Phone #	Price	Stars	Closed
Estella	**948+**			
Navarra C. Gustavo de Maeztu, 16	55 10 69	Exp	*	M, Su/d

ARAGÓN AND NAVARRE

	Phone #	Price	Stars	Closed
Olite	*948+*			
Tubal Pl. de Navarra, 2 Tafalla	70 08 52	Mod	***	M, Su/d
Pamplona	*948+*			
Hartza C. Juan de Labrit, 19	22 45 68	Exp	**	M, Su/d
Iruna Pl. del Castillo, 44	22 20 64	Inexp	*	
Josetxo Pl. Principe de Viana, 1	22 20 97	Exp	***	Su
Otano C. San Nicolas, 5	22 70 36	Mod	*	Su/d
Zaragoza	*976+*			
Costa Vasca Teniente Coronel Valen- zuela, 13	21 73 39	Exp	***	Su
Tres Hermanos C. San Pablo, 45	44 10 85	Inexp		T

CATALONIA AND THE LEVANT

	Phone #	Price	Stars	Closed
Barcelona	*93+*			
Agut C. Gignas, 16	315 17 09	Inexp	*	M, Su/d
Agut d'Avignon C. Trinitat, 3	302 60 34	Exp	**	
Azulete Via Augusta, 281	203 59 43	Exp	***	Su, S/l
Botafumeiro C. Mayor de Gràcia, 81	218 42 30	VExp	****	M, Su/d
Brasserie Flo C. Jonqueres, 10	319 31 02	Mod	**	
Café de l'Academie C. Lledo, 1	315 00 26	Inexp		Dinners

CATALONIA AND THE LEVANT

	Phone #	Price	Stars	Closed
Caracoles, La P. Escudellers, 14	302 31 85	Mod	*	
Dama, La Avinguda Diagonal, 423	202 06 86	Exp	***	
Dorada Petit, El C. Dolors Monserda, 51	204 51 53	VExp	****	Su
Egipte C. Jerusalem, 12	317 74 80	Inexp	*	Su
Font del Gat P. Santa Madrona	424 02 24	Mod		M
Neichel Av. de Pedralbes, 16bis	203 84 08	VExp	*****	Su
Odisea, La C. Copons, 7	302 36 92	Exp	***	Su, S/I
Pitarra C. d'Avinyò, 56	301 16 47	Inexp		Su
Raim D' or Can Maxim C. Bonsucces, 8	302 02 34	Inexp		Su
Senyor Parellada Carrer Argentería, 37	315 40 10	Mod	**	Su
Set Portes Passeig Isabel II, 14	319 30 33	Mod	**	
Via Venito C. Ganduxer, 10	200 72 44	VExp	***	Su, S/I

Costa Blanca

	Phone #	Price	Stars	Closed
Alicante	96+			
Delfin Expanada de España, 12	521 49 11	Exp	**	
Rincón Castellano Calle Manero Molla, 12	521 90 02	Mod	*	Th
Altea	96+			
Monte Molar Caretera Valencia	584 15 81	Exp	**	W
Moraira	96+			
Girasol, El Moraira	574 43 73	Exp	***	M

CATALONIA AND THE LEVANT

	Phone #	Price	Stars	Closed
Costa Brava				
Cadaqués	972+			
Galiota, La C. Narciso Monturiol, 9	25 81 87	Exp	**	
Sant Feliú de Guíxols	972+			
Can Toni C. Sant Martiria, 29	32 10 26	Exp	***	M
Eldorado Petit, El Rambla Vidal, 23	32 18 18	Exp	***	W
Costa Dorada				
Cambrils de Mar	977+			
Can Gatell P. Miramar, 27	36 03 31	Exp	**	T, M/d
Casa Gatell P. Miramar, 26	36 00 57	Exp	**	M, Su/d
Tarragona	**977+**			
Galería, La Rambla Nova, 16	23 61 43	Mod	*	W, Su
Puda, La Muelle Pescadores, 25	21 15 11	Mod	**	
Valencia	**96+**			
Plat, El C. Conde de Altea, 41	35 15 11	Exp	**	M, Su/d
Rio Sil C. Mosén Femades, 10	352 97 64	Exp	*	
Romeral, El Gran Vía Marquês del Turia, 62	395 15 17	Inexp	*	M
Timonel, El C. Felix Pizcueta, 13	352 63 00	Mod	*	M

PORTUGAL

NORTHERN AND CENTRAL PORTUGAL				
	Phone #	Price	Stars	Closed
Aveiro	**034+**			
Centenario Largo do Mercado, 9	227 98	Mod	**	T
Braga	**053+**			
Abade de Priscos Pr. Mousinho de Albuquer- que, 7		Mod	**	
Inácio, O Campo das Hortas, 4	61 32 25	Mod	*	T
Bragança	**073+**			
Lá em Casa Rua Marquês de Pombal	221 11	Mod		M
Plantório Estrada Cantarias	224 26	Mod		
Coimbra	**039+**			
Alfredo, O Av. João das Regras, 32	44 15 22	Inexp	*	
Dom Pedro Av. Emidio Navarro, 58	291 08	Inexp		M
Pedro dos Leitões Mealhada	220 62	Inexp	*	
Trovador Largo da Sé Velha, 17	254 75	Inexp	*	M
Elvas	**068+**			
Don Quizote On N-4	62 20 14	Mod	*	
Estalgem Don Sancho II Pr. da República, 20	62 26 86	Inexp	*	
Pousada de Santa Luzia Av. de Badajoz	62 21 94	Mod	*	
Évora	**066+**			
Cozinha de Santo Humberto Rua da Moeda, 39	242 51	Mod		Th

NORTHERN AND CENTRAL PORTUGAL

	Phone #	Price	Stars	Closed
Fialho Travessa das Mascarenhas, 14	230 79	Mod	*	M
Guião Rua da República, 81	224 27	Mod		M
Figeira da Foz 033+				
Tamargueira Estrada do Cabo Mondeo	225 14	Mod	*	
Tubarão Av. 25 de Abril	234 45	Mod	*	
Guarda 071+				
Filipe Rua Vasco da Gama, 9	21 26 58	Mod	*	
Guimarães 053+				
Pousada de Santa Maria da Oliveira Rua Santa Maria	51 41 57	Mod	*	
Marvão 045+				
Pousada de Santa Maria Rua 24 de Janeiro, 7	932 01	Mod	***	
Oporto 02+				
Aquário Marisqueiro Rua Rodriques Sampaio, 179	200 22 31	Mod	*	Su
Chez Lapin Cais da Ribeira, 42	264 18	Inexp	*	
Escondidinho, O Rua de Passos Manuel, 144	200 10 79	Mod		Su
Mesa Antiga Rua de Santo Ildefonso, 208	200 64 32	Mod	*	S
Portucale Rua da Alegria, 598	57 07 17	Exp	***	
Standard Bar Rua Infante Dom Henrique, 43	239 04	Inexp	*	Su
Taverna de Bebobos Cais da Ribeira, 25	31 35 65	Inexp	**	Su

NORTHERN AND CENTRAL PORTUGAL

	Phone #	Price	Stars	Closed
Tomar	**049+**			
Chez Nous Rua Dr. Joaquim Jacinto, 31	31 47 43	Mod	*	T
Chico Elias Algarvias	310 67	Mod	**	T
Viana do Castelo	**058+**			
3 Potes, Os Beco dos Fornos, 7	82 99 28	Mod	**	M
Viseu	**032+**			
Cacimbo Rua Alexandre Herculano, 95	228 94	Inexp	*	
Cortiço, O Rua Augusto Hilário, 43	42 38 53	Mod	*	
Trave Negra Rua dos Loureiros, 40	261 38	Mod	*	

LISBON AND ITS ENVIRONS

	Phone #	Price	Stars	Closed
Batalha	**044+**			
Pousada do Mestre Afonso Domingues Batalha	962 60	Mod		
Lisbon	**01+**			
Aviz R. Serpa Pinto, 12-B	32 83 91	Exp	*	Su, S/l
Bonjardim Traversa de Santo Antõa, 11	342 74 24	Inexp	*	
Bota Alta Travessa da Queimada, 35	32 79 59	Inexp	*	Su
Casa da Comida Travessa das Amoreiras, 1	388 53 76	Exp	****	Su, S/l
Cervejaria da Trindade R. Nova de Trindade, 20-B	342 35 06	Inexp	*	

LISBON AND ITS ENVIRONS

	Phone #	Price	Stars	Closed
Comida de Santo Calçada do Eng. Miquel Pais, 39	396 33 39	Mod	*	
Conventual Pr. das Flores, 45	60 91 96	Exp	***	Su, S/l
Gambrinus R. das Portas de Santo Antão, 25	32 14 66	Exp	**	
Great American Disaster Pr. Marquês de Pombal, 1	51 61 45	Inexp		
Pap'Acorda R. da Atalaya, 57	346 48 11	Mod	*	Su
Pastelaria Bénard R. Garrett, 104	347 31 33	Inexp	*	Su
Restaurante 33 R. Alexandre Herculano, 33A	54 60 79	Mod	*	Su, S/l
Sancho Travessa da Gloria, 14	346 97 80	Mod	*	Su
Sua Excelencia R. do Conde, 42	60 36 14	Mod	**	W, S/l
Tágide Largo da Academia Nacio- nal de Belas Artes, 18	347 18 80	Exp	****	Su, S/d
Xêlê Bananas Pr. des Flores, 29	395 25 15	Inexp	*	Su, S/l

Praia do Guincho
01+   (See also Cascais and Estoril)

	Phone #	Price	Stars	Closed
Porto de Santa Maria Estrada do Guincho	487 02 40	Exp	***	M

Nazaré   062+

	Phone #	Price	Stars	Closed
Beira-Mar Av. da República, 40	56 13 58	Inexp		
Mar Bravo Pr. Sousa Oliveira, 75	55 11 80	Inexp		

Óbidos   062+

	Phone #	Price	Stars	Closed
Alcaide R. Direita	95 92 20	Mod	*	M

LISBON AND ITS ENVIRONS

	Phone #	Price	Stars	Closed
Sintra	**01+**			
Alcobaça R. da Padarias, 7	923 16 51	Inexp	*	W
Galeria Real R. Tude de Sousa	923 16 61	Mod	*	M

ALGARVE

	Phone #	Price	Stars	Closed
Albufeira	**089+**			
A Ruína Cais Herculano	51 20 94	Mod	*	
Montinho, O Montechoro	51 39 59	Mod	**	Su
Faro	**089+**			
Cidade Velha Rua Domingos Guieiro, 19	271 45	Exp	**	Su, S/l
Réserve, La Estrada do Esteval	902 34	Exp	***	T
Lagos	**082+**			
Alpendre Rua António Barbosa Viana, 17	76 27 05	Exp		
Dom Sebastião Rua 25 de Abril 20, 20-2	76 27 95	Mod		
Sagres	**082+**			
Fortaleza do Beliche Cabo Vicente	641 34	Mod	*	

INDEX

S

Introducing the 1994 Fielding Travel Guides— fresh, fascinating and fun!

An incisive new attitude and an exciting new look! All-new design and format. In-depth reviews. Fielding delivers travel information the way frequent travelers demand it—written with sparkle, style and humor. Candid insights, sage advice, insider tips. No fluff, no filler, only fresh information that makes the journey more fun, more fascinating, more Fielding. Start planning your next great adventure today!

Australia 1994	**$16.95**
Belgium 1994	**$16.95**
Bermuda/Bahamas 1994	**$16.95**
Brazil 1994	**$16.95**
Britain 1994	**$16.95**
Budget Europe 1994	**$16.95**
Caribbean 1994	**$16.95**
Europe 1994	**$16.95**
Far East 1994	**$16.95**
France 1994	**$16.95**
The Great Sights of Europe 1994	**$16.95**
Hawaii 1994	**$16.95**
Holland 1994	**$16.95**
Italy 1994	**$16.95**
Mexico 1994	**$16.95**
New Zealand 1994	**$16.95**
Scandinavia 1994	**$16.95**
Spain & Portugal 1994	**$16.95**
Switzerland & the Alpine Region 1994	**$16.95**
Worldwide Cruises 1994	**$16.95**
Shopping Europe	**$12.95**

To place an order: call toll-free
1-800-FW-2-GUIDE
add $2.00 shipping & handling, allow 2-6 weeks.

FIELDING'S
TRAVEL
SECRETS

For Travel Insiders Only!

FIELDING'S TRAVEL SECRETS is the insider's travel guide, available only to travel professionals and a very limited number of Fielding Travel Guide readers. Created by Fielding's experienced staff of writers and released in six bi-monthly installments per year, the insider's report is packed with timely travel information, trends, news, tips and reviews. Enroll now and you will also receive a variety of significant discounts and special preview information.

Due to the sensitive nature of the information contained in these reports, subscriptions available to non-travel industry individuals are limited to the first 10,000 subscribers. The annual price for all six installments is $60. This offer also comes with an unconditional money-back guarantee if you are not fully satisfied.

To Reserve Your Subscription
1-800-FW-2-GUIDE

Favorite People, Places & Experiences

ADDRESS:	NOTES:

Name

Address

Telephone

Name

Address

Telephone

Name

Address

Telephone

Name

Address

Telephone

Name

Address

Telephone

Name

Address

Telephone

Name

Address

Telephone

Favorite People, Places & Experiences

ADDRESS:	NOTES:

Name

Address

Telephone

Name

Address

Telephone

Name

Address

Telephone

Name

Address

Telephone

Name

Address

Telephone

Name

Address

Telephone

Name

Address

Telephone

Favorite People, Places & Experiences

ADDRESS:	NOTES:

Name

Address

Telephone

Name

Address

Telephone

Name

Address

Telephone

Name

Address

Telephone

Name

Address

Telephone

Name

Address

Telephone

Name

Address

Telephone